On Sense and Direct Reference

READINGS IN THE PHILOSOPHY OF LANGUAGE

MATTHEW DAVIDSON

California State University—San Bernardino

Boston Burr Ridge, IL Dubuque, IA Madison, WI New York
San Francisco St. Louis Bangkok Bogotá Caracas Kuala Lumpur
Lisbon London Madrid Mexico City Milan Montreal New Delhi
Santiago Seoul Singapore Sydney Taipei Toronto

Higher Education

ON SENSE AND DIRECT REFERENCE: READINGS IN THE PHILOSOPHY OF LANGUAGE

1 2 3 4 5 6 7 8 9 0 DOC/DOC 0 9 8 7

ISBN: 978-0-07-353561-6

MHID: 0-07-353561-3

Vice president and Editor-in-chief: *Emily Barrosse*
Publisher: *Mary Lyn Uhl*
Sponsoring Editor: *Jon-David Hague/Mark Georgiev*
Editorial Coordinator: *Sora Kim*
Marketing manager: *Pamela Cooper*
Production supervisor: *Randy Hurst*
Production editor: *Mel Valentin*
Design manager: *Kim Menning*
Cover designer: *Kim Menning*
Interior designer: *Valerie Brewster*
Compositor: *ITC*
Typeface 10/13 Miller
Printer: *RR Donnelley*

Library of Congress Cataloging-in-Publication Data

On sense and direct reference readings in the philosophy of language [edited by] Matthew Davidson.
    p. cm.
   Includes bibliographical references.
   ISBN 13: 978-0-07-353561-6 (alk. paper)
   MHID: 0-07-353561-3 (alk. paper)
   1. Language and languages—Philosophy. I. Davidson, Matthew, 1972–
P107.O5 2006
401—dc22

                                              2006046789

http://www.mhhe.com

For
Claudia Davidson
Harold Davidson
Mark Davidson

with love.

CONTENTS

PREFACE

The 20th Century saw the development of substantive philosophical positions concerning the nature of reference. Very broadly, two competing camps emerged: Those who follow Frege in thinking that the semantic content of a referring term determines its reference and is distinct from its reference; and those who follow Mill (roughly) in thinking that the semantic content of a referring term (names and indexical expressions in particular) is the referent of the term. This anthology in the philosophy of language focuses exclusively on the debate between "Millians" or "neo-Russellians" and "Fregeans" or "neo-Fregeans." It came to be after I put together one course packet too many in teaching contemporary issues in philosophy of language. There are other excellent extant anthologies in the philosophy of language. But none of them focus only on what is arguably the most important debate in the philosophy of language—that over reference. I sincerely hope that this collection will prove helpful to philosophers who wish to focus on reference in their philosophy of language classes and seminars, as well as to those who wish to have a collection of many of the important papers concerning the nature of reference.

I am grateful to many who provided significant help to me in putting together this volume. My editor at McGraw-Hill, Jon-David Hague, exhibited every virtue one might hope for in an editor. His patience, encouragement, and advice were invaluable. I appreciate the suggestions I received from colleagues from all parts of the globe. Special thanks go to Nathan Salmon (for very many things, including yet another deft turn of phrase on his part in suggesting the title), Scott Soames, Jay Atlas, Gordon Barnes, Ben Caplan, David Chalmers, Graeme Forbes, David Kaplan, Jeffery King, Mark Richard, Tony Roy, Jennifer Saul, and Alan Sidelle. I also am grateful to Scott Soames for writing a piece specially for this volume, David Kaplan for granting permission to reprint some of the very best works that exist in philosophy of language (and analytic philosophy, more broadly), and Ben Caplan for providing an unpublished paper (of the same name as the volume) to serve as an excellent overview to the issues in the book. Finally, the path to production of this book would have been much bumpier without the diligent efforts of my research assistant, Katrina Krallis.

Matthew Davidson
California State University, San Bernardino

FOREWORD
Matthew Davidson, ed., *On Sense and Direct Reference*

By Nathan Salmon

One of the most important achievements in philosophy in the second half of the last century has been a movement in the philosophy of language, spilling over into metaphysics, epistemology, and the philosophy of mind. This movement is known as the *theory of direct reference*. The present reader is the best extant introduction to this theory.

A French speaker uttering the words '*La neige est blanche*' asserts the same thing as an German speaker uttering '*Schnee ist weiß*'. The thing asserted, as distinct from the words uttered, is a *proposition:* that snow is white. The fundamental semantic role of a declarative sentence is to *express* a proposition, which is the *semantic content* of the sentence. The proposition component semantically correlated with an expression is the expression's *semantic content*. Proper names, like 'Shakespeare' and 'London', are generally classified along with definite descriptions, individual variables, pronouns, and some other indexicals, as *singular terms—* expressions whose semantic function, when used in a particular context, is to *refer to* (denote, designate), i.e. to stand for, a single thing. The thing to which a singular term refers is the term's *referent*. The principal philosophical controversy regarding singular terms concerns the question: What are their semantic contents?

The theories of John Stuart Mill (1806–1873), Bertrand Russell (1872–1970), and Gottlob Frege (1848–1925) provide the classical rival answers. Despite a fundamental disagreement over the matter of whether ordinary referents can play the role of semantic contents, there is common ground between Russell and Frege in regard to ordinary proper names. Both held that names are *descriptional—* expressing a descriptive content, or sense (Frege's *Sinn*), whereby the term's referent or denotation is whatever uniquely fits (or best fits) that descriptive content. In fact, both held a strong version of the theory. On their view, if 'St. Anne' is analyzable as 'the mother of Mary', it must be analyzable even further, since 'Mary' is also supposed to be descriptional. But even 'the mother of the mother of Jesus' must be in this sense further analyzable. If α is a non-descriptional singular term referring to Mary, then we may say that the result of writing 'the mother of' followed by α is *descriptional relative to* Mary. A *thoroughly descriptional* term is one that is descriptional but not descriptional relative to anything. The orthodox theory, shared by Russell and Frege, is the theory that proper names and similar devices are either thoroughly descriptional or descriptional relative only to items entirely

viii

contained within one's consciousness. Frege held the stronger thesis that proper names are thoroughly descriptional. The orthodox theory stood in sharp contrast to Mill's theory that whereas definite descriptions are descriptional, proper names, by contrast, are altogether non-descriptional (except relative to themselves).

During the first half of the 20th century, the orthodox account of meaning and reference reigned supreme. Then some philosophers—notably Keith Donnellan, David Kaplan, Ruth Barcan Marcus, Hilary Putnam, and especially Saul Kripke—began exposing how badly the Fregean picture fit certain sorts of terms. Especially and most obviously, the Fregean account did not seem to fit the logician's individual variables 'x', 'y', and 'z'. But it failed also for such common expressions as proper names, demonstratives, pronouns, natural-kind terms, and more—perhaps most, or even all, simple (or single-word) terms. Donnellan's 1966 classic "Reference and Definite Descriptions"—spot-lighting its famous distinction between the *referential* and the *attributive* uses of definite descriptions—is an early and important version of the direct-reference theory, in its contemporary incarnation. Ironically, Donnellan argues there for a direct-reference theory on its least promising turf: definite descriptions. Even these, Donnellan argued, are not correctly accounted for by the orthodox theory.

The theory of direct reference holds with Mill that proper names and similar devices are non-descriptional. Importantly, this theory does not deny that particular names may exhibit any or all aspects of a Fregean sense. What is denied is that the conceptual representation carried by a name also secures the referent. But the direct-reference theory is significantly stronger than a simple denial of Russell's doctrine that ordinary names are abbreviated definite descriptions. The theory holds that insofar as definite descriptions are descriptional, names are not even similar to definite descriptions. An immediate consequence is that a great many definite descriptions fail to be thoroughly descriptional or descriptional relative only to items of direct acquaintance, since many contain names of ordinary individuals.

Three main kinds of arguments have been advanced in favor of the direct-reference theory. The modal and epistemological arguments are due chiefly to Kripke. Suppose for simplicity that the name 'Shakespeare' simply means "the English playwright who wrote *Hamlet, Macbeth* and *Romeo and Juliet*." If the orthodox theory of names is correct, then the sentence,

> Someone is Shakespeare iff he is an English playwright who is sole author of Hamlet, Macbeth, and Romeo and Juliet,

should express a necessary, *a priori* truth. On the contrary, however, it might have come to pass that Shakespeare elected to enter a profession in law instead of becoming a writer. Furthermore, it is possible, and is not ruled out solely by semantic reflection, that Francis Bacon should go on to write these plays. These intuitions are supported by a complementary intuition: that 'Shakespeare' continues to refer to the same person even with respect to non-actual possible worlds in which Shakespeare lacks the distinguishing characteristics that we actually use to identify him—i.e., even in discourse about such a counterfactual scenario. One important consequence of the direct-reference theory is that any proper name is a *rigid designator* (Kripke), i.e. it designates the same thing with respect to every possible world in which that thing exists and does not designate anything else with respect to other possible worlds.

One example of the semantic arguments for the direct-reference theory comes from Donnellan: According to the orthodox theory, the semantic content of the name 'Thales' is determined by a description such as 'the Greek philosopher who held that all is water'. But suppose that the man referred to by writers from whom our use of the name 'Thales' derives never genuinely believed that all is water but was thought to, owing to some error or hoax, and that, by coincidence, there was a Greek hermit who did hold this bizarre view, though he bears no historical connection to us. Contrary to the orthodox theory, our name 'Thales' would nevertheless refer to the first of the two. This argument seems to reveal also that the surrounding settings in which speakers find themselves, and not merely the concepts evoked in them, are crucial to determining the referents of the names they use. In a word, the securing of a referent for a name is a *contextual* phenomenon. Donnellan and Kripke have provided partial accounts of the securing of a referent for a name by means of historical chains of communication. Putnam has given a similar account of certain terms designating something by means of a "division of linguistic labor." Because of these accounts the direct-reference theory is sometimes called the *causal theory of reference*. Further exploration of direct reference and related notions—rigid designation, social linguistic networks, context—has led to important advances in cognate fields (for example, the recognition that not only linguistic meaning but also psychological or cognitive content is determined socially or contextually).

Important though it has proved itself to be, the theory of direct reference is not without its detractors. Difficult problems arise in connection with attributions of propositional attitude and in connection with non-referring names. Many language philosophers see these problems as sufficiently serious to warrant the rejection of direct reference. Many urge some version or variant of the orthodox theory. Most important, direct-reference theory still leaves us with our original question: What, then, is the semantic content of a name?

The present anthology gives a very lively sense of the continuing development of direct-reference theory and of the continuing intriguing debate concerning content and direct reference.

Santa Barbara, California

ON SENSE AND DIRECT REFERENCE*

Ben Caplan

1. Millianism and Fregeanism

There is a connection between language and the world. For example, we can use sentences to say things about the world. There is also a connection between language and thought. For example, we can use sentences to express things that we think. These two connections suggest two broad pictures about how language gets it content, about how sentences can be used to say the things and express the thoughts that they are used to do. The first picture focuses on the connection between language and the world. According to this first picture, language gets its content directly from the world: it is the objects, properties, and relations in the world that determine what the content of language is. The second picture, by contrast, focuses on the connection between language and thought. According to this second picture, language gets its content from thought: it is the things that we think that determine what the content of language is. It is natural to think of two competing views in the philosophy of language—namely, Millianism and Fregeanism—as being developments of these two contrasting pictures.

Millianism and Fregeanism agree that sentences express—that is, semantically express—propositions, where propositions are abstract objects that are the primary bearers of truth-values and that are the objects of attitudes such as believing and asserting.[1] Millianism and Fregeanism also agree that propositions are structured. This means that the proposition expressed by

(1) Cary is debonair.

—for example—can be represented as the ordered pair ⟨C, *being debonair*⟩, where C is something that corresponds to 'Cary'.[2]

But Millianism and Fregeanism disagree about the propositions expressed by sentences that contain names.[3] According to Millianism, sentences that contain names express singular propositions (if they express any propositions at all). This means that, in the proposition expressed by (1), C is Cary himself. According to

---

* This essay overlaps Caplan forthcoming a, b. For comments and discussion, thanks to David Braun, Michael Glanzberg, and David Sanson. For funding in the form of a Standard Research Grant (410-04-0702), thanks to the Social Sciences and Humanities Research Council of Canada (SSHRC).

[1] On propositions, see, for example, Cartwright 1962, 1968. On structured propositions, see, for example, Kaplan 1989, Soames 1987a. A list of named (or numbered) sentences is provided in the appendix.

[2] In the text, complications about what goes in the non-C slot are glossed over; it is assumed that what goes in that slot is a property: namely, *being debonair*. Other complications about other slots are also glossed over elsewhere in the text.

[3] Millianism and Fregeanism also disagree about the propositions expressed by sentences that contain demonstratives and indexicals; but, for the most part, in the text those expressions will be ignored in favor of names.

Millianism, the proposition expressed by (1) can thus be represented as ⟨Cary, *being debonair*⟩. This captures the idea that it is entities in the world—for example, Cary—that determine what the content of language is.[4] By contrast, Fregeanism denies that sentences that contain names express singular propositions. According to Fregeanism, in the proposition expressed by (1), C is not Cary himself; rather, C is a mode of presentation of Cary, $MP_{'Cary'}$, something that is a way of thinking about Cary or that captures an agent's perspective on Cary. According to Fregeanism, the proposition expressed by (1) can thus be represented as ⟨$MP_{'Cary'}$, *being debonair*⟩. This captures the idea that it is what we think that determines what the content of language is.[5]

Different versions of Fregeanism disagree about what modes of presentation are. On the one hand, according to Fregean Descriptivism modes of presentation are descriptive: that is, they pick out objects by describing them as having certain properties. As a result, according to Fregean Descriptivism a sentence that contains a name expresses a descriptive proposition: that is, a proposition that contains a descriptive mode of presentation. For example, according to Fregean Descriptivism $MP_{'Cary'}$ might pick out Cary by describing him as having the property *being the actor who played C. K. Dexter Haven in* The Philadelphia Story; and (1) might express the same descriptive proposition as

> (1D) The actor who played C. K. Dexter Haven in *The Philadelphia Story* is debonair.[6]

On the other hand, according to Fregean Nondescriptivism modes of presentation are nondescriptive: that is, they pick out objects, but not by describing them as having certain properties. For example, according to Fregean Nondescriptivism $MP_{'Cary'}$ might be an abstract object that is individuated by an agent's cognitive abilities,[7] or something that contains the linguistic expression 'Cary',[8] or a *sui generis* entity of some other kind. Fregean Nondescriptivism and Fregean Descriptivism agree that, since it is singular, the proposition represented as ⟨Cary, *being debonair*⟩ is the wrong sort of proposition to be the proposition expressed by (1). But, unlike Fregean Descriptivism, Fregean Nondescriptivism says that, since it is descriptive, the proposition expressed by (1D) is also the wrong sort of proposition to be the proposition expressed by (1).

Since Millianism and Fregeanism disagree about the propositions expressed by sentences that contain names, Millianism and Fregeanism disagree about the contents of names, where the content of a name is what it contributes to the propositions expressed by sentences that contain it. According to Millianism,

---

[4] On Millianism, see, for example, Kaplan 1989; Salmon 1986; Soames 1987a, 1987b, 2002. The view is named after John Stuart Mill (see Mill 1843), although he probably wasn't a Millian.

[5] On Fregeanism, see, for example, Frege 1892; McDowell 1977; Dummett 1981; Evans 1982; Peacocke 1983, 1986, 1992.

[6] 'D' is for 'descriptive'. On Fregean Descriptivism, see, for example, Dummett 1981, Stanley 1997, Jackson 1998, Sosa 2001.

[7] See, for example, McDowell 1977; Evans 1982; Peacocke 1983, 1986, 1992.

[8] See, for example, Richard 1990.

names are directly referential. This means that the content of a name is nothing other than the object that it refers to. For example, according to Millianism the content of 'Cary' is Cary himself.[9] By contrast, Fregeanism denies that names are directly referential. According to Fregeanism, the content of a name is not the object that it refers to; rather, the content of a name is a mode of presentation of that object. For example, according to Fregeanism the content of 'Cary' is $MP_{\text{'Cary'}}$, a mode of presentation that presents Cary. This mode of presentation is also known as a sense.

2. Millian Problems

2.1. The Problems

Although Millianism seems to many to be an attractive view about the connection between language and the world, Millianism faces several well-known problems.[10] Here's one. For example, it seems that

(2) Cary is Cary.

and

(3) Cary is Archie.

differ in cognitive value: (2) is trivial, uninformative, and *a priori;* whereas (3) is nontrivial, informative, and *a posteriori.* But 'Cary' and 'Archie' corefer. ('Cary Grant' is the screen name of Archibald Alexander Leach.) So, according to Millianism, (2) and (3) express the same singular proposition: one that can be represented as the ordered triple ⟨Cary, the identity relation, Cary⟩.[11] As a result, it seems that Millianism cannot account for the apparent difference in cognitive value between (2) and (3). Let's call this *The Problem of Cognitive Value for Simple Sentences.*[12]

Here's another. For example, it seems that

(2Bel) George believes that Cary is Cary.

and

(3Bel) George believes that Cary is Archie.

---

[9] Millianism is also known as 'the direct reference theory' or 'neo-Russellianism'. Unlike 'the direct reference theory', 'Millianism' is sometimes reserved for a claim about names—say, the claim that the semantic function of a name is exhausted by its having the bearer that it does—that doesn't presuppose the existence of propositions. Since not everyone who is willing to accept the claim about names is willing to accept the existence of propositions, it is sometimes handy to have a name for that claim. Although the existence of proposition is not beyond dispute, it is assumed in the text that propositions do exist. In keeping with that assumption, 'Millianism' is used in the text for a claim that presupposes the existence of propositions.

[10] These problems can be traced back to Frege 1892.

[11] This ordered triple is ⟨Cary, the identity relation, Archie⟩, or ⟨Archie, the identity relation, Cary⟩, or ⟨Archie, the identity relation, Archie⟩.

[12] A simple sentence is simply a sentence that doesn't contain propositional-attitude verbs, modal operators, or other nonextensional fancy stuff.

can differ in truth-value: (2Bel) can be true even if (3Bel) is false.[13] (2Bel) expresses a proposition, about George and the proposition expressed by (2), to the effect that he bears a propositional attitude—namely, the belief relation—to it; and (3Bel) expresses a proposition, about George and the proposition expressed by (3), to the effect that he bears that propositional attitude to it. And, according to Millianism, (2) and (3) express the same proposition. So, according to Millianism, (2Bel) and (3Bel) also express the same proposition, one that can be represented as the ordered triple ⟨George, the belief relation, ⟨Cary, the identity relation, Cary⟩⟩.[14] As a result, it seems that Millianism cannot account for the apparent difference in truth-value between (2Bel) and (3Bel). Let's call this *The Problem of Truth-Value for Propositional-Attitude Ascriptions.*

Empty names pose a host of further problems for Millianism.[15] An empty name is a name that doesn't refer to anything. For example, suppose that Katharine introduces the name 'Sparkie' to refer to the lighter in her pocket, if there is one, and to nothing otherwise. If it turns out that Katharine's pockets are empty, then 'Sparkie' is also empty. The source of the problems that empty names pose for Millianism is that it seems that Millianism entails that a sentence that contains an empty name doesn't express any proposition at all. According to Millianism, propositions are structured; so, if

(4) Sparkie doesn't exist.

—for example—expresses a proposition, then that proposition can be represented as the ordered pair ⟨S, *not existing*⟩, where S is something that corresponds to 'Sparkie'. And, according to Millianism, sentences that contain names express singular propositions, if they express any propositions at all; so, if (4) expresses a proposition represented as ⟨S, *not existing*⟩, then S is the object that 'Sparkie' refers to. But, since 'Sparkie' is empty, there is no object that it refers to. So there is no object in the S slot in ⟨S, *not existing*⟩. As a result, it seems that there is no singular proposition for (4) to express and hence that, according to Millianism, (4) doesn't express any proposition at all. Let's call the view that sentences that contain empty names don't express any proposition at all *The No Proposition View.*

The No Proposition View apparently has a number of consequences that are apparently counterintuitive. Here's one. You might think that a sentence is meaningful only if it expresses a proposition. If that's right, then The No Proposition View entails that (4), for example, is meaningless. But (4) doesn't seem meaningless. Let's call this *The Problem of Meaningfulness for Sentences That Contain Empty Names.* Here's another. You might think that a sentence

---

[13] 'Bel' is for 'belief'.

[14] This ordered triple is ⟨George, the belief relation, ⟨Cary, the identity relation, Archie⟩⟩, or ⟨George, the belief relation, ⟨Archie, the identity relation, Cary⟩⟩, or ⟨George, the belief relation, ⟨Archie, the identity relation, Archie⟩⟩.

[15] These problems are nicely catalogued in Braun forthcoming. See also Caplan forthcoming a.

inherits its truth-value from the proposition it expresses. If that's right, then The No Proposition View entails that, for example, (4) and

(4Bel) Katharine believes that Sparkie doesn't exist.

have no truth-value. But (4) and (4Bel) seem true. Let's call this *The Problem of Truth-Value for Sentences That Contain Empty Names*. And here's a third. You might think that a person can sincerely and assertively utter a sentence only if she believes the proposition that it expresses. If that's right, then The No Proposition View entails that no one can sincerely and assertively utter (4), for example. But it seems that someone could sincerely and assertively utter (4). Let's call this *The Problem of Belief and Sincere Assertive Utterance for Sentences That Contain Empty Names*. Let's call these problems—namely, The Problem of Meaningfulness for Sentences That Contain Empty Names, The Problem of Truth-Value for Sentences That Contain Empty Names, and The Problem of Belief and Sincere Assertive Utterance for Sentences That Contain Empty Names—*The Problems for Sentences That Contain Empty Names*. Because of The Problem of Cognitive Value for Simple Sentences, The Problem of Truth-Value for Propositional-Attitude Ascriptions, and The Problems for Sentences That Contain Empty Names, many philosophers have concluded that Millianism should be rejected in favor of Fregeanism.

2.2. Fregean Solutions

Fregeanism can solve just about all of the problems that beset Millianism.[16] According to Fregeanism, 'Cary' and 'Archie' have different contents: the content of 'Cary' is one mode of presentation, $MP_{\text{'Cary'}}$; whereas the content of 'Archie' is a distinct mode of presentation, $MP_{\text{'Archie'}}$. (If modes of presentation are descriptive, then $MP_{\text{'Cary'}}$ might be something that presents someone as being the actor who played C. K. Dexter Haven in *The Philadelphia Story*, whereas $MP_{\text{'Archie'}}$ might be something that presents someone—the same person, as it turns out—as having been the boy from Bristol who ran away to join an acrobatic troupe.) In that case, (2) and (3) express different propositions: (2) expresses a proposition that can be represented as the ordered triple ⟨$MP_{\text{'Cary'}}$, the identity relation, $MP_{\text{'Cary'}}$⟩, whereas (3) expresses a proposition that can be represented as the ordered triple ⟨$MP_{\text{'Cary'}}$, the identity relation, $MP_{\text{'Archie'}}$⟩. According to Fregeanism, (2) and (3) differ in cognitive value, because they express different propositions. This is a Fregean solution to The Problem of Cognitive Value for Simple Sentences.

According to Fregeanism, (2Bel) and (3Bel) express different propositions: (2Bel) expresses a proposition that can be represented as the ordered triple ⟨George, the belief relation, ⟨$MP_{\text{'Cary'}}$, the identity relation, $MP_{\text{'Cary'}}$⟩⟩; whereas (3Bel) expresses a proposition that can be represented as ⟨George, the belief relation, ⟨$MP_{\text{'Cary'}}$, the identity relation, $MP_{\text{'Archie'}}$⟩⟩. And these propositions can differ in truth-value, because George can bear the belief relation to the proposition

---

[16] These solutions can be traced back to Frege 1892.

represented as $\langle MP_{\text{'Cary'}}$, the identity relation, $MP_{\text{'Cary'}}\rangle$ without bearing that relation to the proposition represented as $\langle MP_{\text{'Cary'}}$, the identity relation, $MP_{\text{'Archie'}}\rangle$. Since the propositions that (2Bel) and (3Bel) express can differ in truth-value, so can (2Bel) and (3Bel) themselves. This is a Fregean solution to The Problem of Truth-Value for Propositional-Attitude Ascriptions.

Fregeanism doesn't entail The No Proposition View. Fregeanism and Millianism agree that the proposition expressed by (4) can be represented as $\langle S,$ *not existing*$\rangle$. But, according to Fregeanism, S isn't the object that 'Sparkie' refers to; rather, S is a mode of presentation, $MP_{\text{'Sparkie'}}$, that corresponds to 'Sparkie'. If $MP_{\text{'Sparkie'}}$ is a descriptive mode of presentation, then it might be something that would pick out the unique object that has the property *being a lighter in Katharine's pocket*, if there were such an object; but perhaps $MP_{\text{'Sparkie'}}$ is a non-descriptive mode of presentation instead.[17]

Since it doesn't entail The No Proposition View, Fregeanism can solve many of The Problems for Sentences That Contain Empty Names. First, Fregeanism can solve The Problem of Meaningfulness for Sentences That Contain Empty Names: (4) is meaningful, because it expresses the proposition represented as $\langle MP_{\text{'Sparkie'}},$ *not existing*$\rangle$. Second, Fregeanism can solve The Problem of Truth-Value for Sentences That Contain Empty Names, at least for propositional-attitude ascriptions like (4Bel): (4Bel) can be true, because Katharine can believe the proposition represented as $\langle MP_{\text{'Sparkie'}},$ *not existing*$\rangle$. And, third, Fregeanism can solve The Problem of Belief and Sincere Assertive Utterance for Sentences That Contain Empty Names: speakers can sincerely and assertively utter (4), because they can believe the proposition represented as $\langle MP_{\text{'Sparkie'}},$ *not existing*$\rangle$.

But Fregeanism doesn't straightforwardly solve The Problem of Truth-Value for Sentences That Contain Empty Names when it comes to sentences like (4). For (4) is true if and only if the proposition that it expresses, the proposition represented as $\langle MP_{\text{'Sparkie'}},$ *not existing*$\rangle$, is true; and that proposition is true if and only if the object that $MP_{\text{'Sparkie'}}$ presents has the property *not existing*. But there is no object that $MP_{\text{'Sparkie'}}$ presents and hence it is not the case that the object that $MP_{\text{'Sparkie'}}$ presents has the property *not existing*. So (4) isn't true (either because it's false or because it lacks a truth-value altogether). Still, many philosophers think that, overall, Fregeanism fares better than Millianism in handling the problems that beset Millianism.

2.3. Sense Millianism

To solve the problems that beset Millianism, Fregeanism appeals to propositions that contain modes of presentation. But Millian views can appeal to modes of

---

[17] If there is such a mode of presentation as MP'Sparkie', then there can be empty modes of presentation: that is, modes of presentation that don't actually present anything. The existence of empty modes of presentation isn't particularly controversial if Fregean Descriptivism is true. But some Fregean Nondescriptivists reject the existence of empty modes of presentation. See, for example, McDowell 1977, Evans 1982. In the text, it is assumed that empty modes of presentation exist.

presentation, too. Let's call any Millian view that appeals to modes of presentation a *Sense Millian* view.[18] According to one Sense Millian view, sentences that contain names express singular propositions (if they express any propositions at all); but, when they use those sentences, speakers communicate—that is, nonsemantically communicate (or assert, or convey, or implicate)—propositions that contain modes of presentation.[19] For example, according to this Millian view, (1) expresses the singular proposition represented as ⟨Cary, *being debonair*⟩; but, when they use (1), speakers communicate the proposition represented as ⟨$MP_{'Cary'}$, *being debonair*⟩. Perhaps this proposition is descriptive (for example, the proposition expressed by (1D)); perhaps not. Sense Millians disagree about what modes of presentation are.[20,21]

According to Millianism, (2) and (3) express the same singular proposition: namely, the proposition represented as ⟨Cary, the identity relation, Cary⟩. But, according to Sense Millianism, when they use (2) and (3) speakers communicate different propositions: when they use (2), they communicate the proposition represented as ⟨$MP_{'Cary'}$, the identity relation, $MP_{'Cary'}$⟩; whereas, when they use (3), they communicate the proposition represented as ⟨$MP_{'Cary'}$, the identity relation, $MP_{'Archie'}$⟩. Because speakers communicate different propositions when they use (2) and (3), (2) and (3) seem to differ in cognitive value. This is a Sense Millian solution to The Problem of Cognitive Value for Simple Sentences.

According to Sense Millianism, (2Bel) and (3Bel) express the same proposition: namely, the proposition represented as ⟨George, the belief relation, ⟨Cary, the belief relation, Cary⟩⟩. But, according to Sense Millianism, when they use (2Bel) and (3Bel) speakers communicate different propositions: when they use (2Bel), they communicate the proposition represented as ⟨George, the belief relation, ⟨$MP_{'Cary'}$, the identity relation, $MP_{'Cary'}$⟩⟩; whereas, when they use (3Bel), they communicate the proposition represented as ⟨George, the belief relation, ⟨$MP_{'Cary'}$, the identity relation, $MP_{'Archie'}$⟩⟩. (2Bel) seems true, because speakers believe the proposition that they communicate when they use it (namely, the proposition represented as ⟨George, the belief relation, ⟨$MP_{'Cary'}$, the identity relation, $MP_{'Cary'}$⟩⟩);

---

[18] It is tempting to call these views *Sensible Millian* views, but that carries the unwanted suggestion that other Millian views aren't sensible.

[19] This sort of view can be found in Soames 2002, Thau 2002, and—perhaps—Salmon 1986. This sort of view coupled with the claim that modes of presentation are descriptive has been called *Millian Descriptivism*. See Caplan forthcoming b.

[20] For a Sense Millian view on which modes of presentation are descriptive, see Thau 2002. For a Sense Millian view on which at least some modes of presentation are descriptive, see Soames 2002. For a Sense Millian view on which modes of presentation are not descriptive, see Salmon 1986. For more on Salmon's view, see note 21.

[21] There are other Sense Millian views. For example, according to another Sense Millian view, sentences that contain names express singular propositions (if they express any propositions at all); but agents' cognitive relations to those propositions are mediated by modes of presentation. (This sort of view can be found in Braun 1998, 2002. Parts of this view can be found in Salmon 1986.) In the text, these other Sense Millian views are ignored in favor of the view that, when they use sentences that contain names, speakers communicate propositions that contain modes of presentation.

but (3Bel) doesn't seem true, because speakers don't believe the proposition that they communicate when they use it (namely, the proposition represented as ⟨George, the belief relation, ⟨MP$_{\text{'Cary'}}$, the identity relation, MP$_{\text{'Archie'}}$⟩⟩). This is a Sense Millian solution to The Problem of Truth-Value for Propositional-Attitude Ascriptions.

Sense Millianism can also solve The Problems for Sentences That Contain Empty Names. First, Sense Millianism can solve The Problem of Meaningfulness for Sentences That Contain Empty Names: (4) seems meaningful, because speakers use it to communicate a proposition (namely, the proposition represented as ⟨MP$_{\text{'Sparkie'}}$, *not existing*⟩). Second, Sense Millianism can solve The Problem of Truth-Value for Sentences That Contain Empty Names: (4) seems true, because speakers use it to communicate a proposition (namely, the proposition represented as ⟨MP$_{\text{'Sparkie'}}$, *not existing*⟩) that they believe; and (4Bel) seems true, because speakers also use it to communicate a proposition (namely, the proposition that can be represented as the ordered triple ⟨Katharine, the belief relation, ⟨MP$_{\text{'Sparkie'}}$, *not existing*⟩⟩) that they believe. And, third, Sense Millianism can solve The Problem of Belief and Sincere Assertive Utterance for Sentences That Contain Empty Names: speakers can sincerely and assertively utter (4), because they can believe the proposition represented as ⟨MP$_{\text{'Sparkie'}}$, *not existing*⟩.

3. Fregean Problems

3.1. The Problems

Although Fregeanism seems to many to be an attractive view about the connection between language and thought, Fregeanism faces problems of its own. Here's one.[22] Suppose that George assertively utters (1). In that case, it seems that

(1Bel) George believes that Cary is debonair. is true.

It also seems that

(5Bel) George believes that you are debonair.
(6Bel) George believes that he is debonair.
(7Bel) George believes that I am debonair.

are true in the appropriate contexts: when one is speaking to Cary, when one is speaking about Cary, and when Cary is speaking, respectively. According to Fregeanism, (1) and

(5) You are debonair.
(6) He is debonair.
(7) I am debonair.

express different propositions (even in the appropriate contexts): the proposition expressed by (1) contains a mode of presentation—namely, MP$_{\text{'Cary'}}$, which corresponds to 'Cary'—that presents Cary in one way; whereas the propositions

---

[22]See, for example, Soames 1987b, Braun 1998.

expressed by (5)–(7) contain distinct modes of presentation—namely, modes of presentation that correspond to 'you', 'he', and 'I'—that present Cary in other ways.[23] (1Bel) and (5Bel)–(7Bel) express propositions, about George and the propositions expressed by (1) and (5)–(7), to the effect that he bears the belief relation to those propositions. According to Fregeanism, (1) and (5)–(7) express different propositions; so (1Bel) and (5Bel)–(7Bel) express different propositions, too. As a result, it seems that Fregeanism cannot account for the apparent sameness of truth-value among (1Bel) and (5Bel)–(7Bel). Let's call this *The Reverse Problem of Truth-Value for Propositioned-Attitude Ascriptions.*

Fregean Descriptivism, in particular, also faces several well-known problems.[24] Here's one. For example, it seems that

(8) Peano is Italian.

is true. But the descriptive mode of presentation that speakers associate with 'Peano' might be given by 'the discoverer of the Peano axioms', and that descriptive mode of presentation picks out Richard Dedekind rather than Giuseppe Peano. In that case, assuming that the descriptive mode of presentation that is the content of a name is the descriptive mode of presentation that speakers associate with that name, Fregean Descriptivism entails that (8) expresses the proposition that the discoverer of the Peano axioms is Italian; and that proposition is false, since Dedekind is not Italian. So it seems that Fregean Descriptivism cannot account for the apparent truth-value of (8). Let's call this *The Problem of Truth-Value for Simple Sentences.* (In the literature, this problem is known as the semantic argument against Fregean Descriptivism.)

Here are two others. For example, it seems that

(9) If Cary exists, then Cary is an actor.

is neither necessary nor *a priori:* Cary might have existed without ever becoming an actor; and, independently of sense experience, one cannot be justified in believing that Cary is an actor if he exists. But the descriptive mode of presentation that speakers associate with 'Cary' might be given by 'the actor who played C. K. Dexter Haven in *The Philadelphia Story*'. In that case, assuming again that the descriptive mode of presentation that is the content of a name is the descriptive mode of presentation that speakers associate with that name, Fregean Descriptivism entails that (9) expresses the proposition that, if the actor who played C. K. Dexter Haven in *The Philadelphia Story* exists, then the actor who played C. K. Dexter Haven in *The Philadelphia Story* is an actor; and that proposition is necessary *a priori.* (9) doesn't seem necessary; but, according to Fregean Descriptivism, the proposition it expresses might be; so it seems that Fregean Descriptivism cannot account for the modal profile of (9), where the modal profile

---

[23]Here Fregeanism is being extended from names like 'Cary' to demonstratives and indexicals like 'you', 'he', and 'I'.

[24]These problems come from Kripke 1972 and Kaplan 1989, among other places. See also Salmon 1981; Soames 2002, 2004.

of a sentence includes information about whether it's necessary or contingent. Let's call this *The Problem of Modal Profile for Simple Sentences.* (In the literature, this problem is known as the modal argument against Fregean Descriptivism.) Similarly, (9) doesn't seem *a priori;* but, according to Fregean Descriptivism, the proposition it expresses might be; so it seems that Fregean Descriptivism cannot account for the epistemic profile of (9) either, where the epistemic profile of a sentence includes information about whether it's *a priori* or *a posteriori.* Let's call this *The Problem of Epistemic Profile for Simple Sentences.* (In the literature, this problem is known as the epistemic argument against Fregean Descriptivism.) Because of The Reverse Problem of Truth-Value for Propositional-Attitude Ascriptions, some philosophers doubt that Fregeanism is true. And, because of The Problem of Truth-Value for Simple Sentences, The Problem of Modal Profile for Simple Sentences, and The Problem of Epistemic Profile for Simple Sentences, many philosophers have concluded that Fregean Descriptivism, in particular, is false.

3.2. Millian Solutions

Millianism can solve the problems that beset Fregeanism in general and Fregean Descriptivism in particular. Millianism can solve The Reverse Problem of Truth-Value for Propositional-Attitude Ascriptions. According to Millianism, (1) and (5)–(7) express the same proposition (in the appropriate contexts).[25] So (1Bel) and (5Bel)–(7Bel) also express the same proposition (in the appropriate contexts). As a result, (1Bel) and (5Bel)–(7Bel) have the same truth-value, as desired.

Millianism can also solve The Problem of Truth-Value for Simple Sentences. According to Millianism, (8) expresses a singular proposition that can be represented as ⟨Peano, *being Italian*⟩. Even if speakers think that Peano is the discoverer of the Peano axioms, it is not the case that that proposition is true if and only if the discoverer of the Peano axioms has the property *being Italian;* rather, that proposition is true if and only if Peano has the property *being Italian.* And Peano does have that property, so the proposition represented as ⟨Peano, *being Italian*⟩ is true, as desired.

And Millianism can solve The Problem of Modal Profile for Simple Sentences and The Problem of Epistemic Profile for Simple Sentences. According to Millianism, (9) express a conditional proposition whose antecedent is a singular proposition that can be represented as the ordered pair ⟨Cary, *existing*⟩ and whose consequent is a singular proposition that can be represented as the ordered pair ⟨Cary, *being an actor*⟩. Let's call this conditional proposition *Condie.* Unlike the proposition that, if the actor who played C. K. Dexter Haven in *The Philadelphia Story* exists, then the actor who played C. K. Dexter Haven in *The Philadelphia Story* is an actor, Condie is neither necessary nor *a priori.* Since it is possible that Cary exists without having the property *being an actor,* it is possible that Condie's antecedent—namely, the singular proposition represented as ⟨Cary, *existing*⟩—is

---

[25] Here Millianism is also being extended from names like 'Cary' to demonstratives and indexicals like 'you', 'he', and 'I'.

true and its consequent—namely, the singular proposition represented as ⟨Cary, *being an actor*⟩—is false; so it is not necessary that Condie is true. And, independently of sense experience, one cannot be justified in believing that, if the proposition represented as ⟨Cary, *existing*⟩ is true, then so is the proposition represented as ⟨Cary, *being an actor*⟩; so Condie is not *a priori* either.

3.3. Object Fregeanism

To solve the problems that beset Fregean Descriptivism, in particular, a number of technical views have been proposed: for example, that the descriptive mode of presentation that is the content of a name is given by an 'actually'-rigidified definite description like 'the x such that x is actually the actor who played C. K. Dexter Haven in *The Philadelphia Story*,' or that the definite description that gives the content of a name must take wide scope with respect to modal operators (even in the metalanguage).[26] But the possibility of Sense Millianism, which co-opts Fregean resources (namely, modes of presentation) to solve the problems that beset Millianism, suggests a simpler solution. To solve the problems that beset Fregean Descriptivism, Millianism appeals to singular propositions, which contain objects. But Fregean views can appeal to objects and the singular propositions that contain them, too. Let's call any Fregean view that appeals to objects or singular propositions an *Object Fregean* view.[27] According to one Object Fregean view, sentences that contain names express propositions that contain modes of presentation; but, when they use those sentences, speakers communicate singular propositions. For example, according to this Object Fregean view, (1) expresses the proposition represented as ⟨MP$_{\text{'Cary'}}$, *being debonair*⟩; but, when they use (1), speakers communicate the singular proposition represented as ⟨Cary, *being debonair*⟩. This Object Fregean view is just like the Sense Millian view discussed above, except that the proposition expressed by the sentence and the proposition communicated by the speaker have been swapped.[28]

Object Fregeanism can solve The Problem of Truth-Value for Simple Sentences: even if (8) expresses a proposition that is false, (8) seems true, because

---

[26]*Pro* the rigidity view, see, for example, Plantinga 1978, Nelson 2002. *Contra* the rigidity view, see, for example, Soames 2002, Everett 2005. *Pro* the wide scope view, see, for example, Dummett 1981, Sosa 2001, Hunter 2005. *Contra* the wide scope view, see, for example, Soames 2002, Caplan 2005, Everett 2005.

[27]It is tempting to call these views *Singular Fregean* views, but that carries the unwanted suggestion that these views are odd. Perhaps these views are indeed odd, but that need not be reflected in their name.

[28]See Bach 1987. There could be other Object Fregean views. For example, according to another Object Fregean view, sentences that contain names express propositions that contain modes of presentation; but, when they bear cognitive relations to those propositions, agents have some object directly in mind. In the text, these other views are ignored in favor of the view that, when they use sentences that contain names, speakers communicate singular propositions.

when they use it speakers communicate a proposition (namely, the singular proposition represented as ⟨Peano, *being Italian*⟩) that they believe.[29]

Object Fregeanism can also solve The Problem of Modal Profile for Simple Sentences and The Problem of Epistemic Profile for Simple Sentences: even if (9) expresses a proposition that is necessary *a priori*, (9) seems neither necessary nor *a priori*, because when they use it speakers communicate a proposition (namely, Condie, the conditional proposition whose antecedent is the singular proposition represented as ⟨Cary, *existing*⟩ and whose consequent is the singular proposition represented as ⟨Cary, *being an actor*⟩) that they believe—correctly—to be neither necessary nor *a priori*.

In addition to solving the problems that beset Fregean Descriptivism in particular, Object Fregeanism can solve The Reverse Problem of Truth-Value for Propositional-Attitude Ascriptions: even if (1Bel) and (5Bel)–(7Bel) express different propositions, they seem to have the same truth-value, because when speakers use those sentences they communicate the same singular proposition (namely, the proposition represented as ⟨George, the belief relation, ⟨Cary, *being debonair*⟩⟩).

Object Fregeanism is not discussed much in the literature.[30] Perhaps that is because Object Fregeanism mimics Sense Millianism, and Fregeans tend to think that Sense Millianism doesn't work. Or perhaps it is because Object Fregeanism appeals to objects, and Fregeans tend to think that one can't have objects directly in mind. But Sense Millians cannot dismiss Object Fregeanism for these reasons.

4. Conclusion

Sense Millianism and Object Fregeanism both appeal to modes of presentation to solve problems about one group of cases (namely, those that concern intuitions about the cognitive value of simple sentences, about the truth-value of some propositional-attitude ascriptions, or about sentences that contain empty names); and both appeal to objects or singular propositions to solve problems about another group of cases (namely, those that concern intuitions about the truth-value of simple sentences, about the modal and epistemic profile of simple sentences, or about the truth-value of other propositional-attitude ascriptions). One further problem for both views is to explain, in a principled way, why one level (the propositions expressed by sentences that contain names, according to Object Fregeanism; something else, according to Sense Millianism) matters in the first group of cases but not in the second; and, conversely, why another level (the propositions expressed by sentences that contain names, according to Sense

---

[29] This solution is the converse of the Sense Millian solution to The Problem of Truth-Value for Propositional-Attitude Ascriptions: even if it is true, (3Bel) doesn't seem true, because when they use it speakers communicate a proposition (namely, the proposition represented as ⟨George, the belief relation, ⟨MP'$_{Cary}$, the identity relation, MP'$_{Archie}$⟩⟩) that they don't believe.

[30] But see Bach 1987.

Millianism; something else, according to Object Fregeanism) matters in the second group of cases but not in the first. This further problem is, it seems, pressing and difficult for both views.[31]

Whatever the prospects for their viability are, the possibility of Sense Millianism and Object Fregeanism suggests that the dispute between Millianism and Fregeanism should be understood, not as a debate about *whether* there are modes of presentation, but rather as a debate about *where* there are such modes of presentation.[32] Fregeanism says that such modes of presentation are contained in the propositions expressed by sentences that contain names, whereas Millianism says they're not—although they might be contained in the propositions that speakers communicate when they use sentences that contain names (or they might otherwise mediate agents' cognitive relations to singular propositions).

APPENDIX: NAMED SENTENCES

(1)   Cary is debonair.

(1D)   The actor who played C. K. Dexter Haven in *The Philadelphia Story* is debonair.

(1Bel) George believes that Cary is debonair.

(2)   Cary is Cary.

(2Bel) George believes that Cary is Cary.

(3)   Cary is Archie.

(3Bel) George believes that Cary is Archie.

(4)   Sparkie doesn't exist.

(4Bel) Katharine believes that Sparkie doesn't exist.

(5)   You are debonair.

(5Bel) George believes that you are debonair.

(6)   He is debonair.

(6Bel) George believes that he is debonair.

(7)   I am debonair.

(7Bel) George believes that I am debonair.

(8)   Peano is Italian.

(9)   If Cary exists, then Cary is an actor.

---

[31] This sort of problem is pressed against one version of Sense Millianism—namely, Millian Descriptivism (see note 19)—in Everett 2003, McKinsey 2005, Sider and Braun forthcoming, Caplan forthcoming b.

[32] This assumes that it isn't the case that too much is built into the notion of a mode of presentation. Among other things, this assumes that it is not built into the notion of a mode of presentation that it is the sort of thing that is the content of a name or that it is the sort of thing that is contained in propositions expressed by sentences that contain names.

BIBLIOGRAPHY

Bach, Kent. 1987. *Thought and Reference*. Oxford: Clarendon.

Braun, David. 1998. "Understanding Belief Reports." *Philosophical Review* 107.4 (Oct.): 555–595.

———. 2002. "Cognitive Significance, Attitude Ascriptions, and Ways of Believing Propositions." *Philosophical Studies* 108.1–2 (March):65–81.

———. forthcoming. "Empty Names, Mythical Names, Fictional Names." *Noûs*. Caplan, Ben. 2005. "Against Widescopism." *Philosophical Studies* 125.2 (Aug.):167–190.

———. forthcoming a. "Empty Names." *The Encyclopedia of Language and Linguistics*. 2nd ed. Ed. Keith Brown. *(Philosophy and Language* vol., ed. Robert Stainton and Alex Barber.) Oxford: Elsevier.

———. forthcoming b. "Millian Descriptivism." *Philosophical Studies*. Cartwright, Richard. 1962. "Propositions." 1961. *Analytical Philosophy*. Ed. R. J. Butler. Oxford: Blackwell. 81–103. Reprinted (with addenda) in Cartwright 1987:33–53.

———. 1968. "Propositions Again." *Noûs* 2.3 (Aug.):229–246. Reprinted in Cartwright 1987:55–70.

———. 1987. *Philosophical Essays*. Cambridge, MA: MIT Press.

Dummett, Michael A. E. 1981. *Frege: Philosophy of Language*. 1973. 2nd ed. Cambridge, MA: Harvard University Press.

Evans, Gareth. 1982. *The Varieties of Reference*. Ed. John McDowell. Oxford: Clarendon.

Everett, Anthony. 2003. "Empty Names and 'Gappy' Propositions." *Philosophical Studies* 116.1 (Oct.):1–36.

———. 2005. "Recent Defenses of Descriptivism." *Mind and Language* 20.1 (Feb.): 103–139.

Frege, Gottlob. 1892. "Über Sinn und Bedeutung" ["On Sense and Reference"]. *Zeitschrift für Philosophie und philosophische Kritik* 100:25–50. Trans. by Max Black as "On Sense and Meaning" in Frege 1980:56–78.

———. 1980. *Translations from the Philosophical Writings of Gottlob Frege*. 1952. 3rd ed. Ed. Peter T. Geach and Max Black. Oxford: Blackwell.

Hunter, David. 2005. "Soames and Widescopism." *Philosophical Studies* 123.3 (April): 231–241.

Jackson, Frank. 1998. "Reference and Description Revisited." In *Philosophical Perspectives*. Vol. 12 *(Language, Mind, and Ontology)*. Ed. James E. Tomberlin. Boston, MA: Blackwell. 201–218.

Kaplan, David. 1989. "Demonstratives: An Essay on the Semantics, Logic, Metaphysics, and Epistemology of Demonstratives and Other Indexicals." 1977. In *Themes from Kaplan*. Ed. Joseph Almog, John Perry, and Howard Wettstein. Oxford: Oxford University Press. 481–563.

Kripke, Saul A. 1972. "Naming and Necessity." 1970. In *Semantics of Natural Language*. Ed. Donald Davidson and Gilbert Harman. Synthese Library 40. Dordrecht: Reidel. 253–355, 763–769. Reprinted (with preface) as Kripke 1980.

———. 1980. *Naming and Necessity*. Cambridge, MA: Harvard University Press.

McDowell, John. 1977. "On the Sense and Reference of a Proper Name." *Mind* 86.342 (April):159–185. Reprinted in McDowell 1998:171–198.

———. 1998. *Meaning, Knowledge, and Reality*. Cambridge, MA: Harvard University Press.

McKinsey, Michael. 2005. "Critical Notice of Scott Soames, *Beyond Rigidity.*" *Canadian Journal of Philosophy* 35.1 (March):149–168.

Mill, John Stuart. 1843. *A System of Logic, Ratiocinative and Inductive: Being a Connected View of the Principles of Evidence, and Methods of Scientific Investigation.* London: Parker.

Nelson, Michael. 2002. "Descriptivism Defended." *Noûs* 36.3 (Sept.):408–435.

Peacocke, Christopher. 1983. *Sense and Content: Experience, Thought, and Their Relations.* Oxford: Clarendon.

——. 1986. *Thoughts: An Essay on Content.* Aristotelian Society 4. New York, NY: Blackwell.

——. 1992. *A Study of Concepts.* Representation and Mind. Cambridge, MA: MIT Press.

Plantinga, Alvin. 1978. "The Boethian Compromise." *American Philosophical Quarterly* 15.2 (April):129-138. Reprinted in Plantinga 2003:122–138.

——. 2003. *Essays in the Metaphysics of Modality.* Ed. Matthew Davidson. Oxford: Oxford University Press.

Salmon, Nathan. 1981. *Reference and Essence.* Princeton, NJ: Princeton University Press.

——. 1986. *Frege's Puzzle.* Bradford. Cambridge, MA: MIT. Press.

Sider, Theodore, and David Braun. forthcoming. "Kripke's Revenge." *Philosophical Studies.*

Soames, Scott. 1987a. "Direct Reference, Propositional Attitudes, and Semantic Content." 1983-1984. *Philosophical Topics* 15.1 (Spring):44–87.

——. 1987b. "Substitutivity." *On Being and Saying: Essays for Richard Cartwright.* Ed. Judith Jarvis Thomson. Cambridge, MA: MIT Press. 99–132.

——. 2002. *Beyond Rigidity: The Unfinished Semantic Agenda of Naming and Necessity.* New York, NY: Oxford University Press.

——. 2004. *Reference and Description: The Case against Two-Dimensionalism.* Princeton, NJ: Princeton University Press.

Sosa, David. 2001. "Rigidity in the Scope of Russell's Theory." *Noûs* 35.1 (March):1–38.

Stanley, Jason. 1997. "Names and Rigid Designation." In *A Companion to the Philosophy of Language.* Ed. Bob Hale and Crispin Wright. Oxford: Blackwell. 555–585.

Thau, Michael. 2002. *Consciousness and Cognition.* Philosophy of Mind. Oxford: Oxford University Press.

ON SENSE AND REFERENCE

Gottlob Frege

Identity[1] gives rise to challenging questions which are not altogether easy to answer. Is it a relation? A relation between objects, or between names or signs of objects? In my *Begriffsschrift*[A] I assumed the latter. The reasons which seem to favor this are the following: $a = a$ and $a = b$ are obviously statements of differing cognitive value; $a = a$ holds a priori and, according to Kant, is to be labeled analytic, while statements of the form $a = b$ often contain very valuable extensions of our knowledge and cannot always be established a priori. The discovery that the rising sun is not new every morning, but always the same, was of very great consequence to astronomy. Even today the identification of a small planet or a comet is not always a matter of course. Now if we were to regard identity as a relation between that which the names "a" and "b" designate, it would seem that $a = b$ could not differ from $a = a$ (i.e., provided $a = b$ is true). A relation would thereby be expressed of a thing to itself, and indeed one in which each thing stands to itself but to no other thing. What is intended to be said by $a = b$ seems to be that the signs or names "a" and "b" designate the same thing, so that those signs themselves would be under discussion; a relation between them would be asserted. But this relation would hold between the names or signs only insofar as they named or designated something. It would be mediated by the connection of each of the two signs with the same designated thing. But this is arbitrary. Nobody can be forbidden to use any arbitrarily producible event or object as a sign for something. In that case the sentence $a = b$ would no longer refer to the subject matter, but only to its mode of designation; we would express no proper knowledge by its means. But in many cases this is just what we want to do. If the sign "a" is distinguished from the sign "b" only as object (here, by means of its shape), not as sign (i.e., not by the manner in which it designates something), the cognitive value of $a = a$ becomes essentially equal to that of $a = b$, provided $a = b$ is true. A difference can arise only if the difference between the signs corresponds to a difference in the mode of presentation of that which is designated. Let a, b, c be the lines connecting the vertices of a triangle with the midpoints of the opposite sides. The point of intersection of a and b is then the same as the point of intersection of b and c. So we have different designations for the same point, and these names ("Point of intersection of a and b," "Point of intersection of b and c") likewise indicate the mode of presentation; and hence the statement contains true knowledge.

It is natural, now, to think of there being connected with a sign (name, combination of words, letter), besides that to which the sign refers, which may be called the referent of the sign, also what I would like to call the *sense* of the sign,

---

[1] I use this word strictly and understand "$a = b$" to have the sense of "a is the same as b" or "a and b coincide."

[A] The reference is to Frege's *Begriffsschrift, eine der arithmetischen nachgebildete Formelsprache des reinen Denkens* (Halle, 1879).

wherein the mode of presentation is contained. In our example, accordingly, the referents of the expressions "the point of intersection of a and b" and "the point of intersection of b and c" would be the same, but not their senses. The referent of "evening star" would be the same as that of "morning star," but not the sense.

It is clear from the context that by "sign" and "name" I have here understood any designation representing a proper name, whose referent is thus a definite object (this word taken in the widest range), but no concept and no relation, which shall be discussed further in another article.[B] The designation of a single object can also consist of several words or other signs. For brevity, let every such designation be called a proper name.

The sense of a proper name is grasped by everybody who is sufficiently familiar with the language or totality of designations to which it belongs;[2] but this serves to illuminate only a single aspect of the referent, supposing it to exist. Comprehensive knowledge of the referent would require us to be able to say immediately whether every given sense belongs to it. To such knowledge we never attain.

The regular connection between a sign, its sense, and its referent is of such a kind that to the sign there corresponds a definite sense and to that in turn a definite referent, while to a given referent (an object) there does not belong only a single sign. The same sense has different expressions in different languages or even in the same language. To be sure, exceptions to this regular behavior occur. To every expression belonging to a complete totality of signs, there should certainly correspond a definite sense; but natural languages often do not satisfy this condition, and one must be content if the same word has the same sense in the same context. It may perhaps be granted that every grammatically well-formed expression representing a proper name always has a sense. But this is not to say that to the sense there also corresponds a referent. The words "the celestial body most distant from the earth" have a sense, but it is very doubtful if they also have a referent. The expression "the least rapidly convergent series" has a sense; but it is known to have no referent, since for every given convergent series, another convergent, but less rapidly convergent, series can be found. In grasping a sense, one is not certainly assured of a referent.

If words are used in the ordinary way, one intends to speak of their referents. It can also happen, however, that one wishes to talk about the words themselves or their sense. This happens, for instance, when the words of another are quoted. One's own words then first designate words of the other speaker, and only the latter have

---

[B] See his "Über Begriff und Gegenstand" in *Vierteljahrsschrift für wissenschaftliche Philosophie* (XVI [1892], 192–205).

[2] In the case of an actual proper name such as "Aristotle" opinions as to the sense may differ. It might, for instance, be taken to be the following: the pupil of Plato and teacher of Alexander the Great. Anybody who does this will attach another sense to the sentence "Aristotle was born in Stagira" than will a man who takes as the sense of the name: the teacher of Alexander the Great who was born in Stagira. So long as the referent remains the same, such variations of sense may be tolerated, although they are to be avoided in the theoretical structure of a demonstrative science and ought not to occur in a complete language.

their usual referents. We then have signs of signs. In writing, the words are in this case enclosed in quotation marks. Accordingly, a word standing between quotation marks must not be taken as having its ordinary referent.

In order to speak of the sense of an expression "A" one may simply use the phrase "the sense of the expression 'A.'" In reported speech one talks about the sense—e.g., of another person's remarks. It is quite clear that in this way of speaking words do not have their customary referents but designate what is usually their sense. In order to have a short expression, we will say: In reported speech, words are used *indirectly* or have their *indirect* referents. We distinguish accordingly the *customary* from the *indirect* referent of a word; and its *customary* sense from its *indirect* sense. The indirect referent of a word is accordingly its customary sense. Such exceptions must always be borne in mind if the mode of connection between sign, sense, and referent in particular cases is to be correctly understood.

The referent and sense of a sign are to be distinguished from the associated conception. If the referent of a sign is an object perceivable by the senses, my conception of it is an internal image,[3] arising from memories of sense impressions which I have had and activities, both internal and external, which I have performed. Such a conception is often saturated with feeling; the clarity of its separate parts varies and oscillates. The same sense is not always connected, even in the same man, with the same conception. The conception is subjective: One man's conception is not that of another. There result, as a matter of course, a variety of differences in the conceptions associated with the same sense. A painter, a horseman, and a zoologist will probably connect different conceptions with the name "Bucephalus." This constitutes an essential distinction between the conception and the sign's sense, which may be the common property of many and therefore is not a part or a mode of the individual mind. For one can hardly deny that mankind has a common store of thoughts which is transmitted from one generation to another.[4]

In the light of this, one need have no scruples in speaking simply of *the* sense, whereas in the case of a conception one must precisely indicate to whom it belongs and at what time. It might perhaps be said: Just as one man connects this conception and another that conception with the same word, so also one man can associate this sense and another that sense. But there still remains a difference in the mode of connection. They are not prevented from grasping the same sense; but they cannot have the same conception. *Si duo idem faciunt, non est idem.*

If two persons conceive the same, each still has his own conception. It is indeed sometimes possible to establish differences in the conceptions, or even in

---

[3] We can include with the conceptions the direct experiences in which sense-impressions and activities themselves take the place of the traces which they have left in the mind. The distinction is unimportant for our purpose, especially since memories of sense-impressions and activities always help to complete the conceptual image. One can also understand direct experience as including any object, in so far as it is sensibly perceptible or spatial.

[4] Hence it is inadvisable to use the word "conception" to designate something so basically different.

the sensations, of different men; but an exact comparison is not possible, because we cannot have both conceptions together in the same consciousness.

The referent of a proper name is the object itself which we designate by its means; the conception, which we thereby have, is wholly subjective; in between lies the sense, which is indeed no longer subjective like the conception, but is yet not the object itself. The following analogy will perhaps clarify these relationships. Somebody observes the moon through a telescope. I compare the moon itself to the referent; it is the object of the observation, mediated by the real image projected by the object glass in the interior of the telescope, and by the retinal image of the observer. The former I compare to the sense, the latter to the conception or experience. The optical image in the telescope is indeed one-sided and dependent upon the standpoint of observation; but it is still objective, inasmuch as it can be used by several observers. At any rate it could be arranged for several to use it simultaneously. But each one would have his own retinal image. On account of the diverse shapes of the observers' eyes, even a geometrical congruence could hardly be achieved, and a true coincidence would be out of the question. This analogy might be developed still further, by assuming A's retinal image made visible to B; or A might also see his own retinal image in a mirror. In this way we might perhaps show how a conception can itself be taken as an object, but as such is not for the observer what it directly is for the person having the conception. But to pursue this would take us too far afield.

We can now recognize three levels of difference between words, expressions, or whole sentences. The difference may concern at most the conceptions, or the sense but not the referent, or, finally, the referent as well. With respect to the first level, it is to be noted that, on account of the uncertain connection of conceptions with words, a difference may hold for one person, which another does not find. The difference between a translation and the original text should properly not overstep the first level. To the possible differences here belong also the coloring and shading which poetic eloquence seeks to give to the sense. Such coloring and shading are not objective, and must be evoked by each hearer or reader according to the hints of the poet or the speaker. Without some affinity in human conceptions art would certainly be impossible; but it can never be exactly determined how far the intentions of the poet are realized.

In what follows there will be no further discussion of conceptions and experiences; they have been mentioned here only to ensure that the conception aroused in the hearer by a word shall not be confused with its sense or its referent.

To make short and exact expressions possible, let the following phraseology be established:

A proper name (word, sign, sign combination, expression) *expresses* its sense, *refers to* or *designates* its referent. By means of a sign we express its sense and designate its referent.

Idealists or skeptics will perhaps long since have objected: "You talk, without further ado, of the moon as an object; but how do you know that the name 'the moon' has any referent? How do you know that anything whatsoever has a referent?" I reply that when we say "the moon," we do not intend to speak of our conception of the moon, nor are we satisfied with the sense alone, but we presuppose a referent. To assume that in the sentence "The moon is smaller than the earth" the conception of the moon is in question, would be flatly to misunderstand the sense. If this is what the speaker wanted, he would use the phrase "my conception of the moon." Now we can of course be mistaken in the presupposition, and such mistakes have indeed occurred. But the question whether the presupposition is perhaps always mistaken need not be answered here; in order to justify mention of the referent of a sign it is enough, at first, to point out our intention in speaking or thinking. (We must then add the reservation: provided such a referent exists.)

So far we have considered the sense and referents only of such expressions, words, or signs as we have called proper names. We now inquire concerning the sense and referent of an entire declarative sentence. Such a sentence contains a thought.[5] Is this thought, now, to be regarded as its sense or its referent? Let us assume for the time being that the sentence has a referent! If we now replace one word of the sentence by another having the same referent, but a different sense, this can have no influence upon the referent of the sentence. Yet we can see that in such a case the thought changes; since, e.g., the thought of the sentence "The morning star is a body illuminated by the sun" differs from that of the sentence "The evening star is a body illuminated by the sun." Anybody who did not know that the evening star is the morning star might hold the one thought to be true, the other false. The thought, accordingly, cannot be the referent of the sentence, but must rather be considered as the sense. What is the position now with regard to the referent? Have we a right even to inquire about it? Is it possible that a sentence as a whole has only a sense, but no referent? At any rate, one might expect that such sentences occur, just as there are parts of sentences having sense but no referent. And sentences which contain proper names without referents will be of this kind. The sentence "Odysseus was set ashore at Ithaca while sound asleep" obviously has a sense. But since it is doubtful whether the name "Odysseus," occurring therein, has a referent, it is also doubtful whether the whole sentence has one. Yet it is certain, nevertheless, that anyone who seriously took the sentence to be true or false would ascribe to the name "Odysseus" a referent, not merely a sense; for it is the referent of the name which is held to be or not to be characterized by the predicate. Whoever does not consider the referent to exist, can neither apply nor withhold the predicate. But in that case it would be superfluous to advance to the referent of the name; one could be satisfied with the sense, if one wanted to go no further than the thought. If it were a question only of the sense of the sentence, the thought, it would be unnecessary to bother with the referent of a part of the sentence; only the sense, not the referent, of the part is relevant to the sense of the whole sentence. The thought remains the same whether "Odysseus" has a referent or not. The fact that we concern ourselves at all about the referent of a part of the sentence indicates that we generally recognize

---

[5] By a thought I understand not the subjective performance of thinking but its objective content, which is capable of being the common property of several thinkers.

and expect a referent for the sentence itself. The thought loses value for us as soon as we recognize that the referent of one of its parts is missing. We are therefore justified in not being satisfied with the sense of a sentence, and in inquiring also as to its referent. But now why do we want every proper name to have not only a sense, but also a referent? Why is the thought not enough for us? Because, and to the extent that, we are concerned with its truth value. This is not always the case. In hearing an epic poem, for instance, apart from the euphony of the language we are interested only in the sense of the sentences and the images and feelings thereby aroused. The question of truth would cause us to abandon aesthetic delight for an attitude of scientific investigation. Hence it is a matter of indifference to us whether the name "Odysseus," for instance, has a referent, so long as we accept the poem as a work of art.[6] It is the striving for truth that drives us always to advance from the sense to the referent.

We have seen that the referent of a sentence may always be sought, whenever the referents of its components are involved; and that this is the case when and only when we are inquiring after the truth value.

We are therefore driven into accepting the *truth value* of a sentence as its referent. By the truth value of a sentence I understand the circumstance that it is true or false. There are no further truth values. For brevity I call the one the true, the other the false. Every declarative sentence concerned with the referents of its words is therefore to be regarded as a proper name, and its referent, if it exists, is either the true or the false. These two objects are recognized, if only implicitly, by everybody who judges something to be true—and so even by a skeptic. The designation of the truth values as objects may appear to be an arbitrary fancy or perhaps a mere play upon words, from which no profound consequences could be drawn. What I mean by an object can be more exactly discussed only in connection with concept and relation. I will reserve this for another article.[C] But so much should already be clear, that in every judgment,[7] no matter how trivial, the step from the level of thoughts to the level of referents (the objective) has already been taken.

One might be tempted to regard the relation of the thought to the true not as that of the sense to the referent, but rather as that of subject to predicate. One can, indeed, say: "The thought, that 5 is a prime number, is true." But closer examination shows that nothing more has been said than in the simple sentence "5 is a prime number." The truth claim arises in each case from the form of the declarative sentence, and when the latter lacks its usual force, e.g., in the mouth of an actor upon the stage, even the sentence "The thought that 5 is a prime number is true" contains only a thought, and indeed the same thought as the simple "5 is a

---

[6] It would be desirable to have a special term for signs having only sense. If we name them, say, representations, the words of the actors on the stage would be representations; indeed the actor himself would be a representation.

[C] See his "Über Begriff und Gegenstand" in *Vierteljahrsschrift für wissenschaftliche Philosophie* (XVI [1892], 192–205).

[7] A judgment, for me, is not the mere comprehension of a thought, but the recognition of its truth.

prime number." It follows that the relation of the thought to the true may not be compared with that of subject to predicate. Subject and predicate (understood in the logical sense) are indeed elements of thought; they stand on the same level for knowledge. By combining subject and predicate, one reaches only a thought, never passes from a sense to its referent, never from a thought to its truth value. One moves at the same level but never advances from one level to the next. A truth value cannot be a part of a thought, any more than say the sun can, for it is not a sense but an object.

If our supposition that the referent of a sentence is its truth value is correct, the latter must remain unchanged when a part of the sentence is replaced by an expression having the same referent. And this is in fact the case. Leibniz explains: "*Eadem sunt, quae sibi mutuo substitui possunt, salva veritate.*" What else but the truth value could be found, that belongs quite generally to every sentence concerned with the referents of its components and remains unchanged by substitutions of the kind in question?

If now the truth value of a sentence is its referent, then on the one hand all true sentences have the same referent and so, on the other hand, do all false sentences. From this we see that in the referent of the sentence all that is specific is obliterated. We can never be concerned only with the referent of a sentence; but again the mere thought alone yields no knowledge, but only the thought together with its referent, i.e., its truth value. Judgments can be regarded as advances from a thought to a truth value. Naturally this cannot be a definition. Judgment is something quite peculiar and incomparable. One might also say that judgments are distinctions of parts within truth values. Such distinction occurs by a return to the thought. To every sense belonging to a truth value there would correspond its own manner of analysis. However, I have here used the word "part" in a special sense. I have in fact transferred the relation between the parts and the whole of the sentence to its referent, by calling the referent of a word part of the referent of the sentence, if the word itself is a part of the sentence. This way of speaking can certainly be attacked, because in the case of a referent the whole and one part do not suffice to determine the remainder, and because the word part is already used in another sense of bodies. A special term would need to be invented.

The supposition that the truth value of a sentence is its referent shall now be put to further test. We have found that the truth value of a sentence remains unchanged when an expression is replaced by another having the same referent: But we have not yet considered the case in which the expression to be replaced is itself a sentence. Now if our view is correct, the truth value of a sentence containing another as part must remain unchanged when the part is replaced by another sentence having the same truth value. Exceptions are to be expected when the whole sentence or its part is direct or indirect quotation; for in such cases, as we have seen, the words do not have their customary referents. In direct quotation, a sentence designates another sentence, and in indirect quotation a thought.

We are thus led to consider subordinate sentences or clauses. These occur as parts of a sentence structure, which is, from the logical standpoint, likewise a sentence. But here we meet the question whether it is also true of the subordinate sentence that its referent is a truth value. Of indirect quotation we already know the opposite. Grammarians view subordinate clauses as representatives of parts of sentences and divide them accordingly into noun clauses, adjective clauses, adverbial clauses. This might generate the supposition that the referent of a subordinate clause was not a truth value but rather of the same kind as the referent of a noun or adjective or adverb—in short, of a part of a sentence, whose sense was not a thought but only a part of a thought. Only a more thorough investigation can clarify the issue. In so doing, we shall not follow the grammatical categories strictly, but rather group together what is logically of the same kind. Let us first search for cases in which the sense of the subordinate clause, as we have just supposed, is not an independent thought.

The case of an abstract^D noun clause, introduced by "that," includes the case of indirect quotation, in which we have seen the words to have their indirect referents coinciding with what is customarily their sense. In this case, then, the subordinate clause has for its referent a thought, not a truth value; as sense not a thought, but the sense of the words "the thought, that . . . ," which is only a part of the thought of the entire complex sentence. This happens after "say," "hear," "be of the opinion," "be convinced," "conclude," and similar words.[8] Otherwise, and indeed somewhat complicated, is the situation after words like "perceive," "know," "fancy," which are to be considered later.

That in the cases of the first kind the referent of the subordinate clause is in fact the thought can also be recognized by seeing that it is indifferent to the truth of the whole whether the subordinate clause is true or false. Let us compare, for instance, the two sentences "Copernicus believed that the planetary orbits are circles" and "Copernicus believed that the apparent motion of the sun is produced by the real motion of the earth." One subordinate clause can be substituted for the other without harm to the truth. The main clause and the subordinate clause together have as their sense only a single thought, and the truth of the whole includes neither the truth nor the untruth of the subordinate clause. In such cases it is not permissible to replace one expression in the subordinate clause by another having the same customary referent, but only by one having the same indirect referent, i.e., the same customary sense. If somebody were to conclude: The referent of a sentence is not its truth value, "For then it could always be replaced by another sentence of the same truth value," he would prove too much; one might just as well claim that the referent of "morning star" is not Venus, since one may not always say "Venus" in place of "morning star." One has the right to conclude only that the referent of a sentence is *not always* its truth value, and that "morning star" does not always refer to the planet Venus, namely when the word has its indirect referent. An exception of such a kind occurs in the subordinate clause just considered whose referents are thoughts.

---

^{D} A literal translation of Frege's "abstracten Nennsätzen," whose meaning eludes me.

[8] In "A lied in saying he had seen B," the subordinate clause designates a thought which is said (1) to have been asserted by A (2) while A was convinced of its falsity.

If one says "It seems that . . ." one means "It seems to me that . . ." or "I think that. . . ." We therefore have the same case again. The situation is similar in the case of expressions such as "to be pleased," "to regret," "to approve," "to blame," "to hope," "to fear." If, toward the end of the battle of Waterloo,[E] Wellington was glad that the Prussians were coming, the basis for his joy was a conviction. Had he been deceived, he would have been no less pleased so long as his illusion lasted; and before he became so convinced he could not have been pleased that the Prussians were coming—even though in fact they might have been already approaching.

Just as a conviction or a belief is the ground of a feeling, it can, as in inference, also be the ground of a conviction. In the sentence "Columbus inferred from the roundness of the earth that he could reach India by traveling towards the west," we have as referents of the parts two thoughts, that the earth is round, and that Columbus by traveling to the west could reach India. All that is relevant here is that Columbus was convinced of both, and that the one conviction was a ground for the other. Whether the earth is really round, and whether Columbus could really reach India by traveling to the west are immaterial to the truth of our sentence; but it is not immaterial whether we replace "the earth" by "the planet which is accompanied by a moon whose diameter is greater than the fourth part of its own." Here also we have the indirect referents of the words.

Adverbial clauses of purpose beginning with "in order to" also belong here; for obviously the purpose is a thought; therefore: indirect referents for the words, subjunctive mood.

A subordinate clause with "that" after "command," "ask," "forbid," would appear in direct speech as an imperative. Such a clause has no referent but only a sense. A command, a request, are indeed not thoughts, yet they stand on the same level as thoughts. Hence in subordinate clauses depending upon "command," "ask," etc., words have their indirect referents. The referent of such a clause is therefore not a truth value but a command, a request, and so forth.

The case is similar for the dependent question in phrases such as "doubt whether," "not to know what." It is easy to see that here also the words are to be taken to have their indirect referents. Dependent clauses expressing questions and beginning with "who," "what," "where," "when," "how," "by what means," etc., seem at times to approximate very closely to adverbial clauses in which words have their customary referents. These cases are distinguished linguistically by the mood of the verb. In the case of the subjunctive, we have a dependent question and indirect reference of the words, so that a proper name cannot in general be replaced by another name of the same object.

In the cases so far considered the words of the subordinate clauses had their indirect referents, and this made it clear that the referent of the subordinate clause itself was indirect, i.e., not a truth value but a thought, a command, a request, a question. The subordinate clause could be regarded as a noun, indeed one could say: as a proper name of that thought, that command, etc., which it represented in the context of the sentence structure.

[E] Frege uses the Prussian name for the battle—"Belle Alliance."

We now come to other subordinate clauses, in which the words do have their customary referents without however a thought occurring as sense and a truth value as referent. How this is possible is best made clear by examples.

He who discovered the elliptic form of the planetary orbits died in misery.

If the sense of the subordinate clause were here a thought, it would have to be possible to express it also in a separate sentence. But this does not work, because the grammatical subject "he" has no independent sense and only mediates the relations with the consequent clause "died in misery." For this reason the sense of the subordinate clause is not a complete thought, and its referent is Kepler, not a truth value. One might object that the sense of the whole does contain a thought as part, namely, that there was somebody who first discovered the elliptic form of the planetary orbits; for whoever takes the whole to be true cannot deny this part. This is undoubtedly so but only because otherwise the subordinate clause "he who discovered the elliptic form of the planetary orbits" would have no referent. If anything is asserted there is always an obvious presupposition that the simple or compound proper names used have referents. If one therefore asserts "Kepler died in misery," there is a presupposition that the name "Kepler" designates something; but it does not follow that the sense of the sentence "Kepler died in misery" contains the thought that the name "Kepler" designates something. If this were the case the negation would have to run not

Kepler did not die in misery

but

Kepler did not die in misery, or the name "Kepler" has no referent.

That the name "Kepler" designates something is just as much a presupposition for the assertion

Kepler died in misery

as for the contrary assertion. Now languages have the fault of containing expressions which fail to designate an object (although their grammatical form seems to qualify them for that purpose) because the truth of some sentences is a prerequisite. Thus it depends on the truth of the sentence

There was someone who discovered the elliptic form of the planetary orbits

whether the subordinate clause

He who discovered the elliptic form of the planetary orbits

really designates an object or only seems to do so while having in fact no referent. And thus it may appear as if our subordinate clause contains as a part of its sense the thought that there was somebody who discovered the elliptic form of the planetary orbits. If this were right the negation would run:

Either he who discovered the elliptic form of the planetary orbits did not die in misery or there was nobody who discovered the elliptic form of the planetary orbits.

This arises from an incompleteness of language, from which even the symbolic language of mathematical analysis is not altogether free; even there combinations of symbols can occur which appear to refer to something having (at any rate so far) no referent, e.g., divergent infinite series. This can be avoided, e.g., by means of the special stipulation that divergent infinite series shall refer to the number 0. A logically complete language *(Begriffsschrift)* should satisfy the conditions, that every expression grammatically well constructed as a proper name out of signs already introduced shall in fact designate an object, and that no new sign shall be introduced as a proper name without having a referent assured. The logic books contain warnings against logical mistakes arising from the ambiguity of expressions. I regard as no less pertinent a warning against apparent proper names having no referents. The history of mathematics supplies errors which have arisen in this way. This lends itself to demagogic abuse as easily as ambiguity—perhaps more easily. "The will of the people" can serve as an example; for it is easy to establish that there is at any rate no generally accepted referent for this expression. It is therefore by no means unimportant to eliminate the source of these mistakes, at least in science, once and for all. Then such objections as the one discussed above would become impossible, because it could never depend upon the truth of a thought whether a proper name had a referent.

With the consideration of these noun clauses may be coupled that of types of adjective and adverbial clauses which are logically closely related to them.

Adjective clauses also serve to construct compound proper names even if, unlike noun clauses, they are not sufficient by themselves for this purpose. These adjective clauses are to be regarded as equivalent to adjectives. Instead of "the square root of 4 which is smaller than 0," one can also say "the negative square root of 4." We have here the case of a compound proper name constructed from the predicate expression with the help of the singular definite article. This is at any rate permissible if the predicate applies to one and only one single object.[9]

Predicate expressions can be so constructed that characteristics are given by adjective clauses as, in our example, by the clause "which is smaller than 0." It is evident that such an adjective clause cannot have a thought as sense or a truth value as referent, any more than the noun clause could. Its sense, which can also be expressed in many cases by a single adjective, is only a part of a thought. Here, as in the case of the noun clause, there is no independent subject and therefore no possibility of reproducing the sense of the subordinate clause in an independent sentence.

Places, instants, stretches of time, are, logically considered, objects; hence the linguistic designation of a definite place, a definite instant, or a stretch of time is to be regarded as a proper name. Now adverbial clauses of place and time can be used for the construction of such a proper name in a manner similar to that which we have seen in the case of noun and adjective clauses. In the same way, predicate

---

[9] In accordance with what was said above, an expression of the kind in question must actually always be assured of a referent, by means of a special stipulation, e.g., by the convention that 0 shall count as its referent, when the predicate applies to no object or to more than one.

expressions containing reference to places, etc., can be constructed. It is to be noted here also that the sense of these subordinate clauses cannot be reproduced in an independent sentence, since an essential component, namely the determination of place or time, is missing and is only indicated by a relative pronoun or a conjunction.[10]

In conditional clauses, also, there may usually be recognized to occur an indefinite indicator, having a similar correlate in the dependent clause. (We have already seen this occur in noun, adjective, and adverbial clauses.) Insofar as each indicator refers to the other, both clauses together form a connected whole, which as a rule expresses only a single thought. In the sentence

> If a number is less than 1 and greater than 0, its square is less than 1 and greater than 0

the component in question is "a number" in the conditional clause and "its" in the dependent clause. It is by means of this very indefiniteness that the sense acquires the generality expected of a law. It is this which is responsible for the fact that the antecedent clause alone has no complete thought as its sense and in combination with the consequent clause expresses one and only one thought, whose parts are no longer thoughts. It is, in general, incorrect to say that in the hypothetical judgment two judgments are put in reciprocal relationship. If this or something similar is said, the word "judgment" is used in the same sense as I have connected with the word "thought," so that I would use the formulation: "A hypothetical thought establishes a reciprocal relationship between two thoughts." This could be true only if an indefinite indicator is absent;[11] but in such a case there would also be no generality.

If an instant of time is to be indefinitely indicated in both conditional and dependent clauses, this is often achieved merely by using the present tense of the verb, which in such a case however does not indicate the temporal present. This grammatical form is then the indefinite indicator in the main and subordinate

---

[10] In the case of these sentences, various interpretations are easily possible. The sense of the sentence, "After Schleswig-Holstein was separated from Denmark, Prussia and Austria quarreled" can also be rendered in the form "After the separation of Schleswig-Holstein from Denmark, Prussia and Austria quarreled." In this version, it is surely sufficiently clear that the sense is not to be taken as having as a part the thought that Schleswig-Holstein was once separated from Denmark, but that this is the necessary presupposition in order for the expression "after the separation of Schleswig-Holstein from Denmark" to have any referent at all. To be sure, our sentence can also be interpreted as saying that Schleswig-Holstein was once separated from Denmark. We then have a case which is to be considered later. In order to understand the difference more clearly, let us project ourselves into the mind of a Chinese who, having little knowledge of European history, believes it to be false that Schleswig-Holstein was ever separated from Denmark. He will take our sentence, in the first version, to be neither true nor false but will deny it to have any referent, on the ground of absence of referent for its subordinate clause. This clause would only apparently determine a time. If he interpreted our sentence in the second way, however, he would find a thought expressed in it, which he would take to be false, beside a part which would be without reference for him.

[11] At times an explicit linguistic indication is missing and must be read off from the entire context.

clauses. An example of this is: "When the sun is in the tropic of cancer, the longest day in the northern hemisphere occurs." Here, also, it is impossible to express the sense of the subordinate clause in a full sentence, because this sense is not a complete thought. If we say: "The sun is in the tropic of cancer," this would refer to our present time and thereby change the sense. Just as little is the sense of the main clause a thought; only the whole, composed of main and subordinate clauses, is such. It may be added that several common components in the antecedent and consequent clauses may be indefinitely indicated.

It is clear that noun clauses with "who" or "what" and adverbial clauses with "where," "when," "wherever," "whenever" are often to be interpreted as having the sense of conditional clauses, e.g., "who touches pitch, defiles himself."

Adjective clauses can also take the place of conditional clauses. Thus the sense of the sentence previously used can be given in the form "The square of a number which is less than 1 and greater than 0 is less than 1 and greater than 0."

The situation is quite different if the common component of the two clauses is designated by a proper name. In the sentence:

> Napoleon, who recognized the danger to his right flank, himself led his guards against the enemy position

two thoughts are expressed:

1. Napoleon recognized the danger to his right flank
2. Napoleon himself led his guards against the enemy position.

When and where this happened is to be fixed only by the context, but is nevertheless to be taken as definitely determined thereby. If the entire sentence is uttered as an assertion, we thereby simultaneously assert both component sentences. If one of the parts is false, the whole is false. Here we have the case that the subordinate clause by itself has a complete thought as sense (if we complete it by indication of place and time). The referent of the subordinate clause is accordingly a truth value. We can therefore expect that it may be replaced, without harm to the truth value of the whole, by a sentence having the same truth value. This is indeed the case; but it is to be noticed that for purely grammatical reasons, its subject must be "Napoleon," for only then can it be brought into the form of an adjective clause belonging to "Napoleon." But if the demand that it be expressed in this form be waived, and the connection be shown by "and," this restriction disappears.

Subsidiary clauses beginning with "although" also express complete thoughts. This conjunction actually has no sense and does not change the sense of the clause but only illuminates it in a peculiar fashion.[12] We could indeed replace the conditional clause without harm to the truth of the whole by another of the same truth value; but the light in which the clause is placed by the conjunction might then easily appear unsuitable, as if a song with a sad subject were to be sung in a lively fashion.

---

[12] Similarly in the case of "but," "yet."

In the last cases the truth of the whole included the truth of the component clauses. The case is different if a conditional clause expresses a complete thought by containing, in place of an indefinite indicator, a proper name or something which is to be regarded as equivalent. In the sentence

If the sun has already risen, the sky is very cloudy

the time is the present, that is to say, definite. And the place is also to be thought of as definite. Here it can be said that a relation between the truth values of conditional and dependent clauses has been asserted, namely such that the case does not occur in which the antecedent clause refers to the true and the consequent to the false. Accordingly, our sentence is true when the sun has not yet risen, whether the sky is very cloudy or not, and also when the sun has risen and the sky is very cloudy. Since only truth values are here in question, each component clause can be replaced by another of the same truth value without changing the truth value of the whole. To be sure, the light in which the subject then appears would usually be unsuitable; the thought would easily seem distorted; but this has nothing to do with its truth value. One must always take care not to clash with the subsidiary thoughts, which are however not explicitly expressed and therefore should not be reckoned in the sense. Hence, also, no account need be taken of their truth values.[13]

The simple cases have now been discussed. Let us review what we have learned!

The subordinate clause usually has for its sense not a thought, but only a part of one, and consequently no truth value as referent. The reason for this is either that the words in the subordinate clause have indirect reference, so that the referent, not the sense, of the subordinate clause is a thought; or else that, on account of the presence of an indefinite indicator, the subordinate clause is incomplete and expresses a thought only when combined with the main clause. It may happen, however, that the sense of the subsidiary clause is a complete thought, in which case it can be replaced by another of the same truth value without harm to the truth of the whole—provided there are no grammatical obstacles.

An examination of all the subordinate clauses which one may encounter will soon provide some which do not fit well into these categories. The reason, so far as I can see, is that these subordinate clauses have no such simple sense. Almost always, it seems, we connect with the main thoughts expressed by us subsidiary thoughts which, although not expressed, are associated with our words, in accordance with psychological laws, by the hearer. And since the subsidiary thought appears to be connected with our words of its own accord, almost like the main thought itself, we want it also to be expressed. The sense of the sentence is thereby enriched, and it may well happen that we have more simple thoughts than clauses. In many cases the sentence must be understood in this way, in others it may be

---

[13] The thought of our sentence might also be expressed thus: "Either the sun has not risen yet or the sky is very cloudy"—which shows how this kind of sentence connection is to be understood.

doubtful whether the subsidiary thought belongs to the sense of the sentence or only accompanies it.[14] One might perhaps find that the sentence

> Napoleon, who recognized the danger to his right flank, himself led his guards against the enemy position

expresses not only the two thoughts shown above, but also the thought that the knowledge of the danger was the reason why he led the guards against the enemy position. One may in fact doubt whether this thought is merely lightly suggested or really expressed. Let the question be considered whether our sentence be false if Napoleon's decision had already been made before he recognized the danger. If our sentence could be true in spite of this, the subsidiary thought should not be understood as part of the sense. One would probably decide in favor of this. The alternative would make for a quite complicated situation: We would have more simple thoughts than clauses. If the sentence

> Napoleon recognized the danger to his right flank

were now to be replaced by another having the same truth value, e.g.,

> Napoleon was already more than 45 years old

not only would our first thought be changed, but also our third one. Hence the truth value of the latter might change—namely, if his age was not the reason for the decision to lead the guards against the enemy. This shows why clauses of equal truth value cannot always be substituted for one another in such cases. The clause expresses more through its connection with another than it does in isolation.

Let us now consider cases where this regularly happens. In the sentence

> Bebel mistakenly supposes that the return of Alsace-Lorraine would appease France's desire for revenge

two thoughts are expressed, which are not however shown by means of antecedent and consequent clauses, viz.:

(1) Bebel believes that the return of Alsace-Lorraine would appease France's desire for revenge
(2) the return of Alsace-Lorraine would not appease France's desire for revenge.

In the expression of the first thought, the words of the subordinate clause have their indirect referents, while the same words have their customary referents in the expression of the second thought. This shows that the subordinate clause in our original complex sentence is to be taken twice over, with different referents, of which one is a thought, the other a truth value. Since the truth value is not the whole referent of the subordinate clause, we cannot simply replace the latter by another of equal truth value. Similar considerations apply to expressions such as "know," "discover," "it is known that."

---

[14] This may be important for the question whether an assertion is a lie, or an oath a perjury.

By means of a subordinate clause of reason and the associated main clause we express several thoughts, which however do not correspond separately to the original clauses. In the sentence

Because ice is less dense than water, it floats on water

we have

(1) Ice is less dense than water;
(2) If anything is less dense than water, it floats on water;
(3) Ice floats on water.

The third thought, however, need not be explicitly introduced, since it is contained in the remaining two. On the other hand, neither the first and third nor the second and third combined would furnish the sense of our sentence. It can now be seen that our subordinate clause

because ice is less dense than water

expresses our first thought, as well as a part of our second. This is how it comes to pass that our subsidiary clause cannot be simply replaced by another of equal truth value; for this would alter our second thought and thereby easily alter its truth value.

The situation is similar in the sentence

If iron were less dense than water, it would float on water.

Here we have the two thoughts that iron is not less dense than water, and that something floats on water if it is less dense than water. The subsidiary clause again expresses one thought and a part of the other.

If we interpret the sentence already considered

After Schleswig-Holstein was separated from Denmark, Prussia and Austria quarreled

in such a way that it expresses the thought that Schleswig-Holstein was once separated from Denmark, we have first this thought, and secondly the thought that at a time, more closely determined by the subordinate clause, Prussia and Austria quarreled. Here also the subordinate clause expresses not only one thought but also a part of another. Therefore it may not in general be replaced by another of the same truth value.

It is hard to exhaust all the possibilities given by language; but I hope to have brought to light at least the essential reasons why a subordinate clause may not always be replaced by another of equal truth value without harm to the truth of the whole sentence structure. These reasons arise:

(1) when the subordinate clause does not refer to a truth value, inasmuch as it expresses only a part of a thought;
(2) when the subordinate clause does refer to a truth value but is not restricted to so doing, inasmuch as its sense includes one thought and part of another.

The first case arises:

(a) in indirect reference of words

(b) if a part of the sentence is only an indefinite indicator instead of a proper name.

In the second case, the subsidiary clause may have to be taken twice over, viz., once in its customary reference, and the other time in indirect reference; or the sense of a part of the subordinate clause may likewise be a component of another thought, which, taken together with the thought directly expressed by the subordinate clause, makes up the sense of the whole sentence.

It follows with sufficient probability from the foregoing that the cases where a subordinate clause is not replaceable by another of the same value cannot be brought in disproof of our view that a truth value is the referent of a sentence having a thought as its sense.

Let us return to our starting point!

If we found "$a = a$" and "$a = b$" to have different cognitive values, the explanation is that for the purpose of knowledge, the sense of the sentence, viz., the thought expressed by it, is no less relevant than its referent, i.e., its truth value. If now $a = b$, then indeed the referent of "b" is the same as that of "a," and hence the truth value of "$a = b$" is the same as that of "$a = a$." In spite of this, the sense of "b" may differ from that of "a," and thereby the sense expressed in "$a = b$" differs from that of "$a = a$." In that case the two sentences do not have the same cognitive value. If we understand by "judgment" the advance from the thought to its truth value, as in the above paper, we can also say that the judgments are different.

OF NAMES

John Stuart Mill

I. Names Are Names of Things, Not of Our Ideas

"A name," says Hobbes, "is a word taken at pleasure to serve for a mark which may raise in our mind a thought like to some thought we had before, and which, being pronounced to others, may be to them a sign of what thought the speaker had before in his mind." This simple definition of a name as a word (or set of words) serving the double purpose of a mark to recall to ourselves the likeness of a former thought and a sign to make it known to others appears unexceptionable. Names, indeed, do much more than this, but whatever else they do grows out of and is the result of this, as will appear in its proper place. . . .

III. General and Singular Names

All names are names of something, real or imaginary, but all things have not names appropriated to them individually. For some individual objects we require and, consequently, have separate distinguishing names; there is a name for every person and for every remarkable place. Other objects of which we have not occasion to speak so frequently we do not designate by names of their own; but when the necessity arises for naming them, we do so by putting together several words, each of which, by itself, might be and is used for an indefinite number of other objects, as when I say, "this stone": "this" and "stone" being, each of them, names that may be used of many other objects besides the particular one meant, though the only object of which they can both be used at the given moment, consistently with their signification, may be the one of which I wish to speak.

Were this the sole purpose for which names that are common to more things than one could be employed, if they only served, by mutually limiting each other, to afford a designation for such individual objects as have no names of their own, they could only be ranked among contrivances for economising the use of language. But it is evident that this is not their sole function. It is by their means that we are enabled to assert *general* propositions, to affirm or deny any predicate of an indefinite number of things at once. The distinction, therefore, between *general* names and *individual* or *singular* names is fundamental, and may be considered as the first grand division of names.

A general name is, familiarly defined, a name which is capable of being truly affirmed, in the same sense, of each of an indefinite number of things. An individual or singular name is a name which is only capable of being truly affirmed, in the same sense, of one thing.

Thus, *man* is capable of being truly affirmed of John, George, Mary, and other persons without assignable limit, and it is affirmed of all of them in the same sense, for the word "man" expresses certain qualities, and when we predicate it of those persons, we assert that they all possess those qualities. But *John* is only capable of being truly affirmed of one single person, at least in the same sense. For, though there are many persons who bear that name, it is not conferred upon them to indicate any qualities or any thing which belongs to them in common, and cannot be said to be affirmed of them in any *sense* at all, consequently not in the same sense. "The king who succeeded William the Conqueror" is also an individual name. For that there cannot be more than one person of whom it can be truly affirmed is implied in the meaning of the words. Even "*the* king," when the occasion or the context defines the individual of whom it is to be understood, may justly be regarded as an individual name. . . .

It is necessary to distinguish *general* from *collective* names. A general name is one which can be predicated of *each* individual of a multitude; a collective name cannot be predicated of each separately, but only of all taken together. "The seventy-sixth regiment of foot in the British army," which is a collective name, is not a general but an individual name, for though it can be predicated of a multitude of individual soldiers taken jointly, it cannot be predicated of them severally. We may say, "Jones is a soldier, and Thompson is a soldier, and Smith is a soldier," but we cannot say, "Jones is the seventy-sixth regiment, and Thompson is the seventy-sixth regiment, and Smith is the seventy-sixth regiment." We can only say, "Jones, and Thompson, and Smith, and Brown, and so forth (enumerating all the soldiers) are the seventy-sixth regiment."

"The seventy-sixth regiment" is a collective name, but not a general one; "a regiment" is both a collective and a general name—general with respect to all individual regiments of each of which separately it can be affirmed, collective with respect to the individual soldiers of whom any regiment is composed.

IV. Concrete and Abstract

The second general division of names is into *concrete* and *abstract*. A concrete name is a name which stands for a thing; an abstract name is a name which stands for an attribute of a thing. Thus *John, the sea, this table* are names of things. *White*, also, is a name of a thing, or rather of things. Whiteness, again, is the name of a quality or attribute of those things. Man is a name of many things; humanity is a name of an attribute of those things. *Old* is a name of things; *old age* is a name of one of their attributes. . . . By *abstract,* then, I shall always, in logic proper, mean the opposite of *concrete;* by an abstract name, the name of an attribute; by a concrete name, the name of an object.

Do abstract names belong to the class of general or to that of singular names? Some of them are certainly general. I mean those which are names not of one single and definite attribute but of a class of attributes. Such is the word *color,* which is a name common to whiteness, redness, etc. Such is even the word *whiteness,* in respect of the different shades of whiteness, to which it is applied in common; the word *magnitude,* in respect of the various degrees of magnitude and the various dimensions of space; the word *weight,* in respect of the various degrees of weight. Such also is the word *attribute* itself, the common name of all particular attribute. But when only one attribute, neither variable in degree nor in kind, is designated by the name—as visibleness, tangibleness, equality, squareness, milk-whiteness— then the name can hardly be considered general; for though it denotes an attribute of many different objects, the attribute itself is always conceived as one, not many. To avoid needless logomachies, the best course would probably be to consider these names as neither general nor individual, and to place them in a class apart.

It may be objected to our definition of an abstract name that not only the names which we have called abstract, but adjectives which we have placed in the concrete class, are names of attributes; that *white,* for example, is as much the name of the color as *whiteness* is. But (as before remarked) a word ought to be considered as the name of that which we intend to be understood by it when we put it to its principal use, that is, when we employ it in predication. When we say "snow is white," "milk is white," "linen is white," we do not mean it to be understood that snow or linen or milk is a color. We mean that they are things having the color. The reverse is the case with the word *whiteness;* what we affirm to *be* whiteness is not snow but the color of snow. Whiteness, therefore, is the name of the color exclusively, white is a name of all things whatever having the color, a name, not of the quality whiteness, but of every white object. It is true, this name was given to all those various objects on account of the quality, and we may therefore say, without impropriety, that the quality forms part of its signification; but a name can only be said to stand for, or to be a name of, the things of which it can be predicated. We shall presently see that all names which can be said to have any signification, all names by applying which to an individual we give any information respecting that individual, may be said to *imply* an attribute of some sort, but they are not names of the attribute; it has its own proper abstract name.

V. Connotative and Non-Connotative

This leads to the consideration of a third great division of names, into *connotative* and *non-connotative,* the latter sometimes, but improperly, called *absolute*. This is one of the most important distinctions which we shall have occasion to point out and one of those which go deepest into the nature of language.

A non-connotative term is one which signifies a subject only, or an attribute only. A connotative term is one which denotes a subject and implies an attribute. By a subject is here meant anything which possesses attributes. Thus John, or London, or England are names which signify a subject only. Whiteness, length, virtue, signify an attribute only. None of these names, therefore, are connotative. But *white, long, virtuous,* are connotative. The word *white* denotes all white things, as snow, paper, the foam of the sea, etc., and implies, or in the language of the schoolmen, *connotes,* the attribute *whiteness.* The word *white* is not predicated of the attribute, but of the subjects, snow, etc.; but when we predicate it of them, we convey the meaning that the attribute whiteness belongs to them. The same may be said of the other words above cited. Virtuous, for example, is the name of a class which includes Socrates, Howard, the Man of Ross, and an undefinable number of other individuals, past, present, and to come. These individuals, collectively and severally, can alone be said with propriety to be denoted by the word; of them alone can it properly be said to be a name. But it is a name applied to all of them in consequence of an attribute which they are supposed to possess in common, the attribute which has received the name of virtue. It is applied to all beings that are considered to possess this attribute, and to none which are not so considered.

All concrete general names are connotative. The word *man,* for example, denotes Peter, Jane, John, and an indefinite number of other individuals of whom, taken as a class, it is the name. But it is applied to them because they possess, and to signify that they possess, certain attributes. These seem to be corporeity, animal life, rationality, and a certain external form which, for distinction, we call the human. Every existing thing which possessed all these attributes would be called a man; and anything which possessed none of them, or only one, or two, or even three of them without the fourth, would not be so called. For example, if in the interior of Africa there were to be discovered a race of animals possessing reason equal to that of human beings but with the form of an elephant, they would not be called men. Swift's Houyhnhnms would not be so called. Or if such newly discovered beings possessed the form of man without any vestige of reason, it is probable that some other name than that of man would be found for them. How it happens that there can be any doubt about the matter will appear hereafter. The word *man,* therefore, signifies all these attributes and all subjects which possess these attributes. But it can be predicated only of the subjects. What we call men are the subjects, the individual Stiles and Nokes, not the qualities by which their humanity is constituted. The name, therefore, is said to signify the subjects *directly,* the attributes *indirectly;* it *denotes* the subjects, and implies, or involves, or indicates, or, as we shall say henceforth, *connotes,* the attributes. It is a connotative name.

Connotative names have hence been also called *denominative,* because the subject which they denote is denominated by, or receives a name from, the attribute which they connote. Snow and other objects receive the name white because they possess the attribute which is called whiteness; Peter, James, and others receive the name man because they possess the attributes which are considered to constitute humanity. The attribute, or attributes, may, therefore, be said to denominate those objects or to give them a common name.

It has been seen that all concrete general names are connotative. Even abstract names, though the names only of attributes, may, in some instances, be justly considered as connotative, for attributes themselves may have attributes ascribed to them, and a word which denotes attributes may connote an attribute of those attributes. Of this description, for example, is such a word as *fault,* equivalent to *bad* or *hurtful quality.* This word is a name common to many attributes and connotes hurtfulness, an attribute of those various attributes. When, for example, we say that slowness in a horse is a fault, we do not mean that the slow movement, the actual change of place of the slow horse, is a bad thing, but that the property or peculiarity of the horse, from which it derives that name, the quality of being a slow mover, is an undesirable peculiarity.

In regard to those concrete names which are not general but individual, a distinction must be made.

Proper names are not connotative; they denote the individuals who are called by them, but they do not indicate or imply any attributes as belonging to those individuals. When we name a child by the name Paul or a dog by the name Caesar, these names are simply marks used to enable those individuals to be made subjects of discourse. It may be said, indeed, that we must have had some reason for giving them those names rather than any others, and this is true, but the name, once given, is independent of the reason. A man may have been named John because that was the name of his father; a town may have been named Dart-mouth because it is situated at the mouth of the Dart. But it is no part of the signification of the word John that the father of the person so called bore the same name, nor even of the word Dart-mouth to be situated at the mouth of the Dart. If sand should choke up the mouth of the river or an earthquake change its course and remove it to a distance from the town, the name of the town would not necessarily be changed. That fact, therefore, can form no part of the signification of the word; for otherwise, when the fact confessedly ceased to be true, no one would any longer think of applying the name. Proper names are attached to the objects themselves and are not dependent on the continuance of any attribute of the object.

But there is another kind of names, which, although they are individual names—that is, predicable only of one object—are really connotative. For, though we may give to an individual a name utterly unmeaning, unmeaningful which we call a proper name—a word which answers the purpose of showing what thing it is we are talking about, but not of telling anything about it; yet a name peculiar to an individual is not necessarily of this description. It may be significant of some attribute or some union of attributes which, being possessed by no object but one, determines the name exclusively to that individual. "The sun" is a name of this description; "God," when used by a monotheist, is another. These, however, are scarcely examples of what we are now attempting to illustrate, being, in strictness of language, general, not individual names, for, however they may be *in fact* predicable only of one object, there is nothing in the meaning of the words themselves which implies this; and, accordingly, when we are imagining and not affirming, we may speak of many suns; and the majority of mankind have believed, and still believe, that there are many gods. But it is easy to produce words which are real instances of connotative individual names. It may be part of the meaning of the connotative name itself, that there can exist but one individual possessing the attribute which it connotes, as, for instance, "the *only* son of John Stiles"; "the *first* emperor of Rome." Or the attribute connoted may be a connection with some determinate event, and the connection may be of such a kind as only one individual could have, or may, at least, be such as only one individual actually had, and this may be implied in the form of the expression. "The father of Socrates" is an example of the one kind (since Socrates could not have had two fathers), "the author of the Iliad," "the murderer of Henri Quatre," of the second. For, though it is conceivable that more persons than one might have participated in the authorship of the Iliad or in the murder of Henri Quatre, the employment of the article *the* implies that, in fact, this was not the case. What is here done by the word *the* is done in other cases by the context; thus, "Caesar's army" is an individual name if it appears from the context that the army meant is that which Caesar commanded in a particular battle. The still more general expressions, "the Roman army," or "the Christian army," may be individualized in a similar manner. Another case of frequent occurrence has already been noticed; it is the following: The name, being a many-worded one, may consist, in the first place, of a *general* name, capable therefore, in itself, of being affirmed of more things than one, but which is, in the second place, so limited by other words joined with it that the entire expression can only be predicated of one object, consistently with the meaning of the general term. This is exemplified in such an instance as the following: "the present prime minister of England." "Prime Minister of England" is a general name; the attributes which it connotes may be possessed by an indefinite number of persons, in succession, however, not simultaneously, since the meaning of the name itself imports (among other things) that there can be only one such person at a time. This being the case, and the application of the name being afterward limited, by the article and the word *present,* to such individuals as possess the attributes at one indivisible point of time, it becomes applicable only to one individual. And, as this appears from the meaning of the name without any extrinsic proof, it is strictly an individual name.

From the preceding observations it will easily be collected that whenever the names given to objects convey any information—that is, whenever they have properly any meaning—the meaning resides not in what they *denote* but in what they *connote.* The only names of objects which connote nothing are *proper* names, and these have, strictly speaking, no signification.

As a proper name is said to be the name of the one individual which it is predicated of, so (as well from the importance of adhering to analogy as for the other reasons formerly assigned) a connotative name ought to be considered a name of all the various individuals which it is predicable of, or, in other words, *denotes,* and not of what it connotes. But by learning what things it is a name of, we do not learn the meaning of the name; for to the same thing we may, with equal propriety, apply many names, not equivalent in meaning. Thus I call a certain man by the name Sophroniscus; I call him by another name, the father of Socrates. Both these are names of the same individual, but their meaning is altogether different. They are applied to that individual for two different purposes: the one merely to distinguish him from other persons who are spoken of; the other to indicate a fact relating to him, the fact that Socrates was his son. I further apply to him these other expressions: a man, a Greek, an Athenian, a sculptor, an old man, an honest man, a brave man. All these are, or may be, names of Sophroniscus, not, indeed, of him alone, but of him and each of an indefinite number of other human beings. Each of these names is applied to Sophronicus for a different reason, and by each whoever understands its meaning is apprised of a distinct fact or number of facts concerning him, but those who knew nothing about the names except that they were applicable to Sophroniscus would be altogether ignorant of their meaning. It is even possible that I might know every single individual of whom a given name could be with truth affirmed and yet could not be said to know the meaning of the name. A child knows who are its brothers and sisters long before it has any definite conception of the nature of the facts which are involved in the signification of those words. . . . Since, however, the introduction of a new technical language as the vehicle of speculations on subjects belonging to the domain of daily discussion is extremely difficult to effect and would not be free from inconvenience even if effected, the problem for the philosopher, and one of the most difficult which he has to resolve, is, in retaining the existing phraseology, how best to alleviate its imperfections. This can only be accomplished by giving to every general concrete name which there is frequent occasion to predicate a definite and fixed connotation in order that it may be known what attributes, when we call an object by that name, we really mean to predicate of the object. And the question of most nicety is how to give this fixed connotation to a name with the least possible change in the objects which the name is habitually employed to denote, with the least possible disarrangement, either by adding or subtraction, of the group of objects which, in however, imperfect a manner, it serves to circumscribe and hold together, and with the least vitiation of the truth of any propositions which are commonly received as true.

This desirable purpose of giving a fixed connotation where it is wanting is the end aimed at whenever any one attempts to give a definition of a general name already in use, every definition of a connotative name being an attempt either merely to declare, or to declare and analyze, the connotation of the name. And the fact that no questions which have arisen in the moral sciences have been subjects of keener controversy than the definitions of almost all the leading expressions is a proof how great an extent the evil to which we have adverted has attained.

ON DENOTING

Bertrand Russell

By a "denoting phrase" I mean a phrase such as any one of the following: a man, some man, any man, every man, all men, the present King of England, the present King of France, the centre of mass of the Solar System at the first instant of the twentieth century, the revolution of the earth round the sun, the revolution of the sun round the earth. Thus a phrase is denoting solely in virtue of its *form*. We may distinguish three cases: (1) A phrase may be denoting, and yet not denote anything; *e.g.,* "the present King of France." (2) A phrase may denote one definite object; *e.g.,* "the present King of England" denotes a certain man. (3) A phrase may denote ambiguously; *e.g.,* "a man" denotes not many men, but an ambiguous man. The interpretation of such phrases is a matter of considerable difficulty; indeed, it is very hard to frame any theory not suscep- tible of formal refutation. All the difficulties with which I am acquainted are met, so far as I can discover, by the theory which I am about to explain.

The subject of denoting is of very great importance, not only in logic and mathematics, but also in theory of knowledge. For example, we know that the centre of mass of the Solar System at a definite instant is some definite point, and we can affirm a number of propositions about it; but we have no immedi- ate *acquaintance* with this point, which is only known to us by description. The distinction between *acquaintance* and *knowledge about* is the distinction between the things we have presentations of, and the things we only reach by means of denoting phrases. It often happens that we know that a certain phrase denotes unambiguously, although we have no acquaintance with what it denotes; this occurs in the above case of the centre of mass. In perception we have acquaintance with the objects of perception, and in thought we have acquaintance with objects of a more abstract logical character; but we do not necessarily have acquaintance with the objects denoted by phrases composed of words with whose meanings we are acquainted. To take a very important instance: There seems no reason to believe that we are ever acquainted with other people's minds, seeing that these are not directly perceived; hence what we know about them is obtained through denoting. All thinking has to start from acquaintance; but it succeeds in thinking *about* many things with which we have no acquaintance.

The course of my argument will be as follows. I shall begin by stating the theory I intend to advocate;[1] I shall then discuss the theories of Frege and Meinong, showing why neither of them satisfies me; then I shall give the grounds in favour of my theory; and finally I shall briefly indicate the philosophical consequences of my theory.

My theory, briefly, is as follows. I take the notion of the *variable* as fundamental; I use "$C(x)$" to mean a proposition[2] in which x is a constituent, where x, the variable, is essentially and wholly undetermined. Then we can consider the two notions "$C(x)$ is always true" and "$C(x)$ is sometimes true."[3] Then *everything* and *nothing* and *something* (which are the most primitive of denoting phrases) are to be interpreted as follows:—

C(everything) means "$C(x)$ is always true";

C(nothing) means "'$C(x)$ is false' is always true";

C(something) means "It is false that '$C(x)$ is false' is always true."[4]

Here the notion "$C(x)$ is always true" is taken as ultimate and indefinable, and the others are defined by means of it. *Everything, nothing,* and *something,* are not assumed to have any meaning in isolation, but a meaning is assigned to *every* proposition in which they occur. This is the principle of the theory of denoting I wish to advocate: that denoting phrases never have any meaning in themselves, but that every proposition in whose verbal expression they occur has a meaning. The difficulties concerning denoting are, I believe, all the result of a wrong analysis of propositions whose verbal expressions contain denoting phrases. The proper analysis, if I am not mistaken, may be further set forth as follows.

---

[1] I have discussed this subject in *Principles of Mathematics,* chapter v., and §476. The theory there advocated is very nearly the same as Frege's, and is quite different from the theory to be advocated in what follows.

[2] More exactly, a propositional function.

[3] The second of these can be defined by means of the first, if we take it to mean, "It is not true that '$C(x)$ is false' is always true."

[4] I shall sometimes use, instead of this complicated phrase, the phrase "$C(x)$ is not always false," or "$C(x)$ is sometimes true," supposed *defined* to mean the same as the complicated phrase.

Suppose now we wish to interpret the proposition, "I met a man." If this is true, I met some definite man; but that is not what I affirm. What I affirm is, according to the theory I advocate:—

"'I met x, and x is human' is not always false."

Generally, defining the class of men as the class of objects having the predicate *human*, we say that:—

"C(a man)" means "'C(x) and x is human' is not always false."

This leaves "a man," by itself, wholly destitute of meaning, but gives a meaning to every proposition in whose verbal expression "a man" occurs.

Consider next the proposition "all men are mortal." This proposition[5] is really hypothetical and states that *if* anything is a man, it is mortal. That is, it states that if x is a man, x is mortal, whatever x may be. Hence, substituting 'x is human' for 'x is a man,' we find:—

"All men are mortal" means "'If x is human, x is mortal' is always true."

This is what is expressed in symbolic logic by saying that "all men are mortal" means "'x is human' implies 'x is mortal' for all values of x." More generally, we say:—

"C(all men)" means "'If x is human, then C(x) is true' is always true."

Similarly

"C(no men)" means "'If x is human, then C(x) is false' is always true."

"C(some men)" will mean the same as "C(a man,"[6] and

"C(a man)" means "It is false that 'C(x) and x is human' is always false."

"C(every man)" will mean the same as "C(all men)."

It remains to interpret phrases containing *the*. These are by far the most interesting and difficult of denoting phrases. Take as an instance "the father of Charles II. was executed." This asserts that there was an x who was the father of Charles II. and was executed. Now *the*, when it is strictly used, involves uniqueness; we do, it is true, speak of "*the* son of So-and-so" even when So-and-so has several sons, but it would be more correct to say "*a* son of So-and-so." Thus for our purposes we take *the* as involving uniqueness. Thus when we say "x was *the* father of Charles II." we not only assert that x had a certain relation to Charles II., but also that nothing else had this relation. The relation in question, without the assumption of uniqueness, and without any denoting phrases, is expressed by "x begat Charles II." To get an equivalent of "x was the father of Charles II." we must add, "If y is other than x, y did not beget Charles II.," or, what is equivalent, "If y

---

[5] As has been ably argued in Mr. Bradley's *Logic*, book i., chap. ii.

[6] Psychologically "C(a man)" has a suggestion of *only one*, and "C(some men)" has a suggestion of *more than one*; but we may neglect these suggestions in a preliminary sketch.

begat Charles II., y is identical with x." Hence "x is the father of Charles II."
becomes "x begat Charles II.; and 'if y begat Charles II., y is identical with x' is
always true of y."

> Thus "the father of Charles II. was executed" becomes:—"It is not always false of
> x that x begat Charles II. and that x was executed and that 'if y begat Charles II.,
> y is identical with x' is always true of y."

This may seem a somewhat incredible interpretation; but I am not at present giving reasons, I am merely *stating* the theory.

To interpret "C(the father of Charles II.)," where C stands for any statement
about him, we have only to substitute $C(x)$ for "x was executed" in the above.
Observe that, according to the above interpretation, whatever statement C may
be, "C(the father of Charles II.)" implies:—

> "It is not always false of x that 'if y begat Charles II., y is identical with x' is always
> true of y,"

which is what is expressed in common language by "Charles II. had one father and
no more." Consequently if this condition fails, *every* proposition of the form "C(the
father of Charles II.)" is false. Thus *e.g.* every proposition of the form "C(the present King of France)" is false. This is a great advantage in the present theory. I shall
show later that it is not contrary to the law of contradiction, as might be at first
supposed.

The above gives a reduction of all propositions in which denoting phrases
occur to forms in which no such phrases occur. Why it is imperative to effect such
a reduction, the subsequent discussion will endeavour to show.

The evidence for the above theory is derived from the difficulties which seem
unavoidable if we regard denoting phrases as standing for genuine constituents of
the propositions in whose verbal expressions they occur. Of the possible theories
which admit such constituents the simplest is that of Meinong.[7] This theory
regards any grammatically correct denoting phrase as standing for an *object*. Thus
"the present King of France," "the round square," etc., are supposed to be genuine
objects. It is admitted that such objects do not *subsist*, but nevertheless they are
supposed to be objects. This is in itself a difficult view; but the chief objection is
that such objects, admittedly, are apt to infringe the law of contradiction. It is contended, for example, that the existent present King of France exists, and also does
not exist; that the round square is round, and also not round; etc. But this is intolerable; and if any theory can be found to avoid this result, it is surely to be
preferred.

The above breach of the law of contradiction is avoided by Frege's theory. He
distinguishes, in a denoting phrase, two elements, which we may call the *meaning*
and the *denotation*.[8] Thus "the centre of mass of the Solar System at the beginning

---

[7] See *Untersuchungen zur Gegenstandstheorie und Psychologie*, Leipzig, 1904, the first three
  articles (by Meinong, Ameseder and Mally respectively).
[8] See his "Über Sinn und Bedeutung," *Zeitschrift für Phil. und Phil. Kritik*, vol. 100.

of the twentieth century" is highly complex in *meaning,* but its *denotation* is a certain point, which is simple. The Solar System, the twentieth century, etc., are constituents of the *meaning;* but the *denotation* has no constituents at all.[9] One advantage of this distinction is that it shows why it is often worth while to assert identity. If we say "Scott is the author of *Waverly,*" we assert an identity of denotation with a difference of meaning. I shall, however, not repeat the grounds in favour of this theory, as I have urged its claims elsewhere (*loc. cit.*), and am now concerned to dispute those claims.

One of the first difficulties that confront us, when we adopt the view that denoting phrases *express* a meaning and *denote* a denotation,[10] concerns the cases in which the denotation appears to be absent. If we say "the King of England is bald," that is, it would seem, not a statement about the complex *meaning* "the King of England," but about the actual man denoted by the meaning. But now consider "the King of France is bald." By parity of form, this also ought to be about the denotation of the phrase "the King of France." But this phrase, though it has a *meaning* provided "the King of England" has a meaning, has certainly no denotation, at least in any obvious sense. Hence one would suppose that "the King of France is bald" ought to be nonsense; but it is not nonsense, since it is plainly false. Or again consider such a proposition as the following: "If u is a class which has only one member, then that one member is a member of u," or, as we may state it, "If u is a unit class, *the u* is a *u.*" This proposition ought to be *always* true, since the conclusion is true whenever the hypothesis is true. But "the u" is a denoting phrase, and it is the denotation, not the meaning, that is said to be a u. Now if u is *not* a unit class, "the u" seems to denote nothing; hence our proposition would seem to become nonsense as soon as u is not a unit class.

Now it is plain that such propositions do *not* become nonsense merely because their hypotheses are false. The King in "The Tempest" might say, "If Ferdinand is not drowned, Ferdinand is my only son." Now "my only son" is a denoting phrase, which, on the face of it, has a denotation when, and only when, I have exactly one son. But the above statement would nevertheless have remained true if Ferdinand had been in fact drowned. Thus we must either provide a denotation in cases in which it is at first sight absent, or we must abandon the view that the denotation is what is concerned in propositions which contain denoting phrases. The latter is the course that I advocate. The former course may be taken, as by Meinong, by admitting objects which do not

---

[9] Frege distinguishes the two elements of meaning and denotation everywhere, and not only in complex denoting phrases. Thus it is the *meanings* of the constituents of a denoting complex that enter into its *meaning,* not their *denotation.* In the proposition "Mont Blanc is over 1,000 metres high," it is, according to him, the meaning of "Mont Blanc," not the actual mountain, that is a constituent of the *meaning* of the proposition.

[10] In this theory, we shall say that the denoting phrase *expresses* a meaning; and we shall say both of the phrase and of the meaning that they *denote* a denotation. In the other theory, which I advocate, there is no *meaning,* and only sometimes a *denotation.*

subsist, and denying that they obey the law of contradiction; this, however, is to be avoided if possible. Another way of taking the same course (so far as our present alternative is concerned) is adopted by Frege, who provides by definition some purely conventional denotation for the cases in which otherwise there would be none. Thus "the King of France," is to denote the null-class; "the only son of Mr. So-and-so" (who has a fine family of ten), is to denote the class of all his sons; and so on. But this procedure, though it may not lead to actual logical error, is plainly artificial, and does not give an exact analysis of the matter. Thus if we allow that denoting phrases, in general, have the two sides of meaning and denotation, the cases where there seems to be no denotation cause difficulties both on the assumption that there really is a denotation and on the assumption that there really is none.

A logical theory may be tested by its capacity for dealing with puzzles, and it is a wholesome plan, in thinking about logic, to stock the mind with as many puzzles as possible, since these serve much the same purpose as is served by experiments in physical science. I shall therefore state three puzzles which a theory as to denoting ought to be able to solve; and I shall show later that my theory solves them.

(1) If *a* is identical with *b*, whatever is true of the one is true of the other, and either may be substituted for the other in any proposition without altering the truth or falsehood of that proposition. Now George IV. wished to know whether Scott was the author of *Waverley;* and in fact Scott *was* the author of *Waverley.* Hence we may substitute *Scott* for *the author of* "*Waverley,*" and thereby prove that George IV. wished to know whether Scott was Scott. Yet an interest in the law of identity can hardly be attributed to the first gentleman of Europe.

(2) By the law of excluded middle, either "A is B" or "A is not B" must be true. Hence either "the present King of France is bald" or "the present King of France is not bald" must be true. Yet if we enumerated the things that are bald, and then the things that are not bald, we should not find the present King of France in either list. Hegelians, who love a synthesis, will probably conclude that he wears a wig.

(3) Consider the proposition "A differs from B." If this is true, there is a difference between A and B, which fact may be expressed in the form "the difference between A and B subsists." But if it is false that A differs from B, then there is no difference between A and B, which fact may be expressed in the form "the difference between A and B does not subsist." But how can a non-entity be the subject of a proposition? "I think, therefore I am" is no more evident than "I am the subject of a proposition, therefore I am," provided "I am" is taken to assert subsistence or being,[11] not existence. Hence, it would appear, it must always be self-contradictory to deny the being of anything; but we have seen, in connexion with Meinong, that to admit being also sometimes leads to contradictions.

---

[11] I use these as synonyms.

Thus if A and B do not differ, to suppose either that there is, or that there is not, such an object as "the difference between A and B" seems equally impossible.

The relation of the meaning to the denotation involves certain rather curious difficulties, which seem in themselves sufficient to prove that the theory which leads to such difficulties must be wrong.

When we wish to speak about the *meaning* of a denoting phrase, as opposed to its *denotation,* the natural mode of doing so is by inverted commas. Thus we say:—

> The centre of mass of the Solar System is a point, not a denoting complex;
>
> "The centre of mass of the Solar System" is a denoting complex, not a point.

Or again,

> The first line of Gray's Elegy states a proposition.

"The first line of Gray's Elegy" does not state a proposition. Thus taking any denoting phrase, say C, we wish to consider the relation between C and "C," where the difference of the two is of the kind exemplified in the above two instances.

We say, to begin with, that when C occurs it is the *denotation* that we are speaking about; but when "C" occurs, it is the *meaning.* Now the relation of meaning and denotation is not merely linguistic through the phrase: there must be a logical relation involved, which we express by saying that the meaning denotes the denotation. But the difficulty which confronts us is that we cannot succeed in *both* preserving the connexion of meaning and denotation and preventing them from being one and the same; also that the meaning cannot be got at except by means of denoting phrases. This happens as follows.

The one phrase C was to have both meaning and denotation. But if we speak of "the meaning of C," that gives us the meaning (if any) of the denotation. "The meaning of the first line of Gray's Elegy" is the same as "The meaning of 'The curfew tolls the knell of parting day,'" and is not the same as "The meaning of 'the first line of Gray's Elegy.'" Thus in order to get the meaning we want, we must speak not of "the meaning of C," but of "the meaning of 'C,'" which is the same as "C" by itself. Similarly "the denotation of C" does not mean the denotation we want, but means something which, if it denotes at all, denotes what is denoted by the denotation we want. For example, let "C" be "the denoting complex occurring in the second of the above instances." Then C = "the first line of Gray's Elegy," and the denotation of C = The curfew tolls the knell of parting day. But what we *meant* to have as the denotation was "the first line of Gray's Elegy." Thus we have failed to get what we wanted.

The difficulty in speaking of the meaning of a denoting complex may be stated thus; The moment we put the complex in a proposition, the proposition is about the denotation; and if we make a proposition in which the subject is "the meaning of C," then the subject is the meaning (if any) of the denotation, which was not intended. This leads us to say that, when we distinguish meaning and denotation, we must be dealing with the meaning: the meaning has denotation and is a complex, and there is not something other than the meaning, which can be called the complex, and be said to *have* both meaning and denotation. The right phrase, on the view in question, is that some meanings have denotations.

But this only makes our difficulty in speaking of meanings more evident. For suppose C is our complex; then we are to say that C *is* the meaning of the complex. Nevertheless, whenever C occurs without inverted commas, what is said is not true of the meaning, but only of the denotation, as when we say: The centre of mass of the Solar System is a point. Thus to speak of C itself, *i.e.*, to make a proposition about the meaning, our subject must not be C, but something which denotes C. Thus "C," which is what we use when we want to speak of the meaning, must be not the meaning, but something which denotes the meaning. And C must not be a constituent of this complex (as it is of "the meaning of C"); for if C occurs in the complex, it will be its denotation, not its meaning, that will occur, and there is no backward road from denotations to meanings, because every object can be denoted by an infinite number of different denoting phrases.

Thus it would seem that "C" and C are different entities, such that "C" denotes C; but this cannot be an explanation, because the relation of "C" to C remains wholly mysterious; and where are we to find the denoting complex "C" which is to denote C? Moreover, when C occurs in a proposition, it is not *only* the denotation that occurs (as we shall see in the next paragraph); yet, on the view in question, C is only the denotation, the meaning being wholly relegated to "C." This is an inextricable tangle, and seems to prove that the whole distinction of meaning and denotation has been wrongly conceived.

That the meaning is relevant when a denoting phrase occurs in a proposition is formally proved by the puzzle about the author of *Waverley*. The proposition "Scott was the author of *Waverley*" has a property not possessed by "Scott was Scott," namely the property that George IV. wished to know whether it was true. Thus the two are not identical propositions; hence the meaning of "the author of *Waverley*" must be relevant as well as the denotation, if we adhere to the point of view to which this distinction belongs. Yet, as we have just seen, so long as we adhere to this point of view, we are compelled to hold that only the denotation can be relevant. Thus the point of view in question must be abandoned.

It remains to show how all the puzzles we have been considering are solved by the theory explained at the beginning of this article.

According to the view which I advocate, a denoting phrase is essentially *part* of a sentence, and does not, like most single words, have any significance on its own account. If I say "Scott was a man," that is a statement of the form "x was a man," and it has "Scott" for its subject. But if I say "the author of *Waverley* was a man," that is not a statement of the form "x was a man," and does not have "the author of *Waverley*" for its subject. Abbreviating the statement made at the beginning of this article, we may put, in place of "the author of *Waverley* was a man," the following: "One and only one entity wrote *Waverley*, and that one was a man." (This is not so strictly what is meant as what was said earlier; but it is easier to follow.) And speaking generally, suppose we wish to say that the author of *Waverley* had the property ϕ, what we wish to say is equivalent to "One and only one entity wrote *Waverley*, and that one had the property ϕ."

The explanation of *denotation* is now as follows. Every proposition in which "the author of *Waverley*" occurs being explained as above, the proposition "Scott was the author of *Waverley*" (*i.e.*, "Scott was identical with the author of *Waverley*") becomes "One and only one entity wrote *Waverley*, and Scott was identical with that one"; or, reverting to the wholly explicit form: "It is not always false of x that x wrote *Waverley*, that it is always true of y that if y wrote *Waverley* y is identical with x, and that Scott is identical with x." Thus if "C" is a denoting phrase, it may happen that there is one entity x (there cannot be more than one) for which the proposition "x is identical with C" is true, this proposition being interpreted as above. We may then say that the entity x is the denotation of the phrase "C." Thus Scott is the denotation of "the author of *Waverley*." The "C" in inverted commas will be merely the *phrase*, not anything that can be called the *meaning*. The phrase *per se* has no meaning, because in any proposition in which it occurs the proposition, fully expressed, does not contain the phrase, which has been broken up.

The puzzle about George IV's curiosity is now seen to have a very simple solution. The proposition "Scott was the author of *Waverley*," which was written out in its unabbreviated form in the preceding paragraph, does not contain any constituent "the author of *Waverley*" for which we could substitute "Scott." This does not interfere with the truth of inferences resulting from making what is *verbally*, the substitution of "Scott" for "the author of *Waverley*," so long as "the author of *Waverley*" has what I call a *primary* occurrence in the proposition considered. The difference of primary and secondary occurrences of denoting phrases is as follows:—

When we say: "George IV. wished to know whether so-and-so," or when we say "So-and-so is surprising" or "So-and-so is true," etc., the "so-and-so" must be a proposition. Suppose now that "so-and-so" contains a denoting phrase. We may either eliminate this denoting phrase from the subordinate proposition "so-and-so," or from the whole proposition in which "so-and-so" is a mere constituent. Different propositions result according to which we do. I have heard of a touchy owner of a yacht to whom a guest, on first seeing it, remarked, "I thought your yacht was larger than it is"; and the owner replied, "No, my yacht is not larger than it is." What the guest meant was, "The size that I thought your yacht was is greater than the size your yacht is"; the meaning attributed to him is, "I thought the size of your yacht was greater than the size of your yacht." To return to George IV. and *Waverley*, when we say, "George IV. wished to know whether Scott was the author of *Waverley*," we normally mean "George IV. wished to know whether one and only one man wrote *Waverley* and Scott was that man"; but we *may* also mean: "One and only one man wrote *Waverley*, and George IV. wished to know whether Scott was that man." In the latter, "the author of *Waverley*" has a *primary* occurrence; in the former, a *secondary*. The latter might be expressed by "George IV. wished to know, concerning the man who in fact wrote *Waverley*, whether he was Scott." This would be true, for example, if George IV. had seen Scott at a distance, and had asked "Is that Scott?" A *secondary* occurrence of a denoting phrase may be defined as one in which the phrase occurs in a proposition p which is a mere constituent of the proposition we are considering, and the substitution for the denoting phrase is to be effected in p, not in the whole proposition concerned. The ambiguity as between primary and secondary occurrences is hard to avoid in language; but it does no harm if we are on our guard against it. In symbolic logic it is of course easily avoided.

The distinction of primary and secondary occurrences also enables us to deal with the question whether the present King of France is bald or not bald, and generally with the logical status of denoting phrases that denote nothing. If "C" is a denoting phrase, say "the term having the property F," then

> "C has the property ϕ" means "one and only one term has the property F, and that one has the property ϕ."[12]

If now the property F belongs to no terms, or to several, it follows that "C has the property ϕ" is false for *all* values of ϕ. Thus "the present King of France is bald" is certainly false; and "the present King of France is not bald" is false if it means

> "There is an entity which is now King of France and is not bald,"

but is true if it means

> "It is false that there is an entity which is now King of France and is bald."

That is, "the King of France is not bald" is false if the occurrence of "the King of France" is *primary*, and true if it is *secondary*. Thus all propositions in which "the King of France" has a primary occurrence are false; the denials of such propositions are true, but in them "the King of France" has a secondary occurrence. Thus we escape the conclusion that the King of France has a wig.

We can now see also how to deny that there is such an object as the difference between A and B in the case when A and B do not differ. If A and B do differ, there is one and only one entity x such that "x is the difference between A and B" is a true proposition; if A and B do not differ, there is no such entity x. Thus according to the meaning of denotation lately explained, "the difference between A and B" has a denotation when A and B differ, but not otherwise. This difference applies to true and false propositions generally. If "a R b" stands for "a has the relation R to b," then when a R b is true, there is such an entity as the relation R between a and b; when a R b is false, there is no such entity. Thus out of any proposition we can make a denoting phrase, which denotes an entity if the proposition is true, but does not denote an entity if the proposition is

---

[12] This is the abbreviated, not the stricter, interpretation.

false. *E.g.*, it is true (at least we will suppose so) that the earth revolves round the sun, and false that the sun revolves round the earth; hence "the revolution of the earth round the sun" denotes an entity, while "the revolution of the sun round the earth" does not denote an entity.[13]

The whole realm of non-entities, such as "the round square," "the even prime other than 2," "Apollo," "Hamlet," etc., can now be satisfactorily dealt with. All these are denoting phrases which do not denote anything. A proposition about Apollo means what we get by substituting what the classical dictionary tells us is meant by Apollo, say "the sun-god." All propositions in which Apollo occurs are to be interpreted by the above rules for denoting phrases. If "Apollo" has a primary occurrence, the proposition containing the occurrence is false; if the occurrence is secondary, the proposition may be true. So again "the round square is round" means "there is one and only one entity x which is round and square, and that entity is round," which is a false proposition, not, as Meinong maintains, a true one. "The most perfect Being has all perfections; existence is a perfection; therefore the most perfect Being exists" becomes:—

> "There is one and only one entity x which is most perfect; that one has all perfections; existence is a perfection; therefore that one exists." As a proof, this fails for want of a proof of the premises "there is one and only one entity x which is most perfect."[14]

Mr. MacColl (MIND, N.S., No. 54, and again No. 55, p. 401) regards individuals as of two sorts, real and unreal; hence he defines the null-class as the class consisting of all unreal individuals. This assumes that such phrases as "the present King of France," which do not denote a real individual, do, nevertheless, denote an individual, but an unreal one. This is essentially Meinong's theory, which we have seen reason to reject because it conflicts with the law of contradiction. With our theory of denoting, we are able to hold that there are no unreal individuals; so that the null-class is the class containing no members, not the class containing as members all unreal individuals.

It is important to observe the effect of our theory on the interpretation of definitions which proceed by means of denoting phrases. Most mathematical definitions are of this sort: for example, "$m - n$ means the number which, added to n, gives m." Thus $m - n$ is defined as meaning the same as a certain denoting phrase; but we agreed that denoting phrases have no meaning in isolation. Thus what the definition really ought to be is: "Any proposition containing $m - n$ is to mean the proposition which results from substituting for '$m - n$' the number which, added to n, gives m.'" The resulting proposition is interpreted according

---

[13] The propositions from which such entities are derived are not identical either with these entities or with the propositions that these entities have being.

[14] The argument can be made to prove validly that all members of the class of most perfect Beings exist; it can also be proved formally that this class cannot have *more* than one member; but, taking the definition of perfection as possession of all positive predicates, it can be proved almost equally formally that the class does not have even one member.

to the rules already given for interpreting propositions whose verbal expression contains a denoting phrase. In the case where m and n are such that there is one and only one number x which, added to n, gives m, there is a number x which can be substituted for $m - n$ in any proposition containing $m - n$ without altering the truth or falsehood of the proposition. But in other cases, all propositions in which "$m - n$" has a primary occurrence are false.

The usefulness of *identity* is explained by the above theory. No one outside a logic-book ever wishes to say "x is x," and yet assertions of identity are often made in such forms as "Scott was the author of *Waverley*" or "thou art the man." The meaning of such propositions cannot be stated without the notion of identity, although they are not simply statements that Scott is identical with another term, the author of *Waverley*, or that thou art identical with another term, the man. The shortest statement of "Scott is the author of *Waverley*" seems to be: "Scott wrote *Waverley*; and it is always true of y that if y wrote *Waverley*, y is identical with Scott." It is in this way that identity enters into "Scott is the author of *Waverley*"; and it is owing to such uses that identity is worth affirming.

One interesting result of the above theory of denoting is this: when there is anything with which we do not have immediate acquaintance, but only definition by denoting phrases, then the propositions in which this thing is introduced by means of a denoting phrase do not really contain this thing as a constituent, but contain instead the constituents expressed by the several words of the denoting phrase. Thus in every proposition that we can apprehend (*i.e.,* not only in those whose truth or falsehood we can judge of, but in all that we can think about), all the constituents are really entities with which we have immediate acquaintance. Now such things as matter (in the sense in which matter occurs in physics) and the minds of other people are known to us only by denoting phrases, *i.e.,* we are not *acquainted* with them, but we know them as what has such and such properties. Hence, although we can form propositional functions C(x) which must hold of such and such a material particle, or of So-and-so's mind, yet we are not acquainted with the propositions which affirm these things that we know must be true, because we cannot apprehend the actual entities concerned. What we know is "So-and-so has a mind which has such and such properties" but we do not know "A has such and such properties," where A *is* the mind in question. In such a case, we know the properties of a thing without having acquaintance with the thing itself, and without, consequently, knowing any single proposition of which the thing itself is a constituent.

Of the many other consequences of the view I have been advocating, I will say nothing. I will only beg the reader not to make up his mind against the view—as he might be tempted to do, on account of its apparently excessive complication—until he has attempted to construct a theory of his own on the subject of denotation. This attempt, I believe, will convince him that, whatever the true theory may be, it cannot have such a simplicity as one might have expected beforehand.

SELECTION FROM THE FREGE–RUSSELL CORRESPONDENCE*

I. Excerpt from Frege to Russell, 13 November 1904

Jena

13 November 1904

Dear Colleague,

... Mont Blanc with its snowfields is not itself a component part of the thought that Mont Blanc is more than 4,000 metres high.... The sense of the word 'moon' is a component part of the thought that the moon is smaller than the earth. The moon itself (i.e., the denotation of the word 'moon') is not part of the sense of the word 'moon'; for then it would also be a component part of that thought. We can nevertheless say: 'The moon is identical with the heavenly body closest to the earth.' What is identical, however, is not a component part but the denotation of the expressions 'the moon' and 'the heavenly body closest to the earth.' We can say that 3 + 4 is identical with 8 − 1; i.e., that the denotation of '3 + 4' coincides with the denotation of '8 − 1.' But this denotation, namely the number 7, is not a component part of the sense of '3 + 4.' The identity is not an identity of sense, nor of part of the sense, but of denotation....

Yours sincerely

G. Frege

II. Excerpt from Russell to Frege, 12 December 1904

Ivy Lodge

Tilford, Farnham

12 December 1904

Dear Colleague,

... Concerning sense and denotation, I see nothing but difficulties which I cannot overcome.... I believe that in spite of all its snowfields Mont Blanc itself is a component part of what is actually asserted in the proposition 'Mont Blanc is more than 4,000 metres high.' We do not assert the thought, for this is a private psychological matter: we assert the object of the thought, and this is, to my mind, a certain complex (an objective proposition, one might say) in which Mont Blanc is itself a component part. If we do not admit this, then we get the conclusion that we know nothing at all about Mont Blanc. This is why for me the *denotation* of a proposition is not the true, but a certain complex which (in the given case) is true. In the case of a simple proper name like 'Socrates,' I cannot distinguish between sense and denotation; I see only the idea, which is psychological, and the object. Or better: I do not admit the sense at all, but only the idea and the denotation. I

---

* The translation is Hans Kaal's, except that *Bedeutung* is here translated as "denotation."

see the difference between sense and denotation only in the case of complexes whose denotation is an object, e.g., the values of ordinary mathematical functions like $\xi + 1$, ξ^2, etc. . . .

Yours sincerely
BERTRAND RUSSELL

INTRODUCTION TO MATHEMATICAL LOGIC

Alonzo Church

00. Logic

Our subject is *logic*—or, as we may say more fully, in order to distinguish from certain topics and doctrines which have (unfortunately) been called by the same name, it is *formal logic*.

   Traditionally, (formal) logic is concerned with the analysis of sentences or of propositions[1] and of proof[2] with attention to the *form* in abstraction from the *matter*. This distinction between form and matter is not easy to make precise immediately, but it may be illustrated by examples.

   To take a relatively simple argument for illustrative purposes, consider the following:

> I   Brothers have the same surname; Richard and Stanley are brothers; Stanley has surname Thompson; therefore Richard has surname Thompson.

Everyday statement of this argument would no doubt leave the first of the three premisses[3] tacit, at least unless the reasoning were challenged; but for purposes of logical analysis all premisses must be set down explicitly. The argument, it may be held, is valid from its form alone, independently of the matter, and independently in particular of the question whether the premisses and the conclusion are in themselves right or wrong. The reasoning may be right though the facts be wrong,

---

[1] See §04.

[2] In the light both of recent work and of some aspects of traditional logic we must add here, besides proof, such other relationships among sentences or propositions as can be treated in the same manner, i.e., with regard to form in abstraction from the matter. These include (e.g.) disproof, compatibility; also partial confirmation, which is important in connection with inductive reasoning (cf. C. G. Hempel in *The Journal of Symbolic Logic*, vol. 8 (1943), pp. 122–143).

   But no doubt these relationships both can and should be reduced to that of proof, by making suitable additions to the object language (§07) if necessary. E.g., in reference to an appropriate formalized language as object language, disproof of a proposition or sentence may be identified with proof of its negation. The corresponding reduction of the notions of compatibility and confirmation to that of proof apparently requires modal logic—a subject which, though it belongs to formal logic, is beyond the scope of this book.

[3] Following C. S. Peirce (and others) we adopt the spelling *premiss* for the logical term to distinguish it from *premise* in other senses, in particular to distinguish the plural from the legal term *premises*.

and it is just in maintaining this distinction that we separate the form from the matter.

For comparison with the foregoing example consider also:

II Complex numbers with real positive ratio have the same amplitude; $i - \sqrt{3}/3$ and ω are complex numbers with real positive ratio; ω has amplitude $2\pi/3$; therefore $i - \sqrt{3}/3$ has amplitude $2\pi/3$.

This may be held to have the same form as I, though the matter is different, and therefore to be, like I, valid from the form alone.

Verbal similarity in the statements of I and II, arranged at some slight cost of naturalness in phraseology, serves to highlight the sameness of form. But, at least in the natural languages, such linguistic parallelism is not in general a safe guide to sameness of logical form. Indeed, the natural languages, including English, have been evolved over a long period of history to serve practical purposes of facility of communication, and these are not always compatible with soundness and precision of logical analysis.

To illustrate this last point, let us take two further examples:

III I have seen a portrait of John Wilkes Booth; John Wilkes Booth assassinated Abraham Lincoln; thus I have seen a portrait of an assassin of Abraham Lincoln.

IV I have seen a portrait of somebody; somebody invented the wheeled vehicle; thus I have seen a portrait of an inventor of the wheeled vehicle.

The argument III will be recognized as valid, and presumably from the logical form alone, but IV as invalid. The superficial linguistic analogy of the two arguments as stated is deceptive. In this case the deception is quickly dispelled upon going beyond the appearance of the language to consider the meaning, but other instances are more subtle, and more likely to generate real misunderstanding. Because of this, it is desirable or practically necessary for purposes of logic to employ a specially devised language, a *formalized language* as we shall call it, which shall reverse the tendency of the natural languages and shall follow or reproduce the logical form—at the expense, where necessary, of brevity and facility of communication. To adopt a particular formalized language thus involves adopting a particular theory or system of logical analysis. (This must be regarded as the essential feature of a formalized language, not the more conspicuous but theoretically less important feature that it is found convenient to replace the spelled words of most (written) natural languages by single letters and various special symbols.)

01. Names

One kind of expression which is familiar in the natural languages, and which we shall carry over also to formalized languages, is the *proper name*. Under this head we include not only proper names which are arbitrarily assigned to denote in a certain way—such names, e.g., as "Rembrandt," "Caracas," "Sirius," "the Mississippi," "The Odyssey," "eight"—but also names having a structure that expresses some analysis of the way in which they denote.[4] As examples of the latter we may cite: "five hundred nine," which denotes a certain prime number, and in the way expressed by the linguistic structure, namely as being five times a hundred plus nine; "the author of *Waverley*," which denotes a certain Scottish novelist, namely Sir Walter Scott, and in the particular way expressed by the linguistic structure, namely as having written *Waverley;* "Rembrandt's birthplace"; "the capital of Venezuela"; "the cube of 2."

The distinction is not always clear in the natural languages between the two kinds of proper names, those which are arbitrarily assigned to have a certain meaning (primitive proper names, as we shall say in the case of a formalized language), and those which have a linguistic structure of meaningful parts. E.g., "The Odyssey" has in the Greek a derivation from "Odysseus," and it may be debated whether this etymology is a mere matter of past history or whether it is still to be considered in modern English that the name "The Odyssey" has a structure involving the name "Odysseus." This uncertainty is removed in the case of a formalized language by fixing and making explicit the formation rules of the language (§07).

There is not yet a theory of the meaning of proper names upon which general agreement has been reached as the best. Full discussion of the question would take us far beyond the intended scope. . . . But it is necessary to outline briefly the theory which will be adopted here, due in its essentials to Gottlob Frege.[5]

The most conspicuous aspect of its meaning is that a proper name always is, or at least is put forward as, a *name of* something. We shall say that a proper name

---

[4] We extend the usual meaning of *proper name* in this manner because such alternative terms as *singular name* or *singular term* have traditional associations which we wish to avoid. The single word *name* would serve the purpose except for the necessity of distinguishing from the *common names* (or *general names*) which occur in the natural languages, and hereafter we shall often say simply *name*.

We do use the word *term*, but in its everyday meaning of an item of terminology, and not with any reference to the traditional doctrine of "categorical propositions" or the like.

[5] See his paper, "Über Sinn und Bedeutung," in *Zeitschrift für Philosophie und philosophische Kritik,* vol. 100 (1892), pp. 25–50. (There are an Italian translation of this by L. Geymonat in *Gottlob Frege, Aritmetica e Logica* (1948), pp. 215–252, and English translations by Max Black in *The Philosophical Review,* vol. 57 (1948), pp. 207–230, and by Herbert Feigl in *Readings in Philosophical Analysis* (1949), pp. 85–102. See reviews of these in *The Journal of Symbolic Logic,* vol. 13 (1948), pp. 152–153, and vol. 14 (1949), pp. 184–185.)

A similar theory, but with some essential differences, is proposed by Rudolf Carnap in his recent book *Meaning and Necessity* (1947).

A radically different theory is that of Bertrand Russell, developed in a paper in *Mind,* vol. 14 (1905), pp. 479–493; in the Introduction to the first volume of *Principia Mathematica* (by A. N. Whitehead and Bertrand Russell, 1910); and in a number of more recent publications, among them Russell's book, *An Inquiry into Meaning & Truth* (1940). The doctrine of Russell amounts very nearly to a rejection of proper names as irregularities of the natural languages which are to be eliminated in constructing a formalized language. It falls short of this by allowing a narrow category of proper names which must be names of sense qualities that are known by acquaintance, and which, in Fregean terms, have *Bedeutung* but not *Sinn*.

denotes[6] or *names*[7] that of which it is a name. The relation between a proper name and what it denotes will be called the *name relation,*[8] and the thing[9] denoted will be called the *denotation*. For instance, the proper name "Rembrandt" will thus be said to denote or name the Dutch artist Rembrandt, and he will be said to be the denotation of the name "Rembrandt." Similarly, "the author of *Waverley*" denotes or names the Scottish author, and he is the denotation both of this name and of the name "Sir Walter Scott."

   That the meaning of a proper name does not consist solely in its denotation may be seen by examples of names which have the same denotation though their meanings are in some sense different. Thus "Sir Walter Scott" and "the author of *Waverley*" have the same denotation; it is contained in the meaning of the first name, but not of the second, that the person named is a knight or baronet and has the given name "Walter" and surname "Scott";[10] and it is contained in the meaning of the second name, but not of the first, that the person named wrote *Waverley* (and indeed as sole author, in view of the definite article and of the fact that the phrase is put forward as a proper name). To bring out more sharply the difference in meaning of the two names let us notice that, if two names are *synonymous* (have the same meaning in all respects), then one may always be

------

[6] In the usage of J. S. Mill, and of others following him, not only a singular name (proper name in our terminology) but also a common or general name is said to denote, with the difference that the former denotes only one thing, the latter, many things. E.g., the common name "man" is said to denote Rembrandt; also to denote Scott; also to denote Frege; etc.

   In the formalized languages which we shall study, the nearest analogues of the common name will be the *variable* and the *form* (see §02). And we prefer to use a different terminology for variables and forms than that of denoting—in particular because we wish to preserve the distinction of a proper name, or constant, from a form which is concurrent to a constant (in the sense of §02), and from a variable which has one thing only in its range. In what follows, therefore, we shall speak of *proper names only* as denoting.

   From another point of view common names may be thought of as represented in the formalized languages, not by variables or forms, but by proper names of classes (class constants). Hence the usage has also arisen according to which a proper name of a class is said to denote the various members of the class. We shall not follow this, but shall speak of a proper name of a class as denoting the class itself. (Here we agree with Mill, who distinguishes a singular collective name, or proper name of a class, from a common or general name, calling the latter a "name of a class" only in the distributive sense of being a name of each individual.)

[7] We thus translate Frege's *bedeuten* by *denote* or *name*. The verb *to mean* we reserve for general use, in reference to possible different kinds of meaning.

[8] The name relation is properly a ternary relation, among a language, a word or phrase of the language, and a denotation. But it may be treated as binary by fixing the language in a particular context. Similarly one should speak of the denotation of a name *with respect to a language,* omitting the latter qualification only when the language has been fixed or when otherwise no misunderstanding can result.

[9] The word *thing* is here used in its widest sense, in short for anything namable.

[10] The term *proper name* is often restricted to names of this kind, i.e., which have as part of their meaning that the denotation is so called or is or was entitled to be so called. As already explained, we are not making such a restriction.

   Though it is, properly speaking, irrelevant to the discussion here, it is of interest to recall that Scott did make use of "the author of *Waverley*" as a pseudonym during the time that his authorship of the Waverley Novels was kept secret.

substituted for the other without change of meaning. The sentence, "Sir Walter Scott is the author of *Waverley*," has, however, a very different meaning from the sentence, "Sir Walter Scott is Sir Walter Scott": for the former sentence conveys an important fact of literary history of which the latter gives no hint. This difference in meaning may lead to a difference in truth when the substitution of one name for the other occurs within certain contexts.[11] E.g., it is true that "George IV once demanded to know whether Scott was the author of *Waverley*"; but false that "George IV once demanded to know whether Scott was Scott."[12]

Therefore, besides the denotation, we ascribe to every proper name another kind of meaning, the *sense*,[13] saying, e.g., that "Sir Walter Scott" and "the author of *Waverley*" have the same denotation but different senses.[14] Roughly, the sense is what is grasped when one understands a name,[15] and it may be possible thus to grasp the sense of a name without having knowledge of its denotation except as being determined by this sense. If, in particular, the question "Is Sir Walter Scott the author of *Waverley?*" is used in an intelligent demand for new information, it must be that the questioner knows the senses of the names "Sir Walter Scott" and "the author of *Waverley*" without knowing of their denotations enough to identify them certainly with each other.

---

[11] Contexts, namely, which render the occurrences of the names *oblique* in the sense explained below.

[12] The particular example is due to Bertrand Russell; the point which it illustrates, to Frege.
    This now famous question, put to Scott himself in the indirect form of a toast "to the author of *Waverley*" at a dinner at which Scott was present, was met by him with a flat denial, "Sire, I am not the author of *Waverley*." We may therefore enlarge on the example by remarking that Scott, despite a pardonable departure from the truth, did not mean to go so far as to deny his self-identity (as if he had said "I am not I"). And his hearers surely did not so understand him, though some must have shrewdly guessed the deception as to his authorship of *Waverley*.

[13] We adopt this as the most appropriate translation of Frege's *Sinn*, especially since the technical meaning given to the word *sense* thus comes to be very close indeed to the ordinary acceptation of the sense of an expression. (Russell and some others following him have used "meaning" as a translation of Frege's *Sinn*.)

[14] A similar distinction is made by J. S. Mill between the denotation and the connotation of a name. And in fact we are prepared to accept *connotation* as an alternative translation of *Sinn*, although it seems probable that Frege did not have Mill's distinction in mind in making his own. We do not follow Mill in admitting names which have denotation without connotation, but rather hold that a name must always point to its denotation *in some way*, i.e., through some sense or connotation, though the sense may reduce in special cases just to the denotation's being called so and so (e.g., in the case of personal names), or to its being what appears here and now (as sometimes in the case of the demonstrative "this"). Because of this and other differences, and because of the more substantial content of Frege's treatment, we attribute the distinction between sense and denotation to Frege rather than to Mill. Nevertheless the discussion of names in Mill's *A System of Logic* (1843) may profitably be read in this connection.

[15] It is not meant by this to imply any psychological element in the notion of sense. Rather, a sense (or a concept) is a postulated abstract object, with certain postulated properties. These latter are only briefly indicated in the present informal discussion; and in particular we do not discuss the assumptions to be made about equality of senses, since this is unnecessary for our immediate purpose.

We shall say that a name *denotes* or *names* its denotation and *expresses*[16] its sense. Or less explicitly we may speak of a name just as *having* a certain denotation and *having* a certain sense. Of the sense we say that it *determines* the denotation, or *is a concept*[17] of the denotation.

Concepts[17] we think of as non-linguistic in character—since synonymous names, in the same or different languages, express the same sense or concept—and since the same name may also express different senses, either in different languages or, by equivocation, in the same language. We are even prepared to suppose the existence of concepts of things which have no name in any language in actual use. But every concept of a thing is a sense of some name of it in some (conceivable) language.

The possibility must be allowed of concepts which are not concepts of any actual thing, and of names which express a sense but have no denotation. Indeed such names, at least on one very plausible interpretation, do occur in the natural languages such as English: e.g., "Pegasus,"[18] "the king of France in A.D. 1905." But, as Frege has observed, it is possible to avoid such names in the construction of formalized languages.[19] And it is in fact often convenient to do this.

---

[16] This is our translation of Frege's *drückt aus*. Mill's term *connotes* is also acceptable here, provided that care is taken not to confuse Mill's meaning of this term with other meanings which it has since acquired in common English usage.

[17] This use of *concept* is a departure from Frege's terminology. Though not identical with Carnap's use of *concept* in recent publications, it is closely related to it, and was suggested to the writer by correspondence with Carnap in 1943. It also agrees well with Russell's use of *class-concept* in *The Principles of Mathematics* (1903)—cf. §69 thereof.

[18] While the exact sense of the name "Pegasus" is variable or uncertain, it is, we take it, roughly that of the winged horse who took such and such a part in such and such supposed events—where only such minimum essentials of the story are to be included as it would be necessary to verify in order to justify saying, despite the common opinion, that "Pegasus did after all exist."

   We are thus maintaining that, in the present actual state of the English language, "Pegasus" is not just a personal name, having the sense of who or what was called so and so, but has the more complex sense described. However, such questions regarding the natural languages must not be supposed always to have one final answer. On the contrary, the present actual state (at any time) tends to be indeterminate in a way to leave much debatable.

[19] For example, in the case of a formalized language obtained from one of the logistic systems of Chapter X (or of a paper by the writer in *The Journal of Symbolic Logic*, vol. 5 (1940), pp. 56–68) by an interpretation retaining the principal interpretation of the variables and of the notations λ (abstraction) and ( ) (application of function to argument), it is sufficient to take the following precautions in assigning senses to the primitive constants. For a primitive constant of type o or ι the sense must be such as—on the basis of accepted presuppositions— to assure the existence of a denotation in the appropriate domain, $\mathfrak{D}$ (of truth-values) or $\mathfrak{I}$ (of individuals). For a primitive constant of type $\alpha\beta$ the sense must be such as—on the same basis—to assure the existence of a denotation which is in the domain $\mathfrak{U}\mathfrak{B}$, i.e., which is a function from the (entire) domain $\mathfrak{B}$ which is taken as the range of variables of type β, to the domain $\mathfrak{U}$ which is taken as the range of variables of type α.

   Then every well-formed formula without free variables will have a denotation, as indeed it must if such interpretation of the logistic system is to accord with formal properties of the system.

   As in the case, e.g., of $\imath_\alpha(o_\alpha)$, it may happen that the most immediate or naturally suggested interpretation of a primitive constant of type $\alpha\beta$ makes it denote a function from a proper part of the domain $\mathfrak{B}$ to the domain $\mathfrak{U}$. In such a case the definition of the function must be extended, by artificial means if necessary, over the remainder of the domain $\mathfrak{B}$, so as to obtain a function having the entire domain $\mathfrak{B}$ as its range. The sense assigned to the primitive constant must then be such as to determine this latter function as denotation, rather than the function which had only a proper part of $\mathfrak{B}$ as its range.

To understand a language fully, we shall hold, requires knowing the senses of all names in the language, but not necessarily knowing which senses determine the same denotation, or even which senses determine denotations at all.

In a well constructed language of course every name should have just one sense, and it is intended in the formalized languages to secure such univocacy. But this is far from being the case in the natural languages. In particular, as Frege has pointed out, the natural languages customarily allow, besides the *ordinary* (*gewöhnlich*) use of a name, also an *oblique* (*ungerade*) use of the name, the sense which the name would express in its ordinary use becoming the denotation when the name is used obliquely.[20]

Supposing univocacy in the use of names to have been attained (this ultimately requires eliminating the oblique use of names by introducing special names to denote the senses which other names express[21]), we make, with Frege, the following assumptions, about names which have a linguistic structure and contain other names as constituent parts: (1) when a constituent name is replaced by another having the same sense, the sense of the entire name is not changed;

---

[20] For example, in "Scott is the author of *Waverley*" the names "Scott," "*Waverley*," "the author of *Waverley*" have ordinary occurrences. But in "George IV wished to know whether Scott was the author of *Waverley*" the same three names have oblique occurrences (while "George IV" has an ordinary occurrence). Again, in "Schliemann sought the site of Troy" the names "Troy" and "the site of Troy" occur obliquely. For to seek the site of some other city, determined by a different concept, is not the same as to seek the site of Troy, not even if the two cities should happen as a matter of fact (perhaps unknown to the seeker) to have had the same site.

According to the Fregean theory of meaning which we are advocating, "Schliemann sought the site of Troy" asserts a certain relation as holding, not between Schliemann and the site of Troy (for Schliemann might have sought the site of Troy though Troy had been a purely fabulous city and its site had not existed), but between Schliemann and a certain concept, namely that of the site of Troy. This is, however, not to say that "Schliemann sought the site of Troy" means the same as "Schliemann sought the concept of the site of Troy." On the contrary, the first sentence asserts the holding of a certain relation between Schliemann and the concept of the site of Troy, and is true; but the second sentence asserts the holding of a like relation between Schliemann and the concept of the concept of the site of Troy, and is very likely false. The relation holding between Schliemann and the concept of the site of Troy is not quite that of having sought, or at least it is misleading to call it that—in view of the way in which the verb *to seek* is commonly used in English.

(W. V. Quine—in *The Journal of Philosophy*, vol. 40 (1943), pp. 113–127, and elsewhere—introduces a distinction between the "meaning" of a name and what the name "designates" which parallels Frege's distinction between sense and denotation, also a distinction between "purely designative" occurrences of names and other occurrences which coincides in many cases with Frege's distinction between ordinary and oblique occurrences. For a discussion of Quine's theory and its differences from Frege's see a review by the present writer, in *The Journal of Symbolic Logic*, vol. 8 (1943), pp. 45–47; also a note by Morton G. White in *Philosophy and Phenomenological Research*, vol. 9, no. 2 (1948), pp. 305–308.)

[21] As an indication of the distinction in question we shall sometimes (as we did in the second paragraph of footnote 20) use such phrases as "the concept of Sir Walter Scott," "the concept of the author of *Waverley*," "the concept of the site of Troy" to *denote* the same concepts which are *expressed* by the respective names "Sir Walter Scott," "the author of *Waverley*," "the site of Troy." The definite article "the" sufficiently distinguishes the phrase (e.g.) "the concept of the site of Troy" from the similar phrase "a concept of the site of Troy," the latter phrase being used as a common name to refer to any one of the many different concepts of this same spot.

This device is only a rough expedient to serve the purpose of informal discussion. It does not do away with the oblique use of names because, when the phrase "the concept of the site of Troy" is used in the way described, it contains an oblique occurrence of "the site of Troy."

(2) when a constituent name is replaced by another having the same denotation, the denotation of the entire name is not changed (though the sense may be).[22]

We make explicit also the following assumption (of Frege), which, like (1) and (2), has been implicit in the foregoing discussion: (3) The denotation of a name (if there is one) *is a function of* the sense of the name, in the sense of §03 below; i.e., given the sense, the existence and identity of the denotation are thereby fixed, though they may not necessarily therefore be known to every one who knows the sense.

02. Constants and Variables

We adopt the mathematical usage according to which a proper name of a number is called a *constant,* and in connection with formalized languages we extend this usage by removing the restriction to numbers, so that the term *constant* becomes synonymous with *proper name having a denotation.*

However, the term *constant* will often be applied also in the construction of uninterpreted calculi—logistic systems in the sense of §07—some of the symbols or expressions being distinguished as constants just in order to treat them differently from others in giving the rules of the calculus. Ordinarily the symbols or expressions thus distinguished as constants will in fact become proper names (with denotation) in at least one of the possible interpretations of the calculus.

As already familiar from ordinary mathematical usage, a *variable* is a symbol whose meaning is like that of a proper name or constant except that the single denotation of the constant is replaced by the possibility of various *values* of the variable.

Because it is commonly necessary to restrict the values which a variable may take, we think of a variable as having associated with it a certain non-empty range of possible values, the *range of* the variable as we shall call it. Involved in the meaning of a variable, therefore, are the kinds of meaning which belong to a proper name of the range.[23] But a variable must not be identified with a proper name of its range, since there are also differences of meaning between the two.[24]

The meaning which a variable does possess is best explained by returning to the consideration of complex names, containing other names as constituent parts. In such a complex name, having a denotation, let one of the constituent names be replaced at one or more (not necessarily all) of its occurrences by a variable, say x. To avoid complications, we suppose that x is a variable which does not otherwise

---

[22]To avoid serious difficulties, we must also assume when a constituent name has no denotation that the entire name is then likewise without denotation. In the natural languages such apparent examples to the contrary as "the myth of *Pegasus*," "the search by Ponce de Leon for *the fountain of youth*" are to be explained as exhibiting oblique occurrences of the italicized constituent name.

[23]Thus the distinction of sense and denotation comes to have an analogue for variables. Two variables with ranges determined by different concepts have to be considered as variables of different kinds, even if the ranges themselves should be identical. However, because of the restricted variety of ranges of variables admitted, this question does not arise in connection with any of the formalized languages which are actually considered below.

[24]That such an identification is impossible may be quickly seen from the point of view of the ordinary mathematical use of variables. For two proper names of the range are fully interchangeable if only they have the same sense; but two distinct variables must be kept distinct even if they have the same range determined by the same concept. E.g., if each of the letters x and y is a variable whose range is the real numbers, we are obliged to distinguish the two inequalities $x(x + y) \geqq 0$ and $x(x + x) \geqq 0$ as different—indeed the second inequality is universally true, the first one is not.

occur,[25] and that the denotation of the constituent name which x replaces is in the range of x. The resulting expression (obtained from the complex name by thus replacing one of the constituent names by a variable) we shall call a *form*.[26] Such a form, for each value of x within the range of x, or at least for certain such values of x, has a *value*. Namely, the value of the form, for a given value of x, is the same as the denotation of the expression obtained from the form by substituting everywhere for x a name of the given value of x (or, if the expression so obtained has no denotation, then the form has no value for that value of x).[27]

---

[25]This is for momentary convenience of explanation. We shall apply the name *form* also to expressions which are similarly obtained but in which the variable x may otherwise occur, provided the expression has at least one occurrence of x as a free variable (see footnote 28 and the explanation in §06 which is there referred to).

[26]This is a different use of the word *form* from that which appeared to §00 in the discussion of form and matter. We shall distinguish the latter use, when necessary, by speaking more explicitly of *logical form*.

Our present use of the word *form* is similar to that which is familiar in algebra, and in fact may be thought of as obtained from it by removing the restriction to a special kind of expressions (polynomials, or homogeneous polynomials). For the special case of propositional forms (see §04), the word is already usual in logic in this sense, independently of its use by algebraists—see, e.g., J. N. Keynes, *Formal Logic*, 4th edn., 1906, p. 53; Hugh MacColl in *Mind*, vol. 19 (1910), p. 193; Susanne K. Langer, *Introduction to Symbolic Logic*, 1937, p. 91; also Heinrich Scholz, *Vorlesungen über Grundzüge der Mathematischen Logik.*, 1949 (for the use of *Aussageform* in German).

Instead of the word *form*, we might plausibly have used the word *variable* here, by analogy with the way in which we use *constant*. I.e., just as we apply the term *constant* to a complex name containing other names (constants) as constituent parts, so we might apply the term *variable* to an appropriate complex expression containing variables as constituent parts. This usage may indeed be defended as having some sanction in mathematical writing. But we prefer to preserve the better established usage according to which a variable is always a single symbol (usually a letter or letter with subscripts).

The use, by some recent authors, of the word *function* (with or without a qualifying adjective) for what we here call a form is, in our opinion, unfortunate, because it tends to conflict with and obscure the abstract notion of a function which will be explained in §03.

[27]It follows from assumption (2), at the end of §01, that the value thus obtained for the form is independent of the choice of a particular name of the given value of x.

The distinction of sense and denotation is, however, relevant here. For in addition to a *value* of the form in the sense explained in the text (we may call it more explicitly a *denotation value*), a complete account must mention also what we may call a *sense value* of the form. Namely, a sense value of the form is determined by a concept of some value of x, and is the same as the sense of the expression obtained from the form by substituting everywhere for x a name having this concept as its sense.

It should also be noted that a form, in a particular language, may have a value even for a value of x which is without a name in that language: it is sufficient that the given value of x shall have a name in some suitable extension of the language—say, that obtained by adding to the vocabulary of the language a name of the given value of x, and allowing it to be substitutable for x wherever x occurs as a free variable. Likewise a form may have a sense value for a given concept of a value of x if some suitable extension of the language contains a name having that concept as its sense.

It is indeed possible, as we shall see later by particular examples, to construct languages of so restricted a vocabulary as to contain no constants, but only variables and forms. But it would seem that the most natural way to arrive at the meaning of forms which occur in these languages is by contemplating languages which are extensions of them and which do contain constants—or else, what is nearly the same thing, by allowing a temporary change in the meaning of the variables ("fixing the values of the variables") so that they become constants.

A variable such as x, occurring in the manner just described, is called a *free variable*[28] of the expression (form) in which it occurs.

Likewise suppose a complex name, having a denotation, to contain two constituent names neither of which is a part of the other, and let these two constituent names be replaced by two variables, say x and y respectively, each at one or more (not necessarily all) of its occurrences. For simplicity suppose that x and y are variables which do not occur in the original complex name, and that the denotations of the constituent names which x and y replace are in the ranges of x and y respectively. The resulting expression (obtained by the substitution described) is a *form*, with two *free variables* x and y. For certain pairs of values of x and y, within the ranges of x and y respectively, the form has a *value*. Namely, the value of the form, for given values of x and y, is the same as the denotation of the expression obtained from the form by substituting everywhere for x and y names of their respective values (or, if the expression so obtained has no denotation, then the form has no value for these particular values of x and y).

In the same way forms with three, four, and more free variables may be obtained. If a form contains a single free variable, we shall call it a *singulary*[29] form, if just two free variables, *binary*, if three, *ternary*, and so on. A form with exactly n different free variables is an *n-ary* form.

Two forms will be called *concurrent* if they agree in value—i.e., either have the same value or both have no value—for each assignment of values to their free variables. (Since the two forms may or may not have the same free variables, all the variables are to be considered together which have free occurrences in either form, and the forms are concurrent if they agree in value for every assignment of values to these variables.) A form will be called *concurrent* to a constant if, for every assignment of values to its free variables, its value is the same as the denotation of the constant. And two constants will be called *concurrent* if they have the same denotation.

Using the notion of concurrence, we may now add a fourth assumption, or principle of meaning, to the assumptions (1)–(3) of the last two paragraphs of §01. This is an extension of (2) to the case of forms, as follows: (4) In any constant or form, when a constituent constant or form is replaced by another concurrent to it,

---

[28] We adopt this term from Hilbert (1922), Wilhelm Ackermann (1924), J. v. Neumann (1927), Hilbert and Ackermann (1928), Hilbert and Bernays (1934). For what we here call a free variable the term *real variable* is also familiar, having been introduced by Giuseppe Peano in 1897 and afterward adopted by Russell (1908), but is less satisfactory because it conflicts with the common use of "real variable" to mean a variable whose range is the real numbers.

As we shall see later (§06), a free variable must be distinguished from a *bound variable* (in the terminology of the Hilbert school) or *apparent variable* (Peano's terminology). The difference is that an expression containing x as a free variable has values for various values of x, but an expression, containing x as a bound or apparent variable only, has a meaning which is independent of x—not in the sense of having the same value for every value of x, but in the sense that the assignment of particular values to x is not a relevant procedure.

[29] We follow W. V. Quine in adopting this etymologically more correct term, rather than the presently commoner "unary."

the entire resulting constant or form is concurrent to the original one.[30] The significance of this principle will become clearer in connection with the use of operators and bound variables, explained in §06 below. It is to be taken, like (2), as a part of our explanation of the name relation, and thus a part of our theory of meaning.

As in the case of *constant*, we shall apply the terms *variable* and *form* also in the construction of uninterpreted calculi, introducing them by special definition for each such calculus in connection with which they are to be used. Ordinarily the symbols and expressions so designated will be ones which become variables and forms in our foregoing sense under one of the principal interpretations of the calculus as a language (see §07).

It should be emphasized that a variable, in our usage, is a symbol of a certain kind[31] rather than something (e.g., a number) which is denoted or otherwise meant by such symbol. Mathematical writers do speak of "variable real numbers," or oftener "variable quantities," but it seems best not to interpret these phrases literally. Objections to the idea that real numbers are to be divided into two sorts or classes, "constant real numbers" and "variable real numbers," have been clearly stated by Frege[32] and need not be repeated here at length.[33] The fact is that a

---

[30]For completeness—using the notion of sense value explained in footnote 27 and extending it in obvious fashion to *n*-ary forms—we must also extend the assumption (1) to the case of forms, as follows. Let two forms be called *sense-concurrent* if they agree in sense value for each system of concepts of values of their free variables; let a form be called *sense-concurrent* to a constant if, for every system of concepts of values of its free variables, its sense value is the same as the sense of the constant; and let two constants be called *sense-concurrent* if they express the same sense. Then: (5) In any constant or form, when a constituent constant or form is replaced by another which is sense-concurrent to it, the entire resulting constant or form is sense-concurrent to the original one.

[31]Therefore, a variable (or more precisely, particular instances or occurrences of a variable) can be written on paper—just as the figure 7 can be written on paper, though the number 7 cannot be so written except in the indirect sense of writing something which denotes it.

And similarly constants and forms are symbols or expressions of certain kinds. It is indeed usual to speak also of numbers and physical quantities as "constants"—but this usage is not the same as that in which a constant can be contrasted with a variable, and we shall avoid it in this book.

[32]See his contribution to *Festschrift Ludwig Boltzmann Gewidmet*, 1904. (Frege's theory of functions as "ungesättigt," mentioned at the end of his paper, is another matter, not necessarily connected with his important point about variables. It will not be adopted in this book, but rather we shall take a function—see §03—to be more nearly what Frege would call "Werthverlauf einer Function.")

[33]However, we mention the following parallel to one of Frege's examples. Shall we say that the usual list of seventeen names is a complete list of the Saxon kings of England, or only that it is a complete list of the constant Saxon kings of England, and that account must be taken in addition of an indefinite number of variable Saxon kings? One of these variable Saxon kings would appear to be a human being of a very striking sort, having been, say, a grown man named Alfred in A.D. 876, and a boy named Edward in A.D. 976.

According to the doctrine we would advocate (following Frege), there are just seventeen Saxon kings of England, from Egbert to Harold, and neither a variable Saxon king nor an indeterminate Saxon king is to be admitted to swell the number. And the like holds for the positive integers, for the real numbers, and for all other domains abstract and concrete. Variability or indeterminacy, where such exists, is a matter of language and attaches to symbols or expressions.

satisfactory theory has never been developed on this basis, and it is not easy to see how it might be done.

The mathematical theory of real numbers provides a convenient source of examples in a system of notation[34] whose general features are well established. Turning to this theory to illustrate the foregoing discussion, we cite as particular examples of constants the ten expressions:

$$0, -\frac{1}{2}, e, -\frac{1}{2\pi}, \frac{1-4+1}{4\pi}, 4e^4, e^8, e-e, -\frac{\pi}{2\pi}, \frac{\sin \pi/7}{\pi/7}.$$

Let us say that x and y are variables whose range is the real numbers, and m, n, r are variables whose range is the positive integers.[35] The following are examples of forms:

$$y, -\frac{1}{y}, -\frac{1}{x}, -\frac{1}{2x}, \frac{1-4+1}{4x}, 4e^x, xe^x, x^x,$$

$$x-x, n-n, \frac{x}{2x}, \frac{r}{2r}, \frac{\sin x}{x}, \frac{\sin r}{r},$$

$$ye^x, -\frac{y}{xy}, -\frac{r}{xr}, \frac{x-m+1}{m\pi}.$$

The forms on the first two lines are singularly, each having one free variable, $y, x, n,$ or r as the case may be. The forms on the third line are binary, the first two having x and y as free variables, the third one x and r, the fourth one x and m.[36]

---

[34] We say "system of notation" rather than "language" because only the specifically numerical notations can be regarded as well established in ordinary mathematical writing. They are usually supplemented (for the statement of theorems and proofs) by one or another of the natural languages, according to the choice of the particular writer.

[35] Every positive integer is also a real number. I.e., the terms must be so understood for purposes of these illustrations.

[36] To illustrate the remark of footnote 28, following are some examples of expressions containing bound variables:

$$\int_0^2 x^x dx, \quad \lim_{x\to 0}\frac{\sin x}{x}, \quad \sum_{n=1}^\infty \prod_{m=1}^{m=n} \frac{x-m+1}{m\pi}.$$

The first two of these are constants, containing x as a bound variable. The third is a singularly form, with x as a free variable and m and n as bound variables.

A variable may have both free and bound occurrences in the same expression. An example is $\int_0^x x^x dx$, the double use of the letter x constituting no ambiguity. Other examples are the variable Δ_x in $(D_x \sin x)\Delta_x$ and the variable x in $xE(k)$, if the notations $D_x \sin x$ and $E(k)$ are replaced by their equivalents

$$\lim_{\Delta x\to 0}\frac{\sin(x+\Delta x)-\sin x}{\Delta x}$$

and

$$\int_0^1 \frac{\sqrt{1-k^2x^2}}{\sqrt{1-x^2}}dx$$

respectively.

The constants

$$-\frac{1}{2\pi} \quad \text{and} \quad \frac{1 - 4 + 1}{4\pi}$$

are not identical. But they are concurrent, since each denotes the same number.[37] Similarly the constants $e - e$ and 0, though not identical, are concurrent because the numbers $e - e$ and 0 are identical. Similarly $-\pi/2\pi$ and $-1/2$.

The form xe^x, for the value 0 of x, has the value 0. (Of course it is the number 0 that is here in question, not the constant 0, so that it is equally correct to say that the form xe^x, for the value 0 of x, has the value $e - e$; or that, for the value $e - e$ of x, it has the value 0; etc.) For the value 1 of x the form xe^x has the value e. For the value 4 of x its value is $4e^x$, a real number for which (as it happens) no simpler name is in standard use.

The form ye^x, for the values 0 and 4 of x and y respectively, has the value 4. For the values 1 and 1 of x and y it has the value $1e^1$; or, what is the same thing, it has the value e.

The form $-y/xy$, for the values e and 2 of x and y respectively, has the value $-1/e$. For the values e and e of x and y, it has again the value $-1/e$. For the values e and 0 of x and y it has no value, because of the non-existence of a quotient of 0 by 0.

The form $-r/xr$, for the values e and 2 of x and r respectively, has the value $-1/e$. But there is no value for the values e and e of x and r, because e is not in the range of r (e is not one of the possible values of r).

The forms

$$-\frac{1}{2x} \quad \text{and} \quad \frac{1 - 4 + 1}{4x}$$

are concurrent, since they are both without a value for the value 0 of x, and they have the same value for all other values of x. The forms $-1/x$ and $-y/xy$ fail to be concurrent, since they disagree for the value 0 of y (if the value of x is not 0). But the forms $-1/x$ and $-r/xr$ are concurrent.

The forms $-1/y$ and $-1/x$ are not concurrent, as they disagree, e.g., for the values 1 and 2 of x and y respectively.

The forms $x - x$ and $n - n$ are concurrent to the same constant, namely 0,[38] and are therefore also concurrent to each other.

The forms $-x/2x$ and $-r/2r$ are non-concurrent because of disagreement for the value 0 of x. The latter form, but not the former, is concurrent to a constant, namely to $-1/2$.

---

[37]Whether these two constants have the same sense (as well as the same denotation) is a question which depends for its answer on a general theory of equality of senses, such as we have not undertaken to discuss here—cf. footnote 15. It is clear that Frege, though he formulates no complete theory of equality of senses, would regard these two constants as having different senses. But a plausible case might be made out for supposing that the two constants have the same sense, on some such ground as that the equation between them expresses a necessary proposition or is true on logical grounds alone or the like. No doubt there is more than one meaning of "sense," according to the criterion adopted for equality of senses, and the decision among them is a matter of convention and expediency.

[38]Or also to any other constant which is concurrent to 0.

03. Functions

By a *function*—or, more explicitly, a *one-valued singulary* function—we shall understand an operation[39] which, when applied to something as *argument*, yields a certain thing as the *value* of the function *for* that argument. It is not required that the function be applicable to every possible thing as argument, but rather it lies in the nature of any given function to be applicable to certain things and, when applied to one of them as argument, to yield a certain value. The things to which the function is applicable constitute the *range of* the function (or the *range of arguments of* the function) and the values constitute the *range of values of* the function. The function itself consists in the yielding or determination[39] of a value from each argument in the range of the function.

As regards equality or identity of functions we make the decision which is usual in mathematics. Namely, functions are identical if they have the same range and have, for each argument in the range, the same value. In other words, we take the word "function" to mean what may otherwise be called a *function in extension*. If the way in which a function yields or produces its value from its argument is altered without causing any change either in the range of the function or in the value of the function for any argument, then the function remains the same; but the associated *function concept*, or concept determining the function (in the sense of §01), is thereby changed.

We shall speak of a function *from* a certain class *to* a certain class to mean a function which has the first class as its range and has all its values in the second class (though the second class may possibly be more extensive than the range of values of the function).

To denote the value of a function for a given argument, it is usual to write a name of the function, followed by a name of the argument between parentheses. And of course the same notation applies (*mutatis mutandis*) with a variable or a form in place of either one or both of the names. Thus if f is a function and x belongs to the range of f, then $f(x)$ is the value of the function f for the argument x.[40]

This is the usual notation for application of a function to an argument, and we shall often employ it. In some context . . . we find it convenient to alter the notation by changing the position of the parentheses, so that we may write in the altered notation: if f is a function and x belongs to the range of f, then (fx) is the value of the function f for the argument x.

So far we have discussed only *one-valued singulary functions* (and have used the word "function" in this sense). Indeed no use will be made in this book of

---

[39]Of course the words "operation," "yielding," "determination" as here used are near-synonyms of "function" and therefore our statement, if taken as a definition, would be open to the suspicion of circularity. Throughout this Introduction, however, we are engaged in informal explanation rather than definition, and, for this purpose, elaboration by means of synonyms may be a useful procedure. Ultimately, it seems, we must take the notion of function as primitive or undefined, or else some related notion, such as that of a class. . . .

[40]This sentence exemplifies the use of variables to make general statements, which we assume is understood from familiar mathematical usage, though it has not yet been explained in this Introduction. (See the end of §06.)

many-valued functions,[41] and the reader must always understand "function" to mean a one-valued function. But we go on to explain functions of more than one argument.

A *binary function*, or function *of two arguments*,[42] is characterized by being applicable to two arguments in a certain order and yielding, when so applied, a certain value, the *value of* the function *for* those two arguments in that order. It is not required that the function be applicable to every two things as arguments; but rather, the function is applicable in certain cases to an ordered pair of things as arguments, and all such ordered pairs constitute the *range of* the function. The values constitute the *range of values of* the function.

Binary functions are identical (i.e., are the same function) if they have the same range and have, for each ordered pair of arguments which lies in that range, the same value.

To denote the value of a binary function for given arguments, it is usual to write a name of the function and then, between parentheses and separated by a comma, names of the arguments in order. Thus if f is a binary function and the ordered pair of x and y belongs to the range of f, then $f(x, y)$ is the value of the function f for the arguments x and y in that order.

In the same way may be explained the notion of a ternary function, of a quaternary function, and so on. In general, an n-ary function is applied to n arguments in an order, and when so applied yields a value, provided the ordered system of n arguments is in the range of the function. The value of an n-ary function for given arguments is denoted by a name of the function followed, between parentheses and separated by commas, by names of the arguments in order.

Two binary functions ϕ and ψ are called *converses*, each of the other, in case the two following conditions are satisfied: (1) the ordered pair of x and y belongs to the range of ϕ if and only if the ordered pair of y and x belongs to the range of ψ; (2) for all x, y such that the ordered pair of x and y belongs to the range of ϕ,[43]

$$\phi(x, y) = \psi(y, x).$$

---

[41]It is the idea of a many-valued (singular) function that, for a fixed argument, there may be more than one value of the function. If a name of the function is written, followed by a name of an argument between parentheses, the resulting expression is a common name (see footnote 6) denoting the values of the function for that argument.

Though many-valued functions seem to arise naturally in the mathematical theories of real and complex numbers, objections immediately suggest themselves to the idea as just explained and are not easily overcome. Therefore it is usual to replace such many-valued functions in one way or another by one-valued functions. One method is to replace a many-valued singular function by a corresponding one-valued binary propositional function or relation (§04). Another method is to replace the many-valued function by a one-valued function whose values are classes, namely, the value of the one-valued function for a given argument is the class of the values of the many-valued function for that argument. Still another method is to change the range of the function, an argument for which the function has n values giving way to n different arguments for each of which the function has a different one of those n values (this is the standard role of the Riemann surface in the theory of complex numbers).

[42]Though it is in common use we shall avoid the phrase "function of two variables" (and "function of three variables" etc.) because it tends to make confusion between *arguments* to which a function is applied and *variables* taking such arguments as values.

[43]The use of the sign = to express that things are identical is assumed familiar to the reader. We do not restrict this notation to the special case of numbers, but use it for identity generally.

A binary function is called *symmetric* if it is identical with its converse. The notions of converse and of symmetry may also be extended to *n*-ary functions, several different converses and several different kinds of symmetry appearing when the number of arguments is three or more (we need not stop over details of this).

We shall speak of a function *of* things of a certain kind to mean a function such that all the arguments to which it is applicable are of that kind. Thus a singulary function of real numbers, for instance, is a function from some class of real numbers to some (arbitrary) class. A binary function of real numbers is a binary function whose range consists of ordered pairs of real numbers (not necessarily all ordered pairs of real numbers).

We shall use the phrase "___ is a function of ___," filling the blanks with forms,[44] to mean what is more fully expressed as follows: "There exists a function *f* such that

$$ \underline{\quad} = f(\underline{\quad}) $$

for all ___," where the first two blanks are filled, in order, with the same forms as before, and the third blank is filled with a complete list of the free variables of those forms. Similarly we shall use "___ is a function of ___ and ___," filling the three blanks with forms, to stand for: "There exists a binary function *f* such that

$$ \underline{\quad} = f(\underline{\quad}, \underline{\quad}) $$

for all ___," where the first three blanks are filled, in order, with the same forms as before, and the last blank is filled with a complete list of the free variables of those forms.[45] And similar phraseology will also be used where the reference is to a function *f* of more than two arguments.

The phraseology just explained will also be used with the added statement of a condition or restriction. For example, "___ is a function of ___ and ___ if ___," where the first three blanks are filled with forms, and the fourth is filled with the statement of a condition involving some or all of the free variables of those forms,[46] stands for: "There exists a binary function *f* such that

$$ \underline{\quad} = f(\underline{\quad}, \underline{\quad}) $$

for all ___ for which ___," where the first three blanks are filled, in order, with the same forms as before, the fourth blank is filled with a complete list of the free

---

[44]Our explanation assumes that neither of these forms has the particular letter *f* as one of its free variables. In the contrary case, the explanation is to be altered by using in place of the letter *f* as it appears in the text some variable (with appropriate range) which is not a free variable of either form.

[45]The theory of real numbers again serving as a source of examples, it is thus true that $x^3 + y^3$ is a function of $x + y$ and xy. But it is false that $x^3 + x^2y - xy^2 + y^3$ is a function of $x + y$ and xy (as is easily seen on the ground that the form $x^3 + x^2y - xy^2 + y^3$ is not symmetric). Again, $x^4 + y^4 + z^4 + 4x^3y + 4xy^3 + 4x^3z + 4xz^3 + 4y^3z + 4yz^3$ is a function of $x + y + z$ and $xy + xz + yz$. But $x^4 + y^4 + z^4$ is not a function of $x + y + z$ and $xy + xz + yz$.

[46]Thus with a *propositional form*, in the sense of §04 below.

variables of those forms, and the fifth blank is filled in the same way as the fourth blank was before.[47]

Also the same phraseology, explained in the two preceding paragraphs, will be used with common names[48] in place of forms. In this case the forms which the common names represent have to be supplied from the context. For example, the statement that *"The density of helium gas* is a function of *the temperature* and *the pressure"* is to be understood as meaning the same as *"The density of h* is a function of *the temperature of h* and *the pressure of h,"* where the three italicized forms replace the three original italicized common names, and where *h* is a variable whose values are instantaneous bits of helium gas (and whose range consists of all such). Or to avoid introducing the variable *h* with so special a range, we may understand instead: "The density of *b* is a function of the temperature of *b* and the pressure of *b* if *b* is an instantaneous bit of helium gas." Similarly the statement at the end of §01 that the denotation of a name is a function of the sense means more explicitly (the reference being to a fixed language) that there exists a function *f* such that

$$\text{denotation of } N = f(\text{sense of } N)$$

for all names *N* for which there is a denotation.

It remains now to discuss the relationship between *functions*, in the abstract sense that we have been explaining, and *forms*, in the sense of the preceding section (§02).

If we suppose the language fixed, every singulary form has corresponding to it a function *f* (which we shall call the *associated function* of the form) by the rule that the value of *f* for an argument *x* is the same as the value of the form for the value *x* of the free variable of the form, the range of *f* consisting of all *x*'s such that the form has a value for the value *x* of its free variable.[49] But, still with reference

---

[47] Accordingly it is true, for example, that: $x^3 + x^2y - xy^2 + y^3$ is a function of $x + y$ and xy if $x \geqq y$. For the special case that the variables have a range consisting of real or complex numbers, a geometric terminology is often used, thus: $x^3 + x^2y - xy^2 + y^3$ is a function of $x + y$ and xy in the half-plane $x \geqq y$.

[48] See footnotes 4, 6.

[49] For example, in the theory of real numbers, the form $\frac{1}{2}(e^x - e^{-x})$ determines the function sinh as its associated function, by the rule that the value of sinh for an argument *x* is $\frac{1}{2}(e^x - e^{-x})$. The range of sinh then consists of all *x*'s (i.e., all real numbers *x*) for which $\frac{1}{2}(e^x - e^{-x})$ has a value. In other words, as it happens in this particular case, the range consists of all real numbers.

Of course the free variable of the form need not be the particular letter *x*, and indeed it may be clearer to take an example in which the free variable is some other letter.

Thus the form $\frac{1}{2}(e^y - e^{-y})$ determines the function sinh as its associated function, by the rule that the value of sinh for an argument *x* is the same as the value of the form $\frac{1}{2}(e^y - e^{-y})$ for the value *x* of the variable *y*. (I.e., in particular, the value of sinh for the argument 2 is the same as the value of the form $\frac{1}{2}(e^y - e^{-y})$ for the value 2 of the variable *y*; and so on for each different argument *x* that may be assigned.)

Ordinarily, just the equation

$$\sinh(x) = \frac{1}{2}(e^x - e^{-x})$$

is written as sufficient indication of the foregoing. And this equation may even be called a *definition* of sinh. . . .

to a fixed language, not every function is necessarily the associated function of some form.[50]

It follows that two concurrent singular forms with the same free variable have the same associated function. Also two singular forms have the same associated function if they differ only by alphabetic change of the free variable,[51] i.e., if one is obtained from the other by substituting everywhere for its free variable some other variable with the same range—with, however, the proviso (the need of which will become clearer later) that the substituted variable must remain a free variable at every one of its occurrences resulting from the substitution.

As a notation for (i.e., to denote) the associated function of a singular form having, say, x as its free variable, we write the form itself with the letters λx prefixed. And of course likewise with any other variable in place of x.[52] Parentheses are to be supplied as necessary.[53]

As an obvious extension of this notation, we shall also prefix the letters λx (λy, etc.) to any constant as a notation for the function whose value is the same for

---

[50]According to classical real-number theory, the singular functions from real numbers to real numbers (or even just the analytic singular functions) are non-enumerable. Since the forms in a particular language are always enumerable, it follows that there is no language or system of notation in which every singular function from real numbers to real numbers is the associated function of some form.

Because of the non-enumerability of the real numbers themselves, it is even impossible in any language to provide proper names of all the real numbers. (Such a thing as, e.g., an infinite decimal expansion must not be considered a *name* of the corresponding real number, as of course an infinite expansion cannot ever be written out in full, or included as a part of any actually written or spoken sentence.)

[51]E.g., as appears in footnote 49, the forms $\frac{1}{2}(e^x - e^{-x})$ and $\frac{1}{2}(e^y - e^{-y})$ have the same associated function.

[52]Thus the expressions $\lambda x(\frac{1}{2}(e^x - e^{-x}))$, $\lambda y(\frac{1}{2}(e^y - e^{-y}))$, sinh are all three synonymous, having not only the same denotation (namely the function sinh), but also the same sense, even under the severest criterion of sameness of sense.

(In saying this we are supposing a language or system of notation in which the two different expressions sinh and $\lambda x(\frac{1}{2}(e^x - e^{-x}))$ both occur. However, the very fact of synonymy shows that the expression sinh is dispensable in principle: except for considerations of convenience, it could always be replaced by the longer expression $\lambda x(\frac{1}{2}(e^x - e^{-x}))$. In constructing a formalized language, we prefer to avoid such duplications of notation so far as readily possible. . . .

The expressions $\lambda x(\frac{1}{2}(e^x - e^{-x}))$ and $\lambda y(\frac{1}{2}(e^y - e^{-y}))$ contain the variables x and y respectively, as *bound* variables in the sense of footnotes 28, 36 (and of §06 below). For, according to the meaning just explained for them, these expressions are constants, not singular forms. But of course the expression $\frac{1}{2}(e^x - e^{-x})$ is a singular form, with x as a free variable.

The meaning of such an expression as $\lambda x(y e^z)$, formed from the binary form $y e^x$ by prefixing λx, now follows as a consequence of the explanation about variables and forms in §02. In this expression, x is a bound variable and y is a free variable, and the expression is a singular form whose values are singular functions. From it, by prefixing λy, we obtain a constant, denoting a singulary function, and the range of values of this singulary function consists of singulary functions.

[53]In constructing a formalized language, the manner in which parentheses are to be put in has to be specified with more care. As a matter of fact this will be done, as we shall see, not by associating parentheses with the notation λx, but by suitable provision for parentheses (or brackets) in connection with various other notations which may occur in the form to which λx is prefixed.

all arguments and is the denotation of the constant, the range of the function being the same as the range of the variable x.[54] This function will be called an *associated singulary function* of the constant, by analogy with the terminology "associated function of a form," though there is the difference that the same constant may have various associated functions with different ranges. Any function whose value is the same for all arguments will be called a *constant function* (without regard to any question whether it is an associated function of a constant, in some particular language under consideration).[55]

Analogous to the associated function of a singulary form, a binary form has two associated binary functions, one for each of the two orders in which the two free variables may be considered—or better, one for each of the two ways in which a pair of arguments of the function may be assigned as values to the two free variables of the form.

The two associated functions of a binary form are identical, and thus reduce to one function, if and only if they are symmetric. In this case the binary form itself is also called *symmetric*.[56]

Likewise an n-ary form has $n!$ associated n-ary functions, one for each of the permutations of its free variables. Some of these associated functions are identical in certain cases of symmetry.

Likewise a constant has associated m-ary functions, for $m = 1, 2, 3, \ldots$, by an obvious extension of the explanation already made for the special case $m = 1$. And by a still further extension of this we may speak of the associated m-ary functions of an n-ary form, when $m > n$. In particular a singulary form has not only an associated singulary function but also associated binary functions, associated ternary functions, and so on. (When, however, we speak simply of *the* associated function of a singulary form, we shall mean the associated singulary function.)

The notation by means of λ for the associated functions of a form, as introduced above for singulary functions, is readily extended to the case of m-ary functions,[57] but we shall not have occasion to use such extension in this book. The passage from a form to an associated function (for which the λ-notation provides a symbolism) we shall speak of as *abstraction* or, more explicitly, *m-ary functional abstraction* (if the associated function is m-ary).

---

[54]Thus in connection with real-number theory we use $\lambda x\, 2$ as a notation for the function whose range consists of all real numbers and whose value is 2 for every argument.

[55]Note should also be taken of expressions in which the variable after λ is not the same as the free variable of the form which follows; thus, for example, $\lambda y(\frac{1}{2}(e^x - e^{-x}))$ As is seen from the explanation in §02, this expression is a singulary form with x as its free variable, the values of the form being constant functions. For the value 0 of x, e.g., the form $\lambda y(\frac{1}{2}(e^x - e^{-x}))$ has as its value the constant function $\lambda y 0$.

In both expressions, $\lambda y(\frac{1}{2}(e^x - e^{-x}))$ and $\lambda y 0$, y is a bound or apparent variable.

[56]We have already used this term, as applied to forms, in footnote 45, assuming the reader's understanding of it as familiar mathematical terminology.

[57]This has been done by Carnap in *Notes for Symbolic Logic* (1937) and elsewhere.

Historically the notion of a function was of gradual growth in mathematics, and its beginning is difficult to trace. The particular word "function" was first introduced by G. W. v. Leibniz and was adopted from him by Jean Bernoulli. The notation $f(x)$, or fx, with a letter such as f in the role of a function variable, was introduced by A. C. Clairaut and by Leonhard Euler. But early accounts of the notion of *function* do not sufficiently separate it from that of an expression containing free variables (or a *form*). Thus Euler explains a *function of a variable quantity* by identifying it with an analytic expression,[58] i.e., a form in some standard system of mathematical notation. The abstract notion of a function is usually attributed by historians of mathematics to G. Lejeune Dirichlet, who in 1837 was led by his study of Fourier series to a major generalization in freeing the idea of a function from its former dependence on a mathematical expression or law of circumscribed kind.[59] Dirichlet's notion of a function was adopted by Bernhard Riemann (1851),[60] by Hermann Hankel (1870),[61] and indeed by mathematicians generally. But two important steps remained to be taken by Frege (in his *Begriffsschrift* of 1879 and later publications): (i) the elimination of the dubious notion of a variable quantity in favor of the variable as a kind of symbol;[62] (ii) the admission of functions of arbitrary range by removing the restriction that the arguments and values of a function be numbers. Closely associated with (ii) is Frege's introduction of the *propositional function* (in 1879), a notion which we go on to explain in the next section.

---

[58] *"Functio quantitatis variabilis est expressio analytica quomodocunque composita ex illa quantitate variabili et numeris seu quantitatibus constantibus.* Omnis ergo expressio analytica, in qua praeter quantitatem variabilem z omnes quantitates illam expressionem componentes sunt constantes, erit functio ipsius z . . . *Functio ergo quantitatis variabilis ipsa erit quantitas variabilis."* Introductio in Analysin Infinitorum (1748), p. 4; Opera, ser. 1, vol. 8, p. 18. See further footnote 62.

[59] See his *Werke*, vol. 1, p. 135. It is not important that Dirichlet restricts his statement at this particular place to continuous functions, since it is clear from other passages in his writings that the same generality is allowed to discontinuous functions. On page 132 of the same volume is his well-known example of a function from real numbers to real numbers which has exactly two values, one for rational arguments and one for irrational arguments.

Dirichlet's generalization had been partially anticipated by Euler in 1749 (see an account by H. Burkhardt in *Jahresbericht der Deutschen Mathematiker-Vereinigung*, vol. 10 part 2 (1908), pp. 13–14) and later by J. B. J. Fourier (see his *Oeuvres*, vol. 1, pp. 207, 209, 230–232).

[60] *Werke*, pp. 3–4.

[61] In a paper reprinted in the *Mathematische Annalen*, vol. 20 (1882), pp. 63–112.

[62] The passage quoted from Euler in footnote 58 reads as if his *variable quantity* were a kind of symbol or expression. But this is not consistent with statements made elsewhere in the same work which are essential to Euler's use of the notion of function—e.g., *"Si fuerit y functio quaecunque ipsius z, tum vicissim z erit functio ipsius y"* (Opera, p. 24), "Sed omnis transformatio consistit in alio modo eandem functionem exprimendi, quemadmodum ex Algebra constat eandem quantitatem per plures diversas formas exprimi posse" (Opera, p. 32).

04. Propositions and Propositional Functions

According to grammarians, the unit of expression in the natural languages is the *sentence*, an aggregation of words which makes complete sense or expresses a complete thought. When the complete thought expressed is that of an assertion, the sentence is called a *declarative sentence*. In what follows we shall have occasion to refer only to declarative sentences, and the simple word "sentence" is to be understood always as meaning a declarative sentence.[63]

We shall carry over the term *sentence* from the natural languages also to the formalized languages. For logistic systems in the sense of §07—uninterpreted calculi—the term *sentence* will be introduced by special definition in each case, but always with the intention that the expressions defined to be sentences are those which will become sentences in our foregoing sense under interpretations of the calculus as a formalized language.[64]

In order to give an account of the meaning of sentences, we shall adopt a theory due to Frege according to which sentences are names of a certain kind. This seems unnatural at first sight, because the most conspicuous use of sentences (and indeed the one by which we have just identified or described them) is not barely to name something but to make an assertion. Nevertheless it is possible to regard sentences as names by distinguishing between the assertive use of a sentence on the one hand, and its non-assertive use, on the other hand, as a name and a constituent of a longer sentence (just as other names are used). Even when a sentence is simply asserted, we shall hold that it is still a name, though used in a way not possible for other names.[65]

An important advantage of regarding sentences as names is that all the ideas and explanations of §§01–03 can then be taken over at once and applied to sentences, and related matters, as a special case. Else we should have to develop independently a theory of the meaning of sentences; and in the course of this, it seems, the developments of these three sections would be so closely paralleled that in the end the identification of sentences as a kind of names (though not demonstrated) would be very forcefully

---

[63]The question may be raised whether, say, an interrogative or an imperative logic is possible, in which interrogative or imperative sentences and what they express (questions or commands) have roles analogous to those of declarative sentences and propositions in logic of ordinary kind. And some tentative proposals have in fact been made towards an imperative logic, and also towards an optative logic or logic of wishes. But these matters are beyond the scope of this book.

[64]Cf. the explanation in §02 regarding the use in connection with logistic systems of the terms *constant, variable, form*. An analogous explanation applies to a number of terms of like kind to be introduced below—in particular, *propositional variable, propositional form, operator, quantifier, bound variable, connective*.

[65]To distinguish the non-assertive use of a sentence and the assertive use, especially in a formalized language, Frege wrote a horizontal line, —, before the sentence in the former case, and the character ⊢ before it in the latter case, the addition of the vertical line thus serving as a sign of assertion. Russell, and Whitehead and Russell in *Principia Mathematica*, did not follow Frege's use of the horizontal line before non-asserted sentences, but did take over the character ⊢ in the role of an assertion sign.

(Frege also used the horizontal line before names other than sentences, the expression so formed being a false sentence. But this is a feature of his notation which need not concern us here.) . . .

suggested as a means of simplifying and unifying the theory. In particular we shall require variables for which sentences may be substituted, forms which become sentences upon replacing their free variables by appropriate constants, and associated functions of such forms—things which, on the theory of sentences as names, fit naturally into their proper place in the scheme set forth in §§02–03.

Granted that sentences are names, we go on, in the light of the discussion in §01, to consider the denotation and the sense of sentences.

As a consequence of the principle (2), stated in the next to last paragraph of §01, examples readily present themselves of sentences which, though in some sense of different meaning, must apparently have the same denotation. Thus the denotation (in English) of "Sir Walter Scott is the author of *Waverley*" must be the same as that of "Sir Walter Scott is Sir Walter Scott," the name "the author of *Waverley*" being replaced by another which has the same denotation. Again the sentence "Sir Walter Scott is the author of *Waverley*" must have the same denotation as the sentence "Sir Walter Scott is the man who wrote twenty-nine Waverley Novels altogether," since the name "the author of *Waverley*" is replaced by another name of the same person; the latter sentence, it is plausible to suppose, if it is not synonymous with "The number, such that Sir Walter Scott is the man who wrote that many Waverley Novels altogether, is twenty-nine," is at least so nearly so as to ensure its having the same denotation; and from this last sentence in turn, replacing the complete subject by another name of the same number, we obtain, as still having the same denotation, the sentence "The number of counties in Utah is twenty-nine."

Now the two sentences, "Sir Walter Scott is the author of *Waverley*" and "The number of counties in Utah is twenty-nine," though they have the same denotation according to the preceding line of reasoning, seem actually to have very little in common. The most striking thing that they do have in common is that both are true. Elaboration of examples of this kind leads us quickly to the conclusion, as at least plausible, that all true sentences have the same denotation. And parallel examples may be used in the same way to suggest that all false sentences have the same denotation (e.g., "Sir Walter Scott is not the author of *Waverley*" must have the same denotation as "Sir Walter Scott is not Sir Walter Scott").

Therefore, with Frege, we postulate[66] two abstract objects called *truth-values*, one of them being *truth* and the other one *falsehood*. And we declare all true sentences to denote the truth-value truth, and all false sentences to denote the truth-value falsehood. In alternative phraseology, we shall also speak of a sentence as *having* the truth-value truth (if it is true) or *having* the truth-value falsehood (if it is false).[67]

---

[66]To Frege, as a thoroughgoing Platonic realist, our use of the word "postulate" here would not be acceptable. It would represent his position better to say that the situation indicates that *there are* two such things as truth and falsehood (*das Wahre* and *das Falsche*).

[67]The explicit use of two truth-values appears for the first time in a paper by C. S. Peirce in the *American Journal of Mathematics*, vol. 7 (1885), pp. 180–202 (or see his *Collected Papers*, vol. 3, pp. 210–238). Frege's first use of truth-values is in his *Funktion und Begriff* of 1891 and in his paper of 1892 which is cited in footnote 5; it is in these that the account of sentences as names of truth-values is first put forward.

The sense of a sentence may be described as that which is grasped when one understands the sentence, or as that which two sentences in different languages must have in common in order to be correct translations each of the other. As in the case of names generally, it is possible to grasp the sense of a sentence without therefore necessarily having knowledge of its denotation (truth-value) otherwise than as determined by this sense. In particular, though the sense is grasped, it may sometimes remain unknown whether the denotation is truth.

Any concept of a truth-value, provided that being a truth-value is contained in the concept, and whether or not it is the sense of some actually available sentence in a particular language under consideration, we shall call a *proposition*, translating thus Frege's *Gedanke*.

Therefore a proposition, as we use the term, is an abstract object of the same general category as a class, a number, or a function. It has not the psychological character of William of Ockham's *propositio mentalis* or of the traditional *judgment:* in the words of Frege, explaining his term *Gedanke*, it is "nicht das subjective Thun des Denkens, sondern dessen objectiven Inhalt, der fähig ist, gemeinsames Eigenthum von Vielen zu sein."

Traditional (post-Scholastic) logicians were wont to define a proposition as a judgment expressed in words, thus as a linguistic entity, either a sentence or a sentence taken in association with its meaning.[68] But in non-technical English the word has long been used rather for the meaning (in our view the sense) of a sentence,[69] and logicians have latterly come to accept this as the technical meaning of "proposition." This is the happy result of a process which, historically, must have been due in part to sheer confusion between the sentence in itself and the meaning of the sentence. It provides in English a distinction not easily expressed in some other languages, and makes possible a translation of Frege's *Gedanke* which is less misleading than the word "thought."[70]

According to our usage, every proposition determines or is a concept of (or, as we shall also say, has) some truth-value. It is, however, a somewhat arbitrary decision that we deny the name *proposition* to senses of such sentences (of the natural

---

[68]E.g., in Isaac Watts's *Logick*, 1725: "A *Proposition* is a Sentence wherein two or more *Ideas* or *Terms* are joined or disjoined by one Affirmation or Negation. . . . In describing a *Proposition* I use the Word *Terms* as well as *Ideas*, because when mere Ideas are join'd in the Mind without Words, it is rather called a *judgment*; but when clothed with Words, it is called a *Proposition*, even tho' it be in the Mind only, as well as when it is expressed by speaking or Writing." Again in Richard Whately's *Elements of Logic*, 1826: "The second part of Logic treats of the *proposition;* which is, '*Judgment expressed in words.*' A Proposition is defined logically 'a sentence indicative,' i.e., affirming or denying; (this excludes *commands* and *questions*.)" Here Whately is following in part the Latin of Henry Aldrich (1691). In fact these passages show no important advance over Petrus Hispanus, who wrote a half millennium earlier, but they are quoted here apropos of the history of the word "proposition" in English.

[69]Consider, for example, the incongruous result obtained by substituting the words "declarative sentence" for the word "proposition" in Lincoln's Gettysburg Address.

[70]For a further account of the history of the matter, we refer to Carnap's *Introduction to Semantics*, 1942, pp. 235–236; and see also R. M. Eaton, *General Logic*, 1931.

languages) as express a sense but have no truth-value.[71] To this extent our use of *proposition* deviates from Frege's use of *Gedanke*. But the question will not arise in connection with the formalized languages which we shall study, as these languages will be so constructed that every name—and in particular every sentence—has a denotation.

A proposition is then *true* if it determines or has the truth-value truth, *false* if it has the truth-value falsehood. When a sentence expressing a proposition is asserted we shall say that the proposition itself is thereby *asserted*.[72]

A variable whose range is the two truth-values—thus a variable for which sentences (expressing propositions) may appropriately be substituted—is called a *propositional variable*. We shall not have occasion to use variables whose values are propositions, but we would suggest the term *intentional propositional variable* for these.

A form whose values are truth-values (and which therefore becomes a sentence when its free variables are replaced by appropriate constants) is a *propositional form*. Usage sanctions this term[73] rather than "truth-value form," thus

----

[71] By the remark of footnote 22, such are sentences which contain non-obliquely one or more names that express a sense but lack a denotation—or so, following Frege, we shall take them. Examples are: "The present king of France is bald"; "The present king of France is not bald"; "The author of *Principia Mathematica* was born in 1861." (As to the last example, it is true that the phrase "the author of *Principia Mathematica*" in some appropriate supporting context may be an ellipsis for something like "the author of *Principia Mathematica* who was just mentioned" and therefore have a denotation; but we here suppose that there is no such supporting context, so that the phrase can only mean "the one and only author of *Principia Mathematica*" and therefore have no denotation.)

To sentences as a special case of names, of course the second remark of footnote 22 also applies. Thus we understand as true (and containing oblique occurrences of names) each of the sentences: "Lady Hamilton was like Aphrodite in beauty"; "The fountain of youth is not located in Florida"; "The present king of France does not exist." Cases of doubt whether a sentence has a truth-value or not are also not difficult to find in this connection, the exact meaning of various phraseologies in the natural languages being often insufficiently determinate for a decision.

[72] Notice the following distinction. The statement that a certain proposition was asserted (say on such and such an occasion) need not reveal what language was used nor make any reference to a particular language. But the statement that a certain sentence was asserted does not convey the meaning of the transaction unless it is added what language was used. For not only may the same proposition be expressed by different sentences in different languages, but also the same sentence may be used to assert different propositions according to what language the user intends. It is beside the point that the latter situation is comparatively rare in the principal known natural languages; it is not rare when all possible languages are taken into account.

Thus, if the language is English, the statement, "Seneca said that man is a rational animal," conveys the proposition that Seneca asserted but not the information what language he used. On the other hand the statement, "Seneca wrote, 'Rationale enim animal est homo,'" gives only the information what succession of letters he set down, not what proposition he asserted. (The reader may guess or know from other sources that Seneca used Latin, but this is neither said nor implied in the given statement—for there are many languages besides Latin in which this succession of letters spells a declarative sentence and, for all that thou and I know, one of them may once have been in actual use.)

[73] Cf. footnote 26.

naming the form rather by what is expressed, when constants replace the variables, than by what is denoted.

A propositional form is said to be *satisfied by* a value of its free variable, or a system of values of its free variables, if its value for those values of its free variables is truth. (More explicitly, we should speak of a system of values of variables as satisfying a given propositional form *in a given language,* but the reference to the particular language may often be omitted as clear from the context.) A propositional form may also be said to be *true* or *false* for a given value of its free variable, or system of values of its free variables, according as its value for those values of its free variables is truth or falsehood.

A function whose range of values consists exclusively of truth-values, and thus in particular any associated function of a propositional form, is a *propositional function.* Here again, established usage sanctions "propositional function"[74] rather than "truth-value function," though the latter term would be the one analogous to, e.g., the term "numerical function" for a function whose values are numbers.

A propositional function is said to be *satisfied by* an argument (or ordered system of arguments) if its value for that argument (or ordered system of arguments) is truth. Or synonymously we may say that a propositional function *holds for* a particular argument or ordered system of arguments.

From its use in mathematics, we assume that the notion of a *class* is already at least informally familiar to the reader. (The words *set* and *aggregate* are ordinarily used as synonymous with *class,* but we shall not follow this usage, because in connection with the Zermelo axiomatic set theory we shall wish later to give the word *set* a special meaning, somewhat different from that of *class.*) We recall that a class is something which has or may have *members,* and that classes are considered identical if and only if they have exactly the same members. Moreover it is usual mathematical practice to take any given singulary propositional form as having associated with it a class, namely the class whose members are those values of the free variable for which the form is true.

In connection with functional calculi . . ., or rather, with the formalized languages obtained from them by adopting one of the indicated principal interpretations (§07), it turns out that we may secure everything necessary about classes by just identifying a class with a singulary propositional function, and membership in the class with satisfaction of the singulary propositional function. We shall consequently make this identification, on the ground that no purpose is served by maintaining a distinction between classes and singulary propositional functions.

---

[74]This statement seems to be on the whole just, though the issue is much obscured by divergencies among different writers as to the theory of meaning adopted and in the accounts given of the notions of function and proposition. The idea of the propositional function as an analogue of the numerical function of mathematical analysis originated with Frege, but the term "propositional" function is originally Russell's. Russell's early use of this term is not wholly clear. In his introduction to the second edition of *Principia Mathematica* (1925) he decides in favor of the meaning which we are adopting here, or very nearly that.

We must add at once that the notion of a class obtained by thus identifying classes with singulary propositional functions does not quite coincide with the informal notion of a class which we first described, because it does not fully preserve the principle that classes are identical if they have the same members. Rather, it is necessary to take into account also the *range-members* of a class (constituting, i.e., the range of the singulary propositional function). And only when the range-members are given to be the same is the principle preserved that classes are identical if they have the same members. This or some other departure from the informal notion of a class is in fact necessary, because, as we shall see later, the informal notion—in the presence of some other assumptions difficult to avoid—is self-inconsistent and leads to antinomies. (The *sets* of Zermelo set theory preserve the principle that sets having the same members are identical, but at the sacrifice of the principle that an arbitrary singulary propositional form has an associated set.)

Since, then, a class is a singulary propositional function, we speak of the *range of* the class just as we do of the propositional function (i.e., it is the same thing). We think of the range as being itself a class, having as members the range-members of the given class, and having the same range-members.

In any particular discussion hereafter in which classes are introduced, and in the absence of any indication to the contrary, it is to be understood that there is a fixed range determined in advance and that all classes have this same range.)

Relations may be similarly accounted for by identifying them with binary propositional functions, the relation being said to *hold between* an ordered pair of things (or the things being said to *stand in* that relation, or to *bear* that relation one to the other) if the binary propositional function is satisfied by the ordered pair. Given that the ranges are the same, this makes two relations identical if and only if they hold between the same ordered pairs, and to indicate this we may speak more explicitly of a *relation in extension*—using this term as synonymous with *relation*.

A *property*, as ordinarily understood, differs from a class only or chiefly in that two properties may be different though the classes determined by them are the same (where the class determined by a property is the class whose members are the things that have that property). Therefore we identify a property with a *class concept*, or concept of a class in the sense of §01. And two properties are said to *coincide in extension* if they determine the same class.

Similarly, a *relation in intension* is a *relation concept*, or concept of a relation in extension.

To turn once more for illustrative purposes to the theory of real numbers and its notations, the following are examples of propositional forms:

$$\sin x = 0, \qquad \sin x = 2$$
$$e^x > 0, \qquad e^x > 1, \qquad x > 0,$$
$$\varepsilon > 0, \qquad \varepsilon < 0,$$
$$x^3 + y^3 = 3xy, \qquad x \neq y,$$
$$|x - y| < t, \qquad |x - y| < \varepsilon,$$
$$\text{if } |x - y| < \delta \text{ then } |\sin x - \sin y| < \varepsilon.$$

Here we are using x, y, t as variables whose range is the real numbers, and ε and δ as variables whose range is the positive real numbers. The seven forms on the first three lines are examples of singular propositional forms. Those on the fourth line are binary, on the fifth line ternary, while on the last line is an example of a quaternary propositional form.

Each of the singular propositional forms has an associated class. Thus with the form $\sin x = 0$ is associated the class of those real numbers whose sine is 0, i.e., the class whose range is the real numbers and whose members are 0, π, $-\pi$, 2π, -2π, 3π, and so on. As explained, we identify this class with the propositional function $\lambda x(\sin x = 0)$, or in other words the function from real numbers to truth-values which has for any argument x the value $\sin x = 0$.

The two propositional forms $e^x > 1$ and $x > 0$ have the same associated class, namely, the class whose range is the real numbers and whose members are the positive real numbers. This class is identified with either $\lambda x(e^x > 1)$ or $\lambda x(x > 0)$, these two propositional functions being identical with each other by the convention about identity of functions adopted in §03.

Since the propositional form $\sin x = 2$ has the value falsehood for every value of x, the associated class $\lambda x(\sin x = 2)$ has no members.

A class which has no members is called a *null class* or an *empty class*. From our conventions about identity of propositional functions and of classes, if the range is given, it follows that there is only one null class. But, e.g., the range of the null class associated with the form $\sin x = 2$ and the range of the null class associated with the form $\varepsilon < 0$ are not the same: the former range is the real numbers, and the latter range is the positive real numbers.[75] We shall speak respectively of the "null class of real numbers" and of the "null class of positive real numbers."

A class which coincides with its range is called a *universal class*. For example, the class associated with the form $e^x > 0$ is the universal class of real numbers; and the class associated with the form $\varepsilon > 0$ is the universal class of positive real numbers.

The binary propositional forms $x^3 + y^3 = 3xy$ and $x \neq y$ are both symmetric and therefore each have one associated binary propositional function or relation. In particular, the associated relation of the form $x \neq y$ is the relation of diversity between real numbers; or in other words the relation which has the pairs of real numbers as its range, which any two different real numbers bear to each other, and which no real number bears to itself.

---

[75]According to the informal notion that classes with the same members are identical, it would be true absolutely that there is only one null class. The distinction of null classes with different ranges was introduced by Russell in 1908 as a part of his theory of types. . . . The same thing had previously been done by Ernst Schröder in the first volume of his *Algebra der Logik* (1890), though with a very different motivation.

The ternary propositional forms $|x - y| < t$ and $|x - y| < \varepsilon$ have each three associated ternary propositional functions[76] (being symmetric in x and y). All six of these propositional functions are different; but an appropriately chosen pair of them, one associated with each form, will be found to agree in value for all ordered triples of arguments which are in the range of both, differing only in that the first one has the value falsehood for certain ordered triples of arguments which are not in the range of the other.

---

[76]We may also occasionally use the term *ternary relation* (and *quaternary relation*, etc). But the simple term *relation* will be reserved for the special case of a binary relation, or binary propositional function.

IDENTITY AND NECESSITY[1]

Saul Kripke

A problem which has arisen frequently in contemporary philosophy is "How are *contingent* identity statements possible?" This question is phrased by analogy with the way Kant phrased his question "How are synthetic a priori judgments possible?" In both cases, it has usually been taken for granted in the one case by Kant that synthetic a priori judgments were possible, and in the other case in contemporary philosophical literature that contingent statements of identity are possible. I do not intend to deal with the Kantian question except to mention this analogy: After a rather thick book was written trying to answer the question how synthetic a priori judgments were possible, others came along later who claimed that the solution to the problem was that synthetic a priori judgments were, of course, impossible and that a book trying to show otherwise was written in vain. I will not discuss who was right on the possibility of synthetic a priori judgments. But in the case of contingent statements of identity, most philosophers have felt that the notion of a contingent identity statement ran into something like the following paradox. An argument like the following can be given against the possibility of contingent identity statements:

> First, the law of the substitutivity of identity says that, for any objects x and y, if x is identical to y, then if x has a certain property F, so does y:
>   (1) $(x)(y) [(x = y) \supset (Fx \supset Fy)]$
> On the other hand, every object surely is necessarily self-identical:
>   (2) $(x) \square (x = x)$
> But
>   (3) $(x)(y) (x = y) \supset [\square (x = x) \supset \square (x = y)]$
> is a substitution instance of (1), the substitutivity law. From (2) and (3), we can conclude that, for every x and y, if x equals y, then, it is necessary that x equals y:
>   (4) $(x)(y) ((x = y) \supset \square (x = y))$
> This is because the clause $\square (x = x)$ of the conditional drops out because it is known to be true.

This is an argument which has been stated many times in recent philosophy. Its conclusion, however, has often been regarded as highly paradoxical. For example, David Wiggins, in his paper "Identity-Statements," says,

---

[1] This paper was presented orally, without a written text, to the New York University lecture series on identity. . . . The lecture was taped, and the present paper represents a transcription of these tapes, edited only slightly with no attempt to change the style of the original. If the reader imagines the sentences of this paper as being delivered, extemporaneously, with proper pauses and emphases, this may facilitate his comprehension. Nevertheless, there may still be passages which are hard to follow, and the time allotted necessitated a condensed presentation of the argument. (A longer version of some of these views, still rather compressed and still representing a transcript of oral remarks, will appear elsewhere.) Occasionally, reservations, amplifications, and gratifications of my remarks had to be repressed, especially in the discussion of theoretical identification and the mind-body problem. The footnotes, which were added to the original, would have become even more unwieldy if this had not been done.

Now there undoubtedly exist contingent identity-statements. Let $a = b$ be one of them. From its simple truth and (5) [= (4) above] we can derive '$\Box (a = b)$'. But how then can there be any contingent identity statements?[2]

He then says that five various reactions to this argument are possible, and rejects all of these reactions, and reacts himself. I do not want to discuss all the possible reactions to this statement, except to mention the second of those Wiggins rejects. This says,

> We might accept the result and plead that provided 'a' and 'b' are proper names nothing is amiss. The consequence of this is that no contingent identity-statements can be made by means of proper names.

And then he says that he is discontented with this solution and many other philosophers have been discontented with this solution, too, while still others have advocated it.

What makes the statement (4) seem surprising? It says, for any objects x and y, if x is y, then it is necessary that x is y. I have already mentioned that someone might object to this argument on the grounds that premise (2) is already false, that it is not the case that everything is necessarily self-identical. Well, for example, am I myself necessarily self-identical? Someone might argue that in some situations which we can imagine I would not even have existed and therefore the statement "Saul Kripke is Saul Kripke" would have been false or it would not be the case that I was self-identical. Perhaps, it would have been neither true nor false, in such a world, to say that Saul Kripke is self-identical. Well, that may be so, but really it depends on one's philosophical view of a topic that I will not discuss, that is, what is to be said about truth values of statements mentioning objects that do not exist in the actual world or any given possible world or counterfactual situation. Let us interpret necessity here weakly. We can count statements as necessary if whenever the objects mentioned therein exist, the statement would be true. If we wished to be very careful about this, we would have to go into the question of existence as a predicate and ask if the statement can be reformulated in the form: For every x it is necessary that, if x exists, then x is self-identical. I will not go into this particular form of subtlety here because it is not going to be relevant to my main theme. Nor am I really going to consider formula (4). Anyone who believes formula (2) is, in my opinion, committed to formula (4). If x and y are the same things and we can talk about modal properties of an object at all, that is, in the usual parlance, we can speak of modality *de re* and an object *necessarily* having certain properties as such, then formula (1), I think, has to hold. Where x is any property at all, including a property involving modal operators, and if x and y are the same object and x had a certain property F, then y has to have the same property F. And this is so even if the property F is itself of the form of necessarily having some other property G, in particular that of necessarily being identical to a certain object. Well, I will not discuss the formula (4) itself because by itself it

---

[2] R. J. Butler, ed., *Analytical Philosophy, Second Series*, Basil Blackwell, Oxford, 1965, p. 41.

does not assert, of any particular true statement of identity, that it is necessary. It does not say anything about *statements* at all. It says for every *object* x and *object* y, if x and y are the same object, then it is necessary that x and y are the same object. And this, I think, if we think about it (anyway, if someone does not think so, I will not argue for it here), really amounts to something very little different from the statement (2). Since x, by definition of identity, is the only object identical with x, "$(y)(y = x \supset Fy)$" seems to me to be little more than a garrulous way of saying 'Fx', and thus $(x)(y)(y = x \supset Fx)$ says the same as $(x)Fx$ no matter what 'F' is—in particular, even if 'F' stands for the property of necessary identity with x. So if x has this property (of necessary identity with x), trivially everything identical with x has it, as (4) asserts. But, from statement (4) one may apparently be able to deduce various particular statements of identity must be necessary and this is then supposed to be a very paradoxical consequence.

Wiggins says, "Now there undoubtedly exist contingent identity statements." One example of a contingent identity statement is the statement that the first Postmaster General of the United States is identical with the inventor of bifocals, or that both of these are identical with the man claimed by the *Saturday Evening Post* as its founder (*falsely* claimed, I gather, by the way). Now some such statements are plainly contingent. It plainly is a contingent fact that one and the same man both invented bifocals and took on the job of Postmaster General of the United States. How can we reconcile this with the truth of statement (4)? Well, that, too, is an issue I do not want to go into in detail except to be very dogmatic about it. It was I think settled quite well by Bertrand Russell in his notion of the scope of a description. According to Russell, one can, for example, say with propriety that the author of Hamlet might not have written "Hamlet," or even that the author of Hamlet might not have been the author of "Hamlet." Now here, of course, we do not deny the necessity of the identity of an object with itself; but we say it is true concerning a certain man that he in fact was the unique person to have written "Hamlet" and secondly that the man, who in fact was the man who wrote "Hamlet," might not have written "Hamlet." In other words, if Shakespeare had decided not to write tragedies, he might not have written "Hamlet." Under these circumstances, the man who in fact wrote "Hamlet" would not have written "Hamlet." Russell brings this out by saying that in such a statement, the first occurrence of the description "the author of 'Hamlet'" has large scope.[3] That is, we say "The author of 'Hamlet' has the following property: that he might not have written 'Hamlet.'" We *do not* assert that the following statement might have been the case, namely that the author of "Hamlet" did not write "Hamlet," for that is not true. That would be to say that it might have been the case that someone wrote "Hamlet" and yet did not write "Hamlet," which would be a contradiction. Now, aside from the details of Russell's particular formulation of it, which depends on his theory of descriptions, this seems to be the distinction that any theory of descriptions has to make. For example, if someone were to meet the President of Harvard and take him to be a Teaching Fellow, he might say: "I took the President of Harvard for a Teaching Fellow." By this he does not mean that he took the proposition "The President of

---

[3] The second occurrence of the description has small scope.

Harvard is a Teaching Fellow" to be true. He could have meant this, for example, had he believed that some sort of democratic system had gone so far at Harvard that the President of it decided to take on the task of being a Teaching Fellow. But that probably is not what he means. What he means instead, as Russell points out, is "Someone is President of Harvard and I took him to be a Teaching Fellow." In one of Russell's examples someone says, "I thought your yacht is much larger than it is." And the other man replies, "No, my yacht is not much larger than it is."

Provided that the notion of modality *de re*, and thus of quantifying into modal contexts, makes any sense at all, we have quite an adequate solution to the problem of avoiding paradoxes if we substitute descriptions for the universal quantifiers in (4) because the only consequence we will draw,[4] for example, in the bifocals case, is that there is a man who both happened to have invented bifocals and happened to have been the first Postmaster General of the United States, and is necessarily self-identical. There is an object x such that x invented bifocals, and as a matter of contingent fact an object y, such that y is the first Postmaster General of the United States, and finally, it is necessary, that x is y. What are x and y here? Here, x and y are both Benjamin Franklin, and it can certainly be necessary that Benjamin Franklin is identical with himself. So, there is no problem in the case of descriptions if we accept Russell's notion of scope.[5] And I just dogmatically want to drop that question here and go on to the question about names

---

[4] In Russell's theory $F(\imath xGx)$ follows from $(x)Fx$ and $(\exists!x)Gx$, provided that the description in $F(\imath xGx)$ has the entire context for its scope (in Russell's 1905 terminology, has a "primary occurrence"). Only then is $F(\imath xGx)$ "about" the denotation of '$\imath xGx$'. Applying this rule to (14), we get the results indicated in the text. Notice that, in the ambiguous form $\Box(\imath xGx = \imath xHx)$, if one or both of the descriptions have "primary occurrences" the formula does not assert the necessity of $\imath xGx = \imath xHx$; if both have secondary occurrences, it does. Thus in a language without explicit scope indicators, descriptions must be construed with the smallest possible scope—only then will $\sim A$ be the negation of A, $\Box A$ the necessitation of A, and the like.

[5] An earlier distinction with the same purpose was, of course, the medieval one of *de dicto–de re*. That Russell's distinction of scope eliminates modal paradoxes has been pointed out by many logicians, especially Smullyan.

So as to avoid misunderstanding, let me emphasize that I am of course not asserting that Russell's notion of scope solves Quine's problem of "essentialism"; what it does show, especially in conjunction with modern model-theoretic approaches to modal logic, is that quantified modal logic need not deny the truth of all instances of $(x)(y)(x = y \cdot \supset \cdot Fx \supset Fy)$, nor of all instances of '$(x)(Gx \supset Ga)$' (where 'a' is to be replaced by a nonvacuous definite description whose scope is all of 'Ga'), in order to avoid making it a necessary truth that one and the same man invented bifocals and headed the original Postal Department. Russell's contextual definition of descriptions need not be adopted in order to ensure these results; but other logical theories, Fregean or other, which take descriptions as primitive must somehow express the same logical facts. Frege showed that a simple, non-iterated context containing a definite description with small scope, which cannot be interpreted as being "about" the denotation of the description, can be interpreted as about its "sense." Some logicians have been interested in the question of the conditions under which, in an intensional context, a description with small scope is equivalent to the same one with large scope. One of the virtues of a Russellian treatment of descriptions in modal logic is that the answer (roughly that the description be a "rigid designator" in the sense of this lecture) then often follows from the other postulates for quantified modal logic; no special postulates are needed, as in Hintikka's treatment. Even if descriptions are taken as primitive, special postulation of when scope is irrelevant can often be deduced from more basic axioms.

which Wiggins raises. And Wiggins says he might accept the result and plead that, provided a and b are proper names, nothing is amiss. And then he rejects this.

Now what is the special problem about proper names? At least if one is not familiar with the philosophical literature about this matter, one naively feels something like the following about proper names. First, if someone says "Cicero was an orator," then he uses the name 'Cicero' in that statement simply to pick out a certain object and then to ascribe a certain property to the object, namely, in this case, he ascribes to a certain man the property of having been an orator. If someone else uses another name, such as say 'Tully', he is still speaking about the same man. One ascribes the same property, if one says "Tully is an orator," to the same man. So to speak, the fact, or state of affairs, represented by the statement is the same whether one says "Cicero is an orator" or one says "Tully is an orator." It would, therefore, seem that the function of names is *simply* to refer, and not to describe the objects so named by such properties as "being the inventor of bifocals" or "being the first Postmaster General." It would seem that Leibniz's law and the law (1) should not only hold in the universally quantified form, but also in the form "if $a = b$ and Fa, then Fb," wherever 'a' and 'b' stand in place of names and 'F' stands in place of a predicate expressing a genuine property of the object:

$$(a = b \cdot Fa) \supset Fb$$

We can run the same argument through again to obtain the conclusion where 'a' and 'b' replace any names, "if $a = b$, then necessarily $a = b$." And so, we could venture this conclusion: that whenever 'a' and 'b' are proper names, if a is b, that it is necessary that a is b. Identity statements between proper names have to be necessary if they are going to be true at all. This view in fact has been advocated, for example, by Ruth Barcan Marcus in a paper of hers on the philosophical interpretation of modal logic.[6] According to this view, whenever, for example, someone makes a correct statement of identity between two names, such as, for example, that Cicero is Tully, his statement has to be necessary if it is true. But such a conclusion *seems* plainly to be false. (I, like other philosophers, have a habit of understatement in which "it seems plainly false" means "it is plainly false." Actually, I think the view is true, though not quite in the form defended by Mrs. Marcus.) At any rate, it seems plainly false. One example was given by Professor Quine in his reply to Professor Marcus at the symposium: "I think I see trouble anyway in the contrast between proper names and descriptions as Professor Marcus draws it. The paradigm of the assigning of proper names is tagging. We may tag the planet Venus some fine evening with the proper name 'Hesperus'. We may tag the same planet again someday before sunrise with the proper name 'Phosphorus'." (Quine thinks that something like that actually was done once.) "When, at last, we discover that we have tagged the same planet twice, our discovery is empirical, and not because the proper names were descriptions." According to what we are told,

---

[6] "Modalities and Intensional Languages," *Boston Studies in the Philosophy of Science*, Vol. 1, Humanities Press, New York, 1963, pp. 71 ff. See also the "Comments" by Quine and the ensuing discussion.

the planet Venus seen in the morning was originally thought to be a star and was called "the Morning Star," or (to get rid of any question of using a description) was called 'Phosphorus'. One and the same planet, when seen in the evening, was thought to be another star, the Evening Star, and was called "Hesperus." Later on, astronomers discovered that Phosphorus and Hesperus were one and the same. Surely no amount of a priori ratiocination on their part could conceivably have made it possible for them to deduce that Phosphorus is Hesperus. In fact, given the information they had, it might have turned out the other way. Therefore, it is argued, the statement 'Hesperus is Phosphorus' has to be an ordinary contingent, empirical truth, one which might have come out otherwise, and so the view that true identity statements between names are necessary has to be false. Another example which Quine gives in *Word and Object* is taken from Professor Schrödinger, the famous pioneer of quantum mechanics: A certain mountain can be seen from both Tibet and Nepal. When seen from one direction it was called 'Gaurisanker'; when seen from another direction, it was called 'Everest'; and then, later on, the empirical discovery was made that Gaurisanker *is* Everest. (Quine further says that he gathers the example is actually geographically incorrect. I guess one should not rely on physicists for geographical information.)

Of course, one possible reaction to this argument is to deny that names like 'Cicero', 'Tully', 'Gaurisanker', and 'Everest' really are proper names. "Look," someone might say (someone has said it: his name was 'Bertrand Russell'), "just because statements like "Hesperus is Phosphorus" and "Gaurisanker is Everest" are contingent, we can see that the names in question are not really purely referential. You are not, in Mrs. Marcus' phrase, just "tagging" an object; you are actually describing it. What does the contingent fact that Hesperus is Phosphorus amount to? Well, it amounts to the fact that *the* star in a certain portion of the sky in the evening is *the* star in a certain portion of the sky in the morning. Similarly, the contingent fact that Gaurisanker is Everest amounts to the fact that the mountain viewed from such and such an angle in Nepal is the mountain viewed from such and such another angle in Tibet. Therefore, such names as 'Hesperus' and 'Phosphorus' can only be abbreviations for descriptions. The term 'Phosphorus' *has* to mean "the star seen . . . ," or (let us be cautious because it actually turned out not to be a star), "the *heavenly body* seen from such and such a position at such and such a time in the morning," and the name 'Hesperus' has to mean "the heavenly body seen in such and such a position at such and such a time in the evening." So, Russell concludes, if we want to reserve the term "name" for things which really just name an object without describing it, the only real proper names we can have are names of our own immediate sense data, objects of our own "immediate acquaintance." The only such names which occur in language are demonstratives such as "this" and "that." And it is easy to see that this requirement of necessity of identity, understood as exempting identities between names from all imaginable doubt, can indeed be guaranteed only for demonstrative names of immediate sense data; for only in such cases can an identity statement between two different names have a general immunity from Cartesian doubt. There are some other things Russell has sometimes allowed as objects of acquaintance, such as one's self; we need not go into details here. Other philosophers (for example, Mrs. Marcus in her reply, at least in the verbal discussion as I remember it—I do not know if this got into print, so perhaps this should not be 'tagged' on her[7]) have said, "If names are really just tags, genuine tags, then a good dictionary should be able to tell us that they are names of the same object." You have an object *a* and an object *b* with names 'John' and 'Joe'. Then, according to Mrs. Marcus, a dictionary should be able to tell you whether or not 'John' and 'Joe' are names of the same object. Of course, I do not know what ideal dictionaries should do, but ordinary proper names do not seem to satisfy this requirement. You certainly *can*, in the case of ordinary proper names, make quite empirical discoveries that, let's say, Hesperus is Phosphorus, though we thought otherwise. We can be in doubt as to whether Gaurisanker is Everest or Cicero is in fact Tully. Even now, we could conceivably discover that we were wrong in supposing that Hesperus was Phosphorus. Maybe the astronomers made an error. So it seems that this view is wrong and that if by a name we do not mean some artificial notion of names such as Russell's, but a proper name in the ordinary sense, then there can be contingent identity statements using proper names, and the view to the contrary seems plainly wrong.

In recent philosophy a large number of other identity statements have been emphasized as examples of contingent identity statements, different, perhaps, from either of the types I have mentioned before. One of them is, for example, the statement "Heat is the motion of molecules." First, science is supposed to have discovered this. Empirical scientists in their investigations have been supposed to discover (and, I suppose, they did) that the external phenomenon which we call "heat" is, in fact, molecular agitation. Another example of such a discovery is that water is H_2O, and yet other examples are that gold is the element with such and such an atomic number, that light is a stream of photons, and so on. These are all in some sense of "identity statement" identity statements. Second, it is thought, they are plainly contingent identity statements, just because they were scientific discoveries. After all, heat might have turned out not to have been the motion of molecules. There were other alternative theories of heat proposed, for example, the caloric theory of heat. If these theories of heat had been correct, then heat would not have been the motion of molecules, but instead, some substance suffusing the hot object, called "caloric." And it was a matter of course of science and not of any logical necessity that the one theory turned out to be correct and the other theory turned out to be incorrect.

So, here again, we have, apparently, another plain example of a contingent identity statement. This has been supposed to be a very important example because of its connection with the mind-body problem. There have been many philosophers who have wanted to be materialists, and to be materialists in a particular form, which is known today as "the identity theory." According to this theory, a certain mental state, such as a person's being in pain, is identical with a

---

[7] It should. See her remark on p. 115, *op. cit.*, in the discussion following the papers.

certain state of his brain (or, perhaps, of his entire body, according to some theorists), at any rate, a certain material or neural state of his brain or body. And so, according to this theory, my being in pain at this instant, if I were, would be identical with my body's being or my brain's being in a certain state. Others have objected that this cannot be because, after all, we can imagine my pain existing even if the state of the body did not. We can perhaps imagine my not being embodied at all and still being in pain, or, conversely, we could imagine my body existing and being in the very same state even if there were no pain. In fact, conceivably, it could be in this state even though there were no mind "back of it," so to speak, at all. The usual reply has been to concede that all of these things might have been the case, but to argue that these are irrelevant to the question of the identity of the mental state and the physical state. This identity, it is said, is just another contingent scientific identification, similar to the identification of heat with molecular motion, or water with H_2O. Just as we can imagine heat without any molecular motion, so we can imagine a mental state without any corresponding brain state. But, just as the first fact is not damaging to the identification of heat and the motion of molecules, so the second fact is not at all damaging to the identification of a mental state with the corresponding brain state. And so, many recent philosophers have held it to be very important for our theoretical understanding of the mind-body problem that there can be contingent identity statements of this form.

To state finally what *I* think, as opposed to what seems to be the case, or what others think, I think that in both cases, the case of names and the case of the theoretical identifications, the identity statements are necessary and not contingent. That is to say, they are necessary if *true;* of course, false identity statements are not necessary. How can one possibly defend such a view? Perhaps I lack a complete answer to this question, even though I am convinced that the view is true. But to begin an answer, let me make some distinctions that I want to use. The first is between a *rigid* and a *nonrigid designator.* What do these terms mean? As an example of a nonrigid designator, I can give an expression such as 'the inventor of bifocals'. Let us suppose it was Benjamin Franklin who invented bifocals, and so the expression, 'the inventor of bifocals', designates or refers to a certain man, namely, Benjamin Franklin. However, we can easily imagine that the world could have been different, that under different circumstances someone else would have come upon this invention before Benjamin Franklin did, and in that case, *he* would have been the inventor of bifocals. So, in this sense, the expression 'the inventor of bifocals' is nonrigid: Under certain circumstances one man would have been the inventor of bifocals; under other circumstances, another man would have. In contrast, consider the expression 'the square root of 25'. Independently of the empirical facts, we can give an arithmetical proof that the square root of 25 is in fact the number 5, and because we have proved this mathematically, what we have proved is necessary. If we think of numbers as entities at all, and let us suppose, at least for the purpose of this lecture, that we do, then the expression 'the square root of 25' necessarily designates a certain number, namely 5. Such an expression I call "a *rigid* designator." Some philosophers think that anyone who even uses the notions of rigid or nonrigid designator has already shown that he has fallen into a certain confusion or has not paid attention to certain facts. What do I mean by "rigid designator"? I mean a term that designates the same object in all possible worlds. To get rid of one confusion which certainly is not mine, I do not use "might have designated a different object" to refer to the fact that language might have been used differently. For example, the expression 'the inventor of bifocals' might have been used by inhabitants of this planet always to refer to the man who corrupted Hadleyburg. This would have been the case, if, first, the people on this planet had not spoken English, but some other language, which phonetically overlapped with English; and if, second, in that language the expression 'the inventor of bifocals' meant the 'man who corrupted Hadleyburg'. Then it would refer, of course, in their language, to whoever in fact corrupted Hadleyburg in this counterfactual situation. That is not what I mean. What I mean by saying that a description might have referred to something different, I mean that in *our* language as *we* use it in describing a counterfactual situation, there might have been a different object satisfying the descriptive conditions *we* give for reference. So, for example, we use the phrase 'the inventor of bifocals', when we are talking about another possible world or a counterfactual situation, to refer to whoever in that counterfactual situation would have invented bifocals, not to the person whom people *in* that counterfactual situation would have called the inventor of bifocals'. *They* might have spoken a different language which phonetically overlapped with English in which 'the inventor of bifocals' is used in some other way. I am *not* concerned with that question here. For that matter, they might have been deaf and dumb, or there might have been no people at all. (There still could have been an inventor of bifocals even if there were no people—God, or Satan, will do.)

Second, in talking about the notion of a rigid designator, I do not mean to imply that the object referred to has to exist in all possible worlds, that is, that it has to necessarily exist. Some things, perhaps mathematical entities such as the positive integers, if they exist at all, necessarily exist. Some people have held that God both exists and necessarily exists; others, that He contingently exists; others, that He contingently fails to exist; and others, that He necessarily fails to exist:[8] all four options have been tried. But at any rate, when I use the notion of rigid designator, I do not imply that the object referred to necessarily exists. All I mean is that in any possible world where the object in question *does* exist, in any situation where the object *would* exist, we use the designator in question to designate that object. In a situation where the object does not exist, then we should say that the designator has no referent and that the object in question so designated does not exist.

As I said, many philosophers would find the very notion of rigid designator objectionable per se. And the objection that people make may be stated as follows: Look, you're talking about situations which are counterfactual, that is to say, you're talking about other possible worlds. Now these worlds are completely disjoint, after all, from the actual world which is not just another possible

---

[8] If there is no deity, and especially if the nonexistence of a deity is *necessary*, it is dubious that we can use "He" to refer to a deity. The use in the text must be taken to be non-literal.

world; it is the actual world. So, before you talk about, let us say, such an object as Richard Nixon in another possible world at all, you have to say which object in this other possible world would *be* Richard Nixon. Let us talk about a situation in which, as *you* would say, Richard Nixon would have been a member of SDS. Certainly the member of SDS you are talking about is someone very different in many of his properties from Nixon. Before we even can say whether this man would have been Richard Nixon or not, we have to set up criteria of identity across possible worlds. Here are these other possible worlds. There are all kinds of objects in them with different properties from those of any actual object. Some of them resemble Nixon in some ways, some of them resemble Nixon in other ways. Well, which of these objects is Nixon? One has to give a criterion of identity. And this shows how the very notion of rigid designator runs in a circle. Suppose we designate a certain number as the number of planets. Then, if that is our favorite way, so to speak, of designating this number, then in any other possible worlds we will have to identify whatever number is the number of planets with the number 9, which in the actual world is the number of planets. So, it is argued by various philosophers, for example, implicitly by Quine, and explicitly by many others in his wake, we cannot really ask whether a designator is rigid or nonrigid because we first need a criterion of identity across possible worlds. An extreme view has even been held that, since possible worlds are so disjoint from our own, we cannot really say that any object in them is the *same* as an object existing now but only that there are some objects which resemble things in the actual world, more or less. We, therefore, should not really speak of what would have been true of Nixon in another possible world but, only of what "counterparts" (the term which David Lewis uses[9]) of Nixon there would have been. Some people in other possible worlds have dogs whom they call "Checkers". Others favor the ABM but do not have any dog called Checkers. There are various people who resemble Nixon more or less, but none of them can really be said to be Nixon; they are only *counterparts* of Nixon, and you choose which one is the best counterpart by noting which resembles Nixon the most closely, according to your favorite criteria. Such views are widespread, both among the defenders of quantified modal logic and among its detractors.

All of this talk seems to me to have taken the metaphor of possible worlds much too seriously in some way. It is as if a 'possible world' were like a foreign country, or distant planet way out there. It is as if we see dimly through a telescope various actors on this distant planet. Actually David Lewis's view seems the most reasonable if one takes this picture literally. No one far away on another planet can be strictly identical with someone here. But, even if we have some marvelous methods of transportation to take one and the same person from planet to planet, we really need some epistemological criteria of identity to be able to say whether someone on this distant planet is the same person as someone here.

---

[9] David K. Lewis, "Counterpart Theory and Quantified Modal Logic," *Journal of Philosophy* 65 (1968), pp. 113 ff.

All of this seems to me to be a totally misguided way of looking at things. What it amounts to is the view that counterfactual situations have to be described purely qualitatively. So, we cannot say, for example, "If Nixon had only given a sufficient bride to Senator X, he would have gotten Carswell through" because that refers to certain people, Nixon and Carswell, and talks about what things would be true of them in a counterfactual situation. We must say instead "If a man who has a hairline like such and such, and holds such and such political opinions had given a bride to a man who was a senator and had such and such other qualities, then a man who was a judge in the South and had many other qualities resembling Carswell would have been confirmed." In other words, we must describe counterfactual situations purely qualitatively and then ask the question, "Given that the situation contains people or things with such and such qualities, which of these people is (or is a counterpart of) Nixon, which is Carswell, and so on?" This seems to me to be wrong. Who is to prevent us from saying "Nixon might have gotten Carswell through had he done certain things"? We are speaking of *Nixon* and asking what, in certain counterfactual situations, would have been true of *him*. We can say that if Nixon had done such and such, he would have lost the election to Humphrey. Those I am opposing would argue, "Yes, but how do you find out if the man you are talking about is in fact Nixon?" It would indeed be very hard to find out, if you were looking at the whole situation through a telescope, but that is not what we are doing here. Possible worlds are not something to which an epistemological question like this applies. And if the phrase "possible worlds" is what makes anyone think some such question applies, he should just *drop* this phrase and use some other expression, say "counterfactual situation," which might be less misleading. If we say "If Nixon had bribed such and such a Senator, Nixon would have gotten Carswell through," what is *given* in the very description of that situation is that it is a situation in which we are speaking of Nixon, and of Carswell, and of such and such a Senator. And there seems to be no less objection to *stipulating* that we are speaking of certain *people* than there can be objection to stipulating that we are speaking of certain *qualities*. Advocates of the other view take speaking of certain qualities as unobjectionable. They do not say, "How do we know that this quality (in another possible world) is that of redness?" But they do find speaking of certain *people* objectionable. But I see no more reason to object in the one case than in the other. I think it really comes from the idea of possible worlds as existing out there, but very far off, viewable only through a special telescope. Even more objectionable is the view of David Lewis. According to Lewis, when we say "Under certain circumstances Nixon would have gotten Carswell through," we really mean "Some man, other than Nixon but closely resembling him, would have gotten some judge, other than Carswell but closely resembling him, through." Maybe that is so, that some man closely resembling Nixon could have gotten some man closely resembling Carswell through. But *that* would not comfort either Nixon or Carswell, nor would it make Nixon kick himself and say "*I* should have done such and such to get Carswell through." The question is whether under certain circumstances Nixon *himself* could have gotten *Carswell* through. And I think the objection is simply based on a misguided picture.

Instead, we can perfectly well talk about rigid and nonrigid designators. Moreover, we have a simple, intuitive test for them. We can say, for example, that the number of planets might have been a different number from the number it in fact is. For example, there might have been only seven planets. We can say that the inventor of bifocals might have been someone other than the man who *in fact* invented bifocals.[10] We cannot say, though, that the square root of 81 might have been a different number from the number it in fact is, for that number just has to be 9. If we apply this intuitive test to proper names, such as for example 'Richard Nixon', they would seem intuitively to come out to be rigid designators. First, when we talk even about the counterfactual situation in which we suppose Nixon to have done different things, we assume we are still talking about Nixon himself. We say, "If Nixon had bribed a certain Senator, he would have gotten Carswell through," and we assume that by 'Nixon' and "Carswell' we are still referring to the very same people as in the actual world. And it seems that we cannot say "Nixon might have been a different man from the man he in fact was," unless, of course, we mean it metaphorically: He might have been a different *sort* of person (if you believe in free will and that people are not inherently corrupt). You might think the statement true in that sense, but Nixon could not have been in the other literal sense a different person from the person he, in fact, is, even though the thirty-seventh President of the United States might have been Humphrey. So the phrase "the thirty-seventh President" is non-rigid, but 'Nixon', it would seem, is rigid.

Let me make another distinction before I go back to the question of identity statements. This distinction is very fundamental and also hard to see through. In recent discussion, many philosophers who have debated the meaningfulness of various categories of truths, have regarded them as identical. Some of those who identify them are vociferous defenders of them, and others, such as Quine, say they are all identically meaningless. But usually they're not distinguished. These are categories such as 'analytic', 'necessary', 'a priori', and sometimes even 'certain'. I will not talk about all of these but only about the notions of a prioricity and necessity. Very often these are held to be synonyms. (Many philosophers probably should not be described as holding them to be synonyms; they simply *use* them interchangeably.) I wish to distinguish them. What do we mean by calling a statement *necessary?* We simply mean that the statement in question, first, is true, and, second, that it could not have been otherwise. When we say that something

---

[10] Some philosophers think that definite descriptions, in English, are ambiguous, that sometimes 'the inventor of bifocals' rigidly designates the man who in fact invented bifocals. I am tentatively inclined to reject this view, construed as a thesis about English (as opposed to a possible hypothetical language), but I will not argue the question here.

What I do wish to note is that, contrary to some opinions, this alleged ambiguity cannot replace the Russellian notion of the scope of a description. Consider the sentence, "The number of planets might have been necessarily even." This sentence plainly can be read so as to express a truth; had there been eight planets, the number of planets would have been necessarily even. Yet without scope distinctions, both a 'referential' (rigid) and a non-rigid reading of the description will make the statement false. (Since the number of planets is nine, the rigid reading amounts to the falsity that nine might have been necessarily even.)

The 'rigid' reading is equivalent to the Russellian primary occurrence; the non-rigid, to innermost scope—some, following Donnellan, perhaps loosely, have called this reading the 'attributive' use. The possibility of intermediate scopes is then ignored. In the present instance, the intended reading of $\Diamond\Box$ (the number of planets is even) makes the scope of the description $\Box$ (the number of planets is even), neither the largest nor the smallest possible.

is *contingently* true, we mean that, though it is in fact the case, it could have been the case that things would have been otherwise. If we wish to assign this distinction to a branch of philosophy, we should assign it to metaphysics. To the contrary, there is the notion of an *a priori truth*. An a priori truth is supposed to be one which can be *known* to be true independently of all experience. Notice that this does not in and of itself say anything about all possible worlds, unless this is put into the definition. All that it says is that it can be known to be true of the actual world, independently of all experience. It may, by some philosophical argument, follow from our knowing, independently of experience, that something is true of the actual world, that it has to be known to be true also of all possible worlds. But if this is to be established, it requires some philosophical argument to establish it. Now, *this* notion, if we were to assign it to a branch of philosophy, belongs, not to metaphysics, but to epistemology. It has to do with the way we can know certain things to be in fact true. Now, it may be the case, of course, that anything which is necessary is something which *can* be known a priori. (Notice, by the way, the notion a priori truth as thus defined has in it *another* modality: it *can* be known independently of all experience. It is a little complicated because there is a double modality here.) I will not have time to explore these notions in full detail here, but one thing we can see from the outset is that these two notions are by no means trivially the same. If they are coextensive, it takes some philosophical argument to establish it. As stated, they belong to different domains of philosophy. One of them has something to do with *knowledge,* of what can be known in certain ways about the *actual* world. The other one has to do with *metaphysics,* how the world *could* have been; given that it is the way it is, could it have been otherwise, in certain ways? Now I hold, as a matter of fact, that neither class of statements is contained in the other. But, all we need to talk about here is this: Is everything that is necessary knowable a priori or known a priori? Consider the following example: the Goldbach conjecture. This says that every even number is the sum of two primes. It is a mathematical statement, and if it is true at all, it has to be necessary. Certainly, one could not say that though in fact every even number is the sum of two primes, there could have been some extra number which was even and not the sum of two primes. What would that mean? On the other hand, the answer to the question whether every even number *is* in fact the sum of two primes is unknown, and we have no method at present for deciding. So we certainly do not know, a priori or even a posteriori, that every even number is the sum of two primes. (Well, perhaps we have some evidence in that no counterexample has been found.) But we certainly do not know a priori anyway, that every even number is, in fact, the sum of two primes. But, of course, the definition just says "*can* be known independently of experience," and someone might say that if it is true, we *could* know it independently of experience. It is hard to see exactly what this claim means. It might be so. One thing it might mean is that if it were true we could *prove* it. This claim is certainly wrong if it is generally applied to mathematical statements and we have to work within some fixed system. This is what Godel proved. And even if we mean an "intuitive proof in general" it might just be the case (at least, this view is as clear and as probable as the contrary) that though the statement is true, there is just no way the human mind could ever prove it. Of course, one way an *infinite* mind might be able to prove it is by looking through each natural number one by one and checking. In this sense, of course, it can, perhaps, be known a priori, but only by an infinite mind, and then this gets into other complicated questions. I do not want to discuss questions about the conceivability of performing an infinite number of acts like looking through each number one by one. A vast philosophical literature has been written on this: Some have declared it is logically impossible; others that it is logically possible; and some do not know. The main point is that it is not trivial that just because such a statement is necessary it can be known a priori. Some considerable clarification is required before we decide that it can be so known. And so this shows that even if everything necessary is a priori in some sense, it should not be taken as a trivial matter of definition. It is a substantive philosophical thesis which requires some work.

Another example that one might give relates to the problem of essentialism. Here is a lectern. A question which has often been raised in philosophy is: What are its essential properties? What properties, aside from trivial ones like self-identity, are such that this object has to have them if it exists at all,[11] are such that if an object did not have it, it would not be this object?[12] For example, being made of wood, and not of ice, might be an essential property of this lectern. Let us just take the weaker statement that it is not made of ice. That will establish it as strongly as we need it, perhaps as dramatically. Supposing this lectern is in fact made of wood, could this very lectern have been made from the very beginning of its existence from ice, say frozen from water in the Thames? One has a considerable feeling that it could *not*, though in fact one certainly could have made a lectern of water from the Thames, frozen it into ice by some process, and put it right there in place of this thing. If one had done so, one would have made, of course, a *different* object. It would not have been *this very lectern,* and so one would not have a case in which this very lectern here was made of ice, or was made from water from the Thames. The question of whether it could afterward, say in a minute from now, turn into ice is something else. So, it would seem, if an example like this is correct—and this is what advocates of essentialism have held—that this lectern could not have been made of ice, that is in any counterfactual situation of which we would say that this lectern existed at

---

[11] This definition is the usual formulation of the notion of essential property, but an exception must be made for existence itself; on the definition given, existence would be trivially essential. We should regard existence as essential to an object only if the object necessarily exists. Perhaps there are other recherché properties, involving existence, for which the definition is similarly objectionable. (I thank Michael Slote for this observation.)

[12] The two clauses of the sentence footnoted give equivalent definitions of the notion of essential property, since $\Box((\exists x)\,(x = a) \supset Fa)$ is equivalent to $\Box(x)\,(\sim Fx \supset x \neq a)$. The second formulation, however, has served as a powerful seducer in favor of theories of 'identification across possible worlds'. For it suggests that we consider 'an object *b* in another possible world' and test whether it is identifiable with *a* by asking whether it lacks any of the essential properties of *a*. Let me therefore emphasize that, although an essential property is (trivially) a property without which an object cannot be *a*, it by no means follows that the essential, purely qualitative properties of *a* jointly form a sufficient condition for being *a*, nor that *any* purely qualitative conditions are sufficient for an object to be *a*. Further, even if necessary and sufficient qualitative conditions for an object to be Nixon may exist, there would still be little justification for the demand for a purely qualitative description of all counterfactual situations. We can ask whether Nixon might have been a Democrat without engaging in these subtleties.

all, we would have to say also that it was not made from water from the Thames frozen into ice. Some have rejected, of course, any such notion of essential property as meaningless. Usually, it is because (and I think this is what Quine, for example, would say) they have held that it depends on the notion of identity across possible worlds, and that this is itself meaningless. Since I have rejected this view already, I will not deal with it again. We can talk about *this very object,* and whether it could have had certain properties which it does not in fact have. For example, it could have been in another room from the room it in fact is in, even at this very time, but it could not have been made from the very beginning from water frozen into ice.

If the essentialist view is correct, it can be correct only if we sharply distinguish between the notions of a posteriori and a priori truth on the one hand, and contingent and necessary truth on the other hand, for although the statement that this table, if it exists at all, was not made of ice, is necessary, it certainly is not something that we know a priori. What we know is that first, lecterns usually are not made of ice, they are usually made of wood. This looks like wood. It does not feel cold and it probably would if it were made of ice. Therefore, I conclude, probably this is not made of ice. Here my entire judgment is a posteriori. I could find out that an ingenious trick has been played upon me and that, in fact, this lectern is made of ice; but what I am saying is, given that it is in fact not made of ice, in fact is made of wood, one cannot imagine that under certain circumstances it could have been made of ice. So we have to say that though we cannot know a priori whether this table was made of ice or not, given that it is not made of ice, it is *necessarily* not made of ice. In other words, if P is the statement that the lectern is not made of ice, one knows by a priori philosophical analysis, some conditional of the form "if P, then necessarily P." If the table is not made of ice, it is necessarily not made of ice. On the other hand, then, we know by empirical investigation that P, the antecedent of the conditional, is true— that this table is not made of ice. We can conclude by *modus ponens:*

$$P \supset \Box P$$
$$\frac{P}{\Box P}$$

The conclusion—'$\Box P$'—is that it is necessary that the table not be made of ice, and this conclusion is known a posteriori, since one of the premises on which it is based is a posteriori. So, the notion of essential properties can be maintained only by distinguishing between the notions of a priori and necessary truth, and I do maintain it.

Let us return to the question of identities. Concerning the statement 'Hesperus is Phosphorus' or the statement 'Cicero is Tully', one can find all of these out by empirical investigation, and we might turn out to be wrong in our empirical beliefs. So, it is usually argued, such statements must therefore be contingent. Some have embraced the other side of the coin and have held "Because of this argument about necessity, identity statements between names have to be knowable a priori, so, only a very special category of names, possibly, really works as names; the other things are bogus names, disguised descriptions, or something of the sort. However, a certain very narrow class of statements of identity are known a priori, and these are the ones which contain the genuine names." If one accepts the distinctions that I have made, one need not jump to either conclusion. One can hold that certain statements of identity between names, though often known a posteriori, and maybe not knowable a priori, are in fact necessary, if true. So, we have some room to hold this. But, of course, to have some room to hold it does not mean that we should hold it. So let us see what the evidence is. First, recall the remark that I made that proper names seem to be rigid designators, as when we use the name 'Nixon' to talk about a certain man, even in counterfactual situations. If we say, "If Nixon had not written the letter to Saxbe, maybe he would have gotten Carswell through," we are in this statement talking about Nixon, Saxbe, and Carswell, the very same men as in the actual world, and what would have happened to them under certain counterfactual circumstances. If names are rigid designators, then there can be no question about identities being necessary, because 'a' and 'b' will be rigid designators of a certain man or thing x. Then even in ever possible world, a and b will both refer to this same object x, and to no other, and so there will be no situation in which a might not have been b. That would have to be a situation in which the object which we are also now calling 'x' would not have been identical with itself. Then one could not possibly have a situation in which Cicero would not have been Tully or Hesperus would not have been Phosphorus.[13]

Aside from the identification of necessity with a priority, what has made people feel the other way? There are two things which have made people feel the other way.[14] Some people tend to regard identity statements as metalinguistic statements, to identify the statement "Hesperus is Phosphorus" with the metalinguistic statement, "'Hesperus' and 'Phosphorus' are names of the same heavenly body." And that, of course, might have been false. We might have used the terms 'Hesperus' and 'Phosphorus' as names of *two* different heavenly bodies. But, of course, this has nothing to do with the necessity of identity. In the same sense "2 + 2 = 4" might have been false. The phrases "2 + 2" and "4" might have been used to refer to two different numbers. One can imagine a language, for example, in which "+," "2," and "=" were used in the standard way, but "4" was used as the name of, say, the square root of minus 1, as we should call it, "i." Then "2 + 2 = 4" would be false, for 2 plus 2 is not equal to the square root of minus 1. But this is not what we want. We do not want just to say that a certain statement which we in fact use to express something true

---

[13] I thus agree with Quine, that "Hesperus is Phosphorus" is (or can be) an empirical discovery; with Marcus, that it is necessary. Both Quine and Marcus, according to the present standpoint, err in identifying the epistemological and the metaphysical issues.

[14] The two confusions alleged, especially the second, are both related to the confusion of the metaphysical question of the necessity of "Hesperus is Phosphorus" with the epistemological question of its a prioricity. For if Hesperus is identified by its position in the sky in the evening, and Phosphorus by its position in the morning, an investigator may well know, in advance of empirical research, that Hesperus is Phosphorus if and only if one and the same body occupies position x in the evening and position y in the morning. The a priori material equivalence of the two statements, however, does not imply their strict (necessary) equivalence. (The same remarks apply to the case of heat and molecular motion below.) Similar remarks apply to some extent to the relationship between "Hesperus is Phosphorus" and "'Hesperus' and 'Phosphorus' name the same thing." A confusion that also operates is, of course, the confusion between what *we* would say of a counterfactual situation and how people *in* that situation would have described it; this confusion, too, is probably related to the confusion between a prioricity and necessity.

could have expressed something false. We want to use the statement in *our* way and see if it could have been false. Let us do this. What is the idea people have? They say, "Look, Hesperus might not have been Phosphorus. Here a certain planet was seen in the morning, and it was seen in the evening; and it just turned out later on as a matter of empirical fact that they were one and the same planet. If things had turned out otherwise, they would have been two different planets, or two different heavenly bodies, so how can you say that such a statement is necessary?"

Now there are two things that such people can mean. First, they can mean that we do not know a priori whether Hesperus is Phosphorus. This I have already conceded. Second, they may mean that they can actually imagine circumstances that they would call circumstances in which Hesperus would not have been Phosphorus. Let us think what would be such a circumstance, using these terms here as *names* of a planet. For example, it could have been the case that Venus did indeed rise in the morning in exactly the position in which we saw it, but that on the other hand, in the position which is in fact occupied by Venus in the evening, Venus was not there, and Mars took its place. This is all counterfactual because in fact Venus is there. Now one can also imagine that in this counterfactual other possible world, the earth would have been inhabited by people and that they should have used the names 'Phosphorus' for Venus in the morning and 'Hesperus' for Mars in the evening. Now, this is all very good, but would it be a situation in which Hesperus was not Phosphorus? Of course, it is a situation in which people would have been able to *say*, truly, "Hesperus is not Phosphorus"; but we are supposed to describe things in our language, not in theirs. So let us describe it in our language. Well, how could it actually happen that Venus would not be in that position in the evening? For example, let us say that there is some comet that comes around every evening and yanks things over a little bit. (That would be a very simple scientific way of imagining it: not really too simple—that is very hard to imagine actually.) It just happens to come around every evening, and things get yanked over a little bit. Mars gets yanked over to the very position where Venus is, then the comet yanks things back to their normal position in the morning. Thinking of this planet which we now call 'Phosphorus', what should we say? Well, we can say that the comet passes it and yanks Phosphorus over so that it is not in the position normally occupied by Phosphorus in the evening. If we do say this, and really use 'Phosphorus' as the name of a planet, then we have to say that, under such circumstances, Phosphorus in the evening would not be in the position where we, in fact, saw it; or alternatively, Hesperus in the evening would not be in the position in which we, in fact, saw it. We might say that under such circumstances, we would not have called Hesperus 'Hesperus' because Hesperus would have been in a different position. But that still would not make Phosphorus different from Hesperus; but what would then be the case instead is that Hesperus would have been in a different position from the position it in fact is and, perhaps, not in such a position that people would have called it 'Hesperus'. But that would not be a situation in which Phosphorus would not have been Hesperus.

Let us take another example which may be clearer. Suppose someone uses 'Tully' to refer to the Roman orator who denounced Cataline and uses the name

'Cicero' to refer to the man whose works he had to study in third-year Latin in high school. Of course, he may not know in advance that the very same man who denounced Cataline wrote these works, and that is a contingent statement. But the fact that this statement is contingent should not make us think that the statement that Cicero is Tully, if it is true, and it is in fact true, is contingent. Suppose, for example, that Cicero actually did denounce Cataline, but thought that this political achievement was so great that he should not bother writing any literary works. Would we say that these would be circumstances under which he would not have been Cicero? It seems to me that the answer is no, that instead we would say that, under such circumstances, Cicero would not have written any literary works. It is not a necessary property of Cicero—the way the shadow follows the man— that he should have written certain works; we can easily imagine a situation in which Shakespeare would not have written the works of Shakespeare, or one in which Cicero would not have written the works of Cicero. What may be the case is that we *fix the reference* of the term 'Cicero' by use of some descriptive phrase, such as 'the author of these works'. But once we have this reference fixed, we then use the name 'Cicero' *rigidly* to designate the man who in fact we have identified by his authorship of these works. We do not use it to designate whoever would have written these works in place of Cicero, if someone else wrote them. It might have been the case that the man who wrote these works was not the man who denounced Cataline. Cassius might have written these works. But we would not then say that Cicero would have been Cassius, unless we were speaking in a very loose and metaphorical way. We would say that Cicero, whom we may have identified and come to know by his works, would not have written them, and that someone else, say Cassius, would have written them in his place.

Such examples are not grounds for thinking that identity statements are contingent. To take them as such grounds is to misconstrue the relation between a *name* and a *description used to fix its reference*, to take them to be *synonyms*. Even if we fix the reference of such a name as 'Cicero' as the man who wrote such and such works, in speaking of counterfactual situations, when we speak of Cicero, we do not then speak of whoever in such counterfactual situations *would* have written such and such works, but rather of Cicero, whom we have identified by the contingent property that he is the man who in fact, that is, in the actual world, wrote certain works.[15]

---

[15] If someone protests, regarding the lectern, that it *could* after all have *turned out* to have been made of ice, and therefore could have been made of ice, I would reply that what he really means is that *a lectern* could have looked just like this one, and have been placed in the same position as this one, and yet have been made of ice. In short, I could have been in the *same epistemological situation* in relation to *a lectern made of ice* as I actually am in relation to *this* lectern. In the main text, I have argued that the same reply should be given to protests that Hesperus could have turned out to be other than Phosphorus, or Cicero other than Tully. Here, then, the notion of 'counterpart' comes into its own. For it is not this table, but an epistemic 'counterpart', which was hewn from ice; not Hesperus-Phosphorus-Venus, but two distinct counterparts thereof, in two of the roles Venus actually plays (that of Evening Star and Morning Star), which are different. Precisely because of this fact, it is not *this table* which could have been made of ice. Statements about the modal properties of *this table* never refer to counterparts. However, if someone confuses the epistemological and the metaphysical problems, he will be well on the way to the counterpart theory Lewis and others have advocated.

I hope this is reasonably clear in a brief compass. Now, actually I have been presupposing something I do not really believe to be, in general, true. Let us suppose that we do fix the reference of a name by a description. Even if we do so, we do not then make the name *synonymous*, with the description, but instead we use the name *rigidly* to refer to the object so named, even in talking about counter-factual situations where the thing named would not satisfy the description in question. Now, this is what I think in fact is true for those cases of naming where the reference is fixed by description. But, in fact, I also think, contrary to most recent theorists, that the reference of names is rarely or almost never fixed by means of description. And by this I do not just mean what Searle says: "It's not a single description, but rather a cluster, a family of properties which fixes the reference." I mean that properties in this sense are not used *at all*. But I do not have the time to go into this here. So, let us suppose that at least one half of pre-vailing views about naming is true, that the reference is fixed by descriptions. Even were that true, the name would not be synonymous with the description, but would be used to *name* an object which we pick out by the contingent fact that it satisfies a certain description. And so, even though we can imagine a case where the man who wrote these works would not have been the man who denounced Cataline, we should not say that that would be a case in which Cicero would not have been Tully. We should say that it is a case in which Cicero did not write these works, but rather that Cassius did. And the identity of Cicero and Tully still holds.

Let me turn to the case of heat and the motion of molecules. Here surely is a case that is contingent identity! Recent philosophy has emphasized this again and again. So, if it is a case of contingent identity, then let us imagine under what circumstances it would be false. Now, concerning this statement I hold that the circumstances philosophers apparently have in mind as circumstances under which it would have been false are not in fact such circumstances. First, of course, it is argued that "Heat is the motion of molecules" is an a posteriori judgment; scientific investigation might have turned out otherwise. As I said before, this shows nothing against the view that it is necessary—at least if I am right. But here, surely, people had very specific cir-cumstances in mind under which, so they thought, the judgment that heat is the motion of molecules would have been false. What were these circumstances? One can distill them out of the fact that we found out empirically that heat is the motion of molecules. How was this? What did we find out first when we found out that heat is the motion of molecules? There is a certain external phenomenon which we can sense by the sense of touch, and it produces a sensation which we call "the sensation of heat." We then discover that the external phenomenon which produces this sensation, which we sense, by means of our sense of touch, is in fact that of molecular agitation in the thing that we touch, a very high degree of molecular agitation. So, it might be thought, to imagine a situation in which heat would not have been the motion of mol-ecules, we need only imagine a situation in which we would have had the very same sensation and it would have been produced by something other than the motion of molecules. Similarly, if we wanted to imagine a situation in which light was not a stream of photons, we could imagine a situation in which we were sensitive to some-thing else in exactly the same way, producing what we call visual experiences, though not through a stream of photons. To make the case stronger, or to look at another side of the coin, we could also consider a situation in which we *are* concerned with the motion of molecules but in which such motion does not give us the sensation of heat. And it might also have happened that we, or, at least, the creatures inhabiting this planet, might have been so constituted that, let us say, an increase in the motion of molecules did not give us this sensation but that, on the contrary, a slowing down of the molecules did give us the very same sensation. This would be a situation, so it might be thought, in which heat would not be the motion of molecules, or, more precisely, in which temperature would not be mean molecular kinetic energy.

But I think it would not be so. Let us think about the situation again. First, let us think about it in the actual world. Imagine right now the world invaded by a number of Martians, who do indeed get the very sensation that we call "the sensation of heat" when they feel some ice which has slow molecular motion, and who do not get a sensation of heat—in fact, maybe just the reverse—when they put their hand near a fire which causes a lot of molecular agitation. Would we say, "Ah, this casts some doubt on heat being the motion of molecules, because there are these other people who don't get the same sensation"? Obviously not, and no one would think so. We would say instead that the Martians somehow feel the very sensation we get when we feel heat when they feel cold and that they do not get a sensation of heat when they feel heat. But now let us think of a counterfactual situation.[16] Suppose the earth had from the very beginning been inhabited by such creatures. First, imagine it inhabited by no creatures at all: then there is no one to feel any sensations of heat. But we would not say that under such circumstances it would necessarily be the case that heat did not exist; we would say that heat might have existed, for example, if there were fires that heated up the air.

Let us suppose the laws of physics were not very different: Fires do heat up the air. Then there would have been heat even though there were no creatures around to feel it. Now let us suppose evolution takes place, and life is created, and there are some creatures around. But they are not like us, they are more like the Martians. Now would we say that heat has suddenly turned to cold, because of the way the creatures of this planet sense it? No, I think we should describe this situation as a situation in which, though the creatures on this planet got our sensation of heat, they did not get it when they were exposed to heat. They got it when they were exposed to cold. And that is something we can surely well imagine. We can imagine it just as we can imagine our planet being invaded by creatures of this sort. Think of it in two steps. First there is a stage where there are no creatures at all, and one can certainly imagine the planet still having both heat and cold, though

---

[16] Isn't the situation I just described also counterfactual? At least it may well be, if such Martians never in fact invade. Strictly speaking, the distinction I wish to draw compares how we *would* speak *in* a (possibly counterfactual) situation, *if* it obtained, and how we *do* speak *of* a counterfactual situation, knowing that it does not obtain—i.e., the distinction between the language we would have used in a situation and the language we *do* use to describe it. (Consider the description: "Suppose we all spoke German." This description is in English.) The former case can be made vivid by imagining the counterfactual situation to be actual.

no one is around to sense it. Then the planet comes through an evolutionary process to be peopled with beings of different neural structure from ourselves. Then these creatures could be such that they were insensitive to heat; they did not feel it in the way we do; but on the other hand, they felt cold in much the same way that we feel heat. But still, heat would be heat, and cold would be cold. And particularly, then, this goes in no way against saying that in this counterfactual situation heat would still *be* the molecular motion, *be* that which is produced by fires, and so on, just as it would have been if there had been no creatures on the planet at all. Similarly, we could imagine that the planet was inhabited by creatures who got visual sensations when there were sound waves in the air. We should not therefore say, "Under such circumstances, sound would have been light." Instead we should say, "The planet was inhabited by creatures who were in some sense visually sensitive to sound and, maybe even visually sensitive to light." If this is correct, it can still be and will still be a necessary truth that heat is the motion of molecules and that light is a stream of photons.

To state the view succinctly: we use both the terms 'heat' and 'the motion of molecules' as rigid designators for a certain external phenomenon. Since heat is in fact the motion of molecules, and the designators are rigid, by the argument I have given here, it is going to be *necessary* that heat is the motion of molecules. What gives us the illusion of contingency is the fact we have identified the heat by the contingent fact that there happen to be creatures on this planet—(namely, ourselves) who are sensitive to it in a certain way, that is, who are sensitive to the motion of molecules or to heat—these are one and the same thing. And this is contingent. So we use the description, 'that which causes such and such sensations, or that which we sense in such and such a way', to identify heat. But in using this fact we use a contingent property of heat, just as we use the contingent property of Cicero as having written such and such works to identify him. We then use the terms 'heat' in the one case and 'Cicero' in the other *rigidly* to designate the objects for which they stand. And of course the term 'the motion of molecules' is rigid; it always stands for the motion of molecules, never for any other phenomenon. So, as Bishop Butler said, 'everything is what it is and not another thing." Therefore, "Heat is the motion of molecules" will be necessary, not contingent, and one only has the *illusion* of contingency in the way one could have the illusion of contingency in thinking that this table might have been made of ice. We might think one could imagine it, but if we try, we can see on reflection that what we are really imagining is just there being another lectern in this very position here which was in fact made of ice. The fact that we may identify this lectern by being the object we see and touch in such and such a position is something else.

Now how does this relate to the problem of mind and body? It is usually held that this is a contingent identity statement just like "Heat is the motion of molecules." That cannot be. It cannot be a contingent identity statement just like "Heat is the motion of molecules" because, if I am right, "Heat is the motion of molecules" is not a contingent identity statement. Let us look at this statement. For example, "My being in pain at such and such a time is my being in such and such a brain state at such and such a time," or, "Pain in general is such and such a neural (brain) state."

This is held to be contingent on the following grounds. First, we can imagine the brain state existing though there is no pain at all. It is only a scientific fact that whenever we are in a certain brain state we have a pain. Second, one might imagine a creature being in pain, but not being in any specified brain state at all, maybe not having a brain at all. People even think, at least prima facie, though they may be wrong, that they can imagine totally disembodied creatures, at any rate certainly not creatures with bodies anything like our own. So it seems that we can imagine definite circumstances under which this relationship would have been false. Now, if these circumstances are circumstances, notice that we cannot deal with them simply by saying that this is just an illusion, something we can apparently imagine, but in fact cannot in the way we thought erroneously that we could imagine a situation in which heat was not the motion of molecules. Because although we can say that we pick out heat contingently by the contingent property that it affects us in such and such a way, we cannot similarly say that we pick out pain contingently by the fact that it affects us in such and such a way. On such a picture there would be the brain state, and we pick it but by the contingent fact that it affects us as pain. Now that might be true of the brain state, but it cannot be true of the pain. The experience itself has to be *this experience,* and I cannot say that it is contingent property of the pain I now have that it is a pain.[17] In fact, it would seem that both the terms, 'my pain' and 'my being in such and such a brain state' are, first of all, both rigid designators. That is, whenever anything is such and such a pain, it is essentially that very object, namely, such and such a pain, and wherever anything is such and such a brain state, it is essentially that very object, namely, such and such a brain state. So both of these are rigid designators. One cannot say this pain might have been something else, some other state. These are both rigid designators.

---

[17] The most popular identity theories advocated today explicitly fail to satisfy this simple requirement. For these theories usually hold that a mental state is a brain state, and that what makes the brain state into a mental state is its 'causal role', the fact that it tends to produce certain behavior (as intentions produce actions, or pain, pain behavior) and to be produced by certain stimuli (e.g., pain, by pinpricks). If the relations between the brain state and its causes and effects are regarded as contingent, then *being such-and-such-a-mental* state is a contingent property of the brain state. Let X be a pain. The causal-role identity theorist holds (1) that X is a brain state, (2) that the fact that X is a pain is to be analyzed (roughly) as the fact that X is produced by certain stimuli and produces certain behavior. The fact mentioned in (2) is, of course, regarded as contingent; the brain state X might well exist and not tend to produce the appropriate behavior in the absence of other conditions. Thus (1) and (2) assert that a certain pain X might have existed, yet not have been a pain. This seems to me self-evidently absurd. Imagine any pain: is it possible that *it itself* could have existed, yet not have been a pain?

If $X = Y$, then X and Y share all properties, including modal properties. If X is a pain and Y the corresponding brain state, then *being a pain* is an essential property of X, and *being a brain state* is an essential property of Y. If the correspondence relation is, in fact, identity, then it must be *necessary* of Y that it corresponds to a pain, and *necessary* of X that it correspond to a brain state, indeed to this particular brain state, Y. Both assertions seem false; it *seems* clearly possible that X should have existed without the corresponding brain state; or that the brain state should have existed without being felt as pain. Identity theorists cannot, contrary to their almost universal present practice, accept these intuitions; they must deny them, and explain them away. This is none too easy a thing to do.

Second, the way we would think of picking them out—namely, the pain by its being an experience of a certain sort, and the brain state by its being the state of a certain material object, being of such and such molecular configuration—both of these pick out their objects essentially and not accidentally, that is, they pick them out by essential properties. Whenever the molecules *are* in this configuration, we *do* have such and such a brain state. Whenever you feel *this,* you do have a pain. So it seems that the identity theorist is in some trouble, for, since we have two rigid designators, the identity statement in question is necessary. Because they pick out their objects essentially, we cannot say the case where you seem to imagine the identity statement false is really an illusion like the illusion one gets in the case of heat and molecular motion, because that illusion depended on the fact that we pick out heat by a certain contingent property. So there is very little room to maneuver; perhaps none.[18] The identity theorist, who holds that pain is the brain state, also has to hold that it necessarily is the brain state. He therefore cannot concede, but has to deny, that there would have been situations under which one would have had pain but not the corresponding brain state. Now usually in arguments on the identity theory, this is very far from being denied. In fact, it is conceded from the outset by the materialist as well as by his opponent. He says, "Of course, it *could* have been the case that we had pains without the brain states. It is a contingent identity." But that cannot be. He has to hold that we are under some illusion in thinking that we can imagine that there could have been pains without brain states. And the only model I can think of for what the illusion might be, or at least the model given by the analogy the materialists themselves suggest, namely, heat and molecular motion, simply does not work in this case. So the materialist is up against a very stiff challenge. He has to show that these things we think we can see to be possible are in fact not possible. He has to show that these things which we can imagine are not in fact things we can imagine. And that requires some very different philosophical argument from the sort which has been given in the case of heat and molecular motion. And it would have to be a deeper and subtler

---

[18] A brief restatement of the argument may be helpful here. If "pain" and "C-fiber stimulation" are rigid designators of phenomena, one who identifies them must regard the identity as necessary. How can this necessity be reconciled with the apparent fact that C-fiber stimulation might have turned out not to be correlated with pain at all? We might try to reply by analogy to the case of heat and molecular motion; the latter identity, too, is necessary, yet someone may believe that, before scientific investigation showed otherwise, molecular motion might have turned out not to be heat. The reply is, of course, that what really is possible is that people (or some rational sentient beings) could have been in the *same epistemic situation* as we actually are, and identify *a phenomenon* in the same way we identify heat, namely, by feeling it by the sensation we call "the sensation of heat," without the phenomenon being molecular motion. Further, the beings might not have been sensitive to molecular motion (i.e., to heat) by any neural mechanism whatsoever. It is impossible to explain the apparent possibility of C-fiber stimulations not having been pain in the same way. Here, too, we would have to suppose that we could have been in the same epistemological situation, and identify something in the same way we identify pain, without its corresponding to C-fiber stimulation. But the way we identify pain is by feeling it, and if a C-fiber stimulation could have occurred without our feeling any pain, then the C-fiber stimulation would have occurred without there *being* any pain, contrary to the necessity of the identity. The trouble is that although 'heat' is a rigid designator, heat is picked out by the contingent property of its being felt in a certain way; pain, on the other hand, is picked out by an essential (indeed necessary and sufficient) property. For a sensation to be *felt* as pain is for it to *be* pain.

argument than I can fathom and subtler than has ever appeared in any materialist literature that I have read. So the conclusion of this investigation would be that the analytical tools we are using go against the identity thesis and so go against the general thesis that mental states are just physical states.[19]

The next topic would be my own solution to the mind-body problem, but that I do not have.

---

[19] All arguments against the identity theory which rely on the necessity of identity, or on the notion of essential property, are, of course, inspired by Descartes' argument for his dualism. The earlier arguments which superficially were rebutted by the analogies of heat and molecular motion, and the bifocals inventor who was also Postmaster General, had such an inspiration; and so does my argument here. R. Albritton and M. Slote have informed me that they independently have attempted to give essentialist arguments against the identity theory, and probably others have done so as well.

The simplest Cartesian argument can perhaps be restated as follows: Let 'A' be a *name* (rigid designator) of Descartes' body. Then Descartes argues that since he could exist even if A did not, $\lozenge$ (Descartes $\neq A$), hence Descartes $\neq A$. Those who have accused him of a modal fallacy have forgotten that 'A' is rigid. His argument is valid, and his conclusion is correct, provided its (perhaps dubitable) premise is accepted. On the other hand, provided that Descartes is regarded as having ceased to exist upon his death, "Descartes $\neq A$" can be established without the use of a modal argument; for if so, no doubt A survived Descartes when A was a corpse. Thus A had a property (existing at a certain time) which Descartes did not. The same argument can establish that a statue is not the hunk of stone, or the congery of molecules, of which it is composed. Mere non-identity, then, may be a weak conclusion. (See D. Wiggins, *Philosophical Review*, Vol. 77 (1968), pp. 90 ff.) The Cartesian modal argument, however, surely can be deployed to maintain relevant stronger conclusions as well.

PROPER NAMES AND IDENTIFYING DESCRIPTIONS*

Keith S. Donnellan

I

There is an extremely plausible principle about proper names that many philosophers up to the present have either assumed or argued for. I will call it the principle of identifying descriptions. One illustration of it is in this passage from Strawson's *Individuals:*

> . . . it is no good using a name for a particular unless one knows who or what is referred to by the use of the name. A name is worthless without a backing of descriptions which can be produced on demand to explain the application.[1]

---

* I am indebted to students and colleagues for comments and suggestions, in particular Professor John Perry and Mr. Theodore Budlong. I believe also that some departure from the traditional alternatives in theories about reference and proper names is "in the air" and that views along some of the lines I take in this paper I may share with others, although the view I attack is still the dominant one. I believe that Saul Kripke has a very similar position, at least insofar as denial of the prevalent theories go. And, indeed, I think I may owe one of my counter-examples to him through a second-hand source (although I did not understand the relevance until much later). David Kaplan's paper, "Quantifying In," *Synthese* **19** (1969) 178–214, also seems to me to be in the same vein, though I am not sure I agree with a variety of details and the main purpose of the paper is not to mount an assault on theories of proper names.

[1] P. F. Strawson, *Individuals,* Methuen & Co. Ltd., London, 1959, p. 20.

The "backing of descriptions" Strawson speaks of supposedly functions as the criterion for identifying the referent of a name, if it has one, or, alternatively, for deciding that there is no referent. If I say, for example, 'Homer is my favorite poet', then, roughly speaking, the descriptions I could supply in answer to the question, 'Who is Homer?', provide the 'backing of descriptions'. And these in turn either pick out a single individual as the referent of the name (as it occurs in my utterance) in virtue of his fitting these descriptions or make it true that there is no referent—that Homer did not exist.

While this initial statement of the principle needs refinement and the acknowledgement of variants, it seems at first sight almost indisputable that some such principle governs the referential function of proper names. Must not a user of a proper name know to whom or what he is referring? And what can this knowledge consist in if not the ability to describe the referent uniquely?

Nevertheless, I believe the principle to be false. In the first sections of the paper I will state the principle more precisely and fill in some of the details of how it would have to operate. The exercise of trying to make it more precise and giving various needed qualifications is enough, I think, to rob it of some of its initial attractiveness. I will then, however, meet it head-on by means of counter-examples. I will argue that (a) a proper name may have a referent even though the conditions laid down by the principle are not satisfied and (b) where the conditions are satisfied, the object that ought to be the referent according to the principle need not be the true referent. In the course of this I will suggest certain positive things about how the referent of a name is determined, though these will not amount to an alternative principle.

II

What I call the 'principle of identifying descriptions' should not be thought of as expressing the thesis that proper names have a sense (or meaning or connotation). (That thesis, I think, suffers in any case from vagueness about what is to count as showing that an expression has a sense.) Anyone who holds that proper names have a sense almost certainly subscribes to the principle, but the converse is doubtful. In his influential paper, "Proper Names,"[2] John Searle begins with the question, 'Do proper names have senses?', and he ends by saying that in a sense they do and in a sense they do not. Searle, however, though he would not without heavy qualification ascribe senses to proper names, is one of the prime examples of a philosopher who defends the principle I have in mind. In this he is in company with Frege who would have no reluctance in talking about the sense of a proper name.

The simplest application of the principle, to be sure, can be found in the view of someone such as Russell who holds that proper names are concealed definite descriptions. Russell says, ". . . the name 'Romulus' is not really a name [that is, in the 'narrow logical sense'] but a sort of truncated description. It stands for a person

---

[2] *Mind* **67** (1958) 166–173.

who did such-and-such things, who killed Remus, and founded Rome, and so on."[3] And again, "When I say, e.g., 'Homer existed', I am meaning by 'Homer' some description, say 'the author of the Homeric Poems'. . . ."[4] Russell associates with the use of a name some definite description for which the name is a simple substitute—the same proposition would be expressed by a sentence containing the name as by the sentence formed from it by substituting the associated description for the name.

This tight connection between proper names and definite descriptions was rightly challenged by Searle in "Proper Names." Yet Searle still retains the backing of descriptions and these serve, as they would also for Russell, as criteria for identifying the referent, albeit in a looser and more complicated manner:

> Suppose we ask the users of the name "Aristotle" to state what they regard as certain essential and established facts about him. Their answers would be a set of uniquely referring descriptive statements. Now what I am arguing is that the descriptive force of "This is Aristotle" is to assert that a sufficient but so far unspecified number of these statements are true of this object.[5]

Without doubt this departs significantly from Russell's simplistic view. It allows for (what surely we should allow for) the possibility, for example, of discovering that Aristotle was not the teacher of Alexander the Great without having to deny Aristotle's existence, which would be impossible on Russell's view if that description was part of the associated description for our use of 'Aristotle'. Only a 'sufficient number' of the things we believe about Aristotle need be true of some individual for him to be Aristotle.

But the flexibility introduced is limited. Vague and indeterminate as we may leave the notion of 'sufficient number', behind our use of a name a set of descriptions still operates to determine the referent. The formulation of the principle of identifying descriptions I shall give will allow both for Searle's looser and Russell's tighter connection between names and descriptions.

I should like to make one more general comment about the issue I am concerned with. The importance of the principle in question is not confined to a narrow issue about how proper names refer. It also has a bearing on the general problem of reference. For proper names constitute something like a test case for theories of reference. A peculiar feature of the situation is that two classical but opposing paradigms for referring expressions can both lead one to adopt the same theory about proper names. The model referring expression has been for many philosophers of language, I believe, a definite description (used 'attributively' in the terminology I used elsewhere[6]). An object is referred to in virtue of possessing uniquely the properties mentioned in the definite description. It is not hard to see how this standard leads to adopting the principle of identifying descriptions for

---

[3] "Lectures on Logical Atomism" in *Logic and Knowledge* (ed. by Robert C. Marsh), George Allen & Unwin Ltd., London, 1956, p. 243.

[4] *Ibid.*, p. 252.

[5] "Proper Names," *op. cit.*, p. 171.

[6] In "Reference and Definite Descriptions," *The Philosophical Review* **75** (1966):281–304, and "Putting Humpty Dumpty Together Again," *The Philosophical Review* **77** (1968):203–215.

proper names. Proper names are referring expressions, yet on the surface fail to exhibit any descriptive content. Given definite descriptions as the paradigm, one is forced to look under the surface (which amounts to looking into the user(s) of the name) for the 'backing of descriptions' that must be there.

The major alternative to a definite description as the paradigm of a referring expression is represented by Russell's and Wittgenstein's (in the *Tractatus*) notion of a name in the 'narrow logical sense'. Ordinary names, of course, are not names at all in this sense; they cannot meet the austere requirements of referring in some mysterious, unanalysable and absolutely direct way to their referents. And given this notion of 'genuine' names, Russell adduces very good reasons why no such ordinary name as 'Homer' or 'Aristotle' can be a genuine name. But some account has to be given of how ordinary names function. Russell saw no alternative but to treat them as concealed definite descriptions, what they name, if anything, being whatever is denoted by the concealed description. (Had he thought of Searle's perhaps more sophisticated view, there seems no reason why he should not have adopted that for 'ordinary' proper names.)

Strangely enough, then, two antagonistic models of what a genuine referring expression is like lead their proponents to the principle of identifying descriptions. Demonstrating that that principle is mistaken would not irrevocably descredit either model, but it would, I think, take away much of the motivation for adopting either. Ordinary proper names may not have as much claim to being genuine referring expressions as Russell's names 'in the strict logical sense' (could we but understand what those are and discover some of them), but as against definite descriptions it is hard to see how they could come out second best. If their mode of functioning, however, is not captured by the principle of identifying descriptions, if, that is, they do not name in much the same way a definite description denotes,[7] then can definite descriptions possibly be model referring expressions?

And on the other side, if ordinary proper names are neither names 'in the strict logical sense', as they surely are not, nor concealed descriptions, then some other relationship will have to be recognized as holding between some singular expressions and what they stand for. In that case, much of the reason for supposing that there are such things as names 'in the strict logical sense' will be gone. For it is clear from Russell's writings, at least, that these are introduced in part because he felt that definite descriptions not *really* being referring expressions (but only denoting expressions), some other sort expression must serve the purpose of allowing us to talk directly about things in the world. If (ordinary) proper names do not function via the relationship of denoting nor through whatever relationship Russell's names are supposed to enjoy, then perhaps the way they do function represents the alternative Russell was seeking.[8]

---

[7] I assume here Russell's definition of denoting, which I think makes it a well-defined relation and ought always to be kept in mind in discussions of reference so that other relations may be compared with it: An entity X is denoted by a definite description, 'the ϕ', just in case X uniquely possesses the property designated by 'ϕ'.

[8] Although I do not have space to develop it, my account of proper names in this paper seems to me to make what I called 'referential' definite descriptions (as discussed in "Reference and Definite Descriptions," *op. cit.*) a close relative of proper names.

III

The principle of identifying descriptions is a two-stage thesis, the second stage depending upon the first. It states, in the first place, that (with some qualifications to be noted later) the user(s) of a proper name must be able to supply a set of, as I shall call them, 'non-question-begging' descriptions in answer to the question, 'To whom (or what) does the name refer?' The important qualifier, 'non-question-begging', I will explain later.[9] I will call these descriptions that speakers supposedly must be able to supply 'the set of identifying descriptions'.

Secondly, the principle states that the referent of a proper name (as used by a speaker in some particular utterance), if there is one, is that object that uniquely fits a 'sufficient' number of the descriptions in the set of identifying descriptions. As a corollary, when no entity (or more than one) satisfies this condition, the name has no referent and a negative existential statement expressible by a sentence of the form '*N* does not exist' (where '*N*' is the name in question) will be true.

I have tried to state the principle so as to make it possible for alternative positions still to embody it. I should like to show that we ought not to accept *any* of the versions of it to be found in the literature. Thus, for reasons that will emerge, I leave it open in the first part whether the set of identifying descriptions is to be formed from what *each* speaker can supply or from what speakers collectively supply. In the second part, the 'sufficient number' of descriptions that an object must satisfy to be the referent might be *all* of them, as in Russell's view, or some *indeterminate number* of them, as in Searle's.

The counter-examples I later give are directed against the second part of the principle; they are designed to show that *even if* the user(s) of a name must be able to supply a set of identifying descriptions, as laid down by the first part, these descriptions do not provide necessary and sufficient conditions for what shall count as the referent. But the first part of the principle is not without difficulties. To strengthen my case against the principle I want first to point out some of these while formulating some of the needed qualifications to the principle as I have just stated it.

IV

There are two views on the source of the set of identifying descriptions that supposedly must back up the use of a proper name.

We find in Russell and Frege[10] the idea that different speakers who use the same name in an otherwise identical propositional context will most likely not express the same proposition (or thought, in Frege's terminology). This happens because very probably they do not associate with the name the same set of descriptions. The propositions might have different truth-values, because the

---

[9] Below, Section VI.

[10] E.g., in "The Thought: A Logical Inquiry" (translated by A. M. and Marcelle Quinton), *Mind* **65** (1956) 289–311. Also in P. F. Strawson (ed.), *Philosophical Logic*, Oxford Readings in Philosophy, Oxford University Press, Oxford, 1967, pp. 17–38.

speakers, with different sets of identifying descriptions, may be referring to different things.[11] Russell and Frege, in other words, look to the individual speaker for the set of identifying descriptions.

In contrast, Searle tells us that the set of identifying descriptions is formed from the descriptions users of the name give of what they refer to. And Strawson, in discussing this question,[12] imagines a situation in which a name is used by a group in which each member "knows some distinguishing fact or facts, not necessarily the same ones, about Socrates, facts which each is prepared to cite to indicate whom he now means or understands, by 'Socrates'." He then suggests that we form a "composite description incorporating the most frequently mentioned facts" and continues, "Now it would be too much to say that the success of term-introduction within the group by means of the name requires that there should exist just one person of whom all the propositions in the composite description are true. But it would not be too much to say that it requires that there should exist one and only one person of whom some reasonable proportion of these propositions is true."[13] Given this difference of opinion, I allowed for alternatives in the statement of the principle.

Both means of determining the set of identifying descriptions contain difficulties. To take the Russell-Frege view first, it seems to me, though evidently not to them, absurd to suppose that a beginning student of philosophy, who has learned a few things about Aristotle, and his teacher, who knows a great deal, express different propositions when each says 'Aristotle was the teacher of Alexander'. Even if this can be swallowed, there are very unpleasant consequences. Given the second part of the principle of identifying descriptions the student and teacher possess different criteria for identifying Aristotle and even for establishing his existence. For the student Aristotle would be a person satisfying (substantially) some fairly small number of descriptions; for the scholar of philosophy a much larger number would determine the existence and identity of Aristotle. This means that if each affirm Aristotle's existence there is the theoretical possibility, at least, that one is correct and the other wrong. Yet suppose that the smaller supply of descriptions available to the student turns out generally to be incorrect (we can imagine him to be unfortunate enough to have been told mostly things about Aristotle that historians of Greek philosophy are mistaken about). Would he really be in error in saying that Aristotle existed? Should we say to him, if we uncover the errors, 'Your Aristotle doesn't exist, though Professor Smith's does'?

Worse still, suppose that the few things the student has "learned" about Aristotle are not only not true of the individual his teacher refers to, but turn out substantially to be true of, say, Plato. He has been told, perhaps, that Aristotle wrote the *Metaphysics* when, in fact, Plato wrote it and Aristotle cribbed it, etc.

---

[11] That is to say, *if* what they refer to is a function of the set of identifying descriptions each possesses. In that case there would be the logical possibility of each speaker's set picking out different objects, each possessing the properties one speaker would attribute to the referent, but not those the other would.

[12] *Individuals, op. cit.*, pp. 191–192.

[13] *Loc. cit.*

Should we say that he has all along been referring to Plato, though his teacher, for whom these few descriptions are not the only source of criteria for what the referent is, continues to refer to Aristotle? The principle of identifying descriptions seems to lead to that result when interpreted in this way.

The more liberal view that utilizes descriptions suppliable by users of the name, in the plural, is not in much better shape. In the first place, what group of speakers is to form the reference set from which the "composite description" is to be drawn? Searle speaks of properties "commonly" attributed to Aristotle. Commonly attributed by whom? By contemporary speakers? One thing seems certain: the speakers in question cannot be *all* those who have ever used the name 'Aristotle' to refer to Aristotle. Aside from the appearance, at least, of circularity, none of us would likely ever be in a position to know what properties that group would attribute to Aristotle. Childhood friends of Aristotle, who did not follow his subsequent career, would have a quite different set of descriptions of him from ours. I doubt that we shall ever know what those were. Using this *total* class of those who have ever spoken of Aristotle is a practical impossibility and can hardly form the basis for our use. (It would also seem to do violence to the motivation behind the principle of identifying descriptions—that users of a name should be able to supply criteria for identifying the referent.)

On the other hand, to limit the group of speakers whose descriptions will generate the "composite description" to, say, those at a particular time yields consequences similar to those of the Russell-Frege view. Different times and ages might have different beliefs about Aristotle. And in conjunction with the second part of the principle of identifying descriptions it would be possible that the affirmation that Aristotle existed should have different truth-values from one time to another. Or, because of the particular beliefs they held, we could imagine that the people of one age, unknown to any of us, referred to Plato when they used the name 'Aristotle'. On the Frege-Russell view any two people using the same sentence containing the name 'Aristotle' and believing that they are referring to the same person, etc., very likely do not express the same proposition. The more liberal view only expands this possibility to different groups of people.

V

The first part of the principle of identifying descriptions tells us that users of a name must be in a position to supply a set of identifying descriptions. (For the sake of argument I will at times allow that this is so, although what positive remarks I make will imply that there is no necessity involved.) How are we to understand this? Strawson says, ". . . When I speak of 'preparedness to substitute a description for a name', this requirement must not be taken too literally. It is not required that people be very ready articulators of what they know."[14] I think he is surely right to allow us this latitude. Small children and even adults often use names without literally being able to describe the referent in sufficient detail to guarantee unique identification.

---

[14] *Ibid.*, p. 182, footnote 1.

I imagine the reason philosophers who have discussed proper names so often use historical figures such as Aristotle, Homer, etc. is just that these names are introduced into our vocabulary via descriptions of facts about their bearers and most of us are prepared to give something like uniquely denoting descriptions. But it is less clear that we are ready to describe our friends, people we have met here and there, or even public figures of our times whose images have not yet been crystallized into a few memorable attributes. At the very least it would be an effort to insure that a description of someone we know fairly well and whose name we use often is both accurate and unique. The first part of the principle, then, seems to require of us a high level of ability—unless what counts as having the ability is very broad indeed. (Even though it is hardly like being able to describe the referent, the ability to *point* to the referent is usually included as if it were simply a variant.)

Construe it as broadly as you will, is there really a requirement that the user of a name be able to identify by description (or even by pointing) what the name refers to? The following example, which anticipates a bit some later results, may cast doubt on this. Suppose a child is gotten up from sleep at a party and introduced to someone as 'Tom', who then says a few words to the child. Later the child says to his parents, "Tom is a nice man." The only thing he can say about 'Tom' is that Tom was at a party. Moreover, he is unable to recognize anyone as 'Tom' on subsequent occasions. His parents give lots of parties and they have numerous friends named 'Tom'. The case could be built up, I think, so that nothing the child possesses in the way of descriptions, dispositions to recognize, serves to pick out in the standard way anybody uniquely. That is, we cannot go by the denotation of his descriptions nor whom he points to, if anyone, etc. Does this mean that there is no person to whom he was referring? It seems to me that his parents might perfectly well conjecture about the matter and come up with a reasonable argument showing that the child was talking about this person rather than that. For example, they might reason as follows: "He's met several people named 'Tom' at recent parties, but only Tom Brown did something that might make him say, 'Tom is a nice man'. Of course, Tom Brown isn't nice and he was just indulging in his usual sarcasm when he told him, 'You have a nice pair of parents', but the sarcasm wouldn't have registered."[15]

If this is a reasonable example, it seems the question of what a speaker referred to by using a name is not foreclosed by his inability to describe or even to recognize or point to the referent. The reasoning of the parents in this example is not aimed at finding out what descriptions the child could give, if only he were able to articulate them. I used a child in the example to sharpen the picture of someone with no descriptions or other means of identifying the referent uniquely; but adults also sometimes conjecture about other adults concerning what person they were referring to in using a name. Is it beyond doubt that in such instances the inquiry must ultimately be concerned with what descriptions the user of the

---

[15] The last part of the remark is there simply to indicate that the parents need not even consider what the child says to be *true;* not only does the child not have a "backing of descriptions," but the predicate in the sentence he uses need not apply. This connects up with the position suggested later in the paper.

name could supply? The examples later on will challenge this, yet even now examples such as the one I have given seem to me to make the requirement that every use of a name have behind it a backing of descriptions highly suspicious (even without relying on what appears to me beyond question, that no one has yet given a clear account of what the ability to describe a referent amounts to).

VI

Before turning to counter-examples one more preliminary issue should be settled. In stating the principle of identifying descriptions, I inserted the condition that the descriptions that "back up" the use of a name should not be "question-begging." The qualification has vital significance because there are certain descriptions that a user of a name (providing he can articulate them) could always provide and which would always denote the referent of the name uniquely (providing there is one). No argument could be devised to show that the referent of a name need not be denoted by these descriptions. At the same time anyone who subscribes to the principle of identifying descriptions would hardly have these descriptions in mind or want to rely on them in defence of the principle. Some examples of what I shall count as "question-begging" are the following:

(a) 'the entity I had in mind'
(b) 'the entity I referred to'
(c) 'the entity I believe to be the author of the *Metaphysics*'.

I think it is clear about (a) and (b) and only a little less so about (c) that if descriptions such as these are included in the "backing of descriptions" the principle would become uninteresting.

Strawson, in fact, explicitly excludes descriptions such as (a): "[the speaker] cannot, for himself, distinguish the particular which he has in mind by the fact that it is the one he has in mind. So, there must be some description he could give, which need not be the description he does give, which applies uniquely to the one he has in mind and does not include the phrase, 'the one he has in mind'."[16] Although Strawson mentions a particular description, it is certain that he would exclude from consideration similar ones. In particular, (b) above surely would not count for him. The point of the "backing of descriptions" is to explain how an object gets referred to by a proper name. Descriptions that fit the referent simply in virtue of the fact that the speaker did, in fact, refer to it or had it in mind as the object he meant to refer to are question-begging in answer to the question, 'who (or what) did you refer to?' in the same way that 'What I have in my hand' would be question-begging in answer to the question, 'What are you holding in your hand?'

It is only a little bit less obvious that descriptions of the form, 'the object I believe to be ϕ', such as (c) above, must likewise be excluded from the set of identifying descriptions.

---

[16] *Individuals, op. cit.*, p. 182.

Call descriptions such as 'the author of the *Metaphysics' primary* descriptions; call those such as 'the man I believed to be the author of the *Metaphysics' secondary* descriptions. Suppose that all primary descriptions the user(s) of a name can supply are false of everything. The backing of secondary descriptions would be useless in the same way that 'the object I had in mind' would be. For if I cannot rely on my primary descriptions to pick out uniquely what I refer to, trying to identify the referent via a description of the form 'the one I believed to be (though it is not) φ' would amount to no more than trying to identify *the object I had in mind* when I held that belief.

In what follows, then, I will count what I have called "secondary" descriptions as question-begging.

VII

In the next sections I construct counter-examples to the principle of identifying descriptions. To do this I must show that there are possible situations in which the referent of a name does not satisfy the conditions the principle lays down or situations in which an entity satisfying those conditions is not the referent. The principle tells us that the referent of a name, if there is one, is that entity that fits some sufficient number of a certain set of descriptions, namely the set suppliable by the user(s) of the name. It is important to note that in denying this, one need not deny that there are some constraints on what the referent of a name may be—*some* description which it must fit. But this is only to allow that there may be a 'backing of descriptions' that serve as *necessary* conditions, while the principle tells us that such a backing of descriptions also serves as sufficient conditions.

Thus, I should want to argue, for example, that *theoretically* Aristotle might turn out to be a person who did *not* write the *Metaphysics,* was *not* the teacher of Alexander, etc.; that is to say, a person who does not fit "a sufficient number" of the descriptions we, as users of the name, would now supply. But I need not argue that even theoretically he could turn out to be, say, a fishmonger living in Hoboken or Plato's dog (although in incautious moments I am inclined to believe in even this outlandish theoretical possibility). If anyone wants to maintain that our use of the name is such that being a human being or not living in modern times, etc. are *necessary* for being the referent of the name, I have no objection here to offer against a "backing of descriptions" in that weaker sense. Such an attenuated backing would not *uniquely* identify the referent.

A word about the nature of the counter-examples is required, because they will undoubtedly seem artificial and possibly taken on their own not wholly convincing. Their artificiality is in part forced on me by the fact that I want to question not only the simple view of, say, Russell that sees a name as a simple substitute for a description, but also the looser and vaguer view of Searle and Strawson. The latter, however, uses the notion of an ill-defined "sufficient" number of descriptions. Since the notion of "sufficient" is ill-defined, it is necessary to invent examples in which, for instance, the referent of a name fits *no* description which is both unique to it and available to the speaker (other than "question-begging" descriptions). Otherwise, a defender of the view might take refuge in those descriptions. To make sure that there are no remaining contaminating descriptions, the examples have to be fairly extreme ones in which the user(s) of a name are radically deceived about the properties of what they are talking about.

But if these "pure" examples are in order in everything except their artificiality, then the fact that I do not tell more true-to-life stories should not be an objection. For however vague "sufficient number" is left, one thing is certain: the Searle-Strawson view cannot be that the referent of a name is any entity that fits uniquely any *one* of the descriptions suppliable by the user(s) of the name. The whole purpose of this variant (as opposed to the stronger Russell view) is to allow that we could discover, e.g., that Aristotle did not teach Alexander without having to deny Aristotle's existence or that *someone else* was the teacher of Alexander. But if any *one* of the descriptions in the set of identifying descriptions counts always as "sufficient," there will be an overwhelming number of cases in which there cannot be a unique referent for a name we use—all those instances in which we ascribe to the referent two or more properties which in fact are unique properties of more than one person.

VIII

The first counter-example is the most artificial (but perhaps the most pure). It is a situation in which a speaker uses a name to refer to something though what is referred to is not picked out uniquely by the descriptions available to the speaker. As well, there is something the speaker's descriptions denote uniquely, but that is not the referent.

Imagine the following circumstances: Perhaps in an experiment by psychologists interested in perception a subject is seated before a screen of uniform color and large enough to entirely fill his visual field. On the screen are painted two squares of identical size and color, one directly above the other. The subject knows nothing of the history of the squares—whether one was painted before the other, etc. Nor does he know anything about their future. He is asked to give names to the squares[17] and to say on what basis he assigns the names. With one complication to be noted later, it seems that the only way in which he can distinguish the squares through description is by their relative positions. So he might respond that he will call the top square 'alpha' and the bottom square 'beta'.

The catch in the example is this: Unknown to the subject, he has been fitted with spectacles that invert his visual field. Thus, the square he sees as apparently on top is really on the bottom and *vice versa*. Having now two names to work with we can imagine the subject using one of them to say something about one of the squares. Suppose he comes to believe (whether erroneously or not doesn't matter)

---

[17] In the example as presented I have the subject of the experiment introduce the names. Nothing hinges on this. The experimenters could just as well use the names and give the subjects "identifying descriptions." Nor is there any importance in the fact that the example contains people, the experimenters, "in the know." For all that, everyone concerned might have the inverting spectacles on that I introduce.

that one of the squares has changed color. He might report, 'Alpha is now a different color'. But which square is he referring to? He would describe alpha as the square on top. And if this is the only uniquely identifying description at his command then according to the principle I am attacking, he would have referred to the square that is on top. But given our knowledge of the presence and effect of the inverting spectacles and the ignorance of the subject about that, it seems clear that we should take him as referring to, not the square on top, but the one that seems to him erroneously to be on top—the one on the bottom. We know why he describes 'alpha' the way he does; we expect changes in the square on the bottom to elicit from him reports of changes in alpha, etc. I think it would be altogether right to say that although *he* does not know it, he is talking about the square on the bottom even though he would *describe* it as 'the square on top'. If this is right, we seem to have a case in which the speaker's descriptions of what he is referring to when he uses a name do not yield the true referent so long as we stick to what is denoted by the descriptions he gives. The referent is something different and the thing actually denoted is not the referent.

This counter-example to the principle of identifying descriptions depends upon the supposition that the subject's only description that could serve to pick out the referent uniquely is the one in terms of relative position. But it must be admitted that I have so far neglected a description of alpha that he could supply, that is not question-begging, and that would in fact uniquely identify alpha despite the operation of the glasses. The subject could describe alpha as, 'the square that *appears* to me to be on top'. We must take 'appears' here in its phenomenological sense. If 'that appears to me to be on top' means 'that I believe to be on top' we would have a question-begging description. But in its phenomenological sense, alpha is the one that *appears* to him to be on top and, indeed, it is just because the square on the bottom is the one that appears to him to be on top that it is the referent of 'alpha'.

There is more than one way to modify the example in order to take care of this objection to it, but an easy way is by having the subject use the name 'alpha' a bit later having forgotten how alpha appeared to him, but recalling the position he took it really to have. Of course in our example as presented the subject would have no reason to suppose that there might be a discrepancy between the actual position of alpha and what position it appeared to him to have and so long as he remembered it as being the one on top, he would presumably say that that was also the way it appeared to him. What is needed is something to make him doubt that his recollection of what position he took alpha to have is an accurate guide to how it appeared to him.

Suppose then that our subject is an old hand at experiments of this sort and knows that inverting lenses are sometimes put into the spectacles he wears. Erroneously he believes he has a method of detecting when this happens. He goes through the experiment as previously described but with the mistaken belief that his spectacles have not been tampered with and that the squares have the position they appear to him to have. Later on he makes some statement such as, 'Alpha changed color at one point'. But while he remembers his judgment that alpha was the top square (and has absolute confidence in it), he cannot remember how alpha appeared to him at the time nor whether he had based his judgment on the assumption that his visual field was inverted or not. The subject's set of identifying descriptions thus no longer contains the *appearance* description, and only the erroneous description of alpha as being the square on top remains as a uniquely identifying description.

IX

If the preceding counter-example was persuasive, then it will also suggest something positive. Its moral might be put this way: When a person describes something, as when he describes what he is referring to, *we* are not limited to looking for something that fits his descriptions uniquely (or fits them better than anything else). We can also ask ourselves, "What thing would be *judge* to fit those descriptions, even if it does not really do so?" That question will utilize his descriptions, but will not be decided on the rigid basis of what is denoted, if anything, uniquely by them. In this particular example the influence of inverting spectacles was a deciding factor. We had to know *both* how he described the referent and, what he did not know, that the spectacles would influence his descriptions in a certain way. The role of his set of "identifying descriptions" in determining the referent of his use of a name is not that which the principle of identifying descriptions gives it. It had its part, but the question asked about it was different: "What do these descriptions denote uniquely (or best)?" vs. "Why should he describe the referent in that way?"

The next counter-example[18] provides a somewhat different insight into how proper names function.

A student meets a man he takes to be the famous philosopher, J. L. Aston-Martin. Previously, the student has read some of the philosopher's works and so has at his command descriptions such as, "the author of 'Other Bodies'" and "the leading expounder of the theory of egocentric pluralism." The meeting takes place at a party and the student engages the man in a somewhat lengthy conversation, much of it given over, it turns out, to trying to name cities over 100,000 in population in descending order of altitude above sea-level. In fact, however, although the student never suspects it, the man at the party is not the famous philosopher, but someone who leads the student to have that impression. (We can even imagine that by coincidence he has the same name.)

Imagine, then, a subsequent conversation with his friends in which the student relates what happened at the party. He might begin by saying, "Last night I met J. L. Aston-Martin and talked to him for almost an hour." To whom does he refer at this point? I strongly believe the answer should be, 'to the famous philosopher', and not, 'to the man he met at the party'. What the student says is simply false; a friend "in the know" would be justified in replying that he did not

---

[18] The idea behind this example originated with me from a conversation with Rogers Albritton in 1966 and may derive from Saul Kripke, who has, I believe, a view about proper names not dissimilar to the one in this paper.

meet J. L. Aston-Martin, but someone who had the same name and was no more a philosopher than Milton Berle.

Suppose, however, that the audience contains no such doubting Thomases, and that the rest of party was of sufficient interest to generate several more stories about what went on. The student might use the name 'J. L. Aston-Martin', as it were, incidently. For example: ". . . and then Robinson tripped over Aston-Martin's feet and fell flat on his face" or "I was almost the last to leave—only Aston-Martin and Robinson, who was still out cold, were left."

In these subsequent utterances to whom was the speaker referring in using the name, 'Aston-Martin'? My inclination is to say that here it was to the man he met at the party and not to the famous philosopher. Perhaps the difference lies in the fact that in the initial utterance the speaker's remark would only have a point if he was referring to the famous philosopher, while in the later utterances it is more natural to take him to be referring to the man at the party, since what happened there is the whole point.[19]

If in such examples as this there are *two* references made (or even if there is a strong inclination to say that there are) this is something unaccounted for by the principle of identifying descriptions.

To see this we need only ask what the student's set of identifying descriptions consists in each time he uses the name, first when he claims to have met Aston-Martin and later when he recounts events at the party that incidently involve the man he met there. In both cases the set of identifying descriptions would be the same. It will include, first of all, those descriptions of Aston-Martin he would have given prior to the party—the author of certain works, propounder of certain doctrines, etc. In addition, it would now contain various descriptions derived from meeting the spurious famous man at the party—the man who played the game about cities, whose feet Robinson tripped over, etc.

The full set of descriptions, available to him when he later talks about the party, would be the same whether he was asked, 'Who is Aston-Martin?', at the outset when he claims to have met Aston-Martin at the party or later on when the name occurs in recounting other events involving the man met at the party. *We* may say that the referent changes during the course of his conversation, but the speaker would not. And his full account, i.e., all the descriptions at his command, of who it is he refers to would remain the same. It would contain, for

---

[19] For the purpose of keeping the example within limits, I compress the two uses of the name, that I claim refer, unknown to the speaker, to two different people, into one conversation. I have sometimes, however, found it useful to make the case stronger intuitively by supposing that the person met at the party, for example, who is not the famous philosopher, becomes a longer term acquaintance of the speaker (who continues under the illusion that he is the famous man). In subsequent conversations perhaps months or years later and after his friends have met the bogus philosopher, his use of the name is even more clearly a reference to the man he met at the party and whom he continues to see. Yet if he claimed to know, as in my example, J. L. Aston-Martin, in circumstances where it is clear that the point of the remark has to do with claiming to know a famous man, I still think we would suppose him to have referred to Aston-Martin, the famous philosopher, and not to man he met at the party, who later is one of his close acquaintances.

example, both "the author of 'Other Bodies'" and "the man I talked to at the party about cities."

This result, however, is inconsistent with the principle of identifying descriptions. On that principle, the *same* set of identifying descriptions can determine at most *one* referent. But in this example we seem to have two referents and only one set of identifying descriptions.

We extracted from the first counter-example the idea that the question we should ask is, 'What would the user(s) of the name describe in this way?' rather than, 'What (substantially) fits the descriptions they give?' Though these questions may usually have the same answer, the counter-example showed that they need not.

The present example, however, shows that even this distinction is not enough. It would do no good to ask about his set of identifying descriptions, 'Who would the speaker describe that way?' In the example the same set of identifying descriptions is related to two different referents. It seems then that the ultimate question is rather, 'What would the speaker describe in this way on this occasion?', where 'describe in this way' does not refer to his set of identifying descriptions, but to the predicate he ascribes to the referent; e.g., in the example, we might ask on one occasion, 'Who would he claim to have met at the party?', on another, 'Who would he want us to believe Jones tripped over at the party?'. And although *his* answer, gleaned from his set of identifying descriptions, would be the same in either case, *we* may have reason to answer differently to each question.

X

It is instructive to look at the use of proper names in historical contexts if only to see why so many philosophers who discuss proper names appeal to examples of it. In general, our use of proper names for persons in history (and also those we are not personally acquainted with) is parasitic on uses of the names by other people—in conversation, written records, etc. Insofar as we possess a set of identifying descriptions in these cases they come from things said about the presumed referent by other people. My answer to the question, 'Who was Thales?' would probably derive from what I learned from my teachers or from histories of philosophy. Frequently, as in this example, one's identifying descriptions trace back through many levels of parasitic derivation. Descriptions of Thales we might give go back to what was said, using that name, by Aristotle and Herodotus. And, if Thales existed, the trail would not end there.

The history behind the use of a name may not be known to the individual using it. I may have forgotten the sources from whence I got my descriptions of Thales. Even a whole culture could lose this history. A people with an oral tradition in which names of past heroes figure would probably not be able to trace the history back to original sources. Yet, for all that, they may be telling of the exploits of real men in the past and they may possess knowledge of them and their deeds.

Yet, in such cases the history is of central importance to the question of whether a name in a particular use has a referent and, if so, what it is. The words of others, in conversation, books and documents can, like the inverting spectacles in a previous example, distort our view of what we are naming. But at the same time it can, to one who knows the facts, provide the means of uncovering the referent, if there is one.

The role of this history leading up to a present use of a name has almost always been neglected by those who accept the principle of identifying descriptions. The sort of description generally mentioned as helping to pick out, say, Thales, is such as 'the Greek philosopher who held that all is water'. Nothing is made of the fact that such descriptions are given by us derivatively. We might be pardoned if we supposed that the referent of 'Thales' is whatever ancient Greek happens to fit such descriptions uniquely, even if he should turn out to have been a hermit living so remotely that he and his doctrines have no historical connection with us at all.

But this seems clearly wrong. Suppose that Aristotle and Herodotus were either making up the story or were referring to someone who neither did the things they said he did nor held the doctrines they attributed to him. Suppose further, however, that fortuitously their descriptions fitted uniquely someone they had never heard about and who was not referred to by any authors known to us. Such a person, even if he was the only ancient to hold that all is water, to fall in a well while contemplating the stars, etc., is not 'our' Thales.

Or, to take the other possible outcome according to the principle of identifying descriptions, suppose no one to have held the ridiculous doctrine that all is water, but that Aristotle and Herodotus were referring to a real person—a real person who was not a philosopher, but a well-digger with a reputation for saying wise things and who once exclaimed, "I wish everything were water so I wouldn't have to dig these damned wells." What is the situation then regarding our histories of philosophy? Have they mentioned a non-existent person or have they mentioned someone who existed but who did not have the properties they attribute to him? My inclination is to say the latter. Yet ignoring the history of these uses of the name 'Thales', the principle of identifying descriptions would tell us that Thales did not exist. But then to whom were Aristotle and Herodotus referring? Surely we cannot conclude, 'to no one'. It seems to me to make sense that we should discover that Thales was after all a well-digger and that Aristotle and Herodotus were deceived about what he did. That would not make sense, however, if we are forced to conclude in such a case that he did not exist. That is, if we neglect the fact that there is a history behind our use of the name 'Thales' or 'Aristotle' and concentrate only upon the descriptions we would supply about their life, their works and deeds, it is possible that our descriptions are substantially wrong without the consequence being that we have not been referring to any existent person.

It is significant that descriptions of the form 'N was referred to by A' should assume central importance in the case of uses of names that are parasitic on their use by others. Not only does the principle of identifying descriptions, as it has usually been defended, fail to prepare us for the special role of one type of description, but we now see that there is a quite ordinary sense in which a person might be ignorant of the nature of the entity he has referred to in using a name. While I do not want to classify descriptions of this form as "question-begging" in the way in which 'the entity *I* have in mind' is question-begging, it seems nevertheless natural to say that in knowing only that Thales was a man referred to by Aristotle and Herodotus, I'm not in a position to *describe* the man Thales; that is, there is, I think, an ordinary use of 'describe' in which to say only 'the man referred to by Aristotle and Herodotus' is not yet to *describe* Thales. So it seems that we could be in the position of having referred to someone in using the name 'Thales', the same person in fact referred to by Aristotle and Herodotus, although we are not in the position of being able to describe him correctly.

Nevertheless, so long as the user of a name can fall back on such a description as 'the person referred to by Aristotle', the principle of identifying descriptions may be salvaged even if at expense of having to elevate one type of description to special status. But it is not at all clear that such descriptions will in general be available to the user of a name or that without them the failure of his other descriptions to identify the referent uniquely must mean that the name has no referent. In the case of individual people there are surely many who would, for example, identify Thales as the presocratic philosopher who held that all is water, but who do not know that he was referred to by Aristotle and Herodotus. And in fact they may not know even the immediate sources of their use of the name; that, for example, Thales was referred to by Mr. Jones, their freshman philosophy instructor. In case Thales was in fact the presocratic philosopher with that doctrine, such people surely know something about Thales and, in using the name, they have referred to him. But if, in fact, the attribution of this view to Thales is wrong and they are left without any descriptions that uniquely fit Thales, I do not believe it follows that they have not referred to anyone or that (in their use of the name) Thales did not exist. To be sure, they may have available to them some such description of Thales as, 'The one who is commonly believed to have been a presocratic philosopher who held that all is water'. But even this may not be true. Everyone may have come to believe that Thales did not have that doctrine. One could continue along these lines, I think, to deny an individual any identifying descriptions, even of the form 'The one referred to by so-and-so' that will serve uniquely to pick out Thales, without the consequence that he has not referred to anyone.

XI

The previous examples have concentrated on individuals and the set of descriptions they could supply. But I think there is no reason to suppose that, with a bit more stretching of the imagination, the same results could not be gotten for the whole of some group in which a name is used. Thus, those who would form the 'set of identifying descriptions' from a collective effort at description seem no better off to me.

Thus, we could imagine a future time, for example, when the plays we attribute to Shakespeare are available and it is believed that Shakespeare was their author, but little else is known about him—perhaps only that he was an actor in

Elizabethan times—and, in particular, nothing about the documentation we rely upon in attributing the plays to him has survived. As we now view it, the people of this future generation would be correct in saying that Shakespeare wrote *Hamlet*. But suppose in fact the Baconian hypothesis is correct—Francis Bacon wrote those plays. What should an omniscient being who sees the whole history of the affair conclude about one of these future beings saying that Shakespeare wrote *Hamlet?* (Surely not that as they use 'Shakespeare' it refers to Bacon— Bacon was not an actor and they may know a great deal about Bacon, enough to insure that he could not have been an actor.) It seems to me that the correct conclusion should be that (perhaps because we did not pay enough attention to the cryptologists who claim to find this message in the plays) we and they have made a mistake—we both believe that Shakespeare wrote the plays, though it was rather Bacon and not Shakespeare who is the Bard.

XII

As I have admitted, my counter-examples are necessarily somewhat artificial because of the vagueness of the position I want to attack. Yet, it seems to me that even artificial examples are sufficient because I take the principle of identifying descriptions to be a doctrine about how reference via proper names *must* take place. If these examples show that there are other possibilities for identifying the referent, they do their job. It is the idea that *only* a backing of descriptions identifying the referent by its fitting them (or some sufficient number of them) could serve to connect an object with a name that I question.

On the positive side my view is that what we should substitute for the question, 'What is the referent?' is 'What would the speaker be attributing that predicate to on this occasion?' Thus, in an early example, the parents of a child ask, 'Who would he say was a nice man at a party of ours,? when the child has said, 'Tom was a nice man'. *How* we answer such questions I do not have a general theory about. It seems clear to me that in some way the referent must be historically, or, we might say, causally connected to the speech act. But I do not see my way clear to saying exactly how in general that connection goes. Perhaps there is no exact theory.

The shift of question, however, seems to be important. One can explain why the principle of identifying descriptions has seemed so plausible, for example, while denying its validity. If a speaker says '*a* is *ϕ*', where '*a*' is a name, and we ask, "To what would he on this occasion attribute the predicate '*ϕ*'?," asking him for descriptions would *normally* be the best strategy for finding out. Generally we know numbers of correct and even uniquely identifying descriptions of the referent of names we use. So others would naturally first rely on these and look for what best fits them.

To illustrate this, we can imagine the following games: In the first a player gives a set of descriptions and the other players try to find the object in the room that best fits them. This is analogous to the role of the set of identifying descriptions in the principle I object to. In the other game the player picks out some object in the room, tries to give descriptions that characterize it uniquely and the other players attempt to discover what object he described. In the second game the problem set for the other players (the audience in the analogue) is to find out what is being described, not what best fits the descriptions. Insofar as descriptions enter into a determination of what the referent of a name is, I suggest that the second game is a better analogy. In that game, on the normal assumption that people are unlikely to be badly mistaken about the properties of an object they are describing, the other players would usually first look for an object best fitting the descriptions given. But that need not always be the best tactics. They may notice or conjecture that the circumstances are such that the describer has unintentionally *mis*-described the object, the circumstances being such as distortions in his perception, erroneous beliefs he is known to hold, etc.

One final point: I earlier questioned whether we can really expect that there must be a backing of descriptions behind the use of a proper name. Insofar as I offer an alternative to the principle of identifying descriptions, it has the merit of not requiring such a backing. If a speaker says '*a* is *ϕ*', where '*a*' is a name, the question of what he referred to does not hinge on what he can supply in the way of descriptions—though what descriptions he does give, if any, can constitute an important datum. It may be possible to answer the question, "To what would he on this occasion attribute the predicate 'is *ϕ*'?," without any backing of descriptions.

DESIGNATION

Michael Devitt

. . . We could sum up the discussion so far by saying that description theories require us to have beliefs that we do not in fact have. A more striking defect is that these theories seriously underestimate the number of *false* beliefs we have. Public opinion surveys show that many people are quite mistaken about famous and historical figures. Many will say, for example, that Columbus was the first person to think that the earth was round and that Einstein invented the atomic bomb. Often the *only* (nontrivial) belief held by someone about an object is a false one. Yet it is clear that the truth or falsity of remarks by such a person using 'Columbus' do not depend on the properties of some ancient Greek but on the properties of *Columbus*.

Suppose that a person intent on misleading his audience launches on a narrative without making it clear that he is story-telling. Or, to avoid deliberate deception, suppose the person tells something that is in fact a vivid dream but which he, deluded as he is, thinks is true. The audience believes the narrative and later passes it on to others. Now it turns out that there are some people, none of whom the narrator could have known, who fit the descriptions of his characters (or mostly fit them). *Must* we say that he (and hence his audience) was talking about those people? Of course, if the parallels were striking enough, we *might* say this; some of us might see it as a case of extrasensory perception. There is another alternative, however; we might say that the parallelism was *purely a matter of chance*—that, despite the fact that the descriptions used pick out those people, the narrator did not designate them.

Even identification by means of demonstratives can be mistaken. It is *possible*, indeed it is likely, that our memories of many people would be so dim that we would point out the wrong person in a crowd for many names we use. The object we identify for a name may thus be quite irrelevant to the truth conditions of statements containing the name.

This discussion reveals further hazards to reference borrowing as a way for the ignorant to get by. The reference lender may be misidentified. Or *he* may be mistaken: Someone who rightly thinks that Einstein discovered the Theory of Relativity may, when pressed to identify the designatum of 'Einstein', place his trust in a close (easily identifiable) friend who wrongly thinks Einstein invented the atomic bomb.

To sum up, we have earlier seen that we may fail to associate any appropriate definite description with a name. We see now that we may associate one that identifies the wrong object. . . .

THE MEANING OF "MEANING"[1]

Hilary Putnam

Language is the first broad area of human cognitive capacity for which we are beginning to obtain a description which is not exaggeratedly oversimplified. Thanks to the work of contemporary transformational linguists,[2] a very subtle description of at least some human languages is in the process of being constructed. Some features of these languages appear to be *universal*. Where such features turn out to be "species-specific"—"not explicable on some general grounds of functional utility or simplicity that would apply to arbitrary systems that serve the functions of language"—they may shed some light on the structure of mind. While it is extremely difficult to say to what extent the structure so illuminated will turn out to be a universal structure of *language*, as opposed to a universal structure of innate general learning strategies,[3] the very fact that this discussion can take place is testimony to the richness and generality of the descriptive material that linguists are beginning to provide, and also testimony to the depth of the analysis, insofar as the features that appear to be candidates for "species-specific" features of language are in no sense surface or phenomenological features of language, but lie at the level of deep structure.

---

[1] First published in K. Gunderson, ed., (1975).

[2] The contributors to this area are now too numerous to be listed; the pioneers were, of course, Zellig Harris and Noam Chomsky.

[3] For a discussion of this question, see Putnam (1967) and Noam Chomsky (1971), especially chapter 1.

The most serious drawback to all of this analysis, as far as a philosopher is concerned, is that it does not concern the meaning of words. Analysis of the deep structure of linguistic forms gives us an incomparably more powerful description of the *syntax* of natural languages than we have ever had before. But the dimension of language associated with the word "meaning" is, in spite of the usual spate of heroic if misguided attempts, as much in the dark as it ever was.

In this essay, I want to explore why this should be so. In my opinion, the reason that so-called semantics is in so much worse condition than syntactic theory is that the *prescientific* concept on which semantics is based—the prescientific concept of *meaning*—is itself in much worse shape than the prescientific concept of syntax. As usual in philosophy, skeptical doubts about the concept do not at all help one in clarifying or improving the situation any more than dogmatic assertions by conservative philosophers that all's really well in this best of all possible worlds. The reason that the prescientific concept of meaning is in bad shape is not clarified by some general skeptical or nominalistic argument to the effect that meanings don't exist. Indeed, the upshot of our discussion will be that meanings don't exist in quite the way we tend to think they do. But electrons don't exist in quite the way Bohr thought they did, either. There is all the distance in the world between this assertion and the assertion that meanings (or electrons) "don't exist."

I am going to talk almost entirely about the meaning of words rather than about the meaning of sentences because I feel that our concept of word-meaning is more defective than our concept of sentence-meaning. But I will comment briefly on the arguments of philosophers such as Donald Davidson who insist that the concept of word-meaning *must* be secondary and that study of sentence-meaning must be primary. Since I regard the traditional theories about meaning as myth-eaten (notice that the topic of "meaning" is the one topic discussed in philosophy in which there is literally nothing but "theory"—literally nothing that can be labeled or even ridiculed as the "commonsense view"), it will be necessary for me to discuss and try to disentangle a number of topics concerning which the received view is, in my opinion, wrong. The reader will give me the greatest aid in the task of trying to make these matters clear if he will kindly assume that *nothing* is clear in advance.

Meaning and Extension

Since the Middle Ages at least, writers on the theory of meaning have purported to discover an ambiguity in the ordinary concept of meaning, and have introduced a pair of terms—*extension* and *intension,* or *Sinn* and *Bedeutung,* or whatever—to disambiguate the notion. The *extension* of a term, in customary logical parlance, is simply the set of things the term is true of. Thus, "rabbit," in its most common English sense, is true of all and only rabbits, so the extension of "rabbit" is precisely the set of rabbits. Even this notion—and it is the *least* problematical notion in this cloudy subject—has its problems, however. Apart from problems it inherits from its parent notion of *truth,* the foregoing example of "rabbit" *in its most common English sense* illustrates one such problem: strictly speaking, it is not a term, but an ordered pair consisting of a term and a "sense" (or an occasion of use, or something else that distinguishes a term in one sense from the same term used in a different sense) that has an extension. Another problem is this: a "set," in the mathematical sense, is a "yes–no" object; any given object either definitely belongs to S or definitely does not belong to S, if S is a set. But words in a natural language are not generally "yes–no": there are things of which the description "tree" is clearly true and things of which the description "tree" is clearly false, to be sure, but there are a host of borderline cases. Worse, the line between the clear cases and the borderline cases is itself fuzzy. Thus the idealization involved in the notion of *extension*—the idealization involved in supposing that there is such a thing as the set of things of which the term "tree" is true—is actually very severe.

Recently some mathematicians have investigated the notion of a *fuzzy set*—that is, of an object to which other things belong or do not belong with a given probability or to a given degree, rather than belong "yes–no." If one really wanted to formalize the notion of extension as applied to terms in a natural language, it would be necessary to employ "fuzzy sets" or something similar rather than sets in the classical sense.

The problem of a word's having more than one sense is standardly handled by treating each of the senses as a different word (or rather, by treating the word as if it carried invisible subscripts, thus: "rabbit$_1$," animal of a certain kind; "rabbit$_2$,"—coward; and as if "rabbit$_1$" and "rabbit$_2$" or whatever were different words entirely). This again involves two very severe idealizations (at least two, that is): supposing that words have discretely many senses, and supposing that the entire repertoire of senses is fixed once and for all. Paul Ziff has recently investigated the extent to which both of these suppositions distort the actual situation in natural language;[4] nevertheless, we will continue to make these idealizations here.

Now consider the compound terms "creature with a heart" and "creature with a kidney." Assuming that every creature with a heart possesses a kidney and vice versa, the extension of these two terms is exactly the same. But they obviously differ in meaning. Supposing that there is a sense of "meaning" in which meaning = extension, there must be another sense of "meaning" in which the meaning of a term is not its extension but something else, say the "concept" associated with the term. Let us call this "something else" the *intension* of the term. The concept of a creature with a heart is clearly a different concept from the concept of a creature with a kidney. Thus the two terms have different intension. When we say they have different "meaning," meaning = intension.

Intension and Extension

Something like the preceding paragraph appears in every standard exposition of the notions "intension" and "extension." But it is not at all satisfactory. Why it is not satisfactory is, in a sense, the burden of this entire essay. But some points can be made at the very outset: first of all, what evidence is there that "extension" is a sense of the word "meaning"? The canonical explanation of the notions "intension" and

---

[4] This is discussed by Ziff (1972), especially chapter VIII.

"extension" is very much like "in one sense 'meaning' means *extension* and in the other sense 'meaning' means *meaning*." The fact is that while the notion of "extension" is made quite precise, relative to the fundamental logical notion of *truth* (and under the severe idealizations remarked above), the notion of intension is made no more precise than the vague (and, as we shall see, misleading) notion "concept." It is as if someone explained the notion "probability" by saying: "in one sense 'probability' means frequency, and in the other sense it means *propensity*." "Probability" *never* means "frequency," and "propensity" is at least as unclear as "probability."

Unclear as it is, the traditional doctrine that the notion "meaning" possesses the extension/intension ambiguity has certain typical consequences. Most traditional philosophers thought of concepts as something *mental*. Thus the doctrine that the meaning of a term (the meaning "in the sense of intension," that is) is a concept carried the implication that meanings are mental entities. Frege and more recently Carnap and his followers, however, rebelled against this "psychologism," as they termed it. Feeling that meanings are *public* property—that the *same* meaning can be "grasped" by more than one person and by persons at different times—they identified concepts (and hence "intensions" or meanings) with abstract entities rather than mental entities. However, "grasping" these abstract entities was still an individual psychological act. None of these philosophers doubted that understanding a word (knowing its intension) was just a matter of being in a certain psychological state (somewhat in the way in which knowing how to factor numbers in one's head is just a matter of being in a certain very complex psychological state).

Second, the timeworn example of the two terms "creature with a kidney" and "creature with a heart" does show that two terms can have the same extension and yet differ in intension. But it was taken to be obvious that the reverse is impossible: two terms cannot differ in extension and have the same intension. Interestingly, no argument for this impossibility was ever offered. Probably it reflects the tradition of the ancient and medieval philosophers who assumed that the concept corresponding to a term was just a conjunction of predicates, and hence that the concept corresponding to a term must *always* provide a necessary and sufficient condition for falling into the extension of the term.[5] For philosophers like Carnap, who accepted the verifiability theory of meaning, the concept corresponding to a

---

[5] This tradition grew up because *the* term whose analysis provoked all the discussion in medieval philosophy was the term "God," and the term "God" was thought to be defined through the conjunction of the terms "Good," "Powerful," "Omniscient," etc.—the so-called "Perfections." There was a problem, however, because God was supposed to be a Unity, and Unity was thought to exclude His essence being complex in *any* way—i.e., "God" was defined through a conjunction of terms, but God (without quotes) could not be the logical product of properties, nor could He be the unique thing exemplifying the logical product of two or more *distinct* properties, because even this highly abstract kind of "complexity" was held to be incompatible with His perfection of Unity. This is a theological paradox with which Jewish, Arabic, and Christian theologians wrestled for centuries (e.g., the doctrine of the Negation of Privation in Maimonides and Aquinas). It is amusing that theories of contemporary interest, such as conceptualism and nominalism, were first proposed as solutions to the problem of predication in the case of God. It is also amusing that the favorite model of definition in all of this theology—the conjunction-of-properties model—should survive, at least through its consequences, in philosophy of language until the present day.

term provided (in the ideal case, where the term had "complete meaning") a *crite-rion* for belonging to the extension (not just in the sense of "necessary and suffi-cient condition," but in the strong sense of *way of recognizing* if a given thing falls into the extension or not). Thus these positivistic philosophers were perfectly happy to retain the traditional view on this point. So, theory of meaning came to rest on two unchallenged assumptions:

(I)   That knowing the meaning of a term is just a matter of being in a cer-tain psychological state (in the sense of "psychological state," in which states of memory and psychological dispositions are "psychological states"; no one thought that knowing the meaning of a word was a con-tinuous state of consciousness, of course).

(II) That the meaning of a term (in the sense of "intension") determines its extension (in the sense that sameness of intension entails sameness of extension).

I shall argue that these two assumptions are not jointly satisfied by *any* notion, let alone any notion of meaning. The traditional concept of meaning is a concept which rests on a false theory.

"Psychological State" and Methodological Solipsism

In order to show this, we need first to clarify the traditional notion of a psycho-logical state. In one sense a state is simply a two-place predicate whose arguments are an individual and a time. In this sense, *being 5 feet tall, being in pain, know-ing the alphabet,* and even *being a thousand miles from Paris* are all states. (Note that the time is usually left implicit or "contextual"; the full form of an atomic sen-tence of these predicates would be "*x is five feet tall at time t,*" "*x is in pain at time t,*" etc.) In science, however, it is customary to restrict the term state to properties which are defined in terms of the parameters of the individual which are funda-mental from the point of view of the given science. Thus, being five feet tall is a state (from the point of view of physics); being in pain is a state (from the point of view of mentalistic psychology, at least); knowing the alphabet might be a state (from the point of view of cognitive psychology), although it is hard to say; but being a thousand miles from Paris would *not* naturally be called a *state*. In one sense, a psychological state is simply a state which is studied or described by psy-chology. In this sense it may be trivially true that, say *knowing the meaning of the word "water"* is a "psychological state" (viewed from the standpoint of cognitive psychology). But this is not the sense of psychological state that is at issue in the above assumption (I).

When traditional philosophers talked about psychological states (or "mental" states), they made an assumption which we may call the assumption of method-ological solipsism. This assumption is the assumption that no psychological state, properly so called, presupposes the existence of any individual other than the sub-ject to whom that state is ascribed. (In fact, the assumption was that no psycho-logical state presupposes the existence of the subject's *body* even: if *P* is a psychological state, properly so called, then it must be logically possible for a "disembodied mind" to be in P.) This assumption is pretty explicit in Descartes, but it is implicit in just about the whole of traditional philosophical psychology. Making this assumption is, of course, adopting a *restrictive program*—a program which deliberately limits the scope and nature of psychology to fit certain mentalistic preconceptions or, in some cases, to fit an idealistic reconstruction of knowledge and the world. Just *how* restrictive the program is, however, often goes unnoticed. Such common or garden variety psychological states as *being jealous* have to be reconstructed, for example, if the assumption of methodological solipsism is retained. For, in its ordinary use, *x is jealous of y* entails that *y* exists, and *x is jealous of y's regard for z* entails that both *y* and *z* exist (as well as *x*, of course). Thus *being jealous* and *being jealous of someone's regard for someone else* are not psychological states permitted by the assumption of methodological solipsism. (We shall call them "psychological states in the wide sense" and refer to the states which are permitted by methodological solipsism as "psychological states in the narrow sense.") The reconstruction required by methodological solipsism would be to reconstrue *jealousy* so that I can be jealous of my own hallucinations, or of figments of my imagination, etc. Only if we assume that psychological states in the narrow sense have a significant degree of causal closure (so that restricting ourselves to psychological states in the narrow sense will facilitate the statement of psychological *laws*) is there any point in engaging in this reconstruction, or in making the assumption of methodological solipsism. But the three centuries of failure of mentalistic psychology is tremendous evidence against this procedure, in my opinion.

Be that as it may, we can now state more precisely what we claimed at the end of the preceding section. Let A and B be any two terms which differ in extension. By assumption (II) they must differ in meaning (in the sense of "intension"). By assumption (I), *knowing the meaning of A* and *knowing the meaning of B* are psychological states *in the narrow sense*—for this is how we shall construe assumption (I). *But these psychological states must determine the extension of the terms A and B just as much as the meanings "intensions" do.*

To see this, let us try assuming the opposite. Of course, there cannot be two terms A and B such that *knowing the meaning of A* is the same state as *knowing the meaning of B* even though A and B have different extensions. For *knowing the meaning of A* isn't just "grasping the intension" of A, whatever that may come to; it is also knowing that the "intension" that one has "grasped" is the intension of A. Thus, someone who knows the meaning of "wheel" presumably "grasps the intension" of its German synonym *Rad;* but if he doesn't know that the "intension" in question is the intension of Rad he isn't said to "know the meaning of Rad." If A and B are different terms, then *knowing the meaning of A* is a different state from *knowing the meaning of B* whether the meanings of A and B be themselves the same or different. But by the same argument, if I_1 and I_2 are different *intensions* and A is a term, then *knowing that I_1 is the meaning of A* is a different psychological state from *knowing that I_2 is the meaning of A*. Thus, there cannot be two different logically possible worlds L_1 and L_2 such that, say, Oscar is in the *same* psychological state (in the narrow sense) in L_1 and in L_2 (in all respects), but in L_1 Oscar understands A as having the meaning I_1 and in L_2 Oscar understands A as having the meaning I_2. (For, if there were, then in L_1 Oscar would be in the psychological state *knowing that I_1 is the meaning of A* and in L_2 Oscar would be in the psychological state *knowing that I_2 is the meaning of A,* and these are different and even—assuming that A has just *one* meaning for Oscar in each world—incompatible psychological states in the narrow sense.)

In short, if S is the sort of psychological state we have been discussing—a psychological state of the form *knowing that I is the meaning of A,* where I is an "intension" and A is a term—then the *same* necessary and sufficient condition for falling into the extension of A "works" in *every* logically possible world in which the speaker is in the psychological state S. For the state S *determines* the intension I, and by assumption (II) the intension amounts to a necessary and sufficient condition for membership in the *extension.*

If our interpretation of the traditional doctrine of intension and extension is fair to Frege and Carnap, then the whole psychologism/Platonism issue appears somewhat a tempest in a teapot, as far as meaning-theory is concerned. (Of course, it is a very important issue as far as general philosophy of mathematics is concerned.) For even if meanings are "Platonic" entities rather than "mental" entities on the Frege-Carnap view, "grasping" those entities is presumably a psychological state (in the narrow sense). Moreover, the psychological state uniquely determines the "Platonic" entity. So whether one takes the "Platonic" entity or the psychological state as the "meaning" would appear to be somewhat a matter of convention. And taking the psychological state to be the meaning would hardly have the consequence that Frege feared, that meanings would cease to be public. For psychological states are "public" in the sense that different people (and even people in different epochs) can be in the *same* psychological state. Indeed, Frege's argument against psychologism is only an argument against identifying concepts with mental particulars, not with mental entities in general.

The "public" character of psychological states entails, in particular, that if Oscar and Elmer understand a word A differently, then they must be in different psychological states. For the state of *knowing the intension of A to be,* say, I is the *same* state whether Oscar or Elmer be in it. Thus two speakers cannot be in the same psychological state in all respects and understand the term A differently; the psychological state of the speaker determines the intension (and hence, by assumption (II), the extension) of A.

It is this last consequence of the joint assumptions (I), (II) that we claim to be false. We claim that it is possible for two speakers to be in exactly the *same* psychological state (in the narrow sense), even though the extension of the term A in the idiolect of the one is different from the extension of the term A in the idiolect of the other. Extension is not determined by psychological state.

This will be shown in detail in later sections. If this is right, then there are two courses open to one who wants to rescue at least one of the traditional assumptions; to give up the idea that psychological state (in the narrow sense) determines *intension*, or to give up the idea that intension determines extension. We shall consider these alternatives later.

Are Meanings in the Head?

That psychological state does not determine extension will now be shown with the aid of a little science-fiction. For the purpose of the following science-fiction examples, we shall suppose that somewhere in the galaxy there is a planet we shall call Twin Earth. Twin Earth is very much like Earth; in fact, people on Twin Earth even speak *English*. In fact, apart from the differences we shall specify in our science-fiction examples, the reader may suppose that Twin Earth is *exactly* like Earth. He may even suppose that he has a *Doppelgänger*—an identical copy—on Twin Earth, if he wishes, although my stories will not depend on this.

Although some of the people on Twin Earth (say, the ones who call themselves "Americans" and the ones who call themselves "Canadians" and the ones who call themselves "Englishmen," etc.) speak English, there are, not surprisingly, a few tiny differences which we will now describe between the dialects of English spoken on Twin Earth and Standard English. These differences themselves depend on some of the peculiarities of Twin Earth.

One of the peculiarities of Twin Earth is that the liquid called "water" is not H_2O but a different liquid whose chemical formula is very long and complicated. I shall abbreviate this chemical formula simply as *XYZ*. I shall suppose that *XYZ* is indistinguishable from water at normal temperatures and pressures. In particular, it tastes like water and it quenches thirst like water. Also, I shall suppose that the oceans and lakes and seas of Twin Earth contain *XYZ* and not water, that it rains *XYZ* on Twin Earth and not water, etc.

If a spaceship from Earth ever visits Twin Earth, then the supposition at first will be that "water" has the same meaning on Earth and on Twin Earth. This supposition will be corrected when it is discovered that "water" on Twin Earth is *XYZ*, and the Earthian spaceship will report somewhat as follows:

> "On Twin Earth the word 'water' means *XYZ*."

(It is this sort of use of the word "means" which accounts for the doctrine that extension is one sense of "meaning," by the way. But note that although "means" does mean something like *has as extension* in this example, one would *not* say

> "On Twin Earth the meaning of the word 'water' is *XYZ*."

unless, possibly, the fact that "water is *XYZ*" was known to every adult speaker of English on Twin Earth. We can account for this in terms of the theory of meaning we develop below; for the moment we just remark that although the verb "means" sometimes means "has as extension," the nominalization "meaning" *never* means "extension.")

Symmetrically, if a spaceship from Twin Earth ever visits Earth, then the supposition at first will be that the word "water" has the same meaning on Twin Earth and on Earth. This supposition will be corrected when it is discovered that "water" on Earth is H_2O, and the Twin Earthian spaceship will report

"On Earth[6] the word 'water' means H_2O."

Note that there is no problem about the extension of the term "water." The word simply has two different meanings (as we say) in the sense in which it is used on Twin Earth, the sense of water$_{TE}$, what *we* call "water" simply isn't water; while in the sense in which it is used on Earth, the sense of water$_E$, what the Twin Earthians call "water" simply isn't water. The extension of "water" in the sense of water$_E$ is the set of all wholes consisting of H_2O molecules, or something like that; the extension of water in the sense of water$_{TE}$ is the set of all wholes consisting of *XYZ* molecules, or something like that.

Now let us roll the time back to about 1750. At that time chemistry was not developed on either Earth or Twin Earth. The typical Earthian speaker of English did not know water consisted of hydrogen and oxygen, and the typical Twin Earthian speaker of English did not know "water" consisted of *XYZ*. Let Oscar$_1$ be such a typical Earthian English speaker, and let Oscar$_2$ be his counterpart on Twin Earth. You may suppose that there is no belief that Oscar$_1$ had about water that Oscar$_2$ did not have about "water." If you like, you may even suppose that Oscar$_1$ and Oscar$_2$ were exact duplicates in appearance, feelings, thoughts, interior monologue, etc. Yet the extension of the term "water" was just as much H_2O on Earth in 1750 as in 1950; and the extension of the term "water" was just as much *XYZ* on Twin Earth in 1750 as in 1950. Oscar$_1$ and Oscar$_2$ understood the term "water" differently in 1750 *although they were in the same psychological state,* and although, given the state of science at the time, it would have taken their scientific communities about fifty years to discover that they understood the term "water" differently. Thus the extension of the term "water" (and, in fact, its "meaning" in the intuitive preanalytical usage of that term) is *not* a function of the psychological state of the speaker by itself.

But, it might be objected, why should we accept it that the term "water" has the same extension in 1750 and in 1950 (on both Earths)? The logic of natural-kind terms like "water" is a complicated matter, but the following is a sketch of an answer. Suppose I point to a glass of water and say "this liquid is called water" (or "this is called water," if the marker "liquid" is clear from the context). My "ostensive definition" of water has the following empirical presupposition that the body of liquid I am pointing to bears a certain sameness relation (say, *x is the same liquid as y,* or *x is the same$_L$ as y*) to most of the stuff I and other speakers in my linguistic community have on other occasions called "water." If this presupposition is false because, say, I am without knowing it pointing to glass of gin and not a glass of water, then I do not intend my ostensive definition to be

---

[6] Rather, they will report: "On Twin Earth (*the Twin Earthian name for Terra*—H. P.), the word 'water' means H_2O."

accepted. Thus the ostensive definition conveys what might be called a defeasible necessary and sufficient condition: the necessary and sufficient condition for being water is bearing the relation same$_L$ to the stuff in the glass; but this is the necessary and sufficient condition only if the empirical presupposition is satisfied. If it is not satisfied, then one of a series of, so to speak, "fallback" conditions becomes activated.

The key point is that the relation same$_L$ is a *theoretical* relation whether something is or is not the same liquid as *this* may take an indeterminate amount of scientific investigation to determine. Moreover, even if a "definite" answer has been obtained either through scientific investigation or through the application of some "common sense" test, the answer is *defeasible:* future investigation might reverse even the most "certain" example. Thus, the fact that an English speaker in 1750 might have called *XYZ* "water," while he or his successors would not have called *XYZ* water in 1800 or 1850 does not mean that the "meaning" of "water" changed for the average speaker in the interval. In 1750 or in 1850 or in 1950 one might have pointed to, say, the liquid in Lake Michigan as an example of "water." What changed was that in 1750 we would have mistakenly thought that *XYZ* bore the relation same$_L$ to the liquid in Lake Michigan, while in 1800 or 1850 we would have known that it did not (I am ignoring the fact that the liquid in Lake Michigan was only dubiously water in 1950, of course).

Let us now modify our science-fiction story. I do not know whether one can make pots and pans out of molybdenum; and if one can make them out of molybdenum, I don't know whether they could be distinguished easily from aluminum pots and pans (I don't know any of this even though I have acquired the word "molybdenum"). So I shall suppose that molybdenum pots and pans *can't* be distinguished from aluminum pots and pans save by an expert. (To emphasize the point, I repeat that this could be true for all I know, and *a fortiori* it could be true for all I know by virtue of "knowing the meaning" of the words *aluminum* and *molybdenum.*) We will now suppose that molybdenum is as common on Twin Earth as aluminum is on Earth, and that aluminum is as rare on Twin Earth as molybdenum is on Earth. In particular, we shall assume that "aluminum" pots and pans are made of molybdenum on Twin Earth. Finally, we shall assume that the words "aluminum" and "molybdenum" are *switched* on Twin Earth: "aluminum" is the name of *molybdenum* and "molybdenum" is the name of *aluminum.*

This example shares some features with the previous one. If a spaceship from Earth visited Twin Earth, the visitors from Earth probably would not suspect that the "aluminum" pots and pans on Twin Earth were not made of aluminum, especially when the Twin Earthians *said* they were. But there is one important difference between the two cases. An Earthian metallurgist could tell very easily that "aluminum" was molybdenum, and a Twin Earthian metallurgist could tell equally easily that aluminum was "molybdenum." (The shudder quotes in the preceding sentence indicate Twin Earthian usages.) Whereas in 1750 no one on either Earth or Twin Earth could have distinguished water from "water," the confusion of aluminum with "aluminum" involves only a part of the linguistic communities involved.

The example makes the same point as the preceding one. If Oscar$_1$ and Oscar$_2$ are standard speakers of Earthian English and Twin Earthian English respectively, and neither is chemically or metallurgically sophisticated, then there may be no difference at all in their psychological state when they use the word "aluminum"; nevertheless we have to say that "aluminum" has the extension *aluminum* in the idiolect of Oscar$_1$ and the extension *molybdenum* in the idiolect of Oscar$_2$. (Also we have to say that Oscar$_1$ and Oscar$_2$ mean different things by "aluminum," that "aluminum" has a different meaning on Earth than it does on Twin Earth, etc.) Again we see that the psychological state of the speaker does *not* determine the extension (*or* the "meaning," speaking preanalytically) of the word.

Before discussing this example further, let me introduce a *non*-science-fiction example. Suppose you are like me and cannot tell an elm from a beech tree. We still say that the extension of "elm" in my idiolect is the same as the extension of "elm" in anyone else's, viz., the set of all elm trees, and that the set of all beech trees is the extension of "beech" in *both* of our idiolects. Thus "elm" in my idiolect has a different extension from "beech" in your idiolect (as it should). Is it really credible that this difference in extension is brought about by some difference in our *concepts?* My concept of an elm tree is exactly the same as my concept of a beech tree (I blush to confess). (This shows that the identification of meaning "in the sense of intension" with *concept* cannot be correct, by the way.) If someone heroically attempts to maintain that the difference between the extension of "elm" and the extension of "beech" in *my* idiolect is explained by a difference in my psychological state, then we can always refute him by constructing a "Twin Earth" example—just let the words "elm" and "beech" be switched on Twin Earth (the way "aluminum" and "molybdenum" were in the previous example). Moreover, I suppose I have a *Doppelgänger* on Twin Earth who is molecule for molecule "identical" with me (in the sense in which two neckties can be "identical"). If you are a dualist, then also suppose my *Doppelgänger* thinks the same verbalized thoughts I do, has the same sense data, the same dispositions, etc. It is absurd to think *his* psychological state is one bit different from mine: yet he "means" *beech* when he says "elm" and *I* "mean" *elm* when I say elm. Cut the pie any way you like, "meanings" just ain't in the *head!*

A Sociolinguistic Hypothesis

The last two examples depend upon a fact about language that seems, surprisingly, never to have been pointed out: that there is *division of linguistic labor*. We could hardly use such words as "elm" and "aluminum" if no one possessed a way of recognizing elm trees and aluminum metal; but not everyone to whom the distinction is important has to be able to make the distinction. Let us shift the example: consider *gold*. Gold is important for many reasons: it is a precious metal, it is a monetary metal, it has symbolic value (it is important to most people that the "gold" wedding ring they wear *really* consist of gold and not just *look* gold), etc. Consider our community as a "factory": in this "factory" some people have the "job" of *wearing gold wedding rings*, other people have the "job" of *selling gold wedding rings*, still other people have the "job" of *telling whether or not something is really gold.* It is not at all necessary or efficient that everyone who wears a gold ring (or a gold cufflink, etc.), or discusses the "gold standard," etc., engage in buying and selling gold. Nor is it necessary or efficient that everyone who buys and sells gold be able to tell whether or not something is really gold in a society where this form of dishonesty is uncommon (selling fake gold) and in which one can easily consult an expert in case of doubt. And it is *certainly* not necessary or efficient that everyone who has occasion to buy or wear gold be able to tell with any reliability whether or not something is really gold.

The foregoing facts are just examples of mundane division of labor (in a wide sense). But they engender a division of linguistic labor: everyone to whom gold is important for any reason has to *acquire* the word "gold"; but he does not have to acquire the *method of recognizing* if something is or is not gold. He can rely on a special subclass of speakers. The features that are generally thought to be present in connection with a general name—necessary and sufficient conditions for membership in the extension, ways of recognizing if something is in the extension ("criteria"), etc.—are all present in the linguistic community *considered as a collective body;* but that collective body divides the "labor" of knowing and employing these various parts of the "meaning" of "gold."

This division of linguistic labor rests upon and presupposes the division of *non*linguistic labor, of course. If only the people who know how to tell if some metal is really gold or not have any reason to have the word "gold" in their vocabulary, then the word "gold" will be as the word "water" was in 1750 with respect to that subclass of speakers, and the other speakers just won't acquire it at all. And some words do not exhibit any division of linguistic labor: "chair," for example. But with the increase of division of labor in the society and the rise of science, more and more words begin to exhibit this kind of division of labor. "Water," for example, did not exhibit it at all prior to the rise of chemistry. Today it is obviously necessary for every speaker to be able to recognize water (reliably under normal conditions), and probably every adult speaker even knows the necessary and sufficient condition "water is H_2O," but only a few adult speakers could distinguish water from liquids which superficially resembled water. In case of doubt, other speakers would rely on the judgment of these "expert" speakers. Thus the way of recognizing possessed by these "expert" speakers is also, through them, possessed by the collective linguistic body, even though it is not possessed by each individual member of the body, and in this way the most recherché fact about water may become part of the *social* meaning of the word while being unknown to almost all speakers who acquire the word.

It seems to me that this phenomenon of division of linguistic labor is one which it will be very important for sociolinguistics to investigate. In connection with it, I should like to propose the following hypothesis:

HYPOTHESIS OF THE UNIVERSALITY OF THE DIVISION OF LINGUISTIC LABOR: Every linguistic community exemplifies the sort of division of linguistic labor just described: that is, possesses at least some terms whose associated "criteria" are known only to a subset of the speakers who acquire the terms, and whose use by the other speakers depends upon a structured cooperation between them and the speakers in the relevant subsets.

It would be of interest, in particular, to discover if extremely primitive peoples were sometimes exceptions to this hypothesis (which would indicate that the division of linguistic labor is a product of social evolution), or if even they exhibit it. In the latter case, one might conjecture that division of labor, including linguistic labor, is a fundamental trait of our species.

It is easy to see how this phenomenon accounts for some of the examples given above of the failure of the assumptions (I), (II). Whenever a term is subject to the division of linguistic labor, the "average" speaker who acquires it does not acquire anything that fixes its extension. In particular, his individual psychological state *certainly* does not fix its extension; it is only the sociolinguistic state of the collective linguistic body to which the speaker belongs that fixes the extension.

We may summarize this discussion by pointing out that there are two sorts of tools in the world: there are tools like a hammer or a screwdriver which can be used by one person; and there are tools like a steamship which require the cooperative activity of a number of persons to use. Words have been thought of too much on the model of the first sort of tool.

Indexicality and Rigidity[7]

The first of our science-fiction examples—"water" on Earth and on Twin Earth in 1750—does not involve division of linguistic labor, or at least does not involve it in the same way the examples of "aluminum" and "elm" do. There were not (in our story, anyway) any "experts" on water on Earth in 1750, nor any experts on "water" on Twin Earth. (The example *can* be construed as involving division of labor *across time*, however. I shall not develop this method of treating the example here.) The example *does* involve things which are of fundamental importance to the theory of reference and also to the theory of necessary truth, which we shall now discuss.

There are two obvious ways of telling someone what one means by a natural-kind term such as "water" or "tiger" or "lemon." One can give him a so-called ostensive definition—"this (liquid) is water"; "this (animal) is a tiger"; "this (fruit) is a lemon"; where the parentheses are meant to indicate that the "markers" *liquid, animal, fruit,* may be either explicit or implicit. Or one can give him a *description*. In the latter case the description one gives typically consists of one or more markers together with a *stereotype*—a standardized description of features of the kind that are typical, or "normal," or at any rate stereotypical. The central features of the stereotype generally are *criteria*—features which in normal situations constitute ways of recognizing if a thing belongs to the kind or, at least, necessary conditions (or probabilistic necessary conditions) for membership in the kind. Not all criteria used by the linguistic community as a collective body are included in the stereotype, and in some

---

7 The substance of this section was presented at a series of lectures I gave at the University of Washington (Summer Institute in Philosophy) in 1968, and at a lecture at the University of Minnesota.

cases the stereotypes may be quite weak. Thus (unless I am a very atypical speaker), the stereotype of an elm is just that of a common deciduous tree. These features are indeed necessary conditions for membership in the kind (I mean "necessary" in a loose sense; I don't think "elm trees are deciduous" is *analytic*), but they fall far short of constituting a way of recognizing elms. On the other hand, the stereotype of a tiger does enable one to recognize tigers (unless they are albino, or some other atypical circumstance is present), and the stereotype of a lemon generally enables one to recognize lemons. In the extreme case, the stereotype may be *just* the marker: the stereotype of molybdenum might be *just* that molybdenum is a *metal*. Let us consider both of these ways of introducing a term into someone's vocabulary.

Suppose I point to a glass of liquid and say "*this* is water," in order to teach someone the word "water." We have already described some of the empirical presuppositions of this act, and the way in which this kind of meaning-explanation is defeasible. Let us now try to clarify further how it is supposed to be taken.

In what follows, we shall take the notion of "possible world" as primitive. We do this because we feel that in several senses the notion makes sense and is scientifically important even if it needs to be made more precise. We shall assume further that in at least some cases it is possible to speak of the same individual as existing in more than one possible world.[8] Our discussion leans heavily on the work of Saul Kripke, although the conclusions were obtained independently.

Let W_1 and W_2 be two possible worlds in which I exist and in which this glass exists and in which I am giving a meaning explanation by pointing to this glass and saying "this is water." (We do *not* assume that the *liquid* in the glass is the same in both worlds.) Let us suppose that in W_1 the glass is full of H_2O and in W_2 the glass is full of *XYZ*. We shall also suppose that W_1 is the actual world and that *XYZ* is the stuff typically called "water" in the world W_2 (so that the relation between English speakers in W_1 and English speakers in W_2 is exactly the same as the relation between English speakers on Earth and English speakers on Twin Earth). Then there are two theories one might have concerning the meaning of "water":

(1) One might hold that "water" was *world-relative* but *constant* in meaning (i.e., the word has a *constant relative meaning*). In this theory, "water" *means the same* in W_1 and W_2; it's just that water is H_2O in W_1 and water is *XYZ* in W_2.

(2) One might hold that water is H_2O in all worlds (the stuff called "water" in W_2 isn't water), but "water" doesn't have the same meaning in W_1 and W_2.

If what was said before about the Twin Earth case was correct, then (2) is clearly the correct theory. When I say "*this* (liquid) is water," the "this" is, so to speak, a

---

[8] This assumption is not actually needed in what follows. What *is* needed is that the same *natural kind* can exist in more than one possible world.

de re "this"—i.e., the force of my explanation is that "water" is whatever bears a certain equivalence relation (the relation we called "same$_L$" above) to the piece of liquid referred to as "this" *in the actual world.*

We might symbolize the difference between the two theories as a "scope" difference in the following way. In theory (1), the following is true:

(1') (For every world W) (For every x in W) (x is water $\equiv x$ bears same$_L$ to the entity referred to as "this" in W_1)

while on theory (2):

(2') (For every world W) (For every x in W) (x is water $\equiv x$ bears same$_L$ to the entity referred to as "this" *in the actual world W_1*).

(I call this a "scope" difference because in (1') "the entity referred to as 'this'" is within the scope of "For every world W"—as the qualifying phrase "in W" makes explicit, whereas in (2') "the entity referred to as 'this'" means "the entity referred to as 'this' *in the actual world*," and has thus a reference *independent* of the bound variable "W.")

Kripke calls a designator "rigid" (in a given sentence) if (in that sentence) it refers to the same individual in every possible world in which the designator designates. If we extend the notion of rigidity to substance names, then we may express Kripke's theory and mine by saying that the term "water" is *rigid.*

The rigidity of the term "water" follows from the fact that when I give the ostensive definition "*this* (liquid) is water" I intend (2') and not (1').

We may also say, following Kripke, that when I give the ostensive definition "this (liquid) is water," the demonstrative "this" is *rigid.*

What Kripke was the first to observe is that this theory of the meaning (or "use," or whatever) of the word "water" (and other natural-kind terms as well) has startling consequences for the theory of necessary truth.

To explain this, let me introduce the notion of a *cross-world relation.* A two-term relation R will be called *cross-world* when it is understood in such a way that its extension is a set of ordered pairs of individuals *not all in the same possible world.* For example, it is easy to understand the relation *same height* as a cross-world relation: just understand it so that, e.g., if x is an individual in a world W_1 who is five feet tall (in W_1) and y is an individual in W_2 who is five feet tall (in W_2), then the ordered pair x, y belongs to the extension of *same height as.* (Since an individual may have different heights in different possible worlds in which that same individual exists, strictly speaking it is not the ordered pair x, y that constitutes an element of the extension of *same height as,* but rather the ordered pair *x-in-world-W_1, y-in-world-W_2*.)

Similarly, we can understand the relation *same$_L$* (same liquid as) as a cross-world relation by understanding it so that a liquid in world W_1 which has the same important physical properties (in W_1) that a liquid in W_2 possesses (in W_2) bears *same$_L$* to the latter liquid.

Then the theory we have been presenting may be summarized by saying that an entity x, in an arbitrary possible world, is *water* if and only if it bears the relation same$_L$ (construed as a cross-world relation) to the stuff *we* call "water" in the *actual* world.

Suppose, now, that I have not yet discovered what the important physical properties of water are (in the actual world)—i.e., I don't yet know that water is H_2O. I may have ways of *recognizing* water that are successful (of course, I may make a small number of mistakes that I won't be able to detect until a later stage in our scientific development) but not know the microstructure of water. If I agree that a liquid with the superficial properties of "water" but a different microstructure *isn't really water*, then my ways of recognizing water (my "operational definition," so to speak) cannot be regarded as an analytical specification of *what it is to be* water. Rather, the operational definition, like the ostensive one, is simply a way of pointing out a standard—pointing out the stuff *in the actual world* such that for *x* to be water, in *any* world, is for *x* to bear the relation *same$_L$* to the *normal* members of the class of *local* entities that satisfy the operational definition. "Water" on Twin Earth is not water, even if it satisfies the operational definition, because it doesn't bear *same$_L$* to the *local* stuff that satisfies the operational definition, and local stuff that satisfies the operational definition but has a microstructure different from the rest of the local stuff that satisfies the operational definition isn't water either, because it doesn't bear *same$_L$* to the *normal* examples of the local "water."

Suppose, now, that I discover the microstructure of water—that water is H_2O. At this point I will be able to say that the stuff on Twin Earth that I earlier *mistook* for water isn't really water. In the same way if you describe not another planet in the actual universe, but another possible universe in which there is stuff with the chemical formula *XYZ* which passes the "operational test" for *water,* we shall have to say that that stuff isn't water but merely *XYZ*. You will not have described a possible world in which "water is *XYZ*," but merely a possible world in which there are lakes of *XYZ*, people drink *XYZ* (and not water), or whatever. In fact, once we have discovered the nature of water, nothing counts as a possible world in which water doesn't have that nature. Once we have discovered that water (in the actual world) is H_2O, *nothing counts as a possible world in which water isn't* H_2O. In particular, if a "logically possible" statement is one that holds in some "logically possible world," *it isn't logically possible that water isn't H_2O.*

On the other hand, we can perfectly well imagine having experiences that would convince us (and that would make it rational to believe that) water *isn't* H_2O. In that sense, it is conceivable that water isn't H_2O. It is conceivable but it isn't logically possible! Conceivability is no proof of logical possibility.

Kripke refers to statements which are rationally unrevisable (assuming there are such) as *epistemically necessary.* Statements which are true in all possible worlds he refers to simply as necessary (or sometimes as "metaphysically necessary"). In this terminology, the point just made can be restated as: a statement can be (metaphysically) necessary and epistemically contingent. Human intuition has no privileged access to metaphysical necessity.

Since Kant there has been a big split between philosophers who thought that all necessary truths were analytic and philosophers who thought that some necessary truths were synthetic *a priori*. But none of these philosophers thought that a (metaphysically) necessary truth could fail to be *a priori:* the Kantian tradition was as guilty as the empiricist tradition of equating metaphysical and epistemic necessity. In this sense Kripke's challenge to received doctrine goes far beyond the usual empiricism/Kantianism oscillation.

In this paper our interest is in theory of meaning, however, and not in theory of necessary truth. Points closely related to Kripke's have been made in terms of the notion of *indexicality*.[9] Words like "now," "this," "here," have long been recognized to be *indexical,* or *token-reflexive*—i.e., to have an extension which varied from context to context or token to token. For these words no one has ever suggested the traditional theory that "intension determines extension." To take our Twin Earth example: if I have a *Doppelgänger* on Twin Earth, then when I think "I have a headache," *he* thinks "I have a headache." But the extension of the particular token of "I" in his verbalized thought is himself (or his unit class, to be precise), while the extension of the token of "I" in *my* verbalized thought is *me* (or my unit class, to be precise). So the same word, "I," has two different extensions in two different idiolects; but it does not follow that the concept I have of myself is in any way different from the concept my *Doppelgänger* has of himself.

Now then, we have maintained that indexicality extends beyond the *obviously* indexical words and morphemes (e.g., the tenses of verbs). Our theory can be summarized as saying that words like "water" have an unnoticed indexical component: "water" is stuff that bears a certain similarity relation to the water *around here*. Water at another time or in another place or even in another possible world has to bear the relation $same_L$ to our "water" *in order to be water*. Thus the theory that (1) words have "intensions," which are something like concepts associated with the words by speakers; and that (2) intension determines extension—cannot be true of natural-kind words like "water" for the same reason the theory cannot be true of obviously indexical words like "I."

The theory that natural-kind words like "water" are indexical leaves it open, however, whether to say that "water" in the Twin Earth dialect of English has the same *meaning* as "water" in the Earth dialect and a different extension (which is what we normally say about "I" in different idiolects), thereby giving up the doctrine that "meaning (intension) determines extension"; or to say, as we have chosen to do, that difference in extension is *ipso facto* a difference in meaning for natural-kind words, thereby giving up the doctrine that meanings are concepts, or, indeed, mental entities of *any* kind.

It should be clear, however, that Kripke's doctrine that natural-kind words are rigid designators and our doctrine that they are indexical are but two ways of making the same point. We heartily endorse what Kripke says when he writes:

> Let us suppose that we do fix the reference of a name by a description. Even if we do so, we do not then make the name synonymous with the description, but instead we use the name rigidly to refer to the object so named, even in talking

---

[9] These points were made in my 1968 lectures at the University of Washington and the University of Minnesota.

about counterfactual situations where the thing named would not satisfy the description in question. Now, this is what I think is in fact true for those cases of naming where the reference is fixed by description. But, in fact, I also think, contrary to most recent theorists, that the reference of names is rarely or almost never fixed by means of description. And by this I do not just mean what Searle says: "It's not a single description, but rather a cluster, a family of properties that fixes the reference." I mean that properties in this sense are not used at all.

Let's Be Realistic

I wish now to contrast my view with one which is popular, at least among students (it appears to arise spontaneously). For this discussion, let us take as our example of a natural-kind word the word *gold*. We will not distinguish between "gold" and the cognate words in Greek, Latin, etc. And we will focus on "gold" in the sense of gold in the solid state. With this understood, we maintain: "gold" has not changed its *extension* (or not changed it significantly) in two thousand years. Our methods of *identifying* gold have grown incredibly sophisticated. But the extension of χρυσὸζ in Archimedes's dialect of Greek is the same as the extension of *gold* in my dialect of English.

It is possible (and let us suppose it to be the case) that just as there were pieces of metal which could not have been determined *not* to be gold prior to Archimedes, so there were or are pieces of metal which could not have been determined not to be gold in Archimedes's day, but which we can distinguish from gold quite easily with modern techniques. Let X be such a piece of metal. Clearly X does not lie in the extension of "gold" in standard English; my view is that it did not lie in the extension of χρυσὸζ in Attic Greek, either, although an ancient Greek would have *mistaken X* for gold (or, rather, χρυσὸζ).

The alternative view is that "gold" *means* whatever satisfies the *contemporary* operational definition of gold. "Gold" a hundred years ago meant whatever satisfied the "operational definition" of *gold* in use a hundred years ago; "gold" now means whatever satisfies the operational definition of *gold* in use in 1973; and χρυσὸζ meant whatever satisfied the operational definition of χρυσὸζ in use *then*.

One common motive for adopting this point of view is a certain skepticism about *truth*. In the view I am advocating, when Archimedes asserted that something was gold (χρυσὸζ) he was not just saying that it had the superficial characteristics of gold (in exceptional cases, something may belong to a natural kind and *not* have the superficial characteristics of a member of that natural kind, in fact); he was saying that it had the same general *hidden structure* (the same "essence," so to speak) as any normal piece of local gold. Archimedes would have said that our hypothetical piece of metal X was gold, but he would have been wrong. But who's to say he would have been wrong?

The obvious answer is: *we are* (using the best theory available today). For most people either the question (*who's to say?*) has bite, and our answer has no bite, or our answer has bite and the question has no bite. Why is this?

The reason, I believe, is that people tend either to be strongly antirealistic or strongly realistic in their intuitions. To a strongly antirealistic intuition it makes little sense to say that what is in the extension of Archimedes's term χρυσὸζ is to be determined using *our* theory. For the antirealist does not see our theory and Archimedes's theory as two approximately correct descriptions of some fixed realm of theory-independent entities, and he tends to be skeptical about the idea of "convergence" in science—he does not think our theory is a *better* description of the *same* entities that Archimedes was describing. But if our theory is *just* our theory, then to use *it* in deciding whether or not X lies in the extension of χρυσὸζ is just as arbitrary as using Neanderthal theory to decide whether or not X lies in the extension of χρυσὸζ. The only theory that it is *not* arbitrary to use is the one the speaker himself subscribes to.

The trouble is that for a strong antirealist *truth* makes no sense except as an intra-theoretic notion. The antirealist can use truth intra-theoretically in the sense of a "redundancy theory"; but he does not have the notions of truth and reference available *extra-theoretically*. But *extension is tied to the notion of truth.* The extension of a term is just what the term is true of. Rather than try to retain the notion of extension via an awkward operationalism, the antirealist should reject the notion of extension as he does the notion of truth (in any extra-theoretic sense). Like Dewey, for example, he can fall back on a notion of "warranted assertibility" instead of truth (relativized to the scientific method, if he thinks there is a *fixed* scientific method, or to the best methods available at the time, if he agrees with Dewey that the scientific method itself evolves). Then he can say that "X is gold (χρυσὸζ)" was warrantedly assertible in Archimedes's time and is not warrantedly assertible today (indeed, this is a *minimal* claim, in the sense that it represents the minimum that the realist and the antirealist can agree on); but the assertion that X was in the extension of χρυσὸζ will be rejected as meaningless, like the assertion that "X is gold (χρυσὸζ)" was *true.*

It is well known that narrow operationalism cannot successfully account for the actual use of scientific or common-sense terms. Loosened versions of operationalism, like Carnap's version of Ramsey's theory, agree with, if they do not account for, actual scientific use (mainly because the loosened versions agree with any possible use!), but at the expense of making the communicability of scientific results a *miracle*. It is beyond question that scientists use terms as if the associated criteria were not *necessary and sufficient conditions,* but rather *approximately* correct characterizations of some world of theory-independent entities, and that they talk as if later theories in a mature science were, in general, *better* descriptions of the *same* entities that earlier theories referred to. In my opinion the hypothesis that this is *right* is the only hypothesis that can account for the communicability of scientific results, the closure of acceptable scientific theories under first-order logic, and many other features of the scientific method.[10] But it

---

[10] For an illuminating discussion of just these points, see R. Boyd's *Realism and Scientific Epistemology* (unpublished: Xerox draft circulated by the author, Cornell Department of Philosophy).

is not my task to argue this here. My point is that if we are to use the notions of truth and extension in an extra-theoretic way (i.e., to regard those notions as defined for statements couched in the languages of theories other than our own), then we should accept the realist perspective to which those notions belong. The doubt about whether *we* can say that X does not lie in the extension of "gold" as *Jones* used it is the *same* doubt as the doubt whether it makes sense to think of Jones's statement that "X is gold" as *true or false* (and not just "warrantedly assertible for Jones and not warrantedly assertible for us"). To square the notion of truth, which is essentially a realist notion, with one's antirealist prejudices by adopting an untenable theory of meaning is no progress.

A second motive for adopting an extreme operationalist account is a dislike of unverifiable hypotheses. At first blush it may seem as if we are saying that "X is gold (χρυσὸς)" was false in Archimedes's time although Archimedes could not *in principle* have known that it was false. But this is not exactly the situation. The fact is that there are a host of situations that *we* can describe (using the very theory that tells us that X isn't gold) in which X would have behaved quite unlike the rest of the stuff Archimedes classified as gold. Perhaps X would have separated into two different metals when melted, or would have had different conductivity properties, or would have vaporized at a different temperature, or whatever. If we had performed the experiments with Archimedes watching, he might not have known the theory, but he would have been able to check the empirical regularity that "X behaves differently from the rest of the stuff I classify as χρυσὸς in several respects." Eventually he would have concluded that "X may not be gold."

The point is that even if something satisfies the criteria used at a given time to identify gold (i.e., to recognize if something is gold), it may behave differently in one or more situations from the rest of the stuff that satisfies the criteria. This may not *prove* that it isn't gold, but it puts the hypothesis that it may not be gold in the running, even in the absence of theory. If, now, we had gone on to inform Archimedes that gold had such and such a molecular structure (except for X), and that X behaved differently because it had a different molecular structure, is there any doubt that he would have agreed with us that X isn't gold? In any case, to worry because things may be *true* (at a given time) that can't be *verified* (at that time) seems to me ridiculous. In any reasonable view there are surely things that are true and can't be verified at *any* time. For example, suppose there are infinitely many binary stars. *Must* we be able to verify this, even in principle?

So far we have dealt with *metaphysical* reasons for rejecting our account. But someone might disagree with us about the empirical facts concerning the intentions of speakers. This would be the case if, for instance, someone thought that Archimedes (in the *Gedankenexperiment* described above) would have said: "it doesn't matter if X *does* act differently from other pieces of gold; X is a piece of gold, because X has such-and-such properties and that's all it takes to be gold." While, indeed, we cannot be certain that natural-kind words in ancient Greek had the properties of the corresponding words in present-day English, there cannot be any serious doubt concerning the properties of the latter. If we put philosophical prejudices aside, then I believe that we know perfectly well that no operational definition does provide a necessary and sufficient condition for the application of any such word. We may give an "operational definition," or a cluster of properties, or whatever, but the intention is never to "make the name *synonymous* with the description." Rather "we use the name *rigidly*" to refer to whatever things share the *nature* that things satisfying the description normally possess.

Other Senses

What we have analyzed so far is the predominant sense of natural-kind words (or, rather, the predominant *extension*). But natural-kind words typically possess a number of senses. (Ziff has even suggested that they possess a *continuum* of senses.)

Part of this can be explained on the basis of our theory. To be water, for example, is to bear the relation $same_L$ to certain things. But what is the relation $same_L$?

X bears the relation $same_L$ to y just in case (1) x and y are both liquids, and (2) x and y agree in important physical properties. The term "liquid" is itself a natural-kind term that I shall not try to analyze here. The term "property" is a broad-spectrum term that we have analyzed in previous papers. What I want to focus on now is the notion of *importance*. Importance is an interest-relative notion. Normally the "important" properties of a liquid or solid, etc., are the ones that are *structurally* important: the ones that specify what the liquid or solid, etc., is ultimately made out of—elementary particles, or hydrogen and oxygen, or earth, air, fire, water, or whatever—and how they are arranged or combined to produce the superficial characteristics. From this point of view the characteristic of a typical bit of water is consisting of H_2O. But it may or may not be important that there are impurities; thus, in one context "water" may mean *chemically pure water*, while in another it may mean the stuff in Lake Michigan. And a speaker may sometimes refer to XYZ as water if one is *using* it as water. Again, normally it is important that water is in the liquid state; but sometimes it is unimportant, and one may refer to a single H_2O molecule as water, or to water vapor as water ("water in the air").

Even senses that are so far out that they have to be regarded as a bit "deviant" may bear a definite relation to the core sense. For example, I might say "did you see the lemon," meaning the *plastic* lemon. A less deviant case is this: we discover "tigers" on Mars. That is, they look just like tigers, but they have a silicon-based chemistry instead of a carbon-based chemistry. (A remarkable example of parallel evolution!) Are Martian "tigers" tigers? It depends on the context.

In the case of this theory, as in the case of any theory that is orthogonal to the way people have thought about something previously, misunderstandings are certain to arise. One which has already arisen is the following: a critic has maintained that the *predominant* sense of, say, "lemon" is the one in which anything with (a sufficient number of) the superficial characteristics of a lemon is a lemon. The same critic has suggested that having the hidden structure—the genetic code—of a lemon is necessary to being a lemon only when "lemon" is used as a term of *science*. Both of these contentions seem to me to rest on a misunderstanding, or, perhaps, a pair of complementary misunderstandings.

The sense in which literally *anything* with the superficial characteristics of a lemon is necessarily a lemon, far from being the dominant one, is extremely deviant. In that sense something would be a lemon if it looked and tasted like a lemon, even if it had a silicon-based chemistry, for example, or even if an electron-microscope revealed it to be a *machine*. (Even if we include growing "like a lemon" in the superficial characteristics, this does not exclude the silicon lemon, if there are "lemon" trees on Mars. It doesn't even exclude the machine-lemon; maybe the tree is a machine too!)

At the same time the sense in which to be a lemon something has to have the genetic code of a lemon is *not* the same as the technical sense (if there is one, which I doubt). The technical sense, I take it, would be one in which "lemon" was *synonymous* with a description which *specified* the genetic code. But when we said (to change the example) that to be *water* something has to be H_2O we did not mean, as we made clear, that the *speaker* has to *know* this. It is only by confusing *metaphysical* necessity with *epistemological* necessity that one can conclude that, if the (metaphysically necessary) truth-condition for being water is being H_2O, then "water" must be synonymous with H_2O—in which case it is certainly a term of science. And similarly, even though the predominant sense of "lemon" is one in which to be a lemon something has to have the genetic code of a lemon (I believe), it does not follow that "lemon" is synonymous with a description which specifies the genetic code explicitly or otherwise.

The mistake of thinking that there is an important sense of "lemon" (perhaps the predominant one) in which to have the superficial characteristics of a lemon is at least *sufficient* for being a lemon is more plausible if among the superficial characteristics one includes *being cross-fertile with lemons*. But the characteristic of being cross-fertile with lemons presupposes the notion of being a lemon. Thus, even if one can obtain a sufficient condition in *this* way, to take this as inconsistent with the characterization offered here is question-begging. Moreover the characterization in terms of *lemon*-presupposing "superficial characteristics" (like being cross-fertile with *lemons*) gives no truth-condition which would enable us to decide which objects in other possible worlds (or which objects a million years ago, or which objects a million light-years from here) are lemons. (In addition, I don't think this characterization, question-begging as it is, is *correct*, even as a sufficient condition. I think one could invent cases in which something which was not a lemon was cross-fertile with lemons and looked like a lemon, etc.)

Again, one might try to rule out the case of the machine-lemon (lemon-machine?) which "grows" on a machine-tree (tree-machine?) by saying that "growing" is not really *growing*. That is right; but it's right because *grow* is a natural-kind *verb*, and precisely the sort of account we have been presenting applies to *it*.

Another misunderstanding that should be avoided is the following: to take the account we have developed as implying that the members of the extension of a natural-kind word necessarily *have* a common hidden structure. It could have turned out that the bits of liquid we call "water" had *no* important common physical characteristics *except* the superficial ones. In that case the necessary and sufficient condition for being "water" would have been possession of sufficiently many of the superficial characteristics.

Incidentally, the last statement does not imply that water could have failed to have a hidden structure (or that water could have been anything but H_2O). When we say that it could have *turned out* that water had no hidden structure what we mean is that a liquid with no hidden structure (i.e., many bits of different liquids, with nothing in common *except* superficial characteristics) could have looked like water, tasted like water, and have filled the lakes, etc., that are actually full of water. In short, we could have been in the same epistemological situation with respect to a liquid with no hidden structure as we were actually with respect to water at one time. Compare Kripke on the "lectern made of ice."

There are, in fact, almost continuously many cases. Some diseases, for example, have turned out to have no hidden structure (the only thing the paradigm cases have in common is a cluster of symptoms), while others have turned out to have a common hidden structure in the sense of an etiology (e.g., tuberculosis). Sometimes we still don't know; there is a controversy still raging about the case of multiple sclerosis.

An interesting case is the case of *jade*. Although the Chinese do not recognize a difference, the term "jade" applies to two minerals: jadeite and nephrite. Chemically, there is a marked difference. Jadeite is a combination of sodium and aluminum. Nephrite is made of calcium, magnesium, and iron. These two quite different microstructures produce the same unique textural qualities!

Coming back to the Twin Earth example, for a moment; if H_2O and *XYZ* had both been plentiful on Earth, then we would have had a case similar to the jade/nephrite case: it would have been correct to say that there were *two kinds of* "*water.*" And instead of saying that "the stuff on Twin Earth turned out not to really be water," we would have to say "it turned out to be the *XYZ kind of water.*"

To sum up: if there is a hidden structure, then generally it determines what it is to be a member of the natural kind, not only in the actual world, but in all possible worlds. Put another way, it determines what we can and cannot counterfactually suppose about the natural-kind ("water could have all been vapor?" yes/"water could have been *XYZ*" no). But the local water, or whatever, may have two or more hidden structures—or so many that "hidden structure" becomes irrelevant, and superficial characteristics become the decisive ones.

Other Words

So far we have only used natural-kind words as example, but the points we have made apply to many other kinds of words as well. They apply to the great majority of all nouns, and to other parts of speech as well.

Let us consider for a moment the names of artifacts—words like "pencil," "chair," "bottle," etc. The traditional view is that these words are certainly defined by conjunctions, or possibly clusters, of properties. Anything with all of the properties in the conjunction (or sufficiently many of the properties in the cluster, on the cluster model) is necessarily a *pencil, chair, bottle,* or whatever. In addition, some of the properties in the cluster (on the cluster model) are usually held to be *necessary* (on the conjunction-of-properties model, *all* of the properties in the conjunction are necessary). Being an artifact is supposedly necessary, and belonging to a kind with a certain standard purpose—e.g., "pencils are artifacts," and "pencils are standardly intended to be written with" are supposed to be necessary. Finally, this sort of necessity is held to be *epistemic* necessity—in fact, analyticity.

Let us once again engage in science-fiction. This time we use an example devised by Rogers Albritton. Imagine that we someday discover that *pencils are organisms*. We cut them open and examine them under the electron microscope, and we see the almost invisible tracery of nerves and other organs. We spy upon them, and we see them spawn, and we see the offspring grow into full-grown pencils. We discover that these organisms are not imitating other (artifactual) pencils—there are not and never were any pencils except these organisms. It is strange, to be sure, that there is *lettering* on many of these organisms—e.g., BONDED *Grants* DELUXE made in U.S.A. No. 2.—perhaps they are intelligent organisms, and this is their form of camouflage. (We also have to explain why no one ever attempted to manufacture pencils, etc., but this is clearly a possible world, in some sense.)

If this is conceivable, and I agree with Albritton that it is, then it is epistemically possible that *pencils could turn out to be organisms*. It follows that *pencils are artifacts* is not epistemically necessary in the strongest sense and, *a fortiori,* not analytic.

Let us be careful, however. Have we shown that there is a possible world in which pencils are organisms? I think not. What we have shown is that there is a possible world in which certain organisms are the *epistemic counterparts* of pencils (the phrase is Kripke's). To return to the device of Twin Earth: imagine this time that pencils on Earth are just what we think they are, artifacts manufactured to be written with, while "pencils" on Twin Earth are organisms à la Albritton. Imagine, further, that this is totally unsuspected by the Twin Earthians—they have exactly the beliefs about "pencils" that we have about pencils. When we discovered this, we would not say: "some pencils are organisms." We would be far more likely to say: "the things on Twin Earth that pass for pencils aren't really pencils. They're really a species of organism."

Suppose now the situation to be as in Albritton's example both on Earth and on Twin Earth. Then we would say "pencils are organisms." Thus, whether the "pencil-organisms" on Twin Earth (or in another possible universe) are really *pencils* or not is a function of whether or not the *local* pencils are organisms or not. If the local pencils are just what we think they are, then a possible world in which there are pencil-organisms is *not* a possible world in which *pencils are organisms;* there are *no* possible worlds in which pencils are organisms in this case (which is, of course, the actual one). That pencils are artifacts *is* necessary in the sense of true in all possible worlds—metaphysically necessary. But it doesn't follow that it's epistemically necessary.

It follows that "pencil" is not *synonymous* with any description—not even loosely synonymous with a *loose* description. When we use the word "pencil," we intend to refer to whatever has the same *nature* as the normal examples of the local pencils in the actual world. "Pencil" is just as *indexical* as "water" or "gold."

In a way, the case of pencils turning out to be organisms is complementary to the case we discussed some years ago of cats turning out to be robots (remotely controlled from Mars). . . . Katz argues that we misdescribed this case: that the case should rather be described as its *turning out that there are no cats in this world*. Katz admits that we might *say* "Cats have turned out not to be animals, but robots"; but he argues that this is a semantically deviant sentence which is glossed as "the things I am referring to as 'cats' have turned out not to be animals, but robots." Katz's theory *is* bad linguistics, however. First of all, the explanation of how it is we can *say* "Cats are robots" is simply an all-purpose explanation of how we can say *anything*. More important, Katz's theory predicts that "Cats are robots" is *deviant,* while "There are no cats in the world" is nondeviant, in fact standard, in the case described. Now then, I don't deny that there *is* a case in which "There are not (and never were) any cats in the world" would be standard: we might (speaking epistemically) discover that we have been suffering from a collective hallucination ("Cats" are like pink elephants.) But in the case I described, "Cats have turned out to be robots remotely controlled from Mars" is surely nondeviant, and "There are no cats in the world" is highly deviant.

Incidentally, Katz's account is not only bad linguistics; it is also bad as a rational reconstruction. The reason we *don't* use "cat" as synonymous with a description is surely that we know enough about cats to know that they do have a hidden structure, and it is good scientific methodology to use the name to refer rigidly to the things that possess that hidden structure, and not to whatever happens to satisfy some description. Of course, if we *knew* the hidden structure we could frame a description in terms of *it;* but we don't at this point. In this sense the use of natural-kind words reflects an important fact about our relation to the world: we know that there are kinds of things with common hidden structure, but we don't yet have the knowledge to describe all those hidden structures.

Katz's view has more plausibility in the "pencil" case than in the "cat" case, however. We think we *know* a necessary and sufficient condition for being a *pencil,* albeit a vague one. So it is possible to make "pencil" synonymous with a loose description. We *might* say, in the case that "pencils turned out to be organisms" *either* "Pencils have turned out to be organisms" *or* "There are no pencils in the world"—i.e., we might use "pencil" either as a natural-kind word or as a "one-criterion" word.[11]

On the other hand, we might doubt that there *are* any true one-criterion words in natural language, apart from stipulative contexts. Couldn't it turn out that pediatricians aren't doctors but Martian spies? Answer "yes," and you have abandoned the synonymy of "pediatrician" and "doctor specializing in the care of children." It seems that there is a strong tendency for words which are introduced as "one-criterion" words to develop a "natural-kind" sense, with all the

---

[11] The idea of a "one-criterion" word, and a theory of analyticity based on this notion, appears in Putnam [(1975a), chapter 2].

concomitant rigidity and indexicality. In the case of artifact-names, this natural-kind sense seems to be the predominant one.

(There is a joke about a patient who is on the verge of being discharged from an insane asylum. The doctors have been questioning him for some time, and he has been giving perfectly sane responses. They decide to let him leave, and at the end of the interview one of the doctors inquires casually, "What do you want to be when you get out?" "A teakettle." The joke would not be intelligible if it were literally inconceivable that a person could be a teakettle.)

There are, however, words which retain an almost pure one-criterion character. These are words whose meaning derives from a transformation: *hunter = one who hunts.*

Not only does the account given here apply to most nouns, but it also applies to other parts of speech. Verbs like "grow," adjectives like "red," etc., all have indexical features. On the other hand, some syncategorematic words seem to have more of a one-criterion character. "Whole," for example, can be explained thus: *The army surrounded the town* could be true even if the *A* division did not take part. *The whole army surrounded the town* means every part of the army (of the relevant kind, e.g., the *A* division) took part in the action signified by the verb.[12]

Meaning

Let us now see where we are with respect to the notion of meaning. We have now seen that the extension of a term is not fixed by a concept that the individual speaker has in his head, and this is true both because extension is, in general, determined *socially*—there is division of linguistic labor as much as of "real" labor—and because extension is, in part, determined *indexically*. The extension of our terms depends upon the actual nature of the particular things that serve as paradigms,[13] and this actual nature is not, in general, fully known to the speaker. Traditional semantic theory leaves out only two contributions to the determination of extension—the contribution of society and the contribution of the real world!

We saw at the outset that meaning cannot be identified with extension. Yet it cannot be identified with "intension" either, if intension is something like an individual speaker's *concept*. What are we to do?

There are two plausible routes that we might take. One route would be to retain the identification of meaning with concept and pay the price of giving up the idea that meaning determines extension. If we followed this route, we might say that "water" has the same *meaning* on Earth and on Twin Earth, but a different *extension*. (Not just a different *local* extension but a different *global* extension. The *XYZ* on Twin Earth isn't in the extension of the tokens of "water" that I utter, but it is in the extension of the tokens of "water" that my *Doppelgänger* utters, and this isn't just because Twin Earth is far away from me, since molecules of H_2O are

---

[12] This example comes from an analysis by Anthony Kroch (in his M.I.T. doctoral dissertation, 1974, Department of Linguistics).

[13] I *don't* have in mind the Flewish notion of "paradigm" in which any paradigm of a *K* is *necessarily* a *K* (in reality).

in the extension of the tokens of "water" that I utter no matter how far away from me they are in space and time. Also, what I can counterfactually suppose water to be is different from what my *Doppelgänger* can counterfactually suppose "water" to be.) While this is the correct route to take for an *absolutely* indexical word like "I," it seems incorrect for the words we have been discussing. Consider "elm" and "beech," for example. If these are "switched" on Twin Earth, then surely we would *not* say that "elm" has the same meaning on Earth and Twin Earth, even if my *Doppelgänger's* stereotype of a beech (or an "elm," as he calls it) is identical with my stereotype of an elm. Rather, we would say that "elm" in my *Doppelgänger's* idiolect means *beech*. For this reason, it seems preferable to take a different route and identify "meaning" with an ordered pair (or possibly an ordered *n-tuple*) of entities, *one of which is the extension*. (The other components of the, so to speak, "meaning vector" will be specified later.) Doing this makes it trivially true that *meaning determines extension* (i.e., difference in extension is *ipso facto* difference in meaning), but totally abandons the idea that if there is a difference in the meaning my *Doppelgänger* and I assign to a word, then there *must* be some difference in our concepts (or in our psychological state). Following this route, we can say that my *Doppelgänger* and *I mean something different* when we say "elm," but this will not be an assertion about our psychological states. All this means is that the tokens of the word he utters have a different extension than the tokens of the word I utter; but this difference in extension is not a reflection of any difference in our individual linguistic competence considered in isolation.

If this is correct, and I think it is, then the traditional problem of meaning splits into two problems. The first problem is to account for the *determination of extension*. Since, in many cases, extension is determined socially and not individually, owing to the division of linguistic labor, I believe that this problem is properly a problem for sociolinguistics. Solving it would involve spelling out in detail exactly how the division of linguistic labor works. The so-called "causal theory of reference," introduced by Kripke for proper names and extended by us to natural-kind words and physical-magnitude terms, falls into this province. For the fact that, in many contexts, we assign to the tokens of a name that I utter whatever referent we assign to the tokens of the same name uttered by the person from whom I acquired the name (so that the reference is transmitted from speaker to speaker, starting from the speakers who were present at the "naming ceremony," even though no fixed *description* is transmitted) is simply a special case of social cooperation in the determination of reference.

The other problem is to describe *individual competence*. Extension may be determined socially, in many cases, but we don't assign the standard extension to the tokens of a word W uttered by Jones *no matter how* Jones uses W. Jones has to have some particular ideas and skills in connection with W in order to play his part in the linguistic division of labor. Once we give up the idea that individual competence has to be so strong as to actually determine extension, we can begin to study it in a fresh frame of mind.

In this connection it is instructive to observe that nouns like "tiger" or "water" are very different from proper names. One can use the proper name

"Sanders" correctly without knowing anything about the reference except that he is called "Sanders"—and even that may not be correct. ("Once upon a time, a very long time ago now, about last Friday, Winnie-the-Pooh lived in a forest all by himself under the name of Sanders.") But one cannot use the word tiger correctly, save *per accidens*, without knowing a good deal about tigers, or at least about a certain conception of tigers. In this sense concepts *do* have a lot to do with meaning.

Just as the study of the first problem is properly a topic in sociolinguistics, so the study of the second problem is properly a topic in psycholinguistics. To this topic we now turn.

Stereotypes and Communication

Suppose a speaker knows that "tiger" has a set of physical objects as its extension, but no more. If he possesses normal linguistic competence in other respects, then he could use "tiger" in *some* sentences: for example, "tigers have mass," "tigers take up space," "give me a tiger," "is that a tiger?", etc. Moreover, the *socially determined* extension of "tiger" in these sentences would be the standard one, i.e., the set of tigers. Yet we would not count such a speaker as "knowing the meaning" of the word *tiger*. Why not?

Before attempting to answer this question, let us reformulate it a bit. We shall speak of someone as having *acquired* the word "tiger" if he is able to use it in such a way that (1) his use passes muster (i.e., people don't say of him such things as "he doesn't know what a tiger *is*," "he doesn't know the meaning of the word 'tiger'," etc.); and (2) his total way of being situated in the world and in his linguistic community is such that the socially determined extension of the word "tiger" in his idiolect is the set of tigers. Clause (1) means, roughly, that speakers like the one hypothesized in the preceding paragraph don't count as having acquired the word "tiger" (or whichever). We might speak of them, in some cases, as having *partially acquired* the word; but let us defer this for the moment. Clause (2) means that speakers on Twin Earth who have the same linguistic habits as we do, count as having acquired the word "tiger" only if the extension of "tiger" in their idiolect is the set of tigers. The burden of the preceding sections of this paper is that it does *not* follow that the extension of "tiger" in Twin Earth dialect (or idiolects) is the set of tigers merely because their linguistic habits are the same as ours: the nature of Twin Earth "tigers" is also relevant. (If Twin Earth organisms have a silicon chemistry, for example, then their "tigers" aren't really tigers, even if they look like tigers, although the linguistic habits of the lay Twin Earth speaker exactly correspond to those of Earth speakers.) Thus clause (2) means that in this case we have decided to say that Twin Earth speakers have not acquired our word "tiger" (although they have acquired another word with the same spelling and pronunciation).

Our reason for introducing this way of speaking is that the question "does he know the meaning of the word 'tiger'?" is biased in favor of the theory that acquiring a word is coming to possess a thing called its "meaning." Identify this thing with a concept, and we are back at the theory that a sufficient condition for acquiring a word is associating it with the right concept (or, more generally, being in the right psychological state with respect to it)—the very theory we have spent all this time refuting. So, henceforth, we will "acquire" words, rather than "learn their meaning."

We can now reformulate the question with which this section began. The use of the speaker we described does not pass muster, although it is not such as to cause us to assign a nonstandard extension to the word "tiger" in his idiolect. Why doesn't it pass muster?

Suppose our hypothetical speaker points to a snowball and asks, "is that a tiger?" Clearly there isn't much point in talking tigers with *him*. Significant communication requires that people know something of what they are talking about. To be sure, we hear people "communicating" every day who clearly know nothing of what they are talking about; but the sense in which the man who points to a snowball and asks "is that a tiger?" doesn't know anything about tigers is so far beyond the sense in which the man who thinks that Vancouver is going to win the Stanley Cup, or that the Vietnam War was fought to help the South Vietnamese, doesn't know what he is talking about as to boggle the mind. The problem of people who think that Vancouver is going to win the Stanley Cup, or that the Vietnam War was fought to help the South Vietnamese, is one that obviously cannot be remedied by the adoption of linguistic conventions; but not knowing what one is talking about in the second, mind-boggling sense can be and is prevented, near enough, by our conventions of language. What I contend is that speakers are *required* to know something about (stereotypical) tigers in order to count as having acquired the word "tiger"; something about elm trees (or anyway, about the stereotype thereof) to count as having acquired the word "elm"; etc.

This idea should not seem too surprising. After all, we do not permit people to drive on the highways without first passing some tests to determine that they have a *minimum* level of competence; and we do not dine with people who have not learned to use a knife and fork. The linguistic community too has its minimum standards, with respect both to syntax and to "semantics."

The nature of the required minimum level of competence depends heavily upon both the culture and the topic, however. In our culture speakers are required to know what tigers look like (if they acquire the word "tiger," and this is virtually obligatory); they are not required to know the fine details (such as leaf shape) of what an elm tree looks like. English speakers are *required by their linguistic community* to be able to tell tigers from leopards; they are not required to be able to tell elm trees from beech trees.

This could easily have been different. Imagine an Indian tribe, call it the Cheroquoi, who have words, say *uhaba'* and *wa'arabi* for elm trees and beech trees, respectively, and who make it *obligatory* to know the difference. A Cheroquoi who could not recognize an elm would be said not to know what an *uhaba'* is, not to know the meaning of the word *uhaba'* (perhaps, not to know the word, or not to *have* the word); just as an English speaker who had no idea that tigers are striped would be said not to know what a tiger is, not to know the meaning of the word "tiger" (of course, if he at least knows that tigers are large felines we might say he knows part of the meaning, or partially knows the meaning), etc. Then the translation of *uhaba'* as "elm" and *wa'arabi* as "beech" would, in our view, be only *approximately* correct. In this sense there is a real difficulty with radical translation,[14] but this is not the abstract difficulty that Quine is talking about.[15]

What Stereotypes Are

I introduced the notion of a "stereotype" in my lectures at the University of Washington and at the Minnesota Center for the Philosophy of Science in 1968. The subsequently published "Is semantics possible?" follows up the argumentation, and in the present essay I want to introduce the notion again and to answer some questions that have been asked about it.

In ordinary parlance a "stereotype" is a conventional (frequently malicious) idea (which may be wildly inaccurate) of what an X looks like or acts like or is. Obviously, I am trading on some features of the ordinary parlance. I am not concerned with malicious stereotypes (save where the language itself is malicious); but I am concerned with conventional ideas, which may be inaccurate. I am suggesting that just such a conventional idea is associated with "tiger," with "gold," etc., and, moreover, that this is the sole element of truth in the "concept" theory.

In this view someone who knows what "tiger" means (or, as we have decided to say instead, has acquired the word "tiger") is *required* to know that *stereotypical* tigers are striped. More precisely, there is *one* stereotype of tigers (he may have others) which is required by the linguistic community as such; he is required to have this stereotype, and to know (implicitly) that it is obligatory. This stereotype must include the feature of stripes if his acquisition is to count as successful.

The fact that a feature (e.g., stripes) is included in the stereotype associated with a word X does not mean that it is an analytic truth that all X's have that feature, nor that most X's have that feature, nor that all normal X's have that feature, nor that some X's have that feature.[16] Three-legged tigers and albino tigers are not logically contradictory entities. Discovering that our stereotype has been based on nonnormal or unrepresentative members of a natural kind is not discovering a logical contradiction. If tigers lost their stripes they would not thereby cease to be tigers, nor would butterflies necessarily cease to be butterflies if they lost their wings.

(Strictly speaking, the situation is more complicated than this. It is possible to give a word like "butterfly" a sense in which butterflies would cease to be butterflies if they lost their wings—through mutation, say. Thus one can find *a* sense of "butterfly" in which it is analytic that "butterflies have wings." But the most

---

[14] The term is due to Quine (in *Word and Object*): it signifies translation without clues either from shared culture or cognates.

[15] For a discussion of the supposed impossibility of uniquely correct radical translation see Putnam (1975a), chapter 9.

[16] This is argued in Putnam (1975a), chapter 8.

important sense of the term, I believe, is the one in which the wingless butterflies would still be butterflies.)

At this point the reader may wonder what the value to the linguistic community of having stereotypes is, if the "information" contained in the stereotype is not necessarily correct. But this is not really such a mystery. Most stereotypes do in fact capture features possessed by paradigmatic members of the class in question. Even where stereotypes go wrong, the way in which they go wrong sheds light on the contribution normally made by stereotypes to communication. The stereotype of gold, for example, contains the feature *yellow* even though chemically pure gold is nearly white. But the gold we see in jewelry is typically yellow (due to the presence of copper), so the presence of this feature in the stereotype is even useful in lay contexts. The stereotype associated with *witch* is more seriously wrong, at least if taken with existential import. Believing (with existential import) that witches enter into pacts with Satan, that they cause sickness and death, etc., facilitates communication only in the sense of facilitating communication internal to witch-theory. It does not facilitate communication in any situation in which what is needed is more agreement with the world than agreement with the theory of other speakers. (Strictly speaking, I am speaking of the stereotype as it existed in New England 300 years ago; today that witches aren't *real* is itself part of the stereotype, and the baneful effects of witch-theory are thereby neutralized.) But the fact that our language has *some* stereotypes which impede rather than facilitate our dealings with the world and each other only points to the fact that we aren't infallible beings, and how could we be? The fact is that we could hardly communicate successfully if most of our stereotypes weren't pretty accurate as far as they go.

The "Operational Meaning" of Stereotypes

A trickier question is this: how far is the notion of stereotype "operationally definable." Here it is necessary to be extremely careful. Attempts in the physical sciences to *literally* specify operational definitions for terms have notoriously failed; and there is no reason the attempt should succeed in linguistics when it failed in physics. Sometimes Quine's arguments against the possibility of a theory of meaning seem to reduce to the demand for operational definitions in linguistics; when this is the case the arguments should be ignored. But it frequently happens that terms do have operational definitions not in the actual world but in idealized circumstances. Giving these "operational definitions" has heuristic value, as idealization frequently does. It is only when we mistake operational definition for more than convenient idealization that it becomes harmful. Thus we may ask: what is the "operational meaning" of the statement that a word has such and such a stereotype, without supposing that the answer to this question counts as a theoretical account of what it is to be a stereotype.

The theoretical account of what it is to be a stereotype proceeds in terms of the notion of *linguistic obligation;* a notion which we believe to be fundamental to linguistics and which we shall not attempt to explicate here. What it means to say that being striped is part of the (linguistic) stereotype of "tiger" is that it is *obligatory* to acquire the information that stereotypical tigers are striped if one acquires "tiger," in the same sense of "obligatory" in which it is obligatory to indicate whether one is speaking of lions in the singular or lions in the plural when one speaks of lions in English. To describe an idealized experimental test of this hypothesis is not difficult. Let us introduce a person whom we may call the linguist's *confederate*. The confederate will be (or pretend to be) an adult whose command of English is generally excellent, but who for some reason (raised in an alien culture? brought up in a monastery?) has totally failed to acquire the word "tiger." The confederate will say the word "tiger" or, better yet, point to it (as if he wasn't sure how to pronounce it), and ask "What does this word mean?" or "What is this?" or some such question. Ignoring all the things that go wrong with experiments in practice, what our hypothesis implies is that informants should typically tell the confederate that tigers are, *inter alia*, striped.

Instead of relying on confederates, one might expect the linguist to study children learning English. But children learning their native language aren't taught it nearly as much as philosophers suppose; they learn it but they aren't taught it, as Chomsky has emphasized. Still, children do sometimes ask such questions as "What is a tiger?" and our hypothesis implies that in these cases too informants should tell them, *inter alia*, that tigers are striped. But one problem is that the informants are likely to be parents, and there are the vagaries of parental time, temper, and attention to be allowed for.

It would be easy to specify a large number of additional "operational" implications of our hypothesis, but to do so would have no particular value. The fact is that we are fully competent speakers of English ourselves, with a devil of a good sense of what our linguistic obligations are. Pretending that we are in the position of Martians with respect to English is not the route to methodological clarity; it was, after all, only when the operational approach was abandoned that transformational linguistics blossomed into a handsome science.

Thus if anyone were to ask me for the meaning of "tiger," I know perfectly well what I would tell him. I would tell him that tigers were feline, something about their size, that they are yellow with black stripes, that they (sometimes) live in the jungle, and are fierce. Other things I might tell him too, depending on the context and his reason for asking; but the above items, save possibly for the bit about the jungle, I would regard it *obligatory* to convey. I don't have to experiment to know that this is what I regard it as obligatory to convey, and I am sure that approximately this is what other speakers regard it as obligatory to convey too. Of course, there is some variation from idiolect to idiolect; the feature of having stripes (apart from figure-ground relations, e.g., are they black stripes on a yellow ground, which is the way I see them, or yellow stripes on a black ground?) would be found in all normal idiolects, but some speakers might regard the information that tigers (stereotypically) inhabit jungles as obligatory, while others might not. Alternatively, some features of the stereotype (big-cathood, stripes) might be regarded as obligatory, and others as *optional*, on the model of certain syntactical features. But we shall not pursue this possibility here.

Quine's "Two Dogmas" Revisited

In "Two dogmas of empiricism" Quine launched a powerful and salutory attack on the currently fashionable analytic-synthetic distinction. The distinction had grown to be a veritable philosophical man-eater: analytic *equalling* necessary *equalling* unrevisable in principle *equalling* whatever truth the individual philosopher wished to explain away. But Quine's attack itself went too far in certain respects; some limited class of analytic sentences can be saved, we feel. More important, the attack was later construed both by Quine himself and by others, as implicating the whole notion of meaning in the downfall of the analytic-synthetic distinction. While we have made it clear that we agree that the traditional notion of meaning has serious troubles, our project in this paper is constructive, not destructive. We come to revise the notion of meaning, not to bury it. So it will be useful to see how Quine's arguments fare against our revision.

Quine's arguments against the notion of analyticity can basically be reduced to the following: that no behavioral significance can be attached to the notion. His argument (again simplifying somewhat) was that there were, basically, only two candidates for a behavioral index of analyticity, and both are totally unsatisfactory although for different reasons. The first behavioral index is *centrality:* many contemporary philosophers call a sentence analytic if, in effect some community (say, Oxford dons) holds it immune from revision. But, Quine persuasively argues maximum immunity from revision is no exclusive prerogative of analytic sentences. Sentences expressing fundamental laws of physics (e.g., the conservation of energy) may well enjoy maximum behavioral immunity from revision, although it would hardly be customary or plausible to classify them as analytic. Quine does not, however, rely on the mere implausibility of classifying all statements that we are highly reluctant to give up as analytic; he points out that "immunity from revision" is, in the actual history of science, a *matter of degree.* There is no such thing, in the actual practice of rational science, as *absolute* immunity from revision. Thus to identify analyticity with immunity from revision would alter the notion in two fundamental ways: analyticity would become a matter of degree, and there would be no such thing as an absolutely analytic sentence. This would be such a departure from the classical Carnap-Ayer-et al. notion of analyticity that Quine feels that if *this* is what we mean to talk about, then it would be less misleading to introduce a different term altogether, say, *centrality.*

The second behavioral index is *being called "analytic."* In effect, some philosophers take the hallmark of analyticity to be that trained informants (say, Oxford dons) *call* the sentence analytic. Variants of this index are: that the sentence be deducible from the sentences in a finite list at the top of which someone who bears the ancestral of the graduate-student relation to Carnap has printed the words "Meaning Postulate"; that the sentence be obtainable from a theorem of logic by substituting synonyms for synonyms. The last of these variants looks promising, but Quine launches against it the question, "what is the criterion of synonymy?" One possible criterion might be that words W_1 and W_2 are synonymous if and only if the biconditional (x) (x is in the extension of W_1 <= => x is in the extension of W_2) is *analytic;* but this leads us right back in a circle. Another might be that words W_1 and W_2 are synonymous if and only if trained informants *call* them synonymous; but this is just our second index in a slightly revised form. A promising line is that words W_1 and W_2 are synonymous if and only if W_1 and W_2 are interchangeable (i.e., the words can be switched) *salva veritate* in all contexts of a suitable class. But Quine convincingly shows that this proposal too leads us around in a circle. Thus the second index reduces to this: a sentence is analytic if either it or some expression, or sequence of ordered pairs of expressions, or set of expressions, related to the sentence in certain specified ways, lies in a class to all the members of which trained informants apply a certain *noise:* either the *noise* ANALYTIC, or the *noise* MEANING POSTULATE, or the *noise* SYNONYMOUS. Ultimately, this proposal leaves "analytic," etc., *unexplicated noises.*

Although Quine does not discuss this explicitly, it is clear that taking the intersection of the two unsatisfactory behavioral indexes would be no more satisfactory; explicating the analyticity of a sentence as consisting in centrality *plus* being called ANALYTIC is just saying that the analytic sentences are a subclass of the central sentences without in any way telling us wherein the exceptionality of the subclass consists. In effect, Quine's conclusion is that analyticity is either centrality misconceived or it is nothing.

In spite of Quine's forceful argument, many philosophers have gone on abusing the notion of analyticity, often confusing it with a supposed highest degree of centrality. Confronted with Quine's alternatives, they have elected to identify analyticity with centrality, and to pay the price of classifying such obviously synthetic-looking sentences as "space has three dimensions" as analytic, and the price of undertaking to maintain the view that there is, after all, such a thing as absolute unrevisability in science in spite of the impressive evidence to the contrary. But this line can be blasted by coupling Quine's argument with an important argument of Reichenbach's.

Reichenbach showed that there exists a *set* of principles each of which Kant would have regarded as synthetic *a priori*, but whose conjunction is incompatible with the principles of special relativity and general covariance. (These include normal induction, the continuity of space, and the Euclidean character of space.) A Kantian can consistently hold on to Euclidean geometry come what may; but then experience may force him to give up normal induction or the continuity of space. Or he may hold on to normal induction and the continuity of space come what may; but then experience may force him to give up Euclidean geometry (this happens in the case that physical space is not even homeomorphic to any Euclidean space). . . .

Applied to our present context, what this shows is that there are principles such that philosophers fond of the overblown notion of analyticity, and in particular philosophers who identify analyticity with (maximum) unrevisability, would classify them as analytic, but whose conjunction has testable empirical consequences. Thus either the identification of analyticity with centrality must be given up once and for all, or one must give up the idea that analyticity is closed under conjunction, or one must swallow the unhappy consequence that an analytic sentence can have testable empirical consequences (and hence that an *analytic* sentence might turn out to be *empirically false*).

It is no accident, by the way, that the sentences that Kant would have classified as synthetic *a priori* would be classified by these latter-day empiricists as analytic; their purpose in bloating the notion of analyticity was precisely to dissolve Kant's problem by identifying *apriority* with analyticity and then identifying analyticity in turn with truth by convention. (This last step has also been devastatingly criticized by Quine, but discussion of it would take us away from our topic.)

Other philosophers have tried to answer Quine by distinguishing between *sentences* and *statements:* all *sentences* are revisable, they agree, but some *statements* are not. Revising a sentence is not changing our mind about the statement formerly expressed by that sentence just in case the sentence (meaning the syntactical object together with its meaning) after the revision is, in fact, not synonymous with the sentence prior to the revision, i.e., just in case the revision is a case of meaning change and not change of theory. But (1) this reduces at once to the proposal to explicate analyticity in terms of synonymy; and (2) if there is one thing that Quine has decisively contributed to philosophy, it is the realization that meaning change and theory change cannot be sharply separated. We do not agree with Quine that meaning change cannot be defined at all, but it does not follow that the dichotomy "meaning change or theory change" is tenable. Discovering that we live in a non-Euclidean world *might* change the meaning of "straight line" (this would happen in the—somewhat unlikely—event that something like the parallels postulate was part of the stereotype of straightness, but it would not be a *mere* change of meaning. In particular it would not be a change of *extension:* thus it would not be right to say that the parallels postulate was "true in the former sense of the words." From the fact that giving up on sentence *S* would involve meaning change, it does not follow that *S* is *true*. Meanings may not fit the world; and meaning change can be forced by empirical discoveries.

Although we are not, in this paper, trying to explicate a notion of analyticity, we are trying to explicate a notion that might seem closely related, the notion of meaning. Thus it might seem that Quine's arguments would also go against our attempt. Let us check this out.

In our view there is a perfectly good sense in which being striped is part of the meaning of "tiger." But it does not follow, in our view, that "tigers are striped" is analytic. If a mutation occurred, all tigers might be albinos. Communication presupposes that I have a stereotype of tigers which includes stripes, and that you have a stereotype of tigers which includes stripes, and that I know that your stereotype includes stripes, and that you know that my stereotype includes stripes, and that you know that I know . . . (and so on, à la Grice, forever). But it does not presuppose that any particular stereotype be *correct*, or that the majority of our stereotypes remain correct forever. Linguistic obligatoriness is not supposed to be an index of unrevisability or even of truth; thus we can hold that "tigers are striped" is part of the meaning of "tiger" without being trapped in the problems of analyticity.

Thus Quine's arguments against identifying analyticity with centrality are not arguments against identifying a feature's being "part of the meaning" of X with its being obligatorily included in the stereotype of X. What of Quine's "noise" argument?

Of course, evidence concerning what people *say,* including explicit metalinguistic remarks, is important in "semantics" as it is in syntax. Thus, if a speaker points to a *clam* and asks "is that a tiger?" people are likely to guffaw. (When they stop laughing) they might say "he doesn't know the meaning of 'tiger'," or "he doesn't know what tigers are." Such comments can be helpful to the linguist. But we are not *defining* the stereotype in terms of such comments. To say that being "big-cat-like" is part of the meaning of tiger is not merely to say that application of "tiger" to something which is not big-cat-like (and also not a tiger) would provoke certain *noises.* It is to say that speakers acquire the information that "tigers are (stereotypically) big-cat-like" as they acquire the word "tiger" and that they feel an obligation to guarantee that those to whom they teach the use of the word do likewise. Information about the minimum skills required for entry into the linguistic community is significant information; no circularity of the kind Quine criticized appears here.

Radical Translation

What our theory does not do, by itself at any rate, is solve Quine's problem of "radical translation" (i.e., translation from an alien language/culture). We cannot translate our hypothetical Cheroquoi into English by matching stereotypes, just because finding out what the stereotype of say, *wa'arabi* is involves translating Cheroquoi utterances. On the other hand, the constraint that each word in Cheroquoi should match its image in English under the translation-function as far as stereotype is concerned (or approximately match, since in many cases exact matching may not be attainable), places a severe *constraint* on the translation function. Once we have succeeded in translating the basic vocabulary of Cheroquoi, we can start to elicit stereotypes, and these will serve both to constrain future translations and to check the internal correctness of the piece of the translation-function already constructed.

Even where we can determine stereotypes (relative, say, to a tentative translation of "basic vocabulary"), these do not suffice, in general, to determine a unique translation. Thus the German words *Ulme* and *Buche* have the same stereotype as elm; but *Ulme* means "elm" while *Buche* means "beech." In the case of German, the fact that *Ulme* and "elm" are cognates could point to the correct translation (although this is far from foolproof—in general, cognate words are not synonymous); but in the case of Greek we have no such clue as to which of the two words ὀξύα, πτελέα means *elm* and which *beech;* we would just have to find a Greek who could tell elms from beeches (or *oxya* from *ptelea*). What this illustrates is that it may not be the *typical* speakers' dispositions to assent and dissent that the linguist must seek to discover; because of the division of linguistic labor, it is frequently necessary for the linguist to assess who are the experts with respect to *oxya,* or *wa'arabi,* or *gavagai,* or whatever, before he can make a guess at the socially determined extension of a word. Then this socially determined extension *and* the stereotype of the *typical* speaker, inexpert though he is, *will* both function as constraints upon the translation-function. Discovery that the stereotype of *oxya* is wildly different from the stereotype of "elm" would disqualify the translation of *oxya* by "elm" in all save the most extensional contexts; but the discovery that the *extension* of *oxya* is not even approximately the class of elms would wipe out the translation altogether, in all contexts.

It will be noted that we have already enlarged the totality of facts counted as evidence for a translation-function beyond the ascetic base that Quine allows in *Word and Object.* For example, the fact that speakers say such and such when the linguist's "confederate" points to the word *oxya* and asks "what does this mean?" or "what is this?" or whatever is not allowed by Quine (as something the linguist can "know") on the ground that this sort of "knowledge" presupposes already having translated the query "what does this word mean?" However, if Quine is willing to assume that one can *somehow* guess at the words which signify *assent* and *dissent* in the alien language, it does not seem at all unreasonable to suppose that one can somehow convey to a native speaker that one does not understand a word. It is not necessary that one discover a locution in the alien language which literally means "what does this word mean?" (as opposed to: "I don't understand this word," or "this word is unfamiliar to me" or "I am puzzled by this word," etc.). Perhaps just saying the word *oxya,* or whatever, with a tone of puzzlement would suffice. Why should *puzzlement* be less accessible to the linguist than *assent?*

Also, we are taking advantage of the fact that segmentation into *words* has turned out to be linguistically universal (and there even exist tests for word and morpheme segmentation which are independent of meaning). Clearly, there is no motivated reason for allowing the linguist to utter whole sentences and look for assent and dissent, while refusing to allow him to utter words and morphemes in a tone of puzzlement.

I repeat, the claim is not being advanced that enlarging the evidence base in this way solves the problem of radical translation. What it does is add further constraints on the class of admissible candidates for a correct translation. What I believe is that enlarging the class of constraints can determine a unique translation, or as unique a translation as we are able to get in practice. But constraints that go beyond linguistic theory proper will have to be used, in my opinion; there will also have to be constraints on what sorts of beliefs (and connections between beliefs, and connections of beliefs to the culture and the world) we can reasonably impute to people. Discussion of these matters will be deferred to another paper.

A Critique of Davidsonian Semantic Theory

In a series of publications, Donald Davidson has put forward the interesting suggestion that a semantic theory of a natural language might be modeled on what mathematical logicians call a *truth definition* for a formalized language. Stripped of technicalities, what this suggestion comes down to is that one might have a set of rules specifying (1) for each word, under what conditions that word is true of something (for words for which the concept of an extension makes sense; all other words are to be treated as syncategorematic); (2) for sentences longer than a single word, a rule is given specifying the conditions under which the sentence is true as a function of the way it is built up out of shorter sentences (counting words as if they were one-word sentences, e.g., "snow" as "that's snow"). The choice of one-word sentences as the starting point is my interpretation of what Davidson intends; in any case, he means one to start with a *finite* stock of *short* sentences for which truth conditions are to be laid down *directly*. The intention of (2) is not that there should be a rule for each sentence not handled under (1), since this would require an infinite number of rules, but that there should be a rule for each sentence *type*. For example, in a formalized language one of the rules of kind (2) might be: if S is $(S_1 \& S_2)$ for some sentences S_1, S_2, then S is true if and only if S_1, S_2, are both true.

It will be noticed that, in the example just given, the truth condition specified for sentences of the sentence type $(S_1 \& S_2)$ performs the job of specifying the meaning of "&." More precisely, it specifies the meaning of the structure (___ & ___). This is the sense in which a truth definition can be a theory of meaning. Davidson's contention is that the *entire* theory of meaning for a natural language can be given in this form.

There is no doubt that rules of the type illustrated can give the meaning of some words and structures. The question is, what reason is there to think that the meaning of most words can be given in this way, let alone all?

The obvious difficulty is this: for many words, an extensionally correct truth definition can be given which is in no sense a theory of the meaning of the word. For example, consider *"Water" is true of x if and only if x is H_2O*. This is an extensionally correct truth definition for "water" (strictly speaking, it is not a truth definition but a "truth of" definition—i.e., a *satisfaction*-in-the-sense-of-Tarski definition, but we will not bother with such niceties here). At least it is extensionally correct if we ignore the problem that water with impurities is also called "water," etc. Now, suppose most speakers don't *know* that water is H_2O. Then this formula in no way tells us anything about the *meaning* of "water." It might be of interest to a chemist, but it doesn't count as a theory of the meaning of the term "water." Or, it counts as a theory of the *extension* of the term "water," but Davidson is promising us more than just that.

Davidson is quite well aware of this difficulty. His answer (in conversation, anyway) is that we need to develop a theory of *translation*. This he, like Quine, considers to be the real problem. Relativized to such a theory (relativized to what we admittedly don't yet have), the theory comes down to this: we want a system of truth definitions which is simultaneously a system of translations (or approximate translations, if perfect translation is unobtainable). If we had a theory which specified what it is to be a good translation, then we could rule out the above truth definition for "water" as uninteresting on the grounds that x is H_2O is not an acceptable translation or even near-translation of x is *water* (in a prescientific community), even if water = H_2O happens to be true.

This comes perilously close to saying that a theory of meaning is a truth definition plus a theory of meaning. (If we had ham and eggs we'd have ham and eggs—*if* we had ham and *if* we had eggs.) But this story suffers from worse than promissoriness, as we shall see.

A second contention of Davidson's is that the theory of translation that we don't yet have is necessarily a theory whose basic units are *sentences* and not *words* on the grounds that our *evidence* in linguistics necessarily consists of assent and dissent from sentences. Words can be handled, Davidson contends, by treating them as sentences ("water" as "that's water," etc.).

How does this ambitious project of constructing a theory of meaning in the form of a truth definition constrained by a theory of translation tested by "the only evidence we have," speakers' dispositions to use sentences, fare according to the view we are putting forward here?

Our answer is that the theory cannot succeed in principle. In special cases, such as the word "and" in its truth-functional sense, a truth definition (strictly speaking, a clause in what logicians call a "truth definition"—the sum total of all the clauses is the inductive definition of "truth" for the particular language) can give the meaning of the word or structure because the stereotype associated with the word (if one wants to speak of a stereotype in the case of a word like "and") is so strong as to actually constitute a necessary and sufficient condition. If all words were like "and" and "bachelor" the program could succeed. And Davidson certainly made an important contribution in pointing out that linguistics has to deal with inductively specified truth conditions. But in the great majority of words, the requirements of a theory of truth and the requirements of a theory of meaning are mutually incompatible, at least in the English–English case. But the English–English case—the case in which we try to provide a significant theory of the meaning of English words which is itself couched in English—is surely the basic one.

The problem is that in general the only expressions which are both coextensive with X and have roughly the same stereotype as X are expressions containing X itself. If we rule out such truth definitions (strictly speaking, clauses, but I shall continue using "truth definition" both for individual clauses and for the whole system of clauses, for simplicity) as

> *"X is water" is true if and only if X is water*

on the grounds that they don't say anything about the meaning of the word "water," and we rule out such truth definitions as

> *"X is water" is true if and only if X is H_2O*

on the grounds that what they say is wrong as a description of the *meaning* of the word "water," then we shall be left with nothing.

The problem is that we want

> *W is true of x if and only if ___*

to satisfy the conditions that (1) the clause be extensionally correct (where ___ is to be thought of as a condition containing "x," e.g., "x is H_2O"); (2) that ___ be a *translation* of *W*—on our theory, this would mean that the stereotype associated with *W* is approximately the same as the stereotype associated with; (3) that ___ not contain *W* itself, or syntactic variants of *W*. If we take *W* to be, for example, the word "elm," then there is absolutely no way to fulfill all three conditions simultaneously. Any condition of the above form that does not contain "elm" and that is extensionally correct will contain a ___ that is absolutely terrible as a *translation* of "elm."

Even where the language contains two exact synonyms, the situation is little better. Thus,

> *"Heather" is true of x if and only if x is gorse*

is true, and so is

> *"Gorse" is true of x if and only if x is heather*

—*this* is a *theory* of the *meaning* of "gorse" and "heather"?

Notice that the condition (3) is precisely what logicians do *not* impose on *their* truth definitions.

> *"Snow is white" is true if and only if snow is white*

is the paradigm of a truth definition in the logician's sense. But logicians are trying to give the extension of "true" with respect to a particular language, not the meaning of "snow is white." Tarski would have gone so far as to claim he was giving the *meaning* (and not just the extension) of "true"; but he would never have claimed he was saying *anything* about the meaning of "snow is white."

It may be that what Davidson really thinks is that a theory of meaning, in any serious sense of the term, is impossible, and that all that is possible is to construct translation-functions. If so, he might well think that the only "theory of meaning" possible for English is one that says "'elm' is true of *x* if and only if *x* is an elm." "'water' is true of *x* if and only if *x* is water," etc., and only rarely something enlightening like "S_1 & S_2 is true if and only if S_1, S_2 are both true." But if Davidson's "theory" is just Quininean an skepticism under the disguise of a positive contribution to the study of meaning, then it is a bitter pill to swallow.

The contention that the only evidence available to the linguist is speakers' dispositions with respect to whole sentences is, furthermore, vacuous on one interpretation, and plainly false on the interpretation on which it is not vacuous. If dispositions to say certain things *when queried about individual words or morphemes or syntactic structures* are included in the notion of dispositions to use sentences, then the restriction to dispositions to use sentences seems to rule out nothing whatsoever. On the nonvacuous interpretation, what Davidson is saying is that the linguist cannot have access to such data as what informants including the linguist himself) say when asked the meaning of a word or morpheme or syntactic structure. No reason has ever been given why the linguist cannot have access to such data, and it is plain that actual linguists place heavy reliance on informants' testimony about such matters, in the case of an alien language, and upon their own intuitions as native speakers, when they are studying their native languages. In particular, when we are trying to translate a whole sentence, there is no reason why we should not be guided by our knowledge of the syntactic and semantic properties of the constituents of that sentence, including the deep structure. As we have seen, there are procedures for gaining information about individual constituents. It is noteworthy that the procedure that Quine and Davidson claim is the only *possible* one—going from whole sentences to individual words— is the *opposite* of the procedure upon which every success ever attained in the study of natural language has been based.

Critique of California Semantics

I wish now to consider an approach to semantic theory pioneered by the late Rudolf Carnap. Since I do not wish to be embroiled in textual questions, I will not attribute the particular form of the view I am going to describe to any particular philosopher but will simply refer to it as "California semantics."

We assume the notion of a *possible world*. Let f be a function defined on the "space" of all possible worlds whose value $f(x)$ at any possible world x is always a subset of the set of entities in x. Then f is called an intension. A term T has meaning for a speaker X if X associates T with an intension f_T. The term T is *true of* an entity e in a possible world x if and only if e belongs to the set $f(x)$. Instead of using the term "associated," Carnap himself tended to speak of "grasping" intensions; but, clearly, what was intended was not just that X "grasp" the intension, but that he grasp *that f is the intension of T*—i.e., that he *associate f* with T is some way.

Clearly this picture of what it is to understand a term disagrees with the story we tell in this paper. The reply of a California semanticist would be that California semantics is a description of an *ideal* language; that actual language is *vague*. In other words, a term T in actual language does not have a single precise intension; it has a set—possibly a fuzzy set—of intensions. Nevertheless, the first step in the direction of describing natural language is surely to study the idealization in which each term T has exactly one intension.

(In his book *Meaning and Necessity*, Carnap employs a superficially different formulation: an intension is simply a *property*. An entity e belongs to the extension of a term T just in case e has whichever property is the intension of T. The later formulation in terms of functions f as described above avoids taking the notion of *property* as primitive.)

The first difficulty with this position is the use of the totally unexplained notion of *grasping* an intension (or, in our reformulation of the position, *associating* an intension with a term). Identifying intensions with set-theoretic entities f provides a "concrete" realization of the notion of intension in the current mathematical style (relative to the notions of possible world and set), but at the cost of making it very difficult to see how anyone could have an intension in his mind, or what it is to think about one or "grasp" one or "associate" one with anything. It will not do to say that thinking of an intension is using a word or functional substitute for a word (e.g., the analogue of a word in "brain code," if, as seems likely, the brain "computes" in a "code" that has analogies to and possibly borrowings from language;

or a thought form such as a picture or a private symbol, in cases where such are employed in thinking) which *refers* to the intension in question, since *reference* (i.e., being in the extension of a term) has just been defined in terms of *intension*. Although the characterization of what it is to think of an abstract entity such as a function or a property is certainly correct, in the present context it is patently circular. But no noncircular characterization of this fundamental notion of the theory has ever been provided.

This difficulty is related to a general difficulty in the philosophy of mathematics pointed out by Paul Benacerraf. Benacerraf has remarked that philosophies of mathematics tend to fall between two schools: either they account for what mathematical objects are and for the necessity of mathematical truth and fail to account for the fact that people can *learn* mathematics, can *refer to* mathematical objects, etc., or else they account for the latter facts and fail to account for the former. California semantics accounts for what intensions *are*, but provides no account that is not completely circular of how it is that we can "grasp" them, associate them with terms, think about them, *refer* to them, etc.

Carnap may not have noticed this difficulty because of his Verificationism. In his early years Carnap thought of understanding a term as possessing the *ability to verify* whether or not any given entity falls in the extension of the term. In terms of intensions: "grasping" an intension would amount, then, to possessing the ability to verify if an entity e in any possible world x belongs to $f(x)$ or not. Later Carnap modified this view, recognizing that, as Quine puts it, sentences face the tribunal of experience collectively and not individually. There is no such thing as the way of verifying that a term T is true of an entity, in general, independent of the context of a particular set of theories, auxiliary hypotheses, etc. Perhaps Carnap would have maintained that something like the earlier theory was correct for a limited class of terms, the so-called "observation terms." Our own view is that the verifiability theory of meaning is false both in its central idea and for observation terms, but we shall not try to discuss this here. At any rate, if one is *not* a verificationist, then it is hard to see California semantics as a theory at all, since the notion of *grasping* an intension has been left totally unexplained.

Second, if we assume that "grasping an intension" (associating an intension with a term T) is supposed to be a *psychological state* (in the narrow sense), then California semantics is committed to both principles (1) and (2) that we criticized in the first part of this paper. It must hold that the psychological state of the speaker determines the intension of his terms which in turn determines the extension of his terms. It would follow that if two human beings are in the same total psychological state, then they necessarily assign the same extension to every term they employ. As we have seen, this is totally wrong for natural language. The reason this is wrong, as we saw above, is in part that extension is determined socially, not by individual competence alone. Thus California semantics is committed to treating language as something private—to totally ignoring the linguistic division of labor. The extension of each term is viewed by this school as totally determined by something in the head of the individual speaker all by himself. A second reason this is wrong, as we also saw, is that most terms are *rigid*.

In California semantics every term is treated as, in effect, a *description*. The *indexical* component in meaning—the fact that our terms refer to things which are similar, in certain ways, to things that we designate *rigidly*, to *these* things, to the stuff we call "water," or whatever, *here*—is ignored.

But what of the defense that it is not actual language that the California semanticist is concerned with, but an idealization in which we "ignore vagueness," and that terms in natural language may be thought of as associated with a set of intensions rather than with a single well-defined intension?

The answer is that an *indexical* word cannot be represented as a vague family of non-indexical words. The word "I," to take the extreme case, is *indexical* but not *vague*. *T* is not synonymous with a *description;* neither is it synonymous with a fuzzy set of descriptions. Similarly, if we are right, "water" is synonymous neither with a description nor with a fuzzy set of descriptions (intensions).

Similarly, a word whose extension is fixed socially and not individually is not the same thing as a word whose extension is *vaguely* fixed individually. The reason my individual "grasp" of "elm tree" does not fix the extension of elm is not that the word is vague—if the problem were simple vagueness, then the fact that my concepts do not distinguish elms from beeches would imply that elms are beeches, as I use the term, or, anyway, borderline cases of beeches, and that beeches are elms, or borderline cases of elms. The reason is rather that the extension of "elm tree" in my dialect is not fixed by what the average speaker "grasps" or doesn't "grasp" at all; it is fixed by the community, including the experts, through a complex cooperative process. A language which exemplifies the division of linguistic labor cannot be approximated successfully by a language which has vague terms and no linguistic division of labor. Cooperation isn't vagueness.

But, one might reply, couldn't one replace our actual language by a language in which (1) terms were replaced by coextensive terms which were *not* indexical (e.g., "water" by "H_2O," assuming "H_2O" is not indexical); and (2) we eliminated the division of linguistic labor by making every speaker an expert on every topic.

We shall answer this question in the negative; but suppose, for a moment, the answer were "yes." What significance would this have? The "ideal" language would in no sense be similar to our actual language; nor would the difference be a matter of "the vagueness of natural language."

In fact, however, one can't carry out the replacement, for the very good reason that *all* natural-kind words and physical-magnitude words are indexical in the way we have described, "hydrogen," and hence "H_2O," just as much as "water." Perhaps "sense data" terms are not indexical (apart from terms for the self), if such there be; but "yellow" as a *thing* predicate is indexical for the same reason as "tiger"; even if something *looks* yellow it may not *be* yellow. And it doesn't help to say that things that look yellow in normal circumstances (to normal perceivers) are yellow; "normal" here has precisely the feature we called indexicality. There is simply no reason to believe that the project of reducing our language to nonindexical language could be carried out in principle.

The elimination of the division of linguistic labor might, I suppose, be carried out "in principle." But, if the division of linguistic labor is, as I conjectured, a linguistic universal, what interest is there in the possible existence of a language which lacks a constitutive feature of *human* language? A world in which every one is an expert on every topic is a world in which social laws are almost unimaginably different from what they now are. What is the *motivation* for taking such a world and such a language as the model for the analysis of *human* language?

Incidentally, philosophers who work in the tradition of California semantics have recently begun to modify the scheme to overcome just these defects. Thus it has been suggested that an intension might be a function whose arguments are not just possible worlds but, perhaps, a possible world, a speaker, and a nonlinguistic context of utterance. This would permit the representation of some kinds of indexicality and some kinds of division of linguistic labor in the model. As David Lewis develops these ideas, "water," for example, would have the same *intension* (same function) on Earth and on Twin Earth, but a different extension. (In effect, Lewis retains assumption (1) from the discussion in the first part of this paper and gives up (2); we chose to give up (1) and retain (2).) There is no reason why the formal models developed by Carnap and his followers should not prove valuable when so modified. Our interest here has been not in the utility of the mathematical formalism but in the philosophy of language underlying the earlier versions of the view.

Semantic Markers

If the approach suggested here is correct, then there is a great deal of scientific work to be done in (1) finding out what sorts of items can appear in stereotypes; (2) working out a convenient system for representing stereotypes, etc. This work is not work that can be done by philosophical discussion, however. It is rather the province of linguistics and psycholinguistics. One idea that can, I believe, be of value is the idea of a *semantic marker*. The idea comes from the work of J. Katz and J. A. Fodor; we shall modify it somewhat here.

Consider the stereotype of "tiger" for a moment. This includes such features as being an animal; being big-cat-like; having black stripes on a yellow ground (yellow stripes on a black ground?); etc. Now, there is something very special about the feature *animal*. In terms of Quine's notion of *centrality* or *unrevisability*, it is qualitatively different from the others listed. It is not impossible to imagine that tigers might not be animals (they might be robots). But spelling this out, they must always have been robots; we don't want to tell a story about the tigers being *replaced* by robots, because then the robots wouldn't be tigers. Or, if they weren't always robots, they must have *become* robots, which is even harder to imagine. If tigers are and always were robots, these robots mustn't be too "intelligent," or else we may not have a case in which tigers aren't animals—we may, rather, have described a case in which some robots are animals. Best make them "other directed" robots—say, have an operator on Mars controlling each motion remotely. Spelling this out, I repeat, is difficult, and it is curiously hard to think of the case to begin with, which is why it is easy to make the mistake of thinking that it is "logically impossible" for a tiger *not* to be an animal. On the other hand, there is no difficulty in imagining an individual tiger that is not striped; it might be an albino. Nor is it difficult to imagine an individual tiger that doesn't look like a big cat: it might be horribly deformed. We can even imagine the whole species losing its stripes or becoming horribly deformed. But tigers ceasing to be animals? Great difficulty again!

Notice that we are not making the mistake that Quine rightly criticized, of attributing an absolute unrevisability to such statements as "tigers are animals," "tigers couldn't change from animals into something else and still be tigers." Indeed, we can describe far-fetched cases in which these statements would be given up. But we maintain that it is *qualitatively* harder to revise "all tigers are animals" than "all tigers have stripes"—indeed, the latter statement is not even true.

Not only do such features as "animal," "living thing," "artifact," "day of the week," "period of time," attach with enormous centrality to the words "tiger," "clam," "chair," "Tuesday," "hour"; but they also form part of a widely used and important *system of classification*. The centrality guarantees that items classified under these headings virtually never have to be reclassified; thus these headings are the natural ones to use as category-indicators in a host of contexts. It seems to me reasonable that, just as in syntax we use such markers as "noun," "adjective," and, more narrowly, "concrete noun," "verb taking a person as subject and an abstract object," etc., to classify words, so in semantics these category-indicators should be used as markers.

It is interesting that when Katz and Fodor originally introduced the idea of a semantic marker, they did not propose to exhaust the meaning—what we call the stereotype—by a list of such markers. Rather, the markers were restricted to just the category-indicators of high centrality, which is what we propose. The remaining features were simply listed as a "distinguisher." Their scheme is not easily comparable with ours, because they wanted the semantic markers *plus* the distinguisher to always give a necessary and sufficient condition for membership in the extension of the term. Since the whole thing—markers and distinguisher—was supposed to represent what every speaker implicitly knows, they were committed to the idea that every speaker implicitly knows of a necessary and sufficient condition for membership in the extension of "gold," "aluminum," "elm"—which, as we have pointed out, is not the case. Later Katz went further and demanded that *all* the features constitute an *analytically* necessary and sufficient condition for membership in the extension. At this point he dropped the distinction between markers and distinguishers; if all the features have, so to speak, the infinite degree of centrality, why call some "markers" and some "distinguishers"? From our point of view, their original distinction between "markers" and "distinguisher" was sound—provided one drop the idea that the distinguisher provides (together with the markers) a necessary and sufficient condition, and the idea that any of this is a theory of *analyticity*. We suggest that the idea of a semantic marker is an important contribution, when taken as suggested here.

The Meaning of "Meaning"

We may now summarize what has been said in the form of a proposal concerning how one might reconstruct the notion of "meaning." Our proposal is not the only one that might be advanced on the basis of these ideas, but it may serve to encapsulate some of the major points. In addition, I feel that it recovers as much of ordinary usage in common sense talk and in linguistics as one is likely to be able to conveniently preserve. Since, in my view something like the assumptions (I) and (II) listed in the first part of this paper are deeply embedded in ordinary meaning talk, and these assumptions are jointly inconsistent with the facts, no reconstruction is going to be without some counterintuitive consequences.

Briefly, my proposal is to define "meaning" not by picking out an object which will be identified with the meaning (although that might be done in the usual set-theoretic style if one insists), but by specifying a normal form (or, rather, a *type* of normal form) for the description of meaning. If we know what a "normal form description" of the meaning of a word should be, then, as far as I am concerned, we know what meaning is in any scientifically interesting sense.

My proposal is that the normal form description of the meaning of a word should be a finite sequence, or "vector," whose components should certainly include the following (it might be desirable to have other types of components as well): (1) the syntactic markers that apply to the word, e.g., "noun"; (2) the semantic markers that apply to the word, e.g., "animal," "period of time"; (3) a description of the additional features of the stereotype, if any; (4) a description of the extension.

The following convention is a part of this proposal: the components of the vector all represent a hypothesis about the individual speaker's competence, *except the extension*. Thus the normal form description for "water" might be, in part:

Syntactic Markers	Semantic Markers	Stereotype	Extension
mass noun; concrete;	natural-kind; liquid;	colorless; transparent; tasteless; thirst-quenching; etc.	H_2O (give or take impurities)

—this does not mean that knowledge of the fact that water is H_2O is being imputed to the individual speaker or even to the society. It means that (*we* say) the extension of the term "water" as *they* (the speakers in question) use it is *in fact* H_2O. The objection "who are *we* to say what the extension of *their* term is in fact" has been discussed above. Note that this is fundamentally an objection to the notion of *truth*, and that extension is a relative of truth and inherits the family problems.

Let us call two descriptions *equivalent* if they are the same except for the description of the extension, and the two descriptions are coextensive. Then, if the set variously described in the two descriptions is, *in fact,* the extension of the word in question, and the other components in the description are correct characterizations of the various aspects of competence they represent, *both* descriptions count as correct. Equivalent descriptions are both correct or both incorrect.

This is another way of making the point that, although we have to use a *description* of the extension to *give* the extension, we think of the component in question as being the *extension* (the *set*), not the description of the extension.

In particular the representation of the words "water" in Earth dialect and "water" in Twin Earth dialect would be the same except that in the last column the normal form description of the Twin Earth word "water" would have *XYZ* and not H_2O. This means, in view of what has just been said, that we are ascribing the *same* linguistic competence to the typical Earthling/Twin Earthian speaker, but a different extension to the word, nonetheless.

This proposal means that we keep assumption (II) of our early discussion. Meaning determines extension—by construction, so to speak. But (I) is given up; the psychological state of the individual speaker does not determine "what he means."

In most contexts this will agree with the way we speak, I believe. But one paradox: suppose Oscar is a German–English bilingual. In our view, in his total collection of dialects, the words "beech" and *Buche* are *exact synonyms*. The normal form descriptions of their meanings would be identical. But he might very well not know that they are synonyms! A speaker can have two synonyms in his vocabulary and not know that they are synonyms!

It is instructive to see how the failure of the apparently obvious "if S_1 and S_2 are synonyms and Oscar understands both S_1 and S_2 then Oscar knows that S_1 and S_2 are synonyms" is related to the falsity of (I), in our analysis. Notice that if we had chosen to omit the extension as a component of the "meaning-vector," which is David Lewis's proposal as I understand it, then we would have the paradox that "elm" and "beech" have the *same meaning* but different extensions!

On just about any materialist theory, believing a proposition is likely to involve processing some *representation* of that proposition, be it a sentence in a language, a piece of "brain code," a thought form, or whatever. Materialists, and not only materialists, are reluctant to think that one can believe propositions *neat*. But even materialists tend to believe that, if one believes a proposition, *which* representation one employs is (pardon the pun) immaterial. If S_1 and S_2 are both representations that are *available* to me, then if I believe the proposition expressed by S_1 under the representation S_1, I must also believe it under the representation S_2—at least, I must do this if I have any claim to rationality. But, as we have just seen, this isn't right. Oscar may well believe that *this* is a "beech" (it has a sign on it that says "beech"), but not believe or disbelieve that this is a "*Buche*." It is not just that belief is a process involving representations; he believes the proposition (if one wants to introduce "propositions" at all) under one representation and not under another.

The amazing thing about the theory of meaning is how long the subject has been in the grip of philosophical misconceptions, and how strong these misconceptions are. Meaning has been identified with a necessary and sufficient condition by philosopher after philosopher. In the empiricist tradition, it has been identified with a method of verification, again by philosopher after philosopher. Nor have these misconceptions had the virtue of exclusiveness; not a few philosophers have held that meaning = method of verification = necessary and sufficient condition.

On the other side, it is amazing how weak the grip of the facts has been. After all, what have been pointed out in this essay are little more than home truths about the way we use words and how much (or rather, how little) we actually know when we use them. My own reflection on these matters began after I published a paper in which I confidently maintained that the meaning of a word was "a battery of semantical rules," and then began to wonder how the meaning of the common word "gold" could be accounted for in this way. And it is not that philosophers had never considered such examples: Locke, for example, uses this word as an example and is not troubled by the idea that its meaning is a necessary and sufficient condition!

If there is a reason for both learned and lay opinion having gone so far astray with respect to a topic which deals, after all, with matters which are in everyone's experience, matters concerning which we all have more data than we know what to do with, matters concerning which we have, if we shed preconceptions, pretty clear intuitions, it must be connected to the fact that the grotesquely mistaken views of language which are and always have been current reflect two specific and very central philosophical tendencies: the tendency to treat cognition as a purely *individual* matter and the tendency to ignore the *world*, insofar as it consists of more than the individual's "observations." Ignoring the division of linguistic labor is ignoring the social dimension of cognition; ignoring what we have called the *indexicality* of most words is ignoring the contribution of the environment. Traditional philosophy of language, like much traditional philosophy, leaves out other people and the world; a better philosophy and a better science of language must encompass both.

BIBLIOGRAPHY

Almog, J.; Perry, J.; and Wettstein, H., eds. (1989). *Themes from Kaplan*. Oxford: Oxford University Press.

Aquila, R. (1977). *Intentionality: A Study of Mental Acts*. University Park: Pennsylvania State University Press.

Ayers, M. (1972). "Some Thoughts." *Proceedings of the Aristotelian Society* LXXIII: 69–96.

Bach, K. "*De Re* Belief and Methodological Solipsism." In Woodfield (1982).

———. (1988). "Burge's New Thought-Experiment: Back to the Drawing Room." *The Journal of Philosophy* 85:88–97.

Bell, D., and Cooper, N., eds. (forthcoming). *The Analytic Tradition*. New York: Blackwell.

Benacerraf, P. (1973). "Mathematical Truth." *The Journal of Philosophy* 70:661–79.

Bilgrami, A. (1985). "Comments on Loar." In Grimm and Merrill, eds. (1988).

———. (1987). "An Externalist Account of Psychological Content." *Philosophical Topics* 15.

———. (1991). "Thought and Its Objects." E. Villanueva, ed. *Consciousness*. New Jersey: Rowman & Littlefield.

———. (1992). *Belief and Meaning*. Oxford: Blackwell Press.

Blackburn, S. (1984). *Spreading the Word*. Oxford: Clarendon Press.

Block, N., ed. (1981). *Readings in the Philosophy of Psychology*, 2 vols. London: Methuen.

———. (1987). "Functional Role and Truth Conditions." *Proceedings of the Aristotelian Society Supplementary Volume* 61:157–81.

Bogdan, R., ed. (1986). *Belief*. Oxford: Oxford University Press.

Brueckner, A. (1986). "Brains in a Vat." *The Journal of Philosophy* LXXXIII, 3:148–67.

Burge, T. (1977). "Belief *De Re*." *The Journal of Philosophy* 74:338–62.

———. (1978). "Belief and Synonymy." *The Journal of Philosophy* 75:119–38.

———. (1979a). "Individualism and the Mental." In French *et al.* (1979).

———. (1982). "Other Bodies." In Woodfield (1982).

———. (1982a). "Two Thought Experiments Reviewed." *Notre Dame Journal of Formal Logic* 23.

———. (1986). "Individualism and Psychology." *Philosophical Review* 95, 1:3–45.

———. (1986a). "Cartesian Error and the Objectivity of Perception." In McDowell and Pettit (1986).

———. (1986b). "Intellectual Norms and the Foundations of Mind." *The Journal of Philosophy* 83:697–720.

———. (1988). "Perceptual Individualism and Authoritative Self-Knowledge." In Grimm and Merrill (1988).

———. (1988a). "Individualism and Self-Knowledge." *The Journal of Philosophy* 85:649–63.

———. (1989). "Individuation and Causation in Psychology." Manuscript, UCLA.

———. (1989a): "Wherein Is Language Social?" In George (1989).

———. (forthcoming). "Frege on Sense and Linguistic Meaning." In Bell and Cooper (forthcoming).

Butterfield, J. (1986a). "Content and Context." In Butterfield (1986b).

———. (1986b). *Language, Mind and Logic*. Cambridge: Cambridge University Press.

Carruthers, P. (1987). "Russellian Thoughts." *Mind* 96:18–35.

Castaneda, H. N. (1966). "'He': A Study in the Logic of Self-Consciousness." *Ratio* 8:130–57.

———. (1967). "Indicators and Quasi-Indicators." *American Philosophical Quarterly* 4:85–100.

———. (1968). "On the Logic of Attributions of Self-Knowledge to Others." *The Journal of Philosophy* 65:439–56.

Chomsky, N. (1971). *Problems of Knowledge and Freedom*. New York.

Churchland, P. S., and Churchland, P. M. (1983). "Stalking the Wild Epistemic Engine." *Nous* 17:5–18.

Crane, T. (1990). "The Language of Thought: No Syntax Without Semantics." *Mind and Language* 5.

Crane, T., and Mellor, D. H. (1990). "There Is No Question of Physicalism." *Mind* 99:185–206.

Davidson, D. (1970). "Mental Events." Reprinted in *Essays on Actions and Events*. Oxford: Oxford University Press.

———. (1984). *Inquiries into Truth and Interpretation*. Oxford: Clarendon Press.

———. (1984a). "First Person Authority." *Dialectic* 38, 2–3:101–11.

———. (1987). "On Knowing One's Own Mind." *Proceedings and Addresses of the American Philosophical Association* 60:441–58.

——. (1988). "Reply to Burge." *The Journal of Philosophy* 85:664–65.

——. (1991). "What Is Present to the Mind." E. Villanueva, ed. *Consciousness*. New Jersey: Rowman & Littlefield.

Davies, M. (1986). "Externality, Psychological Explanation, and Narrow Content; Reply to Jerry Fodor's 'Individualism and Supervenience'." Paper delivered to the Joint Session of the Aristotelian Society and the Mind Association, July 1986.

Dennett, D. (1969). *Content and Consciousness*. London: Routledge & Kegan Paul.

——. (1978). *Brainstorms*. Cambridge: MIT Press.

——. (1982). "Beyond Belief." In Woodfield (1982), pp. 1–95.

——. (1984c). "Cognitive Wheels: The Frame Problem of AI." C. Hookway, ed. *Minds, Machines and Evolution*. Cambridge: Cambridge University Press.

——. (forthcoming). "Out of the Armchair and into the Field." *Poetics Today* (Israel).

Devitt, M. (1974). "Singular Terms." *The Journal of Philosophy* 71:183–205.

——. (1976). "Semantics and the Ambiguity of Proper Names." *Monist* 59:404–23.

——. (1979). "Against Incommensurability." *Australasian Journal of Philosophy* 57:29–50.

——. (1981). *Designation*. New York: Columbia University Press.

Devitt, M., and Sterelny, K. (1987). *Language and Reality*. Cambridge: Basil Blackwell.

Donnellan, K. (1966). "Reference and Definite Descriptions." *Philosophical Review* 75:281–304.

——. (1970). "Proper Names and Identifying Descriptions." *Synthese* 21:335–58.

——. (1974). "Speaking of Nothing." *Philosophical Review* 83:3–31.

——. (1977). "The Contingent: A Priori and Rigid Designators." P. French *et al.*, eds. *Midwest Studies in Philosophy Vol. II*.

Dretske, F. (1981). *Knowledge and the Flow of Information*. Cambridge: MIT Press.

——. (1986). "Misrepresentation." In Bogdan (1986).

Dummett, M. (1973). *Frege: Philosophy of Language*. London: Duckworth.

——. (1974). "Postscript." *Synthese* 27:523–34.

Dupte, John. (1981). "Natural Kinds and Biological Taxa." *Philosophical Review* 90:66–90.

Enc, B. (1976). "The Reference of Theoretical Terms." *Nous* 10:261–82.

Evans, G. (1977). "The Causal Theory of Names." In Schwartz (1977).

——. (1973). "The Causal Theory of Names." *Aristotelian Society Supplementary Volume* XLVII:187–208.

——. (1980). "Understanding Demonstratives." H. Parret and J. Bouveresse, eds. *Meaning and Understanding*, New York and Berlin: De Gruyter.

——. (1982). *The Varieties of Reference*. Oxford: Oxford University Press.

Feyerabend, P. (1962). "Explanation, Reduction, and Empiricism." H. Feigl and G. Maxwell, eds. *Minnesota Studies in the Philosophy of Science* 3:28–97.

——. (1970). "Consolations for a Specialist." I. Lakatos and A. Musgrave, eds. *Criticism and the Growth of Knowledge*. Cambridge: Cambridge University Press, pp. 197–230.

Field, H. (1972). "Tarski's Theory of Truth." *The Journal of Philosophy* 69:347–75.

——. (1973). "Theory Change and the Indeterminacy of Reference." *The Journal of Philosophy* 70:462–81.

——. (1975). "Conventionalism and Instrumentalism in Semantics." *Nous* 9:375–405.

——. (1978). "Mental Representation." Reprinted in Block (1981).

Fine, A. (1975). "How to Compare Theories: Reference and Change." *Nous*: 17–32.

Fodor, J. A. (1975). *The Language of Thought*. Harvester.

——. (1980). "Methodological Solipsism Considered as a Research Strategy in Cognitive Psychology." *The Behavioral and Brain Sciences* 3:63–109. Reprinted in Fodor (1981).

——. (1981). *Representations*. Cambridge: MIT Press.

——. (1981a): "Methodological Solipsism as a Research Strategy in Cognitive Science." Reprinted in Fodor (1981).

——. (1982). "Cognitive Science and the Twin Earth Problem." *Notre Dame Journal of Formal Logic* 23.

——. (1986). "Individualism and Supervenience I." *Proceedings of the Aristotelian Society,* Supp. Vol. LX: 235–62.

——. (1987). *Psychosemantics*. Cambridge: MIT Press.

French, P.; Uehling, T.; and Wettstein, H., eds. (1979). *Midwest Studies in Philosophy Vol. IV.* Minneapolis: University of Minnesota Press.

Geach, P. T. (1969). *God and the Soul*. London: Macmillan.

George, A., ed. (1989). *Reflections on Chomsky*. Oxford: Blackwell.

Gibson, E. (1969). *Principles of Perceptual Learning and Development*. New York: Appleton-Century-Crofts.

Goodman, N. (1961). "About." *Mind* 71:1–24.

——. (1978). *Ways of Worldmaking*. Indianapolis: Hackett.

Grimm, R., and Merrill, D., eds. (1988). *Contents of Thought (Proceedings of the 1985 Oberlin College Colloquium in Philosophy)*. Tucson: Arizona University Press.

Gunderson, K., ed. (1975). *Language, Mind and Knowledge*. Minnesota Studies in the Philosophy of Science, Vol. VII. Minneapolis: University of Minnesota Press.

Haldane and Ross, eds. (1955). *The Philosophical Works of Descartes, Vol. I*. New York: Dover.

Hampshire, S. (1975). *Freedom of the Individual*. Expanded edition. Princeton: Princeton University Press.

Harman, G. (1973). *Thought*. Princeton: Princeton University Press.

Haugeland, J. (1985). *Artificial Intelligence: The Very Idea*. Cambridge, MA, and London: MIT Press.

Heil, J., and Mele, A., eds. (1993). *Mental Causation*. Oxford: Clarendon Press.

Hintikka, J. (1962). *Knowledge and Belief*. Ithaca: Cornell University Press.

Hofstadter, D. (1979). *Gödel, Escher, Bach: An Eternal Golden Braid*. New York: Basic Books.

Hofstadter, D., and Dennett, D. (1981). *The Mind's I: Fantasies and Reflections on Mind and Soul*. New York: Basic Books.

Hornsby, J. (1986). "Physicalist Thinking and Behavior." In Pettit and McDowell (1986).

Jackson, F., and Pargetter, R. (forthcoming). "Causal Statements." *Philosophical Topics*.

Jackson, F., and Pettit, P. (1988). "Functionalism and Broad Content." *Mind* 97:381–400.

James, W. (1890). *The Principles of Psychology*.

Kaplan, D. (1968). "Quantifying In." *Synthese* 19:178–214.

——. (1978). "Dthat." P. Cole, ed. *Syntax and Semantics*. New York: Academic Press.

——. (1977). "Demonstratives." In Almog, Perry, and Wettstein (1989).

——. (1980). "Demonstratives." The John Locke Lectures, Oxford University.

Kitcher, P. (1978). "Theories, Theorists and Theoretical Change." *Philosophical Review* 87:519–47.

Kripke, S. (1971). "Identity and Necessity." M. Munitz, ed. *Identity and Individuation*. New York: New York University Press, pp. 135–64.

——. (1972). "Naming and Necessity." D. Davidson and G. Harman, eds. *Semantics of Natural Languages*. New York: Humanities, pp. 253–355.

——. (1979). "A Puzzle About Belief." A. Margalit, ed. *Meaning and Use*. Dordrecht: Reidel, pp. 239–83.

——. (1980). *Naming and Necessity*. Oxford: Blackwell.

Kuhn, T. (1962). *The Structure of Scientific Revolutions*. Chicago: University of Chicago Press.

——. (1970). "Reflections on My Critics." I. Lakatos and A. Musgrave, eds. *Criticism and the Growth of Knowledge*. Cambridge: Cambridge University Press, pp. 231–78.

Lewis, D. (1972b). "Psychophysical and Theoretical Identifications." *Australasian Journal of Philosophy* 50.

——. (1973). *Counterfactuals*. Oxford: Blackwell.

——. (1974). "Radical Interpretation." *Synthese* 27.

——. (1978). "Truth in Fiction." *American Philosophical Quarterly* 15:37–46.

——. (1979). "Attitudes *De Dicto* and *De Se*." *Philosophical Review* 78:513–43.

——. (1981). "What Puzzling Pierre Does Not Believe." *Australian Journal of Philosophy* 59:283–89.

——. (1983). "New Work for a Theory of Universals." *Australasian Journal of Philosophy* 61:343–77.

——. (1986). "Causal Explanation." Reprinted in *Philosophical Papers*, Vol. 2. Oxford: Oxford University Press.

Loar, B. (1982). "Must Beliefs Be Sentences?" P. Asquith and T. Nickles, eds. *PSA 1982: Proceedings of the 1982 Biennial Meeting of the Philosophy of Science Association*. East Lansing: Philosophy of Science Association, pp. 627–42.

——. (1987). "Names in Thought." *Philosophical Studies* 51:169–85.

——. (1988). "Social Content and Psychological Content." R. Grimm and D. Merrill, eds. *Contents of Thought*. Tucson: University of Arizona Press, pp. 99–110.

McCarthy, J., and Hayes, P. (1969). "Some Philosophical Problems from the Standpoint of Artificial Intelligence." B. Meltzer and D. Michie, eds. *Machine Intelligence*. Edinburgh: Edinburgh University Press.

McCulloch, G. (1986). "Scientism, Mind and Meaning." In Pettit and McDowell (1986).

——. (1989). *The Game of the Name*. Oxford: Clarendon Press.

McDowell, J. (1984). "*De Re* Senses." *The Philosophical Quarterly* 36:283–94.

——. (1986). "Singular Thought and Inner Space." In Pettit and McDowell (1986).

——. (1991). "Intentionality and Interiority in Wittgenstein." In Puhl (1991), pp. 148–69.

McGinn, C. (1977). "Charity, Interpretation, and Belief." *The Journal of Philosophy* LXXIV.

——. (1982). "The Structure of Content." In Woodfield (1982).

——. (1989). *Mental Content*. Oxford: Basil Blackwell.

McKinsey, M. (1978). "Names and Intentionality." *Philosophical Review* 87:171–200.

——. (1986). "Mental Anaphora." *Synthese* 66:159–75.

——. (1987). "Apriorism in the Philosophy of Language." *Philosophical Studies* 52:1–32.

——. (1991). "The Internal Basis of Meaning." *Pacific Philosophical Quarterly* 72: 143–69.

Mellor, D. H. (1977). "Natural Kinds." *British Journal for the Philosophy of Science* 28:299–312.

——. (1981). *Real Time*. Cambridge: Cambridge University Press.

——. (1989). "I and Now." *Proceedings of the Aristotelian Society* 89:79–94.

Morton, A. (1975). "Because He Thought He Had Insulted Him." *The Journal of Philosophy* LXXII:5–15.

Musgrave, A. (1976). "Why Did Oxygen Supplant Phlogiston?" C. Howson, ed. *Method and Appraisal in the Physical Sciences*. Cambridge: Cambridge University Press.

Nagel, T. (1986). *The View from Nowhere*. Oxford: Oxford University Press.

Neisser, U. (1976). *Cognition and Reality*. San Francisco: Freeman.

Nelson, R. (1978). "Objects of Occasion Beliefs." *Synthese* 39:105–40.

Noonan, H. (1984). "Fregean Thoughts." *The Philosophical Quarterly* 36:205–24.

——. (1986). "Russellian Thoughts and Methodological Solipsism." In Butterfield (1986b).

Nozick, R. (1981). *Philosophical Explanations*. Cambridge: Harvard University Press.

Owens, J. (1987). "In Defense of a Different Doppelgänger." *Philosophical Review*: 521–54.

Papineau, D. (1979). *Theory and Meaning*. Oxford: Clarendon Press.

Parfit, D. (1984). *Reasons and Persons*. Oxford: Oxford University Press.

Pearce, G., and Maynard, P., eds. (1973). *Conceptual Change*. Dordrecht: D. Reidel.

Perry, J. (1977). "Frege on Demonstratives." *Philosophical Review* 86:474–97.

——. (1979). "The Problem of the Essential Indexical." *Nous* 13:3–21.

Pettit, P. (1986). "Broad-Minded Explanation and Psychology." In Pettit and McDowell (1986).

Pettit, P., and McDowell, J., eds. (1986). *Subject, Thought, and Context*. Oxford: Oxford University Press.

Puhl, K., ed. (1991). *Meaning Skepticism*. Berlin and New York: De Gruyter.

Putnam H. (1967). "The 'Innateness' Hypothesis and Explanatory Models in Linguistics." *Synthese* 17:12–22.

——. (1973). "Meaning and Reference." *The Journal of Philosophy* LXX, 19:699–711.

——. (1974). "Comment on Wilfred Sellars." *Synthese* 27.

——. (1975). "The Meaning of 'Meaning'." Reprinted in Putnam (1975a).

——. (1975a). *Mind, Language, and Reality: Philosophical Papers, Vol. 2*. New York: Cambridge University Press.

——. (1975b). "The Meaning of 'Meaning'." K. Gunderson, ed. *Language, Mind, and Knowledge*. Minneapolis: University of Minnesota Press.

——. (1975c). "Explanation and Reference." In Putnam (1975a).

——. (1975d). *Mathematics, Matter and Method: Philosophical Papers, Vol. 1*. New York: Cambridge University Press.

——. (1975e). "Is Semantics Possible!" In Putnam (1975a).

——. (1978). *Meaning and the Moral Sciences*. Boston: Routledge & Kegan Paul.

——. (1981). *Reason, Truth and History*. Cambridge: Cambridge University Press.

——. (1988). *Representation and Reality*. Cambridge: MIT Press.

——. (1990). *Realism with a Human Face*. Cambridge: Harvard University Press.

Pylyshyn, Z. (1979). "Complexity and the Study of Artificial and Human Intelligence." M. Ringle, ed. *Philosophical Perspectives in Artificial Intelligence*. New Jersey: Humanities Press.

Quine, W. V. O. (1960). *Word and Object.* Cambridge: MIT Press.

Ramsey, F. (1928). "Universals of Law and of Fact." In *Philosophical Papers.* Cambridge: Cambridge University Press, 1990.

——. (1929). "General Propositions and Causality." In *Philosophical Papers.* Cambridge: Cambridge University Press, 1990.

Reichenbach, H. (1965). *The Theory of Relativity and A Priori Knowledge.* California.

Rosenberg, J., and Travis, C., eds. (1971). *Readings in the Philosophy of Language.* Englewood Cliffs: Prentice Hall.

Schiffer, S. (1978). "The Basis of Reference." *Erkenntnis* 13:171–206.

Schilpp, P., ed. (1951). *Albert Einstein Philosopher-Scientist.* New York.

Schlesinger, G. (1963). *Method in the Physical Sciences.* London: Routledge & Kegan Paul.

Schwartz, S., ed. (1977). *Naming, Necessity, and Natural Kinds.* Ithaca: Cornell University Press.

Searle, J. (1958). "Proper Names." *Mind* 67:166–73.

——. (1979). *Expression and Meaning.* Cambridge: Cambridge University Press.

——. (1979a). "Referential and Attributive." *The Monist* 62:190–308.

——. (1983). *Intentionality,* Cambridge: Cambridge University Press.

Segal, G. (1989a). "The Return of the Individual." *Mind* 98:39–57.

——. (1989b). "Seeing What Is Not There." *The Philosophical Review* 97:189–214.

Shoemaker, S. (1984). *Identity, Cause and Mind.* Cambridge: Cambridge University Press.

Smart, J. (1959). "Sensations and Brain Processes." *The Philosophical Review*: 141–56.

Stalnaker, R. (1984). *Inquiry.* Cambridge: MIT Press.

Sterelny, K. (1981). "Davidson on Truth and Reference." *Southern Journal of Philosophy* 19:95–117.

Stich, S. (1978a). "Autonomous Psychology and the Belief-Desire Thesis." *The Monist* 61:571–91.

——. (1983). *From Folk Psychology to Cognitive Science: The Case Against Belief.* Cambridge: MIT Press.

Ullman, S. (1979). *The Interpretation of Visual Motion.* Cambridge: MIT Press.

Van Gulick, R. (1989). "Metaphysical Arguments for Internalism and Why They Don't Work." S. Silvers, ed. *Rerepresentation.* Boston: Kluwer.

Wallas, Graham. *The Art of Thought.*

White, S. (1982). "Partial Character and the Language of Thought." *Pacific Philosophical Quarterly* 63:347–65.

Winograd, T. (1972). *Understanding Natural Language.* New York: Academic Press.

Wittgenstein, L. (1953). *Philosophical Investigations.* Oxford: Blackwell.

Woodfield, A., ed. (1982). *Thought and Object: Essays on Intentionality.* Oxford: Clarendon Press.

Wright, C. (1989). "Wittgenstein's Later Philosophy of Mind: Sensation, Privacy and Intention." *The Journal of Philosophy* 86.

Zemach, E. (1976). "Putnam's Theory on the Reference of Substance Terms." *The Journal of Philosophy* 73:116–27.

Ziff, P. (1972). *Understanding Understanding.* New York.

TAKING THE FREGEAN SERIOUSLY

Mark Richard

> *My taste is for keeping open house for all sorts of conditions*
> *of entities, just so long as when they come in they help with*
> *the housework.*
>
> —H. P. Grice

1. Introduction

According to the Fregean, 'that'-clauses in attitude ascriptions name senses; the main verb of an ascription names a relation which one may bear to a sense. An ascription *a V's that S* is true iff the referent of *a* bears the relation named by *V* to the sense named by its 'that'-clause.

According to Frege, there really is no such thing as *the* sense of sentence.[1] Different people may associate different senses with the same proper name, while using it to refer to the same person. Likewise, presumably, different people may associate different senses with the same predicate, while using it to refer to the same property.[2] The point is distinct from the now familiar one that sentences containing demonstratives and indexicals must vary in sense from use to use. Since, presumably, any proper name might suffer from intersubjective variations in sense, even eternal sentences such as '2 + 2 = 4' may vary in sense from person to person.

What does a 'that'-clause (t-clause) which has no one sense associated with it name, when it occurs in an attitude ascription? This is a serious question for Fregeanism, taken as a doctrine about the semantics of natural language. It has received surprisingly little attention.[3] In this paper, I argue that the Fregean is unable to give a satisfactory answer to the question. I try to show that no semantical account which makes t-clauses name Fregean senses gives an acceptable account of the truth conditions of, and entailment relations among, attitude ascriptions.

My arguments are largely indifferent to how one construes the nature of senses. I make no large assumptions about senses, beyond the assumption that the sense associated with a sentence may vary intersubjectively, without a variation in the ordinary references of the sentence's component expressions. I do assume that sense determines reference, since the Fregean assumes this, but I

---

[1] See, for example, the second footnote to Frege [1952], where Frege claims that the sense of 'Aristotle' may vary from person to person.

[2] The idea that the reference of a predicate is a property (in some sense of property) which does not allow for the individuation of properties in terms of their this worldly extensions is not universal among Fregeans. Frege himself would not have accepted the view. Herb Heidelberger once claimed that we ought to identify the sense of a predicate for Frege with a property. A number of contemporary Fregeans nonetheless subscribe to the view that properties are the referents of predicates, and I shall assume that here. None of the arguments of the paper requires this assumption.

[3] Kripke mentions this problem in Kripke (1979); he considers only the solution in 2.2., below. The only Fregean I am aware of who has given the problem extended consideration is Forbes, in Forbes (unpublished) and Forbes (1987). His solution is, in effect, the solution of section 4.

make no heavy weather about this. The problems which I raise will arise, even if familiar criticisms of the doctrine that sense determines reference should fail.

2. Three Obvious Answers

2.1

The most obvious answer to our question is that in an ascription

> a V's that S

the t-clause names the sense which the referent of *a* associates with *S*. (Qualifications must be made for demonstratives and indexicals, of course. But the literature is already rich with suggestions as to how the Fregean might treat these.)

This will quite obviously not do. Nebuchadnezzar associated no sense whatsoever with 'Hesperus is not Phosphorus'. So, on this proposal, 'that Hesperus is not Phosphorus' names nothing in

> (1) Nebuchadnezzar believed that Hesperus is not Phosphorus.

So, the ascription is not true. Not good.

2.2

No better is the proposal that in an attitude ascription a t-clause names its sense for the person making the ascription. At least this is no better, given that the relations named by propositional attitude verbs are the relations we would naturally think them to name. I suppose we have some handle on what these relations are supposed to be; call the relation we would naturally take 'believes' to name 'Belief'. If 'believes' names Belief, and, in (1), the t-clause names my sense for 'Hesperus is not Phosphorus', (1) still is, most probably, not true. For Nebuchadnezzar quite probably did not grasp precisely the sense which I associate with this sentence. On a more pedestrian level, if your sense for 'Aristotle' has a different conceptual content than mine, as it did for the two men in Frege's example, I will most likely not speak truly, if I try to ascribe to you a belief about Aristotle.

2.3

Perhaps the Fregean could say that proper names are special, in that they do something like 'always take wide scope' in attitude contexts. On this proposal, ascription (1) would be equivalent to something like

> (2) $(\exists x)(\exists y)(C(x, \text{Hesperus}) \,\&\, C(y, \text{Phosphorus}) \,\&\,$ Nebuchadnezzar believed that ^{s}x is not y^s)

where 'C(x, y)' names the relation a sense bears to what it presents, and the "s" 's are 'sense quotes'.

There are certain advantages to this treatment of proper names in attitude ascriptions. For example, given a standard Fregean treatment of *de re* attitude ascriptions—ascriptions of the form suggested by

> (3) a believes, with respect to b, that she is F

—the wide scope treatment of names facilitates a Fregean explanation of the validity of the inference from something of the form of

(4) a believes that b is F

to (3), when b is a proper name. By 'a standard Fregean account of *de re* ascriptions', I intend those which regiment sentences of the form suggested by (3) by ones of the form suggested by

(5) $(\exists x)(P(x, b)$ & (a believes $^s x$ is F^s)

where 'P(x, y)' indicates a relation which entails that named by 'C(x, y)', but is perhaps more restrictive. Call such a relation 'presentation'. If the Fregean feels that the sense of a name always presents its bearer, he may then give names a wide scope treatment in attitude ascriptions, regimenting sentences whose form is suggested by

(6) a believes that $A(t_1, \ldots, t_n)$

(where the t_i's are precisely the proper names in the t-clause) by sentences whose form is suggested by

(7) $(\exists x_1) \ldots (\exists x_n)\{P(x_1, t_1)$ & $\ldots$ & $P(x_n, t_n)$ & a believes $^s A(x_1, \ldots, x_n)^s\}$.

This automatically validates inferences such as that from (4) to (3).

My primary objection to this is that it robs Fregeanism of much of its interest, as a doctrine about the semantics of English. First of all, there is a clear sense in which this 'Fregean solution' is not really Fregean. For it gives up the idea that the t-clauses of most attitude ascriptions *refer* to senses. To construe (1) as (2) is to give up the idea that there is some sense, p, such that 'that Hesperus is not Phosphorus', as it occurs in (1), refers to p.

Secondly, on this account of attitude ascriptions, most substitution of co-referential proper names in attitude ascriptions preserves truth. This wipes out what was supposed to be one of the primary virtues of Fregeanism over rival accounts, which assign simpler, more grossly individuated semantic values to expressions. Finally, the Fregean can hardly stop with the exportation of names. Presumably, much the same treatment must be extended to predicate expressions, since the senses of these will vary intersubjectively. We end up exporting pretty much all of the nonlogical vocabulary in the t-clauses of attitude ascriptions. From the perspective of the truth conditions the theory ascribes to sentences, this makes Fregeanism appear to be little more than a baroque version of a Russellian treatment of attitude ascriptions.[4]

---

[4] I do not mean to altogether dismiss this sort of view; in fact, the approach suggested in the text is close to the view which I suggested in Richard (1987) and Richard (1983). The trouble with such views, to repeat what is said in the text, is that they seem hardly Fregean.

3. An Obvious Solution Reconsidered

3.1

Perhaps we were too hasty in rejecting solution 2.1. We might think that a sentence such as "Hesperus rises in the morning" has associated with it some function from individuals to senses. The function takes me to my sense for the sentence, Willy Brandt to his sense for some German equivalent thereof, Nebuchadnezzar to the sense of some Babylonian equivalent. Of course, we need to be told just how this function operates, when there are multiple 'equivalents' of a sentence for a particular individual. And there are problems about what such a function would do with an individual who had beliefs that would naturally be ascribed with a sentence, no equivalent of which he understands. Even waiving such problems, I do not think that this is a satisfactory solution. I will develop two objections to this sort of view.

3.2

Let us consider certain turgid details; in particular, how the Fregean will treat multiple embeddings such as

(8) Janie Marr believes that Barbara believes that Anne is married.

(I will often abbreviate this sentence as the extended-first-orderese 'jBbBMa'. I will analogously abbreviate its constituent expressions as 'j', 'bBMa', and so on. Each 'B' should be understood as having absorbed a term-forming 'that'.) One wants to know how many levels of sense the Fregean will postulate on this approach, how indirect senses (if postulated) are related to other senses, and exactly what the sense and reference of embedded expressions in sentences such as (8) will turn out to be.

Let us begin with the most straightforward story about the reference of multiple embeddings No matter how many verbs of propositional attitude intervene between e and e' in an ascription of the form

e V's that . . . e' . . .

(V a verb of propositional attitude), e' refers, therein, to its sense for the referent of e. (Of course, talk about the sense of e' for the referent of e must be just a *façon de parler*, given the Nebuchadnezzar objection in section 2.1. Such talk is harmless enough, provided we realize that it must eventually be replaced with a definition of the function which maps an embedded sentence to its embedded referent.)

The problem with this suggestion is as follows. Just as sense can vary intersubjectively, so, it would seem, one person may associate different senses with two expressions while another associates the same sense with those expressions. For example, Barbara might associate different senses with 'Hesperus is Hesperus' and 'Hesperus is Phosphorus', while Anne associates the same sense with both sentences. Let us suppose that this is so, and that Anne's sense for both sentences is the same as the sense Barbara associates with 'Hesperus is Hesperus'.

Suppose that Barbara can say truly

> (9) I believe that Hesperus is Hesperus; I don't believe that Hesperus is Phosphorus.

Intuitively, Anne ought to be able to report this accurately by saying

> (10) Barbara believes that Hesperus is Hesperus; Barbara doesn't believe that Hesperus is Phosphorus.

And on the account under consideration, she can say this. For in (10), the embedded sentences refer to Barbara's, not Anne's senses for those sentences.

So far, all is well. But it seems that not only can Anne truly say that Barbara believes that Hesperus is Hesperus, she could come to know that Barbara believes this. And if she can know this, she can say that she knows it, in a straightforward way, by saying

> (11) I know that Barbara believes that Hesperus is Hesperus.

And it is here that the problem arises. For 'Hesperus is Hesperus' in (11), on the proposal we are considering, refers to Anne's sense for this sentence. So its reference in (11) is the same as the reference of 'Hesperus is Phosphorus' in a use of

> (12) I know that Barbara believes that Hesperus is Phosphorus.

by Anne. So, by the principle that a difference in truth value requires a difference in reference, Anne's use of (12) must be true, too. But if Anne's uses of (10) and (12) would be true, so would her use of

> (13) Barbara doesn't believe that Hesperus is Phosphorus, but I know that Barbara believes that Hesperus is Phosphorus.

I take it that this final result is clearly unacceptable. Since the assumptions powering this argument seem quite reasonable, not to mention being Fregean in spirit, I think it best that we pursue other ways of working out the details of this approach.

On the last strategy, a t-clause changed its reference with each new embedding. Let us consider a strategy on which multiple embedding does not effect the reference of a t-clause or its constituents. One might say that an embedded sentence always refers to the sense it has for the subject of the 'closest' verb of propositional attitude. On this strategy, 'Anne' in

> (14) Janie Marr believes that Barbara believes that Anne is married.

would refer to its sense for Barbara, not for Janie Marr.

Let us develop this strategy.[5] A particularly simple version of the strategy postulates two levels of sense for each expression e: (i) customary senses (pluralized, since sense varies intersubjectively); (ii) for each person u, a sense which presents

---

[5] This strategy is suggested in Parsons (1981). None of what follows should be taken to be critical of Parsons, who is concerned with problems quite different from those being considered here.

the customary sense of e for u. I'll suppose that this latter sense is expressed by e whenever e refers to the customary sense of e for u. The straightforward justification of this last assumption is by appeal to the Fregean principle that sense determines reference.

Let's suppose that associated with each (atomic) expression is a function from individuals to pairs of senses; the function associated with e is named by bracketing e. [Hesperus] is a function which, applied to u, yields a pair whose first member is the sense which u associates with 'Hesperus' (or some other sense, in case u does not use 'Hesperus'); the second member of the pair is a sense which presents the first member. We write such things as '$[\text{Verdi}]^1_{Ed}$' for the first value of $[\text{Verdi}]$ applied to Ed, and '$[\text{Rossini}]^2_{Lucia}$' for the second value of $[\text{Rossini}]$ applied to Lucia.

Define the head of an occurrence o of an expression in a sentence as the term which is the subject of the verb of propositional attitude which immediately dominates o. (Thus, not all occurrences have heads.) In (14), for example, the head of 'b' is 'j', the head of 'Ma' is 'b', and 'j' has no head. According to the approach we are sketching, an embedded occurrence o of an expression e refers to $[e]^1_u$ and expresses $[e]^2_U$, where u is the referent of o's head.[6] Complex expressions will refer to (express) the results of applying their referents (senses expressed) to one another. We assume that it is obvious how such modes of composition can be read off of the syntax of the embedded sentence. Thus, a use of

(15) Barbara believes that Anne is married.

by Janie Marr would have as reference

(16) $\text{Belief}(b, [M]^1_b([a]^1_b))$

and would express

(17) $[B]^1_j([b]^1_j, [M]^2_b([a]^2_b))$

(Here it is assumed that an unembedded use of an expression e by u expresses $[e]^1_u$.) A use of (14) by Ralston would refer to

(18) $\text{Belief}(j, [B]^1_j([b]^1_j, [M]^1_b([a]^1_b)))$

---

[6] Actually, this will not quite work as it stands. As the reader can work out, this requires 'Robbie is sleeping', in the true ascription 'Virginia believes that Santa knows that Robbie is sleeping', to refer to Santa's sense for 'Robbie is sleeping'. Since this exists no more than does Santa, the ascription to Virginia would be false because of reference failure.

This can be remedied by making the associated functions operate on the senses, instead of the references, of the heads. (Somewhat *ad hoc* strictures are then required on the functions to insure the validity of the inference pattern

> a believes that S
> a = b
> ---
> Hence, b believes that S.)

The resulting treatment is more complicated, but no more satisfactory, than the one discussed in the text.

while it would express

(19) $[B]^1_{\text{Ralston}}([j]^1_{\text{Ralston}}, [B]^2_j([b]^2_j, [M]^2_b([a]^2_b)))$

This treatment of attitude ascriptions has unacceptable results. (14), presumably, ascribes to Janie Marr the thought she expresses when she utters (15). Thus the sense of her utterance of (15)—(17), that is—in the reference of (15), as it occurs in (14). That is, (17) is identical with

(20) $[B]^1_j([b]^1_j, [M]^1_b([a]^1_b))$

Thus, when she thought (17), Janie Marr thought a thought among whose constituents were Barbara's ways of thinking of marriage and of Anne. But this seems odd, since there is no reason to think that Janie Marr is able to grasp Barbara's sense for 'Anne'. Of course, Janie Marr may be able to refer to this sense. In fact, she did refer to it, when she uttered sentence (15). But referring to a sense is not using it in a thought. The identity of (17) and (20) seems to imply that Janie Marr is able to think of Anne in whatever way Barbara does. But surely this need not be true, in order that the sentences (14) and (15) be true.

The fact that (17) is identical with (20) thus runs afoul of a sort of constituency principle If sense *s* is a constituent of thought *p*, then anyone who thinks *p* is able to grasp *s*. One would have thought that the Fregean would subscribe to such a principle.

Perhaps the Fregean will simply disown the principle. He may still, of course, endorse a watered down version of the principle, one which might be worded: If *x* has a thought *p*, then there is some complete set *T* of constituents for *p* such that *x* is able to grasp each member of *T*.[7]

But denying the constituency principle puts the Fregean account of *de re* belief ascriptions into jeopardy. The problem is this. According to the Fregean, to have a *de re* belief about *u* that it's so and so, it is necessary and sufficient to believe a thought which has, as a constituent, a sense which presents *u*. (Recall the discussion in section 2.3.) This is all well and good, provided that one can have such a belief only by grasping a sense which presents *u*—only, to put it intuitively, by thinking about *u*. The constituency principle makes it reasonable to think that this is so. Once it is abandoned, we run the following sort of risk: For some *s*, *s'*, *u*, *v*, and *p*, *s* presents *u*; *s'* applied to *s* yields *p*; *v* believes *p*; there is no sense which presents *u* which *u* grasps. In this case, *v*, according to the Fregean, has a *de re* belief about *u*, even though, in a quite straightforward sense, he is unable to think about him!

---

[7] I say that in a sense *s* is a constituent of a sense *s'* iff *s* is *s'* or there is a collection *T* of senses such that (i) by applying members of *T* to one another, it is possible to generate *s'*; (ii) no proper subset of *T* generates *s'*, and; (iii) *s* is in *T*. (I assume that senses, when they can be combined at all to yield another sense, combine as function and argument. Below, when I speak of a complete set of constituents for a thought *s'*, I mean a set *T* which satisfies conditions (i) through (iii).)

Indeed, we run into something like this problem in the case under consideration. Suppose that Janie Marr does not grasp Barbara's sense of Anne, but does think that Barbara thinks that Anne is married. We may, for example, suppose that Barbara thinks of Anne as the mother of Emily—her senses for 'Anne' and 'the mother of Emily' are in fact identical; Janie Marr, on the other hand, has never even heard of Emily. In this case, it seems clear that neither

(14*) Janie Marr believes that Barbara believes that the mother of Emily is married.

nor

(14**) Janie Marr believes, with respect to Emily, that Barbara believes that her mother is married.

is true. But the truth of (14), along with the fact that

$$[a]^1_b = [g]^1_b([e]^1_b)$$

(here, 'g' is proxy for 'mother of'; 'e' for 'Emily') guarantees the truth of (14*) and (14**), on the current approach. For the reference side of (14*) would be

(18) Belief(j, $[B]^1_j([b]^1_j, [M]^1_b([a]^1_b))$)

with the right side of the above identity substituted for the left. In the case in question, (18) is the true, since it is the reference of the true

(14) Janie Marr believes that Barbara believes that Anne is married.

Using a Fregean account of *de re* attitude ascriptions, (14**) would be regimented as

($\exists s$) {s presents Emily & Belief(j, $[B]^1_j([b]^1_j, [M]^1_b([g]^1_b(s))$)}

which must name the true, if (18) and the identity above do.

This approach to attitude ascriptions will not do. It violates the constituency principle, which, as I just argued, a Fregean ought not to violate. Furthermore it (speaking loosely) allows us to substitute one expression for another *salva veritate*, whenever the expressions have the same customary sense for their head. It is this fact that makes (14) and (14*) agree in truth value, given only that 'Anne' and 'the mother of Emily' have the same sense for Barbara. It should be clear that this is not sufficient for substitutivity. The fact that the expressions have the same sense for Barbara seems irrelevant to the question of whether (14) and (14*) must agree in truth value.

There is one more way to treat multiple embeddings Let them refer to a mode of presentation of what they refer to when singly embedded. Using the notation developed above, the proposal is that a single embedding of e refers to $[e]^1_u$, while in a multiple embedding it refers to $[e]^2_u$ where u is the referent of its head. (This would seem, incidentally, to force the Fregean to admit at least a third level of sense.[8]) On this proposal, the reference side of (14) cashes out to

(21) Belief (j, $[B]^1_j([b]^1_j, [M]^2_b([a]^2_b)))$.

This proposal, however, makes our practices of *de re* belief ascription somewhat strange. For just as we are inclined to infer 'Anne is such that Barbara believes her to be married' from (15), so we are inclined to infer

(22) Anne is such that Janie Marr believes that Barbara believes that she is married

from (14), thereby ascribing a belief *de re* about Anne to Janie Marr. Given the proposal concerning multiple embeddings now under consideration, and the Fregean treatment of *de re* ascriptions, we would regiment (22) as

(23) $(\exists x) \{P(x, a)$ & Belief$(j, [B]^1_j([b]^1_j, [M]^2_b(x)))\}$.

But this doesn't even follow from (21). $[a]^2_b$ isn't a mode of presentation of Anne, but of a mode *of* presentation of Anne.

We began this section supposing that some way could found to avoid the obvious objection to the view that a singly embedded sentence referred to its sense for the person to whom an attitude is ascribed. We proceeded to consider accounts, on this view, of the reference of multiply embedded sentences. There seemed to be three possibilities: they referred to their senses for the overall subject of the ascription; they referred to their senses for the referents of their heads; they referred to modes of presentation of their senses for the referents of their heads. In each case, the account we arrived at was unacceptable. Since there seems no other choice for the referent of such sentences, I conclude that the view in question cannot give an acceptable account of multiple embeddings. This seems an adequate reason for rejecting it.

3.3

In developing the above objections, I have tacitly assumed that the reference to a sense made by an embedded expression would be 'more or less direct'. By this, I mean that an expression when embedded would be more or less directly assigned its reference on a Fregean semantics, and would not be treated as a truncation of an elaborate description of a sense.

It might be possible to avoid the above criticisms, if one is willing to treat the constituents of a 'that'-clause, as well as the clause itself, as elaborate descriptions of senses. If 'Anne' in 'Barbara believes that Anne is married' is a truncation of something like "the mode of presentation of Anne which Barbara expresses with 'Anne'," and analogously for the other embedded expressions, the above objections need not go through. (The description must be one which refers to

---

[8] More properly, this forces a third level of sense, given the Fregean principles (A) if two occurrences of expressions have the same senses, then the expressions, on those occurrences, have the same reference; (B) an ascription of attitude is true iff the subject of the ascription has the relevant attitude towards the reference of the ascription's t-clause; along with harmless empirical assumptions.

Anne, and not merely mentions her name, if the problems about *de re* ascriptions are not to arise again.)

Thus, it is important to see that there is a much more serious problem with the proposal we are considering: it makes 'that'-clauses flaccid in an unacceptable way. What a t-clause like 'that Billy is riding a moped' names depends upon its linguistic environment (and not just on such features as the time and location of the speaker, what she is demonstrating, the causal chains between names and individuals, etc.). Such a clause will typically switch reference as it moves from 'Rusty believes that' to 'Emily believes that'; it behaves somewhat like 'his own dog'.

It seems clear that t-clauses in English do not behave in this way. Arguments of the form

> Rusty believes that Billy is riding a moped.
> Emily believes everything which Rusty believes.
> _____
> Hence, Emily believes that Billy is riding a moped.

are obviously valid. They would not be, on the proposal under consideration. It would seem that this proposal is committed to treating the argument as being of the form

> rBa
> $(p)(rBp \rightarrow eBp)$
> _____
> Hence, eBa

But since a is flaccid in the way observed above, this turns out no more valid than the inference: Rusty spit on his own dog; Stevie spit on everything Rusty did; hence, Stevie spit on his own dog.

This objection assumes that the quantifier in the second premiss of the argument is objectual. If the quantifier were substitutional, the argument would be valid, even though the 'that'-clause is flaccid in the way noted.[9] Could a determined Fregean evade this objection, by insisting that quantification over senses is substitutional, not objectual?

It should be observed that there is something disingenuous about such a response. Surely a hallmark of Fregeanism is its commitment to the claim that *there is* (objectual quantifier) something identical with the thought that snow is white, or, at least, that for each person who can think that snow is white, *there is* (objectual) something which is the sense that person thinks, when they think that snow is white. Since the Fregean is thus committed to objectual quantification over senses in any case—just to explain his position—why would he reject the claim that quantification in English over the objects of attitudes is itself objectual?

In any case, I am inclined to think that appeal to substitutional quantification will not do the job here. Consider the sentence

> If there is always someone who is the mayor, then there is someone who is the mayor and is such that it is always true that he is mayor.

_____
[9] I am indebted to Graeme Forbes for pointing this out.

It is natural to suppose that the form of this sentence is indicated by

$$A((\exists x)(x = \text{the mayor}) \rightarrow (\exists x)(x = \text{the mayor} \,\&\, A(x = \text{the mayor}))).$$

Here 'A' is the tense operator 'It is always the case that'.

I take it that the sentence is not a logical truth. Thus, if we were to interpret the existential quantifier here substitutionally, we would have to be careful to specify that its substitution class was limited to terms which are 'temporally rigid'. In particular, we would want to bar the term 'the mayor' from the quantifier's substitution class. Otherwise, we would make the sentence valid.[10]

The general point is that in treating a natural language quantifier substitutionally, one must be quite careful about specifying its substitution class, if one is to get truth conditions and entailment relations right. Not only must one generally introduce new expressions to form the substitution class (in order to get the quantifier to 'range' over all the things intuitively in the quantifier's 'domain'), but one must also carefully circumscribe the substitution class, to ensure that the members of the substitution class are appropriately rigid with respect to the class of operators with which the quantifier can interact.

It would seem that most 'that'-clauses of English are temporally flaccid, in the sense that they express different propositions on different occasions of utterance. (The first Fregean was quite explicit on this.[11]) Because of this, a substitutional interpretation of propositional quantification does not square well with the seeming invalidity of arguments such as

> Emily believed that Billy was riding a moped.
> Emily still believes all she once did.
> _____
> Hence, Emily believes that Billy is riding a moped.

I assume that the form of this argument is given by

> $P\{eB((\exists x)(Mx \,\&\, Rbx))\}$
> $(p)(P(eBp) \rightarrow eBp)$
> _____
> Hence, $eB((\exists x)(Mx \,\&\, Rbx))$

where the 'P' is the past tense operator, and '$(\exists x)(Mx \,\&\, Rbx)$' is a representation of 'Billy is riding a moped'. *No matter what* semantics we ascribe to the past tense operator, this comes out valid on a substitutional interpretation of the universal quantifier, as long as '$(\exists x)(Mx \,\&\, Rbx)$' is in the substitution class of the quantifier. So, since the argument in question is invalid, we must exclude the 'that'-clause in question from the quantifier's substitution class.

But once this clause is excluded from the substitution class, we no longer have an explanation of why the original problem argument is valid. For the

---

[10] I assume, of course, that the eternal truth of '$(\exists x)(x = \text{the mayor})$' implies the eternal truth of 'the mayor = the mayor'.

[11] See, for example, Frege's discussion of fruit trees in Frege (1977).

claim that the propositional quantifier was substitutional explained the validity of the argument only on the assumption that the t-clause was a part of its substitution class.

Of course, this also suggests that practically no English t-clause will be a member of the substitution class of the propositional quantifier. One wonders what, then, would be the quantifier's substitution class. I conclude that we ought not take this quantifier to be substitutional. The objection stands.

4.   Another Obvious Solution Reconsidered

4.1

Perhaps the Fregean should jettison the idea that a belief ascription ascribes Belief in what its t-clause names. Instead, the Fregean might assign another relation to the verb 'believes', the relative product of some relation R and Belief. If he did this, and was clever in selecting R, he might be able to revive the solution of section 2.2, allowing t-clauses to name the sense their user associates with them. An ascription of the form *a believes that S*, as used by an individual u, would be true iff (what) a (names) Believes a thought which bears R to the thought which u expresses with S.

I cannot pretend to consider every plausible candidate for R. I will instead discuss what seem the most likely candidates, relations of similarity.[12] Once again, I attempt to keep the argument as general possible My goal is to show that serious problems arise, no matter how we construe similarity of sense.

---

[12] Forbes, in Forbes (unpublished), develops this approach. All of the criticisms developed here seem applicable to his view. Forbes has tried to try to avoid counterintuitive consequences, like that involving the echo principle, by postulating an ambiguity in belief ascriptions involving names, between a "wide scope" reading such as that discussed in section 2, and the reading which is the subject of this section.

The use of the postulation to defend this solution will be convincing only if it is accompanied by an account which allows us to tell which of the readings of an ambiguous expression a speaker intends, when he uses such an expression. (Otherwise, the claim that, in such and such a case, a speaker is using the wide scope reading, will seem pretty *ad hoc*.) But such an account can't appeal to intentions (beliefs, etc.) of the speaker, to use (about using, etc.) one sense instead of the other—it seems that only very sophisticated speakers have anything resembling beliefs or intentions which would thus separate *de dicto* from *de re* readings.

But then off what could such an account work? Perhaps one could make appeal to (implicit?) beliefs, about whether the person to whom we ascribe a belief associates the same sense with their terms as we do—if we believe she does, we are using the *de dicto* sense of an ascription involving those terms; otherwise, we are using the *de re* sense.

I don't believe that this will work. I don't have any idea what sense Nebuchadnezzar associated with (the Babylonian version of) 'Hesperus' and 'Phosphorus', but I'm sure it's not the one I associate with the terms. This means that I should be using a wide scope reading when I say 'Nebuchadnezzar believed that Hesperus was Phosphorus'. But on a wide scope reading, this is true, since there are senses s and s' which presented Hesperus, etc. Intuitively, though, the ascription is false.

Similarity accounts are not liable to the objection raised at the end of the last section. Such accounts will ascribe to the problem argument of the last section the form ascribed to it there:

$$rBa$$
$$\frac{(p)(rBp \rightarrow eBp)}{\text{Hence, } eBa}$$

But now, as long as we evaluate premises and conclusion relative to the same context, the term 'a' cannot switch reference from premiss to conclusion. So, there's no context, relative to which all of the premises of the argument are true, although the conclusion isn't. The argument is valid.

I will present four objections to this sort of account.

4.2

Similarity proposals would appear to face a dilemma. Let us suppose that the sense of a term presents an individual; that of a predicate, a property. Then we can define a notion of referential similarity for thought. Speaking very crudely 'atomic thoughts' are referentially similar if their constituent senses present the same things (taken in the appropriate order, of course); conjunctive thoughts are referentially similar if the thoughts of which they are conjunctions are referentially similar; and so on.[13] For example, if Ann's senses for 'Twain' and 'Clemens' are the same, she can truly say, 'Whoever believes that Twain is Twain, believes that Twain is Clemens'. And if Barbara's sense for 'Twain' is Ann's, she can truly say 'Barbara believes that Twain is Twain'.

Call the kind of similarity appealed to in the truth definition of belief ascriptions *overall* similarity. Either referential similarity of thoughts is sufficient for overall similarity or it isn't. If it is, then a similarity proposal reduces to the obvious solution of section 2.3, which makes the notion of sense semantically otiose. But if it's not, then we would seem to lose a principle which we might call the 'echo principle': If you and I both use a sentence S in such a way that its constituents, when we use it, refer to the same things, then, if you can express a belief using S, I can use S to ascribe that belief to you.[14] It would seem to be the truth of such a principle which justifies my saying 'Ralston thinks Aunty Baba is waddling', having heard Ralston say 'Aunty Baba is waddling',

---

[13] It would be difficult to give a full-scale definition of such a notion, without introducing a notion like that of logical complexity for thoughts. The notion suggested in the text should be understood in such a way that to say that a sense s presents x is to say something stronger than that it simply is a concept of x. This makes thoughts like those expressed by me with 'Twain is dead' and 'Clemens is dead' referentially similar, although neither would be referentially similar to that I express with 'The author of *Huck Finn* is dead'.

[14] This is reminiscent of Kripke's disquotational principle. But it is considerably weaker, since it is built into the antecedent of this principle that your assent to S expresses belief, while the disquotational principle allows us to infer (and ascribe) your belief on the basis of your assent.

and thinking him sincere; it underlies the feeling that Emily's part in the dialogue

> Rusty: Billy is quivering.
>
> Emily: If Rusty just said something that he believes, then he believes that Billy is quivering.

couldn't be false. If referential similarity doesn't suffice for overall similarity, then presumably there will be cases of exchanges like the above in which Rusty's thought is not overall similar to the one Emily expresses with 'Billy is quivering', and so Emily is, on a similarity account, wrong.

Indeed, natural accounts of the nature of senses and of overall similarity suggest that it would be quite common for referentially similar thoughts to fail to be similar overall, even referentially similar thoughts expressed by different uses of (orthographically) the same sentence. Suppose that a sense is composed of some conceptual content (which might be expressible by means of a definite or indefinite description) along with a causal 'tail' which determines reference. It would be natural to suppose that similarity was to be determined by the conceptual part of a sense (with the proviso that senses whose tails led to different individuals aren't similar).[15] But then senses of terms, one thinks, would often fail to be similar overall: to think of Aristotle as the most famous student of Plato would not be overall similar to thinking of him as the principal teacher of Alexander; to think of Cicero as some Latin poet would not be similar to thinking of him as some famous speaker, maybe an Italian.[16]

4.3

A related problem for similarity proposals arises once it is acknowledged that one person might associate the same sense with distinct expressions, while others might associate referentially similar but distinct senses with the expressions. Schematically: Suppose that A and B use t and t' as names for u; that A associates s with both t and t', while B associates s with t, s' with t', for distinct s and s'. In this case, the sense which A associates with sentences of the form

---

[15] The reader will notice that I have shifted from talk of the similarity of thoughts to the similarity of senses of terms. This is mostly for the sake of expository convenience. I do assume that a similarity account of the semantics of belief ascriptions would countenance talk of similarity of the senses of terms, and that such similarity would be relevant to the similarity of thoughts of which the term senses were constituents.

    I have been guided here by the intuition that if a rational person could associate the conceptual part of two senses with two different terms and think it not only false but unlikely that the identity formed with the two terms was true, then the senses are not overall similar.

[16] An advantage of taking senses in the way I have suggested, of course, is that it allows the conceptual part of senses to be filled with bad information—bad in that it isn't accurate information about the referent of the term. It seems to me a that a serious Fregean must allow such senses, in the face of criticisms of the notion of sense such as Kripke's. At least, he must do this, if he is to retain even a ghost of the idea, that the sense of an expression is something which the speaker grasps.

$F(t, t')$ will be identical with the sense which B associates with the corresponding sentence of the form $F(t, t)$. (I assume, of course, that the senses each
associate with the predicate are the same.) Assuming that identity suffices for
overall similarity, this leads to counterintuitive consequences. For example, we
may be forced to say that whoever believes that the United Nations was
founded when the United Nations was founded, believes that the United
Nations was founded when the U.N. was founded. Likewise, we would have to
say that whoever thinks that the U.N. is located in New York believes that the
United Nations is located in New York.

4.4

Consider a monolingual French speaker, F, and a monolingual English speaker, E,
and their respective senses, for 'London' and 'Londres'. It would be grotesque to
suppose that our sense for 'London' was not overall similar to both of these senses.
For surely we can successfully ascribe to F and E their mundane beliefs about
London's pulchritude, unemployment rate, and so on, using 'London'. If E has a
belief he can express with 'London is not pretty', we can ascribe it to him with that
sentence; if F has a belief he can express with 'Londres est jolie', we can ascribe it
to her with 'London is pretty'.

The Fregean may be tempted here by the grotesque. He may insist that the
thought that F expresses with 'Londres est jolie' may be stunningly different from
our own. She may, for example, think that London is a tiny town, where no one
speaks English, etc. Do we really want to say, the Fregean may ask, that F thinks
what we do, when we think that London is pretty? If not, the Fregean presses,
then surely there is merit to the claim that we cannot truly say that F thinks that
London is pretty.

Three points should be made here. First of all, in such a case, we all would
without hesitation say 'F believes that London is pretty'. We might allow that
F thinks of London somewhat differently than we do. But we do not infer from
that that F fails to think that London is pretty. Secondly, it is worth pointing
out that such a case is *naturally* described as one in which F thinks that
London is tiny, that London has few English speakers, etc. We feel no embarrassment over this; it would never occur to a normal speaker to deny the truth
of such a claim. The position we are discussing would deny the truth of such
claims. Finally, the strategy seems particularly unacceptable, in the case of
ascriptions of assertion, which, the Fregean would say, are ascriptions of relations to senses. It is difficult to see any merit at all in a view which insists that,
because F has a different conception of London than do we, we are unable to
truthfully say that F said that London was not pretty, when F assertively utters
'Londres n'est pas jolie'.

That we can *obviously* ascribe beliefs to the monolingual F with 'London' in
this way seems to constitute compelling evidence against the account we are considering. At least it does, in the company of the reasonable principle that if a
rather large collection of sentences are obviously true, a semantic theory should

not make their truth at best unobvious. For it is not obvious that others have senses of London and of other objects which are overall similar to our own. Indeed, on reflection, it seems rather obvious that they do not.

Thus far, my remarks suggest an epicycle on the objection I gave above which involved the echo principle. However, these observations also form the basis for a somewhat different objection. Return to the monolingual *E* and *F*, and their respective senses for 'London is not pretty' and 'Londres est jolie'. It would seem that, in general, no irrationality attaches to a system of beliefs which includes a pair of beliefs which would be expressed by sentences of the forms of *t is not pretty* and *t' is pretty*, where *t* and *t'* express, respectively, *E*'s sense for 'London' and *F*'s sense for 'Londres'. This is part of the lesson of Kripke's story of Pierre. Let *H* be a person with such beliefs. These two beliefs of *H*'s are identical, respectively, with beliefs we have already seen to be overall similar to those we would ascribe to *E* with 'London is not pretty' and to *F* with 'London is pretty'. So the ascriptions 'H believes that London is pretty' and 'H believes that London is not pretty' will both be true, on a similarity account. Indeed, if overall similarity 'projects up' conjunction (so if *a* is overall similar to *a'*, *b* to *b'*, then the conjunction of *a* and *b* is overall similar to that of *a'* and *b'*), the ascription 'H believes that London is not pretty and London is pretty' will be true.

If you think that Kripke has presented a genuine problem about belief, and that the ascription of contradictory beliefs to Pierre is clearly wrong, then this alone should dissuade you from similarity accounts. Even if you do not think this, this result should give you some pause.

If a similarity account is to be in accord with our general practices of ascribing beliefs, it will have to make similarity judgments like that concerning the monolinguals *E* and *F*. There we had a pair of beliefs which it would be rational to hold simultaneously, which were respectively judged overall similar with a thought and its negation. This means that in a goodly number of hard cases, a similarity account will be no more responsive to our intuitions than will be accounts which eschew senses for 'simpler' semantic values: just like the advocates of 'direct reference', the Fregean will wind up committed to ascribing contradictory beliefs, when the sentences the believer assents to are perfectly consistent. It is thus not at all clear, that the Fregean will be able to give an account of the truth conditions of attitude ascriptions, which is substantially more in accord with our intuitions than that given by advocates of direct reference and other theories with relatively simple semantic values. Once more, the notion of sense begins to appear, from a semantic perspective, otiose.

4.5

It is perhaps worth raising a last problem about the similarity relation. Almost no acceptable candidate for the similarity relation will be transitive. This, along with plausible demands that similarity 'project' across sentential connectives, causes trouble: in certain cases, we will be unable to say of a person, all of whose beliefs are true, that all of his beliefs are true.

To see this, suppose that similarity breaks down, among *a*, *b*, and *c*, with respect to a sentence *S*. That is, although *a* and *b* have overall similar senses for the sentence, as do *b* and *c*, *a*'s sense for *S* is not overall similar to *c*'s. This means, assuming that *a* and *b* express beliefs with *S*, that *b* can truly say 'a believes that S'; *c* can truly say 'b believes that S', but *c* cannot truly say 'a believes that S'.

What should we say in such a case about the senses which *b* and *c* associate with 'a believes that S'—are these senses overall similar or not? Consistent with everything we have said so far is the supposition that *b* and *c* have the same sense for 'a' and 'believes'. And the breakdown in transitivity, in moving from *a* to *c*, should not prevent *b* and *c*'s senses for *S* from being as similar as you like, short of identity.

If similarity projects across 'believes', *b* and *c*'s senses for *S* ought to be similar. And on most natural construals of the notion of similarity, the two thoughts would appear to be very similar indeed. Speaking somewhat roughly, it turns out that component by component, the thoughts are either identical or pretty much as close to identity as you like.

But if they are overall similar, odd things happen. Suppose that *b* can express a belief with *S*. Suppose, that this belief, along with all the rest of his beliefs, is true. It then turns out that *c* can not say that all of *b*'s beliefs are true. For on the similarity account, the argument

> b believes that a believes that S.
> Everything that b believes is true.
> Hence, a believes that S.

is valid.[17] If the senses of *S* are overall similar for *b* and *c*, and *c* can say that everything *b* believes is true, he will have to be able to use truly the conclusion of the argument. *Ex hypothesi*, he cannot.

5. CONCLUSION

I have argued that the Fregean is unable to supply an adequate answer to the question, What does a 'that'-clause in an attitude ascription name?, once he takes his own view, that senses vary intersubjectively, seriously. From a semantic perspective the notion of sense doesn't seem able to do very much work.[18]

---

[17] I assume that the form of the argument is

> bBp
> $$\underline{(x)(bBx \rightarrow Tx)}$$
> Hence, Tp

I further assume that, provided that *S* expresses a thought, a use of *S* is true iff a use of the sentence *It is true that S* is itself true.

[18] I am not arguing that the Fregean's notion of sense is completely otiose. It might be that such a notion is of use in some theory other than a theory whose business is to give the truth

Admittedly, I have offered no proof that only the answers I've considered to our question about t-clauses are open to the Fregean. Perhaps some ingenious Fregean can provide a more adequate answer than any considered here. Until then, I suggest, we try to do without the appeal to Fregean senses, in analyzing the semantics of attitude ascriptions in natural language.[19]

Tufts University

BIBLIOGRAPHY

Forbes, Graeme (1987), "Indexicals and Intensionality: A Fregean Perspective," *The Philosophical Review* **XCVI** (January) 3–31.

Forbes, Graeme (unpublished), "Indirect Contexts in Unideal Languages."

Frege, Gottlob (1952), "On Sense and Reference," reprinted in P. Geach and M. Black, eds., *Translations from the Philosophical Writings of Gottlob Frege* (Oxford: Basil Blackwell).

Frege, Gottlob (1977), "The Thought," in *Logical Investigations* (New Haven, CT: Yale University Press).

Kripke, Saul (1979), "A Puzzle about Belief," in A. Margalit, ed., *Meaning and Use* (Dordrecht: D. Reidel Pub. Co.).

Parsons, Terence (1981), "Frege's Hierarchies of Indirect Senses and the Paradox of Analysis," in P. French *et al.*, eds., *Midwest Studies in Philosophy* **VI** (Minneapolis: University of Minnesota Press).

Richard, Mark (1983), "Direct Reference and Ascriptions of Belief," *Journal of Philosophical Logic* **12** 425–452.

Richard, Mark (1987), "Quantification and Leibniz' Law," *Philosophical Review* **XCVI** (October) 555–578.

---

conditions of attitude ascriptions and other sentences of natural languages. The notion of sense might, for example, be of use in theories in philosophy of psychology, or even a psychological theory.

Since it seems to me that there is some confusion among philosophers on this issue, let me make this point in another way. Suppose, for the sake of argument, that 'believes' in English belief ascriptions expresses a relation. The argument of this paper is, in effect, that there is no very good reason to think that the range of this relation must consist of Fregean senses; a range of things much more "Russellian", one suspects, might turn out to be better choices.

I do not say that it follows from this, that there are no such things as Fregean senses. Of course, no such thing follows. Consistent with everything in this paper is the claim that underlying (in some important sense of 'underlying') the relation named by 'believes' is a relation to Fregean senses. It might even be that only by studying this relation will we be able to explain puzzles about the relation named by 'believes'. (I don't myself assert that this is so.)

It seems to me that only confusion can result, if we do not carefully keep separate questions about the semantics of propositional attitude verbs and questions about the nature of the relations which may underlie (in an important if obscure sense of 'underlie') whatever relations such verbs name.

[19] I am indebted to Nathan Salmon for comments; to Graeme Forbes for comments, discussions, correspondence, and showing me drafts of unpublished work. Forbes remains unconvinced. This essay is dedicated to Ed Gettier.

A MILLIAN HEIR REJECTS THE WAGES OF SINN

Nathan Salmon[1]

It is argued, in sharp contrast to established opinion, that the linguistic evidence arising out of propositional-attitude attributions strongly supports Millianism (the doctrine that the entire contribution to the proposition content of a sentence made by a proper name is simply the name's referent) without providing the slightest counter-evidence. This claim is supported through a semantic analysis of such *de re* attributions as 'Jones believes of Venus that it is a star'. The apparent failure of substitutivity of co-referential names in propositional-attitude attributions is shown to be evidentially irrelevant through consideration of analogous phenomena involving straightforward synonyms.

I

In *Frege's Puzzle* [157] I defended a Millian theory of the information contents of sentences involving proper names or other simple (noncompound) singular terms. The central thesis is that ordinary proper names, demonstratives, other single-word indexicals or pronouns (such as 'he'), and other simple singular terms are, in a given possible context of use, Russellian "genuine names in the strict logical sense."[2] Put more fully, I maintain the following anti-Fregean doctrine: that the contribution made by an ordinary proper name or other simple singular term to securing the information content of, or the proposition expressed by, declarative sentences (with respect to a given possible context of use) in which the term occurs (outside of the scope of nonextensional operators, such as quotation marks) is just the referent of the term, or the bearer of the name (with respect to that context of use). In the terminology of *Frege's Puzzle* [157], I maintain that the *information value* of an ordinary proper name is just its referent.[3]

Another thesis that I maintain in *Frege's Puzzle* [157]—and which both Frege and Russell more or less accepted—is that the proposition that is the information content of a declarative sentence (with respect to a given context) is structured in a certain way, and that its structure and constituents mirror, and are in some way

---

[1] The present essay has benefitted from discussions with Mark Richard and Stephen Schiffer, from comments by Graeme Forbes and Timothy Williamson, and from discussions at Birkbeck College, London and Oxford University (where portions of the essay were presented as talks in May 1988), and at the University of Minnesota conference on Propositional Attitudes: The Role of Content in Logic, Language, and Mind, October 1988.

[2] See Russell's "Knowledge by Acquaintance and Knowledge by Description" [152] and "The Philosophy of Logical Atomism" [153].

[3] Throughout this essay, I use the term 'Millian' broadly to cover any theory that includes this doctrine. (The term derives from Kripke, "A Puzzle About Belief" [96].) I do not use the term in the more restricted sense of a theory that includes the (apparently stronger) thesis that the reference of a simple singular term completely exhausts the "linguistic function" of the term (whatever that means). John Stuart Mill himself was almost certainly not a Millian, strictly speaking, but his philosophical view of proper names is very much in the spirit of Millianism—enough so for genuine Millians, such as I, to be counted his heirs.

readable from, the structure and constituents of the sentence containing that proposition.[4] By and large, a simple (noncompound) expression contributes a single entity, taken as a simple (noncomplex) unit, to the information content of a sentence in which the expression occurs, whereas the contribution of a compound expression (such as a phrase or sentential component) is a complex entity composed of the contributions of the simple components.[5] Hence, the contents of beliefs formulatable using ordinary proper names, demonstratives, or other simple singular terms, are on my view so-called *singular propositions* (David Kaplan), i.e., structured propositions directly about some individual, which occur directly as a constituent of the proposition. This thesis (together with certain relatively uncontroversial assumptions) yields the consequence that *de re* belief (or *belief of*) is simply a special case of *de dicto* belief *(belief that)*. To believe *of* an individual *x*, *de re*, that it (he, she) is *F* is to believe *de dicto* the singular proposition about (containing) *x* that it (he, she) is *F*, a proposition that can be expressed using an ordinary proper name for *x*. Similarly for the other propositional attitudes.

Here I will elaborate and expand on certain apects of my earlier defense of Millian theory, and present some new arguments favoring Millianism. It is commonly held that Millianism runs afoul of common-sense belief attributions, and other propositional-attitude attributions, in declaring intuitively false attributions true. Ironically, the main argument I shall propose here essentially relies on common-sense belief attributions and the semantics of the English phrase 'believes

---

[4] This separates the theory of *Frege's Puzzle*, together with the theories of Frege, Russell, and their followers, from contemporary theories that assimilate the information contents of declarative sentences with such things as sets of possible worlds, or sets of situations, or functions from possible worlds to truth values, etc.

Both Frege and Russell would regard declarative sentences as typically reflecting only *part of* the structure of their content, since they would insist that many (perhaps even most) grammatically simple (noncompound) expressions occurring in a sentence may (especially if introduced into the language by abbreviation or by some other type of explicit "definition") contribute complex proposition-constituents that would have been more perspicuously contributed by compound expressions. In short, Frege and Russell regarded the prospect of expressions that are grammatically simple yet semantically compound (at the level of content) as not only possible but ubiquitous. Furthermore, according to Russell's Theory of Descriptions, definite and indefinite descriptions ('the author of *Waverley*', 'an author', etc.) behave grammatically but not semantically (at the level of content) as a self-contained unit, so that a sentence containing such an expression is at best only a rough guide to the structure of its content. Russell extends this idea further to ordinary proper names and most uses of pronouns and demonstratives. This makes the structure of nearly any sentence only a very rough guide to the structure of the sentence's content. The theory advanced in *Frege's Puzzle* sticks much more closely to the grammatical structure of the sentence.

[5] There are well-known exceptions to the general rule—hence the phrase 'by and large'. Certain nonextensional operators, such as quotation marks, create contexts in which compound expressions contribute themselves as units to the information content of sentences in which the expression occurs. Less widely recognized is the fact that even ordinary temporal operators (e.g., 'on April 1, 1986' + past tense) create contexts in which some compound expressions (most notably, open and closed sentences) contribute complexes other than their customary contribution to information content. See "Tense and Singular Propositions" [159]. In addition, compound predicates are treated in *Frege's Puzzle* as contributing attributes, as single units, to the information contents of sentences.

that'. I shall argue, in sharp contrast to established opinion, that the seemingly decisive evidence against Millianism from the realm of propositional-attitude attributions is no evidence at all, and is in fact evidentially irrelevant and immaterial. If I am correct, common-sense propositional-attitude attributions, insofar as they provide any evidence at all, strongly support Millianism without providing even the slightest counter-evidence (in the way that is commonly supposed).

Historically, the most influential objection to the sort of theory I advocate derives from Frege's notorious 'Hesperus'-'Phosphorus' puzzle. The sentence 'Hesperus is Phosphorus' is informative; its information content apparently extends knowledge. The sentence 'Hesperus is Hesperus' is uninformative; its information content is a "given." According to my theory, the information content of 'Hesperus is Hesperus' consists of the planet Venus, taken twice, and the relation of identity (more accurately, the relation of identity-at-t, where t is the time of utterance). Yet the information content of 'Hesperus is Phosphorus', according to this theory, is made of precisely the same components, and apparently in precisely the same way.[6] Assuming a plausible principle of compositionality for propositions, or pieces of information—according to which if p and q are propositions that involve the very same constituents arranged in the very same way, then p and q are the very same proposition—the theory ascribes precisely the same information content to both sentences. This seems to fly in the face of the fact that the two sentences differ dramatically in their informativeness.

This puzzle is easily transformed into an argument against Millian theory, by turning its implicit assumptions into explicit premises. The major premise, which I call *Frege's Law*, connects the concept of informativeness (or that, in Frege's words, of "containing a very valuable extension of our knowledge") with that of cognitive information content (what Frege called *"Erkenntniswerte,"* or "cognitive value"):

> If a declarative sentence S has the very same cognitive information content as a declarative sentence S', then S is informative if and only if S' is.

A second premise is the compositionality principle for propositions. A third critical premise consists in the simple observation that whereas 'Hesperus is Phosphorus' is informative, 'Hesperus is Hesperus' is not. Assuming that the information contents of 'Hesperus is Phosphorus' and 'Hesperus is Hesperus' do not differ at all in structure or mode of composition, it follows that they differ in their constituents.[7] This points to a difference in information value between the names 'Hesperus' and 'Phosphorus'. Since these names are co-referential, it cannot be that the information value of each is simply its referent.

---

[6] It has been argued, however, that the information content of a sentence is a function not only of the information-values and the sequential order of the information-valued parts but also of the very logical structure of the sentence as a whole, and that therefore, since the two identity sentences differ in logical structure, the modes of composition of the information values of their parts are different from one another. See Putnam [131], especially note 8 (also in [160], pp. 157n10). For response, see Church [29]; Scheffler [162] (pp. 42n7); Soames [177]; and Salmon [157] (pp. 164–165n4).

[7] See the previous note. There is considerable conflict, however, between Putnam's stance described therein and his more recent concession in his "Comments" on Kripke's "A Puzzle about Belief" [135] (p. 285), that "certainly Frege's argument shows meaning cannot just *be* reference."

As I pointed out in *Frege's Puzzle* [157] (pp. 73–76), there is a very general difficulty with this Fregean argument: an exactly similar argument can be mounted against any of a wide variety of theories of information value, including Frege's own theory that the information value of a term consists in an associated purely conceptual representation. It happens that I, like Hilary Putnam, do not have the slightest idea what characteristics differentiate beech trees from elm trees, other than the fact that the English term for beeches is 'beech' and the English term for elms is 'elm'.[8] The purely conceptual content that I attach to the term 'beech' is the same that I attach to the term 'elm', and it is a pretty meager one at that. My concept of elm wood is no different from my concept of beech wood. Nevertheless, an utterance of the sentence 'Elm wood is beech wood' would (under the right circumstances) be highly informative for me. In fact, I know that elm wood is not beech wood. At the same time, of course, I know that elm wood is elm wood. By an argument exactly analogous to the one constructed from Frege's puzzle about the informativeness of 'Hesperus is Phosphorus' we should conclude that the information value of 'elm' or 'beech' is not the conceptual content.[9]

---

[8] This particular example is due to Putnam, whose botanical ignorance cannot possibly exceed my own. See "Meaning and Reference" [133] (p. 704).

[9] I had made this same general point earlier in a review of Leonard Linsky's *Names and Descriptions* [154] (p. 451). There, however, I labored under the illusion that the original Fregean argument is sound.

It may be objected that my concept of elm trees includes the concept of being called 'elms' in English, and perhaps even the concept of being a different genus from the things called 'beeches' in English, making the purely conceptual contents different after all. Even setting aside the question of whether such differences can show up in a purely conceptual representation, this objection is mistaken. In the relevant sense of "conceptual content," such concepts as that of being called 'elm' in English are not part of the conceptual content I attach to the term 'elm'. Not everything one believes about elms can be part of the information value of the term 'elm', or of the conceptual representation attached to the term 'elm', as the notion of conceptual representation is intended in Fregean theory. Otherwise, every sentence S that is sincerely uttered by someone and that involves the word 'elm' (not in the scope of quotation marks or other such devices) would be such that the conditional ⌜If there are any elms, then S⌝ is analytically true for the speaker. One could not acquire new beliefs expressed by means of the term 'elm', and hence one could not change one's mind about anything expressed in terms of 'elm' (e.g., that Jones is standing by an elm tree), without literally changing the subject. In particular, there are compelling reasons for denying that any concept like that of being called such-and-such in English can be part of the information value of terms like 'elm' and 'beech'. It is not analytic, for example, that elms are called 'elm' in English. (That 'elm' applies to elms in English is a nontrivial piece of information about English. Things might have been otherwise, and it is not "given" or known *a priori* what the expression 'elm' applies to in English.) Whatever the information value of 'elm' is, there are terms in other languages that have the same information value—e.g., the German words '*Ulme*' and '*Rüster*'. The information value of these German terms does not include any concept of what things of that kind are called in English. A German speaker may know what an elm is—may have a concept of an elm tree—without having the foggiest idea what elms are called in English. Also, for most terms, such as 'tree', 'table', 'anthropologist', 'green', etc., it is distinctly implausible to suppose that the information value of the term includes the concept of being so-called in English. Each is perfectly translatable into any number of languages. The typical German speaker knows what a tree is—has the concept of a tree—even if he or she does not have any opinion as to the English term for a tree. There is no reason why 'elm' should be different from 'tree' in this respect. See Kripke, *Naming and Necessity* [95] (pp. 68–70) and "A Puzzle about Belief" [96] (note 12), and my *Frege's Puzzle* [157] (pp. 163–164n2).

This argument employs the same general strategy, and mostly the very same premises (including Frege's Law and the compositionality principle for propositions), as the original Fregean argument in connection with 'Hesperus' and 'Phosphorus'. This generalized Fregean strategy may be applied against virtually any minimally plausible and substantive theory of information value. In this particular application of the generalized strategy, the relevant informative identity statement is not even true, but that does not matter to the general strategy. The truth of an informative identity statement is required only in the application of the general argument against theories that locate information value, at least in part, in reference. In the general case, only informativeness is required. False identity statements are always informative—so informative, in fact, as to be misinformative. Thus, virtually any substantive theory of information value imaginable reintroduces a variant of Frege's puzzle (or else it is untenable on independent grounds, such as Kripke's modal arguments against orthodox Fregean theory).

The sheer scope of the generalized Fregean strategy—the fact that, if sound, it is applicable to virtually any substantive theory of information value—would seem to indicate that the strategy involves some error. That the generalized strategy does indeed involve some error can be demonstrated through an application of the generalized strategy to a situation involving straightforward (strict) synonyms for which it is uncontroversial that information value is exactly preserved. Suppose that foreign-born Sasha learns the words 'ketchup' and 'catsup' not by being taught that they are perfect synonyms, but by actually consuming the condiment and reading the labels on the bottles. Suppose further that, in Sasha's idiosyncratic experience, people typically have the condiment called 'catsup' with their eggs and hash browns at breakfast, whereas they routinely have the condiment called 'ketchup' with their hamburgers at lunch. This naturally leads Sasha to conclude, erroneously, that ketchup and catsup are different condiments that happen to share a similar taste, color, consistency, and name. He thinks to himself, "Ketchup is a sandwich condiment, but no one in his right mind would eat a sandwich condiment with eggs at breakfast; so catsup is not a sandwich condiment." Whereas the sentence 'Ketchup is ketchup' is uninformative for Sasha, the sentence 'Catsup is ketchup' is every bit as informative as 'Hesperus is Phosphorus'. Applying the generalized Fregean strategy, we would conclude that the terms 'catsup' and 'ketchup' differ in information value for Sasha. But this is clearly wrong. The terms 'ketchup' and 'catsup' are perfect synonyms in English. Some would argue that they are merely two different spellings of the very same English word.[10] Most of us who have learned these words (or these spellings of the single word) probably learned one of them in an ostensive definition of some sort, and the other as a strict synonym (or as an alternative spelling) of the first. Some of us learned 'ketchup' first and 'catsup' second; for others the order was the reverse. Obviously, it does not matter which is learned first and which second. Either word (spelling) may be learned by ostensive definition. If either may be learned by

---

[10] Indeed, a similar example could be constructed using the American and British spellings of 'color', or even differing *pronunciations* of 'tomato'.

ostensive definition, then both may be. Indeed, Sasha has learned both words (spellings) in much the same way that nearly everyone else has learned at least one of them: by means of a sort of ostensive definition. This manner of acquiring the two words (spellings) is unusual, but not impossible. Sasha's acquisition of these words (spellings) prevented him from learning at the outset that they are perfect synonyms, but the claim that he therefore has not learned both is highly implausible. Each word (spelling) was learned by Sasha in much the same way that some of us learned it. Even in Sasha's idiolect, then, the two words (spellings) are perfectly synonymous, and therefore share the same information value. Since this contradicts the finding generated by the generalized Fregean strategy, the generalized Fregean strategy must involve some error. This discredits the original Fregean argument.[11]

What is the error? It is tempting to place the blame on Frege's Law. In Sasha's case, the sentences 'Catsup is ketchup' and 'Ketchup is ketchup' have the very same information content, yet it seems that the first is informative and the second is not. This would be a mistake. A sentence is *informative* in the sense invoked in Frege's Law only insofar as its information content is a "valuable extension of our knowledge," or is knowable only *a posteriori,* or is not already "given," or is non-trivial, etc. There is some such property *P* of propositions such that a declarative sentence *S* is informative in the only sense relevant to Frege's Law if and only if its information content has *P*. Once the informativeness or uninformativeness of a sentence is properly seen as a derivative semantic property of the sentence, one that the sentence has only in virtue of encoding the information that it does, Frege's Law may be seen as a special instance of Leibniz's Law, the doctrine that things that are the same have the same properties: if the information content of *S* is the information content of *S'*, then the information content of *S* has the informative-making property *P* if and only if the information content of *S'* does. Since Frege's Law is a logical truth, it is unassailable.

By the same token, the sentence 'Catsup is ketchup' is definitely not informative *in this sense.* The proposition it semantically contains is just the information that ketchup is ketchup, a proposition that clearly lacks the relevant informative-making

---

[11] The argument given here involving the terms 'ketchup' and 'catsup' is related to Kripke's "proof" of substitutivity using two Hebrew words for Germany, and to his argument involving 'furze' and 'gorse', in the conclusion section of "A Puzzle about Belief" [96]. All of these arguments are closely related to Church's famous arguments from translation. (See especially "Intensional Isomorphism and Identity of Belief" [29].) For further discussion of the relation between the position taken in Kripke's article on belief and the position defended here see *Frege's Puzzle* [157] (pp. 129–132), and "Illogical Belief" [158].

The example of Sasha, like the 'beech'-'elm' example, demonstrates that the difficulty involved in Frege's puzzle is more general than it appears, arising not only on my own theory of information value but equally on a very wide range of theories, including various Fregean theories. This is not peculiar to Frege's puzzle. Although I will not argue the case here, a great many criticisms that have been levelled against the sort of account I advocate—perhaps most—are based on some difficulty or other that is more general in nature than it first appears, and that equally arises on virtually any substantive theory of information value in connection with the example of Sasha's understanding of the synonyms 'ketchup' and 'catsup'. (Cf. "Illogical Belief" [158].) Perhaps I will elaborate on this matter in later work.

property *P*. The sentence 'Catsup is ketchup', unlike the sentences 'Ketchup is ketchup' and 'Catsup is catsup', is "informative" in various other senses. If uttered under the right circumstances, the former can convey to someone like Sasha that the sentence itself is true, and hence that the words (or spellings) 'ketchup' and 'catsup' are English synonyms, or at least co-referential. To someone who already understands 'ketchup' but not 'catsup', an utterance of the sentence can convey what 'catsup' means. These pieces of linguistic information about English do have the informative-making property *P*, but in order for a sentence to be informative in the relevant sense its very information content itself must have the informative-making property *P*. It is not sufficient that utterances of the sentence typically impart information that has *P*, if that imparted information is not included in the semantic information content of the sentence. The question of information value concerns semantically contained information, not pragmatically imparted information.

Exactly analogously, once the word 'informative' is taken in the relevant sense, thereby rendering Frege's Law a truth of logic, one of the other crucial premises of the original Fregean argument against Millian theory is rendered moot. Specifically, with the word 'informative' so understood, and with a sharp distinction between semantically contained information and pragmatically imparted information kept in mind, the assumption that the sentence 'Hesperus is Phosphorus' is informative *in the relevant sense* requires special justification. To be sure, an utterance of the sentence typically imparts information that is more valuable than that typically imparted by an utterance of 'Hesperus is Hesperus'. For example, it may impart the nontrivial linguistic information about the sentence 'Hesperus is Phosphorus' itself that it is true, and hence that the names 'Hesperus' and 'Phosphorus' are co-referential. But presumably this is not semantically contained information. The observation that 'Hesperus is Phosphorus' can be used to convey information that has the informative-making property *P* does nothing to show that the sentence's semantic content itself has the property *P*. It is by no means obvious that this sentence, stripped naked of its pragmatic impartations and with only its properly semantic information content left, is any more informative in the relevant sense than 'Hesperus is Hesperus'. I claim that the information content of 'Hesperus is Phosphorus' is the trivial proposition about the planet Venus that it is it—a piece of information that clearly lacks the informative-making property *P*. It is by no means certain, as the original Fregean argument maintains, that the difference in "cognitive value" we seem to hear between 'Hesperus is Hesperus' and 'Hesperus is Phosphorus' is not due entirely to a difference in pragmatically imparted information. Yet, until we can be certain of this, Frege's Law cannot be applied and the argument does not get off the ground. In effect, then, the original Fregean argument begs the question, by assuming that the typical impartations of 'Hesperus is Phosphorus' that have the informative-making property *P* are included in the very information content. Of course, if one fails to draw the distinction between semantically contained and pragmatically imparted information (as so many philosophers have), it is small wonder that information pragmatically imparted by 'Hesperus is Phosphorus' may be mistaken for semantically contained information. If the strategy of the original Fregean argument is ultimately to succeed, however, a further argument must be given to show that the information imparted by 'Hesperus is Phosphorus' that makes it seem informative is, in fact, semantically contained. In the meantime, Frege's 'Hesperus'-'Phosphorus' puzzle is certainly not the conclusive refutation of Millian theory that it has been taken to be. For all that the Fregean strategy achieves, some version of Millianism may be the best and most plausible theory available concerning the information value of proper names.

II

What evidence is there in favor of the Millian theory? One extremely important consideration comes by way of the paradigms of nondescriptional singular terms: individual variables. A related consideration involves pronouns. Consider the following so-called *de re* (as opposed to *de dicto*), or *relational* (as opposed to *notional*), propositional-attitude attribution, expressed in the formal mode by way of quantification into the nonextensional context created by the nonextensional operator 'that':

(1) $(\exists x)[x =$ the planet Venus & Jones believes that x is a star].

Such a *de re* locution might be expressed less formally in colloquial English as:

(1′) Jones believes of the planet Venus that it is a star.

What is characteristic of these *de re* locutions is that they do not specify how Jones conceives of the planet Venus in believing it to be a star. It is left open whether he is thinking of Venus as the first heavenly body visible at dusk, or as the last heavenly body visible at dawn, or instead as the heavenly body he sees at time t, or none of the above. The Fregean (or "neo-Fregean") theorist contends that this lack of specificity is precisely a result of the fact that the (allegedly sense-bearing) name 'Venus' is positioned outside of the scope of the oblique context created by the nonextensional operator 'believes that', where it is open to substitution of co-referential singular terms and to existential generalization. What is more significant, however, is that another, non-sense-bearing singular term is positioned within the scope of the nonextensional context: the last bound occurrence of the variable 'x' in (1), the pronoun 'it' in (1′). Consider first the quasi-formal sentence (1). It follows by the principles of conventional formal semantics that (1) is true if and only if its component open sentence

(2) Jones believes that x is a star

is true under the assignment of the planet Venus as value for the variable 'x'—or in the terminology of Tarski, if and only if Venus *satisfies* (2). The open sentence (2) is true under the assignment of Venus as value of 'x' if and only if Jones believes the proposition that is the information content of the complement open sentence

(3) x is a star

under the same assignment of Venus as the value of 'x'.

A parallel derivation proceeds from the colloquial *de re* attribution (1′). Sentence (1′) is true if and only if its component sentence

(2′) Jones believes that it is a star

is true under the anaphoric assignment of Venus as referent for the pronoun 'it'. As with the open sentence (2), sentence (2′) is true under the assignment of Venus as the referent of 'it' if and only if Jones believes the information content of

(3′) It is a star

under this same assignment.

Now, the fundamental semantic characteristic of a variable with an assigned value, or of a pronoun with a particular referent, is precisely that its information value is just its referent. The referent-assignment provides nothing else for the term to contribute to the information content of sentences like (3) or (3′) in which it figures. In fact, this is precisely the point of using a variable or a pronoun rather than a definite description (like 'the first heavenly body visible at dusk') within the scope of an attitude verb in a *de re* attribution. A variable with an assigned value, or a pronoun with a particular referent, does not have in addition to its referent a Fregean sense—a conceptual representation that it contributes to semantic content. If it had, (3) and (3′) would semantically contain specific general propositions, under the relevant referent-assignments, and (2) and (2′) would thus be notional rather than relational. If (2) and (2′), used with reference to Venus, are to be relational—if they are to fail to specify how Jones conceives of Venus—the contents of (3) and (3′) under the assignments of Venus to 'x' and 'it' can only be the singular proposition about Venus that it is a star, the sort of proposition postulated by the Millian theory. This means that the information value of the variable or the pronoun must be its referent.

What is good for the variable or the pronoun, under an assigned referent, is good for the individual constant. Indeed, the only difference between a variable and a constant is that the variable varies where the constant stands fast. The semantics for a given language fixes the reference of its individual constants. It happens that some particularly useful operators, included in the usual mathematical languages, operate simultaneously on a certain kind of simple singular term and a formula, by surveying the various truth values that the operand formula takes on when the operand singular term is assigned different referents (and the rest of the sentence remains fixed), and then assigning an appropriate extensional value to the whole formed from the operator and its two operands. (Technically, the extension of such an operator is a function from the extension of its operand formula with respect to its operand term to an appropriate extension for the compound formed by attaching the operator to an appropriate term and a formula—where the extension of a formula S_v *with respect to* a term v is a function that assigns to any assignment of a referent to v the corresponding truth value of S_v under that referent-assignment.) If a given language includes operators of this sort, it is natural for it to include also special singular terms that are not coupled with a particular referent to which they remain faithful, and that are instead allowed to take on any value from a particular domain of discourse as temporary referent. These special singular terms are the individual variables, and the operators that induce their presence are the variable-binding operators. Individual variables are singular terms that would be individual constants but for their promiscuity. Conversely, then, individual constants are singular terms that would be variables but for their monogamy. The variability of a variable has nothing whatsoever to do with the separate feature that the variable's information value, under an assignment of a referent, is just the assigned referent. It is the simplicity of the variable that gives it the latter feature; the variability only guarantees that the information value also varies. Once the variable is assigned a particular value, the variable becomes, for all intents and purposes pertaining to that assignment, a constant. Hence, if the open sentence (3), under the assignment of Venus as the value of 'x', semantically contains the singular proposition about Venus that it is a star, then the closed sentence

> a is a star,

where 'a' is an individual constant that refers to Venus, semantically contains this same proposition. Assuming that the individual constants of natural language are the proper names, single-word indexical singular terms, and other (closed) simple singular terms, the considerations raised here support the Millian theory.[12]

There is an alternative way of looking at the same result. All of us are accustomed to using special variables or pronouns that have a restricted domain over which they range. In ordinary English, the pronoun 'he' often ranges only over males, the pronoun 'she' only over females. Among special-purpose technical languages, some variables range only over numbers, some only over sets, some only over times. The domain over which a variable ranges (at least typically) must be non-empty, but it can be quite small in size. In standard extensional second-order logic, for example, the range of the second-order variables 'p', 'q', and 'r' is the pair set consisting of (representatives of) the two truth values. Could there be variables whose range is a unit set? Of course there could. Why not? Except that it would be odd to call such terms "variables." Their range is too restrictive to allow for genuine

---

[12] The foregoing argument is closely related to a somewhat different argument advanced in *Frege's Puzzle* [157] (pp. 3–7) for the conclusion that so-called *de re* propositional-attitude attributions, such as (1) and (1′), attribute attitudes toward singular propositions. (This is not a premise of the argument; it is a conclusion.) The latter argument was derived from a similar argument of David Kaplan's involving modality in place of propositional attitudes. The new argument is an argument by analogy: Individual constants are relevantly analogous to individual variables and pronouns, differing only in their constancy; hence, so-called *de dicto* propositional-attitude attributions involving proper names also attribute attitudes toward singular propositions. This argument by analogy to variables and pronouns occurred to me sometime in late 1980, and although it is not proffered in *Frege's Puzzle*, it was this argument more than any other that actually convinced me of the highly contentious thesis that the information value of a proper name, or any other closed simple singular term, is simply its referent and nothing more. The argument of the following section occurred to me immediately thereafter. (Cf. *Frege's Puzzle* [157], p. ix.) A version of the latter of these is proffered in *Frege's Puzzle* (pp. 84–85, 114–118, and *passim*).

variation, in an ordinary sense; they are maximally restricted. Let us not call them "variables," then. What should we call them? We could call them "invariable variables." (This has the advantage that it emphasizes the exact analogy with the less restrictive variables.) Alternatively, we could call them "constants." In fact, we do. The proper names and demonstratives of ordinary language might be seen as nothing other than the hypothesized "invariable variables." Proper names and unrestricted variables are but the opposite limiting cases of a single phenomenon.[13]

III

This sort of consideration favoring the sort of account I advocate is complemented by a new application of a general form of argument that has been suggested, and usefully exploited, by Saul Kripke.[14]

What compelling evidence is there that the proper names of ordinary language are not simply the hypothesized invariable variables? We have seen that the original Fregean argument from the alleged informativeness of 'Hesperus is Phosphorus' is illegitimate, or at least seriously incomplete. What other evidence is there? An alternative argument against Millian theory derives from the apparent failures of substitutivity in propositional-attitude attributions. Consider the familiar story of Jones and his ignorance concerning the planet Venus. Jones sees a bright star in the dusk sky, before any other heavenly body is visible, and is told that its name is 'Hesperus'. Subsequently he sees another bright star in the dawn sky, later than any other heavenly body is visible, and is told that its name is 'Phosphorus'. What Jones is not told is that these are one and the very same heavenly body, the planet Venus. Although Jones believes the proposition that Hesperus is

---

[13] I know of no convincing evidence that proper names (and natural-language simple singular terms generally, other than pronouns) are not invariable pronominals. The fact that proper names do not seem to be grammatically bindable by quantifier (or other) antecedents cannot be taken as conclusive refutation of the thesis that names are maximally restricted variables. Since quantification employing such variables would not differ in truth value from the unquantified open sentence, binding such variables would serve no useful purpose; the natural evolution of language would have little reason to introduce a device for binding these special invariable pronominals. In any event, the general argument in the text does not require the premise that proper names are variables of a special sort (maximally restricted); it requires only the premise that names are sufficiently *analogous* to (unrestricted) variables— together with the usual semantics governing existential quantification, conjunction, and identity (or the natural semantics governing anaphora in English locutions of the form ⌜Of *a*, . . . it . . .⌝), and the further premise that a (closed or open) sentence of the form (*a* believes that *S*' is true (under an assignment of values to variables) if and only if the referent of *a* believes the information content of *S*. See the previous note.

[14] Cf. Kripke, *Naming and Necessity* [95] (pp. 108). Kripke's general methodological observation is given in more detail in "Speaker's Reference and Semantic Reference" [97] (especially p. 16). Kripke does not explicitly consider applying the general strategy specifically to substitutivity-failure objections to Millianism. Whereas he clearly regards such objections as inconclusive at best (see his "A Puzzle about Belief" [96]), I am not certain that he would endorse this particular application of the "schmidentity" strategy to showing the substitutivity phenomena evidentially irrelevant. (I hope that he would.)

Hesperus, he seems not to believe (and indeed to disbelieve) the proposition that Hesperus is Phosphorus. That is, upon substitution of 'Phosphorus' for the second occurrence of 'Hesperus' in the true sentence

(4) Jones believes that Hesperus is Hesperus

we obtain the evidently false sentence

(5) Jones believes that Hesperus is Phosphorus.

The apparent failure of substitutivity in propositional-attitude attributions is generally taken by philosophers to constitute a decisive refutation of the sort of account I advocate. But the very phenomena that appear to show that substitutivity fails would arise even if the Millian theory were absolutely correct (for standard English) and substitutivity of co-referential proper names in propositional-attitude attributions were uniformly valid. In particular, the same feeling of invalidity in connection with substitution in such attributions as (4) would arise even in a language for which it was stipulated—say, by an authoritative linguistic committee that legislates the grammar and semantics of the language, and to which all speakers of the language give their cooperation and consent—that the theory of *Frege's Puzzle* is correct. Suppose, for example, that such a committee decreed that there are to be two new individual constants, 'Schmesperus' and 'Schmosphorus'. (I am deliberately following the genius as closely as possible.) It is decreed that these two words are to function exactly like the mathematician's variables 'x', 'y', and 'z' as regards information value, except that they are to remain constant (with whatever other differences this key difference requires)—the constant value of the first being the first heavenly body visible at dusk and the constant value of the second being the last heavenly body visible at dawn. Suppose further that some English speakers—for example, the astronomers—are aware that these two new constants are co-referential, and hence synonymous. Nevertheless, even if our character Jones were fully aware of the legislative decree in connection with 'Schmesperus' and 'Schmosphorus', he would remain ignorant of their co-reference. Jones would dissent from such queries as 'Is Schmesperus the same heavenly body as Schmosphorus?' Would those who are in the know—the astronomers—automatically regard the new constants as completely interchangeable, even in propositional-attitude attributions? Almost certainly not. English speakers who use 'ketchup' and 'catsup' as exact synonyms but who do not reflect philosophically on the matter—and even some who do reflect philosophically—may be inclined to assent to the sentence 'Sasha believes that ketchup is a sandwich condiment, but he does not believe that catsup is'.[15] On reflection, however, it emerges that this sentence expresses a logical impossibility, since the proposition that catsup is a sandwich condiment just is the proposition that ketchup is a sandwich condiment. Similarly, speakers who agree to abide by the legislative committee's decree about 'Schmesperus' and 'Schmosphorus' and who recognize

---

[15] For similar claims, see for example Burge's "Belief and Synonymy" [10]. Burge explicitly disagrees with my contention that such claims express logical impossibilities.

that these two terms are co-referential—especially if these speakers do not reflect philosophically on the implications of the decree in connection with such *de re* constructions as (1)—might for independent pragmatic reasons be led to utter or to assent to such sentences as 'Jones believes that Schmesperus appears in the evening, but he does not believe that Schmosphorus does' and 'Jones believes that Schmesperus is Schmesperus, but he does not believe that Schmesperus is Schmosphorus'. The astronomers may be led to utter the latter sentence, for example, in order to convey (without knowing it) the complex fact about Jones that he agrees to the proposition about Venus that it is it, taking it in the way he would were it presented to him by the sentence 'Schmesperus is Schmesperus' but not taking it in the way he would were it presented to him by the sentence 'Schmesperus is Schmosphorus'. The astronomers would thus unknowingly speak in a way that conflicts with the usage to which they have agreed. This, in turn, would lead to their judging such belief attributions as 'Jones believes that Schmesperus is Schmosphorus' not only inappropriate but literally false, and to the unmistakable feeling that substitution of 'Schmosphorus' for (some occurrences of) 'Schmesperus' in such attributions as 'Jones believes that Schmesperus is Schmesperus' is logically invalid. Insofar as the same phenomena that give rise to Frege's puzzle about identity sentences and to the appearance of substitutivity failure would arise even in a language for which the theory advanced in *Frege's Puzzle* was true by fiat and unanimous consent (and do in fact arise with respect to such straightforward strict synonyms as 'ketchup' and 'catsup'), these phenomena cannot be taken to refute the theory.

IV

The anti-Millian argument deriving from the apparent failure of substitutivity is closely related to the original Fregean argument about the informativeness of 'Hesperus is Phosphorus'. The analogue of the questionable premise that 'Hesperus is Phosphorus' is informative is the assertion that (5) is false (or that 'Hesperus is Phosphorus' does not correctly give the content of one of Jones's beliefs, etc.). This premise too, I claim, is incorrect.[16] However, this premise, unlike its analogue in the original Fregean argument, does not simply beg the question. The intuition that (5) is false (according to the story) is strong and universal. We have seen that this

---

[16]I do not deny the initial intuitive force of the premises that 'Hesperus is Phosphorus' is informative and that (5) is false; I argue that they are nevertheless erroneous, and I propose an explanation for their initial pull. My rejection of these premises is by no means a standard position among Millians. A more common Millian reaction is to concede these premises, and to challenge instead the relevant analogue of Frege's Law—for example, the common and extremely plausible assumption that if 'Hesperus' has the same information value as 'Phosphorus' (as Millianism requires), then (4) is true if and only if (5) is. (The assumption has been challenged merely on the grounds that Millianism is not committed to it. Such a reaction misjudges the force of the Fregean argument: the assumption is independently compelling, and taken in conjunction with the other premises, it precludes Millianism. The Millian is under the gun to reject either this premise or one of the others as untrue, and to motivate his or her rejection of the offending premise.) It has been argued, for example, that

intuition cannot be regarded as decisive—or even evidentially relevant—regarding the question of the actual truth value of (5), since (for some reason) the intuition of falsity would arise in any case. But there are forceful reasons for deeming (5) false, and the intuition of falsity must be addressed and explained. A full reply to the objection from the apparent failure of substitutivity involves greater complexities.[17]

In *Frege's Puzzle*, I propose the sketch of an analysis of the binary relation of belief between believers and propositions (sometimes Russellian singular propositions). I take the belief relation to be, in effect, the existential generalization of a ternary relation, *BEL*, among believers, propositions, and some third type of entity. To believe a proposition *p* is to adopt an appropriate favorable attitude toward *p* when taking *p* in some relevant *way*. It is to agree to *p*, or to assent mentally to *p*, or to approve of *p*, or some such thing, when taking *p* a certain way. This is the *BEL* relation. The third relata for the *BEL* relation are perhaps something like *modes* of acquaintance or familiarity with propositions, or *ways* in which a believer may take a given proposition. The important thing is that, by definition, they are such that if a fully rational believer adopts conflicting attitudes (such as belief and disbelief, or belief and suspension of judgment) toward propositions *p* and *q*, then the believer must take *p* and *q* in different ways, by means of different modes of acquaintance, in harboring the conflicting attitudes towards them—even if *p* and *q* are in fact the same proposition. More generally, if a fully rational agent construes objects *x* and *y* as distinct (or even merely withholds construing them as one and the very same—as might be evidenced, for example, by the agent's adopting conflicting beliefs or attitudes concerning *x* and *y*), then for some appropriate notion of a *way* of taking an object, the agent takes *x* and *y* in different ways, even if in fact *x* = *y*.[18] Of course, to use a distinction of Kripke's,

---

whereas (5) attributes belief of a proposition, it does not attribute belief of the very content of 'Hesperus is Phosphorus' (i.e., the singular proposition about Venus that it is it). This merely evades the general problem. Consider instead the parallel assumption that if 'Hesperus is Phosphorus' has the same information (proposition) content as 'Hesperus is Hesperus', then the former correctly gives the content of one of Jones's beliefs if and only if the latter does. This assumption is virtually as certain as Frege's Law. Yet common sense dictates that 'Hesperus is Hesperus' does, and 'Hesperus is Phosphorus' does not, correctly give the content of one of Jones's beliefs (since Jones sincerely and reflectively assents to the first while dissenting from the second, etc.). Cf. *Frege's Puzzle* [157] (pp. 5–6, 87–92, and *passim*).

[17] I provide only an outline of my reply here. See *Frege's Puzzle* [157] (especially pp. 80–118) for the details.

[18] An appropriate notion of a way of taking an object is such that if an agent encounters a single object several times and each time construes it as a different object from the objects in the previous encounters, or even as a different object *for all he or she knows*, then each time he or she takes the object in a new and different way. This is required in order to accommodate the fact that an agent in such circumstances may (perhaps *inevitably will*) adopt several conflicting attitudes toward what is in fact a single object. One cannot require, however, that these ways-of-taking-objects are rich enough by themselves to determine the object so taken, without the assistance of extra-mental, contextual factors. Presumably, twin agents who are molecule-for-molecule duplicates, and whose brains are in exactly the same configuration down to the finest detail, may encounter different (though duplicate) objects, taking them in the very same way. Likewise, a single agent might be artificially induced through brain manipulations into taking different objects the same way. Cf. *Frege's Puzzle* (p. 173n1).

this formulation is far too vague to constitute a fully developed *theory* of ways-of-taking-objects and their role in belief formation, but it does provide a *picture* of belief that differs significantly from the sort of picture of propositional attitudes advanced by Frege or Russell, and enough can be said concerning the *BEL* relation to allow for at least the sketch of a solution to certain philosophical problems, puzzles, and paradoxes involving belief.[19]

In particular, the *BEL* relation satisfies the following three conditions:

(a) *A* believes *p* if and only if there is some *x* such that *A* is familiar with *p* by means of *x* and *BEL(A, p, x)*;[20]

(b) *A* may believe *p* by standing in *BEL* to *p* and some *x* by means of which *A* is familiar with *p* without standing in *BEL* to *p* and all *x* by means of which *A* is familiar with *p*;

(c) In one sense of "withhold belief", *A* withholds belief concerning *p* (either by disbelieving or by suspending judgment) if and only if there is some *x* by means of which *A* is familiar with *p* and not-*BEL(A, p, x)*.

These conditions generate a philosophically important distinction between withholding belief and failure to believe (i.e., not believing). In particular, one may both withhold belief from and believe the very same proposition simultaneously. (Neither withholding belief nor failure to believe is to be identified with the related notions of disbelief and suspension of judgment— which are two different ways of withholding belief, in this sense, and which may occur simultaneously with belief of the very same proposition in a single believer.)

It happens in most cases (though not all) that when a believer believes some particular proposition *p*, the relevant third relatum for the *BEL* relation is a function of the believer and some particular *sentence* of the believer's language. There is, for example, the binary function *f* that assigns to any believer *A* and sentence *S* of *A*'s language, the *way A* takes the proposition contained in *S* (in *A*'s language with respect to *A*'s context at some particular time *t*) were it presented to *A* (at *t*) through the very sentence *S*, if there is exactly one such way of taking the proposition in question. (In some cases, there are too many such ways of taking the proposition in question.)

---

[19] The *BEL* relation is applied to additional puzzles in "Reflexivity" [156].

[20] I do not claim that a sentence of the form ⌜*A believes p*⌝ is exactly synonymous with the existential formula on the right-hand side of the 'if and only if' in condition (a). I do claim that condition (a) is a (metaphysically) necessary, conceptually *a priori* truth. (See note 5 above concerning the contents of predicates. It may be helpful to think of the English verb 'believe' as a *name* for the binary relation described by the right-hand side of (a), i.e., for the existential generalization on the third argument-place of the *BEL* relation.) My claim in [157] (p. 111) that belief may be so "analyzed" is meant to entail that condition (a) is a necessary *a priori* truth, not that the two sides of the biconditional are synonymous. (My own view is that something along these lines is all that can be plausibly claimed for such purported philosophical "analyses" as have been offered for ⌜*A knows p*⌝, ⌜*A perceives B*⌝, ⌜*A* (nonnaturally) means *p* in uttering *S*⌝, etc.)

According to this account, (5) is true in the story of Jones and the planet Venus, since Jones agrees to the proposition that Hesperus is Phosphorus when taking it in a certain way—for example, if one points to Venus at dusk and says (peculiarly enough) "That is that," or when the proposition is presented to him by such sentences as 'Hesperus is Hesperus' or 'Phosphorus is Phosphorus'. That is,

BEL[Jones, that Hesperus is Phosphorus, f(Jones, 'Hesperus is Hesperus')].

Jones also withholds belief concerning whether Hesperus is Hesperus. In fact, according to my account, he believes that Hesperus is not Hesperus! For he agrees to the proposition that Hesperus is not Hesperus, taking it in the way he would were it presented to him by the sentence 'Hesperus is not Phosphorus'. That is,

BEL[Jones, that Hesperus is not Hesperus, f(Jones, 'Hesperus is not Phosphorus')].

and hence, assuming Jones is fully rational, it is not the case that

BEL[Jones, that Hesperus is Hesperus, f(Jones, 'Hesperus is Phosphorus')].

As noted above, these consequences of my account do not conform with the way we actually speak. Instead it is customary when discussing Jones's predicament to say such things as "Jones does not realize that Hesperus is Phosphorus; in fact, he believes that Hesperus is *not* Phosphorus." It is partly for this reason that the anti-Millian's premise that (5) is false does not simply beg the question. Yet, according to my account, what we say when we deny such things as (5) is literally false. In fact, (5)'s literal truth conditions are, according to the view I advocate, conditions that are plainly fulfilled (in the context of the Jones story). Why, then, do we not say such things, and instead say just the opposite? Why is it that substitution of 'Phosphorus' for 'Hesperus'—or even of 'Schmosphorus' for 'Schmesperus'—*feels* invalid in propositional-attitude attributions? Some explanation of our speech patterns and intuitions of invalidity in these sorts of cases is called for. The explanation I offer in *Frege's Puzzle* is somewhat complex, consisting of three main parts. The first part of the explanation for the common disposition to deny or to dissent from (5) is that speakers may have a tendency to confuse the content of (5) with that of

(5′) Jones believes that 'Hesperus is Phosphorus' is true (in English).

Since sentence (5′) is obviously false, this confusion naturally leads to a similarly unfavorable disposition toward (5). This part of the explanation cannot be the whole story, however, since even speakers who know enough about semantics to know that the fact that Hesperus is Phosphorus is logically independent of the fact that the sentence 'Hesperus is Phosphorus' is true, and who are careful to distinguish the content of (5) from that of (5′), are nevertheless unfavorably disposed toward (5) itself—because of the fact that Jones demurs whenever the query 'Is Hesperus the same heavenly body as Phosphorus?' is put to him.

The second part of my explanation for (5)'s appearance of falsity is that its denial is the product of a plausible but mistaken inference from the fact that Jones sincerely dissents (or at least does not sincerely assent) when queried 'Is Hesperus Phosphorus?', while fully understanding the question and grasping its content, or (as Keith Donnellan has pointed out) even from his expressions of preference for the Evening Star over the Morning Star. More accurately, ordinary speakers (and even most nonordinary speakers) are disposed to regard the fact that Jones does not agree to the proposition that Hesperus is Phosphorus, when taking it in a certain way (the way it might be presented to him by the very sentence 'Hesperus is Phosphorus'), as sufficient to warrant the denial of sentence (5). In the special sense explained in the preceding section, Jones withholds belief from the proposition that Hesperus is Phosphorus, actively failing to agree with it whenever it is put to him in so many words, and this fact misleads ordinary speakers, including Jones himself, into concluding that Jones harbors no favorable attitude of agreement whatsoever toward the proposition in question, and hence does not believe it.

The third part of the explanation is that, where someone under discussion has conflicting attitudes toward a single proposition that he or she takes to be two independent propositions (i.e., in the troublesome 'Hesperus'-'Phosphorus', 'Superman'-'Clark Kent' type cases), there is an established practice of using belief attributions to convey not only the proposition agreed to (which is specified by the belief attribution) but also the way the subject of the attribution takes the proposition in agreeing to it (which is no part of the semantic content of the belief attribution). Specifically, there is an established practice of using such a sentence as (5), which contains the uninteresting proposition that Jones believes the singular proposition about Venus that it is it, to convey furthermore that Jones agrees to this proposition *taking it in the way he would were it presented to him by the very sentence 'Hesperus is Phosphorus' (assuming he understands this sentence)*. That is, there is an established practice of using (5) to convey the false proposition that

BEL[Jones, that Hesperus is Phosphorus, *f* (Jones, 'Hesperus is Phosphorus')].

V

An unconventional objection has been raised by some self-proclaimed neo-Fregeans against versions of Millianism of the sort advanced in *Frege's Puzzle*. It is charged that such theories are, at bottom, versions of a neo-Fregean theory.[21] Ironically, this unorthodox criticism is invariably coupled with the further, standard criticism that such versions of Millianism are problematic in some way or other that neo-Fregean theory is not (for example, in counting sentence (5) true). The fact that this more familiar criticism is directly contrary to the newer criticism is all but completely ignored. More importantly, this more recent criticism betrays a serious misunderstanding of the gulf that separates Frege's theory from that of Mill or Russell.

---

[21]The charge has been made both in oral discussion and in print. See Forbes [57] (pp. 456–457), Smith [174], and Wagner [184] (p. 446). A very similar charge was apparently first made by Gareth Evans, in Section VI of his "Understanding Demonstratives" [49] (pp. 298–300). Although Evans's criticism was aimed at John Perry's views on demonstratives, a great deal of my reply to my own critics extends to Evans's criticism of Perry.

It should be said that the theory of *Frege's Puzzle* does indeed follow Frege's theoretical views in a number of significant respects. First and foremost, the theory sees the information value (contribution to proposition-content) of such compound expressions as definite descriptions as complexes whose constituents are contributed by the component expressions and whose structure parallels the syntactic structure of the compound itself. Although my theory has been called "neo-Russellian," it departs radically from the theory of Russell in treating definite descriptions as genuine singular terms, and not as contextually defined "incomplete symbols" or quantificational locutions. In addition to this, a semantic distinction is observed, following Frege's distinction of *Bedeutung* and *Sinn*, between a definite description's referent and the description's information value. A similar distinction is maintained for predicates, sentential connectives, quantifiers, other operators, and even for whole sentences. The referent of a predicate is taken to be its semantic characteristic function from (sequences of) objects to truth values; the information value is taken to be something intensional, like an attribute or concept. Sentences are viewed entirely on the model of a definite description that refers (typically nonrigidly) to a truth value. The content ("information value") of a sentence is taken to be a proposition—the sort of thing that is asserted or denied, believed or disbelieved (or about which judgment is suspended), etc., something that is never-changing in truth value. The account of predicates, sentences and the rest as referring to their extensions is defended by means of the principle of extensionality (the principle that the referent of a compound expression is typically a function solely of the referents of the component expressions and their manner of composition). In all of these respects, the theory advanced in [157] self-consciously follows Frege.

There remains one crucial difference, however: the information value of a simple singular term is identified with its referent. This major plank makes the theory Millian (or "neo-Russellian"), and hence severely and deeply anti-Fregean.

Although a great deal of attention has been paid to the differences between Russell and Frege over the question of whether it is false that the present king of France is bald, their disagreement on this question is dwarfed in significance by their disagreement over the information values of simple proper names. This primary bone of contention emerged in correspondence in 1904, even before Russell came to herald his Theory of Descriptions, which later supplemented his Millianism.[22] Russell answered Frege's protest that Mont Blanc with its snowfields cannot be a constituent of the "thought," or information, that Mont Blanc is more than 4000 meters high, arguing that unless we admit that Mont Blanc is indeed a constituent of the content of the sentence 'Mont Blanc is over 4000 meters high' we obtain the absurd conclusion that we know nothing at all concerning Mont Blanc. Although Frege apparently made no attempt at a response (Russell did not seem to be fully apprehending Frege's remarks), one can be certain that he did not regard Russell's vision of the proposition that Mont Blanc is

---

[22]In Frege's *Philosophical and Mathematical Correspondence* [62] (pp. 163, 169–170; also in [160], pp. 56–57) and this volume.

over 4000 meters high as merely a minor departure from his own sense-reference theory. There can be no real doubt that Frege would have vigorously denounced all versions of Millianism as completely inimical to his theoretical point of view.[23]

What, then, is the rationale for the charge that my version of Millianism is, at bottom, a neo-Fregean theory? My critics have not been absolutely clear on this point. The charge appears to stem from my acknowledgment of something like *ways of taking objects,* and my reliance on them to explain away the appearance of falsity in connection with such propositional-attitude attributions as (5). To this somewhat

---

[23]The (allegedly) neo-Fregean charge that my account is ultimately Fregean is sometimes coupled with (and perhaps predicated on) an extraordinary interpretation of Frege, advanced by Evans (in "Understanding Demonstratives" [49], and in *The Varieties of Reference* [50] (pp. 22–30 and *passim*), on which Frege is supposed to have held that typical nonreferring proper names have no Fregean sense and that declarative sentences involving such names (in ordinary extensional contexts, or in "purely referential position"), while they appear to express thoughts, do not really do so. This highly unorthodox interpretation is based heavily on what seems a tendentious reading of an ambiguous passage in Frege's *Posthumous Writings* [61] (p. 30). Evans and his followers may have been misled by Frege's unfortunate term 'mock thought' (the translators' rendering of Frege's '*Scheingedanke*,' which might also be translated as 'sham thought' or 'pseudo-thought'), and by his habitual use of the term 'fiction' in an artificially broad sense—roughly, as a term for any piece of discourse or line of thought (whether of fiction, in the ordinary sense, or otherwise) in which senses occur without *Bedeutungen* and/or in which sentences or their thought contents occur that are either without truth value or not put forward as true. (This use of 'fiction' is not especially remarkable for a mathematician/ logician/philosopher keenly interested in truth and its properties.) Evans evidently thought that Frege regarded any such discourse on the model of genuine fiction, and as only seeming to have cognitive content.

In the same work by Frege appear numerous passages that unambiguously preclude Evans's unconventional interpretation. Cf., for example, pp. 118, 122, 194, and especially 191–192, 225. Similar remarks occur in "*Über Sinn und Bedeutung*," in English in [63], pp. 162–163. Curiously, Evans dismisses these passages as "dubiously consistent with the fundamentals" of Frege's post-1890 philosophy of semantics, although Evans fails to cite any passage which is uncontroversially post-1890 and in which Frege unambiguously asserts something straightforwardly inconsistent with these passages (something that uncontroversially entails that the sense of an ordinary proper name depends for its existence on the object it determines). This interpretive stance makes it difficult to imagine what Evans and his followers would accept as convincing evidence that Frege did not hold the theory they attribute to him. (In fact, Frege's use of the phrase 'mock proper name' or 'pseudo proper name'—for nonreferring but nevertheless real singular terms—in the central passage cited by Evans would, even by itself, tend to indicate that Evans's reading of this very passage is not faithful to Frege's intent. Cf. also Frege's "Thoughts" [60] (p. 38), where Frege speaks of "mock assertions" made either by actors on the stage—"it is only acting, only fiction"—or in poetry, where "we have the case of thoughts being expressed without being actually put forward as true," not for lack of the thoughts themselves but for lack of "the requisite seriousness" on the speaker's part.) In any event, Frege unambiguously denied (*Posthumous Writings* [61], pp. 187, 225) that the referent of a proper name like 'Mont Blanc' or 'Etna' is involved in any way in the name's information value; Frege's *explicit* theory (whether internally consistent or not, and whether compatible with any secret doctrines or not) is therefore diametrically opposed to Millianism. (Cf. Salmon, *Reference and Essence* [155] (pp. 9–23), and *Frege's Puzzle* [157] (pp. 46–50, 63–65, 78). John McDowell, who appears to follow Evans's misreading of Frege, nevertheless disagrees with Evans's notational-variant charge on these, or related, grounds. See McDowell's "Engaging with the Essential" [120] (p. 61), and "*De Re* Senses" [121] (especially p. 104*n*15).) The important point as far as the present discussion is concerned is that (whatever Frege's real views were) my own view is a form of genuine Millianism.

vague and general criticism, a specific and detailed response was offered in [157].[24]
To begin with, my ways-of-taking-objects do not have all of the features that characterize Fregean senses. (See below.) Even if they had, however, they play a significantly different role in my theory. My analogy to the philosophy of perception (pp. 122–125) illustrates the anti-Fregean nature of my view (despite its acknowledgment of sense-like entities): Whereas my theory is analogous to the naïve theory that we perceive external objects—apples, tables, chairs—Fregean theory is analogous to the sophisticated theory that the only objects of genuine perception are percepts, visual images, auditory images, and so on. The naïve theorist of perception sees the 'sees' in 'Jones sees the apple' as expressing a relation between perceivers and external objects, and its grammatical direct object 'the apple' as occurring in purely referential position and referring there to the apple. By contrast, the sophisticated theorist sees the 'sees' as expressing a relation between perceivers and mental objects, and 'the apple' as referring *in that context* to Jones's visual apple image. The two theories disagree fundamentally over *what is perceived*. The naïve theorist need not deny that internal sensory images play a role in perception. He or she may even propose an analysis of perceptual relations (like seeing) that involves existential generalization over mental objects. Why not? Perception obviously does involve experience; there need be no quarrel over such trivial and extremely general matters. The fundamental disagreement over the objects of perception remains. This disagreement will manifest itself not only in differing interpretations of such sentences as 'Jones sees the apple', but often even in differing judgments concerning its truth value (for instance when Jones is hallucinating).

Likewise, I do not quarrel with Fregeans over the trivial question of whether belief and disbelief involve such things as conceptualizing. Our fundamental disagreement concerns the more substantial matter of *what is believed*—in particular, the question whether what is believed is actually made up entirely of such things as "ways of conceptualizing." The *ways of taking objects* that I countenance are, according to my view, not even so much as mentioned in ordinary propositional-attitude attributions. In particular, on my view, a 'that'-clause makes no reference whatsoever to any way of taking the proposition that is its referent, and a 'that'-clause whose only singular terms are simple (such as the one occurring in (5)) makes no reference whatsoever to any way of taking (or conceiving of, etc.) the individuals referred to by those terms. Consequently, ways-of-taking-objects are not mentioned in (an appropriate specification of) the truth conditions of such an attribution. The only way they come into the picture at all is that in some cases, a certain sort of analysis of the propositional attribute designated by the relevant predicate (e.g., belief) involves existential generalization over them—and even this is not true in all cases. There are many propositional locutions that are not attitudinal as such, and that consequently do not involve ways-of-taking-objects in the

---

[24]A number of passages in *Frege's Puzzle* are devoted to pointing out significant advantages of my version of Millianism over Fregean theory (and hence significant differences between them). Cf. pp. 2–7, 66–71 (and *passim*), and Chapter 9, especially pp. 119–126. See also note 18 above.

way that belief does—for example, "The laboratory test indicates that Mary has contracted the disease' or better still 'It is necessary that Mary is human' (perhaps even 'Jones asserted that Venus is a star'). In short, my ways-of-taking-objects have nothing whatsoever to do with the semantic content of ordinary sentences, and consequently they have nothing whatsoever to do with the semantics of propositional attributions, even attributions of propositional attitude. Ways-of-taking-objects hail from philosophical psychology, not from philosophical semantics.

By contrast, for the Fregean, ways of conceptualizing objects are explicitly referred to in, and pivotal to the truth conditions of, all propositional attributions. I sharply disagree with the Fregean who claims that alethic modality—or even that laboratory tests—involve such things as conceptualizing in just the same way that belief does. (Consider the Fregean account of such valid inferences as "The physician believes whatever the laboratory test indicates, and the test indicates that Mary has contracted the disease; hence the physician believes that Mary has contracted the disease', or 'It is necessary that Mary is human, and Jones believes that Mary is human; hence Jones believes at least one necessary truth'.)[25] My fundamental disagreement with Fregeans over the objects of propositional attitude is manifested not only in our differing interpretations of propositional-attitude attributions, but often even in different judgments concerning their truth value. (Recall the conflict between the charge that my version of Millianism is neo-Fregean, and the more orthodox Fregean criticisms of Millianism.)

Fortunately, Graeme Forbes has provided a somewhat more detailed account of how my view is supposed to "dissolve" into a neo-Fregean theory.[26] It is especially instructive to examine his rationale for this criticism.

Forbes exploits the fact that the neo-Fregean is not shackled by the letter of Frege's specific views, and may preserve the general spirit of Frege's theoretical point of view while departing in various details. Forbes proposes two ways in which a neo-Fregean theory can converge, in certain respects, with my version of Millianism.[27] One thing the neo-Fregean may do is to regard a belief attribution ⌜Jones believes that S⌝, as uttered by a given speaker, as asserting not that Jones stands in the belief relation specifically to P, where P is the "thought" (proposition) that is the sense of S in the speaker's idiolect, but instead that Jones stands in the belief relation to some thought or other that is relevantly *similar* to P.

---

[25]Notice also the relative lack of hesitation in substituting for 'Mary' in 'The test indicates that Mary has contracted the disease' any other proper name Mary may have, or even the pronoun 'she' accompanied by ostension to Mary. Where ways-of-taking-objects obviously play no role, they do not matter to what we say in ascribing attitudes. Notice also our reluctance to substitute 'the woman who spent 17 years studying primate behavior in the wild'. Where ways-of-taking-objects obviously do play a role, they do matter to what we say.

[26]Forbes [57] (p. 457).

[27]Although Forbes does not treat these two proposals as two parts of a single proposal, I shall treat them in unison in this reconstruction of his criticism. Forbes's overall criticism is considerably more effective when his two proposals are united into a single proposal, and I believe that doing so does not necessarily conflict with Forbes's intentions. Either proposal taken alone leaves obvious and significant (not merely notational) differences between the resulting (so-called) neo-Fregean account and my version of Millianism.

In this way, the neo-Fregean might find his or her way to delivering the same (somewhat liberal) verdicts as I do with respect to various controversial propositional-attitude attributions (presumably, such as (5)).

Forbes's second proposal suggests a particular way of fleshing out the similarity relation involved in the first proposal, one that is designed to ensure that the neo-Fregean's verdicts will always coincide exactly with mine. It is well-known that Fregean theory runs into difficulty with such *de re* constructions as (1) or (1′). Although Frege himself was largely tacit concerning constructions involving *belief of,* a number of neo-Fregeans have proposed various ways of accommodating them within the spirit of Fregean theory. The most famous (and I believe the most compelling) of these neo-Fregean proposals is still David Kaplan's from "Quantifying In" [90].[28] For present purposes, we shall modify Kaplan's proposal slightly. As can be gleaned from the previous section, the Fregean's difficulty with such constructions as (1) arises from a lack of genuine Fregean sense in connection with the open sentence (3), taken under an assignment of a value to x. Kaplan's analysis (as here modified) reconstrues (1) in such a way that (3) is no longer regarded as a proper (i.e., semantic) constituent. Specifically, the open sentence (2) is analyzed into the following:

(6) $(\exists\alpha)[\alpha$ represents x to Jones & Jones believes $\ulcorner\alpha$ is a star $\urcorner]$,

where the special representation relation designated in the first conjunct is such as to entail that α is an individual concept (a sense appropriate to a singular term) that determines x as its referent, and where the quasi-quotation marks occurring in the second conjunct are sense-quoting marks that function in a manner analogous to standard quasi-quotation marks with respect to (i.e., without attempting to quote the sense of) the sense variable 'α'.[29] (Think of this analysis as resulting from a contextual definition for open 'that'-clauses, analogous to Russell's contextual definition for definite descriptions—complete with scope distinctions, the definiendum's lack of "meaning in isolation," and all the rest.) It is a (fairly) straightforward matter to extend this analysis of such quasi-formal *de re* constructions as (1) to such informal constructions as (1′): The neo-Fregean analysis of (2′) is obtained from (6) by substituting the pronoun 'it' for the free variable 'x'.[30] Replacing the bound occurrence of (2) in (1) by its analysis (6) (or the scattered occurrence of (2′) in (1′) by a non-scattered occurrence of its analysis), we obtain something equivalent to

(7) $(\exists\alpha)$ [α *represents* Venus to Jones & Jones believes $\ulcorner\alpha$ is a star $\urcorner]$.

---

[28]Kaplan himself has long since given up on neo-Fregean attempts to accommodate the effects of direct reference.

[29]Strictly speaking, different analyses result from different choices for the representation relation.

[30]Notice that the proposed analyses of such constructions as (2) and (2′), if sound, would effectively block the argument given in section II above in connection with (1) and (1′)—by falsifying the premise that an open sentence of the form $\ulcorner a$ believes that $S\urcorner$ is true under an assignment of values to variables if and only if the referent of a, under the assignment, believes the content of S, under the assignment. (See note 13 above.) The argument takes (2) and (2′) at face value, rather than as contextually defined in terms of quantification and quasi-sense-quotation. Kaplan's analysis allows the neo-Fregean to eschew singular propositions altogether, even in the semantics of *de re* constructions. But how plausible is it—independently of the Fregean motivation for the analysis—that (3) is not a (semantic) constituent of (2)?

The neo-Fregean is struck by the fact that this analysis of (1) and (1′) is significantly similar to my proposed analysis of

(8) Jones believes that Venus is a star.

It is a small step to obtain (7) from (8). One need only extend Kaplan's analysis further, to cover all cases in which a simple singular term—whether a variable or pronoun, or even a proper name or demonstrative—occurs free in a propositional-attitude attribution. We thus obtain a special neo-Fregean theory, one according to which (8) asserts that Jones stands in the belief relation to some thought or other to the effect ⌜α is a star⌝, where α is a sense that represents Venus to Jones. Thus (8) is counted true both by this theory and by my version of Millianism. Similarly, (5) is seen on this theory as asserting that Jones stands in the belief relation to some thought or other to the effect ⌜α is β⌝, where each of α and β is a sense that represents Venus to Jones. Thus (5) is also counted true, as with my Millianism. Therefore, Forbes argues, my version of Millianism dissolves, for all intents and purposes, into this special neo-Fregean theory—with my talk of "singular propositions" and "ways of taking objects" merely a notational variant of the neo-Fregean's talk of "representation" and "individual concepts."[31]

----

[31] A full development of this (allegedly) neo-Fregean theory would involve David Kaplan's procedure of *articulation*, described in "Opacity" [93] (p. 270).

I have not followed Forbes's proposal in detail. Forbes (on my reconstruction—see note 27) suggests instead that my Millianism be taken to be a notational variant of a neo-Fregean theory according to which (8) asserts that Jones stands in the belief relation to some thought or other to the effect ⌜α obtains⌝, where α represents the entire singular proposition about Venus that it is a star to Jones. This proposal is thwarted, however, in case Jones believes Venus to be a star (so that (8) is, on my view, true), but—perhaps because of Jones's philosophical skepticism concerning singular propositions in general—he does not also believe this singular proposition to obtain (so that Forbes's suggested construal of (8) is false). An analogous difficulty arises if the belief that the singular proposition obtains is replaced with the belief that Venus has the property of being a star. (Suppose Jones is skeptical of properties.)

Forbes's proposed (alleged) version of neo-Fregeanism follows his own in substituting the singular proposition about Venus that it is a star for its truth value as the referent of the sentence 'Venus is a star', and likewise in substituting the property of being a star for (the characteristic function of) its extension as the referent of the predicate 'is a star'. These planks disqualify Forbes's theory as genuinely neo-Fregean. Furthermore (as Alonzo Church and Kurt Gödel independently showed), assuming extensionality, each plank precludes the conjunction of the following two plausible principles: (a) that a definite description refers to the individual that uniquely answers to it, if there is one; (b) that trivially equivalent expressions are, if not strictly synonymous, at least close enough in meaning as to ensure their having the same referent. Forbes apparently rejects both of these principles. In fact, he adopts a Russellian account both of definite descriptions and of modal contexts. These various anti-Fregean elements strongly invite the countercharge that Forbes's so-called neo-Fregean theory collapses into a neo-Russellian theory. (But see below.)

A more literal reading of Forbes's proposal is that my assertion that "(8) is true if and only if there is a way of taking the singular proposition about Venus that it is a star such that Jones agrees to this proposition when taking it that way" is merely a notational variant of the neo-Fregean's thesis that the *de re* attribution 'Jones believes of the state of affairs of Venus's being a star that it obtains' is true if and only if there is some state-of-affairs concept α that represents Venus's being a star to Jones and Jones believes ⌜α obtains⌝. This interpretation construes my assertions ostensibly assigning truth conditions to (8) as really making disguised

One significant difficulty with this neo-Fregean proposal is that it does not validate such apparently valid inferences as 'Smith believes that Bush will win the presidency, and so does Jones; hence there is something (some proposition) that both Smith and Jones believe'.[32] This constitutes one fairly dramatic difference between the proposed theory and my version of Millianism. But there are more fundamental differences.

Does the proposed neo-Fregean theory even agree with my version of Millianism on every question of propositional-attitude attribution, without exception, as it is designed to do? On my theory, any propositional attribution involving a proper name within the scope of the 'that'-operator is deemed equivalent to the corresponding *de re* construction in which the name is moved outside the scope of the 'that'-operator. (For instance, (8) is true if and only if (1') is.) Thus Forbes's proposed neo-Fregean theory succeeds in echoing the verdicts of my version of Millianism only insofar as neo-Fregean analyses along the lines of Kaplan's succeed in capturing the truth conditions of *de re* constructions. Several direct-reference theorists (including Kaplan) have mounted an impressive case that Kaplan-style neo-Fregean analyses fail in this attempt. Hilary Putnam's Twin-Earth argument suffices to demonstrate the point:[33] Oscar believes his friend Wilbur to be stingy, while Oscar's exact Doppelgänger on Twin Earth, Oscar$_{TE}$, likewise believes his friend Wilbur$_{TE}$ to be stingy. Duplicates in every detail, Oscar and Oscar$_{TE}$ believe the very same Fregean (nonsingular) thoughts. Neither Oscar nor Oscar$_{TE}$ is in possession of any Fregean individual concept (in which only senses occur as constituents) that differentiates between Wilbur and Wilbur$_{TE}$, and consequently neither possesses

---

reference to a different sentence altogether, and as assigning the truth conditions to this other sentence instead of to (8). I find this interpretation incredible, and assume it is not what Forbes intends. More likely, he means that my analysis of belief, together with the neo-Fregean analysis of *de re* locutions, make my use of (8) into a notational variant of the neo-Fregean's use of 'Jones believes of the state of affairs of Venus's being a star that it obtains'. (Analogously, Evans (*Varieties of Reference* [50]) seems to propose that Perry's use of such an attribution as (8) is a notational variant "at best" of the neo-Fregean's use of something like (1').) But this would hardly make my (or Perry's) theory of (8) into a notational variant of the neo-Fregean's theory of *the very same sentence* (8)—we would still disagree concerning its truth conditions— unless the envisaged neo-Fregean goes further and construes (8) as a paraphrase of something like the relevant *de re* attribution. The proposal in the text represents my attempt to construct the strongest possible case for the spirit of Forbes's (and Evans's) criticism while staying as much as possible within the spirit of Fregean theory (and the bounds of plausibility).

[32]Strictly speaking, this depends on the details of Forbes's neo-Fregean proposal. (The proposed theory certainly does not validate the inference 'Smith believes that Bush will win the presidency, and so does Jones; hence there is some proposition to which both Smith and Jones stand in the belief relation'.) Forbes has confirmed, in personal correspondence, that the intended theory does not validate the inference in the text—on the most straightforward reading of its conclusion—and instead allows only the much weaker conclusion that Smith and Jones believe propositions of the same type. (He proposes taking this weaker conclusion as an alternative reading of the conclusion in the text.)

[33]"Meaning and Reference" [133] (pp. 700–704 and *passim*). Cf. *Frege's Puzzle* (pp. 66–67, 70, 176*n*7).

a Fregean sense that determines the relevant friend as referent independently of context. Assuming that the objects of belief (whether Fregean thoughts or Russellian singular propositions) and their constituents determine their objects (truth values, individuals, etc.) independently of context,[34] each believes something *de re* that the other does not. Oscar's belief concerning Wilbur is therefore irreducible to his beliefs of Fregean (nonsingular) thoughts. The sentence 'Oscar believes that Wilbur is stingy', which is true on my theory, is deemed false by the proposed neo-Fregean theory. The theories are thus diametrically opposed on a key issue.

The Twin-Earth thought experiment illustrates a further, and more central, divergence between my theory and Fregean theory. The way in which Oscar takes Wilbur is presumably exactly the same as the way in which $Oscar_{TE}$ takes $Wilbur_{TE}$—despite the fact that Oscar's thought of Wilbur that he is stingy and $Oscar_{TE}$'s thought of $Wilbur_{TE}$ that he is stingy concern different individuals. By contrast, for the Fregean, each individual concept determines a unique object, or nothing at all. Oscar's thought that Wilbur is stingy and $Oscar_{TE}$'s thought that $Wilbur_{TE}$ is stingy, if they were to have such thoughts concerning different individuals, would have to contain different individual concepts; the sense that Oscar attaches to the name 'Wilbur' would have to be different from the sense that $Oscar_{TE}$ attaches to

---

[34]This assumption is shared by both Frege and myself. As Frege noted, propositions, or "complete thoughts," (unlike indexical sentences or their conventional meanings—or their senses-in-abstraction-from-context) do not change in truth value, or in the objects they concern, when placed in different settings within a single possible world. The alternative would be an account that allows that one subject A may believe one and the very same proposition (complete thought) p as another subject B, yet A's belief of p is correct, or concerns C, while B's belief of p is incorrect, or does not concern C—because of their differing contexts. Any such indexical account of propositions (as opposed to sentences or their meanings) evidently gets things wrong. For suppose p is the alleged "indexical thought" believed by both Oscar and $Oscar_{TE}$ to the effect $\ulcorner \alpha$ is stingy$\urcorner$, where α is the relevant (complete) "indexical individual concept." Notice first that p cannot be the thought that Wilbur is stingy, since $Oscar_{TE}$ does not believe that thought (in his context, whatever that means), or any other thought concerning Wilbur. (The thought that Wilbur is stingy has nothing whatever to do with $Wilbur_{TE}$—on Twin Earth or anywhere else. It is definitely *not* indexical.) Nor is p the thought that *this* person here [pointing to Wilbur] is stingy, for precisely the same reason. Evidently, we do not express p (in our dialect) with the words 'Wilbur is stingy' or 'He [pointing to Wilbur] is stingy'. Nevertheless, barring singular propositions, p is supposed to be the thought that Oscar expresses (in his idiolect) with these words (or with these words-accompanied-by-pointing). Similarly for $Oscar_{TE}$—otherwise, they would not have the same nonsingular thoughts, and consequently would not be exact duplicates. Thus, on most theories (including orthodox Fregean theory and most of its contemporary variations), Oscar should be able to utter the words 'My Twin-Earth counterpart believes with me that Wilbur is stingy' truthfully (thereby attributing to $Oscar_{TE}$ a belief of p). But he cannot. The alleged indexical thought p, therefore, does not exist. (The fact that Oscar cannot truthfully say '$Oscar_{TE}$ believes that Wilbur is stingy' might be urged as evidence in favor of the theory described in the text! On that theory, coupled with indexical thoughts, Oscar could truthfully say "$Oscar_{TE}$ does not believe that Wilbur is stingy, but the sentence 'Wilbur is stingy' does correctly give the content, in my idiolect, of one of $Oscar_{TE}$'s beliefs." But taking the argument in this way would be perverse. The point of the argument is precisely that the thought that Oscar expresses with the words 'Wilbur is stingy' in his idiolect is no more indexical than the thought that we express in our dialect.)

the same name. This is made impossible by the fact that Oscar and Oscar$_{TE}$ are exact duplicates.[35] This sort of consideration points up a crucial difference—in many respects *the* crucial difference—between my ways-of-taking-objects (which are not precluded from determining their objects only contextually) and Fregean senses (which, since they are information values, cannot do so). (See note 18 above.)

The neo-Fregean might attempt to remedy this serious difficulty with his or her attempt to accommodate *de re* constructions, by tinkering with the Kaplan-style analysis (for example, by relaxing the determination requirement on representation). I remain doubtful that this can be successfully accomplished in a plausible manner without resorting to singular propositions, or the like. But suppose I am wrong and the neo-Fregean can find Fregeanistically acceptable necessary-and-sufficient conditions for *de re* belief and other *de re* propositional

---

[35]I can find no plausible way out of this problem for the Fregean. A favored response to this difficulty by self-proclaimed neo-Fregeans has been the postulation of special senses the grasping of which leaves no distinctive trace in one's inner (wholly internal, "purely psychological") state of consciousness—so that exact duplicates like Oscar and Oscar$_{TE}$, whose inner states are exactly the same, nevertheless grasp different "individual concepts." This move faces a serious dilemma: Either the postulated "senses" involve nonconceptual objects (presumably the objects they determine, or their surrogates) as constituents—and are thus individuated by their means—or they do not. If the former, the postulation amounts to the adoption of precisely the sort of theory against which Frege (post-1890) rebelled, while misleadingly couching this anti-Fregean theory in Fregean terminology and labelling the theory with the misnomer 'neo-Fregean'. An "object-involving sense"—a Fregean *Sinn* with nonconceptual components—is a *contradiction in adjecto;* the hypothesized theory is the proverbial wolf in sheep's clothing. (See note 23 above. The arguments of the preceding sections apply equally against this anti-Fregean theory. See also *Frege's Puzzle* [157] (pp. 67–70).) If the latter, the response seems little more than a desperate attempt to stipulate or hypothesize what is intuitively impossible, or even conceptually incoherent. The very notion of a concept (*qua* graspable content) seems to include as a necessary condition that those concepts actively grasped or apprehended by someone at any given time, if free of constituents not themselves grasped by the mind, are determined by the grasper's inner state of consciousness—in the sense that such a concept is grasped by someone if and only if it is also grasped by anyone in exactly the same inner state. Actively grasping a purely conceptual concept just *is* a matter of (or, at least, supervenes on) being in a particular inner mental state. Cf. the last paragraph of "Thoughts" [60] (p. 54), where Frege says that grasping or believing a thought is "a process in the inner world of a thinker," and that "when a thought is grasped, it . . . brings about changes in the inner world of the one who grasps it." See also *Reference and Essence* [155] (pp. 56–58, 65–69). If Oscar's believing ⌜α is stingy⌝ is a "process in Oscar's inner world," where α is a purely conceptual individual concept representing Wilbur, and Oscar$_{TE}$ is in exactly the same inner state, how can he fail to believe exactly the same thing? On the other hand, if grasping the postulated individual concepts is not just a matter of being in a particular inner mental state, the entire account becomes quite mysterious. What exactly are these postulated entities—and what is the justification for calling them "senses" or "purely conceptual concepts" that the mind "grasps," when the (alleged) act of grasping them leaves no distinguishing trace in one's inner state? (Contrast our concepts of *blue, down, left*.) Is there any plausible reason to suppose that there are such concepts that are pure yet traceless? What would *grasping* such an entity amount to, over and above one's inner state? Is there any plausible reason to believe that the mind engages in such activity?

attributes, including alethic necessity. (Committed neo-Fregeans might suppose that this *must* be possible.) Would this show that my version of Millianism is simply a notational variant of a suitably designed neo-Fregean theory? Certainly not. Even if (1′) is true with respect to a possible circumstance if and only if Jones believes some Fregean thought or other of such-and-such a sort in that possible circumstance—so that, on my view, (8) is also true exactly on the same Fregean condition—still (8), according to my account, does not *say* that this Fregean condition is fulfilled. On my view, (8) asserts a certain relationship—the belief relationship—between Jones and the singular proposition about Venus that it is a star. It does not merely *characterize* Jones's belief as being of some Fregean thought *or other* of such-and-such a special sort; it *specifies* a particular belief and attributes it to Jones. In short, even if the neo-Fregean's promise can be kept by adjusting the Kaplan-style analysis (a very big 'if'), the suitably designed neo-Fregean theory ascribes to (8) a very different semantic content from that ascribed by my version of Millianism. The neo-Fregean's semantic truth conditions for (8) are, at best, *a priori* and metaphysically necessarily equivalent to my own. They are not identical.

Finally, we must consider whether the suitably designed theory would be neo-Fregean. It is true, of course, that a neo-Fregean need not follow the master in every detail. (I do not know of any follower of Frege, for instance, who has not shied away from Frege's views concerning the concept *horse*.) But there must be some limit as to how much departure still qualifies as neo-*Fregean*. Certainly the theory of Russell, for example, differs too extensively from that of Frege on central issues to qualify as neo-Fregean. (It is worth noting in this connection that Russell too recognized certain nonsemantic elements from philosophical psychology in his correspondence with Frege over the proposition that Mont Blanc is over 4000 meters high. It is highly doubtful that Frege saw this as simply another way of saying what he himself was saying.) The sort of theory that Forbes envisions (on this reconstruction of his criticism) is a theory that denies that the 'that'-operator occurring in (8) is functioning there merely as a device for sense-quotation, in the same way that it functions in 'Jones believes that the first heavenly body visible at dusk is a star'; specifically, it denies that (8) asserts a relationship between Jones and the sense of the sentence 'Venus is a star'. Furthermore, the theory denies that (8) specifies a particular belief and attributes it to Jones, claiming instead that (8) merely characterizes Jones's belief as being one or another of a particular sort. Most significantly, the theory construes any occurrence of a simple singular term (even of a proper name) within the scope of the 'that'-operator in a propositional attribution (even in an attribution of propositional attitude) as completely open to substitution by any co-referential simple singular term. The theory is specifically designed to have the consequence that Jones believes that Hesperus is Hesperus if and only if he also believes that Hesperus is Phosphorus. It draws no significant distinction at all, in fact, between the ostensibly *de dicto* (8) and the patently *de re* (1′). Otherwise it would be very different from my version of Millianism—obviously so—and hence unsuited to support Forbes's charge of mere notational variance. I submit that there is not enough of Frege's overall theoretical point of view left here for this (would-be) theory to warrant the epithet 'neo-Fregean'.[36] The same would be true of any of its notational variants.

Nor is the envisioned theory a version of Millianism exactly. It is more a curious admixture, a strange brew made up of elements of both Fregeanism and Millianism. I do not claim that one (perhaps even an erstwhile Fregean) could not find reason to adopt this strange theory; I claim only that doing so would involve abandoning too much of the spirit of orthodox Fregean theory for the proponent to qualify as a neo-Fregean. Indeed, if (much to my surprise) genuinely Fregean necessary-and-sufficient conditions are eventually found for the *de re*, I would urge any committed anti-Millian to give the envisioned blend of Fregeanism and Millianism serious consideration as a superior alternative to neo-Fregeanism. Given greater flexibility, however, I would strongly advise against its adoption. Some version of genuine Millianism is much to be preferred. (This was the moral of sections II and III above.)

BIBLIOGRAPHY

[1] Anderson, A. R., ed. 1964. *Minds and Machines*. Englewood Cliffs, NJ: Prentice Hall.

[2] Asher, N., 1986. Belief in Discourse Representation Theory. *Journal of Philosophical Logic* 15(2):127–189.

[3] Asher, N. 1987. A Typology of Attitudinal Verbs and Their Anaphoric Properties. *Linguistics and Philosophy* 10(2):125–197.

[4] Austin, J. L. 1962. *Sense and Sensibilia*. New York: Oxford University Press.

[5] Austin, J. L. 1970. *Philosophical Papers*, 2d ed. New York: Oxford University Press.

[6] Barwise, J. 1986. Noun Phrases, Generalized Quantifiers, and Anaphora. Report No. CSLI-86-52. Stanford: CSLI Publications. Also in *Generalized Quantifiers: Linguistic and Logical Approaches*, ed. E. Engdahl and P. Gärdenfors. Dordrecht: D. Reidel.

[7] Blackburn, S. 1975. The Identity of Propositions. In *Meaning, References and Necessity*, ed. S. Blackburn. New York: Cambridge University Press.

[8] Boer, S., and Lycan, W. 1986. *Knowing Who*. Cambridge, MA: MIT Press.

[9] Brody, J. E. 1989. Personal Health: Most Studies Indicate Presence of Aluminum Is the Effect, Not the Cause, of Diseased Brains. *The New York Times, National Edition*, April 6, 1989, p. 22.

---

[36]Essentially this same point is made, on similar grounds, by Mark Richard, "Taking the Fregean Seriously" [149] (pp. 221–222). There, and also in "Attitude Ascriptions, Semantic Theory, and Pragmatic Evidence" [148] (pp. 247–248), Richard makes the related criticism of (something like) the envisaged "neo-Fregean" theory that, since it validates substitution of co-referential names, it lacks one of the primary motivations for the original Fregean theory of senses. (Here Richard also recognizes that the envisaged theory and Millianism assign different, even if equivalent, truth conditions to such propositional-attitude attributions as (8).)

[10] Burge, T. 1978. Belief and Synonymy. *Journal of Philosophy* 75:119–138.

[11] Burge, T. 1979. Individualism and the Mental. In *Midwest Studies in Philosophy, IV: Studies in Metaphysics*, ed. P. French, T. Uehling, and H. Wettstein. Minneapolis: University of Minnesota Press.

[12] Burge, T. 1982. Other Bodies. In *Thought and Object*, ed. A. Woodfield. New York: Oxford University Press.

[13] Burge, T. 1982. Two Thought Experiments Reviewed. *Notre Dame Journal of Formal Logic* 23:284–293.

[14] Burge, T. 1986. Cartesian Error and the Objectivity of Perception. In *Subject, Thought and Context*, ed. P. Pettit and J. McDowell. Oxford: Oxford University Press.

[15] Burge, T. 1986. Individualism and Psychology. *Philosophical Review* 95:3–45.

[16] Burge, T. 1986. Intellectual Norms and Foundations of Mind. *Journal of Philosophy* 83:697–720.

[17] Burge, T. 1986. On Davidson's "Saying That." In *Truth and Interpretation*, ed. E. LePore. Oxford: Basil Blackwell.

[18] Burge, T. 1988. Individualism and Self-Knowledge. *Journal of Philosophy* 85:649–663.

[19] Bylebyl, J. J. 1970. *Cardiovascular Physiology in the Sixteenth and Early Seventeenth Centuries*. Ann Arbor: University Microfilms.

[20] Carnap, R. 1947. *Meaning and Necessity*. Chicago: University of Chicago Press.

[21] Chastain, C. 1975. Reference and Context. In *Mind, Language and Reality*, ed. K. Gunderson. Minneapolis: University of Minnesota.

[22] Chomsky, N. 1965. *Aspects of the Theory of Syntax*. Cambridge, MA: MIT Press.

[23] Chomsky, N. 1980. *Rules and Representations*. Oxford: Basil Blackwell.

[24] Chomsky, N. 1982. *Lectures on Government and Binding*. Dordrecht: Foris.

[25] Chomsky, N. 1986. *Knowledge of Language: Its Nature, Origin, and Use*. New York: Praeger.

[26] Church, A. 1943. Review of Quine's "Notes on Existence and Necessity." *Journal of Symbolic Logic* 8:45–47.

[27] Church, A. 1950. On Carnap's Analysis of Statements of Assertion and Belief. *Analysis* 10:97–99.

[28] Church, A. 1951. A Formulation of the Logic of Sense and Denotation. In *Structure, Method and Meaning: Essays in Honor of Henry M. Sheffer*, ed. P. Henle, H. Kallen, and S. Langer. New York: Liberal Arts Press.

[29] Church, A. 1954. Intensional Isomorphism and Identity of Belief. *Philosophical Studies* 5(5):65–73. Also in *Propositions and Attitudes*, ed. N. Salmon and S. Soames. Oxford: Oxford University Press, 1988.

[30] Churchland, P. M. 1984. *Matter and Consciousness: A Contemporary Introduction to the Philosophy of Mind*. Cambridge, MA: MIT Press.

[31] Davidson, D. 1963. The Method of Extension and Intension. In *The Philosophy of Rudolf Carnap*, ed. P. Schilpp. La Salle: Open Court.

[32] Davidson, D. 1965. Theories of Meaning and Learnable Languages. *Proceedings of the 1964 International Congress for Logic, Methodology, and Philosophy of Science*. Amsterdam: North Holland. Also in *Inquiries into Truth and Interpretation*. New York: Oxford University Press, 1984.

[33] Davidson, D. 1967. Truth and Meaning. *Synthese* 17:304–323. Also in *Inquiries into Truth and Interpretation*. New York: Oxford University Press, 1984.

[34] Davidson, D. 1968. On Saying That. *Synthese* 19:130–146. Also in *Inquiries into Truth and Interpretation*. New York: Oxford University Press, 1984.

[35] Davidson, D. 1969. True to the Facts. *Journal of Philosophy* 66:748–764. Also in *Inquiries into Truth and Interpretation*. New York: Oxford University Press, 1984.

[36] Davidson, D. 1973. Radical Interpretation. *Dialectica* 27:313–328. Also in *Inquiries into Truth and Interpretation*. New York: Oxford University Press, 1984.

[37] Davidson, D. 1974. Belief and the Basis of Meaning. *Synthese* 27:309–323. Also in *Inquiries into Truth and Interpretation*. New York: Oxford University Press, 1984.

[38] Davidson, D. 1976. Reply to Foster. In *Truth and Meaning: Essays in Semantics*, ed. G. Evans and J. McDowell. Oxford: Oxford University Press. Also in *Inquiries into Truth and Interpretation*. New York: Oxford University Press, 1984.

[39] Davidson, D. 1984. *Inquiries into Truth and Interpretation*. New York: Oxford University Press.

[40] Davidson, D. 1987. Knowing One's Own Mind. *Proceedings and Addresses of the American Philosophical Association* 60(3):441–458.

[41] Dennett, D. 1978. *Brainstorms*. Cambridge, MA: MIT Press.

[42] Dennett, D. 1987. *The Intentional Stance*. Cambridge, MA: MIT Press.

[43] Donnellan, K. 1972. Proper Names and Identifying Descriptions. In *Semantics of Natural Language*, ed. D. Davidson and G. Harman. Dordrecht: Reidel.

[44] Dretske, F. 1981. *Knowledge and the Flow of Information*. Cambridge, MA: MIT Press.

[45] Dreyfus, H. L., and Dreyfus, S. E. 1986. *Mind over Machine*. New York: Macmillan.

[46] Dummett, M. 1973. *Frege: Philosophy of Language*. London: Duckworth.

[47] Dummett, M. 1981. *The Interpretation of Frege's Philosophy*. Cambridge, MA: Harvard University Press.

[48] Evans, G. 1980. Pronouns. *Linguistic Inquiry* 11(2):337–362.

[49] Evans, G. 1981. Understanding Demonstratives. In *Meaning and Understanding*, ed. H. Parret and J. Bouveresse. Berlin and New York: De Gruyter.

[50] Evans, G. 1982. *The Varieties of Reference*. Oxford: Oxford University Press.

[51] Evans, G., and McDowell, J., eds. 1976. *Truth and Meaning: Essays in Semantics*. Oxford: Oxford University Press.

[52] Field, H. 1977. Logic, Meaning, and Conceptual Role. *Journal of Philosophy* 74:379–409.

[53] Field, H. 1978. Mental Representation. *Erkenntnis* 13:9–61.

[54] Fine, K. 1989. The Problem of *De Re* Modality. In *Proceedings of the Conference "Themes from Kaplan,"* ed. J. Almog, J. Perry, and H. Wettstein. Oxford: Oxford University Press.

[55] Fodor, J. 1987. *Psychosemantics*, Cambridge, MA: MIT Press.

[56] Fodor, J. Substitution Arguments and the Individuation of Beliefs. Forthcoming.

[57] Forbes, G. 1987. Review of Nathan Salmon's *Frege's Puzzle. The Philosophical Review* 96(3):455–458.

[58] Foster, J. A. 1976. Meaning and Truth Theory. In *Truth and Meaning: Essays in Semantics*, ed. G. Evans and J. McDowell. Oxford: Oxford University Press.

[59] Frege, G. 1892. On Sense and Reference. In *Translations from the Philosophical Writings of Gottlob Frege*, ed. P. Geach and M. Black. Oxford: Basil Blackwell, 1952.

[60] Frege, G. 1918. Thoughts. In *Propositions and Attitudes*, ed. N. Salmon and S. Soames. Oxford: Oxford University Press, 1988. Originally appeared in English in *Mind* 65(1956):289–311.

[61] Frege, G. 1979. *Posthumous Writings*. Ed. H. Hermes, F. Kambartel, and F. Kaulbach. Trans. P. Long and R. White. Chicago: University of Chicago.

[62] Frege, G. 1980. *Philosophical and Mathematical Correspondence*. Ed. G. Gabriel, H. Hermes, F. Kambartel, C. Thiel, and A. Veraart. Chicago: University of Chicago Press.

[63] Frege, G. 1984. *Collected Papers on Mathematics, Logic, and Philosophy*. Ed. Brian McGuinness. Oxford: Basil Blackwell.

[64] Freud, S. 1949. *Outline of Psycho-Analysis*. Trans. James Strachey. London: Hogarth Press.

[65] Gabel, P., and Feinman, J. M. 1982. Contract Law as Ideology. In *The Politics of Law: A Progressive Critique*, ed. D. Kairys. New York: Pantheon Books.

[66] Goldman, A. 1976. Discrimination and Perceptual Knowledge. *Journal of Philosophy* 73:771–791.

[67] Goodman, N. 1968. *The Languages of Art*. New York: Bobbs-Merrill.

[68] Grice, P. 1989. *Studies in the Ways of Words*. Cambridge, MA: Harvard University Press.

[69] Groenendijk, J., and Stokhof, M. 1990 Dynamic Predicate Logic. To appear in *Linguistics and Philosophy*.

[70] Gunderson, K. 1983. Interview with a Robot. *Analysis* 23:136–42.

[71] Gunderson, K. 1984. Leibnizian Privacy and Skinnerian Privacy. *Behavioral and Brain Sciences* 7(4):628–629.

[72] Gunderson, K. 1985. *Mentality and Machines*, 2d ed. Minneapolis: University of Minnesota Press.

[73] Gunderson, K. 1989. Leibniz's Walk-In Machine, Perception, and the Perils of Physicalism. In *Science, Mind, and Psychology*, ed. C. W. Savage and M. L. Maxwell. Lanham, MD: University Press of America.

[74] Haliday, M., and Hasan, R. 1976. *Cohesion in English*. New York: Longman.

[75] Hart, H. L. A., and Honore, H. M. 1959. *Causation in the Law*. New York: Oxford University Press.

[76] Haugeland, J. 1981. Semantic Engines: An Introduction to Mind Design. In *Mind Design*, ed. J. Haugeland. Cambridge, MA: MIT Press.

[77] Haugeland, J. 1985. *Artificial Intelligence—The Very Idea*. Cambridge, MA: MIT Press.

[78] Heidelberger, H. 1975. A Review of Dummett's *Frege: Philosophy of Language*. *Metaphilosophy* 6:35–43.

[79] Heim, I. 1982. *The Semantics of Definite and Indefinite Noun Phrases*. Ph.D. thesis. University of Massachusetts, Amherst.

[80] Higginbotham, J. 1986. Davidson's Program in Semantics. In *Truth and Interpretation*, ed. E. LePore. Oxford: Basil Blackwell.

[81] Hornsby, J. 1977. Saying Of. *Analysis* 37(4):177–185.

[82] Jackendoff, R. 1987. *Consciousness and the Computational Mind.* Cambridge, MA: MIT Press.

[83] Johnston, M. 1988. The End of the Theory of Meaning. *Mind and Language* 3:28–42.

[84] Kadmon, N. 1987. *On Unique and Non-unique Reference and Asymmetric Quantification.* Ph.D. thesis. University of Massachusetts, Amherst.

[85] Kamp, H. 1984. A Theory of Truth and Semantic Representation. In *Truth, Interpretation and Information: Selected Papers from the Third Amsterdam Colloquium,* ed. J. Groenendijk, T. Janssen, and M. Stokhof. Dorsrecht: Foris.

[86] Kamp, H. 1986. What Should Intensional Logic Be For? Lecture delivered at the APA Western Division Meeting, St. Louis.

[87] Kamp, H. 1986. Comments on H. Sluga: Reading, Writing, and Understanding. APA Pacific Division, Los Angeles.

[88] Kamp, H. 1987. Comments on R. Stalnaker: Belief Attribution and Context. In *Contents of Thought,* ed. R. Grimm and R. Merrill. Tucson: University of Arizona.

[89] Kamp, H. and Reyle, U. n.d. *From Discourse to Logic, I.* Forthcoming, Kluwer.

[90] Kaplan, D. 1969. Quantifying In. In *Words and Objections: Essays on the Work of W. V. Quine,* ed. D. Davidson and G. Harman. Dordrecht: Reidel. Also in *Reference and Modality,* ed. L. Linsky. Oxford: Oxford University Press, 1971.

[91] Kaplan, D. 1975. *Demonstratives.* Unpublished manuscript.

[92] Kaplan, D. 1979. On the Logic of Demonstratives. In *Contemporary Perspectives in the Philosophy of Language,* ed. P. French, T. Uehling, and H. Wettstein. Minneapolis: University of Minnesota Press.

[93] Kaplan, D. 1986. Opacity. In *The Philosophy of W. V. Quine,* ed. L. E. Hahn and P. A. Schilpp. La Salle: Open Court.

[94] Kobes, B. 1986. Individualism and the Cognitive Sciences. Unpublished dissertation, University of California at Los Angeles.

[95] Kripke, S. 1972. *Naming and Necessity.* Cambridge, MA: Harvard University Press.

[96] Kripke, S. 1979. A Puzzle About Belief. In *Meaning and Use,* ed. A. Margalit. Dordrecht: Reidel. Also in *Propositions and Attitudes,* ed. N. Salmon and S. Soames. Oxford: Oxford University Press, 1988.

[97] Kripke, S. 1979. Speaker's Reference and Semantic Reference. In *Contemporary Perspectives in the Philosophy of Language,* ed. P. French, T. Uehling, and H. Wettstein. Minneapolis: University of Minnesota Press.

[98] Kuhn, T. S. 1962. *The Structure of Scientific Revolutions.* Chicago: University of Chicago Press.

[99] Lashley, K. 1956. Cerebral Organization and Behavior. In *The Brain and Human Behavior,* ed. H. Solomon, S. Cobb, and W. Penfield. Baltimore: Williams and Wilkins.

[100] LePore, E., and Loewer, B. 1981. Translational Semantics. *Synthese* 48:121–133.

[101] LePore, E., and Loewer, B. 1988. Dual Aspect Semantics. In *Representations,* ed. S. Silvers. Dordrecht: Kluwer Academic Press.

[102] LePore, E., and Loewer, B. In press. What Davidson Should Have Said. In *Information Based Semantics and Epistemology,* ed. E. Villanueva. Oxford: Basil Blackwell.

[103] LePore, E., and Loewer, B. In press. You Can Say That Again. *Midwest Studies in Philosophy.*

[104] Lettvin, J. Y., Maturana, H. R., McCulloch, W. S., and Pitts, W. H. 1959. What the Frog's Eye Tells the Frog's Brain. *Proceedings of the IRE* 47:1940–1951.

[105] Lewis, D. 1969. *Convention.* Cambridge, MA: Harvard University Press.

[106] Lewis, D. 1972. General Semantics. In *Semantics of Natural Language,* ed. D. Davidson and G. Harman. Dordrecht: Reidel.

[107] Lewis, D. 1979. Attitudes De Dicto and De Se. In *Philosophical Review* 88:113–143. Also in Lewis, D., *Philosophical Papers, I.* Oxford: Oxford University Press, 1983.

[108] Lewis, D. 1981. What Puzzling Pierre Does Not Believe. *Australasian Journal of Philosophy* 59:283–289.

[109] Lewis, D. 1983. New Work for a Theory of Universals. *Australasian Journal of Philosophy* 61:343–377.

[110] Lewis, D. 1983. Postscripts to "Radical Interpretation." In *Philosophical Papers,* Vol. I. Oxford: Oxford University Press.

[111] Linsky, L., ed. 1952. *Semantics and the Philosophy of Language.* Urbana: University of Illinois Press.

[112] Linsky, L., ed. 1971. *Reference and Modality.* Oxford: Oxford University Press.

[113] Loar, B. 1976. Two Theories of Meaning. In *Truth and Meaning: Essays in Semantics,* ed. G. Evans and J. McDowell. Oxford: Oxford University Press.

[114] Loar, B. 1987. Subjective Intentionality. *Philosophical Topics* 15(1):89–124.

[115] Loar, B. 1988. Social Content and Psychological Content. In *Contents of Thought,* ed. R. Grimm and D. Merrill. Tucson: University of Arizona Press.

[116] Lycan, W. 1973. Davidson on Saying That. *Analysis* 33:138–139.

[117] Lycan, W. 1987. *Consciousness.* Cambridge, MA: MIT Press.

[118] Marr, D. 1982. *Vision.* San Francisco: W. H. Freeman.

[119] Marx, K. 1963. *Karl Marx: Early Writings,* ed. T. B. Bottomore. London: Watts and Company, Ltd.

[120] McDowell, J. 1981. Engaging with the Essential. *Times Literary Supplement* (January 16, 1981):61–62.

[121] McDowell, J. 1984. De Re Senses. In *Frege: Tradition and Influence,* ed. C. Wright. Oxford: Basil Blackwell.

[122] McGinn, C. 1982. The Structure of Content. In *Thought and Object,* ed. A. Woodfield. Oxford: Oxford University Press.

[123] Millikan, R. 1984. *Language, Thought and Other Biological Categories.* Cambridge, MA: MIT Press.

[124] Namier, L. 1957. *The Structure of Politics at the Accession of George III,* 2d ed. London: Macmillan.

[125] Newell, A., and Simon, H. 1956. The Logic Theory Machine. *IRE Transactions on Information Theory* IT-2(3):61–79.

[126] Owens, J. 1989. Contradictory Belief and Cognitive Access. *Midwest Studies in Philosophy XIV,* ed. P. French, T. Uehling, and H. Wettstein. Notre Dame: University of Notre Dame Press.

[127] Peacocke, C. In press. What Are Senses?

[128] Perry, J. 1977. Frege on Demonstratives. *Philosophical Review* 86:474–497.

[129] Perry, J. 1980. Belief and Acceptance. *Midwest Studies in Philosophy* 5:533–542.

[130] Poulet, G. 1971. The Phenomenology of Reading. In *Critical Theory Since Plato*, ed. H. Adams. New York: Harcourt Brace Jovanovich.

[131] Putnam, H. 1954. Synonymity and the Analysis of Belief Sentences. *Analysis* 14:114–122. Also in *Propositions and Attitudes*, ed. N. Salmon and S. Soames. Oxford: Oxford University Press, 1988.

[132] Putnam, H. 1970. Is Semantics Possible? In *Language, Belief, and Metaphysics*, ed. H. Kiefer and M. Munitz. Albany: State University of New York Press. Also in *Philosophical Papers*, Vol. II. Cambridge: Cambridge University Press, 1975.

[133] Putnam, H. 1973. Meaning and Reference. *Journal of Philosophy* 70:699–711.

[134] Putnam, H. 1975. The Meaning of 'Meaning'. In *Language, Mind and Knowledge*, ed. K. Gunderson. Minneapolis: University of Minnesota Press. Also in *Philosophical Papers*, Vol. II. Cambridge: Cambridge University Press, 1975.

[135] Putnam, H. 1979. Comments. In *Meaning and Use*, ed. A. Margalit. Dordrecht: Reidel.

[136] Putnam, H. 1988. *Representation and Reality*. Cambridge, MA: MIT Press.

[137] Quine, W. V. 1943. Notes on Existence and Necessity. *Journal of Philosophy* 40:113–127. Also in *Semantics and the Philosophy of Language*, ed. L. Linsky. Urbana: University of Illinois Press, 1952.

[138] Quine, W. V. 1951. *Mathematical Logic*. New York: Harper and Row.

[139] Quine, W. V. 1953. Reference and Modality. In *From a Logical Point of View*. New York: Harper and Row.

[140] Quine, W. V. 1956. Quantifiers and Propositional Attitudes. *The Journal of Philosophy* 53(5):177–187. Also in *The Ways of Paradox*. New York: Random House, 1966.

[141] Quine, W. V. 1960. *Word and Object*. Cambridge, MA: MIT Press.

[142] Quine, W. V. 1963. *From a Logical Point of View*. New York: Harper and Row.

[143] Quine, W. V. 1966. *The Ways of Paradox*. New York: Random House.

[144] Quine, W. V. 1969. Reply to Davidson. In *Words and Objections*, ed. D. Davidson and J. Hintikka. Dordrecht: Reidel.

[145] Ramsey, F. P. 1960. General Propositions and Causality. In *The Foundations of Mathematics and Other Logical Essays*, ed. R. B. Braithwaite. Paterson, NJ: Littlefield, Adams.

[146] Ramsey, F. P. 1960. *The Foundations of Mathematics and Other Logical Essays*, ed. R. B. Braithwaite. Paterson, NJ: Littlefield, Adams.

[147] Richard, M. 1983. Direct Reference and Ascriptions of Belief. *Journal of Philosophical Logic* 12:425–452.

[148] Richard, M. 1986. Attitude Ascriptions, Semantic Theory, and Pragmatic Evidence. *Proceedings of the Aristotelian Society* 87:243–262.

[149] Richard, M. 1988. Taking the Fregean Seriously. In *Philosophical Analysis: A Defense by Example*, ed. D. Austin. Dordrecht: Reidel.

[150] Richards, B. 1974. A Point of Reference. *Synthese* 28:361–454.

[151] Rosch, E., and Lloyd, B. 1978. *Cognition and Categorization*. Hillsdale, NJ: Lawrence Erlbaum.

[152] Russell, B. 1911. Knowledge by Acquaintance and Knowledge by Description. Chapter X of *Mysticism and Logic and Other Essays*. London: Longmans, Green. Also in *Propositions and Attitudes*, ed. N. Salmon and S. Soames. Oxford: Oxford University Press, 1988.

[153] Russell, B. 1918. The Philosophy of Logical Atomism. In *Logic and Knowledge,* ed. R. C. Marsh. London: George Allen and Unwin, 1956. Also in *The Philosophy of Logical Atomism,* ed. D. Pears. La Salle: Open Court, 1985.

[154] Salmon, N. 1979. Review of Leonard Linsky's *Names and Descriptions. Journal of Philosophy* 76(8):436–452.

[155] Salmon, N. 1981. *Reference and Essence.* Princeton: Princeton University Press, and Oxford: Basil Blackwell.

[156] Salmon, N. 1986. Reflexivity. *Notre Dame Journal of Formal Logic* 27(3):401–429. Also in *Propositions and Attitudes,* ed. N. Salmon and S. Soames. Oxford: Oxford University Press, 1988.

[157] Salmon, N. 1986. *Frege's Puzzle.* Cambridge, MA: MIT Press.

[158] Salmon, N. 1989. Illogical Belief. In *Philosophical Perspectives 3: Philosophy of Mind and Action Theory,* ed. J. Tomberlin. Atascadero, CA: Ridgeview.

[159] Salmon, N. 1989. Tense and Singular Propositions. In *Themes from Kaplan,* ed. J. Almog, J. Perry, and H. Wettstein. Oxford: Oxford University Press.

[160] Salmon, N., and Soames, S., eds. 1988. *Propositions and Attitudes.* Oxford: Oxford University Press.

[161] Sartre, J.-P. 1971. Why Write. In *Critical Theory Since Plato,* ed. H. Adams. New York: Harcourt Brace Jovanovich.

[162] Scheffler, I. 1955. On Synonymy and Indirect Discourse. *Philosophy of Science* 22(1):39–44.

[163] Schiffer, S. 1978. The Basis of Reference. *Erkenntnis* 13:171–206.

[164] Schiffer, S. 1987. The 'Fido'-Fido Theory of Belief. *Philosophical Perspectives* 1:455–480.

[165] Schiffer, S. 1987. *Remnants of Meaning.* Cambridge, MA: MIT Press.

[166] Schiffer, S. 1988. Reply to Mark Johnston. *Mind and Language* 3:58–63.

[167] Searle, J. R. 1980. Minds, Brains, and Programs. *The Behavioral and Brain Sciences* 1:417–424.

[168] Searle, J. R. 1980. Intrinsic Intentionality. Reply to criticisms of Minds, Brains and Programs. *The Behavioral and Brain Sciences* 3:450–456.

[169] Searle, J. R. 1983. *Intentionality: An Essay in the Philosophy of Mind.* Cambridge: Cambridge University Press.

[170] Searle, J. R. 1984. Intentionality and Its Place in Nature. *Synthese* 61:3–16.

[171] Searle, J. R. 1984. *Minds, Brains and Science.* Cambridge, MA: Harvard University Press.

[172] Searle, J. R. 1987. Indeterminacy, Empiricism and the First Person. *Journal of Philosophy* 84:123–146.

[173] Segal, G. 1988. A Preference for Sense and Reference. *The Journal of Philosophy* 89:73–89.

[174] Smith, A. D. 1988. Review of Nathan Salmon's *Frege's Puzzle. Mind* 97(385):136–137.

[175] Smith, E., and Medin, D. 1981. *Concepts and Categories.* Cambridge, MA: Harvard University Press.

[176] Soames, S. 1987. Direct Reference, Propositional Attitudes, and Semantic Content. *Philosophical Topics* 15(1):47–87.

[177] Soames, S. 1987. Substitutivity. In *On Being and Saying: Essays for Richard Cartwright,* ed. J. J. Thomson. Cambridge, MA: MIT Press.

[178] Stalnaker, R. 1984. *Inquiry.* Cambridge, MA: MIT Press.

[179]   Stalnaker, R. 1987. Belief Attribution and Context. In *Contents of Thought*, ed. R. Grimm and R. Merrill. Tucson: University of Arizona.

[180]   Stillings, N. 1987. Modularity and Naturalism in Theories of Vision. In *Modularity in Knowledge Representation and Natural-Language Understanding*, ed. J. Garfield. Cambridge, MA: MIT Press.

[181]   Temin, M. 1975. The Relational Sense of Indirect Discourse. *The Journal of Philosophy* 72:287–306.

[182]   Thomason, R. H. 1979. Home Is Where the Heart Is. In *Contemporary Perspectives in the Philosophy of Language,* ed. P. French, T. Uehling, and H. Wettstein. Minneapolis: University of Minnesota Press.

[183]   Turing, A. M. 1950. Computing Machinery and Intelligence. *Mind* 59(236):433–460.

[184]   Wagner, S. 1986. California Semantics Meets the Great Fact. *Notre Dame Journal of Formal Logic* 27(3):430–455.

3
The Development of the New Theory

BOB AND CAROL AND TED AND ALICE

David Kaplan

1. The problem

Consider the following:

(1) The last word of (1) is obscene.

(2) The last word of (1) is obscene.

It would appear that (1) cannot be turned into a truth by addition of quotation marks, but that (2) can be so changed—namely, by putting quotation marks around its last word. Yet it would also appear that (1) = (2); and if this is so, then by Leibniz's Law whatever is true of (2) is also true of (1). How is this apparent contradiction to be resolved?[1]

2. Preliminaries

Call the sentence token which occurs in the line indexed above by '(1)', 'Bob'. Call the sentence token which occurs in the line indexed by '(2)', 'Carol'. Bob and Carol are twins. Using 'T' to abbreviate 'the type of', we can express this as follows:

Bob ≠ Carol, but T(Bob) = T(Carol).

Suppose that next Sunday morning I add quotation marks to Carol's last word (token), and the following Monday morning I do the same to Bob. By the following Tuesday morning, they would both look like this:

The last word of (1) is 'obscene'.

Call Bob's descendent 'Ted', and Carol's descendent 'Alice'. Ted and Alice are also twins.

Ted ≠ Alice, but T(Ted) = T(Alice).

In order to decide whether Bob and Carol and Ted and Alice are true we must know to whom they are referring. Clearly the Great Designer, Professor Cartwright, designed them to use '(1)' to refer to the individual dubbed '(1)' by the '(1)' which occurs to the left of Bob. Call that token of '(1)', 'Index-1'. *Our* use of '(1)' is governed by the use of Index-1. A point of the problem is to make *their* use of '(1)' co-referential with ours.[2]

---

[1] The problem is stated thus in *The Journal of Philosophy* **68** (1971), p. 86, where it is attributed to Professor Richard Cartwright. Solutions follow. Certain collateral issues are discussed in a series of appendices of varying interest. Suggestions for further study are given in the homework problems. An Instructor's Manual is in preparation. All of this has been supported by the National Science Foundation.

[2] I shall use 'refers to', 'denotes', 'designates', 'takes as value', etc. indifferently for the standard notion. Though my way of talking may suggest it, Donnellan's *referential use* is not here applicable.

Index-1 occurs as part of an act of dubbing in which what is displayed to the right of Index-1 is dubbed '(1)'. Our dubbings, of Bob and Carol and Ted and Alice and Index-1, have all been by description—"Call the blah blah blah, 'Bob'." But the dubbing which occurs in the line containing Index-1 is a dubbing by demonstration—"Call this: (18') '(1)'." So, Index-1 must refer to whatever is displayed to its right.

Bob is certainly displayed there, but it seems equally appropriate to claim that T(Bob) is displayed there.

3. The Obvious Solution

For this solution we assume that it is always a sentence *type* that is displayed in dubbings of the kind in question. Thus:

$$(1) = T(\text{Bob}) = T(\text{Carol}) = (2).$$

Is it true that in violation of Leibniz's Law (2) can be changed into a truth by the addition of quotation marks but (1) cannot?

Let us begin by discussing (2) in both its actual form, T(Carol), and its potential form, T(Alice). T(Carol) is not true[3] because the last word of (1), namely, the word 'obscene', is not itself obscene. However, T(Alice) is true (allowing for a tacit shift from the 'is' of predication to the 'is' of identity) because the last word of (1) is the word 'obscene'.

But wait a minute! On Sunday morning, when Alice first appears, she (or, if you prefer, her type) is true. However by Monday afternoon, when Ted has replaced Bob, the last word of (1), i.e., the last word of the referent of Index-1, seems to be the word 'obscene'. Thus at that time Alice degenerates to falsity.

Alice's apparent instability is illusory. On Monday morning, when we replace Bob with Ted, we replace the display in a dubbing. Since we neglect to simultaneously replace the name being bestowed, distinct entities are given the same name. Horrors! There is the old (1), T(Bob); and there is (1) Jr., T(Ted).

If at her birth on Sunday, Alice uses '(1)' to refer to T(Bob), then there is no reason to believe that Bob's replacement by Ted should cause her to forget Bob and begin using '(1)' to refer to T(Ted). Indeed, her type and that of her mother are both named '(2)', but this has not caused her to forget her own mother, nor to confuse

---

[3] There is an ellipsis here. The truth of T(Carol) depends on the reference made by T(Carol)'s '(1)'. (Carol may have a remote twin whose '(1)' token is not co-referential with Carol's.) A more explicit form is:

T(Carol) is not true when T(Bob) is taken as referent of '(1)'.

Or, since T(Carol)'s '(1)' is the only word in T(Carol) whose reference is under examination:

T(Carol) is not true with respect to T(Bob).

Or since we have fixed *our* use of '(1)' by means of Index-1:

T(Carol) is not true with respect to (1).

Or, since, as remarked in the preliminaries, it is an assumption of the problem that Carol's use of '(1)' is co-referential with ours:

T(Carol) is not true.

their differently truth valued types. Alice may continue to refer to whichever (1) she referred to on Sunday. This allows that she may—presciently—have referred to T(Ted) all along.

Alice's constancy aside, the conclusion is that so long as the twins refer to the same (1) they have the same truth value.[4]

When (2) is changed, it is changed into a truth with respect to (1), but a falsehood with respect to (1) Jr. *Exactly the same holds when* (1) *is changed!* Thus Leibniz's Law applies without contradiction.

The puzzle was generated by thinking that both (2) and (2) Jr. must refer to (1); whereas both (1) and (1) Jr. must be self-referential. Thus (2) Jr. and (1) Jr. would refer to different sentences. The puzzle is resolved by recognizing that there are two (1)'s and keeping track of which (1) is under discussion.

4. A More Interesting Solution

There is a grave difficulty in the obvious solution. The problem speaks the language of 'turn into' and 'change into', but the solution is couched in a metaphysics of replacement.[5]

We did not *change* the false Carol into the true Alice, we *replaced* the false Carol with the true Alice. Or did we? What really happens when I take my pen to Carol next Sunday morning? Could it be that Alice and Carol, like Hesperus and Phosphorus, are one?

There is every reason to think so. Sentence tokens are physical objects and macro-objects at that. They are created, wear down, fade, are touched up, and sometimes are distorted. Neon sentence tokens frequently malfunction and thereby change type. If sufficiently comical, such transformations are enshrined in *The Reader's Digest*.

I conclude that:

> Carol = Alice and Bob = Ted.

This not only accounts for the critical use of 'changed' in the formulation of the problem, but as we shall see, it also illuminates the respect in which Carol *can* be changed into a truth by the addition of quotation marks while Bob cannot.

Our bookkeeping simplifies. We can make the natural assumption that only two tokens are involved, Bob-Ted and Carol-Alice, and also that only two dubbings are involved, one incorporating Index-1 and one incorporating its colleague, Index-2. Index-1 stands beside the same token, Bob-Ted, throughout the period of interest. In the problem it is (1) and (2) that are 'changed'. So it must be intended that:

> (1) = Bob-Ted, and (2) = Carol-Alice.

---

[4] I waver between Alice and T(Alice) as vehicle of truth. The ambivalence is not critical. The truth value of T(Alice) should, for this problem, be evaluated with respect to the individual referred to by Alice.

[5] Surely on a distinction of such fundamental metaphysical importance, the choice of language in framing the problem was no accident.

With only one (1) to contend with, we can make the natural assumption that throughout the period of interest both Bob-Ted and Carol-Alice use '(1)' to refer to Bob-Ted.

Both (1) and (2) are false at the present time. But their potentialities differ.

(2) *can* be transformed into a truth by putting quotation marks around her last word. In fact, next Sunday morning she *will* be so transformed. Note that this possibility depends on the possibility of making no earlier transformation in (1). When quotation marks are put around the last word in (1), on Monday morning, (2) will again change in truth value. This time not because *she* has changed, but because the world has changed around her and she has viewed it as unchanged.

In contrast, (1) *cannot* be transformed into a truth simply by the addition of quotation marks to his last word. In particular, when those quotation marks are added next Monday morning, his revised self-analysis is true only of his unrevised self. Thus he continues to dissemble. In order to change (1) into a truth, a second change must be made so that (1) looks like this:

> The last word in (1) was 'obscene'.

5. A Complete Solution

The preceding solution, though it adequately accounts for the critical elements of *change* and *self-reference*, is yet only a partial solution to the original problem. A complete solution must, in addition, satisfy all three of the following paradoxical conditions:

> (1) cannot be changed into a truth by addition of quotation marks to its last word.
>
> (2) can be changed into a truth by addition of quotation marks to its last word.
>
> (1) = (2).

According to the preceding solution, (1) = Bob-Ted ≠ Carol-Alice = (2). Thus the preceding solution clearly fails to satisfy the third condition. This is a cheap avoidance of paradox, no more subtle in this respect than the obvious solution, which simply fails to satisfy the first condition.

In order to obtain a complete solution we must abandon our preliminary claim that Index-1 is used to dub some individual displayed to its right. In a dubbing, a proper name is introduced. But treating Index-1 as a proper name, whether of Bob-Ted or Bob-Ted's current type, is what led to the incompleteness of the previous solutions.

Thus, what is required is an analysis which treats Index-1 as semantically complex. Index-1 must refer to a type, but not by naming it as in the obvious solution. Instead Index-1 should be thought of as *describing* its referent, in the manner of the functional expression, 'the type of *this*'. The only *naming* involved is that of the component demonstrative 'this', which names what is displayed—in the present case, the token Bob-Ted. Since we never replace the display, the demonstrative 'this' always refers to Bob-Ted. If we assume that a proper name functions rather like a demonstrative with a fixed demonstratum, we might describe Index-1 as semantically equivalent to 'T(Bob-Ted)'. When Bob-Ted changes, 'T(Bob-Ted)' takes on a new referent.

The treatment of Index-2 clearly should parallel that of Index-1. We can express the strong equivalence of 'T(Bob-Ted)' with the use of '(1)' introduced by Index-1, and of 'T(Carol-Alice)' with the use of '(2)' introduced by Index-2, roughly as follows:

> (a) Necessarily ((1) = T(Bob-Ted)), and
> necessarily ((2) = T(Carol-Alice)).

If the third condition on a complete solution is to be satisfied, Index-1 and Index-2 must refer to types as in the obvious solution. But if the first two conditions are to be satisfied, Index-1 must reflect the self-referential element represented in the more interesting solution. The present treatment is simply the natural way to combine the advantages of each of the previous solutions.

Given this interpretation of '(1)', how shall we treat the predicate "can be changed into a truth by addition of quotation marks"? This too has a simple and natural interpretation.

Consider first an analogous predicate. Let M be a metal bar exactly one meter long. A typical claim for a potential of change is

> (b) M's length can be changed to more than a meter by heating it to 200°.

Change is mentioned, and change is indeed involved. But a change in M, not a change in the length: *one meter*. M, not M's length, is heated; as a consequence, M's former length, one meter, is replaced by a new length, 1.001 meters. Ignoring the subtleties involved in the use of 'can' as opposed to 'would', and also ignoring the presupposition that M's length is not now more than one meter, an approximate equivalent to (b) is

> (c) If M were heated to 200°, then M's length would be more than one meter.

The purpose of this example is to point out the *intensional context* involved in (b).[6]

Returning to the present interpretation of '(1)', we expand the first condition for a complete solution in the style of (c):

> (d) It is not the case that, if quotation marks were put around Bob-Ted's last word, then T(Bob-Ted) would be true.

---

[6] The *subjunctive* conditional is not critical to this example or to the following analysis of the problem. We may suppose that M *will* be heated to 200°, and thereby shift to the simple future tense.

When M is heated to 200°, M's length will be more than one meter. The occurrence of 'M's length' remains oblique; it cannot be replaced by its co-designator, 'one meter'. A similar shift from the subjunctive or modal to the future tense would also not affect the following analysis of the problem. It is interesting to note, in comparison, that no intensional context of any form was involved in the preceding solution to the problem. According to that analysis, it is the *present* referent of Index-1, Bob-Ted himself not one of his types or stages, that becomes true.

To establish that (d) holds, suppose that quotation marks *were* put around Bob-Ted's last word. Bob-Ted would then look like this:

> The last word of (1) is 'obscene'.

Recalling that it is an assumption of the problem that both Bob-Ted and Carol-Alice always use '(1)' as we do, we see, by (a), that T(Bob-Ted) would then be true if and only if the last word of what would then be T(Bob-Ted) were the word 'obscene'. But the last word of what would then be T(Bob-Ted) would be "obscene" not 'obscene'. Hence T(Bob-Ted) would not be true. Hence the subjunctive conditional in (d) does not hold. Hence (d), and thereby the first condition for a complete solution, is satisfied.

The second condition for a complete solution expands as follows:

> (e) If quotation marks were put around Carol-Alice's last word, then
> T(Carol-Alice) would be true.

Arguing as above, we see that (e) is satisfied if and only if the placing of quotation marks around Carol-Alice's last word would leave the last word of T(Bob-Ted) (currently the word 'obscene') unaffected. Since the stability of Bob-Ted surely *is* one of the background conditions to be assumed in evaluating a subjunctive conditional like (e), it follows that (e), and thereby the second condition for a complete solution, is satisfied.

Bob-Ted and Carol-Alice *currently* have the same type. Thus, by (a), the third condition is also satisfied.

Our solution is therefore complete.

Appendix I: The Addition of Quotation Marks

In the preliminaries, quotation marks were added directly to the token Bob, and T(Ted) was taken to be the type so tokened. An alternative is to treat the addition of quotation marks as an operation applied directly to the type T(Bob), and yielding the type T(Ted).

> *Homework Problem #1.* The alternative treatment leads to a solution even less interesting than the obvious solution. What is it?
> *Homework Problem #2.* Can the three solutions given above be reconstructed using the alternative treatment of quotation marks?

Appendix II: Types, Tokens, and Reference

Although in the obvious solution T(Bob) $=$ T(Carol), it did not immediately follow that Bob and Carol share a truth value. Tokens of 'Ari is so clever' in the mouths of Plato and Jackie could differ in truth value. Tokens of 'I am so clever' in the mouths of Plato's Aristotle and Jackie's Aristotle could differ in truth value.

> *Homework Problem #3.* Do the two pairs of twins (of the types 'Ari is so clever' and 'I am so clever') differ in the same way?

Appendix III: A Nonsolution

It might be thought that the original problem could be dissolved simply by claiming that (1) = Bob and (2) = Carol. Then (1) ≠ (2). Hence no application of Leibniz's Law is possible. Hence no paradox. But this leaves unexplained how twins can differ in truth value when they do not differ in the ways discussed in Appendix II. The use of twins to construct the puzzle is, in fact, inessential.

> *Homework Problem #4.* Reconstruct the original problem and discuss its solution using
>   the following:
> (Dick)   My last word is obscene.
> (Helen)   Your last word is obscene.

Appendix IV: Truth and Content

It may be thought that another plausible candidate for the referent of Index-1 is the *content* of Bob—the proposition expressed by *T*(Bob) in the context in which Bob occurs. Indeed, the problem uses language of the form:

  (1) is not true.

How can truth or falsity be predicated directly of either a token or a type? (1) must be a proposition. But the same proposition is expressed by each of the following:

> The last word of (1) is obscene.
> An obscene word is the last word of (1).

So if (1) is a proposition, how can the function *the last word of* be applied directly to (1)?

  To make sense of the conditions of the problem, both of the following must be meaningful:

  (i) the last word of (1)

  (ii) (1) is false.

We have chosen to interpret '(1)' in such a way that (i) has an obvious meaning. (ii) is then accommodated by implicit (and sometimes, explicit) relativization to features which fix the content of a fugitive sentence. Among the features implicitly taken into account are that the language is English. Among the features explicitly accounted for are the referent of the '(1)' contained in (1) (see note 3). In the obvious solution we spoke of (1) Jr. being *true with respect to* (1) but *false with respect to* (1) Jr. Similarly, in the more interesting solution when the tense of (1) became relevant, the notion of truth used was that of (1) being *true on Tuesday morning*.

> *Homework Problem #5.* Construct a solution in which the referent of '(1)' is such that truth is
>   not relativized as above. That is, construct a solution in which the content is built into (1).

Appendix V: The Individuation of Types

I have suggested that the most natural notion of a token allows a token to change its type—in the sense that a token can be so changed that a new type will replace its former type. What principle of individuation should we use for types? It is not really necessary that homographous words should share a type. If a useful notion of type can grant the tokens:

> homographous
> *homographous*

the same type, why should it deny 'yellow' (a color) and 'yellow' (a character) distinct types?

> *Homework Problem #6.* Do the verb 'paint' and the noun 'paint' have distinct types?

Appendix VI: Congruence and Identity

We might have said that although Bob-Ted ≠ Carol-Alice, there are times at which Bob-Ted *is congruent with* Carol-Alice. We could have symbolized this with an explicit three-place predicate:

> Cong(Bob-Ted, Carol-Alice, *t*)

or with a tensed two-place predicate:

> Bob-Ted ≈ Carol-Alice
> Next Sunday morning (Bob-Ted ≉ Carol-Alice)

where 'next Sunday morning' is a temporal operator treated in the standard way.

Instead, in order to achieve a real identity between (1) and (2), we introduced a tensed functor: '*T*'. Thus '*T*(Bob-Ted) = *T*(Carol-Alice)', with tenseless '=', is true at the same times as 'Bob-Ted ≈ Carol-Alice'.

> *Homework Problem #7.* Under what conditions on the three-place congruence relation can the tensed predicate '≈' be traded off for a tensed functor and real (i.e., tenseless) identity?

Appendix VII: What Can Be Displayed?

A dubbing by demonstration takes the form:

> Let us call this: _____ 'McBlank'.

A dubbing by description takes the form:

> Let us call α 'McAlpha',

where the blank is replaced by the individual being dubbed, and 'α' is replaced by a description of the individual being dubbed.

It would be good if dubbings by demonstration and dubbings by description were to correspond respectively to dubbings with the subject present and dubbings in absentia.[7] But first some problems concerning display potentials must be resolved.

---

[7] Anything of which we can frame a definite description can be dubbed by description including, for example, Newman 1 (the first child to be born in the twenty-second century). Thus we might dub by description even when the subject is present, if we are unaware of the fact, or if he is not appropriately 'available', or if we have an ulterior motive.

Some individuals, like the universe, are hard to display all at one place because they are difficult to gather up. Some individuals, like Quine, are hard to display all at once because, as he would protest, "of my hence and ago." Other individuals, like 'Quine' and red are hard to display because they themselves are not within space-time, though their manifestations are. Still other individuals, like nine and the null set, neither are, nor have manifestations, within space-time.

Nine and null can probably only be dubbed by description. But things like Quine, 'Quine', red, and the universe, which have locally presentable aspects or manifestations might be deemed demonstrable in themselves.

There are epistemological reasons for coming to think, as Russell did, that only completely local beings can be demonstrated directly. On this view when I point to Venus and say 'this planet', I am giving a *description* of Venus which incorporates a *demonstration* of one aspect of Venus. Such a treatment provides a Fregean explanation of how a long slow utterance of:

> This planet [pointing to Venus in the morning] = this planet [pointing to Venus in the evening]

can be both informative and true. The denoting phrases are thought of as stylistic variants of 'the planet of which *this* is an aspect'.

On the other hand it seems more natural to think of nice solid continuous four dimensional objects as typical of the kind of thing we point at (directly), and to think of their aspects and stages as somehow derived and abstracted (by description).

> *Homework Problem #8.*   Can Quine be demonstrated or only described?
> *Homework Problem #9.*   Are Quine's aspects and stages like 'Quine's manifestations'?
> *Homework Problem #10.*   Are 'Quine's manifestations' like red's?
> *Homework Problem #11.*   How do we dub nine and null?

Only on a view such as Russell's is it at all reasonable to make it a prerequisite for a dubbing that the dubbor *know,* or stand in some other special epistemological relationship to, the dubbee? Though most pointings are *teleological* (the finger is aimed at a preconceived individual), *blind demonstrations* (as in spin-the-bottle) are also possible and provide an equally satisfactory basis for a dubbing. Descriptions also may be either teleological or blind. A description like 'the first child to be born in the twenty-second century' is near-blind.

> *Homework Problem #12.*   How much was known of Jack the Ripper when he was so dubbed?

Appendix VIII: The Ambiguity of Demonstrations

There are conventions governing what is demonstrated when I point. I cannot aim my finger at you and thereby refer to myself. Even though you and the rest of my auditors know that I have mistaken you for your twin, I cannot aim my finger at you and thereby refer to your twin. But in cases like that of Index-1 and cases where my finger is genuinely aimed at a boy, his jacket, and its zipper the conventions are not completely determinative. The only further resource available to resolve the issue seems to be my intentions, taken in a broad sense to include that which guided my pointing. If we wish to avoid introducing an intentional element into the truth conditions for assertions in which 'this' is completed by a pointing, we might require that 'this' always be accompanied by a common noun phrase—'this boy', 'this zipper', 'this momentary stage of a rabbit surface'. When my finger aims at more (or less) than one such, the demonstrative phrase could be treated in the manner of an improper description. The more general common noun phrases, 'physical object', 'entity', would invariably produce improper demonstrations.

> *Homework Problem #13.* If one points at the center of a pool of blood, is the demonstrative phrase 'this blood' proper or improper?
>
> *Homework Problem #14.* Does the correct solution to the problem—and in particular to the question of what is displayed to the right of Index-1—depend on what Cartwright had in mind?
>
> *Homework Problem #15.* Donnellan's account (1966, 1968, 1970) of the referential use of a description is more along intentional lines. If he were to adapt his account to pointings, what would he say about the mistaken pointing at a twin?

Appendix IX: Rigid Designators

The introduction of an expression which is a simple name syntactically, but a compound description semantically, I call an *abbreviation*—to contrast with the more common form of introduction, a *dubbing*. Proper names are, or at least purport to have been, introduced by dubbings. Since the introduction of a syntactically simple expression, like Index-1, is almost invariably a dubbing, I took special care to point out that in the complete solution I was interpreting the introduction of Index-1 as an abbreviation.

The semantical differences between descriptions like 'the number of planets' and proper names like '9' are already familiar. The description may denote different numbers under different circumstances, but the name always denotes the same number. It has been less widely noticed that in this respect all proper names are like '9'. In fact, the very purpose of introducing a proper name is often to provide an expression free from the vagaries of 'the number of planets'. Kripke (1972) has remarked that proper names are *rigid designators*—the same name designates the same individual in all circumstances. I add that the introduction of a proper name may as well be occasioned by frustration over the flaccidity of a description as by frustration over its length. Discussion of an individual's potentiality to fail to fulfill the description by which he is known, will almost always be facilitated by the introduction of a proper name. The yacht owner's guest who is reported by Russell to have become entangled in "I thought that your yacht was longer than it is" should have said, "Look, let's call the length of your yacht a 'russell'. What I was trying to say is that I thought that your yacht was longer than a russell." If the result of such a dubbing were the introduction of 'russell' as a mere abbreviation for 'the length of your yacht', the whole performance would have been in vain.

Through its use in a dubbing by description, an arbitrary description can produce a name which *rigidly* designates whatever the description *happens* to describe in the context of the dubbing.

> *Homework Problem # 16 (adopted from Kripke).* '100° Centigrade' is *defined* as 'the tempera-
> ture at which water boils at sea level'. Are such definitions dubbings or abbreviations?
> *Homework Problem #17.* The insertion of words like 'present' and 'actual' in a description—
> 'the *present* Queen of England', 'the *actual* length of your yacht'—cause the description to
> take the referent it would have if it were not within the scope of any temporal, modal,
> epistemological, or other intensional operators. In Russell's language, they give the
> description *primary scope.* Thus the insertion of such words fixes the referent
> independently of any intensional operators within whose scope the description lies. Do
> such words convert the description into a rigid designator?

Others, before Kripke, had recognized the rigidity of proper names. His notable contribution has been to indicate a technique for *finding* the referent of a proper name, on a particular occasion of use, which is independent of the knowledge and belief of the user. The technique consists in tracing the history of acquisition of the name from use back to bestowal. It is based on the exceedingly plausible assumption that if a name enters your vocabulary from hearing me use it (you learn the name from me), then your utterances of the name have the same referent as mine. Kripke's technique for finding the referent frees proper names from their supposed dependence on currently associated descriptions[8] and thus eases the way for recognition of their rigidity.

I have attempted to supplement the view by emphasizing the techniques for bestowing a proper name and thus *fixing* reference. I call such acts of bestowal 'dubbings'. (Other terms are available, but they tend to carry a sectarian bias.) The resulting view of the reference of proper names can be encapsulated as follows:

> If α is the proper name used on some particular occasion, then
> (i) α denotes x iff α originated in a dubbing of x and
> (ii) for all possible circumstances w, α denotes x with respect to w iff α denotes x.

It is a corollary that if α did not originate in a successful dubbing (one which is a dubbing of *some x*), α nowhere denotes anything.

This view of the reference of proper names is anti-intentional. It says what the *name* (in use) refers to, not what a *user* refers to, or intends to refer to, or is most plausibly taken to be talking about, in *using* the name. The latter (user's reference) is an important, but different, sense of 'refer'. Suppose the name 'Jaakko Hintikka' is introduced to me by having Julius Moravcsik introduced to me with the lie "This is Jaakko Hintikka." When I later remark, "Hintikka's Finnish accent is a very unusual one," I, no doubt, am talking about Moravcsik. I may even be said to have referred to him. But my *utterance* of the name refers to Hintikka. Thus the sentence token I have uttered is false. (There may be other Hintikka's with unusual Finnish accents, but the Finnish accent of the Hintikka referred to in the lie is

---

[8] There was always something implausible about the idea that the referent of a proper name is determined by the currently associated descriptions. For example, the entry under 'Rameses VIII' in the *Concise Biographical Dictionary* (Concise Publications: Walla, Washington) is 'One of a number of ancient pharaohs about whom nothing is known'.

usual. Remember it was a lie, so the 'this' and the 'Jaakko Hintikka' could not be co-referential.) I see no way, other than speaking carefully, of avoiding the ambiguating effects of this distasteful dualism.

> *Homework Problem #18.* Kaplan (1968, especially §IX) has introduced a peculiar relation between an occurrence of a name and an individual, which he expresses with an italicized '*of*'. To which of the following does his notion correspond: the name's reference, the user's reference, some confused combination of the two, none of the above?

Appendix X: Denotation and Existence

Some have claimed that though a proper name might denote the same individual with respect to any possible world (or, more generally, possible circumstance) in which he exists, it certainly cannot denote him with respect to a possible world in which he does not exist. With respect to such a world there must be a gap in the name's designation, it designates nothing. This is a mistake.[9] There are worlds in which Quine does not exist. It does not follow that there are worlds with respect to which 'Quine' does not denote. What follows is that with respect to such a world 'Quine' denotes something which does not exist in that world. Indeed, Aristotle no longer exists, but 'Aristotle' continues to denote (him).

The view that no expression could name Quine with respect to a possible world in which he does not exist seems to be based on one of two ideas. The first is usually expressed with respect to possible worlds, but I will caricature it with respect to the moments of time.

Individuals are taken to be specific to their moment, thus they are momentary stages of what *we* would call individuals. Variables and constants, when evaluated with respect to a moment *t*, take as values stages occurrent at *t*. *Our* individuals can be constructed from these individuals (which were sliced out of our individuals in the first place) by assembly (or, perhaps, reassembly). The assemblages of stages are used to evaluate quantification into and out of temporal operators. Although you cannot literally step in the same river twice, you can step in two stages of the same assemblage. A variable which recurs within and without a temporal operator will take different values in its different occurrences, but its values will be from the same assemblage.[10] Note that though each stage belongs to one or more assemblages, the values of the variables are not

---

[9] An explicit perpetration occurs in Kaplan (1968, p. 196). But he has not erred alone.

[10] To interpret this theory within a normal one, take the stages to be ordered couples consisting of a moment of time and the coincidence class of one of the normal (continuant) individuals at that time. The coincidence class of a given continuant at a given time is the class of all those continuants which coincide with the given continuant at the given time. The assemblages are determined by the normal individuals. The assemblage corresponding to a normal individual *a* is that function which assigns to each moment of time at which *a* occurs the coincidence class of *a* at that time. Though the value of each occurrence of a variable is a stage, these stages are coordinated by means of assemblages determined by the quantifiers. An existentially quantified formula holds at a given moment if there is an assemblage which has a stage at that moment and which is such that the formula is satisfied by taking as value of each occurrence of the quantified variable the relevant stage of the assemblage. The universal quantifier is, as usual, the dual of the existential. Atomic predicates must also be reinterpreted to apply to the coincidence classes of the continuants to which they originally applied.

assemblages but stages. The individuals are stages. Genidentity, as determined by the assemblages, holds between distinct stages.[11]

> *Homework Problem #19.* Let **T** be the set of moments of time ordered by $<$. The present time is 0. Let $S(t)$, for $t \in T$, be the set of stages occurrent at t; let $F(t)$, for $t \in T$, be the subset of $S(t)$ of which 'F' is true at t; let **A** be the set of assemblages f, where the domain of f is included in **T** and for each t in the domain of f, $f(t) \in S(T)$. The operator 'P' is read 'at some earlier time'. Translate the following sentence, involving a quantification out of a temporal operator, into the metalanguage:
>
> $$P[\forall x(Fx) \rightarrow Fx)$$
>
> (In English: There is a certain time in the past such that all individuals, of that time, who were then female still are.)[12]

According to the foregoing view, at each moment of his lifetime 'Aristotle' denoted a different entity, the Aristotle of the moment. Thus, at the present moment, when no current entity is sufficiently well connected to the other Aristotle stages to be an Aristotle stage, 'Aristotle' denotes nothing. What should it denote, a stage of Quine?[13] But according to this view, there is no real Aristotle to be denoted, only the Aristotles of each moment, so this view, in its pure form, is too bizarre to support the mistake.

A compromise is proposed. Continue to think of things as before, but take the assemblages themselves as the values of the variables and constants. Whenever a term denoted a stage, let it now denote that stage's assemblage (or one of them). Whenever a term denoted nothing (i.e., at those times not in the domain of a relevant assemblage), let it still denote nothing. Here is the mistake in full bloom.

The original view may have been bizarre, but it had its uses in explicating bizarre notions, for example that I might change into twins or that twins might have changed into me.[14] The compromise view does not have one becoming two, instead it has two coincident assemblages diverging. An unusual situation, but one not violative of Leibniz's Law. As individuals, assemblages are quite well behaved. Thus no reason remains not to take them as values of their proper names with respect to moments when they do not exist.[15] If, on the compromise, 'Quine' denotes the same thing yesterday and today, why not let 'Aristotle' denote the same thing 2,300 years ago and today? After all, it does.

---

[11] See Carnap, (1958, esp. §48) for further discussion of genidentity and its topology.

[12] Since the problem of quantifying out has only recently been solved, the solution to Homework Problem #19 is given here, but in a form intended to discourage peeking.

$$[[((0)Ⅎ ∋ (0)f \leftarrow (ʇ)Ⅎ ∋ (ʇ)f) \leftarrow (ʇ)S ∋ (ʇ)f]∀ ∋ fA \lor 0{>}ʇ]⊥ ∋ ʇE$$

[13] There is a tacit prejudice in this argument. Namely, that the value of a constant with respect to a given moment must be among the values of the variables in variable binding operators evaluated with respect to that moment. I shall attempt to exorcise this prejudice in Appendix XII. Even then, what stage of Aristotle should 'Aristotle' now denote? His birthstage? His deathstage? A triumphant middle-age stage?

[14] The bizarre view is adopted in Kaplan (forthcoming) and Lewis (1968), in neither of which, I fear, is the relation to normal theories correctly seen.

[15] No reason remains other than the prejudice alluded to in note 13, and even given the prejudice, why not let the variables themselves take nonoccurrent assemblages as values? How else to express the fact that I now remember someone who is no longer alive?

The second idea that might lead one to doubt that 'Quine' could denote where Quine does not exist is a simple confusion between our language and theirs. For reasons to be adumbrated shortly, ever-unactualized possibilia are extraordinarily difficult to dub. Thus the inhabitants of a world in which Quine never exists would likely have no name for him.[16] So what! He exists here. *We* have a name for him, namely, 'Quine'. It is *our* terms and formulas whose denotation and truth value are being assessed with respect to the possible world in question.

> *Homework Problem #20.* If a horse's tail were called a 'leg', horses would have five appendages called 'legs'. How many legs would a horse have?
>
> *Homework Problem #21.* Does 'Quine' denote Quine with respect to the time of Aristotle's birth? Who was then called 'Quine'?

Appendix XI: Names from Fiction

I have argued that 'Aristotle' denotes something which, at the present time, does not exist. I could now argue that 'Pegasus' denotes something which, in the actual world, does not exist. I shall not. Pegasus does not exist, and 'Pegasus' does not denote. Not here; not anywhere. What makes 'Aristotle' more perfect than 'Pegasus'?

The 'Aristotle' we most commonly use originated in a dubbing of someone,[17] our 'Pegasus' did not. Some rascal just *made up* the name 'Pegasus',[18] and he then pretended, in what he told us, that the name really referred to something. But it did not. Maybe he even told us a story about how this so-called Pegasus was dubbed 'Pegasus'. But it was not true.

Maybe he proceeded as follows. First, he made up his story in Ramsified form: as a single, existentially quantified sentence with the made up proper names ('Pegasus', 'Bellerophon', 'Chimaera', etc.) replaced by variables bound to the pre-fixed existential quantifiers; second, he realized that the result was possible, and that therefore it held in some possible world, and that therefore there was at least one possible individual who played the winged horse in at least one possible world; and third, he tried to dub one of those possible individuals 'Pegasus'. But he would not succeed. How would he pick out just one of the millions of such possible individuals?

> *Homework Problem #22.* Suppose that Quine and Kripke both might have been winged horses of the kind described in the story. Which one, if either, is Pegasus? (Hint: remember that 'Pegasus' is a rigid designator, so whoever might be Pegasus *is* Pegasus.)

I do not assume that there are no proper names which succeed in naming ever-unactualized possibilia (be they individuals, worlds, or circumstances). But the dubbing problem raises serious questions about the content of discourse using

---

[16] Hence, 'the person who both is Quine and is named "Quine"' would not denote anything with respect to such a world.

[17] Like the token Bob-Ted, the name 'Aristotle' may have been somewhat changed in the course of its travels.

[18] I am not sure that this is how our 'Pegasus' originated but let us assume it so.

such putative proper names. I fear that those who would so speak have adopted the logician's *existential instantiation* as a form of dubbing:

> There is at least one cow in yonder barn. Let's call one of them 'Bossie'. Now, how much do you think she weighs?

I am skeptical of such dubbings. The logician is very cautious in *his* use of the names so derived.[19]

The requirement for a successful dubbing is not that the dubbor know who the dubbee is. As remarked in Appendix VII, the dubbor can point with his eyes closed or use a description like 'the first child to be born in the twenty-second century'. The requirement is simply that the dubbee be, somehow, uniquely specified. This our story teller has not succeeded in doing. Probably he did not even try.

Perhaps I am being too harsh on 'Pegasus'. I have treated a myth as if it were pseudo-science, and dismissed it for failure of factuality. Even pseudo-science may have something to offer other than factuality.

Suppose we start out by acknowledging that the Pegasus-myth is FICTION.[20] Still it is, in a sense, possible. Should we not take 'Pegasus' to denote what it denotes in *the world of the myth?* We must be very careful now.

If 'the world of the myth' is meant to refer to the (or even, *a*) possible world with respect to which the myth—taken as pseudo-science—is true, there is an immediate objection. As given, the myth uses the name 'Pegasus'. Thus its truth with respect to a possible world requires a *prior* determination of what, if anything, 'Pegasus' names with respect to the possible world. Suppose we turn, then, to the Ramsified myth. Although it will be true in millions of possible worlds, Ramsification eliminates the very name whose denotatum we seek.

An alternative strategy arises in connection with the Ramsified myth. Wherever it is true, *something* plays Pegasus. If we limit attention to those cases

---

[19] Suppose, for the moment, that we take possible individuals, both actualized and unactualized, seriously enough to quantify over them (thus validating $\ulcorner \Diamond \exists x \phi \rightarrow \exists x \Diamond \phi \urcorner$). It still does not follow from the fact that if the Ramsified myth had been true there would have been an actualized winged horse, that there is some possible individual such that if the Ramsified myth had been true *he* would have been an actualized winged horse. There are simply too many ways (possible worlds) in which the Ramsified myth might have been true. (The critical invalidity is $[(\phi \succ (\psi \vee \chi)) \rightarrow ((\phi \succ \psi) \vee (\phi \succ \chi))]$ where '$\succ$' symbolizes the subjunctive conditional.) Much less does it follow that we could properly speak of *the* possible individual who would have been an actualized winged horse had the Ramsified myth been true. But some such descriptions may be proper. In the most plausible cases we speak of the unique possible individual that would have resulted had a certain closed, developing, deterministic system not been externally aborted. (The possibility of externally induced abortion implies that the system is not completely closed.) Consider, for example, the completely automated automobile assembly line. In full operation, it is, at each moment, pregnant with its next product. Each component: body, frame, motor, etc., lies at the head of its own subassembly line, awaiting only Final Assembly. Can we not speak of the very automobile that would have been produced had the Ecologists Revolution been delayed another 47 seconds?

[20] I will ignore the immediate conjecture that Pegasus symbolizes, and thus 'Pegasus' denotes, *that which man strives for but never fully attains*. Such symbolizations are not reserved to fictional entities; Carnap symbolized the same.

where exactly one thing plays Pegasus, we can refer to it by means of the description ⌜the x $\mathcal{M}$⌝, where $\mathcal{M}$ is the Ramsified myth without the existential quantifier which binds the variable 'x' which replaced all occurrences of 'Pegasus' in the myth as given. Why not take 'Pegasus' to *abbreviate* ⌜the x $\mathcal{M}$⌝?[21] The objection to this wonderfully candid proposal is that the Friend of Fiction is unlikely to accept it. First, 'Pegasus' loses the status which allowed it to function so smoothly in 'Bellerophon hoped that Pegasus . . .' contexts. The expansion of such declarations is awkward at best. Second, there is no fixed individual, Pegasus, denoted by 'Pegasus' with respect to all possible worlds in which he exists. Third, 'Pegasus' still denotes nothing. When the presumed dubbing is disregarded and 'Pegasus' ceases to be a rigid designator, the world of the myth ceases to be of interest.

There is another interpretation of 'the world of the myth' which, I believe, better represents the position of those who take the view that 'Pegasus' finds its denotatum in the world of the myth.[22] The myth is possible in the sense that there is a possible world in which it is truthfully *told*. Furthermore, there are such worlds in which the language, with the exception of the proper names in question, is semantically and syntactically identical with our own. Let us call such possible worlds of the myth, 'M worlds'. In each M world, the name 'Pegasus' will have originated in a dubbing of a winged horse. The Friend of Fiction, who would not have anyone believe the myth (even Ramsified), but yet talks of Pegasus, pretends to be in an M world and speaks its language.

But beware the confusion of our language with theirs! If w is an M world, then *their* name 'Pegasus' will denote something with respect to w, and *our* description 'the x such that x is called 'Pegasus'' will denote the same thing with respect to w, but *our* name 'Pegasus' will still denote nothing with respect to w. Also, in different M worlds, different possible individuals may have been dubbed 'Pegasus'; to put it another way, *our* description 'the x such that x is called 'Pegasus'' may denote different possible individuals with respect to different M worlds.

I do not object to the inhabitants of one of the M worlds remarking that their name 'Pegasus' denotes something with respect to *our* world that does not exist in our world. But I reserve the right to retort that *our* name 'Pegasus' does not even denote with respect to their world.

To summarize. It has been thought that proper names like 'Pegasus' and 'Hamlet' were like 'Aristotle' and 'Newman 1', except that the individuals denoted by the former were more remote. But regarded as names of *our* language—introduced by successful or unsuccessful dubbings, or just made up—the latter denote and the former do not.

> *Homework Problem #23.* Is the foregoing account of proper names deriving from fiction correct? If so, how could its fourth sentence be true?

---

[21] Lewis (1970) would so define theoretical terms of science.

[22] A conversation with my colleague John Bennett caused me to believe this.

Appendix XII: The Universe of Discourse

At the present time, the techniques are available to produce a completely axiomatized formal theory of definite descriptions to fit almost any specification. We should now more carefully distinguish that part of the metalinguistic apparatus which consists of logicians' tricks, adopted for purely instrumental reasons and devoid of philosophical import, from that part which directly realizes the intended interpretation of the object language.

It may be technically convenient to introduce an entity, †, completely alien to the universe of discourse of the object language and to adjust slightly our use of 'denotes' so that we can say that a singular term α does *not* denote, in the following odd way:

> α so-to-speak-denotes †.

We have not lost sight of the fact that α does not really denote, *denotation* and *so-to-speak-denotation* are interdefinable. The use of the latter is fairly described as a logician's trick for smoothing some definitions in the metalanguage. Though it seems unlikely, it may even turn out to be useful to introduce more than one such way of saying that α does not denote.

Definite descriptions are rather special kinds of terms. A definite description ⌜the x ϕ⌝ is proper if among the values of 'x' there is a unique individual satisfying ϕ. As ordinarily conceived, a proper definite description denotes one of the values of the variables, and an improper definite description does not denote at all (though of course it may so-to-speak-denote something). Thus a definite description can denote an individual who fails to exist only if among the values of the variables are things which do not (in the appropriate sense) exist. For example, if among the values of the variable 'x' are all persons who ever lived, and if 'exists' is taken to apply to those persons who are yet alive, then 'the x such that x wrote *Meaning and Necessity*' denotes someone who fails to exist and 'the x such that x wrote *Principia Mathematica*' fails to denote. If the values of the variables are limited to persons now alive, then neither description denotes.

The universe of discourse of a theory need not be limited to the values of the variables. There may well be entities which are not among the values of the variables but which are related to those values in various natural and interesting ways, as books are related to their authors, sets to their members, and ancestors to their surviving descendents. A theory may afford recognition to such entities by mentioning them individually, by name or singular term, without quantifying over them. Much that would otherwise be artificially constrained can thus be treated easily and naturally.

Though our variable binding discourse be limited to natural numbers, we may wish to drop in occasional reference to an unnatural rational, perhaps via the functional expression '$x/2$'. When the values of the variables are so restricted, the following are all true. Why deny them?

$$\exists x \, \forall y \, y \neq x/2$$
$$\forall x \, 2(x/2) = x$$
$$\forall x \, \forall y \, (y = x/2 \leftrightarrow 2y = x)$$

Must '$x/2$' fail to denote when 'x' takes the value 3? Of course not. The reasonable course is to let it then denote 1-1/2. Must 'the y such that $2y = x$' fail to denote when 'x' takes the value 3? Yes.

> *Homework Problem #24.* In Zermelo-Fraenkel set theory the set of all values of the variables is not among those values. This can be expressed as follows:
> $$\sim\exists x\, x = \{y : y = y\}$$
> Must '$\{y : y = y\}$' fail to denote? Must 'the x such that $\forall y(y \in x \leftrightarrow y = y)$' fail to denote?[23]

Usually it is most convenient to allow the values of the variables to comprehend the entire universe of discourse, marking realms of special interest with predicates. Expressibility increases at no apparent cost. Such motivations lead modal logicians to take as values of their variables all *possible* individuals and to add a predicate of actuality. Similar motivations lead logicians of tense to range their variables over past, present, and future individuals, and to add a predicate of occurrence. But this strategy may entail hidden costs. The systematization of a theory that comes with axiomatization may be lost or compromised. Increased expressibility may open the door to the discussion of issues we shun. In addition, a wider range for the variables may engender talk of new entities in a still wider universe of discourse, with the result that the universe of discourse does not yet close with the domain of values of the variables.

> *Homework Problem #25.* What happens if the strategy of expanding the domain of values of the variables to meet the universe of discourse is applied to a set theory with abstracts, $\ulcorner\{x{:}\phi\}\urcorner$, some of which denote sets not among the values of the variables?

We have seen that although our choice of values for the bound variables will restrict the possible values of definite descriptions, there is no sound reason to restrict the values of all terms in the same way. Thus, putting aside the bizarre view of Appendix X, there is nothing to prevent us from treating proper names which denote with respect to some circumstance as denoting the same entity with respect to all possible circumstances, including those in which the entity is not among the values of the variables or, in some other sense, does not exist. The analysis of proper names taken from fiction does not motivate any departure from this practice. I conclude that a proper name either denotes the same individual with respect to every possible circumstance or else denotes nothing with respect to any possible circumstance.

Appendix XIII: The Exclusion of Nondenoting Terms

There is an alternative to so-to-speak-denotation which is equally smooth. We can use so-to-speak definite descriptions. An entity, ∗, is chosen from, or added to, the universe of discourse of the language. A slight alteration is made in the definite description operator; now written 'the∗'. $\ulcorner$the∗ $x\phi\urcorner$ is translated as 'the unique entity among the values of the variable 'x' which satisfies ϕ; or, if there is none, ∗'.[24] It is clear that 'the∗$x(x \neq x)$' denotes∗. Whatever ease of semantical formulation resulted from

---

[23]Hint: re-read Scott (1967). But see Appendix XIII regarding his answer to the second question.

[24]Note that '∗' is a symbol of the metalanguage, and 'the∗' is an operator of the object language.

the adoption of so-to-speak-denotation also accrues to the adoption of 'the*', provided that a similar alteration is made in the meaning of *all* nondenoting terms.[25]

Let α^* be the altered version of α. It is conceptually important to distinguish the following:

α^* denotes $*$.

α so-to-speak-denotes $\dagger$.

The latter is equivalent to saying that α does not denote; the former holds when α does not denote, but also holds when α denotes $*$. Another aspect of the difference comes out when we ask what considerations are relevant to determining the truth values of atomic sentences. When α does not denote, the considerations relevant to determining the truth value of $\ulcorner \Pi\alpha \urcorner$ (for extensional atomic predicates Π) are very different from those relevant to determining the truth value of $\ulcorner \Pi\alpha^* \urcorner$. The truth value of $\ulcorner \Pi\alpha^* \urcorner$ is fixed by the choice of $*$ and its properties. Determination of the truth value of $\ulcorner \Pi\alpha \urcorner$, and even whether it has one, suffers no such constraints. Since $\dagger$ is alien to the universe of discourse of the object language, its properties are irrelevant. If identity is given its standard interpretation, $\ulcorner \alpha^* = \beta^* \urcorner$ *must* be true when neither α nor β denote, since in that case both α^* and β^* denote the same element of the universe of discourse. But the mere interpretation of identity does not yet determine the truth value of $\ulcorner \alpha = \beta \urcorner$ when neither α nor β denotes. Adoption of so-to-speak-denotation may be a consequence of the decision to call $\ulcorner \alpha = \beta \urcorner$ true, but so-to-speak-denotation also has its uses when $\ulcorner \alpha = \beta \urcorner$ is to be neither true nor false.

It is clear from the interdefinability of 'denotes' and 'so-to-speak-denotes' that the use of the latter for the formulation of the semantical rules does not limit the semantical alternatives for treating nondenoting terms. On the other hand, the use of α^* rather than α, avoids the problem of nondenoting terms by confining the object language to terms whose denotation is guaranteed.

Within the systems which exclude nondenoting terms, a variety of altered definite description operators are available. Among those of the form 'the*' some choose $*$ within the values of the variables, some without. An inner choice of $*$ yields a simpler axiomatization of the resulting logic. But it has turned out that the logic resulting from an outer choice of $*$ is much more smoothly axiomatizable than was thought possible twenty years ago. An outer choice of $*$ allows α^* to better simulate α. But the improvement is only to the extent that nondenoting terms are clearly distinguished from terms which denote elements of the domain of values of the variables. The formula $\ulcorner \alpha^* = \text{the}^* x\, x \neq x \urcorner$ does not differentiate nondenoting terms α from those which naturally denote $*$.

There is no general way, within a theory, to absolutely determine whether a term α for which $\ulcorner {\sim}\exists x\, x = \alpha \urcorner$ is true denotes an element of the universe of discourse or only so-to-speak-denotes $\dagger$. The distinction is not in general expressible within the

---

[25] In a generalized theory of descriptions (see Homework Problem # 27) this can be accomplished by treating each term α as semantically equivalent to $\ulcorner$ the $x(\alpha : x = x) \urcorner$ where 'x' is not free in α.

language.[26] Even the difference between a choice of $*$ within or without the domain of values of the variables may be disguised by interdefinable alterations of notation which extend or restrict the range of quantification by just that one element. But the intended semantics may often be inferred from theorems of the form $\ulcorner \alpha = \Delta \urcorner$, where Δ is a term which 'naturally' denotes. For example, within a theory of virtual classes, 'the $x(x \neq x) = \{x{:}x = x\}$' suggests that 'the $x(x \neq x)$' denotes an element of the universe of discourse, whereas such tantalizing assertions as '$\{$the $x(x \neq x)\} = \{x : x \neq x\}$' suggest that 'the $x(x \neq x)$' denotes nothing.

The important question is whether we accept the outer entities (those in the universe of discourse but not in the domain of values of the variables) as *real*, as entering into properties and relations of interest to the object language with as much vigor and independence as do the inner entities, lacking only the characteristic property of the inner entities. If we do, then the choice of $*$ as inner or outer seems of secondary importance. If we do not, then there seems no need for more than one outer entity, and its choice as $*$ amounts to identifying it with †.

> *Homework Problem #26.* Dana Scott has proposed a theory of descriptions according to which the value of an improper description is not an element of the domain of values of the variables.[27] Is he recommending the adoption of so-to-speak-denotation or just an outer choice of $*$?

> *Homework Problem #27.* 'the xFx' denotes the unique inner entity satisfying 'Fx'. If more than one entity satisfies 'Fx', there may still be a unique common value for the functional expression '$g(x)$' whenever the value of 'x' satisfies 'Fx'. Thus in a generalized theory of definite descriptions we may wish an operator of the form 'the $x(g(x){:}Fx)$'. So long as the value of '$g(x)$' is an inner entity, this operator is expressed by 'the $y\exists x(Fx \wedge y = g(x))$'. But if the language includes terms such as '$x/2$', which carry inner entities to outer ones, a new operator must be introduced. We write $\ulcorner$ the $x_0 \ldots x_n (\alpha{:}\phi) \urcorner$ for the generalized definite description. The variables $x_0 \ldots x_n$ are bound by the operator. It is permitted that the value of α may be an outer entity. The familiar $\ulcorner$ the $x\, \phi \urcorner$ is definable by $\ulcorner$ the $x(x{:}\phi) \urcorner$. A single schema characterizes the generalized definite description:
>
> (L) $\beta \neq$ the $x(x{:}x \neq x) \rightarrow$
> $\qquad [\beta = $ the $x_0 \ldots x_n (\alpha{:}\phi) \leftrightarrow \exists\, x_0 \ldots x_n[\forall y_0 \ldots y_n(\exists x_0 \ldots x_n(\phi \wedge \alpha = a_x^y)$
> $\qquad\qquad\qquad \leftrightarrow \alpha = a_x^y) \wedge \alpha = \beta]]$
>
> where a_x^y is the proper substitution of $y_0 \ldots y_n$ for $x_0 \ldots x_n$ in α. Call the schema which results from (L) by restricting attention to the familiar case of the form $\ulcorner$ the $x(x{:}\phi)\urcorner$ '(D)'. Give a simple characterization of the theory of descriptions which results from (D) by adding:
>
> (I) $\exists x(x = $ the $x(x{:}x \neq x))$.
>
> Give a simple characterization of the theory which results from adding the negation of (I) to (D). Show that (D) is equipolent to the disjunction of the two theories as you have characterized them. Is any alteration in (L) called for if 'the $x(x{:}x \neq x)$' is taken as so-to-speak-denoting †?

---

[26]The problem is that a formal isomorphism can be constructed between a model using † and one in which the universe of discourse is enlarged to include a new element $*$. (Barring, of course, the possible decision to treat $\ulcorner \alpha = \alpha \urcorner$ as false, or at least not true, for nondenoting α.) *Given* that the definite description operator of a theory is 'the' not 'the*', the formula $\ulcorner \alpha = $ the $x(x \neq x) \urcorner$, which holds only for nondenoting α, can be used. But lacking some notational sign to distinguish the two operators they are in general indiscernable.

[27]Dana Scott (1967). Also see references to other authors therein.

Appendix XIV: A Last Solution

Take the changing tokens of the more interesting solution and slice them up as in the bizarre view of Appendix X. Now ignore all properties of the slices but their time and type (ignore, for example, their location). We can then reassemble the tokens as in the compromise view of Appendix X. A token can now be thought of as a function which assigns to each moment in its lifetime, its type at that moment. Under this interpretation two tokens with the same type at a given time literally coincide at that time. These tokens are idealized versions of the real tokens (the physical objects afflicted with location and all that) with which we usually deal. To each such real token there corresponds, in the obvious way, an ideal token. Using ideal tokens we can construct a variant of the more interesting solution which is slightly less natural but which may come closer to meeting the adequacy condition: (1) = (2). Treat Index-1 as naming the ideal token which corresponds to Bob-Ted, and similarly for Index-2. The addition of quotation marks becomes an operation directly on the types which constitute the slices of (1) and (2). Otherwise, the argument proceeds as in the more interesting solution. We do not quite achieve the identity of (1) and (2), but almost. At the present time, (1) *coincides* with (2).[28]

Compared to the more interesting solution this solution has the drawback of standing the relation between tokens and types on its head. A consequence of the upside down perspective is that when two real tokens are congruent, their idealizations are coincident. If congruence is as close to identity as coincidence is, then the last solution is no improvement over the more interesting one. From a methodological point of view, however, the last solution is very interesting. Let us look at it as a variant of the complete solution. There, '(2)' was regarded as abbreviating a description which denoted different sentence types at different times. Since applicability of the predicate 'can be changed . . .' depends on the referent of the abbreviated description at times other than the time of utterance (at which time (1) = (2)), it was not surprising that the substitution of '(1)' for '(2)' in this context did not preserve truth. The now common diagnosis of such failures of substitutivity is that substitution in *intensional* contexts like those produced by the

---

[28]My attention was drawn to this solution by Richard Montague's solution (in 'The Proper Treatment of Quantification in Ordinary English', this volume) to Partee's paradox: from the premises 'the temperature is ninety' and 'the temperature is rising', the conclusion 'ninety is rising' would appear to follow by normal principles of logic; yet there are occasions on which both premises are true, but none on which the conclusion is. Montague has 'the temperature' denote the function which assigns to each moment the temperature at that moment, 'ninety' denote the constant function to ninety, and the putative 'is' of identity (in the first premise) denote the relation of coincidence.

An alternative to Montague's solution, in the style of the complete solution, would take 'the temperature' and 'ninety' both to designate a number (the unit, degrees Fahrenheit, is tacit in the terms); the name rigidly and the description flaccidly. The 'is' of the first premise then *is* the 'is' of identity. The predicate 'is rising' must be regarded as producing an intensional context, but it receives the now standard treatment.

The availability of, and some of the consequences of, certain trade-offs between the reference of terms, the intensionality of contexts, and the like is the subject of this appendix.

'can be changed . . .' predicate requires that '(1)' and '(2)' have, not only the same referent, but the same sense.[29] Frege (1952) would agree and go further; within such contexts, '(1)' and '(2)' *refer* to their ordinary sense. When '(1)' and '(2)' are given the interpretation appropriate to their occurrence as subjects of the 'can be changed . . .' predicate, it will be discovered that the purported identity, (1) = (2), is not a true identity but only a matter of coincidence.[30] Thus we see that the interpretation of Index-1 proposed in the last solution accords exactly with the method of Frege, made explicit by Church, for *completing* the complete solution.

Frege exports intensionality by reinterpreting the expressions which lie within an intensional context. Those which would ordinarily be taken to designate different things with respect to different possible circumstances are reinterpreted to take a fixed designatum, the sense, which by itself determines the entire spectrum of former designata. To put it Kripke's way, a flaccid designator is transformed into a rigid one. But in a way very different from the introduction of a proper name through a dubbing by description. A dubbing by the description α introduces a new expression which rigidly designates the same entity as that which happens to be designated by α with respect to the context of the dubbing. Frege's reinterpretation of α has α itself rigidly designating a new entity of a higher level than any of those which it formerly designated.[31] According to Frege, even an expression in an oblique context is open to substitution by an expression whose entire spectrum is determined by means of the same higher level entity (the same sense). Thus the reinterpretation allows free substitution of expressions whose *reinterpreted* designata are the same. But very few pairs of expressions will pass *that* test.

The process of Fregean ascent can be reversed to import intensionality where none is apparent. Any continuant with different stages in different circumstances, can be sliced into its stages. Any rigid designator of such a continuant can be

---

[29] Here I take the sense of an expression to be its *intension* in the sense of Carnap (1947), namely that function which assigns to each possible circumstance the denotatum (called, by Carnap, the *extension*) of the expression with respect to that circumstance. Strictly speaking the sense *determines* the intension. The same intension may be determined (in different ways) by different senses.

[30] If f and g are functions, they coincide at a point if their values are the same at that point. If α and β are terms such that $\ulcorner \alpha = \beta \urcorner$ is true with respect to a given possible world, then the intension of α and the intension of β will coincide at that world. A predicate expressing coincidence is easily definable in Church's (1951) formalization of Frege's semantics.

[31] To regard an expression other than a proper name as a rigid designator need not entail any unwillingness to recognize the distinctive *syntactical* role played by expressions of differing syntactical categories. Not all rigid designators are, prima facie, proper names; not all are, prima facie, names. Designators like the 'red' in 'Your eye is red' and the 'penguin' in 'Peter is a penguin', which would not ordinarily be regarded as proper names, may yet be rigid if regarded as designating the appropriate entities. If 'red' designates the property of being red, it is probably rigid. If it designates the class of red things, it is certainly not rigid. In my own esoteric doctrines, 'red' rigidly designates a third entity, the color red. Similarly, 'penguin' rigidly designates the species penguin (almost all single words other than particles seem to me to be rigid designators). For Frege, even 'the class of red things' and 'the class of penguins', when located within an oblique context, are rigid designators (though not of classes of red things and penguins).

deinterpreted to designate, with respect to a circumstance, only the then occurrent *stage* of the continuant it formerly designated.[32] The unity of the continuant is dissipated, perhaps irretrievably. It survives primarily in the spectra of the vestigial, no longer rigid, designators. Identity becomes a subject demanding serious attention. Distinct things can be 'the same individual'! Coincidence degenerates to identity. Intensionality runs rampant.

Although I *am identical with* my body, one of us will survive the other.

Thus begins the long process of Darwinian descent.[33]

BIBLIOGRAPHY

Ajdukiewicz, K., *Jezyk i Poznanie*, Warsaw 1960.

Austin, J. L., 'Truth' in *Philosophical Papers* (ed. by J. O. Urmson and G. J. Warnock), Oxford 1961.

Austin. J. L., *How To Do Things With Wards*, New York 1965.

Bach, E., 'Nouns and Noun Phrases' in *Universals in Linguistic Theory* (ed. by E. Bach and R. Harms), New York 1968.

Bach, E., "Problominalization", *Linguistic Inquiry* **1** (1970) 121–2.

Bach, E. and Harms, R. (eds.), *Universals in Linguistic Theory*, New York 1968.

Bar-Hillel, Y., 'Logical Syntax and Semantics', *Language* **30** (1954) 230–7.

Bar-Hillel, Y., Gaifman, C., and Shamir. E., 'On Categorial and Phrase-Structure Grammars', *Bulletin of Research on the Council of Israel* **9F** (1960) 1–16.

Becker, E., *An Analysis of Thirty-One Primers*, Unpublished master's thesis, University of Pittsburgh, 1936.

Bell, A., *A State-Process Approach to Syllabicity and Syllable Structure*, Unpublished doctoral dissertation. Stanford University, 1971.

Berman, A., 'Abstract and Agentive Sentences', Unpublished manuscript, Harvard University, 1970.

Bierwisch, M., 'Two Critical Problems in Accent Rules', *Journal of Linguistics* **4** (1968) 173–9.

Binnick, R., Morgan, J., and Greene, C. J., 'Camelot, 1968', Mimeographed manuscript, 1968.

Bolinger, D., 'Stress and Information' in Forms *of English* (ed, by I. Abe and T. Kanekiyo), Cambridge, Mass., 1958.

Bormuth, J. R., 'Readability: A New Approach', *Reading Research Quarterly* **1** (1966) 79–132.

---

[32]Just such a process will transform the last solution back into the complete one.

[33]Sam Darwin is the widely acclaimed ontologist and delicatessen operator who once remarked, "Balonies? I don't believe in them. All there is are *slices* arranged in different ways. They come arranged in one way; my job is to rearrange them in tastier ways." The Sam Darwin Fund supports research on the principle of individuation for balonies (what properties of slices determine them as coming from 'the same baloney'). The Fund reports that a breakthrough may be near based on discoveries made with the help of a recently acquired electron microscope. Related investigations, not sponsored by the Darwin Fund, are reported in Geach (1967b), Perry (1970), Lewis (1971), and Perry (forthcoming).

Braine, M. D. S., 'On Two Types of Models of the Internalization of Grammars' (1971).

Bresnan, J., 'An Argument Against Pronominalization', *Linguistic Inquiry* **1** (1970a) 122–3.

Bresnan, J., 'On Complementizers: Toward a Syntactic Theory of Complement Types', *Foundations of Language* **6** (1970b) 297–321.

Bresnan, J., 'Sentence Stress and Syntactic Transformations', this volume, pp. 3–47.

Bresnan, J., 'The Theory of Complementation in English Syntax', 1971 (in preparation).

Brown, R. and Hanlon, C., 'Derivational Complexity and the Order of Acquisition', in *Cognition and The Development of Language* (ed. by J. R. Hayes), New York 1970.

Burge, T., *Truth and Some Referential Devices*. Unpublished doctoral dissertation, Princeton University, 1971.

Burling, R., 'Language Development of a Garo and English-Speaking Child', *Word* **15** (1959) 45–68.

Carden, G., and Miller, A. G., 'More Problominalizations', *Linguistic Inquiry* **1** (1970) 555–6.

Carnap, R., *Meaning and Necessity*. Chicago 1947, (Enlarged edition 1956).

Carnap, R., 'On Belief Sentences' in *Philosophy and Analysis* (ed. by M, Macdonald), Oxford 1954. Also Appendix C in Carnap (1956).

Carnap, R., *Introduction to Symbolic Logic and Its Applications*, New York 1958 (transl. by W. H. Meyers).

Cartwright, H. M., 'Heraclitus and the Bath Water', *Philosophical Review* **74** (1965) 466–85.

Cartwright, H. M., 'Quantities', *Philosophical Review* **79** (1910) 25–42.

Cartwright, H. M., 'Chappell on Stuff and Things', *Nous* (1971, in press).

Cartwright, R., 'Propositions" in *Analytical Philosophy* (ed. by R. J. Butler), New York, 1962.

Chall, J. S., *Readability. An Appraisal of Research and Application*, Columbus, Ohio, 1958.

Chao, Y. R., *A Grammar of Spoken Chinese*, Berkeley 1968. (Preliminary edition, 1965).

Chapin, P. G., 'Samoan Pronominalization', *Language* **46** (1970) 366–78.

Chomsky, N., 'Logical Syntax and Semantics; Their Linguistic Relevance', *Language* **31** (1955) 36–45.

Chomsky, N., *Syntactic Structures*, The Hague 1957.

Chomsky, N., *Aspects of the Theory of Syntax*, Cambridge, Mass., 1965.

Chomsky, N., 'Linguistics and Philosophy' in *Language and Philosophy: A Symposium*, part II (ed. by S. Hook), New York 1969a.

Chomsky, N., 'Quine's Empirical Assumptions' in *Words and Objections, Essays on the Work of W. V. Quine* (ed. by D. Davidson and K. J. Hintikka), Dordrecht 1969b.

Chomsky, N., 'Some Empirical Issues in the Theory of Transformational Grammar', Indiana University Linguistics Club, 1970a.

Chomsky, N., 'Remarks on Nominalization' in *Readings in English Transformational Grammar* (ed. by R. A. Jacobs and P. S. Rosenbaum), New York 1970b.

Chomsky, N., 'Deep Structure, Surface Structure, and Semantic Interpretation' in *Semantics: An Interdisciplinary Reader* (ed. by D. D. Steinberg and L. A. Jakobovits), Cambridge 1971.

Chomsky, N., and Halle, M., *The Sound Pattern of English*, New York 1968.

Chou, F., *Chung kuo ku-tai yu-fa, Ch'ao chu pien, (A Historical Grammar of Ancient Chinese*, Part I, Syntax), Taipei 1961.

Church, A., 'On Carnap's Analysis of Statements of Assertion and Belief', *Analysis* **10** (1950) 97–9.

Church, A., 'A Formulation of the Logic of Sense and Denotation' in *Structure, Method, and Meaning* (ed. by P. Henle, H. Kallen, and S. Langer), New York 1951.

Church, A., 'Intensional Isomorphism and Identity of Belief', *Philosophical Studies* **5** (1954) 65–73.

Dobson, W. A. C. H., *Late Archaic Chinese*, Toronto 1959.

Dobson, W. A. C. H., *Early Archaic Chinese*, Toronto 1962.

Dobson, W. A. C. H., *Late Han Chinese*, Toronto 1964.

Donnellan, K., 'Reference and Definite Descriptions', *Philosophical Review* **75** (1966) 281–304.

Donnellan, K., 'Putting Humpty Dumpty Together Again', *The Philosophical Review* **77** (1968) 203–15.

Dannellan, K., 'Proper Names and Identifying Descriptions', *Synthese* 21 (1970) 335–58.

Dougherty, R., 'An Interpretive Theory of Pronominal Reference', *Foundations of Language* **5** (1969) 488–519.

Emonds, J., *Root and Structure Preserving Transformations*, Unpublished doctoral dissertation, Massachusetts Institute of Technology, 1970.

Feldman, J., 'Some Decidability Results on Grammatical Inference and Complexity', Memo AI-93, 1969, Stanford University, Artificial Intelligence Project.

Feldman, J., Gips, J., Horning, J., and Reder, S., 'Grammatical Complexity and Inference'. Technical Report N. CS 125, 1969, Stanford University, Department of Computer Science.

Fillmore, C, 'Toward a Modern Theory of Case', *Project on Linguistic Analysis* **13** (1965) 1–24.

Fillmore, C., 'The Case for Case' in *Universals in Linguistic Theory* (ed. by E. Bach and R. Harms), New York 1968.

Fodor, J. D., 'Whose Description?', Unpublished manuscript, Harvard University, 1968.

Frege, G., 'On Sense and Reference' in *Translations from the Philosophical Writings of Gottlob Frege* (ed. by P. T. Geach and M. Black), Oxford 1952.

Frege, G., 'The Thought: A Logical Inquiry' in *Philosophical Logic* (ed, by P. F. Strawson) Oxford 1967.

Friedman, J., 'A Computer System for Transformational Grammar', *Communications of the ACM* **12** (1969) 341–8.

Friedman, J., Bredt, T. H., Doran, R. W., Mariner, T. S. and Pollack, B. W., *A Computer Model of Transformational Grammar*, New York 1971.

Friedman, J. and Myslenski, P., *Computer Experiments in Transformational Grammar: The UCLA English Grammar*, Ann Arbor, Michigan, 1970 (multilith).

Fromkin, V., 'The Non-Anomalous Nature of Anomalous Utterances', *Language* **47** (1971) 27–52.

Gammon, E., *A Syntactical Analysis of Some First-Grade Readers*, Unpublished doctoral dissertation, Stanford University, 1969.

Gates, A, I., *Interest and Ability in Reading*, New York 1930.

Geach, P. T., *Reference and Generality*, Ithaca 1962.

Geach, P. T., 'Assertion', *Philosophical Review* 74 (1965) 449–65.

Geach, P. T., 'Intentional Identity', *Journal of Philosophy* **64** (1967a) 627–32.

Geach, P. T., 'Identity', *The Review of Metaphysics* **21** (1967b) 3–12.

Ginsburg, S. and Partee, B., 'A Mathematical Model of Transformational Grammars'. *Information and Control* **15** (1969) 297–334.

Gleitman, L. and Gleitman, H., *Phrase and Paraphrase*, New York 1971.

Gold, E. M., 'Language Identification in the Limit', *Information and Control* **10** (1967) 447–74.

Goodman, N., *The Structure of Appearance*. Cambridge, Mass., 1951.

Goodman, N. and Leonard, H. S., 'The Calculus of Individuals and Its Uses', *Journal of Symbolic Logic* **5** (1940) 45–55.

Gruber, J. S., *Studies in Lexical Relations,* Unpublished doctoral dissertation. Massachusetts Institute of Technology, 1965.

Hamburger, H., *On the Learning of Three Classes of Transformational Components,* doctoral dissertation, University of Michigan. Ann Arbor, 1971.

Hamburger, H. and Wexler, K., 'Identifiability of a Class of Transformational Grammars', this volume, pp. 153–66.

Harris, Z. S., *Mathematical Structures of Language* (Interscience Tracts in Pure and Applied Mathematics, 21), New York 1968.

Hasegawa, K., 'The Passive Construction in English', *Language* **44** (1968) 230–43.

Hilbert, D. and Bernays, P., *Grundlagen der Mathematik,* I-II, Berlin 1934, 1939.

Hintikka, K. J., *Knowledge and Belief,* Ithaca 1962.

Hintikka, K. J., *Models for Modalities: Selected Essays,* Dordrecht 1969a.

Hintikka, K. J., 'Partially Transparent Senses of Knowing', *Philosophical Studies* **20** (1969b) 5–8.

Hintikka, K. J., 'Knowledge, Belief, and Logical Consequence', *Ajatus* **32** (1970a) 32–47.

Hintikka. K. J., 'Surface Information and Depth Information', in *Information and Inference* (ed. by K. J. Hintikka and P. Suppes). Dordrecht 1970b.

Hintikka, K, J., 'Objects of Knowledge and Belief: Acquaintances and Public Figures', *Journal of Philosophy* **67** (1970c) 869–83.

Hintikka, K. J., 'The Semantics of Modal Notions and the Indeterminacy of Ontology' *Synthese* **21** (1970d) 408–24.

Hintikka, K. J., 'Knowledge by Acquaintance-Individuation by Acquaintance' in *Bertrand Russell (Modern Studies in Philosophy)* (ed. by D. Pears), Garden City, N.Y., 1972a.

Hintikka, K. J., 'On the Different Constructions in Terms of the Basic Epistemological Concepts: A Survey of Some Problems and Proposals' in *Contemporary Philosophy in Scandinavia* (ed. by R. E. Olson and A. M. Paul), Baltimore, 1972b.

Hintikka, K. J., 'Grammar and Logic', this volume, pp. 197–214.

Hockett, J. A., *The Vocabulary and Content of Elementary School Readers.* Sacramento, Calif., 1938,

Hopcroft, J. and Ullman, J., *Formal Languages and Their Relation to Automata.* Reading. Mass., 1969.

Jackendoff, R., *Some Rules of Semantic Interpretation for English,* Unpublished doctoral dissertation, Massachusetts Institute of Technology, 1969.

Jakobson, R., *Child Language, Aphasia, and Phonological Universals,* The Hague 1968.

Jakobson, R., 'Why "Mamma" and "Papa"?' in *Selected Writings of Roman Jakobson.* The Hague 1939, Reprinted in *Child Language: A Book of Readings* (ed. by A. Bar-adon and W. F. Leopold), Englewood Cliffs, N.J., 1970.

Kanger, S., *Provability in Logic,* Stockholm Studies in Philosophy, vol. 1, Stockholm 1957.

Kaplan, D., 'Trans-World Heir Lines', Unpublished manuscript of an address presented to a joint Meeting of the Association for Symbolic Logic and the American Philosophical Association, May 1967.

Kaplan, D., 'Quantifying In', in *Words and Objections: Essays on the Work of W. V. Quine* (ed. by D. Davidson and K. J. Hintikka), Dordrecht 1969. Reprinted from *Synthese* **19** (1968) 178–214.

Karttunen, L., 'Co-Reference and Discourse', presented to the Winter Meeting of the Linguistic Society of America, 1968.

Karttunen, L., 'Pronouns and Variables' in *Papers from the Fifth Regional Meeting, Chicago Linguistic Society,* 1969.

Katz, J. J., *The Philosophy of Language,* New York 1966.

Katz, J. and Postal, P., *An Integrated Theory of Linguistic Descriptions,* Cambridge, Mass., 1964.

Kinball, J. P., 'Predicates Definable over Transformational Derivations by Intersection with Regular Languages', *Information and Control* **11** (1967) 177–95.

Kimball, J. P., 'The Semantic Content of Transformations', *Linguistic Inquiry* (to appear).

Kiparsky, R. P. V. and Kiparsky, C. A. S., 'fact', in *Recent Advances in Linguistics* (ed. by M. Bierwisch and K.-H Heidolph) (forthcoming).

Kleene, S. C., *Introduction to Metamathematics,* Princeton 1952.

Klima, E. S., 'Negation in English', in *The Structure of Language* (ed. by J. Fodor and J. Katz), Englewood Cliffs, N.J., 1964.

Klima, E. S. and Bellugi, U., 'Syntactic Regularities in the Speech of Children' in *Psycho-linguistics Papers* (ed. by J. Lyons and R. Wales), Edinburgh 1966.

Knuth, D. E., 'Semantics of Context-Free Languages', *Mathematical Systems Theory* **2** (1968) 127–31.

Kripke, S. A., 'Semantical Considerations on Modal Logic', *Acta Philosophica Fennica* **16** (1963a) 83–94.

Kripke, S. A., 'Semantical Analysis of Modal Logic: I, Normal Modal Propositional Calculi', *Zeitschrift für mathematische Logik und Grundlagen der Mathematik* **9** (1963b) 67–96.

Kripke, S. A., 'Semantical Analysis of Modal Logic: II, Non-Normal Modal Propositional Calculi', in *The Theory of Models* (ed. by J. W. Addison, L. Henkin, and A. Tarski), Amsterdam 1965.

Kripke, S. A., Naming and Necessity' in *Semantics of Natural Language* (ed. by D. Davidson and G. Harman). Dordrecht 1972.

Kuno, S., 'Some Properties of Non-Referential Noun Phrases' in *Studies in Oriental and General Linguistics* (ed. by R. Jakobson), Tokyo (to appear).

Lakoff, G., *On the Nature of Syntactic Irregularity,* NSF-16, 1965, Indiana University, Mathematical Linguistics and Automatic Translation Report.

Lakoff, G., 'Pronominalization, Negation, and the Analysis of Adverbs', Mimeographed manuscript, 1967.

Lakoff, G., 'Instrumental Adverbs and the Concept of Deep Structure', *Foundations of Language* **4** (1968a) 4–29.

Lakoff, G., 'Counterparts, or the Problem of Reference in Transformational Grammar', presented (under a different title) to the Summer Meeting of the Linguistics Society of America in 1968, 1968b.

Lakoff, G., 'On Derivational Constraints' in *Papers from the Fifth Regional Meeting of the Chicago Linguistics Society* (ed. by R. Binnick *et. al.*), Chicago 1969.

Lakoff, G., 'Repartee', *Foundations of Language* **6** (1970a) 389–422.

Lakoff, G., *Linguistics and Natural Logic* Studies in Generative Semantics, vol. 1., Ann Arbor, Mich., 1970b. (Also appeared in a modified form in *Synthese* **22** (1970–71) 151–271. References in the text pertain to the earlier version whose relevant theoretical theses have been somewhat modified and weakened in the newer version.)

Lakoff, R., 'A Syntactic Argument for Negative Transportation' in *Papers from the Fifth Regional Meeting of the Chicago Linguistics Society* (ed. by R. Binnick *et al.*), Chicago 1969.

Langacker, R., 'Semantic Theory and the Problem of Supposition', Mimeographed manuscript, 1966.

Langacker, R. W., 'Mirror Image Rules', *Language* **45** (1969a) 575–98, 844–62.

Langacker, R. W., 'On Pronominalization and the Chain of Command' in *Modern Studies in English* (ed by S. A. Schane and D. A. Reibel), Englewood Cliffs, N.J., 1969b.

Leech, G. N., *Towards a Semantic Description of English,* Bloomington 1969.

Lees, R., 'A Multiply Ambiguous Adjectival Construction in English', *Language* **36** (1960) 207–21.

Leopold, W. F., *Speech Development of a Bilingual Child.* vol. 1, Evanston 1939.

Lewis, C. I., 'The Modes of Meaning' in *Semantics and the Philosophy of Language* (ed. By L. Linsky), Urbana 1952.

Lewis, D., 'Counterpart Theory and Quantified Modal Logic', *The Journal of Philosophy* **65** (1968) 113–26.

Lewis, D., 'How to Define Theoretical Terms', *The Journal of Philosophy* **67** (1970) 427–46.

Lewis, D., 'Counterparts of Persons and Their Bodies'. *The Journal of Philosophy* **68** (1971) 203–11.

Lewis, D., 'General Semantics', in *Semantics of Natural Language* (ed. by D. Davidson and G. Harman), Dordrecht 1972.

Lyons, J., *Introduction to Theoretical Linguistics,* Cambridge 1969.

McCawley, J., 'Concerning the Base Component of a Transformational Grammar', *Foundations of Languages* **4** (1968) 243–69.

McCawley, J., 'English as a VSO Language', *Language* **46** (1970) 286–99.

MacIver, A. M., 'Demonstratives and Proper Names' in *Philosophy and Analysis* (ed. By M. Macdonald), Oxford 1954.

McKaughan, H., 'Topicalization in Maranao–An Addendum', in *Pacific Linguistic Studies in Honor of Arthur Capell* (ed. by S. A. Wurm and D. C. Laycock), Canberra A.C.T. Australia, 1970.

Marsh, W. and Ritchie, R. W., 'Predictably Enumerable Sets' (to appear).

Mates, B., 'Synonymity' in *Meaning and Interpretation,* Univ. of Calif. Publications in Philosophy **25** (1950) 201–26. Also in *Semantics and the Philosophy of Language* (ed. By L. Linsky), Urbana 1952.

Mehl, M. A., *A Vocabulary Study of First Grade Readers,* Unpublished master's thesis, University of Colorado 1931.

Montague, R., 'Pragmatics' in *Contemporary Philosophy – La Philosophic Contemporaine,* vol. I (ed. by R. Klibansky), Florence 1968.

Montague, R., 'On the Nature of Certain Philosophical Entities', *The Monist* **53** (1969) 161–94.

Montague, R., 'English as a Formal Language' in *Linguaggi netla Società e nella Tecnica* (ed. by B. Visentini *et. al.*), Milan 1970a.

Montague, R., 'Pragmatics and Intensional Logic', *Synthese* **22** (1970b), 68–94.

Montague, R., 'The Proper Treatment of Quantification in Ordinary English', this volume, pp. 221–42.

Montague, R., 'Universal Grammar', *Theoria* **36** (1970, published 1971), 373–98.

Moravcsik, J. M. E., 'Competence, Creativity, and Innateness', *Philosophical Forum* **1** (1969) 407–37.

Moravcsik, J. M, E., 'Subcategorization and Abstract Terms', *Foundations of Language* **6** (1970) 473–87.

Moravcsik, J, M. E., 'Mass Terms in English', this volume, pp. 263–85.

Moskowitz, A. I., 'The Two-Year-Old Stage in the Acquisition of English Phonology', *Language* **46** (1970) 426–41.

Newman, S., 'On the Stress System of English', *Word* **2** (1946) 171–87.

Niyakawa-Howard, A., 'A Psycholinguistic Study: The Whorfian Hypothesis Based on the Japanese Passive', Paper presented to the 13th Annual National Conference in Linguistics. New York, March 1968.

Ousley, O. and Russell, D., *The Pre-Primer Program. My Little Red Story Book, My Little Green Story Book, My Little Blue Story Book*, Boston, Mass., 1957.

Ousley, O. and Russell, D., *The Little White House*, Boston. Mass., 1961.

Pap, A., 'Belief. Synonymity, and Analysis', *Philosophical Studies* **6** (1955) 11–5.

Pap, A., 'Belief and Propositions', *Philosophy of Science* **24** (1957) 123–36.

Parsons, T., 'An Analysis of Mass Terms and Amount Terms', *Foundations of Language* **6** (1970) 363–88.

Partee, B. H., 'Negation, Conjunction, and Quantifiers: Syntax vs. Semantics', *Foundations of Language* **6** (1970a) 153–65.

Partee, B. H., 'Opacity, Conference, and Pronouns', *Synthese* **21** (1970b) 359–85.

Partee, B. H., 'On the Requirement that Transformations Preserve Meaning' in *Studies in Linguistic Semantics* (ed. by C. J. Fillmore and D. T. Langendoen). New York 1971.

Partee, B. H., 'The Semantics of Belief-Sentences', this volume, pp. 309–36.

Perlmutter, D., *Deep and Surface Structure Constraints in Syntax*, New York 1970a.

Perlmutter, D., 'Surface Structure Constraints in Syntax', *Linguistic Inquiry* **2** (1970b) 187–255.

Perry, J., 'The Same F', *The Philosophical Review* **79** (1970) 181–200.

Perry, J., 'Can the Self Divide?' (forthcoming).

Peters, S. and Ritchie, R. W., 'On Restricting the Base Component of Transformational Grammars', *Information and Control* **18** (1971) 483–501.

Peters, S. and Ritchie, R. W., 'On the Generative Power of Transformational Grammars'. *Information Sciences* (1972) (to appear).

Peters, P. S., Jr., and Ritchie, R. W., 'Nonfiltering and Local-Filtering Transformational Grammars', this volume, pp. 180–93.

Postal, P., 'Underlying and Superficial Linguistic Structures', *Harvard Educational Review* **34** (1964) 246–66.

Postal, P. M., 'On So-Called "Pronouns" in English', *Monograph Series on Languages and Linguistics* **19** (1966). Reprinted in *Modern Studies in English* (ed. by D. A. Reibel and S. A. Schane), Englewood Cliffs, N.J., 1969.

Postal, P. M., 'Cross-Over Phenomena' in *Specification and Utilization of a Transformational Grammar*, Yorktown Heights, N.Y., 1968a.

Postal, P. M., *On Coreferential Complement Subject Deletion*, Yorktown Heights, N.Y., 1968b.

Postal, P. M., 'Anaphoric Islands' in *Papers from the Fifth Regional Meeting. Chicago Linguistic Society*, 1969.

Putnam, H., 'Synonymity and the Analysis of Belief-Sentences', *Analysis* **14** (1954) 114–22.

Quine, W. V. O., *From a Logical Point of View*, Cambridge, Mass., 1953.

Quine, W. V. O., *Word and Object*, Cambridge, Mass., 1960.

Quine, W. V. O., 'Quantifiers and Propositional Attitudes', *Journal of Philosophy* **53** (1956) 177–87; reprinted in W. V. O. Quine, *The Ways of Paradox and Other Essays*, New York 1966.

Quine, W. V. O., *Philosophy of Logic*, Englewood Cliffs, N.J., 1970a.

Quine, W. V. O., 'Methodological Reflections on Current Linguistic Theory', *Synthese* **21** (1970b) 386–98.

Ritchie, R. W., 'Classes of Predictably Computable Functions', *Transactions of American Mathematical Society* **106** (1963) 139–73.

Robinson, H. M., Monroe, M., and Artley, A. S., *Sally Dick and Jane*. Chicago 1962a.

Robinson, H. M., Monroe, M., and Artley, A. S., *Second and Third Pre-Primers*, Chicago 1962b.

Robinson, H. M., Monroe, M., and Artley, A. S., *Fun with our Friends*, Chicago 1962c.

Robinson, H. M., Monroe, M., and Artley, A. S., *More Fun with our Friends*, Chicago 1962d.

Ross, J., 'On the Cyclic Nature of English Pronominalization', Unpublished manuscript, 1966.

Ross, J., *Constraints on Variables in Syntax*. Unpublished doctoral dissertation, Massachusetts Institute of Technology, 1967.

Ruddell, R. B., 'The Effect of the Similarity of Oral and Written Patterns of Language Structure on Reading Comprehension', *Elementary English* **42** (1964) 403–10.

Ruddell, R. B., *The Effect of Four Programs of Reading Instruction with Varying Emphasis on the Regularity of Grapheme-Phoneme Correspondences and the Relation of Language Structure to Meaning on Achievement in First Grade Reading*, Berkeley, Calif., 1965.

Russell, D. and Ousley, O., *On Cherry Street*, Boston 1957.

Scheffler, I., 'On Synonymy and Indirect Discourse', *Philosophy of Science* **22** (1955) 39–44.

Scott, D., 'Existence and Description in Formal Logic' in *Bertrand Russell: Philosopher of the Century* (ed. by R. Schoenman), London 1967.

Sellars, W., 'Putnam on Synonymity and Belief'. *Analysis* **15** (1955) 117–20.

Shvachkin, N., 'The Development of Phonemic Speech Perception in Early Childhood' in *Studies of Child Language* (ed. by D. I. Slobin and C. A. Ferguson), New York (to appear).

Slobin, D. I. and Welsh, C. A., 'Elicited Imitation as a Research Tool in Developmental Psycholinguistics'. Working Paper No. 10, University of California, Berkeley, 1968, Language Behavior Research Laboratory.

Spache, G., 'Problems in Primary Book Selection: The Selection of Pre-Primers . . . Supplementary Pre-Primers . . . Primers and Supplementary Primers . . . First and Second Readers', *Elementary English Review* **18** (1941) 5–12, 52–9, 139–48, 175–81.

Stockwell, R. P., Schachter, P., and Partee, B. H., *Integration of Transformational Theories on English Syntax*. Los Angeles 1968–1969, Multilith paper, 1969.

Strawson, P. F., *Individuals,* New York 1963.

Strawson, P. F. (ed.). *Philosophical Logic,* Oxford 1967.

Strickland, R. G., 'The Language of Elementary School Children: Its Relationship to the Language of Reading Textbooks and the Quality of Reading of Selected Children', *Bulletin of the School of Education,* Indiana University **38** (1962) 1–131.

Suppes, P., 'Probabilistic Grammars for Natural Languages', *Synthese* **22** (1970) 95–116.

Suppes, P., 'Semantics of Context-Free Fragments of Natural Languages', this volume, pp. 370–94.

Tarski, A., 'Der Wahrheitsbegriff in den formalisierten Sprachen', *Studio Philosophic* **1** (1935) 261–405.

Urmson, J. O., 'Criteria of Intensionality', *Proceedings of the Aristotelian Society, Supplementary Volume* **42** (1968) 107–22.

Wang, L. (ed.), *Ku-tai han-yu (The Ancient Chinese),* vol. 1, part I, Pelting 1962.

Wang, L. (ed.), *Ku-tai han-yu (The Ancient Chinese),* vol. 1, part II. Peking 1964.

Watt, W. C., '*Review, Aspects of the Theory of Syntax* (2nd ed.), by N. Chomsky', *College Composition and Communication* **21** (1970) 75–81.

Watt, W. C., 'Paradox Lost', Manuscript, 1971a.

Watt, W. C., 'Paradox Regained', Manuscript. 1971b.

Wilson, C, *Statement and Inference,* vol. 1, Oxford 1926.

ON PROPER NAMES IN BELIEF ASCRIPTIONS

Tom McKay

The view that a proper name has no connotation but refers directly, without any semantic contribution from associated properties, has quickly become a commonplace.[1] But recently it has had its detractors, reviving arguments that proper names must have additional connotation if their use in belief contexts is to be understood.[2] In addition, it has been argued that since there are meaningful uses of names lacking reference, it cannot be the case in general that names have no connotation.[3] And Saul Kripke, the leading promoter of the view that names lack connotation, has found the direct reference view contributing to a puzzle about belief.[4]

I will defend direct reference views of proper names against the attacks and solve the puzzle. In doing so, I will defend some views on belief needed to serve as a basis for the defense.

---

[1] This is due principally to Saul Kripke's "Naming and Necessity," in *Semantics of Natural Language,* edited by Donald Davidson and Gilbert Harman (Reidel, 1972).

[2] Alvin Plantinga, "The Boethian Compromise," *American Philosophical Quarterly* 15 (1978), 129–138. Diana Ackerman, "Plantinga, Proper Names and Propositions," *Philosophical Studies* 30 (1976), 409–412; "Proper Names, Propositional Attitudes and Non-descriptive Connotations," *Philosophical Studies* 35 (1979), 55–69, and "Proper Names, Essences and Intuitive beliefs," *Theory and Decision* 11 (1979), 5–26. Leonard Linsky, *Names and Descriptions,* (Chicago, 1977).

[3] Plantinga argues in this way (cf. Section V below) in "The Boethian Compromise." This is a reversal of the position he took in *The Nature of Necessity,* Oxford, 1974. My view is more like his earlier view.

[4] "A Puzzle about Belief," in Meaning and Use, edited by Ashvali Margalit (Dordrecht, 1979).

Since I will argue that proper names can be understood to have many of the characteristics of demonstratives, I will begin by saying some fairly natural things about demonstrative reference.[5] In Section II the discussion will be extended to proper names, in support of the general point that an appropriately similar treatment of demonstratives and proper names can be achieved by rejecting connotative theories of names. The remaining sections answer objections and deal with Kripke's puzzle.

I

Consider these three sentence tokens.[6]

(1) This is a penny.

Jones uses (1) at t_1 in saying to Smith that the object he is demonstrating (we call it 'Charlie') is a penny, and Jones knows that it is a penny.

(2) This is a penny.

Jones uses (2) at t_2 and the context is otherwise exactly like that of (1) (same penny—Charlie, same audience—Smith, same sort of demonstration, etc.).

(3) This is a penny.

Jones uses (3) and t_3 and everything looks the same (to Smith) as for (1) and (2), but this time the object demonstrated is *not* a penny (though it looks like one) and Jones knows this.

Let us further suppose that Smith examines Charlie at t_1 and believes Jones when he utters (1), but, thinking that a switch has been made, Smith disagrees with Jones when Jones utters (2). We can even suppose that Smith closely examines Charlie at t_2 and that he has very good reason to think that, despite all appearances, a trick is occurring, and that what he observes at t_2 differs from what he observed at t_1 and is not a real penny.

Right after Jones utters (1) (and Smith examines Charlie) Smith has a belief about Charlie—that it is a penny. What shall we say about Smith's disagreement with Jones when Jones utters (2)? At t_2 has Jones said something different from what he said at t_1, and does Smith disbelieve what Jones says at t_2? Has Jones said the same thing both times and Smith lost his belief about Charlie? Or has Jones said the same thing, Smith believed the same thing (that Charlie is a penny) and Smith simply made some mistake about his own beliefs? I intend to argue for the third of these options but also to remove some of the sting of the word 'mistake' used in stating it.

---

[5] I will be using distinctions and some terminology developed in work by David Kaplan; "Demonstratives" (unpublished), "Dthat," in *Contemporary Perspectives in the Philosophy of Language*, edited by Peter A. French, Theodore E. Uehling and Howard K. Wettstein (Minneapolis, 1979), 383–400, and "On the Logic of Demonstratives," *Ibid.*, 401–414, (and also Journal of Philosophical Logic (1979)).

[6] I will use '(1)', '(2)' and '(3)' to refer to the sentence tokens described. This differs from standard practice in using sentence reference numbers.

The principal distinction to be employed in considering these examples is a familiar distinction between a sentence (with its 'sentence meaning') and the content of a particular utterance.[7] Utterances (1)–(3) employ the same words combined in the same way. If we understand (1), we need not consult a dictionary (or a grammar) for new meanings in order to understand (3). Yet (1) and (3) are used to make different claims (in particular, claims about different objects). (1) says that Charlie is a penny, but (3) says this about a different object. (1) is true, (3) is false. They have different content because of the difference in the *context* of use, namely that different individuals are demonstrated at t_1 and t_3. The reference of 'this' varies accordingly.

Similarly, suppose that Jones is being attacked by a bear.[8] Jones would inform Smith of this by saying "I am being attacked by a bear," and Smith would inform Jones of this by saying "You are being attacked by a bear". Utterances with different sentence meaning would be used to express the same thing.

Parallel to this distinction between sentence meaning and utterance content there is a distinction between our attitudes towards particular sentences (in a context) and the contents of our beliefs. If each of Jones and Smith had a belief that he could express by "I am being attacked by a bear," then Jones and Smith would have distinct beliefs. Jones would have a belief about Jones, and Smith would have a belief about Smith. If Smith then acquired the belief that he would express by "You are being attacked by a bear" directed at Jones (or by "He is being attacked by a bear" while pointing at Jones), they would share a belief. Thus the content of the utterance expressing the belief is the content of the belief. The same sentence can, in different contexts, determine distinct contents of utterance and distinct contents of belief, whereas distinct sentences can determine the same content of utterance and the same content of belief.

Of course there is a similarity of belief when Jones says "I am being attacked by a bear" and Smith says "I am being attacked by a bear." They have different beliefs that they could express in the same way, I will say that they *accept* the same sentence.[9] The divergence in the content of their beliefs is a natural outcome of the different contexts in which the sentence is accepted—i.e., by different people.

---

[7] More properly, I would wish to draw the distinction between sentence meaning and content or perhaps between character and content (to use David Kaplan's terminology). In particular, I wish to allow that different sentences can have the same sentence meaning—for example 'This is a penny' and 'c'est un penny'. I have no objection to calling the content 'a proposition', although I will avoid that term (and, I hope, at least some controversies that might come with it). Similar distinctions are employed by David Kaplan, *op. cit.*; John Perry, "Frege on Demonstratives," *Philosophical Review* 86 (1977), 474–497, and "The Problem of the Essential Indexical," *Nous* 13 (1979), 3–21, Tyler Burge, "Belief De Re," *Journal of Philosophy* 74 (1977), 338–362. Naturally none of these authors is to be blamed for the employment I make of these distinctions.

[8] This example is borrowed from John Perry, "Frege on demonstratives."

[9] I will speak of accepting a sentence (in a context). A more general theory may require that this point be put in terms of accepting a character (in a context). But for the examples discussed in this paper there is no relevant difference. Chisholm has introduced similar notions of acceptance and belief (in "On the Logic of Purpose," *Midwest Studies in Philosophy* 4 (1979), 223–238) although his use of it differs from mine. Cf. also Perry, "Frege on Demonstratives," 495–496.

Clearly one can accept a sentence in one context without accepting it in other contexts. Few would always accept "Now it is time for dinner," and I will accept "He is the department chairman" in some but not all contexts, depending at least on who I believe is referred to by the use of 'He'. A sentence determines a content in a context, and one will accept it in a particular context when one believe it is used to determine a true content.

Now let us consider (1) and (2). They are sentences of the same type,[10] yet Smith believes Jones when he utters (1) but disagrees when he utters (2). Employing the terminology we have developed, it seems that we should say that Smith accepts (1) at t_1 and does not accept (2) at t_2. (1) and (2) have the same sentence meaning, but if they are used at different times, so that their contents *might* differ, then one can have reason to accept the sentence in one context yet not accept it in another context.

Even though the possibility of a difference in content makes it possible for Smith to reasonably accept (1) at t_1 but not (2) at t_2, that does not provide an adequate basis to claim that Smith changes his belief about Charlie after t_1. If Smith had missed Jones's second performance ((2) at t_2), then we would say that Smith continued to believe that Charlie was a penny. But his witnessing (2) does not *remove* any belief established when he witnessed (1). When Smith rejects (2), a new belief is added, but the old belief is not thereby removed, since Smith believes the new utterance to be irrelevant to the first. He believes Charlie to be a penny and may well continue to hold that belief even when he rejects (2). His beliefs include the content of (1) throughout.[11]

But the content of (1) = the content of (2). Thus in a case in which his presence at (1) induces in Smith the belief that Charlie is a penny, and in which Smith goes on to disagree with (2) because he believes that some different object, a non-penny, is under discussion at t_2, Smith may have contradictory beliefs. He may believe that Charlie is a penny and that Charlie is not a penny. In accepting (1) and rejecting (2), Smith deals coherently with the sentence (since it might have determined distinct contents), but, unluckily for Smith, the contents of his beliefs cannot both be true.

It seems natural to say (in the case of (1) and (2)) that Smith *believes Jones* when he utters (1) but does not *believe him* when he utters (2). But if we ask whether Smith *believes what Jones asserted* when he uttered (2), the answer should be 'yes' (despite Smith's claims to the contrary). In virtue of accepting (1) and rejecting (2) (and of entering into an epistemically suitable relationship with Charlie each time) Smith has contradictory beliefs. Smith may have very good reason to think that tokens (1) and (2) were used to express distinct contents and thus that he can, without contradiction, accept (1) and reject (2); but he is wrong.

---

[10] Perhaps we could worry about whether (1) and (2) have the same content, since they are uttered at different times. We might need a better object, say a cat, and a better sentence, perhaps "From birth to death, this has been and will be a cat." But since the essential points would be the same, I am avoiding that complication.

[11] In "A Puzzle about Belief," Saul Kripke presents a similar argument without endorsing its conclusion.

It takes more than just cleverness in logic to avoid inconsistency in one's beliefs. One must also know which uses of terms are co-referential.

II

Now consider the following performances by Jones, in which the context of (1*) and (2*) is like that of (1) and (2) respectively.

(1*)   I dub this 'Angelo'.

(1**)   Angelo is a penny.

(2*)   I dub this 'Angelo'.

(2**)   Angelo is a penny.

We will assume that (1**) and (2**) are true; that the same penny (Charlie) is dubbed at (1*) and at (2*); and that Smith accepts (1**) but not (2**) (again because he believes a trick is occurring).

It seems clear that Jones uses (1**) and (2**) to say the same thing. Yet Smith believes him the first time and expresses disagreement the second. Must we conclude that because Smith accepts (1**) but not (2**), (1**), and (2**) say something different (differ in semantic content; express different propositions)? Clearly not. Since different utterances of sentences of the same type *can* say different things, Smith might believe that (1**) and (2**) differ in what they say (though he is wrong if he does).

Smith can reasonably accept the utterance (1**) made at t_1 and reject the utterance (2**) made at t_2 as long as he doesn't realize that the name 'Angelo' is being used with the same reference each time. Smith's beliefs are contradictory, but his joint acceptance of (1**) and rejection of (2**) is not unreasonable because (1**) and (2**) might have said something different (if a switch had been made). Since they say the same thing, Smith's acceptance of one and rejection of the other makes his beliefs contradictory.

What we have said about the case in which the same name is employed would seem to apply even more easily if different names are used. Let the context of (1') and (2') be like that of (1*) and (2*).

(1')   I dub this 'Albert'.

(1″)   Albert is a penny.

(2')   I dub this 'Arnold'

(2″)   Arnold is a penny.

Charlie = Albert = Arnold, and thus (1″) and (2″) are true. Smith expresses agreement with Jones when he utters (1″) but expresses disagreement when he utters (2″). (Here Smith need not even be so subtle as to recognize that in distinct contexts a term can have different referents. We have different terms, and Smith might believe that they refer to distinct objects.)

The two uses of 'Angelo' in (1**) and (2**) are no more closely related semantically than the uses of 'Albert' and 'Arnold' in (1″) and (2″). They were introduced by separate dubbings and might, for all Smith knows, refer to distinct objects. Just as we said that (1**) and (2**) have the same content (despite Smith's failure to recognize this), we should say that (1″) and (2″) have the same content. Smith believes the content of (1″) and (2″), but he does not accept (2″) at t_2.

III

In saying that (1″) and (2″) have the same content, so that Smith can believe what one says if and only if he believes what the other says, I am denying a conclusion that Alvin Plantinga, Diana Ackerman and Leonard Linsky have drawn concerning proper names and the sentences in which they occur.[12] Let us now consider their arguments.

The principal argument is based on the Hesperus-Phosphorus example (from Frege via Quine). It is said that since it might be true that

(4) Smith believes that Hesperus is visible in the evening.

yet false that

(5) Smith believes that Phosphorus is visible in the evening.

'Hesperus' and 'Phosphorus' must make different semantic contributions to these sentences. Thus they must differ in semantic content (meaning, connotation). Diana Ackerman has called the operative principle[13] "the propositional attitude principle."

(PA) If α and β are singular terms that are not interchangeable *salva veritate* in propositional attitude contexts, than α and β must have different connotations (i.e., must make different semantic contributions).

I have no quarrel with (PA). I question the claim that the terms are not here interchangeable *salva veritate*. Let us consider

(6) Hesperus is visible in the evening.
(7) Phosphorus is visible in the evening.

Though Smith might accept (6) but not (7), this is not itself sufficient to establish that he believes the content of (6) but not that of (7). Even if (6) and (7) determine the same content, they are different sentences that might have (given appropriate differences in their context of use) determined different contents. A failure to see that (6) and (7) contain references to the same individual might lead one to be mistaken about whether they have the same content. Thus one can fail to accept (7) while still believing its content.

It remains to us to explain why (5) might seem false in the case described. We can do this by giving an account of its inappropriateness that appeals to factors other than its semantic content.

---

[12] Cf. note 2.

[13] In "Proper Names, Essences and Intuitive Beliefs."

A sentence using 'that'-clauses in reporting a belief must give the content of the belief. But usually more is done: a sentence that is *accepted* by the believer is displayed. If "Smith believes that all camels have humps" expresses a truth and Smith is a speaker of English, then ordinarily it is true both that Smith accepts "All camels have humps" and believes its content. Sentence (4) performs nicely, providing the content of Smith's belief and displaying a sentence that Smith accepts. Sentence (5), in so far as it contrasts with (4), is a failure because it displays a sentence that Smith does not accept. The juxtaposition with (4) calls our attention to the differences between these belief attributions—the difference in displayed sentences. We must regard (5) as a *poorer* report of Smith's attitudes because it displays a sentence that Smith does not accept. It is, however, a true report of Smith's belief.

That (5) truly reports Smith's belief can be seen by considering a dicussion with Thompson, who knows only the name 'Phosphorus' for Venus and who does not know that it is visible in the morning.[14] In telling Thompson about the common pastime in which he and Smith engage we might say "Smith also knows that Phosphorus is visible at that place in the sky in the evening and he loves to watch it". We have not given Thompson the whole story. (We haven't told him that Smith, in the evening, wouldn't call it 'Phosphorus'.) But we have not lied either.

In reporting the beliefs of an ordinary speaker of English we can usually give the content of the belief and at the same time display a sentence that he accepts. In non-indexical cases we perform both acts in a single utterance. My claim that co-referential names make the same semantical contribution to content requires the recognition of the secondary non-semantical element—the displayed sentence—in belief attributions. The sentence may be important, but it is not directly relevant to the literal *truth-value* of the belief attribution but only to the common secondary purpose in uses of such sentences, that of displaying something accepted by the believer.

That we should regard the displaying of a sentence as secondary can also be seen by considering the clear cases in which sentence and content do not match up. Our intuition is definite about what we should say. We know that attributions involving indexicals (such as 'I', 'you', 'now', 'here', 'he', etc.) typically give a correct representation of someone's belief only if they employ a sentence (in the that-clause) that is *not* something that the believer accepts. If Smith believes that he is being attacked by a bear he accepts "I am being attacked by a bear" not "He is being attacked by a bear," and even if, in years to come, Smith will believe that now was the best time of his life, there is no time at which he accepts "Now was the best time of his life". In addition, when we attribute beliefs to individuals who do not speak English (foreigners, infants and non-humans) we do so in a way that treats sentences with the same content as attributing the same belief. Thus, if a languageless infant (or a cat) always acts as though he expects Johnson (who goes by the alias 'Robinson') to feed him, I might say either that

---

[14] Thompson could of course learn this name without knowing how its reference was fixed.

he believes that Johnson will feed him or that he believes that Robinson will feed him. There is no difference in the belief attributed.[15] Also, if we meet a foreigner from a (very distant) land in which Hesperus is neither the evening star nor the morning star, and if the foreigner speaks no English and has only one name for the planet—say 'Hesfoss'—then in listing his semantical beliefs I need to list only one of the following

'Hesfoss' refers to Hesperus (not to Mars).

'Hesfoss' refers to Phosphorus (not to Mars).

'Hesfoss' refers to Venus (not to Mars).

The same belief is listed each time. (The claim that he believes that 'Hesfoss' refers to Hesperus but not to Phosphorus or Venus is simply incoherent.)

But in discussing (4) and (5) I have not yet considered the application of (PA) that has been used by Plantinga, Ackerman, Linsky and Frege. They have considered belief attributions involving *identity* claims.

(8) Smith believes that Hesperus = Hesperus

(9) Smith believes that Hesperus = Phosphorus

I claim that if (8) is true, then (given that Hesperus = Phosphorus) (9) must be true as well. That will, no doubt, need further explanation.

Identity claims have a particularly peculiar status. There is little point in noting that someone (say Smith) believes Venus to be self-identical. Mere acquaintance with Venus guarantees this. Yet, if a referential treatment of names is correct, (8) and (9) must both do just that. Since this use of (8) or (9) would be pointless, it is natural to search for other interpretations, and another use for (9) is ready at hand. Most belief attributions serve to display a sentence that a believer accepts as well as to give the content of his belief, so this normally secondary function can become the sole point of a sentence like (9). Thus our intuition that (9) is wrong is on target despite the fact that (9) has an interpretation that is (trivially) true. (9) is worse than (8) because Smith accepts 'Hesperus = Hesperus' and rejects 'Hesperus = Phosphorus'.

The case is similar to one in which I answer a question about someone's enthusiasm for baseball by saying "When he plays the game, *he plays the game!*" or to other uses of 'tautologies' like "Fair is fair," or "A vote for Carter or Reagan is a vote for Carter or Reagan." Literal reading is pushed aside because of the triviality of the claim. A point is being made, and to make it these sentences are used in a way that reaches beyond their standard semantic content.

What is done here is also very much like what is done by a definition. When I learn a definition I *accept* many new sentences involving the defined word. In particular, I accept the definitional sentence itself. It should not be inferred from the non-triviality of accepting definitions that therefore the definiens and

---

[15] Appeal to a de re–de dicto distinction here (or in other discussions involving proper names) is question-begging. The thesis I am defending amounts to the view that in proper name cases there is no real distinction to be made.

the definiendum must differ in meaning. Adding new sentences to the stock of those I accept can be valuable even when these sentences express things I already believe, and even when they express trivial truths. (But perhaps this is another topic.)

IV

Plantinga also argues that the facts about the use of non-denoting proper names like 'Romulus' make the direct reference view of proper names untenable. After all, if Jones can meaningfully say

(10) Romulus founded Rome.

then even if it isn't true it has a meaning. If Jones sincerely utters (10), then Jones certainly means *something* by it. But if 'Romulus' is non-referential, then the direct reference view provides *no* complete meaning for (10), since there is nothing existent for 'Romulus' to refer to. The direct reference view gives us nothing to assert and leaves nothing to believe for someone who really accepts the myth about Rome's founding.

We can begin the response to this by accepting the consequence that no assertion has been made. Jones *seems* to have meant something because he has used 'Romulus' in an ordinary way to try to refer to something. But he has not succeeded. He has failed to do what he tried to do, and there is nothing that he has said (i.e., no content in his utterance), though of course he has produced an utterance that is grammatical, and he intended to assert something in doing so. (He has uttered a sentence he accepts.)

But if we acknowledge that Jones has not succeeded in expressing a complete propositional content because (10) has no complete content, then what Jones believes when he becomes convinced about (10) cannot be the content of (10). Jones accepts (10), but has no belief related to (10) in the way that my belief that Jimmy Carter is president is related to my sincere assertions made with tokens of "Jimmy Carter is president." Of course Jones will also believe some logical consequences of (10) (or, should we say, some things that would be logical consequences of (10) if (10) said anything?). So he will believe that Rome has not always existed, that someone founded Rome, that someone named 'Romulus' founded Rome, etc. But (10) itself expresses nothing that could be the content of his belief.

But then what about negative existentials? Consider Robinson, who is more in the know than Jones and who sincerely utters.

(11) Romulus did not exist.

in order to bring Jones up to date on this matter. Has he said something incoherent, as the direct reference theory seems to require? What does he believe, and what has he informed Jones of?

A standard use of the words of (11) would involve someone in using 'Romulus' in trying to refer to someone but then going on to deny that there was anything to be referred to. Since this is incoherent, we should expect a non-standard use. Robinson uses (11) to inform Jones that the uses of 'Romulus' in the conversation (and in the myth it is based on) are not referential. The use of 'Romulus' in (11) does not play the usual role of a name, that of continuing the history of the individual to whom earlier uses referred. It is a satire rather than a new chapter of history. One who accepts (10) in accepting a myth, not history, and Robinson makes that clear to Jones. When I say of a student "Even when he is in class, he isn't there" or the coach says "It is impossible for our team to beat theirs, so it will take more than the usual effort," we expect the audience to get the point even though what is said is, taken literally, incoherent.

V

I believe that I have shown that the direct reference view has not been overturned by Plantinga's considerations on vacuous names nor by the arguments concerning propositional attitudes and co-reference. In addition, the argument that Plantinga gives for his own view that each name expresses an essence of the thing it names does not fare well when indexicals are considered.

Plantinga argues that since a person could know the proposition expressed by

(12) Mark Twain was a pessimist.

without knowing the proposition expressed by

(13) Samuel Clemens was a pessimist.

these must be different propositions. But then the direct reference theory must be wrong (since Mark Twain = Samuel Clemens). I have given my answer to this, and I want to suggest that this type of argument is wholly implausible in cases involving indexicals. Just as someone might accept (12) but not (13), someone (like Smith in our example) might accept (1) but not (2). But in that case it is implausible in the extreme to say that (1) and (2) express different propositions. One can coherently reject sentences that express propositions that one believes. Acceptance of (12) and rejection of (13) would represent such a case. As things stand, Plantinga's claims about (12) and (13) seem to commit him to very counter-intuitive claims about (1) and (2). Since Smith accepts (1) but not (2), arguments parallel to Plantinga's would seem to lead to the conclusion that (1) and (2) express different propositions and the use of 'this' in (1) expresses a different essence from the use of 'this' in (2).[16] That

---

[16] We can't get out of this simply by saying that Smith does not know what was referred to by the use of 'this' in (2) (and thus does not know what proposition is expressed). Smith can, at t_1 and again at t_2, examine the penny referred to as closely as is needed to make sure that he knows what Jones referred to. He still might accept (1) but not (2). What he doesn't know is that the thing referred to in (2) is the thing referred to in (1) (and (1) and (2) have the same content).

requires explanation at least, since these uses seem to refer to Charlie in precisely the same way (despite Smith's failure to recognize that).[17]

vi

In "A Puzzle about Belief"[18] Kripke considers a slightly different argument against the conclusion that proper names are devices of pure reference in belief contexts. Although he does not endorse the premises, he presents it as part of his puzzle; i.e., as part of the reason for claiming that there is no satisfactory account of belief. But I want to show the weakness of the argument directly, in order to support the account of belief given here.

The argument Kripke considers relies on two principles; the 'disquotational principle'

> D If a normal English speaker, on reflection, sincerely assents to 'p', then he believes that p.[19]

and what I shall call the 'logical perspicuity principle'.

> P A believer with a modicum of logicality will not, after appropriate reflection, accept directly contradictory propositions—of the form 'p' and '$\sim p$'.[20]

Appropriate reflection consists simply in the simultaneous (or closely successive) and attentive consideration of p and $\sim p$.[21]

The argument proceeds by having us consider a normal speaker of English with a modicum of logicality who attentively considers and assents to both of

> (X1) Cicero was bald.

> (X2) Tully was not bald.

---

[17] A problem posed by Kaplan (in "Quantifying" in *Words and Objections,* Davidson and Hintikka (eds.) 1969) for certain views of de re attitudes might seem to apply to my account. I claim that when Smith accepts (1) and rejects (2), he has inconsistent beliefs. But what if Smith then becomes less sure about (2), thinking that it might or might not be true? Since, on my view, he believes what (2) says (i.e., what (1) says) before and after the change of mind, how can we describe this change?

In this case, Smith steps out of the inconsistency of belief by giving up one belief (that Charlie is not a penny). He believes that Charlie is a penny throughout the change, but what he rejects is altered. He now neither accepts nor rejects (2), and in so doing is failing to accept an utterance that expresses one of his beliefs. But at least this is an improvement over rejection of that belief.

(This is discussed in somewhat different terms by Tyler Burge, "Kaplan, Quine and Suspended Belief," Philosophical Studies 31 (1977), 197–203.)

[18] Cf. note 4.

[19] pp. 248–249.

[20] 205–251.

[21] p. 251.

D guarantees that he believes each proposition, and P then guarantees that they are not contradictory. Thus the direct reference view must be wrong if D and P are right, since 'Cicero' and 'Tully' are co-referential.

But I think that we can see that there are no versions of D and P that will be correct that will also support this argument.

D is false as stated, and this can be seen in several ways. For example, consider a normal English speaker who, like other normal English speakers, makes a mistake about some word, say he uses 'chicken' as a term to apply to his pigs. Even though he would, upon emerging from the pig pen, assent to 'the chickens were just fed' we should not attribute to him the belief that he just fed his chickens. We attribute that belief when he comes out of the chicken coop with an empty feed bucket, not when he comes out of the pig pen.

This example is, however, not very enlightening because one could defend the principle by requiring that the individual be a competent speaker *of the sentence in question*. If he misunderstands a word and that misunderstanding is relevant to the case at hand, then the principle does not apply.

But the requirement that the individual be a competent speaker cannot go so far as to require that he know which uses of names are co-referential, otherwise the principle would fail to apply to Kripke's example. A speaker accepting (X1) and (X2) would not know that 'Cicero' and 'Tully' are co-referential. Kripke's argument requires (quite correctly) that this might occur to a normal (and competent) speaker. (It is probably easier to imagine an example with 'Mark Twain' and 'Samuel Clemens', in which a speaker accepts a multitude of true claims including 'Mark Twain' and a multitude of true claims including 'Samuel Clemens'—perhaps he is a relative of Samuel Clemens—yet never knows that the names are co-referential.)

Thus a revised version is more acceptable.

D′ If a normal speaker of English understands a sentence *S* of English and sincerely assents to it, then he believes what *S* expresses.

Even D′ may falter over cases of self-deception,[22] but if we can agree that self-deception is not a factor, then in cases like Kripke's someone's understanding a sentence and sincerely assenting to it would ordinarily show that he believes

---

[22]Smith may sincerely assent to "My Father is a very fine fellow," or the dean may sincerely assent to "Professor Jones is a fine scholar who deserves all of the recognition and encouragement we can give him," yet either might show by his actions that he does not believe what is expressed by the utterance he accepts. Smith might regularly protect himself against his father's deceit and irresponsibility, the dean might regularly exclude Jones from recognition and encouragement. They might be sincere despite this if they have deceived themselves about what their beliefs are. But I would not wish the response to Kripke to rest on these empirical claims about self-deception. So in considering cases of the type already presented in Kripke's paper and in this paper I will assume that such self-deception is not a factor. It is clear that in such cases someone's understanding a sentence and sincerely assenting to it would ordinarily be taken to show that he believes what it expresses.

what it expresses. A speaker's understanding and acceptance of (X1) and (X2), or his understanding and acceptance of (1) and the negation of (2),[23] (1**) and the negation of (2**), or (1″) and the negation of (2″) can be sufficient to guarantee a belief in what is expressed in each case.

Let us then consider P and the standards of consistency of belief it presents.

In supporting the direct reference view of proper names, I have embraced the position that a person can be justified in accepting sentences with contradictory content, and thus can be justified in having contradictory beliefs. But certainly it is sometimes irrational to accept contradictory beliefs, and the fact that beliefs are contradictory is good reason to give up their conjunction.

How can we say when contradictory beliefs are unacceptable if sometimes they are justified? How do we draw the distinction between reasonable and unreasonable acceptance of a contradiction?

Kripke's principle P certainly formulates a standard that we are willing to apply in most cases. To accept the claims "My car burns gas" and "My car does not burn gas" would be incoherent; and to accept "Hesperus is a planet" and "Hesperus is not a planet" would be incoherent, as long as the uses of 'Hesperus' were thought to be co-referential. But the qualification about 'Hesperus' is the very point at issue. When one does not think that the uses of names are co-referential, he may be perfectly justified in accepting tokens which appear superficially to contradict one another. Consider the familiar case of accepting tokens of the types "Aristotle was a philosopher" and "Aristotle was not a philosopher" when the two uses of 'Aristotle' are taken to have different referents. Similarly, if one does not believe that the distinct names are co-referential, then one can be justified in accepting pairs of sentences like (X1) and (X2) which could not both be true if the names were co-referential.

Thus, if principle P is about accepting sentences, it is false. The best we can claim is that

> P′ (1) A believer with a modicum of logicality will not, after appropriate reflection, accept a token of type S and a token of its negation if he takes the words to be used with the same content in both tokens.
>
> (2) If S and S' are alike except that some proper name n in S is replaced by a different proper name n' in S' then a believer with a modicum of logicality will not, after appropriate reflection, accept a token of S and a token of a negation of S' if he takes n and n' to be co-referential and he takes the other words to be used with the same content in both sentences.

---

[23]When I speak of the negation of (2), I am asking your co-operation in imagining a situation just like that in which (2) is uttered, but in which a sentence of the type

(N2) This is not a penny.

is uttered. Similarly for the 'negations' of (2**) and (2″).

But P′ will not guarantee that someone who attentively accepts (X1) and (X2) is not accepting a contradiction. So P′ will not support Kripke's argument.

Of course Kripke's principle P speaks of "directly contradictory propositions—of the form 'p' and '$\sim p$'," and it does not speak of sentences at all. So let us assume that a proposition is something independent of the sentence formulating the proposition and that accepting a proposition is the same as believing that proposition. Then P is false. Consider the man who accepts both (1) and the negation of (2) or the man who accepts both (1**) and the negation of (2**). He accepts a proposition and its negation, and he may do so with appropriate attention. The situation with respect to (1″) and the negation of (2″) or with (X1) and (X2) is, as I have argued, similar. Reflection alone will not reveal the co-reference relationship of the terms or the contradictory character of the propositions. The examples are counter-examples to the strong form of P.

To rescue P, it would appear that one would have to say that a person never accepts a proposition and its negation if he recognizes that the propositions he is accepting bear this relation. But the person who accepts sentences (X1) and (X2) and thereby accepts the propositions expressed has a deficiency in just this respect. He does not recognize that the propositions he has accepted are directly contradictory to one another. If P is revised to require the recognition of a contradiction where it exists, P produces no puzzle.

P can be defended only if one accepts some view that propositions believed show their simple logical relationships in some immediate way. But given D′ and the examples we have considered, that is apparently not true.

Language is a great resource for entertaining propositions, yet in its very virtue, that this can lead us to new beliefs, lies our problem. Language can lead us to contradictory beliefs without providing the immediate resources for removing the contradiction. Our grasp of a name on a particular occasion can be a sufficient basis for a belief about its referent and yet be an insufficient basis for determining all of the co-reference relations of that use with other uses of names that we grasp.[24] In this special case, contradictory belief can be the outcome of conscientious inquiry. Principle P′ is strong enough to cover the cases we most often need to consider. The false principle P can then be discarded without throwing us into the position of being totally unable to say when contradictories are rationally unacceptable.[25]

---

[24] In "Plantinga, Proper names and Propositions," Diana Ackerman has given examples that support this point, though her use of them is very different from mine.

[25] I thank Diana Ackerman, Bill Alston, Jose Benardete, Jonathan Bennett, John Robertson, Alex Rosenberg and Peter van Inwagen for their helpful comments on earlier drafts. The writing of this paper was supported by summer grants from the Syracuse University Senate.

FREGE'S PUZZLE

Nathan Salmon

1. Frege's Puzzle and the Naive Theory

1.1. *Frege's Puzzle and Information Content*

Identity challenges reflection through questions which are connected with it and are not altogether easy to answer. . . . $\ulcorner a = a \urcorner$ and $\ulcorner a = b \urcorner$ are obviously sentences of a different cognitive value [Erkenntniswerte]: $\ulcorner a = a \urcorner$ holds a priori and is according to Kant to be called analytic, whereas sentences of the form $\ulcorner a = b \urcorner$ often contain very valuable extensions of our knowledge and are not always to be grounded a priori. . . . If we then wanted to view identity as a relation between that which the names a and b signify, then $\ulcorner a = b \urcorner$ and $\ulcorner a = a \urcorner$ would seem to be potentially not different, in case, that is, $\ulcorner a = b \urcorner$ is true. There would be thereby expressed a relation of a thing to itself, one in which each thing stands to itself, but no thing stands to another.

With the German equivalent of these words, Frege tortuously poses the problem that gave rise to his celebrated theory of sense: How can $\ulcorner a = b \urcorner$, if true, differ in "cognitive value"—that is, in cognitive information content—from $\ulcorner a = a \urcorner$? Clearly they differ, since the first is informative and a posteriori where the latter is uninformative and a priori. But, assuming that $\ulcorner a = b \urcorner$ predicates the relation of identity between the referent of the name a and the referent of the name b, and that $\ulcorner a = a \urcorner$ predicates the relation of identity between the referent of a and the referent of a, then if $\ulcorner a = b \urcorner$ is true, it predicates the same relation between the same pair of objects as does $\ulcorner a = a \urcorner$. It would seem, then, that $\ulcorner a = b \urcorner$ and $\ulcorner a = a \urcorner$ ought to convey the same piece of information. But clearly they do not. So what gives here?

A number of philosophers have found the identity relation, taken as the relation that "each thing stands in to itself, but no thing stands to another," curious, mysterious, or bogus. In the *Tractatus* (sections 5.53–5.535), Wittgenstein denies that there is any such relation.[1] Earlier, in *Begriffsschrift* (section 8), Frege took a similar tack, proposing an analysis of identity sentences according to which singular terms "display their own selves [appear in propria persona] when they are combined by means of the sign ['='] for identity of content [referent], for this expresses the circumstance of two names [singular terms] having the same content [referent]." Thus the early Frege and Wittgenstein attempted to rid themselves of the puzzle. More recent philosophy has followed Frege's later characterization of the origins of the puzzle as one arising from reflection on the concept of the identity by the use of such epithets as 'Frege's puzzle about identity' or 'Frege's identity problem'. The first point I wish to emphasize about 'Frege's puzzle about

---

[1] See also Wittgenstein, *Philosophical Grammar* (Berkeley: University of California Press, 1974), at pp. 315–318; *Philosophical Investigations* (New York: Macmillan), at p. 216. For a more recent endorsement of the general strategy see Ian Hacking, "Comment on Wiggins," in *Philosophy of Logic*, ed. S. Körner (Berkeley: University of California Press, 1976).

identity' is that, pace Frege, it is not a puzzle about identity. It has virtually nothing to do with identity. Different versions of the very same puzzle, or formally analogous puzzles that pose the very same set of questions and philosophical issues in the very same way, arise with certain constructions not involving the identity predicate or the identity relation. For example, the sentence 'Shakespeare wrote *Timon of Athens*' is informative, whereas 'The author of *Timon of Athens* wrote *Timon of Athens*' is not. The same question arises: How can that be? Given that the first sentence is true, it would seem that both sentences contain the same piece of information; they both attribute the same property (authorship of *Timon of Athens*) to the same individual (Shakespeare). This kind of example is unlike Frege's version of the puzzle in that it involves a definite description, whereas Frege's can involve two proper names and consequently applies pressure against a wider range of semantic theories. It is not difficult, however, to construct further puzzling examples involving two names without using the identity predicate; the sentence 'Hesperus is a planet if Phosphorus is' is informative and apparently a posteriori, whereas the sentence 'Phosphorus is a planet if Phosphorus is' is uninformative and a priori. However, both sentences attribute the same property, *being a planet if Phosphorus is,* to the same entity, the planet Venus. Looked at another way, both sentences attribute the same relation, x *is a planet if y is,* to the same (reflexive) pair of objects. In either case, the two sentences seem to contain the very same information.

It is easy to see from these examples that versions of Frege's Puzzle can be constructed in connection with any predicate whatsoever, not just with the identity predicate. What, then, is the general puzzle about if it is not a puzzle about identity? These same examples provide the answer. The general problem is a problem concerning pieces of information (in a nontechnical sense), such as the information that Socrates is wise or the information that Socrates is wise if Plato is. The various versions of Frege's Puzzle are stated in terms of declarative sentences rather than in terms of information. This is because there is an obvious and intimate relation between pieces of information (such as the information that Socrates is wise) and declarative sentences (such as 'Socrates is wise'). Declarative sentences have various semantic attributes: they are true, or false, or neither; they have semantic intentions (i.e., correlated functions from possible worlds to truth values); they involve reference to individuals, such as Socrates; and so on. But the fundamental semantic role of a declarative sentence is to encode information.[2] I mean the term 'information' in a broad sense to include misinformation (that is,

---

[2] A word of clarification is needed concerning my use of the semantic predicates 'encode' and 'information'. Throughout this book I am concerned with discrete units of information that are specifiable by means of a 'that'-clause, e.g., the information that Socrates was wise. These discrete units are *pieces of information.* I shall generally use the mass noun 'information' as if it were shorthand for the count noun phrase 'piece of information', i.e., as a general term whose extension is the class of pieces of information. Thus, I write 'information that is such-and-such' to mean "pieces of information that are such-and-such," 'the same information' to mean "the same pieces of information," 'different information to mean "different pieces of information," and so on. I use the verb 'encode' in such a way that an unambiguous declarative

(contd.)

inaccurate or incorrect pieces of information), and even pieces of information that are neither true nor false. Pragmatically, we use declarative sentences to communicate or convey information to others (generally, not just the information encoded by the sentence), but we may also use declarative sentences simply to record information for possible future use, and perhaps even to record information with no anticipation of any future use. If for some reason I need to make a record of the date of my marriage, say to recall that piece of information on a later occasion, I can simply write the words 'I was married on August 28, 1980', or memorize them, or repeat them to myself. Declarative sentences are primarily a means of encoding information, and they are a remarkably efficient means at that. Many of their other semantic and pragmatic functions follow from or depend upon their fundamental semantic role of encoding information.

This statement of the semantic relation between declarative sentences and information is somewhat vague, but it is clear enough to convey one of the fundamental presuppositions of Frege's Puzzle. Vague though it may be, it is also obviously correct. Any reasonable semantic theory for declarative sentences ought to allow for some account of declarative sentences as information encoders, at least to the extent of not contradicting it. A conception of sentences as information encoders will be assumed throughout this book. A declarative sentence will be said to *contain* the information it encodes, and that piece of information will be described as the *information content* of the sentence.

Pieces of information are, like the sentences that encode them, abstract entities. Many of their properties can be "read off" from the encoding sentences. Thus, for instance, it is evident that pieces of information are not ontologically simple, but complex. The information that Socrates is wise and the information that Socrates is snub-nosed are both, in the same way, pieces of information directly about Socrates; hence, they must have some component in common. Likewise, the information that Socrates is wise has some component in common with the information that Plato is wise, and that component is different from what it has

---

sentence encodes (with respect to a given possible context c) a *single* piece of information, which is referred to (with respect to c) by the result of prefixing 'the information that' to the sentence and which is to be called 'the information content' of the sentence (with respect to c). A declarative sentence may encode (with respect to a given context) two or more pieces of information, but if it does so it is ambiguous. Pieces of information encoded by the logical consequences of an unambiguous sentence are not themselves encoded, in this sense, by the sentence. The (piece of) information that snow is white and grass is green is different information (a different piece of information) from the (piece of) information that snow is white, though intuitively the latter is included as part of the former. The sentence 'Snow is white and grass is green' encodes only the former, not the latter. This constitutes a departure from at least one standard usage, according to which the information content of a sentence is perhaps something like a class of pieces of information, closed under logical consequence.

I am not concerned in this book with a notion of an *amount* of information, which arises in the mathematical theory of communication or information. The information *that snow is white and grass is green and Socrates is Socrates* may be no more or less information than the information *that both snow is white if and only if grass is green and either snow is white or grass is green*. Nevertheless, general considerations involving Leibniz's Law strongly suggest that they are numerically distinct pieces of information. For instance, the first concerns Socrates whereas the second does not.

in common with the information that Socrates is snub-nosed. Correspondingly, the declarative sentence 'Socrates is wise' shares certain syntactic components with the sentences 'Socrates is snub-nosed' and 'Plato is wise'. These syntactic components—the name 'Socrates' and the predicate 'is wise'—are separately semantically correlated with the corresponding component of the piece of information encoded by the sentence. Let us call the information component semantically correlated with an expression the *information value* of the expression. The information value of the name 'Socrates' is that which the name contributes to the information encoded by such sentences as 'Socrates is wise' and 'Socrates is snub-nosed'; similarly, the information value of the predicate 'is wise' is that entity which the predicate contributes to the information encoded by such sentences as 'Socrates is wise' and 'Plato is wise'. As a limiting case, the information value of a declarative sentence is the piece of information it encodes, its information content.

Within the framework of so-called possible-world semantics, the information value of an expression determines the semantic *intension* of the expression. The intension of a singular term, sentence, or predicate is a function that assigns to any possible world w the *extension* the singular term, sentence, or predicate takes on with respect to w. The extension of a singular term (with respect to a possible world w) is simply its *referent* (with respect to w), i.e., the object or individual to which the term refers (with respect to w). The extension of a sentence (with respect to w) is its truth value (with respect to w)—either truth or falsehood. The extension of an n-place predicate (with respect to w) is the predicate's semantic characteristic function (with respect to w), i.e., the function that assigns either truth or falsehood to an n-tuple of individuals, according as the predicate or its negation applies (with respect to w) to the n-tuple. Assuming bivalence, the extension of an n-place predicate may be identified instead with the class of n-tuples to which the predicate applies.

Since ordinary language includes so-called indexical expressions (such as 'I', 'you', 'here', 'now', 'today', 'yesterday', 'this', 'that', 'he', 'she', 'there', and 'then'), the information value of an expression, and hence also the semantic intension, must in general be indexed, i.e., relativized, to the context in which the expression is uttered. That is, strictly one should speak of the information value of an expression (e.g., the information content of a sentence) with respect to this or that context of utterance, and similarly for the corresponding semantic intension of an expression; the information value and corresponding intension of an expression with respect to one context may be different from the information value and corresponding intension of the same expression with respect to a different context. This generates a higher-level, nonrelativized semantic value for expressions, which David Kaplan calls the *character* of an expression. The character of an expression is a function or rule that determines, for any possible context of utterance c, the information value the expression takes on with respect to c. For example, the character of a sentence is a function or rule that assigns to any possible context of utterance c the piece of information that the sentence encodes with respect to c, that is, the information content of the sentence with respect to c.

In addition to the character of an expression, we may consider a related non-relativized semantic value: the function or rule that determines for any possible context of utterance c the extension (e.g., the referent, the class of application, or the truth value) that the expression takes on with respect to c. Let us call this the *contour* of an expression. The contour of an expression is fully determined by its character, as follows: Given any context c, the character of an expression determines the information value of the expression with respect to c. This, in turn, determines the intension of the expression with respect to c. Applying this intension to the possible world of the context c yields the extension of the expression with respect to c.[3]

In summary, the central and fundamental semantic value of a declarative sentence is its information content, the piece of information encoded. This generates a fundamental semantic value for expressions generally: information value. The information value of an expression determines the expression's semantic intension, which assigns to any possible world a lower-level semantic value for the expression, its extension with respect to that possible world. Since ordinary language includes indexicals, the information value of an expression must be indexed to a context of utterance. This generates a higher-level semantic value for expressions, character, which assigns to any possible context the information value the expression takes on with respect to that context. The character of an expression

---

[3] I use here, and throughout this book, a quasi-technical notion of the *context* of an utterance, which is such that, for any particular actual utterance of any expression by anyone, if any facts had been different in any way, even if they are only facts entirely independent of and isolated from the utterance itself, then the context of the utterance would, ipso facto, be a different context—even if the utterance is made by the very same speaker in the very same way to the very same audience at the very same time in the very same place. To put it another way, although a single utterance occurs in indefinitely many different possible worlds, any particular possible context of an utterance occurs in one and only one possible world, so that, in every possible world in which the same utterance occurs, it occurs in a new and different context—even if the speaker, his or her manner of uttering, the time of the utterance, the location of the speaker, the audience being addressed, and all other such features and aspects of the utterance remain exactly the same. There is a very good reason for using the term 'context' in this way: Suppose, for example, that it will come to pass that a Democrat is elected to the presidency in the year 2000, and consider a possible world W that is exactly like the actual world in every detail up to January 1, 1999, but in which a Republican is elected to the presidency in 2000. Suppose I here and now utter the sentence

Actually, a Republican will be elected to the presidency in A.D. 2000.

In the actual world, I thereby assert a piece of information that is necessarily false. In W, on the other hand, I thereby assert a piece of information that is necessarily true. I utter the very same sequence of words of English, with the very same English meanings, in both possible worlds, yet I assert different things. If we were to use the term 'context' in such a way that the context of my utterance remains the same in both worlds, we should be forced to say, quite mysteriously, that the sentence I uttered is such that it would have encoded different information with respect to the context in which I uttered it if W had obtained even though both its meaning and its context of utterance would remain exactly the same. Using the term 'context' as I shall throughout this book, we may say instead that, although the very same utterance occurs by me both in W and in the actual world, the context of the utterance is different in the two worlds. This allows us to say that the sentence I utter takes on different information contents with respect to *different* contexts of utterance, thereby assimilating this phenomenon to the sort of context sensitivity that is familiar in cases of sentences like 'A Republican is presently president'.

determines the expression's contour, which assigns to any possible context the extension the expression takes on with respect to that context.

The systematic method by which it is secured which information is semantically encoded by which sentence is, roughly, that a sentence semantically encodes that piece of information whose components are the information values of the sentence parts, with these information values combined as the sentence parts are themselves combined to form the sentence.[4] In order to analyze the information encoded by a sentence into its components, one simply decomposes the sentence into its information-valued parts, and the information values thereof are the components of the encoded information. In this way, declarative sentences not only encode but also codify information.

---

[4] The latter clause is needed in order to distinguish 'Bill loves Mary' from 'Mary loves Bill', where the sequential order of composition is crucial. This succinct statement of the rule connecting sentences and their information contents is only an approximation to the truth. A complicated difficulty arises in connection with the latter clause of the rule and with such quantificational locutions as 'someone' in 'Someone is wise'. Grammatically the sentence 'Someone is wise' is analogous to 'Socrates is wise', though logically and semantically they are disanalogous. In 'Socrates is wise', the predicate 'is wise' attaches to the singular term 'Socrates'. This situation is reversed in 'Someone is wise', wherein the restricted quantifier 'someone' attaches to the predicate 'is wise'. Thus, whereas grammatically 'someone' is combined with 'is wise' to form the first sentence in just the same way that 'Socrates' is combined with 'is wise' to form the second sentence, the information values of 'someone' and 'is wise' are combined very differently from the way the information values of 'Socrates' and 'is wise' are combined. (This complication may lie behind at least part of Russell's motivation for claiming that definite descriptions and quantificational locutions generally ("denoting phrases") have no "meaning in isolation." . . .)

A perhaps more important qualification to the general rule is noted in the next paragraph of the text. Yet another important qualification concerns overlaid quantifiers. It is necessary to distinguish between the information contents of such constructions as

    (A) For everyone x there is someone y such that x loves y

and

    (B) For everyone x there is someone y such that y loves x.

One possible method is to include as part of the structure of some propositions *unoccupied positions* as well as some device that connects or links a proposition component, such as the information value of a quantifier, with an unoccupied position within the proposition. Thus, for example, the information value (with respect to a time t) of the open sentence 'x loves y' may be taken to be something like a partially defined ordered triple, with the first two places undefined and the third place filled by the relation of loving: $\langle$___, ___, loving$\rangle$. (Actually the third place would be filled by the temporally indexed relation of *loving at t*: $\langle$___, ___, $\langle$loving, $t\rangle\rangle$. . . .) Entities of this sort may be called *open propositions*. (They are not to be confused with proposition matrices, which will be defined below. A proposition matrix may have the form of a totally defined ordered n-tuple, whereas open propositions always have the form of partially defined ordered n-tuples, or sequences containing partially defined ordered n-tuples as elements, etc.) The information values of the quantifiers 'for everyone' and 'there is someone such that' are certain higher-order properties. (Specifically, they are properties of one-place functions from individuals to truth values.) Let us designate them by 'πone' and 'Σone', respectively. Then, on this method, the information content of sentence A is not merely a sequence of the

(contd.)

One may take it as a sort of general rule or principle that the information value of any compound expression, with respect to a given context of utterance, is made up of the information values, with respect to the given context, of the information-valued components of the compound. This general rule is subject to certain important qualifications, however, and must be construed more as a

information values of the information-valued components of the sentence, but something that is also interconnected. This proposition might be diagrammed thus:

$$\langle\langle\langle \ \underline{\quad\quad} , \ \underline{\quad\quad} , \ \text{loving}\rangle, \Sigma\text{one}\rangle, \Pi\text{one}\rangle$$

The information content of sentence B, on the other hand, would be diagrammed thus:

$$\langle\langle\langle \ \underline{\quad\quad} , \ \underline{\quad\quad} , \ \text{loving}\rangle, \Sigma\text{one}\rangle, \Pi\text{one}\rangle$$

(Strictly accurate diagrams would replace 'loving' with '⟨loving, t⟩'.) The lines of connection, or links, though not strictly "elements" of the propositions, are regarded as essential to the structures of the propositions. They serve both to *close* what would otherwise be open propositions and to distinguish them from each other. See W.V.O. Quine, *Mathematical Logic* (Cambridge, Mass.: Harvard University Press, 1965), at p. 70; Gareth Evans, "Pronouns, Quantifiers and Relative Clauses (I)," in *Reference, Truth and Reality*, ed. M. Platts (London: Routledge and Kegan Paul, 1980).

On this method, the open sentence 'y loves x' has exactly the same information value as 'x loves y'. Hence, on this method, sentences A and B are such that either can be obtained from the other simply by replacing one component—the contained open sentence with two free variables—by another with the same information value. Nevertheless, A and B clearly differ in information content. This result conflicts with a certain compositionality principle, commonly attributed to Frege, according to which the information value of a compound expression such as A or B is a function solely of the information values of its information-valued components. (See Alonzo Church, "Intensional Isomorphism and Identity of Belief," *Philosophical Studies* 5, no. 5 (1954):65–73, for a similar but more sharply articulated principle.) On this method, the connections between the information value of a quantifier and the corresponding unoccupied positions within the information value of the open sentence, as indicated by the containing sentence, must also be taken into account.

A superior method, due to Church and pointed out to me by David Kaplan, eliminates open propositions in favor of Russellian propositional functions, i.e., functions from an individual to a singular proposition involving that individual. (Church himself applies the general method in such a way as to invoke only Fregean functions from pure concepts of individuals to Fregean purely general propositions, although the general method can also accommodate anti-Fregean theories by invoking propositional functions.) On this method, the information content of sentence A is regarded as having the structure of the following ordered pair:

$$\langle(\lambda x)(\lambda y) \ \langle x, y, \text{loving}\rangle, \Sigma\text{one}\rangle, \Pi\text{one}\rangle.$$

general guide or rule of thumb. Exceptions arise in connection with quotation marks and similar devices. The numeral '9' is, in an ordinary sense, a component part of the sentence 'The numeral '9' is a singular term', though the information value of the former is no part of the information content of the latter. I shall argue below that, in addition to quotation marks, there is another important though often neglected class of operators that yield exceptions to the general rule in something like the way that quotation marks do.[5] Still, it may be correctly said of any English sentence free of operators other than truth-functional connectives (e.g., 'If Socrates is wise, then so is Plato') that its information content is a complex made up of the information values of its information-valued components.

It is out of the natural and preliminary analysis presented here of the information contained in (i.e., semantically encoded by) declarative sentences, and not from reflection on the alleged mystique of identity, that Frege's challenging question arises.

1.2. The Naive Theory

What makes Frege's challenging question a puzzle? It poses a serious difficulty for a certain type of semantic theory: one that entails that two sentences involving an n-place predicate and n singular terms have the same information content (encode the same piece of information) if their predicates are semantically correlated with the same attribute (property or relation) and their singular terms, taken in sequence, coincide in reference, respectively. Specifically, the question poses a serious problem for what I, following David Kaplan, shall call the *naive theory*.

The information content of sentence B, on the other hand, is regarded as having the following structure:

$\langle(\lambda x)\rangle\langle(\lambda y)\ \langle x, y, \text{loving}\rangle, \Sigma\text{one}\rangle, \Pi\text{one}\rangle.$

(Here again, for complete accuracy, 'loving' should be replaced by '$\langle \text{loving}, t\rangle$'.) The first element of the former proposition is the propositional function that assigns to each individual x the proposition made up of the propositional function that assigns to each individual y the proposition that x loves y and the second-order property (one. The first element of the latter proposition is the appropriate analogue. A variant of this method (closer to the spirit of the naive and modified naive theories defined below) replaces these propositional functions with the properties of loving someone (at t) and of being loved by someone (at t), respectively. The information content of sentence A may be regarded as the following complex proposition: that the function that assigns truth to an individual x if x loves someone or other, and assigns falsehood otherwise, assigns truth to everyone whatsoever. This powerful method need not assign any information value to an open sentence like 'x loves y', except relative to an assignment of values to its free variables, and hence generates no counterexamples to the original compositionality principle. Even on this method, however, it is not true in general that the information value of a compound expression involving bound variables is a complex made up entirely of the information values of its information-valued components. If the first element of the information content of sentence A is the information value of any component of the sentence—for example, the component 'x there is someone y such that x loves y'—then the information value of that component is not made up of the information values of its information-valued components.

[5] See also . . . note 9 below.

The naive theory is a theory of the information values of certain expressions. According to the naive theory, the information value of a singular term, as used in a possible context, is simply its referent in that context. This is similar to what Gilbert Ryle called the *'Fido'-Fido theory,* according to which the "meaning" or content of a singular term is simply its referent. Elements of this theory can be traced to ancient times. Likewise, the information value of a predicate, as used in a particular context, is identified with something like the semantically associated attribute with respect to that context, that is, with the corresponding property in the case of a monadic predicate or the corresponding n-ary relation in the case of an n-place predicate. On the naive theory, an atomic sentence consisting of an n-place predicate II and n occurrences of singular terms, $a_1, a_2, \ldots, a_n$, when evaluated with respect to a particular possible context, has as its cognitive content in that context a piece of information, called a *proposition,* which is supposed to be a complex consisting of something like the attribute referred to by II with respect to that context and the sequence of objects referred to by the singular terms with respect to that context. For example, the cognitive information content of the sentence 'Socrates is wise' is to be the singular proposition consisting of Socrates and wisdom. On the naive theory, a sentence is a means for referring to its information content by specifying the components that make it up. A sentential connective may be construed on the model of a predicate. The information value of a connective would thus be an attribute (a property if monadic, a relation if polyadic)—not an attribute of individuals like Socrates, but an attribute of pieces of information, or propositions. For example, the information value of the connective 'if and only if' might be identified with the binary equivalence relation between propositions having the same truth value. Similarly, the information value of a quantifier might be identified with a property of properties of individuals. For example, the information value of the unrestricted universal quantifier 'everything' may be the (second-order) property of being a universal (first-order) property, i.e., the property of being a property possessed by every individual. The information value of a sentence, as used in a particular context, is simply its information content, the proposition made up of the information values of the information-valued sentence components.

The naive theory of information value, then, may be thought of as flowing from the following theses:

Thesis I
(Declarative) sentences encode pieces of information, called *propositions.* The proposition encoded by a sentence, with respect to a given context, is its *information content* with respect to that context.

Thesis II
The information content, with respect to a given context, of a sentence is a complex, ordered entity (e.g., a sequence) whose constituents are semantically correlated systematically with expressions making up the sentence, typically

the simple (noncompound) component expressions. Exceptions arise in connection with quotation marks and similar devices.

Thesis III
The information value (contribution to information content), with respect to a given context c, of any singular term is its referent with respect to c (and the time of c and the world of c).

Thesis IV
Any expression may be thought of as *referring*, with respect to a given context, time, and possible world, to its information value with respect to that context.

Thesis V
The information value, with respect to a given context, of an n-place first-order predicate is an n-place attribute (either a property or an n-ary relation)—ordinarily an attribute ascribed to the referents of the attached singular terms. Exceptions arise in connection with quotation marks and similar devices.

Thesis VI
The information value, with respect to a given context, of an n-adic sentential connective is an attribute, ordinarily of the sorts of things that serve as referents for the operand sentences.

Thesis VII
The information value, with respect to a given context, of an n-adic quantifier or second-order predicate is an n-ary attribute, ordinarily of the sorts of things that serve as the referents for the operand first-order predicates.

Thesis VIII
The information value, with respect to a given context, of an operator other than a predicate, a connective, or a quantifier is an appropriate attribute (for sentence-forming operators) of, or operation (for other types of operators) on, the sorts of things that serve as referents for its appropriate operands.

Thesis IX
The information value, with respect to a given context, of a sentence is its information content, the encoded proposition.

Within the framework of the naive theory, the *meaning* of an expression might be identified with the expression's character, i.e., the semantically correlated function from possible contexts of utterance to information values. For example, the meaning of the sentence 'I am busy' will be thought of as a function that assigns to any context of utterance c the singular proposition composed of the agent of the context c (= the referent of 'I' with respect to c) and the property of being busy. . . .

6. The Crux of Frege's Puzzle

6.1. The Minor Premise

There are three main elements in Frege's Puzzle, and in the corresponding strategy: Frege's Law, the compositionality principle, and the further premise that ⌜$a = b$⌝ is informative and a posteriori whereas ⌜$a = a$⌝ is not. I have argued that there is nothing to be gained by challenging the compositionality principle, and that Frege's Law is beyond challenge, since properly understood it is simply a special instance of Leibniz's Law. Still to be considered is the minor premise that ⌜$a = b$⌝ is informative whereas ⌜$a = a$⌝ is not.

Historically, philosophers who have had some inclination toward something like the naive theory, including Frege, Mill, and Russell, have allowed that ⌜$a = b$⌝ is informative and a posteriori whereas ⌜$a = a$⌝ is not. This was thought too obvious to be denied, and other means for coming to grips with Frege's Puzzle were sought and devised. In contemporary philosophy, direct-reference theorists—who should find the naive theory particularly congenial—have typically conceded this point, or something tantamount to it, and have therefore abstained from outright, unequivocal endorsement of the naive theory or any modification of the naive theory. Consider the following remarks:

> [You] see a star in the evening and it's called 'Hesperus'. . . . We see a star in the morning and call it 'Phosphorus'. Well, then we find . . . that Hesperus and Phosphorus are in fact the same. So we express this by 'Hesperus is Phosphorus'. Here we're certainly not just saying of an object that it's identical with itself. This is something that we discovered. (Saul Kripke, *Naming and Necessity*, pp. 28–29)

> [We] do not know a *priori* that Hesperus is Phosphorus, and are in no position to find out . . . except empirically. (ibid., p. 104; see also the disclaimer on pp. 20–21)

> Before appropriate empirical discoveries were made, men might have failed to know that Hesperus was Phosphorus, or even to believe it, even though they of course knew and believed that Hesperus was Hesperus. (Kripke, "A Puzzle about Belief," p. 243—but see p. 281, note 44; see also the disclaimer at p. 273, note 10)

> Certainly Frege's argument shows meaning cannot just *be* reference. . . . (Hilary Putnam, "Comments," p. 285)

> If we distinguish a sentence from the proposition it expresses then the terms 'truth' and 'necessity' apply to the proposition expressed by a sentence, while the terms '*a priori*' and '*a posteriori*' are sentence relative. Given that it is true that Cicero is Tully (and whatever we need about what the relevant sentences express) 'Cicero is Cicero' and 'Cicero is Tully' express the same *proposition*. And the proposition is necessarily true. But looking at the proposition through the lens of the *sentence* 'Cicero is Cicero' the proposition can be seen *a priori* to be true, but through 'Cicero is Tully' one may need an *a posteriori* investigation. (Keith Donnellan, "Kripke and Putnam on Natural Kind Terms," note 2 on p. 88)

> Faced with Frege's identity puzzle, it is difficult indeed to maintain that the names 'Hesperus' and 'Phosphorus' make precisely the same contribution to the information content of sentences that contain either one. Such a claim would be extremist. (Nathan Salmon, *Reference and Essence*, p. 13)

Here is where well-intentioned philosophers have been led astray. It is precisely the seemingly trivial premise that $\ulcorner a = b \urcorner$ is informative whereas $\ulcorner a = a \urcorner$ is not informative that should be challenged, and a proper appreciation for the distinction between semantically encoded and pragmatically imparted information points the way. Recall that Frege's Law is erected into a truth of logic by understanding the word 'informative' in such a way that to say that a sentence is informative is to say something about its information content. By the same token, however, with 'informative' so understood, and with a sharp distinction between semantically encoded information and pragmatically imparted information kept in mind, it is not in the least bit obvious, as Frege's Puzzle maintains, that $\ulcorner a = b \urcorner$ is, whereas $\ulcorner a = a \urcorner$ is not, informative *in the relevant sense*. To be sure, $\ulcorner a = b \urcorner$ *sounds* informative, whereas $\ulcorner a = a \urcorner$ does not. Indeed, an utterance of $\ulcorner a = b \urcorner$ genuinely imparts information that is more valuable than that imparted by an utterance of $\ulcorner a = a \urcorner$. For example, it imparts the nontrivial linguistic information about the sentence $\ulcorner a = b \urcorner$ that it is true, and hence that the names a and b are co-referential. But that is pragmatically imparted information, and presumably not semantically encoded information. . . . It is by no means clear that the sentence $\ulcorner a = b \urcorner$, stripped naked of its pragmatic impartations and with only its properly semantic information content left, is any more informative in the relevant sense than $\ulcorner a = a \urcorner$. Abstracting from their markedly different pragmatic impartations, one can see that these two sentences may well semantically encode the very same piece of information. I believe that they do. At the very least, it is by no means certain, as Frege's Puzzle pretends, that the difference in "cognitive significance" we seem to hear is not due entirely to a difference in pragmatically imparted information. Yet, until we can be certain of this, Frege's law cannot be applied and Frege's Puzzle does not get off the ground. In effect, then, Frege's Strategy begs the question against the modified naive theory. Of course, if one fails to draw the distinction between semantically encoded and pragmatically imparted information, as so many philosophers have, it is small wonder that information pragmatically imparted by (utterances of) $\ulcorner a = b \urcorner$ may be mistaken for semantically encoded information.[6] If Frege's Stategy is ultimately to

---

[6] In claiming that Frege and Russell and their followers have mistaken pragmatically imparted information for semantically encoded information, I do not mean that they would assent to such things as 'The sentence "Hesperus is Phosphorus" expresses in English the information about itself that it is true'. Clearly they would not; in any case, they need not. Nor would someone who mistakes a particular celebrity impersonator for the president of the United States assent to 'The president is the celebrity impersonator'. Philosophers mistake pragmatically imparted information for semantically encoded information in failing to keep the two sharply distinct and consequently judging whether a sentence S is informative partly on the basis of information pragmatically imparted by utterances of S.

Other writers have drawn distinctions similar to the one drawn here between semantically encoded and pragmatically imparted information as part of a defense of something like the original or the modified naive theory, though I came upon the idea independently. See Michael Tye, "The Puzzle of Hesperus and Phosphorus," *Australasian Journal of Philosophy* 56, no. 3 (1978):219–224, at p. 224; Raymond Bradley and Norman Swartz, *Possible Worlds: An Introduction to Logic and Its Philosophy* (Indianapolis: Hackett, 1979), at pp. 191–192;

(contd.)

succeed, a further argument must be made to show that the information imparted by $\ulcorner a = b \urcorner$ that makes it sound informative is, in fact, semantically encoded. In the meantime, Frege's Puzzle by itself is certainly not the final and conclusive refutation of the modified naive theory that the orthodox theorists have taken it to be. For all that Frege's Strategy achieves, the modified naive theory remains the best and most plausible theory available concerning the nature and structure of the information encoded by declarative sentences.

Ironically, . . . Frege was not unaware of the distinction between semantically encoded and merely pragmatically imparted information. He did not fully appreciate the significance of this distinction for his theory of information content. In particular, he failed to notice that the distinction undermines his main argument against the naive theory.

6.2. Substitutivity

The general puzzle, however, is not so easily put to rest. Although the premise that $\ulcorner a = b \urcorner$ is informative whereas $\ulcorner a = a \urcorner$ is not facilitates the derivation of Frege's Puzzle, this premise is not an essential element in the general puzzle. The premise is invoked in conjunction with Frege's Law to establish the result that there are pairs of sentences of the form ϕ_a and ϕ_b that differ in information content from one another—i.e., that encode different pieces of information—even though a and b are co-referential (genuine) proper names, demonstratives, single-word indexical singular terms, or any combination thereof. This is the crux of Frege's Puzzle. One might attempt to establish this result in some more general way, without invoking the suspect premise that $\ulcorner a = b \urcorner$ is informative. As Michael Dummett has stressed, and as Frege's formulation of the puzzle clearly indicates, the notion of *information content* relevant to Frege's Puzzle is closely tied to the ordinary, everyday notions of *knowledge* and *belief.* One intuitively appealing picture that is entrenched in philosophical tradition depicts belief as a type of inward assent, or a disposition toward inward assent, to a piece of information. To believe that p is to concur covertly with, to endorse mentally, to nod approval to, the information that p when p occurs to you. At the very least, to believe that p one must adopt some sort of favorable disposition or attitude toward the information that p. In fact, the adoption of some such favorable attitude toward a piece of

Tom McKay, "On Proper Names in Belief Ascriptions," *Philosophical Studies* 39 (1981): 287–303, at pp. 294–295; R. M. Sainsbury, "On a Fregean Argument for the Distinctness of Sense and Reference," *Analysis* 43 (January 1983):12–14; Takashi Yagisawa, Meaning and Belief, Ph.D. diss., Princeton University, 1981; J. Paul Reddam, Pragmatics and the Language of Belief, Ph.D. diss., University of Southern California, 1982. However, there are subtleties involved in Frege's Puzzle that these writers do not discuss. These subtleties will be developed in chapter 7 of this book with a new and stronger version of the puzzle, for which the solution presented here is simply irrelevant. (McKay comes very close to recognizing some of the finer aspects of the puzzle in his note 17, wherein he discusses an example (due to David Kaplan) involving a case of change of mind to suspension of judgment similar to the example to be presented in section 7.2 of this book. McKay's brief discussion of the example does not bring out the moral of my chapter 8.)

information is both necessary and sufficient for belief. That is just what belief is.[7] To believe that p is, so to speak, to include that piece of information in one's personal inner "data bank." It is to have that information at one's disposal to rely upon, to act upon, to draw inferences from, or to do nothing with. Belief is thus a relation to pieces of information.

These observations suggest the following principal schema, where the substituends for S and S' are declarative English sentences:

> If the information that S = the information that S', then someone believes that S if and only if he or she believes that S'.

Analogous schemata may be written for assertion and the other so-called propositional attitudes of knowledge, hope, and so forth. Like Frege's Law, each of these schemata may be regarded as (formal mode renderings of) so many instances of Leibniz's Law. In fact, Frege's Law can be viewed as a minor variation of one such schema:

> If the information that S = the information that S', then it is informative (knowable only a posteriori, a valuable extension of our knowledge, etc.) that S if and only if it is informative (a posteriori, etc.) that S'.

---

[7] I am not talking here about overt verbal assent to a *sentence*, but about *mental* assent to a proposition.

The conception of belief as inward assent is apparently advanced by Saint Augustine in chapter 5 of *Predestination of the Saints*, where belief is analyzed as "to think with assent." For an illuminating contemporary discussion of the analysis of belief as assent to an entertained proposition, see H. H. Price, *Belief* (London: Allen and Unwin, 1969), especially series I, lectures 8 and 9, and series II, lectures 1–3.

In suggesting that belief might be understood in terms of inward assent, concurrence, or approval, I am not suggesting a reduction of belief to a phenomenological episode (in the style of Hume). By 'inward assent', etc., I do not mean merely a private, subjective experience directed toward or involving the relevant piece of information (such as the experience one typically has when reading or saying the words 'yes, I agree' to oneself, together with a "feeling of understanding" of these words, etc.). Such an analysis would be unacceptable for familiar philosophical reasons: In unusual circumstances someone could have these experiences without believing, and without even grasping, the proposition. By 'inward assent', etc., I mean a state of *cognition*, with everything that this entails.

Furthermore, in speaking of a *disposition* to inward assent, or other favorable *dispositions*, I do not mean merely an inclination, tendency, or propensity to assent, etc. (the usual philosophical use of 'disposition' as in, e.g., 'dispositional property'). Here again, it is possible for someone to have such inclinations without believing the proposition, and vice versa. In saying that someone is favorably "disposed" toward something, I mean that the person harbors a positive, favorable attitude (e.g., agreement, as opposed to disagreement or indifference) toward the thing. Typically, the harboring of this attitude will result in certain inclinations or propensities, but that is not part of the analysis of the attitude, and in extraordinary circumstances the harboring of the favorable attitude may not result in the typical inclinations. Conversely, the inclinations may be present in the absence of the favorable attitude. It is probably best to speak of 'attitudes' rather than 'dispositions'. So understood, the suggested analysis may appear unilluminating, but then at least it is not controversial.

I use the term 'believe', and its cognates, in such a way that one believes that S if one is convinced that S, of the opinion that S, confident that S, persuaded that S, etc., but it is not sufficient that one merely thinks it likely that S, guesses that S, suspects that S theorizes that S, assumes that S, or supposes that S.

The *thesis of the substitutivity of co-informational sentences in propositional attitude contexts* is the thesis that every proper instance of any of these schemata is true. This may be separated into the *thesis of the substitutivity of co-informational sentences in assertion contexts* and so on for each of the attitudes. The thesis, or theses, is virtually a logical consequence of the idea that the object or content of a given belief, piece of knowledge, etc., is a piece of information, or a "proposition," and that a sentence encoding that information thereby gives the content of the belief. This idea, or something like it, is a commonplace in the philosophy of language; it is usually taken for granted without challenge by both sides in philosophical disputes over related issues (such as the question of the logical form of belief attributions). Some philosophers, in an effort to rescue a favored theory of propositions from the pitfalls of propositional attitude contexts, have rejected the thesis of substitutivity of co-informational (or co-propositional) sentences in propositional attitude contexts. But doing so seems both extreme and ad hoc. If the favored theory of propositions conflicts with the thesis, it would be more plausible to reject the theory.[8]

Insofar as some of the substitutivity theses are accepted as plausible principles concerning the relation between the pieces of information contained in a sentence and the content of an attitude (belief, knowledge, etc.) thereby expressed, they yield an important procedure for establishing that two given pieces of information are distinct. One may simply rely on our ordinary, everyday criteria, whatever they happen to be, for correctly saying that someone believes or knows something or does not believe or know it. We do not have to be able to specify these criteria; we need only to be able to apply them correctly in certain paradigm cases.

---

[8] I have in mind theories like that given by Robert Stalnaker in "Assertion," in *Syntax and Semantics 9: Pragmatics*, ed. P. Cole (New York: Academic, 1978). See also Stalnaker, "Indexical Belief," *Synthèse* 49, no. 1 (1981):129–151; David Lewis, "What Puzzling Pierre Believes," *Australasian Journal of Philosophy* 59, no. 3 (1981):283–289. The favored theory of propositions here is one that identifies propositions with sets of possible worlds—a theory on which propositions are even more coarse-grained than on the modified naive theory—though that is largely irrelevant to the main idea behind Stalnaker's account. Stalnaker claims that, in at least some propositional-attitude contexts, a 'that'-clause, $\ulcorner$ that $S \urcorner$, will sometimes refer not to the proposition expressed by the sentence S but instead to a related proposition, which Stalnaker calls 'the diagonal proposition of the propositional concept for S.' This so-called diagonal proposition, if it is a proposition at all, is best identified as the singular proposition about S that it is true—or, more accurate, as the proposition *that the proposition semantically encoded by S, as uttered in a context, is true*. (Stalnaker shows reluctance to so identify the diagonal proposition. The coarse-grainedness of his favored theory of propositions enables him to avoid specifying the relevant proposition in this way; however, from the point of view of a more fine-grained theory (such as the modified naive theory or the Fregean theory), the metatheoretic proposition that S is true is the most plausible candidate for being the diagonal proposition.) I shall not argue the point fully here. For present purposes, it is sufficient that this be one way of understanding what Stalnaker means by 'the diagonal proposition'. In effect, then, on Stalnaker's theory a 'that'-clause $\ulcorner$ that $S \urcorner$ may be ambiguous. It sometimes refers to the proposition encoded by S, and it sometimes refers to a different, metatheoretic proposition about S itself. Rather than postulate this sort of complexity or ambiguity in connection with 'that'-clauses, it would be more plausible to claim that, in some cases, the speaker reporting a propositional attitude strictly speaking misspoke and, for complete accuracy, should have used a more complicated formal-mode 'that'-clause in place of the material-mode 'that'-clause used.

Now, there is no denying that, given the proper circumstances, we say things like 'Lois Lane does not realize (know, believe) that Clark Kent is Superman' and 'There was a time when it was not known that Hesperus is Phosphorus'. Such pronouncements are in clear violation of the modified naive theory taken together with the thesis of substitutivity of co-informational sentences in doxastic and epistemic contexts. When we make these utterances, we typically do not intend to be speaking elliptically or figuratively; we take ourselves to be speaking literally and truthfully. Of course, one could intentionally utter such sentences in a metaphorical vein, or as an ellipsis for something else, but such circumstances are quite different from the usual circumstances in which such utterances are made, which are so familiar to teachers and students of contemporary analytic philosophy. The crucial question, however, is whether when we say such things we are correctly applying the criteria that govern the correct use of propositional-attitude locutions.

Recently a number of philosophers, mostly under the influence of the direct reference theory, have expressed doubt about the literal truth of such utterances in ordinary usage. If someone believes that Hesperus is a planet, they claim, then, strictly speaking, he or she also believes that Phosphorus is a planet, regardless of what the philosophically untutored or unenlightened say about his or her belief state. Whatever fact such speakers are attempting to convey by denying the belief ascription, the fact is not the lack of the ascribed belief but something else—perhaps the lack of a corresponding metalinguistic belief to the effect that a certain sentence is true. It is my view that this general approach to these problems is essentially correct, as far as it has been developed. The major problem with this approach is that it has not been developed far enough. I shall say more about this in due course. First, however, it is important to note a glaring philosophical difficulty inherent in this approach.

It is easy nowadays to get caught up in direct-reference mania, but one should never be blinded to possible departures from standard and generally reliable philosophical method and practice. What is ordinarily said in everyday language about a certain set of circumstances—where we take ourselves to be speaking literally and truthfully, and where the circumstances are judged to constitute a paradigm case of what we are saying, etc.—is often regarded as an important datum, sometimes the only possible datum, relevant to a certain philosophical or conceptual question about the facts in the matter. Of course, what we ordinarily say in everyday language is sometimes misleading, sometimes irrelevant, sometimes just plain wrong, but in cases where the issue concerns the applicability or inapplicability of a certain concept or term ordinary usage is often the best available guide to the facts. Consider, for example, the sorts of considerations invoked by epistemologists in deciding that Edmund Gettier's celebrated examples constitute genuine counterexamples to the traditional analysis of knowledge as justified true belief, or the sorts of considerations invoked by philosophers of perception in deciding that the state of experiencing a visual impression that is in fact caused by and resembles a certain external object is not the same thing as *seeing* the object. In the familiar problem cases, we simply do not say that the subject *knows* the relevant piece of information, or that he or she *sees* the relevant object. That is not the way we speak. Our forbearance in attributing knowledge or visual perception in these cases is rightly taken as conclusive evidence that such attributions are strictly false, given the actual and ordinary meanings of 'know' and 'see'. Philosophical programs such as that of analyzing knowledge or that of analyzing perception are, in a significant sense, at least partly an attempt to specify and articulate the implicit criteria or principles that govern the correct application of such terms as 'know' and 'see'. It is precisely for this reason that philosophers so often consult linguistic intuition in doing epistemology or metaphysics. Ordinary language is relevant because it is, at least to some extent, ordinary language that is under investigation. And ordinary usage is a reliable guide to the principles governing the correct use of ordinary language. When the traditional analyses of knowledge or perception are challenged through thought experiments concerning what we would say in certain problem cases, philosophers are rightly skeptical of the reply that ordinary usage is incorrect and that the subject does indeed know the proposition in question, or see the object in question, even though we typically say that he or she does not. Anyone maintaining this position may well by suspected of protecting an invested interest in the theory being challenged, rather than pursuing in good faith the philosopher's primary purpose of seeking truth no matter where the facts may lead. This is not to disparage such concepts as *justified true belief* and *experiencing a visual impression caused by and resembling an external object*. Such concepts may be epistemologically important. However, they demonstrably do not correspond—at least, they do not correspond exactly—to the everyday criteria that are implicit in ordinary usage for knowing or seeing. These criteria are, in a significant sense, *what are in question*.

Similarly, the claim that Lois Lane does, strictly speaking, believe and even know that Clark Kent is Superman (since she knows that he is Clark Kent) must not be made lightly, lest he or she who makes it be placed under the same suspicion. For here the question concerns, at least partly, the tacit principles governing the correct use of ordinary-language words such as 'believe', and the ordinary-usage evidence against the claim is strong indeed. The plain fact is that we simply do not speak that way. Perhaps we should learn to use a language in which propositional-attitude idioms function in strict accordance with the modified naive theory across the board, including the troublesome 'Hesperus'-'Phosphorus' and 'Cicero'-'Tully' cases, since ordinary language already agrees with the modified naive theory in the other, more commonplace sorts of cases. But that is a question for prescriptive philosophy of language, not one for descriptive philosophy of language. The more immediate and pressing philosophical question concerns the actual criteria that are implicitly at work in the everyday notion of belief, and the other attitudes, in their crude form, as they arise in real life without theoretical or aesthetic alteration.

I maintain that, according to these very criteria (in the standard sort of circumstance), it is, strictly speaking, correct to say that Lois Lane does know that Clark Kent is Superman, and that when ordinary speakers deny this they are typically operating under a linguistic confusion, systematically misapplying the criteria that govern the applicability or inapplicability of their own doxastic and epistemic terms and concepts. Similarly, anyone who knows that Hesperus is Hesperus knows that Hesperus is Phosphorus, no matter how strongly he or she may deny the latter. Moreover, anyone who knows that he or she knows that Hesperus is Hesperus also knows that he or she knows that Hesperus is Phosphorus, no matter how self-consciously he or she may disbelieve that Hesperus is Phosphorus.[9]

---

[9] This consequence of the modified naive theory concerning nesting of propositional-attitude operators often goes unnoticed. In an attempt to soften the blow of the modified naive theory, it is sometimes argued that, for example, though the ancients strictly speaking did believe the proposition that Hesperus is Phosphorus, since this is just the trivial proposition that Hesperus is Hesperus, they did not realize that the proposition that Hesperus is Phosphorus is really the very same proposition as the trivial proposition that Hesperus is Hesperus, and hence they did not realize that they believed that Hesperus is Phosphorus. Similarly, it is sometimes argued that, since the name 'Hamlet' from Shakespeare's fiction actually refers to no one, there is no such thing as a proposition that Hamlet does not exist, and hence the sentence 'Hamlet does not exist' strictly speaking has no information content, but still there is a proposition that there exists no proposition that Hamlet does not exist, and it is true. All of this is inconsistent with the modified naive theory. On the modified naive theory, if a is a single-word singular term (individual constant), then for any sentence ϕ_a containing a, barring quotation marks and other such aberrant devices, the 'that'-clause $\ulcorner$ that $\phi_a \urcorner$ refers to the singular proposition that is the information content of the sentence. It is tempting to think of the 'that'-term as a sort of description of the proposition by specifying its components, like $\ulcorner$ the proposition made up of a and the property of being $\phi \urcorner$, analogous to a set-theoretic abstraction term $\ulcorner \langle a,$ the property of being $\phi \rangle \urcorner$. But this is incorrect. A set-abstraction term $\ulcorner (x)\phi_x \urcorner$ may be regarded as a special sort of definite description, since it is equivalent to $\ulcorner (\imath y)[Set(y) \& (x)(x \in y \equiv \phi_x)] \urcorner$. Thus, a set-abstraction term is descriptional—specifically, descriptional in terms of the property of being a set with such-and-such membership. The 'that'-operator attaches to a sentence to form a singular term referring to the sentence's information content. Since 'that Plato is wise' refers to a different proposition from 'that the author of *The Republic* is wise', however, one cannot see the 'that'-term as referring to its referent proposition by mentioning the components of the referent proposition. Plato is not a component of the proposition that the author of *The Republic* is wise, though he is referred to by the component term 'the author of *The Republic*'. In a word, the 'that'-operator is nonextensional. One should think of the 'that'-operator as analogous to quotation marks, and of a 'that'-term $\ulcorner$ that $S \urcorner$ as analogous to a quotation name, only referring to the information content of S rather than S itself. (See the introduction on the 'that'-operator.) A 'that'-clause, $\ulcorner$ that $\phi_a \urcorner$, then, is a singular term whose information value is the ordered pair of the information value of the 'that'-operator and the information content of ϕ_a, the letter being a singular proposition p about the referent of a. A sentence involving this 'that'-clause, $\ulcorner \psi[$ that $\phi_a] \urcorner$, encodes a singular proposition about the proposition p, to wit, that (the proposition identical with) it is ψ, and the 'that'-clause formed from this sentence, $\ulcorner$ that $\psi[$ that $\phi_a] \urcorner$, refers to this singular proposition about p. If b is any proper name or other single-word singular term co-referential with a, then $\ulcorner$ that $\phi_b \urcorner$ refers to the very same proposition p, and $\ulcorner \psi[$ that $\phi_b] \urcorner$ encodes the same singular proposition about p that (the proposition identical with) it is ψ, so that $\ulcorner$ that $\psi[$ that $\phi_a] \urcorner$ and $\ulcorner$ that $\psi[$ that $\phi_b] \urcorner$ are co-referential. In particular, if the sentence 'Jones realizes that he believes that Hesperus is Hesperus' is true, then what Jones realizes is a certain singular proposition about the proposition that Hesperus is Hesperus, to the effect that he believes it. Since the proposition that Hesperus is Hesperus is, according to the modified naive theory, the same proposition as the proposition that Hesperus is Phosphorus, another way of specifying what Jones realizes, according to the modified naive theory, is 'that Jones believes that Hesperus is Phosphorus'. Hence, on the modified naive theory, if the original sentence is true, so is 'Jones realizes that he believes that Hesperus is

(contd.)

These claims clash sharply with ordinary usage. Whereas it is (as I have argued) extremely important not to lose sight of the tried and true philosophical tool of looking to ordinary usage in such matters, it is equally important to recognize the limitations of that test. Ordinary usage is a reliable guide to correct usage, but it is only a guide. Ordinary usage can sometimes be incorrect usage. Even when the ordinary usage of a certain locution is systematic, it can be systematically incorrect—if, for example, the language is deficient in ways that compel speakers to violate its rules in order to convey what they intend, or if the principles and social conventions governing the appropriateness of certain utterances require certain systematic violations of the principles and rules governing correct and incorrect applications of the terms used. My claim is that ordinary usage with regard to such predicates as 'is aware that Clark Kent is Superman' and 'believes that Hesperus is Phosphorus' conflicts with the criteria governing their correct application in just this way. However inappropriate it may be in most contexts to say so, Lois Lane is (according to the myth) fully aware that Clark Kent is Superman, and anyone who believes that Hesperus is Hesperus does in fact believe that Hesperus is Phosphorus. We do not speak this way; in fact, it is customary to say just the opposite. But if we wish to utter what is true, and if we care nothing about social convention, we should speak this way. The customary way of speaking involves us in uttering falsehoods.

Of course, it is no defense of the modified naive theory simply to make these bold claims. It is incumbent on the philosopher who makes these claims (i.e., me) to offer some reason for supposing that ordinary speakers, in the normal course of things, would be led to distort the rules of language systematically, so that ordinary usage cannot be relied upon in these cases as a guide to the correct-applicability conditions of the relevant terms and concepts. The account I shall offer is complex. The main part of this account will be given in section 8.4. For now, a tentative account is provided by repeating the distinction between semantically encoded and pragmatically imparted information. If one is not careful to keep this distinction in mind, it is altogether too easy to confuse information pragmatically imparted by (utterances of) 'Hesperus is Phosphorus' for semantically encoded information. In saying that A believes that Hesperus is Phosphorus, taken literally, we are merely attributing to A a relation (belief) to a certain piece of information (the information

Phosphorus'. The proposition that Jones believes that Hesperus is Hesperus is the same proposition as the proposition that Jones believes that Hesperus is Phosphorus, and thus if Jones realizes the former he realizes the latter. Similarly, if the nonexistence of Hamlet means that there is no such proposition as the proposition that Hamlet does not exist, then it also means that there is no such proposition as the proposition that the proposition that Hamlet does not exist does not itself exist. Few philosophers—even direct-reference theorists who accede to the modified-naive-theoretical claim that the ancients strictly speaking believed that Hesperus is Phosphorus—have been willing to endorse these further consequences of the modified naive theory. Properly seen, however, they are no more unacceptable than the better-known controversial consequences of the modified naive theory.

These points concerning nested occurrences of 'that'-clauses are important in connection with the modified naive theory's account of Mates's problem concerning nested propositional attitude contexts. . . .

semantically encoded by 'Hesperus is Phosphorus'). The 'that'-clause 'that Hesperus is Phosphorus' functions here as a means for referring to that piece of information. Since the form of words 'Hesperus is Phosphorus' is considerably richer in pragmatic impartations than other expressions having the same semantic information content (e.g., 'Hesperus is Hesperus'), if one is not careful one cannot help but mistake the 'that'-clause as referring to this somewhat richer information—information which A may not believe. . . . Utterances of the locution $\ulcorner a$ believes that $S \urcorner$ may even typically involve a Gricean implicature to the effect that the person referred to by a believes the information that is typically pragmatically imparted by utterances of S. Even so, that is not part of the literal content of the belief attribution. The general masses, and most philosophers, are not sufficiently aware of the effect that an implicature of this kind would have on ordinary usage. It is no embarrassment to the modified naive theory that ordinary speakers typically deny literally true belief attributions (and other propositional-attitude attributions) when these attributions involve a 'that'-clause whose utterance typically pragmatically imparts information which the speaker recognizes not to be among the beliefs (or other propositional attitudes) of the subject of the attribution. In fact, it would be an embarrassment to the modified naive theory if speakers did not do this. With widespread ignorance of the significance of the distinction between semantically encoded and pragmatically imparted information, such violation of the rules of the language is entirely to be expected.

7. More Puzzles

7.1. The New Frege Puzzle

The distinction between semantically encoded and pragmatically imparted information goes a long way toward solving the problems posed by Frege's Puzzle and the apparent failure of substitutivity of proper names and other single-word singular terms in propositional-attitude contexts. There can be little doubt that failure to appreciate the distinction is largely responsible for the relative unpopularity of the modified naive theory in favor of its rivals throughout the history of the theory of meaning. Unfortunately, the distinction does not yield the final word on the general problem. A version of this general problem arises again, this time in a particularly strengthened form, when one takes note of the following fact: Even a speaker who has been fully apprised of the distinction between semantically encoded and pragmatically imparted information, and who has learned to be scrupulously careful about separating out pragmatic impartations when dealing with matters of semantics, may give assent to some sentence S which encodes a certain piece of information and which the speaker fully understands, while the same speaker may fail to give assent, and may even give dissent, to some sentence S' which the speaker also fully understands and which, according to the modified naive theory, encodes the very same information. This can easily happen even if the speaker is perfectly rational, mentally acute (in fact, an ideally perfect thinker), eager to indicate his or her beliefs through verbal assent and dissent, and a firm and dogmatic believer in the modified naive theory!

In saying that someone fully understands a sentence, I mean only that he or she associates the right proposition with the sentence in the right way (that is, unconsciously "computes" the semantically encoded content of the sentence from the recursion rules of semantic composition, or something along these lines—however it is that we get things right when we understand a sentence), and that he or she has a complete grasp of this proposition. In particular, knowing the truth value of the proposition is not required for complete understanding.

For example, suppose that Lois Lane is forced to endure a full academic year of intensive training in the theory of meaning through the writings of a famous Kryptonian philosopher of language. On Krypton (Superman's native planet, according to the myth), the distinction between semantically encoded and pragmatically imparted information was duly appreciated, and the modified naive theory was held in the highest esteem by all but a very small minority of semanticists. The modified naive theory is drilled into her head. She is instructed in the distinction between semantically encoded and pragmatically imparted information, and she is taught to assent to all and only those sentences whose semantically encoded information content she believes and to dissent from all and only those sentences whose negation commands her assent. Now consider the following two sentences:

(5) Superman fights a never-ending battle for truth, justice, and the American way.

(6) Clark Kent fights a never-ending battle for truth, justice, and the American way.

If anyone understands these sentences, Lois does. She fully grasps the proposition encoded by these sentences, and she associates the right proposition with each sentence. One might wonder whether she fully understands sentence 6, but a moment's reflection confirms that she does. For example, she certainly does not misunderstand sentence 6 to mean that Perry White is a tyrant. She correctly understands sentence 6 to mean that Clark Kent fights a never-ending battle for truth, justice, and the American way. Lois grasps this information as well as anyone does. Of course, she wrongly believes it to be misinformation, but getting clearer about its truth value would not enable her to grasp it any deeper. So Lois correctly understands both sentences. Yet she verbally assents to sentence 5 and verbally dissents from sentence 6. The fact that she fails to assent to, and in fact dissents from, sentence 6 when she correctly understands it to mean that Clark Kent fights a never-ending battle for truth, justice, and the American way, is very strong evidence that she does not believe this information. This is especially true if one takes seriously the analysis of belief suggested in the preceding section, whereby belief is identified with inward assent or agreement to a piece of information or with a disposition toward inward assent. Given that Lois sincerely wishes to reveal her opinions through verbal assent and dissent, that she correctly understands what is meant by sentence 6, and that she is a perfectly rational and competent thinker, her verbal dissent from sentence 6 would seem to be as good an indication as one could possibly have that she inwardly dissents from the proposition. If she inwardly assented to the proposition, it would seem, she would outwardly assent to the sentence. Her failure to assent to sentence 6, therefore, provides an extremely compelling reason to suppose that she does not believe what she correctly understands it to mean. Similarly, Lois's assent to sentence 5 provides extremely compelling evidence, evidence as good as one could ever have, that she believes this piece of information. Her combined verbal behavior, then, provides an extremely compelling reason to conclude that she believes that Superman fights a never-ending battle for truth, justice, and the American way, but does not believe that Clark Kent does. No doubt, this is also part of the original justification for saying just this about Lois's beliefs. This characterization of Lois's beliefs flatly contradicts the modified naive theory.

It is no help to appeal here to ignorance of the distinction between semantically encoded and pragmatically imparted information, for both Lois (whose beliefs we are talking about) and we (who are talking about those beliefs) are by now well aware of the distinction. Awareness of the distinction does nothing to obviate the compelling force of the evidence provided by Lois's verbal behavior. In particular, it does nothing to dissipate the extremely compelling grounds, provided by Lois's failure to assent to sentence 6, for concluding that she does not believe that Clark Kent fights a never-ending battle.

These considerations generate another puzzle for the modified naive theory. It was argued that Lois correctly, completely, and fully understands both sentence 5 and sentence 6. In particular, she correctly understands sentence 6 to mean that Clark Kent fights a never-ending battle for truth, justice, and the American way. Which proposition does she take sentence 6 to encode? Given her working knowledge of English, her acquaintance with Clark Kent, and her recent training in the philosophy of language, it can only be the singular proposition about Clark Kent that he fights a never-ending battle for truth, justice, and the American way. Now, according to the modified naive theory, Lois believes this singular proposition, for she believes of Superman that he fights a never-ending battle for truth, justice, and the American way. If anyone is ever in a position to have de re beliefs about Superman, Lois has this particular de re belief about him. On the modified naive theory, the content of this de re belief simply is the very proposition that she correctly takes sentence 6 to encode. Hence, on the modified naive theory, Lois—whom we may suppose to be an ideally rational and competent speaker and who sincerely wishes to reveal her opinions through verbal assent and dissent—correctly identifies which proposition is encoded by sentence 6, and she firmly believes this very proposition. Yet, even on reflection, she fails to assent to sentence 6, and in fact dissents from it. What, on the modified naive theory, can account for her behavior? How can the theory explain away her failure to assent to sentence 6 as grounds for concluding that she does not believe that Clark Kent fights a never-ending battle for truth, justice, and the American way?

Let us take a more familiar example. An ancient astronomer-philosopher, well versed in the modified naive theory and the distinction between semantically encoded and pragmatically imparted information, verbally assents to (his sentence for) the sentence 'Hesperus is Hesperus' without assenting to the sentence

'Hesperus is Phosphorus'. It is not enough to explain this phenomenon by pointing out that the astronomer-philosopher does not realize that the second sentence
encodes information that he believes, or that the two sentences encode the same
information, or that one sentence is true and commands his assent if and only if
the other one is and does. The question is: How can he fail to realize any of this?
We may suppose (1) that he fully grasps the proposition about the planet Venus
and the planet Venus that the former is the latter, (2) that, being an adherent of
the modified naive theory, he takes the first sentence to encode this very proposition and no other, and (3) that it is this very same proposition and no other that
he also takes the second sentence to encode (since this is also the proposition
about Hesperus and Phosphorus that they are identical). How then can he fail to
see that the sentences are informationally equivalent? Moreover, he fully endorses
this proposition, so how, upon reflection, can he fail to be moved to assent to the
second sentence when it is this very proposition—one he fully grasps and believes—
that he takes the second sentence to encode? The situation becomes especially
puzzling for the adherent of the modified naive theory if we suppose that, in
believing the proposition that Hesperus is Hesperus, the ancient astronomer-
philosopher inwardly assents to it, or is so disposed. If he assents inwardly to the
proposition, or is so disposed, why, if he is reflective and eager to reveal his beliefs
through verbal assent, is he not similarly disposed to assent outwardly to a sentence which he takes to encode that very proposition? The distinction between
semantically encoded and pragmatically imparted information sheds no light on
this new problem, for we are supposing that the ancient astronomer-philosopher is
well aware of the distinction and never allows himself to be misled by pragmatic
impartations in matters concerning semantic content. Moreover, we may also suppose that there is nothing whatsoever wrong or imperfect about the astronomer-
philosopher's reasoning or thought processes. We may even suppose him to have
superhuman intelligence (or as much intelligence as is compatible with his not
knowing the truth of 'Hesperus is Phosphorus'). What, then, is preventing him
from making the connection between what he takes the sentence to encode and his
belief of that very information?

It appears that the modified naive theory turns against itself in discourse
involving propositions about singular propositions, for, on the modified naive
theory, these too are singular propositions. . . . If the ancient astronomer-
philosopher believes that 'Hesperus is Phosphorus' encodes the information
that Hesperus is Phosphorus, then, on the modified naive theory, he also
believes that 'Hesperus is Phosphorus' encodes the information that Hesperus
is Hesperus—information which he fully grasps and firmly believes on logical
grounds alone. It seems to follow that the mere understanding of the sentence
should suffice to elicit his unhesitating and unequivocal assent, even if he is
not so intelligent. But, as Frege rightly noted, there was a time when the mere
understanding of this sentence was not sufficient to elicit the assent of
astronomers who understood it, and may even have elicited emphatic dissent.
This is not a particularly bizarre state of affairs: it is perfectly reasonable that
this would be their reaction given the state of ignorance at the time. Yet the

modified naive theory seems to lack the means to give a coherent account of this state of affairs without making it appear quite paradoxical.

What we have here is a new and stronger version of Frege's Puzzle, one that does not rely on the question-begging premise that 'Hesperus is Phosphorus' is (semantically) informative, or that someone may believe that Hesperus is Hesperus without believing that Hesperus is Phosphorus, or indeed any premise involving notions such as informativeness or a priority. The new version of the puzzle makes do instead with a weaker, less philosophical-theory-laden and clearly undeniable premise. The new premise is this:

> Someone who is reflective, without mental defect, and eager to reveal his or her beliefs through verbal assent may correctly identify the information encoded by 'Hesperus is Hesperus', fully grasp that information, indicate concurrence with that information by readily assenting to the sentence, correctly identify the information encoded by 'Hesperus is Phosphorus', fully grasp that information, and yet not feel the slightest impulse to assent to the latter sentence.

In addition, Frege's Law is replaced by the following analogue:

> If a declarative sentence S has the very same cognitive information content (Erkenntniswerte) as a declarative sentence S', then an ideally competent speaker who fully understands both sentences perfectly, reflects on the matter, is without mental defect, is eager to indicate his or her beliefs through sincere verbal assent and dissent, and has no countervailing motives or desires that might prevent him or her from being disposed to assent verbally to a sentence while recognizing its information content as something believed, is disposed to assent verbally to S if and only if he or she is disposed to assent verbally to S'.

Given, further, the compositionality principle for pieces of information, we have all of the makings of a new and more powerful refutation of the modified naive theory. The distinction between semantically encoded and pragmatically imparted information simply has no bearing on this new argument.

7.2. Elmer's Befuddlement

7.2.1. The Example

The new version of Frege's Puzzle derives its additional strength by invoking dispositions to verbal assent in place of informativeness. We can construct a variant of this stronger version of the puzzle directly in terms of belief without invoking dispositions to verbal assent to sentences. One such variant of the new Frege Puzzle is, in some respects, even stronger than the new Frege Puzzle itself, though ironically it also helps to bring out the modified naive theory's means for solving the general problem. This is best demonstrated by means of a paradox generated by an elaborate example, which I shall call *Elmer's Befuddlement*. Rather than present the entire example all at once, it is more instructive to consider a major part of the example first, in order to test our intuitions about this aspect of the example before considering the example in its entirety.

Elmer's Befuddlement (Excerpts)

Elmer, a bounty hunter, is determined to apprehend Bugsy Wabbit, a notorious jewel thief who has so far eluded the long arm of the law. Before setting out after Bugsy, Elmer spends several months scrutinizing the FBI's files on Bugsy, studying numerous photographs, movies, and slides, listening carefully to tape recordings of Bugsy's voice, interviewing people who know him intimately, and so on. After learning as much about Bugsy as he can, on January 1 Elmer forms the opinion that Bugsy is (is now, has always been, and will always be throughout his lifetime) dangerous. . . .

On June 1, Elmer receives further information from the FBI that Bugsy was last seen in a club in uptown Manhattan, walking away from a poker game after a gangster type had accused him of cheating. This further information gives Elmer pause. He thinks to himself: "Maybe Bugsy . . . is harmless after all. I used to believe that he is a dangerous man, but now . . . I don't know what to think. Maybe he's dangerous, maybe not. I'll just have to wait and see."

Here now is a little two-part quiz: (A) Before June 1, did Elmer believe that Bugsy Wabbit is dangerous? (B) If so, does he continue to believe this even after taking into account the further information he received from the FBI on June 1?

Clearly, question A must be answered affirmatively; Elmer believed for a full five months, from January 1 to June 1, that Bugsy is dangerous, right up until he received the further information concerning Bugsy. This must be so on any reasonable theory of the nature of belief, and it is so on the modified naive theory in particular. On the modified naive theory, to believe that Bugsy is dangerous is to believe the singular proposition about Bugsy that he is dangerous, which is the same thing as believing of Bugsy that he is dangerous. Surely, Elmer had this belief about Bugsy before June 1. If anyone can ever be in a position to have beliefs about Bugsy Wabbit without actually meeting him face to face, then surely Elmer was in such a position when he first decided on January 1 that Bugsy is dangerous. He knew as much about Bugsy as anyone did, save perhaps Bugsy himself, and he may even have known a few things about Bugsy that Bugsy himself did not know.

It would appear equally obvious that question B should be answered negatively. Once he takes the new information into account, Elmer suspends judgment about whether Bugsy is dangerous. Hence, he no longer believes that Bugsy is dangerous. If anyone can ever give up a formerly held belief about someone, Elmer's situation on June 1 would appear to be a typical and central case of such an occurrence. This is not to say, of course, that Elmer now believes that Bugsy is not dangerous, for he does not. Elmer has reconsidered the question of whether Bugsy is dangerous, and he now withholds belief as well as disbelief. Having reconsidered the question, he now believes neither that Bugsy is dangerous nor that he is not. That is what it means to say that Elmer now suspends judgment.

But things are not as clear as they seem. Let us turn now to the example in its entirety.

Elmer's Befuddlement (Unabridged)

As already recounted, Elmer the bounty hunter forms the opinion on January 1 that Bugsy is (is now, has always been, and will always be throughout his lifetime) dangerous.

Shortly thereafter, having learned that there is a bounty hunter after him, Bugsy undergoes extensive plastic surgery, so that he looks nothing like his former photographs. He also has his voice surgically altered, adopts an entirely new set of personality traits and mannerisms, and so on. He retains his name, however, since it is such a common name.

Hot on Bugsy's tail, Elmer eventually meets up with the new Bugsy Wabbit. Noting that this man is nothing like the Bugsy Wabbit he is pursuing, Elmer falls for Bugsy's ruse and concludes that this Bugsy Wabbit is simply another person with the same name. Elmer befriends Bugsy, but never learns his true identity.

On April 1, Elmer happens to overhear a dispute (apparently over 24 carrots) between Bugsy and someone, and notices that the other party in the dispute is extremely deferential, almost as if he were positively frightened of Bugsy. Elmer decides then and there that this Bugsy Wabbit is also a dangerous man. He says to himself: "I'd better watch my step with my new friend, for Bugsy is a dangerous fellow. In this one respect, the two Bugsy Wabbits are alike."

On June 1, as already recounted, Elmer receives from the FBI further information that gives him pause. He thinks to himself: "Maybe Bugsy the criminal is harmless after all. I used to believe that he is a dangerous man, but now I'm not so sure. In every other respect he is nothing like my friend Bugsy Wabbit, so perhaps I was a bit hasty in deciding that the two Bugsies are like each other in this one respect. My friend Bugsy is definitely dangerous, I haven't changed my mind about that. But as for the jewel thief, I don't know what to think. Maybe he's dangerous, maybe not. I'll just have to wait and see."

Elmer waits, but he never sees. Even today, Elmer feels certain that his friend Bugsy is dangerous, but still wonders whether Bugsy the criminal is dangerous or not.

The saga of Elmer's pursuit of Bugsy Wabbit presents many of the familiar problems. It is reminiscent of Quine's famous example about Ralph and Bernard J. Ortcutt, as well as Kripke's example about Pierre and London, and it has significant points in common with a number of other examples, including Castañeda's examples concerning belief about oneself. There are special aspects of Elmer's Befuddlement that are not present in these other examples, and I shall focus on these special features to construct a paradox.[10]

---

[10] One special feature of Elmer's Befuddlement is that Elmer knows the relevant individual, Bugsy, by name, and by the same name in both of his guises, and Elmer comes to have his beliefs and his lack of belief concerning Bugsy (at least partly) by means of that name. This removes the wrongheaded temptation to identify the information value of a name with the name itself, for in this example Elmer's conflicting attitudes are directed toward a single sentence, 'Bugsy Wabbit is dangerous', involving a single name, 'Bugsy Wabbit'. Quine gives a name to his corresponding character, Ortcutt, but he frames the problem primarily in terms of definite descriptions—'the man in the brown hat' and 'the man seen at the beach'. This introduces a host of further issues, some of which have tended to distract commentators from the primary philosophical issues involved in situations involving ignorance of an identity.

(contd.)

7.2.2. The Puzzle

Consider again question B: Once Elmer takes account of the further information obtained from the FBI on June 1, how does he stand with respect to the information (or misinformation, as the case may be) that Bugsy Wabbit is dangerous? Does he or does he not believe this piece of information concerning Bugsy?

Let us first consider a simpler question. Roll back the time to April, before Elmer came to have second thoughts about the criminal. Did he believe, at that time, that Bugsy Wabbit is dangerous?

The answer must be that he did. The reasoning that this must be the answer goes as follows: In considering question A, we had already decided that Elmer believed on January 1 that Bugsy is dangerous. We did not yet have the whole story concerning Elmer and Bugsy, but all of the additional information that we have been given concerns events that take place some time after January 1. Hence, the original grounds for claiming that Elmer believes on January 1 that Bugsy is dangerous still obtain. On the modified naive theory in particular, it is still true that Elmer's having familiarized himself with Bugsy's history and appearance in the way he did places him in a position on January 1 to be able to believe at that time of Bugsy that he is dangerous. Now, on April 1 Elmer formed the opinion that his friend Bugsy is dangerous. In doing so Elmer was ignorant of certain critical information concerning Bugsy, but that does not alter the fact that he also steadfastly maintained his view, which he had held since January 1, that Bugsy is dangerous. He did not yet change his mind about Bugsy, first believing him to be dangerous and then giving up that belief. If he believed it before, he believes it still.

Kripke framed his original example concerning Pierre in London using names instead of descriptions, but he used two different syntactic shapes, 'London' and 'Londres', which correspond in the example to two different guises of the city, and which are correct translations of one another. This also has the unfortunate tendency to digress the course of the discussion toward a host of issues concerning translation—issues which are, and which Kripke recognizes to be, entirely irrelevant to the primary philosophical problems raised by the example. In this respect, Elmer's Befuddlement is more like Kripke's more pointed example concerning Paderewski. . . .

The most important aspect of Elmer's Befuddlement is the fact that Elmer has *changed his mind* about something and withholds belief where he once had an opinion. This aspect of the example—the change of mind from having an opinion to suspension of judgment—poses the most pressing and difficult philosophical problems, and is at the same time the most philosophically illuminating feature of the example. The importance of suspension of judgment to issues concerning propositional attitudes, especially de re propositional attitudes, was first noticed by Kaplan in an important and underappreciated argument in section XI of "Quantifying In" (at pp. 139–142 of *Reference and Modality*, ed. L. Linsky (New York: Oxford University Press, 1971). See also Kripke, "A Puzzle about Belief," at p. 258. The similarity of my example involving Elmer and Bugsy, and the use to which I put it, to Kaplan's continuation of Quine's example should be apparent, though I do not argue for exactly the same conclusions as Kaplan. In particular, I do not argue, and I do not believe, that a de re or relational belief is reducible to a de dicto or notional one. . . . Moreover, my proposal below to analyze belief as the existential generalization of a ternary relation among believers, propositions, and something else, unlike Kaplan's analysis in "Quantifying In" of de re belief, allows the formulation of de re belief in the manner of '$(\exists x)[x$ is Elmer's friend & Elmer believes that x is dangerous]', with ordinary unrestricted, objectual quantification into the same believes' predicate used in the formulation of de dicto belief.

There is, it must be admitted, something quite peculiar about Elmer's doxastic state on April 1. There is some sense in which Elmer *comes to* believe on April 1 that Bugsy Wabbit is dangerous (comes to believe of Bugsy that he is dangerous), but there is also some sense in which Elmer believed this about Bugsy since January and never stopped believing it. To give some account of how it is that someone can come to believe something that he or she already believes without ever having ceased to believe it is already a problem for the modified naive theory. I shall not pause here to discuss this. The problem I shall discuss is a sharpened version of this problem, and its solution entails a solution to the present problem. What matters so far is that, however peculiar his doxastic state on April 1, Elmer believed at that time that Bugsy is dangerous.

Now, what about the following summer? Does Elmer continue to believe that Bugsy Wabbit is dangerous even after taking account of the further information from the FBI?

Here no simple 'yes' or 'no' answer by itself is entirely satisfactory. In particular, no simple 'yes' or 'no' answer is satisfactory even if we presuppose the correctness of the modified naive theory. On the one hand, it is critical to the story that in some sense Elmer came to believe on January 1 that Bugsy is dangerous but that Elmer now suspends judgment. Hence, there is an important sense, critical to the story, in which Elmer now believes neither that Bugsy is dangerous nor that he is not dangerous. But it is surely not enough to say that Elmer believes neither that Bugsy is dangerous nor that he is not, and to leave the matter at that, for there is also a very compelling reason to say that Elmer still believes that Bugsy is dangerous: Something exactly analogous to the grounds for holding that Elmer continues to believe on April 1 that Bugsy is dangerous also obtains on June 1. Elmer has not relinquished his opinion that his friend Bugsy is dangerous. If he believed it on April 1, it would seem, he believes it still.

If Elmer had decided on January 1 that Bugsy is dangerous, and had come to have second thoughts on June 1 as he actually did, but had never met Bugsy in the interim and had never formed any further opinion about him, then we would not hesitate to say that Elmer believed on January 1 that Bugsy is dangerous but believes it no longer. Indeed, that is precisely what we did say when we first considered question B, before we knew about Elmer's encounters with Bugsy after January 1. All the information we had given seemed enough to determine that the answer to question B is that Elmer no longer believes that Bugsy is dangerous. Our being given further information concerning Elmer and Bugsy cannot alter what is already determined by the information on hand. If part of the story of Elmer's befuddlement entails that Elmer no longer believes that Bugsy is dangerous, then so does the whole story. (If S entails T, then so does $\ulcorner S$ and $S'\urcorner$.)

In fact, if Elmer had decided on January 1 that Bugsy is dangerous, and had come to have second thoughts on June 1 just as he actually did, but had never met Bugsy in the interim and had never formed any further opinion about him, then it would be true that Elmer no longer believes that Bugsy is dangerous. If anyone can ever give up a formerly held belief about someone, then this would be a typical and central case of such an occurrence. But Elmer is actually in exactly the same state as this, save for the fact that he had met Bugsy in the interim and had formed an opinion about him at that time. Why should Elmer's former beliefs make any difference here? It is just his present doxastic state that we want to capture in specifying his disposition with respect to the information that Bugsy is dangerous. Elmer's present attitude toward this information involves something that ordinarily *constitutes* relinquishing a former opinion. Unless we find some appropriate way to specify Elmer's withholding belief, we leave out of our account a very important element of Elmer's cognitive or doxastic state.

This seems to require us to say that Elmer does not believe that Bugsy is dangerous (or that Bugsy is not dangerous). But that contradicts something which we have also said, and which it appears we are required to say, concerning Elmer's befuddlement. Even during his soliloquy on June 1, Elmer steadfastly remained convinced of his friend's dangerousness. Thus, the facts of the matter in the story of Elmer's befuddlement seem to require us to say that Elmer still believes, at least since April 1, that Bugsy is dangerous, and they also seem to require us to say that Elmer no longer believes, as of June 1, that Bugsy is dangerous. Now, it sometimes happens that a story involves certain inconsistencies. For example, if the author of a series of mystery novels decides to alter some of the biographical facts concerning the detective who is the main character in all the novels (say, his birthdate), then stringing these novels together yields an inconsistent story. But nothing like this is the case with the story of Elmer's befuddlement. Clearly, the story is consistent. There is no logical reason why it could not be a true story. Perhaps some structurally similar befuddlement has actually occurred at some time in the history of intelligent life in the universe, or may yet occur at some time in the future.

Here, then, is the puzzle. Either Elmer believes that Bugsy is dangerous or he does not. Which is it? We seem to be required to say that Elmer does indeed believe that Bugsy is dangerous, for he remains convinced of his friend Bugsy's dangerousness. We also seem to be required to say Elmer does not believe that Bugsy is dangerous, for he now actively suspends judgment concerning the criminal's dangerousness. Yet we are logically prohibited from saying both together. How, then, are we to describe coherently Elmer's doxastic disposition with respect to the information that Bugsy Wabbit is dangerous? How can it be consistent for Elmer to believe that Bugsy is dangerous, on the one hand, and to withhold that belief, on the other?

The same puzzle can be stated with a different emphasis by focusing on the fact that on June 1 Elmer, in some obvious (but so far unclear) sense, changes his mind about whether Bugsy is dangerous. The change of mind is evident in Elmer's soliloquy. He suspends judgment where he used to have an opinion. Before that, at least since January, Elmer believed that Bugsy is dangerous. But there is also some obvious sense in which Elmer does not change his mind on June 1 concerning Bugsy, since he remains convinced of his friend's dangerousness. If we say, then, that Elmer continues to believe even on June 1 that Bugsy is dangerous, we fail to depict his change of mind. We represent him as believing on January 1 that Bugsy is dangerous, believing it still on April 1, and believing it still even on June 1 after taking into account the further information from the FBI. There is nothing in all this about any change of mind. In order to express the fact that Elmer has changed his mind concerning Bugsy's dangerousness, we would like to say that Elmer believed on January 1 that Bugsy is dangerous but by the following summer believes it no longer (and also does not believe that Bugsy is not dangerous). However, we seem to be prevented from saying this; else we lie about Elmer's continued and unwavering conviction concerning his friend's dangerousness. How, then, do we express the important fact about Elmer that he has changed his mind concerning the question of Bugsy Wabbit's dangerousness and has withdrawn his former opinion?

7.2.3. Some Nonsolutions

It is worth mentioning some tempting nonsolutions to the puzzle. First, it is no solution to attribute an inconsistency solely to Elmer and his system of beliefs. At no point in the story does Elmer come to believe both that Bugsy is dangerous and that he is not dangerous. In fact, at no point does Elmer come to believe that Bugsy is not dangerous.[11] Moreover, even if an inconsistency is uncovered among Elmer's beliefs (e.g., that Bugsy ≠ Bugsy), that does not rescue us from the apparent meta-inconsistency concerning Elmer's beliefs to which we seem committed, for it is we who seem committed to saying both that Elmer believes and that he does not believe that Bugsy is dangerous.

One might try to avoid this inconsistency by looking to Elmer's idiolect. It may be argued that in Elmer's idiolect the syntactic sound and shape 'Bugsy Wabbit' represents not one but two different names, just as 'Aristotle' is ambiguous in the public language, functioning sometimes as a name referring to the celebrated philosopher of antiquity and sometimes as a name referring to the late shipping magnate. In Elmer's idiolect, one might argue, there are two distinct sentences corresponding to the syntactic string of the public language 'Bugsy is dangerous'. These two sentences might be represented formally by means of different subscripts on the name 'Bugsy'. We may then say, consistently, that Elmer still believes that $Bugsy_2$ is dangerous but no longer believes that $Bugsy_1$ is dangerous.

There are a number of difficulties with this attempt to solve the puzzle. In effect, it is an attempt to "reduce the problem to the previous case" (i.e., to cases like the 'Hesperus'-'Phophorus' and 'Cicero'-'Tully' examples, where there are distinct names for the same individual). I have been busy arguing that these cases are best treated in accordance with the modified naive theory. In any case, my main concern here is with the ability or inability, as the case may be, of the modified naive theory to remove the puzzle. Accordingly, we should assume here that the modified naive theory is correct. On the modified naive theory, the information values of '$Bugsy_1$' and '$Bugsy_2$' are the same, viz., Bugsy Wabbit himself. Hence, if Elmer believes the information that $Bugsy_2$ is dangerous, ipso facto he also believes that $Bugsy_1$ is dangerous, for they are the same piece of information.

---

[11] This contrasts with Kripke's puzzle about belief, where on the modified naive theory, the subject comes to have incompatible beliefs. . . .

More important, this attempt to solve the puzzle does not even address the relevant question, for we are attempting to describe Elmer's doxastic state and we do not share Elmer's idiolect. In our idiolects, the name 'Bugsy Wabbit' is not ambiguous. We know what Elmer does not know: that there is only a single person of that name throughout the entire story. We use the expression 'Bugsy Wabbit' as a name for that individual. In our idiolects—and in the public language—the syntactic string 'Bugsy Wabbit is dangerous' unambiguously encodes a single piece of information, and the string 'Elmer believes that Bugsy is dangerous' contains the proposition that Elmer believes that information. The question is whether the latter string is true or false as it is used in our idiolects. We are not concerned with the truth value of other strings in other idiolects. We seem to be committed to saying that the relevant string, which is not ambiguous in our idiolects, is both true and false at the same time in our idiolects. But that cannot be right.

Again, one might try to avoid inconsistency by looking to other pieces of information. What Elmer believes, one might claim, is that his friend named 'Bugsy Wabbit' is dangerous, and what he suspends judgment about is whether the notorious criminal named 'Bugsy Wabbit' is dangerous. These are different pieces of information, and there is no contradiction in Elmer's believing the first but failing to believe the second.

This account is correct as far as it goes, but it also fails to address the problem. We are still left wondering what Elmer's doxastic disposition is with respect to the (singular) proposition that Bugsy is dangerous. Never mind what other propositions Elmer may believe or fail to believe; does he believe this proposition about Bugsy? There seems to be every bit as much reason to say that he does as there is to say that he does not, and vice versa. There are compelling reasons on both sides of the question, but taking either side seems utterly inadequate since it omits some critical element of Elmer's cognitive state. If we say that he continues to believe that Bugsy is dangerous, we must give some account of the sense in which Elmer changed his mind and now withholds belief. And, insofar as Elmer withholds belief, he withholds belief concerning this very same singular proposition, whatever other propositions he may also be withholding belief from (e.g., that the criminal named 'Bugsy' is dangerous).[12] Conversely, if we say that Elmer

---

[12] Tyler Burge, in "Kaplan, Quine, and Suspended Belief," *Philosophical Studies* 31 (1977): 197–203, responds to Kaplan's argument concerning suspension of judgment (cited in note 1 above) by observing that suspension of judgment in the face of continued belief, such as Elmer's, can be expressed coherently by means of a certain conjunction—in our case, the conjunction of

Elmer believes that Bugsy is dangerous

with

($\exists \alpha$)[Elmer believes that Bugsy = α, but Elmer does not believe that α is dangerous],

where 'α' ranges over Fregean individual concepts and Russellian intensional entities that are like Fregean individual concepts except for having nonintensional entities as constituents. (I have rephrased Burge's proposal extensively to frame it in the terminology of the present essay and to fit it to the example under discussion, under the presupposition of the

does not believe that Bugsy is dangerous but suspends judgment, we need to give some account of the sense in which Elmer steadfastly retained his opinion formed shortly after meeting Bugsy, which is that he is dangerous. Surely nothing happened since then to deprive Elmer of this belief; today he would sincerely claim to retain this belief if asked.

Does the distinction between semantically encoded and pragmatically imparted information help solve the problem? It might be suggested that, strictly speaking, Elmer does believe the information that Bugsy Wabbit is dangerous, and that the temptation to say that Elmer does not believe this information results from a confusion of this information with further information that is only pragmatically imparted by utterances of 'Bugsy Wabbit is dangerous'. One difficulty with this attempt to solve the puzzle is that it is unclear exactly what information is supposed to be pragmatically imparted but not believed by Elmer. Apparently it is not the metalinguistic information that the relevant sentence is true, as in the previous examples, for whatever reason may be given for supposing that Elmer believes that Bugsy is dangerous may also be given for supposing that Elmer believes that the sentence 'Bugsy is dangerous' is true. Surely he *does* believe that this sentence is true, when it is understood as involving reference to his friend! A case would have to be made

---

correctness of the modified naive theory. I believe that I do not seriously misrepresent the spirit of Burge's original proposal, at least as far as the present discussion is concerned.) Burge goes on to argue that the second conjunct, expressing Elmer's withholding belief regarding his friend's dangerousness, is richer than it needs to be, and he suggests that Elmer's doxastic state can be correctly described by some simpler conjunction like 'Elmer believes Bugsy to be *this* man and that *this* man is dangerous, and Elmer also believes Bugsy to be *that* man, but Elmer does not believe that *that* man is dangerous', using each occurrence of a demonstrative with reference to Bugsy. This I regard as entirely unsatisfactory as a solution to the paradox, but I shall not argue the case here. In any event, this latter proposal clearly involves a rejection of the modified naive theory, and is therefore irrelevant to the present discussion.

Burge's former proposal, as stated, also fails to solve the puzzle. If Elmer is sufficiently clever but unreflective, the second conjunct will be satisfied even if Elmer does not withdraw his former opinion about the criminal's being dangerous. For example, let α be the concept *the x such that x is Bugsy's mother's son's father's son, if Bugsy has no brothers, and x is Bugsy's father's son but not one of Bugsy's brothers, otherwise.* Elmer may know on April 1 that the person so characterized is Bugsy; however, he may never have entertained, and may have no favorable disposition toward, any other proposition involving this concept. This problem can be overcome by strengthening Burge's proposed second conjunct, but even so, the general idea of expressing Elmer's suspension of judgment by way of Elmer's failure to believe some *other* related proposition gives insufficient recognition to the fact that, whatever other propositions Elmer may fail to believe, his recent change of heart and his present cautious attitude toward the very singular proposition about Bugsy that he is dangerous, when he takes it as a proposition about the notorious jewel thief, have all of the signs and trappings of withholding belief and suspension of judgment. His present attitude clearly would *constitute* withheld belief concerning that very proposition had Elmer not formed his earlier opinion about the dangerousness of his friend. Somehow this feature of Elmer's doxastic state—the fact that Elmer has withdrawn his earlier favorable disposition and now adopts a cautious "wait-and-see" attitude that, at least ordinarily, constitutes a suspension of belief toward the relevant singular proposition—must be expressed if we are to capture the gist of Elmer's complex state.

that utterances of the sentence pragmatically impart, say, the information that the notorious jewel thief named 'Bugsy Wabbit' is dangerous. Elmer suspends judgment concerning this information, and that would provide some account of why we are tempted to deny that Elmer believes that Bugsy is dangerous, even though he does have the belief. It is not clear, however, that such a case can plausibly be made. Surely not all utterances of the sentence, by Elmer or anyone else, pragmatically impart this information. Nor is it the case that typical utterances of the sentence, occurring in the context of the story, typically impart this information; some typical utterances, such as those made by Elmer (either aloud or to himself) on April 1, typically do not impart this information.

Even if the case can be made, the general account suggested here so far leaves it mysterious how it was decided that Elmer now believes that Bugsy is dangerous rather than that he suspends judgment. A full account of the situation must recognize somehow that, by summer, Elmer is in a doxastic state that would ordinarily *constitute* no longer believing that Bugsy is dangerous, but suspending judgment. As we have already seen, if Elmer had never met Bugsy in the interim, but had received the further information concerning Bugsy on June 1, just as he actually did, it would be false that Elmer continues to believe that Bugsy is dangerous. The doxastic state of mind that he is actually in would constitute suspension of judgment; being in that state is all that would be required of him for it to be true that he has relinquished the relevant belief. That is just what giving up a belief is. Elmer's actual acquaintance with Bugsy, and Elmer's actual former opinions about him, should not stand in the way of this same state now constituting withheld belief and suspension of judgment.

The puzzle generated by the paradox of Elmer's Befuddlement is, to my mind, among the most difficult problems that arise in connection with propositional attitudes. Nevertheless, a certain extension of the modified naive theory contains the resources for solving this puzzle. The solution, sketched in the following chapter, suggests similar solutions to the new Frege Puzzle, and to many of the familiar philosophical problems that arise in this area.

8. Resolution of the Puzzles

8.1. Attitudes and Recognition Failure

To find a way out of the quandary generated by Elmer's befuddlement, I propose that we take seriously the idea that belief is a favorable attitude or disposition toward a piece of information or a proposition, and that we look more closely at the psychology and the logic of attitudes in general. Other favorable attitudes of the sort I have in mind are such states as that of liking ice cream, finding a certain piece of music pleasant, or loving someone. All of these are analogous in certain respects to belief of a proposition. For example, each seems to be a "standing" state—that is, it does not require the immediate presence of "occurrent" subjective experiences of approval or pleasure directed toward the object of the attitude at every moment while one is in the relevant state; it requires at most only occasional such occurrent experiences (typically when one is confronted with the object of the attitude). If de re belief is belief of a singular proposition, then de re belief about an external object is in certain important respects like loving someone. Both consist chiefly in the subject's adopting a certain favorable or positive attitude toward something external, or, in the case of de re belief, toward an abstract entity—a proposition—made up in part of something external. And in both cases, the adoption of the relevant favorable attitude can depend on the way in which the subject takes the object. If the subject does not recognize the object when it is encountered on different occasions, he or she may adopt the relevant attitude when the object is taken one way yet fail to adopt this attitude, and perhaps even adopt a corresponding unfavorable attitude (hatred or disbelief), when the object is taken another way.

Consider the following story, which is analogous to Elmer's Befuddlement. Suppose that Mrs. Jones does not realize it, but her husband leads a double life. By day he is the drab Mr. Jones, District Attorney, but by night he is Jones the Ripper-Offer (as he is called by the news media), a so-far-unidentified body snatcher who steals corpses from the city morgue. Mrs. Jones has faithfully loved her husband for many years, but recently she has been intrigued and perversely fascinated by the macabre reports of Jones the Ripper-Offer. Stalking him out in the morgue, she eventually meets him but fails to recognize him as the very man she lives with and has lived with for many years. Unable to control her fascination, by April 1 she falls in love with Jones the Ripper-Offer. This bothers her deeply, since she has never fallen out of love with her husband, the DA. Emotionally, she is in that unfortunate state in which some people sometimes find themselves: being in love with (what she takes to be) two different individuals at the same time. Later that summer, her fascination with the demented body snatcher grows so overpowering that she retains no affection toward or emotional attachment to her husband whatsoever. She is now completely and entirely in love with the body snatcher, whom she still takes to be someone other than her drab husband.

Does Mrs. Jones now love Mr. Jones, alias Jones the Ripper-Offer, or doesn't she? Here again no simple 'yes' or 'no' answer by itself is satisfactory. Any attempt to describe Mrs. Jones's present emotional state with respect to Mr. Jones cannot rest only on the claim that she does love him (on the grounds that she remains in love with the grave robber), nor can it rest only on the claim that she does not love him (on the grounds that her emotional attitude toward him changed during the summer when she fell out of love with him). Somehow, both of these seemingly contradictory facts must be accommodated. But how?

Mr. Jones has two distinct personalities, two different guises. Under one of these guises, the happily married district attorney, Mrs. Jones once loved him but loves him no longer. Under his other guise, the demented grave robber,

Mrs. Jones loved him before and loves him still. We do not normally speak of someone loving someone else under this or that guise. We say simply that *A* loves *B* or that *A* does not love *B*. The notion of *loving under a guise* is not the ordinary notion. But the case of Mrs. Jones's emotional attitude toward her husband is by no means a normal circumstance. In order to convey a complete picture of the situation, we must distinguish two ways in which Mrs. Jones can be in love with her husband. In April she loved him twice over, so to speak. By summer she loves him one way but not the other. We can decide to say that Mrs. Jones does love her husband by summer, in the absolute, nonrelativized sense of 'loves', since after all she does still love him in one of these two ways. But if we say only that Mrs. Jones loves Mr. Jones, we leave out of our description of Mrs. Jones's complex emotional attitude toward Mr. Jones the critical fact that she has fallen out of love with him and, in some obvious but unclear sense, loves him no longer. That is, if we allow ourselves only the ordinary, two-place, nonrelativized notion of *loves*, on which *A* simply loves *B* or does not love *B*, the only thing that we can say about Mrs. Jones's present emotional attitude toward her husband—to wit, that she loves him—is seriously misleading at best, if not entirely and simply incorrect. It is only when we explicitly make the distinction between loving Jones qua her husband and loving him qua infamous body snatcher that we can coherently express the seemingly self-contradictory dual fact that Mrs. Jones has fallen out of love but also remains in love with a single man.

I do not claim that a three-place relativized notion of *loving qua*, or loving-in-a-certain-way, or loving-under-a-certain-guise, is philosophically clear or problem free. Surely it is not. What I do claim is that we have some grasp of this notion, and that it is clear in the present instance that Mrs. Jones loves Mr. Jones qua infamous grave robber (in this way, under this guise) but no longer loves him qua her husband (in that way, under that guise). The ordinary and familiar two-place notion of *A loving B* may then be identified with the existential notion of *A loving B in some way or other, or under some guise or other*, or *qua something or other*. At any rate, some such three-place notion of loving-in-a-certain-way or loving-under-a-certain-guise is required to capture all the relevant facts concerning Mrs. Jones's emotional state with respect to Mr. Jones, for in this special case the relevant three-place relation holds among the triple of Mrs. Jones, Mr. Jones, and one such third relatum by which Mrs. Jones is acquainted with Mr. Jones (whatever sort of thing this third relatum is, e.g. a guise), but fails to hold among Mrs. Jones, Mr. Jones, and another equally relevant third relatum. No account framed only in terms of a mere binary relation between Mrs. Jones and Mr. Jones can discriminate the relevant possibilities in this case and do justice to the relevant facts. Trying to get by with only the ordinary two-place notion of *loves* is like trying to specify whether an object is red by saying only whether it is colored, or like trying to convey whether 16 is odd or even allowing yourself only a predicate for being a composite (nonprime) integer.

8.2 Propositional Attitudes and Recognition Failure

Just as Mrs. Jones failed to recognize her husband on April 1 when she fell in love with him a second time, so Elmer failed to recognize Bugsy Wabbit on April 1 when Elmer formed the opinion for a second time that Bugsy is dangerous. But there is something else that Elmer failed to recognize: the information or proposition about Bugsy that he is dangerous.

The very idea of someone's failing to recognize a piece of information or a proposition can be somewhat mysterious. The phenomenon of failing to recognize an individual person or material object is familiar. All of us have had the experience of running into someone who was familiar a long time ago but whose physical appearance has changed in the interim "beyond recognition," that is, to such an extent that we take him or her to be a perfect stranger. Many of us have had the converse experience of being taken for a total stranger by a past acquaintance. These are cases in which an individual goes unrecognized because of a significant objective change in physical appearance. In some cases, a change in physical appearance is induced intentionally for the precise purpose of preventing recognition. We call this 'taking on a disguise'. (Note the 'guise' in 'disguise'.) In our story of Elmer's Befuddlement, Bugsy disguised himself precisely so that Elmer would not recognize him. An object or an individual may also go unrecognized by a subject even though the object's appearance has not undergone any significant change. The subject may be situated with respect to the object in such a way as to prevent recognition, as when a familiar object is too far away for its distinguishing features to be discerned, or the subject's senses may be impaired. In such cases, although the object has not undergone any significant physical change in appearance, there is a change in what might be called its 'subjective appearance' with respect to the subject. This also occurs when the subject who is familiar with an object by having perceived some part of it encounters the same object by perceiving a different part of it, as may happen when a weary traveler passes the front of a building, inadvertently travels in a circle, and approaches the same building from the rear.

What all these cases of recognition failure have in common is that the object goes unrecognized by the subject because of a change in appearance—either objective appearance or subjective appearance. In both types of cases, the change of appearance may be a one-time-only affair, as with Bugsy, or the object may, so to speak, vacillate between two or more appearances, being regularly encountered in both or several of its appearances or guises, as in the case of Mr. Jones and the philosophical legend of the planet Venus. Now I am suggesting that Elmer has failed to recognize not only Bugsy himself but also a piece of information, or a proposition, concerning Bugsy. But propositions do not have *appearances*. We do not perceive propositions through the senses; propositions do not "appear" to us in the way that material objects do. If we "encounter" propositions at all, we do so by grasping or apprehending them—in an act of understanding, an act of the intellect, an act of thought or cognition.

There is no notion of a proposition's *appearance.* Hence, there is no notion of a proposition's *changing its appearance,* and consequently there is no notion of *failing to recognize* a proposition in the way that a subject can fail to recognize some individual because of a change in its objective or subjective appearance.

Of course, one may be said to "fail to recognize" a particular proposition— say, by failing to reidentify it as the very cornerstone of McTaggart's philosophy of time, or as the very proposition to which the United States is said to be dedicated (the proposition that all men are created equal). In such cases, the proposition in question has been selected to some special sort of status, and it is this special status that the subject fails to impute to the proposition. In the same way, one might be said to "fail to recognize" a colleague in one's department by failing to think of him as, say, the world's foremost authority on the history of rock 'n' roll music from 1956 to 1959. This is not a case of mistaking him for a perfect stranger, nor is failing to think of the proposition that all men are created equal as the proposition to which the United States is said to be dedicated a case of mistaking that proposition for some other proposition in the way that I may mistake someone from my past to be a perfect stranger, someone unknown to me, someone with whom I am wholly unacquainted. Any proposition I can apprehend is a proposition that is fully known to me, in the relevant sense, for the only relevant sense in which one may be "acquainted with" a proposition is that one may fully apprehend it. If there is any sense to be made of a notion of "recognizing a proposition," analogous to recognizing a friend or acquaintance upon encountering him or her, it can only be this: that one fully apprehends the proposition. Once a proposition is fully apprehended, there is nothing relevant about the proposition that one is missing or failing to notice. To apprehend a proposition fully is to identify it in the fullest and most complete way that one can.

This objection to the notion of grasping but failing to recognize a proposition flows naturally from the traditional conception of the nature of propositions. In particular, it is the natural reaction of one who is thinking of propositions in accordance with the orthodox theory, that is, in accordance with the theories of Frege and Russell. But this is because one is in the grip of a faulty and misleading picture. On the Fregean conception, every piece of cognitive information, every 'thought,' is made entirely of things like concepts. . . . To apprehend such a "thought" is, it seems, to be fully acquainted with it. There is no changing appearance, no superficial surface concealing the soul, no guise or veil of outward manifestation interceding between the subject and the thing-in-itself. To apprehend it is, as it were, to see through it, to see directly to its very soul. The same is true of a singular proposition whose only constituent other than things like concepts is a particular sensation or visual sense datum, an item of "direct acquaintance." There is no "failing to recognize" a particular pain, for example by mistaking it for someone else's tickle. To have such a sensation or sense datum is to be acquainted with it in the fullest and most complete way possible. But the modified naive theory allows for propositions of a different sort: singular propositions involving external individuals and material objects as constituents. Clearly, the mode of apprehension for such propositions must be more complex than the mere grasping of pure concepts and the experiencing of wholly internal sensations. Apprehending such a proposition cannot be a wholly internal, mental act. The means by which one is acquainted with a singular proposition includes as a part the means by which one is familiar with the individual constituent(s) of the proposition. The mode of acquaintance by which one is familiar with a particular object is part of the mode of apprehension by which one grasps a singular proposition involving that object. For example, if one is familiar with some individual by having read his or her writings, then the reading of these writings is also part of the means by which one is acquainted with a singular proposition about that individual—say, that he or she had an unhappy childhood. One apprehends this proposition in part by having read the words written by the individual the proposition is about. If Elmer is familiar with Bugsy Wabbit by having interacted wi1th him socially, then the social interaction with Bugsy is part of the means by which Elmer grasps the proposition about Bugsy that he is dangerous. Elmer apprehends this proposition in part by having interacted with part of it.

It is a large and difficult problem to specify exactly what sorts of modes of acquaintance with an object are sufficient to place one in a position to entertain singular propositions about that object. Must the mode of acquaintance be causal? Is any causal relation enough? (Consider the case of numbers and mathematical knowledge.) Is it enough simply to have heard the individual mentioned by name? Is it enough simply to be able to refer to the object? (Consider the shortest spy.) Is it enough simply to point at the object, without even looking to see what one is pointing at? Must one have some conception of what kind of thing the object is (a person, an abstract entity, etc.)? Can one have mistaken opinions about the object? How many? Does one have to know who the individual is, or which object the object is, in some more or less ordinary sense of 'know who' or 'know which'? Must one know some feature or characteristic of the object or individual that distinguishes it (or him or her) from all others? Is it sufficient simply to know some distinguishing feature or characteristic (i.e., is what Russell called 'knowledge by description' always enough)? It is not important for the present purpose to have the answers to all of these questions, or even to any of them. What is important is to recognize that, whatever mode of acquaintance with an object is involved in a particular case of someone's entertaining a singular proposition about that object, that mode of acquaintance is part of the means by which one apprehends the singular proposition, for it is the means by which one is familiar with one of the main ingredients of the proposition. This generates something analogous to an "appearance" or a "guise" for singular propositions. If an individual has a certain appearance, either objective or subjective, and through perceiving the individual one comes to have some thought directly about that individual—say, a thought that would be verbalized as 'Gee, is he tall'—then there is a sense in which the cognitive content of the thought may be said to have a certain appearance for the thinker since one of its major components does. This unorthodox conception of the nature of propositions and their apprehension thus allows for the possibility of a notion of "failing to recognize" a proposition by mistaking it for a new and different piece of information. If the subject happens to see the same tall man tomorrow without recognizing that it is the same man, and the subject happens to think 'Gee, is he tall', the subject's thought will have precisely the same cognitive content as the earlier thought, even though the subject does not recognize that this is so.

There is no reason why the modified naive theory should hold that the grasping of a piece of information places one in a position to "see through" the information, so to speak, and to recognize it infallibly as the same information encountered earlier in quite different surroundings under quite different circumstances. In fact, there is every reason to reject this idea.

8.3. Resolution

8.3.1. Elmer's Befuddlement

Now, whatever the necessary and sufficient conditions are for being in a position to entertain a singular proposition, it is clear that Elmer was in such a position on January 1, before he actually met Bugsy, when he first formed the opinion about Bugsy that he is dangerous. Elmer was an expert on Bugsy, well acquainted with his appearance and deeds through reports, photographs, tape recordings, and the rest; all these form a part of the means by which Elmer apprehends the proposition about Bugsy on January 1 that Bugsy is dangerous. Later, when Elmer meets up with Bugsy and forms for a second time the opinion that he is dangerous, Elmer apprehends this same proposition by entirely different means. His new mode of acquaintance with Bugsy, and thereby with the proposition that he is dangerous, involves perceptions of a wholly new appearance. The proposition takes on a new guise for Elmer. In failing to recognize Bugsy, Elmer also fails to recognize the very proposition that he is dangerous. It is precisely for this reason that Elmer is able to form for the second time the opinion that Bugsy is dangerous without having ceased believing this very same piece of information. Elmer took his friend Bugsy to be someone other than the notorious jewel thief. Consequently, he took the information that he is dangerous, when it occurred to him on April 1, to be a different piece of information from the proposition about the jewel thief that he is dangerous (information that Elmer already believed). Elmer's problem stems from the fact that he takes the information that Bugsy Wabbit is dangerous to be two distinct and utterly independent pieces of information. He grasps it by means of two distinct appearances or guises; he takes it in two different ways. When he takes it in one way, Elmer does not recognize this piece of information as the same information that he also takes the other way. On June 1, Elmer adopts conflicting doxastic dispositions with respect to what he takes to be two different pieces of information but what is in fact a single proposition. On the one hand, Elmer has the appropriate favorable attitude toward this information; he is disposed to assent. On the other hand, he does not have an appropriate favorable attitude toward this information. It all depends on how Elmer takes the information.

How do we avoid this apparent contradiction? Does Elmer believe the relevant information, or doesn't he?

I have said that belief is a favorable attitude toward a piece of information, perhaps a disposition to inward assent or agreement. I have not said, however, that there must be a disposition to inward assent or agreement no matter how the information is taken. Elmer assents to the proposition that Bugsy is dangerous; he agrees with this information when he takes it as information concerning his friend. Hence, Elmer does believe this information. The fact that Elmer is no longer so disposed when he takes it as information concerning the notorious jewel thief does not entail that he has no disposition to assent to the proposition whatsoever. Indeed, he *has* such a disposition when he takes the proposition another way. This resolves the contradiction: Strictly speaking, Elmer does believe that Bugsy is dangerous, and it is strictly incorrect to say that he does not believe this, even after his change of mind on June 1.

We can still account for Elmer's change of mind with respect to the proposition that Bugsy is dangerous. When Elmer takes the information that Bugsy is dangerous as the information concerning his friend, he is continuously disposed to inward agreement since April 1. It is for this reason that we say that Elmer continues to believe that Bugsy is dangerous. However, when Elmer takes the proposition to be one about the notorious jewel thief, he agrees with it on January 1 but by the following summer he is no longer so disposed. There is a certain way of taking the proposition that Bugsy is dangerous such that Elmer grasps the proposition by means of it but is no longer disposed to assent to the proposition when taking it that way. In this special sense, Elmer now *withholds belief.* Strictly speaking, this is not to say that he *fails* to believe. Nonetheless, Elmer manifests the central and most significant characteristic of giving up this belief so long as he takes the proposition to be one about the criminal, for then he is disposed to neither inward assent nor inward dissent, neither agreement nor disagreement, with respect to the relevant proposition. The only thing that prevents Elmer from failing to believe altogether is the fact that he happens to harbor a disposition to inward assent when he takes the proposition another way. This, at any rate, is how the modified naive theory can explain the sense in which Elmer may be said to "withhold belief." The fact one attempts to convey is just the fact that Elmer now lacks the appropriate favorable attitude or disposition when he takes the proposition in a certain contextually significant way.

I have argued so far as if belief may be analyzed in terms of a notion of *disposition to inward assent or agreement when taken in such-and-such a way.* It does not matter much whether this is the relevant notion, only that the modified naive theory is compelled to acknowledge some such ternary relation whose existential generalization coincides with the binary relation of belief. The matter can be put more formally as follows: Let us call the relevant ternary relation, whatever it is, *'BEL'*. It is a relation among believers, propositions, and something else (e.g., the relation of disposition to inward agreement when taken in a certain way), such that

> (i) $\ulcorner A$ believes $p \urcorner$ may be analyzed as $(\exists x)[A$ grasps p by means of x & $BEL(A, p, x)]$,
>
> (ii) A may stand in BEL to p and some x by means of which A grasps p, without standing in BEL to p and all x by means of which A grasps p,

and

> (iii) $\ulcorner A$ withholds belief from $p \urcorner$, in the sense relevant to Elmer's befuddlement, may be analyzed as $(\exists x)[A$ grasps p by means of x & $\sim\!BEL(A, p, x)]$.[13]

In the special case of Elmer's Befuddlement, we initially seemed compelled to say both that Elmer believes that Bugsy is dangerous and that Elmer does not believe that Bugsy is dangerous. The grounds for saying that Elmer does believe that Bugsy is dangerous are straightforward. Elmer formed this opinion on April 1 and has remained steadfastly convinced ever since. It is strictly incorrect, therefore, to say that Elmer does not believe that Bugsy is dangerous. How, then, do we express the other side of Elmer's doxastic state resulting from his recent change of mind? The specifics of the story do not allow us to say that Elmer believes that Bugsy is not dangerous, and so we are prevented from transferring the inconsistency from us to Elmer by saying that Elmer believes both that Bugsy is dangerous and that he is not dangerous. What, then, do we say to capture Elmer's apparent withheld belief, which we initially tried to capture by saying that he no longer believes that Bugsy is dangerous? The analysis in terms of BEL uncovers that there is yet a third position in which the negation sign may occur. What we are trying to say when we say, erroneously, that "Elmer does not believe that Bugsy is dangerous" is not

> $\sim(\exists x)[$Elmer grasps *that Bugsy is dangerous* by means of x & $BEL($Elmer, *that Bugsy is dangerous, x*$)]$

(that is, it is not the case that Elmer believes that Bugsy is dangerous). This would saddle us with a contradiction. Nor is it

> $(\exists x)[$Elmer grasps *that Bugsy is not dangerous* by means of x & $BEL($Elmer, *that Bugsy is not dangerous, x*$)]$

---

[13] Withheld belief, as defined here, is compatible with (in fact, perhaps entailed by) disbelief (belief of the negation). One can similarly define suspension of judgment so that its analysis is

$$(\exists x)[A \text{ grasps } p \text{ by means of } x \text{ & } \sim\!BEL(A, p, x) \text{ & }$$
$$\sim\!BEL(A, \sim\!p, \text{Neg}(x))],$$

e.g., under at least one relevant way of taking p, A is disposed neither to inward agreement nor to inward disagreement with respect to p. So understood, suspension of judgment entails withheld belief with respect to both the proposition in question and its negation, but not vice versa. The main idea is to see the various doxastic states of belief, disbelief, withheld belief, and suspension of judgment as existential generalizations of ternary relations relativized to guises, or some such items, so that it is consistent and reasonable for someone to be in conflicting doxastic states (e.g., belief and disbelief, or belief and suspension of judgment) with respect to the very same proposition.

(that is, Elmer believes that Bugsy is not dangerous). This is straightforwardly false. Rather, it is

> ($\exists x$)[Elmer grasps *that Bugsy is dangerous* by means of x & ~*BEL*(Elmer, *that Bugsy is dangerous, x*)]

(that is, Elmer withholds belief about Bugsy's being dangerous). This is at once true, compatible with Elmer's believing that Bugsy is dangerous, and *constitutive* of Elmer's change of mind. There is some relevant third relatum x such that on January 1 Elmer stands in *BEL* to the proposition that Bugsy is dangerous and x but by the following summer Elmer no longer stands in *BEL* to this proposition and x. As in the case of Mrs. Jones's complex emotional attitude with respect to her husband, alias Jones the Ripper-Offer, no attempt to describe Elmer's complex doxastic state with respect to the singular proposition about Bugsy Wabbit that he is dangerous can succeed using only the two-place notion of belief as a binary relation between believers and propositions. Without some relativized, ternary notion, and the resulting distinction between withholding belief and failure to believe, the attempt to describe Elmer's complex doxastic state with respect to the relevant singular proposition breaks down. The only thing one can say using the binary notion of belief—to wit, that Elmer does believe the proposition that Bugsy is dangerous—is highly misleading at best. Thus, by casting singular propositions as objects of belief, the modified naive theory is compelled to acknowledge an analysis of belief as the existential generalization of some three-place relation *BEL* in order to uncover the appropriate position for the negation required by Elmer's change of mind in the face of his continued belief.

8.3.2. The New Frege Puzzle

This modified naive theoretical scheme for solving the problems posed by Elmer's Befuddlement points the way to a similar and related treatment of some of the other problems encountered earlier. Consider again the new and stronger version of Frege's Puzzle: An ancient astronomer-philosopher, who is an ideally competent speaker and thinker and a firm believer in the modified naive theory, unhesitatingly assents to 'Hesperus is Hesperus', but is not in the least disposed to assent to the sentence 'Hesperus is Phosphorus', even though he understands both sentences perfectly and, in fact, associates the very same proposition with each sentence. The explanation now available on the modified naive theory begins with the observation that the astronomer-philosopher does not recognize the proposition he attaches to the second sentence as the very same proposition he attaches to the first sentence, and firmly believes on logical grounds alone. When he reads and understands the sentence 'Hesperus is Phosphorus', he takes the proposition thereby encoded in a way different from the way in which he takes this same proposition when he reads and understands the sentence 'Hesperus is Hesperus'. He grasps the very same proposition in two different ways, by means of two different guises, and he takes this single proposition to be two different propositions. When he takes it as a singular proposition of self-identity between the first heavenly body sometimes visible in such-and-such location at dusk and itself, he unhesitatingly assents inwardly to it. When he takes it as a singular proposition identifying the first heavenly body sometimes visible in such-and-such location at dusk with the last heavenly body sometimes visible in so-and-so location at dawn, he has no inclination to assent inwardly to it, and may even inwardly dissent from it. His verbal assent and his refraining from verbal assent with respect to the two sentences are merely the outward manifestations of his inward dispositions relative to the ways he takes the proposition encoded by the two sentences. In the context of the new Frege Puzzle, this entails a rejection of the analogue of Frege's Law stated in terms of the verbal dispositions of ideally competent speakers. Unlike Frege's Law, this analogue is not a truth of logic but an empirically false hypothesis.

The account of belief as the existential generalization of a ternary relation *BEL* was constructed around the modified naive theory's account of de re belief as a binary relation between believers and singular propositions (see the introduction), so that the modified naive theory could accommodate Elmer's complex cognitive state. The analysis makes room for the modified naive theory's claim that whoever believes that Hesperus is Hesperus also believes that Hesperus is Phosphorus, for whoever agrees inwardly with the singular proposition about the planet Venus that it is it, taking the proposition as an affirmation of self-identity about the first heavenly body sometimes visible at dusk in such-and-such location, stands in *BEL* to the proposition that Hesperus is Phosphorus and some x or other, and hence believes this singular proposition, even if he or she is not so disposed when this same proposition is taken some other way (e.g., as information concerning the last heavenly body sometimes visible at dawn in so-and-so location). It is part of the account that one who stands in the *BEL* relation to the information about Venus that it is it, together with some third relatum x by means of which he or she grasps this information, need not also stand in the *BEL* relation to this same information together with some further relatum y distinct from x and by means of which he or she also grasps the information.

8.4. Why We Speak the Way We Do

This aspect of the account yields another part (promised in section 6.2) of the explanation for the prevailing inclination to say—erroneously, according to the modified naive theory—that the ancient astronomer-philosopher does not believe that Hesperus is Phosphorus, and that Lois Lane is not aware that Superman is Clark Kent. The first part of the explanation was that most speakers, being insufficiently aware of the distinction between semantically encoded and pragmatically imparted information, will inevitably mistake information only pragmatically imparted by utterances of 'Hesperus is Phosphorus' (such as the information that the sentence is true) for part of the information content of the sentence, and hence will mistake the sentence 'The astronomer-philosopher believes that Hesperus is Phosphorus' for an assertion that the astronomer-philosopher believes this imparted information—information we know he does not believe. It was seen, however, that this explanation by itself cannot be the complete story, for, even when one takes care to distinguish semantically encoded and pragmatically imparted information, the astronomer-philosopher's failure to assent to the sentence 'Hesperus is Phosphorus', when he fully understands it and completely grasps the information thereby encoded, provides a compelling reason to suppose that he does not believe this information, and this reason is part of the original justification for denying that he believes that Hesperus is Phosphorus. The existential analysis of belief in terms of the ternary relation *BEL* reveals that this sort of evidence, compelling though it may be, is *defeasible*. When the astronomer-philosopher fails to assent verbally to 'Hesperus is Phosphorus', having fully understood the sentence, he also fails to assent mentally to the information thereby encoded, taking it in the way he does when it is presented to him through that particular sentence. He "withholds belief," in the sense defined earlier. This does not entail that he does not mentally agree with this information however he takes it. In the usual kind of case, one uniformly assents or fails to assent to a single piece of information, however it is taken, by whatever guise one is familiar with it. It is for this reason that failure to assent to a proposition when taking it one way—i.e., withholding belief—is very good evidence for failure to believe. But in this particular case it happens that the astronomer-philosopher is also familiar with the information that Hesperus is Phosphorus under its guise as a trivial truism, the way he takes it when it is presented to him through the sentence 'Hesperus is Hesperus'. Taking it this way, he unhesitatingly assents to it. Hence, he believes that Hesperus is Phosphorus, and his sincere denials constitute defeated, misleading evidence to the contrary. He "withholds belief," in the sense used here, but he also believes, in the sense used everywhere. To say that he does not is to say something false.

The true sentence 'The ancient astronomer believes that Hesperus is Phosphorus' may even typically involve the Gricean implicature, or suggestion, or presumption, that the ancient astronomer believes (his sentence for) the sentence 'Hesperus is Phosphorus' to be true and, under normal circumstances, would verbally assent to it if queried. Since he does not and would not, the implicatures of the sentence would also lead speakers to deny it, even though its literal truth conditions are fulfilled.

The reasons just given why we speak the way we do in cases of propositional recognition failure may still fail to get to the bottom of the problem. In attributing beliefs, we are stating whether the believer is favorably disposed to a certain piece of information or proposition. In the 'Hesperus'-'Phosphorus' and 'Superman'-'Clark Kent' cases, however, the believer in question is favorably disposed toward a certain singular proposition when taking it one way, but fails to recognize this proposition and is not favorably disposed toward it when it is encountered again. Since our purpose in attributing belief is to specify how the believer stands with respect to a proposition, we should, in these cases where the believer's disposition depends upon and varies with the way the proposition is taken, want to specify not only the proposition agreed to but also something about the way the believer takes the proposition when agreeing to it. The dyadic predicate 'believes' is semantically inadequate for this purpose; we need a triadic predicate for the full *BEL* relation, which the belief relation existentially gener-alizes. But there may be no such predicate available in the language. Even if such a predicate is available, it may be inordinately long, or cumbersome, or incon-venient. We are accustomed to speaking with the dyadic predicate, 'believes', and we mean to continue doing so even in these problem cases. How, then, do we convey the third relatum of the *BEL* relation?

In the case of Elmer's believing that Bugsy Wabbit is dangerous, the sentence used to specify the information content of Elmer's belief, 'Bugsy Wabbit is dan-gerous', is itself understood by Elmer, though Elmer understands the sentence in two different ways. He mistakes the sentence to be semantically ambiguous. As one might say, he takes the single sentence to be two different sentences. This is unlike the 'Hesperus'-'Phosphorus' and 'Superman'-'Clark Kent' cases. In these cases, the two ways in which the believer takes the relevant proposition are asso-ciated, respectively, with two different sentences, either of which may be used in specifying the content of the belief in question. The ancient astronomer agrees to the proposition about the planet Venus that it is it when he takes it in the way it is presented to him through the logically valid sentence 'Hesperus is Hesperus', but he does not agree to this same proposition when he takes it in the way it is pre-sented to him through the logically contingent sentence 'Hesperus is Phosphorus'. The fact that he agrees to it at all is, strictly speaking, sufficient for the truth of both the sentence 'The astronomer believes that Hesperus is Hesperus' and the sentence 'The astronomer believes that Hesperus is Phosphorus'. Though the sen-tences are materially equivalent, and even modally equivalent (true with respect to exactly the same possible worlds), there is a sense in which the first is better than the second, given our normal purpose in attributing belief. Both sentences state the same fact (that the astronomer agrees to the singular proposition in question), but the first sentence also manages to convey *how* the astronomer agrees to the proposition. Indeed, the second sentence, though true, is in some sense inappropriate; it is positively misleading in the way it (correctly) specifies the content of the astronomer's belief. It specifies the content by means of a 'that'-clause that presents the proposition in the "the wrong way," a way of taking the proposition with respect to which the astronomer does not assent to it. This does not affect the truth value of the second sentence, for it is no part of the semantic content of the sentence to specify the way the astronomer takes the proposition when he agrees to it. The 'that'-clause is there only to specify the proposition believed. It happens in the 'Hesperus'-'Phosphorus' type of case that the clause used to specify the believed proposition also carries with it a particular way in which the believer takes the proposition, a particular x by means of which he or she is familiar with the proposition. In these cases, the guise or appearance by means of which the believer would be familiar with a proposition at a particular time t were it presented to him or her through a particular sentence is a function of the believer and the sentence. Let us call this function f_t. For example, $f_t(x, S)$ might be the way x would take the information content of S, at t, were it presented to him or her through the very sentence S. In the case of the ancient astronomer, we have

(7) *BEL*[the astronomer, that Hesperus is Hesperus, f_i(the astronomer, 'Hesperus is Hesperus')]

and

(8) *BEL*[the astronomer, that Hesperus is Phosphorus, f_i(the astronomer, 'Hesperus is Hesperus')],

but not

(9) *BEL*[the astronomer, that Hesperus is Hesperus, f_i(the astronomer, 'Hesperus is Phosphorus')]

and not

(10) *BEL*[the astronomer, that Hesperus is Phosphorus, f_i(the astronomer, 'Hesperus is Phosphorus')].

The quasi-symbolizations 7 and 10 reveal that, though one cannot be explicit about the particular third relatum involved in the *BEL* relation using only the dyadic predicate 'believes', one can, so to speak, "fake it" by using as a 'that'-clause a sentence that determines the third relatum in question. If one existentially generalizes on the third argument place in all of sentences 7–10, the first and the fourth, unlike the second and the third, typographically retain all that is obliterated by the variable of generalization—all, that is, but the functor 'f_i' and the quotation marks around and recurrence of its second argument. One can exploit this feature of the sentence 'The astronomer believes that Hesperus is Hesperus' to convey the third relatum of *BEL*. The 'that'-clause, whose semantic function is simply to specify the content of the astronomer's belief, is also used here to perform a pragmatic function involving an autonomous mention-use of the clause. This is the closest one can come to saying by means of the dyadic predicate what can, strictly speaking, be said only by means of the triadic predicate. To borrow Wittgenstein's terminology, one *shows* using 'believes' what one cannot *say* by its means alone.

Since it is our purpose in this case to convey not only what the astronomer agrees to but also how he takes what he agrees to when agreeing to it, the belief attribution 'The astronomer believes that Hesperus is Phosphorus' may typically involve the false (further) implicature (or suggestion, or presumption) that the astronomer agrees to the proposition that Hesperus is Phosphorus when he takes it in the way it is presented to him through the very sentence 'Hesperus is Phosphorus'. If we allowed ourselves the full triadic predicate, we could cancel the implicature without explicitly specifying the third relatum by uttering something like the following:

> The astronomer believes that Hesperus is Phosphorus, although he does not agree that Hesperus is Phosphorus when he takes this information the way he does when it is presented to him through the very sentence 'Hesperus is Phosphorus'.

The second conjunct here—the cancellation clause—is meant to take the sting out of the first conjunct, and the conjunction taken as a whole remains perfectly consistent. However, since the sentence that determines (via the function f_t) the way the astronomer takes the information when agreeing to it is readily available, it is easier and equally efficacious simply to retain the dyadic predicate 'believes' and to deny the literally true but misleading belief attribution 'The astronomer believes that Hesperus is Phosphorus' while asserting an equally true but not misleading attribution. Denying the misleading attribution is the closest one can come, using only the dyadic predicate, to denying proposition 9 (= proposition 10). Hence we are naturally led to say things like 'The astronomer believes that Hesperus is Hesperus, but he does not believe that Hesperus is Phosphorus'. We speak falsely, but the point is taken, and that is what matters. So it is that the modified naive theory, properly extended to acknowledge that believers may fail to recognize the singular propositions they embrace, predicts the sort of usage in propositional attitude discourse that we actually find where propositional recognition failure is involved.[14]

---

[14] There are important limitations to this device inherent in the complexities of 'natural language. Suppose that Jones believes that he is the best logician in the department, so that something like the following obtains:

> BEL[Jones, that he is the best logician in the department, f(Jones, 'I am the best logician in the department')],

where the function $f(x, S)$ is something like the way x takes the proposition encoded by S *with respect to a context in which x is agent* when it is presented to him through the very sentence S. That is, Jones assents to the proposition that he is the best logician in the department when he takes it in the way he does when he presents it to himself through the sentence 'I am the best logician in the department'. It will not do in this case to use for the 'that'-clause the sentence that determines via the function f the way Jones takes the relevant proposition when agreeing to it, since Jones does not believe that I am the best logician in the department. It is quite possible that belief attributions of the form ⌜a believes that he or she is ϕ⌝, understood on the reflexive reading of the pronoun, involve the analogous cancelable implicature, suggestion, or presumption, expressible using 'BEL' by ⌜$BEL[a$, that he or she is $\phi, f(a,$ 'I am ϕ')]⌝, and similarly for other so-called first-person propositional-attitude attributions (i.e., propositional-attitude attributions concerning oneself) and for other indexical or tensed propositional-attitude attributions. Thus, for example, if Jones believed at time t that the meeting was over by *then*, he probably did so by agreeing to that information when taking it the way he would had it been presented to him at t through the present tensed sentence 'The meeting is over by now'. Where the relevant implicature, suggestion, or presumption is false, competent speakers may be inclined, erroneously from the point of view of truth, to deny the attribution, just as in the case of 'The ancient astronomer believes that Hesperus is Phosphorus' or 'The ancient astronomer believes that Hesperus appears at dawn'. This fact may help explain the widespread intuition, tapped by Hector-Neri Castañeda in support of his theory of so-called quasi-indicators and by others in support of equally or even more dramatically philosophical theses, that such attributions are literally false in such cases. See for example Castañeda, "Indicators and Quasi-Indicators," *American Philosophical Quarterly* 4, no. 2 (1967):85–100; "On the Logic of Attributions of Self-Knowledge to Others," *Journal of Philosophy* 65, no. 15 (1968):439–456; Roderick Chisholm, *The First Person* (Minneapolis: University of Minnesota Press, 1981); David Lewis, "Attitudes *De Dicto* and *De Re*," *Philosophical Review* 87 (1979):513–443. For an account of first-person propositional-attitude attributions similar in broad outline and spirit to the one proposed here (although, as David Austin has pointed out, apparently lacking the full resources of the ternary account in terms of the *BEL* relation), see Steven Boër and William Lycan, "Who Me?," *Philosophical Review* 89, no. 3 (1980):427–466.

SUBSTITUTIVITY*

Scott Soames

I

In his 1962 article "Propositions," Richard Cartwright identified propositions with what is said or asserted by assertive utterances of sentences. He distinguished the proposition asserted by an utterance from various things with which it might be confused, including the sentence uttered, its meaning, the act of uttering it, and the sentence token produced. In distinguishing the proposition asserted from the meaning of the sentence used to assert it, Cartwright relied heavily on observations about indexical and context-sensitive sentences.

For example, he pointed out that the meaning of sentence (1) or (2) in what follows cannot be the proposition it is used to assert, for the simple reason that there is no such single proposition.[1]

(1) It is raining.

(2) Botvinnik uses it.

Rather, he noted, the meanings of these sentences allow distinct utterances of them to express different propositions. Although Cartwright did not attempt to provide a systematic characterization of the propositions expressed by these sentences in different contexts of utterance, he did note the importance of contextually determined reference for this task. Thus, in speaking of (1), he says that the fact about its meaning that allows different utterances of it to express different propositions is that one who utters it "speaks correctly only if he refers to the weather at the time of his utterance and in his (more or less) immediate vicinity" (Cartwright 1962, p. 93).

In recent years a conception of semantics has grown up under the influence of David Kaplan and others that preserves Cartwright's central observations.[2] According to this conception the meaning of a sentence is a function from contexts of utterance to propositions expressed in those contexts. Sentences containing indexicals and other context-sensitive elements express different propositions in different contexts. Propositions determine functions from circumstances of evaluation to truth values. These functions give the truth conditions of propositions. The truth conditions of a sentence, as used in a particular context, are the truth conditions of the proposition it expresses in that context.

---

* I would like to thank the Philosophy Department at the University of Washington for use of their facilities during the summer of 1986, when this paper was written. I would also like to thank Ali Akhtar Kazmi for his useful comments on the initial draft.

[1] Following Cartwright, I have spoken of the proposition asserted by an utterance. This is a convenient simplification. Although an unambiguous sentence expresses a single proposition in a context, a speaker who utters it often asserts a number of propositions in addition to the one semantically expressed by the sentence uttered. (See section VIII.) Cartwright's point regarding sentences (1) and (2) is not this one but rather the more fundamental observation that these sentences express different propositions in different contexts.

[2] See, in particular, Kaplan (1977), Salmon (1986a), and Soames (1987).

These points are illustrated by

(3) I am American.

This sentence, as used in a context C, is true with respect to an arbitrary circumstance of evaluation E if and only if the referent of "I" in C is in the extension of "American" in E. Since the referent of "I" in a context is just the designated agent (speaker) in the context, this means that (3) is true with respect to C and E if and only if the agent (speaker) in C is an American in E. Thus an utterance of (3) by Reagan expresses a proposition that is true in a circumstance E if and only if Reagan is an American in E (whether or not he ever speaks in E).

Undoubtedly Reagan thinks of himself as the fortieth president of the United States. This may even be his favorite, most privileged description of himself. Still, the proposition expressed by his utterance of (3) is not the proposition that the fortieth president of the United States is American. Since there are circumstances in which the latter proposition is true but the former proposition is not, they cannot be identical. This result, together with an elementary principle of compositionality, establishes that the contribution made by "I" to the proposition expressed by (3) in the context is not the sense of the description "the fortieth president of the United States."

This reasoning can be extended to all descriptions that denote someone other than Reagan, with respect to some circumstance of evaluation. If, following David Kaplan and Nathan Salmon, we account for the truth conditions of examples such as

(4) In the future I will be dead, but my policies will live on

by taking Reagan's (present) utterance of "I" to denote him even in circumstances in which he does not exist, we can extend the result to descriptions such as "the x: x = Reagan" and "the x: actually x is the fortieth president of the United States" (which denote Reagan in all circumstances in which he exists but denote nothing in circumstances in which he does not).[3] These points are not, of course, restricted to "I" but apply to proper names and other indexicals that designate contingently existing objects. Finally, as David Kaplan (1977), Saul Kripke (1980), and John Perry (1977) have emphasized, the semantic mechanism determining reference with respect to a circumstance for a name or indexical (as used in a context) is not the satisfaction in the circumstance of an associated description. In short, names and indexicals are *nondescriptional* as well as *rigid*.

A singular term is rigid if and only if it refers to the same object in all circumstances with respect to a fixed context of utterance. It is descriptional if and only if its referent with respect to an arbitrary circumstance E (and fixed context C) is, by

---

[3] A description, ⌜the x: Fx⌝, refers with respect to a circumstance E (and context C) to the unique object *in the domain of E* that satisfies ⌜Fx⌝ with respect to E (and C). When ⌜Fx⌝ is ⌜actually Gx⌝, the description refers with respect to E (and C), if at all, to the unique object existing in E that satisfies ⌜Gx⌝ in the circumstance of the context C. See Salmon (1981), chapter 1, for a discussion of these issues plus arguments for the claim that names and indexicals are *nondescriptional* (Salmon's terminology).

definition, the unique satisfier of a condition Sx, with respect to E (and C). There are, of course, rigid descriptions, for example, "the even prime." However, even if a description is rigid and so picks out the same object in every circumstance, its referent is determined in each circumstance by means of satisfaction of an associated condition. By contrast, the referent of a name or indexical is determined just once, in the context. In presenting a semantics, one standardly does define the referent of such a term t with respect to a context C and arbitrary circumstance E. However, given the referent of t in C, there is no further process one invokes to determine reference at alternative circumstances. Rather, one simply *stipulates* that the referent of t with respect to C and an arbitrary circumstance E is its referent in C.

What bearing does this difference in reference determination have on these about the propositional contents of names and indexicals (relative to contexts) and the propositions expressed by sentences containing them? It is easy to proceed incautiously here. Given that propositional content determines reference and that reference of names and indexicals is not determined descriptively, one is tempted to conclude both that the content of a name or indexical (relative to a context) is never the same as the content of a description and that the proposition expressed by $\ulcorner S(n) \urcorner$ (in a context) is never the same as the proposition expressed by $\ulcorner S(d) \urcorner$, where d is a description and n is a name or indexical. However, these inferences are fallacious.

The reason they are is that we have not yet said enough about what propositions and propositional contents are. We have taken propositions to be objects of the attitudes of saying and asserting, as well as bearers of truth values in circumstances of evaluation. Suppose, however, that one were to add that circumstances of evaluation are possible worlds and that the proposition expressed by a sentence (in a context C) is the set of worlds in which it is true (as used in C).[4] On this conception the propositional content of a singular term (relative to C) is the function from worlds W to referents of the term with respect to W (and C). Thus "2" and "the even prime" are assigned the same 'propositional content', and the following (a) and (b) sentences are assigned the same 'proposition'—even though the (b) sentences arise from the (a) sentences by substituting a singular term with one propositional content for a singular term with a different content.[5]

(5a) Reagan is American.

(5b) The actual fortieth president of the United States is American.

(6a) Three squared is less than 10.

(6b) Five is less than 10.

In attempting to distinguish these propositions, one cannot simply stipulate that they are different because they are complexes constructed out of different component parts (the propositional contents of constituent expressions). Although such a view of propositions is, I think, correct, it cannot be established

---

[4] For the sake of simplicity, I assume that a proposition is always either true or false with respect to a world.

[5] I assume that only those who exist (at a given time) in a world are Americans (at that time) in the world.

by semantic fiat. Rather, one must appeal to pretheoretic facts that support it over and against alternative conceptions. This appeal cannot, of course, be restricted to facts about the truth values of propositions in different circumstances of evaluation, for the (a) and (b) propositions do not differ in this respect. What we need are some commonplace observations about propositional attitudes. It is possible to say, assert, or express (believe, consider, or prove) one of the (a) propositions without saying, asserting, or expressing (believing, considering, or proving) the corresponding (b) proposition. Thus the propositions are different.

By appealing to observations of this kind, one can make a plausible case for two negative theses: First, the propositional content of a name or indexical (relative to a context) is never the same as that of a description; second, the proposition expressed by a sentence containing such a term is never the same as the proposition expressed by a sentence that results from substituting a description for the name or indexical. However, these negative conclusions, together with the claim that names and indexicals are rigid, do not add up to a positive specification of their propositional contents (relative to contexts) or of the propositions expressed by sentences containing them.

We may take it that the propositional contents of terms (relative to contexts) determine their referents with respect to circumstances of evaluation (in the sense that two terms with the same content must agree in reference in all circumstances). Still, our conclusions about names and indexicals are compatible with a variety of hypotheses about their contents. For all that has been said so far, the content of such a term (relative to a context) could be its referent: it could be a pair consisting of its referent plus a descriptive condition associated with it by the speaker; it could be a triple consisting of this pair plus the character or linguistic meaning of the term; it could be a quadruple containing all this plus the term itself; or it could be any number of other things.

At issue are the conditions under which substitution of one name or indexical for another in a simple sentence preserves the proposition it expresses. The idea behind the more baroque alternatives is to restrict such substitution by encoding into propositions many of the linguistic and contextual peculiarities of utterances expressing them. This idea is not entirely without foundation in our pretheoretic linguistic practice. For example, when we report in indirect discourse what proposition someone has asserted or expressed, we typically try to keep as close to the person's own words as is feasible, relative to the conversational purposes and standards of accuracy prevailing in the reporting discourse.

However, there are definite limits to this presumption of linguistic fidelity. If someone speaking German utters a sentence containing the name "Deutschland," we can typically report in English the proposition he expressed using the name "Germany." Thus sentences containing different names may express the same proposition. Similarly, two people who utter

(7) Reagan is persistent

may assert the same thing even if they have contrasting views of Reagan and associate radically different descriptive content with his name. Thus utterances of a sentence by speakers who associate different descriptive content with one of its names may express the same proposition.

Finally, utterances of the sentences in (8) may express the same proposition in their respective contexts, provided that the indexicals they contain refer to the same individual in those contexts:

(8a) I am persistent.

(8b) You are persistent.

(8c) He is persistent.

Thus utterances of sentences with different meanings (characters) may express the same proposition. This should not be surprising, since one of the primary functions of indexicals is to allow the expression of the same proposition from different points of view.

In all these cases observations about propositional attitudes (saying, asserting, expressing) are used to identify or distinguish various propositions. These observations provide substantial support for two well-known semantic theses.[6]

> *Thesis 1*
> Names and indexicals are *directly referential;* that is, the propositional content of such a term, relative to a context, is its referent in the context.

> *Thesis 2*
> Simple sentences containing directly referential terms express *singular propositions* (relative to contexts), that is, propositions containing individuals as constituents.

II

What consequences do these theses have for the substitutivity of coreferential names and indexicals? By themselves they have none. However, in conjunction with other plausible principles—some of which were instrumental in establishing them—they have consequences that are profound and wide ranging.

The most obvious of these have to do with simple sentences, free of nonextensional operators. A plausible principle governing such sentences is that substitution of expressions with the same propositional content preserves the proposition expressed.

> *Random Compositionality*
> Let S be a simple, extensional sentence containing one or more occurrences of an expression e. Let S' arise from S by substituting an occurrence of e' for any

---

[6] The term "directly referential" has been used in the literature in two main ways: as it is in Thesis 1 and as a synonym for "nondescriptional." The two conceptions are different and should not be confused. I always use the term in the sense of Thesis 1.

In Soames (1985, 1987), Thesis 1 is used to show that propositions must encode much of the structure of the sentences that express them. A natural way of looking at this is to take propositions to be structured complexes whose constituents are the propositional contents of subsentential expressions, relative to contexts.

(single) occurrence of e in S. If the propositional content of e in context C is identical with the propositional content of e' in context C, then the proposition expressed by S in C is identical with the proposition expressed by S' in C.[7]

The conjunction of this principle with the thesis that names and indexicals are directly referential entails that substitution of coreferential names or indexicals for one another in a simple, extensional sentence preserves the proposition expressed.

This conclusion has a number of consequences, some welcome and some not. Among the former is the intuitively correct result that the sentences in (7) and (8) express the same proposition in contexts in which their names and indexicals are coreferential. Among the latter is the problematic result that the sentence pairs in (9) and (10) also do.

(9a) I am Scott Soames.

(9b) Scott Soames is Scott Soames.

(10a) Tully shaved Cicero.

(10b) Cicero shaved Cicero.

It is important to be clear about what is and what is not problematic about this result. The result does *not* entail that utterances of the sentences in each example convey the same information. In the case of sentence (9a), its meaning guarantees that it is true in the context of utterance if and only if the speaker of the utterance is Scott Soames. Since this is not so for (9b), competent hearers can be expected to find utterances of (9a) informative in a way that utterances of (9b) are not—even if they express the same (trivial) proposition.

The case of (10) is a little more complicated but still analogous. The proposition expressed by sentence (10b) (and, by hypothesis, (10a)) is nontrivial. Thus utterances of both sentences are informative. However, the (total) information conveyed by an utterance of one may differ from that conveyed by an utterance of the other. For example, suppose that x associates one set of descriptive criteria, D, with the name "Tully" and another set, D', with the name "Cicero." It is not important whether D and D' represent information about the referent that is complete or incomplete, accurate or inaccurate. We may suppose that these descriptive criteria are not *semantically* associated with the names at all. Still, if x takes an utterance of (10a) to be true, he will be in a position to conclude that $\ulcorner D$ shaved $D'\urcorner$ is true and hence to acquire a belief in the proposition it expresses. Since this belief would not arise from an utterance of (10b), the utterances convey different information. Similarly, if x takes an utterance of (10b) to be true, he will be in a position to conclude that someone was a self-shaver. Since this belief would not

---

[7] Substitution of e' for multiple occurrences of e are handled by repeated applications of the principle. The terminology "random compositionality" is due to Kaplan (1985). Note that, if the content of e in C is the same as that of e' in C', then the proposition expressed by S in C will be the same as that expressed by S' in C', provided that S does not contain other expressions whose contents vary between C and C'.

arise from an utterance of (10a),[8] the two do not convey the same information—even if they do express the same proposition.

Therefore, what is problematic about the conclusion that the (a) and (b) sentences in (9) and (10) express the same propositions (in their respective contexts) is not a matter of differences in the informativeness of utterances of these sentences. What is problematic about the result arises from the assumption that propositions are the objects of attitudes such as saying, asserting, and expressing (denying, believing, and considering). The conjunction of this assumption with the direct reference thesis and random compositionality entails that it is impossible to assert (deny, etc.) the proposition expressed by one of the sentences in the pair without asserting (denying, etc.) the proposition expressed (in the relevant context) by the other. This is counterintuitive. Ordinarily we are inclined to think that one can deny that I am Scott Soames without denying that Scott Soames is Scott Soames or assert that Cicero shaved Cicero without asserting that Tully did.

So far the only substitutivity results explicitly considered have involved simple, extensional sentences. However, these results have natural corollaries involving complex, nonextensional examples. There is, of course, no reason why substitution of expressions with the same propositional content should always preserve truth value, let alone the proposition expressed. It is easy to specify quotation, or quotationlike, operators that block such substitution. However, substitutivity in sentences containing familiar modal or propositional attitude constructions seems well-nigh irresistible.

In the case of the attitudes the argument leading to this result may be summarized as follows:

Truth-Preserving Substitution in Attitude Constructions

A. Propositions are objects of the attitudes saying, asserting, and expressing (denying, believing, considering, etc.); that is, these attitudes are relations to propositions.

B. The verbs "assert," "deny," "believe," etc. are two-place predicates relating individuals and propositions. An individual i satisfies $\ulcorner x$ asserts (denies, etc.) NP$\urcorner$ in a context C if and only if i asserts (denies, etc.) the proposition denoted by NP in C.[9]

C. An individual i satisfies $\ulcorner x$ asserts (denies, etc.) the proposition that $S\urcorner$ in a context C if and only if i asserts (denies, etc.) the denotation of $\ulcorner$the proposition that $S\urcorner$ in C, that is, the proposition expressed by S in C.

D. An individual i satisfies $\ulcorner x$ asserts (denies, etc.) that $S\urcorner$ in C if and only if i asserts (denies, etc.) the proposition expressed by S in C.

---

[8] Note that this holds even if x associates the same (incomplete) descriptive material—for example, "a famous Roman"—with both names, or associates no descriptive material at all with them. See section VIII, and note 12 of Soames (1985) for further discussion.

[9] Some verbs, such as "believe," take NP arguments other than those denoting propositions, as in "John believes Mary." I put aside such uses for present purposes. Other verbs, such as "say" and "think," do not take full NP arguments at all. For these one moves directly from statement A to statement D.

E. It follows that, if S is a sentence for which random compositionality holds, if S' arises from S by substituting an expression e' for an occurrence of an expression e in S, and if the propositional content of e in a context C is identical with the propositional content of e' in C, then i satisfies $\ulcorner x$ asserts (denies, etc.) that $S\urcorner$ in C if and only if i satisfies $\ulcorner x$ asserts (denies, etc.) that $S'\urcorner$ in C.

F. When Thesis 1, about direct reference, is added, it follows that substitution of coreferential names and indexicals in attitude constructions preserves truth value.

Some of the consequences of F are counterintuitive. However, they are not easily avoided. In particular, direct reference theorists cannot divorce themselves from these consequences by professing agnosticism regarding the supplementary assumptions A through D, used to derive F.[10] It is true that the direct reference thesis does not itself make any claims about attitudes or attitude sentences. However, it is also true that without assumptions about the attitudes the thesis could not have been given its original motivation. To refuse to endorse these assumptions is to jeopardize crucial arguments for the thesis.

But this only makes the problem more acute, for to endorse the assumptions, together with direct reference, is to be committed to some notably counterintuitive conclusions. Thus direct reference theorists seem to be left in an uncomfortable position. The very assumptions that made the direct reference thesis initially compelling lead to substitutivity results that seem to undermine it.

III

Nevertheless, the correct response to these results is not, I think, to give up direct reference. One reason it is not is that essentially the same problems arise in cases in which there is little doubt that the expressions undergoing substitution do have the same content, for example, cases involving garden variety synonymies.[11] Let us assume, for the sake of argument, the following:

(11) "Doctor" and "physician," as well as "fortnight" and "period of fourteen days," are synonymous and hence have the same propositional contents.

The combination of this plus random compositionality yields the conclusion that the (a) and (b) sentences of (12) and (13) express the same proposition.

(12a) Doctors are doctors.

(12b) Physicians are doctors.

(13a) The meeting lasted a period of fourteen days if and only if it lasted a period of fourteen days.

---

[10]This agnostic position seems to be taken by Almog (1985) and Wettstein (1986).

[11] Other cases, noted in Church (1982), Kripke (1979), Salmon (1986), and Soames (1987), involve substitution of coreferential variables (with respect to an assignment) and substitution of a name for its translation ("London"/"Londres," "Peking"/"Beijing").

(13b) The meeting lasted a period of fourteen days if and only if it lasted a
        fortnight.

Many, I think, would find these results counterintuitive—on the grounds that
ordinarily we think it possible to assert (deny, believe, etc.) one of the propositions
in the pair without asserting (denying, believing, etc.) the other.

Following Benson Mates (1950), we can give the problem a further twist.
Consider examples (14a) and (14b):

(14a) Whoever believes (asserts, etc.) that the meeting lasted less than a
        period of fourteen days believes (asserts, etc.) that the meeting lasted
        less than a period of fourteen days.

(14b) Whoever believes (asserts, etc.) that the meeting lasted less than a
        period of fourteen days believes (asserts, etc.) that the meeting lasted
        less than a fortnight.

Sentence (14a) is clearly true. The combination of (11), assumptions A through D,
and random compositionality yields the result that (14b) is also true. However, the
two examples seem to differ markedly in status. It is hard to imagine anyone
doubting proposition (14a); but it seems easy to imagine someone doubting
proposition (14b). Thus, if doubt is an attitude toward a proposition, it would
seem the (a) and (b) sentences must express different propositions. But how can
they, for they differ only in the substitution of one synonym for another?

The force of the question derives from a plausible extension of random compositionality to sentences containing attitude verbs. The conjunction of this
extension with (11) entails that sentences (14a) and (14b) express the same proposition. We also get the conclusion that the examples in (15) have the same truth
value.

(15a) Nobody doubts that (14a).

(15b) Nobody doubts that (14b).[12]

But these results are counterintuitive.

There are two points to notice about this problem. First, the way to deal with
it is not to deny (11). From denials of this sort we would quickly reach the conclusion that no two expressions can have the same content, a conclusion that would
wreak havoc with our intuitions about meaning in general and attitude reports in
particular. Second, the problem confronting us here is analogous to the one in section II involving direct reference—so much so that it seems advisable to look for
a single solution to both. If there is such a solution, it will not turn on denying that
the expressions undergoing substitution have the same content.

---

[12] In these examples, "(14a)" and "(14b)" are abbreviations of the previous examples, rather
    than terms referring to them. The conclusion that (15a) and (15b) have the same truth
    value can be gotten either from an extension of random compositionality to sentences
    containing multiple embeddings of propositional attitude ascriptions or from assumptions
    A through D together with an extension of random compositionality to sentences with a
    single level of embedding.

IV

In 1954 Alonzo Church and Hilary Putnam offered different, but potentially generalizable, solutions to the Mates puzzle. According to Church, (14a) and (14b) express the same proposition, and (15a) and (15b) have the same truth value. The argument for this rested on elementary claims about translation. First, if S' is a proper German translation of a sentence S of English, then S and S' have the same truth values in their respective languages. Second, since "fortnight" has no single-word German translation, its translation is the same as that of "period of fourteen days." Because of this, sentences (15a) and (15b) have the same German translation and hence the same truth value.

According to Church, what makes this result initially counterintuitive is that it is confused with other, metalinguistic, claims that are false. For example, the claim that the sentences in (15) have the same truth value may be confused with the claim that those in (16) or (17) do:

(16a) Nobody doubts that whoever satisfies (in English) the sentential matrix "x believes that the meeting lasted less than a period of fourteen days" satisfies (in English) the sentential matrix "x believes that the meeting lasted less than a period of fourteen days."

(16b) Nobody doubts that whoever satisfies (in English) the sentential matrix "x believes that the meeting lasted less than a period of fourteen days" satisfies (in English) the sentential matrix "x believes that the meeting lasted less than a fortnight."

(17a) Nobody doubts that whoever sincerely assents (in English) to "the meeting lasted less than a period of fourteen days" sincerely assents (in English) to "the meeting lasted less than a period of fourteen days."

(17b) Nobody doubts that whoever sincerely assents (in English) to "the meeting lasted less than a period of fourteen days" sincerely assents (in English) to "the meeting lasted less than a fortnight."

The (a) and (b) sentences in these examples do have different truth values. Thus, if one does not properly distinguish them from their counterparts in (15), one will be led to conclude, incorrectly, that (15a) and (15b) also differ in truth value.

Unlike Church, Putnam did not take the intuition that (15a) and (15b) have different truth values to be based on linguistic confusion; rather, he regarded it as accurate. According to Putnam, (14a) and (14b) have different contents, and (15a) and (15b) have different truth values. Similarly, he held that sentences such as (12a) and (12b) differ in content and that propositional attitude ascriptions in which one of them is substituted for the other may differ in truth value. These conclusions conflict with the combination of claim (11), which Putnam accepted, plus random compositionality, and assumptions A through D about the attitudes. For largely historical reasons, these latter assumptions were not under consideration in Putnam's discussion. However, the discussion can be recast in a way that takes them for granted without affecting the essential dispute over sentences (12) through (15).[13] When this is done, the point at issue becomes random compositionality. In effect, what Putnam noticed was that there might be a good reason to reject this principle.

Random compositionality gains much of its plausibility from the observation that the content of a sentence (in a context) is determined by the contents of its constituent parts (in the context). However, this observation is incomplete. For example, sentences (18a) and (18b) are made up of parts with the same semantic content:

(18a)   John loves Mary.

(18b)   Mary loves John.

However, the sentences have different contents because those parts are put together in different ways. We might express this by saying that the content of a sentence is determined by the contents of its parts plus the way the parts are structured.

It should follow that sentences with the same structure and semantically equivalent parts have the same content. But what counts as sameness of structure? Do the following (a) and (b) sentences have the same or different structures?

(19a)   *Rab.*

(19b)   *Raa.*

(20a)   All *F*'s are *G*'s.

(20b)   All *F*'s are *F*'s.

---

[13] Mates, Putnam, and Church were all responding to Carnap's proposal (1947) that S and S' are synonymous, and express the same belief, if and only if they are intensionally isomorphic. Carnap proposed that an individual i satisfies $\ulcorner x$ believes that $S \urcorner$ in English if and only if there is a language L and sentence S' such that S in English is intensionally isomorphic to S' in L, and i is disposed to assent to S' as a sentence of L. In the subsequent debate three objections were brought against this proposal.

Church (1950) argued that the analysis wrongly characterized the content of ordinary beliefs, such as the belief that the earth is round, as being about sentences. Instead of relating individuals to sentences, belief ascriptions should, Church thought, be analyzed as relating individuals to propositions. Church (1954) argued that, in any case, intensional isomorphism was too weak for Carnap's purposes because it allowed substitution of nonsynonymous constants with the same intension. Mates (1950) argued that, no matter how closely two simple sentences were related, one could always embed them in structures such as (15) in such a way that speakers would assent to one but not the other (and indeed would assent to one and the negation of the other).

Putnam's article (1954) was a defense of Carnap against Church (1950) and Mates (1950). Regarding Mates (1950), Putnam's proposal was that the definition of "intensionally isomorphic" should require S and S' to have the same *logical* structure in the sense discussed at the end of section IV (as well as being made up of constituents with the same intensions). In reconstructing Putnam's proposal, I follow Church in analyzing "believe" as relating individuals to structured propositions and Carnap in taking that relation to hold in virtue of a relation between the individual and a mode of representation that expresses the proposition. In this framework Putnam's proposal requires sentences expressing the same proposition to have the same logical structure.

The answer depends on one's notion of structure. In one sense the pairs have the same structures—in each case they would be assigned the same constituent structure tree by a standard syntax. In another sense, however, they do not. Thus, when doing logic, we say that the sentences have different *logical structures* in virtue of the fact that the (b) sentences contain two occurrences of the same constituent, whereas the (a) sentences contain one occurrence each of different constituents.

Suppose now that this notion of structure is used to determine the content of a sentence from its structure plus the contents of its parts. Under this analysis the (a) and (b) sentences in (19) and (20) may have different contents, even if the contents of their constituents, "*a*" *and* "*b*," "*F*" and "*G*," are the same. According to Putnam, random compositionality fails because substitution in these cases changes structure and, thereby, content. The same may be said for the sentence pairs (12) through (15).

V

We need not at this point try to evaluate the relative merits of the Church and Putnam proposals. However, one initial advantage of Putnam's approach is worth noting. Ordinary speakers do, I think, have pretheoretic intuitions that the examples in (15) may have different truth values and that those in (12) through (14) may represent different beliefs. Putnam's proposal respects these intuitions in a way that Church's does not.

The semantic intuitions of ordinary competent speakers are not, of course, infallible. Thus Putnam's advantage on this score is not in itself a refutation of Church's position. However, the intuitions of such speakers are, in general, the best evidence we have in semantics and so cannot be taken lightly. If there is a way of respecting them in this case that does not run into trouble elsewhere, then it should be preferred.

Another desirable feature of Putnam's suggestion is the way it generalizes. The results involving belief sentences are easily extended to other attitude ascriptions (saying, asserting, expressing, etc.). Putnam's approach also applies to cases involving substitution of directly referential singular terms.

If names and indexicals are directly referential, then the content of "Cicero" is the same as the content of "Tully," and the content of "I" is the same as the content of "Scott Soames" in a context in which I am the agent (speaker). However, substitution of one for the other in (9) and (10) changes logical structure and so, on the Putnam account, changes the proposition expressed. Thus one can preserve the intuition that it is possible to deny that I am Scott Soames without denying that Scott Soames is Scott Soames and to assert that Cicero shaved Cicero without asserting that Tully did. By contrast, substitution of coreferential names and indexicals in (7) and (8) preserves both logical structure and proposition expressed. In this way one retains the positive results about substitutivity that helped motivate the direct reference thesis while avoiding some of the most notorious substitution problems that seemed to undermine it.

This application to direct reference was not, of course, envisioned in 1954.[14] In recent years, however, the idea behind Putnam's proposal has been rediscovered and used in connection with direct reference theory by Mark Richard (1983; forthcoming) and by David Kaplan (1985). The details of their respective proposals differ in several respects that need not concern us here.[15] What is important is whether the apparent difficulties for the direct reference thesis posed by problematic substitutions can be overcome using Putnam's basic idea.

In investigating this question, I adopt assumptions A through D about the attitudes given in section II plus versions of Theses 1 and 2 that extend the direct reference analysis to variables.

Thesis 1*
Names, indexicals, and variables are *directly referential*—the prepositional content of such a term, relative to a context C and assignment f of objects as referents to variables, is its referent relative to C and f.

---

[14]However, Putnam did apply his analysis to certain sentences containing singular terms. For example, although he took '5' and 'V' to be synonymous, he distinguished the contents of '5 is identical with 5' and '5 is identical with V' on the basis of the different logical structures of the two sentences.

[15] Kaplan (1985) accepts assumptions A through D, restricts himself to ascriptions in which the only directly referential terms are names (no indexicals and no quantifying-in), and argues against random compositionality. Richard (1983) holds that beliefs are relations to propositions but maintains that a belief ascription $\ulcorner x$ believes that $S \urcorner$ not only reports the proposition believed but also provides information about the sentence, or representation, acceptance of which is responsible for the agent's belief. This is illustrated by the relationship between the following ascriptions (i) and (ii), in which the terms are variables or indexicals that refer to the same thing (relative to their respective contexts and assignments):

    (i) x believes that ... t ... t ....

    (ii) x believes that ... t ... t' ....

Although the complements of ascriptions (i) and (ii) express the same proposition P, the ascriptions are assigned different truth conditions. In order for ascription (i) to be true, the agent must believe P in virtue of accepting a sentence containing occurrences of directly referential terms (indexicals) with the same character. The truth conditions assigned to ascription (ii) are the same except that the sentence accepted by the agent may contain either occurrences of directly referential terms with the same character or occurrences with different characters. Thus Richard (1983) characterizes the truth of ascription (i) as guaranteeing the truth of ascription (ii), but not vice versa.

The system in Richard (1983) does not cover cases involving names. (Since distinct names t and t' with the same referent have the same character, a simple extension of that system to include them would treat an agent's acceptance of $\ulcorner S(t, t') \urcorner$ as equivalent to the acceptance of $\ulcorner S(t, t) \urcorner$—which Richard does not want.) However, Richard (forthcoming) considers a modification of his 1983 system that accommodates names. On this account ascription (i) is true provided that the sentence accepted by the agent contains two occurrences of a single name; ascription (ii) is true provided that the accepted sentence contains occurrences of different names. Thus, in his forthcoming article neither (i) and (ii) implies the other (where t and t' in (i) and (ii) are either names or variables).

The arguments given in the text bear in slightly different ways on all these proposals. For an argument directed specifically against Richard's claim that the truth of belief ascriptions requires more than a correct report of the proposition believed, see Soames (1987), note 24.

Thesis 2*

Sentences containing names and indexicals, as well as formulas containing free occurrences of variables, express *singular propositions* relative to contexts and assignments.[16]

I further assume that propositions are complexes that reflect the structure of the sentences that express them. In the case of simple sentences the propositions are made up of properties corresponding to predicates and individuals corresponding to directly referential terms. In more complex cases operators such as "and," "or," and "not," definite and indefinite descriptions, and quantifiers contribute higher-order elements to structurally complex propositions whose constituents are (or encode) the semantic contents of the constituents of sentences that express them.[17]

Finally, we need a way of representing in propositions the kinds of distinctions in the logical structures of sentences that are crucial to Putnam's proposal. For example, we must distinguish the propositions expressed by the (a) and (b) sentences in (21) and (22), where t and t' are distinct directly referential terms that refer to the same thing:

(21a) Rt, t'

(21b) $Rt, t.$

(22a) $Ft \wedge Gt'.$

(22b) $Ft \wedge Gt.$

The propositions expressed by the (a) sentences can be represented as follows:[18]

(21a′) $\langle\langle o, o\rangle, R^*\rangle$

(22a′) $\langle \mathrm{Conj}, \langle\langle\langle o\rangle, F^*\rangle, \langle\langle o\rangle, G^*\rangle\rangle\rangle.$

To get the propositions expressed by the (b) sentences, we need to add something that reflects the repeated occurrences of the same term in these examples. There

---

[16] I use

(i) $\exists x\, A$ believes that Fx

to represent the English sentences

(ii) Someone is such that A believes that he is F

(iii) A believes of someone that he is F.

Note that in sentence (i) the occurrence of "x" in the complement does not contribute an object to the proposition expressed. However, the assumption that variables are directly referential plays a crucial role in evaluating its truth value. Sentence (i) is true if and only if there is an object o such that the following is true with respect to an assignment of o to "x":

(iv) A believes that Fx.

Sentence (iv) is true with respect to such an assignment if and only if the referent of "A" believes the proposition expressed by $\ulcorner Fx \urcorner$ with respect to the assignment. Theses 1* and 2* characterize this as a singular proposition.

[17] See Soames (1987) for details.

[18] R^* is the relation expressed by the predicate in (21); F^* and G^* are properties expressed by the predicates in (22); and o is the referent of the directly referential terms.

are, of course, many ways to do this. For the sake of vividness let us think of the (b) propositions as arising from the (a) propositions by adding 'wires' connecting the different occurrences of o in the propositions:[19]

(21b′) $\langle\langle\overline{o, o}\rangle, R^*\rangle,$

(22b′) $\langle\text{Conj}, \langle\langle\langle\overline{o}\rangle, F^*\rangle, \langle\overline{o}\rangle, G^*\rangle\rangle\rangle.$

Multiple occurrences of the same predicates, or other constants, can be similarly represented.

The question at issue, then, is this: Does prepositional encoding of repeated occurrences of the same expression successfully resolve the puzzles involving substitution of expressions with the same content? In particular, does it resolve puzzles involving substitution of names, indexicals, and variables with the same referent? I argue that it does not.

VI

The first point to notice is that the extra-structure idea fails to block some of the most problematic substitutions. For example, since the structure of sentence (23a) is the same as that of (23b), the propositions they express are identified, and the ascriptions (24a) and (24b) are treated as equivalent:[20]

(23a) Superman is stronger than Clark Kent.

(23b) Clark Kent is stronger than Superman.

(24a) Lois Lane said (believed, etc.) that Superman is stronger than Clark Kent.

(24b) Lois Lane said (believed, etc.) that Clark Kent is stronger than Superman.

But these results are no less counterintuitive than those the extra-structure idea is designed to block. In general, interchanging t and t' in (21a) and (22a) is as problematic as substituting one of these terms for the other. It would seem, therefore, that the cases ought to be treated similarly. Making the attitudes sensitive to extra structure does not do this.

---

[19] This picture is due to Kaplan (1985). Another way of encoding the syntax would be to assimilate sentences (21b) and (22b) to

(i) $[\lambda x R x, x]t$

and

(ii) $[\lambda x (F x \wedge G x)]t.$

The predicates formed by lambda abstraction express one-place properties. If we choose to represent these as functions from objects to singular propositions, the propositions expressed would then be (iii) and (iv), where f maps an arbitrary object y onto $\langle\langle y, y\rangle, R^*\rangle$ and h maps y onto $\langle\text{Conj}, \langle\langle\langle y\rangle, F^*\rangle, \langle\langle y\rangle, G^*\rangle\rangle\rangle$:

(iii) $\langle\langle o\rangle, f\rangle,$

(iv) $\langle\langle o\rangle, h\rangle.$

[20] This point was made by David Lewis at the Princeton version of Kaplan (1985).

A similar point holds for examples involving conjunction:

(25a) The ancients said (believed, etc.) that Phosphorus was visible only in the morning and Hesperus was visible only in the evening.

(25b) The ancients said (believed, etc.) that Phosphorus was visible only in the morning and Phosphorus was visible only in the evening.

We may take it that (25a) is true and that the introduction of extra structure into propositions blocks the inference to (25b). However, nothing blocks the move from (25a) to

(25c) The ancients said (believed, etc.) that Phosphorus was visible only in the morning and the ancients said (believed, etc.) that Hesperus was visible only in the evening

and from there to

(25d) The ancients said (believed, etc.) that Phosphorus was visible only in the morning and the ancients said (believed, etc.) that Phosphorus was visible only in the evening

and

(25e) The ancients said (believed, etc.) that Phosphorus was visible only in the morning and that Phosphorus was visible only in the evening.[21]

If the goal is to preserve pretheoretic intuition, there is little to be gained by holding that (25b) is false whereas (25d) and (25e) are true. But this is what the extra-structure approach is committed to. In general, when substitution in a conjunction within the scope of an attitude verb is blocked, substitution in the separate conjuncts is allowed, counterintuitive or not.

Another problem similar to this illustrates the overreliance of the extra-structure approach on accidental matters of syntax. We assume that the semantic content of the directly referential proper name "Phosphorus" is not the same as that of the description "the x: x = Phosphorus." The former is just the planet Venus, whereas the latter is a complex consisting of an operation corresponding to the definite article plus that property of being identical with Venus. Nevertheless, a competent speaker who sincerely assents to sentence (26a) typically will assent to (26b):

(26a) Hesperus is distinct from Phosphorus.

(26b) Hesperus is distinct from the x: x = Phosphorus.

---

[21]I assume that, if $\ulcorner A$ said (believed, etc.) that P and $Q \urcorner$ is true, then so are $\ulcorner A$ *said (believed, etc.) that P* $\urcorner$ and $\ulcorner A$ said (believed, etc.) that $Q \urcorner$. However, the basic point of the argument could be reconstructed without assuming this. (I also take (25e) to be equivalent to (25d).)

Suppose now that we introduce a new syntactically simple term, "Vesperus," which we stipulate to have the same semantic content as the description.[22] Next we substitute "Vesperus" for the description in

(27a) *A* says (believes, etc.) that Hesperus is distinct from the x: $x =$ Phosphorus

to get

(27b) *A* says (believes, etc.) that Hesperus is distinct from Vesperus.

Having derived (27b), we can now substitute "Phosphorus" for "Hesperus" without changing structure to get

(27c) *A* says (believes, etc.) that Phosphorus is distinct from Vesperus.

But this is problematic. Although (27c) comes out true on the extra-structure proposal, intuitively it seems to be on a par with

(27d) *A* says (believes, etc.) that Phosphorus is distinct from the x: $x =$ Phosphorus

which the proposal is designed to block.

So far I have argued that the extra-structure proposal does not carve semantic reality at the joints. For every problematic substitution that it blocks, there are others, intuitively no different, that it allows. Although this does not show that the proposal is false, it does suggest that there is less to be said for it than might first have been imagined.[23]

---

[22]The argument here parallels one given by Church (1954) against Carnap. Church says:

> Again by the Principle of Tolerance it is possible to introduce a predicator constant which shall be synonymous with a specified abstraction expression of the form $(\lambda x)[..x..]$; or to introduce an individual constant synonymous with a specified individual description of the form $(\iota x)[..x..]$. And (unlike the case of synonymous primitive constants) it may be held that something like this actually occurs in formalized languages commonly constructed—namely those in which definitions are treated as introducing new notations into the object language, rather than as metatheoretic abbreviations. But whether or not the process is called definition, it is clear by the Principle of Tolerance that nothing prevents us from introducing (say) a predicator constant R as synonymous with the abstraction expression $(\lambda x)[..x..]$, and taking $R \equiv (\lambda x)[..x..]$ as an axiom. And if this is done, then R must be interchangeable with $(\lambda x)[..x..]$ in all contexts, including belief contexts, being synonymous with $(\lambda x)[..x..]$ by the very construction of the language—by definition, if we choose to call it that. (Church 1954, p. 67)

[23]Richard (1983) deals with examples such as those in (25) by positing a dichotomy between (25b), on the one hand, and sentences (25d) and (25e), on the other. Sentence (25b) is said to be false, whereas sentences (25d) and (25e) are claimed to be true but pragmatically inappropriate or misleading.

Kaplan rejects this dichotomy, hoping for a way to treat all three sentences as false. Although Kaplan (1985) did not contain an explicit semantic mechanism for doing this, he suggested that perhaps a semantics that relativized the truth conditions of attitude ascriptions to a discourse might solve the problem. Roughly put, the idea is that the truth of (25d) would require the existence of a pair of sentences, S and S', accepted or assertively uttered by the agent, expressing the reported propositions, and anchored by a one-one (order-preserving) mapping from names in S and S' to names in the complements of the reports.

(contd.)

In addition to this, there is another, more powerful criticism to be made. The proposal was motivated by the idea that the examples in (28) may differ in truth value even when expressions e and e' have the same semantic content:

(28a) A says (believes, etc.) that . . . e . . . e. . . .

(28b) A says (believes, etc.) that . . . e' . . . e. . . .

The proposal implements this idea by introducing a mechanism that makes such sameness of content an insufficient basis for deriving one from the other. However, it does not preclude the possibility that other factors might bring it about that (28a) and (28b) have the same truth value. Of course, if such factors could always be found, then the proposal would lose its motivation. Given the background assumptions in section V together with some pretheoretic attitude ascriptions, we can show that this is the case.

Consider again the familiar example of Hesperus and Phosphorus. By encoding extra structure into propositions, one can distinguish the proposition expressed by (29a) from the propositions expressed by (29b) and (29c):

(29a) Phosphorus is Phosphorus.

(29b) That (pointing in the morning at Venus) is Phosphorus.

(29c) Hesperus is Phosphorus.

Note, however, that the proposition expressed by (29b) is still identified with the one expressed by (29c).

We may assume that the ancients sincerely and reflectively assented to (translations of) (29a) and dissented from (translations of) (29c). Surely, however, they

---

It might even be thought that the interchange problem illustrated by (24) could be handled in this way. Suppose that the speaker associates descriptions D and D' with the names h and p. One might maintain that sentence (i) can be true only if it is true relative to the discourse (ii):

(i) x believes Rh, p.

(ii) x believes h is D, x believes p is D', x believes Rh, p.

If the agent associated D and D' with h and p, respectively, then this proposal could assign different truth values to (i) and (iii):

(iii) x believes Rp, h.

One problem with the attempt to relativize the semantics of belief ascriptions to discourses is that it seems to give up the independently motivated assumptions A through D analyzing "believe" as a two-place predicate of individuals and propositions. However, even if we put this aside, the proposal for treating the interchange problem gives the wrong results when the descriptive information associated with names by the speaker conflicts with that associated with the names by the agent. For example, if the speaker associates "the first star seen in the evening" with p and "the first star seen in the morning" with h and the agent reverses those associations, the proposal will incorrectly characterize (i) as true and (iii) as false when the agent rejects the complement of (i) and accepts the complement of (iii).

The point here is that, when the names used by the agent appear in the belief report, they should be used as the agent used them. In my opinion this is a pragmatic rather than a semantic fact. In section VII I apply it uniformly to the sentences in (24) and (25).

also produced sincere, reflective utterances of the sort illustrated by (29b). Moreover, the following attitude ascription seems clearly correct:

> (30) The ancients said (believed, etc.) that that (pointing in the morning at Venus) was Phosphorus.

But then, even the extra-structure proposal predicts that ascriptions (31a) and (31b) are true:

> (31a) The ancients said (believed, etc.) that Hesperus was Phosphorus.

> (31b) The ancients said (believed, etc.) that that (pointing in the morning at Venus) was Hesperus.

The point is a general one. Let e and e' be expressions with the same content. Suppose that (28a) is true and that (28b) appears, pretheoretically, to be false. Typically one can find or introduce another expression e^* with the same content as e, such that

> (28b*) A says (believes, etc.) that ... e^* ... e ...

is unproblematically true (because, for example, the agent realizes that e and e^* have the same content). But given the truth of (28b*), the extra-structure proposal is committed to the truth of (28b). Thus, no real progress has been made on examples such as this. Although the proposal makes the move from (28a) to (28b) depend on more than content alone, the ease with which intermediaries of the sort (28b*) can be produced robs the proposal of its intended significance.[24]

A similar moral can be drawn from ascriptions involving quantifying-in. Let us suppose that Lois Lane sees Clark Kent shaving in his office at the *Daily Planet* and on the basis of this sincerely and assertively utters "Clark Kent shaves Clark Kent." Surely, there is someone—Clark Kent—of whom Lois Lane says and believes that he shaves Clark Kent. Thus both sentences (32a) and (32b) are true:

> (32a) Lois Lane says (believes) that Clark Kent shaves Clark Kent.

> (32b) $\exists x[x = $ Clark Kent $\wedge$ Lois Lane says (believes) that x shaves Clark Kent].

According to the extra-structure proposal, (32a) ascribes to Lois the property of standing in a relation to a 'wired proposition', the structure of which incorporates the double occurrence of the name in the complement clause. However, (32b) does not. Instead, it requires that Lois stand in the appropriate attitude relation to the proposition expressed by "x shaves Clark Kent" under an assignment of

---

[24]Examples involving only names, or general terms, can easily be produced. Imagine speakers that have three names for Venus—"Hesperus" and "Venus," which are applied freely and interchangeably to Venus when seen in the evening, and "Phosphorus," which is applied to Venus when seen in the morning. These speakers readily assent to (translations of) "Venus is Hesperus" and dissent from "Hesperus is Phosphorus" and "Venus is Phosphorus." Nevertheless, the extrastructure proposal characterizes them as believing that Hesperus is Phosphorus and that Venus is Phosphorus.

A similar example using general terms can be constructed in a language in which "surgeon," "physician," and "doctor" are synonyms.

Clark Kent as value of "x." Since "x," "Clark Kent," and "Superman" are different terms with the same content (with respect to the assignment of Clark Kent to "x"), it follows that this proposition is the same as that expressed by "Superman shaves Clark Kent." Thus the truth of (32b) guarantees the truth of

> (32c) Lois Lane says (believes) that Superman shaves Clark Kent.

As before, the problem is general. According to the extra-structure approach, (33a) can be true when (33c) is false only when (33b) is also false:

> (33a) A says (believes, etc.) $\ldots t \ldots t \ldots$.
>
> (33b) $\exists x[x = t \wedge A$ says (believes, etc.) $\ldots x \ldots t \ldots]$.
>
> (33c) A says (believes, etc.). $\ldots t' \ldots t$.

However, in a great many cases in which (33a) is true, it seems obvious that (33b) is also. Thus proponents of extra structure face a dilemma. If they grant the truth of (33b), they must countenance ascriptions that their theory was designed to avoid. However, if they reject (33b), they miss an obvious truth.[25]

Similar reasoning applies to the inference from (33c) to (33a). Although the extra-structure proposal does not license it simply on the basis of identical content on the part of t and t', arguments appealing to pretheoretic intuitions can often be found to sanction it. For example, Professor McX, looking through the open back door of the faculty lounge, sees Y walking down the hall and says to a visitor, "He (pointing to Y) is a professor in the department." A few seconds later Y passes by the front door, and McX says, "He (pointing to Y again) is a graduate student in the department." Although McX does not realize that he has pointed twice to the same individual, Y, who has overheard the remarks, can correctly report, "McX said both that I am a professor in the department and that I am a graduate student in the department." A third party may report, "There is someone such that McX said both that he is a professor in the department and that he is a graduate student in the department."

Developing the example further, we can have McX conjoin his remarks:

> (34) Who is in the department? Let me see. He (pointing to Y as he passes the back door) is a professor in the department and (turning) he (pointing to Y as he passes the front door) is a graduate student in the department.

On the basis of this, the following ascriptions seem clearly true:

> (35a) McX says that he (pointing to Y as he passes the back door) is a professor in the department and he (pointing to Y as he passes the front door) is a graduate student in the department.

---

[25] In Richard (1983) the truth of (33a) guarantees the truth of (33c); however, the move from (33c) to (33a) is blocked. This is unattractive. It does not help to be told that the ancients did not believe that Hesperus was not Hesperus, if it is granted that they did believe that Hesperus was not Phosphorus and that Phosphorus was Hesperus. The system in Richard (forthcoming) blocks the move from (33a) to (33c) at the cost of blocking the move to (33b)—which is also unattractive. Quantification is not treated by Kaplan (1985).

(35b) McX says that I am a professor in the department and I am a graduate student in the department. [Uttered by Y]

(35c) $\exists z$[McX says that z is a professor in the department and z is a graduate student in the department].

(35d) McX says that Y is a professor in the department and Y is a graduate
student in the department [where "Y" is a proper name of Y].

Following Kaplan, I take (35a) to contain two different demonstratives: "he"
plus the first demonstration and "he" plus the second demonstration. Thus it has
the same form as (33c). Sentence (35b), on the other hand, has the form (33a).
Since (35b) is clearly true, the extra-structure proposal is again faced with a
dilemma. If it fails to countenance the move from (35a) to (35b), it misses an obvious truth. However, if it allows the move, it predicts that

(35e) McX says that t^* is a professor in the department and l^* is a graduate
student in the department

will be true for any directly referential term t^* that refers to Y—and thereby countenances the ascriptions it was designed to falsify.[26]

VII

For all these reasons it seems to me that the extra-structure proposal fails.
However, its failure is instructive. The examples involving indexicals and variables
point to something important about attitude ascriptions. Typically, when we
report someone's attitudes in indirect discourse, we are expected to keep as close
to the words he or she used, or would use, as is feasible. However, this expectation
of linguistic fidelity is not an absolute semantic requirement but a pragmatic
desideratum that can be outweighed by other factors. This is evident in reports of
assertions or beliefs expressed in other languages. It is also evident in cases in
which indexicals are used.

For example, when one talks about oneself, one is expected to do so in the first,
rather than the third, person. This applies even when reporting someone else's
beliefs or assertions about oneself. Thus, if I were to report Richard Cartwright's
remark, "Scott Soames is one of my former students," in most contexts I would be
expected to use sentence (36a) rather than (36b):

(36a) Richard Cartwright said that I was one of his former students.

(36b) Richard Cartwright said that Scott Soames was one of his former
students.

Here, deviation from the exact words of the agent of the attitude is not only
acceptable but preferred.

---

[26]The system in Richard (1983) would use terms with different characters to represent the two
demonstratives in (34) and (35a). An extension of the system treating assertion on the model
of belief would incorrectly characterize sentences (35b) through (35d) as false. The same is
true of Richard (forthcoming).

The McX and Y example given in section VI exploits this fact. When Y reports McX's remark about him, he has little choice but to use occurrences of "I" in place of the demonstratives used by McX. However, the result of this substitution is striking. Although the sentence used by McX indicates that he took himself to be talking about two individuals,[27] Y's sentence indicates that the assertion concerns a single individual. In short, the logical structures and cognitive perspectives associated with the two sentences are different. Nevertheless, the second is a truthful report of the assertion made by the first. This shows that reports of propositions asserted are not semantically required to preserve the logical structures or cognitive perspectives of the sentences used to assert them.

This result is not limited to cases in which the sentence assertively uttered contains indexicals or in which the subject of the assertion actually reports it. Imagine The Ancient Babylonian looking up in the sky in the morning and uttering (37a) and looking up in the sky in the evening and uttering (37b):

(37a) Phosphorus is a beautiful star visible only in the morning.

(37b) Hesperus is a beautiful star visible only in the evening.

Although Venus cannot report these remarks, this does not stop us from semantically evaluating (38a) and (38b) as true in a context in which Venus is the designated agent:

(38a) The Ancient Babylonian said that I was a beautiful star visible only in the morning.

(38b) The Ancient Babylonian said that I was a beautiful star visible only in the evening.

If The Ancient Babylonian conjoined sentences (37a) and (37b), (38c) would be true in a context with Venus as agent:

(38c) The Ancient Babylonian said that I was a beautiful star visible only in the morning and I was a beautiful star visible only in the evening.

What about (39) and (40)?

(39a) The Ancient Babylonian said that Venus was a beautiful star visible only in the morning.

(39b) The Ancient Babylonian said that Venus was a beautiful star visible only in the evening.

(39c) The Ancient Babylonian said that Venus was a beautiful star visible only in the morning and Venus was a beautiful star visible only in the evening.

(40a) The Ancient Babylonian said that Hesperus was a beautiful star visible only in the morning.

(40b) The Ancient Babylonian said that Phosphorus was a beautiful star visible only in the evening.

---

[27] I take the different demonstrations to be parts of McX's sentence.

(40c) The Ancient Babylonian said that Hesperus was a beautiful star visible only in the morning and Phosphorus was a beautiful star visible only in the evening.

If names are directly referential, then these reports should be true. Why, then, do they seem objectionable?

The answer, I believe, lies in the pragmatic desideratum of being maximally faithful to the words of the agent. When reporting the assertions from the perspective of Venus, the ability to use the first person pronoun allows us to deviate from the agent's words; and the reports sound fine. When reporting from the perspective of a third party, we need some excuse for not using the agent's own words (or strict translations of them). In the case of (39) there may be one—the name "Venus" may be familiar to the speaker and to the speaker's audience, whereas the names "Hesperus" and "Phosphorus" may not be. In such a situation utterances of the sentences in (39) are not only true but pragmatically appropriate.

The examples in (40) seem much worse. Here, the reports contain the names used by the agent. However, the way they are used in the reports conflicts with the way they were used by the agent. Since it is hard to imagine any conversational justification for this, they are naturally heard as incorrect. And they are. However, the principle they violate—remain faithful to the words of the agent unless there is reason to deviate—is pragmatic. Thus, the reports may be true after all. (The same analysis applies to sentences (24) and (32).)

VIII

If this is right, then the intuitions motivating the extra-structure proposal conflate pragmatic inappropriateness with semantic incorrectness. However, there is more motivating the proposal than this—at least in its extension to direct reference theory. An important insight behind it is the observation that a sincere, reflective speaker who assertively uttered a sentence

(41b) Rt, t

would standardly assert (and believe) a proposition that someone who assertively uttered the sentence

(41a) Rt, t'

would not (where t and t' are different, but coreferential, directly referential terms). This observation is correct. However, it does not show that (41a) and (41b) express different propositions.

Someone who assertively utters a sentence standardly asserts the proposition semantically expressed by the sentence in the context. However, the speaker often asserts other propositions as well. For example, someone assertively uttering a conjunction asserts not only the conjunctive proposition but also the propositions expressed by the conjuncts. Similarly, someone who asserts that Hesperus is a planet visible in the evening (standardly) asserts that there is a planet visible in the evening.

Competent conversational participants who recognize the two occurrences of t in sentence (41b) to be occurrences of the same term can be expected to accept (41b) if and only if they accept

(41c) $\lambda[xRx, x]t$

(that is, 't self-R's'). Since conversational participants typically do recognize this, someone who sincerely and assertively utters (41b) can usually be taken to believe, and to have asserted, the proposition expressed by (41c). Moreover, the pragmatic requirement that the reporter be faithful to the words of the agent is responsible for the fact that utterances of

(42) A said (believes) that Rt, t

often give rise to the suggestion that

(43) A said (believes) that $[\lambda xRx, x]t$

is true. All this combines to create the impression that the proposition expressed by (41b) is the same as the proposition expressed by (41c). However, this is an illusion.

Let us first distinguish (41a) from (41c). The former contains a two-place predicate plus occurrences of a pair of terms. The latter contains a compound one-place predicate plus a single occurrence of a term. Corresponding to this difference in structure, the proposition expressed by (41a) attributes the relation R to a pair consisting of an object and itself; the proposition expressed by (41c) attributes the one-place relational property of bearing-R-to-oneself to a single object. Not only are these propositions different, an individual may assert or believe one without asserting or believing the other. For example, one may assert or believe the proposition that Hesperus is not Phosphorus without asserting or believing the proposition that Hesperus is non-self-identical.

What about (41b)? Does it express the same proposition as (41a) or as (41c)? The extra-structure proposal, in effect, equates the proposition expressed by (41b) with the proposition expressed by (41c). I believe this to be a mistake.

First there is the matter of structure. Like (41a), (41b) consists of a two-place predicate plus a pair of occurrences of singular terms. Unlike (41c), (41b) does not contain a one-place predicate expressing the relational property of bearing-R-to-oneself. These differences are significant if, as I have suggested, propositions encode the structure of the sentences that express them. According to this independently plausible conception, (41b) and (41c) express different propositions. If, as I have assumed, the propositions are Russellian, and thus contain the objects designated by occurrences of directly referential terms, then (41b) expresses the same proposition as (41a).

The lambda operator used in (41c) is, of course, not part of standard English. However, English does contain a number of devices that may be used to the same end, for example, reflexive pronouns, the formation of adjectives such as, "self-shaver" from two-place predicates, and the use of conjunctions to connect subsentential constituents. The first two of these are illustrated in (44):

(44a) Reagan shaves himself, and Bush does too.

(44b) Reagan is a self-shaver, and Bush is too.

(44c) Reagan shaves Reagan, and Bush does too.

In each case the proposition expressed by the second conjunct is the same as that expressed by the first, save for the different contributions of the subjects of the two clauses. In (44a) and (44b) the proposition expressed by the second conjunct attributes to Bush the property of shaving oneself. In (44c) that proposition attributes to Bush the property of shaving Reagan. Since these properties are different, the propositions expressed by the respective conjuncts are different. Since these differences are inherited from the first conjuncts, the proposition expressed by the initial conjuncts in (44a) and (44b) differs from that expressed by the initial conjunct of (44c).

Next there is the matter of the attitudes. If truth-preserving inferences from (45a) to (45b) are as common as I have indicated, then similar inferences from (45b) to (45c) must often be blocked—for it seems undeniable that (45a) may be true when (45c) is not:

(45a) A says (believes, etc.) $\ldots t \ldots t' \ldots$

(45b) A says (believes, etc.) $\ldots t \ldots t \ldots$

(45c) A says (believes, etc.) $[\lambda x(\ldots x \ldots x \ldots)]t$.

This is borne out by previous examples.

In the case of McX and Y, McX's utterance of (34) attributed to Y both the property of being a professor in the department and the property of being a graduate student in the department. Thus the ascriptions (35b) through (35d) are true. Similarly, The Ancient Babylonian's utterance of the conjunction of sentences (37a) and (37b) attributed to Venus the property of being a beautiful star visible only in the morning and the property of being a beautiful star visible only in the evening. Thus the ascriptions (38c) and (39c) are true. However, McX did not attribute the uninstantiated property of being a graduate-student-professor-in-the-department to anyone; and The Ancient Babylonian did not attribute the contradictory property of being a beautiful-star-visible-only-in-the-morning-and-only-in-the-evening to anything.

There ought to be a way of reflecting these facts in attitude ascriptions. And there is. The ascriptions that report joint attributions of properties (to Y and to Venus) are of the form (45b)—with occurrences of the same term in different (sentential) conjuncts. These are true. Ascriptions that report attributions of compound properties are represented by (45c). These are false.

The latter are most naturally expressed in English by combining a single occurrence of a directly referential term with a compound subsentential constituent, as in the following examples:

(35*) McX said that Y was (both) a professor and a graduate student in the department—or, McX said that Y was a graduate student professor in the department.

(38*) The Ancient Babylonian said that I was a beautiful star visible in the morning and evening.[28] [Said by Venus]

There is, I think, a significant contrast between these ascriptions and those in (35), (38) and (39). Although the intuitions are delicate and subject to potential pragmatic interference, the ascriptions in (35), (38), and (39) seem, intuitively, to be true, whereas (35*) and (38*) do not. These intuitions support my critique of the extra-structure proposal and provide evidence for the accompanying alternative analysis.[29]

IX

This analysis is, in effect, an extension of Church's treatment of the Mates puzzle to examples involving directly referential singular terms. Like Church, I hold that attitudes are relations to propositions, that ascriptions such as

(46) A says (believes) that S

report relations to the proposition expressed by S (relative to contexts and assignments to variables) and that (random) substitution of expressions with the same (propositional) content in such constructions preserves both truth value and proposition expressed. I differ from Church in taking coreferential names, indexicals, and variables to have the same (propositional) content.

The decision to treat these terms as directly referential leads, in certain cases, to the derivation of problematic attitude ascriptions from unproblematic ones. However, this occurs even without direct reference, as is illustrated by the parallel between (47) and (48):

(47a) A says (believes) that doctors are doctors.

(47b) A says (believes) that physicians are doctors.

(48a) A says (believes) that Phosphorus is Phosphorus.

(48b) A says (believes) that Hesperus is Phosphorus.

Although the (a) sentences may appear to differ in truth value from the (b) sentences, this appearance is due to pragmatic considerations, most notably, the requirement that the reporter be maximally faithful to the words of the agent unless there is reason to deviate. Since in cases like this there often is no such reason, utterances of these sentences will suggest to the hearer that the reporter has been maximally faithful to the agent's own words. In these particular examples this suggestion takes on added significance because of the triviality of the propositions semantically expressed by the complement clauses. Thus it is natural to regard utterances of (47b) and (48b) as incorrect when the suggestions are false.

---

[28] In order to facilitate the conjoining of subsentential constituents, I have simplified the example by eliminating occurrences of "only." This does not affect the main issue.

[29] A thorough and illuminating investigation of the distinction between the simple sentences (41a) through (41c) as well as the ascriptions (42) and (43) is given in Salmon (1986b). These issues are also briefly discussed in Soames (1985), note 12.

Such utterances are incorrect, but that does not mean that the propositions semantically expressed by these sentences are false.

One potential difference between Church's synonyms and my coreferential, directly referential terms is worth noting. There is some plausibility in holding that anyone who understands both "doctor" and "physician" knows that they are synonymous.[30] If one does hold this, one may characterize anyone who rejects sentence (49) as someone who fails to understand one of its terms:

(49) Physicians are doctors.

But, if one fails to understand a term, then one's dispositions to accept or reject sentences containing it will not be reliable indications of whether or not one believes the propositions they express. The same may be true of the relation between one's assertive utterances and one's assertions. Thus a person's dissent from sentence (49) or assertive utterance of its negation might well be taken as proof of linguistic confusion rather than as evidence for the truth of

(50a) A believed (asserted) that physicians are not doctors

and

(50b) A believed (asserted) that doctors are not doctors.

Indeed, there is some plausibility in holding that these examples cannot be true.

The situation is different with directly referential singular terms. There is no plausibility in holding that anyone who understands both "Hesperus" and "Phosphorus" knows that they refer to the same thing. Thus dissent from sentence (51), or assertive utterance of its negation, cannot be taken as showing linguistic confusion but rather must be seen as evidence for the truth of (52a) and (52b):

(51) Hesperus is Phosphorus.

(52a) A believed (asserted) that Hesperus is not Phosphorus.

(52b) A believed (asserted) that Hesperus is not Hesperus.

The counterintuitiveness of utterances of (52b) are, I maintain, due both to violations of the pragmatic principle of fidelity to the words of the agent and to confusion of (52b) with

(52c) A believed (asserted) that Hesperus is non-self-identical.

Despite this possible difference between (50) and (52), the contrast does not represent a general difference between Church-type cases and those involving directly referential terms. The point can be made using Church's example.

(14a) Whoever believes (asserts, etc.) that the meeting lasted less than a period of fourteen days believes (asserts, etc.) that the meeting lasted less than a period of fourteen days.

---

[30]I do not hold this myself. However, for purposes of the present argument, it is not necessary to challenge the view here.

(14b) Whoever believes (asserts, etc.) that the meeting lasted less than a period of fourteen days believes (asserts, etc.) that the meeting lasted less than a fortnight.

(15a) Nobody doubts that (14a).

(15b) Nobody doubts that (14b).

According to Church—and me—the (a) sentences in these examples express the same propositions as the corresponding (b) sentences. However, not everyone who assents to (a) will assent to (b). We know this is true in the case of (15), since Putnam assented to (15a) while dissenting from (15b).[31] Now Putnam is, and was, a sincere, reflective, competent speaker. Certainly, his different treatment of sentences (15a) and (15b) was not evidence that he misunderstood "fortnight" or "period of fourteen days." Nor was it evidence that he did not understand the words "doubt" and "believe"—or the sentences themselves. He may have had the wrong semantic theory about these examples—I think he did—but he understood them in the sense relevant to linguistic competence as well as anyone.

Because of this, his dissent from sentence (15b) and acceptance of its negation cannot be dismissed as unreliable indicators of his attitude toward the propositions they express. Had he assertively uttered both (15a) and the negation of (15b), he would have asserted both propositions. Furthermore, his assertions would have been accurate reflections of his beliefs. Because sentences (15a) and (15b) express the same proposition, this means that Putnam would have asserted and believed both a proposition and its negation—without having made any straightforward logical error. This is just the sort of thing that we find in cases involving direct reference.[32]

If these conclusions are correct, then a widespread picture of our relationship to what we assert and believe is faulty. We are apt to think of this relationship as direct, unmediated, and fully transparent to introspection and observation. It is not. Propositions are contents of various intermediaries with which we are intimately related—sentences, belief states, and other modes of presentation. To assert or believe a proposition P is to stand in the right relation to an appropriate intermediary with P as content.[33] In cases involving language, our ordinary linguistic

---

[31] In point of fact, Putnam's examples involved "Greeks" and "Hellenes" rather than "fortnight" and "period of fourteen days"; but this makes no difference.

[32] The argument can be given at one less level of embedding if we grant, as I believe we should, that a fully competent speaker who understands sentences (14a) and (14b) may sincerely and reflectively assent both to the former and to the negation of the latter. In my view such a speaker asserts and believes the proposition expressed by the negation of (14b). Moreover, he has made no straightforward logical error even though this proposition is also expressed by the negation of a logical truth, namely (14a).

This view apparently conflicts with that of Church, who concludes (1954) by saying that Mates does not really doubt the proposition expressed by (14b)—no matter what he himself may say. If to doubt P is to consider P and take up a skeptical attitude toward it (such as believing its negation), then I think that Church's conclusion is false. However, on this conception of the attitude of doubting, doubting P does not involve not believing P. Although Mates did doubt the proposition expressed by sentence (14b), he also believed it—by virtue of his attitude toward (14a).

[33] This conception is developed in Salmon (1986a) and Soames (1987).

competence ensures that we have a reasonable pretheoretic grasp of when two people have said the same thing or expressed the same belief. However, since linguistic competence does not guarantee the possession of a correct semantic theory, theoretical investigation is capable of yielding some surprising conclusions about our beliefs and assertions.

In undertaking such an investigation, I believe it is crucial to take seriously the notion of a proposition as the information expressed by a sentence. In this respect Richard Cartwright's 1962 article, "Propositions," is a classic. At a time when many philosophers either dismissed or misidentified propositions, Cartwright clarified the strong intuitive case for countenancing them and exposed the misidentifications. With characteristic modesty he concluded the article by indicating that, although he had said what propositions are not, he had not said what they are. "To distinguish them from other things is not by itself to provide either means for their detection or rules for distinguishing one of them from another" (Cartwright 1962, p. 103). There is today a resurgence of interest in propositions and no dirth of attempts to provide rules for distinguishing among them. It would be nice to think that these attempts will be as successful in this part of the task as Cartwright's paper was in its.

REFERENCES

Almog, Joseph. 1985. "Form and content." *Noûs* 19:603–616.

Carnap, Rudolf. 1947. *Meaning and Necessity*. Chicago: University of Chicago Press.

Cartwright, Richard. 1962. "Propositions," in *Analytical Philosophy*, R. J. Butler, ed. Oxford: Basil Blackwell, 81–103.

Church, Alonzo. 1950. "Carnap's analysis of statements of assertion and belief," *Analysis* 10:98–99.

Church, Alonzo. 1954. "Intensional isomorphism and identity of belief." *Philosophical Studies* 5:65–73. To be reprinted in *Propositions and Attitudes*, N. Salmon and S. Soames, eds. (forthcoming).

Church, Alonzo. 1982. "A remark concerning Quine's paradox about modality." *Analisis Filosofico* 2:25–34 (in Spanish). English version to appear in *Propositions and Attitudes*, N. Salmon and S. Soames, eds. (forthcoming).

Kaplan, David. 1977. "Demonstratives." UCLA Department of Philosophy (unpublished). To appear in *Themes from David Kaplan*, J. Almog, J. Perry, and H. Wettstein, eds. (forthcoming).

Kaplan, David. 1985. "Word, object, and belief." Unpublished talks given in May at Princeton University, and in July at the meetings of the Association for Symbolic Logic, Stanford University.

Kripke, Saul. 1980. *Naming and Necessity*. Cambridge, Mass.: Harvard University Press and Basil Blackwell. Originally printed in *Semantics of Natural Language*, D. Davidson and G. Harman, eds. (Dordrecht: Reidel, 1972), 253–355, 763–769.

Kripke, Saul. 1979. "A puzzle about belief," in *Meaning and Use*, A. Margalit, ed. Dordrecht: Reidel, 239–275. To be reprinted in *Propositions and Attitudes*, N. Salmon and S. Soames, eds. (forthcoming).

Mates, Benson. 1950. "Synonymity." *University of California Publications in Philosophy* 25:210–226. Reprinted in *Semantics and the Philosophy of Language,* L. Linsky, ed. (Champaign: University of Illinois Press, 1952), 111–136.

Perry, John. 1977. "Frege on demonstratives." *The Philosophical Review* 86: 474–497.

Putnam, Hilary. 1954. "Synonymity, and the analysis of belief sentences." *Analysis* 14: 114–122.

Richard, Mark. 1983. "Direct reference and ascriptions of belief." *Journal of Philosophical Logic* 12:425–452. To be reprinted in *Propositions and Attitudes,* N. Salmon and S. Soames, eds. (forthcoming).

Richard, Mark. Forthcoming. "Quantification and Leibniz's law." *The Philosophical Review.*

Salmon, Nathan. 1981. *Reference and Essence.* Princeton, N.J.: Princeton University Press.

Salmon, Nathan. 1986a. *Frege's Puzzle.* Cambridge, Mass.: The MIT Press. A Bradford Book.

Salmon, Nathan. 1986b. "Reflexivity." *Notre Dame Journal of Formal Logic* 27: 401–429. To be reprinted in *Propositions and Attitudes,* N. Salmon and S. Soames, eds. (forthcoming).

Soames, Scott. 1985. "Lost innocence." *Linguistics and Philosophy* 8:59–71. To be reprinted in *The Philosopher's Annual,* Vol. 8, P. Grim, C. J. Martin, and P. Athay, eds. (Atascadero, Calif.: Ridgeview Press, forthcoming).

Soames, Scott. (1987). "Direct reference, propositional attitudes, and semantic content." *Philosophical Topics* 15. To be reprinted in *Propositions and Attitudes,* N. Salmon and S. Soames, eds. (forthcoming).

Wettstein, Howard. 1986. "Has semantics rested on a mistake?" *Journal of Philosophy* 83:185–209.

THE PRINCE AND THE PHONE BOOTH: REPORTING PUZZLING BELIEFS*

Mark Crimmins and John Perry

In Mark Twain's *The Prince and the Pauper,* Tom Canty and Edward Tudor decide to change lives for a day, but fate intervenes, and the exchange goes on for a considerable period of time. The whole story turns on what people believe and do not believe about the two boys, and an intelligent reader, unexposed to recent philosophy of language and mind, could probably describe the key facts of the story with some confidence. Such a reader might explain why Miles Hendon, a penniless nobleman who encounters a boy dressed in rags, does not bow to the Prince, by noting:

(1) Miles Hendon did not believe that he was of royal blood.

* This work was supported in part by the System Development Foundation through a grant to the Center for the Study of Language and Information. We would like to thank the Philosophy of Situation Theory group at CSLI; special thanks to David Israel.

And such a reader might ward off the implication that Miles was a fool or ignoramus by noting that Miles shared the dominant conception of Edward Tudor:

> (2) Miles Hendon believed that Edward Tudor was of royal blood.

One of our main claims in this paper is that such a reader would be right on both counts. In this we depart from a recent trend to explain the apparent truth of statements like (1) as an illusion generated by pragmatic features of such claims. Accounts of belief reporting given by Jon Barwise and John Perry,[1] Scott Soames,[2] and Nathan Salmon[3] have employed this strategy of denying the accuracy of our strong intuitions about truth and falsity. Here, we shall present an account that does not ignore pragmatic features, but assigns to them a more honorable role. They do not create an illusion, but help to identify the reality the report is about. Our account honors the intuition that claims (1) and (2) are true.

Since 'Edward Tudor' in (2) and 'he' in (1) both refer to Edward Tudor, this seems to commit us to some version of the doctrine of *opacity*.[4] Specifically, we are committed to the view that, if our reader were to say either of the following, in the same circumstances, he would be incorrect:

> (1') Miles Hendon did not believe that Edward Tudor was of royal blood.
>
> (2') Miles Hendon believed that he was of royal blood.

The doctrine of opacity has been thought incompatible with two others, to which we also are attracted: the first, *direct reference,* is that the utterance of a simple sentence containing names or demonstratives normally expresses a "singular proposition"—a proposition that contains as constituents the individuals referred to, and not any descriptions of or conditions on them; the second, *semantic innocence,* is that the utterances of the embedded sentences in belief reports express just the propositions they would if not embedded, and these propositions are the contents of the ascribed beliefs.[5]

Direct reference and semantic innocence are well-motivated by many considerations in the philosophy of language. But if direct reference and semantic innocence are correct, then it seems that opacity must not be: the substitution of

---

[1] *Situations and Attitudes* (Cambridge: MIT, 1983), pp. 253-264.

[2] "Substitutivity," in *Essays in Honor of Richard Cartwright* (Cambridge: MIT, 1987), pp. 99–132, and "Direct Reference and Propositional Attitudes," in Almog, Perry, Wettstein, eds., *Themes from Kaplan* (New York: Oxford, 1989).

[3] *Frege's Puzzle* (Cambridge: MIT, 1986).

[4] *Opacity* is the claim that substitution of coreferring names and demonstratives in belief reports does not necessarily preserve the truth of those reports (definite descriptions are another matter; it is not nearly as controversial that substituting a description for a coreferring name can influence the truth value of a belief report). What "substitution" comes to with respect to utterances (belief reports), as opposed to sentences (belief sentences), is not at all obvious. Our simple notions of substitutivity, opacity, and so on are really useful only if sentences are (wrongly) taken as the bearers of truth and content. Here, we shall adopt an informal notion of substitution in belief reports, such that the reports (1) and (1'), as well as (2) and (2'), are related by substitution.

[5] For an important qualification, see fn. 14 below.

'Edward Tudor' for 'he' in (1) [or vice-versa in (2)] should be completely legitimate. The name and the demonstrative refer to the same object. There is just one proposition, belief in which is denied by (1) and affirmed by (2), the "singular" proposition, which we shall represent in this way:

⟨⟨Being of royal blood; Edward Tudor⟩⟩

The example is typical of many doxastic puzzle cases in the literature—puzzles because they seem to reveal a conflict among the three very plausible doctrines. We hold all three, however.

I

When we substitute 'Edward Tudor' for 'he', the words change while the proposition expressed by the embedded sentence stays the same. If we think that belief is a relation to propositions and not words, the apparent change in truth value of the whole report seems puzzling. We are likely to focus on the most apparent change, the change in words, as the clue to the mystery.

The most famous doxastic puzzle case, due to Saul Kripke,[6] has nothing to do with substitution, however. Kripke describes a case in which the Frenchman Pierre first hears of London, comes to believe it is pretty, then moves to London, and, not connecting it to the city he has heard about (under the French 'Londres'), comes to believe it is not pretty. He does not change his mind about the city he has heard of, but simply does not connect the "two" cities. We have one sentence

(3) Pierre believes that London is pretty.

that we seem to be able to use, when reflecting on different parts of the story, to say something true and to say something false. The words have not changed. What has?

What changes in this case, and in every other doxastic puzzle case, is what we are talking about. Pierre has two different notions of London, which play very different roles in his beliefs. An assertion of (3) is true if it is about one of them, false if it is about the other. An ordinary doxastic puzzle case uses a change in words to precipitate the change in the subject matter of the utterance. Kripke spells out the details of his case so clearly that our focus gets redirected without a change in the wording of the report. We shall return to these claims about belief reports in the next section.

One of Pierre's beliefs was caused by his acceptance of the stories he heard about London. It has the content that London is pretty, and it leads him to cherish the prospect of someday visiting that city. This belief also causes him to affirm, in French, "Londres est jolie," in discussions about the city he has heard of.

Also, Pierre has a different belief which was caused by his displeasure with his new surroundings, which has the content that London is not pretty and which causes him to affirm, "London is not pretty," in discussions about his home.

---

[6] "A Puzzle about Belief," in A. Margalit, ed., *Meaning and Use* (Dordrecht: Reidel, 1979), pp. 239–283.

It is a commonplace to distinguish these two beliefs. We think it is often not sufficiently appreciated, however, that the beliefs so distinguished are concrete cognitive structures. Focusing on this fact provides the basis for our account of belief and for our solutions to the various doxastic puzzle cases.

These are the key features of our theory of beliefs:

(i) Beliefs are concrete cognitive structures: they are particulars that belong to an agent, come into existence, endure, and go out of existence.

(ii) Beliefs are related to the world and to other cognitive structures and abilities in a way that allows us to classify them by propositional content.

Beliefs, since they are cognitive particulars or "things in the head," are not things that are believed; they are not in any sense the objects of belief. The propositions believed are the objects of belief. An agent believes some proposition in virtue of having a belief with that content. Many agents can believe the same proposition, so propositions are public; they also are abstract. Beliefs are neither public nor abstract; they are concrete particulars that belong to agents just like arms, headaches, and bouts of the flu. A belief comes into existence when an agent forms it; it is not the sort of thing that is around for the agent to adopt. Agents believe the same thing, a proposition p, when each has a belief with p as its content. This is not an analysis of reports of "believing the same thing"—which are not always so simple to unpack—but a clarification of what we mean by objects of belief.

To countenance beliefs as particulars is not to deny that there are interesting systems of abstract objects which might be used to classify them, such as meanings, Fregean senses, intensions, characters, or the like. But in addition to having these abstract features, beliefs, like other concrete particulars, have lots of other features, both intrinsic and relational, many of which can in some cases be relevant to explaining how we talk about beliefs in belief reports. In particular, we often exploit facts about the causes and effects of beliefs, a point to which we shall return.

There are a number of reasons to allow ourselves to speak of particular beliefs, rather than just of a belief relation between a person and an abstract object of some kind. There is, first, the attraction of having entities that can occupy causal roles with respect to perception, reasoning, and action. As Jerry Fodor and others have argued at length, structured concrete particulars or "token" mental entities go a long way toward explaining the roles of belief, desire, and so on in cognition. There is, second, the fact that the most plausible statements of materialist intuitions about the mind are formulated in terms of particular mental entities. And, third, there is the problem that belief puzzles repeatedly have emphasized: it seems that, for any natural way of classifying beliefs with abstract objects, we can find examples in which a single agent, at a single time, is belief-related to one such abstract object twice over. These are cases, we would like to be able to say, in which an agent, at a time, has two beliefs classified by the same sense, meaning, or whatever. Classifying beliefs only with abstract meanings, senses, and so on is like classifying drops of water only with intrinsic properties. Kant argued against Leibniz that intrinsic properties of particulars will not always provide us with sufficient material for their individuation. Kant took it as obvious that there can be two exactly similar drops of water; the puzzle cases make it clear that there can be two beliefs sharing the abstract features which one or another theory of belief claims to be central.[7]

Beliefs, then, are particulars that bear complex causal relations to an agent's perceptions, actions, and other cognitive structures and abilities. The story of the causal properties of beliefs will be closely bound to the story of how and why beliefs can be classified with propositional content. A belief constrains an agent's reasoning and action in a way that is conducive, if the belief's content is true, to the agent's getting what she wants.

The ground-level facts behind belief are simply the facts of agents having beliefs. There is a basic relation $B(a, b, t)$ that holds of an agent, a belief, and a time just in case b is a belief that belongs to the agent a at time t.

Normally, a belief has a propositional content. So there is a partial function $\text{Content}(b, t)$ that, for a belief b and time t at which b exists, yields the content of b. The content of a belief will be determined by the "internal" structural properties of the belief plus its real connections to things and circumstances in the world and to the agent's other cognitive structures and abilities.

If an agent a at time t has as an object of belief the proposition p, then there is a belief b such that:

$$B(a, b, t) \ \& \ \text{Content}(b, t) = p.$$

So much is all that is really needed for a theory of belief adequate for a broad explanation of the doxastic puzzle cases, and so we are tempted to stick with just the minimal theory of beliefs given so far. The minimal theory is compatible with a wide class of views about beliefs, about propositions (or contents), and about central issues in theories of representation, practical reasoning, and inference. The crucial features of the semantics we give for belief reports, and the resulting solutions for the troubling cases, are therefore to some degree theory-neutral. But we want to present a slightly more detailed, if still simple-minded, theory of beliefs which satisfies the demands of the minimal theory and which yields a sufficiently rich account of just how the puzzling belief reports work.

Beliefs are structured entities that contain ideas and notions as constituents. Ideas and notions, like beliefs, are on our view concrete cognitive particulars. So there is no such thing as agents having the same idea or notion, but only similar ones. Admittedly, the technical use we make of these terms involves a departure from what we ordinarily say about 'ideas' and 'notions', or at least represents a choice among the many different ordinary uses of these terms. On our use of the terms, there are no notions and ideas that agents do not have, any more than there

---

[7] For a fuller defense of the particularity of beliefs, see Crimmins, *Talk about Beliefs*, Ph.D. dissertation, Stanford University, 1989.

are headaches that no one has. The difference between notions and ideas is the difference between an agent's "ways of thinking" about individuals versus properties. The properties and things of which ideas and notions are ideas and notions we call their *contents*. We shall explain in a moment how the contents of ideas and notions help determine the contents of beliefs.

What determines the content of an idea or notion? For example, what is it about Miles's notion of the poorly dressed boy which causes it to be a notion of Edward as opposed to another boy? The crucial fact is that it was Edward with whom Miles was confronted when he formed this notion. Edward played the right part in the causal origin of the notion; the notion was formed in order to keep track of information about Edward—that is, what makes him its content. So the content of an idea can depend on its external properties, like facts about its origin. The very same notion might have been a notion of a different person, had someone other than Edward figured in its origin.

There is a close parallel between this view of the contents of ideas and causal views of the semantics of names. A speaker can refer to an individual with a name, it is held, because that individual figured, in the right way, in the speaker's adoption of the name as a tool of reference.[8]

The content of an idea is not always fixed once for all by facts about the circumstances of the idea's origin. Some ideas are *context-sensitive*, in that their contents change with changes in the agent's circumstances. The context sensitivity of ideas is analogous to that of demonstratives in language. David Kaplan[9] has proposed that there is associated with each demonstrative a *character*, a function that specifies how the content of a demonstrative depends on the circumstances surrounding its use. The content of a use of the word 'you', for example, is the person being addressed in the circumstances of the utterance. Analogously, an agent a may have an idea I_{addr} of "being the one I am addressing." The property which is the content of this idea changes with changes in circumstances as follows:

> In any circumstances in which a person b is being addressed by a, the content of a's idea I_{addr} is the property of being b.

Undoubtedly, each of us has a "you" idea, the content of which is determined functionally in this way. We do not share ideas, but we have ideas with the same *semantic role*. An idea's semantic role is the function that determines the idea's content based on the agent's circumstances. Semantic roles for ideas are a bit like characters of expressions; some ideas have semantic roles that are context-sensitive, others have semantic roles that are constant functions—their contents do not vary with changes in context.

---

[8] A speaker can adopt a name (like 'John') more than once, to refer to what may be different individuals. Each such adoption creates a type of use to which the speaker may put the name. So a causal analysis of names should look not at names themselves, but at types of uses of names, as the things for which reference is determined causally. An agent may use 'John' to refer either to John Dupre or to John Etchemendy. What individuates these distinct types of uses of the name 'John'? One answer is that the types of uses of 'John' are tied to distinct notions in the agent.

[9] See "Demonstratives," 1977 manuscript reprinted in *Themes from Kaplan*.

So there are two ways in which an agent's external circumstances might be relevant to determining the content of an idea. First, the facts surrounding the origin of the idea may fix its content once for all. Second, the idea's semantic role may be sensitive to changes in the agent's circumstances—the content of the idea may vary from occasion to occasion. So an idea may exhibit origin sensitivity, context sensitivity, or both.

Miles's idea of red is certainly not context-sensitive. It may be deemed origin-sensitive, whether one supposes that his idea stands for red innately, or because of some original assignment of ideas to colors early in Miles's life. Miles's idea of being past, in contrast, stands for different properties as his life unfolds; at each time t, this idea stands for the property of occurring before t. This idea is certainly context-sensitive, and may or may not be origin-sensitive. And Miles's notion of Prince Edward, formed upon hearing of the new-born Prince, is origin-sensitive, but it is not context-sensitive.

Notions are the things in the mind that stand for things in the world. A notion is a part of each of a collection of beliefs[10] (and of other mental structures, such as desires and intentions) that are internally about the same thing. This is not a definition of 'notion', but just a central fact about notions-sharing a notion is what it is for beliefs to be internally about the same thing. An agent may occasionally (and will in many of the examples) have several notions of a single individual. This can happen in two ways. First, in cases of misrecognition and "failure to place," an agent may have two notions of an individual which he does not link or connect; such an agent is guilty of no internal inconsistency. But also an agent can retain two notions of an individual, while linking them, in the way one does when one recognizes that "two" of one's acquaintances are actually a single individual. Why might two notions be retained when such a recognition takes place? One reason for this would be to allow the possibility of easy revision in case the "recognition" was in error. But an agent can also burn his bridges and merge two notions into a single notion. Two beliefs, then, can be internally about the same thing in two ways: by sharing a notion, and by containing notions that are linked.

For the purposes of this paper, we assume that each belief involves a single k-ary idea and a sequence of k notions.[11] To represent the structure of such a belief, we write:

$$\text{Structure } (b) = \langle \text{Idea}^k, \text{Notion}_1, \ldots, \text{Notion}_k \rangle.$$

Each belief has as its content the proposition that the objects its notions are of have the property or stand in the relation, that its idea is of:

$$\text{Content}(b, t) = \langle\langle \text{Of}(\text{Idea}^k, t); \text{Of}(\text{Notion}_1, t), \ldots, \text{Of}(\text{Notion}_k, t)\rangle\rangle$$

---

[10] There is no mystery as to how a single thing can be a part of many different things at the same time (and at different times). One way, for example, be a member of many different committees or clubs.

[11] This is to consider only beliefs of a certain kind of composition. In a more thorough presentation, a discussion of other kinds of belief structures, perhaps including general beliefs and complex beliefs, might be called for—although the logical connectives and quantifiers can be accommodated within this simple structure. Also, we have chosen to ignore in this paper many subtleties of time and tense.

The structures of beliefs are individuated not simply by the ideas and notions involved in them, but also by which argument places of the ideas the various notions fill. Thus the order of the notions in our representation of the structure of the belief reflects an assignment of notions to the argument places of the associated idea.

To be clear about the relation between beliefs and their contents, we need to introduce some new concepts.

A belief b associates an idea I with a notion n at an argument place pl:

$$\text{Associates}(b, I, n, pl)$$

The belief that Tom fired Mary and the belief that Mary fired Tom differ in which places are associated with which notions, even though the ideas and notions involved are the same.

An argument place of an idea is intimately connected with an argument role of the relation which is the content of the idea, and so with an argument role in the content of the beliefs of which the idea forms a part.[12] If we were to consider complex cases, spelling out this relationship might be a matter of some delicacy, but we shall take it to be straightforward here. We shall say that an argument place pl_I of an idea I generates an argument role r_p of a proposition p (an example below will make this clearer):

$$\text{Generates}(pl_I, r_p)$$

Finally, a notion is responsible for which object occupies an argument role of the content of a belief, when the belief associates it with an idea at the argument place which generates the argument role in the content of the belief:

$$\text{Responsible}(n, r, b) \Leftrightarrow_{def} \exists I, pl \text{ Associates}(b, I, n, pl), \text{ and Generates}(pl, r)$$

When a notion in a belief is responsible for filling an argument role of the belief's content, it fills the role with its own content, the object of which the notion is a notion.

To give an example: Arthur's belief that Yvain smote Kay involves Arthur's idea for smiting, I_s, and his two notions of Yvain and Kay, call these n_Y and n_K. The idea I_s has two argument places, one (pl_+) for the smiter and one (pl_-) for the smitten. In Arthur's belief (call it b), the notion n_Y is associated with argument place pl_+ of I_s, and n_K is associated with pl_-. The content of b is the proposition p, where:

$$p = \langle\langle\text{Smote; Yvain, Kay}\rangle\rangle$$

The relation "smote" has two argument roles, one (r_+) for the smiter and one (r_-) for the smitten; these are also argument roles of the proposition p. In p, Yvain fills r_+ and Kay fills r_- of the "smote" relation. Since b associates pl_+ with n_Y, and pl_+ (the smiter in I_s) generates r_+ (the smiter in p), we say that, in b, n_Y is responsible for filling r_+ in p. Arthur's notion of Yvain is responsible in b for determining who

---

[12] Roughly, an argument role of a relation is also an argument role of a proposition (at least) when, in that proposition, the role of the relation is occupied by an object.

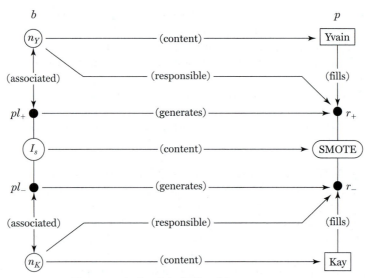

Figure 1: Arthur's belief and its content.

fills the argument role r_+ in p. And n_Y provides its content, Yvain, to fill that argument role. Figure 1 should make this clear.

Notions and ideas are key figures in our commonsense "folk" model of cognition. The recurring appearance in philosophy of such things as concepts, senses, ways of thinking, names in a language of thought, mental file folders, and other such devices reflects a firm intuition about the mind, namely, that having beliefs about an individual means having beliefs involving an internal something that is one's cognitive "fix" on the individual. As we have said, we think the correct way to express this intuition demands reference to cognitive particulars that are involved in beliefs, desires, and so on. Now, this leaves a great deal open about just what kinds of thing our notions and ideas are. For all we have said, notions and ideas might be—or might have been—particular words in a language of thought, physical objects like file folders, or things with more of a dispositional character, like the process underlying the disposition of an agent to have a specific "pattern of neural activation" in certain circumstances. And, whichever of these kinds of thing our notions and ideas are, they certainly may be classifiable with senses, property clusters, intensions, and so on. We want our "notions and ideas" to capture what is in common among all these very different models of cognition: there are things shared by different beliefs which explain the internal way in which beliefs must be about the same object or property.

On this theory, one can have two beliefs with exactly the same content or with diametrically opposed contents, such that there is no significant causal relation between them—because they involve different notions. This is a feature of all of the problematic examples that we shall consider. There is nothing particularly puzzling about this—and in fact there is nothing particularly puzzling about any of the examples that we discuss, so long as we simply consider the beliefs and not the reporting of them. Nevertheless, it is a good idea to go over the examples in some detail, for it is these details which our semantic account pays more attention to than others of which we know.

Consider the Prince and the Pauper. Miles Hendon has two notions of Edward Tudor. They have quite different circumstances of origin. One Miles has had for a long time. It is associated (in his beliefs) with his ideas as being a Prince of England, being named 'Edward Tudor', being rich, not being a pauper, not looking like a pauper, not being likely to run into (me) on an average day, and the like. The beliefs with this notion as a constituent influence Miles's behavior when confronted with ordinary sorts of information about Edward Tudor. When he reads an article in the *Times*, for example, it is beliefs with this notion as a constituent which are affected.

His other notion was formed when he saw Edward being set upon by an angry mob—angry because Edward, dressed in rags, had been proclaiming himself to be Prince. This notion is associated with ideas of being out of his mind, being dressed like a pauper, and not being of royal blood. The beliefs involving this notion, and not those involving his old notion of Edward Tudor, influence Miles's behavior toward Edward and Edward's assertions during the period he is associated with him as a comrade, until that point, toward the end of the story, when Miles merges his two notions and comes to believe that Edward the pauper is Edward the Prince.

Perhaps the ultimate doxastic puzzle case is Mark Richard's[13] puzzle about the woman in the telephone booth:

> Consider A—a man stipulated to be intelligent, rational, a competent speaker of English, etc.—who both sees a woman, across the street, in a phone booth, and is speaking to a woman through a phone. He does not realize that the woman to whom he is speaking—B, to give her a name—is the woman he sees. He perceives her to be in some danger—a run-away steamroller, say, is bearing down upon her phone booth. A waves at the woman; he says nothing into the phone (*ibid.*, p. 439).

The man has two distinct, unlinked notions of the woman. Via one, he believes that she is in danger. This is the notion which arose in virtue of his visual perception of her, and which is associated with an idea of being in grave danger. It is this notion which is involved in the beliefs that motivate his waving out the window. The second notion is an older one, assuming the woman is an old acquaintance. It is associated with an idea of being the person addressed, and not associated with ideas of being the person seen or being in danger. Hence, the beliefs involving this notion do not motivate a warning.

Let us return to Kripke's case. Pierre has the same misfortune as Miles and the man on the phone: he has two notions of the same thing. He has one notion of London which is linked to his memories of the stories and to his use of the word 'Londres'. He has another, unconnected notion of London which is influenced by

---

[13] "Direct Reference and Ascriptions of Belief," *Journal of Philosophical Logic,* XII (1983):425–452.

his perceptions and memories about his present surroundings and which influences his use of the word 'London'. He has a belief associating the former notion with his idea of being pretty, but has no belief associating the latter notion with this idea. In fact, Pierre associates an idea of being ugly with the latter notion.

II

Our basic idea is simple: a belief report claims that an agent has a belief with a certain content. But the basic idea, unembellished, will not allow us to hold the family of views we want to defend. For (2) and (2′) would claim that Miles Hendon had at least one belief with the content

$$\langle\langle\text{Being of royal blood; Edward Tudor}\rangle\rangle$$

while (1) and (1′) would deny this—thus contradicting our truth intuitions and the doctrine of opacity.

But our embellishment is also simple. When we report beliefs, there is always some further condition that a belief with the specified content is claimed to meet. The belief report is true, only if a belief meeting that further condition has the right content. What may be novel is our insistence that this additional requirement is part of the proposition expressed by the belief report. Thus, it is a condition on the truth, not merely the felicity, of the report.

Consider (1). In context, (1) provides an explanation of why Miles Hendon did not treat someone he was looking at in a certain way—a way that would have been compulsory for Miles, given the status of that person. We are interested in the content of only those beliefs which motivated Miles's behavior, the beliefs which involve the notion of Edward which arose when Miles saw him being threatened and which explain Miles's treatment of him. The existence of such a notion is clear from the description of the incident. We know that Miles is perceiving Edward and interacting with him on the basis of what he, Miles, perceives. Our view is that, in reporting beliefs, we quite often are talking about such notions, although our belief reports do not explicitly mention them. The general solution to the puzzles is to allow a condition on particular beliefs, over and above a content condition, to be part of the claim made. The version of this strategy we shall pursue here is to take this further condition always to be a specification of the notions that are supposed to be involved in the ascribed belief.

We shall say that a notion that a belief report is about is an *unarticulated constituent* of the content of the report—it is a propositional constituent that is not explicitly mentioned. We shall distinguish another kind of belief report, and say more about the notion of unarticulated constituents in a moment. But first let us see what the semantics of this sort of belief report looks like.

From our account of beliefs, we have the following concepts:

$B(a, b, t)$: b is a belief that belongs to agent a at time t.

Content(b, t) = p: p is the content of belief b at time t.

Responsible(n, r, b): $\exists I, pl$ Associates (b, I, n, pl), and Generates(pl, r).

We take a belief report to be an utterance u of a belief sentence of the form:

A believes that S

where A is a singular term and S is a sentence. We assume a semantics for the use of the embedded sentence, so that $Con(u_s)$ (the content of u_s) is the proposition expressed by the subutterance of u corresponding to S.[14] Where u is a belief report at t which is about notions $n_1, \ldots, n_k$, and $p = Con(u_s)$,

$$Con(u) = \exists b[B(a, b, t) \wedge \text{Content}(b, t) = p \wedge$$

$$\bigwedge_{r\text{in}p} \text{Responsible } (n_i, r_i, b)]$$

The claim made by the belief report is that the agent a[15] has a belief with the content p, involving the notions $n_1, \ldots, n_k$ (in a certain way).[16] This claim entails the proposition that a has a belief with the content p, but the truth of that proposition is not sufficient for the truth of the report—the report says more than that about the ascribed belief.

We shall say in such cases that the notions that the belief report is about are *provided* by the utterance and its context. Note that the provided constituents of the report's content are not existentially quantified.

---

[14] In accord with our simple version of "semantic innocence," we assume throughout that a belief report specifies the content of the ascribed belief by providing a sentence with the same content, as uttered in the report. The puzzle cases that we consider seem to be ones for which this assumption is correct. There are good reasons, however, to think that things do not always work this way. One way of analyzing, "Barbara believes that the Twin Towers are over a foot tall," would involve quantification over contents of beliefs. Other cases of reporting implicit and tacit beliefs might well work similarly. Another case in which a proposition might be "quantified out" is in the use of, "He believes that Russell's yacht is longer than it is." Also, one can use, "Timmy believes that the Tooth Fairy will make him rich," knowing full well that the embedded sentence does not express any proposition (if in fact it does not). These and other cases make us wary of insisting that a content proposition is always specified in a belief report. The present strategy can be extended in relatively simple ways to account for such cases.

[15] Yet another simplification: we ignore the fact the many uses of singular terms, including terms in the subject position of belief sentences, are not directly referential. "Attributive" uses of definite descriptions really should be handled differently. Note also that we really should treat the idea in a belief in the same way we treat notions here; though the puzzles considered here do not turn on this, others certainly do.

[16] Here one major difference from the "official" belief-report semantics in ch. 10 of Perry's *Situations and Attitudes* (p. 256) is apparent. There, a belief report is true if the agent has any belief with the specified content. There is a further crucial difference that is not so obvious. Barwise and Perry countenance beliefs as real, concrete things, as we do here. But these beliefs are represented as situations of an agent being related to an anchored belief schema. Belief schemas are abstract objects in which what we have called notions are represented by indeterminates. Although the way this all works is quite complicated, in the end beliefs are individuated by belief schemas—abstract objects—and the things in the world to which the indeterminates in the schemas are anchored. But indeterminates are not notions, and, we think, relations to anchored belief schemas are not quite fine-grained enough to individuate beliefs in the ways needed for belief reports. So we suggest two major changes to the account in *Situations and Attitudes:* we give ourselves the theoretical machinery to talk about notions and ideas directly; we then claim that these things are among the subject matter of belief reports (via the mechanism of unarticulated constituents), and are not merely quantified over.

Let us see how this theory works with Miles, Edward, and our intelligent reader. We take our reader to be talking about n_{vis}, the notion Miles acquires of Edward from visually perceiving him on the occasion of the rescue. $Con(u_S)$ is just the proposition $\langle\langle$Being of royal blood; Edward$\rangle\rangle$. So our reader is saying with (1) that there is no belief that associates Miles's idea of the property of being of royal blood with Miles's notion n_{vis}. He is not contradicting any proposition that Miles has some other notion of Edward Tudor which is so associated.

And, in fact, a proposition of this latter kind might be just what our reader intends to claim with (2). Imagine the case in which he reads that Miles Hendon is shouting, while treating Edward as a mad fool, "Prince Edward is a man of royal blood, you fool, who would not dress in rags." Our reader might intend to say, of the notion involved in the beliefs that motivate this behavior, that is both is of Edward Tudor and is associated with the idea of being of royal blood.

If so, our reader would surely be consistent, direct, and innocent. On the one hand, the proposition he in turn denies and affirms Miles's belief in is just the singular proposition that contemporary theories of direct reference assign to the utterances of "Edward Tudor is of royal blood" and "He is of royal blood" in the described contexts. On the other, the denial and affirmation are completely consistent.

III

We have claimed that, in belief reports, an n-ary relation is reported with an n-minus-one-place predicate. On our account, the complex relation invoked in belief reports is a four-place relation: an agent believes a proposition at a time relative to a sequence of notions. But there is no argument place in the 'believes' predicate for the sequence of notions. The notions are unarticulated constituents of the content of the report.

Propositions have constituents. The proposition that Yvain smote Kay has Kay as a constituent—Kay himself is in that claim. When Arthur says, "Yvain smote Kay," there is no great mystery about why Kay, rather than someone else, is part of the claim Arthur makes: Arthur uses the name 'Kay', which, as he uses it, refers to Kay. Kay is the content of Arthur's utterance of 'Kay'. This is what it is to be an articulated constituent of the content of a statement.

It is very common in natural languages for a statement to exploit unarticulated constituents. When we consider the conditions under which such a statement is true, we find it expresses a proposition that has more constituents in it than can be traced to expressions in the sentence that was spoken. Each constituent of the content which is not itself the content of some expression in the sentence is an unarticulated constituent of the content of the statement.

We report the weather, for example, as if raining and snowing and sleeting and dark of night were properties of times, but they are one and all relations between times and places. If I say, "It is raining," you understand me as claiming that it rains at that time at some place the context supplies. It often is, but need not be, the place of utterance. If I am talking to a friend in Kansas City on the phone, or watching news reports about the continuing floods in Berkeley, you may understand me to be talking about those places rather than the place where we both are.

The phenomenon of unarticulated constituency is similar to that of indexicality in the reliance on context. But the two phenomena should not be conflated. If we say, "It's raining *here*," an expression in our statement identifies the place. The place is articulated in a context-sensitive way. In the case of indexicals, expression and context share in the job of identifying the constituent, according to the conventional meaning or character of the indexical. In a case of underarticulation, there is no expression to determine the constituent in this way.

It would be misleading, however, to say that, in the case of unarticulated constituents, the context alone does the job. The whole utterance—the context and the words uttered—is relevant to identifying the unarticulated constituent. Thus, a change in wording can affect the unarticulated constituent, even though it is not a change in an expression that designates that constituent. Suppose I am in Palo Alto talking on the phone to someone in London; we both know that it is morning in Palo Alto and evening in London. If I say, "It's exactly 11 A.M.," I will be taken to be talking about the time in Palo Alto; if I had said, in the same context, "It's exactly 8 P.M.," I would be taken to be talking about the time in London.

The important principle to be learned is that a change in wording can precipitate a change in propositional constituents, even when the words do not stand for the constituents.

Unarticulated constituency is one example of the incrementality of language. In the circumstances of an utterance, there always is a great deal of common knowledge and mutual expectation that can and must be exploited if communication is to take place. It is the function of the expression uttered to provide just the last bit of information needed by the hearer to ascertain the intended claim, exploiting this rich background. What is obvious in context we do not belabor in syntax—we do not articulate it.

This is by no means to transgress the intuition of the systematicity of language which is commonly reflected in principles of "compositionality." Since we finite creatures are able to make and understand a potential infinity of claims, there must be systematic features of our statements which explain our infinite abilities in something like a combinatorial fashion—in terms of our more finite abilities to understand the contributions of specific features of statements toward the claims made. But there is no reason to assume that these features of statements must all involve syntactic expressions. It is just as systematic for a form of speech, like a belief report or a report of rain, to *call for* a propositional constituent that meets, say, certain conditions of relevance and salience, as it is for a form of speech to have a syntactic expression *stand for* a propositional constituent.[17]

Consider our practices of reporting velocity. A claim that an object is moving at a certain velocity makes sense only if it is understood with respect to what the velocity is to be assessed. We say that velocity is relative to an observer, or a frame of reference—we must count something as stationary. But we articulate this additional

---

[17] For more on unarticulated constituents, see Perry, "Thought without Representation," *Proceedings of the Aristotelian Society*, suppl. vol. LX (1986):263–283. There, a systematic semantics for some underarticulated constructions is given, which is connected to a recursive model of syntax in the usual way.

parameter of velocity claims only when it is not obvious what is to count as stationary. We have in English a number of general-purpose constructions for articulating commonly suppressed constituents of a claim. We say, 'with respect to . . .' or 'relative to . . .' or 'in the sense that . . . '. The more likely the unarticulated constituent is to be unclear, the more likely it is that we have a natural way to articulate it.

In the case of belief reports, in which notions are unarticulated, we do have rough and ready ways to clarify just which notions we mean to talk about. We say, for instance, that Miles believes that Edward is a peasant in one way—the way related to the boy in front of him, not in the way related to the Prince. Or we add to the report, "that is, he thinks the boy in front of him, who really is Edward, is a peasant." Or we specify how Miles would or would not "put" his belief. Or we allude to the evidence which led Miles to form the belief, or to the actions it would be likely to bring about. Each of these devices can succeed in distinguishing among the two notions which in context can seem equally relevant, thus eliminating possible confusion about which notion we mean to talk about.

We do not, of course, have a very direct way of specifying the notions we mean to talk about in belief reports. This is due to the fact that it is almost always obvious which notion a speaker is talking about. Where it is not, we either use one of the devices just mentioned, or leave the language of belief reporting altogether and talk instead about what the agent would say or would do.

IV

Unarticulated constituency and direct reference are of a single stripe. In fact, if we take the term 'reference' in the ordinary sense in which it does not require a referring expression, unarticulated constituency can be seen to result from a kind of direct reference-perhaps "tacit" reference. When a speaker claims that "it's raining," she is referring to a place and not to a description of, nor a condition on, a place. In the same way, on our view, a belief reporter refers to an agent's notions. We have chosen not to talk this way in our official account only to avoid being read as claiming that notions are referred to by the reporter's words.

A difficult issue facing all views of direct reference, and ours in particular, is the need to make sense of intuitions about truth and falsity in cases of reference failure. This problem is especially acute for our account in some cases of denials. Consider the following example. A blind man is facing in the direction of a distant building. Someone, unaware of the man's blindness, says, "He believes that that building is far away." One normally would take this report to be about the notion the man has as a result of his current visual perception of the building. The speaker is trying to refer (though not with a word) to such a notion, to provide such a notion for the report to be about. But of course there is no such notion in this case. Is this report false, or, owing to a failure of tacit reference, does it fail to express a proposition? Certainly, we ordinarily would respond not by saying, "You have failed to express a proposition," but "He doesn't believe that"—and we have the strong intuition that this denial would be true.

Compare the following case: an astronaut on the moon[18] says, "It's three o'clock." Typically, this sentence would be used to express the claim that it is three o'clock in Z, where Z is the time zone in which the utterance takes place. The confused astronaut thinks that there are time zones on the moon, and he intends to claim that it is three o'clock in "Z," which is the time zone he is in. But there is no such time zone. So he fails to express a proposition. We feel no qualms, however, about denying his claim: "It's not three o'clock. There are no time zones on the moon, you. . . ."

The present difficulties are often discussed in connection with "negative existential" claims. But the same issues arise with respect to all sorts of denials in which the speaker believes there to be reference failure. A child who sincerely asserts, "Santa will come tonight," fails to refer, and therefore, on most direct reference accounts, fails to express a proposition. But the parent who responds, "Santa will not come tonight," explaining that there is no Santa, makes what seems to be a true claim, despite the fact that the use of 'Santa' does not refer.

Note that these examples would present no trouble for descriptional theories of reference. For if in these cases the original speakers are seen, not as attempting to provide a specific thing to be a propositional constituent, but merely as claiming that there is a thing meeting a certain condition (being the generous elf known as 'Santa', being the local time zone, or being the man's perceptual notion of the building), then the claims are straightforwardly false and the denials are true.

The descriptional theories have even more than this kind of extensional correctness going for them; it is because the cited conditions—call them *providing conditions*—are not satisfied that the denials are true. In the child's use of 'Santa', the providing condition, of being the generous elf known as 'Santa', plays a central semantic role, even though it is not the referent of the child's use of the name. It is a condition that the child expects to be filled as a precondition of successful reference. He expects to refer successfully to a thing in virtue of its meeting the providing condition. His supposed ability to refer to a thing by using the name 'Santa' depends on the condition's being satisfied. Similarly, the astronaut takes it that he can talk directly about a time zone, that he can provide one, because it meets the providing condition of being the local time zone. And, we claim, the belief reporter expects to be able to talk directly about a notion because it satisfies the condition of being the man's perceptual notion of the building.[19]

A normal, successful case of direct reference involves a speaker referring to an object in virtue of that object's satisfying a providing condition. Reference failure involves failure of a presupposition, namely, the presupposition that a providing condition is satisfied. Now, expressions like proper names and underarticulated phrases that normally invoke devices of direct reference are sometimes used where

---

[18]John Etchemendy brought up this version of Wittgenstein's example.

[19]Just which providing conditions are invoked in a given case depends on a wide range of circumstances. Also, there usually is more than one such condition for a given use of a term. Providing conditions for a use u of 'here' by speaker A at location l, for instance, includes the conditions of being the location of the utterer of u, being where A is, and being l. In the 'Santa' case, we have the conditions of being the referent of the utterance of 'Santa', being the relevant thing known as 'Santa', being the generous elf known as 'Santa', and so on.

there is no presupposition that the relevant providing conditions are satisfied. The denials in the cases of the blind man, the astronaut, and Santa are like this. In each of these denials, the speaker does not presuppose that there is a thing meeting the providing condition that is invoked by the utterance. Instead, we claim, the speaker *raises the providing condition to constituency*—he talks about the condition itself rather than about a supposed thing that meets it. The providing condition now plays a semantic role—as a constituent of the proposition expressed in the denial—more central than its usual auxiliary role of providing a propositional constituent.

In particular, the claim expressed by 'Santa will not come tonight' (in the described circumstances)[20] is to the effect that there is no generous elf known as "Santa" who will come tonight. And the proposition expressed by 'It is not three o'clock' is that there is no local time zone such that it is three o'clock there. And the content of 'He does not believe that that building is far away' is the claim that there is no perceptual notion of the building such that the man has a belief involving that notion, with the content that the building is far away. The denials are thus true, and their truth is consistent with our claim that the assertions they deny strictly speaking fail to make claims.

Of course, for each of the original, claimless assertions, there is a proposition closely related to the kind of proposition the speaker intends to express, which we can for most purposes charitably treat as the content of the statement. Specifically, we can take the speaker to have expressed the claim that there is a thing meeting the invoked providing condition, such that so-and-so. In fact, the speaker of such an assertion is pre-assertively committed to this proposition, in virtue of his commitment to the presuppositions that must be satisfied if he is to make a successful claim in the way he intends.

Above we analyzed our reader's utterance of (2) in an imaginary case in which Miles has been shouting about the Prince. In fact, Miles was not shouting, "Edward Tudor is of royal blood," at the time he encountered the boy. The reader actually has no specific actions on Miles's part to which he can tie such a notion of Prince Edward. It is obvious from the general tenor of the novel, however, that Miles would have such a notion. Every full-witted adult in England at the time has a notion of Prince Edward—one they acquired shortly after he was born which motivates their behavior in regard to the Prince of Wales, such as their use of the phrase 'Prince Edward', their decorum when the royal procession goes by, and the like. Our reader may not be able to pick out anything very specific in Miles's behavior to serve as evidence that he has such a normal notion of the Prince. But he has every right to suppose that he has one.[21]

---

[20]In circumstances where it is presupposed that the providing condition is met, the denial expresses just the negation of the proposition (if there is one) expressed by the corresponding assertion.

[21]What counts as being a normal notion certainly depends, we think, not only on what is common in a community, but also on other aspects of the background of the discourse, including facts about what is relevant to the goals of the discourse. We would expect an account of "being a normal notion" to exhibit many of the same features as an appropriate account of "knowing who *b* is," which certainly is background-sensitive in many ways. See, for example, Böer and Lycan, *Knowing Who* (Cambridge: MIT, 1985).

It may seem implausible to suppose that our reader, in using (2), can directly provide a notion for the report to be about, since the reader is not directly acquainted with such a notion. If this intuition is right—an assumption we shall question in a minute—our machinery gives us a natural way of respecting it: this is a case in which, instead of a notion, a providing condition becomes a propositional constituent. What our reader is claiming with (2) is that there is some normal notion via which Miles believes that Edward is royal; that is, the condition of being a normal notion of the Prince is the unarticulated constituent. The report, on this construal, is an example of a second kind of belief report—in which notions are not provided, but instead are constrained by provided conditions; the report is about those conditions in the sense of "about" appropriate to propositional constituents.

For this (supposed) second kind of belief report we can give the following account. Where u is a belief report at t which is about conditions $C_1, \ldots, C_k$, and $p = Con(u_s)$, where u_s is the subutterance of u corresponding to the object sentence S,

$$Con(u) = \exists b[B\,(a,\,b,\,t) \wedge \text{Content}\,(b,\,t) = p\,\wedge$$

$$\exists n_i, \ldots, n_k \wedge {}_{r_i inp}\,(C_i(n_i) \wedge \text{Responsible}\,(n_i,\,r_i,\,b))]$$

So we have room in our framework for two sorts of belief report, corresponding to whether notions are themselves *provided* or merely *constrained* by conditions. Supposing for now that there really are two kinds of belief report, how can we know, for a given report, of which kind it is? One way, surely, is to look at what would happen if the appropriate notions were to fail to exist. If the report would then be false, then it is a case of notion constraint rather than provision; if the report would fail to make a claim, then it is a case of (attempted) notion provision.

Of course, we have seen how, in a case where an attempt to provide a notion fails, a proposition closely related to what the speaker is trying to express takes center stage. This is the false proposition to the effect that the agent has a notion which meets the invoked providing condition and which is involved in a belief with such-and-such content. Given this fact, our intuitions about whether a belief report fails to make a claim or is simply false are in the same boat as our intuitions about the truth value of the child's claim that Santa is coming. The falsity of the closely related propositions, plus the truth of the natural denials of these statements, may well obscure intuitions about the truth of the original claims.

In this paper, we adopt officially the position that there really are belief reports of the second kind (which are about conditions rather than notions). Given our points about providing conditions and propositions to which speakers are pre-assertively committed in cases of direct reference, however, a plausible case can be mounted for the view that, in all successful belief reports, specific notions are provided for the report to be about.[22]

---

[22]This view is argued in Crimmins, *Talk about Beliefs*, though in the end the argument rests precariously on the fact that none of the examples considered as natural candidates for reports of the "second kind" seems clearly to be as required.

Assuming, now, that there are two classes of belief reports, there is no reason to suspect that all reports will fall clearly into one camp or the other. For example, if our reader simply assumes that Miles must have a normal notion of King Henry and expects his audience to do the same, then it makes little difference whether he claims that Miles has a belief involving that notion (notion provision) or just a belief involving a normal notion (notion constraint). Since it makes little difference, our reader need not go to any pains to indicate which of the claims he is making; his report simply can land between the two claims.[23]

v

With that out of the way, let us turn to our examples.

First, a recap of the semantics of (1) and (2). We shall treat (1) as a case of notion provision. The provided notion is Miles's notion of Edward which is connected with his perception of and actions toward Edward in the mob incident. The reader claims that Miles does not have a belief involving that notion, with the content that Edward is of royal blood.

With (2), the reader provides a condition on notions, the condition of being a normal notion of Prince Edward. The reader claims that Miles has a belief involving some normal notion of Edward, with the content that Edward is of royal blood.

In the Pierre case, the sentence (3) gets used in two reports, first in a discussion of Pierre's initial acquaintance with London through stories, then in a discussion about Pierre's thoughts of his adopted home. Call these reports u_3 and Pierre actually has two notions of London, one relevant to each discussion; call the first n and the second n'. The notion n meets the condition C of being a notion germane to the discussion of Pierre's reaction to the stories; the notion n' meets the condition C' of being a notion germane to the discussion of Pierre's new home.

If one of the two analyses is uniquely correct for u_3 and u'_3 it is perhaps the account in terms of notion constraint. The speaker of the former report is claiming that Pierre has a belief involving some notion germane to the current conversation about the stories, with the content that London is pretty. The speaker of the latter report requires that the belief involve some notion relevant to the conversation about Pierre's new home.

If the circumstances of u_3 and u'_3 are such as to make the notions n and n' clear and present to the speakers and their audiences, then the analysis should be in terms of notion provision. If this is the case, then the speaker of u_3 claims that Pierre has a belief involving the notion n with the content that London is pretty; the speaker of u'_3 claims that Pierre has a belief involving the notion n' with the

---

[23]There is another way, also, in which a report can land between the notion-provision and the notion-constraint types of report. It is not hard to concoct cases in which one notion is provided and another is constrained; a natural construal of our reader's report "Miles believed that he (Edward in rags) was less noble than Prince Edward" might go along these lines. So in the general case, both notions and conditions may be provided; there are no difficulties in formalizing this along the lines already given for the pure notion-provision and pure notion-constraint analyses.

content that London is pretty. If the circumstances of the two reports are less clear-cut, as they often are, then, as noted earlier, the claims made by the speakers might fall between those offered by the notion-provision and notion-constraint accounts. There just might be no saying.

Note, though, that any of these analyses constitutes a solution to the puzzle. The claim made in u_3 is simply true, and the claim made in u'_3 is simply false.

Kripke presents the puzzle as arising from a few very plausible principles about belief reports, including:

> Disquotation: If a normal English speaker, on reflection, sincerely assents to 'p', then he believes that p (*op. cit.*, pp. 248/9).

> Translation: If a sentence of one language expresses a truth in that language, then any translation of it into any other language also expresses a truth (*op. cit.*, p. 250).

On our account of belief reporting, neither of these principles is at all plausible in general. Each principle presupposes that it is belief sentences that are true or false. On our view, a single sentence, like (3), can be used in both true and false reports. Kripke assumes that, because of the lack of obviously context-sensitive words, (3) can be considered more or less "eternal." But words are not the only sources of context-sensitivity; the presence of unarticulated constituents also can widen the gap between a sentence and the proposition expressed by a statement of it. And that is what happens in the Pierre case.

Richard lists three sentences considered as uttered by A watching B in the phone booth:

(4) I believe she is in danger.

(5) I believe you are in danger.

(6) The man watching you believes you are in danger.

A uses (4), clearly, to make a true report. His notion n_{vis} of B which stems from his view out the window, which is associated with his idea of being in peril, and which causes his waving is supplied. It is claimed that A has a belief involving n_{vis} with the content that B is in danger. He in fact has such a belief.

The man would not sincerely use (5) over the phone; if sincere, he certainly would deny (5). The natural intuition, we think, is that a use of (5) in the described circumstances would make a false claim. (It is this reaction which Richard sets out to prove mistaken. The very possibility of our semantics shows that his proof is in error.)

The set-up for (6) is as follows. B sees a man, A, in a building across the street waving frantically. Amused, she says (over the phone), "The man watching me believes that I'm in danger." Echoing her, A utters (6). Surely, B's claim is true. And if so, A's use of (6), which is in explicit agreement with her, is true also.

So we hold that the use of (5) is false while that of (6) is true. But how can this be? The two reports are uttered by the same person in the same circumstances, they ascribe beliefs to the same agent, and they use precisely the same embedded sentence, understood in the same way! The only difference is the way in which the man is referred to-in the one case with 'I', in the other with 'the man watching you'.

Difference enough, we think. The pragmatic principle of self-ascription applies to (5) but not to (6):

> Self-Ascription: An utterance of 'I believe that . . . τ . . .' provides (or, is about) the notion that is connected to the speaker's use of 'τ'.

Using 'I' in (5), A thus directs attention to the notion (n_{phone}) that is linked to his use, in (5), of 'you'—the notion of B which is associated with his idea of being the one he is addressing[24] and not associated with his idea of being in danger. So A's use of (5) makes the claim that he has a belief involving n_{phone}, which has the content that B is in danger. He in fact has no such belief.

In (6), A is discussing those beliefs of the man watching B, that is, of A himself, which explain the frantic gestures directed at B. So he claims that the man has a belief involving n_{vis}, the notion linked to his perception out the window and his gestures of warning, which has the content that B is in danger. In fact, A has such a belief.

Richard's case is especially interesting because it shows how a contextual shift can be brought about by a change in wording outside of the embedded sentence in a belief report. This gives added force to our analysis of substitution worries: the wording changes in the usual cases of reluctance to substitute are responsible, not for changes in meaning or explicitly specified content, but for changes in what is provided by context for the reports to be about.

Our semantics allows that, for a given belief sentence, absolutely any of the agent's notions may be provided—there is no semantic restriction on what notions may be provided in a use of a given sentence. But there are many pragmatic principles, like self-ascription, that constrain which notions can be provided in the normal case. It is semantically but not pragmatically possible for a use of 'I believe I am not me' or (normally) 'S, but I do not believe that S' to be true. Although it is semantically possible, in W.V.O. Quine's example, for an utternace of 'Tom believes that Cicero is Tully' to express a true proposition (say, if Tom's 'Cicero' notion is provided twice over), there may be no very natural use of that sentence which in fact expresses the proposition (although surely we can concoct a Richard-ish example to put this point in doubt). In the normal case, the use of different names for Cicero serves as a strong, though perhaps defeasible, indication that the names have some importance to what's being said over and above just standing for Cicero. Such a difference in names requires a sufficient reason— in this case, a difference in which notions are being provided to play the corresponding roles in the ascribed belief.

---

[24]More precisely, with his idea I_{addr}, the idea that has the context-sensitive semantic role picking out the person being addressed.

VI

The relation of the present proposal to Fregean semantics for belief reports should be relatively clear. The broad similarity consists in the agreement that a belief report specifies, in addition to simply which objects the agent is claimed to have a belief about, also just how the agent is cognitively connected to those objects. On our account, the report specifies (or constrains) the particular notions allegedly involved in the belief. On a Fregean account, "senses" are specified.

Two crucial differences separate the accounts. First, we stress the particularity and unsharability of notions. Since notions are full-fledged particulars immersed in the causal order, they have a great array of different features that we can exploit to provide them in our belief reports. They are involved in beliefs, associated (sometimes) with words, formed in specific circumstances, connected to perceptual situations, reasonings, and actions; they survive the formation and abandonment of beliefs in which they are involved; and so on. We can use each of these kinds of fact to give us a handle on a notion, a way of picking it out. This frees us from a problem often noted about the Fregean strategy; it appears that, on most natural construals of what senses are, we often do not know just what sense an agent attaches to an object (we do not grasp it), and so we cannot know just what we are attributing to the agent with a belief report, which, after all, must be about the agent's ways of thinking.

As we have said, there is nothing in our view incompatible with something like Fregean senses, considered as entities which we can use to classify an agent's notions. A Fregean might well take our talk of "notions" as an account of what it takes for an agent to grasp a sense—agents grasp sense in virtue of having appropriate notions.

The second departure from a Fregean account is in our claim that the agent's ways of thinking about things (her notions), though they are specified in a belief report, are not the referents of the words occurring in the embedded sentence. This difference becomes especially important in the analysis of certain kind of reports: those with content sentences containing devices of under-articulation, and those with no content sentences at all, but which instead are completed with the likes of 'what you said', 'the same thing', and 'Church's Thesis'.

VII

The account of belief reports sketched here closes some doors. If, as we claim, a single belief sentence can be used in both true and false reports, then there can be no simple logic of such sentences. The simplest possible rule,

$$\frac{A \text{ believes that } S}{A \text{ believes that } S}$$

does not hold in general, as we learn from Kripke's puzzle.

Even a logic of belief sentences restricted to a single context will prove diffi-cult.[25] Although a relativized version of the above rule with certainly hold, this one,

$$\frac{\begin{array}{ll} A \text{ believes that } S & (\textit{relative to } c) \\ A = B & (\textit{relative to } c) \end{array}}{B \text{ believes that } S \qquad (\textit{relative to } c)}$$

will not, as we learn from Richard's puzzle.

Also closed is the prospect of a strictly compositional semantics for belief sentences. The semantic values of the subexpressions in a belief report, on our analysis, do not provide all the materials for the semantic value of the report itself. Notions and conditions on notions are not articulated, but end up in the contents of reports; so the semantics of belief reports is in an important way noncompositional.

In addition, our account denies what some have seen as a primary desidera-tum for theories of belief: that a belief report claims simply that a binary relation holds between an agent and an object of belief.

And, perhaps worst of all, we have given an account on which it appears to be next to impossible to give a complete, systematic account of which claims are made by which belief reports. We have claimed that belief reports are context-sensitive, that they invoke unarticulated constituents, without offering any gen-eral method for determining what the relevant contextual factors are, and how they give rise to these unarticulated constituents of belief reports.

Tempted as we are to view each of the above results as an insight rather than a drawback, we realize that we have abandoned many of the issues and goals com-monly pursued in this area. But we think the account opens many doors as well.

Whereas there is little possibility of an interesting logic of belief sentences, the logic of beliefs, notions, and ideas is available. Such issues as logical and ana-lytic closure of belief, explicit versus implicit belief, and inferential issues in belief change really belong to the logic of beliefs rather than to the logic of belief sen-tences. We can explore the logic of the relations we have seen as underlying our ordinary talk about beliefs—but this logic will not be a logic of ordinary language.

Of course, we have explained very little about what beliefs, notions, and ideas are. But we think our partial account of them raises obvious questions in theories of representation, action, perception, and the metaphysics of mind.

Our semantics is not compositional, but there is system in the noncomposi-tional mayhem. The ways in which notions and conditions on notions are pro-vided have yet to be explored to any great extent. But the discussions of the belief puzzles suggest several directions from which to look at these mechanisms.

---

[25] Here we mean 'context' in a sense such that various different statements can be made in the same context. One way of taking our claims in this paper would be as denying the general usefulness is semantics of such a restricted notion of context. Taken this way, we have claimed that such things as the words used in a statement can affect the semantically relevant parts of the statement's context.

Last, the move to unarticulated constituents emphasizes the importance of pragmatic facts about language to the study of what seem like purely semantic issues. In order to express claims, we exploit a tremendous variety of facts, conventions, and circumstances, of which the meanings and referents of our terms form just a part. So it is a mistake to relegate pragmatics to matters of felicity and implicature. In the case of belief reports, it is central to understanding content and truth.

ATTITUDES IN CONTEXT

Mark Richard

Why has the semantics of attitude ascription proven so difficult? Some say the fault lies in a contextual shiftiness of sentences like

(P) Pierre believes that London is expensive,

a shiftiness not evident from surface structure, and thus liable to be overlooked. On this view, different uses of (P) convey different information about Pierre's representations of London. But though the information is semantically conveyed, conveyance is not via a sentential constituent whose role is to refer to or otherwise pick out representations about which information is imparted.

I have offered a version of this view on which attitude ascription involves something like translation.[1] In (P), 'that London is expensive' is offered as a representation or translation of one of Pierre's thoughts; a use of (P) is true provided its 'that'-clause is an acceptable translation of such a thought, according to currently prevailing (and contextually shifting) standards of translation. Such standards are keyed to and shift because of our varying interests in agents' differing ways of representing the world to themselves. Thus, in context, (P) will typically be true only if Pierre holds belief using a particular kind of representation.

Another version of the view is offered by Mark Crimmins and John Perry in Crimmins and Perry (1989); it is further developed in Crimmins (1992). According to Crimmins and Perry, a use of (P) may involve "tacit reference" to Pierre's representations, the reference tacit because it is not made via constituents of (P). The representation of Pierre's referred to in a use of (P) varies as do our interests in his representations.

The accounts are different, but, one might think, not all that different. What Crimmins and Perry achieve by positing a tacit reference to a representation, one might say, Richard can achieve by positing a standard of translation involving the type of representation at issue. And vice versa. Is there a reason to prefer my translational account to the referential account, or vice versa? In Crimmins (1992b), Crimmins offers two arguments which he thinks show his account to be

---

[1] See Richard (1990). A brief sketch of the view is given in Richard (1989). Further references to these and other works occur parenthetically in the text.

preferable to mine. One is that a better account of iterated attitude ascriptions is given by taking them as involving reference to representations. The other is that, construing translation (as I do) as a relation between the sentence *type* of a 'that'-clause and the representational *types* of a believer produces mistakes about truth conditions. This objection is related to a difference between myself and Perry/Crimmins about the proper treatment of contextual sensitivity in natural language. Perry and Crimmins, in the tradition of situation semantics, see the object of semantic evaluation as a sentence token or concrete utterance; working in the tradition of Kaplan's *Demonstratives,* I take the object of semantic evalua-tion to be a sentence type, evaluated relative to a Kaplanesque context.

In this paper I respond to Crimmins' objections, and offer reasons to prefer my account of attitude ascriptions to Perry and Crimmins's account. Section 1 quickly reviews the semantics I gave in Richard (1990); Sections 2 and 3 respond to Crimmins' arguments. Section 4 sketches a modification to the framework of Richard (1990) occasioned by the complexities of iterated attitude ascriptions. Finally, Section 5 offers some reasons, having to do with the logical properties of sentences like (P), for preferring the kind of account given here and in Richard (1990) to an account like Crimmins and Perry's.

1

I take beliefs—the psychological states belief ascriptions are about—to involve sentence-like mental representations. Among the ways in which representations are sentence-like is that their parts have the sort of content that Russellians are wont to ascribe to natural language terms, predicates, and the like. If we take a (token) belief-making mental representation and pair off (the types of) its parts with their contents, the result is something along the lines of a Russellian propo-sition, each constituent of which is paired up with something that (in the proper context) represents it. Such interpreted representations seem good candidates for objects of belief. In Richard (1990) I called such representation/content pair-ings *RAM*s; a RAM that is the object of someone's belief I'll refer to as one of the person's *thoughts*.[2]

The point of a belief ascription is to tell us something about a person's thoughts. It always tells us about Russellian content, and it often tells us some-thing about the representations the believer uses to get at this content. How does an ascription do this? I think it's done by letting the words in the ascription's 'that'-clause play two roles. One role is to pick out a Russellian content: One of the things 'Tom' does in 'Jenny believes that Tom is tired' is to pick out Tom. But we also use the words in a 'that'-clause to translate or represent the representations the believer uses to realize his belief. In some uses of 'Jenny thinks that Tom is tired', 'Tom' stands proxy for one of Jenny's representations of Tom. When it does,

---

[2] Crimmins and Perry use *thoughts* for mental representations, not for pairings of these with their (contextually established) interpretations. 'RAM' is acronymous for 'Russellian annotated matrix'.

'Tom' functions as a name of Tom *and* as a translational proxy for one of Jenny's representations of Tom.

Given an ascription of attitude, we can form a RAM from its content sentence, pairing the word (types) in the sentence with their interpretations. In ascribing an attitude, I suggested in Richard (1990), we offer the RAM provided by the ascription's 'that'-clause as a "translation" of one of the believer's thoughts; the ascription is true provided the proffered RAM adequately represents or translates one of the believer's thoughts. The standards for translation shift from occasion to occasion. This explains how it is that sometimes we can truly say that Pierre thinks that London is pretty, and sometimes we cannot, though nothing about Pierre's thoughts has altered.

How does the contextual shifting of standards of translation get reflected in the semantics of attitude ascriptions? On my view, the reflection is in the meaning of the attitude verbs, which are indexical. What's said by 'Jenny believes that Tom is tired' might be made more explicit by saying 'Jenny has-a-thought-that-for-present-purposes-may-be-rendered-as-the-RAM that Tom is tired'. The hyphenated material gives a rough gloss of the attitude verb, and indicates that the content of the verb will shift, as what counts as an acceptable rendering shifts.

Context, on this view, offers constraints on translation or representation. These act as input to the meaning of 'believes'. Given such input, the verb's value in context is a relation $B(u, f, p)$ that a believer u bears to a RAM p and a "translation manual" f just in case f conforms to whatever restrictions on translation the context offers and p translates under f one of u's thoughts. If $B_c(u, f, p)$ is the content of the verb in c, then our running example is true in c iff for some f, B_c (Jenny, f, the RAM that Tom is tired).

"Translation manuals" aren't anything more, in the formalism, than functions that map word/content pairs (which go to make up the RAMs named by 'that'-clauses) to representation/content pairs (which make up thoughts). p translates q under f if we can obtain q from p by replacing parts of p with their image under f. Thus the RAM

$$\langle\langle\text{'is tired'}, \text{being tired}\rangle, \langle\text{'Tom'}, \text{Tom}\rangle\rangle$$

translates the thought

$$\langle\langle\text{Jenny's representation } j_1, \text{being tired}\rangle, \langle\text{Jenny's representation } j_2, \text{Tom}\rangle\rangle$$

under the manual f_1 that maps $\langle\text{'is tired'}, \text{being tired}\rangle$ to $\langle j_1, \text{being tired}\rangle$ and $\langle\text{'Tom'}, \text{Tom}\rangle$ to $\langle j_2, \text{Tom}\rangle$. Given that e translates r only if they have the same Russellian content, we can cheat in describing the manuals, for example describing f_1 as mapping 'is tired' to j_1 and 'Tom' to j_2.

What of the restrictions on translation offered by context? They are, I assume, keyed to individuals, and arise (in part) as a result of our interests in and attention to the ways believers represent individuals in thought and express thoughts in public. An example of such a restriction would be that an ascription to Jenny can use $\langle\text{'Tom'}, \text{Tom}\rangle$ only to represent something of the form $\langle r, \text{Tom}\rangle$, where r is the natural language name 'Tom'. Such a restriction might arise if we were trying to convey the way in which Jenny's thought is or would be expressed in her public language. For brevity I will sometimes compress the statement of such restrictions by writing things like

Jenny: 'Tom' → 'Tom'.[3]

2

To this account, Crimmins objects that

> Since what context provides is sensitive only to name-types, any two uses of the same name-type in a that-clause must be mapped to the same representation if the report is true . . . . [I]n normal contexts this seems right. But I think there are cases in which this result conflicts with strong intuitions. Consider the natural use of

> (R) He's falling for it; Cyril believes that John is John's father.

---

[3] The fact that restrictions are keyed to individuals is of course reflected in the semantic values of attitude verbs. In context c, the semantic value of 'believes' is a function that takes u, p, and f to the set of worlds w such that at w: there's a RAM q that is a thought of u's, and p represents q under f, and f conforms to every restriction c offers that is concerned with u. See Richard (1990), p. 142.

I suggested in the text that translation always preserves Russellian content (*qua* what is picked out by a meaningful expression in context), but this is not quite correct. In particular, when it comes to indexical expressions, there seems to be a continuum, as to whether preserving Russellian content in translation for attitude ascription is obligatory, optional, or at best accidental.

In some cases—terms like first person pronouns are paradigmatic—we are required to preserve content. If Lauben thinks to herself 'Ich bin eine Ärtzin', I cannot report her as thinking that *I* am a doctor. I must in this case preserve reference. Here, preservation of content is mandatory, and thus preservation of meaning, in Kaplan's sense of meaning as function from context to content (*character,* as Kaplan calls it), is usually impossible-save in the relatively unusual case where the speaker is the subject of the ascription.

In other cases, however, preservation of content seems optional; preservation of character instead is apparently permissible. Relatively non-controversial examples are provided by the adjectives 'domestic' and 'foreign', as well as the adjectival 'the local'. Suppose, for example, that I am in America, Martin is in England, and we are on the phone. Martin says "I had some domestic plonk last night; it made me dreadfully sick." I can, I think, report what Martin said by uttering either 'Martin said that he had some domestic wine' or by saying 'Martin said that he had some English wine'. Here, we can preserve character or content, though not, in this situation, both.

Finally, there are cases in which preservation of character is mandatory, and preservation of content is generally barred (save in unusual circumstances when character and content coincide across contexts). Examples are the verbs of propositional attitude. Clearly, if Lauben thinks to herself 'Gottlob glaubt, dass ich ein Mann bin', I can generally correctly report her as believing that Gottlob believes that she is a man. This is so even if her context and mine provide different restrictions on translation, and thus the verb 'believes' has in my context a quite different content from that of 'glaubt' in hers. The difference in content is no bar to the truth of my report if the sort of translation involved in attitude ascription requires that 'believes' translates r when the two share their *character,* not their Russellian content.

In Crimmins (1992), Crimmins calls this aspect of my account *ad hoc*. In Richard (1990), I failed to make the point that there is this sort of continuum of options for translating indexicals.

On Richard's account, unless Cyril is cognitively deficient or a believer in science fiction this statement is false. . . . Richard would hold that (R) is
strictly speaking false, but pragmatically okay. . . . this kind of move is mistaken for the same reason Richard rejects similar moves in the naive
Russellian approach . . . if we do not need to abandon truth intuitions, we
should hang onto them. (Crimmins (1992), 192; Crimmins's numbering has
been altered)

My view is that (R) is on all fours with things like 'Cyril believes that John is his
own father', that would also be naturally used in the sort of situations Crimmins
has in mind. As I see it, 'his own' is a 'reflexivizier", and the proposition that John
is his own father *is* one that only the cognitively deficient or believers in science
fiction believe. If this is right, then the sort of case that Crimmins's objection plays
upon is one in which *everyone* is forced to "abandon truth intuitions", since the
intuition that Cyril believes that John is his own father will be at least as strong as
the intuition that he believes that John is John's father. And as a matter of fact,
intuitions about the two beliefs seem to run roughly in tandem—if you think Cyril
has (or doesn't have) one of the beliefs, you are pretty likely to think he has (does
not have) the other.[4]

   Crimmins suggested (in correspondence) that the truth of 'Cyril believes that
John is his own father' in the sort of case at issue could be explained by granting
'his own' the power to reflexivize, but (speaking very loosely) letting the domain of
the reflexive be the entire sentence, instead of just 'John is his own father.' The
reading of 'Cyril believes that John is his own father' which Crimmins has in mind
is suggested thus

   (R1) x Cyril believes that x is x's father) John;

the reading I have in mind is suggested thus

   (R2) Cyril believes that x (x is x's father) John.[5]

Crimmins claims that by appealing to (R1), one might explain why we take 'Cyril
believes that John is his own father' to be true in a case in which we would not, on
reflection, think that Cyril has a reflexive belief. This is because on Crimmins's
view, although to believe (R1) is to have a reflexive belief, the belief in question is
not that *Cyril* has a reflexive belief.

   The problem with this response is that it does not generalize to cases that
seem perfectly parallel to the sort of case Crimmins has in mind. Consider this
variation on Crimmins's example. We have pointed out John to Cyril and said

---

[4] It may seem puzzling that we so naturally say something that we so obviously know is false.
I have offered an account of how this comes about in this sort of case in Section 4.2 of
Richard (1990).

[5] For present purposes I don't dispute that the sentence has two different readings along
the lines of (R1) and (R2), the difference residing in (as it's put in the text) the domain
of the reflexive. But I would not ascribe a difference in truth conditions to the readings,
since I take the reading suggested by (R1) to be one that is true only if Cyril has a reflexive
belief.

'that's John's father'. Cyril accepts this, and says things like 'that is John's father' while demonstrating John. We now have the following dialogue with a third party:

—Ha! Cyril was taken in. He actually believes it.
—What exactly does he believe?
—That John is his own father.

The last response is in no way strained. And it could be replaced by 'That John is John's father' without affecting the acceptability of the exchange. But by separating the propositional name from the attitude verb as the dialogue does, we block the reading Crimmins has in mind. The obvious and natural—and I think only correct—way to understand this dialogue is to see it as involving the claim that Cyril believes what's expressed by an unembedded use of 'John is his own father'. So the point made above goes though.

The upshot is that saying that (R) would be literally false in a case in which Cyril has a belief he would express by saying 'that [pointing unbeknownst to John] is John's father' doesn't force us to abandon some intuition that there wasn't reason to abandon *quite independently* of whether we adopt my theory, Perry and Crimmins's theory, or some other theory. The issue raised by (R) is whether embedding multiple occurrences of a singular term within the scope of an attitude verb forces the ascription of a "reflexive belief," a belief like that (relatively uncontroversially) ascribed using sentences in which 'self' or 'his own' occurs. So far as I can see, Crimmins does not give us a good reason for thinking that to believe that John is John's father is not to have a reflexive belief.

3

Imagine that Tom knows of Pierre's confusion about London.[6] He knows that Pierre has a sort of representation of London he acquired in France—let us call it *FR*—and another, *ER*, acquired in England; he knows that Pierre fails to connect these appropriately. Tom himself is not confused about London. My account was designed in part to explain how different uses of

(1) Pierre believes that London is pretty

by Tom might have different truth values, without any shift in Pierre's mental state. Suppose Pierre thinks London pretty using FR but not ER. A use of (1) by Tom when the restriction on translation

(R1) Pierre: 'London' → FR

is in effect is true, since the RAM that London is pretty then represents one of Pierre's thoughts under an acceptable translation manual. But a use of (1) in a context in which the restriction

(R2) Pierre: 'London' → ER

---

[6] See Kripke (1979) for details.

is in force would not be true, since Pierre doesn't have a thought of the form ⟨⟨r, being pretty⟩, ⟨ER, London⟩⟩.

Crimmins claims that when we turn to talking about Tom's beliefs about Pierre's beliefs, we run into problems. Crimmins thinks that if Pierre and Tom are as I've described them, there should be two readings of

(2) Tom believes that Pierre believes that London is pretty.

The readings correspond to the two readings just accorded to (1). One of the readings says something that is (roughly) conveyed thus:

(3) Tom thinks that among Pierre's thoughts is one like this: ⟨⟨one or another representation of beauty, being beautiful⟩, ⟨FR, London⟩⟩.

The other reading says something roughly conveyed so:

(4) Tom thinks that among Pierre's thoughts is one like this: ⟨⟨one or another representation of beauty, being beautiful⟩, ⟨ER, London⟩⟩.

Crimmins's second objection involves the two readings just suggested:

> Assume that Tom knows that Pierre has two representations of London, and that Tom himself, not being confused, has only a single representation of London. Corresponding to *Pierre's* two representations of London there should be two readings of . . . 2.: I may mean that Tom's belief is about . . . [FR], or about . . . [ER]. But there is no way for Richard's contextual machinery to distinguish these claims, because there is no constituent in the RAM [that Pierre believes that London is pretty] . . . of which *Tom* has two representations. (Crimmins 1992, 193; numbering altered to conform to present paper)

The passage raises two questions. The first is whether the "machinery" sketched in section 1 can distinguish between the claims (3) and (4)—that is, can it provide the two readings of sentence (2)? The second question is whether on my account both readings of the sentence could be true if Tom had but one (type of) representation of London, and, if so, whether this is undesirable.

The brief answer to the first question is that of course the account can provide both readings. Varying contextual restrictions on translation changes what (2)'s complement may represent, and thus varies the truth conditions of uses of (2) in the way in which Crimmins thinks they should vary. Achieving this sort of variation in truth conditions is part of the point of making 'believes' indexical. Since this may not be completely clear, I will supply a few details.

What would it be like, for Tom to have the belief conveyed by (3)? As I see it, it would be for Tom to be in a mental state in which he thinks of Pierre more or less as follows:

(H) Hmmh. Pierre has a way of thinking of London—he associates it with 'Londres'—and when he thinks that way of London, he thinks that London is pretty.

If this is the way that Tom thinks about Pierre when he thinks the thought that (3) conveys, then when he thinks the sort of thought that (3) conveys certain restrictions on translation are operative in his context. In particular, the restriction (R1) is operative.

Tom is Crimmins's example, and for all I know, Tom thinks in French. So a more precise statement of the last point is this: If Tom has the belief in question, he has it in virtue of *his* using *some* representation, TR1, of London—perhaps 'London', perhaps 'Londres', perhaps 'diese Burgstadt'—to pick out London *and* to function as a representative in Tom's thought of Pierre's representation FR. If, for example, Tom has the belief in virtue of tokening (H), a particular token of 'London', the last one appearing in (H), does this job. In any event, if Tom has the belief in question, the restriction

Pierre: TR1 → FR

is operative in Tom's context. Analagously, if Tom has the other belief, then there must be some representation of Tom's, TR2, such that the restriction

Pierre: TR2 → ER

is operative in Tom's context.[7]

Different readings of (2), corresponding to (3) and (4), presuppose differences in how Tom represents Pierre's beliefs. If I am trying to convey that Tom has one or the other of the beliefs in question, this can only be because I am focusing on one of Tom's putative representations of Pierre's representations, as opposed to the other. If I utter (2) trying to convey (3), I have a picture of Tom on which he has some way, TR, of thinking of London as he thinks of Pierre's thoughts about London. Tom uses TR not just to think of London but to represent Pierre's French representation, FR, of London. Thus making use of TR, Tom thinks that Pierre thinks that London is pretty. Of course, this last representation of Tom's thought processes lets 'London' go proxy for TR—and has it name London, as it always does. That is, in uttering (2) to convey (3), the restriction

Tom: 'London' → a way of thinking of London, TR, of Tom's such that in Tom's situation the restriction: Pierre: TR → FR is operative.

is operative. But if this is so, then my use of (2) is true only if Tom has the sort of belief mentioned in (3). A corresponding restriction will assign to a use of

---

[7] Actually, I think that restrictions are almost always nonspecific about what representations are in their range. The last mentioned restriction, for example, should be replaced by something suggested by

> Pierre: TR2 → representations that would naturally find expression by Pierre with the English 'London'.

(What this indicates is that in ascriptions to Pierre, TR2 can only represent representations in the class picked out by what follows the arrow.) I think this because I think an adequate account of representations will individuate them so finely that direct—as opposed to quantificational—reference to them will turn out to be (practically) impossible. But this difference with Crimmins and Perry is not relevant here, so I have suppressed it.

(2) truth conditions suggested by (4). The upshot is that the account sketched in section 1 provides readings of (2) corresponding to (3) and (4).[8]

Let's turn to the second question Crimmins's objection raises: Suppose Tom expresses a belief with

(1) Pierre believes that London is pretty

while restriction (R1) is in place (so the belief expressed is focused on Pierre's French representations); next he expresses a belief using (1) while restriction (R2) is in place (so the expressed belief focuses on an English representation). Could Tom have these beliefs *simultaneously* if he had but one way of representing London?

There is, in fact, nothing about the account of Richard (1990) that rules this out. Richard (1990) treats 'believes' as an indexical. The relation 'believes' picks out with (R1) in place is quite different from that it picks out with (R2) in place. The first relates Pierre and the RAM that London is pretty to one of Pierre's "French thoughts," but not to an English one; the second relates the RAM to an English thought but not a French one. This variation in what 'believes' picks out allows a single word, 'London', to go proxy for different representations of Pierre's in different uses of (1). So long as Tom can simultaneously represent belief relations that differ as these do, he can have both beliefs with only one representation of London. Nothing in Richard (1990) bars this. Call this the *multiple relation solution.*

While the multiple relation solution is an option for the theory of Richard (1990), it is an option I would prefer to avoid. Here's why. If Tom represents different belief relations—i.e., different possible semantic values of 'believes'—he presumably does so using 'believes'. Thus, for Tom to simultaneously represent different belief relations, different mental tokenings of 'believes' by Tom will have to pick out different relations. But this implies that simultaneous mental tokenings of the verb by Tom occur in different contexts. For if they occurred in the same context, they would have the same semantic value. At least this is true not he Kaplanesque view of indexicals and contexts presupposed by Richard (1990).

Because the multiple relation response requires this sort of multiplication of contexts, it sits somewhat uneasily with the overall view of context sensitivity which Kaplan suggested in Kaplan (1989) and which (I will suggest below) we have good reason to wish to hold on to. A Kaplanesque context is determined by an agent, a time, a place, and a world. It is supposed to provide the resources for

---

[8] I suppose someone might say that my story lacks a certain "psychological reality." Of course I don't mean to suggest that a user of (2) goes through any of the above rigamarol consciously, or even unconsciously. But I do think that it is plausible to think that if (2) has the sorts of readings Crimmins alleges it has, then (a) he who uses (2) to convey one of the readings is in some sense cognitively focused upon how Tom thinks Pierre thinks of London, and (b) the use of (2) involves some sort of "cognitive co-ordination" between the focus in (a) and the embedded use of 'London'. If (a) and (b) are plausible, then, I think, it is not implausible that my psychological state, when using (2) to convey (3), is one that ties my use of 'London' to Tom's representations in a way that induces the last mentioned restriction.

interpreting arbitrary sentences of its language; generally speaking, sentences which are supposed to be "interpreted together" (for example, premises and conclusions of arguments) are to be interpreted within a single context. Switching contexts in the middle of interpreting a sentence is clearly contrary to the spirit, not to speak of the letter, of Kaplan's approach to indexicals. But the multiple relation response employs a notion of a context on which many contexts will correspond to an agent, time, place and world. These contexts seem destined to interpret only specific sentences (or sentence tokens!) of a language; it thus seems that several contexts might be needed to provide the interpretation of an argument's premises and conclusion. And the multiple relation response positively invites us to switch contexts in mid-sentence.

So I fear that the multiple relation response would force us either to abandon a Kaplanesque account of context sensitivity or to provide two accounts of how sentences receive semantic values, when they are used privately to think, and when they are used publically to air thought: A multiple context account for private use, a Kaplanesque one for the public. While I have no reason to think that such a bifurcated account is impossible,[9] such accounts strike me as awkward and as something which, all else equal, are to be avoided. And they *can* be avoided, since there are straightforward responses to the question we are considering besides the multiple relation response.[10]

Couldn't Tom have both of the beliefs mentioned in (3) and (4), though he had only one way of thinking of, or kind of representation of, London? To answer, we need some illumination as to how we are to individuate representational types, since there are many ways of sorting token representations to come up with types. One account identifies ways of thinking or representational types with what correspond to mental files, mental dossiers, or vivid names. On such a view one who accepts an identity—say 'Twain is Clemens'—and thus directs information tagged with either name to a single file, associates the same way of thinking with each name in the identity. This makes for a relatively coarse-grained concept of representation. Much finer grained accounts are, however, quite natural. For example, it is quite natural to think that tokens of distinct, though co-referential, natural language name types—for example, tokens of 'Clemens' and 'Twain'—determine different ways of thinking even for one who understands the terms and knows that the relevant identity is true. That they function as different representations, even for someone who knows that Twain is Clemens, is witnessed by the difference in their function when embedded within 'believes' and other attitude verbs: To think that John doubts that Twain is asleep is not to think that John doubts that

---

[9] We can of course fragment a Kaplanesque context $c = \langle a, t, p, w \rangle$ into a family $c_i = \langle a, t, p, w, v_i \rangle$ for any family of values V; we may then use the fragmented context to interpret sentences in thought, the unfragmented to interpret sentences in public. One would need, if one adopted such a course, some assurance of uniformity of interpretation of a sentence, when it is used privately to think and publically to express what is so thought. I see no reason that one couldn't construct such an account. But it is horribly redundant.

[10] I am grateful to a referee and an editor for urging me to explain why I do not avail myself of the multiple relation response.

Clemens is asleep. That 'Twain' and 'Clemens' can play different roles in thoughts about the beliefs of others while continuing to name Twain makes them different representations of Twain in some (fairly important) sense of 'representation'.

Certainly there is *a* sense of 'representation' in which, provided Tom is not confused, all of Tom's tokenings of 'London' are tokenings of the same type of representation. In this sense of 'representation', Tom doesn't need multiple representations of London to have the two beliefs at issue. But there is no reason that every (singular) representation I have must directly correspond to a natural language term naming what it represents. In particular, to think about what others think when they are confused may require minting new representations of the objects of their thought in order to keep track of their confusion. A natural way to manufacture new representations is to ambiguate existing ones. This is something we clearly do consciously in thinking about puzzle cases—we say that Peter thinks Paderweski-the-musician plays the piano, but not that Paderweski-the-politician does.

To say that Tom has multiple representations of London, in the quasitechnical sense being suggested, is *not* to say what is informally suggested by saying that he has "different ways of conceptualizing" the town. Tokens of different natural language name types of the same thing are, on my view, tokens of different representational types. For example, 'Twain' and 'Clemens' are of different representational types for reasons just rehearsed. But this difference need not and typically is not accompanied by multiple "ways of conceptualizing" Twain.

Let's apply all this to Tom, London, and 'London'. Suppose that Tom thinks that when Pierre thinks of London as he did as a child, he thinks that London is pretty, but that when Pierre thinks of London as he does in adult mode, he doesn't think that London is pretty. Tom has a number of token representations of London that perform different functions in his thoughts about London and Pierre: Some of them represent Pierre's representation FR, others his representation ER. Of course, they are all names of—and therefore representations of—London. It seems not inappropriate to assimilate the difference among these tokens of 'London' to the difference between tokens of 'Twain' and 'Clemens' in my thought. If we do, we will say that these tokens are, in one sense of 'representation', of different representational types. So Tom has different representations of London. We may look upon routines like (H) above—or "mental models" of the belief systems of others which would be partially rehearsed by the likes of (H)—as among other things introducing new representations, or ambiguating old ones. This would have the effect of allowing 'London' to function in one way in its last appearance in (H), and in a different way in its last appearance in

(H′) Hmmh. Pierre has a way of thinking of London—he associates it with 'London'—and when he thinks that way of London, he thinks that London is not pretty.

The suggestion I've just made is, in effect, that (i) there is a way of partitioning a person's token representations of an object *o* that tends to generate finer divisions among representations—i.e., more sets of representations—as the person comes to recognize that others have multiple representations of *o*. Furthermore,

(ii) the way we ascribe beliefs and other attitudes is sensitive to the divisions induced by this way of partitioning representations.

For reasons just rehearsed, it seems appropriate to think of the collections of representations so generated as constituting different ways of thinking of o, and thus as different representations of o. You may find this way of using 'representa- tion' offensive. Then we have a difference about the semantics of 'representation'. But this is merely a difference about the semantics of 'representation'. It does not bear on claims (i) and (ii) in the above paragraph, and thus doesn't constitute an objection to Richard's (1990) view of the semantics of 'believes'.

4

Let us pretend that Tom's language of thought is some extension of English, dif- fering from English only by explicitly ambiguating terms (say by subscripting) in a manner along the lines discussed in the last section. Thus Tom, under the impression that Pierre has two representations of London, extends his language of thought to include terms 'London$_1$' and 'London$_2$' that go proxy for the repre- sentations in ascriptions of attitude to Pierre. Suppose Tom thinks that Marie- Bernard is also confused about London, though her confusions differ in various ways from Pierre's. So Tom has further ambiguated, and uses 'London$_3$' and 'London$_4$' to think about Marie-Bernard's thoughts.

Consider

(5) Tom thinks that Pierre thinks that London is ugly, and Marie-Bernard thinks that London (or: it) is ugly.

(The scope of the second 'thinks' extends to the comma, of the first to the period.) This would normally be taken to be true if Tom could voice a belief using

(6) Pierre thinks that London is ugly; Marie-Bernard thinks that London is ugly, too.

Given the position I took in Richard (1990), one would expect that I would hold that a use of (5) would be true only if Tom accepted a sentence of the form of (6). But it is hard to see how I can hold that, given what I suggested in the last section. For the suggestion seems to require that the thought Tom gives voice to, when he utters (6), is of a form different from (6), because it does not involve multiple occurrences of one name or representation of London; what Tom is giving voice to is really of the form

(6') Pierre thinks that London$_1$ is ugly; Marie-Bernard thinks that London$_3$ is ugly, too.

If you combine this example with Crimmins's example, you have the following problem: Crimmins's example seems to point to the necessity, in the context of my account, of assigning different representations to different occurrences of 'London' in Tom's thought; this example seems to show that one must generally assign a single representation to different occurrences.

Things are not as bad as they appear. After sketching a way of modelling the mental structures underlying beliefs about beliefs, I will use the model to solve the problem.

When I have beliefs about what Pierre believes, I have a mental structure which can be modelled by a table headed by a representation of Pierre—say, 'Pierre'—and then a list of beliefs. Part of the model might look like this:

Pierre: *Beliefs*
   that Paris is lovely
   that London is not lovely
   that PA's consistency is provable in ZFC

The table contributes a number of "sentences" that go to make up my thoughts. Minimally, it contributes 'Pierre believes that Paris is lovely' and two other simple belief ascriptions; perhaps it also contributes sentences ascribing conjunctive beliefs. In combination with other sentences, it will contribute still more. Suppose I have opinions that some of Pierre's beliefs are, or are not, held in a certain way, or tied to certain ways of thinking of or talking about things. That is, suppose I have a mental structure that would be naturally rehearsed by the likes of (H) or (H'). To model this we need something that will encode the information that I believe that Pierre has multiple ways of thinking of one or another object. And we need something that will encode whatever opinions I may have about the multiples.

The first job can be done simply by subscripting. (Subscripting applies to all expressions with a semantic value, but let's keep things simple and just subscript singular terms.) When different subscripts appear upon a term in my table of Pierre's beliefs, as in

Pierre: *Beliefs*
   that Paris is lovely
   that $London_1$ is not lovely
   that $London_2$ is expensive
   that $London_2$ is 425 km from Paris

—this indicates that I do not presuppose that the representations corresponding to the distinct subscripts are "merged" by the subject. Thus, if the above models my opinions of Pierre, I don't believe that Pierre believes that London is 425 km from Paris and not lovely. But I do believe that he believes that London is 425 km from Paris. And I (probably) believe that he believes that London is expensive and 425 km from Paris.[11]

---

[11] *Probably* only because I hesitate to say that one always believes some conjunction corresponding to each pair of beliefs one has.

 I should stress that I see the subscripting and the resulting syntactic distinction among names of London as an artifact of the model. I am suggesting a way of modelling mental states that would naturally be voiced by things like (H) and (H') in the last section. Such structures might be realized in the mind by tokenings of English sentences in which only occurrences of the natural language 'London' were to be found.

The second job mentioned above can be done by devoting a separate section of the table to information, comments, conjectures, and such about the modes of thought and speech that the subscripts track. A full blown Pierre-table might thus contain a section that would be fairly represented with something like

London$_1$: proxy for a way of thinking of London acquired in London

London$_2$: proxy for a way of thinking of London acquired in France

London$_3$: proxy for a way of thinking Martin had in mind yesterday; probably identical with one of the above

I may have opinions about what opinions Pierre has about Marie-Bernard's opinions. We might extend the subscript notation to deal with multiple iterations, generating things like

Pierre: *Beliefs:*
> that London$_1$ is not lovely
>
> . . . .

Marie-Bernard: *Beliefs:*
> that London$_{1,1}$ is pretty
> that London$_{1,2}$ is not pretty

The mental structure modelled by such a table accurately represents Pierre's system of beliefs only if Pierre has a representation of London, L_1, such that (a) he uses it to believe that London is not lovely; (b) he has used it to go proxy for what he takes to be potentially different representations of London of Marie-Bernard's, in the way the user of (H) and (H$'$) uses 'London' as proxy for two of Pierre's representations; (c) analogously to the user of (H) and (H$'$), using L_1, Pierre takes Marie-Bernard to think that London is pretty, and he takes her to think that London isn't pretty.

I have been spelling out a way of modelling the sort of mental structures underlying our thoughts of others' thoughts. Using this model, we can solve the problem posed by the iteration examples in a straightforward way.

Let us henceforth use *representational type* in a fairly narrow sense, so that, for instance, all my thought tokens of 'London' are of a single representational type, given that they are all names of London and that I "take" them to all name the same thing. Call the collection of sentence tokens, table tokens, and so forth that realize my beliefs my *belief text*. The RAMs of Richard's (1990) semantics for attitude ascriptions are constructions based upon the belief text. They are formed by taking a sentence token from the text and pairing the types of its parts with the referents of the token's parts. If the sort of type used in the construction is representational type, we will have trouble with iteration. What we need in this construction is something reflecting not only sameness and difference of representational type, but also the structure, due to opinions about sameness and difference of representational type in the texts of others, reflected by subscripting. Let's call the replacements for representational types *representational paths,* or paths for short.

To construct a path, pick a representation (type)—say, 'London'—and, for each table T in which something of that type occurs, a subscript. If a table T′ is embedded in T, as the Marie-Bernard table is embedded in the Pierre table, we pick for T′ a subscript that extends the subscript chosen for T, as 1,2 extends 1. The result defines a *representational path* through a system of beliefs. A token t is part of such a path if it is of the representational type on which the path is based, and (a) t occurs in the belief text outside of any belief table (so, t is part of a "zero level" belief, like the belief that snow is lovely), or (b) t occurs in a belief table and has the subscript picked for that table.

A representational path is a way of collecting token representations. It collects only representations that are of the same representational type. It also respects the way in which a thinker takes others to represent the world to themselves: If I take *you* to have two representations of London that you fail to connect to one another, a representational path consisting of tokens of 'London' from *my* thought does not contain tokens that go proxy for both of your putative representations.

Suppose we have a sentence S from Tom's belief text, perhaps one formed by "conjoining" various sentences that go to make up the text. For each assignment of representational paths to S's token parts, there will be a RAM among Tom's thoughts. Suppose, for example, that Tom's belief text looks (partially) like this:

(Zero level) London is lovely

Pierre: *Beliefs:*	Marie-Bernard: *Beliefs:*
that $London_2$ is ugly	that $London_3$ is ugly
that $London_1$ is lovely	that $London_4$ is not ugly
that $London_2$ is not lovely	
that $London_1$ is expensive	
that $London_2$ is expensive	

$London_1$: proxy for a French representation
$London_2$: proxy for an English representation

There are a number of paths through this text. One path collects all occurrences of 'London' in the zero level text, all the proxies for the English representation—i.e., the 'London's subscripted with '2'—in the Pierre table, plus all the occurrences of '$London_3$' in the Marie-Bernard table; another collects all the 'London's in the zero level, all the proxies for a French representation in the Pierre table, and all the '$London_3$'s for Marie-Bernard. There are yet more. Call the two paths described p_1 and p_2, respectively.

To construct Tom's thoughts, we take a sentence (possibly a conjunction of subsentences) from his belief text. We then select paths $p_1, \ldots, p_n$ such that for each (atomic) expression (with a semantic value) in the sentence, there is exactly one path in which it occurs. Then, letting the paths play the role of types, we construct a thought by pairing the type of an expression token with the token's Russellian referent.[12] So among the thoughts that Tom has is one corresponding

---

[12] The construction will make the relation between sentences accepted and thoughts one-many. In Richard (1990) (section 4.3) I argue that this will generally be the case; in particular, the proper treatment of puzzles concerning the retention of belief over time requires this.

to the sentence 'Pierre believes that London$_2$ is ugly; Marie-Bernard believes that London$_3$ is ugly', constructed using p_1, and thus constructed so that the two names of 'London' are like-typed. A use of (5) (with no restrictions accompanying it) is true in virtue of the fact that Tom has such a thought.

In Crimmins's example, we need to show that there is a reading of 'Tom believes that Pierre believes that London is expensive' that is true only in virtue of a thought constructed from a path like p_1—and so is true only in virtue of a belief focused on Pierre's representation ER—and another reading of the sentence that is true only in virtue of a thought constructed with a path like p_2. But that is straightforward, once we say, as we shall henceforth, that the restrictions that a context provides for evaluating uses of natural language attitude ascriptions map the word types in a 'that'-clause to ways of thinking that are given by paths. Thus, the first reading of the sentence is induced by a restriction along the lines of

> Tom: 'London' → ways of representing London that, *inter alia,* go proxy in Tom's thought for one of Pierre's English ways of thinking of the town.

The other reading is secured by a corresponding restriction.[13]

There is a faint echo of Frege's hierarchy of indirect senses in all this. Frege is often thought to have held that with each new embedding of 'London' in a sequence such as

> Pierre thinks that London stinks
>
> Tom thinks that Pierre thinks that London stinks
>
> Marie-Bernard thinks that Tom thinks that Pierre thinks that London stinks

'London' shifts its reference, referring to its sense at the previous level, and expresssing a new sense to present the new reference. It is natural to understand such a view as one on which 'London' in the above sequence first names Pierre's way of thinking of London, then Tom's way of thinking of Pierre's way of thinking of London, and then Marie-Bernard's way of thinking of Tom's way of thinking of Pierre's way of thinking of London.

'London', on the view I've outlined, functions as a proxy for different sorts of representations in a way somewhat reminiscent of this progression. Representational paths are ways of following shifts in the proxy function within the belief text of an individual. But there are rather significant differences

---

[13] To complete the picture just sketched, we need an account of when an individual's thoughts are true. The account of section 4.4 of Richard (1990) can be adapted. In generating the appropriate restrictions for evaluating someone's thoughts for truth, we use the appropriate material (for example, things like

London$_1$: proxy for one of Pierre's English representations)

from the tables in which the parts of the path making up the RAM occur. The restrictions in this case must be ones that map paths to paths. (I hope to expand on these cryptic remarks elsewhere.)

between Frege's position and the position sketched here. In particular, in natural language attitude ascriptions, I take 'London', no matter how deeply embedded, to refer to London, while Frege does not. In the progression just displayed I see no variation in the reference or semantic value of 'London'. The contribution of 'London' is always the same, namely the pair ⟨the natural language name type 'London', the city London⟩.

Unlike Frege, I do not see attitude ascription as involving reference to the object that the believer has in her "psychological ken" in belief. This is a good part of the point of describing my position as one on which an attitude ascription involves a *translation* of the object of the target's belief: In translating another's words, we wind up with something that refers, not to their words, but to what they referred to therewith. Analogously, for translating their thoughts.

5

The most salient difference between my account and that of Crimmins and Perry is that they take run-of-the-mill attitude ascriptions to involve reference to representations, while I do not.[14] A (quite simplified) version of their account runs as follows: A speaker who uses a sentence of the form *a believes that T* typically makes "tacit reference" to representations. The tacit reference is tacit, because there is no expression in the sentence uttered which can be identified as the expression with which the reference is made; the tacit reference is reference, since the representations in question are constituents of the proposition expressed by the utterance as a whole. Roughly speaking, and ignoring for the moment iteration of 'believes', the semantic value of an utterance of 'believes that T' on which the representation R is the object of tacit reference is: *believes the Russellian proposition that T using the representation R.*

Crimmins and Perry account for the multiple readings of (2) by holding that Tom's beliefs about Pierre's beliefs are in part about Pierre's representations; in reporting these by using (2) we may make differing references to Pierre's representations. One reading involves reference to FR, the other to ER. If we adopt the Perry/Crimmins account, we can get both readings of (2) without multiplying *Tom's* modes of representing London, or introducing the extra complexity of the notion of a representational path. Why not simply accept the idea that when Tom thinks about Pierre, he refers to Pierre's representations of London, and when we think about Tom, *we* refer to *Pierre's* multiple representations, too?

I think there is a very good reason to resist this idea. This reason is best appreciated, I think, when one appreciates what is perhaps the other major difference between the Crimmins/Perry account and my own. This is not a difference about the semantics of attitude verbs, but about the best way to treat contextual shiftiness in natural language. This difference is marked, though not exhausted,

---

[14] Crimmins and Perry suggest that some attitude ascriptions involve (more or less direct) reference to representations, while other attitude ascriptions may make claims involving quantificational reference to or description of representations. This subtlety doesn't affect the argument of this section, so I propose henceforth to ignore it.

by our choices of objects of semantic evaluation and our accounts of the structure of such evaluation. I have couched my account within the framework suggested by Kaplan (1989), in which the objects that get evaluated semantically are sentence types taken in a context, with contexts being abstractions from and idealizations of actual and possible types of speech situations. Such contexts are conceived as typically supplying (in the way in which a function "supplies" its values) the sorts of parameters and determinants necessary for interpreting any sentence of the language; thus one typically (though not invariably) can interpret arbitrary sets of sentences of the language under study relative to such contexts.

Crimmins and Perry's account, on the other hand, is one that semantically evaluates utterances. It allows for a notion of *context of an utterance,* of course. But the Crimmins/Perry view seems to be one on which contexts should be identified with things that would "really be found in a speech situation." (These are my words, not theirs.) A context of use, on this view, need not provide the material necessary to interpret more than whatever sentence or sentences are in fact used therein. This notion of context is not one designed to accommodate the interpretation of arbitrary collections of sentences of the language of study. And in fact Perry and Crimmins disparage the sort of contexts I employ. Crimmins calls them "donut contexts" (because they are unhealthy? because he and Perry donut use them?); Perry and Crimmins suggest that "[o]ne way of taking our claims would be as denying the general usefulness in semantics of" such a notion of context (Crimmins and Perry 1989, 710).

As Crimmins quite correctly suggests, my treatment of the example in section 2 flows naturally from my decision to make expression types the objects whose semantically relevant properties shift across context. Crimmins, in suggesting alterations of my account, proposes taking utterance parts—uses of expressions— to be objects whose representational properties shift across contexts. He observes (putting things roughly) that if context makes *uses* of expressions representative of the mental representations of others, then in an utterance of (R) the first use of 'John' can represent one (type) of Cyril's representations of John, the second quite another.

If our only interest were in assigning truth conditions or propositions to the uses of sentences, a case could be made that the Crimmins/Perry approach to the matter must be superior to mine. Suppose a satisfactory semantic account of a certain class of sentences uses can be given by assigning types to the sentences used, inventing a collection of contexts relative to which to endow the *types* with semantic properties, and then evaluating the types-as-taken-in-a-context for truth. Certainly we give an equally satisfactory treatment of the class by assigning semantic properties to the *uses,* assigning property p to a use u iff for some t and c, the first approach assigned u to type t, identified c as u's context, and assigned p to t in c. So anything my approach can do, the Crimmins/Perry approach can do as well. But conversions in the opposite direction are not always possible, simply because a token utterance may be made out of tokens of like type.

The point of this argument is not, of course, that sentence types are irrelevant to semantics. Systematic semantics is impossible without a systematic assignment of types to token utterances, if only because there seems no hope of a comprehensive assignment of semantic values unless the assignment is made *via* types. Rather, the point of the argument is that nothing is lost, and apparently some flexibility is gained, if we identify the things to which we are assigning semantic values as the type-bearing tokens, rather than the types-in-a-context.

The argument, however, is conditional upon the assumption that our only interest is the assignment of truth conditions and propositions to sentence uses. Traditionally, we have hoped for more from a semantic account of a language. We have also hoped to extract an account of validity from an account of a language's semantics. Such accounts traditionally proceed by ferreting out types whose tokens are invariably valid: Argument types whose premise tokens guarantee the truth of their conclusion tokens, or sentence types whose tokens enjoy an immunity from falsity or guarantee of truth. Traditionally, it was assumed that logic's types would be identical with or at least parasitic upon the types semantics uses.

Approaching contextual shiftiness *via* the assignment of semantic properties to types in a Kaplanesque context can be thought of as being partially motivated by the desire to cast semantic theory so that it will deliver an account of validity in a form as close to the traditional one as the contextual shiftiness of the language under study will allow. (Certainly this was a primary motivation for the author of *Demonstratives* when he developed the framework to begin with.) In this framework, we can continue to identify the bearers of formal validity with (parasites upon) the syntactic types of the language under study. Validity itself can be identified with the guarantee of being true when taken in any context (Kaplan's definition) or with the guarantee of expressing a necessary truth in any context (an alternative to which I am partial). It is the demands upon the formalism imposed by this approach to validity that require the idealization noted above, on which a context turns out (typically, if not inevitably) to supply the material necessary for interpreting arbitrary sentences of the language.

If the flexibility of assigning semantic values to tokens instead of types is one of which we must avail ourselves, in doing the semantics for a portion of a language, then we will expect the semantic theory for that portion of the language to tell us relatively little about logical properties. For insofar as the assignment of semantic values, and thus truth conditions and propositions, must advert to tokens and not just to types and context, it will not be possible to predict whether the truth of premises guarantees that of a conclusion just by looking at the types of the premises and conclusion. Insofar as semantics is the story of tokens and not types, language has no logic, at least as logic is normally conceived.

Insofar as we have strong intuitions about the logical properties of some portion of a language, we will want our semantic theory to validate these intuitions. When these intuitions are intuitions about formal validity—and surely we do have such intuitions—we shall want our semantic theory, all else being equal, to validate our intuitions by showing that the validity of certain arguments can be seen as a formal matter. What a semantic account says about validity is, in any case, an important test of the theory. One reason for rejecting a semantic theory, after all, is that it sits poorly with, or is outright inconsistent with, particular intuitions of speakers concerning validity and invalidity, or more general logical intuitions, like the intuition that utterances in English that have the form

whatever a Rs is a thing that b Rs, and aRc

commit the utterer to the truth of one of the form of bRc.

How does all this bear on a choice between the account of attitude ascriptions I've offered and that offered by Perry and Crimmins? The idea that Kaplanesque contexts are somehow unfit for doing natural language semantics seems to me unsubstantiated by any argument Crimmins or Perry gives. As I have suggested, one reason for employing a framework in which such contexts figure is to enable us to give straightforward accounts of validity. The account of attitude ascriptions I have given is in part shaped by common intuitions about logical properties of sentences ascribing attitudes. For instance, I see it as a desideratum of a semantics for attitude verbs that it validate our intuition that inferences such as

Whatever Tom doubts Pierre doubts

Tom doubts that London is lovely

So Pierre doubts that London is lovely.

are valid. To this end, my account assigns a semantic value to the predicate type 'doubts that London is lovely' relative to a context, allowing the predicate to be univocal within a context. The initial premise is treated in what seems the most natural way in my framework, as the claim that for any RAM p, if there is an f such that D(Tom, f, p), then there is an f such that D(Pierre, f, p). ('D', of course, names an analogue of the relation B from section 1.) The argument is thus valid in virtue of the principles governing the treatment of the quantifier 'whatever'.[15]

Among the morals Crimmins and Perry draw from their discussion of the attitudes is that "there is little possibility of an interesting logic of belief sentences" (Crimmins and Perry 1987, 711). Their pessimism results from what I have suggested is a primary difference between us: They eschew the kind of account of indexicality I employ because they think that "such things as the words used in a statement can affect the semantically relevant parts of the statement's context."[16]

Even the simplest sorts of apparently valid arguments are rendered invalid on their account. Recall that on their account a speaker who uses a sentence of the form *a believes that T* typically makes "tacit reference" to representations of a's; the semantic value of an utterance of 'believes that T' on which the representation R is the object of tacit reference is: *believes the Russellian proposition that T using the representation R*. Analogous treatment is of course accorded verbs like 'doubts'. On such a treatment, 'doubts that London is lovely' is typically *not* univocal, even within a single context of actual utterance, such as an utterance of

---

[15] See the discussion on pages pp. 141–150 in Richard (1990).

[16] I do not deny that this is so. For example, salience is effected by an utterance and salience is (probably) a semantically relevant "part" of context. What I deny is that the best accounts of the interaction of utterance and context are incompatible with the types-in-a-context method of semantics.

'Tom doubts that London is lovely and Pierre doubts that London is lovely'. For the predicate uses involve tacit reference to token representations. So the predicate involves, when fronted by 'Tom', reference to Tom's representations, not Pierre's; it involves reference to Pierre's representations, not Tom's, when fronted by 'Pierre'.

How would Crimmins and Perry treat quantifications like 'whatever Tom doubts Pierre doubts'? What they say doesn't allow one to confidently generalize.[17] The most natural treatment of 'whatever a doubts b doubts' in their framework is arguably one on which it reads so: for any Russellian p, if there is an r such that a doubts p using r, then there is an r^* such that b doubts p using r^*. But if this is how we should read the initial premise of the argument above, there is apparently no sense in which the argument is valid. Even if we confine our attention to how the premises and conclusion of the argument are interpreted in a single context of utterance, Crimmins and Perry's view seems to commit them to the view that there will be contexts in which uses of the relevant sentences come to something like

> (p)($\exists r$ Tom doubts p under $r \rightarrow \exists r'$ Pierre doubts p under r')
> Tom doubts the proposition that London is pretty under r_1
> So, Pierre doubts the proposition that London is pretty under r_2

with r_1 and r_2 tacitly referred-to representations. This isn't valid. In fact, since one can presumably say that someone doubts a proposition under r when he doesn't (because, say, he in fact believes it under r), there is every reason to think that there will be cases in which the premises are all true while the conclusion is false.

Perhaps there is some way to render the argument in question valid without violating the spirit of the Crimmins/Perry account, but it is not easy to see what it might be. I am inclined to think that the argument in question is valid. In fact, I am inclined to think that there must be some sense in which the argument *form*

> Whatever Tom doubts Pierre doubts
> Tom doubts that A
> So, Pierre doubts that A

is a valid one. It is not as if one is faced with a choice between honoring the intuition about validity and incorporating contextual shiftiness into an account of the semantics of attitude ascriptions: One can do both by giving an account of the sort suggested in Richard (1990).[18]

---

[17] While Crimmins (1992) discusses some plural attitude reports—for example, 'The Egyptians believed that Tut was divine' and 'Ann and Tom believe that Max has fleas', the discussion is fairly tentative. So far as I can see, the approach taken in Crimmins (1992) does not sit easily with the idea that the argument in the text is valid, much less formally so.

[18] Mark Crimmins gave useful comments on an earlier version of this, for which I'm grateful. This paper was written during my tenure as an NEH Fellow; I'm most grateful for the support.

REFERENCES

Crimmins, Mark: 1992, "Context in the Attitudes," *Linguistic and Philosophy* 15, 185–198.

Crimmins, Mark: 1992, *Talk about Beliefs*, MIT Press, Cambridge.

Crimmins, Mark and Perry, John: 1989. "The Prince and the Phone Booth," *Journal of Philosophy* 86, 685–711.

Kaplan, David: 1989, *Demonstratives*, in Almog, Perry, and Wettstein (eds.), *Themes from Kaplan*, Oxford University Press, Oxford.

Kripke, Saul: 1979, "A Puzzle about Belief," in A. Margalit (ed.), *Meaning and Use*, Reidel, Dordrecht, pp. 239–83.

Richard, Mark: 1989, "How I Say What You Think," in P. French et al. (eds.), *Midwest Studies in Philosophy*, Volume XIV, Notre Dame University Press, Notre Dame.

Richard, Mark: 1990, *Propositional Attitudes*, Cambridge University Press, Cambridge.

4

The Response to the New Theory of Reference

BELIEF ASCRIPTION*

Stephen Schiffer

I shall do four things in this paper. First, I shall propose a certain theory of the semantics of belief ascriptions as being the best theory of their semantics relative to a certain assumption. Second, I shall raise three problems for this best theory. Third, I shall make what I hope is an interesting connection between the main issue addressed and the vexing question about the form that a meaning theory for a particular language must take. And, fourth, I shall close with a word about the theoretical situation thus determined.

The assumption in question is the widely accepted one that each natural language has a correct compositional truth theory. A compositional truth theory for a particular language *L* is a finitely axiomatizable theory of *L* that issues in a theorem of the form

> An utterance of '*S*' is true in *L* iff such and such.

for each of the infinitely many truth-evaluable sentences of *L*. For example, a truth theory for English might contain a theorem like

> An utterance of 'She wrote it' is true in English iff the female referred to by the utterance of 'she' wrote the thing referred to by the utterance of 'it'.

If we assume that English has a correct compositional truth theory, then we may ask how a particular class of sentences is to be accommodated in such a theory. This is to ask about the kinds of semantic values that would have to be assigned to the components of those sentences and the kinds of compositional rules that would need to apply to those values in order to crank out a truth condition for each sentence of the class. Roughly speaking, this question of accommodation within a compositional truth theory is what philosophers are concerned with when they ask about the *logical form* of a class of sentences. And this is my cue to restate the first of the things I shall do—namely, to offer what I take to be the best account of the logical form of belief ascriptions. In other words, I shall try to say how belief ascriptions would have to be accommodated in a compositional truth theory on the assumption that English has one.

I. The Hidden-Indexical Theory Baldly Stated

If English has a compositional truth theory, how should belief sentences be accommodated in it? What, that is to ask, is the best theory of the logical form of belief ascriptions on the assumption that they have a logical form? The theory I

---

* I am much indebted to the participants in the seminar I gave on these topics in 1991 at the CUNY Graduate Center. Earlier versions of this paper were read in spring 1991 at the University of Wisconsin/Madison, the University of Chicago, and the SOFIA conference in Salamanca, Spain. I benefited considerably from the discussions at these talks, and especially from the comments of Ned Block, James Higginbotham, Richard Jeffrey, Jaegwon Kim, Ernest LePore, Richard Mendelsohn, and Ernest Sosa.

shall propose in answer to this question is one I shall call the *hidden-indexical theory*. It is a theory whose essential idea must have occurred to almost anyone who has thought seriously about the semantics of belief sentences. I first discussed a version of it in "Naming and Knowing",[1] I discuss it briefly in the form I shall presently give it in "The 'Fido'-Fido Theory of Belief",[2] and a version of the theory is nicely presented and defended in Mark Crimmins's and John Perry's "The Prince and the Phone Booth: Reporting Puzzling Beliefs."[3]

The theory, in my favored version, begins with the claim that believing—the relation expressed by 'believes' in a sentence of the form 'x believes that S'—is a three-place relation, $B(x, p, m)$, holding among a believer x, a certain sort of *structured proposition p*, and a *mode of presentation m* under which x believes p. The idea is that x may believe p under one mode of presentation m, disbelieve p under a second mode of presentation m', *and* suspend judgment altogether under a third mode of presentation m''. Actually, I should have said that believing is a four-place relation, where the fourth place is a time at which x believes p under m, but I shall suppress the temporal reference for simplicity. Let me now explain the notions of a structured proposition and a mode of presentation before moving on to the essence of the theory, its account of the semantics of belief reports.

The sort of proposition I have in mind is a structured entity whose basic components always include at least one property or relation, and may include any sort of contingently existing object. The simplest example of such a structured proposition would be a so-called *singular proposition*, such as the ordered pair ⟨Fido, doghood⟩. This proposition is true just in case Fido instantiates doghood, the property of being a dog; that is to say, just in case Fido is a dog. Interesting technical questions arise about the representation of more complex propositions, but singular propositions will serve present purposes well enough. All that really matters to the hidden-indexical theory is that the propositions we believe are structured entities composed out of the objects and properties we are pretheoretically taken to be talking about when we express our beliefs. I shall call such propositions *Kaplan propositions*, in honor of David Kaplan, who did so much to popularize them.[4]

---

[1] *Midwest Studies in Philosophy*, II (1977):28–41.

[2] *Philosophical Perspectives*, I (1987):455–80.

[3] *Journal of Philosophy*, LXXXVI, 12 (December 1989):685–711.

[4] Let a *singular proposition* be any ordered pair ⟨⟨$x_i, \ldots, x_n$⟩, Φ_n⟩, where ⟨$x_i, \ldots, x_n$⟩ is an n-ary sequence of items and Φ^n is an n-ary property (brackets are customarily dropped for one-membered sequences). Such a proposition is true just in case its n-ary sequence instantiates its n-ary property. One way to go with Kaplan propositions is to treat them all as singular propositions. Thus, the proposition *that Fido is a dog and Pieface is a cat* might be

⟨⟨⟨Fido, doghood⟩, ⟨Pieface, cathood⟩⟩, CONJ⟩

where CONJ is that relation between two propositions that obtains iff both are true; and the proposition that some dogs bark might to a first approximation be represented as

⟨the property of being a dog that barks, SOME⟩

where SOME is that property that a property has iff it is instantiated. And so on.

This brings us to modes of presentation. A mode of presentation of a *proposition* is determined by (a) the modes of presentation of the objects and properties contained in the proposition and (b) the place of those things in the proposition. As a first approximation, you might think of a mode of presentation of a proposition as an n-tuple of modes of presentation of the objects and properties contained in the proposition.

The expression 'mode of presentation', as it was introduced by Gottlob Frege and as it is used today, is a technical notion, and to understand it is to appreciate the need for its introduction. Two little stories should help remind us of that need.[5]

The first is the infamous case of the morning dog and the evening dog. There is a certain dog who begs at Ralph's door every morning. Ralph feeds this dog, whom he has named 'Fido', and has grown attached to it. Ralph believes that Fido is male. There is also a certain dog who begs at Ralph's door every evening. Ralph feeds this dog, too, whom he has named 'Fi Fi', and has also grown quite attached to it. Ralph believes that Fi Fi is female, and he thinks that Fido and Fi Fi would make a really cute couple. Unbeknown to Ralph, Fido *is* Fi Fi.

The second story is that of the spurious natural kind shmoghood. Ralph came upon a race of creatures that he thought constituted a previously unencountered biological species, and he introduced the word 'shmog' to designate members of that species. "A thing shall be called a 'shmog'," Ralph said, "just in case it belongs to the species of these creatures." Unbeknown to him, however, shmoghood is doghood; Ralph had stumbled not upon a new species but upon a new race of dogs, and thus the property that 'shmog' has been introduced as standing for is none other than doghood.

Now, when Ralph says "Fido is male but Fi Fi is female," he is not being irrational in holding the belief which that utterance expresses. But he could not rationally hold the belief that would be expressed by an utterance of 'Fido is and is not male'. Likewise, Ralph is not irrational in holding the two beliefs expressed by a morning utterance of 'This dog is male' and an evening utterance of 'This dog is female', even though the same dog is referred to in both utterances. But Ralph could not rationally hold the belief that would be expressed by a sincere utterance of 'This dog is and isn't male'.

Similarly, when Ralph says "Fido is a dog, not a shmog," and when he says "No dogs are shmogs," he is not being irrational in holding the beliefs those utterances express. But he would be irrational were he to hold the belief that would be expressed by an utterance of 'No dogs are dogs'.

Appeal to the notion of a mode of presentation is designed precisely to accommodate these sorts of data. The intuitive idea, definitive of the notion of a mode of presentation, may be called *Frege's constraint*. Stated informally and in a way that prescinds from the details of any particular theorist's account of belief or of belief-ascribing sentences, Frege's constraint has two parts. First it says that a rational person x may both believe and disbelieve that a certain thing

---

[5] The next couple of paragraphs derive from my "The Mode-of-Presentation Problem," in
  C. Anderson and J. Owens, eds., *Propositional Attitudes* (Stanford: CSLI, 1990).

or property y is such and such only if there are distinct modes of presentation m and m' such that x believes y to be such and such under m and disbelieves it to be such and such under m'. Then it says that there are distinct modes of presentation m and m' such that rational person x believes y to be such and such under m and disbelieves y to be such and such under m' only if x fails to realize that m and m' are modes of presentation of one and the same thing. In other words, you cannot rationally believe and disbelieve something under one and the same mode of presentation, or under modes of presentation that you realize are modes of presentation of the same thing. The notion of a mode of presentation is *functionally defined* by Frege's constraint in that something is a mode of presentation if it plays the role defined by Frege's constraint, and nothing can be a mode of presentation unless it plays that role. *To ask what modes of presentation are is just to ask what things play that role.* Presently I shall raise the question of what modes of presentation might be, but the hidden-indexical theory I shall now describe is so far neutral on the outcome of that question.

As applied to the paradigmatic example

[1] Ralph believes that Fido is a dog.

the hidden-indexical theory says that the logical form of an utterance of this sentence may be represented as

[2] $(\exists m)\,(\Phi^*m \,\&\, B(\text{Ralph}, \langle \text{Fido}, \text{doghood}\rangle, m))$

where Φ^* is an implicitly referred to and contextually determined type of mode of presentation. By a type of mode of presentation I mean merely a property of modes of presentation; Φ^*, for example, might be that property that a propositional mode of presentation has when and only when it requires thinking of Fido as being the dog who appears in the morning and requires thinking of doghood as a property shared by such-and-such similar-looking creatures. The reference to a type of mode of presentation is implicit in that, although the sentence requires the speaker to be referring to a type of mode of presentation whenever the sentence is uttered, there is no word in [1] which refers to that type (whence the 'hidden' in 'hidden-indexical theory'). The reference to the type of mode of presentation is "contextually determined" in that different types may be referred to on different occasions of utterance (whence the 'indexical' in 'hidden-indexical theory').

As we shall see when I stop baldly stating the theory and begin defending it, the reference is to a type of mode of presentation rather than to some particular mode of presentation because we need not be in a position to refer to an actual mode of presentation under which someone believes a proposition. But in a limiting case reference may be to an actual mode of presentation, for the "type" referred to may be one that uniquely picks out a particular mode of presentation, or it may simply be the property of being identical to such-and-such mode of presentation. So at one end of the spectrum, the type referred to may constitute a reference to a unique mode of presentation; at the other end, the type might be vacuous, as when the speaker's import in uttering [1] is merely that Ralph believes the proposition that Fido is a dog under some mode of presentation or other. In between, we have reference to substantial types that do not determine unique modes of presentation.

So the representation of [1] as [2] tells us quite a bit. It tells us that a correct compositional truth theory for English must construe 'believes' as a three-place relational predicate holding among believers, Kaplan propositions, and modes of presentation of those propositions. It tells us that [1]'s 'that'-clause, 'that Fido is a dog', is a referential singular term whose referent is the singular proposition ⟨Fido, doghood⟩, and it tells us that the references of 'Fido' and 'dog' in that 'that'-clause are Fido and doghood, respectively. It tells us that an utterance of the sentence requires reference to a type of mode of presentation, so that an utterance of [1] is true just in case [2], where Φ^* is the mode-of-presentation type referred to in the utterance. And it tells us that this contextually determined reference to a type of mode of presentation is by a "hidden indexical" in that there is no actual indexical in [1] which carries this reference. In this respect, belief ascriptions are like other sentences containing hidden indexicals. For example, in uttering 'It's raining', the speaker must be referring to some place at which it is raining (typically, this is the speaker's location, but it need not be: a speaker in Chicago may reply 'It's raining' when asked about the weather in New York).

II. Remarks in Support of the Hidden-Indexical Theory

According to the hidden-indexical theory, an utterance of the sentence *'A believes that S'* is true just in case the utterer is referring to a type of mode of presentation Φ and the referent of '*A*' believes the Kaplan proposition referred to by 'that *S*' under some mode of presentation of the type Φ. My claim is that this theory provides the best account of how belief ascriptions must be accommodated in a compositional truth theory for English if English has one. A full-scale defense of this claim would outrun a feasible number of pages, but I would like to give *some* sense of what supports the theory.

One very important thing the hidden-indexical theory tells us is that the 'that'-clause in a paradigmatic belief ascription such as [1] is a *referential singular term*. This at least has the *appearance* of being right: [1] does indeed seem to be telling us one of the things Ralph believes—to wit, that Fido is a dog. On the face of it, [1] says that Ralph stands in the belief relation to the referent of the singular term 'that Fido is a dog'. This appearance that [1]'s 'that'-clause, 'that Fido is a dog', is a referential singular term is sustained by the evident validity of arguments such as

> Ralph believes that Fido is a dog, and so does Thelma.
> So, there is something that they both believe (viz., that Fido is a dog).
>
> Ralph believes everything that Thelma says.
> Thelma says that Fido is a dog.
> So, Ralph believes that Fido is a dog.
>
> Ralph believes that Fido is a dog.
> That Fido is a dog is impossible.
> So, Ralph believes something that is impossible (viz., that Fido is a dog).

For how else are we to account for the validity of these inferences other than on the assumption that 'that'-clauses are referential singular terms? I think that the rhetorical force of this question is correct: the best explanation of the way in which these arguments may be valid does presuppose that 'that'-clauses are referential singular terms.[6]

It is obvious that we may give simple and straightforward explanations of the validity in question via hypotheses that entail that 'that'-clauses are referential singular terms. The question is whether validity can be accounted for without that assumption. Perhaps, as I myself argued in *Remnants of Meaning*,[7] the arguments are valid only when their quantifications are read *nonobjectually*, say, as something akin to substitutional quantification. This would entail that 'that'-clauses were *not* referential singular terms. Or perhaps, as Graeme Forbes[8] has argued, we can use some very fancy footwork to account for the validity even though [1]'s 'that'-clause disappears on analysis, leaving us with an existential generalization along the lines of

> ($\exists m$) ($\exists m'$) (m is a mode of presentation of Fido & m' is a mode of presentation of doghood & B(Ralph, the proposition that m has m'))

Or perhaps we could salvage enough validity using Donald Davidson's "paratactic" theory of propositional-attitude ascriptions, wherein the only singular term referring to what Ralph believes is the demonstrative 'that', as it occurs in

> Ralph believes that. Fido is a dog.

when its reference is the utterance that follows it of 'Fido is a dog'.

Perhaps; but I doubt it. I have argued elsewhere[9] against Davidson's proposal, and if it were not for present constraints I would offer to explain why neither Forbes's line nor my former self's nonobjectual-quantification line can be made to succeed.[10] But there are the constraints; so I must ask you provisionally to assume

---

[6] I say 'the way in which these arguments *may* be valid' because of the alleged hidden-indexical nature of belief ascriptions: qua inference *type*,

> Ralph believes that Fido is a dog.

> So, Ralph believes that Fido is a dog.

is no more valid than

> It's raining.

> So, it's raining.

Tokens of these inference types are valid only when premise and conclusion make the same implicit reference.

[7] Cambridge: MIT, 1987.

[8] "The Indispensability of *Sinn*," *The Philosophical Review*, XCIX, 4 (1990):535–63.

[9] *Remnants of Meaning*, ch. 5.

[10] Well, I guess I can afford to mention one especially devastating problem for the Forbes line. Applied to

> Ralph *said* that Fido is a dog.

it yields

> ($\exists m$) ($\exists m'$) (m is a mode of presentation of Fido & m' is a mode of presentation of doghood & S(Ralph, the proposition that m has m'))

The trouble with this is that it is extremely unlikely that Ralph, in his utterance of 'Fido is a dog', will have said any such mode-of-presentation-containing proposition. If he did mean some such proposition, then there would be a specification of what he said that is other than 'that Fido is a dog' and that refers to a mode-of-presentation-containing proposition. But it is clear that there need be no such alternative specification of what he said.

that I have justified the assumption that 'that'-clauses are referential singular terms. Then we may move to the question this assumption invites.

If 'that Fido is a dog' is a referential singular term, then we may ask what its reference is. To what, that is, does it refer? This, however, is easy to answer: 'that Fido is a dog' refers to that Fido is a dog; what 'that Fido is a dog' refers to is that Fido is a dog. But what is this thing, *that Fido is a dog,* which is the referent of the 'that'-clause singular term? Well: (i) it is *abstract,* in that it has no spatial location. That Fido is a dog is not under the kitchen sink or anywhere else. (ii) It is *mind- and language-independent* in that it exists in possible worlds in which there are neither thinkers nor speakers. That Fido is a dog is also language-independent in that, while it may be the content of a sentence of any language, it itself belongs to no language; it is not a linguistic entity. (iii) It has a *truth condition,* and it has its truth condition *essentially,* in contrast to the contingent way sentences have theirs. It is a contingent fact that 'Fido is a dog' is true iff Fido is a dog; if the conventions of English had been different, it might have had a totally different truth condition or none at all. But it is a necessary truth that that Fido is a dog is true iff Fido is a dog. It follows, then, that the referents of 'that'-clauses are *propositions,* in the philosophical sense of that term: abstract, mind- and language-independent objects that have essentially the truth conditions they have.

If the hypothesis that 'that'-clauses are referential singular terms is to cohere with the assumption that English has a compositional truth theory, then we must suppose that each 'that'-clause is a semantically complex singular term whose reference is determined by its syntax and the references, or extensions, of its component words. What, we might then ask, are the references of 'Fido' and 'dog' in 'that Fido is a dog', as it occurs in an utterance of [1]?

For all intents and purposes, there are but two possible answers. One, apparently Frege's, is that the terms in a 'that'-clause refer to modes of presentation and the proposition referred to by the entire 'that'-clause is a structured proposition made up of those modes of presentation. With respect to a particular utterance of [1], the Fregean proposal would be that the token of 'Fido' refers to a particular mode of presentation of Fido while the token of 'dog' refers to a particular mode of presentation of doghood, the utterance of [1] thus enjoying the representation

$$B(\text{Ralph}, \langle m_f, m_d \rangle)$$

$\langle m_f, m_d \rangle$ being the mode-of-presentation-containing proposition referred to by the occurrence of 'that Fido is a dog' in the utterance. This will be true, of course, only if m_f and m_d are ways Ralph has of thinking of Fido and doghood, respectively.

The merit of this proposal is that it allows us to see how the ancient astronomer was able to believe that Hesperus was Hesperus long before she believed that Hesperus was Phosphorus. Its demerit is that it is false. For consider

[3] Everyone who has ever known her has believed that Madonna was musical.

According to the Fregean proposal, there is a particular mode of presentation m of Madonna and a particular mode of presentation m' of the property of being musical such that the foregoing utterance of [3] is true only if everyone who has ever known Madonna has believed the proposition $\langle m, m' \rangle$. Yet this is surely too strong a requirement on the truth of [3]. It requires that everyone who has ever known Madonna shared a single way of thinking of her and a single way of thinking of the property of being musical, and this is most unlikely given that there may have been people who knew her as a child and then died and that someone like Helen Keller may have been among them. If the Fregean proposal were correct, we could prove that [3] was false just on the basis of the virtual certainty that, whatever modes of presentation turn out to be, there will not be one single mode of presentation of Madonna shared by all who ever knew her. But it seems that we cannot disprove [3] in this way, and this because we would count it as true if each person who has ever known Madonna thought of her as being musical *under some mode of presentation or other.*[11]

Our question is: What are the references of 'Fido' and 'dog' in [1]'s 'that'-clause on the assumption that it refers to a proposition that is true just in case Fido is a dog? The second possible answer is that they are Fido and doghood, respectively, $\langle$ Fido, doghood $\rangle$ being the referent of 'that Fido is a dog'.[12] Certainly this offers a proposition with the right truth conditions. The prima facie problem with this proposal is that it is apt to suggest—and has been taken by many to suggest—that the logical form of [1] may be represented as

[4] B(Ralph, $\langle$ Fido, doghood $\rangle$)

And you may be very quickly reminded of the well-known problem with this representation if I momentarily change the example. Surely, Lois Lane does not believe

---

[11] Here is a longer way of showing that 'that'-clauses do not refer to mode-of-presentation-containing propositions. Intuitively, 'believes that Fido is a dog' may be univocally true of people who think of Fido and doghood in radically different ways (you and Helen Keller may be among them) and who do not share any single mode of presentation for either Fido or doghood. This shows that 'that Fido is a dog' makes no context-independent reference to a mode-of-presentation-containing proposition. At the same time, a speaker may truly say that so-and-so believes that Fido is a dog even though she is not in a position to refer to any particular mode of presentation so-and-so has for either Fido or doghood. This shows that the 'that'-clause makes no context-dependent reference to a mode-of-presentation-containing proposition. And if it makes neither a context-independent nor a context-dependent reference to such a proposition, then it makes no reference to one.

[12] Friends of possible-worlds semantics or of counterpart theory will think my rush to singular propositions a bit cavalier. Why not say that the reference of 'Fido' is a function from possible worlds to referents of 'Fido' in those worlds—Fido himself, perhaps, in each world, or variable counterparts of our Fido? First, I think importation of possible worlds is unmotivated, though I cannot argue that here. Second, I think any prima facie plausible theory that used possible worlds and propositions that were constructions based on them would, when the dust settled, simply yield alternative styles of bookkeeping. Third, nothing that I really care about changes if, say, you opt for a version of the hidden-indexical theory wherein 'Fido' in a 'that'-clause refers to that constant function that maps each possible world onto our Fido (but the counterpart theory might be a version of the rejected proposal that the referent is a mode of presentation of Fido).

that Clark Kent flies, though she does believe that Superman flies. But this is impossible according to the present proposal, since, as Clark Kent = Superman, the proposition that Superman flies = the proposition that Clark Kent flies. Likewise, reverting now to the ongoing example, Ralph may believe that Fido is a dog without believing that Fido is a shmog, and he may believe that Fido is male without believing that Fi Fi is male. Yet all this is impossible according to the theory in question, since it implies that the proposition that Fido is a dog = the proposition that Fido is a shmog and that the proposition that Fido is male = the proposition that Fi Fi is male. The problem is even manifested in belief ascriptions involving indexical reference. For example, pointing to one mug shot, Thelma might say, 'I believe that he is the culprit', while pointing to another, she might say, 'I neither believe nor disbelieve that this guy is the culprit; I simply can't tell'. Intuitively, both of her utterances are true, even though, as it may happen, the same man is referred to in each utterance; but this, again, is incompatible with the proposal in question.

Nathan Salmon[13] has tried to defend the extreme 'Fido'-Fido theory of belief that would represent [1] as [4] by trying to explain away the patina of counterintuitiveness adhering to the theory's consequences. But I think he has not succeeded, and in "The 'Fido'-Fido Theory of Belief" I try to show why.[14] We really do need a theory that allows us to see how an utterance of

> Lois believes that Superman flies but doesn't believe that Clark Kent flies.

can be literally true.

Here, then, is our situation. We are motivated to see [1]'s 'that'-clause as a referential singular term whose reference is the proposition that Fido is a dog. Since we are assuming that English has a compositional truth theory, we must hold the reference of this 'that'-clause to be determined by its syntax and the semantic values the words in the 'that'-clause have in it. Those semantic values—those references—cannot be modes of presentation, and the only viable option is that they are Fido, for 'Fido', and doghood, for 'dog'. At the same time, we cannot accept the representation of [1] as [4], for we also want to allow that Ralph does not believe that Fido is a shmog.

Enter now on its white charger the hidden-indexical theory, which satisfies all desiderata. This theory, you will recall, represents the logical form of an utterance of [1] as [2], where Φ^* is an implicitly referred to and contextually determined type of mode of presentation. Thus, 'that Fido is a dog' in [1] as a referential singular term whose referent is the singular proposition $\langle$Fido, doghood$\rangle$, and thus the referents of 'Fido' and 'dog' in that 'that'-clause are Fido and doghood, respectively. At the same time, we can see how an utterance of

[5]   Ralph does not believe that Fido is a shmog.

can also be true, even though, as shmoghood = doghood, 'shmog' in [5] has the same reference as 'dog' in [1], so that the 'that'-clause in each sentence refers to

---

[13] *Frege's Puzzle* (Cambridge: MIT, 1986).

[14] See also Salmon's reply, "Illogical Belief," *Philosophical Perspectives*, III (1989):243–85.

one and the same singular proposition, to wit, ⟨Fido, doghood (i.e., shmoghood)⟩. That the utterances of [1] and [5] can both be true is due, of course, to the hidden-indexical feature: in the normal case, the type of mode of presentation referred to in an utterance of [1] will be different from that referred to in an utterance of [5]. Likewise in the other examples discussed, and likewise as regards the London/Londres and Paderewski examples that puzzled Saul Kripke.[15] These are no puzzles for the hidden-indexical theory.

III. Three Problems for the Hidden-Indexical Theory

So much for what recommends the hidden-indexical theory. I shall now raise three problems for the theory.

The candidate problem. This problem arises for *any* theory that appeals to modes of presentation. It is a problem I have discussed at length elsewhere,[16] and I will say only enough about it now to indicate its nature. In a nutshell, the candidate problem is that there is some question whether there is a plausible candidate for what modes of presentation are.

The notion of a mode of presentation is, we saw, a functionally defined technical notion: a mode of presentation is whatever plays the mode-of-presentation role defined by Frege's constraint. So we may ask what things play that role. This is like asking what genes are, the notion of a gene being functionally defined as whatever is responsible for the transmission of hereditary characteristics. There the answer turned out to be segments of DNA molecules. What, though, is the answer to the mode-of-presentation question? There is no dearth of proposed answers:

> Modes of presentation are *individual concepts,* uniqueness properties of the form *the property of being the unique instantiator of such-and-such property.*
>
> Modes of presentation are simply *general properties* that make no pretense of applying uniquely to the things of which they are modes of presentation.
>
> Modes of presentation are *percept tokens,* actual instances of sensory experience.
>
> Modes of presentation are "*stereotypes,*" perhaps what cognitive psychologists call *prototypes.*
>
> Modes of presentation are "*characters,*" functions from contexts of the utterance of an expression to the expression's contents in those contexts.
>
> Modes of presentation are *public language expressions.*
>
> Modes of presentation are *Mentalese expressions,* formulae in the neural language of thought.
>
> Modes of presentation are *functional roles,* perhaps conceptual roles of Mentalese expressions.
>
> Modes of presentation are *causal chains* linking Mentalese names and predicates to the objects and properties for which they stand.

---

[15] "A Puzzle about Belief," in A. Margalit, ed., *Meaning and Use* (Dordrecht: Reidel, 1979).

[16] "The Basis of Reference," *Erkenntnis*, XIII, 1 (1978):171–206; *Remnants of Meaning*, esp. ch. 3; and "The Mode-of-Presentation Problem."

And finally there is the *no-theory theory of modes of presentation,* which rejects what I have elsewhere called the *intrinsic-description constraint.*[17]

This constraint holds that if a thing is a mode of presentation—if, that is, it plays the mode-of-presentation role—then it must be intrinsically identifiable in a way that does not describe it as a mode of presentation or as a possible mode of presentation. If a thing is a mode of presentation, then it must be intrinsically identifiable as some other kind of thing. Rejecting this constraint, the no-theory theorist of modes of presentation holds that modes of presentation are modes of presentation and there is an end to it. You simply cannot say what they are in any other terms.

But I think the intrinsic-description constraint *is* well-motivated, and I think there are compelling objections against each of the foregoing candidates but one. The exception is the view that modes of presentation are functional roles, perhaps conceptual roles of Mentalese expressions. This view of what modes of presentation are has intrinsic problems and it does not cohere with every theory of the logical form of belief ascription; but its problems do not *refute* it and it does cohere with the hidden-indexical theory.[18] In any case, the hidden-indexical theory entails that believing is a relation among a believer, a proposition, and a mode of presentation of that proposition, which mode of presentation is in turn determined by modes of presentation of the proposition's components. It is hard to see how we can reasonably accept this theory without some well-motivated idea of what these modes of presentation are supposed to be.

The meaning-intention problem. This problem is that one may reasonably doubt that belief ascribers mean what the hidden-indexical theory requires them to mean when they ascribe beliefs. Let me explain.

Floyd's sister calls him in Chicago and asks about the weather. Floyd replies, "It's raining." Here Floyd refers to Chicago, and this by virtue of the fact that in uttering 'It's raining', Floyd *means* that it is raining in Chicago. In other words, Floyd counts as having referred to Chicago because the proposition he meant is about Chicago. Notice that there is no difficulty whatever in ascribing to Floyd the propositional speech act in question: he clearly intended his sister to believe that

---

[17] "The Mode-of-Presentation Problem."

[18] This corrects a flawed argument in "The Mode-of-Presentation Problem" which was intended to show that modes of presentation cannot be conceptual roles of Mentalese expressions. The argument overlooked what must be the intended generalization of the hidden-indexical theory for belief ascriptions with embedded 'that'-clauses—namely, that a belief ascription with n 'that'-clauses embedded in the primary 'that'-clause must be making $n + 1$ implicit references to types of modes of presentation. Thus, the logical form of an utterance of

Floyd believes that Lois believes that Superman flies.

is

$$(\exists m)\,(\varPhi m \,\&\, B(\text{Floyd}, [\exists(m')\,(\varPhi'm' \,\&\, B(\text{Lois}, [\text{Superman flies}], m'))], m))$$

where $\varPhi$ and $\varPhi'$ are implicitly referred to and contextually determined types of modes of presentation (and where '[. . .]' is a singular-term forming operator with the force of 'the proposition that . . . .'). If this inevitable complexity weakens the plausibility of the hidden-indexical theory, then so be it.

it was raining *in Chicago,* and he is quite prepared to tell you that this is what he meant, what he implicitly said, and what he intended her to be informed of. Because these things are so clear, Floyd's utterance is a paradigm of implicit reference.

Now for a different case. During a casual conversation about air-fare bargains, Flora says,

> [6] Harold believes that TWA is offering a New York–Paris return fare for $318.

According to the hidden-indexical theory, there is a property Φ of modes of presentation of the proposition that TWA is offering a New York–Paris return fare for $318 such that Flora referred to Φ in her utterance. If this is true, then, presumably, it is because Flora, in producing her utterance, meant some proposition about Φ in just the way that Floyd, in his utterance, meant some proposition about Chicago. But, we shall see, it is doubtful that Flora meant any such thing.

We had no trouble saying what Floyd meant in uttering 'It's raining': he meant that it was raining in Chicago. But what that implies a reference to a type of mode of presentation does Flora mean in uttering [6]? It must surely be

> [7] that there is something that both has Φ and is such that Harold believes the proposition *that TWA is offering a New York–Paris return fare for $318* under it

for some particular property Φ of modes of presentation of the proposition that TWA is offering a New York–Paris return fare for $318. But—and this is where the trouble begins—neither Flora nor her audience is aware of her meaning any such thing. Floyd is consciously aware of both the *form* of the proposition he meant (he is aware that he meant that it is raining *in* Chicago) and the implicitly referred to thing the proposition is about (he is aware that he meant that it is raining in *Chicago*). But it is doubtful that the nonphilosopher Flora has conscious access to the form of [7], and it is especially doubtful that she has conscious awareness of referring to any mode-of-presentation property. That is to say, if she did mean a proposition of form [7], then she has no conscious awareness of what property Φ that proposition is about, and no conscious awareness, therefore, of what she meant in uttering [6].

Neither we nor Flora can say what mode-of-presentation property was referred to in her utterance of [6]. Just try to say it. The referred-to property, if it exists, would be given by a completion of the form

> The property of being an *m* such that to believe the proposition *that TWA is offering a New York–Paris return fare for $318* under *m* requires thinking of TWA, the offering relation, New York, Paris, the US dollar currency, the number 318 [and so on for the other components of the proposition] in . . . ways, respectively.

But the nonphilosopher Flora has no access even to this *form* of specification, and who among us can offer to replace the three dots? Now, of course, it is in principle possible to have knowledge of such a property even though one cannot specify it in the foregoing way. One might, for example, have knowledge of it under some quite extrinsic description. But I submit that it will be obvious on reflection that Flora has no such alternative way of explicitly picking out a property of modes of presentation to which she is implicitly referring in her utterance of [6].[19] There is no sentence σ such that Flora can say 'I meant that σ', where 'that σ' explicitly refers to a proposition of [7]'s form.

Thus, if the hidden-indexical theory is correct, then Flora has no conscious awareness of what she means, or of what she is saying, in uttering [6], and this is a prima facie reason to deny that she means what the theory is committed to saying she means.

There is more than one way a hidden-indexical theorist might respond to this prima facie problem, but let me go directly to what I think is the theorist's best bet. This response is to concede that Flora is not *aware* of meaning a proposition of form [7] under any mode of presentation, but to insist that she nevertheless meant such a proposition. The idea is to appeal to so-called "tacit belief" and "tacit intention." This idea has its origin, I believe, in Noam Chomsky's controversial claim that speakers know a grammar of their language. To this it was protested that in no ordinary sense of 'know' do speakers know any such thing. When the dust settled, many theorists supposed that the best construal of Chomsky's claim was that the correct theory of language processing implies that a speaker has an internal representation of the grammar of her language, where this internal representation is stored not as a *belief,* but as what Stephen Stich was later to call a *subdoxastic state.*[20] Subdoxastic states are representational states that are belief-like in some respects but differ from paradigmatic beliefs in their unavailability to consciousness and the way they are inferentially isolated from beliefs (for example, if you believe that if p, then q, and believe p, you are likely to infer q; but you will not make this inference if the state representing p is subdoxastic). Now, the notion of a tacit propositional attitude can admit of a spectrum of cases, from the Chomsky-required subdoxastic states at one end, to states that may reasonably be claimed to be subsumable under our current propositional-attitude concepts, at the other. What is evidently unifying about the notion of a tacit prepositional attitude is that a tacit propositional attitude is unavailable to consciousness and that one cannot be made irrational by conflicts between those of one's thoughts which are available to consciousness and those which are merely tacit. At any rate, the present proposal is that it is thanks to her *tacit* beliefs and intentions in uttering [6] that Flora means a proposition of [7]'s form even though she is not aware of meaning any such thing.

One trouble with the tacit-intention proposal is that it induces a rather radical *error theory:* not only do ordinary belief ascribers have no conscious

---

[19] Besides, it is quite against the spirit of the hidden-indexical theory that the type of mode of presentation referred to should be one that the speaker knows only under some nonintrinsic mode of presentation. The idea of the theory is that, though one might not know the particular mode of presentation under which so-and-so believes that such-and-such, still one has access to some interesting *description* that the mode of presentation satisfies.

[20] "Beliefs and Subdoxastic States," *Philosophy of Science,* XLV (1978):499–518.

knowledge of what they are asserting, they also turn out not to have the conscious thoughts they think they have. Flora clearly *thinks* she has conscious knowledge of what she is asserting in uttering [6]. She is quite prepared to say, "Look, what I am saying, and all that I am saying, is that Harold believes that TWA is offering a New York–Paris return fare for $318." In other words, she thinks she is consciously aware of what she is asserting in uttering [6], but the tacit-intention line implies that here she is in error: the only proposition she asserts in uttering [6]—viz., some proposition of form [7]—is not anything of which she is conscious. What makes this error aspect of the tacit-intention proposal problematic is not merely that it riddles the propositional-attitude ascriptions of ordinary speakers with error; it also forces us to qualify our views about first-person authority in an important way. Flora does not have the privileged access to what she consciously means, intends, and believes in uttering [6] which one might reasonably have supposed to be part of a normal person's functional architecture.

A more serious trouble with the tacit-intention proposal actually constitutes a direct objection to the claim that speakers have the meaning intentions the hidden-indexical theory requires them to have, whether or not those intentions are claimed to be tacit. But the objection is best presented here, in response to the tacit-intention proposal, since it is obvious that speakers do not consciously mean what the hidden-indexical theory entails that they mean. The objection takes hold even if it is conceded that ordinary people do have some sort of indirect awareness of modes of presentation, which is all to the good, as it is not out of the question that one could motivate the idea that Flora tacitly *believes* that Harold believes the proposition about TWA under a certain type of mode of presentation. The point to be pressed, however, is that considerably more is required of tacit *meaning*. I shall explain.

Meaning entails audience-directed intentions, and one cannot mean something without intending to be understood. Part of meaning that such and such is intending one's audience to recognize that that is what one meant, and—a corollary—part of referring to a thing is intending one's audience to recognize that reference. Consequently, the present tacit-intention proposal requires there to be some type of mode of presentation Φ such that Flora tacitly means that Harold believes that TWA . . . under a mode of presentation of type Φ, and tacitly intends her audience to recognize (no doubt tacitly) that she means that Harold believes that TWA . . . under a mode of presentation of type Φ. But as James Higginbotham pointed out to me, this puts the implausibility of Flora's *meaning* a proposition of form [7] on a par with that of a certain way of trying to extend the description theory to "incomplete" definite descriptions. The idea there is that, when a speaker utters a sentence like 'The dog has fleas', then there must be some property Φ such that she means the proposition that the thing that is uniquely a dog and Φ has fleas. What makes this so implausible is that there will typically be a number of potentially completing descriptions that are equally salient in the context (e.g., *the dog that I own, the dog we are both looking at, the spotted dog in the green chair,* and so on). Consequently, it is highly implausible that there will be *one* such description such that the speaker intends it to be understood between her and her audience that she means a proposition containing that very description.[21]

Now, just the same problem arises with the meaning claim required by the hidden-indexical theory. For assume that propositions are believed under modes of presentation. If a proposition is believed under one mode of presentation, then it will typically be believed under many modes of presentation. Further, each of those modes of presentation will instantiate infinitely many *types* of modes of presentation, many of which will be equally salient in the communicative context. This makes it extremely implausible that of all the equally salient types of ways that Harold has of believing the proposition about TWA, Flora should mean—and intend to be taken to mean—a proposition about one definite one of them.

A little thought experiment should make the objection vivid. When considering the hypothesis that a certain expression has a certain semantic property, it is often helpful to introduce an expression that has that semantic property by stipulation. Presently in debate is the hidden-indexical theory's claim that one uttering [6] would mean a proposition of the form [7] displays. So let us introduce 'shmelieves' as a term that satisfies the hidden-indexical theory by stipulation: to utter a sentence of the form

> *A* shmelieves that *S.*

with its literal meaning requires a speaker to mean

> that there is something that both has Φ and is such that *A* believes the proposition that *S* under it

for some particular contextually determinate property Φ of modes of presentation of the proposition that *S*. The hidden-indexical theory may or may not be true of '*A believes* that *S*', but it is true by stipulation of '*A shmelieves* that *S*'.

So far so good, but let me now try to use this newly minted coin to make an assertion.

> Placido Domingo shmelieves that Luciano Pavarotti will be arriving at Orly airport today at around 4 PM Paris time.

Very well, what assertion did I make? What is the type of mode of presentation Φ such that I meant that Placido Domingo believes the proposition *that Luciano Pavarotti will be arriving at Orly airport today at around 4 PM Paris time* under a mode of presentation that has Φ? Remember, Φ is made up of types of modes of presentation for each of the constituents of the proposition to which my 'that'-clause refers: Luciano Pavarotti, the arrival relation, Orly airport, the number 4, Paris, etc. The question, of course, cannot be answered. For although 'shmelieves' was stipulatively given a perfectly good hidden-indexical semantics, I was not, in uttering the displayed sentence, in a position assertively to use it, and this because I was not in a position to refer to a contextually determinate type of mode of presentation. None is sufficiently salient to enable you, my audience, to identify it as the one I meant, and

---

[21] See my "Indexicals and the Theory of Reference," *Synthese*, XLIX, 1 (1981):43–100; esp. pp. 77–8.

this notwithstanding the fact that we understand all the concepts involved and everything has been painstakingly raised for us to the level of conscious awareness.

The application to the hidden-indexical theory should be clear. Although I cannot utter the foregoing 'shmelieves' sentence and mean what its literal meaning requires me to mean, there are no such impediments to my uttering 'Placido Domingo *believes* that Luciano Pavarotti will be arriving at Orly airport today at around 4 PM Paris time'. I can perfectly well utter this and hope to have my literal assertion be perfectly well-understood by you. Since 'shmelieves' is by stipulation what 'believes' would be if the hidden-indexical theory were true, this appears to show that the theory is not true. The best account of why neither Flora nor her audience (who understood her perfectly well) is aware of her meaning a proposition of form [7], as the hidden-indexical theory requires her to mean, is not that the requisite meaning intentions have gone tacit; it is that she does not mean any such thing.

The logical-form problem. According to the hidden-indexical theory, 'believes' is a three-place relational predicate. But this might strike one as fishy for the following reason. If 'believes' really were three-place, then it ought to have occurrences where its three-place form is explicit, as the three-placedness of 'gives' is made explicit when we move from 'She gave the house' to 'She gave the house to her husband'. Yet in what analogous way can we make explicit the three-placedness of 'Ralph believes that Fido is a dog'? Perhaps in the way of

[8]   Ralph believes that Fido is a dog *in way w/under mode of presentation m.*

There are, however, two problems with this.

First, this is no ordinary-language specification but technical jargon. If one is told that Mary gave the house, one can ask, "To whom did she give the house?" But what is the corresponding ordinary-language question for 'Ralph believes that Fido is a dog'? Ask a nonphilosopher, "In what way, or under what mode of presentation, does Ralph believe this?" and your best answer will be a puzzled look.

Second, [8] does not look like a specification of a three-place relation. It looks more like a two-place relation with *an adverbial qualifier.* In other words, it is to be assimilated to

Ralph kissed her in the most exciting way.

where 'the most exciting way' is merely part of an adverb, rather than to

[9]   Mary gave the house to her husband.

where 'her husband' is an argument of the verb 'to give'. Evidence for this assimilation comes from well-known constraints in syntactic theory which distinguish between arguments and adverbs in their ability to extract from 'whether'-clauses.[22] Thus, the argument status of 'her husband' in [9] is revealed in the fact that we can answer 'Her husband' in response to the question

To whom did you wonder whether Mary gave the house?

---

[22]See Chomsky, *Barriers* (Cambridge: MIT, 1986). I owe this reference and the point about 'whether'-clauses to Robert Fiengo.

And the nonargument, adverbial status of 'way w/mode of presentation m' in [8] is revealed by the fact that it *cannot* be given in answer to the question

> In what way/under what mode of presentation did you wonder whether Ralph believes that Fido is a dog?

IV. The Importance of the Issue

I have proposed that, if natural languages have compositional truth theories, then the hidden-indexical theory is the correct account of the accommodation of belief ascriptions in them. I have also offered some reason for thinking the hidden-indexical theory is false. If it is both conditionally correct and false, then it follows that natural languages do not have compositional truth theories. This is one reason the issue of the semantics of belief ascriptions is important. There is, however, another reason for the importance of the question of the accommodation of belief ascriptions in a compositional truth theory; it has to do with the bearing of this question on the vexing question about the form that a compositional *meaning* theory for a language must take. I shall explain.

It is commonly assumed that each natural language L has a *compositional meaning theory,* this being a finitely axiomatizable theory of L whose theorems ascribe to each sentence of L its meaning in L. Those who make the assumption reason that without it there will be no explaining either the platitude that the meaning of a sentence is determined by its syntax and the meanings of its component words or the fact that we have the ability to understand indefinitely many novel sentences. But while it is generally agreed that every natural language enjoys a compositional meaning theory, no three philosophers can be made to agree on the form such a theory must take. For a start, it is not even clear what form the *theorems* of a meaning theory would have to take. You might at first blush suppose that a compositional meaning theory for L would generate theorems of the form

> 'S' means in L that such and such.

but this could hardly be the form of a theorem for sentences like 'He was there' or 'Stop singing, you idiot!' and it is anything but clear that the word 'means' should ever be used in saying what a sentence means. After all, to know the meaning of a sentence is to be able to know what a speaker is saying in uttering the sentence; so it is reasonable to suppose that a compositional meaning theory would have to ascribe to each sentence a feature, knowledge of which would enable us to know what would be said in the utterance of any sentence having that feature. But there is no agreement as to what such a feature would be like, or that the word 'meaning' would need to be used to ascribe it.

Those who assume that each natural language has a compositional *meaning* theory typically assume that each natural language also has a compositional *truth* theory, in the sense already glossed. After all, it is part of the *meaning* of 'Snow is white' that an utterance of it is true iff snow is white; so if it is reasonable to think a compositional theory can assign meanings to sentences, then it is reasonable to think one can assign truth conditions to them, too. What we are now in a position to see is that, if we know how to accommodate belief ascriptions in a compositional truth theory, then we will be able to answer the question about the form that a compositional meaning theory must take. This ought at first to seem a little surprising. Merely knowing how to accommodate 'Fido is a dog' in a truth theory would not per se tell us the first thing about how to accommodate that sentence in a *meaning* theory. So how can knowing how to accommodate *belief ascriptions* in a truth theory tell us how to accommodate *any* sentence in a meaning theory?

I shall forego a general answer, but we can see straightway how the hidden-indexical theory of belief ascription constrains the nature of a meaning theory. For what applies to belief ascriptions applies, mutatis mutandis, to all propositional-attitude ascriptions involving 'that'-clauses. What holds for 'Ralph believes that Fido is a dog' also holds for 'Ralph says that Fido is a dog'. The theory tells us that the 'that'-clause in a saying ascription refers to a Kaplan proposition. This means that to know what a speaker said in the utterance of a sentence is to know what Kaplan proposition she said. Since to understand a language is to have the ability to understand utterances in it, and since to understand an utterance is to know what the speaker said in it, we can see that, if the hidden-indexical theory is correct, then the main task of a compositional meaning theory for a language will be the construction of a finitely specifiable correlation that relates each sentence of the language to what Kaplan has called a *character*—a function that, in effect, maps each utterance of the sentence onto the Kaplan proposition that is the propositional object of the primary speech act performed in the utterance.[23] In other words, if the hidden-indexical theory of the accommodation of propositional-attitude ascriptions in a truth theory is correct, then so is the "direct reference" approach to a compositional meaning theory, and in this way we can see how the hidden-indexical theory constrains the nature of a meaning theory.

It may be worth noting that this point I have been laboring reverses the usual procedure of those who argue for the direct reference treatment of 'that'-clauses implied by the hidden-indexical theory. That procedure begins by assuming a direct reference approach to meaning and then draws the consequence as regards the propositional content of propositional-attitude ascriptions, which consequence entails that 'that'-clauses are referential singular terms whose referents are Kaplan propositions. My procedure has been different, and I think less contentious. I started with no assumptions about "content" or meaning. My question was wholly about the *references* that must be assigned to words in a belief ascription on the assumption that languages had compositional *truth* theories, theories whose theorems are of the extensional paradigm

'La neige est blanche' is true in French if snow is white.

---

[23]Kaplan, "Dthat," in P. Cole, ed., *Syntax and Semantics 9: Pragmatics* (New York: Academic, 1978).

It was then argued that, relative to the assumption, 'that'-clauses had to be construed as referential singular terms whose *referents* are Kaplan propositions. Then, in the final step, this premise about *reference* was used to derive the general point about *meaning*.

V. Conclusion

If the hidden-indexical theory is correct, then we not only know how to accommodate belief ascriptions in a compositional truth theory for English, we also know the form that a compositional meaning theory for English must take. But I did not argue that the hidden-indexical theory is correct. I merely argued that it is the correct theory relative to the assumption that natural languages have compositional truth theories, and I proceeded to raise problems for the theory. There are but three possible ways out of this impasse: either the problems can be answered, or the hidden-indexical theory is not the best accommodation of belief sentences in a compositional truth theory, or natural languages such as English do not have compositional truth theories. Elsewhere I have argued that the third option is one that deserves to be taken seriously.[24] Others may disagree; but I hope it will be agreed that the hidden-indexical theory and its obstacles present a challenge that cannot be ignored.

---

[24]*Remnants of Meaning;* "Does Mentalese Have a Compositional Semantics?" in B. Loewer and G. Rey, eds., *Meaning in Mind; Essays on the Work of Jerry Fodor* (Cambridge: Blackwell, 1991); and "Actual-Language Relations," forthcoming in *Philosophical Perspectives,* VII (1993)

WHY SEMANTIC INNOCENCE?
Graham Oppy

Many recent semantic theories have involved explicit acceptance of the following two theses:

1. *Direct Reference* (DR): The utterance of a simple sentence containing names or demonstratives normally expresses a 'singular proposition'—a proposition that contains as constituents the individuals referred to, and not any descriptions or conditions on them.

2. *Semantic Innocence* (SI): The utterances of the embedded sentences in belief reports express just the propositions they would if not embedded, and these propositions are the contents of the ascribed beliefs.[1]

Such theories face a well-known difficulty: they seem to conflict with a third, and apparently obviously true, thesis:

3. *Opacity* (O): Substitution of coreferring names and demonstratives in belief reports does not always preserve the truth of those reports.

---

[1] See, for example: Nathan Salmon, *Frege's Puzzle* (Cambridge: MIT Press, 1986); Scott Soames, "Direct Reference, Propositional Attitudes, and Semantic Content," *Philosophical Topics* 15 (1987) pp. 47–87; and Mark Crimmins and John Perry. "The Prince and the Phone Booth: Reporting Puzzling Beliefs," *The Journal of Philosophy* 86 (1989) pp. 685–711.

In order to meet this difficulty, two different strategies have been proposed.

A. *Conventional implicature*: The first suggestion, adopted by Salmon and Soames, is to claim that O is false: despite appearances, the substitution of core-ferring names and demonstratives in belief reports does preserve the truth of those reports. Now, of course, this suggestion leaves us with a puzzle, namely: why do we ordinarily suppose, and speak as if it were the case, that O is true? Here, Salmon and Soames suggest that belief reports carry *conventional (or gener-alised) implicatures* which can change under substitution of coreferring embed-ded names and demonstratives.

Neither Soames nor Salmon has given any details about the nature of these implicatures. However, they do say that what gets implicated is information about the mode of presentation under which a singular proposition is grasped by a sub-ject. Consequently, it seems hard to resist the suggestion that what they require is a compositional theory according to which implicated modes of presentation associated with sentences are composed of implicated modes of presentation associated with the words which make up those sentences.[2]

But then the question naturally arises why it should not be supposed that these allegedly implicated modes of presentation are actually part of the semantic content of belief reports. Given that we need a theory which associates modes of presentation with words, won't all of this talk about implicated modes of presen-tation be just a pointless and unmotivated complication in the theory?

B. *Unarticulated constituents:* The second suggestion, adopted by Crimmins and Perry, is to deny that the theses DR, SI, and O are inconsistent. This response seems most unpromising. Consider the following quasi-logical principle which connects the notions of truth and semantic value:

4. *Fundamental Semantic Principle* (FSP): If the substitution of expression E_1 for expression E_2 in sentence S (in context C) leads to a change in (literal) truth-value, then this change is due to the semantic values of E_1 and E_2 (in context C).

I take it that this is more or less a definition of what it is to be a semantic value: semantic values are whatever it is that words contribute to the determination of the literal truth-values of sentences in which they occur (upon particular occasions of utterance, or more generally, of tokening of those sentences). Moreover, I take it that it is obvious that FSP entails that if the substitution of a name or demonstra-tive E_1 for a coreferring name or demonstrative E_2 in a sentence S (in a context C) leads to a change in the literal truth-value of S, then it follows—contrary to DR, or SI, or both-that E_1 and E_2 do not have the same semantic content.

---

[2] Salmon has noted that he has not explicitly committed himself to such a view—cf. "Illogical Belief" in James Tomberlin (ed.), *Philosophical Perspectives 3: Philosophy of Mind and Action Theory, 1989* (Atascadero, CA: Ridgeview Press, 1989) pp. 243–285, fn. 26—but he has nowhere canvassed possible alternatives to it. Moreover, it seems to me that the standard reasons for supposing that semantic theories ought to be compositional—e.g., facts about the 'productivity' of speakers—are also reasons for supposing that Salmon's account of the implicatures associated with propositional attitude ascriptions must be compositional.

Not surprisingly, Crimmins and Perry are at least tacitly committed to the rejection of FSP. In their words, their view is as follows:

> It is very common in natural languages for a statement to exploit unarticulated constituents. When we consider the conditions under which such a statement is true, we find it expresses a proposition which has more constituents in it than can be traced to expressions in the sentence that was spoken. Each constituent of the content that is not itself the content of some expression in the sentence, is an unarticulated constituent of the content of the statement. . . . The important principle to be learned is that a change in the wording can precipitate a change in propositional constituents, even when the words do not stand for constituents.[3]

In other words, the 'important principle' to which Crimmins and Perry wish to draw attention is that the substitution of an expression E_1 for an expression E_2 in a sentence S (in a context C) can lead to a change in the semantic content of the sentence S (in the context C) even though E_1 and E_2 have exactly the same semantic content—and this is the denial of FSP.

In order to illustrate the notion of 'unarticulated constituency', Crimmins and Perry consider the example of utterances of:

(1) It's raining.

As they note, if one utters (1), one will be understood to be claiming that it is raining at the time of one's utterance *at some place which is indicated by features of the context of utterance.* (Often this place will be the place of one's utterance, but it needn't be.) Moreover, there is no (surface) expression in (1) which has the place in question as its content.

However, there are two points to note about this example. Firstly, this example does nothing to support the principle that a change in wording can precipitate a change in propositional content even when the words do not stand for the constituents. Rather, this example supports the principle that there can be a change in propositional constituents when there is no change in wording even in the case of sentences which contain no indexical expressions. (In other words: sentences can exhibit an indexicality which is not derived from the indexicality of their component expressions.)

Secondly, and more importantly, the genuine principle which can be derived from cases like (1) does nothing to support the account of belief reports which Crimmins and Perry wish to defend. In their view, the semantic contents of

(2a) Scott believes that Hesperus rises in the morning.

and

(2b) Scott believes that Phosphorus rises in the morning.

in a given context C, may differ because the context contributes different unarticulated constituents to (2a) and (2b). But it is incredible to suppose that cases like

---

[3] *Ibid.*, pp. 699–700.

(1) lend any credence to such a view. In the case of (1), there is no word which can plausibly be connected to the place which forms part of the semantic content of (1). However, in the case of (2a) and (2b) there are obvious candidate words—namely, 'Hesperus' and 'Phosphorus'—which could be semantically associated with the unarticulated constituents of the semantic contents of (2a) and (2b). So why suppose that these constituents of the semantic contents of (2a) and (2b) are not (parts of) the semantic contents of the words 'Hesperus' and 'Phosphorus'?

This mystery is deepened when we note that Crimmins and Perry claim that 'the whole utterance, the context *and the words uttered,* are relevant to identifying the unarticulated constituent'.[4] The point in the first example seemed to be that, since there is no word in (1) which could have the place in question as its semantic value, it is necessary to suppose that the place in question is an unarticulated semantic constituent; but now we are told that in (2a) and (2b) the words 'Hesperus' and 'Phosphorus' are 'relevant to identifying' certain constituents of the semantic contents of (2a) and (2b), and yet that these words can't have those constituents as (parts of) their semantic values.

This time, I take it that the obvious question to ask is: why not suppose that the semantic constituents which Crimmins and Perry claim are unarticulated semantic constituents in propositional attitude reports are actually (parts of) the semantic contents of the names and demonstratives which appear in those reports? Isn't all this talk of unarticulated constituents of belief reports a pointless and unmotivated complication in the theory?

In sum, then, the crucial question for the two types of semantic theory which I have discussed centres on the thesis of semantic innocence. Crimmins and Perry claim that it is "well-motivated by many considerations in the philosophy of language."[5] However, I cannot see that this is so; rather, it seems to me that this thesis is completely unmotivated, and that, in virtue of the above considerations, it is obvious that semantic theory would be better off without it. The point of the rest of this note is to explain why this is so.[6]

I

A useful way to approach this issue is to consider a distinction which has been drawn among various different components of the (allegedly) Fregean notion of sense. Among the senses (or components) of 'sense' which can be distinguished, there are at least the following:

(i) *Sense₁*: a purely conceptual or totally descriptional representation which all fully competent speakers associate with a singular term

---

[4] *Ibid.*, p. 700 (my emphasis).

[5] *Ibid.*, p. 686.

[6] I should not that some people will prefer to reject DR, while others—including Orthodox Fregeans—will wish to reject both DR and SI. Readers who do not share my conviction that DR is correct should read what follows as support for a conditional thesis, viz., given that one adopts DR, one ought then to reject SI.

(ii) *Sense$_2$*: a set or cluster of properties which are mentally represented and which speakers (more or less) idiosyncratically associate with a singular term

(iii) *Sense$_3$*: the mechanism by which the reference of a singular term is semantically determined

(iv) *Sense$_4$*: the information value of a singular term

(v) *Sense$_5$*: the semantic content of hyperintensional occurrences of a singular term (i.e., of occurrences of singular terms which are embedded within the scope of verbs of propositional attitude, etc.)

Moreover, it is useful to note that Frege's own view—or, at least, the view which is most commonly attributed to Frege, and which is taken to be the standard target of 'Direct Reference' (and 'Semantically Innocent') theorists—relies on a notion of sense which is derived from the identification of sense$_1$, sense$_3$, sense$_4$ and sense$_5$ (or perhaps sense$_2$, sense$_3$, sense$_4$ and sense$_5$).

Now, Frege's own view, as thus characterised, has been heavily criticised—especially, and most famously, by Saul Kripke.[7] However, it is important to note that the two main points established in *Naming and Necessity*—viz., (i) that there is no one notion which can plausibly be identified with sense$_1$ + sense$_3$ + sense$_4$ + sense$_5$, and (ii) that names in ordinary language have nothing like sense$_1$—have nothing at all to do with the question whether referring terms in ordinary language have something other than their ordinary referent for sense$_5$. Kripke's criticisms of Frege are arguments for DR, but say nothing at all about SI. (It should also be noted that when David Kaplan[8] introduced the term 'direct reference', what he had in mind was the thesis which denies that sense$_3$ can plausibly be identified with sense$_1$.)

More recently, there have been theorists—e.g., Salmon and Soames, and Crimmins and Perry—who have contended that the only thing that sense$_5$ can be is the referent of the singular term in question. But, as far as I can see, there is very little positive argument which has been given for this view. (I know of only three such arguments; I shall discuss them in a moment.) Rather, the main defence of this view has been that it is hard to see what else sense$_5$ could be.

However, it is important point to note that both the conventional implicature view and the unarticulated constituent view provide the materials for semantic theories in which the sense$_5$ of a name or demonstrative is not simply the usual referent of that term.

On the conventional implicature view, the entity in question would be the ordered pair consisting of the referent of the name or demonstrative (in the context in question) together with the relevant mode[9] of presentation of that referent.

---

[7] See *Naming and Necessity*, 2nd ed. (Cambridge, MA: Harvard University Press, 1980).

[8] See "Demonstratives" in J. Almog, J. Perry, and H. Wettstein (eds.), *Themes from Kaplan* (New York: Oxford University Press, 1988).

[9] Or, perhaps, modes. For the argument of this paper, I do not need to answer the question—which is not addressed by Salmon and Soames or Crimmins and Perry—whether multiply embedded singular terms require more than one mode of presentation. Consequently, I shall henceforth ignore this issue.

On the unarticulated constituent view, the entity in question would be a similar ordered pair, except that the second component would be a contextually supplied condition on modes of presentation of the referent.[10]

In slightly more detail, then, a neo-Fregean reformulation of these views would claim that the semantic content of a sentence which instantiates the schema:

(CS) X #'s that Fa

—where '#' is a propositional attitude verb, 'F' is a simple, unstructured predicate, and 'a' is a non-empty name, indexical, or demonstrative—has the form:

(CS*) $\langle$SOME M_1:$C_1\rangle\langle$SOME M_2:$C_2\rangle\langle X$ #'s $\langle\langle a, M_1\rangle\langle F, M_2\rangle\rangle\rangle$

—where a is the referent of 'a', F is the property denoted by 'F', X is the referent of 'X', #s is the relation denoted by '#s', M_1 and M_2 are variables which range over modes of presentation, and C_1 and C_2 are contextually supplied properties (conditions on modes of presentation). Moreover, a sentence which instantiates (CS) is true provided (i) that X possesses modes of presentation N_1 and N_2 which satisfy the conditions C_1 and C_2, and which are of a and F, respectively; and (ii) that, in virtue of (i), X stands in the #-relation to the state of affairs $\langle a, F\rangle$.

I take it that it is clear that this view is very similar to the views that Salmon and Soames, and Crimmins and Perry defend—but it does not require, and nor is it even compatible with, the acceptance of semantic innocence.

I mentioned earlier that I know of three positive arguments which have been advanced in defence of semantic innocence. These are (i) the appeal to intuition; (ii) the argument from free variables; and (iii) the argument for universal substitutivity. Since two of these arguments—the argument from intuition and the argument for universal substitutivity—are also arguments against opacity, these are not arguments which Crimmins and Perry could espouse (and, indeed, I suspect that they might well agree with the criticisms which I have to make of these arguments). However, it is important that we consider all of the available arguments.

1. The Appeal to Intuition

In his book *Frege's Puzzle*, Nathan Salmon goes to great lengths to proclaim the intuitive appeal of a trio of theories ("The Naive Theory," "The Singly Modified Naive Theory," "The Doubly Modified Naive Theory") which make essential use of semantic innocence. According to Salmon, the natural appeal of these theories

---

[10] Given how little Soames and Salmon say about modes of presentation, it is not clear that these two views are in competition. 'Modes of presentation' can be taken to mean nothing more than 'whatever is required to make the theory of propositional attitude ascriptions come out right'; however, it can also be given a (slightly) more precise interpretation, e.g., 'way of thinking of the referent', etc. Given the more precise reading, then—following the spirit but not the letter of the view developed by Crimmins and Perry—there is good reason to suppose that *contextually supplied conditions on modes of presentation* will be incorporated into the semantic content of propositional attitude ascriptions.

constitutes good evidence of their (close approximation to the) truth. But in what does this "natural appeal" consist? It may be true that "The Naive Theory" (i.e., the most straightforward theory which incorporates the principles DR and SI) is the first theory which one is likely to think of when one comes to theorise about the semantics of natural languages—but this is not much of a proof of the value of the theory. Moreover, it is very important to note that it is not plausible to claim that "The Naive Theory" is the theory which we tacitly employ in our ordinary use of language; for—at least *prima facie*—our ordinary use of propositional attitude ascriptions does not conform to "The Naive Theory." But what other reason can there be to suppose that the 'natural appeal' of these theories is a recommendation of them?

Even if we waive these worries, there is a further point to consider, viz., that—as I have already argued—one can easily convert Salmon's theories into otherwise equally plausible theories which reject SI, but which have the advantage that they get the distribution of truth-values to propositional attitude ascriptions to accord with pre-theoretical intuition. Consequently, it seems that the appeal to intuition does nothing to support semantic innocence.

2. The Argument from Free Variables

In the introduction to their anthological collection *Propositions and Attitudes*,[11] Salmon and Soames claim that semantic innocence is especially compelling in the case of at least one sort of referring expression, viz., free individual variables in open sentences. For example, consider the open sentence:

(3) x is pretty

What more is there for the variable 'x' to contribute to the semantic content of (3) than its referent under an assignment—i.e., how can 'x' be anything other than semantically innocent?

This argument is rather puzzling—for, of course, open sentences belong to formal languages, not to natural languages. So why should we suppose that this argument has any relevance for our present investigation? But, in any case, consider the open sentence:

(4) John believes that x is pretty

Does it now seem right to ask what more there is for the variable 'x' to contribute to the semantic content of (4) than its referent under an assignment? Surely to insist on this would be simply to beg the question.

There is a further argument which can be made in support of the view that the occurrence of 'x' in (4) must be semantically innocent. As Salmon notes in *Frege's Puzzle*, it may seem that the existence of sentences like:

(4a) (∃x)(x = Ted Kennedy & Tom is thinking that x is tall)

---

[11] Oxford: Oxford University Press, 1988.

force the conclusion that the last occurrence of 'x' in (4a) is semantically innocent. As Salmon puts it: "Once it is granted that this sentence is true, it follows by principles of formal semantics that its component open sentence

(4b) Tom is thinking that x is tall

must be true under the assignment of Ted Kennedy as the value of the variable 'x'. . . . [But] the fundamental semantic characteristic of a variable 'x' with an assigned value . . . is that its only semantic value is its referent. There is nothing else for it to contribute to the semantic content of the sentences in which it figures."[12]

This argument can be—and in my opinion should be—resisted. A natural first thought is that in a sentence like (4), the variable 'x' needs to contribute both a referent and a condition on modes of presentation of that referent to the semantic content of the sentence. In order to protect this intuition in the face of examples like (4a), what we need to do is to insist that what an assignment function assigns to an occurrence of a variable depends upon the degree of embedding of that occurrence of the variable within the scope of propositional attitude operators. An unembedded variable simply requires a referent; but an embedded variable requires a package which contains both a referent and a condition on modes of presentation of that referent.[13]

Finally, it should be noted that it is not even clear that there is an argument from the nature of free variables in simple sentences like (3) to the conclusion that a theory which identifies $sense_1$ and $sense_3$ is in error. (In other words—and contrary to what is often supposed—it is not even clear that an argument from the nature of free variables provides good support for the thesis of direct reference.) For it seems that an Orthodox Fregean could claim that the $sense_1$ of a free individual variable—i.e., the description which must be known by any competent user of an open sentence containing that free variable—is embedded in the assignment function. Without the assignment function, (3) has no semantic content—so there is a sense in which the assignment function is 'part of the meaning of (3)'. Of course, this point connects to the initial observation that there are no free individual variables in natural languages.

I conclude that the argument from free variables is unpersuasive.

3. The Argument for Universal Substitutivity

In his paper "Direct Reference, Propositional Attitudes, and Semantic Content," Scott Soames suggests that there are sound arguments involving indexicals and demonstratives which directly support the thesis of semantic innocence. For example, suppose that:

(5) A believes that Ruth Barcan is F is true with respect to a context c_1. Then:

(6) A believes that I am F

---

[12] *Ibid.,* p: 4. (I have changed the numbering of propositions to fit my own scheme.)

[13] As I mentioned earlier, there are many questions of detail which need to be answered, for example: how many senses are required for a variable which is multiply embedded in the scope of verbs of propositional attitude? However, there is surely no reason to suppose that these questions cannot be answered.

will be true in a closely related context c_2 in which Ruth Barcan (= Ruth Marcus) is the agent. (We suppose, for the sake of the example, that 'F' does not contain first-person pronouns or other related devices.) Suppose that the audience in the context c_2 is someone who knows the agent as 'Ruth Marcus'. Then it seems that there will be a further closely related context c_3 in which

(7) A believes that Ruth Marcus is F

is true. "Thus, substitution of one co-referential name or indexical for another preserves truth-value. Since there seems to be nothing special about this example, we have a general argument for [substitutivity as licensed by semantic innocence]."[14]

The problem with this argument is that c_1 is not c_3: for what needs to be shown, in order to justify semantic innocence, is that—with no other contextual changes of any sort—co-referential names, etc. can be substituted in PA-ascriptions without changing the associated semantic content. For all that we have been told, (7) might well have been false in c_1, and so the argument is unsuccessful.

Since these are all the positive arguments for semantic innocence with which I am familiar, I conclude that it is just not true that semantic innocence is well-motivated by many—nor, indeed, by any—considerations in the philosophy of language. However, since—as I mentioned earlier—Crimmins and Perry also reject at least two of the above arguments, there is a further puzzle which now arises, viz., how can it be that Crimmins and Perry claim that semantic innocence is well-motivated by many considerations in the philosophy of language?

The only suggestion that I can offer is that they suppose that it is crucial to any neo-Fregean semantic theory to suppose that 'senses' are descriptions or conditions on referents.[15] Now, of course, this supposition is crucial to Frege's own semantic theory—for Frege wanted to use senses to solve problems about the cognitive significance and potential informativeness of sentences.[16] However, from the conclusion that nothing like Frege's solution to these puzzles can be made to work, it does not follow that nothing like Frege's solution to puzzles about the substitution of coreferring expressions in belief reports can be made to work. And, indeed, if one supposes that 'senses' are descriptions of, or conditions on, ways of thinking of objects and properties, then it is clear that Crimmins and Perry are committed to them—and hence ought to reject the principle of semantic innocence.

There is one final consideration which might be offered against the proposed neo-Fregean reformulation of new theories of reference, viz., that this sort of

---

[14] *Ibid.*, pp. 67.

[15] See their formulations of DR and SI (on p. 686) for evidence that they do make this supposition.

[16] E.g., Frege wanted to use 'senses' to solve what Salmon calls 'Frege's Puzzle': how can 'Hesperus is Hesperus' and 'Hesperus is Phosphorus' differ in cognitive significance?

account won't be able to handle belief reports "with content sentences containing devices of underarticulation, and those with no content sentences at all, but which instead are completed with the likes of 'what you said', 'the same thing', and 'Church's Thesis'."[17] However, if we can give a neo-Fregean reformulation of the semantic theories of Salmon and Soames, and Crimmins and Perry, then it is clear that this objection can be met (at least on the assumption that the original versions of those theories can handle these examples).

In the first sort of case, if there really are devices of underarticulation, then both objects and what I have called 'senses$_5$' could be subject to underarticulation. So, for example, the content of:

(8)　John believes that it's raining

could be

$\langle$ *John, Bel,* $\langle\langle$ *it's raining,* [it's raining]$_c\rangle$ $\langle t,$ [t]$_c\rangle$ $\langle$ *place,* [place]$_c\rangle\rangle\rangle$

where [place]$_c$ is a contextually supplied condition on the notion of that place which is an unarticulated constituent of the content of (8), and where [place]$_c$ is itself an unarticulated constituent of that content. No problem.

What about cases like 'what you said', etc? Well, consider a situation in which I utter:

(9)　Hesperus is visible in the morning

and then you say

(10)　John believes what you said.

If 'what you said' is to be taken as a sort of anaphoric device, then (10) should be taken to have the content:

$\langle$ *John Bel* $\langle\langle$ *Hesperus,* [Hesperus]$_c\rangle$ $\langle$ *visible in the morning,* [visible in the morning]$_c\rangle\rangle\rangle$

If, on the other hand, 'what you said' is taken to be quantificational, then the earlier discussion of quantification shows that there will be no difficulty. (At the very least: if there is a problem, it remains to be discovered.)

I conclude that there is no reason to adopt semantic innocence.[18,19]

---

[17] Crimmins and Perry, *op. cit.,* p. 710.

[18] Moreover, I note that John Perry has had trouble with semantic innocence before—cf. Scott Soames. "Lost Innocence." *Linguistics and Philosophy* 18 (1985) pp. 59–72. I suggest that perhaps it is time he gave it up.

[19] This paper is based on a section of my unpublished doctoral dissertation, *Attitude Problems,* Princeton University, 1990. I would like to thank Gil Harman, David Lewis, Scott Soames. Bas van Fraassen, Richard Holton, Steve Rieber, Allen Hazen, Len Goddard, Kai-Yee Wong, Frank Jackson, Philip Pettit and the editors and reviewers of this *Journal* for helpful comments.

NOTE ON AN ATTEMPTED REFUTATION OF FREGE

Michael Dummett

Since this book went to press, I have had an opportunity to see Saul Kripke's 'Naming and Necessity', in *Semantics of Natural Language*, ed. Harman and Davidson, pp. 253–355. This essay mounts a strong attack on Frege's theory of proper names, in the strict sense of the term (which, for convenience, will alone be used throughout this note), an attack deserving of extended comment. There are a number of distinguishable issues.

(1) Kripke alludes to those, such as Paul Ziff, who hold that proper names have no meaning and are not part of the language, but dissociates himself from them. He attributes to Frege an express declaration that the sense of a proper name is always the same as that of some one definite description, though noting that Frege allowed that a proper name in common use in natural language may have many different such senses associated with it by different speakers. He proceeds to launch an attack on this theory. In fact, Frege made no explicit statement to this effect, and it is extremely dubious that he supposed such a thing. It is true that, in giving examples of possible senses that may be associated with a proper name, Frege expresses these by means of definite descriptions; but this should be considered as merely a device for a brief characterization of a sense, rather than as a means of conveying the thesis which Kripke ascribes to Frege. What is important about Frege's theory is that a proper name, if it is to be considered as having a determinate sense, must have associated with it a specific criterion for recognizing a given object as the referent of the name; the referent of the name, if any, is whatever object satisfies that criterion. Sometimes the criterion may be capable of being conveyed by means of a definite description, in other cases not. It is therefore of importance to note how much of Kripke's criticism depends upon his excessively narrow interpretation of Frege, and how much is unaffected by taking Frege's theory as a 'sense theory' but not necessarily a 'description theory' (in fact, most of it is unaffected by the adoption of the broader interpretation).

Kripke's arguments are quite different from those of Wittgenstein apropos of the name 'Moses'. For Wittgenstein, the sense of a proper name is given, not by a single specific criterion of identification, but by a cluster of such criteria: for an object to be the referent of the name, it is not necessary that it satisfy all these criteria, but only that it satisfy most of them, or, perhaps, merely a suitable number of them. Thus, for Wittgenstein, the sense of a proper name overdetermines its reference, and is, at the same time, elastic, in that we are prepared in advance to drop some of our criteria of identification if they are discovered not to converge with the others. Kripke regards Wittgenstein's modification as a mere variant of Frege's theory, as much subject to his counter-arguments as the original Fregean form.

(2) Kripke's first argument makes play with a distinction of Geach's I cite on p. 168, viz. that a proper name may be *introduced* by means of a definite description without thereby being stipulated as *equivalent* to it. Kripke describes this situation as one in which the definite description is used to 'fix the reference' of the name, but not to 'give its meaning'. He is prepared to allow that a proper name is frequently introduced in this way; he says further that, by stretching the application of 'definite

description', we can force the case of a name introduced by ostension into this mould. Actually, since we do not need to ascribe to Frege the thesis that the sense of a proper name is always that of some definite description, there is no need to go in for any such Procrustean manoeuvre; we may simply say that Kripke agrees with Frege that a proper name is first introduced into the language by associating with it a criterion of identification, but that he differs from him in holding that such a criterion serves merely to fix the reference of the name and not to give its meaning. In fact, Kripke accuses Frege precisely of confusing these two things: he says (p. 277) that Frege uses 'sense' in two senses, both for the way the reference of a term is determined and for its meaning. We shall ask later what Kripke understands by 'meaning'.

Kripke uses various arguments, which will be considered later, to show that the means used to fix the reference of a name on its first introduction does not subsequently remain that which determines its reference. For the time being, however, we are concerned only with that argument of Kripke's which purports to prove that, even where the reference of a name is assumed to be fixed by means of some one definite description, still the description will not give the meaning of the name, i.e. will not be synonymous with it. It is therefore worth while to select an example for which it would generally be agreed that that assumption was true. Among personal proper names (from which, like most writers on proper names, Kripke draws most of his examples), there are very few instances of this; but one is that of the name 'St. Anne'. There are many legends about St. Anne, including an account of her life in one of the apocryphal Gospels; but there is little reason to suppose that any of these stories enshrines a genuine tradition. A due scepticism about these stories is not, however, an obstacle to the acceptance of the existing cult of St. Anne (the celebration of her feast, etc.), although this demands that the object of the cult be taken as having been a genuine historical person. The reference of the name 'St. Anne' can therefore be taken as fixed in essentially only one way, namely by means of the description 'the mother of the Blessed Virgin Mary': but we can claim to know nothing whatever about its referent, save for the obvious facts that she was a married Jewish woman living at the end of the first century B.C., etc. There is not even any presumption that the name she was known by in her lifetime was 'Anne' (Kripke makes pointlessly heavy weather of the fact that a proper name may have a translation from one language into another).

In the next chapter (p. 168), the only substance which is given to Geach's distinction between introducing a name by means of a definite description and stipulating it as equivalent to it concerns the case in which the definite description, and therefore the proper name, in fact proves to lack a referent. In such a case, an atomic sentence containing the definite description would, in accordance with Russell's Theory of Descriptions, be false, whereas the corresponding sentence containing the proper name would be neither true nor false: this shows that the proper name and the definite description would not coincide in sense. Kripke, however, claims to discern a far more striking difference than this between proper names and definite descriptions, which would preclude a proper name's ever being equivalent in meaning to a definite description: their behaviour, namely, in model contexts. It is evidently true, for example, to say, 'The mother of Mary was necessarily a parent', at least where this is understood as meaning, 'It is necessarily true that, if there was such a person as Mary, and there was one and only one woman who was her mother, then that woman was a parent'. But it is not so evident that it would be true to say, 'St. Anne was necessarily a parent', meaning thereby, 'It is necessarily true that, if there was such a woman as St. Anne, then she was a parent'. For surely we can truly say, 'St. Anne might have died in infancy' or 'St. Anne might have remained a virgin all her life'. It appears to follow that 'St. Anne' and 'the mother of Mary' cannot be synonymous.

This part of Kripke's argument has very little force. It bears a certain resemblance to an argument cited by Moore to cast doubt upon the thesis that 'exists' is not a predicate—more specifically, a thesis of Russell's that we cannot meaningfully say, 'This exists'—from the fact that one can usually truly say, 'This might not have existed'. The contrast drawn above between proper names and definite descriptions in modal contexts is not as sharp as there made out. After all, even though there is an intuitive sense in which it is quite correct to say, 'St. Anne might never have become a parent', there is also an equally clear sense in which we may rightly say, 'St. Anne cannot but have been a parent', provided always that this is understood as meaning that, if there was such a woman as St. Anne, then she can only have been a parent. Kripke indeed acknowledges that such a sense exists, although not in connection with personal proper names. He comments on Wittgenstein's example of the standard metre rod in Paris, and insists, as against Wittgenstein, that it is perfectly proper to ascribe to that rod the property of being 1 metre long, on the ground that we can truly say of it that it might not have been 1 metre long. But, in arguing this, he also grants that, in another way, it is a priori true that the standard metre is 1 metre long. Of course, this case is not one to do with what is ordinarily called a proper name: but Kripke wishes to apply his distinction between 'fixing the reference' and 'giving the meaning' to this case also, holding that taking the metre rod as the standard is a way of fixing the reference, but not of giving the meaning, of the word 'metre'. Hence the concession must be taken to apply to proper names in the more usual sense, at least whenever there is something specific which may be taken as fixing the reference.

Conversely, however, there is equally a clear sense in which it is true to say, 'The mother of Mary might not have been a parent', and this Kripke also acknowledges. Thus he says (p. 279) that one might truly say that the man who taught Alexander might not have taught Alexander, but adds that it could not have been true that: the man who taught Alexander didn't teach Alexander. Again, in footnote 25 he says that the teacher of Alexander might not have taught Alexander, and, in such circumstances, would not have been the teacher of Alexander. So far, therefore, no difference between proper names and definite descriptions appears at all. In both cases, there seems to be an ambiguity in modal statements containing them: the very same ambiguity in both cases, which accordingly cannot be used to differentiate the two types of expression.

That the situation as regards proper names appears, so far, exactly like that with definite descriptions is obscured by the fact that Kripke adopts completely different explanations of the ambiguity in the two cases. In the case of definite descriptions, he says that the ambiguity arises because of uncertainties of scope (in the sense in which Russell speaks of the scope of a definite description). If we abbreviate 'x taught Alexander' as 'Tx', the sentence 'The teacher of Alexander might not have taught Alexander' may be written:

$$\Diamond \neg T \, (\iota x : Tx).$$

If we adopt Russell's Theory of Descriptions, the definite description can be eliminated in more than one way, according to what we take its scope to be. If we take it to be '$\neg T(\xi)$', we obtain:

$$\Diamond \exists y \, [\forall x \, (Tx \leftrightarrow x = y) \, \& \, \neg \, Ty].$$

This expresses the sense in which the sentence is false, i.e. the sense in which Kripke means to deny it by saying that it could not have been true that: the teacher of Alexander didn't teach Alexander. The definite description is here within the scope of the modal operator. If, however, we take the modal operator to fall, conversely, within the scope of the description operator, so that the scope of the latter is '$\Diamond \neg T \, (\xi)$', we obtain:

$$\exists y \, [\forall x \, (Tx \leftrightarrow x = y) \, \& \, \Diamond \, \neg \, Ty].$$

This expresses the sense in which the sentence is true, that is, the sense in which Kripke wants to assert that the teacher of Alexander might not have taught Alexander. There is, indeed, nothing special to definite descriptions here; questions of the relative scope of the quantifier and the modal operator arise equally with 'Some teachers might not have been teachers'. It is, admittedly, obvious that anyone who says this must mean

$$\exists x \, (Qx \, \& \, \Diamond \, \neg \, Qx)$$

(where 'Qx' abbreviates 'x is a teacher'), and not

$$\Diamond \exists x \, (Qx \, \& \, \neg \, Qx),$$

since the latter would be such a stupid thing to say; but with, say, 'Some narcotics might not have been harmful', there is a genuine ambiguity.

Kripke is, of course, vividly aware that to invoke the notion of scope in order to account for the ambiguity is explanatory only when it is supplemented by an account of quantification into a modal context: i.e. when we either can explain when the predicate '$\Diamond \neg T \, (\xi)$' is true of an object, or can give a suitable account of the range of the bound variables as being something other than ordinary objects. We shall in due course consider how Kripke thinks this supplementation is to be carried out.

A theory according to which proper names were merely disguised definite descriptions would have no difficulty with the parallel ambiguity that arises when proper names occur in modal contexts: it can give a uniform account of both kinds of ambiguity, in both cases invoking the notion of scope in the same way. For such an account to work, in the case of proper names, it would be unnecessary either to adopt Russell's Theory of Descriptions or to maintain that proper names are always strictly synonymous with definite descriptions. So long as it is acknowledged, as it must be, that definite descriptions may sometimes lack reference, and that the existence or non-existence of a referent will, in general, affect the truth-value of a sentence in which a description occurs, there will be a need to determine the scope of a description in a complex sentence, whether or not Russell's Theory of Descriptions is taken as the right way of determining the truth-value once the scope has been agreed. One may, indeed, adopt some convention which uniquely determines the scope without the need for any special indication of it; but the question is there to be resolved. Likewise, so long as it is allowed that there may be proper names which are meaningful and yet not guaranteed a reference, and that the possession or lack of a reference by a proper name will in general affect the truth-value of a sentence in which it occurs, the question of scope may arise for a proper name. This is quite independent of whether or not it is held that the question whether a given proper name has reference may always be equated with the question whether some definite description does. It is independent also of whether it is held that an atomic sentence containing a proper name without a reference is false, or, with Frege, that it is neither true nor false. Again, the question may be resolved for all contexts by adopting some uniform convention determining the scope; thus Frege may be represented as having adopted the convention that the scope of a proper name or definite description is always to be taken as the widest possible, i.e. the whole sentence. The question was, nevertheless, there to be resolved.

It is thus plain that, so far as the present point is concerned, any theory which represents proper names and definite descriptions as functioning in essentially similar manners has an advantage over one that widens the difference between them, in that it allows a uniform explanation to be given of what appears to be just the same phenomenon—the occurrence of ambiguity in modal contexts—in the two cases. Kripke, on the other hand, wants to give an entirely different explanation of the phenomenon when it relates to proper names. In this case, he acknowledges no role for the notion of scope: and so he explains the ambiguity by saying that we are concerned, under the two interpretations, with different modal notions, different kinds of possibility. The sense in which we can truly say that the standard metre rod could not but be 1 metre long, or that St. Anne can only have been a parent, is an epistemic one. This does not mean that we are in these cases asserting the kind of epistemic necessity usually considered by philosophers, under which 'It must be . . .' means 'It follows from what we know . . .' and 'It may be . . .' means 'It would be consistent with all we know . . .'. In the present case, our knowledge is genuinely a priori knowledge, given in advance of any particular observations or experience relating to the subject-matter of the sentence. It is knowledge derived solely from a grasp of the way in which the words are used, i.e. from the fact that 'the length of the standard metre rod' is used to fix the reference of '1 metre' and 'the mother of Mary' to fix the reference of 'St. Anne'. By contrast, the kind of necessity that we are concerned to deny when we say that the standard metre rod might have been shorter than 1 metre (e.g. if it had been deformed), or that St. Anne might not have been a parent (e.g. if she had never married), does not depend solely upon our grasp of the use of the words: it is a metaphysical necessity. Kripke reserves the phrase 'a priori' for epistemic necessities of the first kind, and the word 'necessary' for metaphysical necessities.

Kripke's views, thus set out, appear implausible. As remarked, we have one and the same phenomenon occurring both for proper names and definite descriptions.

There cannot, therefore, be any argument from this fact alone to the conclusion that a proper name can never be equivalent to a definite description. In the case of definite descriptions, Kripke explains the phenomenon in terms of the notion of scope. For proper names, on the other hand, he considers the notion of scope inapplicable, and therefore invokes a distinction between two kinds of possibility. The argument for saying, in this case, that there are two kinds of possibility seems no stronger than it would be in the case of definite descriptions. When we say that the mother of Mary can only have been a parent, in that sense in which it is true to say this, are we not expressing a priori knowledge, based solely on our understanding of the words, precisely similar to that expressed by saying that the standard metre rod can only be 1 metre long? When, on the other hand, we say that the mother of Mary might not have been a parent, are we not concerned with the very same kind of metaphysical necessity involved in saying that St. Anne might not have been a parent? To explain the ambiguity, in the definite description case, in terms of uncertainty of scope, however, requires that the modal operator be taken as unambiguous: if its sense shifted, we should not need also to suppose that its scope altered, as we pass from one interpretation of the sentence to the other. Quite plainly, these considerations, so far from providing grounds against the assimilation of proper names to definite descriptions, supply substantial evidence in its favour.

This is not to deny that a distinction between the necessary and the a priori is called for. I shall discuss this in detail only in the second volume, when we come to consider Frege's doctrine on analyticity; but for the present we may observe the following. Frege uses both the terms 'analytic' and 'a priori' in an epistemic sense: the status of a sentence, as analytic, synthetic a priori or a posteriori, depends upon the kind of justification that could be given for it (only true sentences are in question): not, indeed, the kind of justification which we in fact possess, if we possess any at all, but that which we should in principle be capable of giving. If, however, we agree with Frege in adopting a realistic interpretation of the sentences of our language, there is room for non-epistemic versions of these notions as well. To adopt a realistic interpretation is to hold that the sense of our sentences is given in such a way as to relate to their determination as true or as false by a reality existing independently of us, and that, in a well-constructed language, every sentence will thus be determined as true or as false, independently of our capacity, even in principle, for recognizing what truth-value it has. Opposed to a realistic interpretation of this kind is any view which holds that the senses of our sentences are always given in terms of the means available to us for recognizing them as true or as false, so that the only notion of truth available to us is one under which a sentence is true only if there is at least some means in principle available to us for recognizing it as true. On any kind of idealistic view of the latter kind, any intelligible notion of necessity must, like the notion of truth, ultimately be of an epistemic character; that is, it must relate to the means by which we could recognize a sentence as true. This is not to say that, from an idealistic standpoint, we might nevertheless not admit several distinguishable kinds of necessity. But, from a realistic standpoint, such as Frege took, the way is open to introduce non-epistemic notions of necessity, although Frege himself did not do so. We may, that is, distinguish sentences as ontically (rather than epistemically) necessary or contingent according to the kind of thing in virtue of which they are true, independently of the means available to us for recognizing them as true; and, within this general notion of ontic necessity, we may be able to distinguish as many varieties as within that of epistemic necessity. A very clear case is precisely one adduced by Kripke. On Frege's view of arithmetic, a provable number-theoretic statement is analytic, in Frege's sense of 'analytic', that is, the epistemic sense. But if we adopt a platonistic view of number theory, i.e. if we interpret it realistically, as Frege did, then the truth of a number-theoretic statement does not depend upon our being able, even in principle, to find a proof of it. Hence it is possible that, say, Fermat's Last Theorem should be true, but not analytic in Frege's sense. It is, how-ever, evident that there would still be an intuitive sense in which it was necessarily, not contingently, true, that is, ontically necessary. In the particular example, this is plain from the consideration that, had it been false, its negation would have been epistemically analytic (since there would be a counterexample which we should be in principle capable of recognizing as such): this is not, of course, to claim that every ontically analytic statement would have this feature.

This distinction should be compared, though perhaps not equated, with that made by Aquinas in rejecting the ontological argument for the existence of God between a statement that is *per se nota* (necessary in itself) and one that is, in addition, *nota quoad nos* (necessary relative to us). The statement that God exists is, he thinks, *per se nota* but not *nota quoad nos*. This means that it is ontically necessary but not epistemically so, and hence there cannot be an a priori proof of it, such as the ontological argument purports to provide. This distinction has been jeered at by those who have argued that, since the language in which the state-ment 'God exists' is expressed is our language, if it is not analytic relative to us, then it cannot be analytic at all, but must be simply contingent; and they have proceeded to attempt to impale theists on the horns of a dilemma. Either the statement 'God exists', if true at all, is contingently so, i.e. there is a God but might not have been one; or it is analytic, in which case various dire, though dubious, consequences are supposed to flow, such as that one cannot base any expectations on one's belief in its truth. The theist rightly fights shy of allowing that there might not have been a God. He may, indeed, be properly suspicious of the consequences alleged to follow from admitting that 'God exists' is analytic, especially in view of the fact that his opponent's philosophical position usually embraces the thesis that all true mathematical statements are analytic; he may, nevertheless, like Aquinas, feel unwilling to allow that God's existence can be known a priori, by reflection merely on the meanings of the words. What his opponent has over-looked is that, even though the language we speak is our language in the sense that it is we that have given to our words the meanings that they bear, it is never-theless part of any realist interpretation of language that that meaning is such that we grasp what it is for a given sentence to be true independently of the means we have for knowing it to be true. Until a realist interpretation is shown to be unten-able, there remains room for the possibility that a statement may not be capable of being known a priori by us, and yet have a meaning such that its truth-conditions could not but be fulfilled.

These remarks do not purport to give definite substance to the notion of ontic necessity, merely to indicate that there is a fairly compelling intuitive content to the notion, and, on any realistic view of language, room for its introduction. A possible way to approach it would be as follows. The simplest statements of our language are those that can be used as reports of observation or of other effective ways of determining their truth or falsity. For such statements, therefore, the realistic and idealistic interpretations coincide: we know what it is for such a statement to be true because we know how to determine it as true. As more complex methods of sentence-formation are introduced into the language, we step outside the range of statements that are even in principle effectively decidable by us. In doing so, however, we retain the capacity for knowing what it is for our statements to be true or false, and our grasp of the fact that they are determinately one or the other. This we do by extending various linguistic devices beyond the range within which we are capable of effectively applying them, by analogy with the more restricted contexts in which we first learned them, and within which we could apply them effectively. The analogy which we implicitly rely on is with a hypothetical observer not subject to the restrictions to which we ourselves are subject. A clear case would be the use of quantification over an infinite domain. We understand the quantifiers in the first place by learning to use them over actually surveyable domains: such a statement as 'Every room in the house has a fireplace' can be checked by inspecting each room in turn, and taking the logical product of the truth-values of the instances so determined. When, now, we use quantification over an infinite totality, say that of the natural numbers, we understand the truth-conditions of a statement involving such quantification by analogy with the primitive case: we tacitly appeal to the notion of an observer who is able to survey the whole infinite domain within a finite time. We ourselves are incapable in principle of doing this, and so, to determine a universally quantified number-theoretic statement as true, we have to have recourse to indirect means, that is, to means which do not directly mirror the way in which the truth-conditions of the statement are given to us. But our understanding of those truth-conditions, and therefore our capacity for conceiving that the statement may be true even though we have no means of recognizing it as such, depend upon the possibility of our transcending in thought the limitations which are, in practice or in principle, imposed upon our intellectual operations.

I do not know whether this is the right account of the matter. I do not even know whether realism can be made plausible, let alone whether, if so, the line just sketched is the right line for the realist to take. But, if it is, then it is clear along what lines the notion of ontic analyticity must be explained. If, for the understanding of a given sentence, it is necessary to invoke the conception of a being whose powers of observation or mental capacities transcended ours in a given respect, then the statement, if true, is was far more dominant, it is to be presumed that, if the discovery had been made then that the calculation of the year of Christ's birth was in error, the dating system would have been adjusted accordingly. So at that time—let us say in 1001 A.D.—it would have been possible, and correct, to assert a priori that Christ was born in 1 A.D., at least if the speaker was prepared to admit that he could be mistaken in supposing that Christ's birth took place 1000 years previously. Would someone who made such an assertion a priori have been expressing a priori knowledge of a contingent fact? Surely not: it may be a contingent matter that Christ was born in the year in which he was, but (given the conventions here being assumed about the dating system) not that he was born *in 1 A.D.* But is it a contingent fact that Christ was born in the year in which he was? I am not here raising a theological question, but could equally well ask: Is it a contingent fact that Shakespeare was born in the year in which he was? Plainly, the answer is 'No', if the question is taken to be whether the sentence, 'Shakespeare was born in the year in which he was born', is only contingently true. In the case of Shakespeare, we may say that this is not the question intended, but rather the question whether the sentence, 'Shakespeare was born in 1564', is only contingently true. But, in the case of Christ, the matter cannot be resolved in this way, or, at least, could not have been in 1001, since the sense, if any, in which it might be questioned whether 'Christ was born in 1 A.D.' was only contingently true has yet to be made out. And this is how it is with the metre rod. If it is a contingent fact that the standard metre rod is 1 metre long, its contingency is not to be accounted for in terms of the a posteriori character of our knowledge of the truth either of the sentence, 'The standard metre rod has the length that it has', or of the sentence, 'The standard metre rod is 1 metre long.'

In a sense, the sentence, 'I am here', is true a priori: that is, any English speaker knows that, whenever he consciously utters the sentence, 'I am here', he will be saying something true. So, if I say, 'I am here', am I expressing a priori knowledge of some contingent fact? By reasoning as Kripke does, the fact must surely be taken as contingent, since I may truly say, 'I might not have been here'. Obviously this is wrong. By saying, 'I am here', I may succeed in telling someone who hears me where I am: but my knowledge that I can always truly say, 'I am here', is quite compatible with my lacking, on a given occasion, the remotest idea where I am. In knowing that I can truly say, 'I am here', I know nothing at all of my own where-abouts. Equally, if someone has no idea at all what length a metre is, save for knowing that it is the length of some rod in Paris which he has never seen, he may still know a priori that the metre rod is 1 metre long, but, in an intuitive sense, he does not know how long the metre rod is, and hence does not give expression, by his remark, to knowledge of any contingent fact. If someone in 1001 understands the dating system, and hence is able to say a priori, 'Christ was born in 1 A.D.', but has no idea whatever what year it is when he says it, then, again, he does not, by his remark, express any contingent fact. It is, indeed, different if he does know the date, for then there is an at least arguably contingent fact which follows from what he says together with the fact, which he has not stated, that it is then 1001 A.D., the fact, namely, that Christ was born 1,000 years before: but then no one would think that he knew this fact simply in virtue of his grasp of the dating system.

It thus does not appear that the statements which Kripke wants to character-ize as both contingent and known a priori can be so described if they are taken unambiguously. In 1001 someone who was ignorant of the principle underlying the dating system but knew what the date was might, if he gave the year of Christ's birth as 1 A.D., be said to know when Christ was born, and to know something sub-stantial thereby; but he would not know the same thing as that known by someone aware of the principle of the dating system but ignorant even what century he was living in. (The improbability of these two extreme cases is beside the point.) We shall note later that it is of crucial importance that two people—these two imaginary individuals, for example—speak the same language and intend to be understood as speaking in that language. (As Quine has in effect pointed out, the situation is not essentially different if they speak different languages, but ones between which there is a generally recognized system of intertranslation.) This fact mitigates the effect of the different ways the two individuals imagined fix the reference of the expression '1 A.D.' Frege would say that they attached different senses to the expression. We are less inclined to describe the situation in this way; and one valid reason for this disinclination is awareness of the relevance of the fact that each intends to be held responsible for using the expression with that reference which is commonly agreed by speakers of the language which they have in common. It is, for this reason, entirely wrong to say that, because they attach different senses to the same expression, they therefore strictly speaking talk different languages. Nevertheless, it is equally wrong to minimize the truth in the contention that they attach different senses to the expression. We are less ready to admit this than we are to concede that they are different facts which they show knowledge of when they say, 'Christ was born in 1 A.D.' But, as has been emphasized several times, Frege's notion of sense is a cognitive one: difference in cognitive value is precisely what requires difference in sense to explain it.

Kripke wants, indeed, to dissociate the necessary/contingent distinction from epistemic considerations altogether. But this he fails to do. The paradox which we are presently engaged in resolving, and which arose from Kripke's thesis that something can be known a priori and yet be contingent, arises precisely from asking how, by merely stipulating a certain means of fixing the reference of an expression, someone could come to know a contingent fact about the world. If the status of a fact, as necessary or contingent, really had no bearing on the way in which it could come to be known, if at all, then this question would no more be paradoxical than the question how someone, by using field-glasses, could come to know an amusing fact.

What, then, is the fact whose contingency we express by saying that the standard metre rod might have been shorter or longer than 1 metre, but which is not expressed when we say a priori that it is 1 metre long or that it has the length which it has? So long as we pose the question in this way, there does not seem to be any satisfactory answer. Rather, it is not so much that some contingent fact obtains, at least, if we understand a fact as something that can be expressed by means of a sentence understood in some specific sense, but that a certain object, namely the standard metre rod, possesses a contingent property, that of being 1 metre long; or perhaps that a certain length, namely a metre, possesses the contingent property of being the length of the standard metre rod. If we refer to the rod as 'the standard metre rod', then we guarantee that (provided we are referring to anything at all) we are referring to a rod 1 metre in length; if we describe the length of the rod as being 1 metre, then, given that the reference of the word 'metre' is fixed as it is, we guarantee that we are referring to a length which is that of the standard metre rod. But that very rod which we refer to might have been of a different length; that very length which we refer to might not have been that of the standard metre. This sort of contingency cannot be grasped in terms of the notion of a contingent *fact*, but only in terms of that of an accidental *property*. And, indeed, Kripke himself strongly emphasizes the importance for his doctrine of the distinction between essential and accidental properties of an object. But what this means is that we cannot attain to the required notion of contingency by concentrating on the linguistic from 'It is contingent (possible, necessary) that . . .', where the gap is to be filled by an entire sentence; we have, instead, to understand the form 'It is contingently (possibly, necessarily) true of ξ that . . . ξ . . .'. We have to explain, not what it is for the sentence, 'The standard metre rod is 1 metre long', to be contingently true, but what it is for the predicate 'ξ is 1 metre long' to be contingently true of an object; equivalently, we have to understand, not the sentence '◇ (the standard metre rod is not 1 metre long)', but the predicate '◇ (ξ is not 1 metre long)'. Just the same will be the case with the contingency which we express by saying that St. Anne might not have been a parent. We cannot understand this as relating directly to the status of the sentence, 'St. Anne was a parent', as this might be used to express something known a priori, but as saying of St. Anne that she possessed the accidental property of being a parent. 'St. Anne might not have been a parent' should not be rendered as 'It is possible that St. Anne was not a parent' but as 'It is true of St. Anne that she was possibly-not-a-parent'. But what this means is that, in order to understand the sort of contingency Kripke alleges to exist in these cases, we are compelled after all to invoke just that notion of scope to which Kripke appealed in the case of definite descriptions. In 'St. Anne might not have been a parent', the name 'St. Anne' must be construed as not being within the scope of the modal operator: precisely this is what is implicit in Kripke's account in terms of accidental and essential properties, as against contingent and necessary facts or statements. It is thus not merely that the uniform explanation, in terms of scope, of the ambiguity that occurs when either definite descriptions or proper names occur in modal contexts is preferable, because more economical, than having, in the latter case, to introduce the a priori/ necessary distinction: it is that, in order to understand the notions of necessity and contingency that Kripke uses, we find ourselves forced to appeal to the notion of scope, for proper names as well as definite descriptions.

It is plain that the distinction between the a priori and the necessary, considered as resting on the contrast between that by which we may know a statement to be true and that which makes it true, is not actually involved at all in Kripke's explanation of the sense in which it may be said of St. Anne that she might not have been a parent. We are not, in fact, concerned at all with what it is that makes the *statement*, 'St. Anne was a parent', true: we are concerned with what makes being a parent an accidental property of the woman we refer to either as 'St. Anne' or as 'the mother of Mary'. Indeed, the notion of accidental properties requires, if it is to be viable, a great deal more discussion than Kripke allots to it, for all the use he makes of it is a mere reliance on intuition is not, in such a case, a guarantee that there really is a clear notion here. But, even granted that this notion can be made out, the upshot of our discussion so far is that no shadow of reason has yet emerged for rejecting even the strongest conceivable version of the theory Kripke is attacking, that version, namely, under which every proper name is equivalent to some specific definite description. We are far from committed to upholding any such extreme version of Frege's theory: but, up to this point, the considerations Kripke adduces, when correctly formulated, serve rather to corroborate the theory than to point to any defect in it.

As we have seen, Kripke does not succeed in disentangling epistemic properties from others as completely as he claims. Properly speaking, Kripke's notions of contingency and necessity do have as little to do with the way a statement is or can be known as that of being amusing; or, better, for him contingency and necessity are not properties of *statements* at all, but of *facts*. His wish to dispense with the notion of sense for proper names leads him to regard a fact as consisting, e.g., in the possession by an object of a certain property, or in two objects' standing to one another in a certain relation. A fact, so conceived, may be taken as forming the content of a particular statement, but it certainly cannot be identified with the thought expressed by the statement, as Frege conceives of it, and hence cannot properly speaking be said to be an object of knowledge at all. The knowledge which someone expresses by means of an assertion (when it is knowledge) is the knowledge that the thought expressed by the sentence used to make the assertion is true; it cannot, properly speaking, be taken to be the knowledge that that fact obtains (in Kripke's sense of 'fact') which is the content of the assertion. Thus, for instance, Kripke's notion of facts leads straight to the conclusion, willingly drawn by Kripke, that the fact which is the content of a true statement of identity is always a necessary one: for it is just the fact that a certain object bears to itself that relation which every object bears to itself and to no other. By adopting Russell's Theory of Descriptions, it is possible for Kripke to refrain from applying this doctrine to identity-statements involving definite descriptions. This, however, has no real bearing on the tenability of Kripke's view; it merely serves to make it less evident that the fact conveyed by a statement, as understood by Kripke, cannot be equated with its cognitive content, and thus to prepare the trap which Kripke falls into when he speaks of someone's knowing a contingent fact.

Kripke expresses reservations about the explanatory character of the treatment of modality in terms of possible worlds very similar to those which will be voiced in Chapter 9: but he nevertheless formulates a great deal of what he has to say in terms of that notion. In these terms, he draws the distinction he sees between proper names and definite descriptions by saying that proper names are rigid designators, while definite descriptions are not. A rigid designator is defined to be a term which stands for the same object in every possible world in which it has a reference at all. Thus the definite description 'the man who led the Jewish people out of Egypt' is not a rigid designator, since there are possible worlds in which it was a different man from Moses who led the Jews out of Egypt; but 'Moses' is a rigid designator, since in every possible world 'Moses' will stand for just that man to whom, in the real world, we refer by means of the name 'Moses', save for those possible worlds in which it has no referent.

Kripke accuses Frege of confusing the meaning of a term with the way in which its reference is fixed. He fails, however, to explain at all the notion of meaning to which he is appealing; in particular, although he holds that the status of a statement, as a priori or a posteriori, depends on how the references of its terms are fixed, he does *not* say that its status as necessary or contingent is correlative to their meanings. If it were, the meaning of a term would have to be a function defined over some or all possible worlds, whose value for any possible world was an object in that world; the worlds for which it was undefined would be those in which the term had no reference. I shall here borrow the term 'connotation' for the meaning of a term, so understood. The connotation of a proper name, or of any rigid designator, would be a constant partial function.

The thesis that proper names are rigid designators is expressed in terms of the metaphor of possible worlds, and hence, to give it substance, we must remove the metaphor. And, as soon as we try to do this, we see that it concerns nothing other than our old notion of the scope of a term in a modal context. For a definite description, the divergence between its meaning and the way its reference is fixed is not apparent; in other words, the way in which the reference of a definite description is determined in the real world is carried over into each particular possible world. The whole point of saying that, for a proper name, its meaning diverges from the way in which its reference is determined is to make clear that the latter is not taken as carrying over into whatever possible world we are concerned with. This must be understood as meaning that, by using a definite description in speaking of hypothetical circumstances, we intend to say what would, in those circumstances, be true of the object to which the description would then apply, but that, by using a name, we intend to say what would be true of that object which we normally use the name to refer to. This is intelligible only if we already understand what it is to say, of some object, that something would be true of it in given circumstances; and this is just to understand what is meant when the term used to refer to the object is construed as lying outside the scope of the subjunctive conditional. If we do not understand this, the metaphor of the name's having the same referent in a possible world as in the real one cannot be interpreted. To assign to a term a reference varying from one possible world to another is just to take it as having, in each possible world, the reference which it would bear in that world; conversely, to assign it a constant reference is to take it as having, in each world, just that reference which it has in the real world. To take a term in the second way is to explain the truth-condition for a sentence containing it as coinciding with that for the sentence that results from removing the term from the scope of the modal operator. When Kripke says it could not be true that: the teacher of Alexander didn't teach Alexander, he is intending to convey that, within any possible world, it would never be true to say, 'The teacher of Alexander didn't teach Alexander'. Here the definite description is taken to have as referent, within each possible world, the unique object (if any) which in that world satisfies the predicate 'ξ taught Alexander'; and we display our adoption of this interpretation by rendering the sentence with the description taken as falling within the scope of the modal operator, namely as:

$$\neg \Diamond \exists y \, \forall x \, [(Tx \leftrightarrow x = y) \, \& \, \neg \, Ty].$$

When, however, we assert that the teacher of Alexander might not have taught Alexander, we are treating the definite description as having, as its constant referent, that referent which it has in the real world, and this is done by taking the description to lie outside the scope of the modal operator.

Kripke's doctrine that proper names are rigid designators and definite descriptions non-rigid ones thus provides a mechanism which both has the same effect as scope distinctions and must be explained in terms of them. We could get the same effect by viewing proper names, in natural language, as subject to a convention that they always have wide scope; Kripke is saved from having to view definite descriptions as non-rigid in some contexts and rigid in others only by explicitly appealing to the mechanism of scope in their case. Such an explanation would not demonstrate the non-equivalence of a proper name with a definite description in any very strong sense: it would simply show that they behaved differently with respect to ad hoc conventions employed by us for determining scope. Kripke's account makes the difference between them seem greater than it is by appealing to different mechanisms to explain comparable phenomena, and by arbitrarily ruling out the use of proper names with narrow scope to yield a sense distinct from the wide-scope reading, save by using a distinct modal operator.

This is not to say that there are no differences between proper names and definite descriptions, of a sort Kripke may be taken as driving at, even in a case of the most favourable kind, such as that of the name 'St. Anne'; and we do not need to look at modal contexts to discern these differences. A large number of definite descriptions are formed from predicates that are significantly present-tensed, and frequently may be true of one object at one time and of another object at another. A consequence of this is that, even when they are so qualified that they could apply to at most one individual, they are still regarded as present-tensed, in such a way as, e.g., to admit the verb 'become' in front of them. Thus we should tend to say that in 1960 Nixon was to be the winner of the 1968 Presidential election, rather than simply that he was the winner; and, in the course of speculating about St. Anne's life, we might say that at a certain age she became the mother of Mary. A definite description will, in general, come to apply to an object at a certain time, even if it is of such a kind that it will continue to apply to it thereafter. (There are, of course, some definite descriptions that apply from the moment the object came into existence.) This is not to deny that a definite description can properly be used to refer to an object at a time before that description became applicable; we can, e.g., quite properly say that the winner of the 1968 Presidential election entered politics in such-and-such a year. By contrast, the condition of being the bearer of a given proper name is not thought of as one that is acquired. This is a point which it is hard to formulate accurately. We may say that, when Miss Smith married Mr. Jones, she became Mrs. Jones, even though the name that she then acquired may be used to refer to her at times before her marriage, e.g. in a sentence like 'Mrs. Jones had a very unhappy childhood'. Here 'Mrs. Jones' appears to function exactly like the definite description 'the wife of Mr. Jones'. But this case should rather be compared to that in which we say that St. Petersburg became Petrograd, and later Leningrad. In this sense, the (tensed) predicate 'ξ became a' is true of an object at the time when the proper name 'a' first came to be used of it, rather than at that at which it first fulfilled the condition by which the reference is fixed. The example of 'Mrs. Jones' confuses us, because in this case the one moment is the same as the other. But we should not say that it was not until St. Anne gave birth to Mary that she became St. Anne. (It may be said that the case of 'Mrs. Jones' is not like that of 'Leningrad', on the ground that, if Miss Smith had married Mr. Jones in secret, so that she continued to be known as 'Miss Smith', it would nevertheless be right to say that, on her marriage, she became Mrs. Jones. What seems to make the difference here is that there is, in our society, a *general* convention regarding the names of married women, whereas what fixes the reference of the name 'St. Anne' is particular to it. On this ground, it might be claimed that appellations like 'Mrs. Jones' are titles rather than proper names.)

These considerations, expressed quite independently of modal contexts or of possible worlds, indeed show that proper names do not function in quite the same way as definite descriptions, even in a case in which there is some one definite description which fixes the reference of a name. If one liked, one might put this by saying that it is not strictly accurate to say that the name 'St. Anne' has the sense of the definite description 'the mother of Mary': rather it has a sense such that it is replaceable either by 'the mother of Mary' or by 'the woman who was to be the mother of Mary', according to context. As already observed, in defending Frege, we are not committed to the thesis that the sense of a name must be expressible as the sense of a definite description, but only to the more general thesis that a proper name has a sense which is that by which its reference is determined, so that there is nothing to trouble us in making the admission that, in the respect described, proper names behave differently from definite descriptions.

What has this difference in the behaviour of proper names and definite descriptions to do with modality? The point turns on Kripke's use of the notion of accidental and essential properties. We may, from the examples he gives, elicit something like the following, which relates to questions of identity, although not to the identification of an object as the bearer of a particular name. Suppose given an object, of some determinate sort; and consider any predicate which is, at some given moment, true of that object (we need not be supposed to know that it is true). There are now two possibilities. It may be ruled out, by the criteria of identity for objects of that kind, that the predicate, being now true of the object, should later cease to be true of it, or it may not. In the former case, we may say that the predicate stands for a presently essential property of the object, in the latter that it stands for a presently accidental one. A presently essential property is one which the object, having acquired, cannot cease to have: for it is ruled out in principle that we should ever subsequently correctly identify an object recognized as then lacking the property with one, of the given sort, recognized as formerly possessing it. Thus it is a presently essential property of President Nixon that he is not a frog, or indeed that he is a human being: for it is ruled out that we should ever in the future correctly identify a frog, or anything other than a human being, as being the former President Nixon. It is likewise a presently essential property of his that he is over 40, that he is of Caucasian race, or that he is the man who won the 1968 election. It is, on the other hand, an accidental property of President Nixon that he is not a circus clown, that he is male, that he is under 100, or that his complexion is what is called 'white'. This distinction between presently essential and presently accidental properties may be used to elucidate one, very weak, use of the modal auxiliary 'might': at any given time, it may be truly said of an object that it might come to satisfy a certain predicate provided that its present failure to satisfy this predicate does not constitute one of its presently essential properties. (This account is certainly not quite watertight, but it is at least as accurate as Kripke's, and will serve its purpose for the present discussion.) We may now define an (absolutely) essential property of an object as one which, at every time during its existence, was a presently essential property of it, and an (absolutely) accidental property to be one which, at some moment during its existence, was a presently accidental property of it. In terms of this notion, we can elucidate the use of 'might have'. It may be truly said of President Nixon, for instance, that he might never have been a politician, because there was a time in his life at which it would have been true to say that he might never become a politician. It is in just this sense that we can say that St. Anne might never have married, or, again, that the star Polaris might have been nowhere near the celestial North Pole (because, e.g., the Earth's axis might have been differently tilted). It is because the kind of possibility in which Kripke is principally interested is to be explained in some such fashion as this that he finds it difficult to provide an example of an essential property of an object of any given sort which other objects of that sort fail to possess, save for the circumstances of its origin. Of Moses as a new-born baby, for example, almost anything that a man could become could have been truly said to be something that that baby might become; and hence, of any such thing, we may say that Moses might have become it. But we cannot push back the moment in respect of which a property is to be characterized as presently accidental behind the point at which the object came into existence: that is why, in the case of a human being, his parentage and even the moment of his conception seem absolutely necessary to his identity, and are virtually the only examples of essential properties, other than those common to all men, which Kripke is able to cite.

We are now in a position to understand the grain of truth in Kripke's doctrine of proper names as rigid designators. For modal contexts in general, there is no relevant difference between proper names and definite descriptions: but the matter stands otherwise when the name or the description is preceded by the verb 'to be' or 'to become'. We may intelligibly say that the mother of Mary might never have become a parent, or even, at a pinch, that the mother of Mary might not have been the mother of Mary; but we cannot say that St. Anne might not have been St. Anne, and, if we say that the mother of Mary might not have been St. Anne, it is still the definite description, and not the name, which lies within the scope of the modal operator, just as when we say that St. Anne might not have been the mother of Mary (though the two statements are not equivalent). The reason we have already seen: it is not a general feature of the behaviour of proper names in modal contexts, but has to do with the fact that we do not regard such a predicate as 'ξ is St. Anne' as standing for a property that can be *acquired*. The mother of Mary did not become St. Anne when she bore Mary: she always had been St. Anne, because she always had been the one who was to be the mother of Mary. Hence being St. Anne is not a candidate for being an accidental property of anybody. And even this, we have seen, needs qualification. There is a sense in which the mother of Mary may be said to have become St. Anne, not indeed at the time when she gave birth to Mary, but when she was recognized by the Church as a saint and her cult established under the name 'Anne'; and in this sense it could be said that St. Anne might not have become St. Anne, and even that the mother of Mary might not have done so.

Doubtless an account of this type does serve to explain quite a range of modal statements, and, equally, a large number of counterfactuals; though, at least as far as counterfactuals go, Kripke's schema of explanation is insufficiently flexible. It certainly appears that the antecedent of a counterfactual has to represent a possible state of affairs, in some meagre sense of 'possible', if the counterfactual is to be assessed at all as true or false, plausible or implausible: and when we speculate, e.g., what would have have happened if Charlemagne had married the Empress Irene, it is true enough that we tacitly suppose the course of history to have gone exactly the same as in reality up to the occurrence of that imaginary event and its immediate preliminaries. But the antecedents of counterfactuals are not restricted to possibilities of the kind Kripke is interested in: we may quite intelligibly discuss, for example, what Lewis Carroll would have achieved if he had been born fifty years later, or wonder what difference it would have made to Franz Kafka's outlook if he had not been of Jewish descent and upbringing.

The explanation of modal statements and of counterfactuals is not here our direct concern, only their bearing on the meanings of proper names and definite descriptions. It is rather natural to think that, while the actual reference of an expression relates only to the real world, its sense must be determined by what its reference would be in every possible world. For instance, must not the sense of a predicate both determine and be determined by what objects it would be true of in all possible circumstances? It therefore seems very plausible that we may identify the sense of an expression with what I called above its 'connotation'. Kripke has since denied that he meant 'connotation' by his use of 'meaning', though the interpretation is hard to avoid. In any case, the notion of connotation remains a non-epistemic one; that is, it does not give an account of what it is that someone knows when he understands a word, which is precisely what the notion of sense, as introduced by Frege, is required to do. In certain cases, it is at least plausible that there will be a one-one correspondence between Frege's senses and our connotations: but that will be so only for words and expressions of which we can say that there is no gap between their meanings and the way in which their reference is determined, as we saw might, in general, be said of definite descriptions. Even in such a case, the notion of 'connotation' is not a credible representation of the knowledge that someone has when he understands the expression: what someone grasps when he understands a predicate is the principle by which we determine whether or not it applies to any given object, not what its actual extension is in each of the infinitely many possible worlds. Still, if 'F(ξ)' is a predicate of which we may say that there is no gap between the way its reference (or application) is determined and its meaning, then two things hold good. First, anyone who grasps the principle by which we determine whether it is true of any given object will be able to say, given a sufficient description of some possible world, whether or not it would be true of a given object in that world. And, secondly, someone who does not fully grasp the sense of the predicate may be able to discover this by describing imaginary circumstances, and asking whether the predicate would or would not be true of given objects in those circumstances. But this breaks down precisely in the case in which there is a gap between the meaning and the way in which the reference is determined, that is to say, in the case of rigid designators. The gap shows itself in the divergence between the answers to the questions, 'Would you call a person "St. Anne" if she proved not to have been the mother of Mary?' and 'Would that person (viz. St. Anne) still have been St. Anne if she had not become the mother of Mary?'; and just for that reason the answer to the latter question is of no help in telling us how the reference of the name 'St. Anne' is determined, i.e. how we should recognize someone as the bearer of the name.

Kripke operates, let us recall, with two notions of possibility, an epistemic and a metaphysical one. The epistemic possibilities are, so to speak, the things that could have turned out to be so, so far as we knew; the metaphysical possibilities are those that are *really* possible, irrespective of our knowledge. There are things that could not have turned out to be so, but are real possibilities nonetheless: e.g. that the standard metre rod might not have been 1 metre long, or that St. Anne might not have been the mother of Mary. Conversely, there are things which could have turned out to be so, but are nevertheless not real possibilities. The Morning Star might have turned out to be a different celestial object from the Evening Star, but this is not a real possibility, since it is an essential property of the planet Venus (as of everything else) that it is identical with itself. Even if this distinction were the right one to draw, it is plain that it is the notion of epistemic possibility that is required if we want to represent sense as a function from possible states of affairs to reference. Sense is (to repeat yet again) a cognitive notion: it relates to our mastery of language, i.e. to the way in which we set about determining the reference of our words. Hence, if we want to get at the sense of an expression by imagining states of affairs and asking what its application would then be, these states of affairs should be taken as those which might turn out to be so, whether also classifiable as real possibilities or not.

Actually, it has been argued here that, although there is a genuine distinction between epistemic and ontic possibility, Kripke misdraws it. The supposed distinction between types of possibility, between what what could have turned out to be so and what might really have been so, which Kripke uses to characterize most of his examples, is much better explained as a variation in scope. To appeal to the notion of scope requires, as we have seen, that the notion of a *statement's* being necessarily or contingently true must be supplemented by that of an *object's* having an essential or accidental property: but this distinction is misrepresented by Kripke as being one between different types of necessity (between being necessary and being a priori) that may independently apply to the same subject, viz. a statement. The notion of a property's being essential to an object does not *compete* with that of a statement's being necessarily true, since they are not ascribed to the same thing. That is why the former may be taken as supplementing the latter, so that we may use both to interpret a modal operator without conferring any ambiguity on that operator: it is this that makes it possible to appeal to the notion of scope at all. All this has, however, as we saw, very little to do with the difference in behaviour of proper names and of definite descriptions: both, in modal contexts, may have wider or narrower scope. If it were correct to say, tout court, that proper names are rigid designators, this would, in our terms, be a way of saying that their scope always included the modal operator. But, as we have seen, the phenomenon Kripke is alluding to is of much more restricted application than he supposes: it relates only to occurrences of proper names after verbs like 'be' and 'become', not to all occurrences in modal contexts. In Kripke's terminology, this means that proper names do not always function as rigid designators; in ours, that they sometimes occur within the scope of a modal operator. Once this is allowed, and once it is recognized that what is relevant is not the (quite genuine) distinction between epistemic and ontic possibility, but the quite different one between a contingent statement and an accidental property, then the way is open to consider even a proper name as a flexible designator: that is, to consider what object, if any, would, in a given possible world, constitute its referent, if that referent were determined in the same way as is done in the real world. ('Possible' here must mean 'epistemically possible': that is the only relevant notion when we are concerned with the epistemic question what we grasp in grasping the use of a word.) With the doctrine thus revised, there would indeed be a one-one correspondence between Fregean senses and Kripkean meanings. It would remain that it was the former of these two notions that was the genuinely explanatory one.

(3) Kripke does not rely solely upon arguments from modal sentences: he claims that, where some definite description is used to fix the reference of a proper name, not only may we say that the bearer of the name might not have satisfied the description, but, in some cases, we may actually discover that he or it does not. Thus, perhaps the way most people would favour to explain the reference of the name 'Kurt Gödel' is by means of the description 'the man who first proved the incompleteness of arithmetic': but, for all that, it is perfectly intelligible to suppose that it might be discovered that Gödel was not the first to prove the incompleteness of arithmetic, or even that he was an impostor and never proved it himself at all.

In this particular example, as Kripke grudgingly admits, the explanatory description is easily amended so as to circumvent the difficulty, namely to 'the man under whose signature a proof of the incompleteness of arithmetic was first published'. Nevertheless, it is quite true that the point is one of some general importance. But, unlike the objection to Frege's account which we considered under (2), the present one, and the related one we shall consider under (4), does not demand a rejection of Frege's account, but only a modification of it along Wittgensteinian lines. If the objection treated under (2) could have been sustained, it would have shown definitely that the sense of a proper name can never be identical with that of a definite description. Admittedly, we rejected Kripke's claim that Frege believed such an identity to hold in the case of every proper name; it remains that it is essential to Frege's account that the sense of a proper name can be that of a definite description, and will be so for any proper name that is introduced by means of a definite description: hence, if the argument had worked, it would have been a flat refutation of Frege's account. To this argument,

Wittgenstein's modification of Frege's account, by replacing a single sharp criterion for identifying the referent by a cluster of alternative ones, of which we are prepared in advance to abandon any fairly small subset, is quite irrelevant. If the argument had worked, it would have told just as much against the modified account as against the original one.

The present objection is entirely different. Not only can it be met by a modification of a Wittgensteinian type, but consideration shows that only such a modification will account for those cases in which the objection fails. For, in so far as a single definite description supplies someone with the only means he has for determining the reference of a name, he cannot treat as intelligible the suggestion that the description does not apply to the bearer of the name. A young child, who has learned of Shakespeare only that he was the author of *Hamlet, King Lear* and other plays, can make nothing of the information that some people think that it was not Shakespeare who wrote them: he is bound, on being told this, to ask, 'Who, then, was Shakespeare?' As Kripke himself points out, in a rather different connection, it would be no use to reply, 'The man generally supposed to have written those plays', for, in order that it be possible to suppose that a particular thing is true of a certain man, there must be some means of identifying that man otherwise than as the man of which that thing is true. If we have all agreed to use the name 'Q' as the name of a document containing sayings of Jesus and drawn upon by the writers of the first and third Gospels, then there is no content whatever to the supposition that there was such a document as Q, but that it contained no mention of Jesus and was unknown to any of the Evangelists.

What makes it possible to entertain the possibility that Gödel might be discovered not to have proved, or not to have been the first to prove, the incompleteness of arithmetic is the fact that there exist other generally accepted ways of determining the reference of the name 'Gödel'. This is always the case with any name about whose bearer a good deal is known by at least some who use the name; and it is never the case with a name about whose bearer practically nothing is known save that it satisfies the description which fixes the reference of the name. Hence something like Wittgenstein's modification of Frege's account is not merely adequate to meet this objection, but is actually called for by the facts. Of course, we can imagine a document being discovered which was identifiable, and identified, as a copy of Q; and we can also imagine that it was later decided by scholars that, despite considerable overlap between sayings recorded in this document and those reported in the Gospels, nevertheless none of the Evangelists had seen this work. In such circumstances, we should be led to assert, what we now cannot regard as intelligible, that there was such a work as Q, but that it was not seen by any Evangelist. But this very fact—that a sentence formerly devoid of content should have been rendered intelligible and, indeed, correct—makes it irresistible to say that, in such a case, the sense of the name 'Q' would have undergone an alteration: from having associated with it a single sharp criterion of identification, it had acquired a different criterion or, perhaps, a cluster of them.

Another of Kripke's examples concerns the name 'Newton': he supposes children to be introduced to the name by being told that Newton was the man who discovered that there is a force pulling things to the earth. He thinks that such children have a false belief *about Newton*; and this shows that a description used to introduce a name not only does not give its sense but may not even fix its reference, as was intended. Even if there were several famous historical characters by the name of 'Newton', and even if the misconception were not a common one, it would be clear enough to us what discovery it was of which the child had been given a garbled version, so that we have a straightforward enough reason for saying that it was of Sir Isaac Newton that he had been given misinformation. But the child himself knows nothing of this reason that we have, so that the fact that it is about Newton that the child has that belief has nothing to do with his grasp of the use of the name. When the true state of affairs is explained to the child, he has to abandon the original description as fixing the reference of the name. There seems no reason at all to deny that, in the process, his understanding of, and thus the sense which he attaches to, the name has changed; unless we are prepared to take the heroic course of saying that someone who had no more than heard the name 'Newton', without having any means of fixing its reference, without knowing anything at all about its bearer, would nevertheless understand it and be capable of using it with the reference commonly attached to it.

These considerations shade into those raised by the fourth point made by Kripke, which, again, is one of very general interest.

(4) All of us frequently use proper names of which we can give no very good explanation: not that none exists, but that we do not know it. One kind of example of which Kripke makes much is the name of a theory or part of a theory, such as 'General Theory of Relativity' or 'Gödel's Theorem'. (The latter is certainly a proper name, and not a description: Gödel has proved many other theorems, and, even if he were later to be found not to have proved the incompleteness theorem, it would almost certainly still be called after him.) Kripke points out that many people employ these names without being anywhere near a capacity to state the theory or the theorem which they designate. Actually, this is too strict a demand. Neither Frege nor anyone else would suppose that one did not attach a sense to the name of, say, a city unless one was familiar with its history, or could draw a street-plan of it or state its population and principal industries. It is sufficient that one have a definite criterion whereby one could correctly identify a city as the bearer of that name. One does not have to be able to state a theory or a theorem in order to attach a sense to its name, just as long as one has adequate means for discovering, of a statement of a theory or theorem, that it is the one denoted by the name; and this identification would not need to go via the person who framed the theory or proved the theorem.

Still, there are certainly cases in which a proper name is used without its user attaching to it anything that Frege would consider a sense. If, when I come home, one of my children says to me, 'Mr. Cunningham telephoned and asked if you would ring him back', the child may no more know the sense or the reference of the name 'Mr. Cunningham', which, let us suppose, he has never heard before, than does a piece of paper on which such a message is written; the child is acting merely as a recording apparatus. But there is no sharp line between such a case and a fully fledged mastery of a name: a whole series of transitional cases stretches from one to the other.

If a person knows of Milan only that it is a city somewhere on the continent of Europe, we should hardly ascribe to him a complete grasp of the name 'Milan'. But how much exactly should he know in order to be said to have such a grasp? If he knows that it is in North Italy, and that Ambrose was once bishop there, even though he could not locate it on a map, is this enough? Are we not all often in a much worse position about the names of less famous places, which we should not hesitate to use, and should be surprised to be told we did not know what they meant?

Suppose that someone, largely ignorant of science, knows of General Relativity that it is that branch of physics in which his nephew specialized at the university. In one respect, he attaches a definite sense to the name 'General Relativity Theory': he has a reasonably precise criterion for identifying some branch of physics as being what the name denotes. Should we say that he has a better grasp of the name than does someone who has no such criterion, but can give a sketchy and inadequate account of the theory?

Of course, this phenomenon is not confined to proper names. Someone may tell, say, a humorous story in which essential use is made of the word 'magenta', although he knows of this word only that it stands for a shade of colour, without any clear idea which: it does not matter to the story.

In a great many such cases, we are exploiting the fact, known to us, that the word we use is part of the common language. We use the name of a town, knowing only that it is a smallish town somewhere in southern Spain, secure in the knowledge that it could be more precisely identified by ourselves or our hearers, when necessary, by means of maps, reference works, road signs or questions addressed to people living in the area. Kripke amuses himself by attributing to his opponents a 'transcendental deduction of the existence of encyclopedias', but the situation would be essentially the same, though far less convenient, if writing had not yet been invented: what we are relying on is the fact that the name is part of established usage. This does not mean that someone so using a name, say 'Stow-on-the-Wold', can be said to attach to it the sense, 'The town known to its inhabitants as Stow-on-the-Wold' or 'The town generally known in English as Stow-on-the-Wold': the sense of a name must provide a criterion of identification independent of any pre-existent use of the name, and similarly with other kinds of words; it must be a sense with which the name could be newly introduced into the language. What it means is, rather, that one of the ways in which it is essential to language that it is a common instrument of communication is that there is no sharp line between the case in which a speaker makes a fully conscious employment of the sense canonically attached to a word and that in which he acts as a recording apparatus. We are able to exploit the fact that a word has a generally recognized sense, which may be discovered by standard means, even when we have only a partial knowledge of that sense; and we do.

At the opposite extreme lies the private use of names, by which I do not mean names in a private language, as this notion is criticized by Wittgenstein, namely as something in principle incommunicable; but, for example, the use of nicknames, as employed by members of a small circle. A man may even employ a special name, for a person or place, for his own use only, e.g. in writing what is to be seen by himself alone, for brevity or out of facetiousness, or for many other reasons. In such cases, it is evident that, unless the user of the name has a perfectly definite criterion for identifying its bearer, then that name has no determinate sense and hence no determinate reference. An intermediate case is that of the private sense for the public word, where, however, the intention is to determine the same referent as that which the word has in its public use. A child, or an adult, may attach to the name 'Innsbruck' only the sense 'that place where Aunt Rosemarie broke her ankle', while realizing perfectly well that the name is the generally accepted name of a place which others identify by quite different means. It is crucial, for the understanding of what someone says, that we know whether he intends a word he uses to be taken as part of the common language or not. When someone uses a private word, knowing it to be such, it is obvious that he does not; and, sometimes, he may use a public word in a sense, private to himself though known to his hearers, which he intends to be followed in case of conflict. Thus, someone may have fallen into the habit of referring to Westminster Abbey as 'Westminster Cathedral', and, even though informed that that is really the name of a quite different building, persist in using the name that way: every time he uses it, he intends his hearers to understand, 'the building that *I* call "Westminster Cathedral"'. (A similar, though more complex, case would be that of deliberate adherence to a widespread, though erroneous, use, as when someone refers to the short poem beginning, 'And did those feet . . . ', as *Jerusalem,* knowing quite well that Blake gave that title to a different and much longer poem.) More usually, in so far as a question arises, a private sense is subordinated to the intention to conform with the publicly agreed reference of the name. Someone who can pick out Innsbruck from among other cities only by the fact that it was there that his Aunt Rosemarie broke her ankle will nevertheless, in using the name 'Innsbruck', intend to be taken as referring to the city for which that name is ordinarily understood as standing; so that, if he happens to be mistaken in supposing that it was in Innsbruck that Aunt Rosemarie broke her ankle, it will nevertheless have been Innsbruck, and not the city where that accident in fact occurred, that he will have been talking about. Such a case is therefore less like that in which someone uses a private nickname, with a precisely delineated sense, than like that of someone who, in the fashion of a recording apparatus, uses a name to which he attaches no definite sense, but of which he knows that, as a word of the common language, it has such a sense, and intends it to be so understood.

It is not possible that none of those who use a name have any criterion for identifying the bearer of the name, that all of them use it with only a partial criterion in mind, but with the intention of referring to the commonly agreed referent: for there would, in such a case, be no commonly agreed referent. It is conceivable, for example, that a wide circle of people were in the habit of using the word 'Easthampton' as the name of a town in England, say with a vague impression that it was somewhere in the East Midlands. In a sense, the name would be part of the English language; it might even appear in a number of dictionaries, with the entry 'town in the East Midlands of England.' Those who used the name would do so with the intention that it be understood as having its commonly agreed referent.

But, if we suppose that there is no single person who knows, and no printed reference-book which supplies, any determinate way of identifying a town as being East-hampton, then the name has no referent and no definite sense.

May it not be possible, however, that there are some speakers who attach to a certain name a purely private sense, although in each case the referent is the same; but that, although the name may be said to belong to the common language, there is no canonical means of identifying its referent, and therefore no public sense attaching to it, as opposed to the many private senses? With a single type of exception, it is hard to fabricate examples: but a case might be that of the name of a wood, seldom visited and in an area which had never been surveyed. Each person would identify the wood as one seen or visited by himself or by some acquaintance on some specific occasion, or as the location of some particular episode; the place is mentioned too rarely and there is too small a common stock of knowledge about it for there to be any commonly agreed method of explaining the reference of the name; but what makes it a word of a common language or dialect is that all, or most, of the divergent explanations of it determine the same referent, and the speakers know that this is so. Such a case is indeed conceivable: what takes the place here of an intended subordination to the commonly accepted sense of the name is an intended subordination to the reference common to all, or to a majority, of those who use the name. In fact, the situation approximates to this whenever the name is one of a person, an animal, a boat, etc., that has not attained any degree of celebrity. In discussing proper names, these tend to be the kinds of names on which philosophers concentrate, so that their special features are too readily generalized: with proper names of other sorts, there is far more often what can be recognized as the sense attached within the language as a whole, one given by a canonical form of explanation of the name. But even in the case where such a public sense does not attach to the name, its reference depends upon there being some speakers who attach a determinate sense to it, that is, a determinate criterion for identifying its bearer, even though none that is uniform from speaker to speaker.

In the use of a proper name which belongs to the language as a whole, and is not the idiosyncratic usage of an individual or group (here of course again the dividing line is blurred), there are two distinguishable features. On the one hand are the senses attached to the name by individual speakers, that is, the particular propensities they have for identifying an object as the bearer of the name. On the other, very often, there is the sense of the name as a word belonging to the common language, that way of determining its reference which constitutes the principle of nomenclature accepted as correct and to which, normally, a speaker intends to subordinate his use of a name even when he does not himself know what its public sense actually is. Dictionaries, encyclopedias, atlases, text-books, etc., do not have to exist; but they do exist, and their existence has its effect on the practice of using language, in that they are recognized as carrying authority though not infallible. In a non-literate culture, the tradition of correct usage, including the correct employment of proper names, will be enshrined in different institutions: in anything properly termed a language, rather than a dialect, there will be such a conception of correct as against incorrect ways of using words. It is a mistake to dismiss that conception as mere snobbery, an attempt by one social class to impose its speech-forms on the others, or to invest them with a spurious cachet (like the drivel about U and non-U terms which was current some years ago). Such an element does, undoubtedly, usually intrude; but it should occasion no surprise that human beings do desire, and strive, to impose upon their language a certain stability, effected by the recognition of standards of correctness, just as they seek to regulate other conventional activities by laws, customs, principles of etiquette, etc. Without agreement, language ceases to function as an instrument of communication; without the recognition of some authority, however imprecise, as to what is and what is not correct, such agreement becomes more difficult to maintain. Compilers of dictionaries who purport to be undertaking a purely descriptive rather than prescriptive task are either the victims of a confusion which denies in principle the possibility of labeling as incorrect anything that anybody says, or else are ignorant of the role which dictionaries do in practice play in literate societies.

Naturally, this is not to deny that language changes, or to pretend that anyone can or hopes to resist all such change. In particular, as already acknowledged, both the public and the private sense attached to a proper name consist, not in a static propensity for identifying something as its bearer, but in one that may be constantly modified by the acquisition of new knowledge about the object named. It is only when problems arise that it becomes desirable to arrest temporarily the process of modification, to fix, for general purposes or for a particular discussion, a precise and determinate sense for a word, proper name or otherwise. Such problems may arise when the existence of a referent comes into doubt, or when criteria of identification appear unexpectedly to diverge; or, as we have noted, they may arise because of a need to systematize knowledge of some topic, or to enquire into the exact justification of what is generally held.

Thus the simple model whereby a proper name possesses a unique and specific sense, common to all users of the name, which determines its reference, requires qualification in many respects before it becomes a realistic picture of our actual employment of names. Frege did not consider it a realistic picture of actual practice: he knew it perfectly well for an idealization, but considered it an idealization that displayed the essential mechanism of language, as well as one to which for scientific purposes we need constantly to try to approximate. In actual practice, senses are blurred, vary from speaker to speaker, fluctuate with time, in all the ways described and doubtless others. In this they are no different from other words: all attacks on the notion of sense, as applied to proper names, may be made with equal justice to extend to very many other classes of words, and, when that extension is made, their force is seen to peter out. What must be resisted is the temptation to think that the need for these multiple qualifications of the simple account in order to do justice to the complexity of actual linguistic practice destroys the utility of the original model, whereby a name has reference in virtue of its sense; for that model displays the only mechanism by which a name could acquire reference, even though the actual working has been simplified for the sake of perspicuity. It is not a choice between Frege's theory and some alternative theory: there is no other theory.

This remark may appear preposterous: has not Kripke supplied just such an alternative theory? Before I attempt to justify the remark, it is worth giving some attention to a part of Kripke's article that lends great force to the rest, because it makes a number of quite just observations which are, however, less closely connected with the other doctrines than he makes it appear.

(5) Kripke applies his notion of a rigid designator to expressions which are not ordinarily thought of as proper names. We have already noted one example of this—a term for a unit of measurement, such as 'metre'. Others are mass terms, such as 'water' and 'gold'; terms for physical phenomena, such as 'heat', 'light' and 'sound'; and words for kinds of organism, such as 'cat' or 'ant'. By Frege's criteria, all of these, in certain of their uses, would count as proper names; and, at least in the case of words for kinds of organism, there is a sense in which such uses are primary. Kripke quite rightly observes that a term like 'tiger' is not applied solely on the basis of purely qualitative criteria. Even if there were found to be on Mars creatures resembling men in every respect, they would not be men, unless, indeed, their presence were due to interplanetary travel that occurred millennia ago; to be a man is not merely to be an animal describable in a certain way, but to be a member of a race, i.e. descended from a common stock. ('Species' would be, as it were, too specific a term to use here: there are many species of ants, but it is nevertheless in accordance with the ordinary meaning of 'ant' to say that white ants are not true ants, because they are not genetically connected with other ants, save in being insects.) Thus the use of the predicate '. . . is a tiger, as applied to individual beasts, is in a sense dependent on the use of 'the tiger' as the proper name of a race of animals (in a sense, that is, which does not require that the latter be actually learned first, or even that it actually exist within the language). Kripke is actually more concerned to insist that we do not determine the application of such terms by purely superficial qualitative criteria, e.g. an animal which to outward appearance was just like a tiger but which was in fact a reptile would not be a tiger. In most cases when we deny a common genetic origin to superficially similar creatures, we do so on the basis of a divergent internal structure, but it is the (presumed) common origin, and not the structural similarity, which is the decisive factor. Kripke's point can thus actually be strengthened, as it has been here: even if creatures *exactly* like men arose from dragons' teeth, they would not be men, because not children of Adam. A dictionary entry under a word like 'tiger' provides, normally, a definition of the word used as the name of a species or broader genetic group: e.g. an entry under 'whale' beginning 'any of various marine mammals of the order Cetacea, . . . ' is to be understood in the sense in which the blue whale is one such mammal, the sperm whale another, not that in which an individual sea-beast can be said to be a mammal. It is tacitly understood that to call an individual beast a 'whale' is to predicate of it membership of any one of the species characterized by the definition.

Somewhat similar remarks apply to mass terms. These can be used as proper names of substances, as in 'Water is a compound', 'Water has a boiling point of

100° C.', etc., but are rather differently used in 'Give me a glass of water', 'He fell into some water', and the like. There is, of course, in their use no reference to common origin; but Kripke is entirely right in saying that it is part of their meaning that they are used to refer to distinguishable *kinds* of stuff. In some few cases, origin is important. I suppose that, even if chemists had succeeded in reproducing the exact structure of silk, what they produced would still be artificial silk and not silk, and similarly with wood. In general, however, we should be inclined to say that what mattered was not superficial appearance but chemical composition. Kripke gives the example of fool's gold, and surely the resemblance could be much closer; something might for everyday purposes be indistinguishable from water, and still not be water, because of a different chemical composition; and, as Kripke says, citing the case of 'heavy water', conversely.

What does all this have to do with Kripke's views on proper names of people, places, etc.? Kripke's idea is that the superficial properties by which we originally identify a race of animals or a kind of material constitute the way in which we 'fix the reference' of the corresponding word. Just as, when we fix the reference of a personal proper name, we do not purport to employ an essential property of the individual named, so these superficial characteristics are not claimed as essential properties of the species or type of substance; just as we may abandon as incorrect the means we first used to fix the reference of a personal name, so we may later allow that these are not really even accidental properties of the species or substance. Gold might not have been yellow: it may not even in fact be yellow (we may all be suffering from an illusion). But it is necessarily an element—no chemically compound substance could be rightly identified as gold, however like gold it appeared—even though, when we first fixed the reference of the term 'gold', we had no idea of its being an element.

All this appears to fit so smoothly into Kripke's technical apparatus that it seems to provide strong reinforcement for his doctrines about proper names, although actually it has very little to do with them. No one supposes that the reference of a proper name is determined solely by qualitative features of the individual either at the time at which the name is used or at the time that is being spoken of, that is, by features whose presence or absence can be determined by examination of the individual at the relevant time. If, to take a crude example, the reference of 'Manhattan Island' is fixed by 'the long narrow island off the Atlantic coast of the United States with all those sky-scrapers, just by the Statue of Liberty', that does not preclude the use of the name at, or of, a time when the island did not yet have, or no longer has, all those features. That is precisely why it is essential to the understanding of a proper name that one knows the criterion of identity associated with it; the sense of a personal proper name requires that its bearer be identified as the same man as the one who, at an appropriate period, fitted some description (if that is how the reference of the name has been fixed). For this reason, if the description by which we attempt to fix the reference of a name is later found not to have a unique application, we do not insist that anyone fitting the description is a referent of the name, but feel bound to change the sense of the name. There is, indeed, as Kripke recognizes, a very good analogy here with names of species or of kinds of substance, which is precisely why Frege is right to classify these as proper names, along with names of individual people, places, stars, etc. In order to grasp the sense of the name of a species, or, more generally, a race of animals, we have to know the criterion of identity for a species or a race, namely a common descent. It is certainly no part of the sense of the name that any individual member of a species have all the features by which the species is picked out (the existence of freaks, sports, etc., is always provided for); it is not even excluded that there may prove to be a whole sub-variety lacking some of these features. Just as someone is the referent of a given name provided that he is the same man as the one who at a given time answered to a certain description, so a beast is (say) a tiger provided that it is of the same species as those which satisfy the characteristic description. Again, just as, when we try to fix the reference of a name, we are aware that we might have failed to do so, so, when we try to pick out a kind of animal, we must be prepared to find that we have confused two genetically distinct kinds. Somewhat similar remarks apply to kinds of substance, although the criteria of identity here are less precise.

All that this shows is that Frege was right to classify such words, in certain of their uses, as proper names, to which must be added the observation that other uses are, in a sense, dependent on these ones; it has no tendency to show that there was anything incorrect about Frege's model of the sense of a name. Kripke's efforts to show that that by which we originally identify the species or the substance might not be true of it at all—'might not', that is, in the sense 'could turn out not to be in the real world', rather than his favoured sense 'might not have been in some other possible world'—are bizarre and quite unconvincing; we need not take seriously his suggestions that it may be that no gold is yellow, that all cats have only three legs, or the like. It really is part of the sense of the word 'gold' that its characteristic examples are yellow, or of 'cat' that it applies to the members of a quadrupedal species. But it is not part of the sense of 'gold' that something white cannot be gold, or of 'cat' that a three-legged monstrosity, born of a cat, is not a cat.

In this discussion, it has nowhere been suggested that Kripke's distinction between essential and accidental properties is untenable or useless. I do not know whether or not it is useful to apply it, as Kripke does, to the genetically significant structural features of animal species, or the underlying chemical structures of substances: but it is certainly no part of my thesis to deny this. All that I am denying is that it is in any way helpful to construe the term 'meaning', as applied to words like 'tiger' or 'water', so as to make this meaning relate solely to the actual structural properties of the species or the substance, regardless of the means by which we identify it, or even of whether we are aware what those properties are. The grain of truth in this contention is one which is fully in accord with Frege's doctrine, viz. that it is part of the sense of such a word that it stands for a species or a kind of substance, not for something recognizable by external appearance alone.

(6) Section (4) ended by my saying that there is no alternative theory of proper names that can be opposed to Frege's. This may be thought grossly unfair. True enough, Kripke himself disclaims possession of a theory: but he claims to give a better and quite different picture. But what is it a picture *of*? Is it a picture of what

a speaker's grasp of the use—his use, or the correct use—of a name consists in? It can hardly be this, because it alludes to matters quite outside the knowledge of the individual speaker, namely the history of the name from the moment of its original introduction to its use by that speaker. In any case, if it were this, it would not stand in the kind of opposition to Frege's account that Kripke represents it as standing; for to grasp the use of a word just is to attach a sense to it. Is it, then, a picture of what reference consists in, for names; that is, an account of what it is for a proper name to stand for an object? It may well be so understood: but only as serving as a kind of stipulative definition of the phrase 'The name . . . stands for the object . . . '. It cannot be an account of what endows a proper name with reference, as Frege understands the term 'reference'. For reference, as it figures in Frege's theory of meaning, has an essential connection with sense: the sense—which is what a speaker knows when he understands the word—must be capable of being exhibited as a means of determining the reference. The notion of reference ought not, that is, to be idle within the theory of meaning. When someone knows the sense of a sentence, what he knows is how the truth-value of the sentence is to be recognized, whenever we are in a position to do so: and if a reference is to be significantly attributed to a word, then, for at least some sentences containing the word, the account of the process of recognizing that such sentences have one or other truth-value must involve the recognition of something as the referent of that word. If this is not so, then, however clearly we may be able to explain the attribution of something which we choose to call 'reference' to that word, the notion of reference we are employing has no role to play within the theory of meaning, as far as it relates to that word. Kripke's account, however, does not describe anything which could be involved in anyone's recognition of an object as the referent of a proper name: hence, though it may succeed in stipulating a sense in which we might, for some purpose or other, choose to say that, by using the name, someone had referred to the object, the sense of 'reference' so stipulated can have no part in any theory of meaning, that is, in a theory of what the use of proper names consists in so far as a mastery of a language requires a mastery of that use. In any case, Kripke himself repudiates any claim that he has provided an account (even stipulative) of what it is for an object to be the referent of a name: for, as he points out, his account itself invokes the notion of reference.

Kripke's account is this. First, there is an initial baptism, i.e. the name is introduction by ostension, or by means of a definite description that fixes its reference, or in some other way. At this initial stage, then, things are just as Frege says (provided that we drop the ascription to Frege of the view that the sense of every proper name must be that of a definite description). Subsequent speakers use the name with the intention of using it with the reference with which it was originally endowed. Later still, yet other speakers pick up the use of the name; and they employ it with the intention that it shall have the same reference as it had in the mouths of those from whom they learned it. This process continues, and so the use of the name is passed from link to link of a chain of communication: what joins each link to the next is its causal connection with it, together with the persistent intention to use the name with the same reference as the previous speaker.

If we ignore the bit about intention, then what we have is something that might be interpreted as an explanation, or stipulation, of what it is for a name to stand for an object: a name stands for an object if the use of the name is causally connected, via a chain of communication, with the original introduction of the name, and, when the name was originally introduced, it was invested for the time being with a sense which determined it as the name of that object. There is, indeed, nothing objectionable in introducing a notion of reference so explained: the question is what use such a notion is. Even if it could be demonstrated that reference, as so explained, coincided extensionally with our intuitive notion of a name's standing for an object, this question is still to be answered; for the proposed explanation in no way serves to give the point of the intuitive notion of reference. Certainly, the notion of reference, as explained in terms of a chain of communication, has no bearing on the way in which we do, as a matter of practice, determine a sentence containing the name as true or as false. We can rarely establish with certainty, and sometimes cannot establish even with probability, the existence of such a chain of communication; we cannot trace the use of the name back in time to its first introduction. And, even when we can, such etymological research plays no part in our ordinary procedure for determining a sentence as true or as false. The notion of reference, explained in this way, bears no relation to our understanding of our language, to our mastery of the practice of using it. Admittedly, one might, by means of a notion of reference as thus explained, give an account of what it is for sentences of our language to be true or false: but this would, again, be a mere stipulation of new notions of truth and falsity, which would have at best an extensional coincidence with the notions of truth and falsity which we employ intuitively or which are needed for a theory of meaning for our language, that is, a systematic account of its actual working.

In any case, there is no reason to suppose that the notion of reference, as explained in terms of a chain of communication, would coincide extensionally with the intuitive notion. As Kripke remarks, if I call my pig 'Napoleon', this may be causally connected with the use of the name for the Emperor, but leads to no identification of the Emperor with the pig. Indeed, the same is true of the use of the name 'Napoleon' for Napoleon III, or of any other dynastic name or any case in which one person or place is called after another. It is for this reason that the qualification is introduced that the use of the name must be made with the intention of effecting the same reference as that from which it was derived; a qualification which of course destroys the possibility of taking the account as an explanation, or even a stipulation, of the notion of reference. This is, however, just the difficulty: we have not been told what the required intention is an intention to do. Each speaker must intend to refer to the same object as the speaker from whom he heard the name: but what is it to refer to an object? We should gain some guidance on this if we were told what it would be to fail in this intention. But apparently the intention is a self-fulfilling one. There are, indeed, self-fulfilling intentions, and ones which occur in connection with reference: if I use the name 'Harold Wilson', and intend thereby not to refer to the leader of the Labour Party but to some other man of that name, then I have not referred to the leader of the Labour Party, although I may be taken as having done so and held accountable for having been so taken. But the existence of such a self-fulfilling intention is intelligible only because it is possible to describe an action which would constitute the fulfillment of that intention independently of the presence of the intention. That is, of course the action could not be correctly described as 'the fulfillment of the intention' unless the intention were present; but it could be described as effecting what the intention was an intention to do. Thus, if I use an expression such as 'Harold Wilson, the archaeologist', or 'Harold Wilson—I don't mean the politician—', then I certainly do bring it about that, if I am referring to anyone, it is not the leader of the Labour Party; and I should do so independently of any intention I might have to achieve such a result—even, if I were in a state of great confusion of mind, if I had the intention thereby to refer to the leader of the Labour Party. It is because we know what it is to refer to something, by the mere use of words (given that the speaker is conscious and in other respects in a normal mental state, etc.), independently of any background intention, that we can allow, in cases of ambiguity, that intention determines reference and is to that extent self-fulfilling. But that is just what we do not know, on Kripke's account. It appears that, if someone uses a name with the intention of referring to the same thing as did the speaker from whom he heard the name, then he cannot but succeed: but we have no idea what it would be to refer to that thing in a way that did not depend upon the presence of such an intention; and so we cannot grasp what intention it is that we are required to have—what it is that we must intend to do—if we are to effect this feat of referring to an object.

In actual practice, it is highly dubious that an intention to effect the same reference as did a previous speaker is always fulfilled: why should it be? We can never trace out in detail a chain of communication of the kind Kripke describes. Often, however, we can, by making a large number of plausible conjectures, render it quite probable that an earlier use is etymologically connected with a present one, though often we cannot go back all the way to the original introduction of the name. But, in the same way, we can sometimes establish with reasonable probability that a name has been unwittingly transferred from one bearer to another. Kripke's account leaves no room for the occurrence of a misunderstanding: since to speak of a misunderstanding would presuppose that the name did in fact have a sense which could be misunderstood. Thus, for instance, there is now a German card game called 'Tarock'. This word is undoubtedly derived etymologically from the same word as formerly employed in Germany, and still in Austria, as the name of the game played with the special form of pack generally known in England as the Tarot pack. A form of this game is still played in part of Germany under the name 'Cego', while the name 'Tarock' is now exclusively used for a distantly related game played with a more ordinary form of pack. It is possible that this change in the reference of the name 'Tarock' is the result of a deliberate transference. But it is equally possible that it is the result of a misunderstanding; that, at each step in the etymological chain, each speaker intended to use the name with the same reference as previous speakers, but that a confusion occurred about what that reference was. (It is easy to see how this could have happened. The game now called 'Tarock' was formerly known as 'bayrischer Tarock', presumably because of its resemblance to the game formerly called 'Tarock';

in the meantime, of the several variants of the latter game, only that known as 'Cego' survived in Germany.) Such a supposition is perfectly intelligible to us, because we have a criterion, although imprecise, for 'the same game', and we have a criterion for determining what game a name is being used as the name of, independently of the historical origin of the name. It is the business of a theory of reference to explain what that criterion is. Kripke's account does not purport to be a theory, in this sense. Still, it would be fatal to its apparent capacity to act at least as a surrogate for such a theory to admit that the existence of a chain of communication, even welded link to link by the presence of the necessary intention to preserve reference, might still not guarantee that the reference was preserved.

In the case of words of other kinds, we should not have the slightest inclination to say that an intention to use a word as others use it would be bound to succeed: a person may quite well be unaware that he is using a word in a different way from others. In the case of a proper name, if we arm ourselves with the Fregean distinction between sense and reference, we can not only explain what determines the reference of a name, but we can admit the possibility that the sense undergoes alteration while the reference remains constant; the multiple ways in which it must be conceded that sense may be incompletely determinate, or may vary from speaker to speaker, do not undermine the account. Kripke wants to throw away the sense/reference distinction in favour of a causal connection backed by the intention to preserve reference. He himself acknowledges that the necessity to invoke this intention disqualifies his account as an explanation of what reference consists in; but, if it is to be explanatory at all, it ought at least to be taken as characterizing persistence of reference. Of course, in some few cases, the intention to achieve the same reference as a previous speaker is an essential ingredient, even a nearly exhaustive one, in the use of a name. If there survives a single text, from some ancient historical source, mentioning a certain individual, about whom the text tells us virtually nothing but his name, then, until more information becomes available, any use of that name can be taken only as referring to whatever man the ancient writer was referring to. Such a case is, however, atypical: it is a mistake to think that, in contemplating it, we have uncovered the true mechanism of reference. Kripke expressly wishes to allow that the association with a name of a description which in fact does not apply to the person or thing for which the name was originally introduced does not deprive that name of reference to that person or thing: it merely reveals a false belief about the referent of the name. There is therefore no room in Kripke's account for a shift of reference in the course of a chain of communication: the existence of such a chain, accompanied all the time by the required intention to preserve reference, must be taken as guaranteeing that reference is in fact preserved. Intuitively, however, there is no such guarantee: it is perfectly possible that, in the course of the chain, the reference has been unwittingly transferred. Once this is conceded, the account crumbles away altogether. We are left with this: that a name refers to an object if there exists a chain of communication, stretching back to the introduction of the name as standing for that object, at each stage of which there was a *successful* intention to preserve its reference. This proposition is indisputably true; but hardly illuminating.

AGAINST DIRECT REFERENCE

Michael Devitt

It is easy nowadays to get caught up in direct-reference mania. (Salmon 1986: 82)

1. The Theories

The origins of the theory of "direct reference" for proper names are alleged to be found in the works of Saul Kripke, Keith Donnellan, and David Kaplan. Sometimes what may seem to be the same theory of names is called "new"; sometimes, "Millian"; sometimes, "causal"; sometimes, "historical."

Despite appearances, there is not one theory covered by these various names but many. My aim is to distinguish these theories and their origins, and to argue against one of them. My own views have the same sources as the views of direct-reference philosophers but differ sharply in concern and content. The implications of this disagreement stretch way beyond the theory of names. Time and again the disagreement comes back to questions about the nature of semantics.

In this section, I set out the theories and some of the relationships between them. In the next section, I focus on the history, examining particularly the extent to which these theories are correctly attributed to Kripke, Donnellan, and Kaplan. In the following sections, I get on with the argument.

The 'Fido'-Fido Theory

The theory that I shall be arguing against is prominent in the discussion of direct reference. It is:

> All there is to the meaning, semantics, information value, or linguistic significance of a name is (standing for)[1] its referent. A name is purely designative or denotative; it is just a tag; it merely labels.

The 'Fido'-Fido theory has problems that have been familiar since Frege and the early Russell:[2] the differing "cognitive values" of '$a = a$' and '$a = b$' which I shall call "the Identity Problem"; the nontriviality of true positive existence statements and the meaningfulness of true negative ones, which I shall call "the Existence Problem"; the meaningfulness of empty names, which I shall call "the Emptiness Problem"; the failure of substitutivity of identicals in thought, or propositional attitude, ascriptions, which I shall call "the Opacity Problem." These problems seem so massive that it is startling to find the 'Fido'-Fido theory revived by able philosophers who are thoroughly aware of the problems.

---

[1] The distinction between the theory with the words in parentheses and without them is unimportant for this paper and will be ignored.

[2] Though Russell rejected the 'Fido'-Fido theory for ordinary proper names, he did of course hold it for logically proper names.

The main reasons for the revival come from the other theories appearing under the banner of direct reference and set out below. My first point against the 'Fido'-Fido theory is that these other reasons are insufficient.

The Nondescription Theory

One of these other theories, often presented in the same breath as the 'Fido'-Fido theory as if it were the same, is as follows:

> A name is nonconnotative. It does not have a Fregean sense determining its reference. It is nondescriptive.

Although the Nondescription theory is entailed by the 'Fido'-Fido theory, it is not the same as that theory. Why might someone think otherwise? Because of the following semantic presupposition:

> SP: The meaning of a name is either descriptive or else it is the name's referent.

SP presupposes that there are no other possible candidates for a name's meaning. So, if the Nondescription theory is right, the meaning of a name must be the name's bearer: the 'Fido'-Fido theory. I shall argue against SP. I think that a name has a certain sort of nondescriptive, hence non-Fregean, sense.

To argue against SP is to take it as a substantive thesis about meaning. However, the discussion of direct reference sometimes proceeds as if SP were true by definition. This would collapse the 'Fido'-Fido theory into the Nondescription theory and leave us without a complete *nontrivial* theory of meaning for names. So, I shall be arguing that 'Fido'-Fido is either false or the result of a trivial addition to Nondescription.

Why do some people behave as if SP were trivial? My diagnosis is that they pay too little attention to what we need a theory of meaning *for*.

The Rigid Designation Theory

A third theory associated with direct reference is as follows:

> A name refers to the same object in every possible world.

We can derive the Rigid Designation theory from the Nondescription theory as follows. First, we need an explanation of "reference in a possible world." Consider a singular term, T, in a sentence, S, in a particular context of utterance. The referent of T in a possible world, W, is whatever object T makes relevant to the truth evaluation of S in W.[3] Second, we need an assumption about what makes reference vary from world to world. Suppose that T were a definite description like 'the President of America in 1989'. It seems obvious that T would vary its reference because different objects would be picked out by the description in different circumstances. The needed assumption is that *only if* T is descriptive can its

---

[3] The apparent commitment to possible worlds in this explanation could be removed. Let 'D' abbreviate a total description of W. To say that x is the referent of T in W is to say that, were it the case that D, x would have to have the attribute specified by S for S to be true.

reference vary. So, given the explanation and this plausible assumption, the Nondescription theory implies that a name refers to the same object in every possible world.

Rigid Designation does not entail either Nondescription or 'Fido'-Fido. So far as Rigid Designation is concerned, a name can have any meaning at all provided only that that meaning does not make any object other than the name's actual referent relevant to evaluations in other possible worlds. This proviso will be met if the name's meaning is the referent, as 'Fido'-Fido holds. But we need further argument to show that this is the *only* way to meet the proviso. Indeed, Alvin Plantinga has shown, ingeniously, that a descriptive name could meet it (1978). Even if we use the Nondescription theory to rule out Plantinga's suggestion, we still need to rule out the possibility of other ways of meeting the proviso. Perhaps a term with a nondescriptive sense would meet it. That possibility could be ruled out by the semantic presupposition, SP, but then if we had SP as well as Nondescription, we wouldn't need Rigid Designation to establish 'Fido'-Fido.

There is no fast and clean route from Rigid Designation and Nondescription to 'Fido'-Fido. I shall examine a slow route later (section 3).

I have deliberately presented these three theories without using two terms that are prominent in the discussion of direct reference: 'proposition' and 'content'. These technical terms are open to various interpretations some of which are appropriate to one of the theories, some to another. The main reason that the discussion is so confusing is that the terms are often inadequately explained and thus tend to blur distinctions between the theories. I will introduce the terms later (section 3).

The Causal Theory

The final theory associated with direct reference is as follows:

> A name designates an object solely in virtue of a certain sort of causal or historical chain connecting the name to the object.

The Causal theory clearly entails the Nondescription theory, because it entails that reference is not determined by a Fregean sense. Further, if we accept the earlier explanation of "reference in a possible world," we can derive Rigid Designation from the Causal theory. A name's causal links to an object in the actual world of its utterance—the links that determine its reference—remain fixed however we vary the world of evaluation. Indeed, the Causal theory *explains* why a name has the semantic property of being rigid.

I am enthusiastic about the Causal theory.[4] So I am very concerned to reject the common assumption that it entails the 'Fido'-Fido theory. Clearly, as it stands,

---

[4] Though I think a few qualifications are necessary. One is needed to allow for "attributive" names; 1974: 196; 1981a: 40–2. Another is needed to allow for the *qua*-problem; 1981a: 60–4; Devitt and Sterelny 1987: 63–5.

it does not, for it says nothing about the meaning, information value, etc., of a name. Indeed, I shall argue that the Causal theory provides the means to reject the 'Fido'-Fido theory, because it provides an explanation of the nondescriptive sense of a name. I have argued this several times before, with no apparent success.[5] In this paper, I hope to do better.

My main aim in this section has been to emphasize that neither the Nondescription theory, the Rigid Designation theory, nor the Causal theory entail the 'Fido'-Fido theory. The most important additional premise to establish that theory is SP. If my argument is good, SP is false.

2. The History

Kaplan introduced the term "direct reference" in the mid-seventies in works that were mainly on the semantics of demonstratives and indexicals (1973; 1975; 1979a, 1979b, 1988a).[6] Neither Kripke nor Donnellan used the term. And neither they, nor Kaplan, called their theories "new."

The 'Fido'-Fido Theory

Insofar as the theory of direct reference is this theory, it is remarkably inappropriate to call it "new" as some do (e.g., Wettstein 1986):[7] 'Fido'-Fido is the oldest theory in the book, going back at least to Plato. Calling it "Millian" is much more appropriate, though strictly it seems not to be what Mill held. The theory has been unpopular for most of this century, but it was by no means dead when the direct-reference philosophers revived it recently.[8]

Who did revive it? Kripke and Donnellan are often mentioned in discussions of direct reference as if they endorsed the 'Fido'-Fido theory. Yet, interestingly enough, nobody makes a serious attempt to cite convincing evidence that they do.[9] Kripke clearly does not endorse it (1980: 20–1). I have been unable to find any decisive evidence that Donnellan does. In one place, he flirts with a view that might seem to come close (1974), but the view seems more appropriately construed as Rigid Designation. Kaplan does, somewhat tentatively, endorse the theory (1988a: 591), although it is not what he *means* when he says that names are directly referential. And names are not his primary concern.

---

[5] 1980: 271–4; 1981a: 152–7; 1981c: 217–8; 1984a: 388, 403–5; 1985: 222–3. I have also argued a similar line to do with natural-kind terms: 1983: 675–7.

[6] Kaplan 1988a, which seems to have made the introduction, circulated widely in an unpublished form from 1977 on. On the semantics of demonstratives and indexicals, see also Perry 1977, 1979.

[7] Stephen Schwartz, who seems to have been first to talk of the "new theory of reference," did not include the 'Fido'-Fido theory as a "main feature" of the new theory (1977b: 20–32).

[8] See, e.g., Smullyan 1947: 140; Marcus 1961: 309–10; 1981.

[9] E.g., Loar 1976 (cf. my 1980); Ackerman 1979a: 58; 1979b: 6; Schiffer 1979 (cf. my 1981c); Marcus 1981: 502; Almog 1984: 482; Baker 1982: 227; Wettstein 1986: 187. So far as I know, Loar was the first to attribute the 'Fido'-Fido theory to Kripke and Donnellan.

'Fido'-Fido has flowered in the work of a "new wave" of philosophers who sail under the banner of direct reference: Joseph Almog, Nathan Salmon, Scott Soames, and Howard Wettstein.[10]

The Nondescription Theory

This theory is entailed by the 'Fido'-Fido theory and it is just as inappropriate to call it "new." It is, however, appropriate to call it "Millian," because Mill is its most famous exponent. There is no doubt that Kripke (1980), Donnellan (1972), and Kaplan (1988a) do subscribe to this theory. Furthermore, Kripke and Donnellan did something importantly new in relation to it. At a time when its opposite, the Description theory, had been the received view for decades, they produced powerful arguments for the Nondescription theory.[11] The Nondescription theory has been enthusiastically embraced by all the direct-reference philosophers.[12]

The Rigid Designation Theory

The Rigid Designation theory has much more claim to be considered "new" though it is, in effect, to be found in Ruth Barcan Marcus (1961).[13] Kripke is famous for urging the theory (1971, 1980). When Kaplan says that names are "directly referential," Rigid Designation is part of what he means.[14] The other part is Nondescription (1988a: 512-6, 521-6). Donnellan did not discuss the Rigid Designation theory in his early articles. However, his idea of a "referential use" of definite descriptions (1966, 1968) was suggestive of the idea, as Kaplan points out (1979a: 383-5). Donnellan did embrace the theory later (1979: 50).

The main interest of the Rigid Designation theory was for logic and formal semantics; in particular, for intensional logic and possible-worlds semantics. The new wave are very interested in the theory.[15]

---

[10] Salmon 1981: 11; 1986; Almog 1984: 482; 1985: 615-6*n*; Wettstein 1986: 185, 192-4. I take the theory to be implicit in Soames 1985, 1987, 1988. John Perry is a direct-reference theorist and is often cited as if he subscribed to 'Fido'-Fido, but I can find no clear evidence that he does; but see, e.g., Barwise and Perry 1983: 165. Though the terms 'proposition' and 'content' often make the discussion confusing (section 1), I do not mean to suggest that the new wave is confused.

[11] The argument that has had the most attention is a modal one, derived from the Rigid Designation theory, and found in Kripke. The other argument, which strikes me as more powerful, is found in Kripke and Donnellan. It points out that people mostly do not have the knowledge of a name's bearer required by the Description theory. I call it "the argument from ignorance and error."

[12] Salmon 1981: 16; 1986; 65-6; Wettstein 1986: 185-6; Almog 1986: 220; Soames 1988: 100.

[13] See also Smullyan 1947; Fitch 1949.

[14] Kaplan has a subtle discussion of a difference between his formulation of Rigid Designation and Kripke's (1988a: 521-2). I have used Kaplan's formulation.

[15] Salmon 1981: ch. 1; 1986: chs. 1-2; Soames 1985, 1987, 1988; Wettstein 1986: 186; Almog 1986.

The Causal Theory

This theory is the one that really is "new." It was discovered by Kripke (1980) and Donnellan (1972) in the late sixties[16] Kaplan seems always to have been impressed with the theory but, in the end, gives it no semantic significance (1988a: 587–92).

The new wave of direct-reference philosophers typically associate their views with the Causal theory but, of the four theories, it clearly *interests* them least.[17] Their concern with the question, 'What determines the reference of a name?', seems to evaporate once they have concluded that the reference is not determined by a Fregean sense.

Consider now the link between the 'Fido'-Fido theory and the Causal theory in the works of the philosophers mentioned. Kaplan and the new wave embrace the 'Fido'-Fido theory but show little interest in the Causal theory. Kripke and Donnellan hold the Causal theory, but the 'Fido'-Fido theory is not to be found in any of their works. So the historical link between the two theories is rather tenuous. It is striking then that the received view seems to be that the Causal theory is a 'Fido'-Fido theory.[18] I am most concerned to break the link between the two theories.

Because of the above history, my term, "the direct-reference theory of names," should be taken as referring to the conjunction of the 'Fido'-Fido theory, the Nondescription theory, and the Rigid Designation theory, but not to the Causal theory. And by "the direct-reference philosophers," I mean Kaplan and the new wave, not Kripke and Donnellan.[19]

In earlier works, I have proposed a theory that developed ideas of Donnellan and Kripke in two ways.[20] First, I drew a distinction at token level, based on Donnellan's distinction at type level, between referential and attributive descriptions,[21] and then I applied this new distinction across the board, covering names, demonstratives, and pronouns, as well a definite descriptions. Second, I gave a

---

[16] See also Chastain 1975, an interesting but neglected article.

[17] Salmon 1981: xiii, 11; Almog 1984; Wettstein 1986: 192–3; 1988: 420.

[18] See references in note 9; also, McGinn 1982: 244; Lycan 1985; Block 1986: 660, 665; LePore and Loewer 1986: 60; Wagner 1986: 452.

[19] I might have included others among the direct-reference philosophers. For example, Lycan subscribes to direct reference and his "paradox of naming" starts from SP (1985). Fodor proposes a "denotational theory" which is, in effect, a direct-reference theory, though he does not mention any of the above literature in his discussion (1987: 72–95). The philosophers I have included are closely related to one another. The detailed discussion of a larger group would have been unmanageable.

[20] I became interested in the semantics of singular terms in discussions with Charlie Martin in Sydney in 1966. Martin had a rigidity thesis for names and demonstratives and a view of definite descriptions that was similar to the view that Donnellan was about to publish (1966, 1968). I first heard the causal theory of proper names from Kripke at Harvard in 1967. I proposed my own theory in my Ph.D. thesis (1972). The following later works were largely based on that: 1974, 1976, 1981a.

[21] This treatment gives Donnellan's distinction a semantic significance that he may not have intended. Kripke thinks that the distinction does not have semantic significance (1979a). My 1981b is a response to Kripke.

causal theory of reference for all the referential tokens.[22] The theory explained their reference in terms of causal chains—I called them "d-chains"—generated by "groundings" in an object[23] and by "reference borrowings" in communication.

In the course of theorizing about the reference of names, I talked also about their meaning. I claimed, in effect,[24] that Frege was right in thinking that a name had a sense which determined its reference—it had a mode of presentation—but wrong in thinking that this sense was descriptive. The sense was a certain type of d-chain (1974: 203–4; 1981a: 153–7). Given the new popular idea that the Causal theory is a 'Fido'-Fido theory, my view about a name's meaning has turned out to be much more radical than I expected. I adopted the view for two reasons. First, a name must have *some* property that determines its reference—it does not refer by magic—and, according to the Causal theory that property is the relational one of being causally linked in a certain way to the referent. In brief, an interest in the *explanation* of reference pointed to a sense of the sort I was proposing. Second, if a name had no sense, it would be impossible to solve the familiar problems that had originally driven people away from the 'Fido'-Fido theory. I took solving those problems to be a requirement on a theory of names (1981a: 6).

The solution to these problems, briefly, is as follows. The Identity Problem: '$a = a$' and '$a = b$' have differing cognitive values because they have different senses; for underlying 'a' and 'b' are different types of d-chain. The d-chains are of different types in virtue of being parts of different "networks" of d-chains. The Existence Problem and the Emptiness Problem: the meaningfulness of a name does not depend on it having a referent; it is meaningful if it has an appropriate network underlying it even if that network is not grounded in a referent. The Opacity Problem: substitutivity does not hold for a name in an opaque thought ascription because the ascription depends for its truth on the sense of the name not on its referent. I shall return to these solutions in section 7.

It follows from my view that SP is false. Fregean senses and referents are not the only candidates for a name's meaning: its meaning is a non-Fregean sense explained in terms of a causal network.

I have already noted the lack of interest of direct-reference philosophers in explaining how names relate to the world. Indeed, though they trace their views

---

[22]Donnellan does not offer a theory of reference for his referential descriptions. In particular, he does not extend his causal theory of names to cover those descriptions (though he does remark in a footnote that such a description is a "close relative" of a proper name; 1972: 378*n*).

[23]It is important to the plausibility of the Causal theory that it allows a name to be *multiply* grounded in its referent, not simply grounded in an initial dubbing (1974: 198–9; 1981a: 56–7).

[24]The qualification is necessary because of my caution with the *word* 'sense' (and the *word* 'meaning'). Initially, I was anxious to emphasize the difference between the Causal theory and the Description theory. This led me to use 'sense' as if it applied only to *Fregean* descriptive senses and hence to deny that names had senses (1974). Later I allowed, tentatively, that we might think of causal modes of presentation as non-Fregean senses (1981a: 236). Had I anticipated the rise of direct reference, I would have emphasized the difference between the Causal theory and the 'Fido'-Fido theory by not being at all tentative about this. I am not tentative now (Devitt and Sterelny 1987: 56–8).

back to Russell, they set aside almost without comment the part of Russell that was an attempt to solve this problem: the theory of acquaintance. Their lack of interest in this ultimate question seems to reflect a narrower view than mine of the scope of semantics.[25]

This difference over the nature of semantics is related to another one. My concern is always with language as a natural phenomenon and so the guide for its investigation is empirical science. The direct-reference philosophers tend to be more concerned with language as an abstract system and so the guide for its investigation is formal logic.

3. Motivating the 'Fido'-Fido Theory

Given the well-known, and apparently overwhelming, problems for the 'Fido'-Fido theory, why has it been revived? The above discussion provides some ideas. In this section I shall develop these ideas in the process of discussing four possible motivations for the theory. Motivations 3 and 4 are certainly influencing the direct-reference philosophers; 1 and 2 probably are too.

1. Suppose that a person starts with the common assumption:

(1) The meaning of a sentence is the proposition it expresses.

The person adds, perhaps under the influence of some reflections on "ordinary language":

(2) The proposition expressed by a sentence is what the sentence says.

(3) A name's contribution to what a sentence containing it says is simply the name's bearer.

From these three premises, it follows that a name's bearer is its contribution to a sentence's meaning. Add in the uncontroversial,

(4) The meaning of the name is its contribution to the meaning of a sentence containing it,

and the person has arrived at the 'Fido'-Fido theory.

The problem with this argument is its first three premises. (1) and (2) identify the meaning of a sentence with what it says. Suppose we accept that. What *does* a sentence say? Our answer must be guided by the truth conditions of indirect speech reports. But then as Quine and others have shown, these truth conditions are tricky. Consider:

Tom said that Cicero is an orator.

---

[25] A lack of interest in this ultimate question has been common among philosophers of language. Consider the long period of rule of the Description theory. Even if the theory had been right, it would not have answered this question. It is essentially incomplete, explaining the reference of one term in terms of the reference of others. But how do *they* refer? Description theories simply pass the referential buck. The buck must stop somewhere with a different sort of theory. This point relates to Putnam's famous arguments for the slogan "Meanings just ain't in the head" (1975: 223–7); see Devitt in press a.

Suppose that the actual words Tom uttered were, "Tully is an orator." Is the report true? According to one popular view, yes and no. It is true if construed transparently. On the basis of that construal, we might feel justified in saying that what is said by "Tully is an orator" is the same as what would have been said by "Cicero is an orator," thus confirming (3). However, if the report is construed opaquely it is false. On the basis of that construal, what is said by the two utterances is not the same, thus falsifying (3). So, for the argument to go through, we have to identify the meaning of a sentence with what is said in the transparent sense. But why should we do that? The traditional problems for the 'Fido'-Fido theory show that this would be a mistake. Perhaps we should identify meaning with what is said in the opaque sense, or with something else altogether. There is no compelling argument here for overlooking the traditional objections.

2. Suppose that a person starts with the popular slogan: "the meaning of a sentence is its truth conditions." This gets interpreted as follows:

> (5) The meaning of a sentence is a possible state of affairs: an arrangement of objects, attributes, and so on.

The meaning of a singular term is simply its contribution to this meaning. Applied to names, this yields (4). But what *does* a term contribute? The easy answer is, its referent: an object, attribute, or whatever, that partly constitutes the state of affairs. The person rejects this answer as too easy, because some terms are complex, picking out their referent partly in virtue of their structure. This structure and the referents of its parts seem relevant to meaning. Thus the meaning of 'the father of Annette' involves the referent of 'father' and 'Annette', and not simply Harry, who *is* the father of Annette. Nevertheless, the person thinks, the answer is on the right track. It is right for a term that is simple, having no structure:

> (6) The meaning of a simple term is its referent.

The Nondescription theory shows that names are simple. The person has reached the 'Fido'-Fido theory.

The traditional problems for the 'Fido'-Fido theory strongly suggest that there is something wrong with truth-referential semantics of the sort reflected in (5) and (6): meaning is not simply a matter of assigning entities to expressions—for example, states of affairs to sentences, and objects to names.[26] Note that this semantics does take *some* account of modes of presentation. *If the term is complex*, then the way in which it presents its referent is important to its meaning. However, if it is simple, only its referent matters. This view could be summed up in a generalization of SP: the meaning of term is either a descriptive structure or else it is the term's referent. The problems suggest, in my view, that modes of presentation are *always* important to meaning; they are important for simple terms as well as complex. The slogan should be understood not as (5) but as: the meaning of a sentence is *a mode of presenting* a possible state of affairs.[27]

---

[26]See Wagner 1986 for a sustained criticism of this sort of semantics.

[27]I am dissatisfied with the attempt at making this point in Devitt and Sterelny 1987: 33.

3. Kaplan came tentatively to the 'Fido'-Fido theory via an argument in possible-world semantics (1988a: 590-1). Kaplan developed this semantics for indexicals and demonstratives. It yields only three candidates for the meaning of an expression: its referent, its "content," and its "character." Applying this to names,

> (7) The meaning of a name is either its referent, its content, or its character.

In Kaplan's semantics the Rigid Designation theory and the Nondescription theory yield,

> (8) The content of a name is its referent.

Kaplan argues further that

> (9) The character of a name is its content.

The 'Fido'-Fido theory follows. "Because of the collapse of character, content, and referent, it is not unnatural to say of proper names that they have no meaning other than their referent" (1988a: 591). This argument is the slow route from Rigid Designation and Nondescription to 'Fido'-Fido mentioned earlier (section 1).

Before assessing this argument, it is worth mentioning a fast, and very dirty, route from possible-worlds semantics to 'Fido'-Fido. The route establishes (8) one way or another, and then simply identifies content with meaning. The problem with this is that "content" is a technical term in the semantics. We need an argument to show that content, *understood in that way,* is appropriately identified with meaning. To suppose that no further argument is needed is to treat the identification as a matter of definition. This would make the 'Fido'-Fido theory trivial.

What is Kaplan's "content"? Consider a sentence in a particular context of utterance. Its content, or the proposition it expresses, is the aspect of it that is evaluated for truth in each possible world. It can be represented by a function from possible worlds to truth values. The content of a singular term in the sentence is its contribution to what is evaluated; it is the aspect of the term that determines its reference in each possible world. It can be represented by a function from possible worlds to objects. According to the Rigid Designation theory, a name refers to the same object in every possible world. So we can represent its content by a *constant* function; it is "fixed" or "stable." A descriptive name *could be* rigid in this way, as Plantinga showed, but the Nondescription theory rules this out. In these circumstances, rather than represent the name's content as a constant function with the actual referent as its value, Kaplan prefers to follow Russell in thinking of the name's content as the referent itself. Hence (8). The content of the sentence containing the name is then a "singular" proposition (pp. 529–31).

What is Kaplan's "character"? The character of an expression "is that which determines the content in varying contexts" of utterance (p. 534). "Indexicals have a *context-sensitive* character" (p. 535). Thus the character of 'he' determines different contents, because it determines different referents, as we vary the context of utterance. "Nonindexicals have a *fixed* character" (p. 535). Thus the character of 'cat' determines the same content, cathood, in all contexts. Kaplan goes on to identify the fixed character of a word with its content (p. 536). All that remains to reach (9) is an argument that names have fixed characters (pp. 587–91).

Kaplan's notions of content and character yield an elegant and plausible semantics for indexicals. And there can be no objection to his applying the notions more widely to yield (8) and (9). The controversial move is (7). The traditional objections to 'Fido'-Fido show that the referent of a name is not a plausible candidate for its meaning. Since the content and character of a name, according to Kaplan's semantics, are identified with the referent, they are not plausible candidates either. We need an argument for (7) that Kaplan does not provide. (7) simply "falls out" of Kaplan's semantics. But that semantics was designed for another purpose. It remains to be argued that it is appropriate for names.[28]

One way of modifying Kaplan's semantics so that the 'Fido'-Fido theory can be dropped would be to broaden the notion of character to cover nondescriptive modes of presentation. Thus, even when the character is fixed, determining the same content in all contexts, it is identified not with the content but with the mode of presenting that content. Character in this broad sense could then be identified with meaning. Another way[29] would be to return to the picture that Kaplan discards: the content of a name is not the referent but a function which always has the referent as value. This function is a mode of presentation and can be identified with meaning.

4. What most motivates the direct-reference philosophers to accept the 'Fido'-Fido theory is that they think that there is no viable alternative. The Nondescription theory has ruled out a descriptive meaning for a name. SP is assumed, and so the name's meaning must be its bearer.

I have proposed that a name has a nondescriptive sense, or mode of presentation, which is identified with the type of causal chain that determines the name's referent. What response do the direct-reference philosophers have to this sort of solution to the problems for the 'Fido'-Fido theory?

(i) Wettstein constructs a view along these lines, which he claims to be based on ideas in Perry and Kaplan. He objects to the view because it has the consequence

> that everyone who uses 'Aristotle' to refer to the ancient Greek philosopher must be thinking of him as "the individual who stands in the appropriate historical relation. . . ." Most competent users of that name have never heard of the Donnellan-Kripke account of names and do not think of the referents of names in such terms. (1986: 194)[30]

The objection is beside the point because the view does not have this consequence. The objection assumes that competent speakers must have propositional knowledge

---

[28] Perhaps Kaplan would agree, for his approach to names *is* tentative. I think that the semantics, as it stands, is also inappropriate for 'cat'.

[29] Which I owe to Georges Rey.

[30] Searle makes a similar point in defending the conclusions he draws from his Chinese-room example (1980:452).

of linguistic rules. This assumption is popular, but nonetheless false. Briefly, a competent speaker's behavior is *governed by* linguistic rules without her being (mostly) *aware of* those rules, just as a pocket calculator's behavior is governed by arithmetic rules without its being aware of those rules. I have argued against the propositional view of competence at length elsewhere[31] and will say no more here.

(ii) Another objection to the proposal runs as follows. "The causal chains that constitute a name's meaning, according to the proposal, are external to the mind. So how could differences in such meanings possibly explain the differing cognitive values of '$a = a$' and '$a = b$'?"[32] It is indeed common for people to think that the Causal theory puts meanings entirely outside the head.[33] But this is simply false. A great deal of the network of d-chains for a name consists in mental processing and functioning. Indeed, it is absurd to think otherwise. For subjects to think about an object as a result of its causal action on them, they must first be appropriately stimulated, and second *must process the results of that stimulus appropriately*. The role of the mind in meaning will be discussed more below.

(iii) Almog rejects something close to my proposal in the context of discussing the problem of ambiguous names (1984: 483–4).[34] His rejection is based solely on his argument that historical chains have, in general, the "presemantic" role of preserving the meanings of words. Thus, he claims that we mean by 'you' what we do because our ancestors meant that and there is a causal chain from them to us. In the case of a name, what is preserved by the chains is reference, because its meaning is its referent (pp. 479–82). The chains solve the ambiguity problem by determining which meaning, hence which referent, a particular token has.

Aside from the 'Fido'-Fido theory, I agree with these claims.[35] Indeed, as Almog says, they are "compatible with a Fregean semantics" (p. 486) and "relatively uncontroversial" (p. 487). I claim that the chains *also* explain what it is for a name to mean what it does. They answer the question: In virtue of what do we, our ancestors included, refer to Aristotle by 'Aristotle'? Almog is uninterested in explaining reference. His story of the preservation of meaning takes the meaning preserved for granted.

That the chains feature in some uncontroversial explanations is not, of course, any reason for thinking that they should not feature also in some other, possibly controversial, explanations.

---

[31] 1981a: 95–110; 1983: 674–5; 1984a: 206–11; Devitt and Sterelny 1987: 146–8; in press.

[32] Some remarks of Evans suggest this objection (1982: 83). I respond to the remarks in my critical notice (1985: 221–3). I have often heard objections along these lines.

[33] See, e.g., Block 1986: 665. Wettstein says that "reference . . . has little to do with the head of the speaker" (1988: 415).

[34] Almog says that an unpublished lecture of Kaplan's in 1971 anticipated the major ideas of his paper (p. 489*n*). See also Kaplan 1988a: 587–92.

[35] I agree also with Almog's criticisms of Fregean attempts to absorb the Causal theory (pp. 484–6). Searle has recently provided a complicated example (1983: ch. 9) which I have criticized (in press a: sec. 5).

(iv) Salmon makes the most striking response to my proposal. He describes it as "ill conceived if not downright desperate . . . widely bizarre . . . a confusion, on the order of a category mistake" (1986: 70–1). He says almost nothing in support of this. David Lewis has remarked that an incredulous stare is hard to argue with (1973: 86). So is an incredulous Salmon. However, I hope that what follows is an argument.

Salmon is also motivated by his criticisms of what he calls "the Generalized Frege Strategy," which I shall discuss later (section 7).[36]

4. The Semantic Task

In the sections that follow I shall sharpen the objections to the 'Fido'-Fido theory (section 5), assess direct-reference strategies for avoiding the problems that generate the objections (section 6), and develop my own solutions to those problems (section 7). All of these discussions depend, to an extent, on a view of what the task is in semantics. So we need to discuss that matter first.

The need is particularly pressing in assessing the strategies for avoiding the problems. For, the main strategies move the problems outside semantics. In considering these export strategies, it is easy to fall into a "merely verbal" disagreement about what we shall *call* "semantics" and "meaning." Thus suppose we ignore empty names (thus ignoring, of course, one of the major problems). Everyone (involved in this debate)[37] will agree that it is semantically significant that 'Cicero' refers to Cicero, 'Reagan' to Reagan, etc. So if 'semantics' is simply *defined* so that everything about a name other than its referent is irrelevant to its meaning or semantics (cf. the fast and dirty argument in section 3), there is no room for substantive disagreement.[38] However, defining away one's problems is clearly too easy an approach to intellectual life. And it has the disadvantage of making the 'Fido'-Fido theory trivial. What the theory needs to avoid this triviality is a justification for export strategies that is based on an independent view of the semantic task. So far as I know, a plausible justification of this sort has not been offered. Indeed, the discussion proceeds with little attention to what semantics is *for*. The view I shall now sketch[39] will be the basis for rejecting the export strategies.

---

[36]Fodor's motive for adopting his denotational semantics is completely different from any of the above (1987). He thinks, rightly in my view, that meaning holism threatens Life As We Know It. He thinks, wrongly in my view, that functional-role semantics leads inevitably to meaning holism. He sees his semantics as the only possible savior.

[37]The qualification is necessary because there are many, most notably those in the French structuralist tradition, who think that reference is irrelevant to meaning. On this see Devitt and Sterelny 1987: ch. 13.

[38]An example of such an approach—not taken by the direct-reference philosophers—would be to appeal to an old division of the study of language according to which syntax deals with expressions alone, semantics deals with expressions together with their referents, and pragmatics with the users of expressions and possible contexts of use. Cf. note 59.

[39]For more details, and some argument, see Devitt and Sterelny 1987.

Philosophers do not approach semantics with virgin minds. They already think about language using the familiar notions of folk theory: *meaning, truth, reference*, and so on. Furthermore, they have been educated to use many further notions: *sense, proposition, possible world*, and so on. In thinking about the task in semantics, it is important to set aside as much of this rich theoretical machinery as possible. Otherwise we are in danger of feeding into the description of the task much that is part of an attempted solution and should perhaps be controversial.[40] We need to get back to basics. What are the phenomena that prompted all this theorizing in the first place?

The phenomena are certain sounds and inscriptions which play strikingly important roles in our lives: people produce them in many circumstances and respond to them in a variety of ways. These token linguistic symbols are not abstract entities: they are datable, placeable parts of the physical world. The initial, and fairly theory-neutral, view of the task is: to describe and explain the properties of linguistic symbols that enable them to play the roles we have indicated.

Early on in our theorizing about linguistic symbols, we are likely to start talking about the mind. Indeed, I think that it is obvious that the role of language in people's lives comes from its relation to their minds.[41] I think that we should follow the folk in our theory by ascribing thoughts to people and in seeing linguistic symbols as the expressions of thoughts. And it is because language expresses thought that people are interested in it. Indeed, it is because it expresses thought that it exists at all.

Why then are we interested in thoughts? I think there are two reasons. First, because we are interested in explaining the behavior of the thinker. Second, because thoughts convey information about the way the world is.[42] So people produce and respond to, say, 'It is raining', partly because of what it shows about the likely behavior of the speaker and partly because of what it shows about the weather. We have arrived at a much less vague, but more theory-laden way, of specifying the roles of linguistic symbols in our lives.

Because of the link between thought and language, we should expect to follow the folk in ascribing many of the same properties to thoughts as to linguistic symbols. I agree with the many philosophers[43] who think that we should ascribe a syntax to thought, thus subscribing to a "language-of-thought" hypothesis. So we can now give a broader, though more theory-laden, description of our semantic task: to describe and explain the properties of linguistic

---

[40] I doubt the need for abstract entities in semantics, particularly propositions; 1976:404–5, 414–6; 1984a: 385–6.

[41] In emphasizing the relevance of the mind to linguistics, I am emphatically not endorsing the view, found for example in Chomsky and Dummett, that the theory of language is a theory of linguistic competence. I have argued against that view elsewhere (1981a: 92–5; Devitt and Sterelny in press). So has Soames (1984a, b).

[42] This is what indicates do. Interrogatives show what the thinker would like to discover about the way the world is. Imperatives show how the thinker would like the world to be. For convenience, I shall ignore nonindicatives.

[43] Including Chastain 1975: 197.

symbols and thoughts that enable them to play their roles in the explanation of behavior and as guides to reality.

It is convenient to use the term 'meaning' as a generic term for the properties of language and thought that are the concern of semantics. The semantic task is then to explain meaning so understood.

5. Sharpening Objections to the 'Fido'-Fido Theory

Against this background, the traditional objections to the 'Fido'-Fido theory seem very powerful.

The Identity Problem is that '$a = a$' and '$a = b$' have strikingly different roles whether in language or in thought.[44] People seldom think and seldomer produce tokens like the former, and there are few signs of consequences or interest when they do. In contrast, people often think and produce tokens like the latter, and there are lots of signs of consequences and interest when they do.[45] The reason for these differences is that the two tokens differ both as guides to reality and as explainers of behavior. I suggest that the strong conviction of the folk that these two differ in meaning—I have never met a beginning student who did not think that they do differ—is the response of folk semantics to these facts.

The Opacity Problem is even more severe. It arises once *truth* has been introduced into the theory of language. Consider, for example, ascriptions of belief in the above identities. It is hard to resist the claim that though Ralph's utterance, 'Flora believes that $a = a$', is certainly true, his utterance, 'Flora believes that $a = b$' may well be false. Yet, according to the 'Fido'-Fido theory if the two names are coreferential the ascriptions have the same meaning and so much have the same truth value; substitutivity of identicals must hold. We shall see that some direct-reference philosophers have managed to convince themselves, against all intuition, that the two ascriptions do have the same truth value (section 6). Yet still the problem does not go away. The two ascriptions differ radically as sources of information about Flora and as explainers of the behavior of Ralph. So they must differ in meaning. Differences in truth values are sufficient for a difference in meaning here, but they are not necessary.

The Opacity Problem makes the Identity Problem worse. If a name's property of referring to a certain object were the only property that was important to its role in identity beliefs and utterances, then it should be the only property of a name relevant to an *ascription* of an identity belief or utterance. If only the referent matters when we are *confronted with* Flora's belief or utterance, then it should be all that matters when we are *informed about* her belief or utterance. But it is not all that matters when we are informed, as the failure of substitutivity shows in the most dramatic way.

---

[44]Salmon (1986: 12) demonstrates neatly that the problem is not peculiar to identity statements; compare the informativeness of 'Phosphorus is a planet if Phosphorus is' and 'Hesperus is a planet if Phosphorus is'.

[45]This picture is too simple; see section 7.

Similarly, if Flora's mode of representing an object often matters when we are informed about her belief or utterance, as I think it does, then that is good evidence that the mode matters when we are confronted with the belief or utterance; it is good evidence that the mode is a property of the name that enables it to play its specified roles.

Ralph's ascriptions of beliefs and utterances to Flora have the same dual roles as his other utterances; explainers of Ralph's behavior and guides to reality. Set aside the first role. What is significant for this debate about Ralph's ascriptions is that the reality they are an immediate guide to is Flora's beliefs and utterances (which may be about anything from quarks to Quakers). Ralph, like everyone else, is interested in the beliefs and utterances of others as guides to reality and explainers of behavior. So his ascriptions to the likes of Flora show what properties of beliefs and utterances are relevant to those interests. So his ascriptions show what properties go into meaning.

That modes matter to our interest in beliefs and utterances as guides to reality is not initially obvious: we need the traditional problems to bring this home to us. That modes matter to our interest in beliefs and utterances to explain behavior does seem initially obvious.[46] The behavior flowing from a belief involving 'Phosphorus', given a certain stimulus, may well be very different from that flowing from a belief involving 'Hesperus', given the same stimulus. This is particularly striking if the stimulus is a verbal one involving one of the names. I suspect that the stubbornness with which the 'Fido'-Fido theory is maintained is partly the result of an exclusive interest in semantic properties as guides to reality rather than as explainers of behavior.

Finally, there are the Existence Problem and the Emptiness Problem. Empty names in existence statements and elsewhere undoubtedly have roles in our lives just as nonempty ones do. So a theory must not deem them meaningless.

6. Avoiding Problems for the 'Fido'-Fido Theory

Direct-reference philosophers have three strategies for avoiding the traditional problems for the 'Fido'-Fido theory. The first is the easiest but has the least to recommend it: ignore the problems. I shall call this "the Ostrich Strategy." The other two are of the export sort already mentioned (section 4): move the problems out of semantics. One, "the Mind Strategy," moves them into the theory of the mind. The other, "the Pragmatics Strategy," moves them into pragmatics.

The Ostrich Strategy

The Ostrich Strategy is bad but underlying it is a sound idea. *All* theories have unsolved problems. Yet it is all right to maintain some theories despite this.

---

[46]See, e.g., Fodor 1980. I think that, for the purpose of explaining behavior, we can abstract from that part of the mode that is outside the skin: only "narrow" meaning matters (in press b). If this is right then, so far as the explanation of behavior is concerned, the referent of a name is not only *not all* of its meaning, it is *not any* of its meaning.

Newton's theory is a striking example: it triumphed for more than two centuries despite many unsolved problems. However, what this shows is not that it is all right to *ignore* problems—the Newtonians did not do so—but rather that in appropriate circumstances it is all right to maintain a theory despite *failing to solve* problems. Briefly, when a theory is justified by an inference to the best explanation, it is all right to be a little bit complacent about it in the face of unsolved problems.

Such complacency about the 'Fido'-Fido theory must rest on the strength of the case for it. I have argued that the case is weak (section 3). This argument rests in part on a rival theory which, I claim, solves the problems and is a better explanation of meaning. That theory will be discussed in more detail in the next section.

It would be unfair to accuse a direct-reference philosopher of following the Ostrich Strategy simply because he has not yet confronted a problem; Rome wasn't built in a day; perhaps he is about to confront it. Nevertheless, it is worth noting that none of the direct-reference philosophers have confronted the Existence Problem or the Emptiness Problem, both of which seem catastrophic for a 'Fido'-Fido theorist who is not prepared to adopt a Meinongian or phenomenalist ontology.[47]

The Mind Strategy

The Mind Strategy exports problems from semantics. The interesting and substantive question in assessing export strategies is whether the very same considerations that make us think that the referent of a name is relevant to its meaning in the first place should also make us think that other factors are relevant. Against the background of my earlier sketch of the semantic task (section 4), I think that the answer, overwhelmingly, is that they should.

The Mind Strategy has been popular for dealing with the Identity Problem. Wettstein has been most explicit.[48] According to him, Frege formulated

> a condition of adequacy for a semantic account of singular terms . . . any such account must provide an answer to a crucial question concerning the cognitive significance of language: the question of how identity sentences in which proper names flank the identity sign can both state truths and be informative. (1986: 185)

Wettstein rejects this "epistemic" condition of adequacy, urging a "radically different conception" of semantics (p. 186). On this conception, cognitive matters are not the concern of semantics.

Wettstein sharply distinguishes between singular propositions and the ways in which those propositions are cognized. He prefers to call those propositions

---

[47]Salmon expresses the hope that the Pragmatic Strategy will work for these problems (1986: 127–8).

[48]See also Almog 1986: 233–5. Kaplan seems to be tempted; 1988a: 558–69, 591–2. Lycan follows the Mind Strategy in treating the computational roles of thoughts, which are relevant to their role in explaining behavior, as not part of their semantics; 1985.

"states of affairs" because they are made up of objects and properties "out in the world." In contrast, the cognizing of them is a mental activity (pp. 197–9). Semantics should be concerned with the former not the latter; with "the uncovering of the semantic rules that govern our linguistic practices" (p. 200), the "institutionalized conventions" (p. 201), and not "with matters cognitive" (p. 201). In the case of names, we should be concerned to "specify the conditions under which an utterance of a name counts as a reference to an individual" (p. 202) and not with the "ways in which speakers think about their referents" (p. 201), not with their "cognitive perspectives" (p. 202).

(1) I have linked the semantics of language closely to the semantics of thought and given the latter a certain priority (section 4). So if linguistic symbols have such semantic properties as being true or referring, they have them because thoughts do also. On this view there can be no question of divorcing cognitive matters from the semantics of language. Wettstein must reject the view, and he does: he denies that "the first step towards understanding how words refer is to understand how thoughts do so" (1988: 421). What are the alternatives to this view? (a) One might accept that thoughts share those semantic properties with linguistic symbols but deny that this is explanatorily significant. This view seems absurd. (b) More promising, but in my view quite mistaken (Devitt and Sterelny 1987: ch. 10), is the view that the direction of explanation should be reversed: language is prior to thought. (c) One might have a generally eliminativist view of the mind, denying that there are any thoughts or, at least, that there are any with those semantic properties. This faces the problem that all eliminativism faces: explaining behavior without minds. Eliminativism in this case faces an even more difficult problem: explaining language in a thoughtless world *without eliminating reference*. For, if reference goes, so does direct reference. In my view, no eliminativist has offered even sketches of a plausible solution to these problems. Wettstein does not say enough about thoughts[49] to make it clear which alternative he favors, though his appeals to Wittgenstein suggest some version of (c).

(2) According to Wettstein, the semantic task for names is to describe, perhaps explain, the convention or rule that links a name referentially to an object. But *why* is that the task? Why is the reference of a name interesting and why is only its reference interesting? An answer might be: we are interested in reference because of its contribution to the truth conditions of sentences (cf. 2 in section 3). But why are we interested in the truth conditions of sentences and only in those? Our discussion of the phenomena that need explaining show that properties of symbols *other* than their reference or truth conditions, namely their modes of presentation, are important to their specified roles in our lives.

---

[49]Wettstein is atypical in saying as much as he does. Direct-reference philosophers typically ignore the semantics of thoughts altogether. For example, Salmon's recent book (1986) does not discuss mental representation or functional- (conceptual-) role semantics, nor does it mention any of the many recent works on this topic (including those by Fodor, thus returning the compliment).

The difference between '$a = a$' and '$a = b$' is not to be set aside as epistemic, cognitive, and unsemantic. We have seen that it is crucial to the role of the two sentences in the explanation of behavior and as guides to reality; it is crucial to what makes us interested in the meanings of the two sentences in the first place.

In the face of this, one can of course insist on applying 'meaning' only to the referential role of a name, but this is an unmotivated verbal manoeuvre that makes the 'Fido'-Fido theory true by definition and uninteresting. What is needed is some account of the point of semantics that justifies the restriction to reference. Wettstein does not provide this.[50]

(3) Wettstein claims that

> there is no reason to suppose that, in general, if we successfully uncover the insti-
> tutionalized conventions governing the references of our terms, we will have cap-
> tured the ways in which speakers think about their referents. (p. 201)

What is involved in uncovering these conventions? Presumably we have not done this for names when we say simply that a name designates an object. Even if we overlook the fact that this is false for some names—the Emptiness Problem—surely semantics should tell us in virtue of what a name refers to a particular referent. That explanation must frequently involve the mind, for there is nothing other than minds and their relations to the external world that *could* establish the conventions of reference. In my view, the mental facts alluded to in this explanation will explain the required difference in cognitive values (section 7).

Wettstein wants to divorce the mind from semantics partly because of his view of the role it would play if it were not divorced. On his view, the meaning of a name would involve the descriptions or concepts that a competent user of the name must associate with it. This association amounts to propositional knowl-edge of the referent sufficient to discriminate the referent from other objects (1986:201–4; 1988). But this is to assume that only the Description theory can provide a "cognitive fix" on the referent. In my view, the Causal theory provides that fix: the fix is a network of d-chains generated by conceptual-role links from thoughts to peripheral stimuli and by links from stimuli to the external world. Little if any of this need be conscious knowledge.

The Pragmatic Strategy

The Pragmatic Strategy is another export strategy. It cannot be dismissed out of hand because there clearly are some linguistic phenomena that are rightly treated as matters for pragmatics not semantics; Gricean conversational implicatures are examples. I suspect that there is not, in general, a theory-neutral way of drawing the line between semantics and pragmatics (1981a: 197–8).

---

[50]Nor does Almog, who seems to apply the Mind Strategy to the Opacity Problem as well as the Identity Problem. Certainly, he thinks that failures of substitutivity in "epistemic contexts" are of no concern to the 'Fido'-Fido theory (1985).

The Pragmatic Stategy has been popular for dealing with the Opacity Problem. Salmon has used it also for the Identity Problem (1986: 77–9).[51]

Salmon's line on the latter is that once we have made the distinction between information that is semantically encoded and information that is pragmatically imparted, it is not obvious that the informativeness of '$a = b$' does not come from what is pragmatically imparted. In the absence of a reason to believe the contrary, Salmon feels justified in putting the Identity Problem aside.

I have argued that when we consider why we ascribe meaning at all—to explain behavior and as a guide to reality—it *is* obvious that the informativeness of '$a = b$' is semantic and not merely pragmatic (section 5). (This is not, of course, to say that the informativeness is not pragmatic at all. Soames demonstrates nicely that it is partly pragmatic; 1988: 104–5.)

Salmon's claims about pragmatics seem to be disastrous for his position that the information semantically encoded by '$a = b$' and by '$a = a$' are equally valuable. He points out that an utterance of S typically pragmatically imparts the information that S is true (1986: 59). Thus the utterance of '$a = b$' imparts the information that that sentence is true and hence, Salmon continues, that the names 'a' and 'b' are coreferential (p. 79). To bring out the disaster, first we express Salmon's view of what is imparted by the identity utterances as follows:

(I1) '$a = b$' is true, hence the referent of 'a' is the same as the referent of 'b'

(I2) '$a = a$' is true, hence the referent of 'a' is the same as the referent of 'a'

Next, consider what Salmon must similarly claim is imparted by the utterances, "Ben is as tall as Saul," and "Ben is as tall as Ben":

(T1) 'Ben is as tall as Saul' is true, hence the referent of 'Ben' is as tall as the referent of 'Saul'

(T2) 'Ben is as tall as Ben' is true, hence the referent of 'Ben' is as tall as the referent of 'Ben'

These claims are precisely analogous to (I1) and (I2). What they show first is that, to someone competent with S,[52] the pragmatically imparted information that S is true *matches in value* the information that S semantically encodes. Indeed, it is *because* S has a certain value that 'S is true' has that value. Further, the value of the pragmatically imparted information about the reference of terms in S reflects the value of the information about the truth of S from which it is derived (with the help of some elementary semantic knowledge), and so is also determined by the value of what S semantically encodes. It is *because* it is interesting to know that Ben is as tall as Saul that it is interesting to know that the referent of 'Ben' is as tall as the referent of 'Saul'. It is *because* it is uninteresting to know that Ben is as tall as Ben that it is uninteresting to know that the referent of 'Ben' is as tall as the

---

[51] So have Soames (1988: 104–5) and Fodor (1987: 85–6). Salmon lists many others who have taken this path before; 1986: 167*n*.

[52] Salmon rightly points out that the Identity Problem is properly posed only of speakers competent with the names in question (p. 60).

referent of 'Ben'. So the additional value of (I1) over (I2) is evidence of precisely what 'Fido'-Fido denies: that '$a = b$' has more information value than '$a = a$'.

Salmon takes the Opacity Problem more seriously. He describes it carefully in a way that demonstrates its enormity for the 'Fido'-Fido theory (pp. 80–81, 87–92).[53] He notes that we always entertain a singular proposition under some "guise." Part of this guise is our "mode of acquaintance" with the object the thought is about (pp. 107–9).[54] He acknowledges that these modes are "similar in some respects to Fregean senses" (p. 120). So Salmon has provided the motivation and the means to adopt a view like mine. But his faith in direct reference does not waiver:

> The ancient astronomer agrees to the proposition about the planet Venus that it is it when he takes it in the way it is presented to him through the logically valid sentence 'Hesperus is Hesperus', but he does not agree to this same proposition when he takes it in the way it is presented to him through the logically contingent sentence 'Hesperus is Phosphorus'. The fact that he agrees to it at all is, strictly speaking, sufficient for the truth of both the sentence 'The astronomer believes that Hesperus is Hesperus' and the sentence 'The astronomer believes that Hesperus is Phosphorus'. (p. 116)

Whatever she says, *Lois Lane really does know that Clark Kent is Superman* (p. 83)![55]

If modes are not relevant to the truth conditions of belief attributions, what is their significance? According to Salmon, they have a "pragmatic function" (p. 117),[56] which makes

> the first [way of attributing the belief to the astronomer] better than the second, given our normal purpose in attributing belief. Both sentences state the same fact . . . but the first sentence also manages to convey *how* the astronomer agrees to the proposition. Indeed, the second sentence, though true, is in some sense inappropriate; it is positively misleading. . . . (p. 116)

Salmon accepts that the astronomer has his belief under a certain mode of acquaintance and not under others. He accepts that the best belief attribution conveys which mode the belief is under. He accepts that conveying this is important "given our normal purpose in attributing belief."[57] *What better evidence could we have that conveying this is part of the meaning of the attribution?* The apparent difference in meaning between the first and second attribution would remain even if they had the same truth value (section 5). However, if conveying information about a mode is part of an attribution's meaning, what better way is there to

---

[53]See also Soames 1988: 105–6.

[54]See also Soames 1988: 125.

[55]See Baker 1982 for a demonstration of the rank implausibility of this view.

[56]See also Soames 1987: 67–9; 1988: 104–5, 117–25.

[57]Wettstein inclines toward this view also. He accepts that substitutivity often does fail for these attributions. He finds the subject "difficult and messy" but seems to think that a context-relative account of these attributions will leave the 'Fido'-Fido theory unscathed (1986: 204–9). See below.

explain the apparent difference than to make the modes relevant to truth conditions? This has the happy result that the first attribution is true and the second false, as everyone always thought. Salmon will have none of this:

> [I]t is no part of the semantic content of the sentence to specify the way the astronomer takes the proposition when he agrees to it. The 'that'-clause is there only to specify the proposition believed. (p. 117)

Salmon offers so little support for these claims that we should suspect that the 'Fido'-Fido theory is being made true by stipulation and hence trivial.

Salmon is well aware that his view flies in the face of ordinary intuition (pp. 83–5). However, his problems are much more serious than that. He agrees that we are interested in modes. Why are we? For the same reason that we are interested in thoughts and utterances at all: to explain people's behavior and to gain information about the world. *The very same considerations that motivate meaning motivate modes.* And if we are interested in the modes of thoughts and utterances, we should *expect* to find attributions of thoughts and utterances informing us about modes (sections 4 and 5). Salmon's theory is guided neither by folk opinion nor by scientific methodology.

On my view, an opaque attribution with a name in the content clause conveys information about modes via the mode (= sense) of the name: the mode in the thinker or utterer must be the same as the mode in the attribution. For singular terms in general, I see a systematic relationship between the mode of the term in the content clause and the mode of the term that would make the attribution true. (For example, roughly, one demonstrative requires another, though not usually the same one.) This is one way for the semantics of an attribution to convey information about modes.

Another view has found favor.[58] On this view, attributions have an implicit indexical reference to some feature of the context—for example, the speaker's intention—which determines which mode makes the attribution true. The view gives no special role to the mode of the term in the content clause in determining truth conditions and so is not as strikingly at odds with the 'Fido'-Fido theory as my view. Nevertheless, it is still at odds because it acknowledges the importance of modes to the significance of thoughts and utterances and hence to their meaning.

Soames's approach to the Opacity Problem is similar to Salmon's, as the notes to the above discussion indicate. He has a further argument for treating the problem as nonsemantic.[59] In the course of a lengthy and subtle discussion of thought and utterance attributions (1985, 1986, 1988), drawing on a paper of Mark

---

[58] E.g., Schiffer 1979. I criticize the view in 1981c.

[59] In a paper defending Tarski and not on direct reference, Soames proposes a division within the study of language between semantics and pragmatics that is reminiscent of the old one mentioned in note 38 (1984c: 425–6). If it were applied here, it would trivialize the disagreement. On Soames' proposal, a language is an abstract object that has its semantic properties essentially; it is a triple consisting of a set of expressions, a domain of objects, and a function assigning objects to expressions. These abstract objects are the concern of semantics.

(contd.)

Richard (1983), Soames offers some reasons for maintaining substitutivity, hence for denying that the attributions are opaque. I have argued that maintaining substitutivity is insufficient to save the 'Fido'-Fido theory (section 5): the evidence will remain that, for example, Salmon's first and second attribution differ in meaning. Nevertheless substitutivity is certainly necessary to save the theory and so I shall consider Soames' reasons.

First, Soames points to some cases where, despite appearances, substitutivity holds, and claims that we can generalize from these (1987: 66–7). However, his discussion overlooks some observations that Quine made long ago.[60] Quine noted that though some thought attributions are opaque, some are transparent; substitutivity holds for them. Transparent attributions can be *obviously* transparent; for example, of the form,

> *b* is such that *a* believes it to be *F*.

However, Quine noted further that the most common forms of attribution are ambiguous between an opaque and a transparent reading; for example,

> *a* believes that *b* is *F*

is ambiguous. In the light of these Quinean observations, the response to Soames's argument is simple: substitutivity does indeed hold in his cases because it is appropriate to construe the attributions transparently. But there is no basis here for Soames's generalization that substitutivity *always* holds.

Quine's view that there are both transparent and opaque attributions is not only supported by our intuitive assignments of truth values to attributions, it is also supported by a consideration of the purposes of these attributions. Take Ralph's attribution of a belief to Flora only as a guide to the reality of Flora's beliefs (not as an explainer of *Ralph's* behavior). If our interest in that reality is for the purposes of explaining Flora's behavior, then an opaque attribution will always be appropriate. On the other hand, if our interest in that reality is as a guide to another reality—what the belief is about—then the transparent form will often better suit our purposes.[61]

Second, Soames has a range of cases involving identity where, he claims, certain substitutions are irresistible. Yet the cases yield the same counter-intuitive

---

Pragmatics is concerned with the contingent question of which language a person or population speaks. Soames' proposal would make the 'Fido'-Fido theory trivial once the Nondescription theory had been adopted for, on this conception of a language, there would then be nothing that could be a name's meaning except its role of referring to its assigned object. The traditional problems for 'Fido'-Fido would not disappear, however. They would become problems for this way of dividing up the subject. Why suppose that the empirically interesting question posed by linguistic phenomena is: Which of *these abstract objects* does *x* speak? The problems suggest that *x*'s use of a name—part of speaking a language—is *not* adequately explained by relating *x* to a pair consisting of the name and an object—part of the abstract object that is supposed to be the language. If language is to be conceived of as an abstract object, the empirically interesting conception must be richer than Soames's.

[60] So does Wettstein's (1986: 205–6) and Salmon's (in press: *n* 12).

[61] For more on this see my 1984a: 394–6; 1984b: 99–101.

results as does the general substitutivity that is so problematic for the 'Fido'-Fido theory. If we are prepared to put up with the results in these cases, why not do so in general?

Soames's most interesting cases are of attributions involving demonstratives. The truth conditions of these are undoubtedly tricky. Soames also has some cases involving general terms. I think that these cases, particularly the demonstrative ones, do provide some solace to direct reference, but nowhere near enough to save it in the face of the considerations I have adduced. However, I must set their discussion aside until another time.[62] I postpone a discussion of Soames's case involving a name until the next section.

7. Solving the Problems

In this section I shall expand on my solutions to the Identity Problem and the Opacity Problem. However, the discussion must still be briefer than the problems deserve. And I shall have nothing more to say about my solutions to the Existence Problem and the Emptiness Problem.[63]

I have argued that the strategies adopted by direct-reference philosophers to avoid the traditional problems for the 'Fido'-Fido theory are all mistaken. If my solutions to those problems are along the right lines, the strategies are also unnecessary. The problems can be solved in semantics by abandoning 'Fido'-Fido.

The Identity Problem

I shall start with a paradigm example of an informative identity statement, 'Hesperus = Phosphorus' soon after the discovery of its truth.

My solution begins with the claim that the two names in this statement have different senses in that underlying them are different types of d-chain.[64] Note that the claim concerns types not tokens. If we located the difference between the names in the different token d-chains that make up their networks, we would be driven to the unfortunate conclusion that every name token differs in sense from every other name token.

How do the d-chains differ in type? They involve different types of groundings: in the one case a set of events in the evening, including the sound of 'Hesperus'; in the other, a set of events in the morning, including the sound of 'Phosphorus'. (I talk of sounds, ignoring other media, for convenience.) They involve different types of reference borrowings: in the one case, communications including the sound of 'Hesperus'; in the other case, communications including the sound of 'Phosphorus'. However, these differences cannot be essential.

Consider two look-alikes who are both named 'George'. Clearly the groundings of these names may be indistinguishable aside from the fact that they involve different objects. But now remove that difference: there is one person leading a

---

[62]There is little discussion of them in my 1981a and 1984a either.

[63]But see 1981a: ch. 6.

[64]For a lot more detail on some aspects of this discussion, see my 1981a: 129–57, 239–40.

double life with such success that everyone wrongly thinks that there are two look-alikes. Intuitively, these two uses of 'George', generating two distinct networks, differ in sense as much as 'Hesperus' and 'Phosphorus'. Certainly they can be part of a very informative identity statement: '(This) George = (that) George'. (So in this highly abnormal situation, a statement of the form '$a = a$' is informative.)[65] So different types of grounding cannot be essential to a difference in sense.

This example shows also that different types of reference borrowings cannot be essential to a difference in sense. Indeed, all reference borrowings involving the sound of 'George' are, in the relevant respect, the same.

What is essential to a difference in sense is that members of the speech community process the input involving the names differently and hence keep the networks distinct; the names are associated with different "files." Evidence of this is that the two names are involved in distinct sets of beliefs.

Suppose that Charles already has the ability to use the sound type 'Gail' to designate a certain object, Gail. So he has a "file" consisting of a set of thoughts that include tokens that dispose him to speak the sound type 'Gail' and that have underlying them d-chains that are grounded in Gail. Suppose now that Charles is in the position to borrow reference from Kate. He hears Kate using tokens of 'Gail' which, in fact, have underlying them d-chains grounded in Gail. If he is to take advantage of Kate's utterance, amending that 'Gail' file, he must process Kate's 'Gail'-sounds so that they are brought to bear on that file. He must process the input as if he had formed the identity belief, 'Gail (the subject of this conversation) = Gail (the subject of these thoughts)'.[66] This processing task may not be easy because he may know several people named 'Gail'. Similarly, if he is to amend his file in a grounding situation as a result of experience of Gail herself, he must process the input as if he had formed the identity belief, 'That person = Gail'. It is in this way that Charles' thoughts prompted by current experience are unified with pre-existing thoughts involving a name. D-chains are of the same type for Charles if his inner processing links them together in this way.

This is the story of sameness of type *for Charles;* of his *personal* network. It is the story of *speaker* sense. We need also the story of sameness of type period, of the community's network. We need the story of *conventional* sense.

When Charles borrowed from Kate, his processing linked his network to hers. And *everybody's doing it,* not always with Kate, but with other members of the community. The union of all these personal networks is the community's network. For two d-chains to be of the same type, and hence for the names they underlie to have the same (conventional) sense, is for them to be linked together by the inner processing of members of the community into the one network and for them to involve tokens of the sound type conventionally part of the network. (Unions can be imperfect, as we shall briefly see.) D-chains are of different types when they have not been so unified.

---

[65]Cf. Salmon's nice example of Aristotle; 1986: 75.

[66]In my 1981a, pp. 134–6, I requiredthat the subject actually from the identity belief. I now think that this yields an over-intellectualized account of the processing.

D-chains of different types normally arise from groundings in different objects. Where they do not, they will almost always involve differences in sound type and different circumstances of use; the case of 'Hesperus' and 'Phosphorous' is an example.[67] Very rarely, differences in d-chain type may arise despite sameness of object and sound type because of different circumstances of use; the case of 'George' above is an example.

The solution to the Identity Problem falls straight out of this. Because 'a' and 'b' differ in sense, '$a = a$' and '$a = b$' differ in role and in the "cognitive value" that Frege drew attention to. The difference in sense is a difference of d-chain type brought about by differences in the processing of tokens of 'a' and 'b'. These processing differences affect our understanding of the two identity statements: understanding the first involves accessing the one file twice whereas understanding the second involves accessing two files. Because of these facts about inner processing, and a mastery of identity, a person knows that the first statement must be true and that the second may be true or false.[68]

I solve the Identity problem by ascribing different meanings to 'a' and 'b' but I do not "give" the meanings. This solution will be a disappointment to those who seek a traditional *a priori* "analysis." In my view, the semantic task does not require such an analysis. The task is to *explain* meaning not give it. Furthermore, I don't think that the meaning of 'a' can be given in other terms. 'a' gives the meaning of 'a' as well as it can be given.[69]

On my view, what is important about a name token, what enables it to play its specified roles, is that it is part of a certain sort of network that links the token to other tokens of a certain sound type (and of a certain inscription type, etc.). Its meaning (information value, etc.) is its property of being so linked. The referent gets into the picture because, if the name is nonempty, the network will be grounded in an object which is the referent.

We can use this discussion to provide a further argument against the 'Fido'-Fido theory. According to that theory the only thing essential to understanding

---

[67]Note that in such cases knowledge of the identity does not lead to amalgamation of files. Thus we process some input to our 'Superman' file and not our 'Clark Kent' file, and vice versa. So the names have different modes of presentation; cf. Schiffer 1987, an interesting criticism of Salmon, to which Salmon in press is a reply.

[68]The story for demonstratives is different. If 'a' and 'b' are such terms, '$a = b$' is usually informative. However, this is not to be explained by the differing senses of the terms, for example the differing senses of 'she' and 'you', but rather by what is common to the senses of all such terms: those senses make the reference of a token depend on a d-chain grounded by the speaker in producing that very token (1981a: 42–3). The possibility of tokens of different terms having different referents is intrinsic to the senses of the terms. Indeed, the possibility of tokens of the same term having different referents is intrinsic to the term's sense with the result that '$a = a$' can be informative.

[69]For more on the place of analysis in semantics, see Devitt and Sterelny 1987, particularly: 231–5. I suspect that the "analytical" view of philosophy lies behind motivation 2 in section 3.
Ackerman's view is like mine in that she ascribes different "non-descriptive connotations" to coreferential names (1979a, b). However, she *does* offer analyses of these connotations as a solution to the Identity Problem. I think the solution will not work for similar reasons to those I offered (1983: 676–7) against her similar view of natural-kind term (1980).

a name token is assigning it the right referent. The case of 'George' shows that this is not so. In that case the name seems to have two meanings but only one referent. Understanding a token requires assigning it the right meaning—in my terms, linking it to the same network that underlies its production. A person who gets this wrong will have misunderstood the token, which may have important consequences for explaining behavior and gaining information about the world. Yet the person may still have assigned the right referent. So assigning the right referent is insufficient for understanding. So having that referent is insufficient for meaning.

We have seen that the 'Fido'-Fido theory is open to refutation by finding a pair of names that share a referent and yet yield an informative identity statement. Salmon calls this "Frege's Strategy." Salmon thinks that if this strategy is good so also is "the Generalized Frege Strategy." Consider the theory that the meaning of a name is its F. The Generalized Strategy is to find a pair of names that share F and yet yield an informative identity statement. Salmon thinks that if the strategy were good, it would work against any plausible theory. So it can't be good. So Frege's Strategy is not good. So the 'Fido'-Fido theory can be retained.[70] I claim that my theory is not open to the Generalized Frege Strategy: it is not possible to find two names that share my sort of senses and yet yield an informative identity statement, for any such names will have underlying them the one causal network.

In assessing this claim, two distinctions are important: first, that between *conventional* senses and *speaker* senses; second, that between what is informative *in general,* and what is informative *to a particular speaker.* I have been primarily discussing the first half of each distinction. I explain informativeness in general by appealing to the differing conventional senses of the names; for the appeal is to the typing of d-chains in the speech community as a whole. However, some individuals may be partly at odds with the community, with the consequence that a name with one conventional sense has two speaker senses for them. They process tokens of the one name as if they were of two names. Then even a thought of the form '$a = a$' would be informative for them, although the names involved share conventional senses. Consider, for example, Ralph, who does not know that Russell the logician is one and the same as Russell the peace marcher; as a result, he does not unify his input from the two sources into one file. 'Russell (the logician) = Russell (the peace marcher)' is informative for him because the names have two speaker senses (though only one conventional sense).[71]

---

[70]Salmon 1986: 73–6. I have adapted the Strategy a little to suit my purposes.

[71]If Ralph's situation were general in a community, the case would be like that of 'George': one referent, one sound type, and yet two conventional senses.

  Ralph might make a more serious mistake: treating tokens from two names as if they were from one. The earlier mistake is failing to unify where he should; this one is unifying where he should not. This mistake leads to a network grounded in two objects and thus to indeterminacy of speaker reference. I discuss this in 1981a: 138–52.

  The Russell case is of the sort that generates Kripke's "Puzzle about Belief" (1979). I have urged a solution making use of the distinction between conventional and speaker senses 1984a: 407–12). I would offer a similar solution to Salmon's case of Elmer (1986: 92–101).

The Opacity Problem

Sometimes substitutivity holds for ascriptions of thought and utterance and so they are transparent. In such cases, the ascriptions pose no *additional* problem for a theory of names. The additional problem comes from the many cases where substitutivity fails and the ascription is opaque: something other than the name's referent is relevant to the truth of the ascription.

The key to my solution is simple: the truth conditions of the ascription depends on the sense of the name in the content clause.[72] The ascription requires that the subject's thought or utterance uses a name with the same sense as the name in the content clause. This talk of senses is to be understood in the causal way set out above. The solution captures the intuitive idea that the ascription requires the subject to use the same name as the ascriber.

This solution demands that we say more about what counts as sameness of sense, and hence sameness of name.

My convenient restriction to the spoken language encourages a simple view: tokens of the same name must sound the same. So the ascription of an utterance to Flora could not be true unless the name she used sounded the same as the one in the content clause of the ascription. Immediately we remove the convenient restriction, we see that this cannot be true. Flora might have been writing, not talking. Indeed, the ascription might be made true by an utterance in any medium at all. Furthermore, what if the ascription is of a thought not a communication? It can be made true by a mental token.

The name in the content clause of an ascription requires that Flora use a token in the same network but not a token in the same medium. However, if Flora's token is not mental, being in the same network is not alone sufficient for the truth of the ascription, because Flora's token might not be in accord with the conventions that have formed the network; it might be aberrant. The truth behind the simple view is that if Flora's token is a sound, it must be of the same sound type as those in the network; if it is an inscription, it must be of the same inscription type; and so on through all the media of communication.

I have written as if tokens of what is intuitively only one sound type, inscription type, and so on, are conventionally part of a network. This may require modification. Consider Soames's example: the names 'Ruth Barcan' and 'Ruth Marcus' (1987: 67). Suppose that the ascriber used a token that sounded like the former, whereas Flora's utterance contained a token that sounded like the latter. In assessing this ascription, it may seem as if these tokens have the same sense. Yet, intuitively, they are of different sound types, at least partly. Let us look at the history. For many years, there were sounds of the type 'Ruth Barcan', but none of the type 'Ruth Marcus', in a network grounded in Ruth Barcan Marcus. When there came to be sounds of the latter type referring to her, were they conventionally in the *same* network? To some degree, probably yes: some people probably treated those sounds as if they were tokens of the

---

[72] For many more details, see my 1981a, chs. 9 and 10, and 1984a.

old name; their processing brought these tokens into the old network. Others almost certainly did not. Doubtless, the same practices go on to this day. So sounds of the two types are partly unified into the one community-wide network and partly not. Unification is always a matter of degree and in this case the degree is well short of what is required for a confident claim that Flora's token and the ascriber's are of the same name type.

So according to the theory, there is some vagueness about sameness of sense. I don't think that this matters to the theory because there is a matching vagueness about the circumstances in which we ordinarily think ascriptions true.

Foreign names pose a similar problem. Tokens of 'London' and 'Londres' normally count as the same for the purposes of thought ascription. Intuitively, they are of different sound types, inscription types, and so on, though not so very different. At first sight, it may seem as if the networks underlying the two types are not unified at all: one network involves English speakers, the other, French speakers. This is a mistake. It overlooks the many situations where an English speaker processes a French speaker's 'Londres' to a 'London' file, and vice versa. If a foreign name has not been unified with an English name in this way, then I think that we would not count an English ascription of a thought to a foreigner true on the strength of a thought involving the foreign name. At least we would not count it true *construed opaquely*. Of course, it might well be true construed transparently.

Soames's example enables us to construct a case of the sort that he likes, discussion of which I postponed (section 6):

(a) Flora believes that Ruth Barcan = Ruth Barcan.
(b) Flora believes that Ruth Barcan = Ruth Marcus.

Soames thinks that the substitution of 'Ruth Marcus' for 'Ruth Barcan' is irresistible: they must have the same meaning. Yet, he claims, (b) still seems much more informative than (a). If everyone has to tolerate this counter-intuitive result, why not tolerate the similarly counter-intuitive results of general substitutivity, thus allowing the 'Fido'-Fido theory to stand?

I bite the bullet here. I think that the substitution is quite resistible. Tokens of 'Ruth Marcus' and 'Ruth Barcan' are not thoroughly unified in the one network. The tendency to favor substitution arises from the partial unification of the networks for the names. Identity of sense is a matter of degree.

8. Conclusions

The theory of direct reference for names is a combination of three distinct but related theories: the 'Fido'-Fido theory, the Nondescription theory, and the Rigid Designation theory. It does not include the Causal theory. I have argued that the 'Fido'-Fido theory does not follow from the three other named theories, lacks adequate motivation, and is false.

The argument against it is a traditional one: it fails to solve the Identity Problem, the Existence Problem, the Emptiness Problem, and the Opacity Problem. Direct-reference philosophers typically try to avoid this argument by exporting the problems into the theory of the mind or pragmatics. A consideration of our purposes in attributing semantic properties to linguistic symbols—explaining behavior and learning about reality—shows that these export strategies fail. The very same considerations that make us think that the reference of a name is semantically significant, make us think that *more than* reference is significant.

A major reason for thinking that the 'Fido'-Fido theory lacks motivation is that there is an alternative. This alternative ascribes to a name a nondescriptive sense, or mode of presentation, that is explained in terms of the reference-determining causal network for the name. Thus, I argue that the Causal theory not only explains a name's reference, it also points to an explanation of the name's meaning that solves the traditional problems for the 'Fido'-Fido theory. Contrary to popular opinion, the Causal theory supplies not an example of the 'Fido'-Fido theory but a way of replacing it.

In my argument, I take the 'Fido'-Fido theory to be a substantive addition to the Nondescription theory. That is, I take its notion of meaning to be the one we need in an empirical theory attempting to explain linguistic phenomena. However, the discussion often proceeds as if 'Fido'-Fido follows from Nondescription by stipulation: nondescriptive meaning is identified with reference *by definition*. This is not a theoretically useful notion of meaning. The move has the further disadvantage of making 'Fido'-Fido the result of a trivial addition to Nondescription.

Why is the 'Fido'-Fido theory maintained in the face of apparently over-whelming objections? Partly, I think, because far too little attention is paid to the question of what we need semantics *for*. As a result, standard views of the nature of semantics, and of the range of alternative theories, are taken for granted. In my opinion, these standard views are mostly unhelpful, if not mistaken.[73,74]

---

[73]Shortly after this paper was sent to the publishers, David Kaplan sent me a copy of his "Afterthoughts" (1988b), in which proper names are discussed at some length. He still favors the 'Fido'-Fido theory (draft pp. 13-9). However, in contemplating a change in his view of a name's character (similar to those I proposed above on his behalf; sec. 3, motivation 3), he seems prepared to bring a name's mechanism of reference into its meaning (draft pp. 30-3). I am in broad agreement with many of his other remarks about names (draft pp. 58-76): on the relation of thought to language (1981a: 83-6; Devitt and Sterelny 1987: 124-8); on being *en rapport* (1981a: ch. 9; 1984a); on naming future objects (1974: 199-200; 1981a: 59-60).

[74]Earlier versions of this paper were given at the University of Sydney (July, 1988), La Trobe University (July, 1988), and Princeton University (October, 1988). The paper has benefited from the discussions it received on those occasions. I am very grateful to the following for helpful comments on a late draft at very short notice: Fiona Cowie, Norbert Hornstein, Bill Lycan, and Georges Rey. Finally, I must thank Nathan Salmon and Scott Soames for comments that removed some misunderstandings and led to other improvements.

REFERENCES

Ackerman, Diana. 1979a. "Proper Names, Propositional Attitudes and Non-Descriptive Connotations." *Philosophical Studies* 35:55–69.

Ackerman, Diana. 1979b. "Proper Names, Essences and Intuitive Beliefs." *Theory and Decision* 11:5–26.

Ackerman, Diana. 1980. "Natural Kinds, Concepts, and Propositional Attitudes." In French, Uehling and Wettstein 1980, 469–85.

Almog, Joseph. 1984. "Semantic Anthropology." In French, Uehling and Wettstein 1984, 479–89.

Almog, Joseph. 1985. "Form and Content." *Noûs* 19:603–16.

Almog, Joseph. 1986. "Naming without Necessity." *Journal of Philosophy* 71:210–42.

Almog, Joseph, John Perry, and Howard Wettstein, eds. 1988. *Themes from Kaplan.* New York.

Baker, Lynne Rudder. 1982. "Underprivileged Access." *Noûs* 16:227–42.

Barwise, Jon, and John Perry. 1983. *Situations and Attitudes.* Cambridge, Mass.

Block, Ned. 1986. "Advertisement for a Semantics for Psychology." In French, Uehling, and Wettstein 1986, 615–78.

Chastain, Charles. 1975. "Reference and Context." In *Language, Mind, and Knowledge: Minnesota Studies in the Philosophy of Science, Volume VII*, edited by Keith Gunderson, Minneapolis

Davidson, Donald, and Gilbert Harman, eds. 1972. *Semantics of Natural Language.* Dordrecht.

Devitt, Michael. 1972. *The Semantics of Proper Names: A Causal Theory*, Harvard Ph.D. thesis.

Devitt, Michael. 1974. "Singular Terms." *Journal of Philosophy* 71:183–205.

Devitt, Michael. 1976. "Semantics and the Ambiguity of Proper Names." *Monist* 59:404–23

Devitt, Michael. 1980. "Brian Loar on Singular Terms." *Philosophical Studies* 37:271–80.

Devitt, Michael. 1981a, *Designation.* New York.

Devitt, Michael. 1981b. "Donnellan's Distinction." In French, Uehling and Wettstein 1981, 511–24.

Devitt, Michael. 1981c. Critical Notice of French, Uehling and Wettstein 1979. *Australasian Journal of Philosophy* 59:211–21.

Devitt, Michael. 1983. "Realism and Semantics," part II of a critical study of French, Uehling and Wettstein 1980. *Noûs* 17:669–81.

Devitt, Michael. 1984a. "Thoughts and Their Ascription." In French, Uehling and Wettstein 1984, 385–420.

Devitt, Michael. 1984b. *Realism and Truth.* Princeton.

Devitt, Michael, 1985. "Critical Notice for Evans 1982." *Australasian Journal of Philosophy* 63:216–32.

Devitt, Michael. In press a. "Meanings Just Ain't in the Head." In *Method, Reason, and Language: Essays in honor of Hilary Putnam*, edited by George Boolos, Cambridge.

Devitt, Michael. In press b. "A Narrow Representational Theory of the Mind." In *Rerepresentation: Readings in the Philosophy of Mental Representation*, edited by Stuart Silvers, Dordrecht. (Reprinted in *Mind and Cognition: A Reader*, edited by William G. Lycan, Oxford.)

Devitt, Michael, and Kim Sterelny. 1987. *Language and Reality: An Introduction to the Philosophy of Language*. Cambridge, Mass.

Devitt, Michael, and Kim Sterelny. In press. "What's Wrong with 'the Right View'." In Tomberlin in press.

Donnellan, Keith S. 1966. "Reference and Definite Descriptions." *Philosophical Review* 75:281–304. (Reprinted in Schwartz 1977a.)

Donnellan, Keith S. 1968. "Putting Humpty Dumpty Together Again." *Philosophical Review* 77:203–15.

Donnellan, Keith S. 1972. "Proper Names and Identifying Descriptions." In Davidson and Harman 1972, 356–79.

Donnellan, Keith S. 1974. "Speaking of Nothing." *Philosophical Review* 83: 3–31. (Reprinted in Schwartz 1977a.)

Donnellan, Keith S. 1979. "The Contingent *A Priori* and Rigid Designation." In French, Uehling and Wettstein 1979, 45–60.

Evans, Gareth. 1982. *The Varieties of Reference*, edited by John McDowell. Oxford.

Fitch, Frederick B. 1949. "The Problem of the Morning Star and the Evening Star." *Philosophy of Science* 16:137–41.

Fodor, Jerry A. 1980. "Methodological Solipsism Considered as a Research Strategy in Cognitive Psychology." *Behavioral and Brain Sciences* 3:63–73.

Fodor, Jerry A. 1987. *Psychosemantics: The Problem of Meaning in the Philosophy of Mind*. Cambridge, Mass.

French, Peter A., Theodore E. Uehling Jr., and Howard K. Wettstein, eds. 1979. *Contemporary Perspectives in the Philosophy of Language*. Minneapolis.

French, Peter A., Theodore E. Uehling Jr., and Howard K. Wettstein, eds. 1980. *Midwest Studies in Philosophy, Volume V: Studies in Epistemology*. Minneapolis.

French, Peter A., Theodore, E. Uehling Jr., and Howard K. Wettstein, eds. 1981. *Midwest Studies in Philosophy, Volume VI: The Foundations of Analytic Philosophy*. Minneapolis.

French, Peter A., Theodore E. Uehling Jr., and Howard K. Wettstein, eds. 1984. *Midwest Studies in Philosophy, Volume IX: Causation and Causal Theories*. Minneapolis.

French, Peter A., Theodore E. Uehling Jr., and Howard K. Wettstein, eds. 1986. *Midwest Studies in Philosophy, Volume X: Studies in the Philosophy of Mind*. Minneapolis.

Kaplan, David. 1973. "Bob and Carol and Ted and Alice." In *Approaches to Natural Language: Proceedings of the 1970 Stanford Workshop on Grammar and Semantics*, edited by K. J. J. Hintikka, J. M. E. Moravcsik and P. Suppes, 490–518. Dordrecht.

Kaplan, David. 1975. "How to Russell a Frege-Church." *Journal of Philosophy* 72:716–29.

Kaplan, David. 1979a. "Dthat." In French, Uehling and Wettstein 1979, 383–400.

Kaplan, David. 1979b. "On the Logic of Demonstratives." In French, Uehling and Wettstein 1979, 401–12.

Kaplan, David. 1988a. "Demonstratives: An Essay on the Semantics, Logic, Metaphysics, and Epistemology of Demonstratives and Other Indexicals." In Almog, Perry and Wettstein 1988, 510–92.

Kaplan, David. 1988b. "Afterthoughts." In Almog, Perry and Wettstein 1988.

Kripke, Saul A. 1971. "Identity and Necessity." In *Identity and Individuation*, edited by Milton K. Munitz, 135–64. New York. (Reprinted in Schwartz 1977a.)

Kripke, Saul A. 1979a. "Speaker's Reference and Semantic Reference." In French, Uehling and Wettstein 1979, 6–27.

Kripke, Saul A. 1979b. "A Puzzle about Belief." In *Meaning and Use*, edited by A. Margalit, 239–83. Dordrecht.

Kripke, Saul A. 1980. *Naming and Necessity*. Cambridge, Mass. (A corrected version of an article of the same name (plus an appendix) in Davidson and Harman 1972, together with a new preface.)

LePore, Ernest, and Barry Loewer. 1986. "Solipsistic Semantics." In French, Uehling and Wettstein 1986, 595–614.

Lewis, David. 1973. *Counterfactuals*. Oxford.

Loar, Brian. 1976. "The Semantics of Singular Terms." *Philosophical Studies* 30: 353–77.

Lycan, William G. 1985. "The Paradox of Naming." In *Analytical Philosophy in Comparative Perspective*, edited by B. K. Matilal and J. L. Shaw, 81–102. Dordrecht.

McGinn, Colin. 1982. "The Structure of Content." In *Thought and Object*, edited by Andrew Woodfield, 207–58. Oxford.

Marcus, Ruth Barcan. 1961. "Modalities and Intensional Languages." *Synthese* 13:303–22.

Marcus, Ruth Barcan. 1981. "A Proposed Solution to a Puzzle about Belief." In French, Uehling and Wettstein 1981, 501–10.

Perry, John. 1977. "Frege on Demonstratives." *Philosophical Review* 86:474–97.

Perry, John. 1979. "The Problem of the Essential Indexical." *Noûs* 13:3–21.

Plantinga, Alvin. 1978. "The Boethian Compromise." *American Philosophical Quarterly*, 15:129–38.

Putnam, Hilary. 1975. *Mind, Language and Reality: Philosophical Papers, Volume 2*. Cambridge.

Richard, Mark. 1983. "Direct Reference and Ascriptions of Belief." *Journal of Philosophical Logic* 12:425–52.

Salmon, Nathan. 1981. *Reference and Essence*. Princeton.

Salmon, Nathan. 1986. *Frege's Puzzle*. Cambridge, Mass.

Salmon, Nathan. In press. "Illogical Belief." In Tomberlin in press.

Schiffer, Stephen. 1979. "Naming and Knowing." In French, Uehling and Wettstein 1979, 61–74.

Schiffer, Stephen. 1987. "The 'Fido'-Fido Theory of Belief." In *Philosophical Perpsectives, 1: Metaphysics, 1987*, edited by James E. Tomberlin, 454-80. Atascadero.

Schwartz, Stephen P., ed. 1977a. *Naming, Necessity, and Natural Kinds*. Ithaca.

Schwartz, Stephen P. 1977b. "Introduction" to Schwartz 1977a, 13–41.

Searle, John R. 1980. "Intrinsic Intentionality." *Behavioral and Brain Sciences* 3:450–6.

Searle, John R. 1983. *Intentionality: An Essay in the Philosophy of Mind*. Cambridge.

Smullyan, Arthur Francis. 1947. Review of W. V. Quine's "The Problem of Interpreting Modal Logic." *Journal of Symbolic Logic* 12:139–41.

Soames, Scott. 1984a. "Linguistics and Psychology." *Linguistics and Philosophy* 7:155–79.

Soames, Scott. 1984b. "Semantics and Psychology." In *The Philosophy of Linguistics*, edited by Jerrold J. Katz, 204–26. London.

Soames, Scott. 1984c. "What Is a Theory of Truth?" *Journal of Philosophy* 81:411–29.

Soames, Scott. 1985. "Lost Innocence." *Linguistics and Philosophy* 8:59–71.

Soames, Scott. 1987. "Direct Reference, Propositional Attitudes, and Semantic Content." *Philosophical Topics* 15:47–87. (A condensed version, "Direct Reference and Propositional Attitudes," is in Almog, Perry and Wettstein 1988, 383–409).

Soames, Scott. 1988. "Substitutivity." In *On Being and Saying: Essays for Richard Cartwright*, edited by J. J. Thomson, 99–132, Cambridge.

Tomberlin, James E., ed. In press. *Philosophical Perspectives, 3: Philosophy of Mind and Action Theory.* Atascadero.

Wagner, Steven J. 1986. "California Semantics Meets the Great Fact." *Notre Dame Journal of Formal Logic* 27:430–55.

Wettstein, Howard. 1986. "Has Semantics Rested on a Mistake?" *Journal of Philosophy* 83:185–209.

Wettstein, Howard. 1988. "Cognitive Significance without Cognitive Content." In Almog, Perry and Wettstein 1988, 410–43.

WHY WATER ISN'T H$_2$O, MUCH LESS ISN'T NECESSARILY H$_2$O?*

Jay David Atlas

I turn to a variation of Putnam's example. Suppose that 'water' in Twin Earth dialect of English refers to D$_2$O, deuterium oxide, deuterium being an isotope of hydrogen, D$_2$O naturally occurring in (Earth) water as approximately 1 part in 6500. My previous sentence is an ordinary as well as scientific way of talking that shows that 'water' in Earth-English does not in fact refer only to H$_2$O, but to H$_2$O and any of its isotopic relatives. (I shall ignore the complexity introduced by the solubility of metallic salts.) In my science-fiction story we are supposing that on Twin Earth the counterpart of (Earth) water in rain, lakes, oceans, etc., is indeed just D$_2$O. On Earth we refer to pure samples of D$_2$O by 'heavy water$_e$'. We refer to pure samples of H$_2$O by 'water$_e$'. We (scientists also) refer to naturally occurring mixtures by 'water$_e$'. Aggregates that Twin Earth speakers call 'water$_{te}$', Earth speakers call 'heavy water$_e$' when pure, and 'water$_e$' if mixed with what Earth speakers also call 'water$_e$'. In sum, on Twin Earth 'water$_{te}$' denotes D$_2$O. On Earth 'water$_e$' denotes X$_2$O, where 'X' ranges over Hydrogen and its isotopes. (Oxygen has isotopes, but that complexity will not change the logic of the argument and can be ignored.)

Putnam supposes that there is phonemic change on Twin Earth so that 'water$_{te}$' in Twin English becomes 'quaxel'. 'Water$_e$' denotes X$_2$O; 'quaxel' denotes D$_2$O. Putnam's argument is then a *reductio*—Supposition: 'Water' and 'quaxel' have the same meaning. Ho, ho, ho, ho, ho! Conclusion: 'Water' and 'quaxel' do not have the same meaning. This argument makes one suspect that its underlying logical form is "'Water' and 'quaxel' do not have the same meaning. Therefore 'water' and 'quaxel' do not have the same meaning."

When in "The Meaning of 'Meaning'" Putnam treats an example like the one I have described, he remarks that 'if H$_2$O and XYZ had both been plentiful on Earth, then . . . it would have been correct to say that there were *two kinds of "water."* And instead of saying that "the stuff on Twin Earth turned out not really to be water," we would have to say "it turned out to be the *XYZ kind of water*" *("From the Meaning of Meaning," this volume, p. 126). D$_2$O is not exactly what Putnam has in mind here;

---

*From *Philosophical Books*, 1980

he envisages lakes of H_2O and lakes of XYZ on Earth. But there is enough similarity to suggest that Putnam should agree that in my story there are at least two kinds of water. Since in fact we use the nomenclature of "heavy water", Putnam's reasoning is confirmed. Heavy water is a kind of water. So far as I can see, what Putnam does not even ask in the case of kinds of water is whether 'water$_e$' and 'water$_{te}$' have the same meaning. What decides the meaning of 'water' on Earth and Twin Earth? Is it that the words denote aggregates belonging to distinct species of the genus water, or that the words denote aggregates of the genus water of whatever kind? If the former, then 'water$_e$' and 'water$_{te}$' have different meanings. If the latter, then 'water$_e$' and 'water$_{te}$' have the same meaning.

In fact, since heavy water is water, 'water$_e$' denotes aggregates of water of whatever kind. *Ex hypothesi* 'water$_{te}$' denotes only D_2O but nothing will have stood in the way of the Twin Earth physicists discovering isotopes and realizing that they could in principle produce "light water$_{te}$." This suffices to show that 'water$_{te}$' is also a term with generic meaning. 'Water$_e$' and 'water$_{te}$' (or equivalently, 'water' and 'quaxel') denote aggregates of different liquids, i.e., they differ in reference, but nonetheless 'water$_e$' and 'water$_{te}$' have the same (generic) meaning. Natural-kind terms are analogous to deictic terms, e.g., 'I', whose referents differ in different indiolects but whose meaning is constant, so the doctrine that differences in reference (extension) entail differences in meaning (intension) is incorrect. My argument will generalize, showing that other natural-kind words are semantically general, e.g., 'man' and 'herring gull'. I conclude that difference in extension is *not, ipso facto*, a difference in meaning for natural-kind words. One prop under Putnam's claim that meanings are not concepts is thereby removed. It may also be worth remarking that another such prop, the Division of Linguistic Labour, the emphasis on which Putnam properly regards as an original feature of his discussion, was anticipated by Wittgenstein in his Division of Epistemic Labour (*On Certainty*, sections 162, 621, *passim*) and Donnellan (Journal of Philosophy 59 (1962)).

THE SEMANTICS OF SINGULAR TERMS

Brian Loar

I

The sentences of a language are correlated in striking ways with certain propositional attitudes of the speakers of the language. For there are regularities which associate the syntactical features of sentences—their structures and constituents—with aspects of the communicative intentions of their conventional utterers. By 'communicative intentions' I mean certain intentions to produce beliefs or actions in one's hearer, which are expected or intended to be out in the open.[1] These regularities create implicit expectations in hearers concerning

---

[1] See H. P. Grice, "Meaning", *Philosophical Review* (1957) 377–388; his "Utterer's Meaning and Intentions," *Philosophical Review* (1969) 147–177; and Stephen R. Schiffer, *Meaning*, Oxford University Press, 1972, Ch. I-III.

the range of intentions with which any given sentence of the language will be uttered. Speakers exploit these expectations when they want to communicate, and consequently they conform to the regularity because they are expected to. Now, a regularity in the actions of a group, which it is mutually known obtains because members expect each other to conform, is a *convention*.[2] So there are conventions which correlate sentences with types of communicative intentions, and which do so according to systematic correlations of the syntactic features of the sentences with aspects of the propositional content, and other features, of the intentions.[3] The sentences of a language form a system of conventional devices for making known communicative intentions.

What is it to give a semantical theory for a language? If we were systematically to pair the sentences of a language with the types of communicative intentions with which they are conventionally correlated, that would include the essentials. We would in effect have recursively defined a function from the sentences of the language to certain entities which, in their way, encapsulate the constraints on what communicative intentions a conventional speaker might have in uttering each sentence. These entities might appropriately be counted as the *meanings* for the sentence-types to which they are assigned by that function—that is, by that language.

To give the semantics of subsentential expressions of a certain kind *qua* expressions of the language (for example, definite descriptions, pronouns or names) is to specify their contribution to the meaning of the sentences in which they occur, in the foregoing sense. So, the basic question is this: What kind of communicative intentions would a conventional utterer of a sentence like 'The cat belongs to Georgina' have? What restrictions do those words impose on what the conventional speaker means?[4]

II

My answer is essentially Frege's: the function of a singular term is to introduce an *individual concept* into what is meant or expressed on its particular uses. Now singular terms on the whole do not, *qua* expressions of the language, express individual concepts in abstraction from particular utterances. The concepts which they do literally express are normally non-individuating class concepts, which we might call their *referential qualifiers;* so, for example, being an oak, and being female, are the referential qualifiers of 'that oak' and 'she'. The task for a

---

[2] For explications of 'convention' along these lines see Schiffer, *op. cit.*, Ch. V, and David K. Lewis, *Convention*, Harvard University Press, 1969, Ch. I–II.

[3] For the form of such conventions, which must be specified in such a way as to allow for non-literal utterances, see my "Two Theories of Meaning," in *Truth and Meaning: Studies in Semantics*, Evans and McDowell (eds.), Oxford University Press, 1976.

[4] I use 'means' in two senses: first, with regard to the speaker's communicative intentions on a given utterance; and secondly, with regard to the semantical properties of a sentence, *qua* sentence of a language, in abstraction from particular utterances.

Fregean theory is then to say what constraints are imposed by the referential qualifier of a singular term on what individual concepts may be meant on its particular uses.

Probably what occurred to many philosophers when they asked how Frege's theory, or Russell's theory of descriptions, accommodates such sentences as 'the wardrobe is walnut' was that the propositions which its utterances express, or which its utterers mean, have the form *the unique such and such wardrobe is walnut*. But the requirement that the individual concept should be a *logical restriction* of the referential qualifier is too strong, as is shown by that broad and central class of conventional uses of definite descriptions, demonstrative phrases, and personal pronouns which Donnellan has called *referential*.[5] For one may utter 'the *F* is *G*' perfectly literally, but in such a way that the object to which one thereby *refers* could happen not to be *F*, the consequence of which seems to be that being the *F* is not essential to what one meant—to what one primarily intended to communicate. The referential qualifier aids somehow in determining what is essential, without itself being so. Hence the Fregean theory which I shall elaborate is more permissive than the classical version. There is a certain non-logical constraint which the referential qualifier imposes on what individual concepts may be meant on the conventional utterances of a singular term.

Semantical theory is part of the psychology of communication, and I shall be emphasizing the question what singular terms contribute to what speakers intend to communicate. But there are, of course, substantial classical considerations as well, not ultimately independent of the psychology of communication, but expressed in the seemingly autonomous concepts of philosophical logic. The Fregean theory permits a natural treatment of: (a) how two utterances can make the same predication of the same object and yet differ in meaning; (b) why failure of reference does not as such destroy sense or understanding; (c) why the final clarification of what is intended to be conveyed naturally takes the form of an individuating description; (d) how negative singular existentials can be true; and (e) why the normal referent of a singular term is, at least sometimes, irrelevant to its contribution to the truth-conditions of opaque contexts.

Description theories, of which the Fregean theory is one kind, have in recent years been sharply attacked along two different lines.[6] First it is claimed that on many actual or possible uses of singular terms, especially of proper names, there are no individual concepts which pick out the referent and are appropriately related to the utterance. My answer to that will be to specify the appropriate relation, and to argue that every normal utterance of a singular term has that relation to some individual concept, and that, moreover, in the suitable sense of 'refers', an object is referred to only if it satisfies that individual concept.

---

[5] Keith S. Donnellan, "Reference and Definite Description," *Philosophical Review* (1966) 281–304.

[6] See Saul Kripke, "Naming and Necessity," in *Semantics of Natural Languages,* Davidson and Harman (eds.), pp. 253–355, and Keith Donnellan, "Proper Names and Identifying Description." *Ibid.,* pp. 356–379.

The second, perhaps more important, line of attack has been to provide a powerful alternative picture of the logical form of 'referential' utterances—that is (to speak roughly) of utterances where it is natural to say that there is a definite, identified, individual about which the speaker intends to communicate something, as contrasted with utterances in which the communicative intention is to say that whoever or whatever uniquely satisfies a certain condition is such and such. It is held that to specify the semantical content—the possible world truth-conditions—of a referential utterance one must specify the referent itself, and that no corresponding individual concept is essential thereto. Hence the semantical content of a referential utterance of 't is G' is, in an abstract way, identified with the ordered pair $\langle G, x \rangle$, where G is the predicated property and x the referent to t. But on other uses of singular terms—the ones, roughly, which Donnellan calls *attributive*—no particular referent is essential to content, for one means that the F, whatever it may be, is G. In assessing the possible world truth-conditions of attributive uses, unlike referential uses, no individual of this world is carried through other worlds, since *the F* has different exemplifications in different worlds.

This *radical two-use theory* (as I shall call it) is normally accompanied by some sort of causal theory of reference; the content of what is said, believed or intended is supposedly often a matter of extra-mental causal connections. Now the two-use theory is, at least in a notional and general way, compatible with the account of the nature of semantical theory I sketched at the outset. For it might be that on a referential use of a singular term the speaker has a sort of irreducibly *de re* intention about the referent, where this may be a matter of the intention's being caused in a certain way by the referent.

I should like now to smooth the way for the Fregean theory by noting (what seem to me to be) serious problems for the two-use theory—problems which, of course, are not unrelated to those matters in which the Fregean theory is most helpful. First, it would seem that there might just as well be two kinds of expression corresponding to the two uses of definite descriptions—the one formed with an *iota*-operator, and the other a sort of demonstrative phrase. One might accept that it is a kind of synchronic accident that we have one kind of expression with two such distinct functions, if the problem were confined to definite descriptions. But personal pronouns would have to be assigned these two uses as well, for they have a sort of 'attributive' use as well as a referential use. For example, upon our discovery of the murdered Smith I might say '*He* is insane', meaning that Smith's murderer, whoever that may be, is insane. So I mean a generalized proposition here, unlike the more referential use of that sentence on which I am supposed to mean something of the form $\langle G, x \rangle$. Now it is not easy to accept that on the more generalizing utterances of 'He is such and such' the 'he' has a different logico-semantical role than it has on its more identifying utterances. On my account, using 'he' and 'the F' to generalize, and using them, as it were, to identify, will turn out to be implementations of a single convention.

Secondly, take any normal referential utterance and imagine a case as like it as possible except that the speaker and hearer are deceived about the existence of the supposed referent. There need be no element of content which the hearer fails to understand. But on the two-use theory the non-existence of the referent should make all the difference. Moreover, the utterance may still have that feature of specific identification of the subject, which, on the two-use theory, is to be explained by the referent's being part of the content. The mere intention to refer does not explain the distinctiveness of the subject in that sort of case.

Thirdly, the radical two-use theory implies that a *sufficient* condition of understanding a referential utterance of '*t* is *G*' is merely correctly identifying the referent of *t* and the property expressed by *G*. But that is not sufficient. Suppose that Smith and Jones are unaware that the man being interviewed on television is someone they see on the train every morning and about whom, in that latter role, they have just been talking. Smith says 'He is a stockbroker', intending to refer to the man on television; Jones takes Smith to be referring to the man on the train. Now Jones, as it happens, has correctly identified Smith's referent, since the man on television is the man on the train; but he has failed to understand Smith's utterance. It would seem that, as Frege held, some 'manner of presentation' of the referent is, even on referential uses, essential to what is being communicated.

Fourthly, the difference between paradigm referential and paradigm attributive utterances is more a matter of degree than the radical two-use theory can make sense of. Consider this range of cases. Case (1): we see a large empty shoe; *S* says about its owner, whoever that may be, 'He's rather big'. This seems not relevantly different from the attributive use of 'He is insane'. Case (2): we see large footprints on the beach; same utterance. Case (3): we see a mound of sand, which we assume covers a man; same utterance. Case (4): like the last case, except that a leg is protruding. Case (5): we see the man directly; *S* says, pointing, 'He's rather big'. This would seem to be a paradigm referential utterance. On the radical two-use theory, somewhere along the line truth-conditions in this range of cases flip over from being a generalized proposition to being a propositional complex. But at what point is that motivated? Of no adjacent pair of these cases is it plausible to suppose that their contents are of such radically different kinds.

III

The objects of my beliefs and utterances are often individuated for me only by virtue of relations in which they uniquely stand to me. So, in a sense, my beliefs about them are beliefs about myself; hence understanding the nature of the individuating conceptions I have of other objects requires some understanding of the nature of my beliefs about myself.

Having a belief about oneself clearly does not require having a purely qualitative individuating conception of oneself: one need only imagine the early stages of amnesia to see that. Nor is my believing myself to be such and such simply a matter of having a *de re* belief about myself. Suppose that Watson sees himself through some sort of mirror device and thinks he is seeing a burglar. He believes of Watson that he is a burglar, but he does not believe himself to be a burglar.

I suggest taking self-ascriptive belief as unanalyzed. If Cynthia believes that she has the flu, then what is true is:

B*(Cynthia, *y has the flu*).

She is related by the self-ascriptive belief relation to that propositional function. If Cynthia believes that the tree she is looking at is a sycamore, then

B*(Cynthia, *the tree which y is looking at is a sycamore.*)

Similarly with *speaker's meaning*. If Cynthia says 'That is a sycamore', she may mean that the tree she is pointing at is a sycamore—that is

M*(Cynthia, *The tree which y is pointing at is a sycamore.*)

So when I say that an individual concept is essential to what is meant I intend that to cover not only complete or saturated fully qualitative individual concepts, but also individual concepts with a gap in them, one-place functions in intension 'like: *whatever is uniquely R to y*. Such an 'individual concept' may be essential to what Cynthia means in the sense that

M*(Cynthia, *whatever is uniquely R to y is G*).

IV

The crux of the contemporary argument against the Fregean theory is the claim that for any individuating description which the speaker might offer of the referent, it could turn out that the description is false of the referent, and hence not essential to the content of what is meant. But that is difficult to accept, given a realistic account of what a normal utterer is intending to communicate on referential utterances. For, among all those descriptions which the speaker might offer as picking out his referent, there is always at least one which is connected in a certain special way with his communicative intentions.

Not surprisingly, it is the attributive use which gives the clue to that special connection. If one utters 'the *F* is *G*' *attributively*, then in response to any discovery of a mistake about the identity or existence of the *F* one would ideally judge: "Nevertheless, what I meant was that the *F*, whatever it may be, is *G*." This is not to say that one would continue to maintain that it is *true* that the *F* is *G*, but merely that that was what one had *meant*. On the attributive utterance of 'Smith's murderer is insane', if the speaker had happened to believe that Jones was the murderer, and then discovered that he wasn't, it would still be appropriate for him to express what he had intended to communicate by uttering the same sentence. What makes the utterance attributive is precisely that that would be the appropriate response to any discovery of a mistake about the identity or existence of Smith's murderer; one would not need to re-express in other terms what had been meant (although one might no longer wish to assert it).

On an intuitively *referential* utterance of 'the *F* is *G*', this, so to speak, *attributive attitude* might be maintained, not towards 'the *F*', but towards some other description, in the following sense. Had this other description—'the H', say—been uttered in attempting to express what the speaker had meant by the utterance of 'the F is G', the speaker would have judged, in response to every discovery of a mistake about the identity or existence of the H, 'Still, what I meant was that the H is G'. Had he chosen to say 'the H is G' in expressing what he had wanted to communicate by saying 'the F is G', then in response to such mistakes he would not have had to choose another description to re-express what he had meant.

Suppose, for example, that 'Smith's murderer is insane' is uttered in reference to the defendant in a trial. When it is discovered that the defendant is not Smith's murderer, the speaker may choose other words to re-express what he had meant. If he chose, say, the description 'the person one can see in that direction', it may then turn out that in response to *every* discovery of a mistake—as a result, e.g., of hallucination, of mistaking a hat-stand for a human, of mistaking that person for the defendant—an appropriate thing for him to say would be 'Nevertheless, what I meant was that the person one can see in that direction is insane'.

No one should want to deny that this may be true in some cases. But I shall make the substantial and controversial further claim that on every normal referential utterance of 't is G' there is some description 'the H' such that the speaker could have expressed what he had meant by saying 'the H is G', and that that utterance would have been attributive.[7] The truth of this counterfactual would indicate a certain feature of the speaker's original communicative intentions; what he had essentially *meant* was that the H—whatever it is—is G. This is the core of the thesis that it is the conventional function of singular terms to introduce individual concepts into what is meant.[8]

Here are some considerations in favor of this claim. First, one might make a small thought-experiment: suppose I were to discover about a certain referential utterance of mine, which had seemed perfectly normal, that my intended referent did not exist. Would I not, after reflection and perhaps some further thought experiments, have a quite good grasp of what *would have verified* what I had intended to communicate? Even so, it might be said, this does not positively support the case, for of course one would know about a referential utterance of 't is G' that, had reference been successful, *the referent's* being G would have verified the utterance. But the point is stronger. One could specify what would have verified one's utterance—what one had primarily intended to communicate—independently of the notion 'the referent of my utterance of t'. The alternative is disconcerting; one would have to think that, on a certain proportion of normal referential utterances, if one discovered that one's intended referent did not exist, one would not be able to say what one had intended to communicate. But normally one would have no

---

[7] This is inspired by an account which Christopher Peacocke gives of the connection between names and definite descriptions, in the context of a rather different kind of overall theory, in an unpublished paper. A related point has been made by Thomas Ricketts in an unpublished paper.

[8] This is not to say that a singular term which is uttered referentially is used somehow inappropriately or non-literally, as will become clearer in the final section.

difficulty in saying what one had meant, within the bounds imposed in general by the vagueness of our propositional attitude ascription.

Secondly, consider how we achieve an intuitive grasp on the referential cases: in them, the individual concept which is connoted by the definite description is not essential to what is meant. But whence this grasp on what is *not* essential to what is meant, except from some awareness of what is essential? A possible reply is that the recognition that a certain individual concept was not essential to what was meant derives merely from one's understanding that one's utterance was referential, and hence that no individual concept was essential. But this does not fit one's grasp of one's own ability to sort out the essential from the inessential. The characteristic experience after reflection is: 'This is not what I meant—for what I meant was that'. It seems that our ability to judge that the referential qualifier was not essential to what was meant stems from being aware of something which was essential.

Thirdly, consider the following exchange:

(A) That tree in front of us is F.

(B) That is no tree; it is part of a stage set.

(A) What I meant was that the tree-like object there in front of us is F.

(B) There's a mirror there; there is no tree-like object in front of us.

(A) What I meant was that the tree-like object which is visible in that direction is F.

(B) I have been deceiving you; you are hallucinating.

Several observations are in order here.

First, the plausibility of A's choice of a new description at any step is somewhat dependent on the predicate F. For example, if the predicate in the above case was 'is a two-thousand year old redwood', his abandonment of 'tree' as essential to what he had meant would be far-fetched. This in general puts severe limitations on the possible lengths of plausible sequences of the above kind.

Secondly, it is difficult to see how such sequences could go on indefinitely without the speaker's substitutions appearing, fairly early on, to be far-fetched and insincere. So I assume that such sequences must terminate in the sense that the speaker, after ideal reflection, can offer no further substitution.

Thirdly, here is the main point. Suppose that in the above case the sequence terminates for A with A's last mentioned reply. It would seem that A is then in one of two positions—namely, either (i) he says after B's last remark something like: "Nevertheless, what I meant was that the tree-like object which is visible in that direction is F"—which is what my account says should happen eventually, or (ii) he is in a state which might best be expressed by his saying: "Then I do not know what I meant"—a state of confusion in which normal speakers would not find themselves on normal referential utterances.

The individual concepts which are essential to what we mean are often *complex,* and *implicit.* That they are complex may be seen from the fact that in many cases one may have the attributive attitude towards more than one individual concept. If, for example, someone addresses us, and I then say 'He looked familiar', I may not be prepared then to reject either 'the person who just appeared to speak to us', or 'the person we just saw in such and such place', as essential to what I had meant. That in such a case it is their *conjunction* which is the essential individual concept is made plausible by the fact that, if through some bizarre contingency those individual concepts (towards both of which one has the attributive attitude) are discovered not to be conjointly instanced, then one will be inclined to think that there is nothing which clearly was one's referent.

This is often the case with regard to beliefs. There may be a certain complex of individual concepts which is essential to how I locate, so to speak, a certain familiar person in my picture of the world. And the discovery of certain kinds of breakdown in the conjoint instancing of key individual concepts would naturally produce the feeling that there really was no person who clearly was the object of at least some of those beliefs.

That this can be true also of our communicative intentions may be somewhat obscured by the fact that, in our causal and unpremeditated utterances, a good deal of the content is implicit—that is, not fully represented in our fully conscious thoughts and intentions. This requires motivation. Consider first the implicitness of what a speaker *believes* about his and his hearer's *mutual beliefs* about some familiar object of conversation. That such implicit beliefs play a central role in the psychology of interpersonal contact I take to be an uncontroversial assumption of any realistic psychology. But the content of our intentions is shot through with the content of our implicit expectations. This is especially operative in just those cases in which a speaker reflectively tries to isolate what was essential to what he had intended to communicate; in effect he consults his background beliefs about mutual beliefs, and decides which individual concept or concepts implicit in those mutual beliefs were such that their recognition was essential to the success of his communication.

V

A difference between the paradigm referential and attributive uses of definite descriptions is that, on the attributive, the referential qualifier—i.e., what is literally expressed—is intrinsic to what is meant—while on the referential it is not. But consider once again the two different uses of 'He is insane'—to mean that whoever murdered Smith is insane, and demonstratively to refer to some identified individual and to say of him that he is insane. One is inclined to assimilate these uses of pronouns respectively to the paradigm attributive and referential uses of definite descriptions. But the distinction there has nothing to do with whether the pronoun literally connotes something which is intrinsic to what is meant.

Let us call the former use of 'he', as well as the paradigm attributive use of definite descriptions, 'generalizing' uses of singular terms. And let us call the latter use of 'he', as well as the referential use of definite descriptions, 'identifying' uses of singular terms. There are then two interesting distinctions between the paradigm referential and attributive uses of definite descriptions: on the former, the use is *identifying*, and it is (as we might call it) *extrinsic*—that is, the referential qualifier is not intrinsic to what is meant; whereas on the latter, the use is *generalizing*, and it is *intrinsic*—that is, the referential qualifier is intrinsic, or essential, to what is meant.

The radical two-use theory attempts to explain the identifying uses of singular terms—where one may think of the utterance as *about* some definite individual—by making the referent itself a constituent of what is meant. Against that I have been maintaining that on all uses of singular terms an individual concept is intrinsic to what is meant. How then do I account for the intuitive distinction between generalizing and identifying uses of singular terms? The short answer is that, on identifying uses of singular terms, the individual concept which is essential to what is meant is 'identifying', in a sense I shall now explain.

Whether a definite description or individual concept identifies an object for us rather depends upon our classificatory interests—on what we want to know. So, relative to an interest in locating him, we learn *who* the secretary of the bridge club is by learning that he is the person standing by the window. Relative to an interest in his name and occupation, we learn who he is by learning that he is Oswald Culbertson, author and ranking player. Relative to an interest in his performance, we may learn who he is by learning that he is the one who bid and made seven spades missing two aces. If we are looking through photographs of famous murderers, we may learn who that ugly character is by learning that he is Smith's murderer. For any *F*, one can specify a set of interests and circumstances relative to which learning that *x* is the *F* is learning who or what *x* is. In that sense, any individual concept may be identifying.

But there are some classes of individual concepts whose members in general have a more central identifying role for us than others. We may feel that we have learned who Smith's murderer is, in a respect which is in general pragmatically important, if we learn that he is: the person whom we see there, or the well known criminal called "Sebastian Moran", or that person, unperceived and nameless as yet, who fits a certain comprehensive dossier. In that same pragmatically important respect, we may feel that we have *not* yet learned who Smith's murderer is if we learn only that he is: the one who left the cigar butt, the person who gave a party for seventeen last week at the Hunam Restaurant, or the first person to swim across the Strait of Magellan. To be sure, those descriptions would be identifying for us relative to certain other interests, but they are not as such identifying relative to certain more central classificatory interests which we generally have with regard to particulars. In all of these cases we may want to know more; but in the former we feel that we have reached a stage of identification which we have not reached in the latter.

Along these lines, I suggest that the following classes of individual concepts are especially important:

(1) those of the form *the such and such which we see (saw, perceived) to be such and such,* which we might call 'perceptual';

(2) those of the form, *the person or object who or which approximately fits such and such comprehensive dossier,* which we might call 'comprehensive';

(3) those of the form, *the such and such which is called N, or the such and such referred to by x,* which we might call 'reference-directed'.

The next step is to take perceptual, reference-directed, and comprehensive individual concepts as forming, perhaps together with a restricted few other classes, the class of those individual concepts which are naturally regarded as identifying *simpliciter* because they are identifying relative to those pragmatically important classificatory interests.

The idea, then, is that a use of a singular term is identifying just in case the individual concept which is intrinsic to what is thereby meant is identifying in the latter sense. The paradigm 'referential' uses of definite descriptions are just those on which the referential qualifier is not intrinsic to what is meant, while the individual concept which is intrinsic is an identifying one. Uses of demonstratives, personal pronouns, and names are then intuitively assimilated to the referential uses of definite descriptions when the corresponding individual concepts are identifying.

The referential-attributive distinction is therefore not the fundamental one. More basic are the distinctions between extrinsic and intrinsic uses, and the distinction between identifying and generalizing uses. While the former is not a matter of degree, the latter is—whence the fact that there seems to be a spectrum of cases, from the central attributive ones to the central referential ones, rather than a sharp distinction. It is a matter of the relative 'identifyingness' of the individual concepts involved; and that perhaps depends upon something like the relative general pragmatic importance of the different identifying classifications. I have nothing more to say here on the subject of identifyingness, but it does seem that it may involve matters of some general philosophical interest.

VI

Now for a complication. Consider any embedding of a singular term within a larger singular term—e.g., 'the daughter of the reporter'. The embedded singular term—'the reporter'—may be being used *extrinsically*—that is, its referential qualifier may not be essential to the individual concept which it is the speaker's more basic communicative purpose to introduce by that term—e.g., something like *the person whom we see there.* That is, if it is pointed out to the speaker that that person is not a reporter, he may say that he really meant to refer to the person whom we see there, and this latter concept may survive the attributive test.

But it will often be the case that this individual concept, which it is the function of the embedded singular term to introduce, is not intrinsic to what is *meant on the whole utterance,* but, rather, is essential to a certain way of determining what is intrinsic to what is meant on the whole utterance—as if it were part of the referential qualifier of the whole singular term.

So, for example, consider 'The daughter of the reporter is a geologist'. If the whole singular term is being used extrinsically—e.g., what is meant is something like 'the such and such person to whom we were earlier introduced is a geologist'—then the individual concept which is introduced by the embedded term 'the reporter'—*the person we see there*—is not itself intrinsic to what is meant on the whole utterance. Rather it functions as part of the concept *daughter of the person we see there,* which we might call a *derived referential qualifier.* Its function is to aid in determining (in the same manner as the literal referential qualifier of a simple singular term) the individual concept which corresponds to the whole singular term and which is intrinsic to what is meant by the whole utterance.

It is, then, the function of a singular term to introduce, on its extrinsic uses, an individual concept either into what is meant by the whole utterance, if the singular term is not embedded, or into the derived referential qualifier of the singular term in which it is immediately embedded. So, when elsewhere in this paper I say that it is the function of a singular term to introduce an individual concept into what is 'meant', that is to be understood as covering both of these. Giving a properly recursive account, to cover unlimited embedding, requires merely some relatively simple technical formulations.[9]

This account is no more complex than the facts. There would be a parallel demand on the radical two-use theory; any developed version of it would have to account for the following. It is only the referent of an *unembedded* singular term which might be counted as intrinsic to truth-conditions. The referents of embedded singular terms would be essential, not to truth-conditions, but to the determination of what *is* essential to truth conditions. A singular term which occurs within a double embedding would function to determine a referent which contributes to the determining of a referent which in its turn contributes to the determining of a referent which is intrinsic to truth-conditions. This is isomorphic to my account; the difference lies solely in the question whether, on referential uses, it is an individual concept or the referent itself which is introduced into the content of what is meant in the broad sense.

---

[9] The relevant semantic structure of a singular term which contains embeddings may be represented as a tree, a nesting of ordered n-tuples—for example, 'that which is R to the F and the G' has as its meaning, at this level of abstraction, the ordered pair $\langle R, \langle F, G \rangle \rangle$ The most embedded referential qualifiers will in particular utterances of that expression aid, together with contextual factors, in determining individual concepts *the H* and *the K.* These are then part of the derived referential qualifier R to the H and the K, which in its turn aids in determining the individual concept introduced by the whole singular term.

VII

What is *to refer?* Explaining the general semantical function of singular terms has not required the notion of referring. Nor has explaining the referential-attributive distinction required it, which is perhaps not so surprising, in view of the fact that an utterance may intuitively be of the referential kind even though reference fails.

Some may be prepared to use 'refers' even of attributive uses, so that x has been referred to merely if x instantiates some perhaps non-identifying individual concept which is intrinsic to what is meant. But many philosophers have wanted to reserve 'refers' for some much more restricted relation than this merely denotational one. The narrower usage has usually been prompted by the idea of a radical semantical distinction between true reference and mere uniqueness generalization, and that is quite against the spirit of my account. Nevertheless, I think that one may capture within my account the intuitive notion with which those philosophers have, in effect, been operating.

A first approximation is this: x refers to y just in case y instantiates some *identifying* individual concept which is intrinsic to what x means. This is not sufficient, for reference has not occurred in the narrow sense unless the singular term admits, in a certain way, of existential generalization.[10] Let us capture this requirement by saying that the singular term (or the individual concept) must occur with widest scope.[11]

I then propose the obvious: x refers to y just in case y instantiates some identifying individual concept which is intrinsic to what x means, and which has widest scope there.[12]

There is a case of Donnellan's which would, if successful, show that those conditions are not *necessary* for referring.[13] A child says to his parents 'Tom is a nice man', but, since the child saw various Toms in various similar circumstances, it happens that there is no individual concept which his parents can infer as being what he means. So, says Donnellan, they naturally take him to be referring to the Tom who was the cause of his use of 'Tom'.

---

[10] In the case of a singular term which occurs referringly but not wholly transparently, the existential proposition which is entailed may not be expressed by the result simply of substituting a variable for the singular term and prefixing an existential quantifier. So 'Giorgione was so-called because of his size' does not entail '$(Ex)x$ was so-called because of x's size', since that makes no sense. But it does entail '$(Ex)x$ was called 'Giorgione' because of x's size'.

[11] Or, in the case of referring but non-transparent occurrences, which are best unpacked as concealing a double occurrence of the term (one transparent and the other non-referring), the requirement should be that a certain one of the relevant occurrences of that term in the *analysans* occurs with widest scope.

[12] The thought might occur that this is not sufficient, because of *predicative* occurrences of singular terms—i.e., as in 'x is the F'. But if 'the F' introduces an identifying individual concept, it is natural to read its predicative occurrences as referring. A singular term occurs *merely* predicatively only if it introduces a non-identifying individual concept.

[13] "Proper Names and Identifying Description," *loc. cit.*, p. 364.

For this to be a problem, there would have to be nothing relevantly in the child's thoughts and intentions which individuates some Tom. But why then say that he has in the appropriate sense referred to someone? The language we use to describe such cases may be misleading. Suppose, for example, that Jones is trying to remember whether he has invited someone besides *A, B* and *C* to dinner; he has the feeling that there may be one or two more. One might say to him: "Whom might you have in mind?'; or 'Whom might you mean?', or even 'To whom might you be referring?' The point is that on other rather more central uses of these expressions, there is in this sort of case no one whom he has in mind, or means, or refers to; he cannot remember.

So we have to be careful not to conflate that use of 'refers', and other such terms, on which we describe a certain kind of *cause* of a vague or indeterminate utterance or state of mind, and that use on which we describe the recoverable *content* or something denotationally related to the content. There is always the danger of forgetting that isolated intuitions about the appropriateness of using 'refers' are not a sufficient basis for semantical theory. The determination of what constitutes referring, in the sense in which that term might be useful in semantical theory, should result from the interaction of intuition with the theory in which that notion is to play a part.

Are those conditions *sufficient* for referring? That is not strictly essential to my principal thesis. For it might be that, while every conventional use of a singular term introduces an individual concept into what is meant, something more than an identifying individual concept's being intrinsic to what is meant and applying to x is necessary for x's having been referred to. For example, some causal connection might also be necessary.

Take this case, for example. Jones has never heard of the real Plato, but has had a detailed dream about a great ancient philosopher called 'Plato' by us. As it happens, the dream did not have the real Plato among its causal antecedents, and, moreover, the dream Plato's biography differs substantially from our Plato's biography. Jones subsequently remembers the dream Plato as if real and (with impressive projection) takes it for granted that Jenkins shares his beliefs. In a conversation with the latter (on the question, say, of ancient anticipations of modern science) he says, 'Plato believed in electrons'. Suppose that the individual concept *the preeminent ancient thinker called, among us, 'Plato'* would alone pass the attributive test. Since I am counting such individual concepts among the identifying ones, it follows from my account that Jones has referred to the real Plato.

But, what Jones intended to communicate was false, and was false, moreover, because of a fact about the real Plato—so why not say that he managed to refer to the real Plato? The trouble is that one does have a strong inclination to deny that Jones referred to, or at least that Jones *was referring to*, the real Plato.

Now I might say, "Very well, I grant you the need for adding some extra condition, a causal one, say, to my explication of 'refers'. Nevertheless my principal thesis stands; it is the function of singular terms to introduce individual concepts into what is meant, and it is a necessary condition of x's being referred to that x to satisfy some such concept."

There is, however, a more fundamental issue at stake. The chief philosophical interest of causal theories of referring consists in their purporting to be theories of semantical *content*. The case under discussion has no tendency to promote causal theories in that sense. The content of what Jones means is clear, and is fully specifiable independently of the causal relations in which his utterance stands. The case would show at most that there is a partially causal sense of 'refers' for which my conditions are not sufficient; but perhaps that notion is not, interestingly, an unmixed *semantical* notion—that is, a notion which is essential to, or definable solely in terms which are essential to, the general account of the semantical function of singular terms.

Is there then another, as it were, purely semantical sense of 'refers' which my definition captures and on which we can say that Jones has referred to the real Plato? I do not mean to suggest that there are in ordinary-cum-philosophical usage several firmly demarcated senses of 'refers'. But my ear is not startled by the suggestion that, given what Jones really meant, he succeeded in referring to something quite different from what he had intended, under a certain description, to refer to. It is compatible with a certain continuous philosophical usage to use 'refers' in that way. The semantical concept of referring is to be knocked down to the highest bidder—that is, the best overall semantical theory.

VIII

There appears to be a conflict between the radical two-use theory and my theory, concerning the possible-world truth-conditions of a referential utterance of 't is G'. On the former, there is a certain item x, the referent of t, such that the utterance is true in a possible world w iff x is G in w. On my theory, however, there is some individual concept F such that the utterance is true in w iff whatever is the F (in w) is G in w. The two are not equivalent since, for non-essential F, x is not the F in every possible world in which x exists.

This conflict is merely apparent, however. For, on the usual form of the two-use theory, the possible world truth-conditions of an utterance are determined by what *statement* is made (or by what is *said*); and supposedly on referential utterances sameness of referent is a necessary condition of sameness of statement. Now, whatever the merits of this claim about how we should individuate statements,[14] it is irrelevant to the question what is *meant* on referential utterances. The notion of the possible-world truth-conditions of a referential utterance is then ambiguous as between what is said and what is meant.

---

[14] If the motivation for the claim is the appropriateness of *de re* reports of what is said on referential utterances, then it is doubtful that ordinary usage justifies this sharp distinction between the kinds of statements made on referential and on attributive utterances, since it permits *de re* reports or the latter as well.

Moreover, the notion of what is said should be regarded as a derivative concept of semantical theory. It is to be explicated partially in terms of the concept of what a sentence means, which is a function of conventional regularities which correlate sentential features with aspects of those communicative intentions which are constitutive of what speakers mean. Consequently it is not to be employed in giving the basic semantics of singular terms.

This brings us to the question of referential occurrences of singular terms within modal contexts. Nothing in my account is incompatible with the idea that in assessing the truth-value of 'Necessarily . . . t . . .' or 'Possibly . . . t . . .', one sometimes, so to speak, carries the real-world referent of t through all possible worlds. For example, one might use 'That is necessarily a spatio-temporal object' in such a way that what is said or meant is true just in case the referent of 'that' is a spatio-temporal object in every possible world in which it exists. That happens if and only if 'that' has *wider scope* than 'necessarily'. It does not follow that there is no individual concept which is thereby introduced; rather, in the proposition which is meant, the individual concept has wider scope than the modal operator: the F is such that necessarily it. . . .

The behavior of referential occurrences of singular terms in *modal* contexts can have a distorting effect on one's theory of their role in *non-modal* contexts if one reasons as follows. First, assume that 'Possibly t is G' (or 't is possibly G') is always to be explicated, even when t occurs referentially, as having the form $\Diamond$ (t is G), that is, as resulting from applying a sentential operator to a complete sentence. Secondly, take $\Diamond S$ as true just in case there is some world at which the proposition which is *independently* expressed by S is true. Thirdly, observe that if t occurs referentially one is inclined to read 'Possibly t is G' as true iff there is some world at which the real-world referent of t is G. Fourthly, conclude that the proposition which is independently expressed by 't is G', with referential t, must somehow incorporate x itself, the real-world referent of t—that is, must be the propositional complex $\langle G, x \rangle$.

The point is that the initial assumption is gratuitous. For modal operators can be quantified into, and it is just as good as hypothesis that some occurrences of singular terms with a modal operator are to be read as quantifiers which have wider scope than the modal operator. Which is the most useful analysis depends upon an independently motivated account of singular terms, in the context of a comprehensive semantical theory.[15]

---

[15] Throughout this paper, I am primarily concerned with that version of the two-use theory on which the referential uses of singular terms (those which supposedly introduce a referent, rather than an individual concept, into semantical content) are *identifying*. But there is a version on which that is not necessary; indeed Kripke's theory would appear to be such. One might envisage two different ways of introducing a proper name: (a) one announces 'When I say "Altissimus is G" I shall be saying that the highest molehill in the world is G'; (b) one announces "The highest molehill in the world, whichever it is, is such that when I say "Altissimus is G" I shall be saying that *it* is G'. On the former, "Altissimus" is a non-rigid designator; on the latter it is supposedly a rigid designator, with the

(contd.)

IX

What I regard as the correct account of proper names has in recent years been unfairly rejected—namely, that the conventional meaning of a name *N* in a certain group of speakers, that is, its meaning in abstraction from any particular utterance, is the same as the conventional meaning of the definite description 'the thing or person called *N*'. Just as a literal use of 'the table' does not imply that there is just one table in the world, so it does not follow that a conventional use of 'Jones' implies that there is just one person called 'Jones'. The definite description 'the table' has as its referential qualifier the non-individuating property *being a table;* similarly, 'Jones' has as its referential qualifier the non-individuating property *being called 'Jones'*. More often perhaps than not, the individual concept which is essential to what is meant on a use of *N* has the form *the F called N,* and since such individual concepts are *identifying,* these uses are intuitively assimilated in that respect to the referential uses of definite descriptions.[16]

There has been a tendency to interpret description theories of names as claiming that, insofar as *N* names *x*, there is some one individual concept which is meant on all uses of *N* to refer to *x*. My thesis is far less dramatic: on each of *N*'s uses in referring to *x* some individual concept or other which is satisfied by *x* is intrinsic to what is thereby meant. There is, of course, a non-arbitrary relation between the name uttered and the individual concept which is meant, but that is just an instance of the general relation which holds between referential qualifier and intrinsic individual concept. The point here is that what is essential to what a speaker means in using *N* as the name of *x* varies among speakers and occasions of utterance, according to what the speaker assumes about the audience's beliefs, and within this assumption, according to what the hearer would have to understand, independently of the existence of the referent, for the utterance to have been a successful communication.

There are some separate issues here which need clarification.

(1) The referential qualifier of *N* is, as I have said, *being called N,* and the occurrence of 'called' here may seem to introduce a circle. By '*x* is called *N*', I mean

---

description 'fixing the referent' of the name in other possible worlds by picking out the thing which satisfies it in this world. (I am indebted to Stephen Schiffer for this perspicuous way of formulating Kripke's theory.)

Now I do not think that (b) has anything to do with the semantics of names or of any singular terms. If someone were first to announce (b) and then to assert 'Altissimus is in Ohio', I would have to interpret him as having *meant* that the highest molehill in the world is in Ohio—i.e., precisely what one would have interpreted him as having meant if he had first announced (a) and then said the same thing. This is not to say that (a) has much to do with the semantics of names either; to which subject I now turn.

[16] There are also *extrinsic* uses of names, some of which are identifying and some generalizing. Of the former we have this example: I point at someone leaning over a balcony and say 'Jenkins is off balance', where it may not be essential to what I mean that the person there is called 'Jenkins'. Of the generalizing extrinsic uses there is this sort of example: We are examining a text attributed to Duns Scotus and I say 'Scotus here reasons badly', meaning the author whoever it was.

to cover these relations: 'x is (commonly) referred to by the use of N', and 'x was dubbed N'. Now the concept of a name is clearly not presupposed in my account of 'refers', and since to dub is to make known a decision or agreement to use a certain vocable to refer to a certain thing, neither does the explication of 'x was dubbed N' presuppose the concept of a name. So, I do not understand why many think that this sort of account threatens circularity. It is not as though one were trying to refer to something by saying 'the referent of this very phrase'; rather, on an intrinsic use of N one means *the F which has been referred to as, or has been dubbed, N;* and there is no more problem with that than there would be had one uttered those very words.

Perhaps it is felt that since an initial dubbing may in some cases be what gives N meaning, it is therefore absurd to suppose that the meaning which N is thereby given is, as it were, *the thing dubbed N*. But, properly understood, this produces no absurdity. We agree that N may be a way of referring to x, knowing that this will be possible because on any particular utterance we may exploit the agreement and mean by N *that which is F and which we agreed we might refer to by uttering N.*

(2) It follows from my account that, strictly speaking, to specify the conventional meaning of N—what it contributes to the literal or conventional meaning of the sentences in which it occurs—does not involve specifying anything of which N is the name. But a strong central tradition in semantics has treated a name as having at least as many distinct literal meanings in a group of speakers as there are bearers of the name for that group. On my account, however, the fact that there are many Smiths no more makes 'Smith' literally ambiguous than the fact that there are many dogs makes 'the dog' literally ambiguous.

The notion of the literal meaning of a name is somewhat technical; it plays a certain role in the account of the relation between the conventional regularities governing expressions, and how these are exploited on particular conventional utterances. There is indeed a conventional name-relation; for it is a conventional, and in its way semantical, fact about a group of speakers that 'George Johnson' names this person and that person and that person. The point is that that conventional property of N, that N names x, is *derivative* from, first, the fact that N has the appropriate literal meaning and, secondly, the fact that there is a practice of referring, or an agreement that one may refer, to x by uttering N in accordance with its literal meaning.

So N is the name of x in a group G just in case it is mutual knowledge among the members of G that it is their practice to (or they have agreed that they may) utter N and thereby refer to x as being called N.

(3) It has been thought to be a problem for 'description theories' of names that our beliefs about a given historical figure may turn out mostly to be false. An example (of Kripke's) is Jonah the prophet; it seems that little of what is said in the book *Jonah* is true of anyone. Nevertheless, it seems that our use of that name does actually refer to a certain Hebrew personage.

But this is a real problem only for description theories which hold that our use of an historical name introduces substantial biographical facts. Recent discussion has amply shown that even the most entrenched beliefs about an historical figure may not be essential to what we intend to communicate when we use that person's name. But that hardly shows that no individual concept is essential. If I am conversing with someone whom I take to have ordinary information, and I say 'Jonah never really visited Nineveh' I would be meaning that the pre-eminent referent of the Biblical use of 'Jonah' never visited Nineveh—or even that that Biblical referent of 'Jonah' who was said to have been ingested by a large fish never visited Nineveh.

(4) A form of argument which gets used against description theories of names is this:

(a) If N were used to mean *the F*, then 'N might not have been the F' would be false.

(b) But 'N might not have been the F' is true.

(c) Therefore, N is not used to mean *the F*.

Of course, if this form of argument works, it works for every non-essential individual concept *the F*: and obviously on my account the individual concepts which are intrinsic to what is meant on the use of a name are non-essential—i.e., contingently applicable.

The argument is defective. Names are normally read as having wider scope than modal operators—and that is why premise (b) is true for the relevant F's. For example, 'Aristotle might not have been the pre-eminent ancient philosopher called "Aristotle"' is true because it asserts of Aristotle that he might not have had that contingent property. But if the N-position in the sentence mentioned in premise (a) is read similarly as having widest scope, then premise (a) is false, as may be seen by substituting 'the F' for N. That 'the pre-eminent ancient philosopher called "Aristotle"' means *the pre-eminent ancient philosopher called 'Aristotle'* does not entail that it is false that the pre-eminent ancient philosopher called Aristotle is such that he might not have had that property.

Kripke anticipates that such a point might be made, and he replies: " . . . we use the term 'Aristotle' in such a way that, in thinking of a counterfactual situation in which Aristotle didn't go into any of the fields and do any of the achievements we commonly attribute to him, still we would say that was a situation in which *Aristotle* did not do those things."[17] Now we would indeed say that, and we would then be giving 'Aristotle' wider scope than the quantifier over counterfactual situations. And if we substitute 'the pre-eminent ancient philosopher called "Aristotle"' and give *it* widest scope we would be entitled to assert the result of that as well.[18] Ordinary particulars are the referents of our

---

[17] *Op. cit.*, p. 279.

[18] This issue is quite distinct from another central point of Kripke's with which I completely agree—namely, that in considering the truth-conditions of 'Hawkins might not have been a taxi-driver', one need not worry about what properties something has to have in another possible world to be Hawkins (or his counterpart). Rather what it means is that there is some world to which our Hawkins stands in the relation *x is not a taxi-driver in w*.

utterances always by virtue of their having contingent individuating properties which are intrinsic to what we mean.

X

The theory so far has these components: (1) corresponding to every use of a singular term, there is an individual concept which is intrinsic to what the speaker means on that occasion; (2) sometimes the individual concept is not a logical restriction of the referential qualifier—that is, of the concept literally connoted by the singular term; such uses are *extrinsic*, the other being *intrinsic;* (3) individual concepts range from the *identifying* to the (more or less) non-identifying or *generalizing;* (4) the so-called referential uses of definite descriptions are extrinsic and identifying; the attributive uses are intrinsic and generalizing; (5) one refers to x by uttering a singular term just in case x instantiates some identifying concept which is intrinsic to what one means and which has widest scope; (6) a proper name N has as its referential qualifier the concept *being called N*. Like other singular terms its uses may be extrinsic or intrinsic, and identifying or generalizing.

One question remains: What constraint is imposed by the referential qualifier of a singular term—by what it literally or conventionally means *qua* expression of the language—on what individual concepts may be essential to what the utterer of that singular term means? This is really the same question as: What conventional regularities in the use of singular terms account for their semantical properties *qua* expressions of English?

On a normal utterance of 'the F', the hearer infers what individual concept is intrinsic to what is meant—*the H*, say—partially from the referential qualifier F, and partially from other facts which the hearer assumes have been taken by the speaker to be mutually believed by them. That is pretty vague, but we can be more specific.

If on an utterance of 'the F is G' the speaker means that the H is G, then normally the speaker assumes that it is mutually believed by him and his hearer that the H is F. For example, if by uttering 'the chair' I mean *the medium-sized object visible in that direction,* I have assumed that it is mutually believed by me and my hearer that the medium-sized object visible in that direction is a chair. This mutual belief is not necessarily epistemically *presupposed;* it may itself be brought about by my utterance, as when I point at something hitherto unnoticed by my audience.

Now, the question is, how does this help the hearer to determine which individual concept is essential to what the speaker means? It is useful, I think, first to consider unqualified indexicals—that is, pronouns which do not have referential qualifiers. Let us pretend that 'it' is unqualified.

How would we, as hearers, normally determine which individual concept was intrinsic to what was meant on an utterance of 'It is F', in a context in which there is no anaphoric reference to another term in the discourse? Virtually *any* fact about the speaker's current interests, motivations, concerns, preoccupations, habits of association, perceptual circumstances, and beliefs in general, including his implicit assumptions about his hearer's beliefs about him and about virtually anything else, may be relevant to the hearer's inference to which individual concept is meant. There are no special pragmatic rules for the interpretation of indexicals, apart from all those psychological generalizations, and specific beliefs about the speaker, which we must assume hearers somehow bring to bear in interpretation. From what he knows, the hearer forms a hypothesis about what the speaker is most likely to have intended to communicate.

Now the point about singular terms which are qualified indexicals is this: the referential qualifier restricts the range of individual concepts which might be meant; and from this class the hearer infers which one is meant. The inference is now just like the inference when the singular term is unqualified, except for the narrower range of possibilities.

The principle of restriction we have in effect already seen. The individual concepts which might be meant on an utterance of 'the F' are not all logical restrictions of the concept F; rather *the H* is among them just in case the speaker assumes that it is mutually believed by him and his hearer that the H is F. In those cases in which *the H* is a logical restriction of F—as *Smith's murderer* is of (the) *murderer*—the looser restriction is obviously satisfied; thus attributive uses of singular terms satisfy the condition just as much as referential uses do. *It is in this that the ultimate univocity of singular terms consists,* in spite of the existence of two such seemingly distinct conventional uses as the referential and the attributive. On an attributive, or intrinsic, use, the individual concept which is intended to be recognized as intrinsic to what is meant is just a logical restriction of the referential qualifier.

So to specify the meaning of a sentence which contains a singular term requires specifying its referential qualifier. And what makes F the referential qualifier of t is just that an utterance of a sentence containing t is in accordance with the conventions only if there is a certain individual concept *the H* such that (a) it is expected by the speaker that (the hearer will believe that) it is mutually believed by speaker and hearer that the H is F, and (b) *the H* is intrinsic to what is meant on that utterance.

Other possible conventions come to mind. Why not, for example, treat referential and other extrinsic uses as extended or non-conventional uses? That would make it possible to simplify the convention: basically, an utterance of 'the F is G' would be conventional only if the speaker means that the F which is H is G. But that is unrealistic. Conventions are not to be introduced merely to simplify semantical theory, to enable us to deal with the complexities of actual communicative practice by casting them into the exterior darkness—into pragmatics. General semantical conventions are regularities, and the referential uses of singular terms are no less frequent than the attributive uses. We can easily imagine, moreover, that English could semantically be just as it is if the referential uses of singular terms were overwhelmingly predominant—even if referential misdescription were the rule. My account of the convention allows for those possibilities. Referential uses of singular terms are literal uses; they are fully in accordance with those regularities which establish the conventional semantical properties of the language.[19]

---

[19] From among the many people discussion with whom has helped me greatly on these matters, I want to mention particularly John Bennett, Lee Bowie, Warren Ingber, Thomas Ricketts, and Stephen Schiffer.

BRIAN LOAR ON SINGULAR TERMS
Michael Devitt

For a hundred years description theories have been the ruling theories of proper names. In the last ten years a movement that rejects such theories has been gathering strength: it claims that the referent of a name is not determined by the descriptions associated with the name but by causal connections of a certain sort. Brian Loar has recently defended the ruling view against this revolution.[1]

Ruling classes, in philosophy as much as in society, typically discredit revolutionists by misrepresenting them. That is the first step in Loar's defense: he incorrectly attributes to the new movement an implausible theory he calls 'the radical two-use theory'. The theory is a straw man. I will show this in section I. Second, against the background of apparent revolutionary failure that this attribution creates, Loar offers a new description theory. In section II, I will show that this new theory is as much open to objection as the classical ones, if not more so.

I

The radical two-use theory has three theses. The works cited by Loar[2] as the basis for the theory are Keith Donnellan's "Reference and Definite Description"[3] and "Proper Names and Identifying Description,"[4] and Saul Kripke's "Naming and Necessity."[5] Oddly enough none of the three theses that constitute the theory are to be found in any of these works.

Two of the theses are as follows: (i) Donnellan's distinction between *referential* and *attributive* uses of definite descriptions is extended to *all* singular terms; (ii) a causal theory of reference is given for all referential uses.[6] The works cited do not support the attribution of either of these theses to Donnellan, and show clearly that the attribution of either to Kripke would be mistaken.

In "Reference and Definite Descriptions" Donnellan describes a distinction between referential and attributive uses of *descriptions* but does not apply the distinction to other singular terms. He does not offer a causal theory of the referential uses.

---

[1] Brian Loar, "The Semantics of Singular Terms," *Philosophical Studies* 30 (1976). pp. 353–377.

[2] *Ibid.*, p. 376, notes 5 and 6.

[3] Keith S. Donnellan, "Reference and Definite Descriptions," *Philosophical Review* (1966), pp. 281–304.

[4] Keith S. Donnellan, "Proper Names and Identifying Descriptions," in: *Semantics of Natural Languages*, Davidson and Harman (eds.) (Reidel, 1972), pp. 356–379.

[5] Saul Kripke, "Naming and Necessity," in: *Semantics of Natural Language*, Davidson and Harman (eds.) (Reidel 1972), pp. 253–355, 763–769.

[6] *Op. cit.*, pp. 355–356. Loar is cautious about (ii), saying that a causal theory 'normally' accompanies the two-use theory. Certainly the 'abnormal' view is unsatisfactory for it promises no plausible *theory* of referential uses. And a causal theory (of names only) is the most prominent positive thesis of two of the three works Loar cites.

In "Naming and Necessity", Kripke offers a causal theory of *names* but does not extend this to other singular terms. He expresses skepticism about Donnellan's distinction in several footnotes.[7]

In "Proper Names and Identifying Description" Donnellan offers a causal theory of names but also does not extend this to other singular terms. The closest he comes to such an extension is his remark in a footnote that a referential definite description is a "close relative" of a proper name.[8]

Though (i) and (ii) are not to be found in Donnellan or Kripke, perhaps Loar is right in attributing them to the new movement: they may seem a natural development of views that are to be found in Donnellan and Kripke. For, *some* names seem tied to descriptions, and a Donnellanish distinction amongst pronouns and demonstratives seems plausible. We apply Donnellan's distinction across the board to singular terms and arrive at (i). *How* does a referential use identify its referent? The question cries out for an answer. The causal theory of names suggests one: referential uses are causally linked to their objects in a certain way. We have arrived at (ii). Certainly this development of the ideas of Donnellan and Kripke seemed natural to me, and I made it in "Singular Terms."[9]

I have no objection, therefore, to the attribution of (i) and (ii) to the movement, though I assume others would have. I object strongly, however, to the attribution of the third thesis.

The third thesis in the two-use theory (iii), is

> [T]he semantical content of a referential utterance of '*t* is *G*' is, in an abstract way, identified with the ordered pair $\langle G, x \rangle$, where *G* is the predicated property and *x* the referent to *t*.[10]

Kripke and Donnellan do not talk of 'semantical content'.[11] Nor do I. What does Loar mean by it? He says initially that it is the utterance's "possible world truth-condition." If this were all there were to it the attribution of this further thesis might seem in order: it would capture the Kripkean view that a name is a 'rigid

---

[7] *Op. cit.*, p. 343, note 3; p. 346, note 22; pp. 348–349, note 37.

[8] *Op. cit.*, p. 378, note 8.

[9] Michael Devitt, "Singular terms," *Journal of Philosophy* (1974), pp. 183–205. So far as I know this is the only work in which even (i) is to be found, though Steven Boër and William G. Lycan come close to it in "Knowing Who," *Philosophical Studies* 28 (1975), pp. 299–344 (see particularly p. 319); they do not mention (ii). I have since modified my views but still subscribe to some version of (i) and (ii); see my *Designation* (Columbia University Press, forthcoming), Secs. 2.5–2.7.

[10] *Op. cit.*, p. 355. Loar says later that this is "the chief philosophical interest of causal theories of referring" (p. 368).

[11] In another paper (not cited by Loar), "Speaking of Nothing," *Philosophical Review* (1974), pp. 3–32. Donnellan flirts dangerously with what he calls 'a natural view' which *is* like Loar's third thesis: a predication is thought to 'express a proposition' like the above semantical content (see pp. 11–12 particularly). However, given (i) that he concludes the paper with some (appropriately) skeptical remarks about the notion of a proposition (p. 32, particularly), and (ii) that he does not seem to assign the notion any theoretical role, his commitment to the 'natural view', and the point of any such commitment, are left indeterminate.

designator': the object in any possible world which is relevant to the truth conditions of an utterance containing the name is the name's referent in the actual world. However Loar's expression, 'semantical content', invites another, stronger, interpretation of the quoted passage. According to this interpretation, *there is nothing more to 'the meaning of a name' (or any other referential use) than its referent: there is nothing semantically significant about it except that.* So interpreted the two-use theory is too implausible to be attributed to anybody without evidence. Loar accepts the invitation of his own terminology and does so interpret the theory.

The problem with such a theory has been obvious since Frege: it makes it impossible to explain the differing 'cognitive values' of '$a = a$' and '$a = b$'. If Kripke is right about names being rigid designators then one way in which statements like these containing names have been thought to differ turns out to be illusory: it has been thought that whereas '$a = a$' is *necessarily* true '$a = b$' is only *contingently* so. However the two-use theorist would be committed to something much stronger: a pair of true statements of this form containing referential terms would not differ in any semantically significant way; they would be 'synonymous'. Such a view has plausibility only if 'a' and 'b' are Russellian 'logically proper names'. It has no plausibility at all as a view of ordinary proper names (as Russell well knew), let alone referential descriptions. And, of course, the two-use theory is supposed to be a theory of such ordinary terms.

Thesis (iii) must be dropped: a causal theorist must put more into the meaning of a name than its referent. I have claimed that Frege was right in supposing that what matters to the meaning, or semantic significance, of a name *is its mode of presenting the referent.* I have claimed further that *this mode is the name's underlying causal network* which, if the name is not empty, is grounded in its referent. The theory I have urged is in fact an amended two-use theory obtained by replacing (iii) by this claim.[12]

That (iii) is understood by Loar in the strong way is shown by two of the four 'serious problems' he finds with the two-use theory. His third problem is that the theory

> implies that a *sufficient* condition of understanding a referential utterance of 't is G' is merely correctly identifying the referent of t and the property expressed by G.[13]

He rightly argues against this claim of sufficiency concluding as follows.

> It would seem that, as Frege held, some 'manner of presentation' of the referent is, even on referential uses, essential to what is being communicated.[14]

I agree. Understanding a referential use of a name involves linking it in a certain way to the right causal network, the network that constitutes the manner in which the name presents the object. The required linking associates the name with the

[12] "Singular Terms," *loc. cit.*, p. 204.

[13] *Op. cit.*, p. 357.

[14] *Op. cit.*, p. 357.

hearer's set of beliefs (and other thoughts) involving the name, and grounded in the right object; those beliefs are part of the causal network.[15] So my amended two-use theory does not imply the above sufficiency claim. Nor would the two-use theory if (iii) concerned only 'possible world truth-conditions' (the amended theory would near enough entail such a theory). Only if (iii) is understood as the strong thesis about the meaning of a name could the two-use theory have that implication.[16]

Loar's second problem also concerns understanding. He rightly points out that a hearer can understand a referential utterance even though deceived about the existence of the referent.

> But on the two-use theory the non-existence of the referent should make all the difference.[17]

Once again this is so only if the two-use theory includes the strong version of (iii). The problem does indeed seem insoluble for that two-use theory. However, for the amended theory, the non-existence of the referent does not make 'all the difference' to understanding because it is consistent with the hearer linking the referential use to the right causal network; even 'empty' referential terms have networks.

I do not suggest that these brief remarks here should remove all worries occasioned by these two problems: lots more needs to be said. The point is rather that Loar has incorrectly, and without proper basis, attributed to the new movement a theory for which these problems *are so serious as to seem insoluble.* In my view the two problems are quite soluble for the amended two-use theory. So also are the other two problems Loar raises[18] This is not the place to attempt to show this.[19] However there should be no presumption that the *real* alternatives to Loar's description theory cannot solve these four problems.

---

[15] "Singular terms", *loc. cit.,* pp. 189–190, see also pp. 201–203 where *mis*understandings are discussed. I discuss understanding in more detail in "Semantics and the Ambiguity of Proper Names," *Monist* (1976), pp. 404–423 (see particularly pp. 410–411).

[16] Strangely enough, in relating causal theories of reference to the two-use theory. Loar says: "the content of what is said, believed or intended is supposedly often a matter of extra-mental causal connections" (*op. cit.,* p. 356), but he never discusses the theory as if that were part of it.

[17] *Op. cit.,* p. 356.

[18] One of these problems, his fourth, seeks to show that "the difference between paradigm referential and paradigm attributive utterances is more a matter of degree than the radical two-use theory can make sense of" (*op. cit.,* p. 357). I discuss this problem briefly in "Singular Terms," *loc. cit.,* p. 192.

[19] I do attempt to show it in *Designation,* forthcoming. In it I develop what I have here called the amended two-use theory. The matters discussed in the pages cited in notes 9, 12, 15 and 18 above are taken up in more detail. So also is the problem of 'empty terms' touched on above. Loar's first problem is that the two-use theory is committed to the unacceptable view that it is 'a synchronic accident' that one expression should have two uses (*op. cit.,* p. 356). Kripke makes a similar criticism of Donnellan in "Speaker's Reference and Semantic Reference," in: *Midwest Studies in Philosophy Volume II: Studies in the Philosophy of Language.* French, Uehling, and Wettstein (eds.) (University of Minnesota, 1977), pp. 255–276. I discuss this criticism in "Donnellan's Distinction," forthcoming.

II

Loar's theory of names is part of a complicated theory of all singular terms involving two distinctions, one between *extrinsic* and *intrinsic* uses, and another between *generalizing* and *identifying* uses.[20] So far as I can see, we can abstract from these complications. Loar regards the paradigm uses of names as intrinsic and identifying. What follows is a discussion of his theory of those names.

First, Loar claims that a speaker's use of a name, N, refers to x only if x instantiates some identifying individual concept which is intrinsic (= essential) to what he means.[21] This is like the classical description theories: the required concept is picked out by an identifying description the speaker associates with N. The special feature of Loar's theory is that the required concept will include, for each speaker, *being called N.*[22] It is this feature that I shall object to.

The appeal of Loar's theory to someone wanting to save description theories in the face of criticisms by Kripke and Donnellan is clear enough. These criticisms have shown how little the user of N may believe about its referent—how *ignorant* he may be—and how many of his central beliefs about the referent may be false—how much in *error* he may be. Yet it is very plausible to claim that users of N all believe that its referent *is called N;* and that belief is true. It may not seem difficult then to build an *identifying* concept around this for each speaker. (Some building is required because typically more than one object is called N.) The arguments from ignorance and error against description theories still apply but they are not nearly no persuasive.

Kripke placed the following condition on a description theory of names:

> (C) For any successful theory, the account must not be circular. The properties which are used in the vote [to determine the name's referent] must not themselves involve the notion of reference in a way that it is ultimately impossible to eliminate.[23]

An obvious violation of condition (C) would be provided by a theory that offered as the identifying description associated with a name N by a speaker, 'the object I refer to by N'. A more interesting violation would be provided by a theory that allowed the following sort of 'reference borrowing'. Speaker a associates the identifying description, 'the object b refers to by N'; b associates 'the object c refers to by N'; c associates 'the object a refers to by N'. We have come a full circle. We have not explained what determines the referent of *any* of these uses of N. A satisfactory description theory that allows for reference borrowings of this sort *must require that some lender can manage reference on his own.*

Though Loar makes no mention of Kripke's condition (C), he seems to be aware of it: he briefly considers and rejects the charge that his theory is circular.[24]

---

[20] *Op. cit.,* pp. 362–363.

[21] *Op. cit.,* pp. 366–367. I am ignoring appearances of the name within opaque contexts.

[22] *Op. cit.,* pp. 370–371.

[23] "Naming and necessity," *loc. cit.,* p. 283.

[24] *Op. cit.,* p. 371.

The briefness of this consideration is surprising given Kripke's detailed discussion of (C)[25] and given that Loar's theory is, on the face of it at least, inconsistent with that discussion.

To see this consider what it is for x to be called N. Loar has two relations in mind. First, it is for x to be (commonly) *referred* to by N. Second, it is for x to have been dubbed N. That dubbing has taken place if a decision or agreement has been made known to use N to *refer* to x.[26] We can sum this up: x's being called N amounts to *a community's present practice of referring to x by N, a practice that may be dependent on a past one.*

Consider first a present practice that is not dependent on a past one. Suppose that the concept a speaker adds to *being called N* to make an identifying concept is *F*: so the full concept is *the F called N*. Given what we have just discovered about being called N, Loar's theory tells us that the speaker of N referred to x because it is an F that the members of his community (a community he must be able to identify) are in the practice of referring to by N. In virtue of what is it x that they are in the practice of thus referring to? Loar tells the same story for each one of them. Each one refers to x only because everyone does. We have no *independent* route to x. This sort of community reference borrowing is no better than the individual borrowing we considered earlier. It violates (C) and is circular.

The situation is not significantly better if the speaker's borrowing takes us back to a past practice of referring to x by N. (In one respect it is worse: the speaker, or one of his fellows, will have to be able to identify the relevant past community, a task that is likely to prove harder than that of identifying the present one.) We do not have immediate circularity in this case because the present community is dependent on the past one but not vice versa. For this reason Kripke seems to regard it as not a violation of condition (C).[27] Nevertheless it is just as objectionable unless we are given some way of eliminating the notion of the *past community's reference*.[28] We need to be told in virtue of what it was x that the *past* community referred to by N.[29] Loar tells us only that each member of it referred to x because all the others did. The circularity has reappeared but in this case it is in the past. This is what we should expect, of course, because there was a time when the past community was a present one like the community above, entirely dependent on its own resources. Reference borrowing from the past simply transfers the problem.

This point about circularity in a theory of a community's reference, whether the present community or the past one on which the present one

---

[25]*Op. cit.*, pp. 283–286, 297, 766–768. See also Donnellan's "Proper Names and Identifying Descriptions," *loc. cit.*, part VI.

[26]*Op. cit.*, pp. 367–369.

[27]*Op. cit.*, p. 766.

[28]If we are not given this we *do* seem to have a violation of (C) despite what Kripke says. (C) requires not only that the account not be circular but also that the notion of reference be ultimately eliminable.

[29]In virtue of what was *Jonah* the biblical referent of 'Jonah' as Loar claims (*op. cit.*, p. 372)?

depends, seems obvious enough. However it is clearly not obvious to Loar. A simple example may help to make it so. Take a community of five each of whom refers to a certain raven by the name 'Oscar'. Suppose that there is no earlier community from which the community borrows this reference. How does Loar's theory explain the reference? Essential to what each of the five means by the name is the concept *the raven called 'Oscar' by this community,* a concept instantiated only by Oscar. Now the concept raven is instantiated by all ravens. For the theory to be satisfactory it must include something that picks Oscar out from amongst all ravens. *Being called 'Oscar'* does this only by making use of the very relationship we are trying to explain. We want to know what makes each of the five's use of 'Oscar' refer to Oscar. Part of the answer is that Oscar is an object the other four refer to by 'Oscar'. But it is the reference of each of the five to Oscar we are trying to explain. *We have been given no way of determining which raven the five do call 'Oscar'.*

Loar has not offered a satisfactory theory of reference. Perhaps his theory can be amended to avoid the circularity. That remains to be seen. A difficulty is that attempts to do so are likely to run a foul of the usual arguments from ignorance and error. I shall not rehearse those arguments but will briefly indicate the difficulty.

Loar's first move to avoid the circularity seems clear enough: *some* members of the community on which we all ultimately depend must be able to refer to x by N *without* relying on the community. How is that requirement to be filled out?

An easy way would be to say that the community rests on *all* those who do not rely on reference borrowing; on *all* those who have an identifying concept which does not include *being called N.* But this easy way leads to disaster. Amongst those courageous enough, or foolhardy enough, to 'go it alone' will be many who are simply *wrong* about x; no single answer will emerge, let alone a correct one. The theory would be open to the arguments from ignorance and error.

The theory must somehow specify *the experts.* How is that to be done? The theory can't, on pain of circularity, say that they are *the people who are expert about what N refers to.* It seems that the theory must require that the members of the community identify the experts. But then we can forget about the community altogether. We are back to reference borrowing from individuals (the experts). That theory must, of course, avoid violating condition (C) (*a* thinks *b* is the expert, *b* thinks *c* is, and *c* thinks *a* is). Still there is the problem that a member of the community may not know the experts; or he may know one but not have an identifying individual concept of him except one that involves *is called* and so raises the same problems; or he may *mis*identify the expert; or he may identify the expert but the expert be *wrong* about the referent. A description theory owes us a solution to these problems of ignorance and error.

I shall conclude with some tentative remarks in diagnosis. At one point Loar contemplates, but finally rejects, the view that the identifying concept may not be *sufficient* for reference (not, of course, on the ground of circularity): a causal condition may have to be added.[30] The discussion suggests that it is *inconceivable* to Loar that a causal chain could be part of the semantical content of a name. Why is this? I suspect it is because of his Gricean interest in *what the speaker means*. It is taken for granted that what he means must be 'descriptive'. Why this prejudice for description over what we might call 'demonstration' or 'designation'? I would say that if a member of the above small community says 'Oscar is black' he is likely to mean simply, *Oscar is black*. He might mean this and yet be able to tell us nothing more about his meaning than that he does mean this. How is it possible that he could mean simply this? His 'communicative intentions' might be linked to a causal network involving others in the community and grounded in Oscar. The network embodies the community's *convention* of referring to Oscar by 'Oscar'. So speaker meaning is to be explained partly in terms of conventional meaning. No good Gricean can accept this line of thought, for it is a central tenet of Griceanism that speaker meaning explains conventional meaning. One way to resist is to assume from the start that speaker meanings *must* be 'descriptive'.

So I see Loar's attachment to description theories as going with his Gricean approach to semantics as a whole. My attachment to causal theories goes with a different approach. A decision about names must be closely connected to a decision about semantics in general.[31] I suspect that it would be most helpful at this time to focus on that connection in discussing names. Nevertheless there is clearly still a need for discussion focused more directly on differing opinions about names. My aim here has been to show that Loar's paper has two important defects as a contribution to this discussion: it misrepresents the opposing view and largely ignores a central criticism.[32]

---

[30]Op. cit

[30]*Op. cit.*, pp. 367–369.

[31]I attempt this in: *Designation.* It can be seen there that I do not regard the above method of resistance as effective.

[32]My thanks to Hartry Field and Bill Lycan for comments on a draft which have led to marked improvements in this paper.

NAMES AND DESCRIPTIONS: A REPLY TO MICHAEL DEVITT

Brian Loar

I do not think that there is a circularity in my description account of names. The theory was of course not: 'if N is the name of x, every use of N to name x involves intrinsically the individual concept *the object that people name when they utter N*'. That is not a very good theory. And naturally I took the reference to *past* uses of the name usually to come into the account. In the vernacular, 'is called' covers at least the recent past. Let me present a very simple history of a name that may serve to get us on the right track.

At time zero, Adam dubs a certain ape 'Arnolfo'. At time one, various persons utter sentences of the form 'Arnolfo is F', meaning thereby that the ape Adam dubbed 'Arnolfo' is such and such. At time two, certain persons, having forgotten Adam's contribution, utter such sentences and mean that the ape that people have been referring to as 'Arnolfo' is such and such. And so through continuous such usage down to the present. I take it that there is no problem in this description.

Devitt writes: 'Loar tells us only that each member of (the past community) referred to x because all the others did'. I suppose that means that I implied something like this: 'At a certain past time t every use of N to name x involved intrinsically the individual concept *the object that people are naming when they utter N at t*'. But nothing I said implied that, as I hope the foregoing history will make clear.

There is no definitional or explicative circularity in my account—nothing circular in the explication of 'refers' or of 'is called N'. Names *could* work as the theory says they do, again as the simple history of 'Arnolfo' shows. So the problem if there is one must be that, as it happens, names do not, or do not all, work like that—that the psychological, linguistic, etc. facts about ordinary real-world uses of names would, as construed by the description theory, lead to the sort of referential circularity that Devitt describes. I think it is fair, at this point, to construe Devitt's critique as posing a dilemma: either accept that there is such a circularity or try to avoid it by introducing 'experts', a move that leads to certain insurmountable problems about error, and about how the experts are to be identified.

Now the very word 'expert' gives the wrong picture of the role of those speakers whose references are drawn upon by other speakers. Suppose that you and I overhear Jones in conversation with Smith say 'Pierre Boulez is my favorite conductor'; and suppose that I comment: 'Pierre Boulez collects tickets on the streetcar Jones rides'. I am drawing upon Jones's reference here, because what I mean is, roughly, *the person whom Jones just referred to as 'Pierre Boulez'*; but am I treating Jones as an *expert?* There is no specific knowledge which I am thereby ascribing to Jones the lack of which would affect the success of *my reference* via that description. All I am supposing is that he referred. I may of course have been wrong in what I then asserted on that basis; Jones could have been speaking of music. But that is neither here nor there. When I depend on Jones's use, I draw on his reference and not on any specific knowledge of his that I have to have in mind; as far as my reference is concerned all that is relevant is my assumption that he thereby referred. The picture is not of Jones pointing to the name 'Pierre Boulez' in the newspaper and asserting authoritatively: 'This fellow "Pierre Boulez" is such and such', and my then relying on his being right. No; the picture is rather of Jones using that name to refer to someone, and my then relying on his having referred. So 'expert' is not the right word; I shall say *'source'* instead.

On a causal theory, just as on my sort of description theory, referential dependence on sources has to be accommodated; I assume this to be uncontroversial. If Jones in that example succeeded in referring to x, then on either account so did I; if he failed, so did I. The description theory of names, as it treats those cases that involve reference to others' references, is the causal theory made self-conscious.

A problem Devitt has raised still needs to be faced—namely, the problem whether speakers are really in a position to specify the relevant sources of their uses of names in cases where the simple shape of the 'Arnolfo' story doesn't apply, which is mostly. Consider the use by a non-expert of the name of someone who is well known but whose biographical details are not. So, for example, suppose that the majority of people who have heard of Alexander Hamilton know little about him. If such a person asserts, on the basis of having just read it, that 'Alexander Hamilton was against the French Revolution', what description might he intend? To say: 'the well known historical figure called "Alexander Hamilton"' raises the question: 'called by whom?'. Should we rely on the historians here? That seems too specific a solution to the general problem, and may even, when it is unpacked, merely push the problem back a stage. I shall now try to show that we do not need such specific characterizations of sources.

On any theory of reference it will presumably be recognized that, lying behind a name in general use like 'Alexander Hamilton', there is a class of past and potentially present users of that name whose use *sustains* the general use and whose reference *determines* the general reference. We might simply call such users of the name the *sources* of the general use and reference of that name. Since any theory of reference needs such a concept, the description theory can surely help itself to it. And ordinary speakers evidently know that names in general use have such sources. So when it is a name in general use that is in question, the intuitive meaning of 'x is called N' can be taken to be: 'x is the referent of uses of N by those who are the sources of N's general use and reference'. To repeat: any theory of reference ought to recognize such sources; so that description must be unproblematic. Any circularity that may be present in Devitt's 'the people who are expert about what N refers to, is absent here. And I hope that it is clear that when I refer to 'the sources of the general use' I do not need to know how those sources managed their reference or how the general use grew up as depending on them, except, of course, minimally: that both happened via descriptions.

Now to the second point. Devitt's diagnosis of my description theory as due to my "Gricean interest in what the speaker means" is in a sense correct, but not for the reason he gave. There is no problem in the abstract possibility of non-description theories within a Gricean framework. The underlying intentions and beliefs behind the use of names might be thought to be directly *de re*. Nothing in the general idea of a communication-intention theory of meaning and reference is incompatible with holding that what makes a belief or intention directly *de a certain re* is some causal relation, and that moreover, with regard to those beliefs and intentions expressed by utterances involving names the general causal relation often obtains by virtue of past practices or conventions involving the use of that name. It would not follow that the concept of speaker's meaning or reference thereby presupposes some concept of conventional meaning; for the notion of conventional meaning need not be an ineliminable part of the explication of what makes a belief directly *de re*, the past practices themselves being described in terms of regularities involving beliefs or communicative intentions. Notice that one could use the notion of past *de re* intentions or beliefs in one's account of what makes a present belief *de* a certain *re,* provided that the general account also provides some way for a communicative intention or belief to be directly *de re* other than by inheritance from other *de re* intentions and beliefs; perception, e.g., would come in.

The sense in which an interest in what the speaker means lies behind my description account of names is rather this. I assumed that the topic of reference was the topic of the use of language to refer; and that that was primarily a matter of communication. Now as it happens the communicative intentions that prompt the use of names are typically formed against a background of beliefs about the hearer that ascribe to the hearer the minimal information required by the description theory; and moreover it appears quite natural to take that information to be part of what the speaker intends the hearer to understand. So it seemed that using merely *de re* intentions to describe what is meant on uses of names leaves out part of what is typically thereby being communicated. If the topic of the semantics of names is in part the topic of the conventional use of names, and if the relevant use is communicative, then the description or individual concept should be brought into the account. Why should that be relevant to the theory of reference? There is no single clear pre-analytic use of 'refers' to be captured. The *utterance-object connections* that are most worth canonizing as reference on a given theory of meaning are those that fall most naturally out of the more basic account of what the whole business of semantic description is about: naturally it is required that it should be intuitively acceptable to say 'refers' in describing the central cases thereby picked out.

I now would present the account within a much expanded framework. For many of the most important questions that have been debated under the label 'theory of reference' are really about the theory of belief and the 'use of language in thought'. An essential part of the theory of reference for beliefs must be a theory of truth-conditions for beliefs. A theory of truth, it seems, cannot take all denotational relations to be directly referential, i.e., not as involving the satisfaction conditions of general concepts. In other words, the theory of truth-conditions will explain the general possibility, in effect, of a belief's being about a thing simply by containing a description of it and not by virtue of some causal relation to it. A description theory of names for beliefs would then simply make use of that account, without denying that beliefs are also about things by virtue of other, direct, causal or functional relations, something I think is true of perceptual beliefs about particulars, for example.

Finally, I quite agree with Devitt that it was wrong to assume that (iii) must be part of any interesting two-use theory. My assumption was of course that understanding an utterance is, roughly speaking, understanding something like a proposition that is appropriately related to the utterance (which is to say, on my account, the proposition that the speaker means). On a theory on which the only relevantly associated proposition is the one determined by what is said, on those utterances on which what is said is identical with a singular proposition, understanding the utterance must amount to something other than identifying the right (singular) proposition, as Devitt explains. Further useful discussion of the relative merits of those two accounts of understanding, and how they bear on the part of the theory of language and thought that is to be called the theory of reference, would seem to require some consideration of what the general point of semantic description should be.

THE CAUSAL THEORY OF NAMES

Gareth Evans

I

1. In a paper which provides the starting-point of this enquiry Saul Kripke opposes what he calls the Description Theory of Names and makes a counter-proposal of what I shall call the Causal Theory.[1] To be clear about what is at stake and what should be the outcome in the debate he initiated seems to me important for our understanding of talk and thought about the world in general as well as for our understanding of the functioning of proper names. I am anxious therefore that we identify the profound bases and likely generalizations of the opposing positions and do not content ourselves with counter-examples.

I should say that Kripke deliberately held back from presenting his ideas as a theory. I shall have to tighten them up, and I may suggest perhaps unintended directions of generalization; therefore his paper should be checked before the Causal Theory I consider is attributed to him.

There are two related but distinguishable questions concerning proper names. The first is about what the name denotes upon a particular occasion of its use when this is understood as being partly determinative of what the speaker strictly and literally said. I shall use the faintly barbarous coinage: *what the speaker denotes* (upon an occasion) for this notion. The second is about *what the name denotes*; we want to know what conditions have to be satisfied by an expression and an item for the first to be the, or a, name of the second. There is an entirely parallel pair of questions concerning general terms. In both cases it is ambiguity which prevents an easy answer of the first in terms of the second; to denote x it is not sufficient merely to utter something which is x's name.

Consequently there are two Description Theories, not distinguished by Kripke.[2] The Description Theory of speaker's denotation holds that a name 'NN' denotes x upon a particular occasion of its use by a speaker S just in case x is uniquely that which satisfies all or most of the descriptions ϕ such that S would assent to 'NN is ϕ' (or '*That* NN is ϕ'). Crudely: the cluster of information S has

---

[1] S. A. Kripke, "Naming and Necessity," in D. Davidson and G. Harman (eds.), *Semantics of Natural Language* (Dordrecht: Reidel, 1972), pp. 253–355 (+ Appendix).

[2] This can be seen in the way the list of theses defining the Description Theory alternate between those mentioning a speaker and those that don't, culminating in the uneasy idea of an idiolect of one. The Description Theorists of course do not themselves distinguish them clearly either, and many espouse both.

associated with the name determines its denotation upon a particular occasion by *fit*. If the speaker has no individuating information he will denote nothing.

The Description Theory of what a name denotes holds that, associated with each name as used by a group of speakers who believe aɪ d intend that they are using the name with the same denotation, is a description or set of descriptions cullable from their beliefs which an item has to satisfy to be the bearer of the name. This description is used to explain the role of the name in existential, identity, and opaque contexts. The theory is by no means committed to the thesis that every user of the name must be in possession of the description; just as Kripke is not committed to holding that every user of the expression 'one metre' knows about the metre rod in Paris by saying that its reference is fixed by the description 'Length of stick S in Paris'. Indeed if the description is arrived at in the manner of Strawson[3]—averaging out the different beliefs of different speakers—it is most unlikely that the description will figure in every user's name-associated cluster.

The direct attack in Kripke's paper passes this latter theory by; most conspicuously the charge that the Description Theory ignores the social character of naming. I shall not discuss it explicitly either, though it will surface from time to time and the extent to which it is right should be clear by the end of the paper.

Kripke's direct attacks are unquestionably against the first Description Theory. He argues:

(a) An ordinary man in the street can denote the physicist Feynman by using the name 'Feynman' and say something true or false of him even though there is no description uniquely true of the physicist which he can fashion. (The conditions aren't necessary.)

(b) A person who associated with the name 'Gödel' merely the description 'prover of the incompleteness of Arithmetic' would none the less be denoting Gödel and saying something false of him in uttering 'Gödel proved the incompleteness of Arithmetic' even if an unknown Viennese by the name of Schmidt had in fact constructed the proof which Gödel had subsequently broadcast as his own. (If it is agreed that the speaker does not denote Schmidt the conditions aren't sufficient; if it is also agreed that he denotes Gödel, again they are not necessary.)

The strong thesis (that the Description Theorist's conditions are sufficient) is outrageous. What the speaker denotes in the sense we are concerned with is connected with saying in that strict sense which logicians so rightly prize, and the theory's deliverance of strict truth conditions are quite unacceptable. They would have the consequence, for example, that if I was previously innocent of knowledge or belief regarding Mr. Y, and X is wrongly introduced to me as Mr. Y, then I must speak the truth in uttering 'Mr. Y is here' since X satisfies the overwhelming majority of descriptions I would associate with the name and X is there. I have grave doubts as to whether anyone has ever seriously held this thesis.

---

[3] P. F. Strawson, *Individuals* (London: Methuen, 1959), p. 191.

It is the weaker thesis—that some descriptive identification is necessary for a speaker to denote something—that it is important to understand. Strictly, Kripke's examples do not show it to be false since he nowhere provides a convincing reason for not taking into account speakers' possession of descriptions like 'man bearing such-and-such a name'; but I too think it is false. It can be seen as the fusion of two thoughts. First: that in order to be saying something by uttering an expression one must utter the sentence with certain intentions; this is felt to require, in the case of sentences containing names, that one be aiming at something with one's use of the name. Secondly—and this is where the underpinning from a certain Philosophy of Mind becomes apparent—to have an intention or belief concerning some item (which one is not in a position to demonstratively identify) one must be in possession of a description uniquely true of it. Both strands deserve at least momentary scrutiny.

We are prone to pass too quickly from the observation that neither parrots nor the wind *say* things to the conclusion that to say that p requires that one must intend to say that p and therefore, so to speak, be able to identify p independently of one's sentence. But the most we are entitled to conclude is that to say something one must intend to say something by uttering one's sentence (one normally will intend to say what it says). The application of the stricter requirement would lead us to relegate too much of our discourse to the status of mere mouthing. We constantly use general terms of whose satisfaction conditions we have but the dimmest idea. 'Microbiologist', 'chlorine' (the stuff in swimming-pools), 'nicotine' (the stuff in cigarettes); these, and countless other words, we cannot define nor offer remarks which would distinguish their meaning from that of closely related words. It is wrong to say that we say nothing by uttering sentences containing these expressions, even if we recoil from the strong thesis, from saying that what we do say is determined by those hazy ideas and half-identifications we would offer if pressed.

The Philosophy of Mind is curiously popular but rarely made perfectly explicit.[4] It is held by anyone who holds that S believes that a is F if and only if

$$\exists\phi \,[S \text{ believes } \exists x \,(\phi x \,\&\, (\forall y) \,(\phi y \to x = y) \,\&\, Fx)) \,\&\, \phi a \,\&$$
$$(\forall y) \,(\phi y \to y = a)]$$

Obvious alterations would accommodate the other psychological attitudes. The range of the property quantifier must be restricted to exclude such properties as 'being identical with a', otherwise the criterion is trivial.[5] The situation in which a thinking, planning or wanting human has some item which is the object of his thought, plan or desire is represented as a species of essentially the same situation as that which holds when there is no object and the thought, plan or desire is, as we might say, purely general. There are thoughts, such as the thought that there

---

[4] See, e.g., J. R. Searle, *Speech Acts* (Cambridge: Cambridge University Press, 1969), p. 87; E. Gellner, "Ethics and Logic," *Proceedings of the Aristotelian Society* 55 (1954–5), pp. 157–78; B. Russell, *Problems of Philosophy* (Oxford: Oxford University Press, paperback 1976), p. 29. E. Sosa criticizes it in "Quantifiers Belief and Sellars," in J. W. Davis, D. J. Hockney, and W. K. Wilson (eds.), *Philosophical Logic* (Dordrecht: Reidel, 1969), p. 69.

[5] I owe this observation to G. Harman.

are eleven-fingered men, for whose expression general terms of the language suffice. The idea is that when the psychological state involves an object, a general term believed to be uniquely instantiated and in fact uniquely instantiated by the item which is the object of the state will figure in its specification. This idea may be coupled with a concession that there are certain privileged objects to which one may be more directly related; indeed such a concession appears to be needed if the theory is to be able to allow what appears an evident possibility: object-directed thoughts in a perfectly symmetrical or cyclical universe.

This idea about the nature of object-directed psychological attitudes obviously owes much to the feeling that there must be something we can say about what is believed or wanted even when there is no appropriate object actually to be found in the world. But it can also be seen as deriving support from a Principle of Charity: so attribute objects to beliefs that true belief is maximized. (I do not think this is an acceptable principle; the acceptable principle enjoins minimizing the attribution of *inexplicable* error and therefore cannot be operated without a theory of the causation of belief for the creatures under investigation.)

We cannot deal comprehensively with this Philosophy of Mind here. My objections to it are essentially those of Wittgenstein. For an item to be the object of some psychological attitude of yours may be simply for you to be placed in a context which relates you to that thing. What makes it one rather than the other of a pair of identical twins that you are in love with? Certainly not some specification blueprinted in your mind; it may be no more than this: it was one of them and not the other that you have met. The theorist may gesture to the description 'the one I have met' but can give no explanation for the impossibility of its being outweighed by other descriptions which may have been acquired as a result of error and which may in fact happen to fit the other, unmet, twin. If God had looked into your mind, he would not have seen there with whom you were in love, and of whom you were thinking.

With that I propose to begin considering the Causal Theory.

2. The Causal Theory as stated by Kripke goes something like this. A speaker, using a name 'NN' on a particular occasion will denote some item x if there is a causal chain of *reference-preserving links* leading back from his use on that occasion ultimately to the item x itself being involved in a name-acquiring transaction such as an explicit dubbing or the more gradual process whereby nicknames stick. I mention the notion of a reference-preserving link to incorporate a condition that Kripke lays down; a speaker S's transmission of a name 'NN' to a speaker S' constitutes a reference-preserving link only if S intends to be using the name with the same denotation as he from whom he in his turn learned the name.

Let us begin by considering the theory in answer to our question about speaker's denotation (i.e., at the level of the individual speaker). In particular, let us consider the thesis that it is *sufficient* for someone to denote x on a particular occasion with the name that this use of the name on that occasion be a causal consequence of his exposure to other speakers using the expression to denote x.

An example which might favourably dispose one towards the theory is this. A group of people are having a conversation in a pub, about a certain Louis of whom

S has never heard before. S becomes interested and asks: 'What did Louis do then?' There seems to be no question but that S denotes a particular man and asks about him. Or on some subsequent occasion S may use the name to offer some new thought to one of the participants: 'Louis was quite right to do that.' Again he clearly denotes whoever was the subject of conversation in the pub. This is difficult to reconcile with the Description Theory since the scraps of information which he picked up during the conversation might involve some distortion and fit someone else much better. Of course he has the description 'the man they were talking about' but the theory has no explanation for the impossibility of its being outweighed.

The Causal Theory can secure the right answer in such a case but I think deeper reflection will reveal that it too involves a refusal to recognize the insight about contextual determination I mentioned earlier. For the theory has the following consequence: that at any future time, no matter how remote or forgotten the conversation, no matter how alien the subject-matter and confused the speaker, S will denote one particular Frenchman—perhaps Louis XIII—so long as there is a causal connection between his use at that time and the long-distant conversation.

It is important in testing your intuitions against the theory that you imagine the predicate changed—so that he says something like 'Louis was a basketball player' which was not heard in the conversation and which arises as a result of some confusion. This is to prevent the operation of what I call the 'mouthpiece syndrome' by which we attach sense and reference to a man's remarks only because we hear someone else speaking through him; as we might with a messenger, carrying a message about matters of which he was entirely ignorant.

Now there is no knock-down argument to show this consequence unacceptable; with pliant enough intuitions you can swallow anything in philosophy. But notice how little *point* there is in saying that he denotes one French king rather than any other, or any other person named by the name. There is now nothing that the speaker is prepared to say or do which relates him differentially to that one king. This is why it is so outrageous to say that he believes that Louis XIII is a basketball player. The notion of saying has simply been severed from all the connections that made it of interest. Certainly we did not think we were letting ourselves in for this when we took the point about the conversation in the pub. What has gone wrong?[6]

The Causal Theory again ignores the importance of surrounding context, and regards the capacity to denote something as a magic trick which has somehow been passed on, and once passed on cannot be lost. We should rather say: in virtue of the context in which the man found himself the man's dispositions were bent towards one particular man—Louis XIII—whose states and doings alone he would count as serving to verify remarks made in that context using the name. And of course that context can persist, for the conversation can itself be

---

[6] Kripke expresses doubts about the sufficiency of the conditions for this sort of reason, see *op. cit.*, p. 303.

adverted to subsequently. But it can also disappear so that the speaker is simply not sensitive to the outcome of any investigations regarding the truth of what he is said to have said. And at this point saying becomes detached, and uninteresting.

(It is worth observing how ambivalent Kripke is on the relation between denoting and believing; when the connection favours him he uses it; we are reminded for example that the ordinary man has a false belief about Gödel and not a true belief about Schmidt. But it is obvious that the results of the 'who are they believing about?' criterion are bound to come dramatically apart from the results of the 'who is the original bearer of the name?' criterion, if for no other reason than that the former must be constructed to give results in cases where there is no name and where the latter cannot apply. When this happens we are sternly reminded that 'X refers' and 'X says' are being used in *technical* senses.[7] But there are limits. One could regard the aim of this paper to restore the connection which must exist between strict truth conditions and the beliefs and interests of the users of the sentences if the technical notion of strict truth conditions is to be of interest to us.)

Reflection upon the conversation in the pub appeared to provide one reason for being favourably disposed towards the Causal Theory. There is another connected reason we ought to examine briefly. It might appear that the Causal Theory provides the basis for a general non-intentional answer to the Problem of Ambiguity. The problem is clear enough: What conditions have to be satisfied for a speaker to have said that p when he utters a sentence which may appropriately be used to say that q and that r and that s in addition? Two obvious alternative answers are:

(a) the extent to which it is reasonable for his audience to conclude that he was saying that p

(b) his intending to say that p

and neither is without its difficulties. We can therefore imagine someone is hoping for a natural extension of the Causal Theory to general terms which would enable him to explain for example how a child who did not have determinative intentions because of the technical nature of the subject-matter may still say something determinate using a sentence which is in fact ambiguous.

I touch upon this to ensure that we are keeping the range of relevant considerations to be brought to bear upon the debate as wide as it must be. But I think little general advantage can accrue to the Causal Theory from thus broadening the considerations. The reason is that it simply fails to have the generality of the other two theories; it has no obvious application, for example, to syntactic ambiguity or to ambiguity produced by attempts to refer with non-unique descriptions, or pronouns. It seems inconceivable that the general theory of disambiguation required for such cases would be inadequate to deal with the phenomenon of shared names and would require *ad hoc* supplementation from the Causal Theory.

---

[7] *Ibid.*, p. 348 fn.

I want to stress how, precisely because the Causal Theory ignores the way context can be determinative of what gets *said*, it has quite unacceptable consequences. Suppose, for example, on a TV quiz programme I am asked to name a capital city and I say 'Kingston is the capital of Jamaica'; I should want to say that I had said something strictly and literally true even though it turns out that the man from whom I had picked up this scrap of information was actually referring to Kingston upon Thames and making a racist observation.

It may begin to appear that what gets said is going to be determined by what name is used, what items bear the name, and general principles of contextual disambiguation. The causal origin of the speaker's familiarity with the name, save in certain specialized 'mouthpiece cases', does not seem to have a critical role to play.

This impression may be strengthened by the observation that a causal connection between my use of the name and use by others (whether or not leading back ultimately to the item itself) is simply not necessary for me to use the name to say something. Amongst the Wagera Indians, for example, "newly born children receive the names of deceased members of their family according to strict rules . . . the first born takes on the name of the paternal grandfather, the second that of the father's eldest brother, the third that of the maternal grandfather."[8] In these and other situations (names for streets in US cities, etc.) a knowledgeable speaker may excogitate a name and use it to denote some item which bears it without any causal connection whatever with the use by others of that name.

These points might be conceded by Kripke while maintaining the general position that the denotation of a name in a community is still to be found by tracing a causal chain of reference preserving links back to some item. It is to this theory that I now turn.

3. Suppose a parallel theory were offered to explain the sense of general terms (not just terms for natural kinds). One would reply as follows:

> There aren't two fundamentally different mechanisms involved in a word's having a meaning: one bringing it about that a word acquires a meaning, and the other—a causal mechanism—which operates to ensure that its meaning is preserved. The former processes are operative all the time; whatever explains how a word gets its meaning also explains how it preserves it, if preserved it is. Indeed such a theory could not account for the phenomenon of a word's changing its meaning. It is perfectly possible for this to happen without anyone's intending to initiate a new practice with the word; the causal chain would then lead back too far.

Change of meaning would be decisive against such a theory of the meaning of general terms. Change of denotation is similarly decisive against the Causal Theory of Names. Not only are changes of denotation imaginable, but it appears that they actually occur. We learn from Isaac Taylor's *Names and Their History* (1898):

> In the case of 'Madagascar' a hearsay report of Malay or Arab sailors misunderstood by Marco Polo . . . has had the effect of transferring a corrupt form of the name of a portion of the African mainland to the great African Island.

---

[8] E. Delhaise, "Les Wagera," *Monogr. Ethnogr.* (1909).

A simple imaginary case would be this: two babies are born, and their mothers bestow names upon them. A nurse inadvertently switches them and the error is never discovered. It will henceforth undeniably be the case that the man universally known as 'Jack' is so called because a woman dubbed some other baby with the name.

It is clear that the Causal Theory unamended is not adequate. It looks as though, once again, the intentions of the speakers to use the name to refer to something must be allowed to count in determination of what it denotes.

But it is not enough to say that and leave matters there. We must at least sketch a theory which will enable 'Madagascar' to be the name of the island yet which will not have the consequence that 'Gödel' would become a name of Schmidt in the situation envisaged by Kripke, nor 'Goliath' a name of the Philistine killed by David. (Biblical scholars now suggest that David did not kill Goliath, and that the attribution of the slaying to Elhannan the Bethlehemite in 2 Sam. 21:19 is correct. David is thought to have killed a Philistine but not Goliath.)[9] For although this has never been explicitly argued I would agree that even if the 'information' connected with the name in possession of an entire community was merely that 'Goliath was the Philistine David slew' this would still not mean that 'Goliath' referred in that community to that man, and therefore that the sentence expressed a truth. And if we simultaneously thought that the name *would* denote the Philistine slain by Elhannan then both the necessity and sufficiency of the conditions suggested by the Description Theory of the denotation of a name are rejected. This is the case Kripke should have argued but didn't.

4. Before going on to sketch such a theory in the second part of this paper let me survey the position arrived at and use it to make a summary statement of the position I wish to adopt.

We can see the undifferentiated Description Theory as the expression of two thoughts.

(a) The denotation of a name is determined by what speakers intend to refer to by using the name.

(b) The object a speaker intends to refer to by his use of a name is that which satisfies or fits the majority of descriptions which make up the cluster of information which the speaker has associated with the name.

We have seen great difficulties with (a) when this is interpreted as a thesis at the micro-level. But consideration of the phenomenon of a name's getting a denotation, or changing it, suggests that there being a community of speakers using the name with such-and-such as the intended referent is likely to be a crucial constituent in these processes. With names as with other expressions in the language, what they signify depends upon what we use them to signify; a truth whose recognition is compatible with denying the collapse of saying into meaning at the level of the individual speaker.

---

[9] H. W. Robinson, *The History of Israel* (London: Duckworth, 1941), p. 187.

It is in (b) that the real weakness lies: the bad old Philosophy of Mind which we momentarily uncovered. Not so much in the idea that the intended referent is determined in a more or less complicated way by the associated information, but the specific form the determination was supposed to take: *fit*. There is something absurd in supposing that the intended referent of some perfectly ordinary use of a name by a speaker could be some item utterly isolated (causally) from the user's community and culture simply in virtue of the fact that it fits better than anything else the cluster of descriptions he associates with the name. I would agree with Kripke in thinking that the absurdity resides in the absence of the causal relation between the item concerned and the speaker. But it seems to me that he has mislocated the causal relation; the important causal relation lies between that item's states and doings and the speaker's body of information—not between the item's being dubbed with a name and the speaker's contemporary use of it.

Philosophers have come increasingly to realize that major concepts in epistemology and the philosophy of mind have causality embedded within them. Seeing and knowing are both good examples.

The absurdity in supposing that the denotation of our contemporary use of the name 'Aristotle' could be some unknown (n.b.) item whose doings are causally isolated from our body of information is strictly parallel to the absurdity in supposing that one might be seeing something one has no causal contact with solely upon the ground that there is a splendid match between object and visual impression.

There probably is some *degree of fit* requirement in the case of seeing which means that after some amount of distortion or fancy we can no longer maintain that the causally operative item was still being seen. And I think it is likely that there is a parallel requirement for referring. We learn, for example, from E. K. Chambers's *Arthur of Britain* that Arthur had a son Anir 'whom legend has perhaps confused with his burial place'. If Kripke's notion of reference fixing is such that those who said Anir was a burial place of Arthur might be denoting a person it seems that it has little to commend it, and is certainly not justified by the criticism he makes against the Description Theory. But the existence or nature of this 'degree of fit' requirement will not be something I shall be concerned with here.

We must allow, then, that the denotation of a name in the community will depend in a complicated way upon what those who use the term intend to refer to, but we will so understand 'intended referent' that typically a *necessary* (but not sufficient) condition for x's being the intended referent of S's use of a name is that x should be the source of causal origin of the body of information that S has associated with the name.

II

5. The aim I have set myself, then, is modest; it is not to present a complete theory of the denotation of names. Without presenting a general theory to solve the problem of ambiguity I cannot present a theory of speaker's denotation, although I will make remarks which prejudice that issue. I propose merely to sketch an

account of what makes an expression into a name for something that will allow names to change their denotations.

The enterprise is more modest yet for I propose to help myself to an undefined notion of speaker's reference by borrowing from the theory of communication. But a word of explanation.

A speaker may have succeeded in *getting it across* or in *communicating* that p even though he uses a sentence which may not appropriately be used to say that p. Presumably this success consists in his audience's having formed a belief about him. This need not be the belief that the speaker intended to say in the strict sense that p, since the speaker may succeed in getting something across despite using a sentence which he is known to know cannot appropriately be used to say that p. The speaker will have referred to a, in the sense that I am helping myself to, only if he has succeeded in getting it across that Fa (for some substitution F). Further stringent conditions are required. Clearly this notion is quite different from the notion of denotation which I have been using, tied as denotation is to saying in the strict sense. One may refer to x by using a description that x does not satisfy; one may not thus denote x.

Now a speaker may know or believe that there is such-and-such an item in the world and intend to refer to it. And this is where the suggestion made earlier must be brought to bear, for *that* item is not (in general) the satisfier of the body of information the possession by the speaker of which makes it true that he knows of the existence of the item; it is rather that item which is causally responsible for the speaker's possession of that body of information, or dominantly responsible if there is more than one. (The point is of course not specific to this intention, or to intention as opposed to other psychological attitudes.) Let us then, very briefly, explore these two ideas: source and dominance.

Usually our knowledge or belief about particular items is derived from information-gathering transactions, involving a causal interaction with some item or other, conducted ourselves or is derived, maybe through a long chain, from the transactions of others. Perception of the item is the main but by no means the only way an item can impress itself on us; for example, a man can be the source of things we discover by rifling through his suitcase or by reading his works.

A causal relation is of course not sufficient; but we may borrow from the theory of knowledge and say something like this. X is the source of the belief S expresses by uttering 'Fa' if there was an episode which caused S's belief in which X and S were causally related in a type of situation apt for producing knowledge that something F-s ($\exists x(Fx)$)—a type of situation in which the belief that something F-s would be caused by something's F-ing. That it is a way of producing knowledge does not mean that it cannot go wrong; that is why X, by smoking French cigarettes, can be the source of the belief S expresses by 'a smokes Greek cigarettes'.

Of course some of our information about the world is not so based; we may deduce that there is a tallest man in the world and deduce that he is over 6 feet tall. No man is the source of this information; a name introduced in relation to it might function very much as the unamended Description Theory suggested.

Legend and fancy can create new characters, or add bodies of sourceless material to other dossiers; restrictions on the causal relation would prevent the inventors of the legends turning out to be the sources of the beliefs their legends gave rise to. Someone other than the ϕ can be the source of the belief S expresses by 'a is the ϕ'; Kripke's Gödel, by claiming the proof, was the source of the belief people manifested by saying 'Gödel proved the incompleteness of Arithmetic', not Schmidt.

Misidentification can bring it about that the item which is the source of the information is different from the item about which the information is believed. I may form the belief about the wife of some colleague that she has nice legs upon the basis of seeing someone else—but the girl I saw is the source.

Consequently a cluster or dossier of information can be dominantly *of* [10] an item though it contains elements whose source is different. And we surely want to allow that persistent misidentification can bring it about that a cluster is dominantly of some item other than that it was dominantly of originally.

Suppose I get to know a man slightly. Suppose then a suitably primed identical twin takes over his position, and I get to know him fairly well, not noticing the switch. Immediately after the switch my dossier will still be dominantly of the original man, and I falsely believe, as I would acknowledge if it was pointed out, that *he* is in the room. Then I would pass through a period in which neither was dominant; I had not misidentified one as the other, an asymmetrical relation, but rather confused them. Finally the twin could take over the dominant position; I would not have false beliefs about who is in the room, but false beliefs about, for example, when I first met the man in the room. These differences seem to reside entirely in the differences in the believer's reactions to the various discoveries, and dominance is meant to capture those differences.

Dominance is not simply a function of *amount* of information (if that is even intelligible). In the case of persons, for example, each man's life presents a skeleton and the dominant source may be the man who contributed to covering most of it rather than the man who contributed most of the covering. Detail in a particular area can be outweighed by spread. Also the believer's reasons for being interested in the item at all will weigh.

Consider another example. If it turns out that an impersonator had taken over Napoleon's role from 1814 onwards (post-Elba), the cluster of the typical historian would still be dominantly of the man responsible for the earlier exploits (α in Diagram 1) and we would say that they had false beliefs about who fought at Waterloo. If however the switch had occurred much earlier, it being an unknown Army Officer being impersonated, then their information would be dominantly of the later man (β in Diagram 2). They did not have false beliefs about who was the general at Waterloo, but rather false beliefs about that general's early career.

---

[10] The term is D. Kaplan's, see "Quantifying In," in D. Davidson and J. Hintikka (eds.), *Words and Objections* (Dordrecht: Reidel, 1969): I think there are clear similarities between my notion of a dominant source and notions he is there sketching. However, I want nothing to do with vividness. I borrow the term *dossier* from H. P. Grice's paper "Vacuous Names" in the same volume.

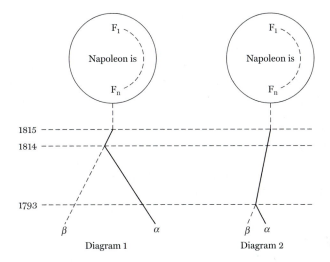

Diagram 1   Diagram 2

I think we can say that *in general* a speaker intends to refer to the item that is the dominant source of his associated body of information. It is important to see that this will not change from occasion to occasion depending upon subject-matter. Some have proposed[11] that if in case 1 the historian says 'Napoleon fought skillfully at Waterloo' it is the imposter β who is the intended referent, while if he had said in the next breath '. . . unlike his performance in the Senate' it would be α. This seems a mistake; not only was what the man said false, what he intended to say was false too, as he would be the first to agree; it wasn't Napoleon who fought skillfully at Waterloo.

With this background, then, we may offer the following tentative definition:

'NN' is a name of x if there is a community C

1. in which it is common knowledge that members of C have in their repertoire the procedure of using 'NN' to refer to x (with the intention of referring to x)
2. the success in reference in any particular case being intended to rely on common knowledge between speaker and hearer that 'NN' has been used to refer to x by members of C and not upon common knowledge of the satisfaction by x of some predicate embedded in 'NN'.[12]

(In order to keep the definition simple no attempt is made to cover the sense in which an unused institutionally approved name is a name.)

---

[11] K. S. Donnellan, "Proper Names and Identifying Descriptions," in Davidson and Harman (eds.), op. cit., p. 371.

[12] For the notion of "common knowledge," see D. K. Lewis, *Convention* (Cambridge, Mass.: Harvard University Press, 1969) and the slightly different notion in S. R. Schiffer, *Meaning* (Oxford: Clarendon Press, 1972). For the notion of "a procedure in the repertoire," see H. P. Grice "Utterer's Meaning, Sentence Meaning, Word Meaning," *Foundations of Language* (1968). Clearly the whole enterprise owes much to Grice but no commitment is here made to any specific version of the theory of communication.

This distinction (between use-because-(we know)-we-use-it and use upon other bases) is just what is needed to distinguish dead from live metaphors; it seems to me the only basis on which to distinguish referential functioning of names, which may grammatically be descriptions, from that of descriptions.[13]

The definition does not have the consequence that the description 'the man we call "NN"' is a name, for *its* success as a referential device does not rely upon common knowledge that *it* is or has been used to refer to x.

Intentions alone don't bring it about that a name gets a denotation; without the intentions being manifest there cannot be the common knowledge required for the practice.

Our conditions are more stringent than Kripke's since for him an expression becomes a name just so long as someone has dubbed something with it and thereby caused it to be in common usage. This seems little short of magical. Suppose one of a group of villagers dubbed a little girl on holiday in the vicinity 'Goldilocks' and the name caught on. However, suppose that there were two identical twins the villagers totally fail to distinguish. I should deny that 'Goldilocks' is the name of either—even if by some miracle each villager used the name consistently but in no sense did they fall into two coherent sub-communities. (The name might denote the girl first dubbed if for some peculiar reason the villagers were deferential to the introducer of the name—of this more below.)

Consider the following case. An urn is discovered in the Dead Sea containing documents on which are found fascinating mathematical proofs. Inscribed at the bottom is the name 'Ib Khan' which is quite naturally taken to be the name of the constructor of the proofs. Consequently it passes into common usage amongst mathematicians concerned with that branch of mathematics. 'Khan conjectured here that . . .' and the like. However, suppose the name was the name of the scribe who had transcribed the proofs much later; a small '*id scripsit*' had been obliterated.

Here is a perfect case where there is a coherent community using the name with the mathematician as the intended referent and a consequence of the definition would be that 'Ibn Khan' would be one of his names. Also, 'Malachi' would have been the name of the author of the biblical work of the same name despite that its use was based upon a misapprehension ('Malachi' means my messenger).[14]

Speakers within such traditions use names under the misapprehension that their use is in conformity with the use of other speakers referring to the relevant item. The names would probably be withdrawn when that misapprehension is revealed, or start a rather different life as 'our' names for the items (cf. 'Deutero Isaiah,' etc.). One might be impressed by this, and regard it as a reason for denying that those within these traditions spoke the literal truth in using the names. It is very easy to add a codicil to the definition which would have this effect.

---

[13] And if Schiffer is right much more as well—see *Meaning*, chap. V.

[14] See O. Eissfeldt, *The Old Testament: An Introduction* (Oxford: Oxford University Press, 1965), p. 441.

Actually it is not a very good reason for denying that speakers within such traditions are speaking the literal truth.[15] But I do not want to insist upon any decision on this point. This is because one can be concessive and allow the definition to be amended without giving up anything of importance. First: the definition with its codicil will still allow many names to change their denotation. Secondly: from the fact that, in our example, the community of mathematicians were not denoting the mathematician it obviously fails to follow that they were denoting the scribe and were engaged in strictly speaking massive falsehood of him.

Let me elaborate the first of these points.

There is a fairly standard way in which people get their names. If we use a name of a man we expect that it originated in the standard manner and this expectation may condition our use of it. But consider names for people which are obviously nicknames, or names for places or pieces of music. Since there is no standard way in which these names are bestowed subsequent users will not in general use the name under any view as to its origin, and therefore when there is a divergence between the item involved in the name's origin and the speakers' intended referent there will be no *mis*apprehension, no latent motive for withdrawing the name, and thus no bar to the name's acquiring a new denotation even by the amended definition. So long as they have no reason to believe that the name has dragged any information with it, speakers will treat the revelation that the name had once been used to refer to something different with the same sort of indifference as that with which they greet the information that 'meat' once meant groceries in general.

We can easily tell the story in case 2 of our Napoleon diagram so that α was the original bearer of the name 'Napoleon' and it was transferred to the counterfeit because of the similarity of their appearances and therefore without the intention on anyone's part to initiate a new practice. Though this is not such a clear case I should probably say that historians have used the name 'Napoleon' to refer to β. They might perhaps abandon it, but that of course fails to show that they were all denoting α. Nor does the fact that someone in the know might come along and say 'Napoleon was a fish salesman and was never at Waterloo' show anything. The relevant question is: 'Does this contradict the assertion that was made when the historians said "Napoleon was at Waterloo"?' To give an affirmative answer to this question requires the prior determination that they have all along been denoting α.

We need one further and major complication. Although standardly we use expressions with the intention of conforming to the general use made of them by the community, sometimes we use them with the *overriding* intention to conform to the use made of them by some other person or persons. In that case I shall say that we use the expression *deferentially* (with respect to that other person or group of persons). This is true of some general terms too: 'viol', 'minuet' would be examples.

I should say, for example, that the man in the conversation in the pub used 'Louis' deferentially. This is not just a matter of his ignorance; he could, indeed,

---

[15] John McDowell has persuaded me of this, as of much else. He detests my conclusions.

have an opinion as to who this Louis is (the man he met earlier perhaps) but still use the expression deferentially. There is an important gap between

> intending to refer to the ϕ and believing that $a =$ the ϕ;
> intending to refer to a

for even when he has an opinion as to who they are talking about I should say that it was the man they were talking about, and not the man he met earlier, that he intended to refer to.

Archaeologists might find a tomb in the desert and claim falsely that it is the burial place of some little known character in the Bible. They could discover a great deal about the man in the tomb so that he and not the character in the Bible was the dominant source of their information. But, given the nature and point of their enterprise, the archaeologists are using the name deferentially to the authors of the Bible. I should say, then, that they denote that man, and say false things about him. Notice that in such a case there is some point to this characterization.

The case is in fact no different from any situation in which a name is used with the overriding intention of referring to something satisfying such-and-such a description. Kripke gives the example of 'Jack the Ripper'. Again, after the arrest of a man a not in fact responsible for the crimes, a can be the dominant source of speakers' information but the intended referent could well be the murderer and not a. Again this will be productive of a whole lot of falsehood.

We do not use all names deferentially, least of all deferentially to the person from whom we picked them up. For example, the mathematicians did not use the name 'Ibn Khan' with the *overriding* intention of referring to whoever bore that name or was referred to by some other person or community.

We must thus be careful to distinguish two reasons for something that would count as 'withdrawing sentences containing the name'

(a) the item's not bearing the name 'NN' ('Ibn Khan', 'Malachi')

(b) the item's not being NN (the biblical archaeologists).

I shall end with an example that enables me to draw these threads together and summarize where my position differs from the Causal Theory.

A youth A leaves a small village in the Scottish highlands to seek his fortune having acquired the nickname 'Turnip' (the reason for choosing a nickname is I hope clear). Fifty or so years later a man B comes to the village and lives as a hermit over the hill. The three or four villagers surviving from the time of the youth's departure believe falsely that this is the long-departed villager returned. Consequently they use the name 'Turnip' among themselves and it gets into wider circulation among the younger villagers who have no idea how it originated. I am assuming that the older villagers, if the facts were pointed out, would say 'It isn't Turnip after all' rather than 'It appears after all that Turnip did not come from this village'. In that case I should say that they use the name to refer to A, and in fact, denoting him, say false things about him (even by uttering 'Here is Turnip coming to get his coffee again').

But they may die off, leaving a homogeneous community using the name to refer to the man over the hill. I should say the way is clear to its becoming his name. The story is not much affected if the older villagers pass on some information whose source is A by saying such things as 'Turnip was quite a one for the girls', for the younger villagers' clusters would still be dominantly of the man over the hill. But it is an important feature of my account that the information that the older villagers gave the younger villagers could be so rich, coherent, and important to them that A could be the dominant source of their information, so that they too would acknowledge 'That man over the hill isn't Turnip after all'.

A final possibility would be if they used the name deferentially towards the older villagers, for some reason, with the consequence that no matter who was dominant they denote who—ever the elders denote.

6. *Conclusion.* Espousers of both theories could reasonably claim to be vindicated by the position we have arrived at. We have secured for the Description Theorist much that he wanted. We have seen that for at least the most fundamental case of the use of names (non-deferentially used names) the idea that their denotation is fixed in a more or less complicated way by the associated bodies of information that one could cull from the users of the name turns out not to be so wide of the mark. But of course that the fix is by causal origin and not by fit crucially affects the impact this idea has upon the statement of the truth conditions of existential or opaque sentences containing names. The theorist can also point to the idea of dominance as securing what he was trying, admittedly crudely, to secure with his talk of the 'majority of' the descriptions, and to the 'degree of fit requirement' as blocking consequences he found objectionable.

The Causal Theorist can also look with satisfaction upon the result, incorporating as it does his insight about the importance of causality into a central position. Further, the logical doctrines he was concerned to establish, for example the non-contingency of identity statements made with the use of names, are not controverted. Information is individuated by source; if a is the source of a body of information nothing else could have been. Consequently nothing else could have been *that a*.

The only theorists who gain no comfort are those who, ignoring Kripke's explicit remarks to the contrary,[16] supposed that the Causal Theory could provide them with a totally *non-intentional* answer to the problem posed by names. But I am not distressed by their distress.

Our ideas also point forward; for it seems that they, or some close relative, must be used in explaining the functioning of at least some demonstratives. Such an expression as 'That mountaineer' in 'That mountaineer is coming to town tonight' may avert to a body of information presumed in common possession, perhaps through the newspapers, which fixes its denotation. No one can be *that* mountaineer unless he is the source of that information no matter how perfectly he fits it, and of course someone can be that mountaineer and fail to fit quite a bit of it. It is in such generality that defence of our ideas must lie.

But with these hints I must leave the subject.

---

[16] Kripke, *op. cit.*, p. 302.

ON EXISTENTIALISM

Alvin Plantinga

According to Jean-Paul Sartre, existentialism is the view that existence precedes essence. As I shall use the term, existentialism is the thesis that existence, even if it does not precede essence, is at any rate not preceded by it. Let me explain.

I. Existentialism Expounded

Suppose we begin by endorsing or at any rate not contesting the view that objects have individual essences. An individual essence E of an object x is a property that meets two conditions: (1) E is essential to x, so that it is not possible that x exists but lacks E, and (2) E is essentially unique to x, so that it is not possible that there should have been an object distinct from x that had E. I believe it is obvious that there are individual essences. Consider, for example, the property of being William F. Buckley or being identical with William F. Buckley. Surely that property is essential to Buckley; he couldn't have existed but lacked it. (Of course he could have lacked the *name* 'William F. Buckley'; no doubt his parents could have named him 'Pico della Mirandola' if they'd wished.) But the property in question is also essentially unique to him; it is not possible that someone distinct from Buckley should have had the property of being identical with William F. Buckley. One kind of essence, then, is the property of being identical with some object— i.e., the property, for some object x, of being identical with x. Following Robert Adams and Duns Scotus, suppose we call such a property a *thisness*, the thisness of an individual is the property of being that individual. It is not necessary that we use proper names to specify or refer to thisnesses; when I use the words "the property of being I" or "the property of being identical with me," the property they denote is a thisness. And consider the meanest man in North Dakota: the property of being identical with *him* is also a thisness.

So objects have thisnesses and thisnesses are essences. One existentialist thesis—a thesis endorsed by Arthur Prior, Robert Adams, Kit Fine, and others— can be stated as follows: thisnesses are ontologically dependent upon their exemplifications. Take any thisness t and the object x of which t is the thisness; t could not have existed if x had not. If Buckley had not existed, then his thisness would not have existed. Every thisness has *essentially* the property of being exemplified by the object that does in fact exemplify it. More exactly, the thesis in question is that it is *necessary* that every thisness has that property; it is not as if there could have been thisnesses that could have lacked the property in question.

This existentialist thesis can be extended. Let's say that a property is *quidditative* if it is either a thisness or involves a thisness in a certain way. We could try to spell out the way in question in formal and recusive detail; but instead let me just give some examples. *Being identical with Nero* or *being Nero* is a quidditative property; but so are *being more blood-thirsty than Nero, being either Nero or Cicero, being either Nero or wise, being possibly wiser than Nero, being believed by Nero to be treacherous*, and *being such that there is someone more bloodthirsty than Nero.* We may contrast the notion of a quidditative property with that of a *qualitative* property. Again, I shall not try to give a *definition* of this notion; but examples would be *being wise, being 14 years old, being angry, being learned, being six feet from a desk,* and the like. If *P* and *Q* are qualitative properties, then so is their conjunction, their disjunction, the complement of each, *being such that there is something that has P,* and *possibly having P.* And the more general existentialist thesis is that while qualitative properties may be necessary beings and exist in every possible world, quidditative properties are ontologically dependent upon the objects whose thisnesses they involve. Of course the thisness of a *necessary* being—God, perhaps, or to use a theologically less dramatic example, the number seven—exists necessarily, just as does the object of which it is a thisness; and the same goes for any quidditative property that involves only thisnesses of necessary beings. But such a quidditative property as *being wiser than Buckley* could not have existed if he had not.

The first existentialist thesis, therefore, is that quidditative properties are ontologically dependent upon the individuals whose thisnesses they involve. And a second existentialist thesis is like unto the first. Consider the propositions

(1) William F. Buckley is wise

and

(2) The Lion of Conservativism is wise.

The first, we might think, involves Buckley in a more direct and intimate way than does the second. The second refers to him, so to say, only accidentally—only by virtue of the fact that he happens to be the Lion of Conservativism. (1), on the other hand, makes a direct reference to him, or to use Arthur Prior's term, is "directly about"[1] him. Now it is not easy to say just what *direct aboutness* is or when a proposition is directly about an object; and for our purposes it isn't crucially important. Instead of trying to explain that notion, I shall say that a proposition directly about some object is a *singular* proposition and give some examples: *Buckley is wise, either Buckley is wise or* 2 + 1 = 3, *possibly Buckley is wise, it's not the case that Buckley is wise, someone is wiser than Buckley, Sam believes that Buckley is wise,* and *possibly Buckley does not exist* are all singular propositions. If we think of propositions as having constituents, we may think of a singular proposition as one that has either at least one individual or at least one quidditative property as a constituent. And the second existentialist thesis—accepted again by Adams, Fine, Prior and others—is this: a singular proposition is ontologically dependent upon the individuals it is directly about. So if Buckley had not existed, then, on this view, none of the above propositions would have so much as seen the light of day.

Existentialism, therefore, is the claim that quidditative properties and singular propositions are ontologically dependent upon the individuals they involve.[2]

---

[1] *Worlds, Times, and Selves* (Amherst: University of Massachusetts Press, 1997), p. 109.

[2] Of course the wholehearted existentialist will add that states of affairs (and hence possible worlds) are also ontologically dependent upon the individuals they involve.

I don't know whether continental *Angst* would be the appropriate reaction to the truth of existentialism, if indeed it were true, but in any event I propose to argue that it is false. First, however, we must try to get a sense of what it is that leads people to accept existentialism.

II. Why Accept Existentialism?

I wish to consider two lines of argument for existentialism, one for each of the two characteristic existentialist theses. But first we must briefly take note of a doctrine presupposed by both lines of argument. As we have learned at our mother's knees, Meinong and his cohorts held that in addition to all the things that exist—houses, horses, men and mice—there are some more things—golden mountains and round squares, perhaps—that do not. I've argued elsewhere[3] that this claim is mistaken; here let's just agree, for purposes of argument, that the claim is false. Let's agree that there neither are nor could have been any nonexistent objects; it's a necessary truth that there aren't any. This view is sometimes called 'actualism'; I shall follow this custom, but with a *caveat*. 'Actualism' is a misleading name for the view in question; it suggests the idea that whatever is, is *actual*. But that is false. There are many states of affairs—for example *London's being smaller than Los Angeles*—that don't obtain, are not actual. Of course these unactual states of affairs *exist* all right—they exist just as robustly as your most solidly actual state of affairs. But they aren't actual. So there are any number of things that aren't actual; what there aren't any of is things that don't *exist*. 'Existentialism' would be a better sobriquet for the view in question, but of course that name has already been preempted; so 'actualism' will have to do. And let's use '*serious* actualism' as a name for the claim that necessarily, no object could have had a property or stood in a relation without existing—the view, that is, that nothing has any properties in any world in which it does not exist.

Now suppose we return to existentialism. We might initially be inclined to reject it by arguing that singular propositions and quidditative properties are abstract objects and therefore exist necessarily. But not all abstract objects are necessary beings; sets with contingent members, for example, are not—not, at least, if serious actualism is correct. For if it is, then if Quine had not existed, Quine's singleton would not have contained him. But surely Quine's singleton could not have existed but been empty (in which case it would have been the null set); neither could it have contained something distinct from Quine. *Containing Quine* and *containing nothing distinct from Quine* are surely essential properties of Quine's singleton; hence there is no possible world in which it exists but he does not. Quine's singleton, then, is just as contingent as is Quine himself. And of course the same goes for other sets that contain him. If Quine had not existed, the set in fact denoted by the phrase 'the set of human beings' would not have existed. Of course that phrase would have denoted a set, even if Quine had not existed— but a *different* set.

---

[3] The Nature of Necessity (Oxford, 1974), pp. 121–63.

So not all abstract objects are necessary beings. Still, what about properties? It is natural to think, indeed, that a crucial difference between sets and properties lies just here. Sets are ontologically dependent upon their members; hence a set with a contingent member is itself contingent. But properties with contingent exemplification typically aren't ontologically dependent upon those exemplifications. The set of dogs—the set that is in fact the set of dogs—would not have existed had my dog Mischa or any other dog failed to exist; but the property *being a dog* can get by perfectly well whether or not there are any dogs at all. Why suppose it is any different with quidditative properties?

Robert Adams offers an argument: "to be the property of being identical with a particular individual is to stand in a unique relationship to that individual. . . . So if there were a thisness of a non-actual individual, it would stand in a relation to that individual. But according to actualism non-actual individuals cannot enter into any relations. It seems to follow that according to actualism there cannot be a thisness of a non-actual individual."[4] But this statement of the issue isn't wholly accurate. The question isn't whether there are thisnesses of non-actual, that is, nonexistent individuals—of course there aren't, because there aren't any nonexistent individuals. In the same way there aren't any shapes of nonexistent individuals—i.e., no shape is the shape of a non-existent individual. The question is rather whether any thisness could have existed if what it is the thisness of had not. The question is whether, for example, my thisness could have existed if I hadn't. Of course if I hadn't existed, the property that is *in fact* my thisness wouldn't have been my thisness; it would not have been related to me by the relation *being the thisness of.* But it doesn't follow that it couldn't have existed if I hadn't. If I hadn't existed, my brother-in-law would not have been my brother-in-law; he would not have had the property of being related to me by the brother-in-law relation. But it doesn't follow that he couldn't have existed if I hadn't. Having that property is not essential to him; he could have existed whether or not I had. And of course the question about me and my thisness is whether the property of being exemplified by me is essential to it. Since we are given that the property *being exemplified by me if at all* is essential to it, the real question is whether being *exemplified* is essential to it: and it isn't in the least obvious that it *is*. Adams holds that an object may have a *qualitative* essence—an essence that doesn't involve a thisness—and the qualitative essence of an object, he thinks, would have existed even if the object hadn't. Of course, if I had not existed, my qualitative essence wouldn't have been my qualitative essence; it wouldn't have been related to me by the *is-the-qualitative-essence-of* relation. But it could have existed even if I hadn't. Why suppose things are different in the case of my thisness?

Taken as an argument, therefore, the above considerations are inconclusive. I suspect, however, that they aren't really intended as an argument; they are more like an appeal to intuition. Isn't it just clear or obvious that the property *being Socrates* could not have existed if Socrates had not existed? What would my thisness have *been,* if I hadn't existed? But it doesn't seem to me, on reflection, to be

---

[4] "Actualism and Thisness," *Synthese* 49 (1981), p. 5.

the least bit obvious. And would my thisness have been, if I hadn't existed? It would have been an unexemplified essence that could have been the thisness of something.

I turn now to the line of argument for the second existentialist thesis—the thesis that singular propositions are ontologically dependent upon the objects they are directly about. Consider again

(1) William F. Buckley is wise

and

(2) The Lion of Conservativism is wise.

On the view in question (1) could have failed to exist, and would have done so if Buckley had not existed. (2), on the other hand, is quite impervious to the harrowing vicissitudes besetting contingent objects, and would have existed no matter what. Why the difference?

One line of argument, or at any rate one "consideration determining the intellect," to use John Stuart Mill's phrase, goes as follows. It is plausible to join Mill in supposing that "Proper Names are not connotative; they denote the individuals who are called by them, but they do not indicate or imply an attribute as belonging to these individuals."[5] Proper names, says Mill, have denotation but no connotation: a proper name denotes its referent but does not express a property. He seems to mean that the sole semantic function performed by a proper name is that of denoting its referent; its semantic function is *exhausted* in denoting its referent. The first premise of this argument, then, is that proper names do not express properties. The second premise is the plausible view that sentences containing proper names do in fact express propositions. And the third premise is that a proposition is an articulated structure containing *constituents* standing in relation to each other. It's not at all clear what a constituent of a proposition is supposed to be; but among the constituents of the proposition *all men are mortal* one would find, presumably, the properties *humanity* and *mortality*.

Now suppose you accept these three premises: what sort of proposition will be expressed by a sentence like (1) if the proper name it contains does not express a property? What would be the constituents of such a proposition—what would be, so to speak, its subject-place constituent? What more natural than to take William F. Buckley himself, that fugleman of the right, as a constituent of the proposition expressed by (1)? On this view, singular propositions include among their constituents not just abstracta, such as Buckley's essence, but concreta, such as Buckley himself. If one holds that propositions have constituents, that proper names do not express properties, and that sentences containing them express propositions, then the view that such propositions contain concrete objects as constituents can seem quite compelling.

Now those who think that propositions have constituents, think of the constituency relation as essential to the constitutee, but not, in the general case, to the

---

[5] *A System of Logic* (New York, 1846), p. 21.

constituent; that is, if *a* is a constituent of *b*, then *b* couldn't exist without having *a* as a constituent, although it is not true in general that *b* could not have existed without being a constituent of *a*. Both William F. Buckley and Paul X. Zwier are constituents of the proposition *Paul Zwier is more conservative than William Buckley,* so if either of them had failed to exist, the same fate would have befallen that proposition. Obviously, however, Buckley could have existed even if Zwier hadn't; accordingly Buckley could have existed even if that proposition hadn't. And hence (given serious actualism) being a constituent of it is not essential to him. So the fourth premise of the argument is: if a concrete object *O* is a constituent of a proposition *P*, then *P* is ontologically dependent upon *O*. To summarize the argument, then: sentences containing proper names express propositions that have concrete and contingent objects as constituents. But the constituency relation is essential to the constituted object; hence singular propositions—many of them, at any rate-are ontologically dependent upon contingent individuals.

Now I think this is at best a weak argument for the existentialist thesis in question; and its weakness results from the obscurity of the premises involving the notion of *constituency.* What exactly, or even approximately, *is* this relationship *being a constituent of ?* Do we know or have reason to suspect that propositions *have* constituents? What can we say about the relation that holds between an object—a concept, property, concrete individual or whatever—and a proposition, when the former is a constituent of the latter? Maybe not much. Some philosophers suggest that the sort of proposition expressed by sentences like (1) can be *represented by* or *taken as* a set-theoretical entity of some sort—an ordered pair, perhaps, whose first member is William F. Buckley and whose second is the property of being wise. Of course if this proposition *were* such an ordered pair, then perhaps we could say what its constituents were: perhaps they would be the members of its transitive closure. Presumably, however, the claim is not that such propositions *really are* ordered pairs, but only that we can fittingly *represent* or *take* them as such, in the way in which for some purposes we can take the natural numbers as sets of one kind or another. We have imbibed with our mother's milk the idea that we can 'identify' the natural numbers with any of various sequences of sets. We can also identify them with other things: for example, we could identify zero with Richard Wagner and the rest of the natural numbers with propositions about him: *Wagner has written just one opera, Wagner has written just two operas,* and so on. All we need for such identification is a countably infinite set of objects together with a recursive relation under which they form a progression. But of course the fact that natural numbers can be thus identified with sets of one sort or another doesn't at all imply that they really *are* sets, or have as constituents the members of the sets with which we identify them. And the same holds for propositions and ordered pairs of the sort mentioned above. Perhaps for some purposes we can identify the former with the latter; but it doesn't follow that the former have as constituents the members of the latter. It is therefore hard to see that the above suggestion—the suggestion that singular propositions can be represented or taken as certain sets—throws any light on the constituency relation.

Of course there clearly is an interesting relationship between the proposition *All men are mortal* and the properties *being a man* and *being mortal*—a relationship that doesn't hold between that proposition and, say, the number seven or the Taj Mahal or the property of being a horse. And no doubt we have something of a grasp—inchoate and groping as it may be—of this relation. So, for example, we can grasp enough of the relation in question to see that a proposition couldn't be a constituent of a person. But could a person be a constituent of a proposition? I feel as if I have a grasp of this notion of constituency when I'm told that, say, wisdom but not beauty is a constituent of the proposition *Socrates is wise;* but when it is added that Socrates himself is also a constituent of that proposition, I begin to lose my sense of what's being talked about. If an abstract object like a proposition has constituents, wouldn't they themselves have to be abstract?

But secondly: if we're prepared to suppose something as initially *outré* as that persons can be constituents of propositions, why insist that a proposition is ontologically dependent upon its constituents? Why boggle at the idea that a proposition could exist even if one of its constituents didn't? Perhaps the proposition expressed by (1) has Buckley as a constituent but would have existed even if he had not. If it had, perhaps it would have been slightly ill-formed or even maimed; but couldn't it exist nonetheless?

This argument, therefore, is inconclusive. It's not at all clear what is being claimed when its claimed that propositions have constituents. Insofar as we have a grasp of that notion, however, it is very hard to see how a person could be a constituent of a proposition. And even if propositions do contain persons as constituents, why suppose that containing a given person as constituent is *essential* to a proposition?

III. An Anti-Existentialist Argument

I want to propose an argument against existentialism—specifically, an argument against the existentialist thesis that singular propositions are ontologically dependent upon contingent objects. The argument begins from an obvious fact. Surely it's possible that Socrates should not have existed; unlike God and the number seven, Socrates is not a necessary being. So the proposition *possibly Socrates does not exist* is true, and the proposition *Socrates does not exist* is possible, that is, possibly true. But that proposition could not have been true without existing. Furthermore, if it *had* been true, Socrates would not have existed. If it had been true, therefore, it would have existed but Socrates would not have existed. It is therefore possible that the proposition *Socrates does not exist* exists when Socrates does not—contrary to the claims of existentialism, according to which that proposition has Socrates as a constituent and hence is ontologically dependent upon him.

Tidying up the argument a bit, we can see it as proceeding from the following five premises:

(3) Possibly Socrates does not exist.

(4) If (3) then the proposition *Socrates does not exist* is possible.

    (5) If the proposition *Socrates does not exist* is possible, then it is possibly true.

    (6) Necessarily, if *Socrates does not exist* had been true, then *Socrates does not exist* would have existed.

and

    (7) Necessarily if *Socrates does not exist* had been true, then Socrates would not have existed.

From (3), (4) and (5) it follows that

    (8) *Socrates does not exist* is possibly true,

i.e., that proposition could have been true; from (6) and (7) it follows that

    (9) Necessarily, if *Socrates does not exist* had been true, then *Socrates does not exist* would have existed and Socrates would not have existed;

and from (8) and (9) it follows that

    (10) It is possible that both Socrates does not exist and the proposition *Socrates does not exist* exists,

which contradicts existentialism.

    Now I take it that premises (3) and (7) are relatively uncontroversial; so the controversial premises, if any, are (4), (5) and (6). (4), I think, is the next least controversial premise. It has been denied, however, by Lawrence Powers.[6] *Powersian Existentialism,* accordingly, is the sort of existentialism that rejects (4). What can be said for that rejection? Now of course we must grant that "possibly" in (3) is an operator rather than a predicate; and we must also grant that certain natural ways of formalizing the attempt to construct the modal operators as predicates of sentences, rapidly come to grief. State (4) is surely not properly rejectable. Suppose we agree that there are such things as propositions and that propositions are the things that are true or false. (We can say that a *sentence* is true if it expresses a true proposition.) Then surely we will regard truth and falsehood as properties of propositions. Furthermore, such a proposition as *It's true that all men are mortal* is true if and only if the proposition *all men are mortal* is true—despite the fact that "It's true that" is an operator, not a predicate. Now surely the same goes for

    (11) Possibly Socrates does not exist.

Possibility, obviously, is a property of propositions; it is an alethic modality, a mode of truth. How could (11) be true if the proposition *Socrates does not exist* were not possible? What proposition would the sentence (11) express, if it didn't express one entailing that *Socrates does not exist* is possible? (11), surely, is true if and only if *Socrates does not exist* is possible. So (4) should be accepted and Powersian Existentialism rejected.

---

[6] In conversation; I'm not certain Powers was altogether serious.

(6)′ I think, is the next least controversial premise; according to (6), *Socrates does not exist* is such that it couldn't have been true without existing. Another way to put the same point: '*Socrates does not exist*' is true entails '*Socrates does not exist*' exists. Still another way to put it: every possible world in which *Socrates does not exist* is true, is one in which it exists. This premise has been denied, at least provisionally, by John Pollock; *Pollockian Existentialism*, therefore, is the sort of existentialism that denies (6).

Now (6) is really a specification of *serious actualism*—the view that no object could have had a property without existing. Stated alternatively, serious actualism is the view that necessarily, for any object x and property P, it's not possible that x should have had P but not existed. Stated in terms of possible worlds, serious actualism is the view that necessarily no object has a property in a world in which it does not exist; that is, it is necessary that for any possible world W and property P and object x, if it is true that if W had been actual, then x would have had P, then it is true that if W had been actual, x would have existed. As our official statement of serious actualism, let's adopt

(12) Necessarily for any object x, possible world W, and property P, if x has P in W, then x exists in W

where an object x has a property P in a world W if and only if it is not possible that W be actual and x fail to have P.

Now it may be tempting to suppose[7] that serious actualism is a corollary of actualism *tout court*. For suppose, in accord with actualism, that

(13) There are no nonexistent objects

is necessarily true and hence true in every possible world. Then the same can be said for

(14) For any property P, there are no nonexistent objects that have P

that is,

(15) Whatever has P, exists.

Now consider Socrates, and let P be any property and W be any world in which Socrates has P. Then

(16) Socrates has P

is true in W; since (15) is also true in W, so is

(17) Socrates exists.

But then it follows that if Socrates has a property P in a world W, Socrates exists in W; and of course the same goes for everything else.

---

[7] As I did in "De essentia," *Grazer Philosophische Studien* (1979), pp. 108–9. I am indebted to John Pollock who helped me see the error of my ways.

Now I said it was tempting thus to infer serious actualism from actualism but the above argument represents at best a bit of flocculent thinking. We can see this as follows. If actualism is true, then

(18) Whatever does *not* exist, exists

is true in every possible world; few would be tempted to infer, however, that if Socrates does not exist in a world W^*, then he exists in that world. The trouble with the argument, obviously, is the following: (15) is indeed true in W, as is (16). To infer that (17) is true in W, however, we must suppose that

(19) If Socrates has P, then Socrates exists

is also true there. One thinks of (19) as following from (15) by Universal Instantiation. (15) says that everything there is—everything that exists and everything else as well, if there is anything else—has a certain property *being such that if it has P, then it exists*. (19) (construed *de re* as *Socrates is such that if he has P then he exists*) says just that Socrates has the property. (15) says everything there is has. But then clearly (19) doesn't follow from (15) alone. Another premise is needed: the premise that Socrates is one of the things there are. Of course this premise is true in fact, but perhaps it isn't true in W. So from the fact that (15) is true in W, we cannot properly infer that (19) is also true in W.

From actualism *tout court*, therefore, we cannot properly infer serious actualism. The latter is a separate thesis and requires separate affirmation. And isn't it just false? For consider any world W^* in which Socrates does not exist: Socrates will not have the property of being wise in W^*; so

(20) Socrates is not wise.

is true in W^*; so Socrates has the property of not being wise in W^*. But of course it won't follow that he exists in W^*. In the same way, Socrates does not exist in W^*. But of course it doesn't follow from *that*, that he exists in W^*. To take another sort of example,

(21) If Socrates is wise, someone is wise

predicates a property of Socrates: *being such that if he is wise, someone is*. But (21) is also necessarily true; Socrates, therefore, has the property (21) predicates of him in every possible world—even those in which he does not exist.

But the answer to these claims is clear; the sentences (20) and (21) are ambiguous. (20) is ambiguous as between

(20*) Socrates is unwise

a proposition predicating of him the complement of *being wise*, and

(20**) It's not the case that Socrates is wise

a proposition that doesn't predicate anything of Socrates but predicates falsehood of the proposition *Socrates is wise*. (20*), we may say, is *predicative* with respect to Socrates; (20**) is *impredicative* with respect to him. A similar comment is to be made about (21). The sentence (21) is ambiguous as between

(21*) Socrates is such that if he is wise, something is

a proposition that is predicative with respect to Socrates and predicates of him the widely shared property of being such that if he is wise, then someone is, and a proposition equivalent to

(21**) The propositions *Socrates is wise* and *someone is wise* are such that if the first is true, then so is the second,

which is impredicative with respect to Socrates. (21*) is predicative with respect to Socrates, and contingent, being false in those possible worlds in which Socrates does not exist. (21**), on the other hand, is necessary, but does not predicate a property of Socrates. Exactly similar comments apply to

(22) Either Socrates is wise or Socrates is not wise.

(23) is ambiguous as between a contingent proposition predicating of Socrates the property *being either wise or not wise,* and a necessary proposition impredicative with respect to Socrates (but predicative with respect to the propositions *Socrates is wise* and *it's not the case that Socrates is wise*). So the proffered examples certainly don't show that serious actualism is false.

Still, isn't there something arbitrary and *ad hoc,* in the present context, about insisting that *Buckley is wise* predicates a property of Buckley while *It's not the case that Buckley is wise* does not? Not really, I think, although *ad hocness* is sufficiently slippery to make it hard to be sure. In any event, let's agree that there are *conditions* as well as properties. For any property *P,* there is the condition of having *P,* and also the condition of not having *P.* Conditions are met by objects, and met by objects in possible worlds. To meet the condition of having *P* in *W,* an object must have *P* in *W;* to meet the condition of not having *P* in *W* an object must not have *P* in *W.* Furthermore, if an object fails to meet the condition of having *P* in *W,* then it meets the condition of failing to have *P* in *W,* although of course it doesn't follow that it meets the condition of having *P* in *W.* Still further, there are such conditions as *having P or not having P,* a condition met by everything in every possible world. Then while it may be the case that no object has any *property* in any world in which it does not exist, an object may perfectly well meet *conditions* in worlds in which it does not exist. And while serious actualism may be *true,* from this perspective it looks considerably less substantial.

Now this maneuver, I think, is fruitless. There *really is* an important distinction between failing to have a property *P* in a world and having its complement in that world; failing to have *P* in *W,* furthermore, is not having *P,* the complement of *P* in *W,* or indeed any other property. The serious actualist claims that an object exists in any world in which it has a property *P,* but of course she doesn't claim that an object exists in every world in which it *doesn't* have *P.* Furthermore, it isn't at all easy to see what sort of thing a *condition* is, or to state the conditions under which an object meets a condition in a world.

But suppose we waive these considerations and agree that there are conditions. Among the conditions there will be *being wise* and *failing to be wise; being unwise* and *failing to be unwise; existing* and *failing to exist.* For any condition *C,* the proposition *everything that meets C exists* is necessarily true; but of course it is not true in general that if an object meets *C* in a world *W,* then it exists in *W.* Now some conditions will be *existence entailing,* they will be such that (necessarily) for any object *x* and world *W,* if *x* meets *C* in *W,* then *x* exists in *W.* Others will not; and the serious actualist will hold that any condition of the sort *has P* (where *P* is a property) is existence entailing, while those of the sort *does not have P* are not. Here the serious actualist is correct, I believe; but for present purposes we needn't argue that general point. For suppose we return to

> (6) Necessarily, if *Socrates does not exist* had been true, then *Socrates does not exist* would have existed

the premise of the anti-existentialist argument that occasioned our excursion into serious actualism. Our question is really whether *being true* is existence entailing. The question is whether there is a proposition *P* and a possible state of affairs *S* such that if *S* had been actual, then *P* would have been true but nonexistent—i.e., *P* would have been true and there wouldn't have been any such thing as *P.* The answer, it seems to me, is obvious. Clearly there is no such state of affairs and proposition. Clearly no proposition could have been true without existing. Clearly every state of affairs which is such that if it had been actual, *P* would have been true, is also such that if it had been true, then *P* would have existed. (6), therefore, ought to be accepted and Pollockian Existentialism, like Powersian, should be rejected.

IV. Priorian Existentialism

Now suppose we turn our attention to

> (5) If the proposition *Socrates does not exist* is possible, then it is possibly true,

the most controversial premise of the anti-existentialist argument. Among those who deny (5) are Arthur Prior,[8] Kit Fine,[9] and Robert Adams.[10] *Priorian Existentialism,* therefore, is the brand of existentialism that denies (5); the Priorian existentialist believes that a proposition can be *possible* without being *possibly true.* This is initially puzzling—*very* puzzling. If possibility, for a proposition, isn't possible truth, what is it? If a proposition could not have been true, how can it be possible? If someone held that there are many possible worlds, but only

---

[8] "Theories of Actuality" in *The Possible and the Actual,* ed. M. Loux (Ithaca: Cornell University Press, 1979), p. 201.

[9] "Postscript" in *World, Times, and Selves,* pp. 116ff.

[10] "Actualism and Thisness" (see also note 4).

the actual world could have been actual, then according to Robert Adams, 'we would be left to wonder in what sense the other possible worlds are possible, since they couldn't have been actual.' But doesn't the same hold for possibility and possible truth when propositions are the topic of discussion? Indeed, it looks as if there aren't *two* concepts here, but only one; it looks as if '*Socrates does not exist* is possible' (in the broadly logical sense) and '*Socrates does not exist* is possibly true' express the very same proposition. Possibility and necessity, after all, are *alethic* modalities-modalities of *truth*. It looks initially as if 'possible' just *means* 'possibly true'; what else *is* there for it to mean? What can Prior, Fine, Adams *et al.* be thinking of?

One way we can understand this alleged contrast between possibility and possible truth has been suggested (perhaps a bit obscurely) by Arthur Prior possibility, as opposed to possible truth, is *possible non-falsehood*. To get a grasp of this notion, we must turn to the idea of essential attribution. An object x has a property P essentially if and only if it is impossible that x exist and lack P—alternatively (given serious actualism), if and only if it is impossible that x have the complement of P. Socrates, for example, has essentially the properties *being a person* and *being self-identical;* it is impossible that Socrates should have existed and lacked these properties, and impossible that he should have had either of their complements. On the other hand, there could have been no such thing as Socrates at all, in which case Socrates would not have had these or any other properties. Accordingly it is possible that Socrates should not have had these properties.

Now suppose we agree, for purposes of argument, that the number nine is a necessary being; it could not have failed to exist. (If you think numbers are contingent beings, substitute your favorite necessary being for the number nine.) Like Socrates, the number nine has some of its properties essentially—*being a number,* for example, and *being composite.* In contrast to Socrates, however, nine could not have failed to exist; and hence it is not possible that nine should have lacked these properties. We might mark this difference by saying that Socrates has the property of being a person *essentially*, but nine has the property of being a number *necessarily.* An object x has a property P necessarily if and only if it is necessary that the former have the latter and only if the state of affairs consisting in x's having P could not have failed to obtain. Alternatively, x has P necessarily if and only if x has P essentially and x is a necessary being. So Socrates has the property of being a person essentially; God, if classical theists are right, has that property necessarily. Everything, trivially, has existence essentially—that is, nothing could have existed but failed to exist. Only such necessary beings as God, however, have existence necessarily.

But now we must not make a similar distinction among propositions. If only some of them are necessary beings, we shall have to distinguish *having truth essentially* from *having truth necessarily.* A proposition p has truth essentially if and only if it is not possible that p should have existed and lacked truth alternatively (given that no proposition can be neither true nor false) if and only if it is not possible that p exist and be false, that is (given (6)), if and only if it is not possible that p be false. A proposition will have truth *necessarily* or *be necessarily true*, however, if and only if it has truth essentially and furthermore exists necessarily, could not have failed to exist. So p is necessarily true if and only if it is not possible that p fail to be true. Every necessary truth is an essential truth; but if the present brand of existentialism is right, the converse does not hold. The proposition *Socrates exists,* for example, could not have been false. It could have failed to exist, however, and hence could have failed to be true; it is therefore essentially but not necessarily true. And now the claim is that to say that *Socrates does not exist* is possible, is only to say that it is possibly non-false—could have failed to be false. But of course that does not entail, say, the Priorian, that it could have been true—that is, is possibly true.

Now I think we can see that Priorian Existentialism, like the Powersian and Pollockian varieties, cannot be right. The fundamental reason is that if it *were* right, propositions like

(23) Socrates does not exist

would not be possible after all; and if we know anything at all about these matters, we know that (23) is possible. Let me explain.

First, the Priorian existentialist will concede or rather insist that (23) is not *possibly true*. (23) would be true only if it existed, which it could do only if Socrates also existed; but then of course it would not be true. Nor, furthermore, is (23) true in some possible world. If there were a possible world in which (23) is true, that would be a world in which Socrates does not exist. But (23) does not exist in any world in which Socrates does not; so if (23) is true in some world, it is true in a world in which it does not exist—which, the Priorian concedes, is impossible.

According to Priorian Existentialism, then, (23) is neither possibly true nor true in some possible world. How, then, can it be thought of as possible? The Priorian will reply, of course, that (23) could have failed to be false. It could not have been true; but it could have failed to be false. There are possible worlds in which it is not false: the worlds in which Socrates does not exist. I said that if we know anything at all about modality, we know that (23) is possible; from the point of view of Priorian Existentialism this intuition does not require possible truth. Possible non-falsehood is possibility enough. But surely this is wrong; possible non-falsehood is not possibility enough. In the first place, entirely too many propositions are possibly non-false: for example,

(24) Socrates is self-diverse

and even such explicit contradictions as

(25) Socrates is wise and Socrates is not wise.

According to the existentialist, (24) and (25) are possibly non-false; they would not have existed and hence would not have been false if there had been no such thing as Socrates. But surely there is no sensible conception of possibility at all in which (24) and (25) are possible.

Second, (24) and (25) imply, respectively,

(26) there is at least one thing that is self-diverse,

and

(27) there is at least one thing that is both wise and not wise

in the first order logic. But (26) and (27) aren't even so much as possibly non-false. Possible non-falsehood is therefore not closed under logical implication—a crucially serious impairment for a candidate for possibility.

But the clinching point, I think, is the following. What was the alleged insight behind existentialism in the first place? That it is impossible that objects of which we might say Socrates is a constituent—singular propositions directly about him, possible worlds containing him, his essences, and the like—should have existed if he had not. If E is any entity of that sort, the idea was that

(28) E exists and Socrates does not

is impossible. This is the central existentialist insight. But note that (28), from the Priorian perspective, is possibly non-false; it would have failed to be false if Socrates had not existed. So if possible non-falsehood is possibility enough, (28) is possible after all. The Priorian existentialist is thus hoist on his own petard. His fundamental insight is that (28) is not possible; he therefore argues that propositions such as (23) are not necessary beings. This apparently conflicts with the obvious truth that such propositions are possible. The proffered resolution consists in claiming that possible non-falsehood is sufficient; but then (28) is possible after all.

The moral to be drawn, I think, is that possibility, for a proposition, is possible truth; there is nothing else for it to be. The alleged distinction between possible truth and possibility is a confusion. According to Prior,[11] Jean Buridan distinguished the *possible* from the *possibly true*. Buridan, however, apparently drew this distinction not for *propositions*, but for *sentences*—more exactly, sentence tokens. And here Buridan is correct. A sentence token is true (or true in English) if it expresses (in English) a true proposition; it is possible (we may say) if it expresses a possible truth—if the proposition it express (in English) is possible, i.e., possibly true. The sentence token

(29) there are not sentence tokens,

then, is possible. It could not have been true (in English), however; for to be true it would have had to exist: in which case it would not have been true. We could therefore say, if we wished, that (29) is possible but not possibly true. But there is no similar distinction in the case of propositions: possibility, for a proposition, is possible truth. Truth and falsehood are the salient characteristics of propositions; it is therefore natural to use 'possible' to abbreviate 'possibly true' (rather than, say, 'possibly existent' or 'possibly Paul's favorite proposition').

---

[11]"The Possibly-True and the Possible," in *Papers in Logic and Ethics* (Amherst: University of Massachusetts Press, 1976), p. 202.

But to argue that (23) is possible on the grounds that it could have failed to be false, is like arguing that Socrates is possibly a number or possibly self-diverse on the grounds that he could have failed to have the properties of being a non-number and being self-identical. Indeed he could have failed to have these properties; had he not existed, Socrates would not have had these or any other properties. It is sheer confusion, however, to conclude that he is possibly a number or possibly self-diverse. Similarly, then, for propositions: if some propositions—e.g., (23)—are contingent objects, then those propositions could have failed to be false. It is sheer confusion, however, to conclude that they are possible.

Priorian Existentialism, therefore, is as unacceptable as the Powersian and Pollockian varieties. The conclusion to be drawn is that the anti-existentialist argument is sound and existentialism must be rejected.

TRANSWORLD IDENTITY, SINGULAR PROPOSITIONS, AND PICTURE-THINKING*

Matthew Davidson

"A picture held is captive. . ."
—Wittgenstein, Philosophical Investigations

I. Transworld Identity

In the late 1960s, the dreaded "problem of transworld identity" arose within the metaphysics of modality. So, we read David Kaplan in 1967:

> I'll even let you peep through my Jules Verne-o-scope [into another possible world G]. Carefully examine each individual, check his fingerprints, etc. The problem is: which one is *our* Bobby Dylan—of course he may be somewhat changed, just as he will be in our world in a few years. . . . Our problem is [to] locate him in G (if he exists there). The task of locating individuals in other worlds is the problem of determining transworld heir lines. I will flatly assert that this problem is the central problem of philosophical interest in the development of intensional logic.

The clearest statements of the "problem" came from those who thought that, ultimately, there was no problem (or at least that it certainly was soluble). Alvin Plantinga (1973) writes:

> [T]he problem may perhaps be put as follows. Let us suppose again that Socrates exists in some world *W* distinct from this one—a world in which let us say, he did not fight in the battle of Marathon. In *W*, of course, he may also lack other properties he has in this world—perhaps in *W* he eschewed philosophy, corrupted no youth, and thus escaped the wrath of the Athenians.

* I would like to thank Tony Roy, Gordon Barnes, Alvin Plantinga, Jay Atlas, and Peter van Inwagen for helpful discussion of these issues.

Perhaps in *W* he lived in Corinth, was six feet tall, and remained a bachelor all his life. But then we must ask ourselves how we could possible *identify* Socrates in that world. How could we *pick him out?* How could we *locate* him there? How could we possibly tell which of the many things contained in *W* is *Socrates?* If we try to employ the properties we use to identify him in *this* world, our efforts may well end in dismal failure—perhaps in that world it is Xenophon or maybe even Thrasymachus that is Plato's mentor and exhibits the splendidly single-minded passion for truth and justice that characterizes Socrates in this. But if we cannot identify him in *W*, so the argument continues, then we really do not understand the assertion that he exists there. . . . In order to make sense of such talk, we must have a *criterion* or *principle* that enables us to identify Socrates from world to world. The criterion must include some property that Socrates has in each world in which he exists. . . . Further, if the property (or property) in question is to enable us to pick him out, it must in some broad sense be "empirically manifest"—it must resemble such properties as having such-and-such a name, address, Social Security number, height, weight, and general appearance in that we can tell by broadly empirical means whether a given object has or lacks it. Now, obviously we do not know of any such property, or even that there is such a property. But then the very idea of transworld identity is not really intelligible. . . . (p. 76)[1]

Saul Kripke says something similar:

Suppose we have someone, Nixon, and there's another possible world where there is no one with all the properties Nixon has in the actual world. Which of these other people, if any, is Nixon? (1980, p. 42).

It now is generally accepted that there was no problem of transworld identity, or if there was a problem of transworld identity, the situation wasn't as dire as some made it out to be. It was a "problem" that arose from bad picture-thinking about possible worlds. Plantinga writes:

The first thing to note about the [problem of transworld identity] is that it seems to arise out of a certain *picture* or *image*. We imagine ourselves somehow peering into another world . . . observe the behavior and characteristics of its denizens and then wonder about which of these, if any, is Socrates. . . . Now perhaps this picture is useful in certain respects; in the present context, however, it breeds nothing but confusion (1973, p. 77).

And Kripke (1980, pp. 43–44):

[T]his depends on the wrong way of looking at what a possible world is. One thinks, in this picture, of a possible world as if it were like a foreign country. One looks upon it as an observer. Maybe Nixon has moved to the other country and maybe he hasn't, but one is given only qualities.

[I]t seems to me not to be the right way of thinking about possible worlds. A possible world isn't a distant country that we are coming across, or viewing through a telescope.

---

[1] The pagination is from Alvin Plantinga. *Essays in the Metaphysics of Modality*, ed. Matthew Davidson (New York: Oxford University Press, 2003).

And Peter van Inwagen (1985, p. 112):

> The problem of transworld identity would seem, therefore, to be a deep and intractable problem. . . . As I have implied, however, this seeming is a mere seeming. It is an illusion one falls into as a consequence of thinking about possible worlds with the aid of pictures . . . drawn according to a convention that represents the *exists-in* relation by the placing of one symbol inside another symbol. This sort of convention encourages one to think of possible worlds as things that have insides, as enormous physical objects. (And if one thinks of possible worlds as enormous physical objects, then one probably will think that 'exists in' means something like 'is located within'.) But possible worlds are not enormous physical objects.[2]

To conclude this short piece of recent philosophical history, philosophers, for the most part, have come to realize that the problem of transworld identity arose from bad metaphysical picture-thinking. We might characterize it with the following diagram:

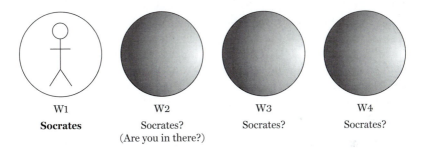

W1	W2	W3	W4
Socrates	Socrates? (Are you in there?)	Socrates?	Socrates?

If you think of possible worlds as entities with things contained inside them—akin to islands or circles on a blackboard—the problem of transworld identity may seem to have force. But once one realizes that possible worlds are abstract objects, and are not spatially located at all, the problem goes away. People took the metaphor of a "world" too seriously, and this led to needless confusion. Thanks to the work of people like Plantinga and Kripke, we have seen the error of our ways.

Or have we? Most no longer think there is a problem of transworld identity, but the very same sort of picture-thinking which gave rise to the problem of transworld identity can be found in a response to a powerful attack on direct reference (see Plantinga, 1983, and Davidson 2000). The attack, briefly, is this. The direct reference theorist thinks that concrete individuals, like Clinton, can be constituents of propositions. The proposition expressed by "Clinton does not exist" has Clinton as a constituent. It is false (now) in the actual world, and it exists in the actual world. But consider a world W where Clinton does not exist. If there is no Clinton, the proposition expressed by "Clinton does not exist" lacks a constituent and so itself does not exist. So, it is not true in W. But it should be true in W; Clinton does not exist there.

---

[2] This, of course, won't be true for David Lewis. But I will take possible worlds to be abstract.

II. Truth and Existence in a World

Before looking at the problem raised in the last paragraph, it is important to note one innocuous sense in which an object may exist in a world or a proposition may be true in a world. These analyses were given by Plantinga (1974), and are very straightforward. We have:

(T$_1$) Necessarily, a proposition p is *true in a world W* iff necessarily, if W is actual, then p is true

and

(E$_W$) Necessarily, an object x *exists in a world W* iff necessarily, if W is actual, then x exists.

So, if we want to talk about an object existing in a world in the sense of (E$_W$), then we're fine. (E$_W$) is easy to understand and unproblematic. Perhaps the terminology here—existence *in* a world is a bit infelicitous; if one is careless one might stray into thinking that worlds are things with insides and outsides. But so long as we keep Plantinga's analyses in mind for truth and existence in a world, we should be able to avoid the sort of bad picture-thinking that led to the problem of transworld identity even if we want to talk about objects in possible worlds.

III. Two Sorts of Truth?

Many philosophers working in the metaphysics of modality have maintained that there are two ways a proposition may be true with respect to a world (see Adams 1981; Fine 1977, 1985; Pollock 1984, 1985; Kaplan 1989a, 1989b; Almog 1985; Fitch 1996; Branquinho 2003). According to these philosophers, not only is there truth *in* a world (in the sense given in our (T$_1$)), but there also is what Robert Adams calls truth *at* a world. If a proposition is true in a world, it exists in that world.[3] However, a proposition may be true at a world without existing *in* that world. Robert Adams writes:

> A world-story [possible world] that includes no singular proposition about me constitutes and describes a possible world in which I would not exist. It represents my possible non-existence, not by including the proposition that I do not exist but simply by omitting me. That I would not exist if all the propositions it includes, and no other actual propositions, were true is not a fact internal to the world that it describes, but an observation that we make from our vantage point in the actual world, about the relation of that world-story to an individual of the actual world.
>
> Let me mark this difference in point of view by saying that the proposition that I never exist is (in the actual world) true *at* many possible worlds, but *in* none. (1981, p. 22)

---

[3] I assume here the truth of *serious actualism,* the claim that necessarily, objects have properties only in worlds where they exist. The term comes from Alvin Plantinga. For discussion of serious actualism see (Plantinga, 1979, 1983, 1985, 2003); Bergmann (1999), and Davidson (2000).

Kit Fine (1985, p. 163) talks about an "inner sense" of truth and an "outer sense" of truth. He says:

> One should distinguish between two senses of truth for a proposition, the *inner* and the *outer*. According to the outer notion, a proposition is true in a possible world regardless of whether it exists in that world; according to the inner notion, a proposition is true in a possible world only if it exists in that world. We may put the distinction in terms of perspective. According to the outer notion, we can stand outside a world and compare the proposition with what goes on in the world in order to ascertain whether it is true. But according to the inner notion, we must first enter with the proposition into the world before ascertaining its truth.

Direct reference theorists take it that singular propositions exist only in worlds where their "subjects" exist. In this way, their ontologies are impoverished with respect to certain possible worlds: those in which certain entities don't exist. It *seems* that propositions to the effect that those entities don't exist should be true in those worlds; but, of course, on this view they can't be. So, at this point the direct reference theorist invokes the true-in vs. true-at distinction. Thus, consider the proposition *Socrates exists*. For a direct reference theorist, it contains the individual Socrates as a constituent. There are possible worlds with respect to which this proposition is false: These will be the worlds in which Socrates does not exist. However, *Socrates does not exist* cannot be true *in* these worlds, it would seem; Socrates doesn't exist in the world to be a constituent of the proposition.

It is at this point that the concept of truth *at* a world arrives to save the day. *Socrates does not exist* is true *in* no worlds. Yet, in some sense "with respect to" worlds where Socrates doesn't exist, there is a strong intuition that *Socrates does not exist* is true. So, a weaker sense of truth with respect to a world than is involved in (T_1) is employed: *Socrates does not exist* is true *at* every world in which Socrates does not exist. So, "truth-at" is an attempt to rescue the "truth" of a proposition which otherwise couldn't be true due to an impoverished ontology.

We see this clearly in David Kaplan, the consummate direct reference theorist (1989b, p. 613):

> I see . . . the importance of a central distinction that I have tried to build into my very nomenclature, the distinction between what *exists* at a given point and what can be 'carried in' to be *evaluated* at that point, though it may *exist* only elsewhere. My 'Circumstances of Evaluation' evaluate contents that may have no native existence at the circumstance but can be expressed elsewhere and carried in for evaluation.

Once again we are given a metaphysical picture involving possible worlds. It is something like this:

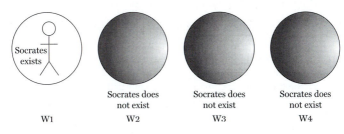

| Socrates exists | Socrates does not exist | Socrates does not exist | Socrates does not exist |
| W1 | W2 | W3 | W4 |

So far, we have one well-defined, pellucid notion of truth with respect to a world, (T_1)—truth-in. It is roughly entailment; a possible world is something like a maximal state of affairs or proposition, and a proposition will be true in this maximal entity iff it is entailed by the maximal entity. It isn't motivated by or based on any sort of metaphysical picture. (Don't let the preposition "in" fool you; the analysis is not motivated by a view where a proposition sits "inside" a world. As I said earlier, Plantinga could have used a different preposition in the place of "in.")

Truth-at, however, looks to be based on an incoherent metaphysical picture. Indeed, it is based on the same sort of picture on which the problem of transworld identity is based. Again, we think of worlds as objects with insides and outsides. However, again, worlds are abstract, and it is incoherent to think of a world as having an "inside" and an "outside." Also, propositions are abstract objects, and can't be "carried" anywhere. Nor can they sit outside (or inside) possible worlds. This is significant, for truth-at is doing important philosophical work for certain ontologically impoverished philosophers (or, strictly, philosophers whose views are ontologically impoverished) like typical direct reference theorists. Indeed, its apparent ability to bring semantic wealth to the ontologically indigent is the main (if only) reason why this notion has gained any purchase in the philosophical literature. If we consider worlds where Socrates doesn't exist, *Socrates does not exist* ought to be true "with respect to" these worlds. But it can't be true *in* the worlds. Socrates does not exist in those worlds. *Socrates does not exist* is true in no worlds where it exists, if it exists in any world at all. Since we can't use our well-defined notion of truth-in in this case, we employ another concept, truth-at, so that the proposition might be true in *some* sense in worlds like w2, w3, and w4.

Indeed, we might set up conditions such that propositions which need to be true with respect to a world W, but can't be true *in* W, wind up true *at* W. Suppose that negative existential propositions like *Socrates does not exist* are the only such propositions we have to worry about; they certainly are an important class of propositions which cause problems (see Plantinga 1983, Crisp 2002, Davidson 2000). So, we could set up conditions that allowed all of these propositions to be true at worlds where the relevant entity doesn't exist. Indeed, some have set up conditions for truth at a world in just this manner. For instance, Robert Adams, the most articulate expositor of this sort of view (1981, p. 23), sets up conditions such that if P is an atomic singular proposition about x, and x does not exist in a world W, then |~P| is true at W.

But have we gained any deeper understanding if we do this? I don't think we have. Imagine the following dialogue between P, someone who understands truth-in and who seeks to understand truth-at. Let A be someone who is a proponent of truth-at, and suppose A is motivated (as all truth-at theorists I know of are) in virtue of his belief that singular propositions exist contingently.[4]

> P: Now, A, it seems to me that you have a problem, for *Socrates does not exist* should be true in any world W where Socrates does not exist. You can't account for this.

---

[4] Direct reference theorists who are presentists arguably will encounter similar issues with singular propositions.

A: You're right to say that I can't say that *Socrates does not exist* is true in any world where Socrates does not exist. But I have this other surrogate relation, *truth-at*, which alleviates the problem. We may hold to the claim that this proposition is *true* with respect to W, it's just true with respect to W in a different manner than propositions that are merely true *in* W.[5]

P: I'm suspicious. What precisely *is* truth *at* a world? What is truth with respect to a world if it's not truth *in* a world? And how does truth at a world help with your problem?

A: Well, a proposition will be true at a world W if it doesn't exist in a world, but should be true in W, or so you claim. In fact, I can lay out formal conditions such that whenever you say a proposition should be true in a world W, I can say that it is true *at* W. A proposition may also be true *in*, W, but even if it's not, it can be true *at* W, and thus true with respect to W.

P: You still haven't told me what this relation, *truth-at* is. I understand truth-*in*. It's analyzed in terms of truth *simpliciter* and entailment. All you've told me is that there is this other relation which, if you'll permit the colloquial speech, happens to come to your rescue whenever *I* say that a proposition p is true in a world W, and your metaphysics won't allow you to agree with me. It is like having a physical theory on which physicists agree predicts a particle will have spin. It turns out that the particle doesn't have spin. "That's OK," you say. "I have this other property, *schwinn*, and anything with spin has it, and this particle also has it. I can give you conditions under which a particle has schwinn, in fact. They will be such that any time a particle has spin, the particle will have *schwinn;* and any time the particle is predicted to have spin, but lacks it on my theory, it has *schwinn*. And, the fact that the particle has *schwinn* is good enough for the purposes of testing my theory, even if it doesn't have spin." This is not the way of true science. If "schwinn" isn't given a *reductive* analysis such that we understand what it is, simply coming up with such a predicate and claiming that the theory is safe because the particle satisfies this other predicate (via stipulation) won't save the original theory. Indeed, we can see how much work picture-thinking involving propositions existing inside and outside worlds is doing for the truth-at theorist: When one constructs an analogous case which isn't bolstered by false pictures, the invocation of surrogate concepts which allow one to hold on to a theory (verbally, at least) seems, at best, bizarre.

---

[5] I recognize that normally *being true in W* is sufficient for *being true at W*, but this doesn't affect the point here.

A: Perhaps this will help. Imagine the following. You have a possible world, and it's full of entities—propositions, concrete individuals, and the like. But it doesn't contain *Socrates does not exist.* But sitting outside the world is the proposition *Socrates does not exist.* Only propositions *inside* the world can be true *in* that world. But if a proposition sits *outside* the world in the right sort of way, it may be *true at* the world. And, although *Socrates does not exist* is true in no worlds, it's true *at* all sorts of them—indeed, at each world where you say it ought to be true *in* that world. And truth-at is truth enough; I give you truth-at, and your insistence that propositions like *Socrates does not exist* be true *in* some worlds thus is seen to be question-begging.

P: But possible worlds don't have insides and outsides. How can a proposition sit *outside* a possible world? Surely you can't take what you've just said to give the sober metaphysical truth of the matter.

A: Well, I don't. But you asked for help understanding truth-at, and truth-at is at its core based on this sort of picture.

P: At its core it's based on an incoherent metaphysical picture?

A: A picture motivates the thinking, but that's not all there is to it. There are the conditions I gave you before.

P: But even with the picture, and the conditions, things still are murky. Or, perhaps this is a better way of putting my concern. You give me conditions for a proposition's being true at a world (conditions which are generated from a false picture, mind you). OK. To this end, I have some sort of a grasp of the relation. But of what relevance is this to the metaphysical questions at hand? How does truth-at help with the fact that it clearly is the case that not only is it true with respect to W (whatever precisely this means), a world in which Socrates does not exist, that *Socrates does not exist;* but it's true *in* W? Surely, if W obtained, *Socrates does not exist* would be true and hence exist. I know your theory won't allow you to say this, but the proper response isn't to produce a made-to-order relation which will allow you to affirm the truth of certain sentences like "*Socrates does not exist* is true with respect to W."

It seems to me that P is exactly right in the above dialogue. It is difficult to see truth-at as anything more than a concept based on a false metaphysical picture (again, one very much like the one which gave rise to the supposed problem of transworld identity, and this connection should raise eyebrows) that exists solely to rescue the truth of some sentences (e.g., ⌜sentences of the form ⌜p is true with respect to W⌝).

Although the problem of transworld identity may be (for the most part) dead, the thinking that motivates it is not. We see it in the notion of truth-at. It is important to note the etiology of these concepts, I think. Once the origin of the problem of transworld identity was noted, it was seen to be a pseudo-problem. Similarly, I think, once we note the same sort of picture-thinking in the genesis of ideas like truth-at, we may see that this notion, like the problem of transworld identity, does not reflect the sober metaphysical truth of the matter. Hence, it cannot be used to save the direct reference theorist from attacks like that of Plantinga's in "On Existentialism" (this volume, previous chapter.)

BIBLIOGRAPHY

Adams, R. M. "Actualism and Thisness." *Synthese* 49 (1981): 3–41.

Almog, J. "Naming without Necessity." *The Journal of Philosophy* 71 (1986): 210–242.

Bergmann, M. "(Serious) Actualism and (Serious) Presentism." *Noûs* 33 (1999): 118–132.

Branquinho, J. "In Defense of Obstinacy." *Philosophical Perspectives* (2003).

Crisp, T. "Presentism." In *The Oxford Handbook of Metaphysics,* ed. D. Zimmerman and Loux. M. Oxford: Oxford University Press, 2002.

Davidson, M. "Direct Reference and Singular Propositions." *American Philosophical Quarterly* 37 (2000).

Fine, K., and A. Prior. *Worlds, Times, and Selves.* Amherst: University of Massachusetts Press, 1977.

Fine, K. "Plantinga on the Reduction of Possibilist Discourse." In *Alvin Plantinga,* ed. J. Tomberlin, and P. van Inwagen. 145–186. Dordrecht: D. Reidel, 1985.

Fitch, G. "In Defense of Aristotelian Actualism." *Philosophical Perspectives: Metaphysics* (1996).

Kaplan, D. 1967 (1976) "Trans-world Heir Lines." In *The Possible and the Actual,* ed. M. Loux. Ithaca: Cornell University Press, 1979.

Kaplan, D. "Bob and Carol and Ted and Alice." In *Approaches to Natural Language,* ed. J. Hintikka, J. Moravcsik, and P. Suppes. Dordrecht: D. Reidel, 1973. Reprinted in this volume.

Kaplan, D. "Afterthoughts." In *Themes from Kaplan,* ed. J. Almog, J. Perry, and H. Wettstein. 565–614. New York: Oxford University Press, 1989b. Reprinted in this volume.

Kaplan, D. "Demonstratives," 1989a.

Kripke, S. *Identity and Necessity.* In *Identity and Individuation,* ed. M. Munitz. (1973). Reprinted in this volume.

Kripke, S. *Naming and Necessity.* Cambridge: Harvard University Press, 1980.

Plantinga, A. "On Existentialism." *Philosophical Studies* (1983). Reprinted in Plantinga 2003 and this volume.

Plantinga, A. "Transworld Identity or Worldbound Individuals." In *Logic and Ontology,* ed. M. Munitz. 193–212. New York: New York University Press, 1973. Reprinted in Plantinga 2003.

Plantinga, A. *The Nature of Necessity.* Oxford: Clarendon Press, 1974.

Plantinga, A. *Essays in the Metaphysics of Modality,* ed. M. Davidson. New York: Oxford University Press, 2003.

Pollock, J. *The Foundations of Philosophical Semantics.* Princeton: Princeton University Press, 1984.

Pollock, J. In *Plantinga on Possible Worlds*, ed. J. Tomberlin, and P. van Inwagen. 145–186. Dordrecht: D. Reidel, 1985.

Salmon, N. *Reference and Essence*. Princeton: Princeton University Press, 1981.

Steinman, R. "Kripke Rigidity versus Kaplan Rigidity." *Mind* (1985):431–442.

Van Inwagen, P. "Plantinga on Transworld Identity." In *Alvin Plantinga*, ed. J. Tomberlin and P. van Inwagen. Dordrecht: D. Reidel, 1985. Reprinted in van Inwagen 2001.

Van Inwagen, P. *Identity, Ontology, and Modality*. Cambridge: Cambridge University Press, 2001.

5

The Rebirth of Fregeanism

THE INDISPENSABILITY OF *SINN*

Graeme Forbes

I

In this paper I propose a neo-Fregean semantic analysis of those belief ascriptions in which names are used to specify the content of the belief.[1] My analysis will justify the intuition that substitution inferences, such as *A*, are invalid rather than merely pragmatically deficient:

A (1) Lois believes that Clark Kent can't fly.

(2) Clark Kent is Superman.

∴ (3) Lois believes that Superman can't fly.[2]

But the reason for substitution failure will not be traced to a shift in the semantic function of the name used in the content specification, as it is in Frege's own account and in quotational analyses. All these agree that the "Clark Kent" of (1) is not performing its usual semantic task of referring to a certain individual. But we can have failure of substitution of coreferential names even when the names are functioning normally, as is clear from Quine's example: Giorgione is so called because of his size, Giorgione is Barbarelli, but it is false that Barbarelli is so called because of his size.[3] In the premise, "Giorgione" surely does no more or less than refer to a certain individual. The problem with the substitution is rather that it changes the reference of "so called," a phrase we may term a *logophor*, since it makes back-reference to a word. The analysis to be developed here will uncover a logophor in belief ascriptions, assimilating the fallacy in *A* to the fallacy in Quine's examples.

Fregean senses, and in particular the senses of names, play a crucial role in the apparatus I employ. Hence my whole project is threatened by the work of a number of philosophers of language who seem to demonstrate that the notion of the Fregean sense of a name is chimerical. For a sense is supposed to determine the reference of the name which expresses it. And are there not examples, particularly due to Kripke, which show that there is no requirement that a reference-determining sense by associated with a name, and examples which show that even in cases where there is a reasonable candidate for the role of the sense of the name, that candidate may determine the *wrong* reference?[4] The force of Kripke's cases

---

[1] The analysis is designed to complement that of ascriptions employing indexicals given in my "Indexicals and Intensionality: A Fregean Perspective," *The Philosophical Review* 96 (1987), pp. 3–33. But the present paper can be read independently.

[2] For the rest of this paper, treat the *Superman* fiction as fact. See Nathan Salmon's *Frege's Puzzle* (Cambridge, Mass.: The MIT Press, 1986), for a defense of the view that the problems with *A* are pragmatic.

[3] See "Reference and Modality," in *From a Logical Point of View* (New York, N.Y.: Harper and Row, 1961), p. 139.

[4] See Saul Kripke, *Naming and Necessity* (Cambridge, Mass.: Harvard University Press, 1980). I have in mind particularly the Gödel/Schmidt case (p. 84) and the Feynman/Gell-Man case (p. 91).

cannot be gainsaid, but I believe the account of the senses of names in section II below is immune to their threat. So I will use that account in section III to formulate a Fregean analysis of name-employing attitude ascriptions. And in section IV, I will apply this analysis to Kripke's well-known "puzzle about belief."

II

My view is that it has not been established that there are no such things as Fregean senses for proper names, but only that "famous deeds" sense theories (Lewis's phrase) are wrong. And not all sense theories need be of this sort. Trivially, the constraint any acceptable account of the senses of names must satisfy is that two names with the same sense are intersubstitutable *salva veritate* in any intensional context (such as an attitude context, or "it is *a posteriori* that," or "it is uninformative that"). In addition, a description should exchange with any name whose sense is the sense of that description, *if* there are any such pairs of expressions. But it is an open question whether there are. I take senses to be theoretical entities with explanatory properties, entities posited by the semantic theorist to explain the semantic intuitions of language understanders. For example, Frege arrives at the notion of sense by elaborating his intuitions about certain identity sentences. The property of a sense which explains our intuitions about propositions of which it is a constituent I call its *cognitive significance*. It is the cognitive significance of a thought which determines that the believer will take a particular attitude to it, given his relations to other thoughts and his sensory input. Cognitive significance is individuated intensionally: thoughts p and q have the same cognitive significance if and only if it is *a priori* that no rational being who grasps both takes an attitude to one at some time which he does not also take to the other at that time. But two expressions whose senses have the same cognitive significance are not *ipso facto* expressions with the same sense. In particular, the sense of a description may *encapsulate* the cognitive significance of the sense of a singular term without there being any literal *sameness* of the senses of the description and the term. This would happen when the sense of the description is structured and the sense of the singular term unstructured. For example, Peacocke has claimed (in my terminology) that "the subject of *this* experience" encapsulates the cognitive significance of the first-person type of mode of presentation (the type tokens of which each of us employs in his or her "I myself" thoughts).[5] Here we have sameness of cognitive significance but not sameness of sense, since in thinking an "I myself" thought one does not *ipso facto* make reference to a present experience, while sameness of sense would require sameness of reference.[6]

---

[5] See Christopher Peacocke, *Sense and Content* (Oxford: England: Oxford University Press, 1983), pp. 109–133. My debt to Peacocke's account of demonstratives in Chapters 5 and 6 is considerable.

[6] If a description merely articulates the cognitive significance of a name, then there is no reason to expect it to be substitutable for the name in *modal* contexts: after all, making the replacement yields a different proposition. But the difference made by such substitution may seem

(Contd.)

The distinction between a sense and the cognitive significance it bears does not by itself circumvent objections to "famous deeds" sense theories, since any reasonable account of the cognitive significance of an expression E should interchange *salva veritate* with E in the context "it is *a priori* that," so long as E is not itself within the scope of further modal or attitude contexts. That is, the substitution should save truth value even if the expressions being exchanged do not have numerically identical senses. To respond to Kripke's critique of sense theories, therefore, we need at least an account of the cognitive significance of the sense of a name which can replace the name in the context "it is *a priori* that" without affecting truth value.

My account is based on the metaphor of a cognitive "operating system" and the following hypothesis about the role of names in it. When we receive what we take to be *de re* information which we have an interest in retaining, our operating system may create a locus, or dossier, where such information is held; and any further information which we take to be about the same object can be filed along with the information about it we already possess.[7] More precisely, the system files what I call "classified conditions"; a condition stands for something an object can satisfy, and the classifier is what specifies the subject's attitude to a certain related proposition. Possible classifiers for conditions are "believed to be true" and "hoped to be true." The role of a name is to identify a file for a particular object—as I shall put it, we use names to "label" dossiers. In sum, then, on coming across a new name, one which is taken to stand for some particular individual, the system creates a dossier labelled with that name and puts those classified conditions into it which are associated with the name.

The hypothesis about cognitive significance which this metaphor suggests is that the sense of a name "NN" has the cognitive significance "the subject of *this* dossier," where the dossier referred to is the one labelled "NN": our way of thinking of NN is *as* the subject of this dossier. Less technically, the cognitive significance of the sense is "the person/thing this body of information is about" (which gives a certain primacy to the "believed to be true" classifier). Such a cognitive significance dovetails with the fact that associated with an ordinary proper name there is no canonical way of thinking of an individual of the sort which "famous deeds" sense theories have posited, not even a way that is canonical merely for a

---

too small for a consequence as large as change of truth value to follow. I should back up my claim that interchangeability in modal contexts is not implied by my approach with a detailed semantics for modal contexts. Such a semantics may be found in my *Languages of Possibility* (Oxford, England: Basil Blackwell, 1989). The leading idea is that a modal operator refers to a function whose argument is not the *sense* of the sentence within its scope but the *type of state of affairs* which the sentence describes (on my approach, states of affairs described by sentences containing non-referential descriptions are quantified, or general, states of affairs, not singular ones). However, a proposition obtains a modal status *derivatively*, from the type of state of affairs of which it is a way of thinking. So despite the different treatments of modality and attitudes, an argument like "B believes that S, □ S, ∴ B believes something necessary," is still correct.

[7] I borrow the term "dossier" from Gareth Evans. See his *The Varieties of Reference* (Oxford, England: Oxford University Press, 1982), p. 399.

particular thinker at a particular time. The hypothesis also explains how an agent reasons with propositions that have the sense of a name as a constituent: if the cognitive significance is "the subject of *this* dossier," then in deciding on an attitude to take towards a currently entertained proposition which would be expressed using the name, a thinker may activate any classified condition in the dossier, he may delete conditions in the light of new evidence or changes in his desires, or he may add new conditions, all without affecting the sense of the name or its cognitive significance. However, it is important that the cognitive significance be explained in terms of the notion of being the *subject* of a dossier. As Kripke's examples show, this is not the same notion as that of being the object which *satisfies* the dossier.[8] Explaining "subject of" is a further task, but I see no reason why the Fregean cannot simply adopt a causal theory of this concept if he finds a plausible one.

This is to say that the causal approach to reference is not at all inimical to a Fregean semantics if the notion of the sense of a name is explained as above. But Frege held that the sense of a name *determines* its reference, and it might seem that I have just abandoned that aspect of his view. I do not think this is so. A sense of the sort that a name might express is a representation of an individual, and there are two ways in which a familiar type of representation, such as a photograph, can reasonably be said to determine an object. In the case of a portrait photograph, there is the object it is of, and (perhaps) the object it *best resembles*. A sense determines an object as the object it is *of*, which, at least in easy cases, is the object at the start of the channel along which the *de re* information in the dossier has flowed to the thinker It is just a prejudice to insist that senses must have qualitative features by which they determine objects via satisfaction, as if we somehow first formulate ways of thinking of things independently of cognitive encounters with the world, and are then faced with the problem of finding entities to fit.[9]

I intend these hypothetical features of the language faculty's architecture to be characteristic of the "standing" *de re* ways of thinking of objects typically expressed by ordinary names, as opposed to the "occasional" *de re* senses of demonstratives and indexicals, and more pertinently, as opposed to the senses of expressions which seem only to express ways of thinking of specific things. Suppose, to adapt Russell's example, that as a result of regaining your confidence in the integrity of electoral processes in Louisiana, you come to believe that the official winner of the next election will in fact be the candidate who gets the most votes. This does not mean that you have a dossier labelled "official winner of the next election" and that you express a sense with the cognitive significance "subject of *this* dossier"

---

[8] Suppose (a) the condition of being F is in B's "NN" dossier, classified as "believed true," and (b) B comes to believe that nothing is F. Then if B's sense for "NN" has the cognitive significance "the satisfier of this dossier," B would have to conclude (if he retains "is F" in the dossier) that there is no such person as NN, or (if he deletes it) that *now* there may be such a person as NN. Either way he cannot make the simple belief revision "NN isn't F after all" which an adequate theory should permit him.

[9] For more on the issues of this paragraph, see John McDowell, *"De Re* Senses," *The Philosophical Quarterly* 35 (1984), pp. 98–109.

when you use that description. There is no specific individual of whom you are thinking when you use that description, and this is something of which you are quite aware. It is for that very reason that no dossier is created you do not take yourself to be having cognitive encounters with a subject of some body of information that is growing as the encounters proceed.[10]

How does my hypothesis about cognitive significance fare with the test of substitutability within the scope of "it is *a priori* that"? It is *a priori* for any subject B who understands the name "NN" that NN is NN. Is it *a priori* for any such B that NN is the subject of *this* dossier, where the reference is to B's "NN"-dossier? The answer to this question may seem to depend in part on what account is given of the cognitive significance of the sense of the demonstrative *"this* dossier." Two possible candidates, between which I will not try to adjudicate here, are "the dossier in which *this* information is stored" and "the dossier *this* name labels." However, neither candidate is of a nature to guarantee that "NN is the subject of *this* dossier" is *a priori* when the demonstrated dossier is labelled "NN," so we ought to consider specific cases in which this proposition is apparently subject to challenge.

There is a kind of situation where one makes the *a posteriori* discovery that NN is *not* the subject of a certain dossier. Suppose that in conversation with others you have picked up a little information about someone called "NN," enough for your mental operating system to have created a dossier labelled "NN" and filed those scraps of information in it. Later you have a number of encounters with someone whom you take to be NN, and your "NN"-dossier rapidly fills with conditions derived from these encounters. After a while, you learn that the person with whom you have had the encounters is in fact MM, not NN. In this situation, it seems reasonable for you to say "NN is not the subject of this dossier" or "NN is not the person whom all this information is about"; you do not seem to be contradicting an *a priori* truth.

I doubt that this is a counterexample to my proposal. Precisely what is going on here depends on the explanation one gives of why "NN is the subject of *this* dossier" is *a priori* for you before you discover your error of identification. According to one account, it is *a priori* for you because "NN" is a name in your idiolect for MM and your dossier is dominated by information about MM, making MM its subject. MM is both the reference of the name and the subject of the dossier because of the role MM played in the processes by which you acquired the bulk of the information in the dossier and which elicit your uses of "NN." On this view, when you learn "this person is MM, not NN," your mental operating system relabels with "MM" the dossier previously labelled "NN" and creates a new dossier labelled "NN" into which is transferred the information for which the now relabelled dossier was first created,

---

[10] I include being told or misinformed about a thing as ways of cognitively encountering it. See *Languages of Possibility,* p. 118 for further discussion of the distinction between *de re* and *de dicto* senses. My use of the phrase "ordinary name" in this paragraph is intended to bracket off the question of descriptive names, which in my view do not express ways of thinking of specific objects (*ibid.,* p. 155) and of empty names which the subject mistakenly takes to be like other ordinary names ("Zeus"). I have no settled view of what to say about names of this sort.

before your encounters with MM. When you now say "NN is not the subject of this dossier" the demonstrative refers to the old dossier which you have relabelled "MM," while "NN" has a new sense and also a new reference (the subject of the newly created dossier). So you are not really controverting the proposition you previously expressed with "NN is the subject of *this* dossier," the proposition which my account implies is a *priori*, since that is not the proposition you now express with these words. Furthermore, once the new dossier has been created, the transfer executed and the labelling done, it is not a *further* empirical discovery that MM is the subject of *this* dossier and NN the subject of *that* one. So the truths of the same form as "NN is the subject of *this* dossier," where the demonstrative refers to the dossier labelled by the displayed name, are a *priori* truths (it would be a *posteriori* that MM is, or is not, the subject of the "NN" dossier).

An alternative explanation of why "NN is the subject of *this* dossier" was previously a *priori* for you, though you can now truly say "NN is not the subject of *this* dossier," involves no change of sense in "NN." On this account, your original introduction to the name "NN" was sufficient to establish its public reference in your mouth. And each time you make an observation of MM and enter "is F" into your "NN" dossier, what you think is: "*that* man is F, and that man is NN, so NN is F." Hence you file a piece of misinformation about NN in your "NN" dossier, a dossier of which NN is the subject simply because you use "NN" in the kind of Identity Elimination illustrated and your introduction to the name automatically brought with it its public reference. When you learn your mistake, you transfer the misinformation out of your "NN" dossier, putting it into a newly created dossier labelled "MM" and leaving only the original information about NN in your "NN" dossier. So you can now truly say "NN is not the subject of *this* dossier so long as "*this* dossier" refers to the newly created "MM" dossier (if it refers to the old dossier, the statement is false). Either way then, "NN is the subject of *this* dossier" is a *priori* true before you discover your error, and afterwards there is both a true proposition you can express with "NN is not the subject of *this* dossier" and an a *priori* proposition you can express with "NN is the subject of *this* dossier."[11]

The example just discussed involves a correct revision of a cognitive filing system prompted by new information to the effect that there are two people where previously you thought there was only one. Mark Richard has raised the question of what happens when we make an incorrect revision based on misinformation that there is only one person where previously you thought (correctly) that there were two. Suppose you already know quite a lot about Mark Twain and quite a lot about Herman Melville and then come to believe that Twain and Melville are the same

---

[11] Since both analyses are consistent with my claims about what is a *priori*. I shall not argue for one over the other. However, my view is that if the second analysis were applied across the board, no explanation of how sense determines reference would have been given. But we can employ Evans's producer/consumer distinction here (*op. cit.*, Chapter 11). Even if it is true that for consumers, introduction to the name brings its public reference with it, the first analysis, with which the position that sense determines reference sits better, would be more appropriate for producers. Since it is they who establish the public reference of a name, sense would determine reference indirectly, via producers, for consumers.

person. Does this mean that two dossiers are merged into one? If so, Richard points out, the description "the subject of *this* dossier" is improper. Furthermore, if in this state of confusion you say "Melville wrote *Huckleberry Finn*," there is an intuition not merely that you *say* that Melville wrote *Huckleberry Finn*, but that you believe this too. Granting the intuition, I therefore conclude that the moral of the example is that pre-existing dossiers are not merged when an identity comes to be accepted, or at least not straight away. Rather, the misinformation "is identical to Melville" is filed in the Twain dossier and the misinformation "is identical to Twain" is filed in the Melville dossier, so that the two names do not come to have the same sense. And when the speaker produces a statement such as "Melville wrote *Huckleberry Finn*" where he would previously have used the other name, he is extracting the believed condition and the identity from his "Twain" dossier and applying Identity Elimination. A kind of cognitive inertia seems to be in effect: when you come to believe that one dossier has been generated by two objects, your cognitive operating system is obliged to restructure your files in order to allow coherent singular thought about what you now take to be two objects. But if you come to believe in the identity of things which you hitherto took to be distinct, your system is not subject to any sanction if it maintains the dossiers as separate, filing conditions more immediately associated with one particular name in that name's dossier only, so long as the system implements Leibniz's Law.

Finally, my approach to names suggests an account of what it is for two names to have the same sense: it is for both names to label the same dossier. This could come about as follows. Add the character of Ralph to the Superman story, Ralph being someone who has never heard of either Superman or Clark Kent, and imaging that Superman encounters Ralph and explains his double life to him, introducing himself by both the names he uses: "I am known both as 'Superman' and as 'Clark Kent.'" It seems reasonable to assume that the system which creates dossiers is governed by the constraint that in setting up new ones for new names it should aim for a one-one correspondence with the purported objects. So Ralph's system would create only a single, double-labelled dossier and so long as Ralph's access to his cognitive system is unimpaired the proposition that Superman is Clark Kent would be as self-evident to him as the proposition that Clark Kent is Clark Kent.[12] A simpler example of the same phenomenon occurs when someone introduces herself with both a real name and a nickname, as in "My name is Kimberley but my friends call me Berry," It would be unmotivated to suppose that in such a situation you create two dossiers. Rather, the two names label the same dossier and consequently have the same sense. For while it is one thing to think of an object *x* as the subject of *this* dossier and a different thing to think of *x* as the subject of *that* one, the difference vanishes if it is the same dossier that is activated

---

[12] I offer an account of how the uninformativeness of such propositions could arise as a consequence of the retrieval procedures of a cognitive operating system in my "Cognitive Architecture and the Semantics of Belief," in *Contemporary Perspectives in the Philosophy of Language II*, ed. P. French et al. (Notre Dame, Ind.: Notre Dame University Press, 1989). The final version of the present paper postdates that one, which is main about the Mates problem. Where the two differ, "Indispensability" states the position I would defend.

when either of two names is processed, provided that the fact that it is the same dossier being readied for action is somehow manifest to the subject. And the manifestness of such features of cognitive operations is in the best explanation of our ability to find some identity statements informative and others uninformative.

I have argued that an approach to the senses of names in terms of cognitive significance, using the metaphor of operating system and dossier, goes some way to filling in the details of a Fregean semantics of names which is not threatened by Kripke's refutation of "famous deeds" theories. So we are free to entertain seriously the thought that it is the Fregean approach, and only it, which provides the machinery to give a semantics for attitude contexts which does justice to our intuitions as language understanders. Hence the title of this paper.

III

Frege abstracted from the phenomenon of intersubjective variation in sense.[13] The analysis of attitude attributions using names that he proposed under this abstraction seems to me to be the best available, once we are reassured of the respectability of the notion of the sense of a name. But we cannot ignore intersubjective variation. If there are ever two names with the same sense for you and different senses for me, then the sense of at least one name varies intersubjectively. And on my own account, while it may be said that names share the same *type* of cognitive significance, their token senses have a private aspect, since only I am in a position to think in a purely demonstrative way about my stores of information, and only you are in a position to think in that way about yours.[14] However, taking account of intersubjective variation raises questions to which the Fregean should have answers. According to Frege, if A utters, "B believes that S," then A uses S to refer to its customary sense.[15] But if S has one customary sense for A and another for B, *which* sense is referred to in A's utterance?

Let us take a concrete example. Treat the Superman story as fact and suppose that Ralph is as described at the end of the last section; that is, for him the names "Superman" and "Clark Kent" have the same sense (or change the example to one involving nicknames if you did not like that case). Despite the fact that for Ralph the two names have the same sense, he can still truly say such things as:

(4) Lois believes that Superman can fly and Clark Kent can't.

---

[13] He thought no such variation would arise in "the theoretical structure of a demonstrative science." See his "On Sense and Reference," in *Philosophical Writings of Gottlob Frege*, ed. P. Geach and M. Black (Oxford, England: Basil Blackwell, 1970), p. 58n.

[14] Here I may be violating Frege's publicity requirement on senses, but I am not violating its point, which is to ensure the possibility of communication. Senses with a private aspect are a bar to communication only if grasp of another's proposition implies the ability to use its constituent senses in thoughts of one's own. But there is no reason to think that every acceptable account of communication must have this implication. See "Indexicals and Intensionality," pp. 20–21.

[15] I explain the rationale for Frege's "customary reference displacement" thesis in "Indexicals and Intensionality," p. 5.

If Frege's "reference-shift" analysis of intensional contexts is to be applied when we are allowing intersubjective variation in sense then the problem is to identify the proposition to which "Superman can fly and Clark Kent can't" refers in (4). Specifically, the question is whether the names (a) refer to the senses Lois customarily expresses when she uses them, or (b) refer to the sense Ralph customarily expresses when *he* uses them, or (c) perform some other function. On the *believer-oriented* view, the names refer to their respective senses for Lois, while on the *ascriber-oriented* view they refer to their sense for Ralph. I will now argue that neither of these options is satisfactory. But the moral I draw from this is not that Frege's account of intensional contexts is fundamentally flawed. It is rather that when we drop the idealization of intersubjective constancy of linguistic senses, the basic elements of the Fregean approach have to be deployed in a less straightforward way to get plausible semantic analyses of belief attributions. It goes without saying that when we move away from a fairly extreme idealization towards something more like the real world, we should *expect* applications of a theory to lose the stark simplicity they had when only the idealization was under consideration.

The ascriber-oriented view is refuted by the case of Ralph, for whom "Superman" and "Clark Kent" express the same sense. There is a clear intuition that Ralph can utter (4) and say something true; yet the propositions *Ralph* expresses by "Superman can fly" and "Clark Kent can't" are explicitly contradictory, though Lois does not believe an explicit contradiction. So Ralph is not referring to his own propositions. Perhaps the example will be challenged on the grounds that if the names express the same sense for Ralph, then he cannot utter (4) truly. But why could he not use (4) to express a truth? (4) is just a fact about Lois and it is hard to see why Ralph should be prevented from expressing this fact in virtue of *superior* knowledge of what is the case.[16]

On the believer-oriented view, the idea is that when Ralph comes out with (4) he "aims" at Lois's two senses with his uses of "Clark Kent" and "Superman." The problem, of course, is to explain the mechanism by which he hits them. How is the reference accomplished? After all, Ralph may not have stood to Lois's sense for either name in any of the familiar relations which bestow a capacity to think of an object; for example, he need not have demonstratively identified either sense. But without a mechanism, the believer-oriented view makes the capacity to refer to a sense seem like magic.

Perhaps there *is* some mechanism at work in (4) as the believer-oriented view requires, even if it is difficult to see precisely what it might be. But I shall not pursue this possibility, since I think the believer-oriented view has other drawbacks.

---

[16] The truth of the ascription follows from what Richard calls the Echo Principle. See his "Taking the Fregean Seriously," in *Philosophical Analysis: A Defence by Example*, ed. David Austin (Dordrecht, The Netherlands: D. Reidel, 1988), pp. 219–239. Nathan Salmon has argued that cases with (what I would describe as) the general structure "one sense for the ascriber, two or more for the believer" constitute difficulties of principle for the Fregean approach (see *Frege's Puzzle*, Chapter 9.1). I believe the account in this paper solves the problems to which Salmon points.

First, it suffers from a difficulty dual to the one (4) presents for the ascriber-oriented view. The believer-oriented view implies that if Lois says of Ralph "He believes Clark Kent is Superman," she is attributing belief in an obviously true proposition to him, since Ralph attaches the same senses to the two names. But intuitively, she is not. A further difficulty for the believer-oriented view arises from a case where Ralph says:

(5) Lois believes Matti Nykaenen can fly

while in fact Lois has never heard of the great Finnish ski jumper and does not even know of the sport of ski jumping. Then (5) is false. However, the reason it is false seems to me to be that (5) requires that Lois believe a certain proposition which in fact she does not believe, whereas the believer-oriented view would have to say that (5) is false because the embedded sentence fails to refer to any complete proposition. This does not seem right in itself, and it also generates some difficulties over negation. The negation of (5) is straightforwardly true, but a semantics in a Fregean spirit usually embodies the principle that failure of reference is contagious: if a sub-expression of a sentence S fails to refer then any expression containing S, in particular $\ulcorner {\sim} S \urcorner$, is infected in the same way as S is, and also fails to refer. Hence it is unclear that the believer-oriented view could find a well-motivated way of ascribing the truth value *True* to the negation of (5).

So it seems to me that neither of the two straightforward accounts I distinguished has much ability to deal with a wide range of cases. One might say that attitude ascriptions are ambiguous between believer-oriented and ascriber-oriented views, with disambiguation being achieved by context and charity. But I cannot find any intuitive support for the idea that (4) or (5) is ambiguous and awaits some kind of contextual input before it can be evaluated. I would prefer to find a single style of semantic analysis of belief ascriptions which works for all the cases we have considered, reserving the ambiguity hypothesis for an account of last resort.

To see our way forward, let us consider again the case where Ralph hears Lois assert "Clark Kent can't fly" and on that basis says:

(6) Lois believes Clark Kent can't fly.

A proposal which cuts through our difficulties here is that Ralph is referring neither to his own nor to Lois's sense with "Clark Kent" all he means by (6) is:

(7) Clark Kent is someone Lois believes can't fly.

Let us use "B" for the belief relation which holds between thinkers and propositions, corners for sense quotes, and "$^$" for the following mode of combination (partially defined function) of the senses of two expressions: if S-followed-by-S' is a meaningful expression, then Sense(S)$^$Sense(S') is the sense of the expression S-followed-by-S'. In these terms, (7) is analyzed as:

(8) $(\exists\alpha)(\alpha$ is a way of thinking of Clark Kent & B(Lois, α, $\ulcorner$ can't fly $\urcorner$))

(in words: for some way of thinking of Clark Kent, Lois believes the proposition consisting in that way of thinking in construction with the sense of "can't fly").[17] It is not difficult to find problems with this construal of (6). For example, Ralph ought to be willing to infer "So Lois believes Superman can't fly," since on the same style of semantic analysis, it follows from (6) and the identity. But he won't be willing to infer this, and it is not obvious how to motivate analyzing his judgment "Lois believes Superman can fly" one way, and his judgment (6) a very different way, when both are based just on hearing Lois utter the associated sentences.

Reflection on this case and the previous ones indicates that the *actual name* the ascriber uses in making his ascription plays a role that none of the proposals canvassed so far has managed to capture. When Ralph says (6) he uses the name "Clark Kent" because that is the name he *heard Lois use* to express her belief. But Ralph is not using that name to refer to Lois's sense for it, since we have already seen that this claim runs into difficulties with other cases (recall (5)). Rather, when Ralph comes out with (6), he is surmising something roughly to the effect that for Lois there is some body of classified conditions concerning Clark Kent (that is, concerning Superman) which she *associates with the name "Clark Kent"* and which includes the condition "can't fly" classified "believed to be true." I suggest that this is *all* he need surmise, and that it provides the material for the semantic analysis of his belief ascriptions. In other words, these ascriptions must be represented as adverting in some way to the name the believer would use in expressing the belief.[18]

If dossiers are labelled by names, then the sense which a name expresses may also be said to be labelled by that name, since in articulating the cognitive significance of the sense we make a reference to a dossier which has the name as a label. In addition, a sense may be said to be labelled by any name which is a *linguistic counterpart* of the name used by the ascriber in specifying the proposition. I explain the notion of t' *being* a linguistic counterpart of t more fully below; for now, I need only say that it requires sameness of customary reference and it is always relativized to a pair of thinkers, (ascriber) A and (believer) B: I write "t' is a linguistic counterpart$_{<B,A>}$ of t," where t is the name the ascriber uses and t' the name the believer employs. Within the context of a use of a name "NN" by A in a belief ascription to B, a sense is then said to be *to labelled* if and only if the

---

[17] See "Indexicals and Intensionality" for this kind of regimentation. Richard justly criticizes the analysis illustrated here, *op. cit.,* p. 237, n. 12.

[18] A case where a name is used by A in a belief ascription to B and B has no name for the relevant object is a case where analysis in the style of (8) *is* called for. But B's willingness to use a name should be distinguished from his having one in thought: B may be subject to a religious prohibition against writing or uttering the name "NN," but that is no bar to A's using it to specify the contents of B's beliefs in a way that (8) does not adequately capture. Alternatively, B may have the capacity to recognize an object x over and over again, though he has no name for it. Such a way of thinking of x does not seem to me to be "namelike," since it appears to give a special role to descriptively specifiable characteristics of x. If A uses a name to specify B's beliefs in this case, analysis in the style of (8) would be appropriate, and substitution permissible.

articulation of the cognitive significance of that sense demonstratively identifies a dossier of B's labelled by a name which is a linguistic counterpart$_{<B,A>}$ of "NN." This allows the following *logophoric* analysis of (6):

> (9) Clark Kent is such that for Lois's so-labelled way of thinking of him α,
> $B(\text{Lois}, \alpha \wedge \ulcorner \text{can't fly} \urcorner)$.

(9) modifies (8) to introduce allusion to the salient name, but we have done this in such a way that (9) does not entail that Lois believes Superman can't fly. For Lois need not possess a dossier labelled "Superman" containing "can't fly" classified "believed true even though she possesses such a dossier labelled "Clark Kent." The objectionable feature of (8) is therefore avoided.

The phrase "Lois's so-labelled way of thinking" embodies a definite description as well as a logophor ("the so-labelled way of thinking employed by Lois"), and a full regimentation of (6) would require some decisions about the syntax and semantics of descriptions. For precision, where it matters I will take a definite description to be a binary restrictive quantifier, in view of the significant structural and semantics parallels between "the F is G," "an F is G," "few Fs are G," etc. But I will not complicate my regimentations by injecting the binary quantifier formalism.[19]

The logophoric analysis gives the right results for the cases we have considered. For example, I analyze Lois's ascription to Ralph of the belief that Clark Kent is Superman as

> (10) Clark Kent is such that for Ralph's so-labelled (way of thinking of him) α, Superman is such that for Ralph's so-labelled β, B (Ralph, $\alpha \wedge \ulcorner = \urcorner \wedge \beta$).

In the example, Ralph uses the two names with the same sense, and (10) is true when that sense is assigned to both sense variables. But we agreed that Lois's ascription is not the ascription of an obvious belief. The analysis (10) makes plain why this is so.

Second, for

> (5) Lois believes that Matti Nykaenen can fly

we have the analysis (suppressing "way of thinking of him")

> (11) Matti Nykaenen is such that for Lois's so-labelled α, B(Losis, $\alpha \wedge \ulcorner \text{can fly} \urcorner$)

which is straightforwardly false, provided the semantics for the description quantifier preserves the Russellian equivalence between "the F is G" and "there

---

[19] For a full account and persuasive arguments for the quantifier treatment of definite descriptions, see Martin Davies, *Meaning, Quantification and Necessity* (Boston, Mass.: Routledge and Kegan Paul, 1981), Chapter VII, Section 1. On this account, definite descriptions do not *refer* to objects, though one can speak loosely of an object being "characterized" or "picked out" by the description.

is exactly one F and it is G": Lois is in the belief relation to no proposition with the constituents required to make (11) true (hence the external negation of (11) is true).[20]

In each of these cases, the linguistic counterpart of the name in the ascription is the name itself. A less trivial application of the linguistic counterpart relation is to foreign names and their translations. For example, an analysis of "Plato believed Aristotle showed promise" in the style of (9), (10) and (11) will ascribe the right truth value since "Aristotle" and "Ἀριστὀτελης" are each other's linguistic counterparts relative to the typical English speaking ascriber of this belief and Plato.[21] A general principle which this case falls under is: if the ascriber and the believer each has exactly one dossier for the object x, then the ascriber can use any name labelling his dossier for x to report a belief the believer would express using one of the names labelling his dossier for x. On the other hand, the previous cases motivate the principle that if the ascriber has one dossier for x labelled with names $N_1, \ldots, N_n$ and the believer has n dossiers D_i each labelled uniquely with N_i, then the linguistic counterpart$_{<B,A>}$ relation on this domain relative to these two thinkers is the set of pair N_i, N_1. Evidently, these principles cover only a fraction of the interesting examples. In the next section, I will discuss one of the hard cases, due to Kripke.[22]

---

[20] It may seem that the analytic strategy illustrated by these examples will lead to excessively baroque complete analyses of "B believes that S": if all words in S are genuinely in the semantic scope of "believes," then they will all be exported and linked to a sense description involving a logophor. However, the underlying idea here can be implemented in a non-baroque way. Exploiting my modification of Frege's views about sentence reference (see note 6), the general form of the analysis would roughly be: the state of affairs that S is such that for B's so-labelled way of thinking of it, B believes that way of thinking. I hope to pursue this in a future paper.

[21] Cross-language application of the linguistic counterpart relation affords a response to a Church-style objection put to me by Salmon. The Greek translation of (a) Plato believed Aristotle showed promise, is be πλατον ωηθην τον Αριστοτελη μεγα δυνασθαι. Now the translation of the analysis of (a) ought to be the analysis of the translation of (a), that is the analysis of (b). But the logophors in the analyses of (a) and (b) refer to an English and a Greek word respectively. However, if, as in the normal case, the counterparts of the former are exactly the counterparts of the latter, the translation of the analysis of (a) and the analysis of the translation of (a) specify the same truth condition.

[22] Richard has raised the following case. B is a bilingual who has knowledge he expresses with "NN = NN," where "NN" is the Mandarin name of China's capital and "=" is the ideogram for "is," but B thinks that Beijing and Peiping are different cities (he says so in English). Why does my analysis not have the false consequence that B believes that Beijing is Peiping? This would require that B's Mandarin name "NN" is a linguistic counterpart$_{<B,A>}$ of both "Beijing" and "Peiping" (the ascriber's names). Suppose that "NN" and "Beijing" have the same sense for B and that "Beijing" and "Peiping" have the same sense for the ascriber. By the principle in the text, we then have that "Beijing" is a linguistic counterpart$_{<B,A>}$ of "Beijing" and "Peiping" is a linguistic counterpart$_{<B,A>}$ of "Peiping." Since "B believes that Beijing is Peiping" is false, we should conclude that "NN" is a linguistic counterpart$_{<B,A>}$ of "Beijing" but not "Peiping"; as one might expect, "NN" is associated only with the English name whose sense it shares. The methodology I use to settle the extension of the linguistic counterpart$_{<B,A>}$ relation follows Lewis's procedure for determining the similarity relation on worlds which fixes the truth values of counterfactuals (see his "Counterfactual Dependence and Time's Arrow," *Noûs* 13 (1979), pp. 455–476): we use our intuitions about which Belief ascriptions are true and which false to settle what is a counterpart of what.

The logophoric analysis also has other attractive features. Special cases like fiction aside, we are intuitively reluctant to make an ascription of the form B(x, *that c is F*) if we believe *c* is a name which lacks a referent (an atheist who says "Mary believes God will forgive her" speaks archly). The analysis justifies this reluctance, since someone who makes such an ascription is, by (11), himself purporting to use the name to refer to an individual. Another advantage of the analysis is that it makes it easy to understand how anaphoric reference to the customary bearer of a name is effected, as by the "he" in "Lois believes Clark Kent can't fly, but in fact he can," where it is hard for a traditional Fregean approach to explain how "he" can refer to Clark if "Clark Kent" refers to a sense. These features of the analysis are aspects of a more general point. However plausible Frege's reference-shift doctrine seems in the abstract, it is difficult to escape the impression that in making an attitude ascription using a name, the ascriber makes a reference to the name's customary bearer, in addition to specifying a proposition. Appropriately, this is exactly what my account portrays the ascriber as doing. The departure from the historical Frege lies in the fact that we are not *completely* specifying the proposition the believer is said to believe; but this departure is simply what is required to accommodate the intersubjective variation from which Frege abstracted.[23]

It may be asked in what sense (9) is an *analysis* of (6). After all, (6) gives little evidence of the presence of a description of a sense. I have no general theory of the nature of the relationship which holds between *analysandum* and *analysans* here. But the non-conservatism of (9) relative to (6) is quite in line with other familiar proposals in contemporary philosophy of language; consider, for example, Davidson's semantic analysis of adverbial modification, which uncovers quantification over events, or Barwise and Perry's approach to seeing.[24] The main claim I wish to make about (9) is that it correctly articulates the way the world has to be if (6) is to be made true: it explains what constitutes the truth of (6). But in addition I know of no compelling reason why such regimentations as (9) could not be accurate depictions of mental representations on which the human language faculty operates.

---

[23]Castañeda's Guise Theory takes a completely different approach to these problems; see, for example, his "Method, Individuals and Guise Theory," in *Agent, Language and the Structure of the World: Essays Presented to Hector-Neri Castañeda*, ed. J. Tomberlin (Indianapolis, Ind.: Hackett, 1983), pp. 329–353. According to my analysis, the suspect principle of Guise Theory is that by removing a name from the content sentence in a belief ascription, one obtains something true of the individual to whom that name refers (pp. 338–339).____ is such that for B's so-labelled sense . . . ." is not purely a condition true of individuals, since co-designative names cannot replace each other in the blank *salva veritate*, though it is undeniable that any name put in the blank performs just its usual semantic function of referring to an individual. It is also referred to by another term in the same sentence, but that is not its semantic *function*.

[24]See D. Davidson, "The Logical Form of Action Sentences," in *The Logic of Decision and Action*, ed. N. Rescher (Pittsburgh, Penn.: Pittsburgh University Press, 1974), and J. Barwise and J. Perry, *Situations and Attitudes* (Cambridge, Mass.: The MIT Press), Chapter 7. There is a congenial account of the nature of this sort of analysis in Chapter 3 of *Events in the Semantics of English* by Terence Parsons (Cambridge, Mass.: The MIT Press, 1990).

The parallel with Davidson's semantics for adverbs is useful in other respects. It is often objected to Fregean approaches to attitude ascriptions which use quantification where singular reference to a sense might have been expected, that they cannot validate intuitively correct first-order reasoning about beliefs.[25] And my own approach appears vulnerable to this charge. Consider the argument:

B (12)   Ralph believes Superman can fly.

(13)   Lois believes Superman can fly.

∴ (14)   There is something Ralph and Lois both believe.

If we give (14) its *prima facie* regimentation, "$(\exists p)(B(R, p)\ \&\ B(L, p))$," we see that it is not a logical consequence of (12) and (13) as I analyze them, since each of (12) and (13) has its own description quantifier over senses. But intuitively, (14) does follow from (12) and (13); therefore the logophoric analyses are wrong.

My reply to this is that B is exactly analogous to the following argument:

C (15)   Ralph buttered some toast in the kitchen after midnight.

(16)   Lois buttered some toast in the kitchen after midnight.

∴ (17)   There is something Ralph and Lois both did.

The intuition that C is a good argument is just as firm as the corresponding intuition for B (even if it is not the same kitchen or the same night that is intended in the two premises). *Of course* there is something Ralph and Lois both did: they both buttered toast in the kitchen after midnight. But if (17) is given the regimentation "$(\exists e)\ (\text{Act}(e)\ \&\ \text{Doer}(e, \text{Ralph})\ \&\ \text{Doer}(e, \text{Lois}))$" analogous to (14), it does not follow logically from the Davidsonian analyses of (15) and (16), each of which has its own existential quantifier over events. Like (14) on its suggested analysis, (17) is not even true (unless we allow arbitrary concoctions of events to be events). I suppose one could take this to be a refutation of Davidson's account of action sentences, but in view of everything which that account has going for it, I would not regard *modus tollens* as a serious option here.

Besides, it is not difficult for a Davidsonian unafflicted with nominalist scruples to explain why we judge C to be a good argument. When we say that (17) is true we are taking the quantifier to range over not particular events, but types of events, abstractions from event tokens. Thus (17) says there is an event type of a certain nature which has tokens one of which has Ralph as agent and another of which has Lois as agent. And I think that something similar is true of (14). Though Ralph and Lois do not stand in the belief relation to one and the same Fregean proposition, there are propositions they believe which are significantly similar, each involving the sense of "can fly" and a way of thinking of Superman labelled "Superman." I take the English quantifier in (14) to range over such abstractions from token Fregean propositions. Hence (14) is true, and follows

---

[25]See George Bealer, *Quality and Concept* (Oxford, England: Oxford University Press, 1982), p. 38, and Chapter 2 of Richard's forthcoming *Attitudes*.

from (12) and (13), whose analyses explicitly reveal that the two beliefs are "abstractly the same."[26] So I do not think that the phenomenon illustrated by B is a real problem, and I suspect that those who do are being simplistic in their interpretations of natural language quantifier locations.[27]

IV

Throughout this paper I have been presupposing commonsense evaluations of belief ascriptions: Lois *does* believe that Superman can fly, that Clark Kent can't, does *not* believe that Clark Kent can fly, and so on. Broadly speaking, these evaluations are arrived at by taking Lois's linguistic behavior, her assents and dissents, at face value. So once this aspect of our ordinary practice of belief ascription is accepted, we have to reject substitution of co-referential names, since this can carry us from truths to what our ordinary practice decrees to be falsehoods. It then becomes a condition of adequacy on any semantics of belief ascription that it explain why substitution fails. And it is a powerful argument for Fregean approaches that they provide the most plausible explanations.

   This argument would be entirely undercut if our normal procedure of taking a subject's assents and dissents at face value could be shown to be of dubious reliability in the kinds of cases we have been considering, since it would then be dubious that substitution is in fact taking us from truths to *falsehoods*. Kripke has developed a family of cases in which our ordinary practices of belief ascription, apparently *by themselves*, lead to ascriptions which are counterintuitive in the same way as (3).[28] He also claims (*ibid.*, p. 268) that his cases are essentially like the standard ones, such as that of Lois, and concludes that an argument for a

---

[26]An alternative view is that the quantifiers in B and C are substitutional. Despite criticisms of this view in Chapter 2 of Richard's *Attitudes* I would regard it as viable if I regarded substitutional quantification as viable. But I share van Inwagen's doubts about its intelligibility; see his "Why I Don't Understand Substitutional Quantification," *Philosophical Studies* 39 (1981), pp. 281–285. Note that on my account of B and C neither is *logically* valid. But the conclusions do follow logically from the premises together with trivial principles guaranteeing that the events and propositions in question are of the same type.

[27]To hold this paper to a reasonable length, I ignore many other interesting issues, particularly having to do with iterated contexts, which I hope to address elsewhere. But I should respond to an objection put to me by Michael Woods about the parallel with action sentences. According to Wood, if we ask what it was that Ralph and Lois both did, the answer butter some toast in the kitchen after midnight, actually *looks* like a specification of an action type, whereas if we ask what they both believe, the answer, that Superman can fly, appears to be a specification of a proposition *token*. But in this linguistic context, the second answer is elliptical for "Ralph and Lois both believe that Superman can fly," which in turn expands into the conjunction "Ralph believes that . . . and Lois believes that . . . ," the logophoric analysis applying to each conjunct separately. So the original answer to the question specified a proposition type after all, or else had a kind of systematic ambiguity. In the same vein, we can apply the parallel with action sentences to an example suggested by Stephen Schiffer, in which there is apparently explicit singular reference to token propositions: (a) My theory is that Frege was right; (b) You believe that Frege was right; ∴ (c) You believe my theory. An appropriate parallel is (a) What I did was to butter toast in the kitchen; (b) You buttered toast in the kitchen; ∴ (c) You did what I did (or "You did the same as me").

[28]See "A Puzzle about Belief," in *Meaning and Use*, ed. A. Margalit (Dordrecht, The Netherlands: D. Reidel, 1979). The quotation below is from p. 265, except that I have altered the numbering.

Fregean approach from "failure of substitution" is far too quick: since it is taking the subject's words at face value that leads to problematic ascriptions in his cases, and since this practice is relied on in the standard cases, it may be this practice itself, rather than substitution, which is questionable in the standard cases.

In this final section, I will use the logophoric analysis to argue that the appearance of paradox in the ascriptions we make if we take the subject's words at face value in Kripke's cases is superficial. By contrast, the ascriptions to which substitution leads are genuinely objectionable, so an argument for a Fregean approach from failure of substitution is well founded. Here is Kripke's central example:

> Peter . . . may learn the name 'Paderewski' with an identification of the person named as a famous pianist . . . and we can infer
> (18) Peter believes that Paderewski had musical talent.
> Later, in a different circle, Peter learns of someone called 'Paderewski' who was a Polish . . . Prime Minister . . . . Peter assents to 'Paderewski had no musical talent'. . . . Should we infer
> (19) Peter believes that Paderewski had no musical talent
> or should we not?

I have one preliminary comment. Kripke presents this puzzle as a puzzle about the beliefs of a certain individual. But from the Fregean perspective, there is no puzzle about Peter's *beliefs:* Peter stands in the belief relation to a proposition consisting in a way of thinking of Paderewski coupled with the sense of "had musical talent," and he also stands in the belief relation to a proposition consisting in a *different* way of thinking of Paderewski coupled with the sense of "had no musical talent." Thus his dossier-object map is many-one as regards Paderewski, like Lois's as regards Clark; the novel element of the case is just that Peter's two dossiers are labelled by coreferential homonyms.[29]

What this gives rise to is not a puzzle about belief but a quandary about belief *ascription:* how should someone who only has one name with a single sense express the facts about Peter's beliefs? One problem is that if we assert both (18) and (19), we make Peter sound foolish, though we know that he does not have contradictory beliefs. The other difficulty is that if we assert both (18) and:

> (20) Peter does not believe Paderewski had musical talent,

we seem to involve *ourselves* in a contradiction. On the other hand, aren't (18) and (20) both true?

At first sight, the logophoric analysis does not seem to hold out much promise of illumination here. For it implies that all of (18)–(20) are defective, because the definite descriptions implicit in their meanings are improper. Thus (18) would be analyzed as

> (21) Paderewski is such that for Peter's so-labelled α, B(Peter, α ^ ⌜had no musical talented⌝)

---

[29]For a recent clear account of this kind of Fregean perspective on Kripke's cases, see W. Taschek's "Would a Fregean Be Puzzled by Pierre?" *Mind* 97 (1988), pp. 99–104.

but we cannot speak of "Peter's so-labelled way of thinking of Paderewski," since Peter has two such ways of thinking. Granted Russellian truth conditions, then, (18) and (19) are false, and (20) is true so long as the description is within the scope of the negation. Yet these verdicts are quite unnatural. Those who know the story are inclined to say, if tentatively, that (18) and (19) are both true, and to waver over, perhaps eventually to reject, (20). It seems that our attachment to ordinary practice inclines us to ascribe contradictory beliefs where we should not and even to make contradictory ascriptions. And the logophoric analysis simply passes these phenomena by.

However, a more sensitive application of the analysis explains why we would assent to both (18) and (19) and has the added bonus of showing that in doing so we need not be ascribing contradictory beliefs. Definite descriptions are rarely, if ever, evaluated without any reference to context: a request to take the dog for a walk does not really carry the implication that there is exactly one dog in the universe. Rather, the context and the content of a discourse determine which of the various objects satisfying the restrictive condition in the description is relevant. And one feature of the procedure involved in this is that when the content of what is said together with features of the surrounding circumstances do not completely determine choice of object, we prefer a choice which makes best sense, psychologically, of the speaker, given what we know he knows.[30] Suppose, for example, that Peter's situation is known to the ascriber, we know this, and we have to evaluate (18), (19) and (20) without reference to any particular occasion of utterance by Peter (there are many variations of the initial conditions which could be considered, but they can all be dealt with by the method I use for this situation). In evaluating (18), we may then take the description "Peter's so-labelled way of thinking of Paderewski" to determine that way of thinking which is a constituent of a belief of Peter's to the effect that Paderewski had musical talent, since that selection makes (18) express a truth which we know the ascriber knows. This is how the tentative thought that (18) is true arises. Correspondingly, and for parallel reasons, when (19) is asserted, we may take the description "Peter's so-labelled way of thinking of Paderewski" to pick out that different way of thinking which is a constituent of a belief of Peter's to the effect that Paderewski had no musical talent. Since the ways of thinking are different, (18) and (19) do not ascribe contradictory beliefs.[31] And we waver over (20) because on the one hand we have already asserted its contradictory, while on the other, there is an available alternative selection of a way of thinking which allows (20) to express a truth which we know

---

[30] Here I have been influenced by David Lewis's "Scorekeeping in a Language Game," *The Journal of Philosophical Logic* 8 (1979), pp. 339–359.

[31] It is not unprecedented for attitude ascriptions which clearly seem to impute contradictory beliefs to turn out on a closer look not to do so. Consider "John believes that you are a philosopher" and "John believes that you are not a philosopher" relative to the *same* context (same speaker, same time, same "you"). According to me, the first ascription means the same as "You are someone John believes to be a philosopher" and the second the same as "You are someone John believes not to be a philosopher," and this pair of ascriptions does not impute belief in a contradiction. See "Indexicals and Intensionality," pp. 13–15.

is known to the ascriber, rather than a falsehood which we know he knows is false. Someone who does wish to agree to (20) is more influenced by this second consideration, and so is not contradicting himself in also endorsing (18).

If this is a plausible reconstruction of the underlying mechanics of how someone who knows the whole story goes about evaluating the ascriptions, it means that such a person is doing more than just taking Peter's linguistic behavior at face value. Principles for resolving *prima facie* improper sense descriptions are also being employed. Such principles will always play a role in Kripke's cases, where there is either a single name labelling two of the believer's dossiers and only one of the ascriber's, or else there are two names labelling distinct dossiers of the believer, names which have an equally good claim to be a linguistic counterpart of a single name of the ascriber's (cf., "London" and "Londres"). And we have just seen that the effect of such principles is to dispel the air of contradiction that hangs over (18)–(20). But improper descriptions play no role in standard cases: there is a stark contrast between the fact that (18) and (19) need not constitute ascription of contradictory beliefs and the fact that someone who assents to both (1) and "Lois believes Clark Kent can fly" does ascribe contradictory beliefs. This is why I reject Kripke's claim to find a significant theoretical parallel between his cases and standard ones: in his cases, we do not ultimately find any results that suggest there is something wrong with taking the believer's linguistic behavior at face value. So no reason has been given to think that it is this practice which is at the root of the trouble in standard cases when substitution is made.

I said earlier that Kripke's puzzle is really a puzzle about how to *describe* Peter's beliefs. For although we can arrive at definite interpretations of (18)–(20), the procedure involves much uncertainty. However, there is a remedy for this, and the logophoric analysis explains nicely how it works. The core of the problem we face in describing Peter's beliefs is one of the *expressive inadequacy* of the range of senses we can express by our words relative to the range Peter expresses with his. Now the obvious way to overcome an expressive inadequacy in a language is simply to extend the language's expressive resources. And it appears to me that this is exactly what we do in such cases as Peter's, without being guided by any philosophical theory. There is in English a way of qualifying singular terms which one naturally reaches for in discussing Peter's beliefs: one can qualify a term by attaching "the F" to it, where F is some salient predicate. Kripke does this himself, apparently without attributing any significance to the maneuver, when he writes: "Before [Peter] hears of 'Paderewski-the-statesman', it would appear that . . . [his] dialect can be translated homophonically into our own" ("A Puzzle about Belief," p. 279, n. 37). If we apply this qualification strategy to (18)–(20), replacing occurrences of "Paderewski" with "Paderewski the pianist" and "Paderewski the Prime Minister" so as to make every ascription true, all appearance of contradiction vanishes: Peter believes Paderewski the pianist had musical talent and Paderewski the Prime Minister had no musical talent, and does not believe that Paderewski the Prime Minister had musical talent.

I think it is a pretheoretic datum that by replacing occurrences of "Paderewski" with "Paderewski the pianist" and "Paderewski the Prime Minister" we are in some way *clarifying* our statements about Peter's beliefs. The clarification is like disambiguation in that it settles an interpretation which was previously unsettled. Some examples of standard uses of a phrase "the F" to disambiguate a term are "the emperor Julian," "Santa Claus: The Movie," "the proposition that Clark Kent is Superman," and "the fact that Clark Kent is Superman." In these examples, the function of "the F" is to determine the customary reference of the (ambiguous) following term. But clarification by using "Paderewski the pianist," etc., cannot be construed as disambiguation of customary reference, since Paderewski the pianist *is* Paderewski the Prime Minister. Rather, the use of qualified names leads to replacement in the ascription analyses of improper by proper definite descriptions, such as "Peter's so-labelled way of thinking of Paderewski the pianist." (The qualification works, of course, only on the supposition that the qualifying condition determines just one of the believer's dossiers.)[32] The effect of augmenting one's language by adding the two names "Paderewski the pianist" and "Paderewski the Prime Minister" is to adjust the linguistic counterpart relation: one of Peter's names "Paderewski" becomes the linguistic counterpart of the ascriber's "Paderewski the pianist" and the other the linguistic counterpart of "Paderewski the Prime Minister." Note that there is no requirement that the conditions "pianist" and "Prime Minister" should actually occur in the labels on Peter's dossiers. Their role is simply to determine which of Peter's labels "Paderewski" shall be the linguistic counterpart of a particular name the ascriber uses. In terms of the functioning of descriptions, what the qualifier does is to eliminate our reliance on our knowledge of what the ascriber knows about Peter in selecting that way of thinking of Peter's which is germane to the evaluation of the ascription. The relevant way of thinking is now fixed by the content of the ascription itself, so that if the ascriber were to say, "Peter believes Paderewski the Prime Minister had musical talent," his statement would be uncontroversially false.

If this is correct, some moves Kripke makes against the Fregean should be resisted. Kripke insists that we answer the question (*ibid.*, p. 259), "Does Peter, or does he not, believe that Paderewski had musical talent?" But if the interpretation of this question is uncertain, then we are under no obligation to answer it. The situation would be comparable to one where someone asks, "Was Aristotle wealthy?" in a context where it is unclear if it is the philosopher or the shipping magnate who is meant. The correct response is to ask which interpretation of the question is intended, and only then to answer it. I suggest that the response should be the same if the question is underspecified in that it leaves the interpreter too much work to do in deciding which way of thinking is relevant: one is entitled to ask the questioner to qualify his uses of the name "Paderewski." Thus it is entirely reasonable to reply to Kripke's question about Peter with: is the question whether Peter believes Paderewski *the pianist,* or Paderewski *the Prime Minister,* had musical talent? That is, there is a case to be made for rejecting the question as Kripke formulates it.

---

[32]If no such condition can be found (see Kripke, "A Puzzle about Belief," p. 260) then perhaps the best we could do in reporting Peter's beliefs is "He believes a Paderewski is F and a Paderewski is not-F."

The main moral Kripke urges for his examples is that we should not take "absurd" conclusions such as "Lois has all along believed that Clark Kent is Superman" as evidence that interchange of co-designative names in belief contexts is illegitimate. I have argued in reply that the reasons Kripke gives for thinking that the difficulty lies elsewhere (in "the nature of the realm being entered"— *ibid.*, p. 206) are ineffective: upon a closer look, and against the background of a realistic account of how descriptions function in natural language as opposed to the logician's abstraction, the belief ascriptions in his examples are seen to be not so problematic. Their worst feature is that they suffer from uncertainty of interpretation, but this can be eliminated by replacing occurrences of "Paderewski" with qualified versions of the name. If we *then* wish to produce effects comparable to the results of substitution in ascriptions of beliefs to Lois, it is precisely substitution that we have to apply. For instance, on the basis of the fact that Paderewski the pianist is Paderewski the Prime Minister, we could infer that Peter believes that Paderewski the Prime Minister had musical talent, though we are already committed to saying that he believes Paderewski the Prime Minister had no musical talent. But without using the identity fact, nothing counterintuitive can be obtained from these belief ascriptions. That is, the only way of generating problems from belief ascriptions made in an expressively adequate language requires substitution on the basis merely of identity of customary reference. The results are "unpalatable" and "absurd," to use Kripke's words; and apart from substitutivity, there is no other principle about propositional attitudes which bids so strongly for the role of culprit.[33]

---

[33]In writing and revising this paper I have benefited from discussion and correspondence with Nicholas Asher, John Campbell, Martin Davies, Kit Fine, Ed Johnson, Ruth Marcus, Michael Martin, Jon Oberlander, Ian Rumfit, Nathan Salmon, Stephen Schiffer, Gene Schlossberg, William Taschek, Timothy Williamson, Michael Woods and Takashi Yagisawa. Part of my research was supported by a grant from Tulane University's Committee on Research, for which I express my sincere appreciation. I am especially grateful to Ali Akhtar Kazmi and in particular Mark Richard. Finally, for resources placed at my disposal I thank both the Institute for Advanced Studies in the Humanities and the Centre for Cognitive Science at Edinburgh University.

THE BOETHIAN COMPROMISE

Alvin Plantinga

Russell held that ordinary proper names—such names as "Socrates," "Aristotle" and "Muhammad Ali"—are really truncated definite descriptions; "Socrates" for example, may be short (in a given person's use) for something like, say, "the snub-nosed Greek philosopher who taught Plato."[1] If so, the result of replacing a name in a sentence by the right description will ordinarily express the same proposition; descriptions can be substituted for names *salva propositione*. On

---

[1] Bertrand Russell, "The Philosophy of Logical Atomism," in *Logic and Knowledge,* ed. Robert Marsh (London 1956), p. 200.

this view, proper names are *semantically equivalent* to descriptions. Frege's view is both more subtle and less clear; but he too held that in many contexts a proper name such as "Aristotle" has the same sense as such a definite description as "the pupil of Plato and teacher of Alexander the Great," so that the sentence "Aristotle was born in Stagira" expresses the same thought as the result of replacing "Aristotle" therein by that description.[2] Let us call such views of proper names *Fregean* views.

According to John Stuart Mill, on the other hand, "Proper Names are not connotative; they denote the individuals who are called by them, but they do not indicate or imply an attribute as belonging to these individuals."[3] More recently, Keith Donnellan,[4] Saul Kripke,[5] David Kaplan[6] and others have joined Mill against Frege and Russell. As they quite properly point out, no description of the sort Russell and Frege had in mind is semantically equivalent to a name like "Socrates." Clearly "the snub-nosed teacher of Plato," for example, will not fill the bill, since

(1) The snub-nosed teacher of Plato never taught Plato

or better

(2) the snub-nosed teacher of Plato was a non-teacher

expresses an impossible proposition, unlike

(3) Socrates was a non-teacher.

But the heart and soul of Fregean views is not that proper names are semantically equivalent to descriptions (after all, the right sort of description might not be available), but that they *have sense*, or *descriptive content*, or that they *"indicate or imply an attribute"*: more briefly, that they *express properties*. And the denial of this claim is the heart and soul of the anti-Fregean views. How then, on these views, *do* proper names function? Mill says proper names have denotation but no connotation; a proper name denotes without expressing a property. He seems to mean that the sole semantic function performed by a proper name is that of denoting its referent; its semantic function is *exhausted* in denoting its referent. The crucial contrast, then, between Fregean and anti-Fregean views is that on the former proper names express properties; on the latter they do not. In what follows I shall first argue that the anti-Fregeans are mistaken; I shall then suggest an alternative in the Fregean spirit.

---

[2] Gottlob Frege, "On Sense and Reference," in *Translations from the Philosophical Writings of Gottlob Frege*, ed. P. T. Geach and M. Black (Oxford, 1952), p. 58.

[3] *A System of Logic* (New York, 1846), p. 21.

[4] "Speaking of Nothing," *The Philosophical Review*, vol. 85 (1976):11–12.

[5] "Naming and Necessity," in *Semantics of Natural Language*, ed. D. Davidson and G. Harman (Dordrecht, 1972), pp. 320, 327; "Identity and Necessity," in *Identity and Individualion*, ed. M. Munitz (New York, 1971), p. 140.

[6] "Demonstratives," his hitherto unpublished address to the Pacific Division of the American Philosophical Association (March, 1976).

I

Russell instructs us to test a logical and semantical theory by "its capacity for dealing with puzzles."[7] His own theory of ordinary proper names nicely passes muster with respect to three such puzzles: those presented by empty proper names, by negative existentials containing proper names, and by propositional identity in the context of propositional attitudes. On the other hand the anti-Fregean view, as I shall argue, founders on these rocks.

(i) If, as the anti-Fregeans claim, proper names do not express properties and do no more than denote their referents, then how shall we understand such sentences as

(4) Romulus founded Rome

as used by someone who believes the legend and is intending to assert part of what he believes? In his use "Romulus" denotes nothing at all. But then what proposition, on the anti-Fregean view, does (4) express? It is hard to see, on this view, how such a sentence could express any proposition at all. If a proper name does not express a property but serves merely to denote its referent, then when it fails to have a referent it presumably performs no semantic function at all—in which case (4) would express no proposition at all. Faced with these considerations, Donnellan suggests that sentences like (4) (under the envisaged conditions) do indeed fail to express propositions:

> [A] true negative existence statement expressed by using a name involves a name with no referent and the corresponding positive existence statement, if false, will also. But in other contexts, when a name is used and there is a failure of reference, then no proposition has been expressed—certainly no true proposition. If a child says, 'Santa Claus will come tonight,' he cannot have spoken the truth, although, for various reasons, I think it better to say that he has not even expressed a proposition.[8]

He adds, via a footnote, "Given that this is a statement about reality and that proper names have no descriptive content, then how are we to represent the proposition expressed?"

But surely this is wrong. Someone who utters (4), intending to tell the sober truth, has surely asserted *something*. What he asserts entails, for example, that Rome has not always existed but had a founder. If so, however, (4) does express a proposition, under these conditions, and the semantic function of "Romulus," therein, can't be that of denoting its referent, since it has no referent to denote. But then there will be no adequate anti-Fregean account of an empty proper name as used by someone who mistakenly believes it non-empty and intends to predicate a property of what it denotes.

(ii) A second difficulty for the anti-Fregean is presented by negative existentials. How, on this view, are we to understand such a sentence as

(5) Romulus did not exist?

---

[7] "On Denoting" (Marsh, *op. cit.*), p. 47.

[8] "Speaking of Nothing," p. 22.

Here, of course, we cannot sensibly say that the sentence expresses no proposition; clearly it expresses a truth. But *what* truth? And how does the name "Romulus" there function? Obviously it does not denote an *existent* object; so if it denotes anything at all, it denotes a *non-existent* object. Accordingly, one can give an anti-Fregean account of (5) only by holding that "Romulus" denotes a non-existent object therein, the rest of the sentence quite properly predicating non-existence of that object. In addition to the things that exist, there are, on this view, some more that do not. The above-mentioned anti-Fregeans show little inclination toward this view, and for (as I see it) good reason: the view is clearly false.[9] So "Romulus" denotes nothing at all in (5). Clearly enough, however, (5) expresses a proposition (since it expresses a truth); hence "Romulus" plays a semantical role of *some* sort therein, though not that of denoting its referent. But how then *does* it function? Is it semantically equivalent in this special existential case to a description? No, says Donnellan:

> . . . [O]n any view we must, I think, accept the following:
> (E) That Socrates did not exist entails that it is not true that Socrates was snub-nosed.

> Our theory tells us that the second occurrence of 'Socrates' in (E) is not a concealed definite description. But then neither can the first occurrence be one. For if we take some definite description such as the one suggested as what the first occurrence of 'Socrates' stands for, rejection of the principle of identifying descriptions for the second occurrence means that it *could* be true that Socrates was snub-nosed even though no unique individual existed who satisfied that description. That is to say, if "Socrates" in "Socrates did not exist" is a concealed definite description, but is not in "Socrates was snub-nosed," then the antecedent of (E) could be true while the consequent is false. Since we want to accept the entailment expressed by (E) our theory cannot treat "Socrates" as a concealed description in existential statements. (p. 22)

How then *are* we to understand (5) and the function of "Romulus" therein? Donnellan's "Speaking of Nothing" (1976) is the most explicit published treatment of existentials by an anti-Fregean; but he tells us little, there, about the function of empty proper names in sentences like (5), and less about the propositions expressed by such sentences. What he gives is a "rule for negative existential statements . . . that purports to give the truth conditions for negative existential statements containing a name. . . .:

> (R) if *N* is a proper name that has been used to predicative statements with the intent to refer to some individual, then "*N* does not exist" is true if and only if the history of those uses ends in a block. (p. 25)

I refer you to Donnellan's piece for the idea of a block. What is important to see in the present context is that a rule like (R) could function in more than one way. On the one hand it could give logically necessary and sufficient conditions for the truth of the *proposition* ordinarily expressed by "*N* does not

---

[9] See my *The Nature of Necessity* (Oxford, 1974), chs. 7 and 8.

exist," in which case it would identify that proposition up to logical equivalence. But (R) does not function in that way. If it did, the proposition

(6) Socrates does not exist

would be equivalent to

(7) The history of (some specific use of) "Socrates" ends in a block.

But clearly (6) is not equivalent to (7): clearly Socrates could have existed no matter what the history of anyone's use of "Socrates"; he could have had another name or no name at all. Hence (7) is true but (6) is false in those worlds where, let us say, Socrates exists but is named "Muhammad Ali," and the history of the appropriate uses of "Socrates" exists in a block. (6) is logically independent of such propositions as (7) that detail the history of "Socrates."

If so, however, (R) does not give necessary and sufficient conditions for such propositions as (5) and (6). What then does it do? Presumably it tells us, not under what conditions the *propositions* (5) and (6) are true, but under what conditions the *sentences* (5) and (6) express true propositions. These, of course, are quite different enterprises. The sentence (6) expresses a truth in just those situations in which the history of certain uses of the name "Socrates" ends in a block; and, as we have seen, these are not the same situations as those in which Socrates does not exist—that is, they are not the same situations as those in which the proposition in fact expressed by (6) is true. So Donnellan's (R) does not give truth conditions for the *propositions* expressed by (5) and (6); nor does he tell us what those propositions *are*. The question therefore becomes acute: how, from the anti-Fregean vantage point, shall we understand sentences like (5) and (6) when they contain empty proper names? What proposition is expressed by such a sentence? The answer is unclear. What is clear, however, is that the anti-Fregean cannot properly stick to his anti-Fregean principles for proper names in existential sentences.

(iii) The third difficulty is presented by propositional identity. If we think, with the anti-Fregeans, that a proper name typically exhausts its semantic role in denoting its referent, then presumably the result of replacing it in a sentence like

(8) Mark Twain was a pessimist

or

(9) Mark Twain is the same person as Samuel Clemens

by another name of the same object will express the same proposition. In other words, the anti-Fregean seems committed to the principle that codesignative proper names in such contexts are intersubstitutable *salva propositione*. Donnellan,[10] indeed, explicitly endorses this principle; and it certainly seems to follow from the views of Mill seconded by Kripke. But surely it is wrong. Clearly a person could know the proposition expressed by (8) without knowing that expressed by

(9.5) Samuel Langhorne Clemens was a pessimist

---

[10] "Speaking of Nothing," p. 28.

just as Lois Lane knows, of course, that Superman is faster than a speeding bullet but does not know that the same goes for Clark Kent. There are various expedients that might tempt anti-Fregeans here; none, I believe, is satisfactory. I don't have the space to pursue the matter here; some of these problems are clearly brought out in Diana Ackerman's "Recent Work in the Theory of Reference."[11]

In what follows I shall suggest a view that (dare I say it?) displays the virtues of both Fregean and anti-Fregean views, but the vices of neither. The first principle of this view is that proper names do indeed express properties. But what is it, exactly, for a singular term to express a property? The anti-Fregeans deny that proper names express properties; precisely what is it they are anti? We might make a beginning as follows. Suppose we agree that such a singular term as "the shortest spy" expresses at least one property: that of being the shortest spy. It is because that term expresses this property that the sentence.

(10) The shortest spy is a non-(shortest spy)

expresses an impossible proposition, as does

(11) The shortest spy is a non-spy.

This suggests the following initial attempts to capture the notion of property expression. Let's suppose we know what it is for a predicate, such as "is a spy" to express a property, such as *being a spy*. Then we might say that

(12) A singular term *t* expresses a property *P* (with respect to a given context of use) if the sentence (*t* is expresses a necessary falsehood (with respect to that context of use)

where $\mathscr{P}$ is a predicate that expresses *P* and $\ulcorner \mathscr{P} \urcorner$ is its complement. It is then clear that "the shortest spy" expresses the properties *being a spy* and *being a shortest spy*, while "Paul J. Zwier" does not, despite the fact that Paul J. Zwier *is* the shortest spy. On the other hand, it is obvious, given (12), that proper names do express *some* properties—those, for example, like *self-identity* or *being unmarried, if a bachelor*, that are trivially essential to everything. Clearly the sentence

(13) Quine is self-diverse

(where "is self-diverse" expresses the complement of *self-identity*) expresses a necessarily false proposition; hence "Quine" expresses self-identity. It also expresses a more interesting property: (13) is impossible; but so is

(14) Quine is diverse from Quine.

But then "Quine" expresses identity-with-Quine as well as self-identity. The former, of course, is distinct from the latter; *everything*, naturally enough, has self-identity, but Quine alone has identity-with-Quine. Some philosophers find this property somehow objectionable; but the fact (as it seems to me) is that identity-with-Quine is a perfectly intelligible property. In any event it is gratifyingly easy

[11] *American Philosophical Quarterly*, forthcoming.

to state the conditions under which an object has it: x has identity-with-Quine if and only if x is Quine.

Identity-with-Quine is an *individual essence*[12] (individual concept, haecceity) of Quine. Let's say that a property P is *essential* to an object x iff it is not possible that x have its complement—equivalently, iff there is no possible world in which x exists but lacks P.[13] Then an essence of Quine is a property that he has essentially and is such that it is not possible that there be an object distinct from him that has it. In terms of possible worlds, an essence of Quine is a property he has in every world in which he exists, and one such that in no possible world is there an object distinct from him that has it. The view that proper names express individual essences has impressive historical credentials: it goes back to Scotus and, before him, to Boethius, who put the matter thus:

> For were it permitted to fabricate a name, I would call that certain quality, singu-lar and incommunicable to any other subsistent, by its fabricated name, so that the form of what is proposed would become clearer. For let the incommunicable property of Plato be called "Platonity". For we can call this quality 'Platonity' by a fabricated word, in the way in which we call the quality of man 'humanity'. Therefore, this Platonity is one man's alone, and this not just anyone's but Plato's. For 'Plato' points out a one and definite substance, and property, that cannot come together in another.[14]

So far as I know, this is the first explicit recognition that proper names express essence; let us therefore call this view "Boethianism." On the Boethian conception, an essence of Plato is a property he has essentially; it is, furthermore, "incommu-nicable to any other" in that it is impossible that something distinct from him should have had it.

The second principle of the present view, then, is that proper names express essences. It is crucially important to see, furthermore, that an object typically has *several* essences. This is evident as follows. Suppose we say that Plato has the *world-indexed* property P-in-W if and only if W includes Plato's having P (if and only if, that is, it is not possible that W be actual and Plato not have P). Now consider any property P that Plato has—*being erudite* for example—and note that the world-indexed property *being-erudite-in-*α (where 'α' is a proper name of the actual world) is essential to him. For while indeed there may be worlds in which Plato is not erudite, there are none in which it is not the case that α includes Plato's being erudite. World-indexed properties are *non-contingent:* for any object x and world-indexed property P-in-W, x has P-in-W essentially, or x has its complement essentially.[15] Where P is a property, let's say that the α-transform of P (call "$P\alpha$") is the world-indexed property P-in-α; and if $\mathscr{P}$ is a

---

[12] See *The nature of Necessity*, ch. 5.

[13] *Ibid.* p., 35.

[14] *In Librum de Interprelatione editio secunda*, PL 64, 462d–464c. Quoted in H. N Casteñeda, "Individuation and Non-Identity: A New Look," *American Philosophical Quarterly*, vol. 12 (1975): 135–36.

[15] See *The Nature of Necessity*, pp. 62–63.

predicate expressing P, its α-transform $\mathscr{P}\alpha$ expresses $P\alpha$. And now consider a property Plato alone has—*being Socrates' best student,* for example, or *being born at P, T* where 'P' names the place and 'T' the time at which he was born. The α-transforms of these properties are *essences* of Plato. All of Plato's world-indexed properties are essential to him; hence these two are. There is no possible world, furthermore, in which there is an object distinct from Plato that has either of these properties[16]; they are therefore among his essences. But (*being Socrates' best student*) α is certainly not the same property as (*being born at P, T*)α; for clearly a person could know of the first that Plato has it without knowing of the second that he has it. They are therefore (by Leibniz's Law) distinct properties; hence Plato has several distinct essences.

The several essences of Plato, furthermore, are logically but not epistemically equivalent. They are logically equivalent: for any such essences E and E^* there is obviously no possible world in which E is exemplified by an object that does not exemplify E^*. On the other hand, they are epistemically inequivalent: it is clearly possible to know or believe that an object has E without knowing or believing that it has E^*. I might know, for example, that Plato has the α-transform of *being Socrates' best student* without knowing that he has the α-transform of *being Aristotle's teacher.* This multiplicity of essences, furthermore, is crucially important to the Boethian view I want to suggest. For if Plato has several distinct essences, then distinct proper names of Plato can express distinct essences. But then (just as Frege and Russell thought) the result of replacing an ordinary proper name in a simple sentence S by a codesignative proper name need not express the same proposition as S. The Boethian view is an improvement on Frege and Russell, however, in that on the former but not the latter proper names express only *essential* properties of the objects they denote. Boethius therefore deserves credit for making an important improvement on the Frege-Russell view and for offering a more subtle, adequate, and up-to-date version of it.

But if we are to hold that different proper names of an object express different essences, we shall need a more discriminating account of property expression than that provided by (12). According to (12) a term expresses any property entailed[17] by any property it expresses; but then if a proper name expresses an essence of an object, it will express every property essential to that object and hence all of its essences.[18] How can we achieve a more discriminating notion?

We must begin by noting that the sentence

(15) 3^2 is odd

expresses a different proposition from that expressed by

(16) $\frac{27}{8} \int_0^2 x^2$ is odd;

---

[16] For argument, see *ibid.*, p. 72.

[17] Where a property P entails a property Q iff it is not possible that there be an object that exemplifies P but not Q.

[18] See *The Nature of Necessity*, pp. 72–73.

clearly one might know the one without knowing the other. Indeed, those of us with an imperfect grasp of the calculus may know the first proposition but not even possess the concepts necessary to apprehend the second, thus being unable to *believe* it, let alone know it. (15) and (16), therefore, express different propositions; and this is due to the fact that their singular terms express different properties. "3^2 and "$\frac{27}{8} \int_0^2 x^2$" both express essences of 9, but epistemically inequivalent and hence *different* essences. But if these singular terms can express epistemically inequivalent and hence *different* essences, why can't the same be said for proper names? Perhaps, for example, "Phosphorus" expresses something like the α-transform of being *the last heavenly body to disappear in the morning*, while "Hesperus" expresses the α-transform of *being the first heavenly body to appear in the evening*. And perhaps we can state the relevant notion of property expression as follows. Let us suppose, once more, that we know what it is for a predicate to express a property. The predicate "is the square of 3" expresses the property *being the square of three;* it does not express the properties *being* $\sqrt[3]{729}$ or being $\frac{27}{8} \int_0^2 x^2$, despite the fact that anything having one of these properties is obliged to have the others. A definite description $\ulcorner$the $\mathscr{P}\urcorner$ then expresses the same property as $\ulcorner$is the sole $\mathscr{P}\urcorner$; and a proper name N expresses (in English) a property P if there is a definite description D (in English or some extension of English) such that D expresses P and N and D are intersubstitutable *salva propositions* in sentences of the form "t is $\mathscr{P}$."

The third principle, then, of the Boethian view I advocate is this: different proper names of an object can express logically equivalent but epistemically inequivalent essences of that object. This view, I believe, displays at least three important virtues. First, it enables us to accommodate the insights of the anti-Fregeans within a Fregean context. Second, the Boethian view succeeds where the anti-Fregean view fails: (a) it enables us to see how such sentences as

(17) Hesperus is the evening star

and

(18) Phosphorus is the evening star

can express epistemically inequivalent propositions, and how

(19) Hesperus is identical with Phosphorus

can express an informative proposition; (b) it enables us to see what propositions are expressed by sentences containing empty proper names; and (c) it enables us to see what propositions are expressed by existential sentences containing proper names. Finally, as a sort of bonus, the Boethian view enables us to see that proper names in existential sentences function in just the way they do in singular sentences generally.

(i) One of the insights of the anti-Fregeans, of course, is that proper names do not express the sorts of properties Frege, Russell, and their followers take them to. More specifically, in criticizing Frege and Russell, what they really point out (although they don't always but it this way themselves) is that proper names do not express properties *inessential* to their bearers.[19] With this, of course, the Boethian enthusiastically concurs; a use of a proper name of Socrates expresses an essence of Socrates and hence does not express any property inessential to him. But the anti-Fregeans have other insights. Kripke states one as follows:

> A rough statement of a theory might be the following: an initial baptism takes place. Here the object may be named by ostension, or the reference may be fixed by description. When the name is 'passed from link to link' the receiver of the name must, I think, intend when he learns it to use it with the same reference as the man from whom he heard it.[20]

And according to Donnellan:

> The main idea is that when a speaker uses a name intending to refer to an individual and predicate something of it, successful reference will occur when there is an individual that enters into the historically correct explanation of who it is that the speaker intended to predicate something of. That individual will then be the referent and the statement made will be true or false depending upon whether it has the property designated by the predicate.[21]

Donnellan and, less explicitly, Kripke hold that proper names do not express properties; and we might suppose that this is a consequence of their view as to how the reference of a proper name is determined. But it isn't. It is entirely possible both that the reference of a proper name is determined in the way they say it is and that proper names express essences. For consider that complex historical relation R, whatever exactly it is, that on the Kripke-Donnellan view holds between an object and the names that name it. There is an initial complication: the same proper name may name different objects. So what an objects stands in R to is not a name *simpliciter* but a name in a given use—in the case of "Socrates," perhaps its use in Plato's *Dialogues* and in history books and philosophy classes. But suppose we ignore this complication, or deal with it by pretending that such names are homonymous: for each person named "Socrates" there is a different name spelled "Socrates." Now of course.

(20) The person that stands in R to "Socrates" was wise

does not express the same proposition as

(21) Socrates was wise

(21) but not (20) is true in a world where Socrates is wise but no one is named "Socrates." So "Socrates" does not express the property *being the person that stands in R to "Socrates."* But perhaps it can express the α-transform of that property. If the fact is Socrates alone *does* stand in R to "Socrates" then (*being*

---

[19] See, e.g., Kripe, *loc. cit.*

[20] "Naming and Necessity," p. 302.

[21] *Ibid.*, p. 302.

the person that stands in R to "Socrates") α is an essence of Socrates, so that the proposition expressed by

(22) the (person that stands in R to "Socrates") α was wise is at least equivalent to (23). And if "Socrates" does express this property, then the reference of "Socrates" is determined in the way Kripke and Donnellan say it is; for then "Socrates" refers to an object x if and only if x stands in R to "Socrates." Thus from our Boethian vantage point we see how it could be both that proper names express essences and that their reference is determined in the way the anti-Fregeans say it is.

And now consider John Searle's Fregean view. Searle holds, roughly, that the name "Socrates" expresses the property *being the person who had enough of the* S_i, where the S_i are the identity criteria associated with that name.[22] "Socrates," however, does not express *that* property:

(23) Socrates had scarcely any of the S_i

and

(24) the person who had enough of the S_i had scarcely any of the S_i

do not express equivalent propositions; the proposition expressed by (24) is necessarily false, while that expressed by (23) is true in those possible worlds where, let's say, Socrates meets with a fatal accident at the age of 6 months, thus having scarcely any of the properties that constitute the identity criteria we associate with "Socrates." But the fact is Socrates alone did have enough of the S_i, so that the α-transform of *being the person that had enough of the* S_i is an essence of Socrates. Hence

(25) the (person who had enough of the S_i) α had scarcely any of the S_i

expresses a contingent proposition equivalent to (23). "Socrates" can't express the property Searle says it does; but there's no reason why it can't express the α-transform of that property.

According to Frege, a proper name of a person may express different properties in the mouths of different persons or in the mouth of the same person on different occasions; perhaps the truth, then, is that "Socrates" serves on some occasions to express the α-transform of *being the person who stands in R to "Socrates"* and on others to express the α-transform of *being the person who had enough of the* S_i. In this way we can bring about a *rapprochement* between the Fregeans and the anti-Fregeans—a sort of group marriage, California style, among Donnellan, Frege, Kaplan, Kripke, Russell, Searle, and anyone else who is interested, with Boethius as presiding clergyman. On the Boethian compromise, proper names express properties, just as the Fregeans hold; but their references, in at least some cases, are determined in the way the anti-Fregeans suppose. We can then see the Fregean—anti-Fregean dispute as a relatively minor domestic

---

[22]See his "Proper Names," *Mind*, vol. 67 (1958): 171, and *Speech Acts* (Cambridge, 1969), p. 169.

quarrel as to just which essence of an object its name expresses. Perhaps the truth is: sometimes one, sometimes another.

(ii) Secondly, let us note how the Boethian view copes with the difficulties besetting the anti-Fregeans.

(a) In *The Nature of Necessity* I unwisely conceded that if proper names express essences, then it is plausible to suppose that different proper names of the same object express the same essence—in which case

(19) Hesperus = Phosphorus

expresses the same proposition as

(26) Hesperus = Hesperus.

If so, however, we shall have to say that the ancient Babylonians, despite their sincere protestations to the contrary, knew all along that Hesperus is identical with Phosphorus. After all, they knew the truth expressed by (26); but that is the very truth expressed by (19). They knew the truth expressed by (19) and (26); what they didn't know was that (19) and (26) express the same truth. They were thus deceived about the *sentence* (19) (or its counterpart in Ancient Babylonian) thinking it expressed a proposition distinct from that expressed by (26).

Now perhaps this is not wholly implausible; it does have about it, however, a certain air of the arcane.[23] In any event, a better explanation is available, once we recognize that different names of the same object may express different essences. For then we can say simply and straightforwardly that the Babylonians knew (26) but did not know (19). This, after all, coincides with their own claims and seems to be no more than the simple truth. On our Boethian account the sentence (19) expresses something like

(19*) the (morning star) α = the (evening star) α

or perhaps

(19**) the (heavenly body last visible in the morning) α = the (heavenly body first visible in the evening) α;

and we can see how the Babylonians could have gone wrong with respect to such items as (19*) and (19**). Here their situation is like that of one who knows, of course, that

(27) $3^2 = 3^2$

but doesn't believe that

(28) $3^2 = \frac{27}{8} \int_0^2$

"3^2" and "$\frac{27}{8} \int_0^2$" both express essences of 9, but *different* essences; and it is easy enough to fail to realize that these essences are exemplified by the same

---

[23]See Diana Ackerman's "Plantinga, Proper Names and Propositions," *Philosophical Studies*, vol. 28 (1976): 409–12.

object. (27) and (28) thus express epistemically inequivalent propositions. But the same goes for (19) and (26); since "Hesperus" and "Phosphorus" express epistemically inequivalent essences of Venus, (19) and (26) express epistemically inequivalent propositions, so that (19) can be informative. And of course exactly similar considerations apply to

(29) Hesperus is visible in the morning

and

(30) Phosphorus is visible in the morning;

these also express epistemically inequivalent propositions. Surely this is the natural and intuitively plausible position; surely a person could believe (26) and (29) without believing either (19) or (30).[24]

The second and third difficulty for the anti-Fregean, you recall, are presented by empty proper names and by proper names in existential sentences. It is extremely difficult, on anti-Fregean principles, to see what propositions are expressed by sentences containing empty proper names; it is equally hard to see what propositions are expressed by simple existential sentences containing proper names—in particular, true negative existentials or false affirmative existentials. The Boethian view encounters no difficulty at all here; its felicitous account of these matters, indeed, is one of its strengths. As we have seen, in the typical case where a proper name occurs in such a sentence as

(31) Leigh Ortenburger is the author of *The Climber's Guide to the Grand Tetons*

the name expresses an essence. (31) expresses a truth, furthermore, if and only if Leigh Ortenburger has the property of being the author of *The Climber's Guide to the Grand Tetons*—if and only if, that is, the essence expressed by that name is coexemplified with that property. More generally, where N is a non-empty proper name and F a predicate that expresses a property, a singular sentence of the form "N is F" expresses a proposition that is true in just those possible worlds where the essence expressed by N is coexemplified with the property expressed by F.

But the case of the existential sentence is just a special case.

(32) Leigh Ortenburger exists

expresses a proposition true in just those possible worlds where the essence expressed by "Leigh Ortenburger" is coexemplified with existence; these, of course, are the worlds where that essence is exemplified. If "Leigh Ortenburger" expresses *being the (author of The Climber's Guide to the Tetons)* α, then (32) expresses the same proposition as

(33) the (author of *The Climber's Guide to the Tetons*) α exists

---

[24]This corrects the account of the Babylonian intellectual economy given in *The Nature of Necessity*, pp. 83–87.

which is equivalent to

(34) There exists just one (author of *The Climber's Guide to the Tetons*) α

And of course the denial of (32), namely

(35) Leigh Ortenburger does not exist

is true in those worlds where (32) is false.

But now suppose N is empty. Suppose you come to doubt the existence of Ortenburger. How, you say, could any one man know as much about the Tetons as the *Climber's Guide* contains? You come to believe that the Stanford mathematics department collaborated on the *Guide*—and that, inspired by the example of Bourbaki, they invented Ortenburger out of whole cloth, playfully ascribing the *Climber's Guide* to him. And now let's add that you are right. When you assert (35) and I assert (32), do I predicate a property of some object? And is there an essence E such that what I say is true if and only if E is exemplified? How shall we understand a negative existential sentence like

(5) Romulus did not exist

where the proper name is empty?

Here we must recognize, as Boethians, that proper names display a certain subtlety of function. The name "Romulus," on the Boethian view, expresses the α-transform of such a property as *being the thing that stands in R to "Romulus."* But this property is unexemplified; so its α-transform is unexemplified in α. But if a world-indexed property *having-P-in-W* is not exemplified in W, then it is not exemplified in any possible world at all. We saw earlier that the α-transform of an exemplified singular[25] property is an essence; we now see that the α-transform of an unexemplified singular property is incapable of exemplification. But then "Romulus" in (5) expresses an impossible property. The proposition expressed by (5), however, is true if and only if the property expressed by "Romulus" is not coexemplified with existence—if and only if, that is, it is not exemplified. (5), therefore, expresses a necessary truth and its negation,

(36) Romulus existed

a necessary falsehood.[26]

Take another example: suppose Socrates had never existed—suppose he'd been frivolously invented by Plato, Xenophon, and Aristophanes, the rest of us having been quite unaware of the hoax. What property would have been expressed by "Socrates"? In fact, that name expresses an essence—perhaps the α-transform

---

[25] A property that is possibly exemplified, but not possibly exemplified by more than one object.

[26] But can't we easily imagine possible circumstances under which (36) would have been true? Isn't it possible that there should have been someone who was named "Romulus," collaborated with his brother in the founding of Rome, and so on for all the rest of the properties depicted in the story? That is indeed possible; those circumstances, however, are ones under which the *sentence* (36) would have expressed a truth; they are not ones under which the proposition (36) *does* express would have been true.

of some such property as *standing in R to "Socrates."* But if Socrates had not existed, some world β distinct from α would have been actual; our name "Socrates" would have expressed a property not exemplified in any possible world; and the sentence

(37) Socrates existed

would have expressed a necessarily false proposition. It follows, of course, that (37) would not have expressed the proposition it does *in fact* express; for *that* proposition is contingently true and hence not necessarily false in any possible world. So if Socrates had not existed, (37) would not have expressed the proposition it *does* express, but a necessary falsehood instead. On the Boethian account, therefore, a proper name N in an existential sentence $\ulcorner N$ exists$\urcorner$ expresses the α-transform $P\alpha$ of a singular property. If N is non-empty. $P\alpha$ is an essence and $\ulcorner N$ exists$\urcorner$ expresses a proposition true in just those worlds where $P\alpha$ is exemplified. If N is empty, $P\alpha$ will be an impossible property and $\ulcorner N$ exists$\urcorner$ will express an impossible proposition.

I said empty proper names display a certain subtlety of function in existential sentences; but this subtlety does not distinguish existentials from other sentences. For consider, again,

(4) Romulus founded Rome

This sentence expresses a proposition true in just those worlds where the property expressed by "Romulus" is coexemplified with the property expressed by "founded Rome." But here, as in (36), "Romulus" expresses the α-transform of an unexemplified property such as *standing in R to "Romulus"* or *having enough of the R_i.* Hence (4) expresses a necessarily false proposition and

(38) it is not the case that Romulus founded Rome

a necessary truth. We thus see what propositions are expressed by simple sentences containing empty proper names. Such a name expresses the α-transform of an unexemplified singular property and therefore expresses an impossible property; as a consequence, a sentence like (4) expresses a necessary falsehood and one like (38) a necessary truth. And it is thus clear that proper names function in existential sentences in just the way they do in predicative sentences generally.

By way of summary: on the Boethian view I mean to suggest, a sentence of the form "N is F" (where N is a proper name and F expresses a property) typically expresses a proposition true in the worlds where the property expressed by N is coexemplified with the property expressed by F. If N is non-empty, then it expresses an essence, and $\ulcorner N$ is $F\urcorner$ expresses a proposition true in the worlds where that essence is coexemplified with the property expressed by F. If N is empty, then it expresses not an essence but an impossible property, so that $\ulcorner N$ *is* $F\urcorner$ expresses a necessary falsehood. Singular existential sentences of the form $\ulcorner N$ exists$\urcorner$ present the special case where F is "exists." If N is non-empty, then $\ulcorner N$ exists$\urcorner$ expresses a proposition true in just those worlds where the essence expressed by N is coexemplified with existence: the worlds, that is where this essence is exemplified. If N is empty, then it expresses an impossible property, so that $\ulcorner N$ exists$\urcorner$ expresses a necessary falsehood and its denial a necessary truth.

These, then, are the essentials of the Boethian view: proper names express essences, and different proper names of the same object (or the same name on different occasions of use) can express different and epistemically inequivalent essences. In an effort to promote amity, I have suggested that proper names sometimes express the α-transforms of such properties as *stands in R to "Socrates"* and *has enough of the S_i*. But they can also express other essences. According to Frege[27] and Chisholm[28] each of us has a property that he alone can grasp or apprehend. Perhaps they are right; perhaps for each person there is an essence he alone grasps, an essence expressed by his own use of his name but not by anyone else's. Perhaps in dubbings by description, as Kaplan calls them,[29] the name in question expresses the α-transform of the description; if I say "Let's name the shortest spy 'Shorty,'" perhaps "Shorty" expresses the α-transform of *being the shortest spy*. If, furthermore, I name someone in full view "Sam," it may be that "Sam" expresses (in my idiolect) a property such that my only alternative means of expressing it then is by way of some such description as 'that person right there', where this latter is accompanied by an appropriate pointing. (There are further subtleties here, but I don't have the space to explore them here.) By way of conclusion, then, I repeat the essential points of the Boethian account: proper names express essences, and different names of the same object may express epistemically inequivalent essences.

---

[27] See "The Thought: A Logical Inquiry," trans. A. M. and Marcelle Quinton, *Mind*, vol. 65 (1956): 298.

[28] Roderick Chisholm, *Person and Object* (London, 1976), p. 37.

[29] "Bob and Carol and Ted and Alice" in *Approaches to Natural Language*, ed. Hintikka, Moravesic, and Suppes (Dordrecht, 1973), p. 499.

ON SENSE AND INTENSION*

David J. Chalmers

1. Introduction

What is involved in the meaning of our expressions? Frege suggested that there is an aspect of an expression's meaning—the expression's *sense*—that is constitutively tied to the expression's role in reason and cognition. Many contemporary philosophers have argued that there is no such aspect of meaning. I think that Frege was closer to the truth: one can articulate an aspect of meaning with many,

---

* I am grateful to audiences at ANU, Florida, Miami, Michigan, and at the "Language, Mind, and World" conference in Tlaxcala for discussion. Thanks especially to Josh Dever, Chris Evans, Mike Harnish, Kirk Ludwig, Marga Reimer, and Jason Stanley for comments.

although not all, of the properties that Frege attributed to sense. This aspect of meaning is what I will call an expression's *epistemic intension*. I will argue that epistemic intensions can serve as quasi-Fregean semantic values, and that this claim is undefeated by the major contemporary arguments against Fregean sense.

The simplest aspect of an expression's meaning is its *extension*. We can stipulate that the extension of a sentence is its truth-value, and that the extension of a singular term is its referent. The extension of other expressions can be seen as associated entities that contribute to the truth-value of a sentence in a manner broadly analogous to the way in which the referent of a singular term contributes to the truth-value of a sentence. In many cases, the extension of an expression will be what we intuitively think of as its referent, although this need not hold in all cases, as the case of sentences illustrates. While Frege himself is often interpreted as holding that a sentence's referent is its truth-value, this claim is counterintuitive and widely disputed. We can avoid that issue in the present framework by using the technical term 'extension'. In this context, the claim that the extension of a sentence is its truth-value is a stipulation.

Different sorts of expressions have different sorts of extensions. By the stipulation above, the extension of a singular term is an individual: the extension of 'France' is a particular country (France), and the extension of 'Bill Clinton' is a particular person (Clinton). Analogously, the extension of a general term is plausibly seen as a class: the extension of 'cat' is a particular class of animals (the class of cats). The extension of a kind term can be seen as a kind: the extension of 'water' is a particular substance (water). The extension of a predicate can be seen as a property or perhaps as a class: the extension of 'hot' is a particular property (hotness) or a particular class (the class of hot things).

The extension of a complex expression usually depends on the extensions of the simpler expressions that compose it. This applies most obviously to the truth-values of sentences. For example, 'Sydney is in Australia' is true, and it is true because the extension of 'Sydney' (a particular city) is located in the extension of 'Australia' (a particular country). 'Michael Jordan is short' is false, and it is false because the individual who is the extension of 'Michael Jordan' does not have the property that is the extension of 'short'. The same applies to typical complex expressions other than sentences: for example, it is not implausible that the complex singular term 'the greatest cricket player' has an extension (Don Bradman), and that this extension depends on the extensions of its parts.[1] Certain expressions (such as those involving belief attributions, to be discussed later) may provide an exception to this rule, but it is plausible that the dependence holds in a very wide range of cases.

There are various complexities here, and there are corresponding choices to be made. For example, some terms (e.g., 'Santa Claus') appear to have no referent:

---

[1] In this paper I will assume for ease of discussion that descriptions are true singular terms. Nothing important turns on this: the main points of this paper carry over to a Russellian analysis on which definite descriptions are complex quantifiers. One simply needs to apply the framework to the appropriately regimented logical form.

in such a case, one might say that they lack extension, or one might say that they have a null extension. In some cases (e.g., 'greatest' above), it appears that the extension of an expression can depend on context: for this reason, we may wish to assign extensions to expression tokens, or to expression types in contexts, rather than to expression types alone. In general, the truth-value of a sentence will be determined by the extensions of its parts within a regimented *logical form* (or perhaps some other underlying form), along with corresponding principles for determining truth-value of a regimented sentence from its logical form and the extensions of its parts; and the regimented sentence may look quite different from the original sentence, with different basic constituents and a more complex structure. Different semantic theories may assign extensions to expressions and logical forms to sentences in different ways.

Many of these complexities will not concern us here. The discussion that follows should be general over many specific proposals concerning logical form, extensions of simple terms, and compositional determination. I will simply take it for granted that sentences have a logical form and contain simple terms that have an extension; that these simple terms compose complex terms, which compose the sentence; and that the extension of a complex expression (including a sentence) is at least in many cases determined by its logical form and the extensions of its parts.

To clarify terminology: on my usage, an "expression" is any linguistic entity that has an extension or that is a candidate for extension. For ease of discussion, I will say that when an expression is of the sort that is a candidate for an extension, but appears to lack extension, it has a null extension. A "term" is any expression other than a sentence. Complex expressions are expressions (including sentences) that are composed of other expressions. Simple expressions are expressions that are not composed of other expressions.

2. Sense and Extension

A simple and attractive view of meaning ties the meaning of an expression to its extension. On such a view (e.g., Mill 1843, Salmon 1986), the meaning of a simple term is its extension, and the meaning of a complex expression is determined by the extensions of its parts. On the strongest version of this view, the meaning of a complex expression is its extension. On a slightly weaker version, the meaning of a complex expression is a complex structure involving the extensions of the simple terms that are parts of the expression. Either way, all meaning is grounded in extension.

There are three traditional reasons for doubting this simple view of meaning. First: some simple terms (such as 'Santa Claus' and 'phlogiston') appear to lack extension. On the view above, these terms will lack meaning, or they will all have the same trivial meaning, corresponding to the null extension. But intuitively it seems clear that these terms have *some* meaning, and that their meanings differ from each others'. If so, then meaning is more than extension.

Second: in some sentences, the role of a word in determining a sentence's truth-value appears to go beyond its extension. This applies especially to sentences about beliefs and related matters. For example, it is plausible that 'John believes that Cary Grant is an actor' could be true, while 'John believes that Archie Leach is an actor' is false, even though 'Cary Grant' and 'Archie Leach' have the same extension. If so, then either the truth-value of the sentence is not determined by the meanings of the terms, or there is more to meaning than extension.

Third: there is often more than one term referring to the same thing. In such cases, the terms often seem intuitively to have different meanings. Witness 'Hesperus', the ancients' name for the evening star, and 'Phosphorus', their name for the morning star. Or take 'water' and 'H_2O', both of which refer to the same substance. If 'water' and 'H_2O' refer to the same thing, and if reference is all there is to meaning, then 'water' and 'H_2O' refer to the same thing. But intuitively, 'water' and 'H_2O' have *different* meanings. If that is so, then reference cannot be all there is to meaning.

In "Über Sinn und Bedeutung" (1892), Frege lays out the central issue roughly as follows. The sentence 'Hesperus is Hesperus' is *trivial*. It can be known a priori, or without any appeal to experience. The knowledge that Hesperus is Hesperus requires almost no cognitive work at all, and gives us no significant information about the world. By contrast, the sentence 'Hesperus is Phosphorus' is *nontrivial*. It can only be known a posteriori, by appeal to empirical evidence. The knowledge that Hesperus is Phosphorus requires much cognitive work, and gives us significant information about the world.

As Frege put it, 'Hesperus is Phosphorus' is *cognitively significant* whereas 'Hesperus is Hesperus' is not. Intuitively, this difference in cognitive significance reflects a difference in the meanings of 'Hesperus' and 'Phosphorus'. When a subject comes to know that 'Hesperus is Phosphorus', what she learns depends on what she means by 'Hesperus' and by 'Phosphorus'. It seems plausible that the subject learns something different when she learns that Hesperus is Phosphorus than when she learns that Hesperus is Hesperus. If these two claims are correct, then 'Hesperus' and 'Phosphorus' have different meanings, and meaning involves more than extension.

If meaning involves more than extension, then what is the further element? Frege held that in addition to extension (or reference), an expression also has a *sense*. 'Hesperus' and 'Phosphorus' have the same referent, but different senses. 'Water' and 'H_2O' have the same referent, but different senses. 'Cary Grant' and 'Archie Leach' have the same referent, but different senses. For all such cases, the intuitive difference in cognitive significance among pairs of terms such as these is reflected in a difference in the terms' senses.

The notion of sense has a number of important features, which I discuss in what follows. The discussion is intended as a broad and informal outline of a Fregean view, rather than as a faithful representation of every feature of Frege's own view. More precise versions of some of the following claims will be given later in this paper.

(1) *Every expression that has an extension has a sense.*

In "Über Sinn und Bedeutung," Frege concentrated mostly on the senses of names, holding that all names have a sense. It is natural to hold that the same considerations apply to any expression that has an extension. Two general terms can have the same extension and different cognitive significance; two predicates can have the same extension and different cognitive significance; two sentences can have the same extension and different cognitive significance. So general terms, predicates, and sentences all have senses as well as extensions. The same goes for any expression that has an extension, or is a candidate for extension.

(2) *Sense reflects cognitive significance.*

The central feature of sense is that it is tied constitutively to cognitive significance. In the case of singular terms, Frege set out this connection as follows: two referring expressions 'a' and 'b' have different senses if and only if an identity statement 'a = b' is cognitively significant.[2] So 'Hesperus' and 'Phosphorus' have different senses, since 'Hesperus is Phosphorus' is cognitively significant. 'Hesperus is Hesperus', by contrast, is cognitively insignificant, and the two sides of the identity correspondingly have the same sense.

Frege's test for difference in sense is limited to singular terms, but one can naturally generalize it to other expressions, by suggesting that a pair of expressions of the same type have different senses when a statement of their coextensiveness is cognitively significant.[3] In the case of kind terms, one can apply the same test as before: 'a' and 'b' have different senses if and only if an identity statement 'a = b' is cognitively significant. So 'water' and 'H_2O' have different senses, since 'water is H_2O' is cognitively significant. In other cases, the test will be slightly different. For general terms, one can say that 'a' and 'b' have different senses when 'All a's are b's and all b's are a's' is cognitively significant: so 'renate' (creature with a kidney) and 'cordate' (creature with a heart) have different senses. For predicates, one can say that 'A' and 'B' have different senses when 'For all x, x is A iff x is B' is cognitively significant: so 'has a kidney' and 'has a heart' have different senses. For sentences, one might suggest that S and T have different senses when 'S iff T' is cognitively significant: so 'Hesperus is a planet' and 'Phosphorus is a planet' have different senses.

It is possible for two different expressions to have the same sense. When two words are intuitively synonymous—as with 'lawyer' and 'attorney', perhaps—an identity between them is cognitively insignificant. The truth of 'lawyers are attorneys' is arguably trivial: it is knowable a priori, requires no cognitive work, and gives no significant information about the world. If so, then 'lawyer' and 'attorney' have the same sense. In a similar way, it is plausible that the sentences 'Vixens are rare' and 'Female foxes are rare' are trivially equivalent. If so, the two sentences have the same sense.

---

[2] Throughout this paper, I use single quotes where some might use corner quotes, and I allow context to disambiguate whether symbols for linguistic expressions invoke use or mention of that expression.

[3] This extension beyond the case of singular terms goes beyond what is explicit in Frege. In various passages that touch on the equivalence of senses of sentences, Frege gives a number of criteria that are not obviously equivalent to each other. Some of these criteria closely resemble the criteria in the text, while others are related but are not obviously equivalent.

We can think of the sense of an expression as mirroring the expression's role in reason and cognition. When two expressions are trivially equivalent, they will play almost the same role in reason and cognition, and will have the same sense. When two expressions are not trivially equivalent, they will play different roles in reason and cognition, and will have different senses. In this way, we can think of an expression's sense as capturing its cognitive significance, and as representing the "cognitive value" or "cognitive content" of the expression.

(3) *The sense of a complex expression depends on the senses of its parts.*

We saw before that the extension of a sentence (such as 'John is hot and Mary is cold') at least typically depends on the extension of the expressions it contains and on its logical form. In a similar way, the sense of a sentence at least typically depends on the senses of the expressions it contains and its logical form. The same goes for complex terms, such as 'the greatest cricket player': insofar as its extension depends on the extensions of its parts, its sense depends on the sense of its parts.

This dependence of an expression's sense on the senses of its part may closely reflect the dependence of an expression's extension on the extensions of its parts. To determine the sense of a complex expression, we first determine the logical form of a complex expression, then determine the senses of the basic terms involved, and then compose these senses in a way that depends on the logical form. Just how this composition works is not entirely clear, but I will say more about it in what follows.

(4) *Sense determines extension.*

Frege held that the extension of a word, a complex expression, or a sentence is determined in some way by its sense. The sense of an expression is not in general determined by its extension. 'Hesperus' and 'Phosphorus' have the same extension but different senses, so it seems that there is no path from extension to sense. If the determination thesis is correct, however, then there is a path from sense to extension.

It is not entirely clear how the determination thesis is to be understood. We might say that sense *strongly* determines extension if sense determines extension on its own, without any further contribution from the world. In contemporary terms, we might say that sense strongly determines extension if any two possible expressions that have the same sense have the same extension. On this view, it seems that an expression's extension must somehow be present at least implicitly within its sense. While there are some indications of this sort of view in Frege, this idea arguably stands in tension with the idea that sense reflects cognitive significance. For example, the two terms 'the morning star' and 'the evening star' have the same extension, but this sameness of extension does not seem to be implicit in the cognitive roles of the terms. It is natural to suppose that someone in a different environment might use a term with the same cognitive role but a different extension. Similarly, it is not clear how the truth of a statement such as 'There are 90 chemical elements that occur in nature' could be determined by its cognitive role alone.

Alternatively, we can say that sense *weakly determines* extension if extension is determined by sense in conjunction with the world. It is natural to suppose that the sentence just mentioned is true not just because of its sense, but because of the way the world is. Likewise, it seems plausible that a term such as 'the morning star' refers to the planet Venus not just because of its sense, but because of the way the world is. Formulating the weak determination thesis so that it is both plausible and nontrivial is not easy: after all, is not everything determined by the way the world is? But there is at least an intuitive idea to keep in mind here, which we can return to later.

Frege also held some further theses concerning sense. These are not quite as crucial to a broadly Fregean view as the theses above, but they will be relevant to our discussion.

(5) *In indirect contexts, expressions refer to their customary senses.*

As we saw before, there are cases in which the truth-value of a sentence seems not to be determined by the extensions of its parts. This happens especially with sentences involving belief, and related ascriptions of attitudes. If 'John believes that Cary Grant is an actor' is true and 'John believes that Archie Leach is an actor' is false, and if 'Cary Grant' and 'Archie Leach' have the same extension, then the truth value of these sentence cannot be determined by the extensions of their parts. The same goes for many other constructions involving indirect contexts, a context where words appear inside a "that"-clause (such as 'that Cary Grant is an actor').

To deal with these cases, Frege suggested that in indirect contexts, an expression inside the "that"-clause does not have its usual extension. Instead, its extension is what is usually its *sense*. So inside such a clause, 'Cary Grant' does not refer to a person, but to the (customary) sense of 'Cary Grant'. In this way, we can see that 'Cary Grant' and 'Archie Leach' have *different* extensions within these sentences, so the thesis that truth-value depends on extension is preserved.

(6) *The sense of a sentence has an absolute truth-value.*

For Frege, the sense of a sentence is a special sort of entity, a "thought." A Fregean "thought" is not a mental entity. It is more like what many philosophers call a proposition, capturing the content that a sentence expresses, when stripped of the accidental clothing of a particular language. (I will use this terminology instead of Frege's in what follows.) Just as a sentence can be true or false, a proposition can be true or false. Frege held that propositions are the primary bearers of truth, and that sentences are true or false derivatively: a sentence is true if and only if the proposition that it expresses is true. Further, Frege held that a proposition is true or false *absolutely*. On his view, it is not possible for the same proposition to be true or false, for example at different times. If two sentences, uttered by any subjects at any times, express the same proposition, they will have the same truth-value.

This has strong consequences for the notion of sense. Many sentences can be true when uttered on one occasion, and false when uttered on another. For example, 'It is raining here now' will be false if I utter it now, but it would have been true if I had uttered it at this time yesterday. One might have been tempted to say that both of these utterances had the same sense. But if senses are propositions with absolute-truth value, this cannot be so. The two sentences must have different senses, and must express different propositions.

(7)   *The sense of an expression can vary between occasions of use.*

It is tempting to hold that the sense of an expression is a *universal* feature of that expression: that is, that every token of an expression type has the same sense. If this were right, then the sense of an expression could be seen as built into the language of which the expression is a part. On Frege's view, however, sense is not always universal in this fashion. One reason for this is given above: on Frege's view, the sense of a sentence such as 'It is raining here now' differs between different occasions of use. One can presumably trace this difference to differences in the sense of expressions such as 'here' and 'now' between occasions of use. Another quite different reason is tied to names. Frege (1892, second footnote) says that two different users of a name such as 'Aristotle' might associate a different sense with it. He says that this should not happen in a 'perfect language', but it does happen in natural languages.

For reasons like these, Frege's view entails that one cannot always attach sense to expression *types*. To handle cases like this, one has to attach sense to expression *tokens* (or to expression types as used in specific contexts, or to something else that is tied to an occasion of use). It follows that on Frege's understanding, the sense of an expression should not be identified with its *linguistic meaning*, where the latter is required to be common to all tokens of an expression type.

To sum up: on a Fregean view, expressions have senses that satisfy theses (1)–(7). In recent years, many philosophers have doubted this. It has been widely argued that expressions do not have Fregean senses, and there is no notion that can play the role that sense is intended to play. In particular it is widely believed that it is difficult to satisfy thesis (2), and that it is impossible to simultaneously satisfy theses (1)–(4).

To flag my conclusions: I think there is a viable notion of sense such that expressions have senses that satisfy slightly modified versions of the core requirements (1)–(4). When sense is interpreted this way, theses (5) and (6) are rejected, but (7) is accepted. I think that such a view can vindicate the spirit, if not the letter, of Frege's view.

3. What Are Senses?

What are senses? I have outlined a number of features that Frege attributed to senses, but this is not yet to say what a sense is. Frege's own discussion leaves the matter somewhat unclear. He says that they are not mental entities, such as the idea or image associated with an expression, and he holds that they are abstract objects of some sort (inhabiting the 'third realm'). But this still leaves their nature open.

One natural suggestion is that senses are *descriptions*. Frege sometimes uses descriptions to specify senses. In talking about the sense of 'Aristotle', for example, Frege says 'It might, for instance, be taken to be the following: the pupil of Plato and teacher of Alexander the great'. One might similarly suggest that the sense of 'Hesperus' is something like 'the brightest object visible in the evening sky', and that the sense of 'Phosphorus' is something like 'the brightest object visible in the morning sky'.

Descriptions, on a natural understanding of the term, are linguistic entities. 'The pupil of Plato and teacher of Alexander the great' is a linguistic entity, a complex expression containing ten words. Senses obviously cannot be descriptions of this sort: descriptions have senses of their own, so we will be left either with descriptions that serve their own sense or endless chains or circles of descriptions. Furthermore, senses of this sort can never break out of the linguistic domain.

A more plausible suggestion is that the sense of an expression is the *sense* of an associated description. Even if this is true, however, it does nothing to tell us what senses *are*. It is also far from clear that associated descriptions of the right sort exist for all expressions. For example, 'knowledge' seems to be a paradigmatic term with a sense: some states qualify as knowledge but others do not, and one might think of the sense as encapsulating a criterion for knowledge. But there famously appears to be no description that captures such a criterion. Gettier showed that 'justified true belief' is inadequate, and all attempts at complex descriptions have failed. Nevertheless, even if there is no linguistic description that captures what it takes to be knowledge, this does not show that 'knowledge' has no sense.

To find a better understanding of sense, it is useful to think about the work that descriptions are doing here. The role of a description is plausibly to give us a *condition on extension:* a condition that an entity in the world must satisfy in order to qualify as an expression's extension, depending on how the world turns out. For example, if 'Hesperus' functions as above, then the associated description will give a condition on its extension. If we discover that the brightest object in the evening sky is Venus, then 'Hesperus' will refer to Venus. If we discover that the brightest object in the evening sky is Jupiter, then 'Hesperus' will refer to Jupiter. And so on.

Here the crucial property of a description is that it gives us a way of identifying an expression's extension, given full knowledge of how the world turns out. It may be that for some expressions (such as 'knowledge'), there is no description that can do this job. It is nevertheless not implausible that the expression's extension depends in *some* fashion on how the world turns out, and in particular that full knowledge of how the world turns out puts a subject in a position to identify the expression's extension. We can then generalize to think of an expression's sense as the relevant condition on extension, whether or not this condition can be captured by a description.[4]

---

[4] Explicit discussion of the idea that a sense corresponds to a condition on extension is surprisingly rare in Frege, but it is present in his *Begriffsschrift*. This strand of Frege's thought is emphasized by Dummett 1973.

What do conditions on extension have to do with cognitive significance? An attractive idea is that when an expression plays a certain cognitive role for a speaker, then it will be associated with certain tacit criteria for identifying the extension of the expression, given sufficient information about the state of the world. It is natural to hope that these criteria will reflect the cognitive role of the expression in some deep respects. In order to tie a condition on extension to cognitive significance in this way, it is important that the relevant condition on extension be understood *epistemically,* in a manner that is closely connected to a speaker's knowledge and cognition. To do this, it is helpful to think about possible states of the world in epistemic terms.

For all we know a priori, there are many ways the world could be. We might live in a world with planets visible in the sky, or we might not. We might live in a world where people play cricket, or we might not. We might live in a world where some objects travel faster than light, or we might not. We might live in a world where the liquid in the oceans is a basic atomic substance, or we might not. We can put this intuitively by saying that there is a space of *scenarios* such that for all we know a priori, any one of these scenarios could be actual. To a first approximation, we can think of a scenario as something like a possible world, though some potential differences will arise later.

This a priori ignorance about the nature of our world reflects a corresponding a priori ignorance about the extensions of our expressions. For a typical expression, such as 'Hesperus', or 'the greatest cricket player', or 'water', we cannot know what the expression refers to without much observation of the world. For all we know a priori, it might be that Hesperus is Jupiter, or that the greatest cricket player is Dennis Lillee, or that water is a basic element. The extensions of our expressions depend on how our world turns out. That is, they depend on which scenario is actual.

Once we know enough about the nature of our world, we are usually in a position to know what our expressions refer to. Once we do enough astronomical work investigating the nature of the objects in the evening sky, we know that 'Hesperus' refers to Venus, not Jupiter. Once we know about the performances of cricket players throughout the history of the game, we know that 'the greatest cricket player' refers to Don Bradman, not Dennis Lillee. Once we know about the chemical makeup of the various substances in our environment, we know that 'water' refers to H_2O, not to a basic element. And so on.

We can think of this as being part of what using a language involves. If a subject uses an expression, then given sufficient information about the world, the subject will be in a position to know the extension of the expression. Furthermore, something like this will be the case *however* the world turns out: for any scenario, given sufficient information about that scenario, the subject will be in a position to determine what the extension of the expression will be *if* that scenario is actual. Of course in some cases the extension may be indeterminate, as it sometimes is in the actual world; but in such a case, the subject will be in a position to determine that, too.

One could put forward a thesis holding that when a subject using an expression is given sufficient information about a scenario, the subject is in a position to know the extension of the expression under the hypothesis that that scenario is actual. A full and precise version of such a thesis would require careful attention that I will not give here, but some things can be said to clarify it.

First, what counts as "sufficient information"? If we allow too much, the thesis becomes trivial: given the information that Hesperus is Phosphorus, one can trivially know that Hesperus is Phosphorus. But it is clear that in this case, no such information is required; neutrally specified information suffices. It is plausible that at least in many cases, 'qualitative' information about the distribution of physical properties, appearances, and mental states (perhaps including some indexical information) in the world suffices to determine an expression's extension. I will not give a precise account of the relevant information here (see Chalmers and Jackson 2001 for a more precise hypothesis). What matters is rather the general idea that there is *some* constrained sort of information such that information of this sort can suffice to determine an expression's extension, and usually in a nontrivial way.

Second, when is a subject "in a position to know" an expression's extension? We can that this is the case when *sufficient reasoning* from information available to the subject will allow the subject to know the expression's extension. Here the reasoning is restricted to a priori reasoning (or to armchair reasoning, if one prefers), so further empirical observation is disallowed. And we idealize away from poor reasoning: it is not a subject's actual reasoning that matters, but rather what the subject could know given unimpaired reasoning. For example, a subject possessing the relevant information might judge that 47 plus 59 is 116, due to a miscalculation, or that Alpha Centauri is the nearest star, because they overlook the sun. But these mistakes can be corrected by better reasoning, so they provide no counterexample to the thesis.

If something like this is right, then a subject using an expression is in a position to know the expression's extension *given* relevant empirical information and sufficient reasoning. The second clause entails that there is a normative element here; but what matters is that the extension is within the reach of reason. This feature of language and thought is responsible for a deep link between meaning, possibility, and rationality.

4. Epistemic Intensions

All this suggests that an expression's sense might be seen as an *intension*: a function from possibilities to extensions. This function takes a given possibility, and associates it with an extension relative to that possibility. The extension will be either an entity present in that possibility, or the null extension. We can say that the intension is *evaluated* at a possibility, and *returns* an extension in that possibility. In what follows, I will make a prima facie case that intensions can be associated with expressions in such a way that they can play much of the role of Fregean sense.

For the Fregean, the possibilities in the domain of an expression's intension will be thought of as *epistemic* possibilities, in a broad sense: ways the world could be, for all we know a priori. These epistemic possibilities are what I called scenarios above: for now, we can think of scenarios as possible worlds. The intension of an expression can be thought of as an *epistemic* intension: it captures (very roughly) the way the extension of the expression depends on which epistemic possibility turns out to be actual. For a sentence S and a scenario W, for example, a useful heuristic is to ask: *if* W is actual, is it the case that S? Or to stress the epistemic nature of this conditional: if W *turns out* to be actual, will it turn out that S? If yes, then the intension of S is true at W.

Take an expression such as 'the greatest cricket player'. Let W_1 be a scenario in which Don Bradman never plays cricket, and in which Phil Tufnell scores more runs and takes more wickets than any other cricket player. Let A be a scenario corresponding to the actual world, where Don Bradman's batting average is 99.94, and where the second highest batting average is around 61. For all we know a priori, scenario W_1 could be actual. For all we know a priori, scenario A could be actual. If scenario W_1 is actual, then the greatest cricket player is Phil Tufnell. So when evaluated at W_1, the intension of 'the greatest cricket player' returns Phil Tufnell. If scenario A is actual (as it is!), then the greatest cricket player is Don Bradman. So when evaluated at A, the intension of 'the greatest cricket player' returns Don Bradman.

What about a term such as 'Hesperus'? Here one can tell a Fregean story in a similar way. Let scenario W_2 be one on which the brightest object visible in the evening is Jupiter, and where the brightest object visible in the morning is Neptune. For all we know a priori, W_2 is actual. If it turns out that W_2 is actual, then it will turn out that Hesperus is Jupiter. So when evaluated at W_2, the intension of 'Hesperus' returns Jupiter. If it turns out that A is actual, then it will turn out that Hesperus is Venus. So when evaluated at A, the intension of 'Hesperus' returns Venus.

The same applies to a term such as 'water'. Let W_3 be a 'Twin Earth' scenario, where the clear, drinkable liquid in the oceans and lakes is XYZ. For all we know a priori, W_3 is actual. If it turns out that W_3 is actual, then it will turn out that water is XYZ. So when evaluated at W_3, the intension of 'water' returns XYZ. If it turns out that A is actual, then it will turn out that water is H_2O. So when evaluated at A, the intension of 'water' returns H_2O.

One can do the same sort of thing for a whole sentence. Just as the extension of a term depends on the way the world turns out, so does the truth-value of a sentence. So a sentence will also be associated with an intension: this time, a function from scenarios to truth-values. This function takes a scenario, and returns a truth-value associated with that sentence in the scenario. This truth-value will be 'true', 'false', or perhaps neither.

Take a sentence such as 'Hesperus is Phosphorus'. One can tell a Fregean story here in a similar way. If it turns out that scenario W_2 above (with Jupiter in the evening and Neptune in the morning) is actual, then it will turn out that Hesperus is not Phosphorus. So when evaluated at W_2, the intension of 'Hesperus is Phosphorus' returns 'false'. When evaluated at the actual scenario A, on the other hand, the intension of 'Hesperus is Phosphorus' returns true.

The intuitive characterization of epistemic intensions using the heuristics I have given here makes a strong prima facie case that expressions have epistemic intensions. Giving a truly precise definition of epistemic intensions involves complexities that I cannot go into here, but it may be useful to say a few words about the foundations of the idea, and about how a more precise definition (in the case of sentences) can be constructed.

The basis for epistemic intensions lies in our ability to describe and evaluate epistemic possibilities. Let us say that it is epistemically possible (in the broad sense) for a speaker that S when the speaker cannot know a priori that S is not the case. Then it is epistemically possible that water is not H_2O. It is also epistemically possible that our world is the XYZ-scenario: that is, that the clear liquid in the oceans and lakes (and so on) is XYZ. And when we reflect on the second, specific epistemic possibility, it reveals itself to us as an instance of the first epistemic possibility. That is, the epistemically possible hypothesis that the XYZ-scenario is actual is a specific version of the epistemically possible hypothesis that water is not H_2O.

We can see, then, that we use language to describe and evaluate epistemic possibilities in a distinctive way. Quite generally, given a specific epistemically possible scenario W and some more general epistemic possible sentence S: a speaker can say, on reflection, that the epistemic possibility that W is actual is an instance of the epistemic possibility that S is the case, or an instance of the epistemic possibility that S is not the case, or is neither. If it is the first, then the epistemic intension of S is true in W. If it is the second, then the epistemic intension of S is false in W. If it is neither, then the epistemic intension of S is indeterminate in W.

Of course any specific scenario must be *described* in order for a speaker to be able to evaluate it as an epistemic possibility. When the speaker considers the epistemic possibility that W is actual, he or she really considers the epistemic possibility that D is the case, where D is a description (in some sense) of W. This raises the issues of what it is to be a description of an epistemically possible scenario, and of whether different descriptions of the same scenario might give different results. I discuss this matter in Chalmers (forthcoming a), isolating a class of canonical descriptions that give equivalent results.[5] For present purposes, the intuitive characterization should suffice.

The epistemic intension of S at W corresponds to a speaker's judgment about whether the epistemic possibility that W is an instance of the epistemic possibility that S, or to the speaker's judgment about whether S is true if W is actual. But it is not the speaker's snap judgment that matters, nor any actual judgment of the

---

[5] See Chalmers forthcoming a. A natural requirement is that a canonical description be epistemically complete, where D is epistemically complete if D is epistemically possible and there is no S such that both $D \wedge S$ and $D \wedge \neg S$ are epistemically possible. If scenarios are understood as possible worlds, one must also require that D use only semantically neutral expressions (roughly, those that are not vulnerable to Twin Earth thought experiments) supplemented by indexicals.

speaker. Rather, it is the speaker's (potential) *rational* judgment that matters. Here we idealize away from poor reasoning, and consider judgments on ideal rational reflection.

An idealization like this can be made in a number of ways. The most obvious way is to invoke the idealization inherent in the notion of apriority. S is a priori not if a speaker knows that S, nor even if a speaker would be able to know that S on reflection, but rather if it would be possible for the speaker to know that S, using the concepts involved in S, on ideal rational reflection. So we can say that the epistemic intension of S is true in W if a priori reasoning by the speaker could reveal the epistemic possibility of W to be an instance of the epistemic possibility that S.

This approach suggests a natural characterization of the epistemic intension of S for a speaker. For a given scenario W, let D be any canonical description of W. Then the epistemic intension of S is true at W iff the material conditional 'D⊃S' is a priori; it is false at W if 'D⊃¬S' is a priori; and it is indeterminate at W if neither is a priori.[6] Other forms of definition are also possible. If someone rejects the notion of apriority, for example, then one can appeal to a different construal of the relevant epistemic status, perhaps by appealing to whether an inference from the hypothesis that D is the case to the conclusion that S is the case would be rational. One also needs to say more about the nature of the relevant scenarios, descriptions, and epistemic status, in order to have a truly precise definition. (For a more precise treatment, and for expression of this treatment to expressions other than sentences, see Chalmers forthcoming a and b.)

It should be noted that to evaluate the epistemic intension of S at W, a token of S need not be present within W. None of the heuristics or definitions that I have given here rely on such a token; rather, they rely on first order claims about epistemic possibility and apriority using an expression present in the actual world. And one can often evaluate expressions at scenarios with no such tokens. For example, there are epistemically possible scenarios in which noone uses language. When one considers such a scenario W, it reveals itself as an instance of the epistemic possibility that no words exist, that there are no novels, and so on. So the epistemic intension of 'words exist' is false at W, and so on. It is even arguably epistemically possible that no-one exists (as long as 'I exist' is not a priori). One can consider and evaluate that epistemic possibility in various ways; for example, the epistemic intension of 'Someone exists' will be false there. Of course some sentences may yield indeterminate results at these epistemic possibilities, but all that matters is that some sentences yield determinate results there.

---

[6] The notion of apriority invoked here will be relative to a speaker, for reasons discussed later in the paper. It is also important that apriority be understood so that sentences such as 'Hesperus is Phosphorus' are not a priori (contrary to some understandings). The easiest way to accommodate these requirements is roughly as follows: a sentence S is a priori relative to a speaker if the sentence as used by that speaker expresses a thought that can be justified independently of experience, on ideal rational reflection. Here a thought is a token propositional attitude such as a belief. This allows that the same sentence type can be a priori for one speaker but not another, and it entails that sentences such as 'Hesperus is Phosphorus' will not generally be a priori, as there will generally be no way to a priori justify the corresponding thought.

This framework is grounded in the fact that when a speaker is given the right sort of information about the actual world, or about an epistemic possibility more generally, then conclusions about extension are within reach of reason, given appropriate reflection. We can use this to articulate a version of the Fregean notion of 'grasping' a sense. We can say that a subject grasps an intension when the subject is in a position to *evaluate* that intension: that is, when sufficient reasoning will allow the subject to determine the value of the intension at any world. Again, this does not require that the subject will actually determine the correct extension when a relevant epistemic possibility is specified, but it does require that the extension is within the grasp of reason. If what I have said here is right, then whenever a subject uses an expression, the expression will be associated with an epistemic intension that the subject grasps.

Occasionally, the epistemic intension of a term will be the same as that of an associated description. For example, the epistemic intension of 'Neptune' as used by Leverrier was arguably the same as that of 'the object causing the perturbation of the orbit of Uranus'; and the epistemic intension of 'bachelor' is arguably the same as that of 'unmarried man'. In these cases, there is a sense in which the epistemic intension can be "captured" by a description.

This does not hold in general. For many or most terms, there may be no description (and certainly no short description) with the same epistemic intension as the term. We saw this in the case of 'knowledge', and the same applies to most names. In these cases, the best one can hope for is a description whose epistemic intension approximates that of the original term: as with 'justified true belief' for 'knowledge', or 'the clear drinkable liquid in the oceans and lakes' for water, and so on. These descriptions may give one a rough and ready sense of how a term's epistemic intension functions, but they do no more than that. Usually there will be at least a small subset of epistemic possibilities (such as the Gettier cases, in the case of 'knowledge') in which the epistemic intension of the original term and of the description come apart.

So there is no reason to think that in general, an epistemic intension can be captured by a description. More generally, there is no reason to think that grasping an epistemic intension requires any sort of descriptive articulation of a concept by a subject. The epistemic intension is a function, not a description. It is revealed in a subject's rational evaluation of specific epistemic possibilities, not in any sort of explicit definition. Even where such a definition exists, a subject need not be able to articulate it to grasp the epistemic intension. Indeed, we usually evaluate the plausibility of such definitions precisely by deploying our prior grasp of a term's epistemic intension, to see how whether the definition gives the right results in specific cases. (Witness the literature on the definition of 'knowledge'.) So epistemic intensions are more basic than descriptions, and should not be assimilated with them.

Epistemic intensions can be associated with any expression that is a candidate for extension. Given the general type of the expression (singular term, general term, etc), it will be constrained to have a certain sort of extension (individual, class, etc). The intension of such an expression will be a function from scenarios to the appropriate sort of extension. So the intension of a singular term is a function from scenarios to individuals; the intension of a general term is a function from scenarios to classes; the intension of a sentence is a function from scenarios to truth-values; and so on.

5. Intensions as Senses

How can we connect intensions as discussed above to the Fregean theses outlined at the start of this paper? We could establish such a connection with the aid of the following four theses about intensions, which are closely related to theses (1)–(4) about sense.

(1*)   *Every expression has an intension, which returns at a scenario an extension of the type appropriate for the expression.*

(2*)   *A sentence is a priori iff its intension is true at all scenarios.*

(3*)   *If the extension of a complex expression E depends by some rule on the extensions of its parts, then at a scenario W, E's intension returns an extension that depends by the same rule on the extensions returned by the intensions of E's parts.*

(4*)   *At a scenario corresponding to the actual world, the intension of E returns the (actual) extension of E.*

These theses all fit naturally with the understanding of epistemic intensions outlined above. (1*) was discussed at the end of the last section. (3*) follows from a natural extension of compositional semantics from the actual world to arbitrary epistemic possibilities. (4*) is a consequence of the claim that given appropriate information about the actual world, a subject will be in a position to determine the expression's actual extension. (2*) also fits naturally with the understanding above, but it raises some tricky issues that I will return to shortly.

Given the theses above and the equation of senses with epistemic intensions, it is not hard to see that versions of the Fregean theses (1), (3), and (4) follow. Requirement (1), that every expression has a sense, follows immediately from (1*). Requirement (3), that the sense of a sentence depends on the sense of its parts, follows from (3*) along with the thesis that the extension of a sentence depends on the extension of its parts. Note that even if there are some cases where the latter thesis fails (such as belief contexts), requirement (3) can still be satisfied as long as the extension of a sentence depends on the extensions *and the intensions* of its parts. For then it is plausible that the extension of a sentence at a scenario will depend on the extension of its parts at a scenario along with the intensions of the parts, so the intension of the sentence will depend on the intensions of the parts.

A version of requirement (4) follows naturally from thesis (4*). Here the relevant version of (4) is the thesis involving weak determination, on which sense determines extension in combination with the world. To determine an expression's extension, one simply evaluates the expression's intension at the actual world. One can naturally think of the intension as supplying *criteria* for determination of extension: in combination with the actual world, these criteria will determine an extension.

What about the crucial requirement (2), that sense reflects cognitive significance? Here matters are complicated by the fact that we lack a precise definition of 'cognitive significance'. There is a natural understanding of cognitive significance that fits well with the intensional framework, however. We can say that a sentence S is cognitively insignificant (for a speaker) when S is knowable a priori (by that speaker, given ideal reflection): that is, when it is knowable with justification independent of experience. And S is cognitively significant when it is not knowable a priori. 'Hesperus is Hesperus' is knowable a priori, so it is cognitively insignificant. 'Hesperus is Phosphorus' is not knowable a priori, so it is cognitively significant.

This understanding of cognitive significance differs from Frege's. On Frege's account, a priori knowledge can be cognitively significant: the knowledge that 59 + 46 is 105 is cognitively significant, for example, because this knowledge requires some cognitive work. It is very hard to articulate this notion of cognitive significance precisely, however, and it is not clear that there is a useful precise notion nearby. The notion of apriority can serve at least as a useful substitute. It is clear that non-apriority entails cognitive significance in the Fregean sense (although not vice versa). Most of Frege's central cases of cognitive significance involve a posteriori knowledge, and are therefore accommodated well on this framework. The main difference is that certain pairs of expressions that Frege counts as cognitively inequivalent (e.g., "59 + 46" and "105") will count as cognitively equivalent on the current framework, because of the rational idealization inherent in the notion of apriority. But this understanding gives at least a first approximation of a Fregean view (one that might later be refined), so it is this understanding that I will work with.

For senses to reflect cognitive significance in this sense, it was required (among other things) that an identity 'a = b' is cognitively significant if and only if 'a' and 'b' have different senses, and that two sentences S and T have the same sense if and only if the material biconditionals 'S iff T' is cognitively insignificant. Recasting these claims in terms of intensions and apriority, we require the following: An identity 'a = b' is a priori if and only if 'a' and 'b' have the same intension; and two sentences S and T have the same intension if and only if the material biconditional 'S iff T' is a priori. For other expression types, such as predicates, general terms, and the like, analogous theses will be required.

It is not hard to see that the relevant requirements will all be entailed by theses (1*)–(4*), with the crucial work being done by thesis (2*): that S is a priori iff its intension is true at all scenarios. This entailment can be illustrated in the case of singular terms and in the case of sentences.

From (2*), it follows that 'a = b' is a priori iff its intension is true at all scenarios. By (3*) and the extensional semantics of identity, the intension of 'a = b' is true at a scenario iff the intensions of 'a' and 'b' return the same extension there. So 'a = b' is a priori iff the intensions of 'a' and 'b' return the same extensions at all scenarios. Equivalently, 'a = b' is a priori iff 'a' and 'b' have the same intensions.

From (2*), it also follows that 'S iff T' is a priori iff its intension is true at all scenarios. By (3*) and the semantics of material conditionals, the intensions of 'S iff T' is true at a scenario iff the intensions of S and T return the same truth-value there. So 'S iff T' is a priori iff the intensions of S and T return the same truth-values at all scenarios. Equivalently, 'S iff T' is a priori iff S and T have the same intensions.

We have seen that from (1*)–(4*), versions of the crucial Fregean requirements (1)–(4) can be satisfied. The question then becomes: is there reason to believe that sentences can be associated with intensions that satisfy (1*)–(4*)? The crucial claim is clearly (2*). Is there reason to believe that expressions can be associated with intensions that satisfy (2*)?

Here, the central reason stems from the Fregean understanding of these intensions and of the associated scenarios. As we saw above, the scenarios represent *epistemic* possibilities: ways the world might be, for all we know a priori. And the intensions are *epistemic* intensions: they capture a subject's idealized judgments about how an expression applies to an epistemic possibility, under the hypothesis that it is actual. On this understanding, a strong connection between intensions and epistemic notions such as apriority is built into the framework.

So consider the left-to-right direction of (2*): if a statement is a priori, its epistemic intension is true at all scenarios. This direction is straightforwardly plausible. If S is a priori, then for *any* epistemic possibility W: if W turns out to be actual, it will turn out that S. We might say that for all W, the epistemic possibility that W is actual is an instance of the epistemic possibility that S. So the epistemic intension of S is true in all scenarios.

This is brought out by cases such as 'Hesperus is Hesperus (if it exists)', 'All bachelors are unmarried men', and even 'The meter stick in Paris is one meter long (if it exists)', assuming that these are a priori. In each of these cases, there is no epistemic possibility of falsehood. No matter how the world turns out, it cannot turn out that Hesperus is not Hesperus, or that the meter stick in Paris is longer or shorter than one meter. So in every epistemic possibility W, the epistemic intensions of these sentences are true.

Something similar applies in the right-to-left direction, which we can consider in the contrapositive form: if S is not a priori, then there is some scenario in which its epistemic intension is not true. This fits the familiar cases. 'Hesperus is Phosphorus' is a posteriori, and its epistemic intension, as we saw above, is false in a scenario W_2 where the objects visible in the morning and evening sky differ. 'Water is H_2O' is a posteriori, and its epistemic intension is false in the 'Twin Earth' scenario W_3. And this is no accident: the aposteriority of these statements seems to be reflected in the existence of scenarios in which the epistemic intension is false.

If S is not a priori, it is clearly epistemically possible that S is not the case. So all we need for the right-to-left direction of (2*) is the following principle: if it is epistemically possible that T, then there is an epistemically possible scenario W in which the epistemic intension of T is true. This principle is suggested very strongly by the above examples. We have seen that even in the case of a posteriori identities involving water, Hesperus, and the like, the principle appears to be satisfied.

The principle is not entirely trivial, however. Someone might hold that if scenarios are understood as possible worlds, there are counterexamples to the claim. For example, it might be held that 'a god exists' is necessary but not a priori, for example. If this view is correct, then 'no god exists' is epistemically possible, but it will plausibly be verified by no possible world. Similarly, it might be held that the Continuum Hypothesis is necessary but not a priori. If this view is correct, then the negation of the Continuum Hypothesis is epistemically possible, but plausibly verified by no possible world. If these views are correct, and if scenarios are understood as possible worlds, then these cases (unlike cases involving water, Hesperus, and so on) provide a counterexample to the principle above, and so to principle (2*).

These claimed counterexamples would be highly controversial, as they presuppose highly controversial views about gods and about mathematics respectively. A Fregean could simply deny these views as contrary to his or her principles, perhaps holding that they tacitly assume a false view of some of the crucial notions: apriority, possibility, intensions. It is useful to probe the basis for such a denial, however. The opposing arguments could be resisted in at least two ways, depending on the relevant conception of possibility.

There are two ways in which the Fregean might understand the space of epistemic possibilities over which epistemic intensions are defined. (See Chalmers forthcoming b.) First, this might be a space of worlds that is *independently characterized*, such as the space of metaphysically possible worlds. In this case, it becomes a substantive thesis that when S is epistemically possible, there is a world in which the epistemic intension of S is false. The thesis is plausible for familiar cases (including 'water' and 'Hesperus' cases), but an opponent might hold that in some cases, it is false. This might happen for reasons such as those in the case above, where an opponent could hold that there are not enough metaphysically possible worlds to go around.

On this understanding, for the Fregean to hold onto principles such as (2*), she will have to deny the opponent's analysis of the cases. She might hold that God's existence cannot be necessary, for example, or perhaps that it is a priori; and she might hold that the Continuum Hypothesis is either a priori or indeterminate. This will require substantive argument. And the postulated connection between the independently characterized space of worlds and epistemic possibility will be a substantive thesis; it will have implications for just what is metaphysically possible, for example. Of course the thesis may nevertheless be plausible. A Fregean might even argue for the thesis directly, perhaps by noting that there are no clear counterexamples, and by arguing that there are constitutive connections between notions of metaphysical and epistemic possibility.

On the second understanding, the possibilities involved are not independently characterized, but are understood as epistemic possibilities from the start. The Fregean might postulate or construct a space of scenarios understood as "maximal epistemic possibilities," for example. (A construction of this sort of discussed in Chalmers forthcoming b.) These might intuitively correspond to maximally specific epistemically possible hypotheses about the way things are, hypotheses from which a priori reasoning can settle everything there is to be settled. This space might be defined quite independently of notions of 'meta-physical possibility'.

On this understanding, a Fregean is free to accept much of the opponent's analysis of the cases above. She is free to accept that 'God exists' is a posteriori but metaphysically necessary, for example. If she accepts this, she will simply insist that there is an epistemically possible scenario in which the epistemic intension of 'God exists' is false. This will follow naturally from the definition of those scenarios. Once epistemic possibility is separated from metaphysical possibility, the opponent will have no obvious reason to deny this. On this understanding, the truth of (2*) does not involve commitment to the substantive theses about metaphysical possibility above, and it will be well-protected from counterexamples.

(A third possibility is that the Fregean could accept both the opponent's analysis of the cases and an independently characterized notion of possibility, and accept that (2*) is not true across the board. It might be held that there are certain special domains where it fails, but that it holds in the most domains, or in certain constrained domains. This view is not out of the question, but I will set it aside here.)

My view is that the Fregean can go in either of these two ways. I think that (2*) is plausible even given an independently constrained notion of metaphysical possibility, and that it can be argued for directly (see Chalmers 2002a); but this is a nontrivial matter. If someone doubts this, however, the second option is available. This has the advantage of making fewer substantive commitments. Here, the main burden is making the case for the relevant space of epistemically possible scenarios. This is also nontrivial, but I think that it can be done in a reasonably straightforward way (see Chalmers forthcoming b).

In any case, we can see that the Fregean is not being unreasonable in accepting (2*). It appears to fit the clear cases, and there are natural ways to respond to one who doubts it. So it seems that the claim that there are intensions of some sort that satisfy (1*)–(4*) is well-motivated. If there are such intensions, then they can function as senses that satisfy (1)–(4).

To clarify what I have and have not done: I have not tried to precisely define epistemic intensions, in the sense of giving a precise recipe for evaluating a sentence S's intension at a scenario W. I have also not tried to give a knockdown argument that (1)–(4) can be satisfied. Rather, I have simply outlined a certain sort of Fregean view, and I have tried to make it plausible that intensions satisfying (1)–(4) exist.

If this is correct, a Fregean can hold that there is at least a prima facie case for a notion of sense that satisfies (1)–(4). But of course there have been numerous arguments *against* Fregean sense in recent years. So we now need to examine these arguments to see whether they have any force against the conception just outlined. I will focus on four main arguments: what we might call the argument from indexicality, the modal argument, the epistemic argument, and the argument from variability.

6. The Argument from Indexicality

The first objection is not so much an explicit argument as a set of considerations put forward by a number of philosophers, especially John Perry (1977). These considerations revolve around Frege's treatment of indexicals, such as 'I', 'here', and 'now'.

Recall that Frege held that the sense of a sentence has an absolute truth-value. This entails that if two utterances of a sentence express the same sense, they must have the same truth-value. But it is clear that certain indexical sentences, such as 'It is now Saturday', can be uttered truly at one time and falsely at another time. So on Frege's picture, these two sentences must have different senses.

If the sense of the sentence depends on the sense of its parts, then some part of the sentence must have a sense that differs between the two occasions of utterance. The obvious source of the difference is the indexical expression 'now'. So Frege's view entails that such an indexical expression has different senses on different occasions of utterance. The same goes for many other indexicals: 'I', 'here', 'today', 'tomorrow', and so on.

It is very hard to see how this is supposed to work. One idea is that the sense of such an expression should build in its referent. If so, my utterance of 'now' today has a sense that builds in a particular Saturday, and my utterance of 'now' tomorrow has a sense that builds in a particular Sunday. Similarly, my utterances of 'I' have a sense that builds in a particular individual, David Chalmers, while your utterances have a sense that builds in a different individual.

It seems that something like this is required to preserve Frege's claims, but it is not clear that this is compatible with the overall spirit of Frege's framework. When I use an expression such as 'now' or 'today', the referent does not seem to be reflected in the cognitive significance of the expression for me. I might have no idea what day today is; and the day might change without it making any special difference to my cognition. So there seems to be some tension between this sort of claim and the thesis that sense reflects cognitive significance.

How will the intensional framework deal with these matters? Let us consider a sentence such as 'It is raining here now'. If such a sentence determines a function from worlds to referents, there is an immediate problem. I can utter the sentence truly today, and falsely yesterday. But both days, I inhabit the same world: at least, the same 'objective' world A. So if the intension of a sentence is a function from (objective) worlds to truth-values, then as before, the two utterances must have different intensions. And as before, the two tokens of 'now' must have different intensions.

It is once again quite unclear how this should work. One might suggest that the epistemic intension of 'now' should pick out a particular time (time t, the specific time of utterance) in all worlds. But then a sentence such as 'It is now time t' will have a necessary epistemic intension. This will not do: the sentence is clearly a posteriori (and cognitively significant), so its epistemic intension must be contingent. It seems that any other proposed intension will have a similar problem.

There is a natural way for the intensional framework to deal with this issue. A proponent of this framework should deny that intensions are functions from objective worlds to extensions. Rather, intensions can be seen as functions from *centered* worlds to extensions. Here, a centered world is a world marked with a 'center', where the center consists of an individual and a time present in that world.

This idea can be motivated in a natural way. On the Fregean intensional framework, scenarios are supposed to represent a sort of maximal epistemic possibility. But it is a familiar idea (this time from the work of Perry (1979), among others) that an objective description of the world leaves some matters epistemically open. When I lie awake in the middle of the night, then even if I had a full objective description of the world, I might still wonder 'what time is it now?', and I might not be able to settle this matter from the information available. Or I might have a full objective description of the world, but not know which individual in that world is *me*. So an objective description of the world is not an epistemically complete description of the world. To make it epistemically complete, the description also needs *locating information*: a 'you are here' marker, indicating which individual is *me* and what time is *now*. This sort of epistemic possibility is best represented by a centered world.

Once epistemic possible scenarios are represented as centered worlds, we can deal with the problem straightforwardly. We can say that the epistemic intension of 'I' picks out the individual marked at the center of any given scenario, and that the epistemic intension of 'now' picks out the time marked at the center. The epistemic intension of 'today' will pick out the day containing the time marked at the center of any given scenario, and the epistemic intension of 'tomorrow' will pick out the following day. These intensions will be common to all occasions of use of these expressions.

When a subject uses an expression, the actual extension of the expression will be given by evaluating the expression's intension at the centered world inhabited by that subject: a scenario corresponding to the actual world centered on that subject and on the time of use. When two different subjects use an indexical expression such as 'I', they will inhabit two different centered worlds: one centered on the first subject, and one on the second. So the epistemic intension of 'I' will pick out different actual extensions for each. For each subject, the intension will pick out himself or herself. Something similar applies to 'now': when this expression is used at different times, the intension will be evaluated at different centered worlds, and will always return the time of use.

Something like this can also help with terms that are not obviously indexical, such as 'water'. If I am given a full objective specification of an epistemic possibility, and am told that it contains a planet where the watery stuff is H_2O and a planet where the watery stuff is XYZ, then I may not be in a position to know what the extension of 'water' is. To know that, I need to know which planet I am on. But if I am also given locating information, in which the center of my world is marked (e.g., on the planet with H_2O), then there is no problem. I am now in a position to know which environment is *my* environment, to know which substances *I* am causally related to, and so on. So as long as I can derive the relevant objective information (about appearance, behavior, distribution of various substances), I will have no problem determining that if this centered world is actual, then water is H_2O. So the epistemic intension of 'water' will return H_2O at this world.

There are a couple of subtleties to the use of centered worlds. One is the following: it is arguably not a priori that I exist (I know this through experience), but the epistemic intension of 'I exist' is true in all centered worlds as defined. To deal with this, one should make the marking of a subject and time *optional*: some scenarios have no marked subject and time, or perhaps mark just one but not both. In a scenario without a marked subject, the epistemic intension of 'I exist' will be false. The other side of this coin is that there may be expressions that require the marking of further entities at the center of a scenario: some demonstratives ('that object') may require marked experiences, for example, and some special cases ('this thought') might require marked thoughts. These cases are not crucial to the current discussion, however, so we can mostly stay with scenarios in which at most a center and a time is marked.

The introduction of centered worlds to the Fregean framework has one major consequence. The sense of a sentence will no longer have an absolute truth-value. When I say 'It is raining here now' yesterday and today, my utterance has the same epistemic intension both times, but it is false yesterday and true today. So the intension is not true absolutely, or false absolutely. It is true or false only relative to a subject and a time. So the Fregean requirement (6) fails.

It is not clear what Frege would have thought of this. The requirement that the sense of a sentence (a 'thought') be an absolute bearer of truth was very important to him. Still, it is widely held that Frege's treatment of indexicals needs major repair. And it seems to me that giving up thesis (6) does not do any significant damage to a broadly Fregean framework, and it allows one to preserve the crucial connection with cognitive significance and the determination of reference. So it may be that giving up this thesis is the best way to preserve a framework that retains the broad spirit of Frege's view.

This adjustment also entails that we must give up on Frege's thesis (5), which holds that expressions in belief contexts refer to their senses. Consider a belief attribution such as 'John believes that I am British'. Here the sense of 'I' is the epistemic intension that picks out the individual at the center of a given scenario, and the sense of 'I am British' is true only in scenarios where the individual at the center has a certain national origin. If John were to entertain a belief with that sense, then he would attribute that national origin to *himself*. But it is clear that this is not what John does when he believes that I am British. So on the current understanding of sense, thesis (5) entails that the wrong sort of belief is attributed to John. So we must give up on thesis (5).

I do not think that this is a high cost to pay. It is widely held that thesis (5) must be rejected, for a number of different reasons. The thesis yields an attractively elegant analysis of belief attributions, but on a close analysis, it seems that belief attributions are more subtle than the thesis suggests. The analysis of belief attributions was only a subsidiary element of Frege's view, however, and it is clear that giving it up preserves the broad spirit of his view. Of course we still need a good analysis of belief attribution, but that is a subject that needs much discussion in its own right.[7]

7. The Modal Argument

Perhaps the best-known argument against a Fregean view of language is the modal argument of Kripke (1980). Kripke's argument is concerned mostly with names, and also with natural kind terms. He is arguing in the first instance against "descriptive" views of reference on which names are semantically akin to descriptions, but the arguments are generally taken to have force against any Fregean view.

Kripke argues as follows that names cannot be equivalent to descriptions. Take any name, such as 'Aristotle', and any description, such as 'the last great philosopher of antiquity'. Then it might have been that Aristotle was not the last great philosopher of antiquity; he might have died while an infant, for example. Something similar applies to any other description D that seems a likely candidate to capture the sense of the name: for any such description D, a judgment 'it might have been that Aristotle was not D' seems correct. So 'Aristotle' is not semantically equivalent to the description D.

Something similar applies in the case of 'Hesperus'. A Fregean might hold that 'Hesperus' is semantically equivalent to 'the brightest object visible in the evening sky', or some such. But Kripke argues that it might have been that Hesperus was not the brightest object visible in the evening; it might have been destroyed millennia ago, or it might have been struck by a comet and left the solar system. So again, it seems that a name is not semantically equivalent to a description.

Kripke uses these considerations to argue that it is not *necessary* that Hesperus is the brightest object visible in the evening sky, since it might have been otherwise. Or as it is sometimes put: it is not *metaphysically necessary* that Hesperus is visible in the evening, and it is *metaphysically possible* that it is not. In a similar way, he argues that there are *possible worlds* in which the evening star is not Hesperus: in a world where Venus was knocked off course by a comet and in which another object is visible in the evening, the evening star is not Hesperus but some other object.

He argues in a similar way that there are no possible worlds in which Hesperus is not Phosphorus. If Venus had been visible only in the morning with something else visible in the evening, this would have been a scenario in which Hesperus was not visible in the evening, and not a scenario in which Hesperus was not Phosphorus. He argues that Hesperus and Phosphorus are the same object (the planet Venus) in all worlds in which they exist. So 'Hesperus is Phosphorus (if they exist)' is necessary.

---

[7] I think that one can give an account of belief ascriptions that exploits epistemic intensions in a somewhat more indirect way. See Chalmers 2002b.

Kripke puts this by suggesting that names are *rigid designators,* picking out the same object in all possible worlds. Most descriptions, in contrast, are not rigid: they pick out different objects in different possible worlds. So names are quite unlike descriptions. Where names are concerned, Kripke's view is closer to the simple view, on which the meaning of a name is its referent, than to the Fregean view, on which the meaning of a name involves an associated sense.

Kripke gives related arguments concerning natural kind terms. These can be illustrated in the familiar case of 'water'. It can be argued that water might have behaved and appeared quite differently from the way in which it actually behaves and appears: it might never have appeared in liquid form, for example (witness the possibility of ice in the actual world). More generally, for any description D of water's macroscopic properties, it can be argued that if H_2O had not satisfied D, water would not have satisfied D. So 'water is D' appears not to be necessary, and it seems that natural kind terms are not equivalent to descriptions.

In a similar way, it can be argued that something might have satisfied any such description D without being water. In Putnam's Twin Earth world (Putnam 1975), a different chemical substance XYZ has all the superficial properties of water. But Putnam argues that this substance is not water. That is, in a counter-factual scenario in which XYZ was watery, XYZ would not be water. Rather, water is necessarily H_2O. If so, 'water' is akin to a rigid designator: it picks out H_2O in all worlds.

Do Kripke's arguments have any force against the intensional framework I have outlined here? Do they show, for example, that names or natural kind terms do not have epistemic intensions that satisfy (1)–(4)? At first glance, one might think so. I have argued that Hesperus has an epistemic intension that picks out something like an object visible in the evening, in any given world. So in a world where Mars rather than Venus is prominent in the evening sky, the epistemic intension will pick out Mars. But Kripke argues that Hesperus picks out Venus in all worlds, and that it need not pick out the evening star, or anything like it.

The conflict is only superficial, however. Kripke takes care to distinguish metaphysical possibility from epistemic possibility. And he allows that it is epistemically possible that Hesperus is not Venus; he simply denies that it is metaphysically possible. Kripke allows that it might *turn out* that Hesperus is not Phosphorus; and he can allow that if it turns out that Venus was never visible in the evening but that Mars was, then it may turn out that Hesperus is not Phosphorus but Mars. So his argument is entirely compatible with 'Hesperus' having an *epistemic* intension that functions roughly as I have suggested. Much the same applies to 'water', and to other relevant terms.

This response is not ad hoc. The sort of possibility that is most relevant to a Fregean view is clearly epistemic possibility. When one thinks about sense in intensional terms, one thinks of it as giving criteria for the extension of an expression *depending on how the world turns out.* If the world turns out one way, it will turn out that water is H_2O; if the world turns out another way, it will turn out that water is XYZ. Nothing in Kripke's modal argument gives any reason to deny this. And the notion of sense was always tied to epistemic notions such as apriority, not to notions such as "metaphysical necessity."[8] These connections are entirely pre-served, even in the light of Kripke's argument.

The other crucial property of sense was that it determines an expression's extension in the actual world. Again, Kripke's argument does nothing to suggest that this is not the case. The epistemic intension determines an expression's actual extension when evaluated at the actual world. For all Kripke has said, it also determines an expression's extension under all epistemically possible hypotheses about the actual world.

What an epistemic intension does not do, if Kripke's arguments are correct, is determine an expression's extension when evaluated in explicitly counterfactual scenarios. When we consider these scenarios, we are not considering them as epis-temic possibilities: as ways things might be. Rather, we are acknowledging that the character of the actual world is fixed, and are considering these possibilities in the subjunctive mood: as ways things might have been. That is, rather than con-sidering the possibilities *as actual* (as with epistemic possibilities), we are consid-ering them *as counterfactual*. If Kripke is right, then evaluation in this sort of explicitly counterfactual context works quite differently from the evaluation of epistemic possibilities. This point still needs explaining.

It is striking that all of Kripke's conclusions concerning modality are grounded in claims concerning what might have been the case, or what could have been the case, or what would have been the case had something else been the case. Kripke is explicit (1980, pp. 36–37) in tying his notion of necessity to these for-mulations, and almost all of his arguments for modal claims proceed via these claims. What all these formulations have in common is that they involve scenar-ios that are acknowledged not to be actual, and that are explicitly considered as counterfactual scenarios.

All these claims are *subjunctive* claims, not in the syntactic sense, but in the semantic sense: they involve hypothetical situations that are considered as coun-terfactual. The paradigm of such a claim is a subjunctive conditional: 'if P had been the case, Q would have been the case'. We can say that all these claims involve a *subjunctive context*, where a subjunctive context is one that invokes counterfac-tual consideration. Such contexts include those created by 'might have', 'would have', 'could have', or 'should have' (on the non-epistemic readings of these phrases), subjunctive conditionals involving 'if/were/would be' or 'if/had/would have', and other phrases. In Kripke's sense of 'possible' and 'necessary', where 'it is possible that P' is equivalent to 'it might have been the case that P', then modal contexts such as 'It is possible that' are themselves subjunctive contexts.

Kripke's central point against the description theory was that names and descriptions function differently in modal contexts: for a name N and a descrip-tion D, 'it is necessary that D is D (if it exists)' is true, but 'it is necessary that N is D' is false. We can put this somewhat more precisely by saying that names and descriptions function differently in subjunctive contexts. And more generally,

---

[8] Dummett 1973 makes a similar point in discussing Kripke's argument.

names and descriptions seem to behave differently under subjunctive evaluation of hypothetical possibilities. How can a Fregean view handle this phenomenon?

I have not argued that names are equivalent to descriptions. I do allow, however, that a name and a description can have the same sense, at least approximately and in some cases, as the case of 'Hesperus' suggests. If so, then if Kripke's point is accepted, we must explain the different truth-value of subjunctive sentences by appealing to something other than a difference in sense. So the question is: why is 'it might have been that Hesperus was not the evening star' true, while 'it might have been that the evening star was not the evening star' is false, given that 'Hesperus' and 'the evening star' have (roughly) the same sense?

There are a number of ways in which one might try to explain this. First, one might appeal to a difference in underlying logical form between subjunctive sentences containing names and descriptions. One could hold that in subjunctive contexts, names always take wide scope, so that the sentence involving 'Hesperus' above has the logical form of 'Hesperus is such that it might not have been the evening star'. Or one could hold that names always involve an unarticulated 'actual', so that the sentence has the logical form of 'it might have been that the actual Hesperus was not the evening star'. Once this logical form is in place, then substituting 'the evening star' for 'Hesperus' yields the same truth-value. On such a view, the difference in the modal status of the sentences is due to a difference in logical form, not a difference in the corresponding expressions' semantic contents. These explanations merit considerable discussion, but I will set them aside here.[9]

The second sort of explanation appeals to a semantic difference between names and descriptions, in some aspect that goes beyond their sense, and that affects how they function in subjunctive contexts. On such a view, a name may have sense and extension, but sense and extension do not *exhaust* the meaning of a name. The simplest addition to the Fregean framework would be a semantic feature that is part of the meaning of all names but not part of the meaning of descriptions, indicating that in counterfactual contexts, the expression contributes its *actual* extension.[10] There will be a corresponding semantics of counterfactual contexts, such that the presence or absence of the feature is relevant to the truth-value of counterfactual statements. This will explain the difference between names and descriptions.

I favor a more general semantic explanation of the second sort. On this account, every expression is associated with *two* intensions: one governing its application to epistemic possibilities, and one governing its application to explicitly counterfactual possibilities. The first of these is the epistemic intension. The second is a *subjunctive intension*. Like the epistemic intension, this is a function from worlds to extensions. But here the worlds in question are seen as counterfactual metaphysical possibilities, and expressions are evaluated in these worlds in the way in which we evaluate counterfactual scenarios.

---

[9] See Dummett 1973, Sosa 2001, and Stanley 1997 for views of this sort, and Soames 1998 for critical discussion.

[10] Recanati (1993) proposes a feature (labeled 'REF') that works something like this, though he conceives of it differently.

Just as the epistemic intension mirrors the way that we describe and evaluate epistemic possibilities, the subjunctive intension captures the way that we describe and evaluate subjunctive possibilities. To evaluate the subjunctive intension of a sentence S in a world W, one can ask questions such as: if W had obtained, would S be the case? For example, if W is a world in which Venus was knocked off course by a comet and in which Mars was prominent in the evening, we can say the following. If W had obtained, Hesperus would not be visible in the evening; if W had obtained, Hesperus would still be Phosphorus, and would still be Venus; if W had obtained, Hesperus would not be Mars. So the subjunctive intension of 'Hesperus is Phosphorus' is true in W.

The same sort of thing applies to a natural kind term, such as 'water'. If W is the Twin Earth world, we can say: if W had obtained, water would still have been H_2O, not XYZ. So the subjunctive intension of 'water is XYZ' is false in that world, and the subjunctive intension of 'water' picks out H_2O in that world. One can tell a related story for a general term such as 'cat', whose subjunctive intension will pick out a class of members of a particular biological species in all worlds, and for a property term such as 'hot', which will arguably pick out a certain sort of molecular motion in all worlds. (Note that at least in the 'cat' case, the extension is a different class in each world, and is not always the actual extension. This can be handled straightforwardly by a subjunctive intension, but it is harder for the other accounts above to handle, as they rely on projecting the actual extension.)

Indexicals such as 'I' can also be accommodated naturally. The epistemic intension picks out the being at the center of a world, but the subjunctive intension does not. The subjunctive intension of my use of 'I' picks out me (David Chalmers) in all worlds. I can say 'if David Chalmers were in a coma, then I would be in a coma', and so on. In evaluating counterfactual scenarios, 'I' always picks out David Chalmers (though of course, he need not be *called* that). So we do not need a center to evaluate the subjunctive intension of 'I'. More generally, the worlds in the domain of subjunctive intensions can be taken to be standard uncentered worlds, not centered worlds.

Just as every expression has an epistemic intension, every expression will have a subjunctive intension. This intension will be a function from worlds to extensions of the appropriate sort: individuals, truth-values, and so on. And as long as the extension of a sentence depends on the extensions of its parts, the subjunctive intension of a sentence will depend on the subjunctive intension of its parts.

A name and a description may have similar epistemic intensions and similar extension, but they may have very different subjunctive intensions. This can be seen by examining world W above. Here we can say that if W were the case, then Hesperus would still be Venus, but the evening star would be Mars. So the subjunctive intensions of 'Hesperus' and 'the evening star' are distinct. The former picks out Venus in all worlds, while the latter picks out something that is visible in the evening in all worlds. More generally, the subjunctive intension of a name picks out its actual extension in all worlds, while the subjunctive intension of a description picks out whichever object satisfies the description in a given world.

The subjunctive intension of a name depends directly on its actual extension. The extension of a name can usually not be known a priori, so the subjunctive intension cannot be known a priori, either. If we lack relevant empirical information about the actual world, we might be unable to evaluate an expression's subjunctive intension at a counterfactual world, even given a detailed specification of that world. For similar reasons, two names (such as 'Hesperus' and 'Phosphorus') may have the same subjunctive intension without the subject knowing that a priori. The same goes for natural kind terms and indexicals. So subjunctive intensions do not reflect the cognitive significance of the expressions involved. This contrasts with the subjunctive intensions of descriptions, which can often be evaluated a priori (at least if the descriptions contain no names, natural kind terms, or indexicals), and it contrasts with epistemic intensions, which can generally be evaluated a priori for any expression.

Subjunctive intensions are most directly relevant to the evaluation of subjunctive sentences. When an expression occurs in a subjunctive context ('it might have been that S'; 'if S had been the case, T would have been the case'; 'if A were B, C would have been D'; and so on), its subjunctive intension is used in evaluating the truth-value of the sentence. For example, 'it might have been that S' (at least in the relevant sense of 'might have been') will be true iff the subjunctive intension of S is true at some world. 'If S had been the case, T would have been the case' is true roughly iff the nearest world that satisfies S's subjunctive intension satisfies T's subjunctive intension. And so on.

Subjunctive intensions are also relevant to the evaluation of modal contexts, at least when these are interpreted the Kripkean way. 'It is necessary that S' will be true iff S's subjunctive intension is true at all worlds. 'Possibly, T' will be true if T's subjunctive intension is true at some world. This is what we would expect, given that 'It is possible that T' will be true precisely when 'It might have been that T' is true.

By analogy, epistemic intensions are relevant to the analysis of corresponding epistemic contexts. The indicative conditionals 'If P is the case, then Q is the case' or 'If it turns out that P, it will turn out that Q' are true (or acceptable) for a subject approximately when the epistemically nearest world that satisfies P's epistemic intension also satisfies Q's epistemic intension, where "epistemically nearest" is defined in a way that depends on the subject's knowledge or perhaps beliefs. (See Chalmers forthcoming.) And 'it is a priori that P' will be true if P has a necessary epistemic intension.

(The material in the remainder of this section is a somewhat more elaborate development of this framework, and can be skipped by those who prefer to move on.)

The subjunctive intension of an expression is always determined by the epistemic intension of the expression and by the character of the actual world. Because of this, it is possible in principle to associate a *two-dimensional intension* with an expression, which captures how its subjunctive intension will vary, depending on which epistemic possibility turns out to be actual. This two-dimensional intension can be thought of as a function from pairs (V, W) of epistemic possibilities and metaphysical possibilities to extensions.

To evaluate the two-dimensional intension of a statement S at a pair of worlds (V, W), one can ask: if V is actual, then if W were the case, would S be the case? This is reflected in some more natural English constructions: for example 'if water is XYZ, then water could not be H_2O'. To determine the truth-value of statements like these, one needs the full two-dimensional intension, as neither epistemic intension nor the subjunctive intension of the terms involved carries information about how to evaluate subjunctive statements under alternative epistemic possibilities. So for a fully general account of sentence's truth-values, one needs at least the full two-dimensional intension, although its full structure will be relevant only in rare cases.

Like an epistemic intension but unlike a subjunctive intension, a two-dimensional intension can be evaluated a priori. One needs no empirical information about the actual world, since all the relevant information is specified in the epistemic possibility. One might hold that the two-dimensional intension represents the true 'cognitive significance' of an expression, if one holds that the difference between the behavior of names and descriptions in counterfactual contexts represents a difference in cognitive significance; so one could hold that the two-dimensional intension is a Fregean 'sense' in some expanded understanding of the term. But we do not need to adjudicate that matter here.

An expression's actual subjunctive intension can be derived from the two-dimensional intension by using the speaker's actual scenario as the epistemic possibility parameter; this cannot be evaluated a priori precisely because we do not know which scenario is actual. It is tempting to reconstruct an expression's epistemic intension as the 'diagonal' of the two-dimensional intension, which results when the same possibility is used as the epistemic possibility parameter and (in an uncentered version) as the metaphysical possibility parameter. This depends on just how epistemically possible scenerios are understood, however.

As before, there are two ways of understanding the class of epistemic possible scenarios. They can be understood in terms of the same worlds that function as metaphysical possibilities, with the addition of a center. Or they can be understood as a separate class defined in purely epistemic terms. The first option is more elegant, but requires a substantive philosophical thesis about possibility. The second option is more complex, but it requires fewer philosophical commitments. A philosopher who holds that the existence of a god is metaphysically necessary but not a priori can embrace the second option but not the first, for example.

If one takes the second option, then one has two distinct classes of possibilities: the epistemically possible scenarios and the metaphysically possible worlds. These possibilities may have certain relations to each other, but the two sets are nevertheless disjoint. One can evaluate a statement in an epistemically possible scenario, yielding the value of its epistemic intension there, and one can evaluate it in a metaphysically possible world, yielding the value of its subjunctive intension there. But because the spaces are distinct, there is no natural way to map epistemic possible scenarios onto metaphysically possible worlds. As a result, one cannot reconstruct an epistemic intension as the 'diagonal' of the two-dimensional intension, and various other elegant properties are removed. This view also has the disadvantage of requiring a strong underlying modal dualism, with distinct modal primitives for each space of worlds.

If one takes the first option, then the scenarios that function as epistemic possibilities are roughly the same as the worlds that function as metaphysical possibilities, with the addition of a center. So epistemic intensions and metaphysical intensions are defined over (almost) the same space. To evaluate an expression's epistemic intension at a world, we consider the world as an epistemic possibility: as a way our world might actually be. To evaluate an expression's subjunctive intension at a world, we consider the world as an explicitly counterfactual possibility: as a way our world might have been, but (probably) is not. One can say that in the first case, we consider the world as actual; in the second case, we consider the world as counterfactual.

The first option is compatible with all the familiar cases. Take the case of 'water', and consider a Twin Earth world where the watery stuff is XYZ (near the center, if required), and where H_2O is not watery. When we consider this world as actual, it is an instance of the epistemic possibility that water is XYZ: if W is actual, then water is XYZ. When we consider this world as counterfactual, it is an instance of the metaphysical possibility that water is H_2O: if W had been actual, then water would still have been H_2O, not XYZ. Something similar applies in all the familiar cases.

One might ask: is W *itself* a world where water is XYZ, or a world where water is H_2O? On a standard philosophical view, it is the latter, not the former. This is because the phrase 'a world in which S' is almost always read as invoking a world W in which the subjunctive intension of S is true, or for which S is true when W is considered as counterfactual. My own view is that this reading is arbitrary, and that the phrase 'a world in which S' is ambiguous between readings that invoke epistemic and subjunctive intensions. If so, there is no determinate answer to the question above. To remove the ambiguity one can define new locutions: for example, when the epistemic intension of S is true in W, then W is a world that *verifies* S; when the subjunctive intension of S is true in W, then W is a world that *satisfies* S. In any case, this terminological issue does not matter too much for our purposes. As long as we are always clear about how we are evaluating statements, and have clear conventions for understanding the relevant phrases, no confusion should result.

If the first option is accepted, various matters become more straightforward. Because there is only one space of worlds (apart from the difference involving centers), one can reconstruct an epistemic intension from the two-dimensional intension as a 'diagonal' intension, where the value of the epistemic intension at W is the value of the two-dimensional intension evaluated at W (considered as actual) and an uncentered version of W (considered as counterfactual). This view is also much simpler metaphysically, since it is compatible with a deep underlying modal monism, with just one space of worlds. Of course there is still a dualism of epistemic and metaphysical possibility in language, but this simply arises from the dual nature of semantic evaluation over a single space of worlds.

Given that any sentence S has an epistemic intension and a subjunctive intension, someone might ask: which of these is the *content* of S? Which of these gives the *truth-conditions* of S? What is the *proposition* expressed by S? My view is that we need not settle these questions one way or another. We can say that the epistemic intension is S's *epistemic content* and that the subjunctive intension is S's *subjunctive content*. As for the content of S (unqualified), this is a complex content that subsumes both of these and possibly more. Similarly, S has *epistemic truth-conditions* (showing how S's truth depends on how the world turns out), and *subjunctive truth-conditions* (showing how S's truth varies across counterfactual hypotheses).

As for propositions, I have avoided this terminology, as it is multiply ambiguous. If one's conception of a proposition is a set of possible worlds (or something similar, such as a structure of intensions), then one could say that S expresses two propositions, an epistemic proposition and a subjunctive proposition. But if one's conception of a proposition is more generally of what remains semantically of S once the arbitrary clothing of a given language is stripped away, then one could say that S expresses a complex proposition that involves at least a two-dimensional structure. One should not run these two conceptions together: for example, the fact that an utterance of S expresses two propositions in the first sense in no way entails that the utterance is ambiguous, since ambiguity would involve expressing two propositions in the second sense. For my part, I prefer to use 'proposition' in the second, more general way; but I will largely avoid the expression here.

It is sometimes objected that the epistemic intension cannot be part of the content expressed by S at all, since it is really a matter of the content that S *would have* expressed had a token of S been present in a different context. This is a mistake. As we saw earlier, the epistemic intension of S can be evaluated in worlds that contain no token of S, and even if a world does contain such a token, its presence is usually irrelevant to evaluating an epistemic intension there. The epistemic intension of S is not defined in terms of counterfactual tokens of S at all. Rather, it is defined in terms of the first-order use of an *actual* expression S in evaluating various epistemic possibilities. This is precisely analogous to the way that the subjunctive intension of S is defined in terms of the first-order use of S in evaluating counterfactual possibilities. So epistemic intensions and subjunctive intensions are on a par here.

One could define the *contextual intension* of S as a function that maps centered worlds containing a token of S at the center to the extension of that token in that world. This might resemble an epistemic intension in some ways, but it would not be an epistemic intension. First, an epistemic intension will be defined over many more worlds. Second, it is unclear just what it takes to be a token of S, and depending on what we require, the contextual intension may give very different results from an epistemic intension. If only orthographic properties are required, then there will be worlds where a token of 'water' refers to horses or to the number two. If the same extension is required, then a token of a name such as 'Hesperus' will pick out the same individual (Venus) in all worlds. Perhaps there is an intermediate requirement that gives roughly the same results as an epistemic intension, but this is not obvious. The obvious suggestion is to presuppose the notion of an epistemic intension, and require that a token of S have the same epistemic intension of S. However one does things, there is not much point in defining such a notion, since we have epistemic intensions to do the job already.

This matter bears on the two-dimensional semantic frameworks developed by Kaplan (1989) and Stalnaker (1974). The framework I have developed here resembles these in obvious respects, and it owes much to them. Epistemic intensions are analogous in certain respects to Stalnaker's "diagonal propositions" and to a version of Kaplan's "character," and subjunctive intensions are much the same as Stalnaker's "propositional content" and Kaplan's "content." But there are crucial differences. First: on Kaplan's and Stalnaker's frameworks, the analogs of epistemic intensions are defined in terms of the analogs of subjunctive intensions, whereas on the framework I have outlined, they are defined quite independently of subjunctive intensions. Second and most important: on Kaplan's and Stalnaker's frameworks, the worlds on the first dimension of evaluation are not considered as epistemic possibilities but as contexts of utterance, where evaluation requires the presence of a token of the expression within the context. As a result, this first dimension of evaluation yields a contextual intension, not an epistemic intension.

These features lead to strong limitations on using these frameworks for epistemic purposes, which both Kaplan and Stalnaker note. Kaplan's framework yields useful epistemic results only for indexicals and demonstratives, and not for names and natural kind terms. This is because the contextual intensions for indexicals and demonstratives behave much like their epistemic intensions, but the contextual intensions for names and natural kind terms behave very differently. (A name arguably picks out the same individual in every context, but it can apply to different individuals within epistemic possibilities.) Stalnaker (1999) argues that his "diagonal proposition" does not reflect matters of apriority directly, partly because of the problems involved in holding the meaning of an utterance constant across contexts. It seems that these frameworks are useful for epistemic purposes precisely to the degree that the notions involved resemble epistemic intensions.

A strong Fregean might criticize this framework from the other side, holding that only epistemic intensions, not subjunctive intensions, are part of the content of a sentence, and the subjunctive behavior can be accounted for by appealing to logical form or to a simpler semantic feature, as above. This matter is not cut and dried, but there are a number of advantages to including subjunctive intensions as an explicit semantic value.

First, subjunctive intensions allow a direct parallel between the treatment of apriority and of necessity, and between epistemic and subjunctive evaluation. Second, subjunctive intensions give a more general account of subjunctive behavior than accounts that rely on actual extension, and consequently can more easily account for the distinctive subjunctive behavior of certain terms, including general kind terms such as 'cat'. Third, we have at least one content (the subjunctive intension) associated with an expression that is "objective" in the way that Frege required. Fourth, people have intuitions about "what is said" by an expression, and sometimes these better reflect subjunctive intensions than epistemic intensions (e.g., when I say 'I am Australian' and you say to me 'You are Australian', there is a sense in which we say the same thing, although our epistemic intensions differ). Fifth, the presence of subjunctive intensions allows for a degree of continuity with current philosophical frameworks in which a central role is played by notion of "propositional content" closely tied to subjunctive intensions; this continuity allows a Fregean to retain some of the insights of this tradition rather than discarding them completely.

The addition of subjunctive intensions certainly goes beyond Frege's view. But it is a supplement to the view rather than a radical overhaul. Senses, or epistemic intensions, are still present and playing the same role they always played. Sense and extension have merely been supplemented by a further semantic value in order to deal with various subjunctive and modal phenomena. Frege did not address these phenomena directly, so it is hard to know how he would have dealt with them. But I think this framework is compatible with the broad spirit of a Fregean view.

8. The Epistemic Argument

Kripke's second central argument against descriptive views of language is an epistemological argument.[11] Kripke recognizes that a description theorist might accept that names are not modally equivalent to descriptions, but might nevertheless hold that names are epistemically equivalent to descriptions. So he raises some quite different considerations to argue that this is not the case. Again, while these arguments are most explicitly aimed at a description theorist, they are generally taken to have force against any broadly Fregean view.

The argument proceeds roughly as follows. The description theorist will hold that a name N (say, 'Gödel'), as used by a given speaker, is epistemically equivalent to some description or cluster of descriptions D (say, 'the person who proved the incompleteness of arithmetic'). On such a view, 'N (if it exists) is D' will be a priori for the speaker. But Kripke argues that for many names N, no such sentence is a priori. In effect, he does this by arguing that for any description D, 'N is not D' is epistemically possible for the speaker. If so, then N is not epistemically equivalent to D.

Take the name 'Gödel'. A speaker may associate a number of descriptions with her use of the name: 'the person who proved the incompleteness of arithmetic', and so on. But Kripke argues that there are (epistemically possible) scenarios in which the name 'Gödel' will turn out to refer to a person who does not satisfy any of the descriptions. So the speaker cannot know a priori that Gödel (if he exists) satisfies any of the descriptions.

---

[11] Some discern a third "semantic argument" in Kripke, closely related to the epistemic argument. The considerations used here to reply to the epistemic argument can also be used to reply to the semantic argument.

One can put the argument strategy as follows. Take the name 'Gödel' and the description 'the man who discovered the incompleteness of arithmetic'. Then there is an epistemically possible scenario in which the incompleteness of arithmetic was discovered by a man named 'Schmidt', and in which the proof was stolen and published by a man named 'Gödel', to whom the proof was thereafter attributed. If this scenario is actual, then the speaker's term 'Gödel' refers to the second man, not to the first. So it is epistemically possible for the speaker that Gödel did not prove the incompleteness of arithmetic, and there is no a priori equivalence between the name and the description.

Kripke argues that the same can be done for any description associated with the name (such as 'the man to whom the discovery of the incompleteness of arithmetic is commonly attributed'). There will always be epistemically possible scenarios such that if they are actual, the speaker's term 'Gödel' refers to someone who does not satisfy the description. (For example, a scenario in which the discovery is now commonly attributed to Hilbert, without the speaker realizing.) If this is right, then the name cannot be equivalent a priori to any description.

Kripke also argues that there are actual cases in which most descriptions that a speaker associates with a name are false of the name's referent. This applies to 'Peano' and 'Jonah', for example: Peano did not discover the axioms associated with him, and Jonah was probably not swallowed by a whale. So here it is not even true, let alone a priori, that the name and the associated description are coextensive. And he also argues that there are some names such that the speaker has *no* associated description that could fix reference: a speaker can use the term 'Feynman' to refer to Feynman while knowing nothing more than that he is a famous physicist, for example, where that description is satisfied by many individuals. So again, it seems that reference is not fixed descriptively.

Does this argument against the description theory yield an argument against the intensional framework I have been outlining? It seems clear that it does not. This argument works with a conception of descriptions on which they correspond to linguistic expressions. When Kripke argues that the speaker the descriptions that the speaker "associates with" the name cannot fix reference, he always invokes linguistic descriptions that the speaker associates with the name, or at least explicit descriptive beliefs of the speaker. But the intensional framework is not committed to the idea that descriptions always correspond to linguistic expressions; in fact, at least part of the motivation of the framework comes from an independent rejection of this idea. And the intensional framework is not even committed to the idea that the intensions associated with a name correspond to explicit beliefs of the speaker. So there is no clear argument against the intensional framework here.

In fact, Kripke's central method of argument seems to be obviously compatible with the intensional framework. A proponent of this framework could accommodate Kripke's argument strategy as follows. We want to show that for a given name N and description D, 'N is D' is not a priori. To do this, we consider a specific epistemically possible scenario W. We then reflect on a question such as the following: 'if W turns out to be actual, will it turn out that N is D?' And we find that the answer is no. If so, the epistemic intension of 'N is D' is false in W. So 'N is D' is not a priori.

On this interpretation, when we think about the Gödel/Schmidt case, for example, we are tacitly evaluating the epistemic intension of 'Gödel' at a world specified as in the example. When we consider that world as an epistemic possibility, it reveals itself as an instance of the epistemic possibility that Gödel did not discover incompleteness. That is, we find that the epistemic intension of 'Gödel' does not pick out the prover in this world; it picks out the publisher. If so, the epistemic intensions of 'Gödel' and of 'the man who discovered the incompleteness of arithmetic' are distinct.

In a way, what is going on here is analogous to what goes on in the analysis of a term such as 'knowledge', as discussed above. Someone might hold that 'knowledge' is equivalent a priori to some description, such as 'justified true belief'. But then we come up with a scenario such that in that scenario, something falls within the extension of 'justified true belief' but not of 'knowledge'. So we conclude that the two are not equivalent a priori. The process repeats itself for other descriptions, suggesting that 'knowledge' is not a priori equivalent to any such description. This suggests that the intension of 'knowledge' cannot be precisely captured in a linguistic description.

In a similar way, Kripke's arguments suggest that the epistemic intension of a name such as 'Gödel' cannot be precisely captured in a linguistic description. But they do nothing to suggest that the epistemic intension does not exist. And the epistemic intension still mirrors the cognitive significance of the name. The identity 'N is D' is a posteriori precisely because the two expressions have different epistemic intensions; that is, precisely because there is an epistemic possibility where they come apart. The subject has the ability to evaluate the name's referent within this epistemic possibility, just as can be done with expressions in general.

The intension of an expression such as 'knowledge' can at least be approximated by certain linguistic descriptions, such as 'justified true belief', and by longer and longer versions that come gradually closer to the true intension. One might wonder whether something similar can be done with a name such as 'Gödel'. Can the epistemic intension of the name in the case above at least be approximated by a linguistic description? This is not compulsory for the intensional framework, but it can at least be enlightening to look. A side benefit is that it provides some sort of at least approximate account of the features of the world in virtue of which the epistemic intension applies.

To answer this question, one needs to consider: when speakers use a name such as 'Gödel' or 'Feynman' in cases such as those above, how do they determine the referent of the name, given sufficient information about the world? For example, if someone knows only that Feynman is a famous physicist and that Gell-Mann is a famous physicist, how will external information allow her to identify the distinct referents of 'Feynman' and 'Gell-Mann'? The answer seems clear: she will look to *others'* use of the name. Further information will allow her to determine that members of their community use 'Feynman' to refer to a certain individual, and that they use 'Gell-Mann' to refer to a different individual. Once she has this information, she will have no problem determining that her own use of 'Feynman' refers to the first, and that her own use of 'Gell-Mann' refers to the second.

This suggests if we want to approximate the epistemic intension of the speaker's use of 'Feynman' in a description, one might start with something like 'the person called 'Feynman' by those from whom I acquired the name'.[12] It certainly seems that if relevant information about others' uses is specified in an epistemic possibility, then this sort of description will usually give the right results. The same goes for the 'Gödel' epistemic possibility. In all these cases, it seems that a name is being used *deferentially*: in using a name, the speaker defers to others who use the name. So maybe the description above is at least a good first approximation.[13]

There are two sorts of objections that might be made to this sort of description. First, it might be held that it does not always give the right results. For example, it may be epistemically possible that the speaker misheard or misremembered the name, and that others were really using the name 'Fireman'. In such an epistemic possibility, the description above will give the wrong results. But this is just the sort of thing that we should expect, given the imperfection of descriptions. As with 'knowledge', we could try to move to closer approximations. Perhaps 'The referent of the relevant name used by the person from whom I acquired the antecedent of my current term "Gödel"' would do a better job. But no doubt there would be further counterexamples, just as with 'knowledge'. But as in all these cases, the most this shows is that any such approximation is imperfect. One refutes these approximations by evaluating the epistemic intension in certain epistemic possibilities and showing that the approximation gives the wrong results; so this sort of argument does nothing to show that the epistemic intension does not exist.

Second, it might be held that this sort of description is "circular," perhaps because it appeals to the notion of reference. The circularity is not obvious, however. If one appealed to the notion of reference in a definition of 'reference', there would be a danger of circularity. But a definition of 'reference' is not being offered here. If the descriptivist were to offer a definition of 'reference' it might be something like 'whatever satisfies a canonical description D associated with N'. This is a general, noncircular definition with no appeal to reference (except in the notion

---

[12] Kripke considers some potential descriptions in this vicinity. He discusses "the man Jones calls 'Gödel'" (1980, p. 92), where the speaker believes he acquired the name from Jones, and dismisses it on the ground that the belief may be false. And he discusses "the man called 'Glumph' by the people from whom I got it (whoever they are), provided that my present determination of the reference satisfies the conditions sketched in *Naming and Necessity* and whatever other conditions need be satisfied" (1980, p. 162), and dismisses this on grounds connected to the second part of the description. Surprisingly, he never considers the obvious intermediate description (e.g., 'the man called "Glumph" by the people from whom I acquired the name') that avoids both of these problems.

[13] Replies to Kripke's epistemic arguments that appeal to metalinguistic descriptions of this general sort are given by Searle 1984, Fumerton 1989, Jackson 1998, and Lewis 1986, among others.

of satisfying a description, which presumably is to be accounted for separately). At worst there is a danger that if a description D involves 'reference', it will not yield a determinate result, since evaluating the description will require evaluating reference, which will require evaluating another description, which will require evaluating reference, and so on. But a descriptivist can reply that this is merely a recursive situation, not a circular one, and that the process will always eventually be grounded in a use of the name whose associated description does not involve 'reference' at all, such as an initial baptism. The descriptivist might even hold that this is a natural way to capture the insights of the causal theory of reference in a descriptivist framework: reference proceeds through recursive deference to others, ultimately grounded in an initial baptism.

In any case, this worry does not arise on the intensional framework. The epistemic intension of a name is simply a function from worlds to individuals that reflects a rational ability to determine a specific individual in a given epistemic possibility. It is not a description, and so makes no use of 'reference'. Perhaps one might worry that if something like the picture above is right, then *evaluating* the epistemic intension of a term like 'Gödel' at a world will require having explicit information about others' reference within that world, and that this would be circular. It is not clear why this would be circular, but in any case, explicit information about reference would not be required. Information about the epistemic intensions that others associate with various names would suffice (along with other information about causal relations, the properties of various objects, and so on). This information might itself be derivable from information about other mental and/or physical states, or it might be some sort of mental primitive; that does not matter. With information about others' epistemic intensions, reference will be determined. And if there is a worry about *evaluating* others' epistemic intensions given that they are deferential also, then knowledge of epistemic intensions across a whole community (including its history) will suffice, since the deference will ultimately be grounded in a nondeferential use.

So given relevant information about the physical and mental states of individuals in the community, there will be no problem evaluating epistemic intensions. And the use of this information is in no way ad hoc; it corresponds to the information that we use in evaluating reference across various epistemic possibilities. In particular, when a name is used deferentially, information about the linguistic and cognitive practices of others will always be relevant.

Of course not every use of a name is a deferential use, so not every epistemic intension will function in this way. When a name is introduced in an initial baptism, there will be no deferential element involved; to evaluate reference in the actual world (and across epistemic possibilities), the speaker will not usually need information about the cognitive states of others. The same goes for some names used for very familiar referents. Say that a wife uses the name 'Fred' for her husband and has done so for years. In such a case, even were the speaker to discover (to her surprise) that no-one else in the community used that name for her husband, she would still reasonably hold that the name she uses refers to the spouse.

If such a situation turned out to be actual, her utterance 'Fred is my husband' would plausibly be true, not false. This suggests that the epistemic intension of her use of the name has no deferential element.

There are also many intermediate cases, where a name is used with some mixture of deferential and nondeferential elements, so that for a speaker to determine reference of the name, relevant information will include both information about others' usage and independent information about properties of the referent (perhaps corresponding to some of the speakers' beliefs involving the name). This sort of intermediate case will be necessary to account for cases such as 'Madagascar' (Evans 1977), where the referent of our use of the name (an island) differs from the referent of the original use (part of mainland Africa). If every use since the initial baptism was entirely deferential, this could not happen. So some uses in the causal chain must have been not entirely deferential, with epistemic intensions that were partly influenced by a speaker's beliefs. It is easy to imagine that even if the beliefs have only a small influence on a given speaker's epistemic intension, the effect of this influence would amplify as a causal chain proceeds. If every speaker in the chain has a small component of influence from the belief, then deference to a speaker whose epistemic intension is also influenced by the belief will increase the effect. In the case of 'Madagascar', the result might be that uses of the name would initially refer to the mainland location, would proceed through a period of divided reference, and would eventually emerge as referring to the island.

(One other subtlety: to evaluate a deferential use of the name in an epistemic possibility, the speaker may need the name itself (as used by her) to be present in an epistemic possibility, so that she can determine where that name was acquired. This suggests that deferential uses are exceptions to the principle that tokens of an expression need not be present within an epistemic possibility. I think that this sort of case is best handled by having one or more optional marked thoughts ('this thought') present at the center of a world, which be used to trace deferential reference in an epistemic possibility.)

Kripke also gives an epistemic argument against descriptive views of natural kind terms (1980, pp. 116–23). He argues that it is not a priori that gold is yellow, or that tigers are striped, and so on, in effect because there are epistemic possibilities in which these statements could turn out to be false (if we were suffering from various illusions, for example). In a similar way, Putnam (1975) argues that it is not a priori that cats are animals, since there are epistemic possibilities in which it would turn out that they are robots from Mars. As before, these arguments do not apply to the intensional account: they proceed by evaluating an epistemic intension at various epistemic possibilities, and they show at most that the epistemic intension is not equivalent to the relevant description. They also suggest that a causal link between the term and the referent plays an important role; so any better descriptive approximation of the intension should give a significant role to this link.

I conclude that Kripke's epistemic arguments have no force against an intensional account of Fregean sense.

9. The Argument from Variability

Another argument against the Fregean view is rarely articulated explicitly,[14] but it may motivate some opposition to the Fregean view. This argument notes that different speakers may associate *different* cognitive significance with the same name. For example, an identity such as "Bill Smith is William Smith" may be cognitively significant for one speaker (e.g., one who has heard of the same person under two names in two different contexts), and cognitively insignificant for another (e.g., the person's partner, who uses both names indiscriminately). So if Fregean sense is to reflect cognitive significance, then the sense of a name must vary between speakers. But if the sense of a name can vary between speakers, it is not part of the *meaning* of the name at all. The same may apply to other expressions, such as natural kind terms: the cognitive significance of such a term is variable, so its sense must be variable, so its sense cannot be part of its meaning.

We need not spend much time on the first part of this argument. On the account I have given, it is clear that the epistemic intension of a name can vary between speakers. We saw this in the discussion just concluded: the first user of a name may use the name with one epistemic intension, and later users may use it with a quite different epistemic intension. When Leverrier introduced the term 'Neptune' as a term for whatever planet was perturbing the orbit of Uranus, then the epistemic intension of his use of the term functioned roughly as described. But the next speaker—perhaps his wife, who knew only that Neptune was an astronomical object for which her husband was searching—might have used it with a different epistemic intension. And later users might well use it in a deferential way (as with 'Feynman' above), with an epistemic intension that reflects this. So different speakers can clearly have different epistemic intensions for the same name.

Something similar may apply to natural kind terms, though this is not quite so clear. For example, two speakers might have been exposed to different forms of water: one has only been exposed to water in liquid form (knowing nothing of a solid form), and the other has been exposed only to water in solid form (knowing nothing of a liquid form). It might be that for the first speaker, the epistemic intension of 'water' functions to pick out (roughly) a substance that takes on a certain liquid form, and that for the second speaker, the epistemic intension of 'water' functions to pick out a substance that takes on a certain solid form. In the actual world, these epistemic intensions both pick out the same substance, but in other scenarios, their extensions will differ. But arguably both are using the same word 'water'. If so, there is no epistemic intension for 'water' that is common across all users of the term.

The same applies in an even stronger way to demonstratives such as 'that'. Here different uses of the same term by the same speaker can have different epistemic intensions. It is plausible that the epistemic intension of 'that' depends at least in part on a speaker's intentions, which may differ between uses of the term: on one occasion, the speaker may intend to refer to an object on her left, and on

---

[14] Frege himself (in "The Thought") addresses objections based on variability, in the context of indexicals rather than names. Burge (1979) stresses that Frege's conception of sense differs from contemporary conceptions of linguistic meaning, in part because of variability.

another occasion, to an object on her right. If so, the epistemic intensions on these different uses may differ. So there is no epistemic intension for 'that' that is common across all uses of the term, even for a single speaker.

This suggests that for a general account, epistemic intensions cannot be assigned to expression *types* but rather must be assigned to expression *tokens* (or perhaps to expression types in contexts of use). There will be some terms for which epistemic intensions are constant across all tokens of an expression type—some descriptive terms and indexicals, for example—in which case an epistemic intension can also be assigned to the type. And for names and natural kind terms, epistemic intensions might be constant at least across an individual speaker's use of an expression (at least within a limited time frame), so there could be an assignment to more limited types. But a fully general account requires that epistemic intensions are assigned to tokens.[15]

What of the second part of the argument: that if epistemic intensions can vary between tokens of a type, then they are not meanings? This issue is largely terminological. If it is stipulated that meanings are constant across all tokens of a type, then epistemic intensions are not meanings. If this is not stipulated, then epistemic intensions might be meanings. We could distinguish 'type meanings' and 'token meanings', and allow that epistemic intensions are not (in the general case) type meanings, but they are token meanings. Or we can use a different term, such as 'content', for the sort of meanings that can vary between tokens of an expression type. It is not clear that a substantive issue remains once the terminological issue is cleared up.

It might be insisted that if epistemic intensions can vary between tokens of a type, then they are not part of *language*, they are not an aspect of *linguistic* content, and that perhaps they do not fall within the domain of the philosophy of language at all. Again, this is a terminological issue. One might say that the epistemic intensions of names are not part of *a language* such as English, where this is considered as what is common between all English speakers. But this is no reason to deny that they are part of language in a broader sense, and they are in the domain of the philosophy of language. Of course these terminological issues are largely sociological in origin; so if someone resists on all these issues, it may help to point to some historical examples.

First, Frege. As we have seen, Frege himself held that the sense of an expression could vary between tokens of a type, in the case of indexicals and names. Frege's theory of sense is generally taken to be one of the most important theories

---

[15] It should be noted that this difference in epistemic intensions between speakers goes along with differences in which sentences are a priori for a given speaker. For example, 'Neptune (if it exists) affects the orbit of Uranus' may be a priori for Leverrier, but not for his wife. Leverrier could use the sentence to express a priori knowledge, but his wife could not. So insofar as the apriority of various sentences is invoked in the analysis of epistemic intensions, it will generally be a speaker-relative notion that is relevant. (This is reflected in Kripke's own discussion (e.g., 1980, p. 73) which usually talks of a sentence being "a priori for a speaker.") Of course the notion is still distinct from the notion of what the speaker knows a priori; it is a notion of what is knowable a priori for a speaker, given ideal rational reflection.

in the philosophy of language, and Frege himself is perhaps the most important figure in the field. To hold that variable semantic values are not part of the content of language would have the odd consequence of excluding Frege's own theory of sense.

Second, Kripke. It is striking that in all his arguments against the Fregean view, Kripke (1980) never mentions an argument from variability. He appears to take it for granted that on a Fregean theory, the descriptive content of a name may vary between speakers (his relevant formulations are all speaker-relative), and does not mention this as an objection. Given the number of other objections that are developed against a Fregean account, this suggests that Kripke assumes that variability alone does not rule out sense as an aspect of language. And it suggests that if the worst problem for a Fregean is variability, then a Fregean view of language would be broadly correct.[16]

Third, Kaplan. Kaplan's theory of character and content (for indexicals and demonstratives) is one of the most important theories in the philosophy of language in recent years. On Kaplan's account, it is clear that both the character and the content of a demonstrative such as 'that' will vary between uses of the term.[17] So if epistemic intensions are not an aspect of language, then neither are character or content.

Someone might object that the epistemic intension of an utterance is not always part of what that utterance *communicates*, since a speaker and a hearer may associate different epistemic intensions with the same expression, and the hearer may not know what the speaker's epistemic intension is. It is true for that this reason, epistemic intensions are not always communicated: a speaker's utterance with a given epistemic intension may cause the hearer to acquire a belief with a different epistemic intension. But it is not clear that this sort of communicative property is a *sine qua non* for any aspect of the content of language. Certainly it is not satisfied by Frege's sense or by Kaplan's character or content, for example. At worst, epistemic intensions are in the same boat as these paradigmatic aspects of linguistic content.

It might also be objected that epistemic intensions are an aspect of "speaker meaning" rather than "semantic meaning." This objection appeals to a distinction that Kripke (1977) exploits to deal with Donnellan's (1966) distinction between the "referential" and "attributive" use of expressions such as 'the man in the corner drinking champagne', used by a speaker intended to refer to a man he is looking at in

---

[16] This helps to defuse a natural objection: that opposition to Fregean theories was only ever intended as opposition to Fregean accounts of linguistic meaning, so that the existence of variable Fregean semantic values is irrelevant. It is clear that this is not how Kripke (the canonical source of recent opposition to the Fregean view) saw the matter.

[17] Kaplan's formal language for demonstratives deals with this issue by holding that tokens of demonstratives that are associated with different intentions or demonstrations are in fact tokens of a different word. But it is extremely plausible that in a natural language such as English, different tokens of a demonstrative such as 'that' are tokens of the same word; so this formal stipulation still leaves character distinct from linguistic meaning in natural language. See Braun 1996 for critical discussions, and for alternative proposals regarding the linguistic meaning of demonstratives.

the corner. If the man in the corner is actually drinking a martini, there is a sense in which the expression refers to him (the referential sense), and a sense in which it does not (the attributive sense). Kripke argues that the attributive reading reflects the "semantic reference" of the expression, while the referential reading is merely an aspect of "speaker's reference." Perhaps something similar applies to epistemic intensions?

I think Kripke's analysis of Donnellan's cases is plausible, but it does not generalize to the case of epistemic intensions. As Kripke says:

> The semantic referent of a designator is given by a *general* intention of the speaker to refer to a certain object whenever the designator is used. The speaker's referent is given by a *specific* intention, on a given occasion, to refer to a certain object.

It is clear that on this definition, the epistemic intension of a name or natural kind term is more akin to semantic reference than to speaker's reference, since it reflects a general intention on the speaker's part, not a specific intention. Indeed, the epistemic intension of 'the man in the corner drinking champagne' in the case above plausibly picks out the semantic referent (no-one), not the speaker's referent (the man in the corner). One might, if one wished, introduce a corresponding difference between "semantic epistemic intension" and "speaker's epistemic intension," where the latter picks out the man who is ostended irrespective of his other properties. But even then, epistemic intensions would be in the same boat as reference, and there would be a clear notion that falls on Kripke's "semantic" side of things.

Perhaps there is some *other* distinction that might be drawn between something one might call "semantic meaning" and something one might call "speaker meaning": for example, if one stipulates that semantic meaning must be constant across all tokens of a type, while speaker meaning can vary between speakers. But that would be a very different distinction from Kripke's, and it would do nothing to suggest that epistemic intensions are in the same boat as Donnellan's "referential" uses of descriptions.

A final objection might be that epistemic intensions are not part of language, since they derive entirely from the contents of thought. On this view, it is the speaker's *concept* of water that has an epistemic intension, and it is the conceptual content that varies between speakers, not any sort of linguistic content. One might respond by accepting that epistemic intensions are associated with concepts and thoughts[18] and that the epistemic intensions of linguistic expressions are derivative in some way on the epistemic intensions of thoughts, while denying that this entails that epistemic intensions are not also part of the content of language. It is not unreasonable to hold that all linguistic content is derivative in some way on mental content (this applies just as much to expressions whose content is constant between speakers as to expressions whose content varies). But if the objection in

---

[18] See Chalmers 2002b, in which epistemic intensions are used to give an account of the "narrow content" of thought.

question were correct, then such a view would be false by definition, or at best, it would entail that there is no linguistic content. Perhaps the view is wrong, but if so, this is a substantive point, not a terminological one. It is also worth noting that Kripke's own discussion above suggests that linguistic content can derive from the mental content inherent in a speaker's intentions. So I think that there is no objection to epistemic intension as a sort of linguistic content here.

Ultimately, the best way to deal with any terminological issue is to reflect on the use to which a term is being put, and to determine which sense of the term is most relevant to a given purpose. It may be that there are some purposes for which the most relevant notion of the "meaning" or "content" of linguistic expressions is one on which meaning and content are required to be constant across all tokens of a type. Such purposes might include those of determining what is built into the semantic structure of a language such as English, giving an account of what is required to competently use an expression of a given type, and perhaps addressing certain questions about what an expression will communicate between arbitrary speakers of a language. For these purposes, one can invoke a notion of meaning on which universality is required. On this conception of meaning, epistemic intensions may be part of the meanings of indexicals and some descriptive terms, but they will not be part of the meanings of names and natural kind terms.

For many other purposes, we do not need such a narrow notion of meaning or content, and we often need a broader notion. This arguably applies to most of the uses to which the philosophy of language and notions of meaning are put in other areas of philosophy: that is, the uses in virtue of which philosophy of language is sometimes said to be "first philosophy." The same also applies to many uses of meaning and content within the philosophy of language itself.

One example: notions of meaning and content are often taken to be central in analyzing questions about necessity and possibility, which in turn play a crucial role in analyzing many metaphysical issues. But for this role, the question of whether meaning or content is constant across speakers is almost entirely irrelevant. It would make very little difference to the deepest issues if there were just one speaker of a language, or if different speakers used terms with different meanings or content. If I use an epistemic intension to reach a metaphysical conclusion about water, the worst possible consequence of variability will be that someone else will not be able to reach a similar conclusion using their term 'water'. This seems unlikely to happen, due to the common referent. But even if it did, it would do nothing to invalidate my conclusion; it would just mean that someone else would have to express the conclusion differently. Once terminological issues are cleared up (as they often need to be), the substantive points will be as before. So if epistemic intensions are otherwise relevant to answering these questions, as I think they are, it is no objection that they can vary between speakers.

The same goes for many or most applications of the philosophy of language in metaphysics, epistemology, the philosophy of mind, the philosophy of science, and other areas. For most of these purposes, a requirement that meaning or content is constant over all tokens of an expression type is at best irrelevant, and is at worst harmful. If a semantic value can otherwise play a useful explanatory role in these domains, then the variability of that semantic value will not be a serious objection. If this is right, then to stipulate that variable semantic values do not qualify as meanings or linguistic contents may be to severely constrain the explanatory role of meaning and linguistic content. To do so would be to compromise the status of the philosophy of language as first philosophy, or to send the burden upstairs to the philosophy of mind.

I think it is best instead to recognize that if variable semantic values can do much of the central work that notions of meaning and linguistic content are introduced to do, then they qualify straightforwardly as aspects of meaning or linguistic content. If so, then the argument from variability has little force against a Fregean view.

10. Conclusion

I have argued that a broadly Fregean account of meaning is tenable. On this account, the notion of an epistemic intension plays the role of a Fregean notion of sense. Epistemic intensions are not the same as Fregean sense in all respects, but they are similar in many respects, and they allow versions of the core Fregean requirements on sense to be satisfied. It may be useful to summarize where the core Fregean theses stand in light of the preceding discussion.

Thesis (1), that every expression has a sense, has been preserved, by allowing that every expression has an epistemic intension. It has also been augmented by a thesis holding that every expression has a subjunctive intension in addition to its epistemic intension.

Thesis (2), that sense reflects cognitive significance, has been preserved in a slightly modified form. In the modified form, cognitive significance is understood as non-apriority. So when an identity is not a priori, the expressions involved have different senses; when two sentences are not equivalent a priori, they have different senses; and so on.

Thesis (3), that the sense of a complex expression depends on the sense of its parts, has been preserved in a modified form. The thesis as it stands holds for all expressions except those involving modal and subjunctive contexts. To handle such expressions, one needs a slightly modified thesis: that the sense of an expression depends on the semantic values of its parts, where the semantic value may include elements (such as subjunctive intension) that go beyond sense. It is also the case that all aspects of semantic value (extension, epistemic intension, subjunctive intension) of a complex expression depends on the semantic values of the parts.

Thesis (4), that sense determines extension, has been preserved in the "weak determination" version that holds that sense determines extension in combination with the world.

Thesis (5), that the sense of a sentence has an absolute truth-value, has been discarded. The sense of a sentence has a truth-value only relative to a subject and a time. Thesis (6), that expressions refer to their senses in indirect contexts, has also been discarded. A more complex account of these contexts is still required. Thesis (7), that the sense of an expression can vary between speakers and between occasions of use, has been preserved.

I have also argued that the most common objections to Fregean theories can be handled by such an account. At most, these objections show that (i) senses are indexical, (ii) senses should be supplemented by a further semantic value, a subjunctive intension, (iii) senses should be understood as intensions, not descriptions, and (iv) the sense of an expression type can vary between speakers and between occasions of use.

I have argued that extension, epistemic intension, and subjunctive intension are all part of the meaning and content of an expression, but I have not argued that these exhaust the meaning or content of an expression. In fact I think that they do not. First, there are plausibly aspects of meaning that have nothing to do with the determination of truth: the difference between 'and' and 'but' is an example. Second, there may be expressions that are a priori equivalent to each other, but that nevertheless have different meaning due to some more fine-grained cognitive difference: the difference between 'equilateral triangle' and 'equiangular triangle' is an example. To handle this last sort of difference, I think that one may need senses of a variety that are more fine-grained than epistemic intensions. The notion of an epistemic intension might be extended to do this (by moving to a more fine-grained space of epistemic possibilities), but this is a separate story (see Chalmers forthcoming b). It may also be that for some purposes, the meanings or contents of complex expressions may need to be taken as structured complexes of extensions and/or intensions; this is quite compatible with the framework I have outlined.

I have also not given a conclusive demonstration that epistemic intensions of expressions exist and have all the properties I have attributed to them. A conclusive demonstration would require some more precise definitions, and a rebuttal of all counterarguments. I have argued that there is a strong prima facie case that epistemic intensions exist and have the properties I have attributed to them, however, and I have argued that the most obvious counterarguments can be rebutted. It may be that there are other arguments against the view; if so, I would be very interested to hear them. In the meantime, I think that a broadly Fregean approach to meaning holds considerable promise.

REFERENCES

Braun, D. 1996. Demonstratives and their linguistic meanings. *Noûs* 30:145–73.
Burge, T. 1979. Sinning against Frege. *Philosophical Review* 58:398–432.
Carnap, R. 1947. *Meaning and Necessity*. University of Chicago Press.
Chalmers, D. J. 2002a. Does conceivability entail possibility? In (T. Gendler and J. Hawthorne, eds.) *Conceivability and Possibility*. Oxford University Press. [consc.net/papers/conceivability.html]
Chalmers, D. J. 2002b. The components of content. In (D. Chalmers, ed.) *Philosophy of Mind: Classical and Contemporary Readings*. Oxford University Press. [consc.net/papers/content.html]

Chalmers, D. J. forthcoming a. The foundations of two-dimensional semantics. [consc.net/papers/foundations.html]

Chalmers, D. J. forthcoming b. The nature of epistemic space. [consc.net/papers/espace.html]

Chalmers, D. J. forthcoming c. The tyranny of the subjunctive. [consc.net/papers/tryanny.html]

Donnellan, K. 1966. Reference and definite descriptions. *Philosophical Review* 75:281–304.

Dummett, M. 1973. *Frege: Philosophy of Language*. Duckworth.

Evans, G. 1973. The causal theory of names. *Proceedings of the Aristotelian Society (Supplementary Volume)* 47:187–208.

Frege, G. 1892. Über Sinn und Bedeutung. Translated in (P. Geach and M. Black, eds.) *Translations from the Philosophical Writings of Gottlob Frege*. Oxford: Blackwell, 1952.

Fumerton, R. 1989. Russelling causal theories of reference. In (C. Savage and C. Anderson, eds.) *Rereading Russell*. University of Minnesota Press.

Jackson, F. 1998. Reference and description revisited. *Philosophical Perspectives* 12:201–18.

Kaplan, D. 1989. Demonstratives. In (J. Almog, J. Perry, and H. Wettstein, eds.) *Themes from Kaplan*. Oxford University Press.

Kripke, S. A. 1977. Speaker's reference and semantic reference. In (P. French, ed.) *Contemporary Perspectives in the Philosophy of Language*. University of Minnesota Press.

Kripke, S. A. 1980. *Naming and Necessity*. Cambridge, MA: Harvard University Press.

Lewis, D. 1979. Attitudes *de dicto* and *de se*. *Philosophical Review* 88:513–43.

Lewis, D. 1986. *Australasian Journal of Philosophy* 62:221–36.

Mill, J. S. 1843. *A System of Logic*. London: Longmans.

Perry, J. 1977. Frege on demonstratives. *Philosophical Review* 86:476–97.

Perry, J. 1979. The problem of the essential indexical. *Nous* 13:3–21.

Putnam, H. 1975. The meaning of 'meaning'. In (K. Gunderson, ed.) *Language, Mind, and Knowledge*. University of Minnesota Press.

Recanati, F. 1993. *Direct Reference*. Blackwell.

Searle, J. 1983. *Intentionality: An Essay in the Philosophy of Mind*. Cambridge University Press.

Soames, S. 1998. The modal argument: Wide scope and rigidified descriptions. *Noûs* 32:1–22.

Sosa, D. 2001. Rigidity in the scope of Russell's theory. *Noûs* 35:1–38.

Stalnaker, R. 1978. Assertion. In (P. Cole, ed.) *Syntax and Semantics: Pragmatics, Vol. 9*. New York: Academic Press.

Stanley, J. 1997. Names and rigid designation. In (C. Wright and R. Hale, eds.) *Companion to the Philosophy of Language*. Blackwell.

RIGID DESIGNATION AND ITS LESSONS FOR THE SEMANTIC CONTENTS OF PROPER NAMES

Scott Soames

This chapter is concerned with Kripke's doctrine that proper names are rigid designators, and the challenges it poses to analyses that treat the meanings of names as given by definite descriptions associated with them by speakers. We will begin with a brief review of Kripke's arguments against descriptivism about names, and with the isolation of one of these arguments—the so-called modal argument—as depending crucially on the claim that names are rigid. After an explanation of this claim and its role in the modal argument, the bulk of the chapter will be devoted to examining and refuting the leading attempts to circumvent the argument and reinstate descriptivism. The main lesson to be drawn from these failures is that the considerations underlying Kripke's original modal argument can be strengthened and extended so as to constitute a decisive objection to all standard forms of descriptivism about the meaning of names, no matter how sophisticated or convoluted. This objection invites the conclusion that no proper names have the semantic contents of definite descriptions. However, it does not quite establish it. Although the conclusion does seem to hold for the great majority of proper names that have attracted the attention of philosophers, at the end of the chapter we will discuss a distinctive class of proper names that may well constitute a special and highly restricted exception to it.

Three Arguments against the Descriptivist Picture

In *Naming and Necessity*, Saul Kripke gives three types of argument against semantic theories that analyze the meaning of proper names, and the manner in which their reference is determined, in terms of the meaning, or denotation, of descriptions associated with those names by speakers. The first type consists of *semantic arguments* designed to show that, typically, the referent of a proper name n, as used by a speaker s, is not linguistically determined to be the denotation of any description, or set of descriptions, associated with n by s. The second type consists of *epistemic arguments* designed to show that what is known or believed by someone who knows or believes that which is expressed by a sentence a containing a proper name n is different from what is known or believed by someone who knows or believes that which is expressed by a sentence which results from substituting a description for n in s. The third type consists of *modal arguments*. These are intended to show that sentences containing names typically have different truth conditions than corresponding sentences containing descriptions, in the sense that sentences of these two types are typically true in different possible states of affairs.

One of Kripke's semantic arguments is based on the observation that in some cases a speaker's use of a name n may uniquely refer to an object o, even though the speaker has no uniquely denoting description at all associated with n.

Names of famous people of whose accomplishments most speakers are only dimly aware provide examples of this type. For example, many people have heard the name *Cicero* and know that it refers to a famous Roman, but know little else about him. Nevertheless, such speakers can use the name to refer to a specific man, even though they are not able to provide any description that picks him out uniquely.

The reason they are able to do this, as Kripke points out, is that the linguistic mechanism determining the reference of a speaker's use of a name is typically the historical chain of transmission in which the speaker stands. The standard case goes roughly as follows: A name is introduced and, once introduced, is passed from one speaker to another. Each time it is passed to a new speaker, the person acquiring the name intends to use it to refer to whomever or whatever that person's sources use it to refer to. Often when this happens, the person acquiring the name picks up substantial information about its referent in the process. However, this is not always so, and in some cases considerable misinformation may be passed along. Because of this, speakers' answers to the question.

> Q.   To whom or what are you using the name n to refer?

are not always reliable. As Kripke has shown, there are cases in which speakers use a name n to refer to an object o even though the descriptions elicited by Q (a) do not pick out any object uniquely,[1] or (b) pick out some unique object other than o.[2] He takes cases like these to refute descriptive theories that claim the referent of an arbitrary proper name n, as used by a speaker s, is linguistically determined to be the unique object (if there is one) satisfying the descriptions that s takes to be definitive of s's use of n.

Some descriptivists have objected that Kripke's conclusion is premature. Although they agree that his semantic arguments show that in most cases the referent of a name for a speaker is not fixed by the descriptions the speaker would most readily give in answer to Q, they insist that there may be other descriptions that fill the bill. Consider, for example, Kripke's own theory about the historical chain of transmission by which reference is normally determined. Surely that theory could be put in the form of a description. But then, if the theory is right, that description fixes reference. And so, it might be claimed, descriptivism is vindicated after all.

However, things are not so simple. First, the historical-transmission account of reference sketched by Kripke leaves many questions unanswered, and falls short of being a complete and explicit theory. For example, we know that sometimes a name is introduced with a certain referent, is passed on to others, and at some stage in the historical chain of transmission loses its initial referent and acquires a new one, without anyone in the chain intending to change the reference

---

[1] For further examples of this type, see Kripke's discussion of the *Feynman* and *Einstein* examples in *Naming and Necessity*, pp. 80–82.

[2] Kripke discusses examples of this type in *Naming and Necessity*, pp. 83–85. See his discussion of *Godel/Schmidt*, *Peano/Dedekind*, and *Columbus*.

of the term.[3] There is nothing in Kripke's discussion that explains precisely how this happens, or that specifies the conditions that have to be met in order for it to occur. This does not, of course, falsify his guiding idea. However, as he was the first to admit, it does show that his idea does not amount to a fully explicit theory that accounts for all instances of a speaker's use of a name referring to an object.[4] Consequently, no description extracted from it constitutes the linguistic mechanism by which the referents of names are definitively determined.

Second, even if one had a complete, explicit theory from which one could extract a definitive reference-fixing description, in order to vindicate descriptivism one would still have to show that ordinary speakers somehow possess this description, and use it to establish the references of names. This problem is by no means trivial. Surely ordinary speakers cannot produce on demand a fully accurate and explicit description that covers all cases. Moreover, even in the unlikely event that they could somehow be shown to implicitly grasp such a description, this would not be enough. Speakers often have many descriptions associated with a name they use. What, if anything, makes one of those descriptions privileged, in the sense not only of managing to apply to what the name really refers to, but also of playing the central role in determining the reference of the name in the first place? Unless the descriptivist can answer this question, there is no vindication of descriptivism.

Finally, the question of how the reference of names is fixed is less important philosophically than related questions about the meaning or semantic content of names, and of sentences containing them. Kripke approaches these questions by investigating the epistemic and modal properties of sentences containing names, and using these properties to argue that the most straightforward versions of descriptivism about the semantic contents of names can't be correct. Unless these arguments can be answered, there will be little to recommend descriptivism.

This brings us to Kripke's *epistemic* arguments against descriptive theories of names. These arguments are designed to show that the epistemic status of (the propositions semantically expressed by) sentences containing names typically is different from the epistemic status of (the propositions semantically expressed by) corresponding sentences containing descriptions. For example, if D is the description associated with a name n by speakers, then the proposition semantically expressed by the sentence *if n exists, then n is D* (or *if there is/was such a thing as n, then n is/was D*) is typically not knowable a priori even though the proposition expressed by *if D exists, then D is D* (or *if there is/was such a thing as D, then D is/was D*) is knowable a priori. This supports the conclusion that D does not, in fact, have the same meaning (semantic content) as n.

One example of this type is provided by the name *Christopher Columbus* and the description *the first European to discover America*. Although this description represents the most important thing that most people think about Columbus, the

---

[3] Gareth Evans describes such a case in his discussion of the name *Madagascar* in "The Causal Theory of Names," Proceedings of the *Aristotelian Society* supp. vol. 47 (1973):187–208. For an illuminating discussion of this example and the general phenomena of reference change, see Alan Berger, "A Theory of Reference Transmission and Reference Change," *Midwest Studies in Philosophy* 14 (1989).

[4] See Kripke, *Naming and Necessity*, pp. 93–94, and 96–97.

claim that if there was such a person as Columbus, then Columbus was the first European to discover America clearly rests on empirical evidence, and thus is the sort of proposition that could, in principle, be shown to be false by further empirical investigation. (In fact, Kripke notes that it may well be false.) Consequently, it is not knowable a priori, and the semantic contents of sentences containing *Columbus* are not the same as the semantic contents of corresponding sentences containing the description *the first European to discover America*. Kripke contends that the same could be said for other descriptions that speakers associate with this name.

The third and final type of argument used by Kripke against description theories of names is the *model argument*. This argument is based on the observation that the modal profile of sentences containing names often differs from the modal profile of corresponding sentences containing descriptions. This fact is used to show that the meanings (semantic contents) of names are not given by the descriptions associated with them by speakers. This argument is both the best-known, and the most criticized, of Kripke's arguments against descriptivism. For this reason it is worth looking at closely.

This argument is encompassed in the following generalized form.

The Modal Argument (Generalized Version)

(1) Proper names are rigid designators.

(2) Therefore proper names do not have the same meanings (semantic contents) as nonrigid descriptions. Thus, if n is a proper name, and D is a nonrigid description, then the sentences **n is F** and **D is F** typically do not have the same meaning (semantic content) or semantically express the same proposition.

(3) Since the descriptions commonly associated with names by speakers are nonrigid, typically the meanings (semantic contents) of names are not given by those descriptions. Thus, if n is a name and D is a description associated with n by speakers, then the sentences **n is F** and **D is F** typically do not have the same meaning (semantic content) or semantically express the same proposition.

The most important step in the argument is the first one, which requires establishing that names are rigid designators. The way this is done can be illustrated using the name *Aristotle*.

To say that *Aristotle* is a rigid designator is to say that it denotes the same thing in (or at, or with respect to) all possible worlds.[5] Before evaluating this claim, I will say a word about what possible worlds are, and what talk about them amounts to. As Kripke understands the notion, a possible world is not another

---

[5] This is a slight simplification of Kripke's own characterization of rigidity. According to Kripke, a singular term t rigidly designates an object o iff t designates o in all worlds in which o exists, and never designates anything other than o in any world. Kripke's cautious formulation leaves room both for rigid designators of o that designate o even in worlds in which o does not exist, and for rigid designators of o that fail to designate anything in worlds in which o does not exist. Except where explicitly indicated in the text, the distinction between these two types of rigid designators will not be relevant to our discussion.

universe; rather, it is a way the universe could have been. Following him, I take a possible world to be a maximally complete property that the universe could have had (instantiated). The actual world is also such a property; it is a maximally complete property that the universe does have. To say that a proposition p is true in (or at, or with respect to, or according to) a possible world w is to say that p would have been true if w had obtained—that is, p would have been true if w had been instantiated. On this conception, talk about possible worlds can be used to illuminate ordinary modal discourse without providing a reductive analysis of it. Ordinary sentences containing modal notions like *could, would, possibly,* and *necessarily* are systematically connected with truth-conditionally equivalent sentences that talk about possible worlds, but since possible worlds themselves are defined as properties the universe could have had, there is no attempt to provide a reductive analysis of ordinary modal notions in terms of nonmodal notions.

The upshot of this is that talk of a possible world need not be thought of as committing one to contentious and implausible metaphysical claims about the existence of real, but nonactual, concrete universes spatiotemporally disconnected from our actual universe, and ordinary statements about what could or could not have been the case need not be thought of an surprising assertions about the goings-on in concrete universes with which we have no connection. Some Philosophers do think of possible worlds, and modal talk in general, in that way. Though I take this to be a mistake, the main arguments I will give in this chapter can be reconstructed from that point of view. What I wish to emphasize is that nothing so elaborate or contentious is either required or intended. My talk of possible worlds is nothing more than talk of ways the universe could have been, which, like Kripke, I take to be relatively innocuous metaphysically.[6]

Back to the modal argument, and to the claim that a name like *Aristotle* is a rigid designator. To say that *Aristotle* is a rigid designator is to say that it denotes the same thing in (or at, or with respect to) all possible worlds. The reason we think it does this is that we think the truth-values, at different worlds, of sentences containing the name always depend on the properties of one and the same individual at those worlds. For example, we take the sentence *Aristotle was a philosopher* to be true at a world (state) w iff a certain individual—the person who was actually Aristotle—was a philosopher in w. Since a sentence α *is F* is true at an arbitrary world (state) w iff the denotation of α at w is in the extension of F at w, we conclude that for any arbitrary world (state) w, *Aristotle* denotes in w the individual who was Aristotle in the actual world (state).

The key point here is the claim that the truth-value of the sentence *Aristotle was a philosopher* at a world (state) w always depends on whether or not the

---

[6] Perhaps it would have been better if, in the development of "possible world semantics," the word 'world' had been reserved for the existing concrete universe, and the phrase 'possible state of the world' had been used to designate maximally complete properties that the universe could have had. Had this terminology been adopted, we would have spoken of claims being true or false relative to *possible states of the world,* rather than relative to the misleadingly shortened *possible worlds.* Though I won't (consistently) adopt this revisionary terminology in the text, the reader is invited to use it to interpret the standard locutions used there.

person we call *Aristotle* in the actual world is a philosopher in w. Why do we think this? Couldn't people in w have given the name *Aristotle* to some other person, and thus taken the sentence to be about him? Of course they could; but that is irrelevant. When we say that the sentence *Aristotle was a philosopher* is true at w, we are saying that the sentence, as we actually understand it, is true when taken as a description of how things stand, according to w. In other words, to say that a sentence is true at a world (state) w is to say that the claim or proposition we actually use the sentence to express would be true if w obtained. Thus, our ultimate ground for thinking that the name *Aristotle* is a rigid designator is our conviction that there is a certain individual x, such that for every possible world (state) w the proposition that Aristotle was a philosopher is true at w iff x was a philosopher at w, and similarly for other proposition.[7] This feature of the name differentiates it from a description like *the teacher of Alexander*. The proposition that the teacher of Alexander was a philosopher is true at an arbitrary world (state) w iff one and only one person taught Alexander at w, and that person was a philosopher at w. Since different people teach Alexander at different worlds, the description *the teacher of Alexander* is not rigid. Hence, by the modal argument, it does not give the meaning (semantic content) of the name *Aristotle*.

---

[7] In order to properly understand the thesis that *Aristotle* is a rigid designator, one must clearly understand how the following two claims are reconciled.

(i) The name *Aristotle* is a rigid designator. Thus, for all possible states of the world w, the name *Aristotle* refers to the same individual—the man Aristotle—in, or at, or with respect to w.

(ii) It is not a necessary truth that Aristotle was named 'Aristotle.' Thus, it could have been the case that the name *Aristotle* did not refer to Aristotle, which means that there is some world-state w such that the claim that the name *Aristotle* did not refer to Aristotle is true in, or at, or with respect to w.

As Kripke would be the first to insist, these claims are both true. At first glance, this might seem puzzling because they might seem to be inconsistent. In fact, they are not. What makes (i) and (ii) seem inconsistent is the tendency to tacitly accept (iii) as something so obvious as to go without saying.

(iii) The three-place relation ___ *refers to* ___ *in, at, or with respect to* ___ holds between the name 'Aristotle,' the man Aristotle, and the world-state w iff it is true in, or at, or with respect to w that the two-place relation ___ *refers to* ___ holds between 'Aristotle' and Aristotle—that is, iff the claim that 'Aristotle' refers to Aristotle is true when taken as a description of w.

Although (iii) might at first seem undeniable, it is false. The three-place relation ___ *refers to* ___ *in, at, or with respect to* ___ holds between a name n, an object o, and a world-state w iff **n, as used by us here and now** *in the actual world, refers to the object o, when our words are taken as descriptions of w.* Because of this, n may refer to o with respect to w even if (a) in, at, or with respect to w there is no name n; or (b) in, at, or with respect to w the name n is not used by speakers to refer to anything; or (c) in, at, or with respect to w, n is used by speakers to refer to something other than o. What, if anything, speakers in w use the name n to refer to is irrelevant to whether n refers to o with respect to w. However, what speakers in w use n to refer to is crucial to determining which pairs of names and objects the two-place relation ___ *refers to* ___ applies to with respect to w. **It is true with respect to w that the name n refers to the object o iff speakers in w use n to refer to o.** Thus, what (ii) says is that there are world-states w such that the speakers in those world-states do not use 'Aristotle' to refer to Aristotle. This is compatible with the claim made by (i)—namely, that the name 'Aristotle,' as we use it here and now in the actual world-state, refers to the man Aristotle when our words are taken as descriptions of any world-state whatsoever.

Descriptivists' Attempts to Circumvent the Modal Argument

As I noted earlier, the modal argument was just one of several arguments given by Kripke against description theories of proper names. As such it was never intended to constitute, all by itself, a decisive refutation of all such theories. Rather, it was intended to be used in conjunction with the other arguments to produce that result. Nevertheless, the modal argument has been the main focus of attention for proponents of descriptivism, who have developed two main strategies for challenging it.

Both strategies claim that names are semantically equivalent to descriptions, but descriptions of a certain special sort. According to the first strategy, names are equivalent to descriptions that are semantically required to take wide scope over modal operators occurring in the same sentence.[8] This strategy amounts to a denial that names are rigid designators, plus an alternative proposal to account for the semantic data on which the doctrine of rigidity is based. According to the second strategy for challenging the modal argument, names are semantically equivalent to rigidified descriptions, and thus are rigid designators. Since speakers have at their disposal the linguistic resources to convert ordinary nonrigid descriptions into corresponding rigid descriptions, proponents of the second strategy take the meanings of proper names to be given by the rigidified descriptions that speakers associate with them.[9] My aim in this chapter will be to examine these two strategies in more detail, to demonstrate that they won't work, and to explain why. Once this is achieved, I will summarize the reasons for thinking (a) that the semantic content of a name is never identical with that of any (nonparasitic, purely qualitative) description, and (b) that the semantic contents of the overwhelming majority of linguistically simple proper names do not even include substantive descriptive elements.

The Analysis of Proper Names as Wide-Scope Descriptions

Recall the conclusion reached earlier about the grounds for thinking that the name *Aristotle* is a rigid designator. We think that *Aristotle* is rigid because we believe that which is expressed by principle (GR).

---

[8] This strategy was suggested by Michael Dummett in *Frege: Philosophy of Language* (New York: Harper & Row, 1973), pp. 110–151. He also defends a variant of the strategy in chapter 9 and appendix 3 of his *The Interpretation of Frege's Philosophy* (London: Duckworth, 1981). The initial (1973) variant of the strategy maintains that the thesis that names are rigid designators is just the thesis that they take wide scope over modal operators (see in particular pp. 128 and 134). In response to Kripke's criticism in the preface of *Naming and Necessity*, Dummett (1981) presents a second variant of the view, which acknowledges that rigidity and wide scope are alternative theoretical notions used by semantic theorists to account for pretheoretic semantic facts and intuitions. What is common to the two variants is the claim that all genuine pretheoretic semantic facts and intuitions bearing on the dispute can be accommodated by treating names as nonrigid descriptions that take wide scope over modal expressions.

A more recent version of the wide-scope position is given by David Sosa in chapter 3, "Russell and Rigidity," of his dissertation, "Representing Thoughts and Language" (Princeton University, 1996).

[9] This strategy is discussed sympathetically by Jason Stanley in section V of his "Names and Rigid Designation," in Bob Hale and Crispin Wright, eds., *A Companion to the Philosophy of Language* (Oxford: Blackwell Press, 1997), pp. 555–585.

GR.   There is a certain individual x, such that for every possible world w, the proposition that Aristotle was a philosopher is true at w iff x was a philosopher at w, . . . and so on for other propositions expressed using the name *Aristotle*.

Note that (GR) contains an occurrence of the name *Aristotle*, embedded under a modal quantifier—one ranging over possible worlds. Suppose we replace this occurrence of the name with a nonrigid description, ***the G*** which denotes the man Aristotle in the actual world, and which is required to take wide scope over all modal predicates, operators, and quantifiers in the same sentence. This replacement of the name *Aristotle* by a wide-scope description gives us a simulated rigidity principle, (SR i), the content of which is explicitly given by (SR ii).[10]

SR.   (i) There is a certain individual x, such that for every possible world w, the proposition that the G was a philosopher is true at w iff x was a philosopher at w, . . . and so on for other propositions expressed using the name *Aristotle*.

(ii) [the y: Gy] (there is a certain individual x, such that for every possible world w, the proposition that y was a philosopher is true at w iff x was a philosopher at w, . . . and so on for other propositions expressed using the name *Aristotle*)

Since the description ***the G*** denotes Aristotle, principle (GR) is true iff (SR) is true. The proponent of the wide-scope analysis now asserts that the name *Aristotle* is synonymous with the wide-scope description ***the G*** that appears in (SR).[11] Thus, he maintains that our original reason for taking the name *Aristotle* to be rigid—namely, (GR)—really is nothing more than (SR), which stimulates rigidity. On this view, the semantic intuitions underlying the original rigidity claim are compatible with a treatment of proper names as having descriptive semantic contents.

Moreover, the proponent of this analysis argues that facts about prepositional attitudes show that names really do have descriptive meanings, and that propositions semantically expressed by sentences containing names are identical with those expressed by sentences containing descriptions. The argument is based on the widely held view that often it is possible to assert or believe the proposition

---

[10] In discussing the wide-scope analysis, I will employ formal representations in which definite descriptions are restricted quantifiers, the scopes of which, like those of other quantifiers, are the formulas to which they are immediately prefixed.

[11] To say that a name is synonymous with a wide-scope description is to say that arbitrary sentences containing the name semantically express the same propositions as corresponding sentences in which the description is substituted for the name and given the appropriate wide scope. This point can also be put in terms of the distinction between "assertive content" and "ingredient sense" drawn by Michael Dummett, in his *Frege: Philosophy of Language*, pp. 446–447, and *The Interpretation of Frege's Philosophy*, pp. 572–573. Roughly speaking, the assertive content of a sentence (in a context of utterance) is the proposition semantically expressed by the sentence (in that context), while the ingredient sense is what the sentence contributes to the assertive contents of larger sentences in which it may be embedded. Dummett claims that there are natural examples in which two sentences, S_1 and S_2, have the same assertive content (express the same proposition) in a context of utterance, but have different ingredient senses because *Operator* S_1 and *Operator* S_2 have different assertive contents (semantically express different propositions) in the relevant context. Phrased in these terms, when I say that according to the wide-scope analysis, names are synonymous with wide-scope descriptions, I am making a claim about the assertive contents of sentences, not about the ingredient senses of sentences or expressions.

semantically expressed by a sentence *a is F* without asserting or believing the proposition semantically expressed by a corresponding sentence *b is F,* even though the two sentences differ only in the substitution of coreferential names. For example, it is widely presumed that one can assert and believe the proposition semantically expressed by the sentence *Hesperus is seen in the evening* without asserting or believing the proposition semantically expressed by the sentence *Phosphorus is seen in the evening,* despite the fact that the names *Hesperus* and *Phosphorus* are coreferential. Proponents of description theories claim that the explanation of this putative fact is that speakers associate the names with different, nonequivalent descriptions, *the E, and the M,* respectively; hence the proposition semantically expressed by *Hesperus is seen in the evening* is just the proposition expressed by *the E is seen in the evening,* and the proposition semantically expressed by *Phosphorus is seen in the evening* is just the proposition expressed by *the M is seen in the evening.* Everyone agrees that one can assert and believe one of these descriptive propositions without asserting or believing the other. According to the descriptivist, a similar treatment can standardly be given to other pairs of coreferential proper names.

The driving force behind the wide-scope analysis is the desire to preserve this explanation of the behavior of names in propositional attitude constructions, while also explaining their behavior in modal constructions. In propositional attitude ascriptions, the different descriptions associated by speakers with codesignative names are invoked to explain the apparent possibility of *substitution failure.* In modal constructions, the wide scope given these descriptions is used to explain the apparent rigidity of names and the accompanying guarantee of *substitution success.*[12]

That, as I see it, is the basic idea behind the wide-scope analysis. I will now to try to state the analysis a bit more precisely. In doing so, we let S(n) be a sentence of English containing an occurrence of a name n; we let d be a description and S(d) be the result of substituting d for each occurrence of n; similarly, we take S(x) to be the result of replacing each occurrence of n with the variable 'x'. According to the analysis, the proposition semantically expressed by S(n) is the proposition expressed by S(d), on an interpretation in which each occurrence of d (that replaces an original occurrence of n in S(n)) is given wide scope over every modal operator, modal predicate, and modal quantifier in S(x), except those for which doing this would involve

---

[12] Where the names *Hesperus* and *Phosphorus* are (semantically) associated with the codesignative descriptions *the heavenly body seen (at a certain place and season) in the evening* and *the heavenly body seen (at a certain place and season) in the morning,* respectively, descriptivists conclude that the ascriptions *Jones believes that Hesperus is so and so* and *Jones believes that Phosphorus is so and so* may have different truth-values since it is possible to believe that the heavenly body seen (at a certain place and season) in the evening is so and so without believing that the heavenly body seen (at a certain place and season) in the morning is so and so (and vice versa). However, since the heavenly body seen (at a certain place and season) in the evening is in fact the heavenly body seen (at a certain place and season) in the morning, the modal sentences *necessarily Hesperus is so and so* and *necessarily Phosphorus is so and so* must have the same (actual) truth-value. That is, since the object which, in the actual world, is both the unique heavenly body seen (at a certain place and season) in the evening and the unique heavenly body seen (at a certain place and season) in the morning, either that object is necessarily so and so (in which case both modal sentences are true) or it is not necessarily so and so (in which case both are false).

removing d from the scope of some propositional attitude verb. When S(n) contains no modal operators, modal predicates, or modal quantifiers, it semantically expresses whatever proposition (or propositions) is (or are) expressed by S(d).[13]

Let us now consider some examples. If the semantic content of the name n is given by the description *the G,* then the proposition semantically expressed by *n is F* is the proposition expressed by *(the x: Gx) Fx*—for example, the proposition that the president of the United States is a Democrat. Similarly, the proposition semantically expressed by *(necessarily) John believes that n is F* is the proposition expressed by *(necessarily) John believes that (the x: Gx) Ex].* However, the propositions semantically expressed by *necessarily n is F* and *necessarily if n is F, then something is both F and G* are the propositions expressed by *(the x: Gx) necessarily [Fx]* and *(the x: Gx) necessarily [Fx ⊃ $ y (Fy & Gy)].*

Finally, two points of clarification. First, the analysis states that sentences of different sorts that contain names semantically express the same propositions as sentences of various kinds containing descriptions. For this reason it is worth saying a word about what I am assuming about propositions. In addition to being expressed by sentences, I assume that propositions are both bearers of truth or falsity and objects of attitudes, such as believing and asserting. To say this is just to say that there are some things that can be asserted and believed, and that what is asserted and believed may also be true or false (either necessarily or contingently). That there are such things seems to be one of the evident commitments of our ordinary, prephilosophical speech. For present purposes, the expression *propositions* is simply a name for these things, whatever they turn out to be. In giving the arguments that follow in this chapter, I will make only the most minimal use of further theoretical assumptions about the structure of propositions and about the nature of the relations, such as belief and assertion, that we bear to them. Thus my arguments will not depend on controversial positions on these issues.

Second, I want to stress that the wide-scope analysis that is the target of these arguments states something more than the claim that names are semantically equivalent to descriptions that may take wide scope in modal constructions. Rather, it states that names are semantically equivalent to descriptions that must take wide scope in modal constructions (of the sort indicated above). The view is not that a modal sentence containing a name is ambiguous, with one reading in which the associated description takes wide scope over the modal operator and another reading in which it does not. Rather, the analysis asserts that such a sentence is unambiguous, having only the reading in which the description takes wide scope. This feature of the analysis is needed to account for certain obvious

---

[13] Since descriptions are often capable of taking different scopes over other operators, S(d) will sometimes express different propositions, depending on the scope of the description—when S(x) is nonatomic. In many cases these scope differences will be irrelevant to my purposes. For this reason, I will adopt a further proviso in the discussion that follows: unless otherwise indicated, an occurrence of a description corresponding to a name that is not required to take wide scope over a modal operator in the same sentence will be interpreted as taking the smallest possible scope. This proviso is heuristic, and is adopted to reduce the number of ambiguities we will have to consider in the examples that follow. This reduction will not affect the force of the criticisms to be developed, since in each case the problem will be that the analysis assigns certain interpretations to sentences, or sequences of sentences, that they do not, in fact, have.

differences between the behavior of names and ordinary descriptions in modal constructions. For example, as Kripke has pointed out, there is clearly a sense in which (i) the teacher of Alexander might not have taught Alexander, and so might not have been the teacher of Alexander, and (ii) someone other than the teacher of Alexander might have been the teacher of Alexander; however, there is no sense in which (i) Aristotle might not have been Aristotle or (ii) someone other than Aristotle might have been Aristotle.[14] In these examples the occurrences of *the teacher of Alexander* that follow the modal operators *might not have been* and *might have been* in the two sentences remain within the scope operator, and the sentences express truths on that interpretation. If *Aristotle* were equivalent to a nonrigid description that could be given any scope, then there would be corresponding senses of *Aristotle might not have been Aristotle* and *Someone other than Aristotle might have been Aristotle* in which they express truths. The fact that these sentences do not have such interpretations shows that any analysis according to which *Aristotle* is analyzed as being equivalent to a nonrigid description, must be one in which the description is not allowed to take small scope in examples like this. It is precisely to account for the lack of ambiguities like this that the wide-scope analysis has been formulated as it has.

With this in mind, we are now ready to criticize the analysis.

Arguments against the Wide-Scope Analysis

The Basic Argument

According to the analysis, the proposition semantically expressed by the sentence **if n is F, then something is both F and G** is the proposition semantically expressed by the sentence **if the G is F, then something is both F and G.** This gives us premise 1 of our argument.

P1.   The proposition that if n is F, then something is both F and G = the proposition that if the G is F, then something is both F and G.

Next we add premise 2.

P2.   The proposition that if the G is F, then something is both F and G is a necessary truth $\square$ [((the x: Gx) Fx) ⊃ ∃y (Fy & Gy)].

Clearly, C ought to follow from P1 and P2.

C.   The proposition that if n is F, then something is both F and G is a necessary truth $\square$ [Fn ⊃ ∃y (Fy & Gy)].

---

[14] See Kripke, *Naming and Necessity*, pp. 48–49, and p. 62, note 25. If pressed, one might force nonliteral, or metaphorical, interpretations on these sentences according to which they convey the claims that Aristotle need not have played the Aristotle role (done the salient things we associate with him), and someone other than Aristotle could have played that role (done those things). But these are forced pragmatic interpretations with different contents in different contexts (depending on what features of Aristotle we are attending to), not different propositions semantically expressed by an ambiguous sentence.

However, on the wide-scope analysis, it does not follow, since, according to the analysis, C is just claim C′.

C′.   The G is such that the proposition that if it is F, then something is both F and G is a necessary truth (the x: Gx) $\square$ [Fx $\supset$ $\exists$y (Fy & Gy)].

The problem for the wide-scope analysis is that whereas the argument from P1 and P2 to C is clearly valid, the analysis wrongly characterizes it as invalid. According to the analysis, both P1 and P2 are true, while C (i.e., C′) may be false (when F and G are unrelated and the property expressed by G is not an essential property of the thing to which G actually applies).

The reason that the wide-scope analysis has this consequence is that it treats linguistic constructions containing modal operators like *necessarily*, or modal predicates like *is a necessary truth*, as inherently shifty. In each case, the modal element combines syntactically with an argument A, a sentence in the case of the operator *necessarily*, a noun phrase in the case of the predicate *is a necessary truth*. When the argument A contains no proper names, the modal element is applied to the proposition expressed, or denoted, by A (depending on whether A is a sentence or a noun phrase). However, when A does contain a proper name, the modal operator, or predicate, is not applied to the proposition expressed or denoted by A; rather, it is applied to a different proposition.[15]

To simplify matters, let us focus simply on the modal predicate *is a necessary truth*. According to the wide-scope analysis, this predicate can be seen as expressing a modal property of propositions. When the predicate is combined with a term α that denotes a proposition p, the resulting sentence α *is a necessary truth* attributes the property of being necessarily true to p, provided that α does not itself contain any proper names. However, when α does contain a proper name, the sentence α *is a necessary truth* does not attribute any property to the proposition denoted by α. For example, if α is the proposition that Fn, and the name n is associated with the description *the G*, then the sentence α *is a necessary truth* is interpreted as saying *there is a unique individual o which is G, and which is such that the (singular, Russellian) proposition that o is F has the property of being a necessary truth.*[16]

This is why the wide-scope analysis of names is forced to treat some arguments with the apparent (grammatical) form (I) as invalid.

I.   (i) $\alpha = \beta$
     (ii) α is a necessary truth
     (iii) β is a necessary truth

---

[15] For an illustrative comparison, see David Kaplan's construal of *Ralph believes that* as a "shifty" operator in section V of "Opacity," in Lewis Edwin Hahn and Paul Arthur Schilpp, eds., *The Philosophy of W. V. Quine* (La Salle Ill.: Open Court, 1986), pp. 229–289.

[16] The parenthetical remark indicates that I here make the assumption that the proposition denoted by *the proposition that Fx*, and expressed by *Fx*, with respect to an assignment of o as value of 'x,' is the singular, Russellian proposition that predicates the property expressed by F of o. Other choices are theoretically possible, but this is by far the most natural and straightforward. Although I believe the choice to be correct, and will maintain the assumption throughout, the overall argument against the wide-scope analysis does not crucially depend on it.

When α contains no proper names but β does, the analysis treats (ii) as predicating the property of being necessarily true of a certain proposition p; the analysis views (i) as identifying p with proposition q; yet the analysis denies that (iii) predicates the property of being necessarily true of q. Because of this, (i) and (ii) may be characterized as true, while (iii) is characterized as false. (An analogous point holds for examples using the operator *necessarily.*)

The lesson to be drawn is clear. The wide-scope analysis purports to provide a correct description of the meanings of English sentences containing proper names, definite descriptions, and modal expressions. The fact that it wrongly characterizes obviously valid arguments as invalid shows that it fails to do this. This failure is not mitigated by the fact that the semantics it provides these sentences is conceptually coherent. There could be a language that worked in the way characterized by the wide-scope analysis, and in such a language many arguments of the (grammatical) form (I) would be invalid. But English as we now understand it is not such a language. It is not even clear that we should be willing to describe such a language as containing proper names in the sense that English does. Because of this, the wide-scope analysis fails to throw light on how names actually function in English or other natural languages.[17]

---

[17] The argument given in this section applies to several positions in the literature, including the two variations of Dummett's views mentioned in note S. In the preface to *Naming and Necessity* (1980), Kripke criticized the identification of rigidity with wide scope by Dummett (1973); acknowledged that some intuitions about the truth-values of modal sentences containing names can be accounted for either by treating names as rigid or by treating them as nonrigid, wide-scope descriptions; and argued that we nevertheless have pretheoretic semantic intuitions about the modal profile of (the propositions expressed by) sentences containing names that cannot be accounted for by the wide-scope analysis. In Appendix 3 of *The Interpretation of Frege's Philosophy*, Dummett responds. He admits that according to the wide-scope analysis, names are not rigid (pp. 594–595), and he maintains that the only genuinely pretheoretic semantic intuitions bearing on his dispute with Kripke concern the conditions under which assertive utterances of sentences express truths. Claims about the modal profile of sentences (relative to contexts)—that is, about the truth-value at alternative possible worlds of that which a sentence expresses in a context)—are decreed not to be directly testable by appeal to pretheoretic intuition, but to be matters of theoretical choice (see, e.g., p. 582). For Dummett this means that we have no pretheoretic intuitions that we can bring directly to bear on the question "Is (that which is expressed by) S true, at all worlds, some worlds, or a certain world w?" Rather, the best we can do is appeal to intuitions that bear on the different, but related, question "Is it the case that **necessarily S, possibly S, or at world w, S** is true?" He asserts that when intuitions are restricted in this way, the wide-scope analysis can explain all of the genuinely pretheoretic semantic intuitions that the rigidity thesis can account for (see pp. 577–579). The argument involving (I) given above indicates that this claim is incorrect, provided that there is a description, **the G,** that gives the content of the name. In that case, the wide-scope analysis will characterize as invalid inferences classified as valid by pretheoretic intuitions (about the conditions under which various sentences express truths) that Dummett presumably deems to be legitimate.

The argument also refutes a different, and more restricted, thesis advocated by Gareth Evans in "Reference and Contingency," *The Monist* 62, no. 2 (April 1979): 161–189, reprinted in his *Collected Papers* (Oxford: Clarendon Press, 1985), pp. 178–213. There Evans is concerned with the special case in which the referent of a name, n, is semantically fixed to be the denotation of a description, **the G,** that is used in a stipulative introduction of the name. Evans argues that in this sort of case (i) and (ii) have the same content—in my terminology, semantically express the same proposition (*Collected Papers*, p. 181).

   i. If there was a unique G, then the G was G.
   ii. If there was a unique G, then n was G.

The argument just given focuses on the modal predicate *is a necessary truth*. The argument shows that names cannot be analyzed as nonrigid descriptions that are required to take wide scope over this modal predicate in sentences of the form *the proposition that S is a necessary truth*. Equivalences like those in E can be used to generalize this result to modal sentences of different but related forms.

Evans notes that there is an obvious objection to this view, which he credits to Kripke. Since the proposition expressed by (i) is necessary and the proposition expressed by (ii) is not, the two sentences cannot express the same proposition (*Collected Papers*, p. 182). Evans responds to this objection as follows: "I agree that sentences containing names embed differently under modal operators than do sentences containing descriptions, but it is perhaps the main point of this paper that the conclusion which Kripke draws from this fact follows only upon a questionable view of the connection between the content of an utterance and its modal properties" (p. 182). Evans then goes on to sketch a semantic theory according to which sentences are assigned both contents (which serve as objects of propositional attitudes) and conditions under which the sentences are true at arbitrary possible worlds (which serve as the arguments for modal operators). It is further maintained that sentences may have the same contents (express the same proposition) even though they are associated with different conditions for being true at arbitrary worlds. Because of this, Evans argues that (i) and (ii) can express the same proposition even though (iii) and (iv), which differ only in the substitution of (ii) for (i), have different truth-values.

    iii. It is necessarily true that if there was a unique G, then the G was G.

    iv. It is necessarily true that if there was a unique G, then n was G.

    The argument involving (I) given in the text—which is essentially just a reworking of Kripke's original objection to Evans—shows that this is incorrect, assuming, as I do, that *it is necessarily true that S, that S is necessarily true,* and *the proposition that S is necessarily true* are equivalent. Like Dummett, Evans gives an empirically incorrect account of the semantics of English, since his position wrongly characterizes certain intuitively valid arguments as invalid. (There are a number of other important errors and confusions in Evans's discussion, some of which are pointed out in my review of his *Collected Papers*, in *Journal of Philosophy* 86, no. 3 [1989]: 141–156, at 148–150.) It should also be noted that although Kripke's original objection to Evan's claim that (i) and (ii) express the same proposition is correct, his own discussion in *Naming and Necessity* contains the seeds of Evans's confusion on this point. There Kripke seems to suggest that one could know the proposition expressed by (ii) a priori, on the basis of a reference-fixing definition of the name. This was naturally taken by many to indicate that knowing the proposition expressed by (i) and knowing the proposition expressed by (ii) come to pretty much the same thing. From here it seemed a short step to identifying the two propositions. My own view is that (ii) is not knowable a priori. See my review of Evans. See also Keith Donnellan, "The Contingent Apriori and Rigid Designators," in P. A. French, T. E. Uehling, Jr., and H. K. Wettstein, eds., *Contemporary Perspectives in the Philosophy of Language* (Minneapolis: University of Minnesota Press, 1979); and Nathan Salmon, "How to Measure the Standard Metre," *Proceedings of the Aristotelian Society* new ser. 88 (1987/1988): 193–217.

    The argument in the text involving (I) also provides strong support for the rigidity thesis RT, questioned by Stanley in "Names and Rigid Designation," and in his "Rigidity and Content," in Richard Heck, ed., *Language, Thought and Logic: Essays in Honor of Michael Dummett.* (Oxford University Press, Oxford, 1997).

RT.   The rigidity of proper names demonstrates that utterances of sentences containing proper names, and utterances of sentences differing from those sentences only in containing nonrigid descriptions in place of proper names, differ in content. [In my terminology: The rigidity of proper names demonstrates that the proposition expressed by a sentence containing a name, relative to a context, differs from the proposition expressed, relative to the same context, by a corresponding sentence in which a nonrigid description is substituted for the name.]

If this principle were false, then for some name and description, we would have (i) and (ii) of the intuitively valid argument (I) characterized as true, while (iii) was characterized as false. Since any semantic theory leading to this result is inadequate, no adequate semantic theory of English falsifies RT.

(E).   (i) The proposition that S(n) is a necessary truth iff that S(n) is a necessary truth
  (ii) That S(n) is a necessary truth iff it is a necessary truth that S(n)
  (iii) It is a necessary truth that S(n) iff it is necessarily true that S(n)
  (iv) It is necessarily true that S(n) iff necessarily S(n)

Any attempt to salvage the wide-scope analysis by blocking the descriptions allegedly associated with names from taking wide scope in sentences of the form *the proposition that S(n) is a necessary truth,* while requiring them to take wide scope in other modal sentences, would force one to deny at least one of the equivalences in E. The obviousness of these equivalences is an argument against any such modification of the wide-scope analysis.

A Variation on the Argument

Before leaving this argument, I would like to call attention to an implicit assumption I have invoked. I have assumed that the descriptive contents attributed by the analysis to proper names are also expressed in English by ordinary descriptive phrases of the form *the G.* This is worth mentioning because some proponents of the wide-scope analysis have denied it.[18] And, of course, if, for some n, there is no synonymous description, *the G,* then we will not be able to formulate any true premise of the form P1, and the above argument will be blocked. In addition, some proponents of the wide-scope analysis have used the possibility that names may have descriptive contents, even if they do not have the same contents as any ordinary descriptive phrases, to support a surprising and mysterious doctrine—namely, that it makes no sense to attribute modal properties to propositions expressed by sentences containing names.

  This mysterious doctrine can be motivated as follows: Suppose that the name n has a wide-scope descriptive content which is not the content of any ordinary descriptive phrase in English. In that case we will not be able to formulate any true claim of the form *'n is F' expresses the proposition that the G is F.* We can say, truly, that *n is F* expresses a proposition, and we can correctly identify that proposition by saying *that proposition is the proposition that n is F.* By using the sentence *n is F,* we can entertain this proposition, and we can make a variety of judgments about it. Strangely, however, we cannot assess its modal profile, its truth or falsity in different possible worlds. For if we try to do this, we find ourselves asking some such question as *Is it the case that in world w, n is F?* But in asking this question we have embedded n under a modal operator, thereby causing the descriptive content of n to "hop over" the content of the operator and take wide scope.

  This has the effect of transforming our question into one different from the one we intended. We intended to ask about the truth-value in w of the proposition expressed by *n is F.* We ended up asking about the truth-value in w of the singular Russellian proposition consisting not of the descriptive content of n together with the property expressed by F, but of the individual denoted by that descriptive

---

[18] See Michael Dummett, *Frege's Philosophy of Language,* appendix to chapter 5, especially pp. 135–137.

content in the actual world, together with the property expressed by F. Moreover, the proponent of the mysterious doctrine asserts, there is no other way in which we can ask the question we intended. Instead, we must face the fact that we simply cannot ask questions about the modal profiles of propositions expressed by sentences. The best we can do is raise questions about the **truth-values** of propositions expressed by larger sentences containing modal operators under which the proper names are embedded.[19]

How should we respond to this strange doctrine? Let us begin by supposing, for the sake of argument, that proper names have nonrigid, wide-scope descriptive contents which are not the contents of any descriptive phrase in English. If so, then propositions expressed by sentences containing names will not be expressible by us in any other way. For example, it may be that the proposition expressed by the sentence *n is F* is not expressed by any other sentence in our language. Still, there is nothing to prevent us from describing that proposition. Indeed, we have already done so—it is the proposition expressed by the sentence *n is F,* a proposition that consists of the descriptive content of the name n together with the property expressed by F. Since we can describe the proposition in this way, nothing prevents us from using our description to ask about its modal profile. For example, we may ask, "What is the truth-value of the proposition expressed by the sentence *n is F* in world w?" This question does, of course, contain a modal phrase. However, since the name n occurs within quotes in the question, it is not given wide scope over that phrase. The alleged descriptive content of the name is not even a constituent of the prepositional content of the question, so there is nothing here to be given wide scope.

Thus we have succeeded in doing what the mysterious doctrine tells us can't be done. We have asked an intelligible question about the modal profile of a proposition expressed by the sentence *n is F.* Moreover, it is not difficult to see how to go about answering it. We know that the proposition expressed by this sentence consists of the allegedly nonrigid descriptive content of the name together with the property F. We also know that, in general, any proposition expressed by a sentence α *is* Φ is true at a world w iff the denotation in w determined by the content of α is something which in w has the property expressed by Φ. Since we have been told that the name n has a descriptive content, we know that the denotation determined by this content at a world is whatever individual, if any, uniquely possesses the relevant descriptive characteristics at that world. Surely this is something that is determinable in many cases-for if it is determinable in the actual world which individual corresponds to the descriptive content of a name, there is no reason the same shouldn't hold true for other possible worlds. But this

---

[19] Dummett holds (i) that, typically, an ordinary proper name does not have the content of any single description; (ii) that it makes no intuitive sense to ask about the modal profile of (the proposition expressed by) a sentence containing a name; and (iii) that our intuitions are restricted to assessing the truth-values of sentences in which names are embedded under modal operators. As will be seen, this position, like the slightly more extreme doctrine presented in the text, provides no effective means of avoiding criticisms of the sort illustrated by (I) above.

just means that often we can determine correct answers to questions about the modal profile of the proposition expressed by **n is F.**

With this in mind, all that remains for us to do is to reformulate the original counterargument (I) against the wide-scope analysis, so that it applies even to those versions of the analysis which maintain that names have wide-scope descriptive contents that are not the contents of any descriptive phrases in English. The first premise of the reformulated argument is P1a, which surely is undeniable.

P1a.   The proposition that n is F = the proposition expressed by the sentence *n is F.*

Next consider claims (1) and (2).[20]

    1.   The proposition expressed by the sentence *n is F* is true at world w.

    2.   The proposition that *n is F* is true at world w.

According to the wide-scope analysis, (1) will be characterized as true iff the descriptive content ascribed to n picks out, at w, an individual that has at w the property expressed by F; (2) will be characterized as true iff that same descriptive content picks out, in the actual world, an individual that has that property at w. If the descriptive sense ascribed to n picks out different individuals at different worlds (as it must, if the appeal to wide scope is to have a point), then for some worlds, the corresponding claims (1) and (2) will be characterized as having different truth-values. Because of this, the wide-scope analysis will fail to characterize the pair of inferences, (i) from P1a and (1) to (2), and (ii) from P1a and (2) to (1), as jointly valid. Since in fact they are both valid, the wide-scope analysis fails.

A Related Confusion

It is illuminating to note that essentially the same failure can be expressed in a slightly different way. As before, we begin with the undeniable premise P1a, to which we add the trivial truth P2a.

P2a.   For all worlds w, the proposition that *n is F* is true at w iff the proposition that n is F is true at w.

From these two premises, Obv is an obvious consequence.[21]

Obv.   For all worlds w, the proposition expressed by the sentence *n is F* is true at w iff the proposition that n is F is true at w.

According to the wide-scope analysis, however, P1a and P2a are true, while Obv is false.

---

[20] Premise P1a is best thought of as a premise schema, instances of which are gotten from substituting particular names for 'n' and particular predicates for 'F.' For purposes of the argument, claims (1) and (2) should also be thought of as schemata. Many of the arguments in the text may be understood in this way.

[21] As before, the premises and conclusions of this argument are schemata.

To see this, imagine that n is synonymous with the wide-scope description, **the G**. (If there is no such ordinary description available in the language, let **the G be the x: x = n,** where the name is taken to have a descriptive content that is uniquely satisfied by different individuals at different worlds.) Then, according to the wide-scope analysis, Obv is equivalent to (3).

3. (the x: Gx) (for all worlds w) [the proposition expressed by *(the x: Gx)* *[x is F]* is true at world w iff the proposition that x is F is true at w]

But when G expresses a property that different objects may have at different worlds, (3) will be false (for some F). Since, according to the wide-scope analysis, (3) is equivalent to Obv, the analysis mischaracterizes it as false (and the inference from P1a and P2a to Obv as invalid).

This failure of the analysis is related to a persistent confusion about its content. A striking feature of the relationship between rigidity and wide scope is the frequency with which the two are confused.[22] In particular, the wide-scope analysis has often been mischaracterized, even by proponents, as claiming that names are rigid. Although this is a mistake, it is an understandable one. Recall our earlier discussion of the name *Aristotle*, in which I mentioned that the wide-scope analysis can account for the truth of the principle GR, which constituted our original grounds for taking the name to be rigid.

GR. There is a certain individual x, such that for every possible world w, the proposition that Aristotle was a philosopher is true at w iff x was a philosopher at w, . . . and so on for other propositions expressed using the name *Aristotle.*

What I did not point out at the time was that in order to get from GR to the claim that *Aristotle* is rigid, we need an instance of Obv involving that name.

Obv$_A$ For all worlds w, the proposition expressed by the sentence *Aristotle was a philosopher* is true at w iff the proposition that Aristotle was a philosopher is true at w; ditto for other examples involving the name.

Together, GR and Obv$_A$ entail R.

R. There is a certain individual x, such that for every possible world w, the proposition expressed by the sentence *Aristotle was a philosopher* is true at w iff x was a philosopher at w, . . . and so on for other propositions expressed using the name *Aristotle.*

This is what is needed for the rigidity of *Aristotle*—for it is R that guarantees that the sentence *Aristotle was a philosopher,* as we now understand it, will be true at a world w iff a certain individual—the person who was actually Aristotle—was

---

a philosopher in w. Given that a sentence **α *is F*** is true at an arbitrary world w iff the denotation of α at w is in the extension of F at w, we conclude that for any arbitrary world w, *Aristotle* denotes in w the individual who was Aristotle in the actual world.

Although the wide-scope analysis accommodates GR, it characterizes Obv$_A$, and R, as false. Thus it wrongly characterizes names like *Aristotle* as nonrigid. The fact that proponents of the analysis have not always recognized this suggests that they, too, may have simply taken Obv for granted, thereby implicitly endorsing as genuine some of the pretheoretic semantic intuitions denied by the analysis.

Argument 2

The second argument against the wide-scope analysis is a simple variation of the first that does not employ any premise explicitly identifying propositions. Instead, it is based on the following scenario: Bill assertively utters the sentence ***If n exists, then n is F,*** where F expresses some essential (but hidden and nonobvious) property of the bearer of the name n—such as the property of originating from a certain bit of genetic material. Suppose further that the bearer of n is the unique object with the property expressed by G, that speakers associate the nonrigid description ***the G*** with n, and that there is no necessary connection between the properties expressed by G and F.[23] In such a case the following premises, P1 and P2, will be true, and recognized as such by the wide-scope analysis.

P1. Bill asserted that if n exists, then n is F.
P2. It is a necessary truth that if n exists, then n is F.

However, C, which in fact follows from P1 and P2, may wrongly be characterized as false.

C. Bill asserted a necessary truth

This is clear when the argument is symbolized (in accord with the wide-scope analysis) as follows:[24]

---

[23]As before, it is not essential to the argument that there be a descriptive phrase in English expressing the descriptive sense attributed to the name. However, the argument is more simply presented if we assume that there is such a phrase.

[24]I assume here that C involves quantification over objects of assertion—that is, propositions, or, in Dummett's terminology, the assertive contents of sentences (in contexts). The argument could, of course, be restated slightly to bring this out.

  P1. Bill asserted the proposition that if n exists, then n is F.
  P2. The proposition that if n exists, then n is F, is necessarily true.
  C. Bill asserted a proposition that is necessarily true.

I assume that English sentences like C cannot be represented adequately by standard substitutional quantification into sentential position.' See Mark Richard, *Propositional Attitudes.* (Cambridge: Cambridge University Press, 1990), pp. 75–78, for a brief sketch of some of the problems facing attempts to treat apparent instances of objectual quantification over propositions in English substitutionally.

P1'.   Bill asserted [that: n exists ⊃ Fn]
P2'.   (the x: Gx) [□ (x exists ⊃ Fx)]
C'.   ∃p [Bill asserted p and p is a necessary truth]

The key point is that, according to wide-scope analysis, P2 does not attribute necessity to that which Bill is said, in P1, to have asserted. According to the analysis, the truth of P2 requires the necessity of that which is expressed by the open formula *(x exists ⊃ Fx)*, relative to an assignment to the variable 'x' of the unique object which actually has the property expressed by G. By contrast, the truth of P1 requires Bill to have asserted that which is expressed by the sentence *(n exists ⊃ Fn)*. But, according to the wide-scope analysis, that which is expressed by this sentence is not identical with that which is expressed by the formula *(x exists ⊃ Fx)*, relative to any assignment of an object to 'x'.[25] Rather, it is a descriptive proposition involving the sense of the name n. Since this proposition is not necessary, C is characterized as false in a situation in which P1 and P2 are characterized as true. As a result, the analysis wrongly characterizes as invalid an argument which is in fact valid. Because of this, the interpretations of sentences provided by the analysis are incorrect.[26]

Argument 3

The third argument against the analysis is based on examples of a slightly different type.

4.   Necessarily, if Bill asserts (believes) that n is F, and n is F, then Bill asserts (believes) something true.

5.   Necessarily, if Bill asserts (believes) that n is F, and everything Bill asserts (believes) is true, then n is F.

Although these sentences express obvious truisms, many of them are wrongly characterized as false by the wide-scope analysis.

---

[25]It may be noted that the wide-scope analysis, as I have stated it, does not require the descriptions associated with occurrences of n in P1 to take narrow scope. If both are given wide scope over the propositional attitude verb, then, it could be argued, P1 and P2 may both be true while logically entailing C. Thus the wide-scope analysis allows a reading in which the argument from P1 and P2 to C is sound. However, it also allows a reading of P1 in which both occurrences of n take smallest scope—surely the natural reading according to the analysis. When P1 is read in this way, the argument from P1 and P2 to C is wrongly characterized as invalid; there simply is no semantic interpretation of this sequence of English sentences in which they are understood in this way. Strictly speaking, the wide-scope analysis allows for a number of other readings of P1 as well. In principle, one occurrence of n can take wide scope relative to the propositional attitude verb while the other takes small scope relative to that verb; and when either occurrence takes small scope relative to the attitude verb, it can take wide or narrow scope relative to the conditional operator in the complement clause. Thus the analysis takes P1 to be many ways ambiguous (on all but one of which the argument from P1 and P2 to C is characterized as invalid). Surely the English sentence is not multiply ambiguous in this way (and the argument itself is not invalid on a multitude of different semantic interpretations).

[26]Like the argument based on (I) above, this argument also applies to the other positions mentioned in note 17.

The problem arises because different occurrences of the name n are assigned different scopes, and so end up being evaluated at different worlds. Note that in each sentence the modal operator takes the entire conditional in its scope. According to the wide-scope analysis, both occurrences of the name are replaced by occurrences of an equivalent descriptions-the G.[27] Since one of these occurrences is in the content clause of a prepositional attitude verb, its scope remains confined to that clause; since the other occurrence is not in the scope of any prepositional attitude verb, it is assigned wide scope over the modal operator.[28]

The resulting symbolizations are the following:[29]

4′. (the x: Gx) □ [(Bill asserts/believes [that: (the y: Gy) Fy] & Fx) ⊃ ∃p [(Bill asserts/believes p) & p is true]]

5′. (the x: Gx) □ [(Bill asserts/believes [that (the y: Gy) Fy] & (p) [(Bill asserts/believes p) ⊃ p is true]) ⊃ Fx]

These examples pose two problems for the wide-scope analysis.

The first is that each asserts the existence in the actual world of a unique individual with the property expressed by G. However, it is not obvious that any such

---

[27]The point made in note 23 applies here as well.

[28]More precisely, the wide-scope analysis requires one of the occurrences of n to take wide scope over the modal operator, while allowing the other occurrence of n to remain within the scope of the attitude verb. As we shall see, according to the analysis, this will produce a reading—surely what, on this analysis, must be regarded as the most natural reading—in which (4) and (5) do not express truisms, but rather are simply false. Since (4) and (5) do not have such readings, the analysis is incorrect. It should also be noted that, as stated, the wide-scope analysis allows additional readings, including one in which both occurrences of n are given wide scope over the modal operator. On this reading (4) and (5) may turn out true, but only if the result of substituting occurrences of any coreferential name for the occurrences of n would also be true. Since one of these is within an attitude construction, the descriptivist can't be happy with the consequence that the only reading allowed by the wide-scope analysis on which (4) and (5) are true is a reading on which substitution of arbitrary coreferential names within attitude constructions is guaranteed to preserve truth-value.

[29]As before, I assume objectual quantification over propositions; however, here this assumption is not needed for the argument. For example, consider the following version of 4′, in which objectual quantification over propositions has been replaced by substitutional quantification into sentential position: *(the x: Gx) □ [(Bill asserts/believes that [(the y: Gy) Fy] & Fx) ⊃ ∃S [Bill asserts/believes that S) & S]].* This sentence is true iff there is a unique individual o that has the property expressed by G, and for all worlds w, if *Bill asserts/believes that [(the y: Gy) Fy] & Fx* is true at w, with respect to an assignment of o to 'x,' then *∃S [(Bill believes that S) & S]* is true at w. Let w be a world in which o has the property that F expresses, in which there is a unique object with the property expressed by G but that object does not have the property expressed by F, and in which Bill asserts the proposition expressed by *the G is F.* Then w is a world at which *Bill asserts/believes that [(the y: Gy) Fy] & Fx* is true (with respect to an assignment of o to 'x'). However, w may also be a world at which *∃S [(Bill asserts/believes that S) & S]* is false. Suppose that *∃S (Bill asserts/believes that S)* is true at w, because the substitution instance *Bill asserts/believes that [(the y: Gy) Fy]* is true at w. Still, the sentence *(the y: Gy) Fy* (or event the sentence *Fn*) is false at w. (Note that in the previous sentence the description and name are mentioned rather than used, and so cannot, on pain of quantifying into quotes, be given wide scope over 'is false at w.') Hence, according to the wide-scope analysis even the substitutional version of 4′ is false.

existential claim is entailed by the original English sentences. More generally, the wide-scope analysis is incompatible with the existence of meaningful proper names that (i) do not denote any individual existing in the actual world, but (ii) sometimes occur embedded under modal operators (outside the scope of prepositional attitude verbs) in true sentences of English. If proper names of this sort exist in English, then the wide-scope analysis is false.[30]

The second problem posed by these symbolizations involves cases in which the description *the G* is a nonrigid designator. For example, suppose that in the actual world o is the unique individual that has the property expressed by G, and that w is a possible world satisfying the following conditions: (i) o has the property expressed by F, but not the property expressed by G, in w; (ii) in w, Bill asserts the proposition expressed by *the G is F;* (iii) Bill doesn't assert anything else (or anything else true) in w; and (iv) either there is no unique object in w having the property expressed by G, or whatever uniquely has that property in w is such that in w it does not have the property expressed by F. The existence of such a world w falsifies (4′). (5′) is falsified by a world w´ in which (i) Bill believes the proposition expressed by *the G is F;* (ii) all of Bill's other beliefs in w′ are true in w′; (iii) there is a unique object in w′ that has the property expressed by G, and, in w′, that object has the property expressed by F; but (iv) in w′ o does not have the property expressed by F. Since (4′) and (5′) are analyses that would be assigned to (4) and (5) by the wide-scope analysis, the analysis incorrectly characterizes these obvious truths of English as false.

On the basis of all these arguments, I conclude that the wide-scope analysis of proper names is incorrect.

The Analysis of Names as Rigidified Descriptions

I now turn to the other main descriptivist challenge to Kripke's modal argument. This is the view that proper names are synonymous with rigidified versions of the descriptions associated with them by speakers. On this view, names are rigid designators; hence no appeal to wide scope is needed to account for the substitutivity of codesignative names in modal constructions. However since codesignative names may be associated with different descriptive information, they are not intersubstitutable everywhere; most notably they are not intersubstitutable in prepositional attitude constructions.

In assessing this view it is crucial to understand how, according to it, names are to be rigidified. There are two main alternatives in the semantic literature, only one of which is promising for the rigidification analysis. The view in question involves using the actuality operator to construct definite descriptions. Syntactically, *actually* combines with a sentence or formula to form a more complex sentence or formula. Semantically, *actually* is an indexical, like 'I', 'now', and 'here'. As such, its content— that which it contributes to propositions expressed by sentences containing it— varies from one context of utterance to another. For example, the sentence *I am*

---

[30] I am indebted to Mike Thau for drawing my attention to this point.

hungry now, used by me at time t, expresses a proposition that is true at an arbitrary world w (and time t*) iff at w Scott Soames is hungry at t; the same sentence used by Saul Kripke at t' expresses a different proposition, one that is true at an arbitrary world (and time) iff Kripke is hungry at t' in that world. Similarly, the sentence *Actually Kripke wrote* <u>Naming and Necessity</u> used by anyone in the actual world, A_w, expresses a proposition that is true at an arbitrary possible world iff in A_w Kripke wrote *Naming and Necessity;* the same sentence used by a speaker at a different world w* expresses a proposition that is true at an arbitrary world iff in w* Kripke wrote *Naming and Necessity.*

It will be apparent from this explanation that whenever S is a true sentence, ***Actually S*** is a necessary truth. The corresponding fact about descriptions is the following: whenever a definite description ***the x: Fx*** denotes an individual o in the actual world, the rigidified description the ***x: actually Fx*** denotes o in all possible worlds in which o exists (and never denotes anything else). This follows directly from the standard semantics of *the* and *actually.* According to the semantics of *the,* the denotation of a description ***the x: Sx*** at an arbitrary world w is the unique object, if any, existing at w that satisfies the open formula Sx at w.[31] Where Sx is the formula ***actually Fx,*** an object satisfies it at w iff in the actual world the object has the property expressed by F.

The position we are considering now claims that ordinary proper names are synonymous with rigidified descriptions of this sort. For example, it might be claimed that the name *Aristotle,* as used by a particular speaker, is synonymous with the description *the actual teacher of Alexander,* which in turn is understood as *the x: actually x taught Alexander.* Several criticisms of this view can be extracted from the existing literature. I will mention them very briefly, and then put them aside in order to focus on a new criticism.

One of these criticisms concerns the question of whether proper names (like variables relative to assignments) designate their referents even with respect to worlds (and times) at which those individuals don't exist. David Kaplan and Nathan Salmon have argued, quite persuasively, that proper names should be understood in this way.[32] The most striking examples employed in their arguments exploit the parallels between temporal and modal semantics, and involve sentences like *Plato is dead* and *Locke anticipated Kripke.* The first of these is a sentence of the form ***n is F.*** On the usual view, such a sentence is true at a time t iff n designates at t something that is in the extension of F at t. But then, since

---

[31] This characterization assumes that the range of the quantifier ***the x: Sx*** at a world w consists of all and only the things existing at w. If the quantifier is allowed to range not just over objects that exist at w but also over objects that are merely possible relative to w, then the description will denote the unique possible object that at w satisfies ***Sx.*** On this possibilist reading of the quantifier, ***the x: actually Fx*** may denote at w the object o denoted at the actual world by ***the x: Fx*** even if o does not exist at w.

[32] David Kaplan, "Bob and Carol and Ted and Alice," in K. J. Hintikka, J. Moravcsik, and P. Suppes, eds., *Approaches to Natural Language* (Dordrecht: Reidel, 1973), appendix X; David Kaplan, "Demonstratives," in *Themes from Kaplan,* section IV; Nathan Salmon, *Reference and Essence* (Princeton, N.J.: Princeton University Press, 1981), pp. 32–40.

Plato is dead is true now, the name *Plato* must now designate something—and what else than the now nonexistent Plato? Kaplan and Salmon generalize this point to cover a variety of cases, including modal examples. If they are right, then proper names are not equivalent to descriptions that have been rigidified using the actuality operator—since these descriptions designate an object at a world only if the object exists at that world.[33]

A second criticism is based on Kripke's original epistemic and semantic arguments against description theories. The epistemic arguments were designed to show that typically the sorts of descriptions D associated by speakers with a name n are such that the proposition expressed by *if n exists, then n is D* is not knowable a priori, even though the proposition expressed by *if D exists, then D is D* is knowable a priori. These arguments illustrate the difficulty of identifying the contributions made by proper names to prepositional attitude ascriptions with the contents of descriptions that speakers typically associate with the names. Since these arguments typically seem to hold even when D is an *actually*-rigidified description, it is difficult to find specific descriptions that allow the analysis to get off the ground.

A third point can be made regarding Kripke's original semantic arguments. For nearly all ordinary proper names, these arguments eliminate the possibility of identifying the semantic content of a name with most of the descriptions speakers typically associate with it, whether rigidified or not. In light of this, a number of theorists seem to have concluded that the only hope of avoiding the standard semantic arguments is to appeal to metalinguistic descriptions that incorporate the insights of Kripke's historical transmission theory of how reference is fixed. Thus, it has sometimes been suggested that the content-giving description associated with a name n is a description of the form ***The x: actually x stands at the beginning of a historical chain of transmission of such and such type ending with this use of the name 'n'.*** (Imagine *such and such type* being filled out with a correct account of the way reference is actually determined, and imagine the referent of ***this use of the name 'n'*** being determined by the context of utterance.) However, it seems clear that no such proposal can be correct, since descriptions of this sort do not, in general, give the contents contributed by names to prepositional attitude ascriptions. If they did, then when I attributed to someone the belief that Venus is a star, I would be attributing to that person a belief about a certain one of my uses of the name *Venus*, as well as a belief about the specific sorts of historical chains that connect uses of names to their bearers. Clearly no such beliefs are being attributed to the ancient Babylonians when I say that they believed Venus was a star.

---

[33]The argument for this conclusion depends on taking sentences containing definite descriptions to make existence claims, and hence on taking the domain of *(the x: Sx)* relative to a world (or circumstance of evaluation) to be a subset of the set of individuals existing at the world (or circumstance). This assumption is explicit in Salmon, "How to Measure the Standard Metre." It is either not made or ignored in David Kaplan, "Afterthoughts," p. 577. If *(the x: Sx)* is given the possibilist interpretation mentioned in note 31, then the argument does not apply.

A fourth criticism that I will simply mention can be extracted from Keith Donnellan's observation that names, unlike definite descriptions (whether rigidified using the actuality operator or not), are routinely exportable from positions within the scope of propositional attitude verbs.[34] For example, if t is a name, such as *Boris*, then (6b) is entailed by (6a) (together, perhaps, with the premise there is such a person as t); however when t is an arbitrary description, such as *the shortest spy* or *the person who is actually the shortest spy,* there often is no such entailment.

> 6a.   Ralph believes that t is a spy.
>
> 6b.   There is someone x such that Ralph believes that x is a spy.

Donnellan's point may also be put by saying that if t is a name, knowledge of the proposition expressed by *t is F* is always *de re* knowledge of the referent of t that it "is F," whereas this is not generally true when t is a definite description. Consequently, no name is synonymous with any description D that fails to support exportation in the manner of (6), or that occurs in a sentence *D is F* that expresses a proposition knowledge of which need not be *de re* knowledge of the denotation of D. In making these points, Donnellan was not concerned with distinguishing names from *actually*-rigidified description.[35] However, since the *actually*-rigidified descriptions standardly proposed as candidates for giving the semantic content of names often fail Donnellan's tests, his observations can be taken to show that these proposals are incorrect.

Considerations like these show that there are strong reasons, independent of special assumptions about the semantics of *actually,* for doubting that names are semantically equivalent to *actually*-rigidified description. I want, however, to waive these difficulties for the moment in order to concentrate on a further problem which, by itself, is sufficient to show that the contents of proper names are not given by rigidified descriptions of the form *the x: actually Fx.* The problem involves the interaction of modal and propositional-attitude constructions; it is based on the elementary observation that not only individuals in the actual world, A_w, but also inhabitants of other worlds, share many of my beliefs. For example, I, along with many others in the actual world, believe that Aristotle was a philosopher; and it is not unreasonable to suppose that we also believe of the actual world, A_w, that Aristotle was a philosopher in it—that is, we believe of the way, A_w, that the concrete universe really is (a maximally complete property the universe instantiates), that relative to it, Aristotle was a philosopher.[36] A similar point holds for a great variety of different possible worlds w. In w, I, along with others, believe that Aristotle was a philosopher; in addition, we may also believe of the

---

[34]Donnellan, "The Contingent Apriori and Rigid Designators," pp. 54–55.

[35]Donnellan's main point was that since knowledge of the proposition expressed by *if n exists, then n is F* is always *de re* knowledge of the referent of n, knowledge of this proposition cannot be a priori even when n is a name that has been introduced by the stipulation that it is to refer (rigidly) to the unique object, if there is one, that has the property expressed by F.

[36]Otherwise put, we believe that the proposition that Aristotle was a philosopher is true with respect to the actual world A_w.

world w that Aristotle was a philosopher in it—that is, we may believe that relative to that way that the universe might have been, Aristotle was a philosopher.[37] However, in w, we need not have any beliefs about the actual world, A_w, which may be different in many respects from w.

This fact provides the basis for the following argument against the analysis of proper names as *actually*-rigidified descriptions.

P1.   It is possible to believe that Aristotle was a philosopher without believing anything about the actual world A_w—that is, about the way the universe really is (the property it really instantiates). In particular, there are worlds w* in which agents believe that Aristotle was a philosopher, without believing of A_w that anything was F in it, and hence without believing of A_w that the unique thing that was F in it was a philosopher.

P2.   Necessarily, one believes that the actual F was a philosopher iff one believes of the actual world, A_w, that the unique thing that was F in it was a philosopher.

C1.   It is not the case that, necessarily, one believes that Aristotle was a philosopher iff one believes that the actual F was a philosopher.

P3.   If the content of *Aristotle*, as used in a context *C*, were identical with the content of ***the actual F,*** as used in C, then (i) the contents of (propositions expressed by) ***Aristotle was G*** and ***The actual F was G*** in C would be the same; (ii) the propositions expressed by ***α believes that Aristotle was G*** and ***α believes that the actual F was G,*** in C, would be necessarily equivalent; and (iii) C1 would be false.

C2.   The content of *Aristotle,* as used in a context, is not the same as the content of ***the actual F*** as used in that context.

Each premise in this argument is true. First consider P1. Surely it is a datum that agents could have believed that Aristotle was a philosopher even if things had been quite different from the way they in fact are. Must these agents also have had beliefs about the actual world—that is, about a certain maximally complete property the universe actually instantiates? In asking this, I am, of course, asking about the world (world-state) that I call 'actual' here and now, the world (world-state) provided by the context for my present remarks. Presumably, in some merely possible world (world-state) the agents there have no direct acquaintance, or epistemic contact, with this world (world-state) that I am now calling 'actual'; nor, in many cases, will they possess any uniquely identifying descriptions of it.[38]

---

[37] Equivalently, we believe that the proposition that Aristotle was a philosopher is true with respect to w.

[38] In thinking about this argument, it is worth keeping in mind the view of possible worlds expressed earlier. Recall that possible worlds are not different concrete universes, but maximally complete properties that the universe could have instantiated. With this conception of worlds it is no objection to P1 to observe that individuals who believe, with respect to certain merely possible worlds, that Aristotle was a philosopher, and individuals who believe this, with respect to the actual world, believe something about the same concrete universe. This observation may be true, but it doesn't show that the merely possible believers have beliefs about the actual world, since the actual world is not the concrete universe, but rather the way that the universe is. (The observation is incompatible with the bizarre but widespread alternative view of possible worlds according to which they are different concrete universes. On that conception P1 would still be taken to be true, but the observation would simply be denied.)

As a result, often there will be no way for them to form beliefs about the actual world.[39]

They may, of course, have beliefs about worlds (world-states) they call 'actual', but that is another matter. An agent who sincerely, and assertively, utters, in a possible world w, a sentence *Actually the earth is round* expresses his belief of w that with respect to it, the earth is round. We may even decide that whenever an agent believes a proposition p, at a world w, he also believes of w that p is true with respect to it. Such a principle would explain how all of us in the actual world have beliefs about the actual world.[40] However, it does not provide a way for agents in other worlds to share those beliefs.

Next consider P2 and P3. These premises are based on the standard Kaplan-style indexical semantics for *actually*,[41] plus an account of propositional attitude ascriptions as reporting relations to the propositions expressed by their content clauses. The relevant semantic ideas are given in (7).[42]

7. For any possible context of utterance C, the sentence **the actual F was G** expresses in C a proposition that says of the world, C_w of C, that the unique thing that "was F" in it "was G." The proposition expressed by **Jones believes that the actual F was G,** in context C, is true when evaluated at an arbitrary world w, iff Jones believes, in w, the proposition expressed by the **actual F was G** in C. Hence, the proposition expressed by **Jones believes that the actual F was G,** in C, is true when evaluated at an arbitrary world w, iff in w, Jones believes of C_w that the unique thing that "was F" in it "was G." It follows that when the actual world, A_w, is the world of the context, the proposition expressed by **Jones believes that the actual F was G** is true at an arbitrary world w iff in w Jones believes, of A_w that the thing that was F in it was also G.

In addition to being highly plausible in itself, (7) is something that the proponent of the view that names are *actually*-rigidified descriptions can scarcely afford to deny. His view requires that *actually* be an operator which rigidifies a description while allowing it to retain its descriptive content. This requirement dictates that the content of **the x: actually Fx,** as used in a context C, be a descriptive condition involving the property expressed by F which, when applied to an arbitrary world w, is satisfied by the unique individual in w that has the property expressed by F somewhere—not in w (unless $w = C_w$), but in the world given by C. Thus, where C_w is the world of the context C, the proposition expressed by **the actual F was G** "says"

---

[39]Even in the unlikely case in which there is an agent in some merely possible world who both believes that Aristotle was a philosopher and has some beliefs about the actual world A_w there is no reason to suppose that included among his beliefs is the belief that whoever was the greatest student of Plato, teacher of Alexander, founder of formal logic, and so on in A_w was a philosopher. (Remember that in the analysis *the F* is the description that we, in the actual world, associate with the name, not necessarily the description that those in other worlds associate with it.)

[40] Whether or not we all employ an indexical actuality operator.

[41]Kaplan, "Demonstratives."

[42]In stating (7) I ignore complications that would result from adding a temporal dimension and taking truth-values to be determined at time/world pairs rather than simply at worlds.

that the unique thing such that it "was F" in C_w "was G," whereas the proposition expressed by *the F was G* "says" something different—namely, that the unique thing that "was F" also "was G." Since it is possible to believe one of these propositions without believing the other, this is enough to establish C1.[43]

---

[43]It should be noted that although P1 and P2 speak of *de re* beliefs about the actual world-that is, believing of the actual world that it is so and so—the argument for C1 can be made quite general. The general argument does not, strictly speaking, require the beliefs to be *de re*, nor does it depend on the resolution of questions of fine detail about the semantic content of *actual* or *actually*. In explaining this, I will first indicate roughly what I take that semantic content to be, and why, if I am right, believing the proposition semantically expressed by a sentence containing *actual* or *actually* should be seen as having a *de re* belief about the actual world. Next I will explain how, even on alternative accounts of semantic contents and the relevant beliefs, the argument from P1 and P2 to C1 can be reconstructed.

First, the picture I favor. As I indicated above, I follow the standard practice of analyzing the description, *the actual F* as *the x: actually Fx.* Like *necessarily* and *possibly*, the expression *actually* combines with an open or closed sentence S to form a more complex sentence. Semantically, the extensions of these operators (relative to a context C and arbitrary world w) can be regarded as mapping the propositions (or the intensions determined by those propositions) expressed by their sentential arguments (relative to assignments of values to free variables) onto truth-values. The extension of *necessarily* (relative to C and w) maps a proposition p onto truth iff p is true in all worlds that are possible relative to w; the extension of *possibly* (relative to C and w) maps p onto truth iff p is true in at least one world that is possible relative to w; and the extension of *actually* (relative to C and w) maps p onto truth iff p is true at C_w—the "actual" world given by the context. What of the semantic contents of these expressions—that which they contribute to propositions expressed by sentences containing them? A number of alternatives are conceivable; they differ primarily on what, for our purposes, may be regarded as matters of inessential detail. One particularly convenient and straightforward approach takes the semantic contents of these expressions (relative to contexts) to be higher-order properties of propositions. Thus, the content of *necessarily* is the property of being true in all possible worlds; the content of *possibly* is the property of being true in some possible world; and the content of *actually* (relative to a context C) is the property of being true in C_w. On this conception, the proposition expressed by *the actual F is G* relative to a context C is, roughly, the proposition that the unique individual x such that the proposition that x is F is true in C_w is G. Here, the "actual" world, C_w, is a constituent of the property of being true in C_w which in turn is a constituent of the proposition expressed in C by *the actual F is G.* Because of this, it is natural to take believing that proposition to involve believing of, or about, C_w—namely, that the unique individual x such that the proposition that x is F is true in, or according to, it is G. The case is analogous to belief in a proposition that attributes the property of being taller than I to my son Greg. Since I am a constituent of the property of being taller than I, which in turn is a constituent of that proposition, believing that proposition involves believing of a certain individual (me) that Greg is taller than that individual. In both of these cases it is plausible to suppose that believing a proposition containing a certain property involves *de re* acquaintance with, and belief about, something that is a constituent of that property.

How much of this picture is needed to establish C1? Not much. In order to establish C1, it is sufficient to observe that it is possible to believe that Aristotle was a philosopher without believing anything about the actual world, whereas it is not possible to believe that the actual F was a philosopher without believing anything about the actual world. As far as the argument is concerned, it does not matter whether the proposition believed—the proposition that the actual F was a philosopher—is about the actual world because it describes it in a certain way, or whether it is about the actual world because it directly involves it without describing it. Surely many agents in merely possible worlds believe that Aristotle was a philosopher even though they have neither any direct epistemic acquaintance with the actual world nor any description that uniquely picks

(Contd.)

In justifying the move from C1 to C2, P3 and (7) embrace an account of the semantics of prepositional attitude ascriptions which has the consequence that expressions with the same content in a content C can be substituted for one another in attitude ascriptions without change in the truth conditions of those ascriptions with respect to C. As before, this view is both plausible in itself and difficult for the descriptivist to deny. His view is that proper names are synonymous with, and hence have the same contents in the same contexts as, *actually-rigidified* descriptions. The main point of appealing to descriptions in the first place was to provide names with the content needed to explain their apparent contributions to attitude ascriptions. This would be lost if the descriptivist were now to deny that expressions with the same content are intersubstitutable in

out the actual world from among all worlds. Because of this, the argument could be reconstructed without invoking *de re* belief about the actual world at all.

My reason for appealing to *de re* belief in formulating the argument is that I think of *actually* as an indexical like 'I' and 'now' that introduces a designated constituent of the context directly into propositions expressed by sentences containing it. In the case of the singular term 'I,' this constituent, the agent of the context, is the referent of the term. In the case of the sentential operator *actually*, this constituent, the world of the context, is a constituent of the property that is the semantic content of *actually* in the context. What we have just seen is that the argument would work just as well if the semantic content of *actually* were a property one of the constituents of which was not the actual world itself, but a descriptive sense that uniquely picked out that world from all other worlds. In this connection it is worth noting that we may have a description of the actual world that uniquely picks it out—namely, *the maximally complete property that the universe instantiates*. (Let us here waive issues about how many such maximally complete properties are in fact instantiated by the universe.) However, this description picks out different properties (worlds) with respect to different worlds, and so is nonrigid. Because of this, its sense is not a constituent of the content of *actually* with respect to a context. This adds plausibility to the directly referential (indexical) analysis.

Finally, the argument could be maintained even if we abstracted still further from my view of the semantic content *actually*. On my view, the content of *actually* relative to C is the higher-order property of propositions of being true in C_w. One might object to this that all we know for sure is that the content of *actually* (relative to C) is some property that is necessarily coextensive with this property. For all we know, some properties necessarily coextensive with the property of being true in C_w may contain as a constituent neither C_w nor any descriptive component designating C_w. And, it might be maintained, believing a proposition involving one of these properties need not involve believing a proposition about the actual world at all. To this I make two responses. First, we need some plausible account of how one particular property gets to be the semantic content of *actually* relative to C. The view I favor, according to which the property is determined demonstratively *(the property of being true in this world)*, gives such an account. If some other property is proposed as an alternative, then we need some equally compelling story of how it gets determined to be the semantic content of *actually* in C. It is not easy to see how this would go. Second, no matter which property P, necessarily coextensive with the property of being true in C_w is selected as the semantic content of *actually* relative to C, when we consider agents in other merely possible worlds, it is hard to see how they could be assured to have the epistemic acquaintance with P needed to believe propositions containing it. After all, P is a property that is intimately related to C_w; it is necessarily coextensive with the property of being true in C_w. Surely arbitrary agents in arbitrary worlds, including some who believe that Aristotle was a philosopher, are not routinely acquainted with P, nor with any property necessarily coextensive with the property of being true in C_w. This is all that is needed to establish C_1.

attitude constructions.[44] As a result, P2 and P3 should be accepted. But then, since the argument is valid, and each of the premises is true, it follows that proper names are not equivalent to descriptions rigidified using the actuality operator.[45] Hence, this version of descriptivism is false.

It is worth noting that this result is robust, and cannot be avoided by appealing to technical variants of the standard actuality operator. Consider, for example, a related operator *actually**, which is just like the operator we have been discussing, except for the fact that occurrences of *actually** can be coindexed with occurrences of standard modal operators, *necessarily* or *it is possible*, when the former occurrences fall within the scope of the latter. When *actually** occurs in a sentence without any such modal operator, the sentence . . . *actually* S* . . . has the same truth conditions, and expresses the same proposition, as . . . *actually S*. . . . However, when another modal operator with which *actually** is coindexed appears, this is not so. For example, the sentence (8a) is understood as making the claim (8b), as opposed to the claim (8c) or (8d).[46]

8a.   Necessarily . . . the x: actually Fx. . . .

8b.   For all worlds w, . . . the x: in w Fx. . . .

8c.   Necessarily . . . the x: actually Fx. . . .

8d.   For all words w . . . the x: in A_w Fx. . . .

---

[44]More precisely, the descriptivist's primary motivation would be lost if he were now to maintain that even though the semantic content of *Aristotle* is the same as *the F in C_w*, this content plays no role in determining the truth conditions of α believes that Aristotle was G. Conceivably, the descriptivist could reject the principle that expressions with the same content are always intersubstitutable in attitude constructions by appealing to something in addition to semantic content to block substitution. For example, he might maintain that an ascription, *α believes that S,* reports a relation between a believer and a thing believed, where the latter is conceived of as a complex consisting of the semantic content of S plus something else. Since on this view the semantic content of S plays a substantial (though partial) role in determining the truth conditions of *α believes that S,* it follows that *α believes that Aristotle was G* is true at a world w only if the referent of α at w bears a substantial epistemic relation to the semantic content: the F in C_w was G. But then, the same considerations that gave us C1 can be invoked to show that, in fact, it **is** possible to believe that Aristotle was G without bearing the necessary epistemic relation to the content: the F in C_w was G. Hence a version of the original argument, sufficient to falsify the analysis of *Aristotle* has an *actually*-rigidified description, can be constructed without invoking the principle of substitutivity for expressions with the same semantic content in attitude ascriptions. All that is necessary for the argument is that semantic content play some substantial role in the determination of the truth conditions of these ascriptions. Since the descriptivist cannot afford to deny this, he cannot avoid the argument.

[45]A related argument, similar in spirit to this one, can be found in G. W. Fitch, "Names and the 'De Re-De Dicto' Distinction," *Philosophical Studies* 39 (1981): 25–34. There Fitch considers the view that a proper name like *Cicero* is synonymous with a description **the x: Fx in this world,** where the demonstrative *this world* is treated as a directly referential term whose content in a context is the possible world of the context. On page 30 he argues that this view is incorrect because it wrongly predicts that speakers in trivially and irrelevantly different possible worlds would express different propositions when they utter *Cicero denounced Catiline*. I would like to thank David Braun for pointing this out to me.

[46]For further discussion of operators of this general sort, see John Burgess and Gideon Rosen, *A Subject with No Object* (Oxford: Clarendon Press, 1997), pp. 143–144 (and the references cited there).

When premise 2 of my argument is reformulated using the coindexed *actuality** operator, rather than the usual *actuality* operator, the true premise, P2, is transformed into premise P2*, which is equivalent to P2**.

P2*.   Necessarily$_1$ one believes that the actually F was a philosopher iff one believes of the actual world, A_w, that the unique thing that was F in it was a philosopher.

P2**.   For all worlds w, in w one believes of w that the unique thing that is F in it was a philosopher iff in w one believes of the actual world, A_w, that the unique thing that was F in it was a philosopher.

Since P2* is false, the proponent of the view that names are synonymous with rigidified descriptions might be tempted to identify the contents of names with those of descriptions rigidified using the indexed *actually** operator, rather than with the contents of descriptions rigidified using the more familiar, unindexed, *actuality* operator. On this modified view, the second premise of my argument fails; as a result, one cannot refute the modified view by deriving corresponding versions of the destructive conclusions C1 and C2.[47]

From the perspective of the descriptivist, the view that proper names are synonymous with *actually** rigidified descriptions has three desirable features. First, like the standard actuality operator, *actually** is a genuine rigidifier in the following sense: if **the x: Fx** is a nonrigid description that denotes o with respect to a context C and world C_w of C, then **the x: actually* Fx** is a rigid designator of o in that it denotes o with respect to C and w, for every world w in which o exists, and never denotes anything other than o. This follows from the fact that (i) the denotation of a description **the x: Sx** with respect to a context C and world w is whatever uniquely satisfies Sx with respect to C and w, and (ii) when **Sx** is **actually* Fx** and *actually** is unindexed, its semantics are just the semantics of the standard actuality operator. Second, like descriptions rigidified using the standard actuality operator, the content of **the x: actually*** Fx includes the descriptive content of F (whether *actually** is indexed or not). Hence, if names are analyzed as synonymous with descriptions of this form, then the different descriptive contents of coreferential proper names may be used to block substitution of coreferential names in attitude ascriptions. Third, unlike belief ascriptions containing the standard actuality operator, some belief ascriptions containing *actually**—namely, those containing occurrences of the operator that are coindexed with occurrences of a modal operator the scope of which includes the entire ascription—may be true even though the believers in question have no beliefs about the actual world. Hence, if names are analyzed as synonymous with descriptions containing the *actually** operator, a sentence like (9a) can be given an interpretation (9b) in which it is equivalent to (9c), and hence is true, even though (9d) is false.

---

[47]Thanks to David Lewis for pointing out this possibility.

9a. Bill could have believed that Aristotle was a philosopher, without believing anything about A_w.

9b. It could have been the case$_i$ that Bill believed that [the x: actually Fx] was a philosopher, without believing anything about A_w.

9c. There is a possible world w such that in w, Bill believes of w that the unique thing that is F in it was a philosopher, without believing anything about A_w.

9d. It could have been the case that Bill believed of A_w that the unique thing that is F in it was a philosopher without believing anything about A_w.

Despite these apparently attractive results, the view that names are synonymous with *actually**-rigidified descriptions is clearly incorrect. Although the view accommodates the fact that (9a) has an interpretation in which it is obviously true, it does so at the expense of assigning (10a) a corresponding interpretation in which it is equivalent to (10b) and (10c), and therefore is false.

10a. There exists an x (Aristotle) such that necessarily one believes that Aristotle was a philosopher only if one believes something that is true iff x was a philosopher.

10b. There exists an x (Aristotle) such that necessarily$_1$ one believes that [the x: actually Fx] was a philosopher only if one believes something that is true iff x was a philosopher.

10c. There exists an x (Aristotle) such that for all worlds w, in w the following is true: one believes of w that the unique thing that was F in it was a philosopher only if in one believes something that is true iff x was a philosopher.

Since (10a) is intuitively true, whereas (10b) and (10c) are false, the view that names are synonymous with *actually**-rigidified descriptions is incorrect. More generally, the view has the unacceptable consequence that when a belief ascription containing a name like *Aristotle* is embedded under a modal operator, the ascription is to be understood in one of two ways: Either *actually** is understood as unindexed, in which case the ascription is true at the relevant worlds only if the agents in those worlds believe certain things of the actual world A_w (and my original argument against such analyses holds), or *actually** is understood as indexed to the modal operator, in which case the ascription may be true at the relevant worlds without the beliefs in question being about one and the same individual— namely, the person who actually was Aristotle. In point of fact, the English belief ascriptions in question don't have either of these interpretations. Instead, they are understood as being true at arbitrary worlds only if the agents' beliefs in those worlds are about the individual who was Aristotle in A_w, even though the beliefs themselves are not about A_w. The view that names are synonymous with *actually**-rigidified descriptions cannot accommodate this fact. Since the same seems to be true of all versions of the view that assimilate names to descriptions rigidified using one or another kind of actuality operator, the lesson to be learned is that names are not synonymous with any descriptions of this kind.

Nevertheless, it must be admitted that there is another possible version of descriptivism that is immune both to Kripke's original modal argument and to all further arguments given here. According to this version, proper names have the same contents as descriptions rigidified using David Kaplan's *dthat*-operator.[48] This operator combines with a singular definite description D to form a singular term **dthat D,** the content of which in a context is just the denotation of D in the context. Rigidified descriptions of this sort designate their referents even in worlds in which the referents do not exist; they also may be used to express propositions that are routinely asserted and believed at alternative possible worlds by agents who have no propositional attitudes about the actual world. This is all to the good. However, the price of this success is too great for any genuine descriptivist to bear. When the *dthat*-operator is applied to a description D, it completely obliterates the descriptive content of D, and leaves the rigidified description **dthat D** with no descriptive semantic content at all. As a result, coreferential *dthat*-rigidified descriptions have the same content, and the goal of distinguishing coreferential names by associating them with different descriptive contents is thwarted.

Conclusion

This concludes my discussion of descriptivist challenges to Kripke's modal argument. If I am right, these challenges are unsuccessful. The original modal argument showed that proper names do not have the meanings (semantic contents) of ordinary nonrigid descriptions. The arguments given here show that they also do not have the meanings (semantic contents) of either wide-scope descriptions or descriptions rigidified using an actuality operator. In addition, these arguments illustrate a general lesson about the importance of paying attention not just to modality, nor just to propositional attitudes, but to the interaction of the two.

The theoretical notion linking these concerns is that of semantic content. The semantic content of a name is that which it contributes to propositions expressed by sentences containing it, relative to contexts of utterance. Since sentences inherit their modal profile (truth conditions) from the propositions they express, which in turn are the objects of assertion and belief, any positive account of the semantic content of a name (relative to a context) is responsible to both modal facts and facts about the attitudes. Looking at the modal facts alone, one can get the impression that the descriptivist's problems can be solved either by rigidifying his descriptions or by giving them wide scope over modal operators. Once the attitudes are added to the picture, it is clear that this is a misimpression. Similarly, if one looks only at Kripke's semantic arguments about how reference is fixed, one can get the impression that a descriptivist account of semantic content might be made to work by identifying the semantic content of a name (relative to a context) with a metalinguistic description based on the historical transmission theory. As before, this can be shown to be a misimpression by looking at a wider range of facts. Not only would such a view be subject to the difficulties inherent in rigidification, but it could not begin to account for the contents of ordinary assertions and beliefs expressed by sentences containing names. In short, when one looks at all the facts, the proper conclusion is that ordinary proper names typically do not have the semantic contents of descriptions.

---

[48] Kaplan, "Demonstratives." See also his "Afterthoughts" for a reconsideration of the viability of the *dthat*-operator.

Does this mean that no name whatsoever has the same the semantic content as any description? Not quite. Nothing we have said up to now rules out the possibility that some names might have semantic contents that are partially descriptive and partially nondescriptive. For example, consider the following possible theory.

A Partially Descriptive Theory

> A partially descriptive name n is semantically associated with both a descriptive property P_D and a referent o. The referent o is determined in part by having the property P_D and in part by the same nondescriptive mechanisms that determine the reference of ordinary nondescriptive names—for instance, by a historical chain of transmission leading back to o. The semantic content of n includes both o and P_D. The proposition expressed by *n is F* is the same as that expressed by *[the x: Dx & x = y] Fx,* relative to an assignment of o to 'y'.[49] This proposition is true at a world w iff o has the properties expressed by D and F at w. To believe this proposition is to believe of o that it has both properties.[50]

According to this theory, the property expressed by D that is included in the semantic content of n need not uniquely pick out the object designated by n, which is determined, in part, nondescriptively—for instance, by the historical chain of transmission of the name from one speaker to another. This feature of the theory allows it to escape some of Kripke's semantic arguments against standard versions of descriptivism. However, the theory is subject to a substantial constraint that seriously limits the range of reasonable candidates for such an analysis: For any given name n and associated description D, the property expressed by D must apply to the object standing at the end of the historical chain of transmission, if there are to be any true sentences of the form *n is F.*

The modal argument further limits the range of potentially acceptable analyses. Here it is useful to consider names like *Trenton New Jersey* and *Princeton University.* Unlike the majority of proper names, these are among the comparatively few cases in which a reasonable argument can be made that understanding them involves associating them with specific and substantial descriptive contents—the property of being located in New Jersey, in the case of *Trenton New Jersey,* and the property of being a university, in the case of *Princeton University.*

---

[49]Interesting questions arise about the semantic contents of partially descriptive names that lack referents. The theory stipulates that in order for an object to be the referent of such a name, it must both have the property P_D and be determined by one of the ordinary nondescriptive processes of reference determination—such as standing at the end of the historical chain of transmission involving the name—which governs the reference-fixing of names generally. When these conditions are not jointly satisfied by any object, the name fails to refer. What is the semantic content of a sentence containing the name in such cases? In the case in which the nondescriptive reference-fixing process—such as the historical chain of transmission—does not lead to any object, the content of *n is F* is the content of *[The x: Dx & x = y] Fx* absent any assignment of an individual to 'y.' In the case in which the nondescriptive reference-fixing process—such as the historical chain of transmission—does lead to an object o, but o doesn't have the property P_D, the content of the sentence *n is F* is the content of *[The x: Dx & x = y] Fx* relative to an assignment of o to 'y.' ....

[50]I here assume without argument that the description is "possibilist" in the sense that its range at a world (and time) is not restricted to the things existing at that world (and time). ...

If this is right, then, according to the partially descriptive theory, the semantic content of the name *Trenton New Jersey* is a propositional constituent incorporating both the property of being located in New Jersey and the city Trenton, whereas the semantic content of *Princeton University* is a propositional constituent that includes both the property of being a university and the well-known institution of higher learning itself.

With this in mind, let us focus on the second of these two cases. Consider a possible world w in which Princeton is founded as a college (as it was in the actual world) but never becomes a university. Is the claim that Princeton University exists true, when taken as a description of w? If so, then *Princeton University* is rigid, and its semantic content cannot be the one ascribed to it by the partially descriptive theory. However, the rigidity intuition does not seem as robust in this case as it does with the great majority of ordinary proper names. Rather, it seems reasonable to suppose that in w there is no such thing as Princeton University, even though the thing which actually is Princeton University exists in w, while being only a college. If this is right, then (11a) may be treated as ambiguous, having one reading in which it is equivalent to the false (11b), and one reading in which it is equivalent to the true (11c).[51]

> 11a.   In w, Princeton University exists.
>
> 11b.   In w, [the x: x is a university and x = p] x exists.
>
> 11c.   [The x: x is a university and x = p] in w, x exists.

Similarly, *Princeton University could have existed without being Princeton University* should be ambiguous, having both a reading in which it is obviously false, and a reading in which it expresses a truth. Admittedly, the latter reading is harder to hear. However, its existence seems to be indicated by the coherence and apparent correctness of *Since Princeton University could have existed even if it had remained a college and never became a university, it (Princeton University) could have existed without being Princeton University.*[52]

---

[51] In these examples, descriptions are treated as restricted quantifiers, *exist* is a predicate, and p is a logically proper name (a pure Millian tag) for the referent of *Princeton University*.

[52] What about the rigidity intuitions expressed by the following dialog?

A: Princeton University gives only undergraduate degrees.

B: That's not true. But it would have been, had Princeton remained a college and not become a university.

Here, B's remarks are naturally interpretable in a way that makes them true. In order for them to be true, B's use of *it* must refer to a proposition asserted by A that would have been true had Princeton remained simply a college. If *Princeton University* is a partially descriptive name, then that proposition can not be the one semantically expressed by the sentence A uttered—since according to the theory the proposition semantically expressed can be true at a world only if Princeton is a university at that world. Suppose, however, that A's assertive utterance resulted in the assertion of more than one proposition. In particular, suppose that when one asserts the proposition expressed by *[The x: Dx & x = y] Fx* relative to an assignment of an individual i to the variable 'y', one is also counted as asserting the singular proposition that i is F. . . . Applying this idea to the case at hand, we get the result that A's assertive utterance resulted in the assertion of the bare singular proposition that Princeton gives only undergraduate degrees, as well as the assertion of the descriptively richer proposition that the university, Princeton, gives only undergraduate degrees. The referent of B's use of *it* in the dialog is taken to be the former proposition.

If this account of the case is correct, then *Princeton University* is not, strictly speaking, a rigid designator. However, according to the partially descriptive theory, it is still namelike in two important respects. First, as with other names, it conforms to the modal principles (12a) and (12b).

> 12a. If n is a name that designates o, then n never designates any object other than o, with respect to any world.
>
> 12b. If n and m are names, and **n = m** is true, then **Necessarily if n and m exist, then n = m** is true.

Second, like other names, it conforms to the epistemic principle (13).

> 13. If n is a name that designates an object o, then believing the proposition semantically expressed by **n is F** involves believing of o that it "is F."

Conformity to these principles is what justifies classifying partially descriptive names as names.

Is the partially descriptive theory acceptable, then, for at least some names? If so, how extensive is its range of application? We have not, as yet, said enough about semantic content to give a definitive answer to these questions. . . . Although speakers often use proper names to assert and convey descriptive information about the referents of those names, in the case of most (linguistically) simple proper names—such as my name, or the names of the readers of this book—there is little or no specific descriptive information that a speaker must associate with a name in order to understand it, or to be a competent user of it; hence there is little or no descriptive information that is part of the semantic content of such a name.[53]

There are, however, apparent exceptions to this rule. For example, it is plausible to suppose that the (linguistically) complex names *Princeton University* and *Trenton New Jersey* are associated with substantial descriptive information that must be grasped by any competent speaker who understands and is able to use them correctly. It is arguable that a similar point might be made about the names *Hesperus* and *Phosphorus*, as well as the name *Superman*—not as we use it to name a fictional character, but as it is used inside the fiction. Certainly, there is some plausibility in the suggestion that anyone who doesn't know that *Hesperus* is associated with the appearance of a celestial body in the evening sky and *Phosphorus* is associated with the appearance of such a body in the morning sky doesn't understand the two names. Similarly, it is not unreasonable to think that any character in the fiction who didn't know that *Superman* names someone with super powers wouldn't count as understanding the name. Because of this, it is an open question—for now—whether the partially descriptive theory fits these special names. . . .

---

[53] It is arguable that in order to understand my name, for example, one must know that it designates a sentient being. Similarly, it might be argued that for most names, competence requires that one must associate some very general sortal with it. If this is so, then some highly attenuated version of the partially descriptive theory may turn out to be true for most names. However, in order to make this plausible, the descriptions must be made so general as to be essentially innocuous. . . .

AMBITIOUS TWO-DIMENSIONALISM
Scott Soames

Three decades ago, a group of philosophers led by Saul Kripke, Hilary Putnam, and David Kaplan ushered in a new era by attacking presuppositions about meaning that occupied center stage in the philosophy of the time. Among these presuppositions were the following:

(i) The meaning of a term is never identical with its referent. Instead, its meaning is a descriptive sense that encodes conditions necessary and sufficient for determining its reference.

(ii) Understanding a term amounts to associating it with the correct descriptive sense. Different speakers who understand a predicate of the common language, or a widely used proper name such as *London*, associate it with essentially the same sense. However, for many names of lesser-known things, the defining descriptive sense associated with the name varies from one speaker to the next.

(iii) Since the meaning of a word, as used by a speaker s, is the descriptive sense that mentally associates with it, meaning is transparent. If two words mean the same thing, then anyone who understands both should be able to figure that out by consulting the sense that he or she associates with them. For similar reasons, word meanings and mental contents are entirely dependent on factors internal to speakers.

(iv) Apriori and necessary truth amount to the same thing. If they exist at all, both are grounded in meaning.

(v) Claims about objects having or lacking properties essentially— independent of how they are described—make no sense. Even if a term t designates o and *Necessarily t is F* is true, there will always be another term t* designating o for which *Necessarily t* is F* is false. Since it would be arbitrary to give either sentence priority in determining the essential properties of o, the idea that objects have, or lack, properties essentially, must be relativized to how they are described.

(vi) Since the job of philosophy is not to come up with new empirical truths, its central task is that of conceptual clarification, which proceeds by the analysis of meaning.

These doctrines and their corollaries provided the framework for much of the philosophy in the analytic tradition prior to the 1970s. Of course, not every analytic philosopher accepted all tenets of the framework, and some, like Quine, rejected the traditional notions of meaning, necessity, and apriority altogether. However, even Quine—the framework's most severe critic—believed that if the traditional notions make sense at all, then they must be related more or less along the lines indicated. What was, for the most part, absent was a recognition that all of these notions do make sense, and are important for philosophy, even though they are mischaracterized by the traditional framework.

That changed with Kripke, Putnam, Kaplan, and the line of research growing out of their work. Today, all doctrines of the framework have been challenged, and replacements have been suggested. However, no new consensus has been reached. Although everyone recognizes the need to take into account the arguments of Kripke and his fellow anti-descriptivists, some continue to believe that the traditional paradigm contained much that was correct, and that a new, more sophisticated version of descriptivism should be put in its place. Even those who reject the idea of a descriptivist revival, and want to push the anti-descriptivist revolution further, have found the task of constructing a positive, nondescriptivist conception of meaning to be daunting. In short, the struggle over the legacy of the original challengers to descriptivism is far from over.

Here, I will discuss an important part of that struggle. In the past 25 years, a systematic strategy has grown up around a technical development called *two-dimensional modal logic*, for reviving descriptivism; reconnecting meaning, apriority, and necessity; and vindicating philosophy as conceptual analysis along recognizably traditional lines. Although the logical and semantic techniques are new, the motivating ideas are old. Since many of these ideas were not without plausibility, it is not surprising that an attempt has been made to reinstate them. But there is more to the attempted revival than this. Anti-descriptivism has brought with it problems of its own. I will begin by explaining how these problems have motivated a cluster of views I call *ambitious two-dimensionalism*. I will then identify what I take to be the shortcomings of these views, and explain why I believe that no version of ambitious two-dimensionalism can succeed.

The Anti-Descriptivist Revolution

First a word about the anti-descriptivist revolution. In *Naming and Necessity*, Kripke offers two main arguments against the view that the meanings of names are given by descriptions associated with them by speakers, plus a further class of arguments against the view that the reference of most names is fixed in this way.[1] The modal argument holds that since sentences containing proper names differ from corresponding sentences containing descriptions regarding the possible world-states in which they are true, names can't mean the same as descriptions. The epistemological argument holds that if names really meant the same as descriptions, then certain sentences containing them would express apriori truths. Since these sentences don't express such truths, names aren't synonymous with descriptions. Finally, Kripke's semantic arguments show that the descriptions speakers would volunteer in answer to the question *To whom, or what, do you use 'n' to refer?* sometimes fail to denote the object to which n really refers, and sometimes denote something to which n doesn't refer.[2] From this he concludes that, except in relatively rare cases, the linguistic rule mastered by speakers for

---

[1] Saul Kripke, *Naming and Necessity* (Cambridge, MA: Harvard University Press, 1980); originally given as lectures in 1970, and originally published in 1972.

[2] Here, and throughout, boldface italics are used as corner quotes.

determining the referent of a name is not that it is to refer to whatever is denoted by a set of associated descriptions. Instead, reference is determined by historical chains of reference transmission connecting later uses to earlier ones, and ultimately to initial baptisms introducing the name. A similar story is told for natural kind terms.

To this David Kaplan added an account of indexicals.[3] On this account, to know the meaning of the first-person, singular pronoun is to know that one who uses it in a sentence—*I am F*—refers to oneself, and says of oneself that one "is F". Similar rules govern other indexicals. These rules both tell us how the referents of indexicals depend on aspects of contexts in which they are used, and implicitly identify the semantic contents of indexicals with their referents. What is semantic content? The semantic content of a sentence is the proposition it expresses. Sentences containing indexicals express different propositions, and so have different contents in different contexts. Nevertheless, the meaning of such a sentence is constant; it is a function from contexts to contents. Kaplan's word for this is *character*. The picture is recapitulated for subsentential expressions. The character of the pronoun *I* is a function that maps an arbitrary context C onto the agent of C, which is its semantic content of *I* in C.

There are two anti-descriptivist implications here. First, the referents of at least some indexicals are not determined by descriptions speakers associate with them. One example involves Kaplan's identical twins, Castor and Pollux, raised in qualitatively identical environments to be molecule-for-molecule identical and so, presumably, to associate the same purely qualitative descriptions with the same terms.[4] Despite this, each twin refers to himself, and not the other, when he uses *I*. Although this leaves open the possibility that some indexicals may have their referents semantically fixed by descriptions containing other indexicals, it precludes the possibility that all indexical reference is determined in this way.

The second anti-descriptivist implication is that since the semantic content of an indexical in a context is its referent, its content is not that of any description. The underlying picture is one in which the proposition expressed by S is a structured complex, the constituents of which are the semantic contents of the words and phrases of S. For example, the proposition expressed by the sentence *I am F* is a complex in which the property expressed by F is predicated on the agent of the context. This is the same proposition that is expressed by the formula *x is F*, relative to an assignment of o to 'x'. A similar story is told for other indexicals. As Kaplan tells it, this story has consequences for propositional attitude ascriptions. Suppose, to adapt Russell's famous example, that on some occasion in which George IV spied Walter Scott, he gave voice to his conviction, saying *He* [gesturing at Scott] *isn't the author of Waverley*. Had he done this, the attitude ascription

---

[3] David Kaplan, "Demonstratives," in J. Almog, J. Perry, and H. Wettstein, eds., *Themes from Kaplan* (New York and Oxford: Oxford University Press, 1989), originally given as lectures in 1971.

[4] "Demonstratives," p. 531.

> The author of *Waverley,* namely Scott, is such that George IV said that he wasn't the author of *Waverley.*

would have been true—as would the ascriptions

> George IV said that you weren't the author of *Waverley.* (said addressing Scott)
>
> George IV said that I wasn't the author of *Waverley.* (said by Scott)

On Kaplan's picture, these reports are true because the semantic content of the sentence George IV uttered (in his context), and so a proposition he asserted, is the same as the content of the complement clauses in the reports of what he said. Whatever descriptions speakers who utter these indexical sentences may happen to associate with the indexicals are irrelevant to the semantic contents of the sentences they utter. When used in attitude ascriptions, indexicals, like variables in cases of quantifying-in, are used to report an agent's attitude toward someone, or some thing, abstracting away from the manner in which the agent thinks of that person, or that thing. All they contribute to the proposition George IV is reported as asserting is the individual Scott. We may express this by saying that for Kaplan indexicals are not only *rigid designators* but also *directly referential.* Some including Nathan Salmon and me, extend this to proper names.[5]

So far, I have talked only about semantics. However, the new view of semantics is closely linked to a view that recognizes the contingent apriori and the necessary aposteriori. Since the latter will be most important for us, we will focus on it. Kripke's route to the necessary aposteriori was simple. He first used the concept of rigid designation to rebut Quine's objection to essentialism.[6] Then, with both a nondescriptive semantics and a rehabilitated conception of essentialism in place, he showed how to generate instances of the necessary aposteriori. If n is a name or indexical that rigidly designates o, and P expresses an essential property of o which is such that knowledge that o has it requires empirical evidence, then the proposition expressed by ***If n exists, then n is P*** is both necessary and knowable only aposteriori.

Reasons for the Descriptivist Revival

So much for anti-descriptivism. We now turn to what some take to be the grounds for a descriptivist revival. First is the conviction that anti-descriptivists have not adequately addressed Frege's puzzle about substitution in attitude ascriptions, and Russell's problem of negative existentials. There is still a widespread belief that these problems show that names can't be directly referential.[7] Although Kripke never asserted that they were, it is hard to see how, if his doctrines are

---

[5] Nathan Salmon, *Frege's Puzzle* (Cambridge, MA: MIT Press, 1986); Scott Soames, *Beyond Rigidity* (New York: Oxford University Press, 2002).

[6] For discussion of Quine's objection and Kripke's rebuttal see pp. 347–54 of my *Philosophical Analysis in the Twentieth Century, Volume 2: The Age of Meaning* (Princeton: Princeton University Press, 2003).

[7] See chapter 1 of my *Reference and Description* (Princeton and Oxford: Princeton University Press, 2005).

correct, they could be otherwise. According to him, the meaning of a name is never that of any description, and the vast majority of names don't even have their referents semantically fixed by descriptions. If these names are so thoroughly nondescriptive, it is hard to see how their meanings could be other than their referents. Consequently, one who takes this Millian view to have been refuted by Frege and Russell may naturally suspect the power of Kripke's arguments to have been exaggerated, and may be motivated to find a way of modifying descriptivism so as to withstand them.

The second factor motivating descriptivists is their conviction that critics like Kripke have focused on the wrong descriptions. To be sure, it will be admitted, for many speakers s and names or natural kind terms n, the descriptions most likely to be volunteered by s in answer to the question *To whom, or what, do you refer when using n?* neither give the meaning of n nor semantically fix its reference. However, the referents of these terms must be determined in some way, and surely, whatever way that turns out to be is one which speakers have some awareness of, and which can be described. So, for each n, there must be some description that correctly picks out its referent—perhaps one encapsulating Kripke's own historical chain picture of reference transmission. Some descriptivists even go so far as to suggest that descriptive theories of reference are, for all intents and purposes, irrefutable.[8] The idea is that any refutation would require an uncontroversial scenario in which n refers to some object o not satisfying the description D putatively associated with n by speakers (or in which n fails to refer to the thing that is denoted by D). However, the very judgment that n refers to o in this scenario (or doesn't refer to what D denotes) is taken by these descriptivists to demonstrate the existence of a different, implicit, description in our minds that does determine reference in the scenarios—even though we can't articulate it.

The third factor motivating descriptivist revival involves the inability of some to see how any single proposition could be either both necessary and aposteriori, or both contingent and apriori, as anti-descriptivists maintain. Again, we focus on the necessary aposteriori. How, some philosophers ask, can empirical evidence about the actual world-state be required to know p, if p is true in every possible state? Surely if such evidence is required, it must have the function of ruling out possible ways in which p could be false. But if p is true in every possible world-state, then there are no such ways to rule out. So, if p is knowable at all, p must be knowable apriori. The idea that p is both necessary and knowable only aposteriori is incoherent, and any nondescriptive semantics that says otherwise must be incorrect.[9]

What gives this reasoning force is a commitment to metaphysical possibility as the only kind of possibility. On this view, there are different metaphysically

---

[8] See, for example, Frank Jackson, "Reference and Description Revisited," *Philosophical Perspectives 12: Language, Mind, and Ontology,* 1998, especially at p. 212.

[9] An analysis of knowledge with this consequence is given by David Lewis in "Elusive Knowledge," originally published in 1996, and reprinted in his *Papers in Metaphysics and Epistemology* (Cambridge: Cambridge University Press, 1999).

possible ways the world could be, but there are no further epistemically possible ways that the world might be. There are no world-states which, though metaphysically impossible, cannot be known by us apriori not to obtain. This restriction of epistemic possibility to metaphysical possibility renders the necessary aposteriori problematic—since it precludes seeing it as involving metaphysically necessary propositions for which empirical evidence is needed to rule out metaphysically impossible, but epistemically possible, world-states in which they are false. When one adds to this the popular analysis of knowing p as having evidence that rules out all relevant possible ways of p's being untrue, one has, in effect, defined propositions that are both necessary and knowable only aposteriori out of existence. A different philosophical commitment that leads to the same result identifies propositions with sets of metaphysically possible world-states.[10] On this view, there is only one necessary proposition, which is known apriori. But then, the anti-descriptivist semantics that leads to the view that there are necessary aposteriori propositions must be mistaken.

The Two-Dimensionalist Strategy for Reviving Descriptivism

I now turn to the strategy of descriptivist revival, which consists of three main elements: (i) the attempt to find reference-fixing descriptions withstanding Kripke's semantic arguments, (ii) the rigidification of those descriptions to avoid the modal argument, and (iii) the use of two-dimensional semantics to explain away putative examples of the necessary aposteriori and the contingent apriori. The most popular strategy for finding reference-fixing descriptions is *causal descriptivism*, which involves extracting a description from Kripke's historical account of reference transmission. This idea is illustrated by the following passage from David Lewis.

> Did not Kripke and his allies refute the description theory of reference, at least for names of people and places? . . . I disagree. What was well and truly refuted was a version of descriptivism in which the descriptive senses were supposed to be a matter of famous deeds and other distinctive peculiarities. A better version survives the attack: *causal descriptivism*. The descriptive sense associated with a name might for instance be *the place I have heard of under the name "Taromeo"*, or maybe *the causal source of this token: Taromeo*, and for an account of the relation being invoked here, just consult the writings of causal theorists of reference.[11]

The second part of the descriptivists' strategy is to rigidify reference-fixing descriptions. The idea is to explain apparent instances of substitution failure involving coreferential names in attitude ascriptions by appealing to descriptive semantic contents of names; while using rigidification to guarantee substitution success when one such name is substituted for another in modal constructions. The final weapon in the descriptivists' arsenal is ambitious two-dimensionalism, which may be illustrated using a putative example of the necessary aposteriori.

---

[10] See Robert Stalnaker, *Inquiry* (Cambridge, MA: MIT Press 1984).

[11] David Lewis, "Naming the Colors," originally published in 1997, reprinted in *Papers in Metaphysics and Epistemology*, fn. 22.

(1) If the x: actually Fx exists, then the x: actually Fx = the x: actually Gx

Here, we let ***the F*** and ***the G*** be contingently codesignative, nonrigid descriptions. The semantics of *actually* guarantees that since (1) is true, it is a necessary truth. Nevertheless, the knowledge reported by (2) is seen as being, at bottom, nothing over and above the knowledge reported by (3).

(2) y knows that if the x: actually Fx exists, then the x: actually Fx = the x: actually Gx

(3) y knows that if the x: Fx exists, then the x: Fx = the x: Gx

Since the latter is aposteriori, so is the former. How can this be?[12]

The two-dimensionalist answer is based on the relationship between the complement sentence, (1), of the ascription (2), and the complement sentence, (4), of the ascription (3).

(4) If the x: Fx exists, then the x: Fx = the x: Gx

(1) and (4) are nonequivalent in that they express different propositions, but equivalent in that they express truths in the same contexts of utterance. Since (4) expresses the same proposition p in all contexts, the two sentences express truths in all and only those contexts in which p is true. By contrast, (1) is semantically associated with two propositions—one which it expresses in our present context, and one which states the conditions a context must satisfy if (1) is to express a truth. The former, called the *secondary proposition*, is necessary, while the latter, called the *primary proposition*, is the contingent, aposteriori truth p that is also expressed by (4).

How does this provide a two-dimensionalist explanation of the putative aposteriori status of (1)? Two main possibilities suggest themselves (between which informal discussions of two-dimensionalism often do not distinguish). The first arises from a semantic theory I call *strong two-dimensionalism*. It holds that although the proposition expressed by (1) is a necessary truth, the knowledge reported by (2) is knowledge, not of this truth, but of the conditions under which (1) expresses a truth. On this view, there is no puzzle explaining how the proposition expressed by (1) can be both necessary and knowable only aposteriori, because it isn't. Instead, the secondary proposition associated with (1) is relevant to its modal status, while its primary proposition is relevant to its epistemic status. All sentences that express different propositions in different contexts are seen as semantically associated with two propositions relative to any single context C:

---

[12]Although it is evident that the proposition expressed by (1) is knowable aposteriori, it is far less clear that it is knowable only aposteriori. For an argument that it is in fact possible to know it apriori (without knowing the proposition expressed by (4)), see my "Understanding Assertion," in J. J. Thomson and A. Byrne, eds., *Content and Modality: Themes from the Philosophy of Robert Stalnaker* (Oxford: Oxford University Press, forthcoming). Although I will return to this point below when assessing ambitious two-dimensionalism, in presenting the view I will temporarily take it for granted that examples like (1), containing the actuality operator, are genuine instances of the necessary aposteriori.

the proposition the sentence expresses in C (its secondary proposition relative to C) and the proposition that states the conditions that must be satisfied by any context in which the sentence expresses a truth (its primary proposition). The primary proposition associated with S provides the argument to the operators *it is knowable apriori* (or *aposteriori*) *that*, as well as *Jones knows (apriori* or *aposteriori) that*. The secondary proposition provides the argument to modal operators like *it is a necessary truth that*. This is the basis for the strong two-dimensionalist's claim that every instance of the necessary aposteriori can be explained along the same lines as (1).

A slightly different explanation arises from a semantic theory I call *weak two-dimensionalism*. As before, sentences that express different propositions in different contexts are semantically associated with primary and secondary propositions. However, according to weak two-dimensionalism, the argument provided by such a sentence to the operators *it is knowable apriori* (or *aposteriori) that* and *Jones knows (apriori* or *aposteriori) that* is not its primary proposition, but its secondary proposition. On this view, (2) reports knowledge of (1)'s necessary, secondary proposition. However, this knowledge is counted as aposteriori because, it is claimed, (1)'s secondary proposition can be known only by virtue of knowing (1)'s primary proposition. As before, what makes the knowledge reported by (2) aposteriori is that (1)'s primary proposition is aposteriori. But whereas the strong two-dimensionalist claims that knowledge of the primary proposition is reported instead of knowledge of the secondary proposition, the weak two-dimensionalist claims that knowledge of the primary proposition counts as knowledge of the secondary proposition. A similar explanation is envisioned for all cases of the necessary aposteriori.

Varieties of Descriptive Two-Dimensionalism

That is the basic idea behind the two-dimensionalist revival of descriptivism. I will now outline several different versions of two-dimensionalism in more detail. I begin with *benign two-dimensionalism*, which is the view that there are two dimensions of meaning—character and content. Character is a function from contexts of utterance to content, which in turn determines a function from circumstances of evaluation to extensions. Characters, which are sometimes called *two-dimensional intensions*, are, as David Kaplan taught us, crucial to the semantics of context-sensitive expressions. It is Kaplan who gave us benign two-dimensionalism. In his sense, "we are all two-dimensionalists now." In recent years, however, the term *two-dimensionalism* has come to stand for something more ambitious—a cluster of views that attempt to use something like the distinction between content and character to explain, or explain away, all instances of the necessary aposteriori and the contingent apriori. I will sketch four versions of ambitious two-dimensionalism—the pragmatic version of Robert Stalnaker's 1978 paper, "Assertion," the strong semantic version suggested in the mid-1990s by Frank Jackson's *From Metaphysics to Ethics* and David Chalmers's *The Conscious Mind*, a weak semantic version which is a natural retreat from strong two-dimensionalism, and a hybrid version suggested by Chalmers in 2002.[13]

Stalnaker's Pragmatic Two-Dimensionalism

In "Assertion," Stalnaker accepted that Kripke's examples of the necessary aposteriori express necessary truths that predicate essential properties of objects. He also recognized that a speaker who assertively utters one of them asserts something that is knowable only aposteriori. However, he maintained that in every such case the proposition asserted is contingent, and so not identical with the proposition semantically expressed by the sentence uttered. He believed he could show this by appealing to a pragmatic model of discourse. According to the model, conversations take place against a background of shared assumptions which rule out certain possible world-states as not obtaining, or "being actual." As the conversation proceeds, new assertions acquire the status of shared assumptions, and the set of world-states compatible with what has been assumed or established shrinks. The aim of further discourse is to continue to shrink this set (called *the context set*) within which the actual state of the world is assumed to be located. The function of assertion is to eliminate from the context set all world-states in which the proposition asserted isn't true.

Stalnaker postulates three rules governing assertion.

R1.   A proposition asserted should always be true in some but not all members of the context set.

R2.   Any assertive utterance should express a proposition relative to each world-state in the context set, and that proposition should have a truth value in each such state.

R3.   The same proposition should be expressed relative to each world-state in the context set.

The rationale for R1 is that a proposition true in all world-states of the context set, or false in all such states, fails to perform the function of assertion—namely, to circumscribe the range of possibilities within which the actual world—state is located. Of course, this rule, like the others, allows for some flexibility in how it applies. If someone seems to say something that violates it, one may sometimes conclude that no violation has really taken place because the context set isn't quite what one originally thought, or because the speaker didn't really assert, or mean, what he at first seemed to assert or mean. In such a case, a speaker may say something the literal interpretation of which would violate the rule, knowing full well that he will be reinterpreted in a way that conforms to it.

---

[13] Robert Stalnaker, "Assertion," *Syntax and Semantics* 9, 1978, reprinted in Stalnaker, *Context and Content* (Oxford: Oxford University Press, 1999); Frank Jackson, *From Metaphysics to Ethics* (Oxford: Clarendon Press, 1998); David Chalmers, *The Conscious Mind* (New York and Oxford: Oxford University Press, 1996); and David Chalmers, "Components of Content," in David Chalmers, ed., *The Philosophy of Mind: Classical and Contemporary Readings* (New York and Oxford: Oxford University Press, 2002).

Stalnaker's rationale for R2 is that if an utterance violates it, then for some world-state w, the utterance won't determine whether w should remain in the context set or not. In explaining the rational for R3, he employs his notion of *the propositional concept associated with an assertion*, which is related to Kaplan's notion of the character of a sentence. For Stalnaker, a propositional concept is a function from world-states, considered as possible contexts of utterance, to propositions—where propositions are nothing more than assignments of truth values to such states. The propositional concept associated with an utterance of S is a function that maps each world-state w of the context set onto such an assignment. This assignment can be thought of, roughly, as the proposition that would be expressed by S, if the context of utterance were to turn out to be w.

D	i	j	k
i	T	T	T
j	F	F	T
k	F	T	T

Example D represents the propositional concept associated with a use of a sentence at a moment in which the context set consists of the world-states i, j, and k. D tells us that if i is the state the world is actually in, then the proposition expressed by the speaker's utterance is the proposition that assigns truth to every world-state of the context set; if j is the actual world-state, then the proposition expressed assigns truth to k and falsity to i and j; and if k obtains, the proposition expressed assigns falsity to i and truth to the other two. Which proposition is expressed depends on which world-state actually obtains. Since the conversational participants haven't agreed on this, they won't know which proposition the speaker is asserting, and so they will be at a loss as to how to update the context set. In this sort of case, we have a violation of R3.

With these rules in place, Stalnaker is ready to explain assertive utterances of Kripkean examples of the necessary aposteriori. The key involves apparent violations of R3. He gives an example of hearing a woman speaking in the next room. I tell you, *That is either Ruth Marcus or Judy Thomson.* Since demonstrative pronouns and proper names are rigid designators, this sentence expresses either a necessary truth or a necessary falsehood, depending on who is in the next room. Let i be a world-state in which the woman speaking is Ruth, j be a state in which it is Judy, and k be a state in which it is Mrs. Clinton. The propositional concept associated with this utterance is then E.

E	i	j	k
i	T	T	T
j	T	T	T
k	F	F	F

E tells us two things: (i) we don't know which proposition is actually expressed by the sentence uttered, because we don't know which context actually obtains; and

(ii) none of the possible propositions expressed would serve a purpose in the conversation. Thus, E violates R3, and any attempt to avoid violation by excluding i, j, or k from the context set would violate R1. So, if we are to avoid violation entirely, and to regard the speaker's utterance as informative, we must take it as asserting something else. What else? Well, whichever world-state turns out to obtain, the speaker will be committed to his utterance expressing a truth. Thus, we take the proposition asserted to be one that is true at any world-state w (of the context set) just in case the proposition expressed by the sentence in w is true at w. This is the assignment of truth values that arises by looking along the diagonal in E to find the value that appears in row w of column w, for each w. Stalnaker calls this the *diagonal proposition*. Since it is neither true in all world-states of the context set nor false in all those states, it can do what asserted propositions are supposed to do. Hence, it is what is really asserted by the speaker's utterance—no matter which member of the context set actually obtains. This is what ⇑E represents, where '⇑' is an operator that maps a propositional concept C1 onto the propositional concept C2 that assigns each potential context the diagonal proposition of C1.

⇑**E**	i	j	k
i	T	T	F
j	T	T	F
k	T	T	F

This example is the prototype for Stalnaker's treatment of the necessary aposteriori. Since the example is supposed to generalize to all such instances, one might get the impression that he thought that all genuine cases of the necessary aposteriori involve indexical sentences, which semantically express different propositions in different contexts. Since many examples of the necessary aposteriori involve only names or natural kind terms, such a view would require analyzing these terms as descriptions rigidified using either the actuality operator, or David Kaplan's *dthat* operator. However, Stalnaker didn't accept any such analysis. This created a problem for his pragmatic model. In order to get the desired results, he needed propositional concepts associated with instances of the necessary aposteriori to assign different propositions to different contexts. However, if the sentences aren't indexical, the needed propositional concepts can't be their characters, since these will be constant functions. But then, it is not evident where the needed propositional concepts will come from, or what interpretation they should be given once we have them. Although Stalnaker tried to finesse this issue, it was a problem.[14] Thus, it is not surprising that later two-dimensionalists took the step of analyzing names and natural kind terms as indexical, rigidified descriptions—thereby transforming the model from a pragmatic to a semantic one.

---

[14] See my "Understanding Assertion" for a discussion of this point.

The standard argument for taking this step goes like this: Imagine finding out that chemists have been wrong about the stuff that falls from the sky as rain, and fills the lakes and rivers. It is not really H_2O but XYZ. What would *water* refer to, if this scenario were to turn out to be actual? XYZ, of course. Although in the world as it really is, we use *water* to rigidly refer to H_2O, in a possible context in which the scenario described is actual, *water* rigidly refers to XYZ. Since the reference of *water* varies in this way from context to context, even though its meaning remains the same, the ambitious two-dimensionalist concludes that it is indexical. Thus, there must be some description implicitly associated with it by speakers that determines its reference in different contexts, which is then rigidified. It may be difficult to determine precisely what this description is, but that there is descriptive content to be rigidified is beyond question. Ditto for every name and natural kind term.[15]

Strong and Weak Two-Dimensionalism

With this we move from Stalnaker's pragmatic model to contemporary semantic versions, ambitious two-dimensionalism. I begin with two versions, which I will call *strong* and *weak*.

Central Tenets of Strong Two-Dimensionalism

ST1.   Each sentence S is semantically associated with a primary intension and a secondary intension. Its primary intension is a proposition which is true with respect to all and only those contexts C to which the character of S assigns a proposition that is true at C. The secondary intension of S at C is the proposition assigned by the character of S to C.

ST2.   Understanding S consists in knowing its character and primary intension. Although this knowledge, plus relevant knowledge of a context C, would give one knowledge of the secondary intension of—i.e., the proposition expressed by—S in C, one does not always have such knowledge of C. However, this does not prevent one from using S correctly in C.

ST3a.   All names and natural kind terms have their reference semantically fixed by descriptive properties which can, in principle, be expressed by descriptions not containing any (ineliminable) names or natural kind terms.

ST3b.   These terms are synonymous with descriptions rigidified using *dthat* or *actually*.

ST4a.   *It is a necessary truth that S* is true with respect to a context C and world-state w iff the secondary intension of S in C is true with respect to all (metaphysically possible) world-states w* that are possible relative to w. Similarly for other modal operators.

ST4b.   *It is knowable apriori that S* is true w.r.t. C and w iff the primary intension of S in C is knowable apriori in w; *x knows/believes (apriori) that S* is true of an individual i w.r.t. C and w iff in w, i knows/believes (apriori) the primary intension of S in C.

---

[15] David Chalmers's use of this line of reasoning is discussed at length in my *Reference and Description*, pp. 209–28.

Sᴛ5a.   S is an example of the necessary aposteriori iff the secondary intension of S (in C) is necessary, but the primary intension of S is contingent and knowable only aposteriori. Such a sentence expresses a necessary truth in our actual context, while expressing falsehoods in other contexts. Its primary intension is not knowable apriori because we require empirical information to determine that our context is not one to which the character assigns a falsehood.

Sᴛ5b.   S is an example of the contingent apriori iff the secondary intension of S (in C) is true, but not necessary, while the primary intension of S is necessary and knowable apriori. Such a sentence expresses a proposition which is false at some world-states, even though it expresses a truth in every context. The primary intension of such a sentence is knowable apriori because no empirical information is needed to determine that its character assigns one's context a truth.

These theses carry with them certain more or less inevitable corollaries, including ST6a.

Sᴛ6a.   There is no proposition that is both necessary and knowable only aposteriori; nor is there any proposition that is contingent yet knowable apriori.

If there were such propositions, then it should be possible to express them using nonindexical sentences, the primary and secondary intensions of which are identical (or at any rate equivalent). Since this is ruled out by ST5, the strong two-dimensionalist has reason to accept ST6a. A similar point holds for the corollary ST6b.

Sᴛ6b.   The necessary aposteriori and the contingent apriori are, in effect, linguistic illusions born of a failure to notice the different roles played by primary and secondary intensions in modal and epistemic sentences.

In what follows, I will take strong two-dimensionalism to include ST6a and ST6b.

One final thesis is ST7, which adds the claim that all necessary truths are knowable.

Sᴛ7.   A proposition is necessary iff it is knowable apriori.

In systems that identify propositions with sets of possible world-states, ST7 is trivial, and already presupposed. In fact, the acceptance by a strong two-dimensionalist of ST7 would seem to go hand in hand with a possible-world-state analysis of propositions. Since it is difficult to imagine another conception of propositions that would justify the claim that all necessary truths are knowable, it is difficult to understand why a strong two-dimensionalist would adopt ST7, unless the theorist wished to adopt that analysis of propositions. Why would such a theorist find such an analysis congenial? Well, consider the standard strong two-dimensionalist explanation of the contingent apriori, which hinges on the necessity of the sentence's primary intension. How does the necessity of this proposition guarantee that it is knowable apriori, unless it is guaranteed that every necessary truth is knowable? And how is this guaranteed unless propositions are just sets of possible world-states? To the extent that two-dimensionalists want simply to take it for granted that necessity of primary intension is enough for apriori truth, they have reason to adopt the possible-world-state analysis of propositions, and with it ST7. In what follows, I will call systems incorporating ST1–ST6 *strong two-dimensionalist*, and those that also include ST7 *very strong two-dimensionalist*. I will take these latter systems to identify propositions with sets of possible world-states.

Before giving a précis of weak two-dimensionalism, I pause over a point of interpretation. Although the analysis of attitude ascriptions given in ST4 is crucial to strong two-dimensionalism, my best examples of strong two-dimensionalism—David Chalmers's *The Conscious Mind* and Frank Jackson's *From Ethics to Metaphysics*—do not explicitly include ST4b, or any other, semantic analysis of attitude ascriptions. Worse, Chalmers repudiates ST4b in "Components of Content," published several years later. Why, then, do I interpret the positions taken in those books as suggesting strong two-dimensionalism? Because they strongly suggest ST4, and because it is difficult without ST4 to maintain other theses to which Chalmers and Jackson are committed. Detailed textual criticism aside, the main interpretive points are these:

(i)   Chalmers and Jackson hold that S is an instance of the necessary aposteriori iff the primary intension of S is contingent (and hence aposteriori) while the secondary intension of S is necessary, and that S is an instance of the contingent apriori iff the primary intension of S is necessary (and hence apriori) while the secondary intension of S is contingent. (These claims are themselves treated as necessary.)

(ii)   Whenever S is an instance of the necessary aposteriori, they endorse *It is not knowable apriori that S.* Whenever S is an instance of the contingent apriori, they endorse *It is knowable apriori that S.* In general, they endorse *It is knowable apriori that S iff the primary intension of 'S' is necessary,* and they take it that (for any context C) the left-hand side expresses a truth (in C) iff the primary intension of S is necessary.

(iii)   From this it is reasonable conclude that, on their view (at the time), *it is knowable apriori that* operates on the primary intension of S, or if it operates on the primary intension of S plus something else, only the primary intension matters.

(iv)   There is no reasonable option to assuming that *know* and *believe* operate on whatever *it is knowable apriori* does.

In effect, this adds up to the analysis given in ST4b.[16]

Next, I will sketch weak two-dimensionalism. Theses WT1–WT4a differ only in minor matters of detail from ST1–ST4a, and for our purposes may be

---

[16] For detailed discussions of the two works see chapters 8 and 9 of *Reference and Description*.

assumed to come to essentially the same thing. The key differences are in WT4b and WT5.[17]

Central Tenets of Weak Two-Dimensionalism

WT1.   Each sentence S is semantically associated with a primary intension and a secondary intension. The former is its Kaplan-style character. The secondary intension of S at a context C is the proposition assigned by its primary intension to C.

WT2.   Understanding S consists in knowing its primary intension. Although, this knowledge, plus relevant knowledge of the context C, would give one knowledge of the proposition expressed by S in C, one does not always have such knowledge of C. However, this does not stop one from using S correctly in C.

WT3.   As before.

WT4a.   As before.

WT4b.   An ascription *x v's that S,* taken in a context C, is true of an individual A w.r.t. a world-state w iff there is some character M such that (i) in w, A bears R to M, and (ii) M assigns the secondary intension of S in C to a related context with A as agent and w as world-state. So propositions are objects of the attitudes, and attitude verbs express two-place relations between agents and propositions. However, this two-place relation holds between A and p in virtue of a three-place relation holding between A, a character, and p. To believe p is to accept a character M that expresses p (and believe that M expresses a truth). To know p is to justifiably accept a character M that expresses p (and know that M expresses a truth).

WT5a.   For all necessary propositions p, p is knowable only aposteriori iff (i) p is knowable by virtue of justifiably accepting some meaning M (and knowing that M expresses a truth)—where (a) M assigns p to one's context, (b) M assigns a false proposition to some other context, and (c) one's justification for accepting M (and believing M to express a truth), requires one to possess empirical evidence—and (ii), p is knowable only in this way.

WT5b.   For all contingent propositions p, p is knowable apriori iff p is knowable by virtue of justifiably accepting some meaning M (and knowing that M expresses a truth)—where (a) M assigns p to one's context, (b) M assigns a truth to every context, and (c) one may be justified in accepting M (and believing M to express a truth) without empirical evidence.

Although some of the differences between strong and weak two-dimensionalism are subtle and far-reaching, others are obvious. For example, whereas strong and weak two-dimensionalists agree that necessary-aposteriori sentences are always associated with two propositions—one necessary and one contingent—the weak two-dimensionalist maintains that the necessary proposition is itself knowable only aposteriori. Because of this, the weak two-dimensionalist cannot identify propositions with sets of possible world-states. Thus, although strong and weak two-dimensionalists both presuppose that whenever a primary intension is necessary, it is knowable apriori, the weak two-dimensionalist does not have the

---

[17] The differences between strong and weak two-dimensionalism are discussed in more detail in chapter 7 of *Reference and Description.*

ready explanation of why this should be so that the very strong two-dimensionalist has. For the latter, it is in the nature of the one necessary proposition that it should be knowable apriori. Since the weak two-dimensionalist cannot say this, a different explanation is needed—of what sort is not obvious. This is one way in which weak two-dimensionalism is initially less attractive than strong two-dimensionalism. However, this initial disadvantage is not decisive, since all three versions of ambitious two-dimensionalism face crippling problems which require their rejection. I will sketch a few of these problems, before turning to the final version of two-dimensionalism to be considered.

Problems with Ambitious Two-Dimensionalism

Critique of Stalnaker's Pragmatic Two-Dimensionalism

Here is one problem for Stalnaker's pragmatic account of the necessary aposteriori. I hold up my briefcase. You look at it closely and ask, *What is it made of? Is it cow leather, some other kind of leather, vinyl, or what?* I answer, *It is made of cow leather.* Let's assume that although you don't know, prior to my utterance, what the briefcase is made of, we both take it for granted that, whatever it is made of, it is an essential property of this briefcase that it be made of that stuff. Since it is, in fact, made of cow leather, my remark is an example of the necessary aposteriori. How would Stalnaker represent the conversation? Well, prior to the utterance he would have different possible world-states in the context set that are compatible with everything we assumed or established up to then. Presumably, these would include a context i in which the one and only briefcase I am holding is made of cow's leather; a context j in which the briefcase I am holding is made of something else, say, pigskin; and context k in which I am holding a briefcase made of something else again—vinyl. So, he would associate my remark with the propositional concept B.

B	i	j	k
i	T	T	T
j	F	F	F
k	F	F	F

His rules for assertion would then yield two conclusions: (i) that on hearing my utterance you had no way of knowing which proposition was expressed, because you didn't know which context—i, j, or k—actually obtained, and (ii) that none of the propositions assigned by B to these world-states would have served a useful purpose. To have asserted a necessary truth would have been uninformative, and to have asserted a necessary falsehood would have been a nonstarter. So, if you were to regard my utterance as informative, you had to take it as asserting some proposition other than any of the candidates assigned to members of the context set by B. Since you knew that whatever the real context turned out to be, I would be committed to my remark expressing a truth, you took me to have asserted the diagonal proposition, which is true at any of i, j, or k iff the proposition B assigns to that world-state is true when evaluated at that state. Since this proposition is neither true at all the world-states, nor false at them all, asserting it does the job that assertion is intended to do.

That is Stalnaker's account. There are two things wrong with it. First, it is wrong to suppose that you had any relevant doubt about what proposition was expressed by my utterance of *It is made of cow leather*. The proposition I expressed is one that predicates being made of cow leather of one particular briefcase—the one I was holding. You knew it was the object you had asked about, and about which I gave my answer. Since you also knew what cow leather was, you knew precisely which property was predicated of which object by my remark. How, then, could you have been in any real doubt about which proposition my sentence expressed?

The second thing wrong with the explanation is that world-states j and k in the context set must either be ones that are not really metaphysically possible (contrary to the assumptions of the model), or ones that are not compatible with all the shared assumptions prior to my utterance (also contrary to the model). What are the world-states i, j, and k? They are total possibilities regarding how the world might be in which I am holding one and only one briefcase, which is both seen by us and the subject of our discourse. The briefcase satisfying these conditions in i is made out of cow leather, whereas the briefcases satisfying them in j and k are made out of pigskin and vinyl, respectively. Which briefcases are these in j and k? If j and k really are metaphysically possible, as Stalnaker insists, then the briefcases there can't be the briefcase I was really holding when I answered your question. Since that briefcase is made out of cow leather in every genuinely possible world-state in which it exists, it is not made out of pigskin in j, or vinyl in k. It follows that j and k must be world-states in which I am holding some other briefcase. But how can that be? Surely, one thing we both knew prior to my remark was that I was holding this very briefcase (imagine me holding it up again now) that we saw and were talking about. But if we did have this *de re* knowledge, or these *de re* beliefs, then Stalnaker's requirement that the world-states in the context set be compatible with everything assumed and established in the conversation must have eliminated all metaphysically possible world-states in which other briefcases were under discussion. But if that is right, then there is no room for the diagonalization required by his explanation, and the account fails.

This example relies on a plausible, but potentially contentious, metaphysical doctrine—the essentiality of origin, or constitution. However, there is nothing special about the particular essential property chosen. Other essential properties or relations (e.g., the property of being non-identical with Saul Kripke, or the relation of non-identity itself) would serve equally well. The important thing is simply that there be such properties (and relations). Given that there are, we can reconstruct different versions of the same problem that don't rely on assumptions about material constitution. For example, if, pointing at a man, David Kaplan, whom we both clearly see and know we have been talking about, you ask *Is he Saul Kripke?* and I reply, *No, he isn't Saul Kripke*, what

I say is knowable only aposteriori, even though the proposition expressed by my sentence is a necessary truth. However, if we try to apply Stalnaker's two-dimensionalist model of discourse to this example, we will run into precisely the same problems we did in the example about my briefcase. Instances of the necessary aposteriori that hinge on the essential properties of things cannot, in general, be explained by the model.

Notice what would happen if we dropped one of the antecedent philosophical commitments used in constructing the model—the restriction of the epistemically possible to the metaphysically possible. The idea is to allow the context set to include world-states that are metaphysically impossible, but epistemically possible—i.e., maximally complete properties that the world couldn't really have had, but which we cannot know apriori that it doesn't have (on analogy with certain properties, like being made of vinyl, that my briefcase couldn't really have had, but which one can't know apriori that it doesn't have). When we allow such world-states, the propositional concept associated with the utterance turns out to be different from what we originally took it to be. On this way of looking at things, i, j, and k are different epistemic possibilities involving the very same object—the briefcase I was actually holding. In i, it is made of cow leather; in j, of pigskin; and in k, of vinyl. This gives us the propositional concept B*.

B*	i	j	k
i	T	F	F
j	T	F	F
k	T	F	F

Since the same proposition is expressed with respect to each possible context, and since that proposition is neither trivially true nor trivially false, diagonalization is irrelevant.[18]

Critique of Strong Two-Dimensionalism

The most obvious problem for strong two-dimensionalism is that its account of the semantics of attitude ascriptions is obviously incorrect. When ordinary indexicals like *I*, *now*, and *he* are involved, their secondary intensions in contexts are crucial for attitude ascriptions in which they occur in the complement clause. Since the thesis ST4b doesn't make room for this, it clearly fails. However, strong two-dimensionalism can be shown to be false, even if these indexicals are put aside.

Here is one argument. Let n be a name. If strong two-dimensionalism were correct, then for some F, n would be synonymous with ***the actual F,*** and hence

---

[18] Stalnaker's two-dimensionalist account of assertion, the objections to it, and the distinction between aspects of it that must be abandoned and those that can be retained are discussed at greater length in my "Understanding Assertion."

would have the same primary intension as *the F*—in which case, the primary intensions of *n is G* and *the F is G* would be the same. If, in addition, attitude ascriptions reported relations to the primary intensions of their complement clauses, then (5a) and (5b) would have the same secondary (as well as primary) intensions, and so would be necessarily equivalent. This would mean that (6a) and (6b) couldn't differ in truth value.

(5a) A believes (knows) that n is G

(5b) A believes (knows) that the F is G

(6a) If it had been the case that . . .; then it would (or would not) have been the case that . . . A believed (knew) that n was G. . . .]

(6b) If it had been the case that . . ., then it would (or would not) have been the case that . . . A believed (knew) that the F was G. . . .]

Of course, pairs of the form (6a) and (6b) can easily differ in truth value, as is shown by (6aa, 6bb).

(6aa) Although John truly believes (knows) that n is F, had the world been in state w, n would not have been F and John would not have believed (known) that n was F.

(6bb) Although John truly believes that the F is F, had the world been in state w, the actual F would not have been F and John would not have believed (known) that the F was F.

The lesson here is that since n is rigid, its referent o is such that, at any world-state w, *n is F* is true iff at w it is a fact that o has the property expressed by F; thus, it ought to be the case that, for any world-state w, *John's belief that n is F* stands for a belief about o—one that is true at w only if, at w, o has the property expressed by F. Incredibly, on strong two-dimensionalism this turns out not to be so; instead "the fact that n is F" and "the belief that n is F" are, wrongly, allowed to be about different individuals.

Here is another argument that makes a similar point. Where n is a name that refers to o, for any world-state w, if *John believes (knows) that n is G* is true with respect to w, then in w John believes (knows) of o that it "is G." In other words, when n designates o, (7b) must be true, if (7a) is.

(7a) In world-state w [A believes (knows) that n is G]

(7b) In world-state w [A believes (knows) that x is G] (relative to an assignment of the referent of n to 'x')

Strong two-dimensionalism can't capture this, since it wrongly allows the ascription *A believes (knows) that n is G* to be about different individuals with respect to different world-states. For reasons like these, it is clear that strong two-dimensionalism is false.[19]

---

[19] For additional arguments, see chapter 10 of *Reference and Description*.

Critique of Weak Two-Dimensionalism

Although the issues here are somewhat more complex, in the interest of economy I will be brief.[20] There are two main points to make. First, the arguments that the reference of names and natural kind terms must be semantically fixed by description are defective, and do nothing to rebut the original Kripkean arguments that the vast majority of such terms do not have their referents fixed in this way. Second, even if we had reference-fixing descriptions, there would be no way of rigidifying them that would meet the needs of the weak two-dimensionalist.

Regarding the first point, about the lack of reference-fixing descriptions, one must distinguish (a) foundational facts that bring it about that terms acquire (and retain) the semantic properties they have from (b) semantic facts about them, known by competent speakers, that constrain what they refer to—in the way that being constrained to refer to a female is part of what must be known in order to understand the demonstrative *she*. When it is claimed by Jackson, Chalmers, and others that the reference of names and natural kind terms must be fixed by description, they are mixing up these two things. For example, when Jackson claims that there must be reference-fixing descriptions associated with names and natural kind terms, because, as he puts it in *From Metaphysics to Ethics*,[21] "it isn't magic" that they refer to what they do, he is pointing to the fact that these expressions—like all others—get to have the semantic properties they do in virtue of some describable empirical features of how they are used. Of course, they do; and, of course, being language users, we are not entirely ignorant of what these features are. However, it doesn't follow that we have complete and accurate knowledge of them. Still less does it follow that such knowledge is part of what a speaker must understand in order to understand the expression. To understand a word you have to know what it means—which in certain cases may amount to knowing its reference—but you don't have to know how the word got to have the meaning or reference it does. So a guarantee that there is some accurate description of how a word got to have its meaning and reference does not provide any guarantee that the word has its reference semantically fixed by a description grasp of which is required for linguistic competence.

This point bears on the suggestion, frequently made by contemporary descriptivists, that what Kripke did in giving his historical-chain account of reference transmission was simply to offer his own version of the description theory of reference-fixing.[22] The idea behind this suggestion is, in simplest terms, that the reference of a name n for a particular speaker is determined by something like the following description: *the individual which the person or persons from whom I acquired n referred to when they used the name*. One of the things that makes this idea seem plausible is the requirement, recognized by Kripke, that in order for a reference-determining chain to be created by passing a name from speaker to

---

[20]For a more complete discussion see chapter 10 of *Reference and Description*.

[21]Page 82.

[22]See, for example, the passage from Lewis referenced in fn. 11.

speaker, the person acquiring the name must intend his reference to be parasitic on the reference of his source(s). The descriptivist proposes simply to state this requirement in terms of a reference-fixing description.

Although the attraction of this idea is evident, when one examines it more closely one finds ample reason to be skeptical. It is not clear that speakers invariably have in mind, among all the different descriptions they associate with a given name, some accurate and precise reference-fixing description for it. Certainly, the description *the referent of the name as it was used by the first person from whom I acquired it* does not always pick out my present referent for it.[23] Since theorists have yet to develop a complete, accurate, and fully explicit historical-chain theory from which the needed description could be extracted, it is not clear which, if any, such description would be sufficient to handle all problematic cases. Even if theorists were to come up with the desired theory, it is far from obvious that ordinary speakers must have had it at their disposal all along, whenever they used a proper name.

We may assume that there is some process of reference-borrowing by which later uses of a name inherit their reference from earlier uses. We may also assume that speakers know that some such process exists, even though they don't know precisely how it works. With this in mind, consider the parasitic, reference-borrowing description D.

D. The thing referred to by those uses—whatever they turn out to be—of the name n from which my present use of n inherits its reference

Since it is plausible to suppose that speakers know, at some level, that the reference of their uses of names is inherited from the use of these names by other speakers—even though they don't know the precise mechanism by which this takes place—it is reasonable to suppose that they implicitly associate D, or something very much like it, with each name n that they use. However, it is important not to be confused by this. Although D does denote the referent of the speaker's use of n, the reference of n is not semantically fixed by D. If it were, then satisfaction of D would be the mechanism by which the speaker's use of n acquired its reference. But this can't be the way in which reference is determined, since D itself presupposes that the speaker's use of n already has a reference, which has been inherited from something else. In order for D to correctly pick out the referent, the speaker's use of n must have acquired that referent in some other way. Thus, the mechanism by which its reference is fixed can't be via satisfaction of D.

---

[23]Suppose, for example, that the person from whom I first picked up the name *Plato* was talking about his neighbor, whom he believed to be very wise. Suppose further that after speaking to this person I had many other conversations in which the name was used to describe Socrates' famous biographer, whom I later started to read about under the name *Plato*. All of this could be true, even if I wrongly assumed that the person from whom I first heard the name was talking about the same individual as everyone else. In this sort of case, I do not refer to the neighbor of my original source when I use the name *Plato*. Instead, I refer to the famous philosopher.

The upshot of all this is that even though the reference-borrowing facts of Kripke's historical-chain account of reference transmission play a foundational role in determining the reference of names and natural kind terms for speakers, there is no reason to think that these facts are among the semantic facts that must be mastered by competent speakers. Since this is precisely what would be required if the referents of these terms were semantically fixed by description, the description theory of reference fixing remains unsupported.

Similar considerations can be used to scotch a familiar two-dimensionalist objection to Kripke's semantic arguments against the description theory of reference fixing. These arguments are based on thought experiments which show that often, in different counterfactual circumstances of use, a name or natural kind term n refers to something other than what is denoted by the descriptions that speakers explicitly associate with n, and that they would offer in answer to the question ***To whom, or what, do you use 'n' to refer?*** From this, Kripke concludes that n does not have its reference fixed by descriptions associated with it by speakers. On the contrary, the two-dimensionalist objects, Kripke's thought experiments undermine his conclusion by covertly presupposing unarticulated reference-fixing descriptions that implicitly guide speakers' judgments.

Here is Frank Jackson:

> Our ability to answer questions about what various words refer to in various possible worlds, it should be emphasized, is common ground with critics of the description theory. The critics' writings are full of descriptions (*descriptions*) of possible worlds and claims about what refers, or fails to refer, to what in these possible worlds. Indeed, their impact has derived precisely from the intuitive plausibility of many of their claims about what refers, or fails to refer, to what in various possible worlds. But if speakers can say what refers to what when various possible worlds are described to them, description theorists can identify the property associated in their minds with, for example, the word 'water': it is the disjunction of the properties that guide the speakers in each particular possible world when they say which stuff, if any, in each world counts as water. This disjunction is in their minds in the sense that they can deliver the answer for each possible world when it is described in sufficient detail, but it is implicit in the sense that the pattern that brings the various disjuncts together as part of the, possibly highly complex, disjunction may be one they cannot state.[24]

Jackson maintains that our ability to identify the reference of terms in imagined Kripkean scenarios presupposes a knowledge of complete and accurate reference-fixing descriptions that is adequate for every scenario. He takes our ability to make these Kripkean judgments to demonstrate that names and natural kind terms must have their reference semantically fixed by these descriptions, that competence with the terms requires mastery of the descriptions, and that the terms themselves have the semantics of (indexical) rigidified descriptions. However, the ability he points to—such as it is—is not sufficient to draw these conclusions.

---

[24]"Reference and Descriptions Revisited," p. 212.

First, there are clear cases in which we have no trouble identifying the referent of a term t, even though it is clear that there is no reference-fixing description associated with t by speakers. David Kaplan's example of the identical twins, Castor and Pollux, discussed earlier, is a case in point. We have no trouble identifying Castor as the referent of his use of *I*, and Pollux as the referent of his, just as we have trouble recognizing ourselves as referents of our own uses. This is so despite the fact that the referent of *I* is not semantically fixed, for any of us, by descriptions we semantically associate with it. If this is true of *I*, it is surely also true of *now*, and may be true of other expressions as well. Second, even in cases in which there may be descriptions picking out the referent of a term that are, in some sense, associated with it by speakers, it remains to be shown that these descriptions play any role in its semantics. One can describe possible scenarios in which our intuitions tell us that speakers use the word *and* to mean disjunction, the material conditional, the property of being a necessary truth, or the property of being a philosopher. Even if one were to grant the assumption that these intuitions arise from an internalized theory T that unconsciously guides us, it would not follow that the meaning of *and*—its character in Kaplan's sense—is one that yields as content in a context whatever satisfies the relevant description extractable from T. Surely not every word is a descriptive indexical in Kaplan's sense. To miss this point is to miss the distinction noted earlier between (a) foundational facts that bring it about that terms acquire (and retain) their semantic properties from (b) semantic facts about them, known by competent speakers, that constrain what they refer to. Whereas the descriptivist needs reference-fixing descriptions arising from (b), Jackson's argument can't exclude the possibility that the only relevant descriptions are those arising from (a). Finally, the claim that our ability to categorize cases in certain ways presupposes the sort of underlying knowledge required by the description theory is tendentious in something like the way that Plato's attribution of apriori knowledge of mathematics to the slave boy in the *Meno* is tendentious. There are other ways to explain the recognition of new facts.

The failure of Jackson's argument on this point is representative of the arguments of two-dimensionalists generally on the subject of descriptive reference fixing. Typically, these arguments do not involve precise and detailed proposals about the descriptions that allegedly fix the referents of specific names or natural kind term. Instead, they attempt to establish, on the basis of very general considerations applying to all such terms, that their reference simply must be fixed descriptively—even if we are not in a position to articulate the crucial descriptions themselves. As the discussion of Jackson has illustrated, these arguments fail for a number of reasons, most notably the failure to distinguish foundational from semantic facts. Once this is recognized, and the Jackson-style arguments are out of the way, full weight can be given both to Kripke's refutations of particular proposals for treating specific descriptions as semantically fixing the reference of particular terms, and to the fact that complete, accurate, and reliable descriptions, known by speakers to fix the reference of typical names and natural kind terms, have not been formulated by anyone.

The next point to be made is that even if reference-fixing descriptions were generally available for names and natural kind terms, the weak two-dimensionalist has no good way of rigidifying them. One of two standard ways of rigidifying a description is by adding the actuality operator. However, this is no help to the weak two-dimensionalist, since it is obvious that neither names nor natural kind terms are equivalent to descriptions rigidified using this operator. For example, *Aristotle* isn't equivalent to **the actual F**, for any F—since it is possible for agents in other possible world-states to know or believe that Aristotle was a genius without knowing or believing anything about our actual world-state—whereas it is not possible for those agents to know or believe that the actual so-and-so was a genius without knowing or believing anything about our actual world-state. In the presence of the defining assumptions of weak two-dimensionalism, this means that the propositions expressed by (i.e., the secondary intensions of) **Aristotle was a genius** and **The actual F was a genius** cannot be the same, no matter what F one chooses.[25]

Thus, if the weak two-dimensionalist is going to take names and natural kind terms as rigidified descriptions, he will have to take them to be descriptions rigidified using David Kaplan's *dthat* operator.[26] However, this choice is also problematic. For one thing, it makes weak two-dimensionalists Millians about semantic contents—and hence subject to the very problems posed by Frege's puzzle and Russell's problem of negative existentials that descriptivists standardly take to refute Millianism, and to motivate descriptivism in the first place. In addition, the weak two-dimensionalist explanations of the necessary aposteriori and the contingent apriori go disastrously awry if one holds (in accord with WT4b) that understanding and justifiably accepting **dthat [the F] is G** is sufficient for knowing the (Russellian) proposition it expresses. It is easy to show that, on this view, the necessary aposteriori will shrink to the vanishing point, and the contingent apriori will bloat to include virtually all contingent propositions involving individuals or kinds.[27]

To block this *reductio ad absurdum*, one must add a condition—knowing *de re* of the denotation of the *dthat*-rigidified description that it is so denoted—to what is required in order for understanding and justifiably accepting **dthat [the F] is G** to count as knowing p, where p is the proposition it expresses. But then there is a further difficulty. The *de re* knowledge mentioned in the condition is itself knowledge of a singular proposition. How does it arise—for all names and natural kind terms for which *dthat*-rigidified descriptions are posited as analyses by weak two-dimensionalists, i.e., for every name and kind term? Since this

---

[25]This argument is elaborated in chapter 2 of my *Beyond Rigidity* (New York: Oxford University Press, 2002). See also pp. 303–6 of *Reference and Description*.

[26]Another reason for weak two-dimensionalists to forsake analyses involving the actuality operator is directly connected to the point made in fn. 12. Given an instance, **n / m**, of the necessary aposteriori, one cannot analyze the names n and m as **the x: actually Nx** and **the x: actually Mx**, unless **~the x: actually Nx = the x: actually Mx** is knowable only aposteriori—something called into question by the argument mentioned there.

[27]*Reference and Description*, pp. 307–10.

knowledge can't typically be explained as the result of understanding and (jus-tifiably) accepting still further indexical sentences, some additional, non-two-dimensionalist, explanation of the crucial *de re* knowledge and belief must be given. If we had such an explanation, however, we could, presumably, apply it directly to paradigmatic Kripkean examples in which we know *de re* of an object that it has an essential property, even though this knowledge can only be apos-teriori. But then we have an instance of the Kripkean necessary aposteriori that can't be forced into the weak two-dimensionalist mold, and the weak two-dimensionalist account of the necessary aposteriori is subject to a falsifying counterexample.[28]

A Hybrid View

Confronted with these objections to existing versions of ambitious two-dimensionalism, one might wonder whether there is some other version that is immune to the problems we have found. I don't think there is. However, the matter is not easily settled, since it is not clear what modifications of two-dimensionalism are possible without abandoning essential features of the program. I will say a word about this by considering a proposal put forward by David Chalmers, in his 2002 paper "The Components of Content," where he sets his sights on solving Frege's puz-zle by treating names and natural kind terms as rigidified descriptions, and making attitude verbs sensitive to both primary and secondary intensions. The new approach implicitly rejects the strong two-dimensionalist analysis of attitude ascrip-tions given by ST4b and the weak two-dimensionalist analysis given by WT4b, in favor of something along the lines of H.

H.   Both the primary and secondary propositions (intensions) associated with S are responsible for necessary conditions on the truth of *x (knows) believes that S,* without providing sufficient conditions. Such an ascription, as used in C, is true of an agent A in a circumstance of evaluation w iff in w, A (justifiably) accepts some (true) sentence or mental representation M which is such that (i) the sec-ondary intension of M in A's context in w is identical with the secondary intension of S in C, and (ii) the primary intension of M is "appropriately related" to the pri-mary intension of S in C.

There are various reasons to doubt the effectiveness of this proposal in solving Frege's puzzle. For one thing, it presupposes that all names and natural kind terms have their referents semantically fixed by description, and so is vul-nerable to the first objection brought against weak two-dimensionalism. For another thing, the most plausible candidates for reference-fixing descriptions that might withstand Kripke's semantic arguments involving error, misdescrip-tion, and failures of uniqueness are metalinguistic descriptions involving the historical chain of reference transmission in which the user of the term stands.

---

[28] *Ibid.,* pp. 310–13.

However, these descriptions are very poor candidates for specifying the contents of the beliefs and assertions one ascribes to others. When I say that the ancient Babylonians believed that Hesperus was a star, I am surely not saying that their mental contents included anything having to do with the chain of reference transmission that brought the name *Hesperus* to me. For these, and other, reasons Chalmers' proposal for solving Frege's problem doesn't seem very promising.[29]

But even if we put Frege's puzzle aside, adopting H is a more effective strategy for challenging ambitious two-dimensionalism than for saving it. Such a strategy threatens the conjunction of two principles, Apriori 1 and Apriori 2, which have been central to the approach.

Apriori 1
A sentence S is an instance of the apriori iff the character of S assigns every context a proposition that is true in that context.

Apriori 2
It is knowable apriori that S is true iff S is an instance of the apriori.

Since the objection against taking names to be descriptions rigidified using the actuality operator within the framework of weak two-dimensionalism remains in force against the hybrid version of the view, the hybridist must analyze names and natural kind terms as *dthat*-rigidified descriptions. But then, by Apriori 1, *If there is a unique F, then n is F* is analyzed as *If there is a unique F, the dthat [the F] is F,* and so is characterized as apriori—when the referent of n is fixed by *the F.* The right-to-left direction of Apriori 2 will then characterize the ascriptions that result from prefixing *it is knowable apriori that* to them as true. However, this can be correct only if *It is knowable apriori that if there is a unique F, then x is F* is true relative to an assignment of the referent of n to 'x'.[30] Since such *de re* knowledge of individuals can't, in general, be apriori, the right-to-left direction of Apriori 2 is in jeopardy. Nor would denying this be of much help, since if such knowledge of individuals can be apriori, then *If there is a unique F, then x is F* (taken relative to an assignment of the referent of n to 'x') will, according to Apriori 2, count as an instance of the apriori, even though, typically, its character (relative to such an assignment) will not assign a truth to every context—thereby falsifying the conjunction of the left-to-right directions of Apriori 1 and Apriori 2.

---

[29] *Ibid.,* 322–24.

[30] It might seem that the defender of H could deny the move from the truth of *It is knowable apriori that if there is a unique F, then n (i.e., dthat [the F]) is F* to the truth of *It is knowable apriori that if there is a unique F, then x is F* relative to an assignment of the referent of n to 'x', on the grounds that the primary intension of the complement clause of the latter is not "appropriately related" to that of the complement clause of the former. However, this would fly in the face of the fact that if n is a name that refers to o, the truth of *α knows/believes (apriori) that . . . n . . .* guarantees the truth of *α knows/believes (apriori) that . . . x . . .,* relative to an assignment of o to 'x'. See pp. 261–62 and 316–18 of *Reference and Description.*

An independent argument against this conjunction can be constructed as follows.

Step 1:   If H is correct, then there will be cases in which an utterance, by a_1 in context C_1, of *A_2 knows that n is F* is true, where (i) the referent a_2 of A_2 justifiably accepts a true sentence *m is F* the secondary intension of which in a_2's context C_2 is the same as the secondary intension of *n is F* in C_1, and (ii) the primary intensions of these two sentences are at least somewhat different because the primary intension of m (as used in C_2) differs slightly from that of n (as used in C_1). Here, n is a name, and m is either a name or an indexical—m may even be the same name as n, provided that one recognizes (as Chalmers knows he must) that different speakers may use it with somewhat different primary intensions in their respective contexts.

Step 2:   If there are cases of the sort indicated in Step 1, then we may suppose that some will be symmetrical in that what a_1 uses *A_2 knows that n is F* to truly report about a_2, the latter can use *A_1 knows that m is F* to truly report about a_1. These reports can be jointly true because the secondary intensions of the two complement clauses are the same in their respective contexts, while the primary intensions of these clauses, though different, are close enough to satisfy constraints imposed by H.

Step 3:   We may assume, with the two-dimensionalist, that the primary intensions of n and m are given by a pair of descriptions D_n and D_m which pick out the same objects in their respective contexts, but which denote different objects with respect to some pairs of contexts. One way for this to happen is for D_n to be like D_m except for containing a conjunct that predicates G of its denotation whereas the corresponding conjunct in D_m predicates n unrelated predicate F.

Step 4:   Now consider a_1's utterance in C_1 of the ascription *A_2 knows that if n exists, then n is F.* For the reasons given in Step 2, this ascription should be true, since a_2 justifiably accepts the true sentence *If m exists, then m is F*, the secondary intension of which in C_2 is the same as the secondary intension of *If n exists, then n is F* in C_1. As before, although the primary intensions of the two sentences (as used in their respective contexts) differ slightly, they should be close enough to satisfy the constraints imposed by H.

Step 5:   Since F is included in the reference-fixing conditions for m, the primary intension of *If m exists, then m is F* (as used in C_2) should be necessary, and so the knowledge correctly attributed to a_2 by a_1's utterance of *A_2 knows that if n exists, then n is F* should (according to ambitious two-dimensionalism) be counted as apriori.

Step 6:   So *A_2 knows apriori that if n exists, then n is F* should be true, as used in context C_1, as should *It is knowable apriori that if n exists, then n is F*—even though the primary intension of *If n exists, then n is F* (as used in C_1) is not necessary (thereby falsifying the conjunction of the left-to-right directions of Apriori 1 and Apriori 2).

What this shows is that Chalmers's explicit proposal H for the attitudes threatens what previously had been a central and defining tenet of ambitious two-dimensionalism—the conjunction of Apriori 1 and Apriori 2. Thus, his proposal may be more of a threat to that view than a way of implementing it.

Be that as it may, there is a final difficulty that the hybrid view shares with other versions of ambitious two-dimensionalism that analyze proper names (and natural kind terms) as *dthat*-rigidified descriptions. The difficulty involves the following acquaintance constraints on names and their potential analyses (as well as similar constraints on natural kind terms).

> The Acquaintance Constraint on Names
> If there is an object o, such that n designates o, and a speaker s understands n, then *x knows that 'n' designates n (if 'n' designates anything at all)* is true of s, as is *There is an object o such that x knows that 'n' designates o (if 'n' designates anything at all)*.

> The Acquaintance Constraint on Descriptive Analyses of Names
> If *dthat [the D]* is the analysis of n, as used by s in C, and *dthat [the D]* designates o (relative to C), and s understands *the D,* then *There is an object o such that x knows that 'the D' designates o (if 'the D' designates anything at all)* is true of s (relative to C).

The problem is that descriptions satisfying the second constraint are not generally available. What is needed are descriptions such that understanding them and correctly believing them to denote puts one in a position to have *de re* beliefs about objects they denote. There are such descriptions. For example, it is arguable that (i) understanding the descriptions *the ancient philosopher that is the referent of the name 'Plato' that I have encountered in the language of my community* and *the ancient philosopher reference to whom is inherited by my use of 'Plato' from standard uses of 'Plato' by speakers of the language of my community* and (ii) correctly believing them to denote, does put me in a position to have *de re* beliefs about Plato expressible using the name. However, this is only because referent of the name, as used in my linguistic community, has already been established *independently* of the satisfaction of these descriptions. Since advocates of descriptivist theories such as ambitious two-dimensionalism require reference to be semantically fixed by virtue of satisfying the descriptive content associated with use of a name, descriptions that presuppose that reference has already been established independently can't play that role. It is doubtful that any other descriptions available to ordinary speakers can do the job.

Conclusion

Having reached this point, we may summarize our results as follows: The versions of ambitious two-dimensionalism we have been able to state precisely—pragmatic two-dimensionalism, plus strong and weak semantic two-dimensionalism—are clearly incorrect.[31] The hybrid version of the view—which is problematic as a solution to Frege's puzzle—both suffers from difficulties that it shares with other descriptivist analyses of names, and threatens principles central to ambitious two-dimensionalist accounts of the necessary aposteriori and the contingent apriori. At present, there is no further version of the view left to consider. If the two-dimensionalist approach is to survive at all, the onus is on those who favor it to formulate a new version that avoids the objections raised here. For that, we will simply have to wait.

---

[31] For a different, but in some respects related, argument for a similar conclusion about the prospects for two-dimensionalism, see George Bealer's discussion in section 2 of "Modal Epistemology and the Rational Renaissance," in Tamar Gendler and John Hawthorne, eds., *Conceivability and Possibility* (Oxford: Oxford University Press, 2002).

DEMONSTRATIVES: AN ESSAY ON THE SEMANTICS, LOGIC, METAPHYSICS, AND EPISTEMOLOGY OF DEMONSTRATIVES AND OTHER INDEXICALS

David Kaplan[1]

Preface

In about 1966 I wrote a paper about quantification into epistemological contexts. There are very difficult metaphysical, logical, and epistemological problems involved in providing a treatment of such idioms which does not distort our intuitions about their proper use and which is up to contemporary logical standards. I did not then, and do not now, regard the treatment I provided as fully adequate. And I became more and more intrigued with problems centering on what I would like to call the *semantics of direct reference.* By this I mean theories of meaning according to which certain singular terms refer directly without the mediation of a Fregean *Sinn* as meaning. If there are such terms, then the proposition expressed by a sentence containing such a term would involve individuals directly rather than by way of the "individual concepts" or "manners of presentation" I had been taught to expect. Let us call such putative singular terms (if there are any) *directly referential terms* and such putative propositions (if there are any) *singular propositions.* Even if English contained no singular terms whose proper semantics was one of direct reference, could we determine to introduce such terms? And even if we had no directly referential terms and introduced none, is there a need or use for singular propositions?

The feverish development of quantified modal logics, more generally, of quantified intensional logics, of the 1960s gave rise to a metaphysical and epistemological malaise regarding the problem of identifying individuals across worlds—what, in 1967, I called the problem of "Trans-World Heir Lines." This problem was really just the problem of singular propositions: those which involve individuals directly, rearing its irrepressible head in the possible-world semantics that were then (and are now) so popular.

It was not that according to those semantical theories any sentences of the languages being studied were themselves taken to express singular propositions, it was just that singular propositions seemed to be needed in the analysis of the nonsingular propositions expressed by these sentences. For example, consider

(0) $\exists x(Fx \wedge \sim\Box Fx).$

[1] This paper was prepared for and read (with omissions) at a symposium on Demonstratives at the March 1977 meetings of the Pacific Division of the American Philosophical Association. The commentators were Paul Benacerraf and Charles Chastain. Much of the material, including the formal system of section XVIII, was originally presented in a series of lectures at the fabled 1971 Summer Institute in the Philosophy of Language held at the University of California, Irvine. © 1977 by David Kaplan.

This sentence would not be taken by anyone to express a singular proposition. But in order to evaluate the truth-value of the component

$\Box Fx$

(under some assignment of an individual to the variable 'x'), we must first determine whether the *proposition* expressed by its component

Fx

(under an assignment of an individual to the variable 'x') is a necessary proposition. So in the course of analyzing (0), we are required to determine the proposition associated with a formula containing a *free* variable. Now free variables under an assignment of values are paradigms of what I have been calling *directly referential* terms. In determining a semantical value for a formula containing a free variable we may be given a *value* for the variable—that is, an individual drawn from the universe over which the variable is taken to range—but nothing more. A variable's first and only meaning is its value. Therefore, if we are to associate a *proposition* (not merely a truth-value) with a formula containing a free variable (with respect to an assignment of a value to the variable), that proposition seems bound to be singular (even if valiant attempts are made to disguise this fact by using constant functions to imitate individual concepts). The point is, that if the component of the proposition (or the step in the construction of the proposition) which corresponds to the singular term is determined by the individual and the individual is directly determined by the singular term—rather than the individual being determined by the component of the proposition, which is directly determined by the singular term—them we have what I call a singular proposition. [Russell's semantics was like the semantical theories for quantified intensional logics that I have described in that although no (closed) sentence of *Principia Mathematica* was taken to stand for a singular proposition, singular propositions are the essential building blocks of all propositions.]

The most important hold-out against semantical theories that required singular propositions is Alonzo Church, the great modern champion of Frege's semantical theories. Church also advocates a version of quantified intensional logic, but with a subtle difference that finesses the need for singular propositions. (In Church's logic, given a sentential formula containing free variables and given an assignment of values to the variables, no proposition is yet determined. An additional assignment of "senses" to the free variables must be made before a proposition can be associated with the formula.) It is no accident that Church rejects *direct reference* semantical theories. For if there were singular terms which referred directly, it seems likely that Frege's problem: how can $\ulcorner \alpha = \beta \urcorner$, if true, differ in meaning from $\ulcorner \alpha = \alpha \urcorner$, could be reinstated, while Frege's solution: that α and β, though referring to the same thing, do so by way of different senses, would be blocked. Also: because of the fact that the component of the proposition is being determined by the individual rather than vice versa, we have something like a violation of the famous Fregean dictum that *there is no road back* from denotation to sense [propositional component]. (Recently, I have come to think that if we countenance singular propositions, a collapse of Frege's intensional ontology into Russell's takes place.)

I can draw some little pictures to give you an idea of the two kinds of semantical theories I want to contrast.

Fregean Picture

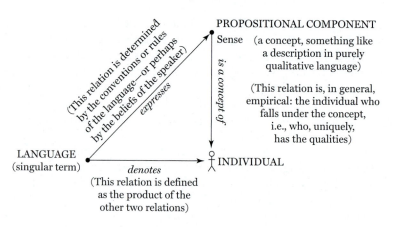

Direct Reference Picture

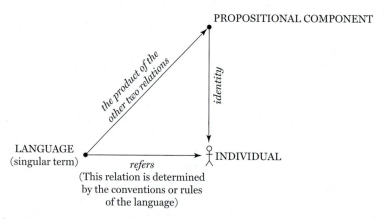

(These pictures are not entirely accurate for several reasons, among them, that the contrasting pictures are meant to account for more than just singular terms and that the relation marked 'refers' may already involve a kind of Fregean sense used to fix the referent.)

I won't go into the pros and cons of these two views at this time. Suffice it to say that I had been raised on Fregean semantics and was sufficiently devout to wonder whether the kind of quantification into modal and epistemic contexts that seemed to require singular propositions really made sense. (My paper "Quantifying In" can be regarded as an attempt to *explain away* such idioms for epistemic contexts.)[2]

But there were pressures from quarters other than quantified intensional logic in favor of a semantics of direct reference. First of all there was Donnellan's fascinating paper "Reference and Definite Descriptions."[3] Then there were discussions I had had with Putnam in 1968 in which he argued with respect to certain natural kind terms like 'tiger' and 'gold', that if their Fregean senses were the kind of thing that one grasped when one understood the terms, then such senses could not determine the extension of the terms. And finally Kripke's Princeton lectures of spring 1970, later published as *Naming and Necessity*,[4] were just beginning to leak out along with their strong attack on the Fregean theory of proper names and their support of a theory of direct reference.

As I said earlier, I was intrigued by the semantics of direct reference, so when I had a sabbatical leave for the year 1970–71, I decided to work in the area in which such a theory seemed most plausible: demonstratives. In fall 1970, I wrote, for a conference at Stanford, a paper "Dthat."[5] Using Donnellan's ideas as a starting point, I tried to develop the contrast between Fregean semantics and the semantics of direct reference, and to argue that demonstratives—although they *could* be treated on a Fregean model—were more interestingly treated on a direct reference model. Ultimately I came to the conclusion that something analogous to Donnellan's referential use of a definite description could be developed using my new demonstrative, "dthat." In the course of this paper I groped my way to a formal semantics for demonstratives rather different in conception from those that had been offered before.

In spring 1971, I gave a series of lectures at Princeton on the semantics of direct reference. By this time I had seen a transcript of *Naming and Necessity* and I tried to relate some of my ideas to Kripke's.[6] I also had written out the formal semantics for my Logic of Demonstratives. That summer at the Irvine Philosophy of Language Institute I lectured again on the semantics of direct reference and repeated some of these lectures at various institutions in fall 1971. And there the matter has stood except for a bit of updating of the 1971 Logic of Demonstratives notes in 1973.

---

[2] David Kaplan, "Quantifying In," *Synthese* 19 (1968):178–214; reprinted in *The Philosophy of Language*, ed. A. P. Martinich (Oxford: Oxford University Press, 1985).

[3] Keith Donnellan, "Reference and Definite Descriptions," *Philosophical Review* 75 (1966): 281–304; reprinted in Martinich, *op. cit.*

[4] Saul Kripke, "Naming and Necessity," in *Semantics of Natural Language,* ed. G. Harman and D. Davidson (Dordrecht: Reidel, 1972); revised edition published as a separate monograph, *Naming and Necessity* (Oxford: Basil Blackwell, 1980). References are to the revised edition.

[5] David Kaplan, "Dthat," in *Syntax and Semantics*, vol. 9, ed. P. Cole (New York: Academic Press, 1978); reprinted in Martinich, *op. cit.*

[6] Although the central ideas of my theory had been worked out before I became familiar with *Naming and Necessity,* I have enthusiastically adopted the "analytical apparatus" and some of the terminology of that brilliant work.

I now think that demonstratives can be treated correctly only on a direct reference model, but that my earlier lectures at Princeton and Irvine on direct reference semantics were too broad in scope, and that the most important and certainly the most convincing part of my theory is just the logic of demonstratives itself. It is based on just a few quite simple ideas, but the conceptual apparatus turns out to be surprisingly rich and interesting. At least I hope that you will find it so.

In this work I have concentrated on pedagogy. Philosophically, there is little here that goes beyond the Summer Institute Lectures, but I have tried, by limiting the scope, to present the ideas in a more compelling way. Some new material appears in the two speculative sections: XVII (Epistemological Remarks) and XX (Adding 'Says'). It is my hope that a theory of demonstratives will give us the tools to go on in a more sure-footed way to explore the *de re* prepositional attitudes as well as other semantical issues.

I. Introduction

I believe my theory of demonstratives to be uncontrovertable and largely uncontroversial. This is not a tribute to the power of my theory but a concession of its obviousness. In the past, no one seems to have followed these obvious facts out to their obvious consequences. I do that. What is original with me is some terminology to help fix ideas when things get complicated. It has been fascinating to see how interesting the obvious consequences of obvious principles can be.[7]

II. Demonstratives, Indexicals, and Pure Indexicals

I tend to describe my theory as 'a theory of demonstratives', but that is poor usage. It stems from the fact that I began my investigations by asking what is said when a speaker points at someone and says, "He is suspicious."[8] The word 'he', so used, is a demonstrative, and the accompanying pointing is the requisite associated demonstration. I hypothesized a certain semantical theory for such demonstratives, and then I invented a new demonstrative, 'dthat', and stipulated that its semantics be in accord with my theory. I was so delighted with this methodological sleight of hand for my demonstrative 'dthat', that when I generalized the theory to apply to words like 'I', 'now', 'here', etc.—words which do *not* require an associated demonstration—I continued to call my theory a 'theory of demonstratives' and I referred to these words as 'demonstratives'.

That terminological practice conflicts with what I preach, and I will try to correct it. (But I tend to backslide.)

The group of words for which I propose a semantical theory includes the pronouns 'I', 'my', 'you', 'he', 'his', 'she', 'it', the demonstrative pronouns 'that', 'this', the adverbs 'here', 'now', 'tomorrow', 'yesterday', the adjectives 'actual', 'present', and

---

[7] Not everything I assert is part of my theory. At places I make judgments about the correct use of certain words and I propose detailed analyses of certain notions. I recognize that these matters may be controversial. I do not regard them as part of the basic, obvious, theory.

[8] See "Dthat," p. 320 in Martinich.

others. These words have uses other than those in which I am interested (or, perhaps, depending on how you individuate words, we should say that they have homonyms in which I am not interested). For example, the pronouns 'he' and 'his' are used not as demonstratives but as bound variables in

> For what is a man profited, if he shall gain the whole world, and lose his own soul?

What is common to the words or usages in which I am interested is that the referent is dependent on the context of use and that the meaning of the word provides a rule which determines the referent in terms of certain aspects of the context. The term I now favor for these words is 'indexical'. Other authors have used other terms; Russell used 'egocentric particular' and Reichenbach used 'token reflexive'. I prefer 'indexical' (which, I believe, is due to Pierce) because it seems less theory laden than the others, and because I regard Russell's and Reichenbach's theories as defective.

Some of the indexicals require, in order to determine their referents, an associated demonstration: typically, though not invariably, a (visual) presentation of a local object discriminated by a pointing.[9] These indexicals are the true demonstratives, and 'that' is their paradigm. The demonstra*tive* (an expression) refers to that which the demon*stration* demonstrates. I call that which is demonstrated the 'demonstratum'.

A demonstrative without an associated demonstration is incomplete. The linguistic rules which govern the use of the true demonstratives 'that', 'he', etc., are not sufficient to determine their referent in all contexts of use. Something else— an associated demonstration—must be provided. The linguistic rules assume that such a demonstration accompanies each (demonstrative) use of a demonstrative. An incomplete demonstrative is not *vacuous* like an improper definite description. A demonstrative *can* be vacuous in various cases. For example, when its associated demonstration has no demonstratum (a hallucination)—or the wrong kind of demonstratum (pointing to a flower and saying 'he' in the belief that one is pointing to a man disguised as a flower[10])—or too many demonstrata (pointing to two intertwined vines and saying 'that vine'). But it is clear that one can distinguish

---

[9] However, a demonstration may also be opportune and require no special action on the speaker's part, as when someone shouts "Stop that man" while only one man is rushing toward the door. My notion of a demonstration is a theoretical concept. I do not, in the present work, undertake a detailed 'operational' analysis of this notion although there are scattered remarks relevant to the issue. I do consider, in XVI below, some alternative theoretical treatments of demonstrations.

[10] I am aware (1) that in some languages the so-called masculine gender pronoun may be appropriate for flowers, but it is not so in English; (2) that a background story can be provided that will make pointing at the flower a contextually appropriate, though deviant, way of referring to a man; for example, if we are talking of great hybridizers; and (3) that it is possible to treat the example as a *referential use* of the demonstrative 'he' on the model of Donnellan's referential use of a definite description (see "Reference and Definite Descriptions"). Under the referential use treatment we would assign as referent for 'he' whatever the speaker *intended to* demonstrate. I intended the example to exemplify a failed demonstration, thus a case in which the speaker, falsely believing the flower to be some man or other in disguise, but having no particular man in mind, and certainly not intending to refer to anything other than that man, says, pointing at the flower, "He has been following me around all day."

a demonstrative with a vacuous demonstration: no referent; from demonstrative with no associated demonstration: incomplete.

All this is by way of contrasting true demonstratives with pure indexicals. For the latter, *no associated demonstration is required, and any demonstration supplied is either for emphasis or is irrelevant.*[11] Among the pure indexicals are 'I', 'now', 'here' (in one sense), 'tomorrow', and others. The linguistic rules which govern *their* use fully determine the referent for each context.[12] No supplementary actions or intentions are needed. The speaker refers to himself when he uses 'I', and no pointing to another or believing that he is another or intending to refer to another can defeat this reference.[13]

Michael Bennett has noted that some indexicals have both a pure *and* a demonstrative use. 'Here' is a pure indexical in

I am in here

and is a demonstrative in

In two weeks, I will be here [pointing at a city on a map].

III. Two Obvious Principles

So much for preliminaries. My theory is based on two obvious principles. The first has been noted in every discussion of the subject.

> PRINCIPLE 1.   *The referent of a pure indexical depends on the context, and the referent of a demonstrative depends on the associated demonstration.*

If you and I both say 'I' we refer to different persons. The demonstratives 'that' and 'he' can be correctly used to refer to any one of a wide variety of objects simply by adjusting the accompanying demonstration.

The second obvious principle has less often been formulated explicitly.

> PRINCIPLE 2.   *Indexicals, pure and demonstrative alike, are directly referential.*

---

[11] I have in mind such cases as pointing at oneself while saying 'I' (emphasis) or pointing at someone else while saying 'I' (irrelevance or madness or what?).

[12] There are certain uses of pure indexicals that might be called 'messages recorded for later broadcast', which exhibit a special uncertainty as to the referent of 'here' and 'now'. If the message: "I am not here now" is recorded on a telephone answering device, it is to be assumed that the time referred to by 'now' is the time of playback rather than the time of recording. Donnellan has suggested that if there were typically a significant lag between our production of speech and its audition (for example, if sound traveled very very slowly), our language might contain two forms of 'now': one for the time of production, another for the time of audition. The indexicals 'here' and 'now' also suffer from vagueness regarding the size of the spatial and temporal neighborhoods to which they refer. These facts do not seem to me to slur the difference between demonstratives and pure indexicals.

[13] Of course it is certain intentions on the part of the speaker that make a particular vocable the first person singular pronoun rather a nickname for Irving. My semantic theory is a theory of word meaning, not speaker's meaning. It is based on linguistic rules known, explicitly or implicitly, by all competent users of the language.

IV. Remarks on Rigid Designators

In an earlier draft I adopted the terminology of Kripke, called indexicals 'rigid designators', and tried to explain that my usage differed from his. I am now shying away from that terminology. But because it is so well known, I will make some comments on the notion or notions involved.

The term 'rigid designator' was coined by Saul Kripke to characterize those expressions which designate the same thing in every possible world in which that thing exists and which designate nothing elsewhere. He uses it in connection with his controversial, though, I believe, correct claim that proper names, as well as many common nouns, are rigid designators. There is an unfortunate confusion in the idea that a proper name would designate nothing if the bearer of the name were not to exist.[14] Kripke himself adopts positions which seem inconsistent with this feature of rigid designators. In arguing that the object designated by a rigid designator need not exist in every possible world, he seems to assert that under certain circumstances what is expressed by 'Hitler does not exist' would have been true, and not because 'Hitler' would have designated nothing (in *that* case we might have given the sentence *no* truth-value) but because that 'Hitler' would have designated—namely Hitler—would not have existed.[15] Furthermore, it is a striking and important feature of the possible world semantics for quantified intensional logics, which Kripke did so much to create and popularize, that variables, those paradigms of rigid designation, designate the same individual in *all* possible worlds whether the individual "exists" or not.[16]

Whatever Kripke's intentions (did he, as I suspect, misdescribe his own concept?) and whatever associations or even meaning the phrase 'rigid designator' may have, I intend to use '*directly referential*' for an expression whose referent, once determined, is taken as fixed for all possible circumstances, i.e., is taken as *being* the propositional component.

For me, the intuitive idea is not that of an expression which *turns out* to designate the same object in all possible circumstances, but an expression whose

---

[14] I have discussed this and related issues in "Bob and Carol and Ted and Alice," in *Approaches to Natural Langauge*, ed. J. Hintikka et al. (Dordrecht: Reidel, 1973), especially appendix X.

[15] Kripke, *Naming and Necessity*, p. 78.

[16] The matter is even more complicated. There are two 'deifnitions' of 'rigid designator' in *Naming and Necessity*, pp. 48–49. The first conforms to what seems to me to have been the intended concept—same designation in *all* possible worlds—the second, scarcely a page later, conforms to the more widely held view that a rigid designator need not designate the object, or any object, at worlds in which the object does not exist. According to this conception a designator cannot, at a given world, designate something which does not exist in that world. The introduction of the notion of a *strongly* rigid designator—a rigid designator whose designatum exists in all possible worlds—suggests that the latter idea was upper most in Kripke's mind. (The second definition is given, unequivocally, on page 146 of "Identity and Necessity," in *Identity and Individuation*, ed. M. K. Munif.) (New York: New York University Press, 1971).) In spite of the textual evidence, systematic considerations, including the fact that variables cannot be accounted for otherwise, leave me with the conviction that the former notion was intended.

semantical *rules* provide *directly* that the referent in all possible circumstances is fixed to be the actual referent. In typical cases the semantical rules will do this only implicitly, by providing a way of determining the *actual* referent and no way of determining any other propositional component.[17]

We should beware of a certain confusion in interpreting the phrase 'designates the same object in all circumstances'. We do not mean that the expression *could not have been used* to designate a different object. We mean rather that given a *use* of the expression, we may ask of *what has been said* whether *it* would have been true or false in various counterfactual circumstances, and in such counterfactual circumstances, which are the individuals relevant to determining truth-value. Thus we must distinguish possible occasions of *use*—which I call *contexts*—from possible circumstances of *evaluation* of what was said on a given occasion of use. Possible circumstances of evaluation I call circumstances or, sometimes, just *counterfactual situations*. A directly referential term *may* designate different objects when used in different *contexts*. But when evaluating what was said in a given context, only a single object will be relevant to the evaluation in all circumstances. This sharp distinction between *contexts of use* and *circumstances of evaluation* must be kept in mind if we are to avoid a seeming conflict between Principles 1 and 2.[18] To look at the matter from another point of view, once we recognize the obviousness of both principles (I have not yet argued for Principle 2) the distinction between contexts of use and circumstances of evaluation is forced upon us.

If I may wax metaphysical in order to fix an image, let us think of the vehicles of evaluation—the what-is-said in a given context—as propositions. Don't think of propositions as sets of possible worlds, but rather as structured entities looking something like the sentences which express them. For each occurrence of a singular term in a sentence there will be a corresponding constituent in the proposition expressed. The constituent of the proposition determines, for each circumstance of evaluation, the object relevant to evaluating the proposition in that circumstance. In general, the constituent of the proposition will be some sort of complex, constructed from various attributes by logical composition. But in the case of a singular term which is directly referential, the constituent of the proposition is just the object itself. Thus it is that it does not just *turn out* that the constituent determines the same object in every circumstance, the constituent (corresponding to a rigid designator) just *is* the object. *There is no*

---

[17] Here, and in the preceding paragraph, in attempting to convey my notion of a directly referential singular term, I slide back and forth between two metaphysical pictures: that of possible worlds and that of structured propositions. It seems to me that a truly semantical idea should presuppose neither picture, and be expressible in terms of either. Kripke's discussion of rigid designators is, I believe, distorted by an excessive dependence on the possible worlds picture and the associated semantical style. For more on the relationship between the two pictures, see pages 724–25 of my "How to Russell a Frege-Church," *The Journal of Philosophy* 72 (1975):716–29.

[18] I think it likely that it was just the failure to notice this distinction that led to a failure to recognize Principle 2. Some of the history and consequences of the conflation of Context and Circumstance is discussed in section VI.

determining to do at all. On this picture—and this is *really* a picture and not a theory—the definite description

(1) The $n[($Snow is slight $\wedge\; n^2 = 9) \vee (\sim$Snow is slight $\wedge\; 2^2 = n + 1)]$[19]

would yield a constituent which is complex although it would determine the same object in all circumstances. Thus, (1), though a rigid designator, is not directly referential from this (metaphysical) point of view. Note, however, that every proposition which contains the complex expressed by (1) is *equivalent* to some singular proposition which contains just the number three itself as constituent.[20]

The semantical feature that *I* wish to highlight in calling an expression *directly referential* is not the *fact* that it designates the same object in every circumstance, but the *way* in which it designates an object in any circumstance. Such an expression is a *device of direct reference*. This does not imply that it has no conventionally fixed semantical rules which determine its referent in each context of use; quite the opposite. There are semantical rules which determine the referent in each context of use—but that is all. *The rules do not provide a complex which together with a circumstance of evaluation yields an object. They just provide an object.*

If we keep in mind our sharp distinction between contexts of use and circumstances of evaluation, we will not be tempted to confuse a rule which assigns an object to each *context* with a 'complex' which assigns an object to each *circumstance*. For example, each context has an *agent* (loosely, a speaker). Thus an appropriate designation rule for a directly referential term would be:

(2) In each possible context of use the given term refers to the agent of the context.

But this rule could not be used to assign a relevant object to each circumstance of evaluation. Circumstances of evaluation do not, in general, have agents. Suppose I say,

(3) I do not exist.

Under what circumstances would *what I said* be true? It would be true in circumstances in which I did not exist. Among such circumstances are those in which no one, and thus, no speakers, no agents exist. To search a circumstance of evaluation for a speaker in order to (mis)apply rule (2) would be to go off on an irrelevant chase.

Three paragraphs ago I sketched a metaphysical picture of the structure of a proposition. The picture is taken from the semantical parts of Russell's *Principles of Mathematics*.[21] Two years later, in "On Denoting,"[22] even Russell rejected that

---

[19] I would have used 'snow is white', but I wanted a contingent clause, and so many people (possibly including me) nowadays seem to have views which allow that 'snow is white' may be necessary.

[20] I am ignoring propositions expressed by sentences containing epistemic operators or others for which equivalence is not a sufficient condition for interchange of operand.

[21] Bertrand Russell, *The Principles of Mathematics* (London: Allen & Unwin, 1903).

[22] Bertrand Russell, "On Denoting," *Mind* 14 (1905):479–93.

picture. But I still like it. It is not a part of my theory, but it well conveys my conception of a directly referential expression and of the semantics of direct reference. (The picture needs *some* modification in order to avoid difficulties which Russell later noted—though he attributed them to Frege's theory rather than his own earlier theory.)[23]

If we adopt a possible worlds semantics, all directly referential terms will be regarded as rigid designators in the *modified* sense of an expression which designates the same thing in *all* possible worlds (irrespective of whether the thing exists in the possible world or not).[24] However, as already noted, I do not regard all rigid designators—not even all strongly rigid designators (those that designate something that exists in all possible worlds) or all rigid designators in the modified sense—as directly referential. I believe that proper names, like variables, are directly referential. They are not, in general, strongly rigid designators nor are they rigid designators in the original sense.[25] What is characteristic of directly referential terms is that the designatum (referent) determines the prepositional component rather than the prepositional component, along with a circumstance, determining the designatum. It is for this reason that a directly referential term that designates a contingently existing object will still be a rigid designator in the

---

[23] Here is a difficulty in Russell's 1903 picture that has some historical interest. Consider the proposition expressed by the sentence, 'The centre of mass of the Solar System is a point'. Call the proposition, '*P*'. *P* has in its subject place a certain complex, expressed by the definite description. Call the complex, 'Plexy'. We can describe Plexy as "the complex expressed by 'the center of mass of the solar system'." Can we produce a directly referential term which designates Plexy? Leaving aside for the moment the controversial question of whether 'Plexy' is such a term, let us imagine, as Russell believed, that we can directly refer to Plexy by affixing a kind of *meaning marks* (on the analogy of quotation marks) to the description itself. Now consider the sentence '^{m}the center of mass of the solar system^m is a point'. Because the subject of this sentence is directly referential and refers to Plexy, the proposition the sentence expresses will have as its subject constituent Plexy itself. A moment's reflection will reveal that this proposition is simply *P* again. But this is absurd since the two sentences speak about radically different objects.

(I believe the foregoing argument lies behind some of the largely incomprehensible arguments mounted by Russell against Frege in "On Denoting," though there are certainly other difficulties in that argument. It is not surprising that Russell there confused Frege's theory with his own of *Principle of Mathematics*. The first footnote of "On Denoting" asserts that the two theories are "very nearly the same.")

The solution to the difficulty is simple. Regard the 'object' places of a singular proposition as marked by some operation which cannot mark a complex. (There always will be some such operation.) For example, suppose that no complex is (represented by) a set containing a single member. Then we need only add $\{\ldots\}$ to mark the places in a singular proposition which correspond to directly referential terms. We no longer need worry about confusing a complex with a prepositional constituent corresponding to a directly referring term because no complex will have the form $\{x\}$. In particular, Plexy $\neq$ $\{$Plexy$\}$. This technique can also be used to resolve another confusion in Russell. He argued that a sentence containing a nondenoting directly referential term (he would have called it a nondenoting 'logically proper name') would be meaningless, presumably because the purported singular proposition would be incomplete. But the braces themselves can fill out the singular proposition, and if they contain nothing, no more anomalies need result than what the development of Free Logic has already inured us to.

[24] This is the *first sense* of footnote 16.

[25] This is the *second sense* of footnote 16.

modified sense. The propositional component need not choose its designatum from those offered by a passing circumstance; it has already secured its designatum before the encounter with the circumstance.

When we think in terms of possible world semantics this fundamental distinction becomes subliminal. This is because the style of the semantical rules obscures the distinction and makes it appear that directly referential terms differ from ordinary definite descriptions only in that the prepositional component in the former case must be a *constant* function of circumstances. In actual fact, the referent, in a circumstance, of a directly referential term is simply *independent* of the circumstance and is no more a function (constant or otherwise) of circumstance, than my action is a function of your desires when I decide to do it whether you like it or not. The distinction that is obscured by the style of possible world semantics is dramatized by the structured propositions picture. That is part of the reason why I like it.

Some directly referential terms, like proper names, may have no semantically relevant descriptive meaning, or at least none that is specific: that distinguishes one such term from another. Others, like the indexicals, may have a limited kind of specific descriptive meaning relevant to the features of a context of use. Still others, like 'dthat' terms (see below), may be associated with full-blown Fregean senses used to fix the referent. But in any case, the descriptive meaning of a directly referential term is no part of the propositional content.

V. Argument for Principle 2: Pure Indexicals

As stated earlier, I believe this principle is uncontroversial. But I had best distinguish it from similar principles which are false. I am *not* claiming, as has been claimed for proper names, that indexicals lack anything that might be called 'descriptive meaning'. Indexicals, in general, have a rather easily statable descriptive meaning. But it is clear that this meaning is relevant only to determining a referent in a context of use and *not* to determining a relevant individual in a circumstance of evaluation. Let us return to the example in connection with the sentence (3) and the indexical 'I'. The bizarre result of taking the descriptive meaning of the indexical to be the propositional constituent is that what I said in uttering (3) would be true in a circumstance of evaluation if and only if the speaker (assuming there is one) of the circumstance does not exist in the circumstance. Nonsense! It *that* were the correct analysis, what I said could not be true. From which it follows that

> It is impossible that I do not exist.

Here is another example to show that the descriptive meaning of an indexical may be entirely *inapplicable* in the circumstance of evaluation. When I say,

> I wish I were not speaking now

The circumstances desired do not involve contexts of *use* and *agents* who are not speaking. The *actual* context of use is used to determine the relevant individual: *me*—and time: *now*—and then we query the various circumstances of evaluation with respect to *that* individual and *that* time.

Here is another example, not of the inapplicability of the descriptive meaning of circumstances but of its irrelevance. Suppose I say at t_0, "It will soon be the case that all that is now beautiful is faded." Consider what was said in the subsentence,

> All that is now beautiful is faded.

I wish to evaluate that content at some near future time t_1. What is the relevant time associated with the indexical 'now'? Is it the future time t_1? No, it is t_0, of course: the time of the context of use.

See how rigidly the indexicals cling to the referent determined in the context of use:

(4) It is possible that in Pakistan, in five years, only those who are actually here now are envied.

The point of (4) is that the circumstance, place, and time referred to by the indexicals 'actually', 'here', and 'now' are the circumstance, place, and time of the *context*, not a circumstance, place, and time determined by the modal, locational, and temporal operators within whose scope the indexicals lie.

It may be objected that this only shows that indexicals always take *primary* scope (in the sense of Russell's scope of a definite description). This objection attempts to relegate all direct reference to implicit use of the paradigm of the semantics of direct reference, the variable. Thus (4) is transformed into,

> The actual circumstances, here, and now are such that it is possible that in Pakistan in five years only those who, in the first, are located at the second, during the third, are envied.

Although this may not be the most felicitous form of expression, its meaning and, in particular, its symbolization should be clear to those familiar with quantified intensional logics. The pronouns, 'the first', 'the second', and 'the third' are to be represented by distinct variables bound to existential quantifiers at the beginning and identified with 'the actual circumstance', 'here', and 'now' respectively.

(5) $(\exists w)(\exists p)(\exists t)\,[w = $ the actual circumstance $\wedge\, p = here \,\wedge\, t = now \wedge \Diamond$ in Pakistan in five years $\forall x\,(x$ is envised $\rightarrow x$ is located at p during t in $w)]$

But such transformations, when thought of as representing the claim that indexicals take primary scope, do not provide an *alternative* to Principle 2, since we may still ask of an utterance of (5) in a context c, when evaluating it with respect to an arbitrary circumstance, to what do the indexicals 'actual', 'here', and 'now' refer. The answer, as always, is: the relevant features of the context c. [In fact, although (4) is equivalent to (5), neither indexicals nor quantification across intensional operators is dispensable in favor of the other.]

Perhaps enough has been said to establish the following.

(T1) *The descriptive meaning of a pure indexical determines the referent of the indexical with respect to a context of use but is either inapplicable or irrelevant to determining a referent with respect to a circumstance of evaluation.*

I hope that your intuition will agree with mine that it is for this reason that:

(T2) *When what was said in using a pure indexical in a context c is to be evaluated with respect to an arbitrary circumstance, the relevant object is
always the referent of the indexical with respect to the context c.*

This is just a slightly elaborated version of Principle 2.

Before turning to true demonstratives, we will adopt some terminology.

VI. Terminological Remarks

Principle 1 and Principle 2 taken together imply that sentences containing pure
indexicals have two kinds of meaning.

VI. (i) Content and Circumstance

What is said in using a given indexical in different contexts may be different. Thus
if I say, today,

> I was insulted yesterday

and you utter the same words tomorrow, what is said is different. If what we say
differs in truth-value, that is enough to show that we say different things. But even
if the truth-values were the same, it is clear that there are possible circumstances
in which what I said would be true but what you said would be false. Thus we say
different things.

Let us call this first kind of meaning—what is said—*content*. The content of a
sentence in a given context is what has traditionally been called a proposition.
Strawson, in noting that the sentence

> The present king of France is bald

could be used on different occasions to make different statements, used 'statement' in a way similar to our use of *content of a sentence*. If we wish to express the
same content in different contexts, we may have to change indexicals. Frege, here
using 'thought' for content of a sentence, expresses the point well.

> If someone wants to say the same today as he expressed yesterday using the word
> 'today', he must replace this word with 'yesterday'. Although the thought is the
> same its verbal expression must be different so that the sense, which would oth-
> erwise be affected by the differing times of utterance, is readjusted.[26]

---

[26]From "The Thought: A Logical Inquiry," *Mind* 65 (1956):289–311. If Frege had only supplemented these comments with the observation that indexicals are devices of direct reference,
the whole theory of indexicals would have been his. But his theory of meaning blinded him to
this obvious point. Frege, I believe, mixed together the two kinds of meaning in what he called
Sinn. A *thought* is, for him, the *Sinn* of a sentence, or perhaps we should say a *complete* sentence. *Sinn* is to contain both "the manner and context of presentation [of the denotation],"
according to "Über Sinn und Bedeutung" (*Zeitschrift für Philosophie und philosophische*

(contd.)

I take *content* as a notion applying not only to sentences taken in a context but to any meaningful part of speech taken in a context. Thus we can speak of the content of a definite description, an indexical, a predicate, etc. It is *contents* that are evaluated in circumstances of evaluation. If the content is a proposition (i.e., the content of a sentence taken in some context), the result of the evaluation will be a truth-value. The result of evaluating the content of a singular term at a circumstance will be an object (what I earlier called 'the relevant object'). In general, the result of evaluating the content of a well-formed expression α at a circumstance will be an appropriate extension for α (i.e., for a sentence, a truth-value; for a term, an individual; for an n-place predicate, a set of n-tuples of individuals, etc.). This suggests that we can represent a content by a function from circumstances of evaluation to an appropriate extension. Carnap called such functions *intensions*.

The representation is a handy one and I will often speak of contents in terms of it, but one should note that contents which are distinct but equivalent (i.e., share a value in all circumstances) are represented by the same intension. Among other things, this results in the loss of my distinction between terms which are devices of direct reference and descriptions which *turn out* to be rigid designators. (Recall the metaphysical paragraph of section IV.) I wanted the content of an indexical to be just the referent itself, but the intension of such a content will be a constant function. Use of representing intensions does not mean I am abandoning that idea—just ignoring it temporarily.

A *fixed content* is one represented by a constant function. All directly referential expressions (as well as all rigid designators) have a fixed content. [What I elsewhere call a *stable* content.)

Let us settle on *circumstances* for possible circumstances of evaluation. By this I mean both actual and counterfactual situations with respect to which it is appropriate to ask for the extensions of a given well-formed expression. A circumstance will usually include a possible state or history of the world, a time, and perhaps other features as well. The amount of information we require from a circumstance is linked to the degree of specificity of contents, and thus to the kinds of operators in the language.

Operators of the familiar kind treated in intensional logic (modal, temporal, etc.) operate on contents. (Since we represent contents by intensions, it is not surprising that intensional operators operate on contents.) Thus an appropriate

---

Kritik 100 (1892); trans. as "On Sense and Nominatum," in *Contemporary Readings in Logical Theory*, ed. Copi and Gould (Macmillan, 1967); mistrans. as "On Sense and Meaning," in Martinich, *op. cit.*). *Sinn* is first introduced to represent the cognitive significance of a sign, and thus to solve Frege's problem: how can $\ulcorner \alpha = \beta \urcorner$ if true differ in cognitive significance from $\ulcorner \alpha = \alpha \urcorner$. However, it also is taken to represent the truth-conditions or *content* (in our sense). Frege felt the pull of the two notions, which he reflects in some tortured passages about 'I' in "The Thought" (quoted below in XVII). If one says "Today is beautiful" on Tuesday and "Yesterday was beautiful" on Wednesday, one expresses the same thought according to the passage quoted. Yet one can clearly lose track of the days and not realize one is expressing the same thought. It seems then that thoughts are not appropriate bearers of cognitive significance. I return to this topic in XVII. A detailed examination of Frege on demonstratives is contained in John Perry's "Frege on Demonstratives," *Philosophical Review* 86 (1977):474–97.

extension for an intensional operator is a function from intensions to extensions.[27]
A modal operator when applied to an intension will look at the behavior of the
intension with respect to the possible state of the world feature of the circumstances of evaluation. A temporal operator will, similarly, be concerned with the
time of the circumstance. If we built the time of evaluation into the contents (thus
removing time from the circumstances leaving only, say, a possible world history,
and making contents *specific* as to time), it would make no sense to have temporal operators. To put the point another way, if *what is said* is thought of as incorporating reference to a specific time, or state of the world, or whatever, it is otiose
to ask whether what is said would have been true at another time, in another state
of the world, or whatever. Temporal operators applied to eternal sentences (those
whose contents incorporate a specific time of evaluation) are redundant. Any
intensional operators applied to *perfect* sentences (those whose contents incorporate specific values for all features of circumstances) are redundant.[28]

---

[27]As we shall see, indexical operators such as "It is now the case that," "It is actually the case
that," and "dthat" (the last takes a term rather than a sentence as argument) are also intensional operators. They differ from the familiar operators in only two ways: first, their extension (the function from intensions to extensions) depends on context, and second, they are
directly referential (thus they have a fixed content). I shall argue below (in Section VIII:
Monsters) that all operators that can be given an English reading are 'at most' intensional.
Note that when discussing issues in terms of the formal representations of the model-
theoretic semantics, I tend to speak in terms of intensions and intensional operators rather
than contents and content operators.

[28]The notion of redundancy involved could be made precise. When I speak of building the
time of evaluation into contents, or making contents specific as to time, or taking what is
said to incorporate reference to a specific time, what I have in mind is this. Given a sentence S: 'I am writing', in the present context c, which of the following should we take as
the content: (i) the proposition that David Kaplan is writing at 10 A.M. on 3/26/77, or
(ii) the 'proposition' that David Kaplan is writing? The proposition (i) is specific as to
time, the 'proposition' (ii) (the scare quotes reflect my feeling that this is not the traditional notion of a proposition) is neutral with respect to time. If we take the content of S
in c to be (ii), we can ask whether it would be true at times other than the time of c. Thus
we think of the temporally neutral 'proposition' as changing its truth-value over time.
Note that it is not just the noneternal sentence S that changes its truth-value over time,
but the 'proposition' itself. Since the sentence S contains an indexical 'I', it will express different 'propositions' in different contexts. But since S contains no *temporal* indexical, the
time of the context will not influence the 'proposition' expressed. An alternative [and
more traditional] view is to say that the verb tense in S involves an implicit temporal
indexical, so that S is understood as synonymous with S': 'I am writing now'. If we take
this point of view we will take the content of S in c to be (i). In this case *what is said* is
eternal; it does not change its truth-value over time, although S will express different
propositions at different times.
 There are both technical and philosophical issues involved in choosing between (i) and
(ii). Philosophically, we may ask why the temporal indexical should be taken to be implicit
(making the proposition eternal) when no modal indexical is taken to be implicit. After
all, we *could* understand S as synonymous with S': 'I am actually writing now'. The content of S'' in c is not only eternal, it is perfect. Its truth changes neither through time nor
possibility. Is there some good philosophical reason for preferring contents which are neutral with respect to possibility but draw fixed values from the context for all other features
of a possible circumstance whether or not the sentence contains an explicit indexical?

(contd.)

What sorts of intensional operators to admit seems to me largely a matter of language engineering. It is a question of which features of what we intuitively think of as possible circumstances can be sufficiently well defined and isolated. If we wish to isolate location and regard it as a feature of possible circumstances we can introduce locational operators: 'Two miles north it is the case that', etc. Such operators can be iterated and can be mixed with modal and temporal operators. However, to make such operators interesting we must have contents which are locationally neutral. That is, it must be appropriate to ask if *what is said* would be true in Pakistan. (For example, 'It is raining' seems to be locationally as well as temporally and modally neutral.)

This functional notion of the content of a sentence in a context may not, because of the neutrality of content with respect to time and place, say, exactly correspond to the classical conception of a proposition. But the classical conception can be introduced by adding the demonstratives 'now' and 'here' to the sentence and taking the content of the result. I will continue to refer to the content of a sentence as a proposition, ignoring the classical use.

Before leaving the subject of circumstances of evaluation I should, perhaps, note that the mere attempt to show that an expression is directly referential requires that it be meaningful to ask of an individual in one circumstance whether and with what properties it exists in another circumstance. If such questions cannot be raised because they are regarded as metaphysically meaningless, the question of whether a particular expression is directly referential (or even, a rigid designator) cannot be raised. I have elsewhere referred to the view that such questions are meaningful as *haecceitism,* and I have described other metaphysical manifestations of this view.[29] I advocate this position, although I am uncomfortable with some of its seeming consequences (for example, that the world might be in a state qualitatively exactly as it is, but with a permutation of individuals).

It is hard to see how one could think about the semantics of indexicals and modality without adopting such a view.

(It may be that the traditional view was abetted by one of the delightful anomalies of the logic of indexicals, namely that S, S', and S'' are all logically equivalent! See Remark 3, p. 547.) Technically, we must note that intensional operators must, if they are not to be vacuous, operate on contents which are neutral with respect to the feature of circumstance the operator is interested in. Thus, for example, if we take the content of S to be (i), the application of a temporal operator to such a content would have no effect; the operator would be vacuous. Furthermore, if we do not wish the iteration of such operators to be vacuous, the content of the compound sentence containing the operator must again be neutral with respect to the relevant feature of circumstance. This is not to say that no such operator can have the effect of *fixing* the relevant feature and thus, in effect, rendering subsequent operations vacuous; indexical operators do just this. It is just that this must not be the general situation. A content must be the *kind* of entity that is subject to modification in the feature relevant to the operator. (The textual material to which this note is appended is too cryptic and should be rewritten.)

[29]"How to Russell a Frege-Church." The pronunciation is: "Heẋ-ee-i-tis-m." The epithet was suggested by Robert Adams. It is not an accident that it is derived from a demonstrative.

VI. (ii) Character

The second kind of meaning, most prominent in the case of indexicals, is that which determines the content in varying contexts. The rule,

> 'I' refers to the speaker or writer

is a meaning rule of the second kind. The phrase 'the speaker or writer' is not supposed to be a complete description, nor it is supposed to refer to the speaker or writer of the *word* 'I'. (There are many such.) It refers to the speaker or writer of the relevant *occurrence* of the word 'I', that is, the agent of the context.

Unfortunately, as usually stated, these meaning rules are incomplete in that they do not explicitly specify that the indexical is directly referential, and thus do not completely determine the content in each context. I will return to this later.

Let us call the second kind of meaning, *character*. The character of an expression is set by linguistic conventions and, in turn, determines the content of the expression in every context.[30] Because character is what is set by linguistic conventions, it is natural to think of it as *meaning* in the sense of what is known by the competent language user.

Just as it was convenient to represent contents by functions from possible circumstances to extensions (Carnap's intentions), so it is convenient to represent characters by functions from possible contexts to contents. (As before we have the drawback that equivalent characters are identified.[31]) This gives us the following picture:

Character: Contexts ⇒ Contents

Content: Circumstances ⇒ Extensions

---

[30] This does not imply that if you know the character and are in first one and then another context, you can *decide* whether the contents are the same. I may twice use 'here' on separate occasions and not recognize that the place is the same, or twice hear 'I' and not know if the content is the same. What I do know is this: if it was the same person speaking, then the content was the same. (More on this epistemological stuff later.)

[31] I am, at this stage, deliberately ignoring Kripke's theory of proper names in order to see whether the revisions in Fregean semantical theory, which seem plainly required to accommodate indexicals (this is the 'obviousness' of my theory), can throw any light on it. Here we assume that aside from indexicals, Frege's theory is correct, roughly, that words and phrases have a kind of descriptive meaning or sense which at one and the same time constitutes their cognitive significance and their conditions of applicability.

Kripke says repeatedly in *Naming and Necessity* that he is only providing a picture of how proper names refer and that he does not have an exact theory. His picture yields some startling results. In the case of indexicals we do have a rather precise theory, which avoids the difficulty of specifying a chain of communication and which yields many analogous results. In facing the vastly more difficult problems associated with a theory of reference for proper names, the theory of indexicals may prove useful; if only to show—as I believe—that proper names are not indexicals and have no meaning in the sense in which indexicals have meaning (namely a 'cognitive content' which fixes the references in all contexts). [The issues that arise, involving token reflexives, homonymous words with distinct character, and homonymous token reflexives with the same character are best saved for later—much later.]

or, in more familiar language,

Meaning + Context $\Rightarrow$ Intension

Intension + Possible World $\Rightarrow$ Extension

Indexicals have a *context-sensitive* character. It is characteristic of an indexical that its content varies with context. Nonindexicals have a *fixed* character. The same content is invoked in all contexts. This content will typically be sensitive to circumstances, that is, the non-indexicals are typically not rigid designators but will vary in extension from circumstance to circumstance. Eternal sentences are generally good examples of expressions with a fixed character.

All persons alive in 1977 will have died by 2077

expresses the same proposition no matter when said, by whom, or under what circumstances. The truth-value of that proposition may, of course, vary with possible circumstances, but the character is fixed. Sentences with fixed character are very useful to those wishing to leave historical records.

Now that we have two kinds of meaning in addition to extension. Frege's principle of intensional interchange[32] becomes two principles:

(F1) The character of the whole is a function of the character of the parts. That is, if two compound well-formed expressions differ only with respect to components which have the same Character, then the Character of the compounds is the same.

(F2) The Content of the whole is a function of the Content of the parts. That is, if two compound well-formed expressions, each set in (possibly different) contexts differ only with respect to components which *when taken in their respective contexts* have the same content, then the content of the two compounds *each taken in its own context* is the same.

It is the second principle that accounts for the often noted fact that speakers in different contexts can say the same thing by switching indexicals. (And indeed they often *must* switch indexicals to do so.) Frege illustrated this point with respect to 'today' and 'yesterday' in "The Thought." (But note that his treatment of 'I' suggests that he does not believe that utterances of 'I' and 'you' could be similarly related!)

Earlier, in my metaphysical phase, I suggested that we should think of the content of an indexical as being just the referent itself, and I resented the fact that the representation of contents as intensions forced us to regard such contents as constant functions. A similar remark applies here. If we are not overly concerned with standardized representations (which certainly have their value for model-theoretic investigations) we might be inclined to say that the character of an indexical-free word or phrase just *is* its (constant) content.

---

[32]See §28 of Rudolf Carnap's *Meaning and Necessity* (Chicago: University of Chicago Press, 1947).

VII. Earlier Attempts: Index Theory

The following picture seems to emerge. The meaning (character) of an indexical is a function from contexts to extensions (substituting for fixed contents). The meaning (content, substituting for fixed characters) of a nonindexical is a function from circumstances to extensions. From this point of view it may appear that the addition of indexicals requires no new *logic*, no sharp distinction between contexts and circumstances, just the addition of some special new *features* ('contextual' features) to the circumstances of evaluation. (For example, an *agent* to provide an interpretation for 'I'.) Thus an enlarged view of intension is derived. The intension of an expression is a function from certain factors to the extension of the expression (with respect to those factors). Originally such factors were simply possible states of the world, but as it was noticed that the so-called tense operators exhibited a structure highly analogous to that of the modal operators the factors with respect to which an extension was to be determined were enlarged to include moments of time. When it was noticed that contextual factors were required to determine the extension of sentences containing indexicals, a still more general notion was developed and called an "index." The extension of an expression was to be determined with respect to an index. The intension of an expression was that function which assigned to every index, the extension at that index.

> The above example supplies us with a statement whose truth-value is not constant but varies as a function of $i \in I$. This situation is easily appreciated in the context of time-dependent statements; that is, in the case where I represents the instant of time. Obviously the same statement can be true at one moment and false at another. For more general situations one must not think of the $i \in I$ as anything as simple as instants of time or even possible worlds. In general we will have
>
> $$i = (w, t, p, a, \ldots)$$
>
> where the index i has many *coordinates*: for example, w is a *world*, t is a *time*, $p = (x, y, z)$ is a (3-dimensional) *position* in the world, a is an *agent*, etc. All these coordinates can be varied, possibly independently, and thus affect the truth-values of statements which have indirect references to these coordinates. [From the *Advice* of a prominent logician.]

A sentence ϕ was taken to be logically true if true at every index (in every 'structure'), and $\Box\phi$ was taken to be true at a given index (in a given structure) just in case ϕ was true at every index (in that structure). Thus the familiar principle of modal generalization: if $\models \phi$ then $\models \Box\phi$, is validated.

This view, in its treatment of indexicals, was technically wrong and more importantly, conceptually misguided.

Consider the sentence

(6) I am here now.

It is obvious that for many choices of index—i.e., for many quadruples $\langle w, x, p, t \rangle$ where w is a possible world history, x is a person, p is a place and t is a time—(6) will be false. In fact, (6) is true only with respect to those indices $\langle w, x, p, t \rangle$ which are such that in the world history w, x is located at p at the time t. Thus (6) fares about on a par with

(7) David Kaplan is in Portland on 26 March 1977.

(7) is empirical, and so is (6).

But here we have missed something essential to our understanding of indexicals. Intuitively, (6) is deeply, and in some sense, which we will shortly make precise, universally, true. One need only understand the meaning of (6) to know that it cannot be uttered falsely. No such guarantees apply to (7). *A Logic of Indexicals* which does not reflect this intuitive difference between (6) and (7) has bypassed something essential to the logic of indexicals.

What has gone wrong? We have ignored the special relationship between 'I', 'here', and 'now'. Here is a proposed correction. Let the class of indices be narrowed to include only the *proper* ones—namely, those $\langle w, x, p, t \rangle$ such that in the world w, x *is* located at p at the time t. Such a move may have been intended originally since improper indices are like impossible worlds; no such contexts *could* exist and thus there is no interest in evaluating the extensions of expressions with respect to them. Our reform has the consequence that (6) comes out, correctly, to be logically true. Now consider

(8) □ I am here now.

Since the contained sentence (namely (6)) is true at every proper index, (8) also is true at every proper index and thus also is logically true. (As would be expected by the aforementioned principle of modal generalization.)

But (8) should not be *logically* true, since it is false. It is certainly *not* necessary that I be here now. But for several contingencies, I would be working in my garden now, or even delivering this paper in a location outside of Portland.

The difficulty, here, is the attempt to assimilate the role of a *context* to that of a *circumstance*. The indices $\langle w, x, p, t \rangle$ that represent contexts must be proper in order that (6) be a truth of the logic of indexicals, but the indices that represent circumstances must include improper ones in order that (8) *not* be a logical truth.

If one wishes to stay with this sort of index theory and blur the conceptual difference between context and circumstance, the minimal requirement is a system of *double* indexing, one index for context and another for circumstance. It is surprising, looking back, that we (for I was among the early index theorists) did not immediately see that double indexing was required, for in 1967, at UCLA, Hans Kamp had reported his work on 'now'[33] in which he had shown that double indexing was required to properly accommodate temporal indexicals along with the usual temporal operators. But it was *four* years before it was realized that this was a general requirement for (and, in a sense, the key to) a logic of indexicals.

However, mere double indexing, without a clear conceptual understanding of what each index stands for, is still not enough to avoid all pitfalls.

---

[33]Published in 1971 as "Formal Properties of 'Now'," *Theoria*.

VIII. Monsters Begat by Elegance

My liberality with respect to operators on content, i.e., intensional operators (any feature of the circumstances of evaluation that can be well defined and isolated) does not extend to operators which attempt to operate on character. Are there such operators as 'In some contexts it is true that', which when prefixed to a sentence yields a truth if and only if in some context the contained *sentence* (not the content expressed by it) expresses a content that is true in the circumstances of that context? Let us try it:

(9) In some contexts it is true that I am not tired now.

For (9) to be true in the present context it suffices that some agent of some context not be tired at the time of that context. (9), so interpreted, has nothing to do with me or the present moment. But this violates Principle 2! Principle 2 can also be expressed in more theory laden way by saying that indexicals always take primary scope. If this is true—and it is—then no operator can control the character of the indexicals within its scope, because they will simply leap out of its scope to the front of the operator. I am not saying we could not construct a language with such operators, just that English is not one.[34] And such operators *could not to be added to it.*

There *is* a way to control an indexical, to keep it from taking primary scope, and even to refer it to another context (this amounts to changing its character). Use quotation marks. If we *mention* the indexical rather than *use* it, we can, of course, operate directly on it. Carnap once pointed out to me how important the difference between direct and indirect quotation is in

Otto said "I am a fool."

Otto said that I am a fool.

Operators like 'In some contexts it is true that', which attempt to meddle with character, I call *monsters*. I claim that none can be expressed in English (without sneaking in a quotation device). If they stay in the metalanguage and confine their attention to sentences as in

In some contexts "I am not tired now" is true

they are rendered harmless and can even do socially useful work (as does, 'is valid' (see below).

I have gone on at perhaps excessive length about monsters because they have recently been begat by elegance. In a specific application of the theory of indexicals there will be just certain salient features of a circumstance of evaluation. So we may represent circumstances by indexed sets of features. This is typical of the model-theoretic way. As already indicated, all the features of a circumstance will generally be required as aspects of a context, and the aspects of a context may all

---

[34]Thomason alleges a counterinstance: 'Never put off until tomorrow what you can do today'. What should one say about this?

be features of a circumstance. If not, a little ingenuity may make it so.[35] We could then represent contexts by the same indexed sets we use to represent circumstances, and instead of having *a logic of contexts and circumstances* we have simply *a two-dimensional logic of indexed sets*. This is algebraically very neat and it permits a very simple and elegant description of certain important classes of characters (for example, those which are true at every pair $\langle i, i \rangle$, though the special significance of the set is somehow diminished in the abstract formulation).[36] But it also permits a simple and elegant introduction of many operators which are monsters. In abstracting from the distinct conceptual roles played by contexts of use and circumstances of evaluation the special logic of indexicals has been obscured. Of course restrictions can be put on the two-dimensional logic to exorcise the monsters, but to do so would be to give up the mathematical advantages of that formulation.[37]

IX. Argument for Principle 2: True Demonstratives

I return now to the argument that all indexicals are directly referential. Suppose I point at Paul and say,

> He now lives in Princeton, New Jersey.

Call *what I said*—i.e., the content of my utterance, the proposition expressed— 'Pat'. Is Pat true or false? True! Suppose that unbeknownst to me, Paul had moved

---

[35]Recall that in a particular formal theory the features of a circumstance must include all elements with respect to which there are content operators, and the aspects of a context must include all elements with respect to which there are indexicals. Thus, a language with both the usual modal operators '$\Diamond$', '$\Box$', and an indexical modal operator 'It is actually the case that' will contain a possible world history feature in its circumstances as well as an analogous aspect in its contexts. If a circumstance is an aspect of a context, as seems necessary for the definition of truth, then we only need worry about aspects of contexts that are not features of circumstances. The most prominent of these is the *agent* of the context, required to interpret the indexical 'I'. In order to supply a corresponding nonvacuous feature to circumstances we must treat contents in such a way that we can ask whether they are true for various agents. (Not *characters* mind you, but contents.) This can be done by representing the agent by a *neutral*—a term which plays the syntactical role of 'I' but gets an interpretation only with respect to a circumstance. Let a be a special variable that is not subject to quantification and let b be a variable not in the language. Our variable a is the neutral. We wish to introduce content operators which affect the agent place and which can be iterated. Let R be a relation between individuals, for example 'aRb' for 'b is an uncle of a'. Then we may interpret the operator $O^R \phi$ as $(\exists b)[aRb \wedge (\exists a) (b = a \wedge \phi)]$. If ϕ is 'a walks', $O^R \phi$ comes to 'an uncle of a walks'. The indexical 'I' can be represented by an operator O^I for which 'aRb' is just 'I $= b$'. The result should be that $O^I \phi$ is equivalent to replacing the neutral a by the indexical 'I'.

[36]See, for example, Krister Segerberg, "Two-dimensional Modal Logic," *Journal of Philosophical Logic* 2 (1973):77–96. Segerberg does metamathematical work in his article and makes no special philosophical claims about its significance. That has been done by others.

[37]There is one other difficulty in identifying the class of contexts with the class of circumstances. The special relationship between the indexicals 'I', 'here', 'now' seems to require that the agent of a context be at the location of the context during the time of the context. But this restriction is not plausible for arbitrary circumstances. It appears that this approach will have difficulty in avoiding the problems of (6) and (8) (section VII).

to Santa Monica last week. Would Pat have then been true or false? False! Now, the tricky case: Suppose that Paul and Charles had each disguised themselves as the other and had switched places. If that had happened, *and* I had uttered as I did, then the proposition I *would have* expressed would have been false. But in that possible context the proposition I *would have* expressed is not Pat. That is easy to see because the proposition I *would have* expressed, had I pointed to Charles instead of Paul—call this proposition 'Mike'—not only *would have* been false but actually is false. Pat, I would claim, would still be true in the circumstances of the envisaged possible context provided that Paul—in whatever costume he appeared—were still residing in Princeton.

IX. (i) The Arguments

I am arguing that in order to determine what the truth-value of a proposition expressed by a sentence containing a demonstrative *would be* under other possible circumstances, the relevant individual is not the individual that *would have* been demonstrated had those circumstances obtained and the demonstration been set in a context of those circumstances, but rather the individual demonstrated in the context which *did* generate the proposition being evaluated. As I have already noted, it is characteristic of sentences containing demonstratives— or, for that matter, any indexical—that they may express different propositions in different contexts. We must be wary of confusing the proposition that would have been expressed by a similar utterance in a slightly different context—say, one in which the demonstratum is changed—with the proposition that was actually expressed. If we keep this distinction in mind—i.e., we distinguish Pat and Mike— we are less likely to confuse what the truth-value of the proposition *actually* expressed would have been under some possible circumstances with what the truth-value of the proposition that *would have been* expressed would have been under those circumstances.

When we consider the vast array of possible circumstances with respect to which we might inquire into the truth of a proposition expressed in some context c by an utterance u, it quickly becomes apparent that only a small fraction of these circumstances will involve an utterance of the same sentence in a similar context, and that there must be a way of evaluating the truth-value of propositions expressed using demonstratives in counterfactual circumstances in which no demonstrations are taking place and no individual has the exact characteristics exploited in the demonstration. Surely, it is irrelevant to determining whether what I said would be true or not in some counterfactual circumstance, whether Paul, or anyone for that matter, *looked* as he does now. All that would be relevant is *where he lives*. Therefore,

(T3) The relevant features of the demonstratum *qua demonstratum* (compare, the relevant features of the x Fx *qua the x Fx*)—namely, that the speaker is pointing at it, that it has a certain appearance, is presented in a certain way—cannot be the essential characteristics used to identify the relevant individual in counterfactual situations.

These two arguments: the distinction between Pat and Mike, and consideration of counterfactual situations in which no demonstration occurs, are offered to support the view that demonstratives are devices of direct reference (rigid designators, if you will) and, by contrast, to reject a Fregean theory of demonstratives.

IX. (ii) The Fregean Theory of Demonstrations

In order to develop the latter theory, in contrast to my own, we turn first to a portion of the Fregean theory which I accept: the Fregean theory of demonstrations.

As you know, for a Fregean the paradigm of a meaningful expression is the definite description, which picks out or denotes an individual, a unique individual, satisfying a condition *s*. The individual is called the *denotation* of the definite description and the condition *s* we may identify with the *sense* of the definite description. Since a given individual may uniquely satisfy several distinct conditions, definite descriptions with distinct senses may have the same denotation. And since some conditions may be uniquely satisfied by no individual, a definite description may have a sense but no denotation. The condition by means of which a definite description picks out its denotation is *the manner of presentation* of the denotation by the definite description.

The Fregean theory of demonstratives claims, correctly I believe, that the analogy between descriptions (short for 'definite descriptions') and demonstrations is close enough to provide a sense and denotation analysis of the 'meaning' of a demonstration. The denotation is the demonstratum (that which is demonstrated), and it seems quite natural to regard each demonstration as presenting its demonstratum in a particular manner, which we may regard as the sense of the demonstration. The same individual could be demonstrated by demonstrations so different in manner of presentation that it would be informative to a competent auditor-observer to be told that the demonstrata were one. For example, it might be informative to you for me to tell you that

> That [pointing to Venus in the morning sky] is identical with that [pointing to Venus in the evening sky].

(I would, of course, have to speak very slowly.) The two demonstrations—call the first one 'Phos' and the second one 'Hes'—which accompanied the two occurrences of the demonstrative expression 'that' have the same demonstratum but distinct manners of presentation. It is this difference between the sense of Hes and the sense of Phos that accounts, the Fregean claims, for the informativeness of the assertion.

It is possible, to pursue the analogy, for a demonstration to have no demonstratum. This can arise in several ways: through hallucination, through carelessness (not noticing, in the darkened room, that the subject had jumped off the demonstration platform a few moments before the lecture began), through a sortal conflict (using the demonstrative phrase $\ulcorner$that $F\urcorner$, where F is a common noun phrase, while demonstrating something which is not an F), and in other ways.

Even Donnellan's important distinction between referential and attributive uses of definite descriptions seems to fit, equally comfortably, the case of demonstrations.[38]

The Fregean hypostatizes demonstrations in such a way that it is appropriate to ask of a given demonstration, say Phos, what *would* it have demonstrated under various counterfactual circumstances. Phos and Hes might have demonstrated distinct individuals.[39]

We should not allow our enthusiasm for analogy to overwhelm judgment in this case. There are some relevant respects in which descriptions and demonstrations are disanalogous. First, as David Lewis has pointed out, demonstrations do not have a syntax, a fixed formal structure in terms of whose elements we might try to define, either directly or recursively, the notion of sense.[40] Second, to different audiences (for example, the speaker, those sitting in front of the demonstration platform, and those sitting behind the demonstration platform) the same demonstration may have different senses. Or perhaps we should say that a single performance may involve distinct demonstrations from the perspective of distinct audiences. ("Exactly like proper names!" says the Fregean, "as long as the demonstratum remains the same, these fluctuations in sense are tolerable. But they should be avoided in the system of a demonstrative science and should not appear in a perfect vehicle of communication.")

IX. (iii) The Fregean Theory of Demonstratives

Let us accept, tentatively and cautiously, the Fregean theory of demonstrations, and turn now to the Fregean theory of demonstratives.[41]

According to the Fregean theory of demonstratives, an occurrence of a demonstrative expression functions rather like a place-holder for the associated demonstration. The sense of a sentence containing demonstratives is to be the result of replacing each demonstrative by a constant whose sense is given as the sense of the associated demonstration. An important aim of the Fregean theory is, of course, to solve Frege's problem. And it does that quite neatly. You recall that the Fregean accounted for the informativeness of

　　　that [Hes] = that [Phos]

---

[38] I have written elsewhere, in appendices VII and VIII of "Bob and Carol and Ted and Alice," of these matters and won't pursue the topic now.

[39] It could then be proposed that demonstrations be individuated by the principle: $d_1 = d_2$ if and only if, for all appropriate circumstances c, the demonstratum of d_1 in c = the demonstratum of d_2 in c. An alternative principle of individuation is that the same demonstration is being performed in two different contexts if the standard audience can't determine, from the demonstration alone, whether the contexts are distinct or identical. This makes the individuation of demonstrations more epistemological than the metaphysical proposal above.

[40] Although recent work on computer perception has attempted to identify a syntax of pictures. See P. Suppes and Rottmayer, "Automata," in *Handbook of Perception*, vol. 1 (New York: Academic Press, 1974).

[41] The Fregean theory of demonstrations is not a part of my obvious and uncontroversial theory of indexicals. On the contrary, it has the fascination of the speculative.

in terms of the distinct senses of Hes and Phos. Now we see that the senses of the two occurrences of 'that' are identified with these two distinct senses so that the ultimate solution is exactly like that given by Frege originally. The sense of the left 'that' differs from the sense of the right 'that'.

IX. (iv) Argument against the Fregean Theory of Demonstratives

Let us return now to our original example:

> He [Delta] now lives in Princeton, New Jersey

where 'Delta' is the name of the relevant demonstration. I assume that in the possible circumstances described earlier, Paul and Charles having disguised themselves as each other, Delta would have demonstrated Charles. Therefore, according to the Fregean theory, the proposition I just expressed, Pat, would have been false under the counterfactual circumstances of the switch. But this, as argued earlier, is wrong. Therefore, the Fregean theory of demonstratives, though it nicely solves Frege's problem, is simply incorrect in associating propositions with utterances.

Let me recapitulate. We compared two theories as to the proposition expressed by a sentence containing a demonstrative along with an associated demonstration. Both theories allow that the demonstration can be regarded as having both a sense and a demonstratum. My theory, the direct reference theory, claims that in assessing the proposition in counterfactual circumstances it is the actual demonstratum—in the example, Paul—that is the relevant individual. The Fregean theory claims that the proposition is to be construed as if the sense of the demonstration were the sense of the demonstrative. Thus, in counterfactual situations it is the individual that *would* have been demonstrated that is the relevant individual. According to the direct reference theory, demonstratives are rigid designators. According to the Fregean theory, their denotation varies in different counterfactual circumstances as the demonstrata of the associated demonstration would vary in those circumstances.

The earlier distinction between Pat and Mike, and the discussion of counterfactual circumstances in which, as we would now put it, the demonstration would have demonstrated nothing, argue that with respect to the problem of associating propositions with utterances the direct reference theory is correct and the Fregean theory is wrong.

I have carefully avoided arguing for the direct reference theory by using modal or subjunctive sentences for fear the Fregean would claim that the peculiarity of demonstratives is not that they are rigid designators but that they always take primary scope. If I had argued only on the basis of our intuitions as to the truth-value of

> If Charles and Paul had changed chairs, then he (Delta) would not now be living in Princeton

such a scope interpretation could be claimed. But I didn't.

The perceptive Fregeans among you will have noted that I have said nothing about how Frege's problem fares under a direct reference theory of demonstratives.

And indeed, if 'that' accompanied by a demonstration is a rigid designator for the demonstratum, then

> that (Hes) = that (Phos)

looks like two rigid designators designating the same thing. Uh oh! I will return to this in my Epistemological Remarks (section XVII).

X. Fixing the Reference vs. Supplying a Synonym[42]

The Fregean is to be forgiven. He has made a most natural mistake. Perhaps he thought as follows: If I point at someone and say 'he', that occurrence of 'he' must refer to the male at whom I am now pointing. It does! So far, so good. Therefore, the Fregean reasons, since 'he' (in its demonstrative sense) means the same as 'the male at whom I am now pointing' and since the denotation of the latter varies with circumstances the denotation of the former must also. But this is wrong. Simply because it is a rule of the language that 'he' *refers* to the male at whom I am now pointing (or, whom I am now demonstrating, to be more general), it does not follow that any synonymy is thereby established. In fact, this is one of those cases in which—to use Kripke's excellent idiom—the rule simply tells us how to *fix the reference* but does not supply a synonym.

Consider the proposition I express with the utterance

> He [Delta] is the male at whom I am now pointing.

Call that proposition 'Sean'. Now Sean is certainly true. We know from the rules of the language that any utterance of that form must express a true proposition. In fact we would be justified in calling the *sentence*

> He is the male at whom I am now pointing.

almost analytic. ('Almost' because of the hypothesis that the demonstrative is *proper*—that I am pointing at a unique male—is needed.)

But is Sean necessary? Certainly not, I might have pointed at someone else.

This kind of mistake—to confuse a semantical rule which tells how to fix the reference to a directly referential term with a rule which supplies a synonym—is easy to make. Since semantics must supply a meaning, in the sense of content (as I call it), for expressions, one thinks naturally that whatever way the referent of an expression is given by the semantical rules, that *way* must stand for the content of the expression. (Church [or was it Carnap?] says as much, explicitly.) This hypothesis seems especially plausible, when, as is typical of indexicals,

> the semantical rule which fixes the reference seems to exhaust our knowledge of the meaning of the expression.

---

[42]I use Kripke's terminology to expound the important distinction he introduces in *Naming and Necessity* for descriptive meaning that may be associated with a proper name. As in several other cases of such parallels between proper names and indexicals, the distinction, and its associated argument, seems more obvious when applied to indexicals.

X. (i) Reichenbach on Token Reflexives

It was from such a perspective, I believe, that Reichenbach built his ingenious theory of indexicals. Reichenbach called such expressions 'token-reflexive words' in accordance with his theory. He writes as follows:

> We saw that most individual-descriptions are constructed by reference to other individuals. Among these there is a class of descriptions in which the individual referred to is the act of speaking. We have special words to indicate this reference; such words are 'I', 'you', 'here', 'now', 'this'. Of the same sort are the tenses of verbs, since they determine time by reference to the time when the words are uttered. To understand the function of these words we have to make use of the distinction between *token* and *symbol*, 'token' meaning the individual sign, and 'symbol' meaning the class of similar tokens (cf. §2). Words and sentences are symbols. The words under consideration are words which refer to the corresponding token used in an individual act of speech, or writing; they may therefore be called *token-reflexive* words.
>
> It is easily seen that all these words can be defined in terms of the phrase 'this token'. The word 'I', for instance, means the same as 'the person who utters this token'; 'now' means the same as 'the time at which this token was uttered'; 'this table' means the same as 'the table pointed to by a gesture accompanying this token'. We therefore need inquire only into the meaning of the phrase 'this token'.[43]

But is it true, for example, that

(10) 'I' mean the same as 'the person who utters this token'?

It is certainly true that

I am the person who utters this token.

But if (10) correctly asserted a synonymy, then it would be true that

(11) If no one were to utter this token, I would not exist.

Beliefs such as (11) could make one a compulsive talker.

XI. The Meaning of Indexicals

In order to correctly and more explicitly state the semantical rule which the dictionary attempts to capture by the entry

I: the person who is speaking or writing

we would have to develop our semantical theory—the semantics of direct reference—and then state that

(D1) 'I' as an indexical, different utterances of which may have different contents

(D3) 'I' is, in each of its utterances, directly referential

(D2) In each of its utterances, 'I' refers to the person who utters it.

---

[43]H. Reichenbach, *Elements of Symbolic Logic* (New York: Macmillan, 1947), p. 284.

We have seen errors in the Fregean analysis of demonstratives and in Reichenbach's analysis of indexicals, all of which stemmed from failure to realize that these words are directly referential. When we say that a word is directly referential are we saying that its meaning *is* its reference (its only meaning is its reference, its meaning is nothing more than its reference)? Certainly not.[44] Insofar as meaning is given by the rules of a language and is what is known by competent speakers, I would be more inclined to say in the case of directly referential words and phrases that their reference is *no* part of their meaning. The meaning of the word 'I' does not change when different persons use it. The meaning of 'I' is given by the rules (D1), (D2), and (D3) above.

Meanings tell us how the content of a word or phrase is determined by the context of use. Thus the meaning of a word or phrase is what I have called its *character*. (Words and phrases with no indexical element express the same content in every context; they have a fixed character.) To supply a synonym for a word or phrase is to find another with the same *character;* finding another with the same *content* in a particular context certainly won't do. The content of 'I' used by me may be identical with the content of 'you' used by you. This doesn't make 'I' and 'you' synonyms. Frege noticed that if one wishes to say again what one said yesterday using 'today', today one must use 'yesterday'. (Incidentally the relevant passage, quoted on page 733, propounds what I take to be a direct reference theory of the indexicals 'today' and 'yesterday'.) But 'today' and 'yesterday' are not synonyms. For two words or phrases to be synonyms, they must have the same content in every context. In general, for indexicals, it is not possible to find synonyms. This is because indexicals are directly referential, and the compound phrases which can be used to give their reference ('the person who is speaking', 'the individual being demonstrated', etc.) are not.

XII. Dthat[45]

It would be useful to have a way of converting an arbitrary singular term into one which is directly referential.

Recall that we earlier regarded demonstrations, which are required to 'complete' demonstratives, as a kind of description. The demonstrative was then treated as a directly referential term whose referent was the demonstratum of the associated demonstration.

---

[44]We see here a drawback to the terminology 'direct reference'. It suggests falsely that the reference is not mediated by a meaning, which it is. The meaning (character) is directly associated, by convention, with the word. The meaning determines the referent; and the referent determines the content. It is this to which I alluded in the parenthetical remark following the lower picture on page 722. Note, however, that the kind of descriptive meaning involved in giving the character of indexicals like 'I', 'now', etc., is, because of the focus on context rather than circumstance, unlike that traditionally thought of as Fregean sense. It is the idea that the referent determines the content—that, contra Frege, there *is* a road back—that I wish to capture. This is the importance of Principle 2.

[45]Pronunciation note on 'dthat'. The word is not pronounced dee-that or duh-that. It has only one syllable. Although articulated differently from 'that' (the tongue begins behind the teeth), the sounds are virtually indistinguishable to all but native speakers.

Now why not regard descriptions as a kind of demonstration, and introduce a special demonstrative which requires completion by a description and which is treated as a directly referential term whose referent is the denotation of the associated description? Why not? Why not indeed! I have done so, and I write it thus:

dthat[α]

where α is any description, or, more generally, any singular term. 'Dthat' is simply the demonstrative 'that' with the following singular term functioning as its demonstration. (Unless you hold a Fregean theory of demonstratives, in which case its meaning is as stipulated above.)

Now we can come much closer to providing genuine synonyms.

'I' means the same as 'dthat [the person who utters this token]'.

(The fact that this alleged synonymy is cast in the theory of utterances rather than occurrences introduces some subtle complications, which have been discussed by Reichenbach.)

XIII. Contexts, Truth, and Logical Truth

I wish, in this section, to contrast an *occurrence* of a well-formed expression (my *technical* term for the combination of an expression and a context) with an *utterance* of an expression.

There are several arguments for my notion, but the main one is from Remark 1 on the Logic of Demonstratives (section XIX below): I have sometimes said that the content of a sentence in a context is, roughly, the proposition the sentence would express if uttered in that context. This description is not quite accurate on two counts. First, it is important to distinguish an *utterance* from a *sentence-in-a-context*. The former notion is from the theory of speech acts, the latter from semantics. Utterances take time, and utterances of distinct sentences cannot be simultaneous (i.e., in the same context). But in order to develop a logic of demonstratives we must be able to evaluate several premises and a conclusion all in the same context. We do not want arguments involving indexicals to become valid simply because there is no possible context in which all the premises are uttered, and thus no possible context in which all are uttered truthfully.

Since the content of an occurrence of a sentence containing indexicals depends on the context, the notion of *truth* must be relativized to a context.

If c is a context, then an occurrence of φ in c is true iff the content expressed by φ in this context is true when evaluated with respect to the circumstance of the context.

We see from the notion of truth that among other aspects of a context must be a possible circumstance. Every context occurs in a particular circumstance, and there are demonstratives such as 'actual' which refer to that circumstance.

If you try out the notion of truth on a few examples, you will see that it is correct. If I now utter a sentence, I will have uttered a truth just in case *what I said*, the content, is true in *these* circumstances.

As is now common for intensional logics, we provide for the notion of a *structure,* comprising a family of circumstances. Each such structure will determine a set of possible contexts. Truth in a structure, is truth in every possible context of the structure. Logical truth is truth in every structure.

XIV. Summary of Findings (so far): Pure Indexicals

Let me try now to summarize my findings regarding the semantics of demonstratives and other indexicals. First, let us consider the nondemonstrative indexicals such as 'I', 'here' (in its nondemonstrative sense), 'now', 'today', 'yesterday', etc. In the case of these words, the linguistic conventions which constitute *meaning* consist of rules specifying the referent of a given *occurrence* of the word (we might say, a given token, or even utterance, of the word, if we are willing to be somewhat less abstract) in terms of various features of the context of the occurrence. Although these rules fix the referent and, in a very special sense, might be said to define the indexical, the way in which the rules are given does not provide a synonym for the indexical. The rules tell us for any possible occurrence of the indexical what the referent would be, but they do *not* constitute the content of such an occurrence. Indexicals are directly referential. The rules tell us what it is that is referred to. Thus, they *determine* the content (the propositional constituent) for a particular occurrence of an indexical. But they are not a *part* of the content (they constitute no part of the propositional constituent). In order to keep clear on a topic where ambiguities constantly threaten, I have introduced two technical terms: *content* and *character* for the two kinds of meaning (in addition to extension) I associate with indexicals. Distinct occurrences of an indexical (in distinct contexts) may not only have distinct referents, they may have distinct meanings in the sense of *content*. If I say "I am tired today" today and Montgomery Furth says "I am tired today" tomorrow, our utterances have different contents in that the factors which are relevant to determining the truth-value of what Furth said in both actual and counterfactual circumstances are quite different from the factors which are relevant to determining the truth-value of what I said. Our two utterances are as different in content as are the sentences "David Kaplan is tired on 26 March 1977" and "Montgomery Furth is tired on 27 March 1977." But there is another sense of meaning in which, absent lexical or syntactical ambiguities, two occurrences of the *same* word or phrase *must* mean the same. (Otherwise how could we learn and communicate with language?) This sense of meaning—which I call *character*—is what determines the content of an occurrence of a word or phrase in a given context. For indexicals, the rules of language constitute the meaning in the sense of character. As normally expressed, in dictionaries and the like, these rules are incomplete in that, by omitting to mention that indexicals are directly referential, they fail to specify the full content of an occurrence of an indexical.

Three important features to keep in mind about these two kinds of meaning are:

1. Character applies only to words and phrases as types, content to occurrences of words and phrases in contexts.

2. Occurrences of two phrases can agree in content although the phrases differ in character, and two phrases can agree in character but differ in content in distinct contexts.

3. The relationship of character to content is something like that traditionally regarded as the relationship of sense to denotation, character is a way of presenting content.

XV. Further Details: Demonstratives and Demonstrations

Let me turn now to the demonstratives proper, those expressions which must be associated with a demonstration in order to determine a referent. In addition to the pure demonstratives 'that' and 'this' there are a variety of demonstratives which contain built-in sortals: 'he' for 'that male', 'she' for 'that female',[46] etc., and there are demonstrative phrases built from a pure demonstrative and a common noun phrase: 'that man drinking a martini', etc. Words and phrases which have demonstrative use may have other uses as well, for example, as bound variable or pronouns of laziness (anaphoric use).

I accept, tentatively and cautiously, the Fregean theory of demonstrations according to which:

(1) A demonstration is a way of presenting an individual.

(2) A given demonstration in certain counterfactual circumstances would have demonstrated (i.e., presented) an individual other than the individual actually demonstrated.

(3) A demonstration which fails to demonstrate any individual might have demonstrated one, and a demonstration which demonstrates an individual might have demonstrated no individual at all.

So far we have asserted that it is not an essential property of a given demonstration (according to the Fregean theory) that it demonstrate a given individual, or indeed, that it demonstrate any individual at all. It is this feature of demonstrations: that demonstrations which in fact demonstrate the same individual might have demonstrated distinct individuals, which provides a solution to the demonstrative version of Frege's problem (why is an utterance of 'that [Hes] = that [Phos]' informative?) analogous to Frege's own solution to the definite description version. There is some theoretical lattitude as to how we should regard such other features of a demonstration as its place, time, and agent. Just to fix ideas, let us regard all these features as accidental. (It

---

[46]'Male' and 'female' are here used in the grammatical sense of gender, not the biological sense.

may be helpful to think of demonstrations as *types* and particular perform-ances of them as their *tokens*). Then,

> (4) A given demonstration might have been mounted by someone other than its actual agent, and might be repeated in the same or a different place.

Although we are not now regarding the actual place and time of a demon-stration as essential to it, it does seem to me to be essential to a demonstration that it present its demonstrata from some perspective, that is, as the individual that looks thusly *from here now*. On the other hand, it does not seem to me to be essential to a demonstration that it be mounted by any agent at all.[47]

We now have a kind of standard form for demonstrations:

> The individual that has appearance A from here now

where an appearance is something like a picture with a little arrow pointing to the relevant subject. Trying to put it into words, a particular demonstration might come out like:

> The brightest heavenly body now visible from here.

In this example we see the importance of perspective. The same demonstration, differently located, may present a different demonstratum (a twin, for example).

If we set a demonstration, δ, in a context, c, we determine the relevant per-spective (i.e., the values of 'here' and 'now'). We also determine the demonstratum, if there is one—if, that is, in the circumstances of the context there is an individual that appears that way from the place and time of the context.[48] In setting δ and c we determine more than just the demonstratum in the possible world of the con-text. By fixing the perspective, we determine for each possible circumstance what, if anything, would appear like that from that perspective. This is to say, we deter-mine a *content*. This content will not, in general, be fixed (like that determined by a rigid designator). Although it was Venus that appeared a certain way from a cer-tain location in ancient Greece, it might have been Mars. Under certain counter-factual conditions, it *would* have been Mars that appeared just that way from just that location. Set in a different context, δ, may determine a quite different content or no content at all. When I look at myself in the mirror each morning I know that I didn't look like that ten years ago—and I suspect that nobody did.

---

[47] If the current speculations are accepted, then in the original discussion of Pat and Mike the emphasis on the counterfactual situation in which the same agent was doing the pointing was misguided and that feature of counterfactual situations is irrelevant. It is the agent of course who focuses your attention on the relevant local individual. But that needn't be done *by* any-one; we might have a convention that whoever is appearing on the demonstration platform is the demonstratum, or the speaker might take advantage of a natural demonstration of oppor-tunity: an explosion or a shooting star.

[48] Since, as remarked earlier, the speaker and different members of the audience generally have different perspectives on the demonstration, it may appear slightly different to each of them. Thus each may take a slightly different demonstration to have been performed. Insofar as the agent and audience of a given context can differ in location, the location of a context is the location of the agent. Therefore the demonstratum of a given demonstration set in a given context will be the individual, if any, thereby demonstrated from the speaker's point of view.

The preceding excursion into a more detailed Fregean theory of demonstrations was simply in order to establish the following structural features of demonstrations:

1. A demonstrations, when set in a context (i.e., an *occurrence* of a demonstration), determines a content.

2. It is not required that an occurrence of a demonstration have a fixed content.

In view of these features, we can associate with each demonstration a *character* which represents the 'meaning' or manner of presentation of the demonstration. We have now brought the semantics of demonstrations and descriptions into isomorphism.[49] Thus, I regard my 'dthat' operator as representing the general case of a demonstrative. Demonstratives are incomplete expressions which must be completed by a demonstration (type). A complete sentence (type) will include an associated demonstration (type) for each of its demonstratives. Thus each demonstrative, d, will be accompanied by a demonstration, δ, thus:

$d[\delta]$

The character of a *complete* demonstrative is given by the semantical rule:

In any context c, $d[\delta]$ is a directly referential term that designates the demonstratum, if any, of δ in c, and that otherwise designates nothing.

Obvious adjustments are to be made to take into account any common noun phrase which accompanies or is built-in to the demonstrative.

Since no immediately relevant structural differences have appeared between demonstrations and descriptions, I regard the treatment of the 'dthat' operator in the formal logic LD as accounting for the general case. It would be a simple matter to add to the syntax a category of 'nonlogical demonstration constants'. (Note that the indexicals of LD are all logical signs in the sense that their meaning [character] is not given by the structure but by the evaluation rules.)

XVI. Alternative Treatments of Demonstrations

The foregoing development of the Fregean theory of demonstrations is not inevitable. Michael Bennett has proposed that only places be demonstrata and that we require an explicit or implicit common noun phrase to accompany the demonstrative, so that:

that [pointing at a person]

becomes

dthat [the person who is there [pointing at a place]].

---

[49]We should not, of course, forget the many disanalogies noted earlier nor fail to note that though a description is associated with a particular character by linguistic *convention*, a demonstration is associated with *its* character by *nature*.

My findings do not include the claim that the—or better, a—Fregean theory of demonstrations is correct. I can provide an alternative account for those who regard demonstrations as nonrepeatable nonseparable features of contexts. The conception now under consideration is that in certain contexts the agent is demonstrating something, or more than one thing, and in others not. Thus just as we can speak of agent, time, place, and possible world history as features of a context, we may also speak of first demonstratum, second demonstratum, . . . (some of which may be null) as features of a context. We then attach subscripts to our demonstratives and regard the n-th demonstrative, when set in a context, as rigid designator of the n-th demonstratum of the context. Such a rule associates a character with each demonstrative. In providing no role for demonstrations as separable 'manners of presentation' this theory eliminates the interesting distinction between demonstratives and other indexicals. We might call it the *Indexical theory of demonstratives*. (Of course every reasonable theory of demonstratives treats them as indexicals of some kind. I regard my own theory of indexicals in general, and the nondemonstrative indexicals in particular, as essentially uncontroversial. Therefore I reserve *Indexical theory of demonstratives* for the controversial alternative to the Fregean theory of demonstrations—the Fregean theory of demonstra*tives* having been refuted.)

Let us call my theory as based on the Fregean theory of demonstrations the *Corrected Fregean theory of demonstratives*. The Fregean theory of demonstrations may be extravagant, but compared with its riches, the indexical theory is a mean thing. From a logical point of view, the riches of the Corrected Fregean theory of demonstratives are already available in connection with the demonstrative 'dthat' and its descriptive pseudodemonstrations, so a decision to enlarge the language of LD with additional demonstratives whose semantics are in accord with the Indexical theory need not be too greatly lamented.

If we consider Frege's problem, we have the two formulations:

that [Hes] = that [Phos]

and

$that_1 = that_2$

Both provide their sentence with an informative character. But the Fregean idea that that very demonstration might have picked out a different demonstratum seems to me to capture more of the epistemological situation than the Indexicalist's idea that in some contexts the first and second demonstrata differ.

The Corrected Fregean theory, by incorporating demonstration types in its sentence types, accounts for more differences in informativeness as differences in meaning (character). It thereby provides a nice Frege-type solution to many Frege-type problems. But it can only forestall the resort to directly epistemological issues, it cannot hold them in abeyance indefinitely. Therefore I turn to epistemological remarks.

XVII. Epistemological Remarks[50]

How do content and character serve as objects of thought? Let us state, once again, Frege's problem

(FP) How can (an occurrence of) $\ulcorner \alpha = \beta \urcorner$ (in a given context), if true, differ in cognitive significance from (an occurrence of) $\ulcorner \alpha = \alpha \urcorner$ (in the same context)?

In (FP) α, β are arbitrary singular terms. (In future formulations, I will omit the parentheticals as understood.) When α and β are demonstrative free, Frege explained the difference in terms of his notion of sense. A notion which, his writings generally suggest, should be identified with our *content*. But it is clear that Frege's problem can be reinstituted in a form in which resort to contents will not explain differences in 'cognitive significance'. We need only ask,

(FPD) How can $\ulcorner$ dthat$[\alpha] = $ dthat $[\beta] \urcorner$ if true, differ in cognitive significance from $\ulcorner$ dthat$[\alpha] = $ dthat$[\alpha] \urcorner$?

Since, as we shall show, for any term γ,

$\ulcorner \gamma = $ dthat$[\gamma] \urcorner$ is analytic

the sentence pair in (FP) will differ in cognitive significance if and only if the sentence pair in (FPD) differ similarly. [There are a few assumptions built in here, but they are O.K.] Note, however, that the *content* of $\ulcorner$ dthat$[\alpha] \urcorner$ and the *content* of $\ulcorner$ d that$[\beta] \urcorner$ are the same whenever $\ulcorner \alpha = \beta \urcorner$ is true. Thus the difference in cognitive significance between the sentence pair in (FPD) cannot be accounted for in terms of content.

If Frege's solution to (FP) was correct, then α and β have different contents. From this it follows that $\ulcorner$ dthat$[\alpha] \urcorner$ and $\ulcorner$ dthat$[\beta] \urcorner$ have different characters. (It doesn't really, because of the identification of contents with intensions, but let it pass.) Is character, then, the object of thought?

If you and I both say to ourselves,

(B) "I am getting bored"

have we thought the same thing? We could not have, because what you thought was true while what I thought was false.

What we must do is disentangle two epistemological notions: *the objects of thought* (what Frege called "Thoughts") and the *cognitive significance of an object of thought*. As has been noted above, a character may be likened to a manner of presentation of a content. This suggests that we identify objects of thought with contents and the cognitive significance of such objects with characters.

> E. PRINCIPLE 1.   *Objects of thought (Thoughts) = Contents*
> E. PRINCIPLE 2.   *Cognitive significance of a Thought = Character*

---

[50]This section has benefited from the opportunity to read, and discuss with him, John Perry's paper "Frege on Demonstratives."

According to this view, the thoughts associated with $\ulcorner\text{dthat}[\alpha] = \text{dthat}[\beta]\urcorner$ and $\ulcorner\text{dthat}[\alpha] = \text{dthat}[\alpha]\urcorner$ are the same, but the thought (not the denotation, mind you, but the *thought*) is *presented* differently.

It is important to see that we have not *simply* generalized Frege's theory, providing a higher order Fregean sense for each name of a regular Fregean sense.[51] In Frege's theory, a given manner of presentation presents the same object to all mankind,[52] But for us, a given manner of presentation—a character—what we both said to ourselves when we both said (B)—will, in general, present different objects (of thought) to different persons (and even different Thoughts to the same person at different times).

How then can we claim that we have captured the idea of cognitive significance? To break the link between cognitive significance and universal Fregean senses and at the same time forge the link between cognitive significance and character we must come to see the *context-sensitivity* (dare I call it ego-orientation?) of cognitive states.

Let us try a Putnam-like experiment. We raise two identical twins, Castor and Pollux, under qualitatively identical conditions, qualitatively identical stimuli, etc. If necessary, we may monitor their brain states and make small corrections in their brain structures if they begin drifting apart. They respond to all cognitive stimuli in identical fashion.[53] Have we not been successful in achieving the same cognitive (i.e., psychological) state? Of course we have, what more could one ask! But wait, they believe different things. Each sincerely says,

My brother was born before I was

and the beliefs they thereby express conflict. In this, Castor speaks the truth, while Pollux speaks falsely. This does not reflect on the identity of their cognitive states, for, as Putnam has emphasized, circumstances alone do not determine extension (here, the truth-value) from cognitive state. Insofar as distinct persons can be in the same cognitive state, Castor and Pollux are.

E. COROLLARY 1.   *It is an almost inevitable consequence of the fact that two persons are in the* same *cognitive state, that they will* disagree *in their attitudes toward some object of thought.*

---

[51] According to Church, such higher order Fregean senses are already called for by Frege's theory.

[52] See his remarks in "On Sense and Nominatum" regarding the "common treasure of thoughts which is transmitted from generation to generation" and remarks there and in "The Thought" in connection with tensed sentences, that "Only a sentence supplemented by a time-indication and complete in every respect expresses a thought."

[53] Perhaps it should be mentioned here, to forestall an objection, that neither uses a proper name for the other or for himself—only 'my brother' and 'I'—and that raising them required a lot of environmental work to maintain the necessary symmetries, or, alternatively, a lot of work with the brain state machine. If proper names are present, and each uses a different name for himself (or, for the other), they will never achieve the same *total* cognitive state since one will sincerely say, "I am Castor" and the other will not. They may still achieve the same cognitive state in its relevant part.

The corollary applies equally well to the same person at different times, and to the same person at the same time in different circumstances.[54] In general, the corollary applies to any individuals x, y in different contexts.

My aim was to argue that the cognitive significance of a word or phrase was to be identified with its character, the way the content is presented to us. In discussing the twins, I tried to show that persons could be in the same total cognitive state and still, as we would say, believe different things. This doesn't prove that the cognitive content of, say, a single sentence or even a word is to be identified with its character, but it strongly suggests it.

Let me try a different line of argument. We agree that a given content may be presented under various characters and that consequently we may hold a propositional attitude toward a given content under one character but not under another. (For example, on March 27 of this year, having lost track of the date, I may continue to hope to be finished by this March 26, without hoping to be finished by yesterday.) Now instead of arguing that character is what we would ordinarily call cognitive significance, let me just ask why we should be interested in the character under which we hold our various attitudes. Why should we be interested in that special kind of significance that is sensitive to the use of indexicals; 'I', 'here', 'now', 'that', and the like? John Perry, in his stimulating and insightful paper "Frege on Demonstratives" asks and answers this question. (Perry uses 'thought' where I would use 'object of thought' or 'content', he uses 'apprehend' for 'believe' but *note that other psychological verbs would yield analogous cases.* I have taken a few liberties in substituting my own terminology for Perry's and have added the emphasis.)

> Why should we care under what character someone apprehends a thought, so long as he does? I can only sketch the barest suggestion of an answer here. *We use the manner of presentation, the character, to individuate psychological states, in explaining and predicting action.* It is the manner of presentation, the character and not the thought apprehended, that is tied to human action. When you and I have beliefs under the common character of 'A bear is about to attack me', we behave similarly. We both roll up in a ball and try to be as still as possible. Different thoughts apprehended, same character, same behavior. When you and I both apprehend that I am about to be attacked by a bear, we behave differently. I roll up in a ball, you run to get help. Same thought apprehended, different characters, different behaviors.[55]

Perry's examples can be easily multiplied. My hope to be finished by a certain time is sensitive to how the content corresponding to the time is presented, as 'yesterday' or as 'this March 26'. If I see, reflected in a window, the image of a man whose pants appear to be on fire, my behavior is sensitive to whether I think, 'His pants are on fire' or 'My pants are on fire', though the object of thought may be the same.

---

[54] The corollary would also apply to the same person at the same time in the same circumstances but in different places, if such could be.

[55] John Perry, "Frege on Demonstratives," p. 494.

So long as Frege confined his attention to indexical free expressions, and given his theory of proper names, it is not surprising that he did not distinguish objects of thought (content) from cognitive significance (character), for that is the realm of *fixed* character and thus, as already remarked, there is a natural identification of character with content. Frege does, however, discuss indexicals in two places. The first passage, in which he discusses 'yesterday' and 'today' I have already discussed. Everything he says there is essentially correct. (He does not go far enough.) The second passage has provoked few endorsements and much skepticism. It too, I believe, is susceptible of an interpretation which makes it essentially correct. I quote it in full.

> Now everyone is presented to himself in a particular and primitive way, in which he is presented to no one else. So, when Dr. Lauben thinks that he has been wounded, he will probably take as a basis this primitive way in which he is presented to himself. And only Dr. Lauben himself can grasp thoughts determined in this way. But now he may want to communicate with others. He cannot communicate a thought which he alone can grasp. Therefore, if he now says 'I have been wounded', he must use the 'I' in a sense that can be grasped by others, perhaps in the sense of 'he who is speaking to you at this moment', by doing which he makes the associated conditions of his utterance serve for the expression of his thought.[56]

What is the particular and primitive way in which Dr. Lauben is presented to himself? What cognitive content presents Dr. Lauben to himself, but presents him to nobody else? Thoughts determined this way can be grasped by Dr. Lauben, but no one else can grasp *that* thought determined in *that* way. The answer, I believe, is, simply, that Dr. Lauben is presented to himself under the character of 'I'.

A sloppy thinker might succumb to the temptation to slide from an acknowledgement of the privileged *perspective* we each have on ourselves—only I can refer to me as 'I'—to the conclusions: first, that this perspective necessarily yields a privileged *picture* of what is seen (referred to), and second, that this picture is what is intended when one makes use of the privileged perspective (by saying 'I'). These conclusions, even if correct, are not forced upon us. The character of 'I' provides the acknowledged privileged perspective, whereas the analysis of the content of particular occurrences of 'I' provides for (and needs) no privileged pictures. There may be metaphysical, epistemological, or ethical reasons why I (so conceived) am especially *important* to myself. (Compare: why *now* is an especially important time to me. It too is presented in a particular and primitive way, and this moment cannot be presented at any other time in the same way.)[57] But the phenomenon noted by Frege—that everyone is presented to himself in a particular and primitive way—can be fully accounted for using only our semantical theory.

Furthermore, regarding the first conclusion, I sincerely doubt that there is, for each of us on each occasion of the use of 'I', a particular, primitive, and incommunicable Fregean self-concept which we tacitly express to ourselves. And regarding

---

[56]Gottlob Frege, "The Thought: A Logical Inquiry," p. 298.

[57]At other times, earlier and later, we can know it only externally, by description as it were. But now we are directly acquainted with it. (I believe I owe this point to John Perry.)

the second conclusion: even if Castor were sufficiently narcissistic to associate such self-concepts with his every use of 'I', his twin, Pollux, whose mental life is qualitatively identical with Castor's, would associate the *same* self-concept with *his* every (matching) use of 'I'.[58] The second conclusion would lead to the absurd result that when Castor and Pollux each say 'I', they do not thereby distinguish themselves from one another. (An even more astonishing result is possible. Suppose that due to a bit of self-deception the self-concept held in common by Castor and Pollux fits neither of them. The second conclusion then leads irresistibly to the possibility that when Castor and Pollux each say 'I' they each refer to a third party!)

The perceptive reader will have noticed that the conclusions of the sloppy thinker regarding the pure indexical 'I' are not unlike those of the Fregean regarding true demonstratives. The sloppy thinker has adopted a *demonstrative theory of indexicals:* 'I' is synonymous with 'this person' (along with an appropriate *subjective* demonstration), 'now' with 'this time', 'here' with 'this place' (each associated with some demonstration), etc. Like the Fregean, the sloppy thinker errs in believing that the sense of the demonstration is the sense of the indexical, but the sloppy thinker commits an additional error in believing that such senses are in any way necessarily associated with uses of pure indexicals. The slide from privileged perspective to privileged picture is the sloppy thinker's original sin. Only one who is located in the exact center of the Sahara Desert is entitled to refer to that place as 'here', but aside from that, the place may present no distinguishing features.[59]

The sloppy thinker's conclusions may have another source. Failure to distinguish between the cognitive significance of a thought and the thought itself seems

---

[58] Unless, of course, the self-concept involved a bit of direct reference. In which case (when direct reference is admitted) there seems no need for the whole theory of Fregean self-concepts. Unless, of course, direct reference is limited to items of direct acquaintance, of which more below.

[59] So far, we have limited our attention to the first three sentences of the quotation from Frege. How are we to account for the second part of Frege's remarks?

Suppose Dr. Lauben wants to communicate his thought without disturbing its cognitive content. (Think of trying to tell a color-blind person that the green light should be replaced. You would have to find another way of communicating what you wanted to get across.) He can't communicate *that* thought with *that* significance, so, he himself would have to attach a nonstandard significance to 'I'. Here is a suggestion. He points at his auditor and uses the demonstrative 'you'. If we neglect fine differences in perspective, the demonstration will have the same character for all present and it certainly will have the same demonstratum for all present, therefore the demonstrative will have the same *character and content* for all present. The indexical 'now' will certainly have the same character and content for all present. Thus 'the person who is speaking to you [points] now' will have a common character and content for all those present. Unfortunately the content is not that of 'I' as Dr. Lauben standardly uses it. He needs a demonstrative like 'dthat' to convert the description to a term with a fixed content. He chooses the demonstrative 'he', with a relative clause construction to make clear his intention. Now, if Dr. Lauben uses 'I' with the nonstandard meaning usually attached to 'he who is speaking to you [points] now' he will have found a way to communicate his original thought in a form whose cognitive significance is common to all. Very clever, Dr. Lauben.

[Perhaps it is poor pedagogy to join this fanciful interpretation of the second part of the passage with the serious interpretation of the first part.]

to have led some to believe that the elements of an object of thought must each be directly accessible to the mind. From this it follows that if a singular proposition is an object of thought, the thinker must somehow be immediately acquainted with each of the individuals involved. But, as we have seen, the situation is rather different from this. Singular propositions may be presented to us under characters which neither imply nor presuppose any special form of acquaintance with the individuals of the singular propositions. The psychological states, perhaps even the epistemological situations, of Castor and Pollux are alike, yet they assert distinct singular propositions when they each say 'My brother was born before me'. Had they lived at different times they might still have been situated alike epistemologically while asserting distinct singular propositions in saying 'It is quiet here now'. A kidnapped heiress, locked in the trunk of a car, knowing neither the time nor where she is, may think 'It is quiet here now' and the indexicals will remain directly *referential*.[60]

E. COROLLARY 2.   *Ignorance of the referent does not defeat the directly referential character of indexicals.*

From this it follows that a special form of knowledge of an object is neither required nor presupposed in order that a person may entertain as object of thought a singular proposition involving that object.

There is nothing inaccessible to the mind about the semantics of direct reference, even when the reference is to that which we know only by description. What allows us to take various propositional attitudes towards singular propositions is not the form of our acquaintance with the objects but is rather our ability to manipulate the conceptual apparatus of direct reference.[61]

The foregoing remarks are aimed at refuting *Direct Acquaintance Theories of direct reference*. According to such theories, the question whether an utterance expresses a singular proposition turns, in the first instance, on the speaker's *knowledge of the referent* rather than on the *form of the reference*. If the speaker lacks the appropriate form of acquaintance with the referent, the utterance cannot express a singular proposition, and any apparently directly referring expressions used must be abbreviations or disguises for something like Fregean descriptions. Perhaps the Direct Acquaintance theorist thought that only a theory like his could permit singular propositions while still providing a solution for Frege's problem. If we could *directly* refer to a given object in nonequivalent ways (e.g., as 'dthat[Hes]' and 'dthat[Phos]'.), we could not—so he thought—explain the difference in cognitive significance between the appropriate instances of $\ulcorner \alpha = \alpha \urcorner$ and $\ulcorner \alpha = \beta \urcorner$. Hence, the objects susceptible to direct reference must not permit such reference in inequivalent ways. These objects must, in a certain sense, be

---

[60] Can the heiress plead that she could not have believed a singular proposition involving the place p since when thinking 'here' she didn't *know*, she was at p, that she was, in fact, unacquainted with the place p? No! Ignorance of the referent is no excuse.

[61] This makes it sound as if an exact and conscious mastery of semantics is prerequisite to having a singular proposition as object of thought. I will try to find a better way to express the point in a succeeding draft.

wholly local and completely given so that for any two *directly* coreferential terms α and β, $\ulcorner \alpha = \beta \urcorner$ will be uninformative to anyone appropriately situated, epistemologically, to be able to use these terms.[62] I hope that my discussion of the two kinds of meaning—content and character—will have shown the Direct Acquaintance theorist that his views are not the inevitable consequence of the admission of directly referential terms. From the point of view of a lover of direct reference this is good, since the Direct Acquaintance theorist admits direct reference in a portion of language so narrow that it is used only by philosophers.[63]

I have said nothing to dispute the epistemology of the Direct Acquaintance theorist, nothing to deny that there exists his special kind of object with which one can have his special kind of acquaintance. I have only denied the relevance of these epistemological claims to the semantics of direct reference. If we sweep aside metaphysical and epistemological pseudo-explanations of what are essentially semantical phenomena, the result can only be healthy for all three disciplines.

Before going on to further examples of the tendency to confuse metaphysical and epistemological matters with phenomena of the semantics of direct reference, I want to briefly raise the problem of *cognitive dynamics*. Suppose that yesterday you said, and believed it, "It is a nice day today." What does it mean to say, today, that you have retained *that* belief? It seems unsatisfactory to just believe the same content under any old character—where is the *retention?*[64] You *can't* believe that content under the same character. Is there some obvious standard adjustment to make to the character, for example, replacing *today* with *yesterday?* If so, then a person like Rip van Winkle, who loses track of time, can't retain any such beliefs.

---

[62]For some consequences of this view with regard to the interpretation of demonstratives see "Bob and Carol and Ted and Alice," appendix VII.

[63]There is an obvious connection between the fix in which the Direct Acquaintance theorist finds himself, and *Kripke's problem:* how can $\ulcorner \alpha = \beta \urcorner$ be informative if α and β differ in neither denotation nor sense (nor, as I shall suggest is the case for proper names, character)?

[64]The sort of case I have in mind is this. I first think, "His pants are on fire." I later realize, "I am he" and thus come to think "My pants are on fire." Still later, I decide that I was wrong in thinking "I am he" and conclude "His pants were on fire." If, in fact, I *am* he, have I *retained* my belief that my pants are on fire simply because I believe the same content, though under a different character? (I also deny that content under the former, but for change of tense, character.) When I first thought "My pants are on fire," a certain singular proposition, call it 'Eek', was the object of thought. At the later stage, both Eek and its negation are believed by me. In this sense, I still believe what I believed before, namely Eek. But this does not capture my sense of *retaining a belief:* a sense that I associate with saying that some people have a very rigid cognitive structure whereas others are very flexible. It is tempting to say that cognitive dynamics is concerned not with retention and change in what is believed, but with retention and change in the characters under which our beliefs are held. I think that this is basically correct. But it is not obvious to me what relation between a character under which a belief is held at one time and the set of characters under which beliefs are held at a later time would constitute retaining the original belief. Where indexicals are involved, for the reasons given below, we cannot simply require that the very same character still appear at the later time. Thus the problem of cognitive dynamics can be put like this: what does it mean to say of an individual who at one time sincerely asserted a sentence containing indexicals that at some later time he has (or has not) *changed his mind* with respect to his assertion? What sentence or sentences must he be willing to assert at the later time?

This seems strange. Can we only *retain* beliefs presented under a fixed character? This issue has obvious and important connections with Lauben's problem in trying to communicate the thought he expresses with 'I have been wounded'. Under what character must his auditor believe Lauben's thought in order for Lauben's communication to have been successful? It is important to note that if Lauben said 'I am wounded' in the usual meaning of 'I', there is no one else who can report what he said, using *indirect* discourse, and convey the cognitive significance (to Lauben) of what he said. This is connected with points made in section VIII, and has interesting consequences for the inevitability of so-called *de re* constructions in indirect discourse languages which contain indexicals. (I use 'indirect discourse' as a general term for the analogous form of all psychological verbs.)

A prime example of the confusion of direct reference phenomena with metaphysical and epistemological ideas was first vigorously called to our attention by Saul Kripke in *Naming and Necessity*. I wish to parallel his remarks disconnecting the *a priori* and the *necessary*.

The form of *a priority* that I will discuss is that of logical truth (in the logic of demonstratives). We saw very early that a truth of the logic of demonstratives, like "I am here now" need not be necessary. There are many such cases of logical truths which are not necessary. If α is any singular term, then

$$\alpha = \text{dthat}[\alpha]$$

is a logical truth. But

$$\Box\,(\alpha = \text{dthat}[\alpha])$$

is generally false. We can, of course, also easily produce the opposite effect.

$$\Box\,(\text{dthat}[\alpha] = \text{dthat}[\beta])$$

may be true, although

$$\text{dthat}[\alpha] = \text{dthat}[\beta]$$

is not logically true, and is even logically equivalent to the contingency,

$$\alpha = \beta$$

(I call ϕ and ψ logically equivalent when $\ulcorner \phi \leftrightarrow \psi \urcorner$ is logically true.) These cases are reminiscent of Kripke's case of the terms, 'one meter' and 'the length of bar x'. But where Kripke focuses on the special epistemological situation of one who is present at the dubbing, the descriptive meaning associated with our directly referential term dthat$[\alpha]$ is carried in the semantics of the language.[65]

---

[65]A case of a seemingly different kind is that of the logical equivalence between an arbitrary sentence ϕ and the result of prefixing either or both of the indexical operators, 'it is actually the case that' (symbolized 'A') and 'it is now the case that' (symbolized 'N'). The biconditional $\ulcorner(\phi \leftrightarrow AN\,\phi)\urcorner$ is logically true, but prefixing either '$\Box$' or its temporal counterpart can lead to falsehood. (This case was adverted to in footnote 28.) It is interesting to note, in this case, that the parallel between modal and temporal modifications of sentences carries over to indexicals.

(contd.)

How can something be both logically true, and thus *certain,* and *contingent* at the same time? In the case of indexicals the answer is easy to see.

> E. COROLLARY 3. *The bearers of logical truth and of contingency are different entities. It is the* character *(or, the sentence, if you prefer) that is logically true, producing a true content in every context. But it is the* content *(the proposition, if you will) that is contingent or necessary.*

As can readily be seen, the modal logic of demonstratives is a rich and interesting thing.

It is easy to be taken in by the effortless (but fallacious) move from certainty (logical truth) to necessity. In his important article "There Grades of Modal Involvement,"[66] Quine expresses his scepticism of the first grade of modal involvement: the sentence predicate and all it stands for, and his distaste for the second grade of modal involvement: disguising the predicate as an operator 'It is necessary that'. But he suggests that no new metaphysical undesirables are admitted until the third grade of modal involvement: quantification across the necessity operator into an open sentence.

I must protest. That first step let in some metaphysical undesirables, falsehoods. All logical truths are analytic, but they can go false when you back them up to '□'.

One other notorious example of a logical truth which is not necessary,

> I exist.

One can quickly verify that in every context, this character yields a true proposition—but rarely a necessary one. It seems likely to me that it was a conflict between the feelings of contingency and of certainty associated with this sentence that has led to such painstaking examination of its 'proofs'. It is just a truth of logic!

Dana Scott has remedied one lacuna in this analysis. What of the premise

> I think

and the connective

> Therefore   ?

His discovery was that the premise is incomplete, and that the last five words

> up the logic of demonstratives

had been lost in an early manuscript version.[67]

The foregoing claims are verified by the formal system (sections XVIII and XIX, see especially Remark 3). Note that the formal system is constructed in accordance with Carnap's proposal that the intension of an expression be that function which assigns to each circumstance, the extension of the expression with respect to that circumstance. This has commonly been thought to insure that logically equivalent expressions have the same intension (Church's Alternative 2 among principles of individuation for the notion of sense) and that logically true sentences express the (unique) necessary proposition. Homework Problem: What went wrong here?

[66] *Proceedings of the XI International Congress of Philosophy,* 14, 65–81; reprinted in W. V. Quine, *The Ways of Paradox* (New York: Random House, 1966).

[67] Again, it is probably a pedagogical mistake to mix this playful paragraph with the preceding serious one.

XVIII. The Formal System

Just to be sure we have not overlooked anything, here is a machine against which we can test our intuitions.

The Language LD

The *Language* LD is based on first-order predicate logic with identity and descriptions. We deviate slightly from standard formulations in using two sorts of variables, one sort for positions and a second for individuals other than positions (hereafter called simply 'individuals').

Primitive Symbols

Primitive Symbols for Two Sorted Predicate Logic

0. Punctuation: (,), [,]
1. Variables:
    (i) An infinite set of individual variables: ν_i
    (ii) An infinite set of position variables: ν_p
2. Predicates:
    (i) An infinite number of m-n-place predicates, for all natural numbers m, n.
    (ii) The 1-0-place predicate: Exist
    (iii) The 1-1-place predicate: Located
3. Functors:
    (i) An infinite number of m-n-place i-functors (functors which form terms denoting individuals)
    (ii) An infinite number of m-n-place p-functors (functors which form terms denoting positions)
4. Sentential Connectives: $\wedge, \vee, \neg, \rightarrow, \leftrightarrow$
5. Quantifiers: $\forall, \exists$
6. Definite Description Operator: the
7. Identity: $=$

Primitive Symbols for Modal and Tense Logic

8. Modal Operators: $\square, \lozenge$
9. Tense Operators:
    F (it will be the case that)
    P (it has been the case that)
    G (one day ago, it was the case that)

Primitive Symbols for the Logic of Demonstratives

10. There 1-place sentential operators:
    N (it is now the case that)
    A (it is actually the case that)
    Y (yesterday, it was the case that)

11. A 1-place functor: dthat
12. An individual constant (o-o-place *i*-functor): I
13. A position constant (o-o-place *p*-functor): Here

Well-Formed Expressions

The *well-formed expressions* are of three kinds: formulas, position terms (*p*-terms), and individual terms (*i*-terms).

1. (i) If $\alpha \in \nu_i$, then α is an *i*-term
    (ii) If $\alpha \in \nu_p$, then α is a *p*-term
2. If π is an *m-n*-place predicate, $\alpha_1, \ldots, \alpha_m$ are *i*-terms, and $\beta_1, \ldots, \beta_n$ are *p*-terms, then $\pi\alpha_1 \ldots \alpha_m\beta_1 \ldots \beta_n$ is a formula
3. (i) If η is an *m-n*-place *i*-functor, $\alpha_1, \ldots, \alpha_m, \beta_1, \ldots, \beta_n$ are as in 2, then $\eta\alpha_1 \ldots \alpha_m\beta_1 \ldots \beta_n$ is an *i*-term
    (ii) If η is an *m-n*-place *p*-functor, $\alpha_1, \ldots, \alpha_m, \beta_1, \ldots, \beta_n$ are as in 2, then $\eta\alpha_1 \ldots \alpha_m\beta_1 \ldots \beta_n$ is an *p*-term
4. If ϕ, ψ are formulas, then $(\phi \wedge \psi), (\phi \vee \psi), \neg\phi, (\phi \rightarrow \psi), (\phi \leftrightarrow \psi)$ are formulas
5. If ϕ is a formula and $\alpha \in \nu_i \cup \nu_p$, then $\forall\alpha\phi$ and $\exists\alpha\phi$ are formulas
6. If ϕ is a formula, then
    (i) if $\alpha \in \nu_i$ then the $\alpha \phi$ is an *i*-term
    (ii) if $\alpha \in \nu_p$ then the $\alpha \phi$ is a *p*-term
7. If α, β are either both *i*-terms or both *p*-terms, then $\alpha = \beta$ is a formula
8. If ϕ is a formula, then $\Box\phi$ and $\Diamond\phi$ are formulas
9. If ϕ is a formula, then $F\phi$, $P\phi$, and $G\phi$ are formulas
10. If ϕ is a formula, then $N\phi$, $A\phi$, and $Y\phi$ are formulas
11. (i) If α is an *i*-term, then dthat[α] is an *i*-term
    (ii) If α is a *p*-term, then dthat[α] is a *p*-term

Semantics for LD

LD Structures

DEFINITION: $\mathfrak{A}$ is an LD structure iff there are $\mathcal{C}, \mathcal{W}, \mathcal{U}, \mathcal{P}, \mathcal{T},$ and $\mathcal{I}$ such that:

1. $\mathfrak{A} = \langle \mathcal{C}, \mathcal{W}, \mathcal{U}, \mathcal{P}, \mathcal{T}, \mathcal{I} \rangle$
2. $\mathcal{C}$ is a nonempty set (the set of contexts, see 10 below)
3. If $c \in \mathcal{C}$, then
    (i) $c_A \in \mathcal{U}$ (the *agent* of *c*)
    (ii) $c_T \in \mathcal{T}$ (the *time* of *c*)
    (iii) $c_P \in \mathcal{P}$ (the *position* of *c*)

    (iv) $c_W \in \mathcal{W}$ (the *world* of *c*)
4. $\mathcal{W}$ is a nonempty set (the set of *worlds*)
5. $\mathcal{U}$ is a nonempty set (the set of all *individuals*, see 9 below)
6. $\mathcal{P}$ is a nonempty set (the set of *positions*, common to all worlds)

7. $\mathcal{T}$ is the set of integers (thought of as the *times,* common to all worlds)

8. $\mathcal{I}$ is a function which assigns to each predicate and functor an appropriate *intension* as follows:

   (i) If π is an *m-n*-predicate, $\mathcal{I}_\pi$ is a function such that for each $t \in \mathcal{T}$ and $w \in \mathcal{W}$, $\mathcal{I}_\pi(t, w) \subseteq (\mathcal{U}^m \times \mathcal{P}^n)$

   (ii) If η is an *m-n*-place *i*-functor, $\mathcal{I}_\eta$ is a function such that for each $t \in \mathcal{T}$ and $w \in \mathcal{W}$, $\mathcal{I}_\eta(t, w) \in (\mathcal{U} (\cup \dagger))^{(\mathcal{U}^m \times \mathcal{P}^n)}$ (Note: † is a completely alien entity, in neither $\mathcal{U}$ nor $\mathcal{P}$, which represents an 'undefined' value of the function. In a normal set theory we can take † to be $\{\mathcal{U}, \mathcal{P}\}$.)

   (iii) If η is an *m-n*-place *p*-functor, $\mathcal{I}_\eta$ is a function such that for each $t \in \mathcal{T}$ and $w \in \mathcal{W}$, $\mathcal{I}_\eta(t, w) \in (\mathcal{P} \cup \{\dagger\})^{(\mathcal{U}^m \times \mathcal{P}^n)}$

9. $i \in \mathcal{U}$ iff $(\exists t \in \mathcal{T})\, (\exists w \in \mathcal{W})(\langle i \rangle \in \mathcal{I}_{\text{Exist}}(t, w))$

10. If $c \in \mathcal{C}$, then $\langle c_A, c_P \rangle \in \mathcal{I}_{\text{Located}}(c_T, c_W)$

11. If $\langle i, p \rangle \in \mathcal{I}_{\text{Located}}(t, w)$, then $\langle i \rangle \in \mathcal{I}_{\text{Exist}}(t, w)$

Truth and Denotation in a Context

We write: $\models^{\mathfrak{A}}_{cfTW} \phi$ for ϕ, when taken in the context c (under the assignment f and in the structure $\mathfrak{A}$), *is true with respect to* the time t and the world w.

We write: $\models^{\mathfrak{A}}_{cfTW}$ for *The denotation of* α, when taken in the context c (under the assignment f and in the structure $\mathfrak{A}$), *with respect to* the time t and the world w

In general we will omit the superscript '$\mathfrak{A}$', and we will assume that the structure $\mathfrak{A}$ is $\langle \mathcal{C}, \mathcal{W}, \mathcal{U}, \mathcal{P}, \mathcal{T}, \mathcal{I} \rangle$.

DEFINITION: f *is an assignment* (with respect to $\langle \mathcal{C}, \mathcal{W}, \mathcal{U}, \mathcal{P}, \mathcal{T}, \mathcal{I} \rangle$) iff:

$$\exists f_1\, f_2\, (f_1 \in \mathcal{U}^{v_i}\ \&\ f_2 \in \mathcal{P}^{v_p}\ \&\ f = f_1 \cup f_2)$$

DEFINITION: $f^\alpha_x = (f \sim \{\langle \alpha, f(\alpha) \rangle\}) \cup \{\langle \alpha, x \rangle\}$ (i.e., the assignment which is just like f except that it assigns x to α)

DEFINITION: For the following recursive definition, assume that $c \in \mathcal{C}$, f is an assignment, $t \in \mathcal{T}$, and $w \in \mathcal{W}$:

1. If α is a variable, $|\alpha|_{cftw} = f(\alpha)$

2. $\models_{cftw} \pi\alpha_1 \ldots \alpha_m \beta_1 \ldots \beta_n$ iff $\langle |\alpha_1|_{cftw} \ldots |\beta_n|_{cftw} \rangle \in \mathcal{T}_\pi(t, w)$

3. If η is neither 'I' nor 'Here' (see 12, 13 below), then

$$|\eta\alpha_1 \ldots \alpha_m \beta_1 \ldots \beta_n|_{cftw} = \begin{cases} \mathcal{I}_\eta(t, w)(\langle |\alpha_1|_{cftw} \ldots |\beta_n|_{cftw} \rangle), \\ \text{if none of } |\alpha_i|_{cftw} \ldots |\beta_n|_{cftw} \text{ are } \dagger; \\ \dagger, \text{ otherwise} \end{cases}$$

4. (i) $\models_{cftw} (\phi \wedge \psi)$ iff $\models_{cftw} \phi$ & $\models_{cftw} \psi$
   (ii) $\models_{cftw} \neg\phi$ iff $\sim \models_{cftw} \phi$ etc.

5. (i) If $\alpha \in v_t$, then $\models_{cftw} \forall\alpha\phi$ iff $\forall_i \in \mathcal{U}, \models_{cf^\alpha_i tw}\phi$

   (ii) If $\alpha \in v_p$, then $\models_{cftw} \forall\alpha\phi$ iff $\forall_p \in \mathcal{P}, \models_{cf^\alpha_i tw}\phi$

   (iii) Similarly for $\exists\alpha\phi$

6. (i) If $\alpha \in v_i$, then:

$$|\text{the } \alpha \ \phi|_{cftw} = \begin{cases} \text{the unique } i \in \mathcal{U} \text{ such that } \models_{cf^\alpha_i tw}\phi, \text{ if} \\ \text{there is such;} \\ \dagger, \text{ otherwise} \end{cases}$$

   (ii) Similarly for $\alpha \in v_p$

7. $\models_{cftw} \alpha = \beta$ iff $|\alpha|_{cftw} = |\beta|_{cftw}$

8. (i) $\models_{cftw} \Box\phi$ iff $\forall w' \in \mathcal{W}, \models_{cftw'}\phi$

   (ii) $\models_{cftw} \Diamond\phi$ iff $\exists w' \in \mathcal{W}, \models_{cftw'}\phi$

9. (i) $\models_{cftw} F\phi$ iff $\exists t' \in \mathcal{T}$ such that $t' > t$ and $\models_{cft'w}\phi$

   (ii) $\models_{cftw} P\phi$ iff $\exists t' \in \mathcal{T}$ such that $t' < t$ and $\models_{cft'w}\phi$

   (iii) $\models_{cftw} G\phi$ iff $\models_{cf(t-1)w}\phi$

10. (i) $\models_{cftw} N\phi$ iff $\models_{cfc_Tw}\phi$

   (ii) $\models_{cftw} A\phi$ iff $\models_{cftc_w}\phi$

   (iii) $\models_{cftw} Y\phi$ iff $\models_{cf(c_T-1)w}\phi$

11. $|\text{dthat}[\alpha]|_{cftw} = |\alpha|_{cfc_Tc_w}$

12. $|\text{I}|_{cftw} = c_A$

13. $|\text{Here}|_{cftw} = c_P$

XIX. Remarks on the Formal System

REMARK 1: Expressions containing demonstratives will, in general, express different concepts in different contexts. We call the concept expressed in a given context the *Content* of the expression in that context. The Content of a sentence in a context is, roughly, the proposition the sentence would express if uttered in that context. This description is not quite accurate on two counts. First, it is important to distinguish an *utterance* from a *sentence-in-a-context*. The former notion is from the theory of speech acts, the latter from semantics. Utterances take time, and utterances of distinct sentences cannot be simultaneous (i.e., in the same context). But to develop a logic of demonstratives it seems most natural to be able to evaluate several premises and a conclusion all in the same context. Thus the notion of ϕ *being true in c* and $\mathfrak{A}$ does not require an utterance of ϕ. In particular, c_A need not be uttering ϕ in c_W at c_T. Second, the truth of a proposition is not usually thought of as dependent on a time as well as a possible world. The time is thought of as fixed by the context. If ϕ is a sentence, the more usual notion of the proposition expressed by ϕ-in-c is what is here called the Content of $N\phi$ in c.

Where Γ is either a term or formula,

we write: $\{\Gamma\}^{\mathfrak{A}}_{cf}$ for   The Content of Γ in the context c (under the assignment f and in the structure $\mathfrak{A}$).

DEFINITION:

(i) If ϕ is a formula, $\{\phi\}_{cf}^{\mathfrak{A}}$ = that function which assigns to each $t \in \mathcal{T}$ and $w \in \mathcal{W}$, Truth, if $\models_{cftw}^{\mathfrak{A}} \phi$, and Falsehood otherwise.

(ii) If α is a term, $\{\alpha\}_{cf}^{\mathfrak{A}}$ = that function which assigns to each $t \in \mathcal{T}$ and $w \in \mathcal{W}$, $|\alpha|_{cftw}$

REMARK 2: $\models_{cftw}^{\mathfrak{A}} \phi$ iff $\{\phi\}_{cf}^{\mathfrak{A}} (t, w) =$ Truth. Roughly speaking, the sentence ϕ taken in context c is *true with respect to t and w* iff the proposition expressed by ϕ-in-the-context-c would be true at the time t if w were the actual world. In the formal development of pages 767, 768, and 769, it was smoother to ignore the conceptual break marked by the notion of *Content in a context* and to directly define *truth in a context with respect to a possible time and world*. The important conceptual role of the notion of Content is partially indicated by the following two definitions.

DEFINITION: ϕ *is true in the context c* (in the structure $\mathfrak{A}$) iff for every assignment f, $\{\phi\}_{cf}^{\mathfrak{A}} (c_\mathrm{T}, c_\mathrm{W}) =$ Truth.

DEFINITION: ϕ *is valid in LD* ($\models \phi$) iff for every LD structure $\mathfrak{A}$, and every context c of $\mathfrak{A}$, ϕ is true in c (in $\mathfrak{A}$).

REMARK 3: $\models(\alpha = \mathrm{dthat}[\alpha])$; $\models(\phi \leftrightarrow AN\phi)$; $\models N(\text{Located I, Here})$; $\models$ Exist I. But, $\sim \models \square(\alpha = \mathrm{dthat}\,[\alpha])$; $\sim \models \square(\phi \leftrightarrow AN\phi)$; $\sim \models \square N(\text{Located I, Here})$; $\sim \models \square (\text{Exist I})$. Also, $\sim \models F(\phi \leftrightarrow AN\phi)$.

In the converse direction (where the original validity has the form $\square\phi$) we have the usual results in view of the fact that $\models(\square\phi \to \phi)$.

DEFINITION: If $\alpha_1, \ldots, \alpha_n$ are all the free variables of ϕ in alphabetical order then *the closure of ϕ* $= AN\forall\alpha_1 \ldots \forall\alpha_n\phi$.

DEFINITION: ϕ *is closed* iff ϕ is equivalent (in the sense of Remark 12) to its closure.

REMARK 4: If ϕ is closed, then ϕ is true in c (and $\mathfrak{A}$) iff for every assignment f, time t, and world w, $\models_{cftw}^{\mathfrak{A}} \phi$.

DEFINITION: Where Γ is either a term or a formula, *the Content of Γ in the context c* (in the structure $\mathfrak{A}$) *is Stable* iff for every assignment f, $\{\Gamma\}_{cf}^{\mathfrak{A}}$ is a constant function (i.e., $\{\Gamma\}_{cf}^{\mathfrak{A}} (t, w) = \{\Gamma\}_{cf}^{\mathfrak{A}} (t', w')$, for all t, t', w, and w' in $\mathfrak{A}$).

REMARK 5: Where ϕ is a formula, α is a term, and β is a variable, each of the following has a Stable Content in every context (in every structure): $AN\phi$, $\mathrm{dthat}[\alpha]$, β, I, Here.

If we were to extend the notion of Content to apply to operators, we would see that all indexicals (including N, A, Y, and dthat) have a Stable Content in every context. The same is true of the familiar logical constants although it does not hold for the modal and tense operators (not, at least, according to the foregoing development).

REMARK 6: That aspect of the meaning of an expression which determines what its Content will be in each context, we call the *Character* of the expression. Although a lack of knowledge about the context (or perhaps about the structure) may cause one to mistake the Content of a given utterance, the Character of each well-formed expression is determined by rules of the language (such as rules 1–13 on page 767 and 768, which are presumably known to all competent speakers. Our notation '$\{\phi\}_{cf}^{\mathfrak{A}}$' for the Content of an expression gives a natural notation for the Character of an expression, namely '$\{\phi\}$'.

DEFINITION: Where Γ is either a term or a formula, *the Character of* Γ is that function which assigns to each structure $\mathfrak{A}$, assignment f, and context c of $\mathfrak{A}$, $\{\Gamma\}_{cf}^{\mathfrak{A}}$.

DEFINITION: Where Γ is either a term or a formula, *the Character of* Γ *is Stable* iff for every structure $\mathfrak{A}$, and assignment f, the Character of Γ (under f in $\mathfrak{A}$) is a constant function (i.e., $\{\Gamma\}_{cf}^{\mathfrak{A}} = \{\Gamma\}_{c'f}^{\mathfrak{A}}$, for all c, c' in $\mathfrak{A}$).

REMARK 7: A formula or term has a Stable Character iff it has the same Content in every context (for each $\mathfrak{A}, f$).

REMARK 8: A formula or term has a Stable Character iff it contains no essential occurrence of a demonstrative.

REMARK 9: The logic of demonstratives determines a sublogic of those formulas of LD which contain no demonstratives. These formulas (and their equivalents which contain inessential occurrences of demonstratives) are exactly the formulas with a Stable Character. The logic of demonstratives brings a new perspective even to formulas such as these. The sublogic of LD which concerns only formulas of Stable Character is not identical with traditional logic. Even for such formulas, the familiar Principle of Necessitation (if $\models \phi$, then $\models \Box\phi$) fails. And so does its tense logic counterpart: if $\models \phi$, then $\models (\neg P \neg \phi \wedge \neg F \neg \phi \ \neg \phi)$. From the perspective of LD, validity is truth in every possible *context*. For traditional logic, validity is truth in every possible *circumstance*. Each possible context determines a possible circumstance, but it is not the case that each possible circumstance is part of a possible context. In particular, the fact that each possible context has an agent implies that any possible circumstance in which no individuals exist will not form a part of any possible context. Within LD, a possible context is represented by $\langle \mathfrak{A}, c \rangle$ and a possible circumstance by $\langle \mathfrak{A}, t, w \rangle$. To any $\langle \mathfrak{A}, c \rangle$, there corresponds $\langle \mathfrak{A}, c_T, c_W \rangle$. But it is not the case that to ever $\langle \mathfrak{A}, t, w \rangle$ there exists a context c of $\mathfrak{A}$ such that $t = c_T$ and $w = c_W$. The result is that in LD such sentences as '$\exists x$ Exist x' and '$\exists x \exists p$ Located x, p' are valid, although they would not be so regarded in traditional logic. At least not in the neotraditional logic that countenances empty worlds. Using the semantical developments of pages 763–767, we can define this traditional sense of validity (for formulas which do not contain demonstratives) as follows. First note that by Remark 7, if ϕ has a Stable Character,

$$\models^{\mathfrak{A}}_{cftw} \phi \text{ iff } \models^{\mathfrak{A}}_{cftw} \phi.$$

Thus for such formulas we can define,

ϕ *is true at t, w (in $\mathfrak{A}$)* iff for every assignment f and every context c, $\models^{\mathfrak{A}}_{cftw} \phi$

The neotraditional sense of validity is now definable as follows,

$\models_T \phi$ iff for all structures $\mathfrak{A}$, times t, and worlds w, ϕ is true at t, w (in $\mathfrak{A}$)

(Properly speaking, what I have called the neotraditional sense of validity is the notion of validity now common for a quantified S5 modal tense logic with individual variables ranging over possible individuals and a predicate of existence.) Adding the subscript 'LD' for explicitness, we can now state some results.

(i)   If ϕ contains no demonstratives, if $\models_T \phi$, then $\models_{LD} \phi$

(ii) $\models_{LD} \exists x$ Exist x, but $\sim \models_T \exists x$ Exist x

Of course '$\Box \exists x$ Exist x' is not valid even in LD. Nor are its counterparts, '$\neg F \neg \exists x$ Exist x', and '$\neg P \neg \exists x$ Exist x'.

    This suggests that we can transcend the context-oriented perspective of LD by generalizing over times and words so as to capture those possible circumstances ($\mathfrak{A}$, t, w) which do not correspond to any possible context ($\mathfrak{A}$, c). We have the following result:

(iii) If ϕ contains no demonstratives,
      $\models_T \phi$ iff $\models_{LD} \Box(\neg F \neg \phi \wedge \neg P \neg \phi \wedge \phi)$.

Although our definition of the neotraditional sense of validity was motivated by consideration of demonstrative-free formulas, we could apply it also to formulas containing essential occurrences of demonstratives. To do so would nullify the most interesting features of the logic of demonstratives. But it raises the questions, can we express our new sense of validity of the nontraditional sense? This can be done:

(iv) $\models_{LD} \phi$ iff $\models_T AN\phi$

REMARK 10: Rigid designators (in the sense of Kripke) are terms with a Stable Content. Since Kripke does not discuss demonstratives, his examples all have, in addition, a Stable Character (by Remark 8). Kripke claims that for proper names α, β it may happen that $\alpha = \beta$, though not a priori, is nevertheless necessary. This, in spite of the fact that the names, α, β may be introduced by means of descriptions α', β' for which $\alpha' = \beta'$ is not necessary. An analogous situations holds in LD. Let α', β' be definite descriptions (without free variables) such that $\alpha' = \beta'$ is not a priori, and consider the (rigid) terms dthat[α'] and dthat[β'] which are formed from them. We know that:

$$\models (\text{dthat}[\alpha'] = \text{dthat}[\beta'] \leftrightarrow \alpha' = \beta').$$

Thus, if $\alpha' = \beta'$ is not a priori, neither is dthat[α'] = dthat[β']. But, since:

$$\models (\text{dthat}[\alpha'] = \text{dthat}[\beta'] \rightarrow \Box(\text{dthat}[\alpha'] = \text{dthat}[\beta']))$$

it may happen that dthat[α'] = dthat[β'] is necessary. The converse situation can be illustrated in LD. Since ($\alpha = \text{dthat}[\alpha]$) is valid (see Remark 3), it is surely capable of being known a priori. But if α lacks a Stable Content (in some context c), $\Box(\alpha = (\text{dthat}[\alpha]))$ will be false.

REMARK 11: Our 0-0 place i-functors are not proper names, in the sense of Kripke, since they do not have a Stable Content. But they can easily be converted by means of the stabilizing influence of 'dthat'. Even dthat[α] lacks a Stable Character. The process by which such expressions are converted into expressions with a Stable Character is 'dubbing'—a form of definition in which context may play an essential role. The means to deal with such context-indexed definitions is not available in our object language.

There would, of course, be no difficulty in supplementing our language with a syntactically distinctive set of 0-0-place i-functors whose semantics requires them to have both a Stable Character and a Stable Content in every context. Variables already behave this way, what is wanted is a class of constants that behave, in these respects, like variables.

The difficulty comes in expressing the definition. My thought is that when a name, like 'Bozo', is introduced by someone saying, in some context c^*, "Let's call the Governor, 'Bozo'," we have a context-indexed definition of the form: $A =_{c^*} \alpha$, where A is a new constant (here, 'Bozo') and α is some term whose denotation depends on context (here, 'the Governor'). The intention of such a dubbing is, presumably, to induce the semantical clause: for all c, $\{A\}_{cf}^{\mathfrak{A}} = \{\alpha\}_{c^*f}$. Such a clause gives A a Stable Character. The context-indexing is required by the fact that the Content of α (the 'definiens') may vary from context to context. Thus the same semantical clause is not induced by taking either $A = \alpha$ or even $A = \text{dthat}[\alpha]$ as an axiom.

I think it is likely that such definitions play a practically (and perhaps theoretically) indispensable role in the growth of language, allowing us to introduce a vast stock of names on the basis of a meager stock of demonstratives and some ingenuity in the staging of demonstrations.

Perhaps such introductions should not be called 'definitions' at all, since they essentially enrich the expressive power of the language. What a nameless man may express by 'I am hungry' may be inexpressible in remote contexts. But once he says "Let's call me 'Bozo'," his Content is accessible to us all.

REMARK 12: The strongest form of logical equivalence between two formulas ϕ and ϕ' is sameness of Character, $\{\phi\} = \{\phi'\}$. This form of synonymy is expressible in terms of validity.

$$\{\phi\} = \{\phi'\} \text{ iff } \vDash \Box[\neg F \neg (\phi \leftrightarrow \phi') \wedge \neg (P \neg (\phi \leftrightarrow \phi') \wedge (\phi \leftrightarrow \phi')]$$

[Using Remark 9 (iii) and dropping the condition, which was stated only to express the intended range of applicability of $\vDash_T$, we have: $\{\phi\} = \{\phi'\}$ iff $\vDash_T$ $(\phi \leftrightarrow \phi')$.] Since definitions of the usual kind (as opposed to dubbings) are intended to introduce a short expression as a mere abbreviation of a longer one, the Character of the defined sign should be the same as the Character of the definiens. Thus, within LD, definitional axioms must take the unusual form indicated above.

REMARK 13: If β is a variable of the same sort as the term α but is not free in α, then $\{\text{dthat}\{\alpha\}\} = \{\text{the } \beta \ AN \ (\beta = \alpha)\}$. Thus for every formula ϕ, there can be constructed a formula ϕ' such that ϕ' contains no occurrence of 'dthat' and $\{\phi\} = \{\phi'\}$.

REMARK 14: Y (yesterday) and G (one day ago) superficially resemble one another in view of the fact that $\vDash (Y \phi \leftrightarrow G\phi)$. But the former is a demonstrative whereas the latter is an iterative temporal operator. "One day ago it was the case that one day ago it was the case that John yawned" means that John yawned the day before yesterday. But "Yesterday it was the case that yesterday it was the case that John yawned" is only a stutter.

Notes on Possible Refinements

1. The primitive predicates and functions of first-order predicate logic are all taken to be extensional. Alternatives are possible.
2. Many conditions might be added on $\mathcal{P}$; many alternatives might be chosen for $\mathcal{T}$. If the elements of $\mathcal{T}$ do not have a natural relation to play the role of $<$, such a relation must be added to the structure.
3. When $\mathcal{K}$ is set of LD formulas, $\mathcal{K} \vDash \phi$ is easily defined in any of the usual ways.
4. Aspects of the contexts other than c_A, c_P, c_T, and c_W would be used if new demonstratives (e.g., pointings, You, etc.) were added to the language. (Note that the subscripts A, P, T, W are external parameters. They may be thought of as functions applying to contexts, with c_A being the value of A for the context c.)
5. Special continuity conditions through time might be added for the predicate 'Exist'.
6. If individuals lacking positions are admitted as agents of contexts, 3(iii) of page 766 should be weakened to: $c_P \in \mathcal{P} \cup \{\dagger\}$. It would no longer be the case that: $\vDash$ Located I, Here. If individuals also lacking temporal location (disembodied minds?) are admitted as agents of contexts, a similar weakening is required of 3(ii). In any case it would still be true that $\vDash$ Exist I.

XX. Adding 'Says'

[This section is not yet written. What follows is a rough outline of what is to come.]

The point of this section is to show, in a controlled experiment, that what Quine called *the relational sense* of certain intensional operators is unavoidable, and to explore the *logical*, as opposed to epistemological, features of language which lead to this result.

I have already mentioned, in connection with Dr. Lauben, that when x says 'I have been wounded' and y wishes to report in indirect discourse exactly what x said, y has a problem. It will not do for y to say 'x said that I have been wounded'. According to our earlier remarks, it should be correct for y to report x's *content* using a character appropriate to the context of the report. For example, accusingly: 'You said that you had been wounded', or quantificationally: '$(\exists x)(Fz \wedge x$ said that z had been wounded)' where x alone satisfied 'Fz'. I will try to show that such constructions are the inevitable result of the attempt to make (third person) *indirect discourse* reports of the person *direct discourse* sayings when those sayings involve indexicals.

The situation regarding the usual epistemic verbs—'believes', 'hopes', 'knows', 'desires', 'fears', etc.—is, I believe, essentially similar to that of 'ways'. Each has, or might have, a *direct discourse* sense in which the character which stands for the cognitive significance of the thought is given (he thinks, 'My God! It is *my* pants that are on fire'), as well as an *indirect discourse* sense in which only the content need be given (he thinks that it is *his* pants that are on fire).[68] If this is correct, and if indexicals are featured in the language of thought (as suggested earlier), then any *indirect* discourse reports of someone's thought (other than first person on the spot reports) must contain those features—*de re* constructions, referential occurrences, quantification in, relational senses— that have no puzzled me, and some others, since the appearance of "Quantifiers and Propositional Attitudes."[69]

What is special and different about the present approach is the attempt to use the distinction between direct and indirect discourse to match the distinction between character and content. Thus when you wonder, 'Is that me?', it is correct to report you as having wondered whether you are yourself. These transformations are traced to the indexical form of your inner direct discourse rather than to any particular referential intentions. The idea is that the full analysis of indirect

---

[68] My notion of "indirect discourse" forms of language is linked to Frege's notion of an *ungerade* (often translated "oblique") context. My terminology is intended to echo his.

[69] Quine, in his "Reply to Kaplan" in *Works and Objections*, ed. D. Davidson et al. (Dordrecht: Reidel, 1969), raises the question—in the idiom of "Quantifiers and Propositional Attitudes" (*Journal of Philosophy* 53 (1956); reprinted in Martinich, op. cit.)—which of the names of a thing are to count as exportable? My point here is that the indexical names must be exportable, not because of some special justification for the transformation from a *de dicto* occurrence to a *de re* occurrence, but because indexicals are devices of direct reference and have no *de dicto* occurrences. I am reminded of the Zen ko-an: How do you get the goose out of the bottle? Answer: It's out!

discourse includes mention of the suppressed character of the direct discourse event which the indirect discourse reports, thus:

> ∃c, C [c is a context ∧ C is a character ∧ x is the agent of c ∧ x direct-discourse-verb C at the time t of c ∧ the content of C in c is that. . .]

approximates a full analysis of

> x indirect-discourse-verb that . . . at t.

Rather than try to include all these semantical ideas in an object language which includes the direct discourse forms of the verbs, the object language will include, *as is usual,* only the indirect discourse forms. The information about the character of the direct discourse event will provide the metalinguistic data against which the truth of object language sentences is tested.[70]

What is not yet clear to me is whether all directly referential occurrences of terms within the scope of indirect discourse epistemic verbs are to be justified *solely* on the basis of a like (though generally distinct) term in the direct discourse event or whether in some cases the English idioms which we symbolize with quantification in (for example, 'There is someone whom Holmes believes to have shot himself') involve some element of *knowing-who* or *believing-who*. To put the question another way: are all the cases that Quine describes, and others similar, which irresistibly suggest the symbolic idiom of quantification in, accounted for by the semantics of direct reference (including indexicals and possibly other expressions as well) as applied to the (putative) direct discourse events? "Quantifying In" suffers from the lack of an adequate semantics of direct reference, but its explicandum includes the epistemological idea of knowing-who, which goes beyond what can be analyzed simply in terms of direct reference. When Ingrid hears someone approaching through the fog and knows 'Someone is approaching' and even knows 'That person is approaching', is it justified to say that there is someone whom Ingrid knows to be approaching? Or must we have, in addition to the indexical 'that person', *recognition* on Ingrid's part of who it is that is approaching? My present thought is that the cases which irresistibly suggest the symbolic idiom of quantification in involve, in an ambiguous way, two elements: *direct reference* (on which we are close to getting clear, I hope) and *recognition*.[71] (The latter is my new term for

---

[70]If this analysis is correct, the suppressed character should wreak its mischief in cases of suspension of belief (I believe, 'that man's pants are on fire' but at the moment neither assent to nor deny 'my pants are on fire') as does its counterpart in section XI of "Quantifying In." Burge, in "Kaplan, Quine, and Suspended Belief," *Philosophical Studies* 31 (1977):197–203, proposes a solution to the problem of section XI which he believes is in the spirit of Quine's formulations. A similar proposal in the present context would seem starkly inappropriate. But there has been a shift in task from "Quantifying In" to the present attempt. In large part the shift is to a course outlined by Burge in the last two pages of the above-mentioned article and urged by him, in conversation, for several years. The point only began to sink in when I came on it myself from a different angle.

[71]There is another form of common speech which may be thought to suggest formalization by quantification in. I call this form the *pseudo de re*. A typical example is, "John says that the lying S.O.B. who took my car is honest." It is clear that John does not say, "The lying S.O.B.

(contd.)

knowing-(or believing)-who. The term is chosen to reflect the idea that the individual in question is identified with respect to some prior or independent information—*re*-cognition—not immediately connected with the current attribution.) Of the two elements the former is semantical; the latter, frankly epistemological. The English idiom 'There is someone such that Ingrid indirect-discourse-propositional-attitude-verb that . . . he . . .' always implies that a singular proposition is the object of Ingrid's thought (and thus that some directly referential term α occurred in her inner direct discourse) and may sometimes imply (or only suggest?) that Ingrid recognized, *who α is.* I offer no analysis of the latter notion.[72]

In the first paragraph, I referred to a controlled experiment. By that I mean the following. Accepting the metaphor of "inner direct discourse events" and "indirect discourse reports" in connection with the usual epistemic verbs, I want to examine the logical relations between these two. But the study is complicated by at least three factors which obscure the issues I wish to bring to light. First, there is no real syntax to the language of thought. Thus, even in the case of the simplest thoughts the relation between the syntax of the sentential complement to the epistemic verb and the structure of the original thought is obscure. Second, in containing images, sounds, odors, etc., thought is richer than the language of the report. Might these perceptual elements play a role in determining logical relations? Third, thought ranges from the completely explicit (inner speech) to the entirely implicit (unconscious beliefs which explain actions) and through a variety of occurrent and dispositional forms. This makes it hard to pin down the whole direct discourse event. These three factors suggest taking as a paradigm of the relation between direct and indirect discourse—direct and indirect discourse!

Even when reporting the (outer) discourse of another, at least three obscure irrelevancies (for our purposes) remain. First, if Christopher speaks in a language different from that of the report, we have again the problem of translation (analogous to, though perhaps less severe than, that of translating the language of thought).

---

who took your car is honest." Does John say $\ulcorner \delta$ is honest$\urcorner$ for some directly referential term δ which the reporter believes to refer to the lying S.O.B. who took his car? Not necessarily. John may say something as simple as, "The man I sent to you yesterday is honest." The reporter has simply substituted his description for John's. What justifies this shocking falsification of John's speech? Nothing! But we do it, and often recognize—or don't care—when it is being done. The form lends itself to strikingly distorted reports. As Church has shown, in his *Introduction to Mathematical Logic* (Princeton: Princeton University Press, 1956), on page 25, when John says "Sir Walter Scott is the author of *Waverley*" use of the *pseudo de re* form (plus a quite plausible synonymy transformation) allows the report, "John says that there are twenty-nine counties in Utah"! I do not see that the existence of the *pseudo de re* form of report poses any issues of sufficient theoretical interest to make it worth pursuing.

[72]There is a considerable literature on this subject with important contributions by Hintikka, Castañeda and others. In connection with the proposal that $\ulcorner a$ knows who α is$\urcorner$ can be symbolized $\ulcorner \exists x(a$ knows that $x = \alpha)\urcorner$, it should be noted that a's knowledge of the logical truth $\ulcorner$dthat$[\alpha] = \alpha\urcorner$ leads, simply by the semantics of direct reference, to $\ulcorner \exists x(a$ knows that $x = \alpha)\urcorner$. This shows only that a *recognition* sense of knowing a singular proposition is not definable, in the obvious way, in terms of a purely *direct reference* sense of knowing a singular proposition.

We control this by assuming the direct discourse to be in the language of the indirect discourse report. Second, as Carnap once pointed out to me, if Christopher's discourse had the form $\ulcorner \phi \wedge \psi \urcorner$ even the strictest court would accept as true the testimony, $\ulcorner$ Christopher said that $\psi \wedge \phi \urcorner$. What logical transformations on the original discourse would be allowed in the report? (If Christopher says '$\exists x\, x$ is round', may we report him as saying that $\exists y\, y$ is round?) We control this by allowing no logical transformations (we are explicating *literal* indirect discourse). Third, if in saying 'The circle can't be squared' Christopher thought that 'can't' was synonymous with 'should not' rather than 'cannot', should he be reported as having said that the circle can't be squared? We control this by assuming that our speakers make no linguistic errors.

What then remains of the logic? Is the move from direct discourse to literal indirect discourse not simply the result of disquotation (and decapitalization) plus the addition of 'that', as in:

> Christopher says 'the world is round'
> ∴ Christopher says that the world is round   ?

But how then are we to report Dr. Lauben's saying, 'I have been wounded'? Certainly not as, 'Dr. Lauben says that I have been wounded'!

Even in this highly antiseptic environment, the logic of *says* should provide us with a full measure of that baffling and fascinating *de re* versus *de dicto*, notional versus relational, etc., behavior. And here, using the conceptual apparatus of the semantics of direct reference, we may hope to identify the source of these antics.

[I also hope to distinguish, in discussing reports of self-attribution, *x says that x is a fool*, from *x says-himself to be a fool*.]

XXI. Russell on Egocentric Particulars and Their Dispensability

In chapter VII of *Inquiry into Meaning and Truth*,[73] Russell gives a series of atrocious arguments for the conclusion that "[indexicals] are not needed in any part of the description of the world, whether physical or psychological." This is a happy no-nonsense conclusion for an argument that begins by remarking "A physicist will not say 'I saw a table', but like Neurath or Julius Caesar, 'Otto saw a table'.": [Why Julius Caesar would be provoked to say 'Otto saw a table', is unexplained.]

Let us examine Russell's conclusion without prejudice to his argument. [What follows is an outline.]

In brief, there are essentially two points. First: if we have both the indexicals and an unlimited supply of unused directly referential proper names, and we can do instantaneous dubbing, then in each context c for any sentence ϕ containing indexicals we can produce a sentence ϕ^* whose character is fixed and whose content is the same as that of ϕ in c. In this sense, if you can describe it with indexicals you can describe it without.[74] There are problems: (i) things can change fast and dubbings take time, (ii) the indexicals retain a kind of epistemic priority.

---

[73] Bertrand Russell (London: Allen & Unwin, 1940).

[74] I assume here that proper names are not indexicals. I argue the point in section XXII.

The second point is: given any *prior* collection of proper names, there will be things, times, places, etc., without a name. How do I say something about these unnamed entities? (E.g., how do I tell you that your pants are on fire—now? It may be that nothing in sight, including us, and no nearby time has a name.)

There are two cases. It seems most likely that without indexicals some entities cannot even be uniquely *described*. In this case we are really in trouble (unless Russell believes in the identity of indescribables—objects lacking uniquely characterizing descriptions) because without indexicals we cannot freely introduce new names. If every entity *can* be uniquely described, there is still the problem of not presenting the right content under the right character required to motivate the right action (recall the discussion on pages 758–759). The proposition expressed by 'the pants belonging to the x Fx are on fire at *the t Gt*' is not the proposition I want to express, and certainly does not have the character I wish to convey.[75]

XXII. On Proper Names

[Some thoughts on proper names from the perspective of the formal system are contained in Remark 11, page 772. What follows is the most hastily written section of this draft. I sketch a view that is mainly negative, without including much supporting argumentation (several of the omitted arguments seem both tedious and tendentious). My current inclination is to drop this whole section from the final draft.]

A *word* is an expression along with its meaning. When two expressions have the same meaning, as with "can't" and "cannot," we call the two words *synonyms*. When two meanings have the same expression, we call the two words *homonyms*. In the latter case we also say that the expression is *ambiguous*. (Probably we would say that the *word* is ambiguous, but accept my terminology for what follows.) In a disambiguated language, semantics can associate meanings with expressions. Even in a language containing ambiguities, semantics can associate a set of meanings with an expression. But given an utterance, semantics cannot tell us what expression was uttered or what language it was uttered in. This is a presemantic task. When I utter a particular vocable, for example, the one characteristic of the first person pronoun of English, you must decide what *word* I have spoken or indeed, if I have spoken any word at all (it may have been a cry of anguish). In associating a word with my utterance you take account of a variety of features of the context of utterance that help to *determine* what I have said but that need not be any *part* of what I have said.

---

[75] Some interesting arguments of a different sort for the indispensability of indexicals are given by Burge in "Belief De Re," *Journal of Philosophy* 74 (1977):338–62, and by Bar-Hillel in his pioneering work, "Indexical Expressions," *Mind* (1954). In connection with the arguments of Burge and Bar-Hillel it would be interesting to check on some related empirical issues involving linguistic universals. Do all languages have a first person singular form? Do they all have all of the standard indexicals?

My egotism, my intonation, my demeanor, may all support the hypothesis that it was the first person pronoun of English. But these aspects of personality, fluency, and mood are no part of any semantic theory of the first person pronoun. The factors I have cited are not, of course, *critical* for the use of the first person pronoun. What are the criteria? What would definitively settle the question? I don't know. I think this is a very difficult question. But among the criteria there must be some that touch on the utterer's intention to use a word in conformity with the conventions of a particular linguistic community. For proper name words, in part because they are so easily introduced, this aspect of the presemantic determination is especially important.

According to the causal chain or chain of communication theory, there are two critical intentions associated with the use of the proper name word. One is the intention to use the word with the meaning given it by the person from whom you learned the word. The other is the contrary intention to create (and perhaps simultaneously use) a proper name word to refer to a given object irrespective of any prior meanings associated with the expression chosen as a vehicle. One who uses a proper name word with the first intention generally (but not always) believes that someone originated the word by using it with the second intention, and—according to the causal chain theory—intends to refer to the given object.[76]

In "Bob and Carol and Ted and Alice," appendix IX, I introduce the notion of a *dubbing* for what I took to be the standard form of introduction of a proper name word. That notion has been mistakenly taken to imply—what I deliberately sought to evoke—a formal public ceremony. What I actually had in mind was a use of a proper name word with the second intention: the intention to originate a word rather than conform to a prior usage. Thus a fleeting "Hi-ya, Beautiful" incorporates all the intentional elements required for me to say that a dubbing has taken place. I believe that my notion here is closely related to Donnellan's notion of a *referential use* of a definite description. Donnellan's distinction between

---

[76]There is disagreement as to how the given object must be given to one who introduces a proper name word with the second intention. Must he be acquainted with the object, directly acquainted, *en rapport,* perceiving it, causally connected, or what? My liberality with respect to the introduction of directly referring terms by means of 'dthat' extends to proper names, and I would allow an arbitrary definite description to *give* us the object we name. "Let's call the first child to be born in the twenty-first century 'Newman 1'." But I am aware that this is a very controversial position. Perhaps some of the sting can be removed by adopting an idea of Gilbert Harman. Normally one would not introduce a proper name or a dthat-term to correspond to each definite description one uses. But we have the means to do so if we wish. Should we do so, we are enabled to apprehend singular propositions concerning remote individuals (those formerly known only by description). Recognizing this, we refrain. What purpose—other than to confound the skeptics—is served by direct reference to whosoever may be the next president of Brazil? The introduction of a new proper name by means of a dubbing in terms of description and the active contemplation of characters involving dthat-terms—two mechanisms for providing direct reference to the denotation of an arbitrary definite description—constitute a form of cognitive restructuring; they broaden our range of thought. To take such a step is an action normally not performed at all, and rarely, if ever, done capriciously. The fact that we have the means—without special experience, knowledge, or whatever—to refer directly to the myriad individuals we can describe, does not imply that we will do so. And if we should have reason to do so, why not?

referential and attributive uses of definite descriptions is easily and naturally extended to referential and attributive uses of proper names. When the intention to conform to a preestablished convention is absent we have the pure referential use. In this case, when a proper name is in question, I take it that an internal, subjective, dubbing has occurred. When a definite description is in question, again the speaker does not intend to give the expression its conventional meaning although he may intend to *make use* of the conventional meaning in conveying who it is that is being referred to or for some other purpose associated with the act of utterance (as in "Hi-ya, Beautiful"). What is important here is that the speaker intends to be creating a meaning for the expression in question rather than following conventions. Dubbings, whether aimed at introducing a relatively permanent sense for the expression or only aimed at attaching a nonce-sense to the expression, are unconventional uses of language. Dubbings create words.

In many, perhaps most, uses of definite descriptions there is a mixture of the intention to follow convention with the intention to refer to a preconceived individual. The same mixture of 'attributive' and 'referential' intentions can occur with a proper name. If I introduce a name into your vocabulary by means of false introduction ("This is Jaakko Hintikka," but it isn't), you are left with an undiscriminated tangle of attributive (to refer to Jaakko Hintikka) and referential (to refer to the person to whom you were introduced) intentions associated with your subsequent uses of the expression "Jaakko Hintikka'. There are several ways in which one might attempt to account for these mixed intentions in a general theory of language. First, we might distinguish two notions: speaker's-reference and semantic-reference. The presence of an attributive intention justifies giving the expressions a conventional meaning and thus allows us to claim that preexisting *words* were used. Whereas the presence of a referential intention (not just a *belief* that the semantic referent is the given object, but an independent intention to refer to the given object) justifies the claim that the speaker is referring to the given object independent of any particular interpretation of the expressions he used as words and independent of whether the utterance has an interpretation as words. A second way of accounting for mixed intentions of this kind is to assume that one of the two intentions must be dominant. If the referential intention dominates, we regard the utterance, on the model of "Hi-ya, Beautiful," as an apt (or inept, as the case may be) introduction of a proper name word (or phrase). Thus, as essentially involving a dubbing. On this way of accounting for mixed intentions, a referential use of an expression would endow the expression with a semantic referent identical with the speaker's referent.[77]

---

[77]This is not an unnatural way to account for the use of the proper name word in the false introduction case, but it does seem a bit strange in the case of a definite description. In that case it involves hypothesizing that the speaker intended the description expression to have a meaning which made the given object its semantic referent, and only *believed* that the conventional meaning would do this, a belief that he is prepared to give up rather than acknowledge that the semantic referent of his words was not the given object. Something like this seems to happen when descriptions grow capitals, as in 'The Holy Roman Empire', and in other cases as well, for example Russell's 'denoting phrases' which do not denote. But it still seems strange.

My aim in the foregoing is to emphasize how delicate and subtle our analysis of the context of utterance must be for the presemantic purpose of determining what words, if any, were spoken. I do this to make plausible my view that—assuming the causal chain theory of reference—proper names are not indexicals. The contextual feature which consists of the causal history of a particular proper name expression in the agent's idiolect seems more naturally to be regarded as determining what word was used than as fixing the content of a single context-sensitive word. Although it is true that two utterances of 'Aristotle' in different contexts may have different contents, I am inclined to attribute this difference to the fact that distinct homonymous words were uttered rather than a context sensitivity in the character of a single word 'Aristotle'. Unlike indexicals like 'I', proper names really are ambiguous. The causal theory of reference tells us, in terms of contextual features (including the speaker's intentions) which word is being used in a given utterance. Each such word is directly referential (thus it has a fixed content), and it also has a fixed character. Therefore, in the case of proper name words, all three kinds of meaning—referent, content, and character—collapse. In this, proper name words are unique. They have the direct reference of indexicals, but they are not context-sensitive. Proper name words are like indexicals that you can carry away from their original context without affecting their content. Because of the collapse of character, content, and referent, it is not unnatural to say of proper names that they have no meaning other than their referent.

Some may claim that they simply use 'indexical' in a wider sense than I (perhaps to mean something like 'contextual'). But we must be wary of an overbroad usage. Is every ambiguous expression an indexical because we look to utterer's intentions to disambiguate? Indeed, is every expression an indexical because it might have been a groan?

If the character and content of proper name words is as I have described it (according to the causal theory), then the informativeness of $\ulcorner \alpha = \beta \urcorner$, with α and β proper names, is not accounted for in terms of differences in either content or character. The problem is that proper names do not seem to fit into the whole semantical and epistemological scheme as I have developed it. I claimed that a competent speaker knows the character of words. This suggests (even if it does not imply) that if two proper names have the same character, the competent speaker knows that. But he doesn't. What is perhaps even more astounding is that I may introduce a new proper name word and send it on its journey. When it returns to me—perhaps slightly distorted phonologically by its trip through other dialects—I can competently take it into my vocabulary without recognizing it as the very same word! Shocking!

In earlier sections of this paper I have tried to show that many of the metaphysical and epistemological anomalies involving proper names had counterparts involving indexicals, and further that in the case of indexicals these wonders are easily explained by an obvious theory. Insofar as I am correct in regarding the anomalies as counterparts, the theory of indexicals may help to break down unwarranted resistance to the causal chain theory. It may also suggest the form of a general semantical and epistemological scheme comprehending both indexicals and proper names. This is not the place to attempt the latter task; my purpose here is simply to show that it is not trivial.[78] Those who suggest that proper names are merely one species of indexical depreciate the power and the mystery of the causal chain theory.

---

[78] The issues to be resolved by "a general semantical and epistemological scheme comprehending . . . proper names" are such as these. Is the work of the causal chain theory presemantic, as I have claimed? Do proper names have a kind of meaning other than reference? Does the causal chain theory itself constitute a kind of meaning for proper names that is analogous to character for indexicals (but which, perhaps, gives all proper names the same meaning in this sense)? Are proper names words of any particular language? Is there synonymy between proper names that are expressed differently (as there is between 'can't' and 'cannot')? How should we describe the linguistic competence of one who does not know that Hesperus is Phosphorus? Is he guilty of linguistic error? Should we say he does not know what words he speaks? Does he know that 'Hesperus' and 'Phosphorus' are different words? Are they? Is it really possible, as I claim, to account for the semantics of indexicals without making use of the full conceptual resources required to account for the semantics of proper names? I raise these issues—and there are others—within the framework of a hypothetical acceptance of the causal chain theory. There are other issues, of a quite different kind, involved in trying to fill out some details of the causal chain theory itself. For example, if one who has received some particular proper name expression, say, "James," hundreds of times, uses that expression attributively as a proper name, and has in mind no particular source, how do we decide which branch to follow back? The first set of issues seems to me to be largely independent of the details of the relevant causal chains.

AFTERTHOUGHTS

David Kaplan[1]

Demonstratives is now being published, after all these years, in the form in which it was written and circulated for all these years.[2] It is manifestly unfinished. It still retains bracketed metacomments like "[My current inclination is to drop this whole section from the final draft.]." So why have I not cleaned it up and finished it?

Two reasons: a small one and a big one. First and least, I don't know exactly how to fix some of the sections that now seem wrong, and I don't yet see exactly

---

[1] © 1989 by David Kaplan.

I am deeply grateful to John Perry, Howard Wettstein, and Joseph Almog, not only for their efforts in planning and executing the conference that resulted in the present volume, but for their patient encouragement of the publication of *Demonstratives* and their good-natured tolerance of the time it has taken me to gather my afterthoughts. Throughout my life, I have had the uncommonly good fortune to fall under the influence of persons of great intelligence, good humor, and tolerance. Principal among these are my wonderful parents, Martha and Irv Kaplan, my inspiring teachers, Rudolf Carnap and Donald Kalish, and my remarkable wife, Renée Kaplan, the *ne plus ultra* of all three qualities.

[2] I have made the following changes to the circulated text of draft #2. Bibliographical references have been added and the footnotes renumbered. In a few places, a word or a bit of punctuation has been added or a phrase has been moved. I have also corrected a few typographical errors. None of the philosophical errors has been touched. (Thanks to Edward Zalta for his logician's help with the corrections, and thanks to Ingrid Deiwiks for her typographical skills.)

how to connect my current thinking, about propositional attitudes and proper names, with indexicals. Last and most, the spirit of the work—the enthusiasm, the confidence, the hesitations—has an integrity that I regard fondly. It reflects its time, the time described in the preface. My own concerns have moved to other topics. I have even felt a resurgence of atavistic Fregeanism. For me to revise *Demonstratives* now would be the intrusion of a third party between the author and his audience.

I had thought of responding to criticism, of which there have been many over the past decade, several in this very volume, and some quite technically challenging. Unfortunately, I do not have the space to agree in detail with all of them. So instead I have decided to try to look more closely at a few of *Demonstratives'* central concepts.

My reflections are divided into four sections, each of which is intended to be more or less coherent (though I must confess that tangent avoidance has never been my strong suit). The separate sections are somewhat disconnected, as one's afterthoughts tend to be.

I. What Is Direct Reference?

Demonstratives was written against my own Fregean upbringing, as was its progenitor "Dthat."[3] I aimed to challenge several tenets of Fregean semantics. In particular, I argued that Fregean *Sinn* conflates elements of two quite different notions of meaning. One, which I called *character*, is close to the intuitive idea of linguistic meaning (and perhaps of cognitive content). Another, which I called *content*, is what is said or expressed by an expression in a particular context of use. The *content* of an utterance of a complete sentence is a truth-bearing proposition. Where indexicals are involved, the difference between character and content is quite clear. The *content* of the sentence "Today is my birthday" will vary with speaker and day of utterance. The *character* of the sentence is the common meaning which each language user can deploy to speak of himself and of the day of utterance. It is this common character that determines how the content adapts in the varying contexts of use.

The idea of Content—the what-is-said on a particular occasion—is central to my account. It is this notion that I saw, and continue to see, as the primary idea behind Frege's *Sinn*.[4] For what I call *directly referential* expressions, among which are indexicals and demonstratives, I argue that the Fregean picture of the relation between *Sinn* (content) and *Bedeutung* (referent) is entirely wrong.

---

[3] "Dthat" was written and read in 1970, published in *Syntax and Semantics*, vol. 9, ed. P. Cole (New York: Academic Press, 1978); and reprinted in *The Philosophy of Language*, ed. A. P. Martinich (Oxford: Oxford University Press, 1985).

[4] My own analysis of the notion, however, is closer to Russell's *signification*, than to Frege's *Sinn*. I have written more recently on the difference between the semantics of Russell and Frege in section VII of "Opacity" (in *The Philosophy of W. V. Quine*, ed. L. E. Hahn and P. A. Schilpp (Illinois: Open Court, 1986)).

Directly referential expressions are said to refer directly without the mediation of a Fregean *Sinn*. What does this mean? There are two things it might mean. It might mean that the relation between the linguistic expression and the referent is not mediated by the corresponding propositional component, the content or what-is-said. This would be directly contrary to Frege, and it *is* what I meant. But it also might mean that *nothing* mediates the relation between the linguistic expression and the individual. So stated, this second interpretation is a wildly implausible idea. And it is contrary to the development of the notion of character which occurs in the text. This is *not* what I meant.[5]

The "direct" of "direct reference" means unmediated by any propositional component, not unmediated *simpliciter*. The directly referential term goes directly to its referent, *directly* in the sense that it does not first pass through the proposition. Whatever rules, procedures, or mechanisms there are that govern the search for the referent, they are irrelevant to the propositional component, to content. When the individual is determined (when *the reference is fixed*, in the language of Saul Kripke[6]), it is loaded into the proposition. It is this that makes the referent prior to the propositional component, and it is this that reverses the arrow from propositional component to individual in the Direct Reference Picture of the Preface to *Demonstratives*.

How Does Rigid Designation Come In?

If the individual is loaded into the proposition (to serve as the propositional component) before the proposition begins its round-the-worlds journey, it is hardly surprising that the proposition manages to find that same individual at all of its stops, even those in which the individual had no prior, native presence. The proposition conducted no search for a native who meets propositional specifications; it simply 'discovered' what it had carried in. In this way we achieve rigid designation. Indeed, we achieve the characteristic, direct reference, form of rigid designation, in which it is irrelevant whether the individual exists in the world at which the proposition is evaluated. In *Demonstratives* I took this to be the fundamental form of rigid designation.

So certain was I that this *was* the fundamental form of rigid designation, that I argued (from "systematic considerations") that it must be what Kripke had *intended* despite contrary indications in his writing.[7]

It was not. In a letter (asking that I take his remarks into account in these afterthoughts), Kripke states that the notion of rigid designation he intended is

---

[5] Nor did I mean that whatever mediation takes place is nondescriptional. The question whether some sort of description can be fashioned to give the correct reference for a term is not decisive for direct reference (but see footnote 24 below).

[6] Saul Kripke, "Naming and Necessity," in *Semantics of Natural Language*, ed. G. Harman and D. Davidson (Dordrecht: Reidel, 1972); revised edition published as a separate monograph, *Naming and Necessity* (Oxford: Basil Blackwell, 1980). References are to the revised edition. Also see Saul Kripke, "Identity and Necessity," in *Identity and Individuation*, ed. M. K. Munitz (New York: New York University Press, 1971).

[7] Footnote 16, *Demonstratives*.

that "a designator d of an object x is *rigid*, if it designates x with respect to all possible worlds where x exists, and *never designates an object other than x with respect to any possible world*." This definition is designed to be neutral with regard to the question whether a designator can designate an object at a world in which the object doesn't exist. It was motivated, he says, by the desire to avoid getting bogged down in irrelevant discussions of the existence question.[8]

My own discussion of rigid designation was motivated by the desire to highlight the features of rigidity that are associated with direct reference. In the first draft of *Demonstratives*. I had actually used the expression "rigid designation" where I now use "direct reference." I thought of my work as delving into the phenomena identified by Donnellan, Putnam, Kripke, and by me in "Dthat." Direct reference was supposed to provide the deep structure for rigid designation, to underlie rigid designation, to explain it. It would never have occurred to me to be 'neutral' about existence.[9] Existence problems would simply disappear when the underlying, direct reference structure was seen. How could rigid designation not be based on some deeper semantic property like direct reference? It couldn't be an *accident* that names were rigid and descriptions were not.[10]

---

[8] The view I thought of as manifest in his texts, what I called "the more widely held view," is stated on page 146 of "Identity and Necessity" (I&N) in the words, "In a situation where the object does not exist, then we should say that the [rigid] designator has no referent and that the object in question so designated does not exist." Kripke asserts that this view should not be attributed to him and that it occurs nowhere, explicitly or implicitly, in *Naming and Necessity* (N&N). Regarding the statement in I&N, he writes that it would be somewhat odd if "there was a mysterious change of position between my explicit view in *Naming and Necessity* and 'Identity and Necessity', delivered a month or so later." (This was the reason I used the remark in I&N to resolve the uncertainties of N&N.) He then questions the accuracy of the language of I&N (quoted above), writing "It is also possible, I think, that the sentence is mistranscribed from the tape of the talk. A simple change of 'and' to 'or' in the sentence would make it entirely consistent with what I said in *Naming and Necessity*. . . . The corrected version would read even better if 'so' were changed to 'though' (an easy mistake in the transcription of an oral presentation)."

It is good to know his mind on this matter, and I regret misrepresenting his views. I cannot, however, feel embarrassed by my reading of the textual evidence. In the course of my discussion of rigid designation in *Demonstratives*, I was careful to cite all the relevant passages. The neutral definition he intended, containing the clause "and never designates an object other than x," does not occur in N&N, I&N, or the new preface to N&N written ten years after the lectures were given. I continue to think that 'the more widely held view', now seen not to be *Kripke's view, is* the more widely held view.

Proper names are the main topic of N&N. Regarding the rigid designation of proper names, Kripke tells us in the new preface that "a proper name rigidly designates its referent even when we speak of counterfactual situations where that referent would not have existed." It is this view of rigid designation that I had thought he intended all along.

[9] That is, to be neutral on such questions as whether a designator can designate an object at a world in which the object doesn't exist or whether a name from fiction such as "Pegasus" might designate a merely possible object that exists in another possible world. I had stated my views strongly on these issues in appendices X and XI of "Bob and Carol and Ted and Alice," in *Approaches to Natural Language*, ed. J. Hintikka et al. (Dordrecht: Reidel, 1973).

[10] It should be noted, of course, that even an accidental difference between the modal behavior of names and descriptions is sufficient to establish that names are not simply abbreviated descriptions.

It all seemed of a piece to me: the singular propositions, the direct reference, the rigid designation. And all of it could be illustrated by the case of indexicals, in which the mechanism of direct reference was understood. When I set out to revise the section distinguishing Kripke's notion from mine, I realized that it is easier to explain the difference between A and B if they are not both named "A." I therefore determined to introduce a new expression, and so coined the phrase "direct reference."

If we call a designator that designates the same object at all worlds, irrespective of whether the object exists there or not, an *obstinately* rigid designator,[11] then in the usual modal semantics, all directly referential terms will be obstinately rigid (though not every obstinately rigid term need be directly referential).[12] It is obstinate rigidity that I took as the fundamental form of rigidity in *Demonstratives*.

The Paradigm of the Variable

This conception of direct reference takes the variable under an assignment of value as its paradigm.[13] In evaluating "Fx" at a world w, we do not ask whether its value exists in w, we only ask what value was *assigned* to the variable before the process of evaluation at w began. Until a value is *assigned* we have nothing to evaluate.[14] Furthermore, and this is important, it is irrelevant *how* "x" gets its value, *how* the assignment is made, how the value of "x" is *described* when it is assigned to "x." All that matters to the evaluation is that "x" *has* a particular value.

Pronouns in natural language have often been analogized to variables. Pronouns are lexically ambiguous, having both an anaphoric and a demonstrative use.[15] An anaphoric use of a pronoun is *syntactically bound* to another phrase occurring elsewhere in the discourse. In meaningful discourse, a pronoun not used anaphorically is used demonstratively. As I saw the matter, a demonstrative use of a pronoun was simply a *syntactically free* use. Like a free occurrence of a variable, it requires something extralinguistic, a *demonstration* as I then termed it, to *assign* it a value. Demonstrative and anaphoric occurrence of pronouns can thus be seen to correspond to free and bound occurrences of variables. What I want to stress is that the difference between demonstrative and anaphoric uses of pronouns need not be

---

[11] Following a suggestion of Nathan Salmon in *Reference and Essence* (Princeton: Princeton University Press, 1981) p. 34.

[12] An example of an obstinately rigid designator that is not directly referential is given in *Demonstratives*, section IV. It has the form:

$$\text{The } n[(P \wedge n^2 = 9) \vee (\sim P \wedge 2^2 = n + 1)].$$

[13] See paragraph 3 of the Preface to *Demonstratives*.

[14] Until a value is assigned, the entity that is to be evaluated at the possible worlds, whether it be thought of as an open formula or as the content of an open formula, is incomplete. There may not yet be enough information available for it to bear a truth-value.

[15] In "Nomoto inscribed his book" and "Each author inscribed his book," we would ordinarily take "his" to be syntactically bound to "Nomoto" and "Each author." Such syntactically bound uses of pronouns are called *anaphoric*. The same form of words can be used with "his" occurring as a demonstrative, for example, if we were to point at a third party when uttering "his."

conceptualized primarily in terms of lexical ambiguity; it can also be seen in terms of the syntactical distinction between free and bound occurrences of terms. I saw the analogy between variables and pronouns as even closer than had been thought.

I believe that the case of the free pronoun, the demonstrative, can take a lesson from the case of the free variable. As in the case of the free variable, the mechanism by which a value is assigned to a demonstrative, *how* a particular demonstration demonstrates its object, is extralinguistic and thus off-the-record, so to speak. It should not figure in the *content* of what was said. (This, of course, still leaves open the possibility that it might figure in the *cognitive value* of the utterance.) All that matters to the evaluation of what is said (content) is that the demonstrative has a particular value.

Thus my vivid talk about loading the referent into the proposition comes down to this: when using a directly referential term, the *mode of presentation of the referent* (if you will allow a lapse into the Frege idiom) is no part of what is said. Only the referent itself figures in content. Directly referential expressions are *transparent*.[16] Though there may be a complex semantical mechanism that mediates the connection between linguistic expression and referent, that mechanism is unseen in what is said.

Taxonomy: Semantics and Metasemantics

The inspiration for direct reference was, as reported in "Dthat," the true demonstratives. One does feel initially that in the use of a true demonstrative, not only is one trying to put the object itself into the proposition (direct reference), but that the connection between demonstrative and object, call this *reference*, is also extraordinarily direct as compared with the connection between a definite description and its denotation. Demonstratives are transparent, whereas descriptions are visibly at work, searching, searching, searching. Despite this, there is an elaborate theory of reference for demonstratives in *Demonstratives*.

How should we organize our total semantical theory so as to take account of the mechanisms of direct reference? Some have questioned whether these mechanisms even belong to semantics. I think that it is quite important to get clear on this and certain related taxonomic questions if we are to improve our understanding of the relation of semantics to thought.[17] And I am quite unclear on the subject.

---

[16] The sense of transparency I wish to evoke has nothing to do with the contrast between Quinean opacity and Russellian transparency (for which see footnote 30 of my "Opacity"). Rather, it is that of the well-designed computer program in which the commands are 'obvious' and the user need not take account of, indeed is usually unaware of, *how* a command is executed. He knows only that to delete you press "Delete." What else?

[17] On my understanding of the controversy between Donnellan and Kripke, just such a taxonomic question is one of the central points at issue. See Keith Donnellan, "Reference and Definite Descriptions," *Philosophical Review* 75 (1966):281–304; reprinted in Martinich, *op. cit.;* Saul Kripke, "Speaker's Reference and Semantic Reference," in *Contemporary Perspectives in the Philosophy of Language*, ed. P. French, T. Uehling, Jr., and H. Wettstein (Minneapolis: University of Minnesota Press, 1977); Keith Donnellan, "Speaker Reference, Descriptions, and Anaphora," also in *Contemporary Perspectives in the Philosophy of Language.*

There are several interesting issues concerning what belongs to semantics. The fact that a word or phrase *has* a certain meaning clearly belongs to semantics. On the other hand, a claim about the *basis* for ascribing a certain meaning to a word or phrase does not belong to semantics. "Ohsnay" means *snow* in Pig-Latin. That's a semantic fact about Pig-Latin. The *reason* why "ohsnay" means *snow* is not a semantic fact; it is some kind of historical or sociological fact about Pig-Latin. Perhaps, because it relates to how the language is *used,* it should be categorized as part of the *pragmatics* of Pig-Latin (though I am not really comfortable with this nomenclature), or perhaps, because it is a fact *about* semantics, as part of the *Metasemantics* of Pig-Latin (or perhaps, for those who prefer working from below to working from above, as part of the *Foundations of semantics* of Pig-Latin). Again, the fact that "nauseous" used to mean *nauseating* but is coming to mean *nauseated* is a historical, semantic fact about contemporary American English. But neither the reason why the change in semantic value has taken place nor the theory that gives the basis for claiming that there has been a change in meaning belongs to semantics. For present purposes let us settle on *metasemantics.*

Does the historical chain theory (or 'picture' as some are wont to say) of what determines the referent of a proper name belong to semantics or to metasemantics? The critical question seems to be: does the theory state a semantic value of proper names, or does it rather tell us the basis for determining a semantic value for a proper name. Those who believe that the semantic function of a name is completely exhausted by the fact that it *has* a particular referent will regard the historical chain theory as a part of metasemantics. Those who believe that a name *means* something like *the individual who lies at the other end of the historical chain that brought this token to me* will regard the historical chain theory as a part of semantics, as *giving* the meaning rather than as telling us how to discover it. In general, if a referent is all the meaning a name has, then any information used to *fix* the referent is metasemantical. *If* names have another kind of meaning, another kind of semantic value (mere cognitive value, if not identified with *Sinn* or with *character,* won't do), then the fact that certain information is used to fix the referent may well belong to semantics.[18]

Now what about the mechanisms of direct reference? In the case of an indexical, it seems clear that the rule that tells us how the referent varies from one context of use to another, for example the rule that tells us that "yesterday" always refers to the day before the day of utterance, is a part of the meaning of the indexical. It is this kind of meaning that I call *character.* To argue that character belongs to metasemantics, one would have to regard indexicals as systematically ambiguous and as having no meaning at all outside a particular context of use. This is a view that seems reasonable for *generic names,* the kind of name that all us Davids have in common. But it is decidedly implausible for indexicals.

---

[18] It is interesting to note that historical chains also have a use in what we might call *metasyntax.* They give the basis for saying that various utterances are utterances of the same word. I will return to historical chains in section IV.

There is also the fact that there is a *logic* of indexicals, a logic whose semantically valid arguments deviate from the classically valid. This in itself seems to argue that the mechanisms by which directly referential expressions determine their referents belong to semantics?[19]

Demonstratives seem to me a less certain case, perhaps because my views about their semantics is less certain. However, I do think that the indexical model—a common meaning for all uses of, say, "you," which then determines a referent in a particular context of use—is closer to the truth than the generic name model according to which "you" would be a meaningless symbol available to use in dubbing whoever one addresses.

This suggests a related reason for wanting to place the mechanisms of direct reference outside of semantics. It is the analogy between these mechanisms, which determine the referent of expressions that already bear meaning, and the methods available to *create* meaningful expressions from empty syntactical forms, by dubbings, definitions, and the like. Especially in the case of a true demonstrative, one may feel—wrongly, I believe—that one is *assigning* a meaning to an otherwise empty form. If content were all there is to meaning, then, since the mechanisms of direct reference do determine content, it would be reasonable to claim that such mechanisms belong to metasemantics. But in general, it is incorrect to equate meaning with content, and it is certainly incorrect in the case of indexicals.[20]

So, as between semantics and metasemantics, I remain of the view that the theory of the mechanisms of direct reference, at least as that theory is developed in *Demonstratives*, in terms of character and content, belongs to semantics.

A second interesting question is whether to call the theory of these mechanisms *semantics* or *pragmatics*. The central role of the notion *context of use* in determining content might incline one to say that the theory of character is semantics, and the theory of content is pragmatics. But *truth* is a property of contents, and one wouldn't want to be caught advocating a pragmatic theory of truth. The problem is that on my analysis, the mechanisms of direct reference operate *before* the familiar semantical notions of truth and denotation come into play. If I continue to think, as Carnap taught me,[21] that the overall theory of a language should be constructed with syntax at the base, semantics built upon that, and pragmatics built upon semantics, I am faced with a dilemma. The mechanisms of direct reference certainly are not *post*semantical. But equally surely they are not syntactical. Thus I put them in the bottom layer of semantics.[22]

---

[19] Or does it? What *does* the fact that there is an interesting logic of indexicals tell us about the taxonomic place of character? If there is no interesting logic of names, does that tell us something?

[20] It may be correct in the case of proper names, though even there I would be more inclined to equate meaning with referent and to say that referent determines content. I will return to the distinction between the assignment of meaning and the evaluation of meaning in the final section.

[21] *Introduction to Semantics* (Cambridge, Mass.: Harvard University Press, 1942), p. 9.

[22] The time may have come to rethink what I think Carnap taught me.

Whether semantics or pragmatics, it is important to emphasize that there are two roads from singular terms to individuals. The road through what is said, through the propositional component, through content. And the direct road, outside of what is said, outside content. Both roads belong to the *rules* of the language, and not to the vagaries of individual difference among language users. Both connect language to the world.

How Do the Two Roads Figure in Names?

In *Demonstratives* I inquire into the semantic mechanisms whereby indexicals and demonstratives are connected to their referents. How might an analogous discussion of names proceed? Without prejudice to any ultimate issues of semantics versus metasemantics, we might begin with a frankly metasemantical inquiry into naming (what I elsewhere[23] call "dubbing") and the process by which a given name can change its referent over time (if, as seems to be the case, it can). These are matters on which, in theory, Fregeans and Direct Reference theorists might agree.

There is a second question: Does the mechanism whereby the referent of a name is determined belong to semantics, as does character, or to metasemantics, as does the mechanism of meaning change? And if the answer is "semantics," there is the third question: Is the mechanism a part of what is said when the name is used? Or, are names transparent so that only the referent itself figures in what is said? It is on this question that direct reference theorists confront Fregeans.[24]

Finally, there is the question: Is the expression a rigid designator? This again is a matter on which we may all agree.

In this last connection it is important to see, as I earlier did not consistently see, that even one who believes that a name is connected to its referent by a description that the speaker associates with the name and who further believes that this description is *included as part of what is said when the name is used* can achieve rigidity, even obstinate rigidity, through the use of rigidifying operators. Thus, a Fregean who takes the name "Aristotle" to have as its sense *the pupil of Plato and teacher of Alexander the Great* need only add something like *actuality* to the content in order to account for the rigidity of proper names. We then have something like *the actual pupil of Plato and teacher of Alexander the Great* as the propositional component. Rigid designation without direct reference.[25] Well . . .

---

[23]In "Bob and Carol and Ted and Alice."

[24]Note that the outcome of the initial discussion may prejudice this tertiary question. Even if the mechanism by which a name is connected to its referent is taken to be a part of semantics, if the mechanism characterizes the referent from the perspective of the context of use, as does the character of an indexical, rather than from a world perspective, it may not be suitable to play the role of propositional constituent. Thus the result of the first inquiry may argue for a direct reference answer to the third question.

[25]I think that this form of rigidity, logical rather than mathematical or metaphysical, falls under what Kripke now calls *de jure* rigidity, which he describes as "the reference of a designator [being] *stipulated* to be a single object, whether we are speaking of the actual world or of a counterfactual situation" (*Naming and Necessity*, footnote 21 to the new Preface). Note that such descriptions can be used to stipulate the constituents of a possible world, as in "Suppose that the actual author had plagiarized the actual plagiarizer."

not quite *entirely* without direct reference, since the rigidifying operator seems to involve some form of direct reference. But certainly the *name* has not come out directly referential.

But are names merely rigid and not transparent? I, of course, believe not. In some cases arguments that have been given for rigidity can be shown actually to support the stronger claim of transparency, but I will not take up those arguments here.

A Generic Argument for Transparency

There is, however, one generic argument for transparency which seems to apply in many cases of alleged direct reference. It is not a *decisive* argument. Rather, it is a challenge to those who maintain a contrary view.

Many users of the so-called directly referential expressions lack a real understanding of the exact mechanism or rule of reference by which the referent is determined. Though we act *in conformity* with some such rule, we do not invariably know the rule in the sense of being able to articulate it.[26] If one could articulate all the cultural rules one conformed to, anthropology would be a much easier discipline. In the case of syntax, it is even more obvious that we act in accordance with a complex set of rules which most of us could not even begin to articulate. Children certainly master the use of indexicals, demonstratives, and proper names well before they develop the rather sophisticated conceptual apparatus needed to undertake explicit semantical investigations. If we don't know what the semantical rule is, how could it be part of what we say when we use the relevant expression?

So long as we were able to cling to the illusion that words like "I" and "Aristotle" abbreviate simple descriptions that are immediately available to introspection, we could think that anyone who used such an expression knew how it secured its reference and might express this knowledge in using the word. But who still thinks that nowadays?

The Notion of Content Is Central to My Account

To recapitulate: the issue is not whether the information used to determine the referent is descriptive or not. It is rather whether the relevant information, of whatever form, is a part of what is said. Opening an alternative semantic road to reference, one that does not run through content but may nevertheless play a role in the analysis of cognition (belief, knowledge, etc.), may in the end help us all, Fregean and non-Fregean alike, to reach a deeper understanding of the puzzling phenomena that challenged Frege.

---

[26]This is contrary to my claim in *Demonstratives* that the character of pure indexicals is known to every competent speaker. There I claimed that Character = Linguistic Meaning. I still believe that Character captures an important sense of Linguistic Meaning, but I have become more sceptical about the competence of competent speakers and about our access to what our words mean.

As is apparent, the notion of content is central to my way of explaining direct reference. I know that there are some who reject the notion of content. I can't prove that my way of organizing the theoretical apparatus is indispensable. Surely it isn't. But there are observations, intuitions if you will, both in the text of *Demonstratives* and in the formal logic, for which every theory must account. This *is* indispensable.

Are Dthat-Terms Directly Referential?

Some semi-technical meditations on dthat-terms may help to illuminate the notions of content and of direct reference.

As parents soon realize, any worthwhile creation quickly becomes autonomous. Recently I have found myself bemused by my own uses of "dthat."

Two Interpretations of the Syntax and Semantics of "Dthat"

The penultimate paragraph of section IV of *Demonstratives* warns that the possible world semantics of the formal system in section XVIII obscures the distinction between direct reference and rigid designation. The representation of content as a function from possible worlds does not allow us to distinguish between a directly referential expression and one that is merely obstinately rigid. Both cases are represented by the same function, a constant function. There are two separate reasons for this. First, in this representation the content of a syntactically complex expression does not reflect that complexity. I call this the problem of *multiplying through,* as when the content of "$4 \times (5 + 4) + 8 \times (7 - 2) + 6$" is represented by a constant function to 82. Second, even for syntactically simple expressions, the functional representation captures only the obstinately rigid designation; there is no further distinction among obstinately rigid designators that marks the directly referential ones.[27]

The representation in possible world semantics tempts us to confuse direct reference and obstinately rigid designation.[28] Could anyone have confused them after the clear warning of section IV? Could I have? Yes.

This is very unfortunate, because I coined the term "direct reference" just in order to keep the distinction clear. I find the confusion most evident in connection with dthat-terms, about whose syntax and interpretation I seem to equivocate. On one interpretation, "dthat" is a directly referential singular term and the content of the associated description is no part of the content of the dthat-term.

---

[27] If, as some have hypothesized, an expression is directly referential if and only if it is syntactically simple and obstinately rigid, then the second problem is spurious.

[28] If so, why use it? First, because the functional representation is *sufficient to do the work* of *Demonstratives,* namely to show that character and content must be distinguished and to develop a coherent theory within which some unconventional claims about logic, belief, and modality could be grounded. Second, because it is a precise and reliable tool, within the scope of its representational limitations.

On another interpretation, "dthat" is syntactically an operator that requires syntactical completion by a description in order to form a singular term.[29]

If "Dthat" Is an Operator

If "dthat" is an operator, and if the description, which constitutes the operand and thus syntactically completes the singular term, induces a complex element into content, then the correct way to describe "dthat" is as a rigidifer. Complete dthat-terms would be rigid, in fact *obstinately* rigid. In this case the proposition would not carry the individual itself into a possible world but rather would carry instructions to run back home and get the individual who there satisfies certain specifications. The complete dthat-term would then be a rigid description which induces a complex 'representation' of the referent into the content; it would not be directly referential. The *operator* "dthat" might still be regarded as *involving* direct reference, though its own referent would not be the individual denoted by the complete dthat-term, but, like that of all operators, would be of an abstract, higher-order functional type.[30]

---

[29]Properly speaking, since descriptions are singular terms rather than formulas, "dthat" would be a functional expression rather than an operator. But I wish I *had* made "dthat" into an operator for *this* usage. I wish I had made it into a variable binding operator for which I would write "dthat x Fx" instead of writing "dthat[the x Fx]." Then there would have been a much clearer distinction between the two uses of "dthat," and I would not have been led into temptation.

  In *Demonstratives* dthat-terms are eliminable in favor of definite descriptions plus the Actually and Now operators (Remark 13, section XIX). It should be noted that this result is not fundamental. It is dependent on the possibilist treatment of variables in the formal semantics. The variables range over all possible individuals, and a primitive predicate of existence is introduced to represent the varying domains of the different possible worlds. This form of language is more expressive than one in which at each world, the variables range only over the individuals of that world and $\ulcorner \beta\ exists \urcorner$ is expressed by $\ulcorner \exists x\ x = \beta \urcorner$. I now incline toward a form of language which preserves the distinction between what *is* (i.e., what the variables range over) and what *exists*, but which does not automatically assume that all possible individuals have *being* (i.e., does not assume that the variables range over all possible individuals).

[30]The operators "it is actually the case that" and "it is now the case that" could also be thought of as rigidifiers on this model. In all three cases I am somewhat uncomfortable calling the *operator* directly referential, thought they certainly seem to contain a directly referential *element*. Perhaps, in view of the highly abstract nature of their content, the content should be thought of as a complex, only one part of which is induced by direct reference. The operator "it is now the case that" would then be seen as a syntactically complex application of the grammatical formative, "it is the case at 12′——that" to the directly referential term "now." And similarly for the operator "it is actually the case that," which would be seen as a syntactical combination involving application of the same grammatical formative to the term "actuality." Such a treatment would comport better with the suggestion that only names, including "now," "actuality," etc., are directly referential.

  Nathan Salmon points out that if one wished to treat species names like "horse" as directly referential, and as having the species *Equus caballus* as referent, it would be required to adopt a similar device regarding the predicate "is a horse," treating it as a syntactically complex application of the grammatical formative "is a" (a kind of copula) to the directly referential term "horse." Salmon is sceptical, but to me this seems natural. The content of the predicate "is a horse" would then be a complex formed of copulation with the species *E. caballus*.

(contd.)

If "Dthat" Is a Demonstrative Surrogate

The operator interpretation is not what I originally intended. The word "dthat" was intended to be a surrogate for a true demonstrative, and the description which completes it was intended to be a surrogate for the completing demonstration. On this interpretation "dthat" is a syntactically complete singular term that requires no *syntactical* completion by an operand. (A 'pointing', being extralinguistic, could hardly be a part of syntax.) The description completes the *character* of the associated occurrence of "dthat," but makes no contribution to content. Like a whispered aside[31] or a gesture, the description is thought of as off-the-record (i.e., off the *content* record). It determines and directs attention to what is being said, but the manner in which it does so is not strictly *part* of what is asserted. The semantic role of the *description* is prepropositonal; it induces no complex, descriptive element into content. "Dthat" is no more an operator than is "I," though neither has a referent unless semantically 'completed' by a context in the one case and a demonstration in the other. The referent of "dthat" is the individual described (rather than an abstract, higher-order function). It is directly referential.

The Operator Interpretation Is More 'Natural' for the Formal System

The predominant interpretation of "dthat" in the text seems to be as demonstrative surrogate except, I am sorry to say, in the formal system. There, the natural interpretation is as rigidifying operator. The reason for this is that the 'completing' description has a syntactical reality within the formal language. It plays an essential role in the logic, for example in the theorem of Remark 13 showing that dthat-terms are eliminable. Although Frege claimed that the context of use was part of "the means of expression" of a thought,[32] he never, to my knowledge, attempted to incorporate "the pointing of fingers, hand movements, glances" into logical syntax. Can an expression such as the description in a dthat-term appear in logical syntax but make no contribution to semantical form? It would seem strange if it did. But there is, I suppose, no strict contradiction in such a language form.

If there are two different interpretations of "dthat" in *Demonstratives*, they seem to be run together in footnote 72. But maybe there aren't. *Probably* there aren't. Probably, I was just farsighted in envisioning yet-to-be-realized forms of

The desire to treat a variety of lexical items as directly referential requires more attention to the distinction between grammatical formatives and those 'pure' lexical items that might be regarded as naming an abstract object, like a species or a color. I would treat "is a bachelor" in the same way as "is a horse." While acknowledging the *metaphysical* differences between a species and *bachelorhood*, the syntactical unity of "horse" and "bachelor" suggests an analogous *semantical* treatment. Keith Donnellan makes this point in "Putnam and Kripke on Natural Kinds," in *Knowledge and Mind*, ed. C. Ginet and S. Shoemaker (Oxford: Oxford University Press, 1983), pp. 84–104, especially section III. Also, I would go further in syntactical decomposition and first form the complex denoting phrase "a horse" (with appropriate content) before forming the predicate "is a horse."

[31] This is how Kripke characterized the description which completes a dthat-term in his lecture at the conference.

[32] Gottlob Frege "The Thought: A Logical Inquiry," *Mind* 65 (1956):296. Original German publication in *Beiträge zur Philosophie des Deutschen Idealismus* (1918–19).

formal semantics. I earlier held that my views were inconsistent. I now deny that my views are inconsistent![33]

II. Do Demonstrations Complete Demonstratives?

In *Demonstratives* I took the demonstration, "typically, a (visual) presentation of a local object discriminated by a pointing," to be criterial for determining the referent of a demonstrative. While recognizing the teleological character of most pointing—it is typically directed by the speaker's intention to point at a perceived individual on whom he has focused—I claimed that the *demonstration* rather than the *directing intention* determined the referent.[34]

I am now inclined to regard the directing intention, at least in the case of perceptual demonstratives, as criterial, and to regard the demonstration as a mere *externalization* of this inner intention. The externalization is an aid to communication, like speaking more slowly and loudly, but is of no semantic significance.[35]

I had rejected this view earlier, in part because it seemed to confound what Donnellan might call the *referential* and the *attributive* uses of a demonstrative. It seemed to me that this should not happen in a proper semantical theory. I recently realized that the distinction still held. In the case of a perceptual demonstrative, the directing intention is aimed at a perceived object. This object may or may not be the object the speaker has in mind. We can distinguish between Donnellan's kind of having-in-mind and perceptual focus.[36]

A benefit of the view that the demonstration is a mere externalization of the perceptual intention, which determines the referent, is that it offers a new perspective on one of Donnellan's most compelling cases of referential use.

> Suppose someone is at a party and, seeing an interesting looking person holding a martini glass, one asks, "Who is the man drinking a martini?" If it should turn out that there is only water in the glass, one has nevertheless asked a question about a particular person.[37]

---

[33]Thanks to Nathan Salmon and Joseph Almog for help with this section.

[34]This view goes back to the case, discussed in "Dthat," of Carnap's picture. I now regard this as a rather complex, atypical case.

[35]I contrast *no* semantic significance with the fundamental idea of direct reference: that there are matters of semantic significance which do not appear in content. In my earlier treatment, I regarded demonstrations as off-the-record in terms of *content*, but as semantically relevant in determining *character*. I now regard them as totally off-the-record in regard to the semantics of demonstratives. I now see demonstrations as playing the same role for true demonstratives as does pointing at oneself when using the first-person pronoun.

We might think of the demonstration on the model of a term in *apposition* to the demonstrative. Such a term appears to duplicate the demonstrative syntactically, but its semantic contribution is to a subordinate, side remark; its semantic contribution to the main clause seems to be only to hold targets for anaphora. (I know of no well-developed semantics of apposition; it seems a topic worth pursuing.)

[36]Just as it is possible to mis*describe* a perceived object, for example, as a martini when it is really only water in a martini glass, so it is also possible to mis*recognize* one. For example, I may have you in mind, and believing that it is you whom I see hiding under the bed, begin berating you. Even if it was not you under the bed, might it not still be you whom I criticized?

[37]Keith Donnellan, "Reference and Definite Descriptions."

Because of the importance of the perceptual element it is tempting to think of this case in terms of demonstratives. Here the directing intention is aimed at the interesting looking person seen holding a martini glass. Had the speaker pointed and said "Who is that man?" the case would have raised no question of referential use. But suppose, having been taught that it is rude to point at people, the normal mode of externalizing the intention is unavailable. What to do? He cannot simply say, "Who is that man?" with *no* externalization. This would baffle his auditor, who would say, "Which man?" To which the original speaker would have to reply, "The man with the martini." So he shortens the dialogue and uses the description "the man with the martini" as a substitute for the demonstration. Here the speaker might equally well have said, "Who is that man with the martini?" or, "Who is that?" followed by an appositive, parenthetical, whispered "(the man with the martial)."

Now according to my new view of what determines the referent of a demonstrative, the demonstration (here, the description) is there only to help *convey* an intention and plays no *semantical* role at all. We might sum up the case by saying the speaker had a demonstrative intention and, constrained by the conventions of polite behavior, substituted a description for the usual pointing.[38] The slight misdescription has no more effect on the determination of the referent of the tacit demonstrative than would a slight error in aim have had on the determination of the referent of a vocalized demonstrative accompanied by a pointing. In both cases the referent is properly determined by the perceptual intention. In neither case is anything semantical at stake in the description or the pointing. All that is at stake is the accuracy of *communicating* what was said.

What makes this analysis especially intriguing is that this classical case of the referential use of a description can be seen as an *attributive* use of a tacit perceptual demonstrative.

Not all of Donnellan's cases can be accounted for in this way. And in any case, as I have already stated, I believe the distinction between referential and attributive uses is fundamental. But still the idea of finding a role for nonsemantic, communication facilitators, and accounting for referential uses of definite descriptions in this way, is appealing. The theory of direct reference, with its prepropositional semantics, seems especially open to such off-the-record elements in language.

Occurrences

As I carefully noted in *Demonstratives*,[39] my notion of an *occurrence* of an expression in a context—the mere combination of the expression with the context—is

---

[38] A quite different summary would deny the demonstrative element and say that the conventions of polite behavior constrain the speaker to use descriptions and not to use demonstratives. This yields Donnellan's original analysis. Accept my summary. (Is there a basis in the speaker's intentions for claiming that a description is, or is not, being used in apposition to a tacit demonstrative?)

[39] Section XIII.

not the same as the notion, from the theory of speech acts, of an *utterance* of an expression by the agent of a context. An occurrence requires no utterance. Utterances take time, and are produced one at a time; this will not do for the analysis of validity. By the time an agent finished uttering a very, very long true premise and began uttering the conclusion, the premise may have gone false. Thus even the most trivial of inferences, *P* therefore *P*, may appear invalid. Also, there are sentences which express a truth in certain contexts, but not if uttered. For example, "I say nothing." Logic and semantics are concerned not with the vagaries of actions, but with the verities of meanings.[40]

Problems with Occurrences of True Demonstratives

On the theory of true demonstratives in *Demonstratives*, a demonstration accompanies every demonstrative and determines its referent. On my current view, the referent of a true demonstrative is determined by the utterer's intention. But if occurrences don't require utterances, how can we be sure that the requisite intention exists in every possible context? We can't!

A version of this problem already existed in a proposal considered in *Demonstratives* for the formal treatment of "you."[41] The idea is that the context simply be enriched by adding a new feature, which we might call the *addressee*. But suppose there is no addressee. Suppose the agent intends no one, e.g., Thomas Jefferson, dining alone, or surrounded by friends but not *addressing* any of them. Or, suppose the agent is hallucinatory and, though addressing 'someone', no one is there.[42] The problem is that there is no *natural* addressee in such contexts, and thus no natural feature to provide within a formal semantics.

A Refined Conception of Context for True Demonstratives

There are really two problems here, calling for separate solutions. The first is the case of the absent intention. In this case one would want to mark the context as *inappropriate* for an occurrence of "you," and redefine validity as truth-in-all-*appropriate*-possible-contexts.[43] The second is the case of the hallucinatory

---

[40] I am unclear even as to what arguments *ought* to come out as utterance-valid (as opposed to occurrence-valid). There are different notions of utterance-validity corresponding to different assumptions and idealizations. With no idealizations, the rules of repetition and double negation become invalid. This seems hopeless. Should we assume then that utterances take no time? (We might imagine writing out premises and conclusion ahead of time and holding up the paper at the moment of assertion.) Should we assume that the agent knows the language? Should we assume that the agent *asserts* the premises and conclusion, that he *believes* them? This last is related to the question: should "*P*, but I don't believe it" (Moore's paradox) come out to be an utterance-contradiction? It certainly is not an occurrence-contradiction.

[41] Possible Refinement 4 of section XIX combined with the 'indexical theory of demonstratives' of section XVI. The idea is considered, not advocated.

[42] I have in mind the classic hallucination involving an imagined person, not a hallucination *of* an actual person who happens not to be present.

[43] The idea, once broached, of defining validity in terms of *appropriate* contexts might also be used to approach utterance-validity.

agent. Here the context seems appropriate enough; the agent is making no *lin-guistic* mistake in using "you." But the occurrence should be given a 'null' referent.[44]

Another proposal I have heard is just to *impose* an intention on the agent whether he has it or not. Put more gently, this is a logician's proposal; just *assign* a referent. There are two problems with this. First, if it is *possible* for the agent to intend the proposed addressee, there will already be a possible context in which he does. So nothing is lost by ignoring the context in which he doesn't. And if it is *not* possible for the agent to intend the proposed addressee, the imposition seems much too heavy handed. (We don't want an impossibility to come out true.) Second, if we are impatient with intention and just want to *assign* away and get on with the logic, we could formulate the expression with free variables instead of demonstratives. And we should. Why pretend that real demonstratives are nothing more than free variables? If the logic of real demonstratives turns out to be identical with the logic of free variables, well . . . that's something that should *turn out*. It shouldn't be presupposed.[45]

We must make one further refinement in our conception of a context for a true demonstrative. The same demonstrative can be repeated, with a distinct directing intention for each repetition of the demonstrative. This can occur in a single sentence, "You, you, you, and you can leave, but you stay," or in a single dis-course, "You can leave. You must stay." Such cases seem to me to involve an exotic kind of ambiguity, perhaps unique to demonstratives (see below). Where different intentions are associated with different syntactic occurrences[46] of a true demon-strative, we would want to use distinct symbols in our formal language in order to avoid equivocation.

Why do we not need distinct symbols to represent different syntactic occur-rences of "today"?[47] If we speak slowly enough (or start just before midnight), a repetition of "today" will refer to a different day. But this is only because the con-text has changed. It is a mere technicality that utterances take time, a technicality that we avoid by studying expressions-in-a-context, and one that might also be avoided by tricks like writing it out ahead of time and then presenting it all at once. It is no part of the *meaning* of "today" that multiple syntactic occurrences must be associated with different contexts. In contrast, the meaning of a demon-strative requires that each syntactic occurrence be associated with a directing intention, several of which may be simultaneous. And if it happened to be true that we never held more than one such intention simultaneously, *that* would be

---

[44] There are several ways to accommodate this in a formal semantics. I am imagining a treatment along the lines of my use of † in section XVIII of *Demonstratives*.

[45] There are morals to be drawn from these arguments. I urge the young author of *Demonstratives* to take them to heart if he wishes to do serious work.

[46] I say *syntactic* occurrence to differentiate from my expression-in-a-context sense of "occurrence."

[47] I choose "today" rather than "now" to avoid the distracting issue of the vagueness of "now."

the mere technicality. In fact, it is not true. In the aforementioned cases ("You, you, you, and you . . ."), in which there is simultaneous perception of all addressees, I think it correct to say that are several distinct, simultaneous, directing intentions, indexed to distinct intended utterances of the demonstrative "you" (which are then voiced one at a time).

The basic fact here is that although we must face life one *day* at a time, we are not condemned to perceive or direct our attention to one *object* at a time. (If we were, the language of thought would be monadic predicate logic.)

Thus within the formal syntax we must have not one demonstrative "you," but a sequence of demonstratives, "you$_1$," "you$_2$," etc., and within the formal semantics the context must supply not a single addressee, but a sequence of addressees, some of which may be 'null' and all but a finite number of which would presumably be marked *inappropriate*.

We will need to be able to formulate sentences of the formal language in which different intentions are associated with different syntactic occurrences of a demonstrative, if we are to face the looming challenge of Frege's Problem, in which one who is simultaneously perceiving two parts of what may or may not be a single object asserts, "That$_1$ is that$_2$."[48]

The Semantic Role of Directing Intentions

What should we think of as the contextual feature relevant to the evaluation of a demonstrative? In the formal semantics, it may be taken to be the demonstratum. But at the preformal level, I think of it as the *directing intention*. The directing intention is the element that differentiates the 'meaning' of one syntactic occurrence of a demonstrative from another, creating the *potential* for distinct referents, and creating the *actuality* of equivocation.[49] It also seems critical for the 'cognitive value' of a syntactic occurrence of a demonstrative, at least for the speaker. Note however that it is neither character, content, nor referent. In the case of the pure indexicals, "today," "here," etc., the relevant contextual feature is always the referent, and there doesn't seem to be any role, let alone a semantic role, for a comparable entity. Curiouser and curiouser!

In *Demonstratives* I accepted "tentatively and cautiously" what I called *the Fregean theory of demonstrations*. The demonstration—a 'manner of presentation' of an individual that was separable from any particular context and could be evaluated at other contexts and circumstances—supplied the character for the associated demonstrative.[50] A reason why I favored the Fregean theory of

---

[48]Consider, for example, a magician performing the 'sawing a woman in half' illusion. The audience sees someone's head sticking out of one end of a box and what appear to be someone's feet sticking out of the other end. "Is that person really *that* person?" they wonder.

[49]I regard it as an equivocation whenever a new directing intention is involved, even if it directs a second syntactic occurrence of a demonstrative to the same referent.

[50]See sections XV and XVI of *Demonstratives*.

demonstrations was that the need for a completing demonstration distinguished the true demonstratratives from the pure indexicals. A second reason was that the Fregean idea that *that very demonstration* might have picked out a different demonstratum, an idea that depended on the separability of a demonstration from a particular context, seemed to track very closely the cognitive uncertainties of "that$_1$ is that$_2$." This cognitive value appears in character, and thus as an aspect of meaning.

The need for a directing intention to determine the referent of a demonstrative still allows us to distinguish the true demonstratives from the pure indexicals. The parameters for the latter are brute facts of the context, like location and time. But if directing intentions are not separable and evaluable at other points (perhaps they are), the cognitive uncertainties of "that$_1$ is that$_2$" may no longer be an aspect of meaning. Should they be?

Linking True Demonstratives

It is interesting to note that in natural language every new syntactic occurrence of a true demonstrative requires not just a referent-determining intention, but a *new* referent-determining intention. When two syntactic occurrences of a demonstrative appear to be linked to a single intention, at least one must be anaphoric. When we wish to refer to the referent of an earlier demonstrative, we do not repeat the demonstrative, we use an anaphoric pronoun, "He [pointing] won't pass unless he [anaphoric pronoun] studies." The fact that demonstrative and anaphoric pronouns are homonyms may have led to confusion on this point. The case is clearer when the demonstrative is not homonymous with the anaphoric pronoun. Contrast, "This student [pointing] won't pass unless he [anaphoric pronoun] studies" with "This student [pointing] won't pass unless this student [pointing a second time at what is believed to be the same person] studies." The awkwardness of the second shows that the way to *secure* a second reference to the referent of a demonstrative is to use an anaphor.

This implies that it is impossible to utter an instance of the rule of Double Negation using a premise containing a demonstrative, "You stay. Therefore, it is not the case that you do not stay." We have a Hobson's choice. We can intend the "you" of the conclusion as anaphoric across the sentential barrier to the "You" of the premise (something we readily do in ordinary discourse, but are ill-prepared to do in formal logic).[51] In which case, the argument is valid, but not really an instance of Double Negation (at least not as we know and love it). Or, we can concentrate, try not to blink, and try to hold our attention on the same

---

[51] It would be good if our formal language allowed variables to be bound to arbitrary terms both within the sentence and across the sentential barrier in the way in which anaphoric reference takes place in natural language. The problem of how to do this in a suitably smooth way seems quite interesting.

addressee, in the hope that we will succeed in targeting the same individual with the second demonstrative. (Can we ever be *certain* that they haven't pulled the old switcheroo?) In this case, the form of argument is really something like, "You$_1$ stay. Therefore, it is not the case that you$_2$ do not stay," and hence not valid. Even if we idealize the speed of speech, so that we are certain that they haven't pulled a switcheroo, the *form* of the argument is still not that of Double Negation because of the equivocation involved in the use of a second demonstrative.

Perhaps we should give up on Double Negation, and claim that the argument is a valid enthymeme with the implicit premise "You$_1$ = you$_2$," the premise we strove to make true by fixing our attention. "All right," said the tortoise to Achilles, "repeat the argument and this time remember to utter the additional premise."

The source of the difficulty is the principle, the correct principle, that every new syntactic occurrence of a demonstrative (one that is not a disguised anaphoric pronoun) requires its own determining intention. The problem, in a nutshell, is that where demonstratives are involved, it doesn't seem possible to *avoid* equivocation. There is an understood, harmless, systematic equivocation built into the semantics of demonstratives in natural language. It is this that I termed "an exotic kind of ambiguity, perhaps unique to demonstratives."

For purposes of logic, on the other hand, it seems essential both to avoid equivocation and to allow any well-formed expression to have multiple syntactic occurrences (in antecedent and consequent, or in premise and conclusion) *without changing its semantical analysis.* The validity of the sentence "If you stay, you stay" (with no anaphors) depends on using the same intention to determine the referent of both occurrences of the demonstrative "you." Just as multiple occurrences of "now" in a single argument must be referenced to the same time parameter, so multiple occurrences of the same demonstrative must be referenced to the same directing intention. Otherwise the language would suffer the same systemic equivocation that natural language does, and there would be no logic, at least none with Double Negation and Repetition and the like. Using the refined conception of context described above, it is easy to write semantical rules that give the same analysis to recurrences of the same demonstrative (what is hard is to write rules that don't). It seems certain that this is how we ought to proceed.

But does it leave our logic vulnerable to a charge of misrepresentation? What is it that we hope to learn from such a logic? I don't think we can regard this as an idealization comparable to that involved in referencing all occurrences of "now" to a single instant. To assume that one intention can drive two occurrences of a demonstrative seems more falsification than idealization.

I hope that there is a key to this problem in my earlier remark that logic and semantics are concerned not with the vagaries of actions, but with the verities of meanings. There is something I'm not understanding here, and it may be something very fundamental about the subject matter of logic.

III. What Is Context?

Context Provides Parameters

Some directly referential expressions, most notably the indexicals, require that the value of a certain parameter be given before a determinate element of content is generated. Context of Use is this parameter. For example, the content of the word "today" is a function of the time of the context of use. If we think of the formal role played by context within the model-theoretic semantics, then we should say that context *provides* whatever parameters are needed.[52] From this point of view, context is a package of whatever parameters are needed to determine the referent, and thus the content, of the directly referential expressions of the language.

An Assignment of Values to Variables Is the Parameter Needed to Determine the Referent of a Variable

Taking context in this more abstract, formal way, as providing the parameters needed to generate content, it is natural to treat the assignment of values to free occurrences of variables as simply one more aspect of context. My point is taxonomic. The element of content associated with a free occurrence of a variable is generated by an assignment. Thus, for variables, the assignment supplies the parameters that determine content just as the context supplies the time and place parameters that determine content for the indexicals "now" and "here."

The assignment, as I am arguing we should conceive of it, is not 'evaluating' the variable at a world; rather it is generating an element of content, and it is the content which is then evaluated at a world.[53] Content is generated at a context, and each context is associated with a particular possible world.[54] The agent, time, and place are all drawn from that world. Similarly, an assignment associated with a particular context may be taken to assign only values that exist in the world of the context. Once such a value is assigned, that is, once a content is determined, the content can, of course, be evaluated at worlds in which the value does not exist.

In arguing that assignments of values to variables play a theoretical role analogous to contexts, I harp upon my theme that free variables can be taken as paradigms of direct reference. Though the theme was stated in *Demonstratives*. I did

---

[52]This, rather than saying that context *is* the needed parameter, which seems more natural for the pretheoretical notion of a *context of use*, in which each parameter has an interpretation as a natural feature of a certain region of the world.

[53]I know, I know! There are other ways to treat assignments, but they obscure my point. Having returned to the semantics of free variables, it may seem that I am obsessed with the topic, but bear with me.

[54]When I revert to the standard "possible worlds" nomenclature rather than the "possible circumstance of evaluation" terminology of *Demonstratives*, it is in order to connect certain points I wish to make with the standard literature. I use the two phrases synonymously.

not then recognize how thoroughgoing it was, because I did not then think of free variables in the robust way I now do, as demonstrative uses of pronouns. Not as real demonstratives, which require a directing intention from the agent of the context, but as a kind of *faux demonstrative,* one which looks real until you check into the origin of its value.

As remarked above, free occurrences of pronouns in meaningful discourse are demonstratives. But a free occurrence of an *anaphoric* pronoun would literally be meaningless. In our logical formalisms, variables play the anaphoric role. Thus a free occurrence of a variable is the mark of an incompletely interpreted expression. The case we are dealing with here is the free occurrence of a variable in a premise or conclusion of an argument. Do not confuse this case, the case with the interpretational gap, with the case in which a *bound* occurrence of a variable *appears* free because we are focusing attention on a subformula. It is the second case, the case of *bound* variables, for which the Tarski apparatus of *satisfaction* and *assignments* was originally designed. In that case there is no interpretational gap; it is the *quantifier* (or other variable binder) that is being interpreted, and we must get it right. So the rules for evaluating *bound* occurrences of variables are another story entirely, and an irrelevant one.

That which is interpretively unconstrained is available for office, and those familiar with logic will be aware that authors of deductive systems have chosen varying paths in their treatment of free variables. Some prohibit them entirely. Some treat them as if they were bound by invisible, outer, universal quantifiers, what is sometimes called the *generality* interpretation. Some treat them as if they were individual constants. My own treatment uses the familiar idea of an *assignment,* taken from the Tarski apparatus for the treatment of bound variables. I even confine the values of the variables to the domain of quantification (assuming the domain of quantification consists of what exists). This seems natural enough. But it does, as will be seen, have surprising consequences.

The discussion of parameters completes the analogy between free variables and indexicals. From an abstract formal point of view, they are highly analogous. Both are *parametric;* their content varies as the parameter varies. If we package all parameters under the heading *context,* an odd but interesting thing to do, we could even claim that content varies with context, the mark of indexicality. (Note that not all directly referential expressions are parametric; proper names are not.)[55]

These formal analogies should not cause us to lose sight of the fundamental difference between free variables and indexicals.[56] Indexicals are real, meaning-bearing elements of language. Free variables are not; they are artifacts of our formalism. Assignments are *stipulative;* they have no fact-of-the-matter parameter

---

[55] Not, at least on my interpretation. One who thought of proper names as *generic* (as standing for any individual so named) until set into a context of use would be thinking of them as parametric.

[56] It should be clear that I am exploring the notion of a content-generating parameter, not insisting on one way of developing the semantics of free variables.

as do the pure indexicals and true demonstratives. Indexicals are *perspectival;* their content is dependent on the speaker's point of view, the context of utterance. Free variables are not *perspectival* in any but the most attenuated metaphorical sense. It is for these reasons that I use the term *parametric* for what indexicals and free variables have in common.[57]

The Rule of Necessitation Fails for Free Variables

One of the things that delighted me about indexicals was the convincingly deviant modal logic. As shown in *Demonstratives,* the rule of Necessitation:

If ϕ is valid, then $\Box\phi$ is also valid

fails in the presence of indexicals.[58] The same rule also fails in the presence of free variables. If our assignments to free variables draw their values from the domain of quantification, then

$$\exists y\ y = x$$

is valid, but if the domain of quantification varies from possible world to world,

$$\Box\exists y\ y = x$$

is not valid.[59]

Harry Deutsch points out a related feature of the logic of free variables. On the present interpretation, although the basic *quantifier* logic for variables is classical, a free logic is simulated within the scope of the necessity operator. Thus, although

$$(\forall xFx \rightarrow Fy)$$

is valid,

$$\Box(\forall xFx \rightarrow Fy)$$

is not. An additional antecedent that is characteristic of free logic is required within the scope of $\Box$:

$$\Box((\exists x\ x = y \wedge \forall xFx) \rightarrow Fy).$$

The failure of the rule of Necessitation in the presence of free variables results from the play between context (if the assignment parameter is taken as part of

---

[57] Perhaps the closest analogy is that developed above (in the subsection: "The Paradigm of the Variable") between the free variable, the 'free' pronoun, and the demonstrative, whose referent must be stipulated by a directing intention. Even in this case, however, there remains the puzzling problem of the seeming semantic role of the directing intention. In the case of an assignment, it is surely only the value that matters.

[58] For example, take ϕ to be "I am here now" or "I exist."

[59] Using a domain of quantification that varies from world to world deviates from the formulation in *Demonstratives*. As noted earlier, in *Demonstratives* I used a fixed domain, thought of as including all 'possible' individuals, along with a predicate "*exists*" whose extension could vary from world to world.

context) and point of evaluation. I view it as indicating that a parametric expression, likely to be directly referential, is at work.[60]

The Actual-World as an Aspect of Context

The world of the context of use—what is taken for model-theoretic purposes to be the *actual-world*—plays a dual role in the logic. It is the parameter that the context provides for the indexical operator "it is actually the case that." It is thus a *generation parameter* required to fix a determinate content for sentences containing the indexical operator. At the same time, and quite independently, it is also an *evaluation parameter* that plays a special role in the notion of validity. The latter is its more fundamental role, a role that would be required even if the language contained no indexicals for which the actual-world was needed as a generation parameter.[61]

Validity is truth-no-matter-what-the-circumstances-were-*in-which-the-sentence-was-used*. As I would put it, *validity* is universal truth in all *contexts* rather than universal truth in all possible worlds. Where indexicals are involved we cannot even speak of truth until the sentence has been set in a context. But it may appear that for a modal language *without* indexicals, without expressions that require a parameter, the notion of a context of use has no bearing. This is not correct. Truth in every model means truth in the 'designated' world of every model. This 'designated' world, the world at which truth is assessed, plays the role of actual-world. It is all that remains of context when the generation parameters are stripped away. But it does remain.

Perhaps this is more easily seen if we add the indexical operator "it is actually the case that" to the language. It is then apparent that the 'actuality' referenced by this operator is what we have become accustomed to refer to as the "designated" world.

The notion of the *actual-world* can be obtained in either of two ways. As I did, by starting from a full-blown language containing indexicals, deriving the notion of a context of use from its role in the semantics of indexicals, and then recognizing that truth, absolute truth in a model, is assessed at the world-of-the-context, i.e., the actual-world; or alternatively, by starting from a modal language *without*

---

[60] There is another, more sceptical, way to view failures of the rule—as an indicator of unclarity regarding the interpretation of free variables. This may be Kripke's outlook in his pellucid discussion of the Barcan formula in "Semantical Considerations on Modal Logic," *Acta Philosophica Fennica* (1963):83–94. His analysis assumes the generality interpretation of free variables (on which the rule of Necessitation does in fact hold). He then shows that an apparent counterinstance to the rule is based on an incorrect formulation of the rule in this environment. As a corrective he proposes to formulate the system of derivation in a way that prohibits free variables in asserted formulas. He does not question the validity of the rule. I, being familiar with other counterinstances to the rule, have no difficulty with an interpretation of free variables that simply makes the rule invalid.

[61] Within the formal system of *Demonstratives*, a content is evaluated at both a world and a time. Within that system, what is said here of the world of the context also holds of the time of the context.

indexicals, recognizing that truth, absolute truth in a model, is assessed at the 'designated' world, and noticing that if we *were* to add the actuality operator this designated world would be the actual-world. Briefly, we can come upon the notion either in its guise as 'world of the context of use' or in its guise as 'designated world'. On either approach, the notion of actual-world plays a special role in validity. It is the indispensable residue of the notion of *context*.

The terminology "context of use" evokes agents and utterances; the terminology "it is actually the case that" does not. There is, however, this common, underlying idea, one which I continue to think of as perspectival—the actual world is where we actually are . . . now. Recognizing that there are these two faces to the one notion makes me want to differentiate the possible worlds that can play the role of actual-world from those that are 'merely' possible, for example, by requiring that the former but not the latter not be empty; but not all will agree that there should be such differentiation. It is, in the end, a question of what you want to *do* with your logic.

Why the Deviant Logic?

The intuitive distinction between the actual-world, in which the content is generated, and all those possible-worlds in which the content can be evaluated,[62] lies at the heart of such interesting logical phenomena as the failure of Necessitation. Any feature of a possible world which flows from the fact that it contains the context of use may yield validity without necessity. Such features need not depend on the contingent existence of individuals. For example, in the actual-world, the speaker, referred to by "I," must be located at the place referred to by "here" at the time referred to by "now." Hence "I am here now" is valid. But this requirement holds *only* in the actual-world, the world in which the content is expressed. Hence, what is expressed by the sentence need not be necessary. No 'existence questions' cloud this case.

I find it useful to think of validity and necessity as *never* applying to the same entity. Keeping in mind that an actual-world is simply the circumstance of a context of use, consider the distinction between:

(V) No matter what the context were, ϕ would express a truth in the circumstances of that context

and:

(N) The content that ϕ expresses in a given context would be true no matter what the circumstances were.

The former states a property of sentences (or perhaps characters): validity; the latter states a property of the content of a sentence (a proposition): necessity.

The nonstandard logic of *Demonstratives* follows from two features of the semantics of context and circumstance. The first is the possibility that a given

---

[62] Joseph Almog emphasizes this distinction in "Naming without Necessity," *Journal of Philosophy* (1986):210–42.

sentence might have a different content in different contexts. It is this that makes "I am here now" a valid *sentence*. And the second is the fact that not every possible circumstance of evaluation is associated with an (appropriate) possible context of use; in other words, not every possible-world is a possible actual-world. Though there may be circumstances in which no one exists, no possible context of use can occur in such circumstances. It is this that makes "Something exists" a valid sentence. Even if no indexical occurs in the language, the second feature puts bite into the notion of the actual-world.

These two features correspond to two kinds of a priori knowledge regarding the actual-world, knowledge that we lack for all other possible worlds. Corresponding to the first feature, there is our knowledge that certain *sentences* always express a truth regarding the world in which they are expressed. Corresponding to the second feature, there is our knowledge that certain *facts* always hold at a world containing a context. The latter is independent of the indexical resources of the language.[63]

A Word for Cognitive Value

The contexts of *Demonstratives* are metaphysical, not cognitive. They reach well beyond the cognitive range of the agent. Any difference in world history, no matter how remote, requires a difference in context.[64]

In *Demonstratives* I tried to get at cognitive value through the notion of character.[65] When the twins, Castor and Pollux, each sincerely say, "My brother was born before I was," they are said to be in the same cognitive state but to believe different things.[66] Though the utterances of the twins have the same cognitive value (same character), they do not bear the same truth-value (nor have the same content). I found it attractive to follow Frege in using a strictly semantical concept (character), needed for other semantical purposes, to try to capture his idea of cognitive value.[67]

As in the case of content, the possible-worlds style of formal semantics in *Demonstratives* represents character as a function, in this case as a function from possible contexts of use. I continue to believe that proper names are not parametric,

---

[63]The preceding material of this section resulted from a conversation with Harry Deutsch and Kit Fine.

[64]As noted, the entire world history is an aspect of context; it is the parameter for the indexical "Actually."

[65]I have been told that "cognitive" is not the right word for what I have in mind. (I have also been told that what I have in mind is not the right idea for what I am trying to do.) I am not committed to the word; I take it from Frege (who probably never used it).

[66]As indicated in *Demonstratives*, my views on this have been influenced by John Perry.

[67]Even granting that we cannot *articulate* the rules of character for all directly referring expressions, we may still recognize a difference in cognitive value when presented with a pair of terms of different character; there may still be a correlation between distinct characters and distinct cognitive values. Joseph Almog suggests that we might express the point by saying that cognitive value *supervenes* on character.

i.e., the *same name*[68] does not vary in referent from context to context.[69] Thus, the characters of two distinct proper names of the same individual would be represented by the same constant function, and thus, under the functional interpretation, coreferential names would not differ in character. Since it is indisputable that distinct proper names have distinct cognitive values,[70] the project of discriminating cognitive values of proper names by character is immediately defeated.[71]

Lately, I have been thinking that it may be a mistake to follow Frege in trying to account for differences in cognitive values strictly in terms of *semantic* values. Can distinctions in cognitive value be made in terms of the message without taking account of the medium? Or does the medium play a central role? On my view, the message—the *content*—of a proper name is just the referent. But the *medium* is the name itself.[72] There are *linguistic* differences between "Hesperus" and "Phosphorus" even if there are no *semantic* differences. Note also that the syntactic properties of "Hesperus" and "Phosphorus," for example, their distinctness as *words*, are surer components of cognition than any purported semantic values, whether objectual or descriptional.

If words are properly individuated, by their world histories rather than by their sound or spelling, a name might almost serve as its own Fregean *Sinn*. The linguistic difference between "Hesperus" and "Phosphorus"—the simple difference between thinking of Venus qua *Hesperus* and thinking of it qua *Phosphorus*—may be all the difference in mode of presentation one needs in order to derive the benefits of sense and denotation theory. Words are undoubtedly denizens of cognition. If, through their history, they also provide the worldly link that determines the referent, then except for serving as content, they do all that Fregean *Sinn* is charged with. But they do it off-the-record, transparently and nondescriptively.[73]

---

[68] A less obvious notion than may appear.

[69] A proposed counterinstance: If a name can change its referent over time, as "Madagascar" is said to have done, then would not that very name have had one referent in an early context and another in a recent context? (For a partial response see the discussion below of logically proper names.)

[70] It is on the rock of distinct cognitive values for distinct names that Frege erected his gossamer theory. Note that Frege's initial argument makes use only of the uninterpreted forms "a = a" and "a = b." The distinction between repetition of a single name and the use of two distinct names is already sufficient to make the points about *cognition* even before any examples (or even the notion of *Sinn*) are introduced.

[71] One could, of course, argue that distinct names do differ in character and abandon the idea that character represents only the *parametric* determination of reference, i.e., how content varies from context to context. The fact that *indexicals* are parametric, that their character can be represented as a function from possible contexts, would then be regarded as a special case. The danger of trying to find characterological differences in distinct proper names is that the notion of *character* either will slip over from semantics to metasemantics or will become an ad hoc pastiche. In either case the dignified reality of character as the fundamental semantical value for indexicals would be seriously diluted.

[72] In the case of indexicals, the character, which I took to represent cognitive value in *Demonstratives* may also be thought of as the medium by which content is generated (though character is semantic rather than syntactic in nature).

[73] Here I echo an idea urged by Felicia (then Diana) Ackerman in "Proper Names, Propositional Attitudes, and Nondescriptive Connotations," *Philosophical Studies* 35 (1979):55–69.

IV. Who Can Say What?

To complete my afterthoughts regarding the semantics of direct reference, I must address certain issues on the border between metasemantics and epistemology.[74] My reflections were driven by a puzzle about Russellian 'logically proper names'. In the end I concluded that the puzzle has a simple answer (to which I will return in the end).[75] But it prompted thoughts on the more controversial issue of constraints on what an agent in a particular epistemological situation can express.

What We Can't Do with Words: The Autonomy of Apprehension

As I understand Frege and Russell, both believed that the realm of propositions accessible to thought, i.e., those capable of being *apprehended,* is independent of and epistemologically *prior to* the acquisition of language. In using language we merely encode what was already thinkable.[76] Therefore, whatever can be expressed using language was already, prelinguistically, an available object of thought.[77]

I see this view of the *autonomy of apprehension* in Russell's claim that

> in every proposition that we can apprehend (i.e., not only in those whose truth and falsity we can judge of, but in all that we can think about), all the constituents are really entities with which we have immediate acquaintance.[78]

Perhaps it accounts for the feeling one has in reading Russell on logically proper names, and even more so in reading Frege, that, like Humpty Dumpty, everyone runs their own language. When we speak, we *assign* meanings to our words; the words themselves do nor *have* meanings. These assignments are, in theory, unconstrained (except by whatever limitations our epistemic situation places on what we can apprehend). In practice, it may be prudent to try to *coordinate* with the meanings others have assigned, but this is only a practical matter.[79]

---

[74] I am indebted to Keith Donnellan for several formative discussions of this material.

[75] It has at least one simple answer; it also has several less simple answers.

[76] Here we may have the foundation for the view that meaning is all in the head, or at least all already directly accessible by the head.

[77] Language, of course, aids communication, and also makes it easier, perhaps even possible, to *reason* using very complex thoughts. But the *manipulation* of thoughts is not what I am getting at here. My interest is in what can be apprehended and what can be expressed.

[78] Bertrand Russell, "On Denoting," *Mind* 14 (1905):479–93.

[79] Prudential considerations of this kind will not, of course, affect a free spirit like H. Dumpty. An analogy: the concept of driving a car in traffic does not imply obedience to the conventions (sometimes called "rules" or "laws") whereby the movement of different drivers is coordinated. But it is usually (often? occasionally?) prudent to so act. Dumpty's friend Dodgson appears to have shared his views. See Lewis Carroll (with an Introduction and Notes by Martin Gardner), *The Annotated Alice* (Cleveland: World Publishing Company, 1963), especially the notes on pages 268–69.

Subjectivist Semantics

We may term this view, *subjectivist* semantics. Although the *entities* which serve as possible meanings may be regarded as objective, in the sense that the same possible meanings are accessible to more than one person,[80] the *assignment* of meanings is subjective, and thus the *semantics* is subjective. Since each individual user must *assign* meanings rather than receiving them with the words, each user's semantics is autonomous. What the language community does make available to each of its members is a syntax, an *empty* syntax to which each user must add his own semantics.

The individual can express only those propositions that were already available to him as thoughts before receiving the benefits of linguistic communion. We cannot enlarge the stock of possible meanings that are available to us by drawing on the total stock of meanings extant in the language community. In this sense there is no semantic sharing. What each user can express is independent of the resources of other members of the language community, and in this sense what each user can express is *independent of language.*

There are differences between Frege and Russell in the way in which one's epistemic situation is seen to influence the propositions one can apprehend. Frege suggests that all mankind has access to the same thoughts. Thus that differences in our experience, our location in space and time, our culture (including in particular our linguistic community), do not affect what propositions we can apprehend.[81]

Russell's view was plainly different. He believed that our idiosyncratic experiences *do* affect what propositions we can apprehend. For Russell one can apprehend a proposition containing an individual x as a component if and only if one is directly acquainted with x. And it is clear that what one is directly acquainted with is a function of one's experience.[82]

A fixed point of all such Russellian theories is that we may be so situated as to be able to *describe* a certain individual x but not to *apprehend* it; whereas a friend may be able to *apprehend* that selfsame individual. The friend can dub x with a logically proper name n, and try to communicate his thought using n. No use. We cannot just accept n with his meaning, we must assign it our own meaning, and in this case his meaning (namely, x) is not available to us for assignment. Sigh![83]

---

[80]This was certainly the view of Frege and sometime the view of Russell.

[81] In "The Thought: A Logical Inquiry," his discussion of the first-person pronoun indicates some ambivalence regarding this view. His suggestion that context of use is a partial determinant of the *Sinn* of an indexical may also indicate ambivalence if it implies (what I believe to be true) that persons in different contexts have access to different (indexical) thoughts.

[82] Let different views of how direct *direct acquaintance* must be reflect different *Theories of Apprehension*. Russell suggests in the beginning of "On Denoting" that we may be acquainted with other people's *bodies* though we are not acquainted with other people's minds "seeing that these are not directly perceived." This suggestion does not accord with Russell's later views, and some think that this was not his *true* view even at the time of "On Denoting."

[83]This is the situation in which we are forced to assign a descriptive meaning to the word our friend used as a name. Bad coordination, but unavoidable according to Russell. Frege's theory of apprehension seems to *permit* perfect coordination, which he urges for scientific discourse while recognizing that we don't always achieve it in ordinary discourse.

Consumerist Semantics

Contrast the view of subjectivist semantics with the view that we are, for the most part, language *consumers*. Words come to us prepackaged with a semantic value. If we are to use *those words*, the words we have received, the words of our linguistic community, then we must defer to *their* meaning. Otherwise we play the role of language *creators*.[84] In our culture, the role of language creators is largely reserved to parents, scientists, and headline writers for *Variety;* it is by no means the typical use of language as the subjectivist semanticists believe. To use language as language, to express something, requires an intentional act. But the intention that is required involves the typical consumer's attitude of compliance, not the producer's assertiveness.[85]

There are two senses of "naming": dubbing and referring. To the consumerist, subjectivist semanticists have not adequately distinguished them.

To some, subjectivist semantics will seem a right and proper conservatism: Practice self-reliance—there is no such thing as a free thought! But it should be recognized that the view is incompatible with one of the most important contributions of contemporary theory of reference: the historical chain picture of the reference of names.

The notion of a historical chain of acquisition by which a name is passed from user to user, was first used to facilitate abandonment of the classical, description theory of proper names found in Frege and Russell.[86] The notion of a historical chain does this by offering an alternative explanation of how a name in local use can be connected with a remote referent, an explanation that does not require that the mechanism of reference is already in the head of the local user in the form of a self-assigned description. In determining the referent of the name "Aristotle," we need not look to the biography's *text,* instead we look to its *bibliography.*

A Role for Language in Thought: Vocabulary Power as an Epistemological Enhancement

There is another, possibly more fundamental, use of the notion: to tilt our perspective on the *epistemology* of language away from the subjectivist views of Frege

---

[84]We may, like the prudent subjectivist semanticist, always attempt to give a known word the same meaning as that *commonly given* to it. We would still be playing the role of language creators, though without the creativity of someone like H. Dumpty.

[85]I would like to formulate the relevant intention as one to use the word with *its* meaning, rather than with the meaning *assigned* by the person from whom the consumer heard (first heard?) the word. The immediate source from which the word was received seems to me to be primarily relevant to the question of which word it is (among homonyms), rather than to the question of what meaning it has.

[86]The idea, and its use in the argument against description theory, first appears in print in Keith Donnellan's "Proper Names and Identifying Descriptions," *Synthese* 21 (1970):335–58; reprinted in *Semantics of Natural Language,* ed. D. Davidson and G. Harman (Humanities Press, 1972). It then appears in Kripke's *Naming and Necessity,* which, coincidentally, was first published in the same collection in which Donnellan's article is reprinted (*Semantics of Natural Language*). Kripke notes, "the historical acquisition picture of naming advocated here is apparently very similar to views of Keith Donnellan" (addenda to *Naming and Necessity,* p. 164).

and Russell and toward a more communitarian outlook.[87] The notion that a referent can be carried by a name from early past to present suggests that the language itself carries meanings, and thus that we can *acquire* meanings through the instrument of language. This frees us from the constraints of subjectivist semantics and provides the opportunity for an *instrumental* use of language to broaden the realm of what can be expressed and to broaden the horizons of thought itself.

On my view, our connection with a linguistic community in which names and other meaning-bearing elements are passed down to us enables us to entertain thoughts *through the language* that would not otherwise be accessible to us. Call this the *Instrumental Thesis*.[88]

The Instrumental Thesis seems to me a quite important, though often tacit, feature of contemporary theories of reference, and one that distinguishes them from many earlier views. It urges us to see language, and in particular semantics, as more autonomous, more independent of the thought of individual users, and to see our powers of apprehension as less autonomous and more dependent on our vocabulary.[89]

Contrary to Russell, I think we succeed in thinking about things in the world not only through the mental residue of that which we ourselves experience, but also vicariously, through the symbolic resources that come to us through our language. It is the latter—*vocabulary power*—that gives us our apprehensive advantage over the nonlinguistic animals. My dog, being color-blind, cannot entertain the thought that I am wearing a red shirt. But my color-blind colleague can entertain even the thought that Aristotle wore a red shirt.

One need not fall in love to speak of love. One need not have grieved to speak of grief. The poet who has never felt or observed love may yet speak of it *if he has heard of it*. The fact that the language to speak of it and to enable us to have heard of it exists may show that *someone* once felt love. But it need not be the poet. And as with love, so with Samarkand (and red, and Aristotle). Our own individual experience may play a dominant role in providing the conceptual resources with which we address the world, but it does not play the whole role.[90]

---

[87] The two uses of the notion of a historical chain of communication are related. It is hard to see how to avoid some version of a description theory of proper names, at least for names of individuals we are not acquainted with, if one maintains a subjectivist semantics. Thus the attack on description theory (by which I mean not just the attack on *classical* description theory but the claim that descriptions are not even required as reference fixers) is *a fortiori* an attack on subjectivist semantics.

[88] Given the wide acceptance of some version of the historical chain explanation for the mechanism of reference for proper names, it is surprising that there has been so little explicit discussion of the epistemological issues to which the Instrumental Thesis is addressed. A notable exception is the discussion of Leverrier's original use of "Neptune" in Keith Donnellan's "The Contingent *A Priori* and Rigid Designation," in *Contemporary Perspectives in the Philosophy of Language*, ed. P. French, H. Uehling, and H. Wettstein (Minneapolis: University of Minnesota Press, 1979).

[89] How could Putnam have apprehended the dismaying thought that he couldn't tell a Beech from an Elm, without the help of his linguistic community? Could one *have* such a thought without having the *words*?

[90] My grand instrumentalist views regarding red and love go beyond a more cautious version of the Instrumental Thesis that would be limited to names like "Aristotle" and "Samarkand." I note this at the urging of friends who characterize the cautious view as "persuasive" and my view as "shocking."

So how shall I apprehend thee? Let me count the ways. I may apprehend you by (more or less) direct perception. I may apprehend you by memory of (more or less) direct perception. And finally, I may apprehend you through a sign that has been created to signify you.

Does a Name Put Us in Causal Contact with the Referent?

I should add that I do not believe that the third category can be subsumed under the first. Apprehension through the language is not a very indirect form of perception that yields a very indirect form of acquaintance—like hearing a scratchy recording of Caruso or perhaps viewing his letters to his manager. Names are not, in general, among the casual effects of their referents. Perhaps a name should be regarded as among the casual effects of the person who *dubbed* the referent, but only in unusual cases will this *be* the referent.

Even if we granted the referent a causal role in a typical dubbing by ostension, we can introduce a name by *describing* the referent (e.g., as the ratio of the circumference of a circle to its diameter). Such names are still directly referential and, in my view, still have the capacity to enlarge what we can express and apprehend. If we were to discover that Aristotle had been predicted and dubbed one year before his birth, or had been dubbed "Aristotle" only in medieval times, the names, like "π," would still be a *name*, with all its attendant powers.[91]

I recognize that some will find my tolerance for nonostensive dubbings unacceptable, and may insist that the mere reception of a name *is* the reception of a causal signal from the referent. The name is likened to a lock of hair, a glimpse of one far distant, uninformative, but evocative. If names were like this, if there were a simple, natural (i.e., nonintentional) relation between name and named as there is between hair and behaired, the theory of reference for proper names would be a simple thing . . . and it isn't.[92]

On my view, acquisition of a name does not, in general, put us *en rapport* (in the language of "Quantifying In") with the referent. But this is not required for us to use the name in the standard way as a device of direct reference. Nor is it required for us to apprehend, to believe, to doubt, to assert, or to hold other *de dicto* attitudes toward the propositions we express using the name.[93]

The *de dicto* hedge reflects my current view that *de dicto* attitudes, even those toward propositions expressed using directly referential terms, cannot easily be translated into *de re* attitudes.[94] The reason for this lies in part with the problems

---

[91] Howard Wettstein points out that whereas dubbing by ostension has a special Russellian flavor, dubbing by description seems the paradigm for Frege. Since both adhere to subjectivist semantics, *they* believe that their dubbings are strictly for home use and will never go on the open market. (Did either have children?)

[92] Those who see names as among the causal effects of the thing named seem to me to be insufficiently appreciative of Grice's distinction between nonnatural and natural meaning. H. P. Grice, "Meaning," *Philosophical Review* 66 (1957):377–88.

[93] It is required, however, that we *use* the name. I would suppose that with some very exotic names we might forbear their use in favor of their mention, and conceive of the referent only as *the referent of that name.*

[94] This represents a change from the view expressed in footnote 69 of *Demonstratives.*

that led to my original claim that we need to be *en rapport* with those toward whom we hold *de re* attitudes and in part with technical problems involving reflexivity.[95]

The proponents of connectivity urge that although the language enables us to *express* contents that would otherwise be inaccessible (thus contradicting subjectivist semantics), something more, something like being *en rapport* with the components of the content, is required to *apprehend* the content (and thus to hold attitudes toward it).[96] I think of the proposal as a requirement that we have *knowledge of* the components. This certainly does not require direct acquaintance with the components, but it may require a natural connection to the components that is stronger than that provided by a name introduced into the language by one who did not himself have *knowledge of* the object (for example, a name now introduced for the first child to be born in the twenty-first century, or for the next president of Brazil, whosoever that may be).[97] The suggestion seems to be that all names (including perhaps names of colors, natural and unnatural kinds, etc.), however introduced, carry their referent as meaning; but not all names carry *knowledge of* their referent. Those names that were properly introduced, by ostension or based on some other form of knowledge of the referent, carry and transmit the requisite epistemic connection. But in a tiny fraction of cases the connection is absent—semantics (or metasemantics) does not require it—and in these cases we have direct reference, and expressibility, but no apprehension.[98]

In theory, this is a dramatic weakening of the instrumental Thesis, since it urges that more than a *semantic* connection needs to be established between a name and its referent before a name can attain its full powers. In practice, because only a tiny fraction of our vocabulary would lack the requisite connection, it may be almost no weakening at all.[99]

---

[95]The first sort of problem involves understanding the conditions under which we correctly ascribe to Holmes, for example, the *de re* attitude that there is someone whom he believes to have committed the murder. It seems clear that the mere fact that the murderer has given himself a *nom de crime* and leaves a message using this name should not suffice. (In fact, I suspect that there are no fixed conditions, only conditions relative to the topic, interests, aims, and presuppositions of a particular discourse.)

The second sort of problem is discussed in "Opacity," appendix B: The Syntactically *De Re*.

[96]A version of this view can be found in my "Quantifying In," *Synthese* 19 (1968):175–214; reprinted in A. P. Martinich, *op. cit.* Others have espoused more sophisticated versions.

[97]The second example shows that what is required is that the *knowledge of* the individual play a special role in the dubbing. It must be intended to dub the individual *as known*. If someone I know well were to turn out, to my astonishment, to be the next president of Brazil, that would not qualify. Donnellan might say that in a dubbing by description, the description must be used referentially to dub an individual that one *has in mind*.

[98]A name may later take on the required epistemic connection when the referent appears upon the scene and is recognized as the named object.

[99]My own hesitations regarding *de re* attitudes (the *de dicto* hedge) can also be seen as a limit on the scope of the Instrumental Thesis, a limit comparable to that proposed by those who suggest that an epistemic connection is required. If those who demand an epistemic connection identify *de dicto* attitudes toward propositions expressed using names (singular propositions) with *de re* attitudes (as I did in *Demonstratives*), it may even be that their qualms are really qualms about *de re* attitudes. But I had better not speak for others' qualms.

I am not entirely unsympathetic to this view.[100] We do distinguish knowledge from belief in part by the way in which we are connected to the object of knowledge. And thus insofar as one needs *to know what it is* that one apprehends, *to know what it is* that one believes, doubts, asserts, etc., the demand for epistemic connection may seem reasonable in analogy to that demanded for knowledge of facts (knowing-that). Note that on this view what gives us *knowledge of* the content of a name is *just* the connection, not any (new) beliefs. In fact, in this sense of knowing-what-we-apprehend, no beliefs at all are involved, only a well-connected name. In any case, a caveat must be added. To know what one apprehends is not to be able to *individuate* it. The Babylonians knew what Hesperus was, and knew what Phosphorus was, but didn't know that they were the same. Similarly, one might apprehend the proposition that Hesperus is a planet, and apprehend the proposition that Phosphorus is a planet, without knowing that they are the same proposition (if they are).

Naming the Nonexistent

There are certain categories of objects which clearly have no causal effects upon us. If such objects can be given names, the view that names are among the causal effects of their referents cannot be correct. I have in mind future individuals and merely possible individuals. Such putative entities are *nonexistent*.[101]

If we can give a name to the person who *once* occupied this body ("John Doe #256"), why should we not be able to give a name to the person who *will*, in fact, arise from this fertilized egg? And if we possess an actual knock-down lectern kit, containing instructions for assembly and all materials (form and matter), why should we not be able to name the unique, merely possible lectern that *would have* been assembled, if only we had not procrastinated until the need was past.

The sceptics, who take the position that an individual cannot be dubbed until it comes into existence, would insist that there is no naming the baby until the end of the first trimester (or whenever the current metaphysical pronouncements from the Supreme Court may indicate). One may, of course, express an intention to dub *whatever first satisfies certain conditions* with a particular name. Perhaps one may even *launch* the dubbing before the referent arrives. But the naming doesn't *take*, the name doesn't *name* it, one cannot *use* the name to refer to it (at least not to refer directly to it in the way names are said to refer by direct reference theorists) until the referent comes into existence.

A difficulty in the skeptical position is that in planning and in other forward-looking activities, we often wish to speak *about* such unnameables, perhaps through the use of descriptions.[102] In my experience, those who protest the possibility

---

[100] Not *entirely*, though I do still maintain the view of footnote 76 of *Demonstratives*.

[101] We certainly can't get *en rapport* with such individuals. Past individuals are also, in my view, nonexistent, but they do affect us causally. Some abstract objects, like numbers, do not, I think, affect us causally (in the appropriate sense), and they surely can be given names. I do not consider them because of qualms about the objectivity of such objects.

[102] Or other 'denoting phrases' as Russell termed them.

of *naming* the first child to be born in the twenty-first century often accept the view that the description is—how shall I put it—not *vacuous*.

Perhaps they accept quantification over such entities and just object to the practice of introducing *names* on the basis of arbitrary descriptions (for names they want connectivity). It would then be natural to add a *narrow existence predicate* to distinguish the robust being of true local existents, like you and me, from the more attenuated being of the nonexistents.

If such quantification is *not* accepted, the position seems odd. Is it assumed that there are clever ways to reformulate any sentence in which such descriptions occur so as to 'eliminate' those that appear outside the scope of a temporal operator?[103] It is not obvious to me how to do this. How would the *de dicto* sentence, "Katie owes her first-(to be)born child to Rumpelstiltskin" be reformulated?[104]

What sounds like skepticism with regard to naming the nonexistent, may merely be the quite different concern that the description of the intended dubbee is insufficiently specific to select a unique nonexistent individual. Such may be the case of the possible fat man in the doorway.

Insufficient specificity seems to be Kripke's qualm in *Naming and Necessity* regarding the merely possible species Unicorn and a merely possible referent for

---

[103] I note that if there is such a method, then there is probably a similar method for eliminating descriptions of past individuals that no longer exist.

[104] Using "*Fy*" for "y is a first-born child of Katie," and "*Ox*" for "Katie owes x to Rumpelstiltskin," we might try the following 'elimination' of the definite description from what is roughly "*O(the x)Fx*" (ignoring the 'if any' aspect of the description "her first-born"),

$$\text{Future } \exists x \, (\text{Always } \forall y (Fy \leftrightarrow y = x) \land \text{Now } Ox).$$

This symbolization would be correct for "Katie *will give* her first-born child to Rumpelstiltskin," but not for "*owes*." The problem is that "owes" (like "needs" and "seeks") is an intensional verb with respect to its grammatical object. Even if it turns out that Katie's first-born child is her ugliest child, *Always* $\forall y (Fy \leftrightarrow Uy)$, she does not now owe Rumpelstiltskin her ugliest child. (However, if she *will give* her first-born child, then she will give her ugliest child.) The 'elimination' of the definite description transforms the predication from *de dicto* to a quantification in. And this leads to incorrect results for intensional verbs. (Note that the same sort of 'elimination' occurs automatically whenever we use first-order logic to symbolize a sentence with an indefinite description as grammatical object. Compare the symbolizations of "Katie owes a bushel of gold to Rumpelstiltskin" and "Katie will give a bushel of gold to Rumpelstiltskin." The interesting problem about indefinite descriptions as grammatical objects of intensional verbs is how to 'uneliminate' them.)

So long as there are no intensional verbs, the eliminations are not plainly incorrect. Intensional *operators*, so long as they are *sentential* operators, do not create a problem, because definite and indefinite descriptions can be eliminated from predicates while remaining within the scope of the operator.

Some think that "*owes*" can be paraphrased to produce a sentential complement where the grammatical object of "owes" appears, for example, as "Katie is now obligated that at some future time she gives her first (to have been) born child to Rumpelstiltskin." This allows a tense operator ("at some future time") to be inserted between the new sentential operator and the old grammatical object of "owes." If you are of this view, try "Katie is thinking about her first (to be) born child," and read appendix A: Paraphrasing into Propositional Attitudes from "Opacity."

My aim here is to indicate that there is a substantial technical problem faced by those who hope to achieve the effect of quantification over future individuals through the use of temporal operators.

"Sherlock Holmes."[105] However, his discussion of what he calls "the epistemological thesis" (that the discovery that there were animals with all the features attributed to Unicorns in the myth does not establish that there were Unicorns) suggests an entirely different argument, namely that *the way in which these particular names arose* (from pure myth and pure fiction) makes it impossible for *them* to name merely possible entities.[106] This argument is independent of the degree of specificity in the myth or in the fiction.[107]

Neither insufficient specificity nor the objections concerning extant names from fiction or myth apply to the case of the first child to be born in the twenty-first century or to the case of the possible lectern, in both of which a frank attempt is made to dub what is recognized as a nonexistent object.

Logically Proper Names

The question that prompted all my thoughts on subjectivist semantics, the Instrumental Thesis, and vocabulary power is this: How should Russellian 'logically proper names' be accommodated in the semantics of Context and Circumstance?

Using "name" for what he sometimes called a "logically proper name," Russell writes,

> a *name* . . . is a simple symbol, directly designating an individual which is its meaning, and having this meaning in its own right, independently of the meanings of all other words.[108]

---

[105] Addenda, pp. 156–58.

[106] As Harry Deutsch puts it, *reference is no coincidence.*

[107] In lecture, Kripke has made the intriguing suggestion that there are abstract but actual (not merely possible) *fictional individuals* that serve as the referents of names like "Sherlock Holmes." The admission of such entities might be accompanied by a narrow existence predicate to distinguish the fictional from the non. I am not aware of Russell's views on future individuals, but he expressed himself in opposition to fictional entities in *Introduction to Mathematical Philosophy.*

> If no one thought about Hamlet, there would be nothing left of him; if no one thought about Napoleon, he would have soon seen to it that someone did. The sense of reality is vital in logic, and whoever juggles with it by pretending that Hamlet has another kind of reality is doing a disservice to thought.

Despite Russell's rhetorical power, I must confess to having been persuaded by Kripke's analysis. (As Joseph Almog points out, it is not clear that Russell's insistence that Hamlet does not have "another kind of reality" would apply to what I take to be Kripke's view that Hamlet, though not a *person*, exists as a *fictional character* in *our* reality.)

If Kripke is correct, it would seem to settle the case in which an author creates a fiction 'out of whole cloth' but specifies one of the characters, which he names "Woody," to have particular characteristics, which, though nothing does in fact *have* the characteristics, our favorite theory of essentialism tells us that there is exactly one possible object that *could* have them (e.g., the characteristic of having been assembled from a certain lectern kit). "Woody" would name an actual fictional entity, not a merely possible nonfictional entity.

Or should we say instead that the author made up a story *about* a particular merely possible nonfictional entity? The fairly plain distinction between an individual, *x, having the properties* of a character in a story and the story being *about x,* grows dim when *x* is merely possible. And if we add the difficulties of the distinction between being *about x* and being *modeled on x* (a hard enough distinction for real *x*), I lose discriminability.

[108] From chapter 15 of *Introduction to Mathematical Philosophy* (London: Allen & Unwin, 1919), reprinted in Martinich, *op. cit.*

It is hard to resist the idea that for Russell, such names are directly referential. However, his ideas about the existence predicate are baffling. He continues,

> The proposition "the so-and-so exists" is significant, whether true or false: but if *a* is the so-and-so (where "*a*" is a name), the words "*a* exists" are meaningless. It is only of descriptions—definite or indefinite—that existence can be significantly asserted; for, if "*a*" is a name, it *must* name something: what does not name anything is not a name, and therefore, if intended to be a name, is a symbol devoid of meaning.

His claim that it is meaningless to predicate existence of a logically proper name is plainly a mistake.[109] Far from being meaningless, such propositions are required as the objects of what Russell called *prepositional attitudes,* "I regret that this pain exists," "I am pleased that Nixon exists" (taking "Nixon" and "this pain" to be logically proper names). These assertions are by no means either trivial or meaningless.

The requirement that a logically proper name *name* something seems to have the result that "*a* exists" ("*a*" a logically proper name) cannot be used to express a proposition that is false. But unless "*a*" names a necessary existent, the proposition expressed would not be necessary. Thus we have a seeming failure of the rule of Necessitation. This, along with Russell's epistemological ideas, which emphasize the special situation of the agent who uses the name, is highly reminiscent of my analysis of indexicals.

These reflections made logically proper names seem a natural topic for the apparatus I had developed in *Demonstratives,* and this drew me in deeper.

When I attempted to apply the apparatus, I was surprised by the results. I was faced with a puzzle. The principles governing logically proper names seemed to imply that a logically proper name *must* name something that exists in its context of use, but need not name a *necessary* existent. But if the referent is not a necessary existent, then there must be a world and time at which it does not exist, and if *c* is a context of use in such a world at such a time, what would be named by an "occurrence" of the name in the context *c*? Briefly, how can every possible occurrence of a name have an existent referent, if the referent isn't a necessary existent?

---

[109] I do not understand why Russell did not recognize that the intolerable existence predicate could be defined by forming the indefinite description, "an individual identical with *a*," and then predicating existence of the indefinite description in the way Russell finds so commendable, "$\exists x\, x = a$."

The problem with empty names should not have dissuaded him. If such names are taken to be (disguised) definite descriptions, as he usually claimed they were, then (where *a* is now a definite description), "$\exists x\, x = a$" is again equivalent to "*a* exists" according to Russell's own theory of descriptions. (As a sidelight, it is interesting to note that even if an empty name is taken to be "a symbol devoid of meaning," it is possible to develop a rigorous semantics according to which "$\exists x\, x = a$" is again equivalent to "*a* exists." Russell was not aware of this.)

It is not my claim that the notion of *existence* is captured by the existential quantifier; variables can have any domain. My argument is *ex concessis.* Insofar as existence can be "significantly asserted" of indefinite descriptions, it can be significantly asserted of names.

To make things definite, consider the puzzling case of Nixon. Suppose that I name a certain pain with which I am directly acquainted, "Nixon." We agree that Nixon does not have necessary existence. So there must be a happier world (or time) in which Nixon does not exist.[110] If I were to utter "Nixon" in this happier circumstance, what existent would I be referring to? If "Nixon exists" cannot be used to express a proposition that is false, an occurrence of "Nixon" in such circumstances must name something that exists there. This cannot be Nixon, *ex hypothesi*. What could it be?

Be clear that I am not raising questions about how to *evaluate* at the happier circumstance what is expressed by an occurrence of "Nixon exists" in the painful context of dubbing. No problem there; it's false (again, *ex hypothesi*). The question is: What is *expressed* by an occurrence of "Nixon exists" in a context in the happier circumstance? And how can it be true there?

So what *is* the referent of "Nixon" when it occurs in a context in a world and time in which Nixon doesn't exist?

We can be certain that names do not enter vocabularies through a transworld chain of communication. If the world is one in which Nixon never exists, how is the agent of the context able to use the term "Nixon"; was the name introduced there to dub a merely possible entity? Not likely.

The solution to the puzzle is, I think, independent of all the issues surrounding subjectivist versus consumerist semantics. As was emphasized earlier, our notion of an *occurrence* of an expression in a context does not require an *utterance* of the expression nor even that the agent of the context have the use of the expression. The apparatus of Context, Character, and Circumstance is designed to help articulate the semantics of an *interpreted* language, one for which meanings, *however derived*, are already associated with the expressions. It takes account of what the meanings are, not of how they came about. Given an interpreted language, a sentence is valid if it expresses a truth in every context, including those contexts in which the language doesn't or couldn't exist, or doesn't or couldn't have that interpretation. Thus the objection that certain meanings *could not arise* or *could not be used* in certain contexts is, strictly speaking, irrelevant to our issue: What is the content in such contexts of an expression which already carries a certain meaning?

So the answer is: Nixon. (Just as you knew all along.) The intuition that "Nixon exists" must be logically valid whenever "Nixon" is a logically proper name, is in error in tacitly assuming that to *evaluate* our language in a foreign context, the language, with its interpretation, must exist there.[111]

---

[110] For example, the next day, when Nixon has subsided into nonexistence. Or, if you think that pains like Nixon never cease to 'exist' (in some sense) once they appear, take the day *before* Nixon came into existence. Or, better yet, take some possible world in which Nixon *never* comes into existence.

[111] This, however, suggests that there may be another interesting analysis of the puzzle about logically proper names in terms of utterance-validity. And another using the notion, from the discussion of contexts for demonstratives, of a context *appropriate* for a particular expression. These considerations may throw light on a kind of metasemantical analyticity, not the usual: truth solely in virtue of what the meaning is, but instead: truth in virtue of having come to have that meaning.

I see here a reaffirmation of the importance of a central distinction that I have tried to build into my very nomenclature, the distinction between what *exists* at a given point and what can be 'carried in' to be *evaluated* at that point, though it may *exist* only elsewhere. My 'Circumstances of Evaluation' evaluate contents that may have no native existence at the circumstance but can be expressed elsewhere and carried in for evaluation. What is crucial to the puzzle about "Nixon" is that my 'Contexts of Use' are also points of evaluation; they evaluate characters (meanings) that may have no native existence at the context but can also be created elsewhere and carried in for evaluation.

Where within the formal theory do I take account of the locus of *creation of character*, the assignment of meanings that is presupposed in the notion of an interpreted language? Where within the formal theory do I take account of such metasemantical matters as constraints on the kinds of dubbings allowed? I do not.[112]

---

[112]In addition to assistance specifically acknowledged, I have been much helped (provided one includes expressions of dismay as *help*) by Joseph Almog, Harry Deutsch, Keith Donnellan, Kit Fine, John Perry, Elisabetta Fava, Nathan Salmon, and Howard Wettstein.

FREGE ON DEMONSTRATIVES[1]

John Perry

In "The Thought," Frege briefly discusses sentences containing such demonstratives as "today," "here," and "yesterday," and then turns to certain questions that he says are raised by the occurrence of "I" in sentences (T, 24–26). He is led to say that, when one thinks about oneself, one grasps thoughts that others cannot grasp, that cannot be communicated. Nothing could be more out of the spirit of Frege's account of sense and thought than an incommunicable, private thought. Demonstratives seem to have posed a severe difficulty for Frege's philosophy of language, to which his doctrine of incommunicable senses was a reaction.

In the first part of the paper, I explain the problem demonstratives pose for Frege, and explore three ways he might have dealt with it. I argue that none of these ways provides Frege with a solution to his problem consistent with his philosophy of

---

[1] The following abbreviations are used for works cited in the text. 'T' for Gottlob Frege, "The Thought: A Logical Inquiry," reprinted in P. F. Strawson *Philosophical Logic* (Oxford, 1967), 17–38. This translation, by A. M. and Marcelle Quinton, appeared originally in *Mind*, Vol. 65 (1956), pp. 289–311. The original, "Der Gedanke. Eine logische Untersuchung," appeared in *Beiträge zur Philosophie des deutschen Idealismus*, I (1918), 58–77. 'SR' for Frege, "On Sense and Reference," in Max Black and Peter Geach (eds.), *Translations from the Philosophical Writings of Gottlob Frege* (Oxford, 1960). Translated by Max Black. The original, "Über Sinn und Bedeutung," appeared in *Zeitschrift für Philosophie und philosophische Kritik*, L. (1892), 25–50. 'CT' for "Compound Thoughts," in E. D. Klemke (ed.), *Essays on Frege*. Translated by R. H. Stoothoff. The original, "Gedankenfuge," appeared in *Beiträge zur Philosophie des deutschen Idealismus*, III (1923), 36–51. 'F' for Michael Dummett, *Frege* (London, 1973).

language. The first two are plausible as solutions, but contradict his identification of the sense expressed by a sentence with a thought. The third preserves the identification, but is implausible. In the second part, I suggest that Frege was led to his doctrine of incommunicable senses as a result of some appreciation of the difficulties his account of demonstratives faces, for these come quickly to the surface when we think about "I." I argue that incommunicable senses won't help. I end by trying to identify the central problem with Frege's approach, and sketching an alternative.

I

Before explaining the problem posed by demonstratives, certain points about Frege's philosophy of languages need to be made.

In "On Sense and Reference," Frege introduces the notion of sense, in terms of the cognitive value of sentences. He then goes on to make two key identifications. First, he identifies the sense of a sentence with the thought it expresses. Then, he identifies the thought expressed by a sentence, and so the sense it has, with the indirect reference of the sentence in the scope of a cognitive verb.

The phrases "the sense of a sentence," "the thought expressed by a sentence," and "the indirect reference of a sentence," are not mere synonyms. They have different senses, though, if Frege's account is correct, they have the same reference. In particular, each is associated, as Frege introduces it, with a separate criterion of difference.

Sense

In the beginning of "On Sense and Reference," Frege introduces the notion of sense as a way of accounting for the difference in cognitive value of the senses of "$a = a$" and "$a = b$," even when both are true, and so made up of coreferential expressions (SR, 56–58). So a criterion of difference for sense is,

> If S and S have differing cognitive value, then S and S' have different senses.

Dummett's explanation of sense will help us to convert this to something more helpful. He emphasizes that sense is linked to understanding and truth. The sense of an expression is "what we know when we understand it," and what we know when we understand it is something like an ideal procedure for determining its reference (F, 293, 589ff.). In the case of a sentence, whose reference is a truth value, the sense is that we know when, roughly, we know what would have to be done—whether or not this is humanly possible—to determine whether or not it is true.

What Frege seems to have in mind at the beginning of "On Sense and Reference," then, is a situation in which some person A who understands both "$a = a$" and "$a = b$," accepts the first while rejecting, or being unsure about, the second. The assumption seems to be, that if A associated just the same ideal procedures with both sentences, he would accept the second if he accepted the first. So he must not associate the same ideal procedures with both sentences, and so, since he understands them, their senses differ. So we have:

> If A understands S and S', and accepts S as true while not accepting S', then S and S' have different senses.

This criterion of difference allows that sentences might have different senses, though provably or necessarily equivalent. A complex true mathematical equation might be provably equivalent to "2 + 3 = 5," and yet a perfectly competent speaker might accept the latter and reject the former, having made an error in calculation. To know an ideal procedure for determining reference, is not necessarily to have carried it out, or even to be able to.

Thought

"Thought" is not just a term introduced by Frege as another way of saying, "sense of a sentence." The notion derived from Frege's untangling of the jumbled notion of a judgment, into act, thought, and truth value. The thought is, first and foremost, "that for which the question of truth arises" (T, 20–22). This is clearly intended to be a criterion of difference for thoughts:

If S is true and S' is not, S and S' express different thoughts.

Indirect Reference

Consider a report of a belief: "Copernicus believed that the planetary orbits are circles." On Frege's analysis, this is relational. "Believed that" stands for a relation, which is asserted to hold between Copernicus and whatever it is that "the planetary orbits are circles" refers to as it occurs in this sentence. Standing alone, "the planetary orbits are circles" would refer to the False, but here it clearly does not have that ordinary reference. If it did, the substitution of any false sentence at all should preserve truth of the whole report (SR, 66–67). The notion of the indirect reference of "the planetary orbits are circles," is just whatever it is, that this sentence has as reference here. (The phrase is first used in connection with indirect discourse [SR, 59].) Now if "*a R b*" is true, and "*a R c*" is not, *b* is not *c*. So we have a clear criterion of difference:

If 'A believes S' is true, and 'A believes S'' is not, then S and S' do not have the same indirect reference.

So we have three separable criterion of difference. But Frege, as noted, identifies the sense of *S*, the thought expressed by *S*, and the indirect reference of *S*. So we are led to a further principle:

S and S' have different senses, if and only if they express different thoughts, and if and only if they have different indirect references.

Sense Completers

Frege takes the structure of language as a suggestive guide to the structure of senses and objects. Just as he views the sentence,

two plus two equals four

as the result of combining the complete

two

with the incomplete

() plus two equals four,

so he sees the sense of "two plus two equals four" as determined by the sense of "two" and the sense of "( ) plus two equals four." The sense of the latter is incomplete; the sense of the former completes it, to yield the complete sense of "two plus two equals four."

"( ) plus two equals four" could also be made into a sentence by writing "something" in the blank; similarly the sense of "( ) plus two equals four" can be completed with the sense of "something." The sense of "something," however, unlike the sense of "two," is itself also incomplete. Where "two" refers to an object, "something" refers to a concept. Two appropriately related incomplete senses can combine to form a complete sense; two complete senses cannot combine at all (CT, 538).

Thus the class of *sense completers* for a given incomplete sense is hybrid, containing both complete and incomplete senses. But the term will be useful in what follows.

Sense Had and Sense Expressed

The structure of language is not always a sure guide to the structure of senses. Not everything we count as a sentence has a complete sense. Consider (1),

(1) Russia and Canada quarrelled when Nemtsanov defected.

"Russia and Canada quarrelled," as it occurs as a clause in (1), does not have a complete sense (SR, 71; T, 37). It refers to a concept of times and thus must have an incomplete sense. "When Nemtsanov defected" refers to a time; the sentence is true if the time referred to falls under the concept referred to. Thus the sense of "when Nemtsanov defected" is a sense completer for the sense of "Russia and Canada quarrelled."

So the sense of the sentence "Russia and Canada quarrelled" is not a thought. Not any sentence, but only a sentence "complete in every respect" expresses a thought (T, 37).

Now "Russia and Canada quarrelled" could be used, without a dependent clause, to express a thought. If it appeared alone, we might take it to express, *on that occasion*, the sense of

At some time or other, Russia and Canada quarrelled. In another setting, for example after the question, "What happened when Nemtsanov defected?" the sentence would express the sense of (1). So we must, even before considering demonstratives, distinguish between the sense a sentence *has* on each occasion of use and the senses it *expresses* on various occasions of use. For an "eternal" sentence, one that really is "complete in every respect," the two will be the same; for a sentence like "Russia and Canada quarrelled," the sense *had* is incomplete; the sense *expressed* on a given occasion will be the result of completing that sense, with some sense completer available from the context of utterance. It is clearly only the sense expressed on such occasions, that Frege wants to identify with a thought.

The Problem Posed by Demonstratives

We are now in a position to see why demonstratives pose a problem for Frege.

I begin by quoting the passage in "The Thought" in which Frege discusses demonstratives in general.

> [O]ften . . . the mere wording, which can be grasped by writing or the gramophone, does not suffice for the expression of the thought. . . . If a time indication is needed by the present tense [as opposed to cases in which it is used to express timelessness, as in the statement of mathematical laws] one must know when the sentence was uttered to apprehend the thought correctly. Therefore, the time of utterance is part of the expression of the thought. If someone wants to say the same today as he expressed yesterday using the word 'today', he must replace this word with 'yesterday'. Although the thought is the same its verbal expression must be different so that the sense, which would otherwise be affected by the differing times of utterance, is readjusted. The case is the same with words like 'here' and 'there'. In all such cases the mere wording, as it is given in writing, is not the complete expression of the thought, but the knowledge of certain accompanying conditions of utterance, which are used as means of expressing the thought, are needed for its correct apprehension. The pointing of fingers, hand movements, glances may belong here too. The same utterance containing the word 'I' will express different thoughts in the mouths of different men, of which some may be true, others false. (T. 24)

Consider (2),

(2) Russia and Canada quarrelled today.

The sentence "Russia and Canada quarrelled" has in (2), as in (1), only an incomplete sense. So presumably "today" in (2) must somehow do what "when Nemtsanov defected" does in (1), and supply us with a completing sense. But it does not seem to do this at all.

If I uttered (2) on August 1, I expressed something true, on August 2, something false. If "today" had the same sense on August 1 as on August 2, then (2) in its entirety must have had the same sense on both occasions. If so, the sense of (2) must be incomplete, for if it were complete, its truth value could not change.

So, if "today" provides a completing sense on both days, its sense must change just at midnight. But what we know when we understand how to use "today" doesn't seem to change from day to day.

When we understand a word like "today," what we seem to know is a rule taking us from an occasion of utterance to a certain object. "Today" takes us to the very day of utterance, "yesterday" to the day before the day of utterance, "I" to the speaker, and so forth. I shall call this the *role* of the demonstrative. I take a context to be a set of features of an actual utterance, certainly including time, place, and speaker, but probably also more. Just what a context must include is a difficult question, to be answered only after detailed study of various demonstratives. The object a demonstrative takes us to in a given context, I shall call its value in that context or on that occasion of use. Clearly, we must grant "today" a role, the same on both occasions of use. And we must, as clearly, give it different values on the two occasions.

Any reasonable account has to recognize that demonstratives have roles. The role of a demonstrative does not seem reducible to other notions available from Frege's philosophy. Senses do not carry us from context to references, but directly to references, the same on each occasion of use. One might suppose that "yesterday" could be thought to have just the sense of "the day before." But,

> (3) Russia and Canada quarrelled the day before does not have the same sense as (4).
>
> (4) Russia and Canada quarrelled yesterday.

If I ask on August 5, "Did Russia and Canada quarrel August 2?" (3) would imply that they quarrelled on August 1, (4) that they quarrelled on August 4. If (3) were uttered when no day had already been mentioned, it would not express anything complete, but simply give rise to the question, "before what?" An utterance of (4) would still be fully in order.

Frege recognizes that demonstratives have roles, or at least that the context of utterance is crucial when dealing with demonstratives. He does not talk about the sense of "today" or "I" so he also seems to have recognized that the role of a demonstrative is not just a sense, as he has explained senses.

But Frege clearly thinks that, given knowledge of the accompanying conditions of utterance, we can get from an utterance of a sentence like (2) or (4) to a thought. He must have thought, then, that the demonstrative provides us not simply with an object—its value on the occasion of utterance—but with a *completing sense*. This is puzzling. Neither the unchanging role of "today," or its changing value, provides us with a completing sense. A day is not a sense, but a reference corresponding to indefinitely many senses (SR, 71). There is no route back from reference to sense. So how do we get from the incomplete sense of "Russia and Canada quarrelled," the demonstrative "today," and the context to a thought? This is the problem demonstratives pose for Frege.

I shall first describe two options Frege might have taken, which would have excused him from the necessity of finding a completing sense. I shall argue that Frege did not take these options, and could not, given his identification of sense expressed and thought.

Sense as Roles?

Let $S(d)$ be a sentence containing a demonstrative d. Without the demonstrative, we have something, $S(\ )$, that has an incomplete sense, and so refers to a concept. This may actually still be a sentence, as when we remove "today" from (2), or it may look more like it should, as when we remove the "I" from "I am wounded."

The following scheme gives us a rule for getting from a particular context, to a truth value, for any such sentence $S(d)$.

> $S(d)$ is true when uttered in context c, if and only if the value of d in c falls under the concept referred to by $S(\ )$.[2]

---

[2] Here and elsewhere I assume, for the sake of simplicity of exposition, that we are considering sentences containing no more than one demonstrative. Given the notion of a sequence of

(contd.)

Such a rule is the *role of S(d)*. It is just an extension of the notion of the role of a demonstrative. Roles take us from contexts to objects. In the case of a sentence, the object is a truth value.

Thus (4) is true as uttered on August 2, if and only if August 1 is a day that falls under the concept referred to by "Russia and Canada quarrelled." "I am ill" as uttered by Lauben is true if and only if Lauben falls under the concept referred to by "( ) is ill."

The role of a sentence containing a demonstrative is clearly analogous in many ways to the sense of a sentence not containing a demonstrative. The role is a procedure for determining truth value, just as the sense is. The difference is that the role is a procedure which starts from a context.

This analogy suggests an option, which Frege might have taken. He might have identified the sense expressed by a sentence containing a demonstrative with its role. This would amount to a generalization of the notion of sense. On this view, an incomplete sense like that of "Russia and Canada quarrelled," could be completed in two ways. A sense completer, such as the sense of "when Nemtsanov defected," gives us a complete sense of the old sort. A demonstrative, like "today," yields a sense of the new sort, a role. No complete sense of the old sort is involved at all in the utterance of a sentence containing a demonstrative, so no completing sense need be found.

But this cannot have been Frege's view. For it is clear that he thinks a thought has been expressed in the utterance of a sentence containing a demonstrative. The role of the sentence cannot be identified with the thought, for a sentence could express the same role on different occasions while having different truth-values. So by the criteria of difference for thoughts, roles are not thoughts. By the identification of the sense expressed by a sentence and the thought expressed, roles are not the senses expressed by a sentence.

Thoughts as Information?

We can put the problem this way. (2), as uttered on August 1st, with the role of "today" fully mastered, seems to yield just this information:

> (*i*)   an incomplete sense, that of "Russia and Canada quarrelled";
>
> (*ii*)   an object, the day August 1st, 1976.

(*i*) and (*ii*) do not uniquely determine a thought, but only an equivalence class of thoughts. Belonging to this equivalence class will be just those thoughts obtainable by completing the sense of "Russia and Canada quarrelled" with a sense completer which determines, as reference, August 1st, 1976. I shall call thoughts related in this manner *informationally equivalent*.[3]

---

objects, there would be no difficulties in extending various suggestions and options for the general case. In some of the examples I use, additional demonstratives are really needed. 'Lauben is wounded', for example, still needs a time indication.

[3] This notion is taken from A. W. Burks, "Icon, Index, and Symbol," *Philosophy and Phenomenological Research*, Vol. IX (1949), p. 685. In this pioneering and illuminating work on demonstratives, Burks emphasizes the ineliminability of demonstratives.

The second option I shall discuss, is introducing a new notion of a thought, corresponding to such a class of informationally equivalent thoughts. Since the information in (i) and (ii) is sufficient to identify such a class, without identifying any one of its members, this would explain how we can get from (i) and (ii) to a thought, without needing a completing sense.

On this view, an utterance of $S(d)$ in context c, and $S'(d')$ in context c', will express the same thought if the (incomplete) senses of $S(\ )$ and $S'(\ )$ are the same, and if the value of d in c is the same as the value of d' in c'. Thus (2), uttered on August 1, and (4), uttered on August 2, would express the same thought. Dummett interprets Frege in this way (F, 384). Frege's remark,

> If someone wants to say the same today as he expressed yesterday using the word 'today', he must replace this with 'yesterday'. Although the thought is the same its verbal expression must be different. . . .

But this cannot have been Frege's view. This criterion actually introduces a new kind of thought, corresponding to informationally equivalent classes of thoughts of the old kind. The thought expressed by Lauben when he says "I am wounded" to Leo Peter, cannot be identified with the thought expressed by any nondemonstrative completion of the same incomplete sense in which the singular term refers to Lauben, such as

> The man born on the thirteenth of September, 1875, in N.N. is wounded.
>
> The only doctor who lives in the house next door to Rudolf Lingens is wounded.

These express different thoughts, so the thought Lauben expresses with "I am wounded" cannot be identified with *the* thought they both express; there just isn't any such thought. There is no more reason to identify it with the one than with the other, or with any other such thought. Nor can thoughts of this new type be identified with classes of thoughts of the old, for in different possible circumstances the pair, Dr. Lauben and the incomplete sense of "( ) am ill," would correspond to different sets of Fregean thoughts. If Lauben had moved, the two Fregean thoughts in question would not be informationally equivalent. We have here a radically new kind of thought, of which Frege would not have approved, even if he had seen its necessity. We have in effect made the value of the demonstrative a part of the thought. But Frege insists that only senses can be parts of senses.

Dummett remarks,

> It is, of course, quite unnecessary to suppose that a thought expressible by the utterance on a particular occasion of a sentence containing a token reflexive expression can also be expressed by some 'eternal' sentence containing no such expressions. (F, 384)

But it is not only unnecessary, but impossible, on this account, that the thought should be expressed by an eternal sentence. It is not the right kind of thought for an eternal sentence to express.

Second, and closely related, this notion of a thought would violate the criteria of difference.

Suppose I am viewing the harbor from downtown Oakland; the bow and stern of the aircraft carrier *Enterprise* are visible, though its middle is obscured by a large building. The name *"Enterprise"* is clearly visible on the bow, so when I tell a visitor, "This is the *Enterprise*," pointing towards the bow, this is readily accepted. When I say, pointing to the stern clearly several city blocks from the bow, "That is the *Enterprise*," however, she refuses to believe me. By the criterion of difference, a different sense was expressed the first time than the second. On the present suggested criterion of identity for thoughts, the same thought was expressed; the incomplete sense was the same in both cases, and the value of the demonstratives was the *Enterprise* in both cases. To adopt this notion of a thought, Frege would have to give up the identification of sense expressed and thought expressed.

This is, of course, simply a variation on Frege's own Morning Star example. Suppose I point to Venus in the morning, and again in the evening, saying "That's the Morning Star." My listener may accept what I say the first time, and continue to think I was right, while rejecting what I say the second time. Here the *same* sentence has a different cognitive value at different times—for my listener has not changed her mind. The sentence does not have different cognitive values because the words have undergone a change of meaning, but because the sentence alone does not express the complete sense. Some supplementation is needed; here the gestures toward Venus provide it. But just what supplementation do they provide? If the supplementation were merely taken to be Venus, itself—which is what the present proposal amounts to—then the sense of the sentence would have been supplemented in the same way on both occasions. But then we would have the same sense expressed in both occasions, in violation of the criterion of difference for senses.

Frege does not explicitly mention the demonstratives "this" and "that." So it is worth pointing out that examples can be constructed using demonstratives he does mention. For example, I might accept what you say at 11:50 p.m. when you utter "Russia and Canada quarrelled today," but disbelieve you at 12:15 a.m. when you utter "Russia and Canada quarrelled yesterday," having lost track of time.

Of course, Frege may have meant to introduce such a new notion of a thought at this point. That he does not explain it, counts against this interpretation. And what he goes on to say, in the next paragraphs, seems to make it totally implausible. There he discusses proper names, and arrives at a point where he has all the materials for this notion of a thought in his hand, so to speak, and yet passes up the opportunity to mold them into the new notion. He describes a situation in which two men express different thoughts with the sentence "Gustav Lauben has been wounded," one knowing him as the unique man born a certain day, the other as the unique doctor living in a certain house. He recognizes that these different thoughts are systematically equivalent:

> The different thoughts which thus result from the same sentence correspond in their truth-value, of course; that is to say, if one is true then all are true, and if one is false then all are false.

But he insists,

> Nevertheless their distinctness must be recognized.

His reason here is clearly a complex example he has just constructed, in which sentences expressing such informationally equivalent thoughts have different cognitive value:

> It is possible that Herbert Garner takes the sense of the sentence 'Dr. Lauben has been wounded' to be true while, misled by false information, taking the sense of 'Gustav Lauben has been wounded' to be false. Under the assumptions given these thoughts are therefore different. (T, 25)

If demonstratives had driven Frege, three paragraphs before this, to the introduction of a class of thoughts, corresponding to a class of informationally equivalent thoughts of the old sort, I think he would have employed it, or at least mentioned it, here.

Senses, considered to be roles, cannot be thoughts. Thoughts, considered as information, cannot be senses. If Frege is to keep his identification of sense expressed by a sentence, with thought expressed by a sentence, he must find, somewhere, a completing sense.

Demonstratives as Providing a Completing Sense

How can we extract from a demonstrative, an appropriate completing sense? Such a sense, it seems, would have to be intimately related to, the sense of a unique description of the value of the demonstrative in the context of utterance. But where does such a description come from? "Today" seems to get us only to a day. And a day does not provide a particular description of itself.

In the case of proper names, Frege supposes that different persons attach different senses to the same proper name. To find the sense a person identifies with a given proper name, we presumably look at his beliefs. If he associates the sense of description D with Gustav Lauben, he should believe,

> Gustav Lauben is D.

Perhaps, with demonstratives too, Frege supposes that speakers and listeners, in grasping the thought, provide the demonstrative with an appropriate sense. To understand a demonstrative, is to be able to supply a sense for it on each occasion, which determines as reference the value the demonstrative has on that occasion.[4] This is, I think, as near as we are likely to come to what Frege had in mind.

There is a problem here, with no analog in the case of proper names. One can attach the same sense to a proper name, once and for all. But, since the demonstrative takes a different value on different occasions, different senses must be supplied. So the demonstrative could not be regarded as an abbreviation, or something like an abbreviation, for some appropriate description.

---

[4] This interpretation was suggested to me by Dagfinn Føllesdal.

But still, can we not say that for each person, the sense of the demonstrative "today" for that person on a given day, is just the sense of one of the descriptions *D* (or some combination of all the descriptions) such that on that day he believes,

> Today is *D*.

One objection to this, is that we seem to be explaining the senses of sentences containing demonstratives in terms of beliefs whose natural expressions contain demonstratives. But there are three more serious problems.

The first problem might be called the *irrelevancy of belief*.[5] The sense I associate with my use of a demonstrative, do not determine the thought expressed by a sentence containing that demonstrative.

Suppose I believe that today is the fourteenth of October, 1976. From that it does not follow that, when I utter

> Today is sunny and bright

I express the thought

> The fourteenth of October is sunny and bright.

For suppose today is really the fifteenth, cloudy, and dull. Then what I have said is wrong, whatever the weather was like on the fourteenth.

The second problem, we might call the *non-necessity of belief*. I can express a thought with "Today is sunny and bright"—that is, say something for which the question of truth arises—whether or not I associate any correct sense at all with "today." I may have no idea at all what day it is, and not be able, without recourse to "today" or other demonstratives, to say anything about today at all, that does not describe dozens of other days equally well.

Both of these problems are illustrated by Rip Van Winkle. When he awakes on October 20, 1823, and says with conviction,

> Today is October 20, 1803

the fact that he is sure he is right doesn't make him right, as it would if the thought expressed were determined by the sense he associated with "today." And, what is really the same point from a different angle, he doesn't fail to be wrong, as would be the case if "today" had to be associated with a completing sense which determined the value of "today" as reference, before the question of truth arose for sentences in which it occurs.

---

[5] In the three problems that follow, and the balance of the paper, I am much in debt to a series of very illuminating papers by Hector-Neri Castañeda. The fullest statement of his view is in "Indicators and Quasi-Indicators," *American Philosophical Quarterly*, Vol. 4 (1967):85–100. See also "'He': A Study in the Logic of Self-Consciousness," *Ratio*, VIII (1966):130–157, and "On the Logic of Attributions of Self-Knowledge to Others," *Journal of Philosophy*, LXV (1968):439–456. All the examples of what I later call "self locating knowledge" are adaptations from Castañeda, and the difficulties they raise for Frege's account are related to points Castañeda has made.

To state my third objection, the *nonsufficiency of belief,* I shall shift to an example using the demonstrative "I." I do so because the objection is clearest with respect to this demonstrative, and because some awareness of this problem might help explain how consideration of "I" led Frege to incommunicable senses.

Let us imagine David Hume, alone in his study, on a particular afternoon in 1775, thinking to himself, "I wrote the *Treatise.*" Can anyone *else* apprehend the thought he apprehended by thinking this? First note that what he thinks is true. So no one could apprehend the same thought, unless they apprehended a true thought. Now suppose Heimson is a bit crazy, and thinks himself to be David Hume. Alone in his study, he says to himself, "I wrote the *Treatise.*" However much his inner life may, at that moment, resemble Hume's on that afternoon in 1775, the fact remains: Hume was right, Heimson is wrong. Heimson cannot think the very thought to himself that Hume thought to himself, by using the very same sentence.

Now suppose Frege's general account of demonstratives is right. Then it seems that, by using the very same sense that Hume supplied for "I," Heimson should be able to think the same thought, without using "I," that Hume did using "I." He will just have to find a true sentence, which expresses the very thought Hume was thinking, when he thought to himself, "I wrote the *Treatise.*" But there just does not seem to be such a thought.

Suppose Heimson thinks to himself, "The author of the *Inquiries* wrote the *Treatise.*" This is true, for the sense used to complete the sense of "( ) wrote the *Treatise*" determines Hume not Heimson as reference. But it seems clear that Hume could acknowledge "I wrote the *Treatise*" as true, while rejecting, "The author of the *Inquiries* wrote the *Treatise.*" He might have forgotten that he wrote the *Inquiries;* perhaps Hume had episodes of forgetfulness in 1775. But then the thought Heimson thinks, and the one Hume apprehended, are not the same after all, by the identification of thoughts with senses, and the criterion of difference for senses.

One might suppose that, while there is no particular sentence of this sort that must have had, for Hume, the same cognitive value as "I wrote the *Treatise,*" there must be some such sentence or other that would have had the same cognitive value for him.

But I see no reason to suppose this is so. For now we have reached just the point where the first objection takes hold. There is no reason to believe we are on each occasion each equipped with some nondemonstrative equivalent of the demonstratives we use and understand. This goes for "I" as well as "today." After all, as I am imagining Heimson, he does not have any correct demonstrative free description of himself at hand. Every correct demonstrative free description he is willing to apply to himself refers to Hume instead. I'm not at all sure that I have one for myself.

To keep the identification between thought and sense intact, Frege must provide us with a completing sense. But then his account of demonstratives becomes impausible.

II

Frege follows his general discussion of demonstratives by saying that "I" gives rise to certain questions. He then makes the point, with the examples concerning Dr. Lauben discussed above, that various persons might associate various senses with the same proper name, if the person were presented to them in various ways. This discussion seems intended to prepare the way for the startling claim about thoughts about ourselves,

> Now everyone is presented to himself in a particular and primitive way, in which he is presented to no-one else. So, when Dr. Lauben thinks that he has been wounded, he will probably take as a basis this primitive way in which he is presented to himself. And only Dr. Lauben himself can grasp thoughts determined in this way. But now he may want to communicate with others. He cannot communicate a thought which he alone can grasp. Therefore, if he now says 'I have been wounded', he must use the 'I' in a sense which can be grasped by others, perhaps in the sense of 'he is speaking to you at this moment', by doing which he makes the associated conditions of his utterance serve for the expression of his thought. (T, 25–26)

Frege's doctrine appears to be this. When I use "I" to communicate, it works like other demonstratives, and perhaps could even be replaced by some phrase which included only other demonstratives. The sense would be completed in whatever way is appropriate for sentences containing these demonstratives. When I use "I" to think about myself, however, it has an incommunicable sense.

This is not quite right, for Frege would not have thought it necessary, in order to think about myself, to use language at all. It is at this point that Frege makes his famous remark, about how the battle with language makes his task difficult, in that he can only give his readers the thought he wants them to examine dressed up in linguistic form.

Nevertheless, it seems clear that Frege thinks there are senses, for each of us, that determine us as reference, which are incommunicable, and which would be the natural sense to associate with "I" if it did happen to be used, not merely to communicate with others, but think about oneself.

I suggest this doctrine about "I" is a reaction to the problems just mentioned, the third in particular. I am not at all certain that this is so. Philosophers have come to hold somewhat similar views about the self, beliefs about oneself, and "I," without thinking as rigorously as Frege did about these matters. Perhaps Frege had adopted some such view independently of his thinking about demonstratives, and simply wished to show he could accommodate it. It seems to me more likely, however, that Frege was led to this view by his own philosophical work, in particular by some realization of the problems I have discussed for his general account, as they apply particularly to "I." All three problems turned on the failure to find a suitable description for the value of the demonstrative, whose sense would complete the sense of the sentence in just the right way. If the sense we are looking for is private and incommunicable, it is no wonder the search was in vain.

But the appeal to private and incommunicable senses cannot, I think, be a satisfactory resolution of the problem.

In the first place, I see no reason to believe that "everyone is presented to himself in a particular and primitive way." Or at least, no reason to accept this, with such a reading that it leads to incommunicable senses.

Suppose M is the private and incommunicable sense, which is to serve as the sense of "I" when I think about myself. M cannot be a complex sense, resulting from the compounding of simpler, generally accessible senses. For it seems clear that it is sufficient, to grasp the result of such compounding, that one grasp the senses compounded. So M will have to be, as Frege says, primitive.

A sense corresponds to an aspect or mode of presentation (SR, 57, 58). There are, I hope, ways in which I am presented to myself, that I am presented to no one else, and aspects of me that I am aware of, that no one else is aware of. But this is not sufficient for Frege's purposes.

Suppose that only I am aware of the scratchiness of a certain fountain pen. Still, "thing which is scratchy" does not uniquely pick out this pen; this pen may not be the only one which falls under the concept this phrase stands for, though perhaps the only one of which I am aware. Similarly, just because there is some aspect, such that only I am aware that I have it, and M is the sense corresponding to that aspect, it does not follow that M determines as reference a concept that only I fall under, or that *the M*, (by which I mean the result of combining the sense of "the" with M), is a sense which determines just me as reference, and can appropriately be associated with my utterances of "I."

What is needed is a primitive aspect of me, which is not simply one that only I am aware of myself as having, but that I alone have. While there are doubtless complex aspects that only I have, and primitive aspects, that only I am aware of myself as having, I see no reason to believe there are primitive aspects, that only I have. Even if there were, if they were incommunicable, I should have no way of knowing there were, since I hardly ask others if they happened to have *mine*. So I shouldn't know that *the M* determined me as reference. But I do know that I am thinking about me, when I use the word "I" in thinking to myself.

My second point in opposition to incommunicable senses, is that the third objection does not merely apply to "I," but to at least one other demonstrative, "now." However one may feel about one's private and unique aspects, Frege's doctrine must appear less plausible when it is seen that it must be extended to other demonstratives.

Suppose the department meeting is scheduled for noon, September 15, 1976. Then only at that time could we say something true with (5).

(5) The meeting starts now.

Now consider any of the informationally equivalent thoughts we might have had the day before, for example (6).

(6) The meeting starts at noon, September 15, 1976.

It seems that one could accept this day before, and continue to accept it right through the meeting, without ever accepting (5), and even rejecting it firmly precisely at noon, simply by completely losing track of time. So (5) and (6) express different senses, and so different thoughts. And it seems this would be true, no matter what nondemonstrative informational equivalent we came up with instead of (6). So with "now," as with "I," it is not sufficient, to grasp the thought expressed with a demonstrative, to grasp an informational equivalent with a complete sense. Frege will have to have, for each time, a primitive and particular way in which it is presented to us at that time, which gives rise to thoughts accessible only at that time, and expressible, at it, with "now." This strikes me as very implausible. An appeal to incommunicable senses won't serve to patch up Frege's treatment.

I will conclude by sketching an alternative treatment of these problems. I try to show just how these recent examples motivate a break between sense and thought, and how, once that break is made, senses can be treated as roles, thoughts as information, and the other examples we have discussed handled.

III

Consider some of the things Hume might have thought to himself,

> I am David Hume.
>
> This is Edinburgh.
>
> It is now 1775.

We would say of Hume, when he thought such things, that he knew *who* he was, *where* he was, and *when* it was. I shall call these self locating beliefs. The objections, posed in the last section to Frege's account of demonstratives, may be put in the following way: Having a self locating belief does not consist in believing a Fregean thought.

We can see that having such beliefs *could* not consist *wholly* in believing Fregean thoughts. Consider Frege's timeless realm of generally accessible thoughts. If Hume's knowing he was Hume, consisted in his believing certain true thoughts in this realm, then it would seem that anyone else could know that *he* was Hume, just by believing those same thoughts. But only Hume can know, or even truly believe, that he is Hume. Analogous remarks apply to his knowing where he was, and when it was.

Either there are some thoughts only Hume can apprehend, and his believing he is Hume consists in believing those thoughts, or self locating knowledge does not consist wholly in believing some true subset of the Fregean thoughts. Frege chose the first option; let's see what happens when we choose the second.

We accept that there is no thought only Hume can apprehend. Yet only he can know he is Hume. It must not just be the thought that he thinks, but the way that he thinks it, that sets him apart from the rest of us. Only Hume can think a true thought, by saying to himself,

> I am Hume.

Self locating knowledge, then requires not just the grasping of certain thoughts, but the grasping of them via the senses of certain sentences containing demonstratives.

To firmly embed in our minds the importance that thinking a thought via one sense rather than another can have, let us consider another example. An amnesiac, Rudolf Lingens, is lost in the Stanford library. He reads a number of things in the library, including a biography of himself, and a detailed account of the library in which he is lost. He believes any Fregean thought you think might help him. He still won't know who he is, and where he is, no matter how much knowledge he piles up, until that moment when he is ready to say,

> *This* place is aisle five, floor six, of Main Library, Stanford.
>
> *I* am Rudolf Lingens.

If self locating knowledge consists not merely in believing certain thoughts, but believing them by apprehending certain senses, then senses cannot be thoughts. Otherwise it would make no sense to say that Hume and Heimson can apprehend all the same thoughts, but Hume can do so by apprehending different senses.

Let us then see how things begin to resolve themselves when this identification is given up. Let us speak of *entertaining* a sense, and apprehending a thought. So different thoughts may be apprehended, in different contexts, by entertaining the same sense (without supposing that it is an incomplete sense, somehow supplemented by a sense completer in the context), and the same thought, by entertaining different senses.

By breaking the connection between senses and thoughts, we give up any reason not to take the options closed to Frege. We can take the sense of a sentence containing a demonstrative to be a role, rather than a Fregean complete sense, and thoughts to be the new sort, individuated by object and incomplete sense, rather than Fregean thoughts. Though senses considered as roles, and thoughts considered as information, cannot be identified, each does its job in a way that meshes with the other. To have a thought we need an object and an incomplete sense. The demonstrative in context gives us the one, the rest of the sentence the other. The role of the entire sentence will lead us to Truth by leading us to a true thought, that is just in case the object falls under the concept determined as reference by the incomplete sense.[6]

Let us see how some of the examples we have discussed are handled.

We must suppose that both Hume and Heimson can entertain the same senses, and think the same thoughts. The difference between them is that they do not apprehend the same thoughts when they entertain the same senses.

---

[6] The notions of the role of a sentence, and of a thought as information, are similar to the concepts of *character* and *context* in David Kaplan's "On the Logic of Demonstratives," xeroxed, UCLA Department of Philosophy. This is no accident, as my approach to these matters was formed, basically, as a result of trying to extract from this work of Kaplan's, and Kaplan himself, answers to questions posed by Castañeda's work. One should not assume that Kaplan would agree with my criticisms of Frege, my treatment of self locating knowledge, or the philosophical motivation I develop for distinguishing between sense and thought.

When Heimson entertains the sense of "I am the author of the *Treatise*" he appre-hends the thought consisting of Heimson and the sense of "( ) is the author of the *Treatise*." This thought is false. When Hume entertains the same sense, he appre-hends the thought consisting of Hume and the sense of "( ) is the author of the *Treatise*," which is true. Hume is right, Heimson is crazy.

Similarly, only at twelve noon can someone think the thought consisting of noon and the sense of "the meeting starts at ( )" by entertaining the sense of "the meeting starts now."

Why should we have a special category of self locating knowledge? Why should we care how someone apprehends a thought, so long as he does? I can only sketch the barest suggestion of an answer here. We use senses to individuate psychological states, in explaining and predicting action. It is the sense entertained, and not the thought apprehended, that is tied to human action. When you and I entertain the sense of "A bear is about to attack me," we behave similarly. We both roll up in a ball and try to be as still as possible. Different thoughts apprehended, same sense enter-tained, same behavior. When you and I both apprehend the thought that I am about to be attacked by a bear, we behave differently. I roll up in a ball, you run to get help. Same thought apprehended, different sense entertained, different behavior. Again, when you believe that the meeting begins on a given day at noon by entertaining, the day before, the sense of "the meeting begins tomorrow at noon," you are idle. Apprehending the same thought the next day, by entertaining the sense of "the meeting begins now," you jump up from your chair and run down the hall.

What of the indirect reference? Is the indirect reference of a sentence contain-ing a demonstrative in the scope of such a cognitive verb, the sense or the thought?

It seems, a priori, that the "believes that" construction (to pick a particular verb) could work either way. That is,

> A believes that *S*

might be designed to tell us the sense *A* entertains, or the thought *A* apprehends. The first seems a little more efficient. If we know the sense entertained, we can compute the thought apprehended, given the believer's context.

Nevertheless, it is surely the thought apprehended that is the indirect reference of a sentence containing a demonstrative in the scope of "believes." Consider (7), (8), and (9),

> (7) I believe that Russia and Canada quarrelled today.
>
> (8) Mary believed that Russia and Canada quarrelled today.
>
> (9) Mary believed that Russia and Canada quarrelled yesterday.

Suppose Mary utters (7) on August 1, and I want to report the next day on what she believed. If I want to report the sense entertained, I should use (8). But this gives the wrong result. Clearly I would use (9). To get from the sentence embed-ded in (9), to the thought Mary apprehended, we take the value of the demon-strative in the context of the belief reporter, not in the context of the believer.

It has been suggested that we try to use the sense entertained by the believer in reporting his belief, whenever possible. What we have just said does not conflict with this. The point is simply that the function of thought identification dominates the function of sense identification, and when we use demonstratives, there is almost always a conflict.

There will be no conflict, when one is dealing with eternal sentences, or when one is reporting one's own current beliefs. The need for distinguishing sense from thought will not be forced to our attention, so long as we concentrate on such cases.

Let us now consider the Morning Star example.

Mary says "I believe that is the Morning Star" in the morning while pointing at Venus, and "I believe that is not the Morning Star" at night while pointing at Venus. It seems that Mary, though believing falsely, has not changed her mind, and does not believe a contradiction.

As long as we think of thoughts as senses, it will seem that anyone who understands the relevant sentences, will not believe both a thought and its negation. So long as we think of senses as thoughts, we shall think that anyone who accepts a sense at one time, and its negation at another, must have changed her mind. The correct principle is simply that no thoughtful person will accept a sense and its negation in the same context, since just by understanding the language, she should realize that she would thereby believe both a thought and its negation.

We should take "believing a contradiction," in the sense in which thoughtful people don't do it, to mean accepting senses of the forms S and not-S, relative to the same context of utterance. Mary doesn't do this; she accepts S in the morning, not-S in the evening. Has she then changed her mind? This must mean coming to disbelieve a thought once believed. We shouldn't take it to mean coming to reject a sense once accepted. I can reject "Today is sunny and bright" today, though I accepted it yesterday, without changing my mind about anything. So Mary hasn't changed her mind, either.

What she does do, is believe a thought and its negation. (Here we take the negation of a thought consisting of a certain object and incomplete sense, to be the thought consisting of the same object, and the negation of the incomplete sense.) I am inclined to think that only the habit of identifying sense and thought makes this seem implausible.

I have tried to suggest how, using the concepts of sense, thought, and indirect reference in a way compatible with the way Frege introduced them, but incompatible with his identifications, sentences containing demonstratives can be handled. I do not mean to imply that Frege could have simply made these alterations, while leaving the rest of his system intact. The idea of individuating thoughts by objects, or sequences of objects, would be particularly out of place in his system. The identification of thought with complete sense was not impulsive, but the result of pressure from many directions. I do not claim to have traced the problems that come to surface with demonstratives back to their ultimate origins in Frege's system.

IV

I have argued that Frege's identification of senses of sentences with thoughts leads to grave problems when sentences containing demonstratives are considered. The utterance of such a sentence in a context seems to yield only an incomplete sense and an object, not a complete sense of the sort a Fregean thought is supposed to be. He probably supposed that context supplies not just an object, but somehow a completing sense. There seems no place for such a sense to be found, save in the mind of the person who apprehends the thought expressed by the sentence. But to understand such a sentence, it is neither necessary nor sufficient to have grasped, and associated with the value of the demonstrative, any such sense. Frege's appeal to incommunicable senses in the case of "I," is probably an implausible attempt to deal with these problems. What is needed is to give up the identification of sense expressed with thought expressed. This would allow us to see the sense as a procedure for determining reference from a context, and the thought as identified by the incomplete sense and the value of the demonstrative. The identification of the thought, with the indirect reference of the sentence is the scope of a cognitive verb, need not be given up.[7]

---

[7] Discussions of these issues with Robert Adams, Michael Bratman, Tyler Burge, Keith Donnellan, Dagfinn Føllesdal, Alvin Goldman, Holly Goldman, David Kaplan, and Julius Moravcsik were enormously helpful. This paper was written while I was a Guggenheim Fellow, and on sabbatical leave from Stanford University. I thank both institutions for their support.

DEMONSTRATING AND NECESSITY*
Nathan Salmon

1

My title is meant to suggest a continuation of the sort of philosophical investigation into the nature of language and modality undertaken in Rudolf Carnap's *Meaning and Necessity* (University of Chicago, 1947, 1956) and Saul Kripke's *Naming and Necessity* (Harvard University Press, 1972, 1980). My topic belongs in a class with meaning and naming. It is *demonstratives*—that is, expressions like '*that* darn cat' or the pronoun 'he' used deictically (in contrast to its use either as a bound variable or as a "pronoun of laziness"). A few philosophers deserve particular credit for advancing our understanding of demonstratives and other

---

* The present paper was written to be delivered in part at the University of San Marino 2001 Conference on David Kaplan's contribution to philosophy. I am grateful to the discussants there, especially Kaplan, for their challenging comments (all of which I believe are answered here), and to the participants in my seminar at UCSB during Fall 2000 for their role as initial sounding board for most of the ideas presented here. I am also grateful to the referees for the *Philosophical Review,* to my audience at an American Philosophical Association, Pacific Division meeting (2002), and especially to my commentator, Ben Caplan, for their insightful reactions and comments.

indexical (that is, context-dependent) words. Though *Naming and Necessity* is concerned with proper names, not demonstratives, it opened wide a window that had remained mostly shut in *Meaning and Necessity* but that, thanks largely to Kripke, shall forevermore remain unbarred. Understanding of demonstrative semantics grew by a quantum leap in David Kaplan's remarkable work, especially in his masterpiece "Demonstratives" together with its companion "Afterthoughts."[1] In contrast to the direct-reference propensities of these two contemporary figures, Gottlob Frege, with his uncompromisingly thoroughgoing intensionalism, shed important light on the workings of demonstratives in *"Der Gedanke"*—more specifically, in a few brief but insightful remarks from a single paragraph concerning tense and temporal indexicality.

Frege and Kaplan are especially concerned with Frege's Puzzle. As it applies to demonstratives, the puzzle may be posed thus: How can 'This is that', if true, differ at all in content from an utterance of 'That is that' while pointing with two hands straight ahead to the same thing? Kaplan lifts much of his theory of demonstratives from Frege's remarks, yet disagrees with Frege concerning the puzzle's solution. This results in a fundamental tension in Kaplan's observations concerning demonstratives.

Kaplan distinguishes among three semantic values for a single expression: *extension, content,* and *character*. Extension is essentially Frege's notion of *Bedeutung*. The extension of a singular term is its *designatum*, that is, the designated object for which the term stands; the extension of a sentence is either truth or falsity. Content corresponds closely to Frege's notion of *Sinn* or sense, and coincides with Russell's notion of what he called "meaning." It also corresponds to Strawson's notion of the statement made in using a sentence. The content of a declarative sentence is the proposition expressed, the content of a singular term is its contribution to the content of sentences in which it occurs. The content of an expression determines its extension with respect to discourse about various scenarios, and in particular, with respect to any possible "circumstance of evaluation"— that is, any possible world at a particular time. Indexicals reveal a need for a third layer of semantic value. An indexical sentence like 'I'm busy now' expresses different propositions on different uses. Some of these propositions may be true and others false. Likewise, when the sentence 'It is rainy today' is uttered one day and again the following day, the propositions asserted are different. Even if the extensions (in this case, the truth values) happen to be the same, the propositions asserted still *might have* differed in truth value—there are possible scenarios in which the same propositions determine different truth values—and even a merely possible divergence in truth value is sufficient to establish the distinctness of the propositions expressed. Yet the sentence uttered is not ambiguous in regard to linguistic meaning; it is univocal. The meaning, which remains constant among different utterances, generates a distinct proposition for each distinct day on which the sentence is uttered, *to wit,* the proposition about that day to the effect

---

[1] In J. Almog, J. Perry, and H. Wettstein, eds., *Themes from Kaplan* (Oxford: Oxford University Press, 1989), 481–614.

that *it* is rainy. The character of an expression determines what content is expressed with respect to any particular context.[2]

A competent speaker need not know the extension of an expression (for example, the truth value of a sentence) in order to understand the expression properly. But neither must a competent speaker always know the content. The detective who stumbles upon an unsigned note containing the words "The loot will be deposited in a Swiss account the day after tomorrow' understands the sentence but cannot know which proposition it was used to express without knowing the extension of 'tomorrow'. What a competent speaker must know to understand the sentence (as opposed to understanding the speaker's speech act) is the character, and it is the character that is best identified with the *meaning*. An expression is *indexical* if its character determines different contents depending on the context.[3]

Among indexicals, Kaplan distinguishes between demonstratives, which require an accompanying demonstration (for example, a finger-pointing or hand gesture), and "pure indexicals," which do not (like 'I' or 'tomorrow').[4] Moreover, according to Kaplan, demonstrations function rather like context-dependent definite descriptions: when performed ("mounted") in a particular context, a demonstration takes on a representational content that determines an object with respect to a possible circumstance. Which content is taken on depends on the context; which object is determined depends on the circumstance. Kaplan calls the demonstrated object the *demonstratum* of the demonstration (in the relevant circumstance)—for example, the person, place, or thing pointed to in an act of ostension.

---

[2] Kaplan's three-tiered theory of character, content, and extension is inadequate. The eternal nature of contents—for example, the fact that a given proposition is unwavering in its truth value—argues in favor of separating the possible world of a circumstance from the time, and drawing a four-way distinction between semantic values by inserting a semantic value—what I call the *content base*—between the levels of character and (proper) content. Content bases of sentences are proposition-like entities except for being non-eternal. Such things are sometimes called *states of affairs*. I call them *proposition matrices*. Kaplan's notion of character is replaced by a semantic value, which I call *program*, that assigns content bases to contexts:

> Level 4: *program*
> Level 3: *content base* with respect to c
> Level 2: *content* with respect to c and t
> Bottom: *extension* with respect to c, t, and w

The content of "I am hungry', when uttered by me at t, is the eternal proposition that I am hungry at t, whereas the content base is a proposition matrix—a recurring state of affairs that, although frequent, is not quite eternal. See my "Tense and Singular Propositions," in *Themes from Kaplan*, 331–92. I will ignore the need for this significant modification of Kaplan's scheme in what follows when there is no danger of any resulting serious confusion of the relevant issues.

[3] More accurately, an indexical determines different *content bases* depending on context. See the preceding note.

[4] In "Afterthoughts" Kaplan proposes replacing demonstrations with "directing intensions" (582–90 and *passim*). Though the distinction remains somewhat unclear, I believe that nothing said here is affected if the proposed replacement is made throughout.

2

As mentioned, Frege made insightful observations concerning tense and indexicality. He wrote:

> [In some cases] the mere wording, which can be made permanent by writing or the gramophone, does not suffice for the expression of the thought. . . . If a time indication is made in present tense, one must know when the sentence was uttered to grasp the thought correctly. Thus the time of utterance is part of the expression of the thought. If someone wants to say today what he expressed yesterday using the word 'today', he will replace this word with 'yesterday'. Although the thought is the same, the verbal expression must be different to compensate for the change of sense which would otherwise be brought about by the different time of utterance. The case is the same with words like 'here' and 'there'. In all such cases, the mere wording, as it can be written down, is not the complete expression of the thought; one further needs for its correct apprehension the knowledge of certain conditions accompanying the utterance, which are used as means of expressing the thought. Pointing the finger, gestures, and glances may belong here too. The same utterance containing the word 'I' will express different thoughts in the mouths of different people, of which some may be true and others false.[5]

Tyler Burge argues that this passage strongly supports an interpretation on which there is a very nearly explicit distinction in Frege's thought about language, very much like Kaplan's—not merely the celebrated dichotomy of sense and designatum, but a distinction between those two and, thirdly, conventional linguistic meaning.[6] Here again, the distinction between these three is said to be revealed by indexicals. Indexical words like 'yesterday', 'there', and the demonstratives express different senses with respect to different contexts of use. The linguistic meaning of an indexical remains constant in different uses, and determines what sense the expression takes on with respect to a possible use, whereas the sense determines what the expression designates. Since the sense shifts with context while the linguistic meaning remains the same, the sense is different from the meaning.

Burge's interpretation is evidently based on a misreading of the quoted passage. Frege explicitly denies that an indexical by itself expresses a sense that determines

---

[5] "*Der Gedanke*," *Beiträge zur Philosophie des deutschen Idealismus* (1918), translated by P. Geach and R. H. Stoothoff as "Thoughts," in Frege's *Logical Investigations* (New Haven: Yale University Press, 1977). An alternative translation of the quoted passage occurs there, at p. 10.

[6] Tyler Burge, "*Sinning* against Frege," *Philosophical Review* 88 (July 1979):398–432. Burge argues that Frege's three-way distinction is partially nonsemantic, because Frege's notion of *sense* is epistemic or cognitive rather than semantic. I am unpersuaded, partly for reasons to be set out shortly. Though Fregean propositions ("thoughts") are mentally apprehended objects of propositional attitude, Frege's notion of sense is no less semantic than Kaplan's notion of content or Alonzo Church's notion of sense. Indeed, the former is a good deal more semantic than, for example, Strawson's notion of the statement made in an utterance (cf. my "Two Conceptions of Semantics," in Z. Szabó, ed., forthcoming). The Fregean sense of an expression is precisely what, on Frege's theory, the expression (as supplemented by various contextual elements) expresses and what, in turn, determines the same expression's *Bedeutung*. The last is a properly semantic notion if anything is.

the relevantly designated object, let alone a different such sense in different contexts. Rather, it is supposed to be the indexical *supplemented by the associated contextual element* that expresses the relevant sense. In an utterance of a sentence involving an indexical, Frege observes, what expresses a proposition (a "thought") is not the sentence itself—the "mere wording" that might be written down or recorded onto an audiocassette—but the wording tan together with certain accompanying elements, like the time of utterance or an ostension, things that cannot be "made permanent" by writing them down or by recording the spoken word. In such cases, the mere wording itself is, in an important sense, essentially incomplete. What expresses the proposition is neither the uttered words nor the conditions accompanying the utterance, but the words and the conditions working in tandem. Indeed, Frege says that the conditions form part of the expression of the proposition, as if what *really* plays the role of a sentence—what actually expresses the proposition—is a hybrid entity made up of syntactic material (words) together with such supplementary contextual material as a time of utterance or a gesture of the hand. According to Frege, the union of sentence and context accomplishes what neither can do without the other. Frege makes his position even clearer in "Logic in Mathematics" (1914):

> I can use the words 'this man' to designate now this man, not that man. . . . The sentences of our everyday language leave a good deal to guesswork. It is the surrounding circumstances that enable us to make the right guess. The sentence I utter does not always contain everything that is necessary; a great deal has to be supplied by the context, by the gestures I make and the direction of my eyes. A concept-word combined with the demonstrative pronoun or definite article often has in this way the logical status of a proper name in that it serves to designate a single determinate object. But then it is not the concept-word alone, but the whole consisting of the concept-word together with the demonstrative pronoun and accompanying circumstances which has to be understood as a proper name.[7]

Let us call these hybrid expressions-*cum*-contextual-elements *supplemented expressions—supplemented words, supplemented sentences*, etc. And let us call the expression that requires supplementation by a contextual element a *mere expression* (a mere word, etc.). Where there is no danger of confusion, we may call the latter entity simply an *expression*—although doing so evidently conflicts to some extent with the spirit of Frege's account, on which it is not the mere indexical sentence but the non-syntactically supplemented sentence that serves as "the expression" of a proposition. Let us call Frege's claim that it is not the mere words themselves but the union of the mere indexical sentence with non-syntactic material that expresses the proposition *the syntactic incompleteness thesis*.

The syntactic incompleteness thesis precludes Burge's interpretation. If a mere indexical does not express a sense that determines the relevantly designated object, and instead only the supplemented indexical does, then neither does the mere indexical have a linguistic meaning that assigns it such senses with respect

---

[7] Frege's *Posthumous Writings*, ed. H. Hermes, F. Kambartel, and F. Kaulbach, trans. P. Long and R. White (Chicago: University of Chicago Press, 1979), 213.

to contexts of use. It is very much in keeping with the spirit of Fregean semantic theory to ascribe linguistic meaning to supplemented expressions. But the same indexical differently supplemented yields *different* supplemented expressions, evidently with different linguistic meanings. The supplemented indexical 'tomorrow' today (the word supplemented by this very day), insofar as it functions as a meaningful expression itself, evidently means something very different from 'tomorrow' tomorrow. As 'tomorrow' is uttered on different days, and the sense that determines the designated day shifts, so the time that supplements the word also shifts; hence so does the supplemented word and its meaning. Conversely, the meaning of 'tomorrow' t is held fixed only by holding the supplementing time t fixed, and hence also the sense that determines the designated day (the day after t). This blurs the line between the linguistic meaning and the sense of a supplemented expression, effectively eliminating any pressure to distinguish between them. If there remains any such distinction here, it threatens to be a distinction without a difference.

If the mere indexical or the mere present tense verb does not express a sense that determines the relevantly designated object, it does not follow that the mere expression does not express any sense at all. Does the mere indexical have a sense on Frege's view? If it does not, then its role is completely *syncategorematic*, that is, it is then a contextually defined "incomplete symbol" having no content itself yet affecting the content of the larger expressions of which it is a part (the supplemented word and the supplemented sentence in which it occurs)—like a right parenthesis or a crucially placed comma. But as a matter of general philosophical policy, Frege eschews syncategorematicity wherever it is not excessively implausible to do so. Instead, Frege very likely viewed mere indexicals as designating *functions*—those "unsaturated" entities in Frege's ontology that stand in need of supplementation—and he regarded the supplementing contextual element, the time of utterance or a hand gesture, as a name of the argument to the designated function.[8] A demonstration functions as a name of its demonstratum, whereas the time of an utterance might serve in the utterance as a name of itself. The mere word 'yesterday' could be taken to designate a function from a time t (which supplements the mere word, designating itself) to the day before t. Correspondingly, the word 'now' would designate the identity function restricted to times, just as a mere demonstrative like 'that' or 'he' would designate the identity function on demonstrata. Accordingly, the sense of the mere demonstrative would be the identity function on the senses of demonstrations.[9] A mere demonstrative would thus express a sense (albeit not a concept, in Alonzo Church's

---

[8] I am indebted to observations made by Kripke, who suggested this interpretation and cited some of these points against Burge's reading of Frege in a seminar at Princeton around 1980.

[9] The time of utterance would have to present itself in a particular way in order to designate itself (perhaps as the current time, the time being, or the *specious present*, etc.), since on Fregean theory all designation is secured by means of a sense. Times of utterance, *qua* self-referential "expressions," would thus provide rare exceptions to the Fregean dictum: *There is no backward road from designatum to sense.*

(contd.)

sense, of the object designated by the supplemented demonstrative), and its sense would remain constant among various utterances, determining the designata for those utterances, precisely as the linguistic meaning intuitively does. This interpretation—which is both a plausible reading of the passage and true to the general spirit of a Fregean philosophy of semantics—does not merely fail to support Burge's attribution to Frege of a three-way distinction like Kaplan's. It strongly suggests that Frege *rejected* the postulation of a level of semantic value distinct from sense that yields a sense for various contexts. By regarding the mere indexical as an expression for an identity function, and contextual elements as separate designating parts of the completed expression, one eliminates the need to postulate an additional semantic value beyond sense and designatum. The task that Kaplan's character was designed to perform is held to be accomplished instead by the context-independent sense of the mere indexical.[10]

A complication arises from Frege's explicit assertion that 'today' yesterday has the same sense as 'yesterday' today. The designated day is the same, but sameness of sense of the supplemented words would require that the sense of 'today' applied to yesterday should yield the very same value as the sense of 'yesterday' applied to today—that is, ∧ today ∧ (yesterday) = ∧ yesterday∧ (today) (where '∧' is a sense-quotation mark). It is difficult (at best) to reconcile this with Frege's tendency to treat the senses of compound expressions as (metaphorically) being *composed* of the senses of the component expressions. (How can the sense of 'yesterday' be a component of the proposition expressed by a sentence using the word 'today'?) On the other hand, as several commentators have noted (including Burge and Kaplan), Frege's assertion seems directly contrary to his original motivation for postulating sense as distinct from designatum. But see note 14 below.

[10] Burge says (399 n.) that his interpretation of Frege as contrasting his notion of sense with the properly semantic notion of linguistic meaning is further supported by the following passage from Frege's "Logik" (probably 1897). But the passage supports, and even strongly suggests, the very different interpretation offered here:

> Words like 'here' and 'now' achieve their full sense always only through the circumstances in which they are used. If someone says 'It is raining' the time and place of utterance have to be supplied. If a sentence of this kind is written down it often no longer has a complete sense because there is nothing to indicate who uttered it, and where and when. . . . [T]he same sentence does not always express the same thought, because the words require supplementation to obtain the complete sense, and this supplementation can vary according to the circumstances. (Frege's *Nachgelassene Schriften*, ed. H. Hermes, F. Kambartel, and F. Kaulbach (Hamburg: Felix Meiner, 1969), at 146. An alternative English translation occurs in Frege's *Posthumous Writings*, at 135.)

Burge also says (400) that his interpretation is neutral concerning whether it is the indexical expression itself (for example, the word 'that') or the accompanying circumstance (a demonstration) that actually expresses the sense that determines the relevant designatum. One way or the other, the sense associated with the indexical relative to the context varies with the context, whereas the meaning of the indexical itself remains constant in all its relevant uses. The reasoning is mistaken. There is more than one sense "associated" with the indexical relative to a context of use: there is the sense of the indexical itself, and there is the sense of the supplemented indexical. Insofar as it might be a third sense, there is also that of the contextual supplement—which, like the supplemented indexical, functions as a distinct expression from the mere indexical. It is irrelevant that different demonstrations will express different senses (as Frege undoubtedly held). Crucial to Burge's interpretation is the claim that the indexical itself ('that') does not, by Frege's lights, express a sense that remains unchanged with variations in context. But Frege is best seen as holding precisely that the mere indexical's sense remains unchanged despite changes in the accompanying contextual elements (and the senses thereby expressed).

3

Although Kaplan's account of indexicals owes much to Frege, it differs from Frege's in important respects. First and foremost, the content of an indexical word is taken to be the designatum itself, rather than a concept of the designatum (in Church's sense). Furthermore, a mere indexical word like 'yesterday' is said by Kaplan to designate the relevant object—in this case, the day before the time of utterance—not a function from times to days. The word takes on, relative to a context of use, a content that determines the designated object with respect to the context. The time of the context serves to determine the content. Though Frege assigns a different designatum to the mere word, he also allows that the supplemented word designates the relevant day. One may wonder whether there is any non-arbitrary way to choose between saying with Frege that the word 'yesterday' *supplemented by* the time of utterance designates the day before the supplementing time, and saying instead with Kaplan that 'yesterday' designates *with respect to* a context the day before the context. Can it make any difference whether we say that a word plus a context designates a given object, or instead that the word designates the object "relative to" or "with respect to" the context?

From a purely formal perspective, the different ways of speaking amount to the same thing. Either way we assert a ternary relation between a word, a context, and an object. But from a broader philosophical perspective, Kaplan's manner of speaking better captures the underlying facts. There are linguistic intuitions governing the situation, and on that basis it must be said that the word 'yesterday' (the *mere* word) designates a particular day—which day depending on the context of utterance—not a function from times to days. The intuition is unshaken even among sophisticates who, through proper training, have acquired the intuition that, for example, the exponentiation in the numerical term '7^2' (and likewise the word 'squared' in 'seven squared') designates a particular mathematical function.[11]

It is preferable, both theoretically and conceptually, to see the ternary relation between word, context, and object as the relativization to context of the binary relation of designation between word and object, rather than as assigning a semantic value to a cross-bred mereological union of word and context. One unwelcome consequence of Frege's syntactic incompleteness thesis is the damage it inflicts on the syntax of an indexical language. The material that supplements the mere word to form the supplemented expression does not itself have a genuine syntax as such. It is not that such entities as times and gestures *could* not have their own syntax. In *"Über Sinn und Bedeutung"* Frege observes that "it is not forbidden to take any arbitrarily produced event or object as a sign for anything." A highly systematic mode of composition of such signs, and with it a generative grammar, could be cleverly devised, or might even evolve through usage. Although the expressions that make up a sign

---

[11] Frege maintained that it is not the exponent itself (and not the word 'squared') that designates the relevant function, but the incomplete expression '__^{2}' (likewise, '____ squared'). On the interpretation suggested here, Frege saw the mere word 'yesterday' as also being incomplete, its argument place to be filled not with a syntactic entity but with the time of utterance (*qua* self-designating "expression").

language, for example, cannot be "made permanent" by writing them down or by audio recording, still sign language itself has its own definite syntax. But as a matter of sociological linguistics, such aids to communication as times of utterance and finger-pointings do not have an obvious and recognizable syntax. On Frege's account, a language with indexicals recruits elements from beyond conventional syntax in order to express propositions. What manages to express a proposition in such a language is not something that can be recorded by writing or the gramophone, at least not in its entirety. It is partly syntactic and partly contextual. Natural-language syntax becomes a fine theoretical mess.

In sharp contrast, one welcome consequence of relativizing the semantic relations of designation, and of expressing a content, to context is the recognition of a third kind of semantic value—Kaplan's character—that at least approximates the intuitive notion of *meaning*. Frege's account avoids the claim that utterances on different days of the word 'yesterday' are of a single univocal expression with different designata, but only at a serious cost: the cost of misinterpretation. Frege imputes univocality by interpreting the word in such a manner that it allegedly designates the same thing on each occasion of use—that designated thing being a function and not an "object," in Frege's sense. Though the word's meaning intuitively remains constant from one use to the next, that same word (not some *other* expression) also *does in fact* have different designata, and therefore also different contents, on different occasions of use.

There is a closely related reason why Kaplan contends that an indexical is monogamous in meaning while promiscuous in designation, a reason pertaining to Frege's Puzzle in connection with indexicals. Frege recognizes that "Today is Smith's birthday', uttered one day, expresses the same proposition as 'Yesterday was Smith's birthday' uttered the next. Yet, as Kaplan notes, Frege apparently overlooks that the two sentences can differ in informativeness or "cognitive value" (*Erkenntniswerte*). Contrary to Frege's assertion, the information conveyed in an utterance at 11:59:59 p.m. of the former sentence is different from that conveyed in an utterance of the latter only seconds later. An auditor who does not keep a close eye on an accurate clock is apt to find the two assertions incompatible. But how can the two utterances differ in cognitive value when the very same proposition is asserted in each?

Kaplan's explanation proceeds in terms of the characters of the two sentences. There is an important yet generally overlooked aspect of character, one that I believe Kaplan invokes in his solution to Frege's Puzzle in connection with indexicals, even if only implicitly. (He does not articulate it in precisely the way I shall here.) It is that the character has a contextual perspective on content. More elaborately, *the character specifies the content with respect to a given context of use in a particular manner, describing the content in terms of its special relation to the context.* To illustrate, the particular English sentence 'I had a fever yesterday' is governed by the following content rule:

(CR1) With respect to any context c the (English) content of 'I had a fever yesterday' is the proposition composed of the (English) contents of 'I', 'had a fever', and 'yesterday' with respect to c.

This rule fixes content for any context. Taking this together with such further English semantic facts as that the content of 'yesterday' with respect to a context is the day before the context, then "multiplying through," one derives a content rule of a rather special form, one that *fixes the character*:

(CR2)   With respect to any context c the (English) content of 'I had a fever yesterday' is the singular proposition about the agent of c, and about the day before c, that the former had a fever on the latter.

I call this rule "character-building." Unlike the content rule (CRI), (CR2) *specifies* the content of the sentence with respect to any context as a particular appropriately nonlinguistic function of the context, instead of merely fixing the content by reference to the semantics of component expressions. It thereby gives the character.[12] Every utterance has a speaker and typically at least one auditor or reader, whom I shall call a "speakee." When a speaker utters 'I had a fever yesterday' in a context c, the speakee who understands the sentence (and thus knows its character-building content rule (CR2)) is thereby presented a particular proposition. The proposition in this case is singular, directly concerning a particular agent (the speaker) and a particular day (the preceding). But the sentence itself, *via* its character, presents the proposition to the speakee "by description" (in Russell's sense), in terms of its relation to the very context c—specifically (and roughly), as *the singular proposition about the agent of this very context, and about the day before this very context, that he/she had a fever that day.* The speakee who has been paying even minimal attention, by knowing which day and agent are in question, easily determines which singular proposition was expressed. The speakee therewith apprehends that proposition. The speakee is acquainted with the proposition, yet that acquaintance is obtained through identification of the objects given in a context-specific description. The meaning of the sentence *describes* a singular proposition in terms of the context, and two separate things occur as a result: the utterance issues in the speaker's assertion of that very proposition; and the attentive speakee thereby makes the acquaintance of the presented proposition.[13]

---

[12] Other specifications of the content, even as a function of context, do not fix the character. There is an exactly analogous distinction between a meta-linguistic biconditional in a theory or definition of truth, like " 'Snow is white' is true-in-English iff 'is white' applies in English to the English designatum of 'snow' ", and those special theorems called 'T'-sentences that appropriately fix the nonsemantic truth conditions. Kaplan represents an expression's character in his formal apparatus by the function-in-extension from contexts to contents fixed by a content rule, but further remarks (e.g., "Demonstratives," 505) suggest that the character is something more like the function-in-intension expressed by the character-building content rule. For present purposes an expression's character may be identified with the meta-proposition expressed by its character-building content rule, as distinguished from the other content rules. One who does not know this meta-proposition does not understand the expression. (David Braun makes a similar observation, but a significantly different positive proposal, in "What Is Character?" *Journal of Philosophical Logic* 24 (1995):227–40.)

[13] Cf. "Demonstratives," 529–32, 597. Kaplan does not articulate the issues concerning knowledge by description and acquaintance as I have. He sees the matter in terms of a supplemented demonstrative's potential for having a different content while retaining its character, in that the same demonstration has different demonstrata in different contexts. I think of the matter instead in terms of the descriptive manner in which the character-building content rule presents

(contd.)

Return now to the utterances of 'Today is Smith's birthday' one day and 'Yesterday was Smith's birthday' the next. The same content is presented differently by the different characters. It is presented in the first context *c* as *the singular proposition about the day at the time of this very context c that it is Smith's birthday*, whereas it—the very same proposition—is presented in the second context *c'* as *the singular proposition about the day before this very context c' that it is Smith's birthday*. The two different descriptions of the same proposition in terms of its relations to two different contexts reflect the different characters' separate contextual perspectives. Kaplan proposes identifying the "cognitive value" ("*Erkenntniswerte*") of an expression with its character—the way the content is presented as a function of context—rather than with the content.[14]

4

As mentioned, Kaplan's attention to Frege's Puzzle also motivates his distinction between demonstratives and the so-called pure indexicals. Since different syntactic

---

the content as a function of context. The difference between the two perspectives is subtle but significant. (See also note 28 below.) To illustrate, Kaplan has introduced the name 'Newman-1' (not an indexical) for whoever will be the first child born in the twenty-second century (in "Quantifying In," *Words and Objections: Essays on the Work of W. V. Quine*, ed. D. Davidson and J. Hintikka (Dordrecht: D. Reidel, 1969), 206–42, at 228–29). Kaplan agrees that 'Newman-1' has no semantic potential for having a different content (unlike the corresponding '*dthat*'-term), since the content is the same no matter the context. Still, its character-building content rule presents that content in a special manner (albeit not as a non-constant function of context):

> With respect to any context *c* the (English) content of 'Newman-1' is whoever will be the first child born in the 22nd century, if there will be a unique such person, and nothing otherwise.

The character's perspective on content underlies the phenomenon that has been called "the essential indexical" in explaining behavior by invoking indexical reports of certain beliefs or other attitudes (for example, the belief that one's pants are on fire). Cf. John Perry, "The Problem of the Essential Indexical," *Noûs* 13 (1979):3–21, reprinted in *Propositions and Attitudes*, ed. N. Salmon and S. Soames (Oxford: Oxford University Press, 1988), 83–101. If I am correct, however, a contextual perspective on content is quite inessential to what is semantically expressed by 'I do believe that my pants are on fire'.

[14] The idea of accounting for cognitive value in terms of meaning rather than content (or the "statement" made) is found in P. F. Strawson, "On Referring," sec. 5.b, where he says:

> [O]ne becomes puzzled about what is being said in these sentences [sentences like 'Today is Smith's birthday' and 'Yesterday was Smith's birthday']. We seem . . . to be referring to the same [thing] twice over and either saying nothing about [it] and thus making no statement, or identifying [it] with [itself] and thus producing a trivial identity.
>
> The bogy of triviality can be dismissed. This only arises for those who think of the object referred to by the use of an expression as its meaning, and thus think of the subject and complement of these sentences as meaning the same because they could be used to refer to the same [thing].

Is Frege stymied here? Perhaps not. If the problem for him cited in note 9 above can be solved, he might accommodate the alleged difference in informativeness between 'Today is Smith's birthday' and 'Yesterday was Smith's birthday' through his doctrine of *indirect sense (ungerade Sinn)*. In fact, Kaplan's identification of the cognitive value of a sentence with its character, *qua* a kind of description of the relevant proposition, is highly reminiscent of Frege's notion of indirect sense. Cf. my "A Problem in the Frege-Church Theory of Sense and Denotation," *Noûs* 27 (1993):158–66, and "The Very Possibility of Language: A Sermon on the Consequences of Missing Church," in *Logic, Meaning and Computation: Essays in Memory of Alonzo Church*, ed. C. A. Anderson and M. Zeleny (Boston: Kluwer, 2001).

occurrences of the same demonstrative can converge on the same designatum (hence the same content) yet differ in cognitive value, Kaplan reasons, the characters of those different occurrences must be different. But how can the characters differ when the two occurrences are of the very same univocal vocable?

Kaplan's solution: It is the same vocable, but different expressions. Kaplan's account of demonstratives, as contrasted with "pure" indexicals, can be summed up in a pair of succinct theses:

KT1. Although incorrect about pure indexicals, Frege's syntactic incompleteness thesis is correct with respect to demonstratives; but

KT2. As with all indexical words, the propositions expressed by sentences invoking supplemented demonstratives are singular rather than general.[15]

The attribution of KT1 is based on numerous passages in "Demonstratives" and in its forerunner, "Dthat."[16] In both of these works, sentences invoking demonstratives are uniformly given with a bracketed specification immediately following the demonstrative of a demonstration. The demonstration that completes the mere demonstrative is typically (not always) performed by the agent of the context, and this demonstration is supposed to serve as a component of the sentence that it accompanies. As Kaplan observes,[17] demonstratives are unlike other indexicals in this respect. A demonstration of oneself is completely superfluous in an utterance of 'I' or 'me', and a demonstration of anything else is completely infelicitous. By contrast, a typical demonstrative is essentially incomplete without an accompanying demonstration. Not vacuous; incomplete. A demonstrative *can* be used vacuously, by performing a demonstration with no unique demonstratum. What designates, or fails to designate, is not the demonstrative itself but a supplemented demonstrative, a demonstrative-*cum*-demonstration.

---

[15] Kaplan sometimes use the term 'utterance' for the supplemented expression, reserving the term 'sentence' for the mere sentence. This terminological difference should not eclipse the fact that on Kaplan's view, as on Frege's, it is the supplemented sentence, not the mere sentence, that expresses a proposition when occurring in a context (see note 33 below).

Kaplan overstates KT2 by saying that "indexicals, pure and demonstrative alike, are directly referential" ("Demonstratives," 492). This statement gives the misleading impression that the fact that indexical words are directly referential (in Russell's terminology, *logically proper names*, in Kripke's, *Millian*) obtains somehow in virtue of their context-sensitivity. Both the statement and the misleading suggestion are refuted by the context-dependence of such nonrigid phrases as 'his wife' and 'my hometown'. Also, indexical sentences typically express contingent truths and falsehoods ('He lives in Princeton, New Jersey'), hence do not rigidly designate their truth value. By contrast, indexical *words* are directly referential not by virtue of their context sensitivity, but presumably because their extensions are not secured through a semantic computation (as with definite descriptions and sentences) but given by a default semantic rule for all simple (for example, single-word) singular terms, indexical or otherwise: the Russellian rule that *designatum* = *content*.

[16] In *Syntax and Semantics*, vol. 9: *Pragmatics*, ed. P. Cole (New York: Academic Press, 1978), 221–43; reprinted in *Contemporary Perspectives in the Philosophy of Language*, ed. P. French, T. Uehling, Jr., and H. Wettstein (Minneapolis: University of Minnesota Press, 1979), 383–400.

[17] "Demonstratives," 490–91.

An unsupplemented demonstrative—the mere word—is not even a candidate for designating. In effect, it is grammatically incomplete. As Kaplan puts it:

> Demonstratives are incomplete expressions which must be completed by a demonstration (type). A complete sentence (type) will include an associated demonstration (type) for each of its demonstratives.[18]

Kaplan tentatively accepts a "Fregean theory of demonstrations," on which demonstrations have a character and express an individual concept as content with respect to a context, and on which the demonstration's content determines a demonstratum with respect to a circumstance (that is, with respect to a world at a time). Demonstrations are, in these respects, exactly like indexical definite descriptions. The demonstration fixes the designatum of the supplemented demonstrative, hence also its content. With this in mind, Kaplan proposes a sanitized demonstration-free model of how the natural-language demonstrative works: a mere indexical, *'dthat'*, which is supplemented not by a demonstration but by a singular term to form a complete singular term. Kaplan's *'dthat'* is intended to represent our natural-language demonstrative 'that', except that it accepts accompanying supplemental specifications of anything whatsoever as demonstratum—even of something that cannot be strictly demonstrated (because, for example, it is nowhere to be found in the context)—as long as the supplemental specification is strictly verbalized:

> *Dthat* [the suspicious-looking guy I saw yesterday wearing a brown hat] is a spy.

The content of this sentence is to be the singular proposition about the suspicious-looking guy the agent saw the day before wearing the relevant brown hat—Bernard J. Ortcutt, to give him a name—that he is a spy.[19] Kaplan writes:

> *'Dthat'* is simply the demonstrative 'that' with the following singular term functioning as its demonstration.[20]
>
> I regard my *'dthat'* operator as representing the general case of a demonstrative. . . . I regard the treatment of the *'dthat'* operator in the formal logic . . . as accounting for the general case.[21]

Though the content of the complete singular term is the designatum (Ortcutt himself), the actual meaning should be given by a character-building content rule. Kaplan suggests the needed content rule by saying that *'dthat'* is "a special demonstrative which requires completion by a description and which is treated as a directly referential term whose referent is the denotation of the associated description."[22] He then liberalizes by allowing the supplemental expression to be

---

[18] *Ibid.*, 527.

[19] A complex demonstrative like 'that man' may be seen as the combination of a mere demonstrative with a sortal term, standing in need of further supplementation by a demonstration that is facilitated by the sortal. Thus, an utterance of 'He is a spy' is a natural-language analogue of:

Dthat [the male x: x is suspicious-looking & x is wearing a brown hat] is a spy.

[20] "Demonstratives," 521–22.

[21] *Ibid.*, 527.

[22] *Ibid.*, 521.

any singular term, definite description or otherwise. Earlier in "Dthat," he wrote: "I would like to count my *verbal* demonstration . . . as part of the sentence type."[23] The content rule suggested by these remarks can be stated thus:

(D) With respect to any context *c* the content of the singular term $\ulcorner dthat[\alpha]\urcorner$ is the designatum with respect to *c*, if there is one, of the component operand singular term α (that is, the designatum, if any, of α with respect to *c* and the particular circumstance c_W-at-c_T of *c*). Otherwise $\ulcorner dthat[\alpha]\urcorner$ has no content.[24]

In effect, (D) constitutes a contextual definition of '*dthat*'. Taking (D) together with such further semantic facts as that 'yesterday' designates the day before the context and "multiplying through," the character-building content rule for the particular term '*dthat* [the suspicious-looking guy I saw yesterday wearing a brown hat]' is obtained:

(CR3) With respect to any context *c* the Kaplish content of '*dthat* [the suspicious-looking guy I saw yesterday wearing a brown hat]' is, if anything, the suspicious-looking guy whom the agent of *c* saw in the possible world of *c* wearing a brown hat on the day before *c*.[25]

The semantic rule (D) also yields the following corollaries:[26]

(D1) The singular term $\ulcorner dthat[\alpha]\urcorner$ is indexical—that is, its content depends on and varies with the context.

(D2) With respect to any context $\ulcorner dthat[\alpha]\urcorner$ is directly referential—that is, its content with respect to a context, if any, is simply its designatum with respect to that context.

(D3) With respect to any context $\ulcorner dthat[\alpha]\urcorner$ rigidly designates the designatum, if any, of α with respect to that context, and is otherwise a rigid non-designator.

Corollary (D3) demonstrates that '*dthat*' is, *inter alia*, an intensional operator. The content and designatum of $\ulcorner dthat[\text{the }\phi]\urcorner$ with respect to a given context *c* and a given circumstance *w*-at-*t* is the designatum of $\ulcorner \text{the }\phi\urcorner$ with respect to the circumstance of *c*, *never mind the given circumstance w-at-t*. The '*dthat*'-operator is thus a *rigidifier*. With respect to any context, '*dthat* [the suspicious-looking guy I saw yesterday wearing a brown hat]' rigidly designates whoever *in that context* is the suspicious-looking guy the agent saw wearing a brown hat on the day before the context. The operator is in this respect analogous to the modal operator 'actually': 'Actually, the suspicious-looking guy I saw yesterday wearing a

---

[23]"Dthat," 237.

[24]Cf. the designation rule 11 of the inductive definition of extension ("truth and denotation") in "Demonstratives," at 545–46.

[25]See note 12 above. The result of instantiating the meta-linguistic variable 'α' in (D) to the quotation-name of 'the suspicious-looking guy I saw yesterday wearing a brown hat' is a content rule that fixes the function-in-extension from contexts to contents, but does not express the actual character. By contrast, the "multiplied through" character-building content rule displayed in the text fixes the intended function-in-intension, thereby expressing the relevant character.

[26]Cf. "Demonstratives," 520–22.

brown hat is a spy' is true with respect to a context c and a possible world w if and only if the suspicious-looking guy that the agent of c saw wearing the relevant brown hat on the day before c is (at the time of c) a spy *in the possible world of c*, even if he is not a spy in w.[27]

As mentioned, Kaplan intends his '*dthat*'-operator as a kind of idealized, thoroughly syntactic model of natural-language demonstratives, which require supplementation by actual demonstrations rather than by singular terms. Kaplan sees in a single deictic utterance of 'that' a pair of component 'expressions": the mere word and the supplemental demonstration. Although the demonstration has a content, that content forms no part of the content of the supplemented sentences in which it figures. The content rule governing supplemented demonstratives is modeled after (D):

(T_K) With respect to any context c the (English) content of the supplemented English demonstrative 'that' δ (where δ is a demonstration) is the demonstratum with respect to c, if there is one, of δ, and nothing otherwise.[28]

Demonstratives on Kaplan's theory are thus content operators, in that the designation of a supplemented demonstrative with respect to a circumstance w-at-t depends not merely on the demonstratum of the supplementing demonstration with respect to w-at-t but on the content. (It is the demonstratum determined by that content with respect to a different circumstance, namely, the circumstance c_W-at-c_T of the context of utterance.) But demonstratives are counterexamples to a strong compositionality principle, on which the content of a compound expression is formed from the contents of the component expressions. This feature of Kaplan's account is brought into focus by (D). The content of '*dthat* [the suspicious-looking guy I saw yesterday wearing a brown hat]' is not formed from the content of its component operand—contrary to what one might have expected on the basis of the general behavior of English compound expressions. The content is the guy himself.

5

By distinguishing supplemented demonstratives in virtue of their demonstrations, Kaplan provides a solution to Frege's Puzzle (as it applies to demonstratives) that builds on the idea that the cognitive value of an indexical is its character rather

---

[27] But see note 33 below.

[28] This rule is stated (slightly differently) in "Demonstratives," at 527, where Kaplan says that it "gives the character" of a supplemented ("complete") demonstrative. The latter assertion contradicts my exposition, on which the instantiation of the variable 'δ' in (T_K) to a particular demonstration yields a content rule that is not character-building. (A character-building rule would specify the content with respect to c as *the such-and-such in c*, where the demonstration's content is: *the such-and-such*. See notes 12 and 25 above.) As I see it, the rule (T_K) itself is instead Kaplan's contextual definition of the mere word 'that'. Have I misinterpreted Kaplan? Or is his claim that (T_K) gives the character of a supplemented demonstrative an oversimplification of his view? (It does *fix* the character, specifying the character by description.)

than its content. A supplemented demonstrative 'that'⁀δ presents its content/designatum in a context c, roughly, as *the such-and-such in this very context*, where the content of the accompanying demonstration δ is: *the such-and-such*. Supplemented demonstratives whose supplementary demonstrations differ in content differ themselves in character, in the way their content/designatum is presented as a function of context. The different completions of the sentence 'That is that', even though they share the same content, differ in informativeness because of a difference in meaning. The same proposition is presented two different ways, by means of different supplemented sentences with different characters: one time as *the singular proposition about the such-and-such in this very context and about the so-and-so in this very context, that they are one and the very same*, and a second time (pointing to the same object simultaneously with two hands) as *the singular proposition about the such-and-such in this very context that it is itself*. The same proposition is given by distinct descriptions of it in terms of different relations that it bears to the same context, descriptions invoking the contents of the distinct accompanying demonstrations.

Kaplan briefly considers an alternative account that does away with Frege's syntactic incompleteness thesis even for demonstratives, treating all indexical words on a par.[29] Kaplan calls this alternative *the Indexical theory of demonstratives*. I shall call it *the Bare Bones Theory*. On this theory, a context of use is regarded as including alongside an agent (to provide content for 'I'), a time ('now'), a place ('here'), and any other such features, a demonstratum—or better yet, a sequence consisting of first demonstratum, second demonstratum, and so on, in case a single demonstrative is repeated in a single context with different designata, as in 'That₁ [pointing to a carton] is heavier than that₂ [a different carton]'. Demonstratives on the Bare Bones Theory function according to a very simple character-building content rule:

(T_n) With respect to any context c the content of the nth occurrence in a sentence of 'that' is the nth demonstratum (if any) of c.

This semantic rule imputes different characters to the demonstrative occurrences in 'That is that', since there are contexts in which the first demonstratum is one thing, the second demonstratum another. According to the Bare Bones Theory, the meaning (character) of a sentence like 'That is heavier than that' presents its content with respect to a context as *the singular proposition about the first and second demonstrata, respectively, of this very context, that the former is heavier than the latter*. This contrasts sharply with Kaplan's theory, on which the content is presented instead by means of the contents of the supplemental demonstration, as *the singular proposition about the such-and-such in this context and about the so-and-so in this context, that the former is heavier than the latter*. The Bare Bones Theory makes no place in semantics for the demonstration that accompanies the use of a demonstrative, and consequently misses the epistemologically significant content-demonstratum distinction. Kaplan favors this distinction as providing a

[29]"Demonstratives," 528–29.

more satisfying solution to Frege's Puzzle with regard to demonstratives, *How can an utterance of 'That₁ is that₂,' if true, differ at all in content from an utterance of 'That₁ is that₁'?* He says:

> The Fregean theory of demonstrations may be extravagant, but compared with its riches, [the Bare Bones Theory] is a mean thing. . . . the Fregean idea that the very demonstration might have picked out a different demonstratum seems to me to capture more of the epistemological situation than the [Bare Bones] Indexicalist's idea that in some contexts the first and second demonstrata differ.[30]

6

We looked at some grounds for favoring an account of indexicals on which contextual features are regarded as indices to which the semantic relations of designation and content are relativized over Frege's idea that such features instead form part of the expression. All of these grounds extend straightforwardly to demonstratives. There is first the damage inflicted upon English syntax. This is the main reason, or at least one very important reason, for the retreat from 'that' to '*dthat*', with the resulting well-behaved syntax of a sort that we students of language have come to treasure. But foremost, there is this: linguistic intuition demands that a demonstrative have a single context-sensitive meaning that assigns different designata, and hence also different contents, on different occasions of use. On Kaplan's theory, in sharp contrast, each utterance of 'that' with a different designatum is an utterance of a different term with a different character or meaning. In fact, as with Frege, each utterance of 'that' accompanied by a different demonstration with a different content is an utterance of *a different term with a different meaning*—even if the demonstrata in that context are exactly the same. (The character is represented by the function that assigns to any context the demonstratum in that context of the particular accompanying demonstration; cf. (D) above.) One might say that the demonstrative 'that' is highly ambiguous on Kaplan's account, its precise meaning depending on the content of the accompanying demonstration. This is not merely somewhat counterintuitive; it is obviously incorrect. As with all indexicals, the designatum of 'that', and therefore also the content, depends on the context, but the English meaning is the same on each occasion of use.[31]

It is not quite correct, however, to say that a demonstrative is ambiguous on Kaplan's account. More accurately, precisely the opposite is true: the mere demonstrative—the word itself—is utterly meaningless in isolation. One feature

---

[30] *Ibid.*

[31] Other writers have made this observation about Kaplan's account—for example, Howard Wettstein, "Has Semantics Rested on a Mistake?" *Journal of Philosophy* 83 (1986):185–209, at 196 n. David Braun presses a related point in "Demonstratives and Their Linguistic Meanings," *Noûs* 30 (1996)):145–73, at 149–50. Braun assumes that Kaplan holds that a mere demonstrative is devoid of character while nevertheless having a univocal meaning, and objects that this is inconsistent with Kaplan's proposed identification of linguistic meaning with character. I provide an alternative interpretation in the next paragraph of the text.

of Kaplan's operator '*dthat*' that is easy to overlook but that makes it a highly implausible model for natural-language demonstratives like 'that' is that the former is, by stipulation, a syncategorematic "incomplete symbol." The content and designatum of the compound term $\ulcorner dthat[\alpha]\urcorner$ is function of the content of its operand α (namely, the designatum thereby determined), but the '*dthat*'-operator itself has no character or content (no "meaning in isolation"). Natural-language demonstratives, in sharp contrast, have a meaning that remains fixed for each use and determines its content in that use.

This is one respect in which Kaplan's account is inferior to Frege's. As we have seen, Frege easily accommodates the fact that a demonstrative has a fixed yet context-sensitive meaning by taking the mere demonstrative to designate a function from features of context to appropriate designata. By contrast, semantically '*dthat*' is not (as its syntax would have us expect) a *functor*. It might appear that Kaplan could improve his account significantly by following Frege's lead and taking '*dthat*' to be a functor for the identity function, and by analogy, taking 'that' to designate the identity function on demonstrata. For numerous reasons, such a modification is not open to Kaplan. One immediate problem—in fact, an immediate *reductio* of Frege's account—is that in the typical case a supplemented demonstrative is, according to that account, a non-rigid designator. Its designatum is simply the demonstratum of the supplementing demonstration, and thus varies from one possible world to the next. This conflicts with Kaplan's thesis KT2 and his semantic corollary (D3).

It might be thought that although Kaplan cannot follow Frege in taking a demonstrative to designate the identity function on demonstrata, this only goes to show that he must seek a different sort of function. As noted above, '*dthat*' is, *inter alia*, an intensional operator. An appropriate designatum for '*dthat*', therefore, cannot operate on the mere designatum of its operand. Analogously, an appropriate designatum for a natural-language demonstrative cannot be a function on the mere demonstratum of the supplementing demonstration. Instead, for any context c there is the aptly suited function $@^i_c$ that assigns to any individual concept (any content suitable for either a definite description or a demonstration) the object determined by that concept in the particular circumstance c_W-at-c_T of c (and to any nonconcept itself). An account of '*dthat*' as designating $@^i_c$ with respect to c could be made to yield exactly the right intension (function from circumstances to designata) for supplemented '*dthat*'-terms. In fact, doing so would make '*dthat*' an indexical modal functor exactly analogous to the sentential operator 'actually' (whose extension with respect to a context c is the function $@^p_c$ that assigns to any proposition its truth value in the particular possible world c_W of c). Kaplan's thesis KT1 virtually cries out for $@^i_c$ to serve as the mere demonstrative's designatum.[32]

---

[32]The character of a demonstrative might be represented on this proposal by the function that assigns to each context c the corresponding function $@^i_c$. Alternatively, the character might be identified with the appropriate function from singular-term characters to directly-referential-singular-term characters (for example, from the character of 'the suspicious-looking guy I saw yesterday wearing a brown hat' to that of the corresponding '*dthat*'-term).

(contd.)

Yet Kaplan is barred from taking '*dthat*' and natural-language demonstratives to be functors. The problem is that the propositions expressed by sentences invoking '*dthat*' could not then be singular propositions—any more than the contents of sentences beginning with 'actually' are truth values rather than propositions (although, again, this could be made to yield exactly the right intension). Instead of Ortcutt himself, the proposition expressed by '*Dthat* [the suspicious-looking guy I saw yesterday wearing a brown hat] is a spy' would include among its constituents, if '*dthat*' were semantically a functor, the content of the operand description 'the suspicious-looking guy I saw yesterday wearing a brown hat' as well as the content of the functor itself (perhaps something like the *operation* of assigning to any such individual concept the individual it determines in the particular circumstance c_W-at-c_T). This violates (D2) and would thus destroy KT2, and therewith tarnish the spirit of Kaplan's general account. The cost of mediation between KT1 and KT2 is not cheap: a demonstrative is regarded as a syncategorematic incomplete symbol, as mere punctuation.[33]

David Braun in "Demonstratives and Their Linguistic Meanings" (see note 31 above) makes a proposal similar to the second identification of characters mentioned above. The similarity is superficial. Braun's specific proposal has at least two significant defects. First, Braun takes the arguments of the functions he identifies with the meanings of demonstratives to be demonstrations themselves rather than their characters. This would be analogous to taking the meaning of 'the mother of' to be a function from its singular-term arguments (instead of their meanings) or the character of 'not' to be a function from sentences. This defect might be forgivable, if demonstrations are arguably part of a universal language (unlike singular terms). More important, Braun's central idea is to assign an additional kind of "meaning" to mere demonstratives: a fourth semantic value beyond character, content, and extension (of the supplemented demonstrative). By contrast, the proposal in the text (to be rejected presently) assigns a character, content, and extension to a mere demonstrative itself. The character of the mere demonstrative determines that of the supplemented demonstrative from that of a given supplemental demonstration, whereas the content or extension of the mere demonstrative determines that of the supplemented demonstrative from the content (in both cases) of the demonstration.

[33] Kaplan explicitly acknowledges some of these points in "Afterthoughts," at 579–82. Discomfort over the cost of mediation seems to have prompted a disorderly retreat from KT1. Kaplan says that, precisely because the singular term is meant to be directly referential, he had intended the designating term to be simply the word '*dthat*', rather than the compound expression ⌜*dthat*[the ϕ]⌝, and that the supplemental description ⌜the ϕ⌝ was to be merely a "whispered aside" that was "off the record" (581; Kaplan adopted these latter phrases from suggestions by Kripke and me, respectively). Since the supplemental term is no part of the term '*dthat*', he says, as originally intended '*dthat*' is not a rigidifier of something else but a term unto itself. He writes:

> The word '*dthat*' was intended to be a surrogate for a true demonstrative, and the description which completes it was intended to be a surrogate for the completing demonstration. On this interpretation '*dthat*' is a syntactically complete singular term that requires no *syntactic* completion by an operand. (A "pointing," being extra-linguistic, could hardly be a part of syntax.) The description completes the *character* of the associated occurrence of '*dthat*', but makes no contribution to content. Like a whispered aside or a gesture, the description is thought of as off-the-record (i.e., off the *content* record). It determines and directs attention to what is being said, but the manner in which it does so is not strictly part of what is asserted. . . . '*Dthat*' is no more an operator than is 'I'. . . . The referent of '*dthat*' is the individual described. . . . It is directly referential.
>
> . . . Although Frege claimed that the context of use was part of "the means of expression" of a thought, he never, to my knowledge, attempted to incorporate "the pointing of fingers, hand movements, glances" into logical syntax. Can an expression such as the

Another problem with Frege's account, inherited by the envisaged account of demonstratives as designating $@^i{}_c$, is that the mere demonstrative is "context-sensitive" on Frege's account only in the sense that its sense and designatum are functions from contextually variant elements. The central insight of Kaplan's account of indexicality is that indexicality is not a matter of expressing functions from contextually variant elements, but a matter of taking on *different contents altogether* in different contexts. This observation goes significantly beyond Hans

---

description in a '*dthat*'-term appear in logical syntax but make no contribution to semantical form? It would be strange if it did. But there is, I suppose, no strict contradiction in such a language form. (581–82)

These remarks are at once curious and maddening. Kaplan's labeling the prospect of a noncompositional compound expression "strange" creates the misimpression that his account of designating demonstratives treats them otherwise. I shall make several points in response and clarification, though I suspect that a much expanded discussion is required. First, Kaplan introduced his expression '*dthat*' in 'Dthat' and again in "Demonstratives" explicitly *stipulating* that it requires completion by a supplemental term, typically a description. He also explicitly said that natural-language demonstratives analogously require completion, by a demonstration instead of a description. (See the quotes supporting the attribution of thesis KT1 and the content rules (D) and (T_K) above.) And indeed, it cannot be merely the expression '*dthat*', but *must* be its union with a supplemental term—thus, a compound expression—that has a character of the appropriate sort. Contrary to Kaplan's remark, the supplemental description makes an essential contribution to content: It *fixes* the content. Without the supplemental term, '*dthat*' is semantically impotent. (Ironically, Kaplan repeatedly acknowledges this point in "Demonstratives," both with regard to '*dthat*'-terms and with regard to natural language (e.g., at 490–91) and even in "Afterthoughts" (e.g., at 588).) To see the point clearly, let the reader attempt to formulate an appropriate content rule like (D) above, except assigning content to the expression '*dthat*' rather than to $\ulcorner dthat[\alpha]\urcorner$, while treating the supplemental term α as neither a component expression nor a component of the context, but instead merely as a "whispered aside" (whatever that would be) that makes no contribution to content. Similarly for (T_K) and the supplemental demonstration. In whatever sense it is true, as Kaplan says above, that the supplemental term α "completes" the character, it is equally true (if not even more so) that '*dthat*' alone is incomplete without a supplemental term and that the complete term has the form $\ulcorner dthat[\alpha]\urcorner$.

All of this is perfectly compatible with the further fact that the content of the supplemental term forms no part of the content of the completed term. Otherwise (D) itself should be formally inconsistent—as should be Kaplan's own informal formulation of this same content rule (521). So too should be (T_K), which Kaplan explicitly endorses (527). In fact, Kaplan's acknowledgment above of the consistency of the envisioned prospect is tantamount to an acknowledgment that there is no valid argument from the noncompositionality of content of a complete '*dthat*'-term to the supplemental term's not being an essential component expression. On the contrary, the envisioned consistent prospect is the very reality Kaplan has produced with his operator. There does seem to be a kind of inconsistency—not in the operator as stipulated, but between the very two paragraphs quoted above. In fact, the very notion of a demonstrative that is on the one hand noncompound and univocal, but on the other variable in character depending on the designata of "whispered asides," is straightforwardly inconsistent.

The remarks in "Afterthoughts" (579–82) fail to provide a coherent interpretation of "Demonstratives." I conclude that Kaplan, on reflection, has misjudged his own original intent for '*dthat*' above (and his own theory of demonstratives!) and that the theory is the one explicitly proffered in "Demonstratives" (at 521–27 and *passim*): that the complete term is the supplemented term comprised by the union of the mere demonstrative with a supplemental demonstration.

Kamp's original insight that indexicality requires *double indexing* of extension both to contexts and to circumstances that may vary independently of context. Not only does the extension, but also the *content,* of an indexical depend upon, and vary with, a context of use.[34] On Frege's account, the content of 'that' is the same in every context: the identity function on demonstration contents. Although "context-sensitive" in one obvious sense—the function in question is a function on a contextually variant element—a mere demonstrative on Frege's account is not indexical in Kaplan's sense. Likewise, although on Frege's account a supplemented demonstrative, 'that'⌢δ, is "context-dependent" in one obvious sense—the argument to the function designated by 'that' is given by the demonstration δ—it is not indexical in Kaplan's sense. It is crucial to Kaplan's account that the supplemented demonstrative be indexical. The content of 'that'⌢δ in any context is the demonstratum of δ *in that context,* and consequently varies with the context. For these various reasons (and more), Kaplan is barred from taking the mere demonstrative—the word itself—to have a meaning in isolation.

But the demonstrative 'that' is surely not meaningless in isolation. It has a definite meaning, one that remains unchanged from one utterance to the next, a meaning that is shared by demonstratives in other languages. And as with any indexical, the meaning of a demonstrative looks to the context to secure a content, and thence, a designatum. Far from being an "incomplete symbol," a demonstrative—the word itself—is a designating singular term if anything is. When Ralph points to Ortcutt and declares, "He is a spy!" the word 'he' surely designates Ortcutt. Furthermore, even if the pointing itself is regarded as somehow designating Ortcutt, intuitively it is the word 'he' *rather than some hybrid consisting of the word and the pointing* that semantically designates Ortcutt. Again, Kaplan's account of demonstratives as syncategorematic punctuation, rather than as fully designating singular terms, is not merely somewhat counterintuitive. It is clearly incorrect.

Does Frege's Puzzle provide adequate grounds to segregate demonstratives from indexical words like 'I' and 'yesterday' in requiring Frege's syntactic incompleteness thesis? Kaplan's complaint concerning the alternative Bare Bones Theory has considerable force. The mere fact that separate occurrences of a demonstrative within a single context frequently differ in their demonstrata is not an adequate explanation of the apparent informativeness of 'That = that', any more than the apparent informativeness of 'Hesperus is Phosphorus' is adequately explained by noting that a single object typically has one name rather than two. Even sophisticated speakers aware of the co-designation of two occurrences of 'that' in a particular context deem it possible to believe that that$_1$ is the same as itself without believing that it is that$_2$. Frege's Puzzle is concerned with the contents of such sentences as 'Hesperus is Phosphorus' and 'This is that' and not merely with their syntax. The puzzle is: How can the expressed propositions differ in the ways that they do from those expressed by 'Hesperus is Hesperus' and by an utterance of 'That = that' while pointing to the same object twice in the

---

[34]So does the content base. (See note 2 above.)

same way—as, perhaps, by pointing simultaneously with both hands?[35] Kaplan's explanation in the case of demonstratives is that the complete sentence is supplemented by distinct demonstrations with distinct contents, and though the two supplemented demonstratives have the same content in the relevant context, they differ in the manner in which they semantically present their common content as a function of context. The Bare Bones Theory also distinguishes the two occurrences of 'that' in regard to meaning, but that difference is described in terms of the different sequential order in which their demonstrations are performed, ignoring the epistemologically crucial contrast between the actual contents of those demonstrations. And, it should be added, the Bare Bones Theory *cannot* provide any explanation in terms of character or content of the *uninformativeness* of an utterance of 'That is that' while pointing with both hands, nor of the *difference* in informativeness between the two utterances of 'That is that', since the sentence is assigned the same character and the same content.

The Bare Bones Theory attempts to solve Frege's Puzzle by postulating distinct words with distinct meanings where there is only one word with one meaning. At bottom, this is the same general strategy employed in both Frege's and Kaplan's solutions. It is a strategy forced on anyone attempting to solve the puzzle in terms of meaning. But it violates a linguistic variation on Occam's Razor: *Thou shalt not multiply meanings beyond necessity.* Worse, it flagrantly violates a further, particularly imposing variation of Occam's Razor: *Thou shalt not multiply expressions beyond plausibility.* Kaplan laments the fact that his preferred solution to the puzzle about 'That$_1$ = that$_2$' does not extend to 'Hesperus is Phosphorus', since the two names, unlike the supplemented demonstratives, share the same character.[36] Rather than contort our linguistic intuitions in order to accommodate an explanation that does not in any event work in the general case, it would be wiser to extract from the case of proper names an important lesson concerning Frege's Puzzle and devices of direct reference generally: *The epistemologically significant ways in which the same proposition is differently presented, or differently taken, are not always a matter of semantics (linguistic meaning).*

The sins of the Bare Bones Theory are not limited to its violation of the linguistic variations on Occam's Razor. That theory ignores demonstrations altogether, and consequently ignores their properly semantic role in the proper use of a demonstrative. One potential problem with the Bare Bones Theory is that *a demonstration's demonstratum need not be active or even present in the context.* This point is illustrated by one of Kaplan's examples (used for a slightly different purpose). I may demonstrate Alonzo Church by pointing to a photograph while uttering 'He was one of the greatest thinkers of the twentieth century'. Regrettably, Church himself is not

---

[35]Cf. my *Frege's Puzzle* (Atascadero, Calif.: Ridgeview, 1986), especially 57–60, 87–92.
    Performing the very same demonstration of the same object twice over in a single utterance of 'That is that' is in fact very difficult to accomplish. For convenience, I assume throughout that pointing simultaneously with both hands is a way of accomplishing this feat (though this assumption is strictly false).

[36]"Demonstratives," 562–63.

present or active in the context; only the photograph is. But the demonstratum is no mere photograph. It is the photograph's subject: Church himself. At most, Church is *present by proxy,* his photograph representing him not merely in the standard way that a picture represents but also standing in for him. The demonstratum of a particular demonstration may be neither present in the context nor an active participant, nor even present by proxy.[37] Consider the following discourse fragment:

(*i*) Do you recall the suspicious-looking guy we saw yesterday wearing a brown hat?

(*ii*) Well, I think: he's a spy.

Although the 'he' in (*ii*) is anaphoric, it is not a variable bound by its grammatical antecedent in (*i*), but a syntactically free term designating Ortcutt. Of course, the pronoun 'he' does not designate Ortcutt no matter what the context. The anaphora here is of a peculiar variety. In effect, the 'he' in (*ii*) is a demonstrative and the definite description in (*i*) plays the role of accompanying demonstration.[38] The demonstratum is entirely absent from, and inactive in, the context; the demonstrative 'he' succeeds all the same. In general, the demonstratum of a particular demonstration need not be present by proxy nor *connected* to the context in any significant ("real") manner, for example, causally. The demonstratum may be *merely* that which is demonstrated—witness Kaplan's '*dthat*'-operator, which may be supplemented by material that designates an object from long, long ago and far, far away, merely "by description" (as in 'Consider whoever was the last

---

[37] I am thinking here of a context as the setting or environment in which an utterance occurs, rather than as the proposition, or set of propositions, assumed by all conversational participants. The case of the answering machine demonstrates that a contextual parameter need not be at the location of the context at the time of the context, since the agent of the utterance of 'I am not here now' is typically asserting a truth. Though the agent of the context of such an utterance is, in some sense, absent from the context, he or she is nevertheless playing an active, or "real," role in the context—there is an assertion *in absentia* by the agent—and I conjecture that it is this fact that warrants including the absent agent as a contextual parameter. By contrast, the demonstratum of a particular demonstration may be entirely passive, utterly inert, a *mere* demonstratum. (Thanks to Ben Caplan for forcing me to be more explicit about this matter.)

The pronouns 'he', 'she', and 'that' may differ in this respect from the special demonstrative 'this', for which the designatum is arguably always present in the context of use (or present by proxy?). If something closely resembling the Bare Bones Theory is applicable to 'this', it is so because of some such special restriction governing its appropriateness. (In effect, the Bare Bones Theory may mistake 'that' for 'this'. Or is it the other way around?)

[38] Contrary to Kaplan's claim (echoing Peter Geach) that anaphoric pronouns may be seen invariably as bound variables ("Demonstratives," 572). Perhaps the issue of whether the 'he' in (*ii*) is a bound variable is to some extent terminological. But the terminology of 'bound' and 'free' is not without constraints. If it is insisted that the 'he' is a bound variable, then what is the variable-binding operator that binds it to its grammatical antecedent? The 'his' in 'No author inscribed his book' is not a designating *occurrence;* it is genuinely a bound variable. By contrast, the 'he' in (*ii*) designates Ortcutt. Nor is the 'he' a "pronoun of laziness" or an abbreviation for the description in (*i*). The speaker's suspicion is not merely a *de dicto* thought to the effect that whoever is a uniquely suspicious-looking guy seen the day before wearing the relevant brown hat is a spy. It is *de re* concerning Ortcutt: that *he* is a spy. All indications are that the 'he' in (*ii*), although anaphoric, is syntactically free, with its grammatical antecedent functioning as a kind of verbalized demonstration.

child born in the nineteenth century. It would have been possible that *he* or *she* be born instead in the twentieth century').

As mentioned, Church's photograph may be employed as a stand in for Church himself. Another feature of the context that is no less relevant to understanding my use of 'he' is my demonstration of Church *via* the photograph. Frege and Kaplan put the demonstration directly into the expression to form a peculiar hybrid: 'he' ⌐pointing-at-the-photograph. But the demonstration does not belong in the expression. I say we take it back. My alternative proposal is that we put the demonstration exactly where it has belonged all along: in the context. Intuitively, the speaker's hand gestures, fingerpointings, and glances of the eye are features of the context of use, every bit as much as the identity of the speaker and the time and place of the utterance. Consider again Frege's insightful observations: "Thus the time of utterance is part of the expression of the thought. . . . The case is the same with words like 'here' and 'there'. In all such cases, the mere wording, as it can be written down, is not the complete expression of the thought; one further needs for its correct apprehension the knowledge of certain conditions accompanying the utterance, which are used as means of expressing the thought. Pointing the finger, gestures, and glances may belong here too." I agree with Frege, as against Kaplan, that gestures and finger-pointings belong together with the time and place of an utterance; I disagree with Frege, and Kaplan, that they go into the expression uttered. Rather, they are equally features of the conditions of an utterance that fix the contents of uttered indexicals. My proposal is that a context of use be regarded as sometimes including a demonstration among its features, along with an agent, a time, a place, and a possible world. Not the bare demonstratum, but the demonstration with all its representational content.[39]

Better yet, since the same demonstrative may recur within a single sentence or stretch of discourse, each time accompanied by a different demonstration ('That one goes between that one and that one'), the context should include an *assignment* of a demonstration for each syntactic occurrence of a demonstrative in a sentence—the first occurrence, the second, and so on.[40] This fuller notion of a context provides a different explanation from that of Frege-Kaplan of the sense in which demonstratives without accompanying demonstrations are *incomplete*. The demonstrative itself is a complete expression, fully assembled and ready to go. Strictly speaking, it is the

---

[39] Kaplan objected (in San Marino) that the demonstration should not go into the context instead of the expression, for otherwise a possible context can include a demonstration completely different from the one performed by the context's agent in the context location at the context time in the context world. This prospect is avoided by restricting the admissible ("proper") contexts to those n-tuples $<c_A, c_T, c_W, \ldots, c_D>$ such that the demonstration c_D is mounted at time c_T in possible world c_W (etc.). It is far from obvious, however, that such a restriction is desirable. Is the sentence 'That object (assuming it exists) is now being demonstrated', for example, to be regarded as true solely by the logic of 'to demonstrate'?

[40] One might wish to let the context assign demonstrations to each demonstrative occurrence in an entire argument. The particular argument 'He is taller than him; hence, he is shorter than him' can be uttered with accompanying demonstrations that ensure the truth of the conclusion given the truth of the premise. ('He$_1$ is taller than him$_2$; hence, he$_2$ is shorter than him$_1$.') Still, the form of words evidently yields an invalid argument. Compare: 'He is taller than him; hence, he is neither shorter than nor the same height as him'.

context that is incomplete. Or if you prefer, it is the *occurrence* of the demonstrative in the defective context that is incomplete, because of a contextual deficiency. It is like the use of 'now' in a timeless universe ("before" the Big Bang?), or the use of 'there' in Oakland, California—fully complete expressions occurring in defective contexts.[41]

The demonstration included in a context need not be an actual finger-pointing, or any action or event in the usual sense. The demonstration can be entirely verbalized—witness the discourse fragment displayed above. Kaplan should formalize this by putting the description from (*i*) directly into (*ii*) thus:

> (*ii*) I think that *dthat* [the male *x*: *x* is a suspicious-looking guy & we saw *x* yesterday wearing a brown hat] is a spy.

If the description in (*i*) is replaced by 'the present Secretary of State', Kaplan would need to make a corresponding adjustment to (*ii′*). But there is no intuitive justification for this dramatic departure from surface syntax. The description in (*i*) does not occur in (*ii*), which is a complete sentence by itself. Instead, (*i*) is part of the context in which (*ii*) occurs ((*i*) is the *verbal* context for the occurrence of (*ii*)), and the description in (*i*) is associated with the 'he' in (*ii*), playing the role of accompanying demonstration. As already mentioned, the description in (*i*) is a verbalized demonstration. If the description is replaced by another, the context for (*ii*) is changed, and hence so too its content. But (*ii*) itself remains the same complete sentence with the same English meaning.[42]

---

[41] Gertrude Stein on seeing her childhood town after it had been torn down: "There is no *there* there."

Braun ("Demonstratives and Their Linguistic Meanings") objects to taking demonstrations as aspects of context on the question-begging grounds that doing so obliterates Kaplan's contrast between demonstratives and the so-called pure indexicals. On the contrary, this is precisely one important reason for putting demonstrations into the context, exactly where they belong. Braun also notes that, unlike other aspects of context (for example, time and place), demonstrations are typically produced under the voluntary control of the agent and are not themselves the contents of the demonstratives they accompany. Here again, these are insufficient grounds to banish demonstrations from their proper place. Demonstrations have important features in common with such contextual aspects as time and place: they are all recognizable as features of the circumstances surrounding an utterance that fix the contents of uttered indexicals.

[42] It is for similar reasons that substitution of 'Barbarelli' for 'Giorgione' fails in 'Giorgione was so called because of his size'. Substitution alters the context for the demonstrative 'so'.

The construction in the text raises particularly perplexing issues. Consider the following variant:

> (*i″*) Consider whoever is the shortest spy in the world; (*ii″*) he or she is a communist.

It seems undeniable that the speaker has asserted *of* the shortest spy, *de re*, that he or she is a communist, since the semantic content of (*ii″*) is precisely that very singular proposition. Kaplan concludes (contradicting his earlier arguments in "Quantifying In"—see note 13 above) that a mastery of the semantics of such directly designating devices as demonstratives enables speakers to form beliefs of singular propositions, and even to gain singular-propositional knowledge a priori (for example, about the shortest spy that he or she is a spy, or about the first child to be born in the twenty-second century that he or she will be born in the twenty-second century), in the absence of any "real" connection to the object in question ("Dthat," 241; "Demonstratives," 560 n.; "Afterthoughts," 605). This conclusion leads almost directly to a form of the controversial thesis of *latitudinarianism* with regard to *de re* belief. But even if *de re* assertion (assertion of the singular proposition) is in fact accomplished through such means, it by no means follows that *de re* belief, let alone *de re* knowledge, follows suit. On the contrary, firm intuitions derived from ordinary language show otherwise. Cf. my "The Good, the Bad, and the Ugly," in Descriptions, ed. A. Bezuidenhout and M. Reimer (Oxford: Oxford University Press, forthcoming.)

Importantly, the distinction between so-called pure indexicals and demonstratives is a matter of incompleteness not in the expressions, but in their contexts. Demonstratives and "pure" indexicals alike are full-fledged indexicals, complete expressions unto themselves. The demonstratives 'this' and 'that' are every bit as complete and purely indexical as 'you' and 'I', as pure as freshly fallen snow. The negative side effects of the syntactic incompleteness thesis are avoided. The strictures of the linguistic variations of Occam's Razor are respected. Forget the Bare Bones Theory. Here is an *Indexical Theory of Demonstratives* worthy of the epithet.

7

As mentioned, this Indexical Theory conforms with the linguistic variations of Occam's Razor that Kaplan's theory flaunts.[43] But how does Frege's Puzzle with regard to demonstratives fare?

The sentence 'That is that' has a single meaning. The sentence is univocal but indexical, expressing different identity propositions in different contexts—some necessarily true, others necessarily false. The invariant meaning presents the content expressed in a given context with its contextual perspective, (roughly) as *the singular proposition about the demonstrata of the separate demonstrations assigned by this very context to the first and second syntactic occurrences of 'that', that they are one and the very same.* One might regard this as a lean and mean way of presenting content as compared with the riches of Kaplan's theory with its multiplicity of demonstration contents. But to see matters thus is to draw a hasty conclusion on the basis of a serious oversight concerning the communicative situation.

One may still appeal to the contents of accompanying demonstrations on the Indexical Theory in an account of *Erkenntniswerte*. The speakee understands the sentence merely by knowing the relevant character-building content rule. But in witnessing the utterance, the attentive speakee observes not only the sentence uttered but also the demonstrations that are assigned to distinct utterances of demonstratives. Indeed, the speakee must observe the demonstrations to grasp the speech act adequately, since knowing which proposition was asserted—knowing what is said—requires knowing which object was demonstrated. Awareness of the context provides the speakee with a special handle on the demonstrations assigned to each utterance. This ancillary empirical knowledge about which demonstrations are performed in the particular context allows the speakee to make

---

[43]Kaplan observes that there is "a kind of standard form for demonstrations" accompanying a typical utterance of a demonstrative: such demonstrations have a character like that of a definite description of the form, *the individual that has appearance A from here now,* where the mentioned appearance is "something like a picture with a little arrow pointing to the relevant subject" (525–26). This is plausible. However, by building excess material into the linguistic meaning of the demonstrative, Kaplan inevitably misclassifies some utterances of synthetic sentences as being utterances of analytic sentences, for example, 'He (if there is such a thing) has appearance A from here now'. Though this sentence is true, a full mastery of its meaning does not by itself give one the knowledge that it is inevitably true, as Kaplan's account implies. Its truth crucially depends on non-linguistic, empirical information: that the demonstrated male appears a particular way from the speaker's perspective at the time of the utterance. This information is supplied with the demonstration; it is built into the context of the utterance, not into the expression uttered. (Cf. note 41 above.)

substitutions into the character-building content rule's mode of presentation of the content, plugging in particular demonstrations, with their particular contents, for the meta-level concept *the demonstration assigned by this very context*. Instead of taking the proposition in terms of its relation to the context, the speakee now takes the proposition in terms of its relation to the particular demonstrations observably included in the context. In effect, the speakee converts knowledge by description of the proposition in terms of the context into knowledge by description in terms of the demonstration, exchanging knowledge by context-specific description for knowledge by demonstration-specific description. The latter, in turn, provides acquaintance with the proposition itself. The epistemic situation is not unlike learning the color of Alonzo Church's hair by being told that Church's hair was the color of snow while simultaneously being shown what snow looks like.

When the speaker utters 'That is that' pointing to the same object with both hands simultaneously, the context assigns the very same demonstration to both syntactic occurrences of 'that'. In such contexts, the proposition expressed is taken by the attentive speakee as a trivial self-identity—in effect, as *the singular proposition about the demonstratum of* δ *that it is itself*. This special way of taking the proposition is given not by the character itself, which presents the proposition in terms of its relation to the context, but by the character in tandem with the context *that includes the observable demonstration* δ. There are other contexts that assign distinct demonstrations that happen to converge on the same demonstratum. In such contexts, the proposition is taken by the attentive speakee as an identification between objects differently demonstrated—as *the singular proposition about both the demonstratum of* δ_1 *and the demonstratum of* δ_2, *that they are one and the very same*. Pairs of contexts, one of each sort, may yield exactly the same singular proposition— resulting in Frege's Puzzle. With regard to such context pairs, the uttered sentence 'That is that' not only expresses the same content but retains the same meaning. The relevant character-building content rule presents the proposition in terms of the same relations to the respective contexts—as a singular proposition about the demonstrata of whatever demonstrations are assigned to utterances of 'that' by the relevant context. In observing those demonstrations, the attentive speakee is enabled to take the proposition in the distinct contexts in terms of its relation to those very demonstrations. The different ways in which the same proposition is taken—what I have elsewhere called *proposition guises*[44]—are provided not by the character-building content rule itself, but in the contents of the demonstrations assigned by the particular context of use. In short, the difference lies not in the semantics but in the contexts, which assign distinct demonstrations to the syntactic occurrences of 'that' and thereby provide the attentive speakee with contrasting perceptual perspectives on what is in fact the same proposition presented *via* the same meaning in the distinct contexts.

---

[44]Cf. my *Frege's Puzzle*, especially chapters 8–9.

This contrasts with Kaplan's account, on which the same mere words are uttered, yet different sentences with different meanings (the different characters resulting from different demonstrations with different contents). While proposition guises can be a matter of linguistic meaning, they are not always so. Where demonstratives are used, they are a matter of ancillary knowledge, of nonlinguistic perceptual perspective. The semantics of demonstratives on the proposed Indexical Theory makes essential reference to demonstrations, which are assigned to syntactic occurrences of demonstratives by the context. But that reference is exclusively by description. The semantics makes no essential reference to the *contents* of those demonstrations, even if they are crucial to the communicative and epistemic situation. The Indexical Theory provides no semantic distinction on which to hang the different ways in which the same proposition might be taken differently in different utterances of "That is that". The various proposition guises are not given in the semantics. They are given in the context—or more accurately, in the union of meaning and context.

In "Afterthoughts," Kaplan says that he accepted the Fregean theory of demonstrations in "Demonstratives" in part because "the Fregean idea that *that very demonstration* might have picked out a different demonstratum, an idea that depended on the separability of a demonstration from a particular context, seemed to track very closely the cognitive uncertainties of 'that$_1$ is that$_2$'. This cognitive value appears in character, and thus as an aspect of meaning" (588). The Indexical Theory I propose demonstrates that the Fregean idea does not require the detachment of the demonstration from context. Nor must the relevant "cognitive uncertainties" be an aspect of meaning. Meaning has a role to play, and an important role it is. But the epistemologically crucial *ways of taking things* are given in the context rather than the character-building content rule. Direct-reference theorists who share my skepticism regarding Frege's Solution to Frege's Puzzle with regard to 'Hesperus' and 'Phosphorus'—including Kaplan[45]—should not be troubled by this aspect of my proposed account. On the contrary, in respecting the strictures of the linguistic variations of Occam's Razor while locating the proposition guises provided through the use of demonstratives in nonsemantic, contextual aspects of their use, the account points the way to a similarly nonsemantic account of the cognitive role played by proper names, natural-kind terms, and other devices of direct reference.[46]

8

I have not argued that Kaplan's operator '*dthat*' could not be added to a natural language like English, or even that it would be undesirable to do so. Quite the contrary, it has already proved itself a very useful addition to philosophical English.

---

[45]"Demonstratives," 562–63, 598.

[46]See note 13 above. A name whose designation is fixed by description has a character of a rather special form. In the case of a typical name, the character-building content rule specifies the content for (every context) by name rather than by description.

What I am asserting is that the operator provides an inaccurate and seriously misleading model of standard uses of the English demonstrative 'that'. Unlike '*dthat*', which is syncategorematic, the English demonstrative 'that' is standardly used as a complete singular term that semantically designates the relevant demonstratum with respect to a context. In other standard uses, the English word 'that' is not itself a singular term but part of a so-called complex demonstrative, 'that *F*', which is a complete, fully designating singular term. It might be better to view the bare demonstrative 'that' as a diminution or abbreviation of the demonstrative phrase 'that object' or 'that thing', making space for the complex phrase 'that *F*' as the underlying general case. There are other uses of phrases of the same surface form as complex demonstratives on which those phrases seem to be instead stylistically altered definite descriptions ("David is still hoping to encounter that pupil who will surpass him"). There may also be uses of words like 'that' and 'she' on which they function nearly enough like '*dthat*'—as perhaps, "A teacher gave Rudolf a low grade and David doubts whether she (the same teacher) graded fairly." Such uses deviate from the standard case.[47]

---

[47] A frequently heard objection to the hypothesis that compound expressions of a given category (for example, definite descriptions) are singular terms is that expressions of the given category can be coherently quantified into (that is, they can contain a variable bound by an external quantifier) while genuine singular terms cannot. The objection evidently originated with Benson Mates, in "Descriptions and Reference," *Foundations of Language* 10 (1973):409–18, at 415, but has been endorsed or echoed by others (for example, Stephen Neale, in *Descriptions* (Cambridge: MIT Press, 1990), at 56 n. 28). The objection typically relies on a λ-abstraction theorem, to the effect that any sentence ϕ_β containing a genuine singular term β in extensional position, and which is the result of uniformly substituting β for the free occurrences of a variable α in the open formula ϕ_α, is true only if the designatum of β satisfies ϕ_α. (The assumed abstraction theorem is not generally stated this precisely, if it is stated at all. Mates may rely on an alternative semantic principle: that any sentence ϕ_β of a restricted class C, and containing a genuine singular term β in extensional position, is true only if β designates. The class C might exclude such problematic formulas as $\ulcorner\beta$ does not exist$\urcorner$.) The objection has been applied to complex demonstratives—for example, by Ernest Lepore and Kirk Ludwig in "The Semantics and Pragmatics of Complex Demonstratives," *Mind* 109 (2000):200–241, at 205–6, 210–22, and *passim* (where something like the assumed abstraction theorem is explicitly applied): "It is difficult to see how to make sense of quantification into complex demonstratives on the assumption that they are referring terms. . . . [The abstraction theorem] renders mysterious how the material in the nominal could interact semantically with the rest of the [quantified] sentence" (205–6). . . . "Examples of apparently coherent quantification into the nominals of complex demonstratives supply some of the most important evidence for denying that they are referring terms" (219). Cf. Jeffrey King, *Complex Demonstratives* (Cambridge: MIT Press, 2001), at 10–11, 20–22.

It should be noted in response that complex demonstratives seem especially immune to this objection, since quantification into them is, at best, odd. If the open phrase 'that man she sees at the podium' is used genuinely demonstratively in 'At least one woman here admires that man she sees at the podium' (not as a stylistically altered definite description), the sentence is indeed true if and only if the relevant demonstratum satisfies the matrix 'At least one woman here admires x', and the objection collapses. (The example is from Lepore and Ludwig.) Cf. Barry Taylor, "Truth-Theory for Indexical Languages," in *Reference, Truth, and Reality*, ed. M. Platts (London: Routledge and Kegan Paul, 1980), 182–98, at 195–96; and Neale, "Term Limits," in *Philosophical Perspectives*, vol. 7: *Language and Logic*, ed. J. Tomberlin (Atascadero, Calif.: Ridgeview, 1993), 89–123, at 107. More importantly, if it were sound, the assumed abstraction principle would establish more generally that the very notion of an *open designator* (a designating

Following Kaplan's lead, I here introduce an artificial operator, '*zat*'. Unlike its predecessor '*dthat*', the '*zat*'-operator does not have the logical form of a functor. But like '*dthat*', neither is it a singular term. Like the logician's inverted iota, it is a variable-binding operator that forms singular terms from open formulas: '(*zat x*) (*x* is a man & *x* looks suspicious)'. It is not required, however, that the open-formula matrix, '*x* is a man & *x* looks suspicious', be uniquely satisfied for the '*zat*'-term to be a "proper" demonstrative, that is, to designate. The meaning of a '*zat*'-term is determined by the following replacement for (D) (as well as for (T_n)):

(Z) With respect to any assignment of values to variables *s* and any context *c*, the content of an occurrence of the demonstrative term $\ulcorner(zat\ \alpha)\ \phi_\alpha\urcorner$ is the demonstratum of the demonstration assigned to that occurrence in *c*, provided there is such a demonstratum and it satisfies ϕ_α with respect to *c* (that is, provided ϕ_α is true under the modified version of *s* that assigns the demonstratum to α and is otherwise the same as *s*, with respect to both *c* and the particular circumstance c_W-at-c_T of *c*). Otherwise $\ulcorner(zat\ \alpha)\phi_\alpha\urcorner$ has no content.[48]

As with '*dthat*', the '*zat*' operator is a content operator, in that the designatum of $\ulcorner(zat\ \alpha)\phi_\alpha\urcorner$ with respect to a circumstance *w*-at-*t* must satisfy the matrix formula ϕ_α with respect to a different circumstance, namely, that of the context. Also like '*dthat*'-terms, '*zat*'-terms are not compositional with regard to content. Though $\ulcorner(zat\ \alpha)\phi_\alpha\urcorner$ is a compound term, the content of its matrix formula ϕ_α (under the assignment of values to its free variables) generally forms no part of the content of the '*zat*'-term itself (under that same value

---

expression containing a free variable) is semantically incoherent. Despite the objection's popularity, ordinary mathematical notation is rife with counterexamples to the abstraction "theorem": '*x* + 3', '*x²*', etc. The most glaring counterexample is the paradigm of an open designator: the individual variable. The objection is in fact based on an elementary confusion. Designation for an open term (whether compound or a variable) is relative to an assignment of values to its free variables. The variable '*y*' is a genuine singular term if anything is. Its designatum (under the assignment of, say, David Kaplan as value) may fail to satisfy the particular open formula '~(*y*) (*y* is a person ⊃ *x* is ingenious)' (let this be ϕ_α, with α = '*x*') even though the sentence that results by substituting '*y*' for '*x*' is true—precisely because the newly introduced occurrence of '*y*' is captured by the quantifier, making its value irrelevant. The mistaken abstraction "theorem" can be corrected, and even generalized:

> An assignment *s* of values to variables satisfies a formula ϕ_β [of the restricted class C] containing a *free occurrence* of a singular term β in extensional position, and which is the result of uniformly substituting *free occurrences* of β for the free occurrences of a variable α in ϕ_α, if and only if the modified value-assignment s' that assigns to α the designatum of β under *s*, and is otherwise the same as *s*, satisfies ϕ_α.

This corrected version effectively blocks the objection. (There is likewise a corrected, generalized version of Mates's apparent assumption: An assignment *s* of values to variables satisfies a formula ϕ_β [of the restricted class C] containing a *free occurrence* of singular term β in extensional position only if β designates under *s*.) Cf. my "Being of Two Minds: Belief with Doubt," *Noûs* 29 (1995):1–20, at 18 n. 26.

[48]By stipulation, '*zat*'-terms are genuine singular terms. Their stipulated content rule (Z) allows for the possibility of quantification in. (See the previous note.)

assignment), which, provided it satisfies the operand, is simply the demonstratum assigned to the term by the context. The semantic rule (Z) yields the following corollaries, analogous to (D1)–(D3) above:

(Z1) The complex demonstrative $\ulcorner(zat\ \alpha)\phi_\alpha\urcorner$ is indexical.

(Z2) With respect to any context $\ulcorner(zat\ \alpha)\phi_\alpha\urcorner$ is directly referential.

(Z3) With respect to any context an occurrence of $\ulcorner(zat\ \alpha)\phi_\alpha\urcorner$ rigidly designates the demonstratum of the demonstration assigned to it in that context, provided such a demonstratum satisfies ϕ_α with respect to c. Otherwise it is a rigid nondesignator.

Accordingly, I propose that Kaplan's content rule (T_K) be replaced with the following as governing standard uses of demonstratives:

(T) With respect to any context c, the (English) content of an occurrence of the complex demonstrative 'that'⌢NP is the demonstratum of the demonstration assigned to that occurrence in c, provided: (i) there is such a demonstratum; and (ii) NP applies to it with respect to c. Otherwise 'that'⌢NP has no content. (NP may be deleted to form a bare demonstrative, in which case condition (ii) is regarded as vacuously fulfilled, or simply deleted.)

This rule yields the same corollaries for natural-language complex demonstratives: 'that' is a content operator; complex demonstratives are not compositional with regard to content; they are indexical, directly referential, rigid.[49] It is

---

[49]Stefano Predelli, in "Complex Demonstratives and Anaphora," *Analysis* 61 (2001):53–59, challenges those who deny that complex demonstratives are compositional with regard to content to explain how the anaphoric pronoun 'her in 'That man talking to Mary admires her' (uttered while pointing to one of several men talking to Mary) obtains its content. It is tempting to suppose that any anaphoric pronoun occurrence whose antecedent is a singular term simply inherits as its content the very content contributed by its antecedent to the content of the sentence in which the antecedent occurs. But according to (T), the antecedent term in this case contributes no component to the content of the complex demonstrative in which it occurs.

In response I note that the naive rule of content inheritance is falsified in cases in which the antecedent is a singular term that is not directly referential, as perhaps in 'The number of planets is such that, necessarily, *it* is odd' and 'Ralph believes of the man seen at the beach that *he* is a spy'. If the naive rule were correct (and if, contrary to Russell, the definite-description antecedents are singular terms), these sentences would be *de dicto* rather than *de re*. A more promising rule of anaphora—applicable even to anaphoric pronouns whose antecedents are singular terms that are not directly referential—is that *a simple (non-reflexive) anaphoric pronoun occurrence whose antecedent is a singular term, if it is not itself a bound variable, typically takes as its content the object customarily designated by its antecedent*. There is no requirement that the antecedent contribute its customary content to the content of the sentence in which the antecedent occurs. Although this rule is also subject to counterexamples, it is applicable to a significantly wider range of cases than the naive rule of content inheritance and it seems likely that some restricted variant is correct. Consider: 'That man talking to the actress honored here tonight admires her'. Although I hold the description 'the actress honored here tonight' does not contribute its customary content to that of the sentence in question, and instead merely contributes toward a restriction on admissible contents for the complex demonstrative, the description itself has a customary designatum (assuming it is a singular term), and it is that customary designatum, though she makes no appearance in the content of the demonstrative itself, that the anaphoric pronoun takes as its content.

presumably Kaplan's intent that his alternative content rule (T_K) is to be extended to cover supplemented complex demonstratives, 'that'⌢NP⌢δ, by including (T)'s condition (ii).[50] This natural extension of (T_K) makes the mere (unsupplemented) complex demonstrative 'that'⌢NP syncategorematic, that is, a contextually defined incomplete symbol.[51] Utterances of the same mere complex demonstrative accompanied by demonstrations of differing content are utterances of strictly different expressions with different meanings. On my alternative proposal, by contrast, a complex demonstrative is a complete singular term each use of which is an utterance of a single expression with a single meaning—though its content varies with context and its use is felicitous only in those contexts in which it is accompanied by a demonstration.

We have already seen numerous philosophically significant consequences of regarding natural-language complex demonstratives in accordance with (T), that is, on the model of '*zat*'-terms: Frege's syntactic incompleteness thesis is rejected; the purity of natural-language syntax is not threatened; complex demonstratives are not syncategorematic; they are both meaningful and univocal; they designate the right object, etc. A treatment of complex demonstratives on the model of '*zat*'-terms yields further philosophically significant consequences. The semantic corollary (Z3) in particular imposes three conditions worthy of special note. Not surprisingly, complex demonstratives are rigid designators.[52] More interesting, a

---

[50] He says of (T_K) that "obvious adjustments are to be made to take into account any common noun phrase which accompanies or is built-in to the demonstrative" ("Demonstratives," 527). Kaplan is interpreted as incorporating condition (ii) by Emma Borg, "Complex Demonstratives," *Philosophical Studies* 97 (2000):229–49, at 242, where a designation rule entailed by my content rule (T) is defended at some length. A similar designation rule, though couched within the Bare Bones Theory, is proffered by David Braun, "Structured Characters and Complex Demonstratives," *Philosophical Studies* 74 (1994):193–219, at 209.

[51] Whereas the mere complex demonstrative 'that'⌢NP is devoid of character, content, and designatum, the content of the completed expression 'that'⌢NP⌢δ is defined to be the demonstratum of δ (in the context), if there is a unique such demonstratum and NP applies to it (with respect to the context), and to be nothing otherwise.

[52] In the sentence 'If there had been an atheist elected to the U.S. Senate, then that Senator's atheism would have been concealed during the political campaign' (on its most natural reading) the phrase 'that Senator' is evidently not correctly formalized using '*zat*'. Yet it is a rigid designator. The sentence seems to have a form something like that of 'For every possible individual i, if i had been an atheist who was elected to the U.S. Senate, then i's atheism would have been concealed during the political campaign'. Though not a demonstrative phrase, the variable 'i' is a rigid designator of its value under any value-assignment. Simple individual variables are rigid designators *par excellence*. (By contrast, see note 38 above.)

The same remark applies to analogous bound-variable uses of pronouns ('. . . , then *he* would have concealed his atheism . . .'; cf. note 49 above). Michael McKinsey, in "Mental Anaphora," *Synthese* 66 (1986):159–75, uses an example like the following to argue that such pronouns are not rigid (161):

An atheist was once elected to the U.S. Senate, but his atheism had been concealed during the political campaign.

According to McKinsey, the pronoun designates different possible individuals with respect to different possible worlds—to wit, whoever in that world is an atheist elected to the U.S.

(contd.)

complex demonstrative 'that F' cannot literally (semantically) designate anything that is not an F. The phrase might be used by a speaker to designate something that is not an F, but this is a matter of "speaker reference" as opposed to "semantic reference." Such a "referential" use is, from the point of view of English semantics, a misuse.[53] More interesting yet, a complex demonstrative 'that F' may designate something with respect to a possible world w even though the designated object is not an F in w, as long as its is *actually* an F—for example, 'If we had not lowered admission standards, then *that graduate student* would not be in graduate school today'.[54] No component of the content of an atomic sentence of the form "That F is G" expresses about the demonstratum that it is F. Yet this is logically entailed. In fact, the sentence presupposes of the demonstratum that it is F, in that unless this is a fact the sentential subject is vacuous and the sentence is without truth value.[55]

There is another noteworthy consequence. The following English sentence is *analytic,* in the sense that it is true by virtue of semantics alone:

S: That graduate student (if there is any such thing) is a graduate student.[56]

Senate. The argument is echoed by Scott Soames, in his review of Gareth Evans's *Collected Papers,* in *Journal of Philosophy* 86 (1989):141–56, at 145, and endorsed by Stephen Neale, in "Descriptive Pronouns and Donkey Anaphora," *Journal of Philosophy* 87 (1990):113–50, at 130, and again in *Descriptions,* at 186. It assumes, following Evans, that such pronoun occurrences (so-called "donkey" pronouns) are unbound singular terms or descriptions. *Pace* Evans, McKinsey, et al., there is every indication that the pronoun here is (as Peter Geach maintains), or at least is naturally taken to be, a bound variable—like the last occurrence of 'i' in 'It was once the case that for some atheist i, i was elected to the U.S. Senate but i's atheism had been concealed during the political campaign'. (In this case the pronoun 'his' might be regarded as bound by the restricted quantifier 'an atheist'. But compare this with the plural pronoun in 'Few current atheists have been elected to the U.S. Senate, and their atheism was concealed during the political campaign'. Though also a bound variable, the 'their' is bound not by the restricted quantifier 'few current atheists' but, as it were, by a related unarticulated restricted universal quantifier. The sentence is true iff; (*i*) few individuals who satisfy the open sentence 'X are current atheists' also satisfy the open sentence 'X have been elected to the U.S. Senate', and (*ii*) those individuals that satisfy both 'X are current atheists' and 'X have been elected to the U.S. Senate' also satisfy the further open sentence 'Their atheism was concealed during the political campaign'.) For any simple pronoun occurrence, if it is a bound variable it is also an occurrence of a rigid designator. Consider: 'A girl sprang from the particular gametes s and e, and it is a necessary truth that whoever sprang from s and e did not spring instead from the entirely different particular gametes s' and e'' us'. 'A girl sprang from the particular gametes s and e, and it is a necessary truth that *she* did not spring instead from s' and e''. Consider also substituting 'that girl' for 'she'. (The foregoing remarks have benefited from discussion with Alan Berger, who realized independently that McKinsey's argument is incorrect.)

[53]Cf. "The Good, the Bad, and the Ugly."

[54]Contrary to Lepore and Ludwig ("Semantics and Pragmatics," 222–26), this is not a matter of demonstrative phrases always, or typically, taking wide scope: 'Consider: *That graduate student* is not in graduate school today. The proposition is, of course, false. But its falsity is quite accidental. Indeed, it would have obtained if we had not lowered our admission standards'.

[55]If the demonstratum is not F, the sentence 'That F does not exist' is a true negative existential. Such things are rare. Cf. my "Nonexistence," *Noûs* 32 (1988):277–319.

[56]I assume here that the parenthetical antecedent is false if the demonstrative 'that graduate student' lacks a designatum.

The analyticity of *S* lies behind the logical validity of the argument, 'Every graduate student is full of angst; therefore that graduate student (assuming he/she exists) is full of angst'.[57] Although analytic, the content of *S* in any context is hardly a necessary truth.[58] Indeed, its contingency is a likely source of considerable anxiety for the demonstrated student. More surprisingly, *S*, although analytic, expresses an a posteriori truth. For consider a typical context in which the demonstratum is a particular graduate student, David. How does one come to know the following *de re* fact about David: that he—that very individual (if he exists at all)—is in graduate school? In any number of ways. One might observe his lifestyle, follow him around the university, confiscate his computer disks, subpoena his transcripts, record his nocturnal mutterings. Not, however, by a priori reflection on the issue.[59]

---

[57] Cf. Borg, "Complex Demonstratives," 239–41. Any theory that assigns logical attributes to propositions rather than to sentences or their meanings (such as is defended by Kripke) is unable to accommodate the validity of this inference, assuming (T), without *S* as an additional premise. Such theories miss the important distinctions illustrated by *S*.

[58] Again, contrary to Lepore and Ludwig ("Semantics and Pragmatics," 213, 222–26). In any context in which the demonstratum is a graduate student, the fact or state of affairs described by *S* could have been otherwise. (Philosophers indoctrinated in the Quinean tradition may have a tendency to misconstrue 'necessary' as a term for analyticity—a semantic notion—rather than for the peculiarly metaphysical notion of a fact or state of affairs that *could not have been otherwise*.)

[59] Kaplan mentions similarly analytic though typically contingent sentences of the form $\ulcorner dthat[\alpha] = \alpha \urcorner$—he specifically mentions 'He is the male at whom I am now pointing' (see note 39 above)—claiming that all such sentences are a priori ("Demonstratives," 518, 538–39). (Braun, "Structured Characters," 211–12, 215–16, considers an example exactly like *S*, correctly deeming it logically valid. Braun does not discuss its epistemological status.) Kaplan offers as an explanation of the existence of such contingent yet (allegedly) a priori truths that alethic modal attributes (metaphysical necessity, possibility, contingency, etc.) are attributes of propositions, whereas apriority and aposteriority are attributes of proposition-characters (that is, of characters that, given a context of use, yield a proposition) or of sentences, not propositions. This confuses epistemological matters (apriority) with properly logico-semantic matters (analyticity), and thus misses one of the important philosophical lessons of demonstratives. Though the sentence '*Dthat* [the only member of the UCSB Philosophy Department born in Los Angeles] is the only member of the UCSB Philosophy Department born in Los Angeles' is analytic-in-Kaplish—and hence, known to be true solely on the basis of pure Kaplish semantics—there is no learning the contingent fact described thereby (to wit, than I am the only UCSB philosopher born in Los Angeles) except through epistemic appeal to experience.

The same considerations apply against Kripke's contention in *Naming and Necessity* (54–56, 63) that 'The Standard Meter is exactly one meter long at t_0' is contingent a priori. See notes 13 and 42 above. Such sentences should be deemed *analytic* even though the facts described are neither necessary nor (*pace* Kaplan and Kripke) a priori. Although the existence of analytic truths that are both contingent and a posteriori is a straightforward consequence of direct-reference theory—*S* is as good an example as any—the aforementioned confusion between epistemological and properly logico-semantic matters has obscured the fact. Cf. my "How to Measure the Standard Metre," *Proceedings of the Aristotelian Society* 88 (1987/1988):193–217, and especially "Analyticity and Apriority," in J. Tomberlin, *Language and Logic*, 125–33.

8
Empty Terms

NONEXISTENCE*

Nathan Salmon

I

Among the most perennial of philosophical problems are those arising from sentences involving nonreferring names. Chief among these problems is that of true singular negative existentials. Consider, for example,

(0)   Sherlock Holmes does not exist,

interpreted not as an assertion within the fiction (as might be made mendaciously by Professor Moriarity in one of the *Sherlock Holmes* stories), but as an assertion about reality outside the fiction. So interpreted, the sentence is evidently true. But how can any sentence with a nonreferring term in subject position be true? It seems as if (0) designates someone (by its subject term) in order to say (by its predicate) that he does not exist. But it entails that there is no such thing to be designated. G. E. Moore put the problem as follows:

> [I]t seems as if purely imaginary things, even though they be absolutely contradictory like a round square, must still have some kind of *being*—must still be in a sense—simply because we can think and talk about them. . . . And now in saying that there is no such thing as a round square, I seem to imply that there *is* such a thing. It seems as if there must be such a thing, merely in order that it may have the property of not-being. It seems, therefore, that to say of anything whatever that we can mention that it absolutely is *not*, were to contradict ourselves: as if everything we can mention must be, must have some kind of being. (*Some Main Problems of Philosophy*, London: George Allen & Unwin, 1953, at p. 289)

In "On Denoting," Russell trumpeted his Theory of Descriptions not only for its explanation (which I believe Russell saw as the theory's principal virtue) of how we gain cognitive access to the world beyond our immediate acquaintance, but also for its ability to handle a variety of puzzles that arise on his theory that the semantic content of a singular term is solely its referent (denotation, designatum).[1] The puzzles are primarily: Frege's Puzzle about $\ulcorner \alpha = \beta \urcorner$; the more general problem of substitution failure in certain contexts, especially those ascribing propositional attitude; the question of content and truth value for sentences

---

* The present essay is a result of the Santa Barbarians Discussion Group's ruminations on fictional objects, during Fall 1996, organized by C. Anthony Anderson. I am grateful to the participants, especially Anderson, for our extremely useful confusions. I also thank Alan Berger, Kevin Falvey, Steven Humphrey, David Kaplan, and Scott Soames for discussion or comments. Portions of the paper were presented at the universities of California, Irvine; California, Los Angeles; Southern California; and Yale. I am grateful to those audiences for their comments. The essay is dedicated to Noman, without whom it would not have been possible.

[1] *Mind*, 14 (1905), pp. 479–493. Page references are to the reprinting in Robert M. Harnish, ed., *Basic Topics in the Philosophy of Language* (Prentice-Hall, 1994), pp. 161–173.

involving nonreferring terms; and as a special case, true negative existentials. In previous writings I have discussed the first two problems from the perspective of *Millianism,* which I endorse, according to which the semantic contents of certain simple singular terms, including at least ordinary proper names and demonstratives, are simply their referents, so that a sentence containing a nonvacuous proper name expresses a *singular proposition,* in which the name's bearer occurs directly as a constituent.[2] It has been objected that the second two problems are sufficient by themselves to refute Millianism even if the first two problems are not. Here I shall discuss the problems of nonreferring names from a Millian perspective, and also from the less committal perspective of the *theory of direct reference,* according to which the semantic content of a name or demonstrative is not given by any definite description. I have also discussed the concept of existence in previous work.[3] I shall draw on these previous discussions.

Russell has us consider the English sentence

    (1) The present king of France is bald,

which, given that France is no longer a monarchy, Russell deems "plainly false" (p. 165). As he points out, if (1) is indeed false, then it would seem that its negation,

    (2) The present king of France is not bald,

ought to be true. But (2) is as wrong as (1), and for the very same reason. By contrast, the singular existential

---

[2] Principally in the following: *Frege's Puzzle* (Atascadero, Ca.: Ridgeview, 1986, 1991); "Reflexivity," *Notre Dame Journal of Formal Logic,* 27, 3 (June 1986), pp. 401–429; "How to Become a Millian Heir," *Noûs,* 23, 2 (April 1989), pp. 211–220; "Illogical Belief," in J. Tomberlin, ed., *Philosophical Perspectives, 3: Philosophy of Mind and Action Theory* (Atascadero, Ca.: Ridgeview, 1989), pp. 243–285; "A Millian Heir Rejects the Wages of *Sinn,*" in C. A. Anderson and J. Owens, eds., *Propositional Attitudes: The Role of Content in Logic, Language, and Mind* (Stanford, Ca.: Center for the Study of Language and Information, Stanford University, 1990), pp. 215–247; "How *Not* to Become a Millian Heir," *Philosophical Studies,* 62, 2 (May 1991), pp. 165–177; "Reflections on Reflexivity," *Linguistics and Philosophy,* 15, 1 (February 1992), pp. 53–63; "Relative and Absolute Apriority," *Philosophical Studies,* 69 (1993), pp. 83–100; and "Being of Two Minds: Beliefs with Doubt," *Noûs,* 29, 1 (January 1995), pp. 1–20.

To correct a common misconception: Millianism does not entail that a proper name has no features or aspects that might be deemed, in a certain sense, intensional or connotive. Unquestionably, some names evoke descriptive concepts in the mind of a user. Some may even have particular concepts conventionally attached. Though the names 'Hesperus' and 'Phosphorus' have the same semantic content (the planet Venus), the former connotes *evening,* the latter *morning.* Barbarelli was called 'Giorgionne' because of his size, though the two names for the Venetian artist are semantically equivalent. There is no reason why there cannot be an operator that operates on this kind of connotation. Kripke mentions the particular construction 'Superman was disguised as Clark Kent'. The second argument position in '____ is disguised as ____' (or 'dressed as', 'appears as', etc.) is semantically sensitive to the physical appearance associated with the name occurring in that position. It does not follow that this connotive aspect of a name belongs to semantics, let alone that it affects the propositions semantically expressed by sentences containing the name.

[3] "Existence," in J. Tomberlin, ed., *Philosophical Perspectives, 1: Metaphysics* (Atascadero, Ca.: Ridgeview, 1987), pp. 49–108.

(3) The present king of France exists

is indeed false, and its negation,

(4) The present king of France does not exist,

is true. In Russell's Theory of Descriptions, (1) is analyzed as:

(1′) $(\exists x)[(y)(\textit{Present-king-of-France}\,(y) \equiv x = y) \wedge \textit{Bald}(x)]$,

in English as "Something is both uniquely a present king of France and bald" (where to say that something is *uniquely* such-and-such is to say that it, and nothing else, is such-and-such). As with (1), Russell says that (1′) is "certainly false" (p. 170). In the English sentence (2), the existential quantifier of (1′) together with its accompanying material joust with negation for dominant position. Sentence (2) may mean either of two things:

(2′) $(\exists x)[(y)(\textit{Present-king-of-France}\,(y) \equiv x = y) \wedge \text{\textasciitilde}\textit{Bald}(x)]$

(2″) $\text{\textasciitilde}(\exists x)\,[(y)(\textit{Present-king-of-France}\,(y) \equiv x = y) \wedge \textit{Bald}(x)]$.

The former is the wide-scope (or *primary occurrence*) reading of (2), on which it expresses that some unique present king of France is not bald. This is false for the same reason as (1′). The latter is the narrow-scope (*secondary occurrence*) reading of (2), on which it expresses that no unique present king of France is bald. This genuinely contradicts (1′) and is therefore true. In *Principia Mathematica*, instead of analyzing (3) by replacing '$\textit{Bald}(x)$' in (1′) with '$(\exists y)\,(x = y)$', Russell and Whitehead analyze it more simply as

(3′) $(\exists x)[(y)(\textit{Present-king-of-France}\,(y) \equiv x = y)$,

i.e., "Something is uniquely a present king of France." This is equivalent to its analysis in the style of (1′), since '$(\exists y)(x = y)$' is a theorem of *Principia Mathematica*. Although Russell did not distinguish two readings for (4), he might as well have. The narrow-scope reading is equivalent to the reading given,

(4′) $\text{\textasciitilde}(\exists x)[(y)(\textit{Present-king-of-France}\,(y) \equiv x = y)$,

while the wide-scope reading is straightforwardly inconsistent, and hence, presumably, cannot be what would normally be intended by (4). Russell extended his solution to sentences involving nonreferring proper names through his thesis that ordinary names abbreviate definite descriptions. The name 'Sherlock Holmes', for example, might abbreviate something like: *the brilliant but eccentric late 19th century British detective who, inter alia, performed such-and-such exploits.* Abbreviating this description instead as 'the Holmesesque detective', (0) is then subject to an analysis parallel to that for (4′), as:

(0′) $\text{\textasciitilde}(\exists x)(y)(\textit{Holmesesque-detective}\,(y) \equiv x = y)$.

Neither (0′) nor (4′) designates anyone in order to say of him that he does not exist.

Frege had defended a very different theory in "*Über Sinn und Bedeutung*" (1892) concerning sentences like (1) and (2).[4] On that theory—later championed in a somewhat different form by Strawson[5]—although the truth of (1) requires that there be a unique present king of France, (1) is not rendered false by the nonexistence of such a monarch. Instead, (1) *presupposes* that there is a unique present king France, in the sense that (1) and (2) each separately entail (3′). Since this entailed proposition is false, neither (1) nor (2) is true. Though meaningful, (1) is neither true nor false.[6] Frege regarded this as a consequence of the Principle of Compositionality for Reference, according to which the referent of a compound expression—and as a special case, the truth value of a sentence—is determined entirely by the referents of the component expressions and their mode of composition. On Frege's view, if a component lacks a referent, so does the whole.

In "Mr. Strawson on Referring," published some 54 years after "On Denoting," Russell responds to the objection that (1) is neither true nor false.[7] Where he had earlier claimed that (1) is "plainly" false, he now says that the issue of whether (1) is false "is a mere question of verbal convenience" (p. 243). Though this seems to indicate a change of heart, I believe it may not actually do so. He goes on to say, "I find it more convenient to define the word 'false' so that every significant sentence is either true or false. This is a purely verbal question; and although I have no wish to claim the support of common usage, I do not think that he [Strawson] can claim it either." Frege can indeed accommodate Russell's verdict that (1) is "plainly false," simply by understanding 'false' as coextensive with 'untrue'. One way for Frege to do this is to invoke a distinction between two types of negation, so-called *choice* and *exclusion* negation.[8] The difference between the two is given by their three-valued truth tables (where 'U' stands for "undefined," i.e., without truth value):

p	$\sim_C p$	$\sim_E p$
T	F	F
F	T	T
U	U	T

Frege's Principle of Compositionality for Reference requires that exclusion negation be seen as an *ungerade* (oblique) operator. Where '$\sim_C$' is concerned with the customary referent of its operand sentence (i.e., its truth value), '$\sim_E$' is concerned instead with the indirect referent of its operand, which is its customary

---

[4] Page references are to the reprinting in Harnish, pp. 142–160.

[5] In "On Referring," *Mind*, 59 (1950), pp. 320–344.

[6] Frege also speaks of a sentence like (1) as presupposing that the expression 'the present king of France' refers to something (pp. 151–152).

[7] In Russell's *My Philosophical Development* (London: Allen & Unwin, 1959), pp. 238–245.

[8] These are called 'internal' and 'external' negation, respectively, in D. A. Bochvar, "On a Three-Valued Calculus and Its Application in the Analysis of the Paradoxes of the Extended Functional Calculus," *Mathematicheskii Sbornik*, 46 (1938), pp. 287–308.

sense. Exclusion negation is definable using choice negation. Let p be the proposition expressed by sentence φ. Then $\ulcorner \sim_E \varphi \urcorner$ means that p is not$_C$ true—or in Fregean terminology, that the thought p does not$_C$ determine the True. Hence, 'The present king of France is not$_E$ bald' may be regarded as shorthand for 'It is not$_C$ true that the present king of France is bald'. One might say this if one wishes to assert, cautiously, that either there presently is no unique king of France, or else there is such and he is not bald—i.e., that (2″).

One may understand the term 'false' so that to call a sentence 'false' is to say that its negation is true, where the relevant notion of the negation of a sentence is syntactic (rather than defined in terms of truth tables). The two notions of negation, choice and exclusion, thereby yield two notions of falsehood. Let us say that a sentence is *F-false*$_1$ (false in the Fregean primary sense) if its choice negation is true, and that it is *F-false*$_2$ (false in the Fregean secondary sense) if its exclusion negation is true. The latter term is coextensive with 'untrue'. By Frege's lights, (1) is neither true nor *F-false*$_1$, and therefore, plainly *F-false*$_2$.

So far so good. But Russell's response to Strawson suggests that not only could Frege and Strawson have chosen an alternative sense for 'false', and deem (1) "false" in that sense, but Russell himself could have chosen a sense for 'false' on which (1′) is neither true nor "false." Only in that case can it rightfully be said that the question of whether (1) is false is entirely terminological.[9] Is there a legitimate sense of 'false' on which (1) is neither true nor false given its analysis on the Theory of Descriptions?

Whatever 'false' means, it is something contrary to truth. Russell, as well as Frege, could understand falsehood as truth of the (syntactic) negation. Except that on Russell's theory, the negation of (1) is ambiguous. Let us restrict our focus for the time being to sentences none of whose definite descriptions occur within the scope of a nonextensional operator (including sentences with no definite descriptions). Let us call the reading of the negation of such a sentence on which each description is given narrowest possible scope the *outermost negation* of the original sentence, and let us call the reading of the negation on which each description is given widest possible scope the *innermost negation*. (Cf. note 8.) Let us say of a sentence of the sort under consideration that it is *R-false*$_1$ if its outermost negation is true, and that it is *R-false*$_2$ if its innermost negation is true. (A multitude of further Russellian notions of falsehood are definable in similar ways.) On the Theory of Descriptions, a sentence none of whose definite descriptions occur in a nonextensional context and all of whose definite descriptions are proper (i.e., such that there is exactly one thing answering to it) is *R*-false$_1$ if and only if it is *R*-false$_2$. Not so for sentences containing improper descriptions. In particular, (1) is *R*-false$_1$ by Russell's lights—and indeed, plainly so in the present absence of a king of France. But (1) is neither true nor *R*-false$_2$.

---

[9] Echoing Russell, Michael Dummett argues, in "Presupposition," *Journal of Symbolic Logic*, 25 (1960), pp. 336–339, that Strawson has not shown that (1) is not false in an antecedently understood sense of the term, but has instead introduced a natural sense of 'false' different from that employed by Russell and on which the term, so understood, does not apply to (1). See also his *Frege: Philosophy of Language* (Cambridge, Mass.: Harvard University Press, 1973, 1981), chapter 12, especially pp. 419–429.

Russell's reply to Strawson has a good deal of merit. It is by no means obvious, however, that the issue of whether (1) is false is entirely verbal. Whereas both Russell and Frege may deem (1) "false" in one sense and not "false" in another, it appears that the particular senses Russell employs are not the same as Frege's. The distinction between innermost and outermost negation is not the same as the distinction between choice and exclusion negation. The Fregean treats (2) as involving a lexical ambiguity; Russell sees (2) instead as involving a scope ambiguity. The terms 'R-false$_1$' and 'R-false$_2$' presuppose the Theory of Descriptions, while 'F-false$_1$' and 'F-false$_2$' presuppose the opposing view (assumed by John Stuart Mill as well as Frege) that definite descriptions are singular terms. Insofar as the term 'false', in its standard sense, is identical in extension, and at least close in meaning, to one of these theoretically loaded terms (or to some appropriate variation), it cannot be close in meaning to any of the remaining three. To decide whether (1) is false in the standard sense, it would seem that one must first make a determination between Russell's theory and the Frege/Strawson view—or (perhaps most likely) in favor of some alternative account.

The nature of the divergence between Russell and Frege emerges more fully at a deeper level of analysis on which the four notions of falsehood are theoretically neutralized, to the extent that this is possible. The notions of R-falsehood$_1$ and R-falsehood$_2$ can be made more or less neutral by taking the former to be truth of the *de dicto* reading of the negation, the latter to be truth of the *de re* reading— where (2) read *de dicto* expresses that it is not true that the present king of France is bald, and read *de re* that the present king of France is such that not bald is *he*. One need not embrace the Theory of Descriptions to recognize the *de re/de-dicto* distinction (problematic though this general distinction is on Fregean theory). R-falsehood$_1$ thus corresponds, closely enough, to F-falsehood$_2$—essentially the notion of untruth. All parties agree that (1) is plainly "false" in this sense. The relationship between R-falsehood$_2$ and F-falsehood$_1$ is not nearly this close. The Fregean agrees that (1) is not R-false$_2$, since it is plainly not true that the present king of France is nonbald. But this is different from the Fregean denial that (1) is F-false$_1$. F-falsehood$_1$ is falsehood in the sense of the 'F' invoked in three-valued truth tables. This notion, though Fregean, is not anti-Russellian. There could be untrue sentences in which all singular terms refer but which lack F-falsehood$_1$ for reasons unrelated to singular-term reference—for example, because of a partially defined predicate, or a category mistake, or a failed presupposition that is not existential in nature. It is perfectly consistent to acknowledge that such sentences are neither true nor F-false$_1$ (i.e., that they are U) while embracing the Theory of Descriptions. A decision would have to be made concerning whether the negation symbol '~' is a sign for choice or exclusion negation, but whichever decision was made (it is customary to use it for choice negation), a second negation sign could be introduced for the other notion. Even if the Russellian were to embrace the Principal of Bivalence—according to which every well-formed declarative sentence is either true or false (Russell says that he finds it convenient to use the term 'false' in such a way as to honor this principle)—this need not represent a rejection of F-falsehood$_1$. It may constitute a thesis that every well-formed sentence is either true or F-false$_1$—even category-mistake sentences and the rest, or that such "sentences" are not well-formed, etc.

F-falsehood$_1$ should be understood not merely as truth of the choice negation, but as truth of the choice negation *construed as the authentic contradictory of the original sentence*—in effect, as truth of the outermost choice negation. Readings or analyses of the choice negation that do not contradict the original sentence, or do not contradict an analysis of it, are irrelevant. If a category-mistake sentence is neither true nor F-false$_1$, then the outermost choice negation of it, and of any analyses of it, are likewise neither true nor F-false$_1$. The question is whether the untrue (1) is F-false$_1$. On Russell's theory, (1) is F-false$_1$ if and only if (2″) is true. The untruth of (2′) is not pertinent. To rebut the objection that (1) is neither true nor F-false$_1$ it is not sufficient for Russell to agree that (1) is neither true nor R-false$_2$. He must argue further that (1) is indeed F-false$_1$, and that in denying this Frege and Strawson have probably confused F-falsehood$_1$ with R-falsehood$_2$.[10]

II

Whereas Frege's Principle of Compositionality for Reference requires that sentences like (1) and (2) lack truth value, his theory of sense and reference explains how such sentences nevertheless semantically express propositions. On the other hand, the same Principle of Compositionality creates a problem for Frege in connection with sentences like (3) and (4). It is natural to take these to be analyzable as:

(3″) $(\exists x)[(\imath y)\ Present\text{-}king\text{-}of\text{-}France\ (y) = x]$

(4″) $\sim(\exists x)[(\imath y)\ Present\text{-}king\text{-}of\text{-}France\ (y) = x]$,

respectively. The intended truth conditions for (3″) and (4″) are given by (3′) and (4′). But since the definite description lacks a referent, (3″) and (4″) must instead

---

[10]An analogous situation obtains in connection with verbs like 'know', 'realize', 'notice', etc. Is the untrue sentence 'Jones knows that the Earth is flat' false, or is it neither true nor false? The analogue of the Russellian view would be that this sentence is analyzable into a conjunction ⌜The Earth is flat & φ⌝, for some sentence φ concerning Jones's epistemic situation (e.g., 'Jones is epistemically justified, in a manner not defeated by Gettier-type phenomena, in believing that the Earth is flat'). This is the standard view in contemporary epistemology. The negation 'Jones does not know that the Earth is flat' may then be subject to an innermost/outermost scope ambiguity. The analogue of the Fregean view would be that the original sentence instead presupposes that the Earth is flat. This alternative to the Russellian view has been discussed by linguists. See Ed Keenan, "Two Kinds of Presupposition in Natural Language" in Charles Fillmore and D. Terence Langendoen, eds., *Studies in Linguistic Semantics* (1971), Paul and Carol Kiparski, "Fact," and Charles Fillmore, "Types of Lexical Information," both in D. D. Steinberg and L. A. Jakobovits, eds., *Semantics* (Cambridge University Press, 1971), and Deirdre Wilson, *Presuppositions and Non-Truth-Conditional Semantics* (Academic Press, 1975). On this view, the negation of the original sentence may be subject to a choice/exclusion lexical ambiguity. Either view may thus regard the negation as true in one sense and untrue in another, making the original sentence false in one sense, unfalse in another. The two views nevertheless differ over the question of whether the original sentence instantiates F-falsehood$_1$. (The similarity between the issues concerning reference and factives can be made more than merely analogous, by taking ⌜α knows that φ⌝ as shorthand for ⌜α knows the fact that φ⌝, with ⌜the fact that φ⌝ a definite description that is proper if and only if φ is true.)

for Frege be neither true nor false—assuming the standard interpretation for existential quantification, identity, and negation (as Frege gave them in connection with his own notation) on which each is fully extensional.

By way of a solution to this difficulty, Frege suggested that (3) and (4) are properly interpreted not by (3″) and (4″), but as covertly quotational. He wrote:

> We must here keep well apart two wholly different cases that are easily confused, because we speak of existence in both cases. In one case the question is whether a proper name designates, names, something; in the other whether a concept takes objects under itself. If we use the words 'there is a ——' we have the latter case. Now a proper name that designates nothing has no logical justification, since in logic we are concerned with truth in the strictest sense of the word; it may on the other hand still be used in fiction and fable. ("A Critical Elucidation of Some Points in E. Schroeder's *Algebra der Logik*," published 1895, translated by Peter Geach in *Translations from the Philosophical Writings of Gottlob Frege*, Oxford: Basil Blackwell, 1970, at p. 104.)

Elsewhere Frege made similar remarks about singular existentials and their negations: "People certainly say that Odysseus is not an historical person, and mean by this contradictory expression that the name 'Odysseus' designates nothing, has no referent (*Bedeutung*)" (from the section on "Sense and Reference" of Frege's 1906 diary notes, "Introduction to Logic," in H. Hermes, F. Kambartel, and F. Kaulbach, eds., *Posthumous Writings*, translated by P. Long and R. White,[11] University of Chicago Press, 1979, at p. 191). Earlier in his "Dialogue with Pünjer on Existence" (pre-1884, also in Hermes, et al.), Frege observed: "If 'Sachse exists' is supposed to mean 'The word "Sachse" is not an empty sound, but designates something', then it is true that the condition 'Sachse exists' must be satisfied [in order for 'There are men' to be inferred from 'Sachse is a man']. But this is not a new premise, but the presupposition of all our words—a presupposition that goes without saying" (p. 60).[12]

The suggestion would appear to be that (3) and (4), at least on one reading (on which the latter is true), are correctly formalized as:

(5) $(\exists x)$['the present king of France' $\text{refers}_{\text{English}}$ to x]

(6) $\sim(\exists x)$['the present king of France' $\text{refers}_{\text{English}}$ to x].

Notice that this semantic-ascent theory of singular existence is not disproved by the success of substitution of coreferential terms in existential contexts—as for example, in 'The author of *Naming and Necessity* exists. 'The author of *Naming and Necessity* is the McCosh Professor of Philosophy at Princeton University; therefore the Princeton McCosh Professor of Philosophy exists'.[13] Although positions

---

[11] Except that I here render '*Bedeutung*' as 'referent'.

[12] Frege also suggests here that there may be an alternative reading for 'Sachse exists', on which it is tantamount to 'Sachse = Sachse', which Frege says in self-evident. He might well have said the same about '$(\exists x)$[Sachse = x]'.

[13] The term 'semantic ascent' is due to W. V. O. Quine. See his *Word and Object* (Cambridge, Mass.: MIT Press, 1960), §56.

within quotation marks are not typically open to substitution of coreferential terms, by the very nature of the particular context $\ulcorner$'___' refers$_{\text{English}}$ to $x\urcorner$ the position within its quotation marks respects such substitution. Assuming, as Frege did, that each instance of the metalinguistic schema

$$(F) \quad (x)([\text{'the'} + \text{NP refers}_{\text{English}} \text{ to } x] \equiv (y)[\phi_y \equiv x = y]),$$

is true where ϕ is a formalization in the notation of first-order logic for the English NP, (5) is true if and only if (3′) is, and (6) is true if and only if (4′) is. Frege can thus attain the same truth conditions for (3) and (4) as does Russell.

Frege's semantic-ascent approach succeeds in capturing information that is indeed conveyed in the uttering of (3) or (4). But, to invoke a distinction I have emphasized in previous work, this concerns what is *pragmatically imparted* in (3) and (4), and not necessarily what is *semantically encoded* or *contained*.[14] Frege does not attain the same semantic content as Russell or even the same modal intension, i.e., the same corresponding function from possible worlds to truth values. Indeed, that the semantic-ascent interpretation of (3) and (4) by (5) and (6), respectively, is incorrect is easily established by a variety of considerations. The semantic-ascent theory of existence is analogous to Frege's account of identity in *Begriffsschrift* (1879). Curiously, Frege evidently failed to see that his objection in "*Über Sinn und Bedeutung*" to the semantic-ascent theory of identity applies with equal force against the semantic-ascent theory of existence. Another objection to semantic-ascent analyses has been raised by Frege's most effective apologist and defender, Alonzo Church.[15] Translating (4) into French, one obtains:

Le roi présent de France n'existe pas.

Translating its proposed analysis into French, one obtains:

'The present king of France' *ne fait référence à rien en anglais.*

These two translations, while both true, clearly mean different things in French. So too, therefore, do what they translate.

A theory of singular existence statements that is equally Fregean in spirit but superior to the semantic-ascent account takes the verb 'exist' as used in singular existentials to be an *ungerade* device, so that both (3) and (4) concern not the phrase 'the present king of France' but its English sense.[16] This is analogous to the semantic-ascent theory of existence, except that one climbs further up to the level

---

[14] *Frege's Puzzle*, pp. 58–60 and elsewhere (especially 78–79, 84–85, 100, 114–115, 127–128). The distinction is developed further in other works cited in note 2 above.

[15] See Church's "On Carnap's Analysis of Statements of Assertion and Belief," *Analysis*, 10, 5 (1950), pp. 97–99. For a defense of the Church-Langford translation argument, see my "The Very Possibility of Language: A Sermon on the Consequences of Missing Church," to appear in C. A. Anderson's and M. Zeleny's, eds., *Logic, Meaning and Computation: Essays in Honor of Alonzo Church* (Boston: Kluwer, 1998).

[16] Church cites the particular sentence (4) as an example of a true sentence containing an *ungerade* occurrence of a singular term ("name"), in *Introduction to Mathematical Logic I* (Princeton University Press, 1956), at p. 27n. See note 58 below.

of intension. On the intensional-ascent theory of existence, (3) and (4) are analyzed thus:

(7) $(\exists x)\ \Delta(^8(\imath y)Present\text{-}king\text{-}of\text{-}France\ (y)^s,\ x)$

(8) $\sim(\exists x)\ \Delta(^s(\imath y)Present\text{-}king\text{-}of\text{-}France\ (y)^s,\ x),$

where 'Δ' is a dyadic predicate for the relation between a Fregean sense and that which it determines (that of which the sense is a concept) and the superscript 's' is a device for sense-quotation (in the home language, in this case a standard notation for first-order logic with 'Δ').[17] Like the semantic-ascent theory, this intensional-ascent account of existence is not disproved by the success of substitution of coreferential terms in existential contexts. On a Fregean philosophy of semantics, sense-quotation marks create an *ungerade* context—one might even say that they create the paradigm *ungerade* context as Frege understood the concept—so that any expression occurring within them refers in that position to its own customary sense, yet the position flanked by them in the particular context $\ulcorner\Delta(^s\underline{\quad}^s,\ x)\urcorner$ remains open to substitution because of the special interplay between sense-quotation and 'Δ'. The intensional-ascent theory is not so easily refuted as the semantic-ascent approach by the Church translation argument.[18] In place of schema (F), we invoke the following:

$(C)\quad (x)[\Delta(^s(\imath y),\phi^s_y,x) \equiv (y)(\phi_y \equiv x = y)],$

thereby attaining the familiar Russellian truth and falsehood conditions for (3) and (4). Unlike (F), every instance of (C) expresses a necessary truth. The intensional-ascent theory of existence thus also obtains the correct modal intensions for (3) and (4).

III

A singular term is *nonreferring* (with respect to a context c, a time t, and a possible world w), in one sense, if and only if there does not exist anything to which the term refers (with respect to c, t, and w). On Millianism, a nonreferring proper name is thus devoid of semantic content. A Millian, like myself, and even a less committal direct-reference theorist like Kripke, may not avail him/herself of the Theory of Descriptions to solve the problems of sentences with nonreferring

---

[17] Cf. my "Reference and Information Content: Names and Descriptions," in D. Gabbay and F. Guenthner, eds., *Handbook of Philosophical Logic IV: Topics in the Philosophy of Language* (Dordrecht: D. Reidel, 1989), chapter IV.5, pp. 409–461, at 440–441 on Fregean sense-quotation. The idea comes from David Kaplan's "Quantifying In," in D. Davidson and J. Hintikka, eds., *Words and Objections: Essays on the Work of W. V. O. Quine* (Dordrecht: D. Reidel, 1969), pp. 178–214; reprinted in L. Linsky, ed., *Reference and Modality* (Oxford University Press, 1971), pp. 112–144, at 120–121. In English, the word 'that' attached to a subordinate clause (as in $\ulcorner$Jones believes that $\phi\urcorner$ or $\ulcorner$It is necessary that $\phi\urcorner$) typically functions in the manner of sense-quotation marks.

[18] On this application of the translation argument, see my "A Problem in the Frege-Church Theory of Sense and Denotation," *Noûs*, 27, 2 (June 1993), pp. 158–166, and "The Very Possibility of Language: A Sermon on the Consequence of Missing Church."

names.[19] If α is a proper name, referring or not, it is not a definite description, nor by the direct-reference theory's lights does it "abbreviate" any definite description. Direct-reference theory thus excludes application of the Theory of Descriptions in connection with the analogues of (1)–(4):

(1α) α is bald

(2α) α is not bald

(3α) α exists

(4α) α does not exist.

For similar reasons, the direct-reference theorist is also barred from using Frege's sense-reference distinction to solve the difficulties. How, then, can the theorist ascribe content to (1α)–(4α)? In particular, how can (4α) express anything at all, let alone something true? The semantic-ascent theory of existence is refuted on the direct-reference theory no less than on Fregean theory by the Church translation argument as well as by modal considerations (among other things). The *ungerade* theory hardly fares much better on direct-reference theory in connection with (3α) and (4α). On the Millian theory, it fares no better at all. Using the superscripted 's' now as a semantic-content quotation mark, the intensional-ascent theory yields

(7α) $(\exists x)\Delta(^s\alpha^s, x)$

(8α) $\sim(\exists x)\Delta(^s\alpha^s, x)$

as purported analyses for (3α) and (4α), respectively. But according to Millianism, if α is a proper name, then $\ulcorner^s\alpha^s\urcorner$ refers to α's bearer. Where α is a nonreferring name, $\ulcorner^s\alpha^s\urcorner$ is equally nonreferring.

Canvassing some alleged cases of true sentences of the form of (4α) with α a nonreferring name reveals that the so-called problem of nonreferring names, on closer examination, frequently vanishes.

First, let the α in (3α) and (4α) be a name for a possible individual that does not actually exist, i.e., for a merely possible individual. Though there is no bald man (we may suppose) in Quine's doorway at this moment, there might have

---

[19] Kripke does not officially endorse or reject Millianism. Informal discussions lead me to believe he is deeply skeptical. (Cf. his repeated insistence in "A Puzzle about Belief" that Pierre does not have inconsistent beliefs—in A. Margalit, ed., *Meaning and Use* (Dordrecht: D. Reidel, 1979) pp. 239–283; reprinted in N. Salmon and S. Soames, eds., *Propositions and Attitudes,* Oxford University Press, 1988, pp. 102–148.) Nevertheless, Kripke believes that a sentence using a proper name in an ordinary context (not within quotation marks, etc.) expresses a proposition only if the name refers. Similarly, Keith Donnellan, in "Speaking of Nothing," *The Philosophical Review,* 83 (January 1974), pp. 3–32 (reprinted in S. Schwartz, ed., *Naming Necessity and Natural Kinds* (Ithaca: Cornell University Press, 1977), pp. 216–244), says, "when a name is used and there is a failure of reference, then no proposition has been expressed—certainly no true proposition. If a child says, 'Santa Claus will come tonight,' he cannot have spoken the truth, although, for various reasons, I think it better to say that he has not even expressed a proposition. [*footnote:* Given that this is a statement about reality and that proper names have no descriptive content, then how are we to represent the proposition expressed?]" (pp. 20–21).

been.[20] I hereby dub the merely possible bald man in Quine's doorway (if there is exactly one there) 'Curly-0'. Even though Curly-0 might have existed, this much should be clear: Curly-0 does not exist. But how can that be?

Contemporary philosophy has revealed that my little naming ceremony was an exercise in futility. For even if we countenance merely possible individuals, at least for the purpose of naming one of them, I have not yet singled any one of them out to be named. There are many different merely possible individuals who might have been bald men standing in Quine's doorway, but none of them are actually bald or standing in Quine's doorway. The problem is to distinguish one of them. Difficult though the task may be, David Kaplan has found a way to do it.[21] Gamete S is a particular male sperm cell of my father's, and gamete E is a partic- ular ovum of my mother's, such that neither is ever actually united with any other gamete. Following Kaplan's instructions, I have given the name 'Noman-0' to the particular possible individual who would have resulted from the union of S and E, had they united in the normal manner to develop into a human zygote.[22] Noman (as I call him for short) is my merely possible brother. He is a definite possible individual who might have been a bald man standing in Quine's doorway. Noman does not exist. But how can that be?

The apparent difficulty here is an illusion. Consider the following analogous situation. Let the α in (4α) be the name 'Socrates'. Then (3α) is true with respect to the year 400 BC, and (4α) false. With respect to the present day, these truth val- ues are reversed. Socrates is long gone. Consequently, singular propositions about him, which once existed, also no longer exist. Let us call the no-longer-existing proposition that Socrates does not now exist, 'Soc'. Soc is a definite proposition. Its present lack of existence does not prevent it from presently being true. Nor does its nonexistence prevent it from being semantically expressible in English. Notice that in 400 BC, the sentence 'Socrates does not exist' evidently did not express anything in English, and hence was not true or false, since the language itself had not yet come into being. Some might argue that the sentence did not yet even exist. Moreover, even if the language had come into being in 400 BC, the English sentence 'Socrates does not exist' might not have had the exactly same semantics then that it has today. Expressing a proposition (or being true or false, etc.) *with respect to* a given time t is not the same thing as expressing that proposition *at t*. Today the sentence 'Socrates does not exist' expresses Soc with respect to the pres- ent time. It does not follow that there exists a proposition that this sentence expresses with respect to the present time. There presently exists no such propo- sition, but there was such a proposition. 'Socrates does not exist' does indeed

---

[20] Cf. "On What There Is," in Quine's *From a Logical Point of View* (New York: Harper & Row, 1953, 1961).

[21] "Bob and Carol and Ted and Alice," in K. J. Hintikka, J. Moravcsik, and P. Suppes, eds., *Approaches to Natural Language* (Dordrecht: D. Reidel, 1973), pp. 490–518, at 516–517n19. Kripke has also described such a procedure.

[22] In "Existence," cited *supra* in note 3, at pp. 49–50. I draw heavily from the discussion there, especially at pp. 90–98, in the remainder of this section.

single out a definite past thing in order to say of it, correctly, that it does not now exist. It does not follow that there presently exists someone designated in the sentence (and said therein not to exist). There presently exists no one to whom the term 'Socrates', as a name for the philosopher who drank the hemlock, refers in English, but there did exist someone to whom the name now refers. The sentence 'Socrates does not exist' *now* expresses Soc, and Soc is now true. And that is why the sentence is now true in English (even though Soc does not now exist). This account of the truth of 'Socrates does not exist' applies *mutatis mutandis* to objects from the future as well as the past. Kaplan has named the first child to be born in the 22nd century 'Newman-1'.[23] There presently exists no proposition expressed by 'Newman-1 does not exist'. But there will exist a particular proposition that is already so expressed, and it is true.

The principal facts about Socrates and Newman-1 are true as well of Noman. I call a nonreferring singular term *weakly nonreferring* if there might have existed something to which the term actually refers, and I call a nonreferring term *very weakly nonreferring* (at a time t) if (at t) there has existed, or is going to exist, something to which the term refers. 'Noman' is weakly nonreferring but not very weakly. There exists no one to whom 'Noman' refers but there might have been a definite someone x such that 'Noman' *actually* refers to x. By the same token, there exists no proposition expressed by 'Noman does not exist', but there might have been a proposition that *actually is* expressed, and it is actually true.

Consider now *la pièce de résistance.* A *strongly nonreferring* term is one such that there could not have existed something to which the term actually refers. Curiously, an extension of the same solution may be made even for some strongly nonreferring terms. To see this, let E_{NS} be the ovum from which I actually sprang. I have introduced the name 'Nothan-0' for the merely possible individual who would have sprang from the union of S and E_{NS} had they been united in the normal manner. Like 'Noman-0', 'Nothan-0' is weakly nonreferring but not very weakly. It seems that Nothan (as I call him) and I are *incompossible;* we could not both exist since we each require the same ovum. Either it is true or it is false that Nothan might have been taller than I actually am. This is a truth-valued singular proposition about a definite pair of possible individuals. But unlike the proposition that Nothan is 6 feet tall, this proposition could not possibly exist; there is no possible world in which its two constituent possible people exist together. The term 'the proposition that Nothan-0 might have been taller than Nathan Salmon actually is' is thus strongly nonreferring. Still, there is in *some* sense a definite impossible thing to which the term actually refers: the very singular proposition in question, which is true if Nothan might have been taller than I actually am and is otherwise false. An analogous situation obtains in connection with the proposition, which I believe, that Plato was taller than I now am. There is no time at which this singular proposition exists. In particular, it

---

[23]In "Quantifying In," p. 135 of Linsky.

does not now exist, yet I now believe it.[24] The negative existential 'The singular proposition that Nothan might have been taller than Nathan Salmon actually is, does not exist' is true, and its subject term is strongly nonreferring. In fact, the proposition expressed by this negative existential could not possibly exist. Yet there is in some sense a definite proposition that is in question, and it is true. Something analogous to this is true also in connection with the pair set {Nothan-0, Nathan Salmon}; there is in some sense a definite set that is actually referred to by this piece of set-theoretic notation (assuming it is properly interpreted), yet that set could not possibly exist. Even if Nothan had existed, {Nothan, me} still could not do so. Neither could the singular proposition about the pair set that it does not exist. Yet that proposition is true, precisely in virtue of the fact that the pair set to which it makes reference does not exist. Analogously again, the pair set {Plato, me} does not exist, never did, and never will. Neither does the proposition that this pair set does not now exist. But it is a definite set with a definite membership, and the proposition is true.

It should be noted that the mentioned impossible objects are not like "the round square," which Alexius Meinong claimed had lower-class ontological status, a sort of being shy of existence due to its incompatible properties of shape.[25] What makes the pair set {Nothan-0, Nathan Salmon} and the proposition that Nothan might have been taller than I actually am impossible is not that they have inconsistent or otherwise incompatible properties. As a matter of pure logic, it is provable that nothing has inconsistent properties. An impossible object, like the mentioned pair set or singular proposition, is a complex entity composed of incompossible things. Any composite entity, even one whose components are incompossible, has a perfectly consistent set of attributes. An impossible object is not a Meinongian inconsistent Object. Though it cannot exist, an impossible object's properties are perfectly coherent.

Some might wish to object to the foregoing that, of the nonreferring names mentioned, only 'Socrates' refers to a definite individual, since the reference of the rest is not fixed by the entire history of the universe up to the present moment. There is not yet any objective fact, says the objector, concerning which

---

[24]The same fate might befall Soc, if (as some believe) the present time did not itself exist when Socrates did. In order to facilitate the exposition I have pretended instead that times (like the present) exist eternally.

The sense in which there is a proposition that Nothan might have been taller than I actually am is troublesome. The fact that it seems to require quantification over objects that could not exist should give one pause. Still, it is difficult to deny that in *some* sense, there are such objects to be quantified over; the proposition that Nothan might have been taller than I actually am is one such. To deny this would be to undertake the burden of explaining how it is either true that Nothan might have been taller than I actually am or true that Nothan could not have been. Either way, the result seems to be a true singular proposition that exists in no possible world. A substitutional interpretation of 'there are' may be called for when impossible objects rear their ugly heads.

[25]"The Theory of Objects," in R. Chisholm, ed., *Realism and the Background of Phenomenology* (Glencoe, Ill.: The Free Press, 1960), pp. 76–117.

future individual the name 'Newman-1' names.[26] This objection involves the issue of future contingencies. While a full response cannot be given here, I will provide a brief response that I think adequate to the task at hand. First, the particular example of Newman-1 could be replaced with the introduction of a name for the future result of an in-progress physically and causally determined process. Second, the objection confuses truth with a concept of unpreventability, which entails truth but is not entailed by it. The fact that 'Socrates' has the particular reference it does is now unpreventable. By contrast, perhaps it is still within our power (at least if free will is assumed) to influence who will be the first child born in the 22nd century. Suppose it is not yet causally (or in some other manner) determined which future person will be born first in the 22nd century. It does not follow that there is no fact of the matter, or that it is as yet neither true nor false that that future person will be born first in the 22nd century. Many facts about the future are as yet causally open, still preventable. Suppose I am about to decide whether to listen to Beethoven or Beatles, but have not yet done so. I will either choose Beethoven or I will not. One of these two disjuncts obtains—one of them is a fact—though which one is not yet settled. There is no incompatibility between its not yet being settled which choice I will make and my eventually choosing Beethoven. On the contrary, it's not yet being settled entails that either I will choose Beethoven and it is not yet settled that I will, or else I will decide against Beethoven and that is not yet settled. Either way, there now is a fact concerning my future choice—as yet still preventable but a fact nonetheless. However I choose, although that future choice is still preventable the fact remains (however preventably) that I will make that decision instead of the other.

What follows from our assumption is that there is no unpreventable fact concerning whom 'Newman-1' now names, not that there is no fact at all. It is not yet *causally* (or in the other manner) fixed which future individual the name names, but the name's reference is *semantically* fixed. There is—or rather there will be—a fact concerning whom the name names, even if it is still preventable. That fact also does not yet exist, but it is already a fact, and eventually (not yet) it will even be unpreventable. Kaplan fixed the reference of 'Newman-1' *semantically* not by means of the description 'the future person who is unpreventably going to be born first in the 22nd century', but by 'the future person who *will* be born first in the 22nd century'. The name's reference is even *causally* fixed to the extent that, given the way in which Kaplan introduced the name, it is already settled that the name now refers to whichever future individual will turn out to be the first child born in the 22nd century if there will be such an individual (and that the name is nonreferring otherwise). This much about the name is unpreventable (although, of course, the name's semantics can be changed from what it currently is). Though it is not yet causally fixed who will be born first in the 22nd century, there already is (or rather, there will exist something that is now) a fact, as yet preventable, concerning who it will be. These two facts—one unpreventable, the other still

---

[26]Ilhan Inan brought this possible objection to my attention.

preventable—entail a third fact, itself as yet preventable, concerning whom the name now names.[27] The possible causal indeterminacy, and our present ignorance, concerning who the first child born in the 22nd century will turn out to be does not impugn the fact that whoever it turns out to be, that one is already the referent of 'Newman-1'. Nor does that future individual's present nonexistence impugn this fact, any more than Socrates's present nonexistence impugns the fact that 'Socrates' refers to him. Socrates's pastness and unpreventability does not bestow on his name any more semantic factuality, or rigidity, than 'Newman-1' enjoys—nor, for that matter, than 'Noman-0' enjoys. There is no more justification for saying that 'Socrates' is semantically superior to "Newman-1" because Newman-1 is preventable and Socrates is not, than there is for saying that 'Newman-1' is semantically superior to 'Socrates' because Socrates is dead and Newman-1 is not.

Followers of Quine dismiss merely possible objects like Noman on the ground of a lack of clear "identity conditions." It is worth noticing that it is causally determined which possible individual would have sprang from gametes S and E, had they united in the normal manner to form a zygote. If causal determination were important to semantic definiteness, the name 'Noman-0', and even the term '{Nothan-0, Nathan Salmon}', should be semantically definite to a greater degree

---

[27]The situation can be illustrated by means of a deductively valid argument:

($P1$) The referent$_{English}$ of 'Newman-1' = the first child to be born in the 22nd century.

($P2$) The first child to be born in the 22nd century = Newman-1.

Therefore,

(C) The referent$_{English}$ of 'Newman-1' = Newman-1.

Assume 'Newman-1' is used as a name of the future person who will be born first in the 22nd century. (This assumption, of course, begs the question against the objector, but let that pass; I wish to clarify the objector's position from the perspective of one who is not persuaded by the objection.) Then the conclusion (C) specifies whom 'Newman-1' names; it states that the name names *that* particular future individual. Think of the argument as consisting not of these sentences, but of the propositions they express. The question at issue is whether (C) (the proposition) is already true. The truth or falsity of ($P2$), we are assuming, is not yet causally (or in some other manner) fixed. Equivalently, the result of prefixing the sentence ($P2$) with a temporal/modal operator 'It is unpreventable that' is false with respect to the present, and likewise the result of prefixing its negation. (Unpreventability is closed under logical consequence.) The objector reasons that since ($P2$) (the proposition) is still preventable, both it and (C) are as yet neither true nor false. (The objector will want to say this about ($P1$) as well.) This wrongly assumes that (for propositions of the class in question) truth is the same thing as unpreventability, thus making $\ulcorner$It is unpreventable that $\phi\urcorner$ truth-functional, equivalent in a three-valued logic to the double exclusion-negation of ϕ, $\ulcorner\sim_E\sim_E\phi\urcorner$. The truth of ($P1$) is already unpreventable. Contrary to the objector, ($P2$) is also true, even though that fact is still preventable. Therefore (C), though preventable, is true.

This same deductive argument illuminates other philosophically interesting issues. I have used it to argue that though ($P1$) is true by semantics alone, and is also known by semantics alone, surprisingly (C)—which is established by this very argument—is neither. See "How to Measure the Standard Metre," *Proceedings of the Aristotelian Society* (New Series), 88 (1987/88), pp. 193–217, at 200–201n10; and "Analyticity and Apriority," in J. Tomberlin, ed., *Philosophical Perspectives* 7, *Language and Logic* (Atascadero, Ca.: Ridgeview, 1993), pp. 125–133, at 133n15.

than 'Newman-1'. Despite its actual nonexistence, there is no problem about the identity conditions of the proposition that Noman does not exist. Nor is there a problem about the identity conditions of Soc. Or at least there is no more problem than there is in the case of the ordered pair consisting of Socrates first, and the temporally indexed property (or concept) of present nonexistence second. A proposition is identical with Soc if and only if it consists of these very same two constituents. Indeed, Soc might even be identified with the ordered pair. If the Principle of Extensionality suffices for giving the "identity conditions" of sets, then an exactly analogous principle is sufficient for propositions, presently existent and not. Quine and his followers also object to such intensional entities as properties and concepts, and on similar grounds. But the particular property of nonexistence creates no special problems. One may take it to be fully definable by means of the purely logical notions of abstraction, universal quantification, negation, and identity thus: $(\lambda x)(y)[x \neq y]$.[28] There is no legitimate reason for allowing a sentence of the form (4α) to be true by virtue of expressing Soc, but to disallow such a sentence from being true by virtue of expressing the analogous proposition about Noman.

Some may balk at my proposal on the grounds that it conflicts with the metaphysical principle that any object must exist in every conceivable circumstance in which that object has any properties. This principle that existence is a precondition for having properties—that existence precedes suchness—underlies the Kantian doctrine that existence is not itself a property (or "predicate"). It, like the Kantian doctrine it supports, is a confused and misguided prejudice. Undoubtedly, existence is a prerequisite for a very wide range of ordinary properties—being blue in color, having such-and-such mass, writing *Waverley*. But the sweeping doctrine that existence universally precedes suchness has very clear counterexamples in which an object from one circumstance has properties in another circumstance in virtue of the properties it has in the original circumstance. Socrates does not exist in my present circumstance, yet he has numerous properties here—for example, being mentioned and discussed by me. Walter Scott, who no longer exists, currently has the property of having written *Waverley*. He did exist when he had the property of writing *Waverley*, of course, but as every author knows, the property of writing something is very different from the property of having written it. Among their differences is the fact that the former requires existence. On the doctrine that existence precedes suchness, Scott lacks the property of having written *Waverley* not because he did not write *Waverley* (since he did), but merely because he does not exist. Once it is conceded that Scott wrote *Waverley*, or that Socrates is admired by Jones, etc., what is gained by denying nevertheless that they have these very properties? To satisfy the prejudice, one may simply insist that objects like Socrates that no longer exist can no longer have properties. To do so is to concede that Socrates does not exist. One thereby falsifies the very position

---

[28]Cf. note 24. The universal quantifier here cannot be substitutional. One of my central tasks in "Existence" was to investigate the viability of an analysis of existence in terms of standard objectual quantification.

insisted upon, by bestowing on Soc the particular property of being conceded (or asserted, agreed upon, presupposed, etc.). As long as it is deemed now true that Socrates does not exist, that is sufficient for the present truth in English of 'Socrates does not exist', granted that 'Socrates does not exist' expresses in English (with respect t) that Socrates does not exist (at t). It matters little whether it is conceded that Soc has the property Truth—or for that matter whether it is conceded that 'Socrates does not exist' has the corresponding property of being a true sentence of English. And it matters not at all that Soc no longer exists.[29]

IV

Though the realm of "logical space" may fail to provide clearly problematic examples of true negative existentials, the realms of fiction and myth may fare better. Let the α in (3α) and (4α) be a name from fiction, for example 'Sherlock Holmes'. It is a traditional view in philosophy, and indeed it is plain common sense, that (3α) is then false and $(4\alpha) = (0)$ true, when taken as statements about reality. For 'Sherlock Holmes', as a name for the celebrated detective, is a *very strongly* or *thoroughly nonreferring* name, one that does not in reality have any referent at all—past, present, future, forever merely possible, or even forever impossible. Bertrand Russell lent an eloquent voice to this common-sense view:

> [M]any logicians have been driven to the conclusion that there are unreal objects. . . . In such theories, it seems to me, there is a failure of that feeling for reality

---

[29]Cf. "Existence," pp. 90–97. Alvin Plantinga calls the doctrine that everything exists in any possible world in which it has properties *serious actualism*, in "De Essentia," in E. Sosa, ed., *Essays on the Philosophy of Roderick M. Chisholm* (Amsterdam: Rodopi, 1979), pp. 101–121, at 108–109. By analogy, *serious presentism* would be the corresponding temporal doctrine that everything exists at any time at which it has properties. The doctrine that existence precedes suchness encompasses both serious actualism and serious presentism. Kripke says that the doctrine that existence is not itself a property but a prerequisite for having any properties, though rather obscure, seems to him in some sense true. The doctrine seems to me erroneous on both counts. What can a precondition for a given property be if not another property?

Joseph Almog, in "The Subject-Predicate Class I," *Noûs*, 25 (1991), pp. 591–619, objects to my view that 'Socrates does not exist' is true in English in virtue of expressing a true singular proposition, on the ground that no sentence can be made true by Soc's being the case since Soc no longer exists. Instead, he asserts (influenced by Donnellan—see note 19) that the sentence is true because 'Socrates' refers to Socrates, who does not exist (pp. 604–607; cf. Donnellan, *op. cit.*, pp. 7–8). Far from solving the problem, skepticism about propositions only makes matters worse: A sentence that mentions Socrates but expresses nothing whatever about him cannot have truth value, let alone truth. In order for a sentence to be true, what it expresses must be the case; this is what truth for sentences consists in. (Curiously, Almog seems to concede this, just one page after objecting to my view.) Further, as Frege and Church argued, 'Jones believes that Socrates does not exist', if true, requires something for Jones to believe. A genuine solution requires genuine semantic content. Worse still, Almog's purported solution is inconsistent. If Soc cannot be true only because it does not exist, then for exactly the same reason Socrates cannot be referred to—the name 'Socrates' *is* nonreferring, however weakly—and we are left with nothing that accounts for the truth in English of 'Socrates does not exist'. But Socrates is referred to, warts and all, and Soc is the case (and in addition is expressed, believed, known, etc.)

which ought to be preserved even in the most abstract studies. Logic, I should maintain, must no more admit a unicorn than zoology can; for logic is concerned with the real world just as truly as zoology, though with its more abstract and general features. To say that unicorns have an existence in heraldry, or in literature, or in imagination, is a most pitiful and paltry evasion. What exists in heraldry is not an animal, made of flesh and blood, moving and breathing of its own initiative. What exists is a picture, or a description in words. Similarly, to maintain that Hamlet, for example, exists in his own world, namely in the world of Shakespeare's imagination, just as truly as (say) Napoleon existed in the ordinary world, is to say something deliberately confusing, or else confused to a degree which is scarcely credible. There is only one world, the "real" world: Shakespeare's imagination is part of it, and the thoughts that he had in writing *Hamlet* are real. So are the thoughts that we have in reading the play. But it is of the very essence of fiction that only the thoughts, feelings, etc., in Shakespeare and his readers are real, and that there is not, in addition to them, an objective Hamlet. When you have taken account of all the feelings roused by Napoleon in writers and readers of history, you have not touched the actual man; but in the case of Hamlet you have come to the end of him. If no one thought about Hamlet, there would be nothing left of him; if no one had thought about Napoleon, he would have soon seen to it that some one did. The sense of reality is vital in logic, and whoever juggles with it by pretending that Hamlet has another kind of reality is doing a disservice to thought. A robust sense of reality is very necessary in framing a correct analysis of propositions about unicorns, golden mountains, round squares, and other such pseudo-objects.[30]

Contemporary philosophy has uncovered that, unlike 'Noman', a name from fiction does not even name a merely possible object. Thus Kripke writes:

> The mere discovery that there was indeed a detective with exploits like those of Sherlock Holmes would not show that Conan Doyle was writing *about* this man; it is theoretically possible, though in practice fantastically unlikely, that Doyle was writing pure fiction with only a coincidental resemblance to the actual man. . . . Similarly, I hold the metaphysical view that, granted that there is no Sherlock Holmes, one cannot say of any possible person, that he *would have been* Sherlock Holmes, had he existed. Several distinct possible people, and even actual ones such as Darwin or Jack the Ripper, might have performed the exploits of Holmes, but there is none of whom we can say that he would have *been* Holmes had he performed these exploits. For if so, which one?
>
> I thus could no longer write, as I once did, that 'Holmes does not exist, but in other states of affairs, he would have existed'. (*Naming and Necessity*, Harvard University Press, 1972, 1980, pp. 157–158)

It is not merely true that Sherlock Holmes does not exist, it is a necessary truth. On Kripke's view, the name 'Sherlock Holmes' is a rigid *non*designator, designating nothing—not even a merely possible thing—with respect to every possible world. In a similar vein, Kaplan says:

---

[30] *Introduction to Mathematical Philosophy* (London: Allen & Unwin, 1919), at pp. 169–170. Cf. Russell's *The Philosophy of Logical Atomism*, D. Pears, ed. (La Salle, Ill.: Open Court, 1918, 1972, 1985), at pp. 87–88.

The myth [of Pegasus] is possible in the sense that there is a possible world in which it is truthfully *told*. Furthermore, there are such worlds in which the language, with the exception of the proper names in question, is semantically and syntactically identical with our own. Let us call such possible worlds of the myth, '*M* worlds'. In each *M* world, the name 'Pegasus' will have originated in a dubbing of a winged horse. The Friend of Fiction, who would not have anyone believe the myth . . . , but yet talks of Pegasus, pretends to be in an *M* world and speaks its language.

But beware the confusion of our language with theirs! If *w* is an *M* world, then *their* name 'Pegasus' will denote something with respect to *w*, and *our* description 'the *x* such that *x* is called 'Pegasus'' will denote the same thing with respect to *w*, but *our* name 'Pegasus' will still denote nothing with respect to *w*. . . .

To summarize. It has been thought that proper names like 'Pegasus' and 'Hamlet' were like 'Aristotle' and 'Newman-1', except that the individuals denoted by the former were more remote. But regarded as names of *our* language—introduced by successful or unsuccessful dubbings, or just made up—the latter denote and the former do not.[31]

The passage closes with a "Homework Problem": If the foregoing account of names deriving from fiction is correct, how could a sentence like (0) be true? Our task is to examine this very problem from a Millian perspective.

We begin with a plausible theory of fiction and its objects. Saul Kripke and Peter van Inwagen have argued, independently, and persuasively, that wholly fictional characters should be regarded as real things.[32] Theirs is not a Meinongian view—one of Russell's targets in the passage quoted above—on which any manner of proper name or definite description, including such terms as 'the golden mountain' and 'the round square', refers to some Object, though the Object may not exist in any robust sense and may instead have only a lower class ontological status (and, as in the case of the round square, may even have inconsistent properties).[33] To be sure, wholly fictional characters like Sherlock Holmes, though real,

---

[31] From appendix XI, "Names from Fiction," of "Bob and Carol and Ted and Alice," *loc. cit.*, at pp. 505–508. Kaplan credits John Bennett in connection with this passage. The same general argument occurs in Donnellan, *op. cit.*, at pp. 24–25, and in Plantinga, *The Nature of Necessity* (Oxford University Press, 1974), section VIII.4, "Names: Their Function in Fiction," at pp. 159–163.

[32] Kripke, *Reference and Existence: The John Locke Lectures for 1973* (Oxford University Press, unpublished); van Inwagen, "Creatures of Fiction," *American Philosophical Quarterly*, 14, 4 (October 1977), pp. 299–308, and "Fiction and Metaphysics," *Philosophy and Literature*, 7, 1 (Spring 1983), pp. 67–77. One possible difference between them is that van Inwagen accepts an ontology of fictional characters whereas Kripke is instead merely unveiling an ontology that he argues is assumed in the way we speak about fiction while remaining neutral on the question of whether this manner of speaking accurately reflects reality. My interpretation of Kripke is based partly on notes I took at his seminars on the topic of reference and fiction at Princeton University during March–April 1981 and on recordings of his seminars at the University of California, Riverside in January 1983. See also Kit Fine, "The Problem of Non-Existence: I. Internalism," *Topoi*, 1 (1982), pp. 97–140; Thomas G. Pavel, *Fictional Worlds* (Harvard University Press, 1986); Amie Thomasson, "Fiction, Modality and Dependent Abstracta," *Philosophical Studies*, 84 (1996), pp. 295–320; Nicholas Wolterstorff, *Works and Worlds of Art* (Oxford University Press, 1980). Various articles on the philosophy and logic of fiction are collected together in *Poetics*, 8, 1/2 (April 1979)—see especially Robert Howell, "Fictional Objects: How They Are and How They Aren't," pp. 129–177—and in Peter McCormick, ed., *Reasons of Art* (University of Ottawa Press, 1985).

[33] Cf. Terence Parsons, "A Meinongian Analysis of Fictional Objects," *Grazer Philosophische Studien*, 1 (1975), pp. 73–86, and *Nonexistent Objects* (New Haven: Yale University Press, 1980).

are not real people. Neither physical objects nor mental objects, instead they are, in this sense, abstract entities. They are not eternal entities, like numbers; they are man-made artifacts created by fiction writers. But they exist just as robustly as the fictions themselves, the novels, stories, etc. in which they occur. Indeed, fictional characters have the same ontological status as the fictions, which are also abstract entities created by their authors. And certain things are true of these fictional characters—for example, that the protagonist of the *Sherlock Holmes* stories was inspired in part by an uncannily perceptive person of Sir Arthur Conan Doyle's acquaintance.

On this theory, a negative existential like (0), taken as making an assertion about the fictional character and taken literally, denies real existence of a real fictional character, and is therefore false. Yes, Virginia, there is a Sherlock Holmes. In fact, Holmes may well be the most famous of all fictional characters in existence. The same sentence, understood as making an assertion about the fictional character, may be open to a more charitable and plausible interpretation, albeit a nonliteral one. Perhaps one may reinterpret the predicate 'exists', for example, to mean *real*, in something like the sense: *not merely a character in the story, but an entity of just the sort depicted.* Then (0) may be understood, quite plausibly, as making an assertion that the character of Sherlock Holmes is a wholly fictional man, not a real one. That is to say, there is a fiction in which Holmes is a man of flesh and blood, but in reality Holmes is merely a fictional character. On this Pickwickian reading, the sentence is indeed true. But it is then not an authentic negative existential, and thus generates no special problem for Millianism, let alone for direct-reference theory.[34]

Our homework problem is not yet solved. How can this talk about the fictional character of Sherlock Holmes as a real entity be reconciled with the passage from Kripke quoted above, in which he appears to agree with Kaplan and Russell that 'Sherlock Holmes' is nonreferring?

On Kripke's account, use of the name 'Sherlock Holmes' to refer to the fictional character is in a certain sense parasitic on a prior, more fundamental use not as a name for the fictional character. Kripke and van Inwagen emphasize that the author of a fiction does not assert anything in writing the fiction. Instead, Kripke, like Kaplan, says that Conan Doyle merely *pretended* to be referring to someone in using the name 'Sherlock Holmes' and to be asserting things, expressing propositions, about him. A fiction purports to be an accurate historical recounting of real events involving real people. Of course, the author typically does not attempt to deceive the audience that the pretence is anything but a pretense; instead the fiction merely goes through the motions (hoaxes like Orson Welles's radio broadcast of H. G. Wells's *The War of the Worlds* and the legend of

---

[34]Cf. Van Inwagen, *op. cit.* at p. 308n11. Kripke argues against any interpretation of (0) on which the name is used as a name of the fictional character but 'exist' receives a Pickwickian interpretation on which the sentence is true. I am somewhat less skeptical. See below, especially note 48. (Van Inwagen's suggestion is neutral between this sort of account and the one proposed below.)

Santa Claus being the exceptions that prove the rule). Frege expressed the basic idea as follows:

> Assertions in fiction are not to be taken seriously: they are only mock assertions. Even the thoughts are not to be taken seriously as in the sciences: they are only mock thoughts. If Schiller's *Don Carlos* were to be regarded as a piece of history, then to a large extent the drama would be false. But a work of fiction is not meant to be taken seriously in this way at all: it's all play.[35]

According to Kripke, as the name 'Sherlock Holmes' was originally introduced and used by Conan Doyle, it has no referent whatsoever. It is a name in the make-believe world of storytelling, part of an elaborate pretense. By Kripke's lights, our language licenses a certain kind of metaphysical move. It postulates an abstract artifact, the fictional character, as a product of this pretense. But the name 'Sherlock Holmes' does not thereby refer to the character thereby postulated, nor for that matter to anything else, and the sentences involving the name 'Sherlock Holmes' that were written in creating the fiction express no propositions, about the fictional character or anything else. They are all part of the pretense, like the actors' lines in the performance of a play. It is only at a later stage when discussing the fictional character from a standpoint outside of the fiction, speaking about the pretense and not within it, that the language makes a second move, this one semantical rather than metaphysical, giving the name a new, nonpretend use as a name for the fictional character. The language allows a grammatical transformation, says Kripke, of a fictional name for a person into a name of a fictional person. Similarly van Inwagen writes, "we have embodied in our rules for talking about fiction a convention that says that a creature of fiction *may* be referred to by what is (loosely speaking) 'the name it has in the story'" (*op. cit.*, p. 307*n*). On this account, the name 'Sherlock Holmes' is ambiguous. In its original use as a name for a human being—its use by Conan Doyle in writing the fiction, and presumably by the reader reading the fiction—it merely pretends to name someone and actually names nothing at all. But in its nonpretend use as a name for the fictional character thereby created by Conan Doyle, it genuinely refers to that particular artifactual entity. In effect, there are two names. Though spelled the same, they would be better spelled differently, as 'Holmes₁' for the man and 'Holmes₂' for the fictional character. Neither names a real man. The latter names an abstract artifact, the former nothing at all. It is the original, thoroughly nonreferring use of 'Sherlock Holmes'—its use in the same way as 'Holmes₁'—that Kaplan, Kripke, and Russell emphasize in the passages quoted.

Kripke's theory involves a complex account of sentences from fiction and myth, like 'Sherlock Holmes plays the violin' and 'Pegasus has wings' (cf. (1α)). I shall call these sentences *object-fictional*, to be contrasted with *meta-fictional* sentences like 'According to the stories, Sherlock Holmes plays the violin'. On

---

[35]"Logic," in Frege's *Posthumous Writings, loc. cit.*, at p. 130. See also Kendall L. Walton, "On Fearing Fictions," *Journal of Philosophy*, 75 (1978), pp. 5–27; and *Mimesis as Make-Believe: On the Foundations of the Representational Arts* (Cambridge, Mass.: Harvard University Press, 1990).

Kripke's view, object-fictional sentences are multiply ambiguous, as a result of the two uses of the names and of differing perspectives from within and without the fiction or myth. Using the name in 'Sherlock Holmes plays the violin' in the manner of 'Holmes$_1$,' as the pretend name of a pretend man, and using the sentence to make a statement not within the pretense and instead about the real world outside the fiction, the sentence expresses nothing and is therefore not literally true. (See note 19.) But object-fictional sentences may also be used from within the fiction, as part of the general pretense of an accurate, factual recounting of real events, not to be mistaken as a "time out" reality check. Interpreted thus, the sentence 'Holmes plays the violin' is a correct depiction, part of the storytelling language-game. So used, the sentence may be counted "true" in an extended sense—truth *in the fiction,* as we might call it—conforming to a convention of counting an object-fictional sentence "true" or "false" according as the sentence is true or false in, or according to, the fiction. This is the sense in which the sentence should be marked "true" on a true-false test in English Lit 101.[36] Alternatively, the name may be used in the manner of 'Holmes$_2$,' as a name for the fictional character. With the name so used, and the sentence used as a statement not about the fiction but about reality, it is false; no abstract entity can play a musical instrument. On the other hand, according to Kripke, we also have an extended use of predicates, on which 'plays the violin' correctly applies to an abstract entity when it is a character from a fiction according to which the corresponding fictional person plays the violin. Giving the name its use as a name of the fictional character, and understanding the predicate 'plays the violin' in this extended sense, the sentence is true. According to the stories, Holmes$_1$ plays the violin. In virtue of that fact we may say that Holmes$_2$ "plays the violin." The truth conditions of the sentence on this reading are exactly the same as the conventional truth-in-the-fiction conditions of the sentence interpreted as 'Holmes$_1$ plays the violin'. But they differ in meaning. The former invokes a new interpretation for both subject and predicate.[37]

---

[36] Kripke recognizes that this is generally equivalent, in some sense, to treating an object-fictional sentence ϕ as implicitly shorthand for the meta-fictional ⌜According to the fiction, ϕ,⌝ and evaluating it as true or false accordingly. But he says that he prefers to regard it as applying 'true' and 'false' in conventionally extended senses directly to object-fictional sentences themselves in their original senses. Cf. David Lewis, "Truth in Fiction," *American Philosophical Quarterly,* 15 (1978), pp. 37–46; reprinted with postscripts in Lewis's *Philosophical Papers: Volume I* (Oxford University Press, 1983), pp. 261–280.

[37] Kripke cautions that when one is merely pretending to refer to a human being in using a name from fiction, that pretense does not in and of itself involve naming a fictional character. On the contrary, such a pretense was involved in the very creation of the as yet unnamed fictional character. He also remarks that an object-fictional sentence like 'Sherlock Holmes plays the violin' would be counted true in the conventionally extended "according to the fiction" sense even if the name had only its 'Holmes$_1$' use and the language had not postulated fictional characters as objects. Van Inwagen (*op. cit.,* pp. 305–306) invokes a notion of a fiction "ascribing" a property to a character, but admits that his terminology is misleading. He does not explain his notion of *ascription* in terms of what sentences within the fiction express, since such sentences on his view (as on Kripke's) do not mention fictional characters and express nothing at all. Nor does he explain this kind of ascription in any other terms. Instead the notion is an undefined primitive of the theory.

Viewing the negative existential (0) on this same model, it has various interpretations on which it is false. Interpreted in the sense of 'Holmes$_1$ does not exist', it is like 'Holmes$_1$ does not play the violin' in pretending to express a proposition that is false in the fiction. The sentence should be marked "false" on a true-false quiz about the *Sherlock Holmes* stories. Interpreted in the sense of 'Holmes$_2$ does not exist', the predicate 'exist' may be given its literal sense, or alternatively it may be given its extended sense on which it applies to a fictional character if and only if according to the relevant fiction the corresponding person exists. Either way the sentence is false. The fictional character exists, and moreover the corresponding person exists according to the stories. But now read (0) again in the sense of 'Holmes$_1$ does not exist', and this time take it not as a statement within the fiction but as a statement about the real world. Then it is significantly unlike 'Holmes$_1$ does not play the violin', which expresses nothing about the real world outside the fiction. For 'Holmes$_1$ does not exist', according to Kripke, is in reality quite true. On this interpretation, the sentence is regarded by Kripke, as by traditional philosophy, as an authentic true negative existential with a thoroughly nonreferring subject term.

This was our primary concern. We have attempted to deal with the problem of negative existentials by concentrating on 'Holmes$_2$ does not exist'. But it is Holmes$_1$, not Holmes$_2$, who literally does not exist. The homework problem requires more work. Kripke says that it is 'perhaps the worst problem in the area.'

By way of a possible solution, Kripke proposes that (0) should not be viewed on the model of 'Holmes$_1$ plays the violin', understood as a statement about the real world—and which thereby expresses nothing—but instead as a special kind of speech act. Consider first the object-fictional sentence 'Sherlock Holmes does not play the violin', in the sense of 'Holmes$_1$ does not play the violin' construed as a statement about reality (cf. (2α)). One may utter this sentence even if one is uncertain whether Holmes$_1$ is a real person, in order to make the cautious claim that either there is no such person as Holmes$_1$ or there is but he does not play the violin. In that case, the assertion is tantamount to saying that either there is no proposition that Holmes$_1$ plays the violin, or there is such a proposition but it is not true. In short, the sentence is interpreted as meaning *there is no true proposition that Holmes$_1$ plays the violin*. A similar cautious interpretation is available whenever negation is employed.

Kripke extends this same interpretation to singular negative existentials. He proposes that whenever one utters any sentence of the form (4α) from the standpoint of the real world, what one really means is better expressed by ⌜There is no true proposition that α exists⌝. What is meant may be true on either of two very different grounds: (*i*) the mentioned proposition is not true; (*ii*) there is no such proposition. If α is 'the present king of France', so that (4α) is (4), then what one is really saying—that there is no true proposition that the present king of France exists—is true for the former reason; it is false that the present king of France exists. If (4α) is (0) with 'Sherlock Holmes' in its 'Holmes$_1$' use, then what one is really saying—that there is no true proposition that Holmes$_1$ exists—is true for the latter reason. Kripke's is not a theory that takes (4α) to express that (3α) is not true$_{\text{English}}$. Semantic-ascent theories are notoriously vulnerable to refutation (as by the Church translation argument). Instead Kripke takes (4α) to express that there is no true proposition of a certain sort, if only because there is no proposition. This is closer to the intensional-ascent theory of existence—with a wink and a nod in the direction of Millianism.

Kripke extends this account to mistaken theories. He explicitly mentions the case of the fictitious intra-Mercurial planet Vulcan, hypothesized and named by Jacques Babinet in 1846 and later thought by Urbain Le Verrier to explain an irregularity in the orbit of Mercury. The irregularity was eventually explained by the general theory of relativity.[38] Though the Vulcan hypothesis turned out to be a mistake, it nevertheless bore existent fruit—not in the form of a massive physical object, but a man-made abstract entity of the same ontological status as Holmes$_2$. Vulcan even has explanatory value. It accounts not for Mercury's perihelion, but for the truth in English of 'A hypothetical planet was postulated to explain Mercury's irregular orbit'. In introducing the name 'Vulcan', Babinet meant to introduce a name for a planet, not an abstract artifact. His intentions were thwarted on both counts. Kripke holds that the dubbing ultimately resulted in two distinct uses of the name—in effect two names, 'Vulcan$_1$' and 'Vulcan$_2$'—the first as a name for an intra-Mercurial planet, and consequently thoroughly nonreferring, the second as a name of Babinet's creation. (Presumably these two uses are supposed to be different from two other pairs of uses, corresponding to the fire god of Roman mythology and Mr. Spock's native planet in *Star Trek*.) When it is said that Vulcan$_1$ does not influence Mercury's orbit, and that Vulcan$_1$ does not exist, what is meant is that there are no true propositions that Vulcan$_1$ influences Mercury or that Vulcan$_1$ exists.

The motivation for Kripke's intensional ascent is obscure. In any event, the account fails to solve the problem. The 'that' clauses 'that Holmes$_1$ plays the violin' and 'that Holmes$_1$ exists' are no less problematic than 'Holmes$_1$' itself. Kripke concedes, in effect, that if α is a thoroughly nonreferring name, then propositional terms like ⌜the proposition that α is bald⌝ are also thoroughly nonreferring. The account thus analyzes a negative existential by means of another negative existential, generating an infinite regress with the same problem arising at each stage: If α is a thoroughly nonreferring name, how can ⌜There is no proposition that α is bald⌝ express anything at all, let alone something true (let alone a necessary truth)? To give an analogy, a proposal to analyze (4α) as ⌜Either {α} is empty or it does not exist⌝ yields no solution to the problem of how (4α) can express anything true. Even if the analysans has the right truth conditions (the first disjunct may be

---

[38] Babinet hypothesized Vulcan for reasons different than Le Verrier's. See Warren Zachary Watson, *An Historical Analysis of the Theoretical Solutions to the Problem of the Perihelion of Mercury* (doctoral dissertation, Ann Arbor, Mich.: University Microfilms, 1969), pp. viii, 92–94; and N. T. Roseveare, *Mercury's Perihelion: From Le Verrier to Einstein* (Oxford University Press, 1982), at pp. 24–27. (Thanks to Alan Berger and Sidney Morgenbesser for bibliographical assistance. I also researched the Vulcan hypothesis on the Internet. When I moved to save material to a new file to be named 'Vulcan', the program responded as usual, only this time signaling a momentous occasion: **Vulcan doesn't exist. Create? Y or N.**)

true if α is an improper definite description, the second is true if α is a nonreferring simple term), it also invokes a disjunct that is of the form of (4α) itself, and it leaves unsolved the mystery of how either disjunct can express anything if α is a thoroughly nonreferring name.[39]

There is more. On the account proposed by Kaplan, Kripke, and van Inwagen, object-fictional sentences, like 'Sherlock Holmes plays the violin', have no genuine semantic content in their original use. This renders the meaningfulness of true meta-fictional sentences like 'According to the *Sherlock Holmes* stories, Holmes plays the violin' problematic and mysterious. (See note 37.) On Kripke's account, it is true that according to the stories Holmes$_1$ plays the violin, and that on Le Verrier's theory Vulcan$_1$ influences Mercury's orbit. But how can this be if there is no proposition that Holmes$_1$ plays the violin and no proposition that Vulcan$_1$ influences Mercury? What is it that is the case according to the stories or the theory? How can Le Verrier have believed something that is nothing at all? If object-fictional sentences like 'Holmes$_1$ plays the violin' express nothing and only pretend to express things, how can they be true with respect (or "according") to the fiction, and how can meta-fictional sentences involving object-fictional subordinate clauses express anything at all, let alone something true?

More puzzling still are such cross-realm statements as 'Sherlock Holmes was cleverer than Bertrand Russell', and even worse, 'Sherlock Holmes was cleverer than Hercule Poirot'. The account as it stands seems to invoke some sort of intensional use of 'Sherlock Holmes', whereby the name is not only ambiguous between 'Holmes$_1$' and 'Holmes$_2$', but also accompanying the former use is something like an *ungerade* use, arising in constructions like 'According to the stories, Holmes$_1$ plays the violin', on which the name refers to a particular concept—presumably something like: *the brilliant detective who performed such-and-such exploits*. Kripke acknowledges this, calling it a "special sort of quasi-intensional use." The account thus ultimately involves an intensional apparatus. Indeed, it appears to involve industrial strength intensional machinery of a sort that is spurned by direct-reference theory, and by the very account itself. Further, the intensionality seems to get matters wrong. First, it seems to give us after all a proposition that Holmes$_1$ plays the violin, a proposition that Vulcan$_1$ influences Mercury, etc.—those things that are the case (or not) according to stories or believed by the theorist. Worse, depending on how the *ungerade* use of 'Holmes$_1$' is explained, it could turn out that if there were someone with many of the attributes described

---

[39]As Kripke intends the construction $\ulcorner$There is no such thing as $\alpha\urcorner$, it seems close in meaning to (8α). In our problem case, α is 'the proposition that Holmes$_1$ exists'. Since the 'that' prefix is itself a device for sense-quotation (see note 17), 'Holmes$_1$' would thus occur in a doubly *ungerade* context. It may be, therefore, that Kripke's intensional-ascent theory presupposes (or otherwise requires) a thesis that proper names have a Fregean *ungerade Sinn*, or *indirect sense*, which typically determines the name's referent, the latter functioning as both customary content and customary referent, but which in the case of a thoroughly nonreferring name determines noting. This would provide a reason for intensional ascent; one hits pay dirt by climbing above customary content. Kripke's theory would then involve Fregean intensional machinery that direct reference scrupulously avoids and Millianism altogether prohibits.

in the *Sherlock Holmes* stories, including various exploits much like those recounted, then there would be *true* propositions that Holmes$_1$ existed, that he played the violin, etc. It could even turn out that if by an extraordinary coincidence there was *in fact* some detective who was very Holmesesque, then even though Holmes$_2$ was purely fictional and not based in any way on this real person, there *are* nevertheless true propositions that Holmes$_1$ existed, played the violin, etc. The theory threatens to entail that the question of Holmes's authenticity (in the intended sense) would be settled affirmatively by the discovery of someone who was significantly Holmesesque, even if this person was otherwise unconnected to Conan Doyle. If the theory has consequences like these, then it directly contradicts the compelling passage of Kripke's quoted above, if not also itself. Kripke expresses misgivings about the theory, acknowledging that the required "quasi-intensional" use of a name from fiction needs explanation.[40]

V

One may well demur from these tenets of Kripke's otherwise compelling account. One need not claim, as Kripke does, that a name like 'Sherlock Holmes' is ambiguous. In particular, there is no obvious necessity to posit a use of the name by

---

[40] Cf. Gareth Evans, *The Varieties of Reference*, J. McDowell, ed. (Oxford University Press, 1982), at pp. 349–352. See also note 2 above. The kind of intensionality required on Kripke's account is not merely pragmatic in nature. Taking account of note 39, the account may be steeped in intensionality. The danger of entailing such consequences as those noted is very real. The theory of fiction in Lewis, *op. cit.*, is similar to Kripke's in requiring something like an *ungerade* use for thoroughly nonreferring names from fiction. Lewis embraces the conclusion that "the sense of 'Sherlock Holmes' as we use it is such that, for any world w where the Holmes stories are told as known fact rather than fiction, the name denotes at w whichever inhabitant of w it is who there plays the role of Holmes" (p. 267 of his *Philosophical Papers, I*). A similar conclusion is also reached in Robert Stalnaker, "Assertion," P. Cole, ed., *Syntax and Semantics, 9: Semantics* (New York: Academic Press, 1978), pp. 315–332, at 329–331. These conclusions directly contradict Kripke's account of proper names as rigid designators. In the first of the Locke Lectures, Kripke argues that uniquely being Holmesesque is not sufficient to be Holmes. Further, Kripke also argues there that the phenomenon of fiction cannot yield considerations against this or that particular philosophico-semantic theory of names, since it is part of the fiction's pretense, for the theorist, that the theory's "criteria for naming, whatever they are, are satisfied." Why should this not extend to the thesis, from direct-reference theory, that names lack Kripke's hypothesized "quasi-intensional use"?

Donnellan, *op. cit.*, regards negative existentials as unlike other object-fictional sentences, though his solution differs significantly from Kripke's and is designed to avoid intensionality. Donnellan provides a criterion whereby if α and β are distinct names from fiction, then (in effect) the corresponding true negative existentials, taken in the sense of $\lceil \alpha_1$ does not exist$\rceil$ and $\lceil \beta_1$ does not exist$\rceil$ as literally true statements about reality, express the same proposition if and only if α_2 and β_2 name the same fictional character. (I have taken enormous liberties in formulating Donnellan's criterion in terms of Kripke's apparatus, but I believe I do not do any serious injustice.) This proposal fails to provide the proposition expressed. In fact, Donnellan concedes that "we cannot . . . preserve a clear notion of what proposition is expressed for existence statements involving proper names" (p. 29; see note 19 above). This fails to solve the original problem, which is even more pressing for Donnellan. How can such sentences be said to "express the same proposition" when by his lights neither sentence clearly expresses any proposition at all? Cf. note 29.

Conan Doyle and his readers that is nonreferring (in any sense) and somehow prior to its use as a name for the fictional character and upon which the latter use is parasitic. There is first a general methodological consideration. Once fictional characters have been countenanced as real entities, why hold onto an alleged use of their names that fails to refer to them? It is like buying a luxurious Italian sports car only to keep it garaged. I do not advocate driving recklessly, but I do advise that having paid for the car one should permit oneself to drive it, at least on special occasions.

There is a more decisive consideration. The alleged use of 'Sherlock Holmes' on which it is thoroughly nonreferring was supposed to be a pretend use, not a real one. In writing the *Holmes* stories, Conan Doyle did not genuinely use the name at all, at least not as a name for a man. He merely pretended to. Of course, Conan Doyle wrote the name down as part of sentences in the course of writing the *Holmes* stories. In that sense he used the name. This is like the use that stage or film actors make of sentences when reciting their lines during the performance of a play or the filming of a movie. It is not a use whereby the one speaking commits him/herself to the propositions expressed. Even when writing 'London' or 'Scotland Yard' in a *Holmes* story, Conan Doyle was not in any robust sense using these names to refer. As J. O. Urmson notes, when Jane Austen, in writing a novel, writes a sentence beginning with a fictional character's name,

> [i]t is not that there is a reference to a fictional object, nor is there the use of a referring expression which fails to secure reference (as when one says "That man over there is tall" when there is no man over there). Jane Austen writes a sentence which has the form of an assertion beginning with a reference, but is in fact neither asserting nor referring; therefore she is not referring to any character, fictional or otherwise, nor does she fail to secure reference, except in the jejune sense in which if I sneeze or open a door I fail to secure reference. Nothing would have counted on this occasion as securing reference, and to suppose it could is to be under the impression that Miss Austen was writing history. . . . I do not say that one cannot refer to a fictional character, but that Miss Austen did not on the occasion under discussion.
>
> What I am saying is that making up fiction is not a case of stating, or asserting, or propounding a proposition and includes no acts such as referring. ("Fiction," *American Philosophical Quarterly*, 13, 2 (April 1976), pp. 153–157 at p. 155)

The pretend use of 'Sherlock Holmes' by Conan Doyle does not have to be regarded as generating a use of the name on which it is nonreferring. *Pace* Kaplan, Kripke, Russell, and traditional philosophy, it *should* not be so regarded. A name semantically refers to this or that individual only relative to a particular kind of use, a particular purpose for which the name was introduced. One might go so far as to say that a pretend use by itself does not even give rise to a real name at all, any more than it gives birth to a real detective. This may be somewhat overstated, but its spirit and flavor is not.[41] Even if one regards a name as something that

---

[41] C. J. F. Williams, in *What Is Existence?* (Oxford University Press, 1981), argues that 'Sherlock Holmes' is not a proper name (pp. 251–255). This is what Kaplan ought to have said, but he did not. See his "Words," *Proceedings of the Aristotelian Society*, 64 (1990), pp. 93–119, especially section II, "What Are Names?" at pp. 110–119.

exists independently of its introduction into language (as is my inclination), it is a confusion to think of a name as referring, or not referring, other than as doing so *on* a particular use. On this view, a common name like 'Adam Smith' refers to different individuals on different uses. The problem with saying that 'Sherlock Holmes' is nonreferring on Conan Doyle's use is that in merely pretending that the name had a particular use, no real use was yet attached to the name on which it may be said to refer or not to refer.

The matter should be viewed instead as follows: Conan Doyle one fine day set about to tell a story. In the process he created a fictional character as the protagonist, and other fictional characters as well, each playing a certain role in the story. These characters, like the story itself, are man-made abstract artifacts, born of Conan Doyle's fertile imagination. The name 'Sherlock Holmes' was originally coined by Conan Doyle in writing the story (and subsequently understood by readers reading the *Holmes* stories) as the fictional name for the protagonist. That thing—in fact merely an abstract artifact—is *according to the story* a man by the name of 'Sherlock Holmes'. In telling the story, Conan Doyle pretends to use the name to refer to its fictional referent (and to use 'Scotland Yard' to refer to Scotland Yard)—or rather, he pretends to be Dr. Watson using 'Sherlock Holmes', much like an actor portraying Dr. Watson on stage. But he does not really so use the name; 'Sherlock Holmes' so far does not really have any such use, or even any related use (ignoring unrelated uses it coincidentally might have had). At a later stage, use of the name is imported from the fiction into reality, to name *the very same thing* that it is the name of according to the story. That thing—now the real as well as the fictional bearer of the name—is according to the story a human being who is a brilliant detective, and in reality an artifactual abstract entity created by Conan Doyle.

The use of 'Sherlock Holmes' represented by 'Holmes$_2$', as the name for what is in reality an abstract artifact, is the same use it has according to the *Holmes* stories, except that according to the stories, that use is one on which it refers to a man. The alleged thoroughly nonreferring use of 'Sherlock Holmes' by Conan Doyle, as a pretend name for a man, is a myth. Contrary to Kaplan, Kripke, et al., there is no literal use of 'Sherlock Holmes' that corresponds to 'Holmes$_1$'—or at least I know of no convincing reason to suppose that there is one. One might say (in the spirit of the van Inwagen–Kripke theory) that there is a mythical use represented by 'Holmes$_1$', an allegedly thoroughly nonreferring use that pretends to name a brilliant detective who performed such-and-such exploits. This kind of use is fictitious in the same way that Sherlock Holmes himself is, no more a genuine use than a fictional detective is a genuine detective. Instead there is at first only the pretense of a use, including the pretense that the name refers to a brilliant detective, a human being, on that use. Later the name is given a genuine use, on which it names the very same entity that it named according to the pretense, though the pretense that this entity is a human being has been dropped.

Literary scholars discussing the *Holmes* stories with all seriousness may utter the name 'Sherlock Holmes' as if to import its pretend use as the name of a man into genuine discourse—as when a Holmes "biographer" says, "Based on the evidence, Holmes was not completely asexual." Even then, the scholars are merely pretending to use the name as a name for a man. There is no flesh-and-blood man for the name to name, and the scholars know that.[42] If they are genuinely using the name, they are using it as a name for the fictional character. The only genuine, nonpretend use that we ever give the name—of which I feel confident—is as a name for the character. And that use, as a name for that very thing, is the very use it has in the story—though according to the story, that very thing is a human being and not an abstract entity. Conan Doyle may have used the name for a period even before the character was fully developed. Even so, this would not clearly be a genuine use of the name on which it was altogether non-referring. For it is at least arguable that if that was a genuine use by Conan Doyle, then it was very weakly nonreferring, in the sense used earlier. There would soon exist a fictional character to which *that* use of the name already referred.[43] In the same way, expectant parents may begin to use a name already decided upon even before the actual birth, perhaps even before conception, and readers of Kaplan may already use the name 'Newman-1' to refer. Once the anticipated referent arrives on the scene, to use the name exactly as before is to use it with reference to that thing. At that point, to use the name in a way that it fails to refer would be to give it a new use.

It seems at least as reasonable as Kripke's account to claim instead that once the name 'Sherlock Holmes' has been imported into genuine discourse, Conan Doyle's sentences involving the name express singular propositions about his character. One might even identify the fiction with a sequence of propositions, about both fictional and nonfictional things (e.g., Scotland Yard). To say this is not to say that Conan Doyle asserted those propositions. He did not—at least not in any sense of 'assert' that involves a commitment to one's assertions. He merely pretended to be Dr. Watson asserting those propositions. In so doing, Conan Doyle pretended (and his readers pretend) that the propositions are true propositions about a real man, not untrue propositions about an abstract artifact. That is exactly what it is to pretend to assert those propositions. To assert a proposition, in this sense, is in part to commit oneself to its truth; so to pretend to assert a

---

[42]What about a foggy headed literary theorist who maintains, as a sophomoric anti-realist or Meinongian philosophical view (or quasi-philosophical view), that Sherlock Holmes is in some sense no less flesh-and-blood than Conan Doyle? The more bizarre is someone's philosophical perspective, the more difficult it is to interpret his/her discourse correctly. Such a case might be assimilated to that of myths. See below.

[43]On the view I am proposing there is a sense in which a fictional character is prior to the fiction in which the character occurs. By contrast, Kripke believes that a fictional character does not come into existence until the final draft of the fiction is published. This severe restriction almost certainly does not accord with the way fiction writers see themselves or their characters. Even if it is correct, it does not follow that while writing a fiction, the author is using the name in such a way that it is thoroughly nonreferring. It is arguable that the name already refers to the fledgling abstract artifact that does not yet exist. There is not already, nor will there ever be, any genuine use of the name as the name of a human being; that kind of use is make-believe.

proposition is to pretend to commit oneself to its truth. And the propositions in question entail that Holmes was not an abstract entity but a flesh-and-blood detective. Taken literally, they are untrue.[44]

This is not quite an offer one can't refuse. Some have reacted to this proposal with a vague feeling—or a definite feeling—that I have conscripted fictional characters to perform a service for which they were not postulated and are not suited. Do I mean to say that *The Hound of the Baskervilles* consists entirely of a sequence of mostly false propositions about mostly abstract entities? Is mine a view on which the essence of fiction is to pretend that abstract entities are living, breathing people? These misgivings stem from a misunderstanding of the nature of fiction and its population. The characters that populate fiction are created precisely to perform the service of being depicted as people by the fictions in which they occur. Do not fixate on the fact that fictional characters are abstract entities. Think instead of the various *roles* that a director might cast in a stage or screen production of a particular piece of fiction. Now think of the corresponding characters as the components of the fiction that *play* or *occupy* those roles in the fiction. It is no accident that one says of an actor in a dramatic production that he/she is playing a "part." The characters of a fiction—the occupants of roles in the fiction—are in some real sense *parts* of the fiction itself. Sometimes, for example in historical fiction, what fictionally plays a particular role is a real person or thing. In other cases, what plays a particular role is the brainchild of the storyteller. In such cases, the role player is a *wholly* fictional character, or what I (following Kripke) have been calling simply a "fictional character." Whether a real person or wholly fictional, the character is that which according to the fiction takes part in certain events, performs certain actions, undergoes certain changes, says certain things, thinks certain thoughts. An actor performing in the role of Sherlock Holmes portrays Holmes$_2$; it is incorrect, indeed it is literally nonsense, to say that he portrays Holmes$_1$, if 'Holmes$_1$' is thoroughly nonreferring.

It is of the very essence of a fictional character to be depicted in the fiction as the person who takes part in such-and-such events, performs such-and-such actions, thinks such-and-such thoughts. Being so depicted is the character's *raison d'être*. As Clark Gable was born to play Rhett Butler in Margaret Mitchell's *Gone with the Wind*, that character was born to be the romantic leading man of that fiction. Mario Puzo's character of Don Corleone is as well suited to be the charismatic patriarch of *The Godfather* as Marlon Brando was to portray the character on film. Except even more so. The character was also portrayed completely convincingly by Robert De Niro. But only that character, and no other, is appropriate to the patriarch role in Puzo's crime saga. Likewise, the butler in Kazuo Ishiguro's *The Remains of the Day* would have been completely inappropriate, in more ways than one, as the

---

[44] See note 37. If my view is correct, then van Inwagen's use of the word 'ascribe' in saying that a fiction ascribes a particular property to a particular fictional character may be understood (apparently contrary to van Inwagen's intent) quite literally, in its standard English meaning.

protagonist of Ian Fleming's *James Bond* novels. It is of the essence of Fleming's character precisely to be the character depicted in the dashing and debonair 007 role in the *James Bond* stories—and not merely in the sense that being depicted thus is both a necessary and a sufficient condition for being the character of Bond in any metaphysically possible world. Rather, this is the condition that defines the character; being the thing so depicted in those stories characterizes exactly *what* the character of James Bond *is*.

In a sense, my view is the exact opposite of the traditional view expressed in Russell's pronouncement that "it is of the very essence of fiction that only the thoughts, feelings, etc., in Shakespeare and his readers are real, and that there is not, in addition to them, an objective Hamlet." To Russell's pronouncement there is Hamlet's own retort: "There are more things in heaven and earth, Horatio, Than are dreamt of in your philosophy." It is of the very essence of Shakespeare's *Hamlet* that there is indeed an object that is Hamlet. I am not urging that we countenance a person who is Hamlet$_1$ and who contemplated suicide according to the classic play but who does not exist. There is no sense in which there is any such person. The objective Hamlet is Hamlet$_2$—what plays the title role in the Bard's drama—and hence not a human being at all but a part of fiction, merely depicted there as anguished and suicidal. It is with the most robust sense of reality prescribed by the Metaphysician that I should urge recognition of this fictionally troubled soul.[45]

It is an offer one shouldn't refuse lightly. Unlike Kripke's theory, a treatment of the sentences of the *Sherlock Holmes* stories on which they literally make reference (although their author may not) to the fictional character, and literally express things about that character (mostly false), yields a straightforward account—what I believe is the correct account—of the meaningfulness and apparent truth of object-fictional sentences like 'Sherlock Holmes plays the violin', and thereby also of the meaning and truth of meta-fictional sentences like 'According to the *Holmes* stories, Holmes plays the violin'. Following Kripke's lead in the possible-world semantics for modality, we say that 'Sherlock Holmes' is a rigid designator, referring to the fictional character both *with respect to the real world* and *with respect to the fiction*. The object-fictional sentence is not true with respect to the real world, since abstract entities make terrible musicians. But it is true with respect to the fiction—or true "in the world of the fiction"—by virtue of being entailed by the propositions, themselves about fictional characters, that comprise the fiction, taken together with

---

[45] In reading a piece of fiction, do we pretend that an abstract entity is a prince of Denmark (or a brilliant detective, etc.)? The question is legitimate. But it plays on the distinction between *de dicto* and *de re*. Taken *de dicto*, of course not; taken *de re*, exactly. That abstract entities are human beings is not something we pretend, but there are abstract entities that we pretend are human beings. Seen in the proper light, this is no stranger than pretending that Marlon Brando is Don Corleone. (It is not nearly so strange as Brando portraying a character in *The Freshman* who, in the story, is the real person on whom the character Marlon Brando portrayed in *The Godfather* was modelled).

supplementary propositions concerning such things as the ordinary physical-causal structure of the world, usual societal customs, etc., that are assumed as the background against which the fiction unfolds.[46] When we speak within the fiction, we pretend that truth with respect to the fiction is truth *simpliciter,* hence that Holmes (=Holmes$_2$) was a human being, a brilliant detective who plays the violin, and so on. Or what is virtually functionally equivalent, we use object-fictional sentences as shorthand for meta-fictional variants. The meta-fictional ⌜According to fiction *f,φ*⌝ is true with respect to the real world if and only if $φ$ is true with respect to the mentioned fiction. In effect, the meta-fictional sentence receives a Fregean treatment on which the object-fictional subordinate clause has *ungerade* reference, referring to a (typically false) proposition about a fictional character. In all our genuine discourse about Holmes, we use the name in the 'Holmes$_2$,' way. One may feign using 'Sherlock Holmes' as the name of a man, but this is only a pretend use. To say that according to the stories Holmes$_1$ plays the violin is to say nothing; what is true according to the stories is that Holmes$_2$ plays the violin.[47]

Consider again sentence (0), or better yet, 'Sherlock Holmes does not really exist; he is only a fictional character'. Taken literally, this sentence expresses the near contradiction that Holmes$_2$ is a fictional character that does not exist. It was suggested above that the existence predicate may instead be given a Pickwickian interpretation on which it means something like: *is the very sort of entity depicted.* This suggestion, however, is questionable. In many cases, Russell's analysis (0′) seems closer to the facts. In uttering (0), the speaker may

---

[46]Cf. John Heintz, "Reference and Inference in Fiction," *Poetics,* 8, 1/2 (April 1979), pp. 85–99. Where the fiction is inconsistent, the relevant notion of entailment may have to be non-standard. Also, the notion may have to be restricted to a *trivial* sort of entailment—on pain of counting arcane and even as yet unproved mathematical theorems true with respect to fiction. Cf. Lewis, *op. cit.,* at pp. 274–278 of his *Philosophical Papers, I.*

[47]Philosophers have sometimes neglected to distinguish among different possible readings of an object-fictional sentence—or equivalently, between literal and extended (fictional) senses of 'true'. See, for example, Richard L. Cartwright, in "Negative Existentials," *Journal of Philosophy,* 57 (1960), pp. 629–639; and Jaakko Hintikka, "*Cogito Ergo Sum:* Inference or Performance," *The Philosophical Review,* 71 (January 1962), pp. 3–32.

When we use an object-fictional sentence $φ$ as shorthand for something meta-fictional, what is the longhand form? Perhaps ⌜There is a fiction according to which $φ$⌝, perhaps ⌜according to the fiction in which he/she/it/they is a character, $φ$⌝, perhaps ⌜According to *that* fiction, $φ$⌝, perhaps something else. Recognizing that we speak of fictional characters in these ways may to some extent obviate the need to posit a nonliteral, extended sense for all predicates. On the other hand, something like Kripke's theory of extended senses may lie behind the use of gendered pronouns ('he') to refer to fictional people even in discourse about reality.

Perhaps the most difficult sentences to account for are those that assert cross-realm relations. Following Russell's analysis of thinking someone's yacht larger than it is, 'Sherlock Holmes was cleverer than Bertrand Russell' may be taken to mean that the cleverness that Holmes$_2$ had according to the stories is greater than the cleverness that Russell had. Cf. my *Reference and Essence* (Princeton University Press and Blackwell, 1981), at pp. 116–135, and especially 147*n.*

intend not merely to characterize Holmes$_2$, but to deny the *existence* of the eccentric detective. It may have been this sort of consideration that led Kripke to posit an ambiguity, and in particular a use of the name in the alleged manner of 'Holmes$_1$', a pretend-referring-but-really-nonreferring use on which the 'Holmes$_2$' use is parasitic (and which generates an intensional *ungerade* use). Kripke's posit, I believe, is also off target. There is a reasonable alternative. We sometimes use ordinary names, especially names of famous people, in various descriptive ways, as when it is said that so-and-so is a Napoleon, or a Nixon, another Hitler, no Jack Kennedy, or even (to segue into the fictional realm) a Romeo, an Uncle Tom, quixotic, Pickwickian, etc. I submit that, especially in singular existential statements, we sometimes use the name of a fictional character in a similar way. We may use 'Sherlock Holmes', for example, to mean something like: *Holmes more or less as he is actually depicted in the stories*, or *Holmes replete with these attributes [the principally salient ones ascribed to Holmes in the stories]*, or best, *the person who is both Holmes and Holmesesque*. In uttering (0), one would then mean that the Holmes of fiction, Holmes as depicted, does not exist in reality, that there is in reality no such person—no *such* person, no person who is both Holmes$_2$ and sufficiently like *that* (as depicted in fiction).

Since this interpretation requires a reinterpretation of the name, it might be more correct to say that the speaker expresses this proposition than to say that (0) itself does. This is not a use of 'Holmes' as a thoroughly nonreferring name, but as a kind of description that invokes the name of the fictional character. In short, the name is used *a là* Russell as a disguised improper definite description. It is very probably a nonliteral, Pickwickian use of the name. It is certainly a nonstandard use, one that is parasitic on the name's more fundamental use as a name for the fictional character, not the other way around. It need not trouble the direct-reference theorist. The disguised-description use is directly based upon, and makes its first appearance in language only after, the standard use in the manner of 'Holmes$_2$' as (in Russell's words) a "genuine name in the strict logical sense." If an artificial expression is wanted as a synonym for this descriptive use, something clearly distinguished from both 'Holmes$_2$' (which I claim represents the standard, literal use of the name) and 'Holmes$_1$' (which represents a mythical use, no genuine use at all) is called for. Let us say that someone is a *Holmesesque-Holmes$_2$* if he is Holmes$_2$ and sufficiently like he is depicted to be, in the sense that he has relevantly many of the noteworthy attributes that Holmes$_2$ has according to the stories. Perhaps the most significant of these is the attribute of being a person (or at least personlike) and not an abstract artifact. Following Russell, to say that *the* Holmesesque-Holmes$_2$ does not exist is to say that nothing is uniquely both Holmes$_2$ and Holmesesque—equivalently (not synonymously), that Holmes$_2$ is not Holmesesque. It is an empirical question whether Holmes$_2$—the character of which Conan Doyle wrote—was in reality like *that*, such-and-such a person, to any degree. The question of Holmes's existence *in this sense* is answered not by seeking whether someone or other was Holmesesque, but by investigating the literary activities of Conan Doyle.[48]

These various considerations, and related ones, weigh heavily in favor of account of names from fiction as unambiguous names for artifactual entities.[49] In its fundamental use that arises in connection with the fiction—and I am inclined to think, its only literal use—'Sherlock Holmes' univocally names a man-made artifact, the handiwork of Conan Doyle. Contra Russell, et al., names from fiction do not have a prior, more fundamental use. They do not yield true negative existentials with thoroughly nonreferring names.

VI

The account suggested here is extendable to sentences that are uttered in debunking myths, like 'Pegasus does not exist'. By 'myth' I shall mean any mistaken theory that has been held true. A mythical object is a hypothetical entity erroneously postulated by a theory. Like a fictional object, a mythical object is an abstract (non-physical, non-mental) entity created by the theory's inventor. The principal difference between myth and fiction is that a myth is believed whereas with fiction there is typically only a pretense.[50] An accidental storyteller, Le

---

[48]The notion of something being *sufficiently* like Holmes$_2$ is depicted may be to some extent interest-relative. Consequently, in some cases the truth value of an assertion made using (3α), with α a name from fiction, may vary with the operative interests. Some scholars tell us, while not believing in vampires, that Bram Stoker's character of Count Dracula really existed. (This aspect of the theory I am suggesting raises a complex hornets' nest of difficult issues. Far from disproving the theory, however, some of these issues may tend to provide confirmation of sorts.)

Kripke argues that the sentence 'Sherlock Holmes does not really exist; he is only a fictional character', properly interpreted, involves an equivocation whereby the name has its original nonreferring use and 'he' is a "pronoun of laziness" referring to the fictional character— so that the sentence means that the man Holmes$_1$ does not exist and the fictional character Holmes$_2$ is just that. Kripke also says that one should be able to assert what is meant in the first clause of the original sentence without mentioning Holmes$_2$ at all. This is precisely what I believe cannot be done. The original may even be paraphrased into 'Sherlock Holmes does not really exist and is only a fictional character'. On my alternative hypothesis, the speaker may mean something like: *The Holmesesque-Holmes$_2$ does not really exist; Holmes$_2$ is only a fictional character.* This is equivalent to: Holmes$_2$ is not Holmesesque but a fictional character. Besides avoiding the putative 'Holmes$_1$' use, my hypothesis preserves an anaphoric-like relation between pronoun and antecedent. (Other possibilities arise if Kripke's theory of extended senses for predicates is applied to 'Holmesesque.')

[49]In later work, and even in the same work cited *supra* in note 32, Kripke argued persuasively against positing ambiguities when an alternative, univocal hypothesis that explains the phenomena equally well is available. Cf. his "Speaker's Reference and Semantic Reference," in P. French, T. Uehling, and H. Wettstein, eds., *Contemporary Perspectives in the Philosophy of Language* (Minneapolis: University of Minnesota Press, 1979), pp. 6–27, especially 19.

[50]Donnellan says that myth is not analogous to fiction (*op. cit.*, at pp. 6–8). Almog agrees, and dismisses the idea of a mythical Vulcan (*op. cit.*, pp. 611, 618*n*13). I am convinced these philosophers are mistaken, and that this myth about myths has also led other philosophers astray. When storytellers tell stories and theorists hypothesize, fictional and mythical creatures abound. (An interesting possibility: Perhaps the myth invented by Babinet no longer exists, now that no one believes it. Can a myth, once it is disproved, continue to exist as merely an unbelieved theory? If not, then perhaps 'Vulcan' is nonreferring after all, though only very weakly.)

Verrier attempted in all sincerity to use 'Vulcan' to refer to a real planet. The attempt failed, but not for lack of a referent. Here as before, there is ample reason to doubt that 'Vulcan$_1$' represents a genuine use of the original name. Le Verrier held a theory according to which there is such a use, and he intended and believed himself to be so using the name. Had the theory been correct, there would have been such a use for the name. But the theory is false; it was all a mistake. Kripke says that in attempting to use the name, 19th century astronomers failed to refer to anything. But this verdict seems to ignore their unintended relationship to the mythical planet. One might just as well judge that the ancients who introduced 'Hesperus' as a name for the first star visible in the dusk sky, unaware that the "star" was in fact a planet, failed to name that planet. Nor had they inadvertently introduced two names, one for the planet and one thoroughly nonreferring. Plausibly, as the ancients unwittingly referred to a planet believing it to be a star, so Le Verrier may have unknowingly referred to Babinet's mythical planet, saying and believing so many false things about it (for example, that it affects Mercury's orbit). There may have been a period during which 'Vulcan' was misapplied to the mythical planet before such application became enshrined as the official, correct use. It does not follow that there is a prior, genuine use of the name on which it is thoroughly nonreferring. I know of no compelling reason to deny that Babinet introduced a single name 'Vulcan' ultimately with a univocal use as a name for his mythical planet.[51] One might say that 'Vulcan$_1$' represents a

---

Kripke extends his account in the natural way also to terms for objects in the world of appearance (e.g., a distant spec or dot), and to species names and other biological-kind terms from fiction and myth, like 'unicorn' and 'dragon'. The theory should be extended also to general terms like 'witch', 'wizard', etc. There is a mythical species designated by 'dragon', an abstract artifact, not a real species. Presumably, if K is the mythical species (or higher level taxonomic kind) of dragons, then there is a corresponding concept or property of being a beast of kind K, thus providing semantic content for the predicate 'is a dragon'. Kripke believes there is a prior use of the term, in the sense of 'dragon$_1$', which has no semantic content. But as before, on this point I find no persuasive reason to follow his lead.

Are there dragons? There are myths and fictions according to which there are dragons, for example the legend of Puff. Is Puff, then, a dragon? No, he is a fictional character—an abstract artifact and not a beast. Fictional dragons like Puff are not real dragons—though they may be said to be "dragons," if by saying that we mean that they are dragons in the story. (Cf. Kripke's hypothesized extended sense of 'plays the violin'.) Is it metaphysically possible for there to have been dragons in the literal (unextended) sense of the word? No; the mythical species K is not a real species, any more than Puff is a real beast, and the mythical species could not have been a species any more than Puff could have been a beast. It is essential to K that it not be a species. *A fortiori* there could not have been such beasts. The reasoning here is very different from that of Kripke's *Naming and Necessity*, at pp. 156–157, which emphasizes the alleged 'dragon$_1$' use (disputed here), on which 'There are dragons' allegedly expresses nothing (hence nothing that is possibly true).

The account of mythical objects as real abstract artifacts also yields a solution to P. T. Geach's famous problem about Hob's and Nob's hypothesized witch, from "Intentional Identity," *Journal of Philosophy*, 74, 20 (1967).

[51] I am assuming throughout that in introducing 'Vulcan', Babinet presupposed the existence of an intra-Mercurial planet to be so named. In some cases of reference fixing, the description employed may have what I call a *Bad mock referential*, or *Ugly*, use—i.e., reference is fixed by an implicit description not coreferential with the description explicitly used. See my "The Good, the Bad, and the Ugly," forthcoming in Paolo Leonardi's festschrift for Keith Donnellan. Cf. Kripke on 'Hesperus', in *Naming and Necessity*, at p. 80n34.

mythical use of the name. As with 'Holmes$_1$', this kind of use is no more a genuine use than a mythical planet is a genuine planet.

It is unclear whether there are significant limitations here, and if so, what they might be. Even Meinong's golden mountain and round square should probably be seen as real mythical objects. Meinong's golden mountain is an abstract entity that is neither golden nor a mountain but as real as Babinet's Vulcan. Real but neither round nor square, Meinong's round square is both round and square according to Meinong's erroneous theory. Should we not also admit and recognize such things as fabrications, figments of one's imagination, and flights of fancy as real abstract entities? Where does it all end?

In the kingdom of France.

If one adopts a very inclusive attitude toward such applicants for Existence as fictional characters, mythical planets, fabricated boyfriends, and flights of fancy, then one is hardly in a position to urge a restrictive admissions policy when it comes to nonreferring names. We know that France has no emperor at present. But we do not know this *a priori*. We could even be mistaken. It is not *a priori* impossible that a fanatic, with the help of an underground army and the unanimous approval of the United Nations, has just seized control of the French government and declared himself the new emperor. I hereby introduce the name 'Nappy' to refer to the new emperor of France, whoever that might be, if there is one, and to refer to nothing otherwise. Take note: I do not introduce 'Nappy' as a name for a particular fictional character that I just created. I am not storytelling and I am not pretending to use 'Nappy' as a name of a person. Nor do I subscribe to any theory to the effect that France now has an emperor. Rather I introduce 'Nappy' as a name for the actual present emperor of France, provided—contrary to my every expectation—that there presently is an emperor of France. Barring a fairly radical skepticism, we know that there is no such person as Nappy. Nappy is not a fictional character, not a mythical character, not a fabrication, not a flight of fancy. There is a very good reason why Nappy is none of these things. Not to put too fine a point on it, Nappy does not exist.

Or consider again the name 'Curly-0', which I introduced above for the merely possible bald man presently standing in Quine's doorway. There is no such merely possible man. But the name itself, so introduced, is real. I introduced it. And it does not refer. It would have been a mistake to suppose that there might have been someone to whom the name actually refers. But I made no such mistake in introducing the name; I knew I had not succeeded in singling out any particular possible individual. This much, then, is not a mistake: Curly-0 does not exist.

Why do the introductions of 'Nappy' and 'Curly-0' result in thoroughly non-referring names when Babinet's introduction of 'Vulcan' results in a name for an existing abstract artifact? Because in inventing his theory, Babinet inadvertently invented a mythical planet, and though Babinet intended to target an independently existing planet, his referential arrow eventually struck the mythical object—not in exactly the same manner as the ancients' arrow that struck Venus despite its not being a star, but close. To the allegation that I have invented a fictional emperor of France, I plead Not Guilty. One should not suppose that to every improper definite description one might conjure up there corresponds a fiction, or mini-fiction, in which the description is proper. Even pulp fiction is not that easy to write.[52]

My contention has not been that there are no true sentences of the form (4α) with α a thoroughly nonreferring name. My point, rather, is that they are rare—and bizarre. The examples are not like an utterance of 'Sherlock Holmes does not really exist' to assert that Holmes$_2$ in reality is not sufficiently like the way he is depicted. The examples are also dissimilar from 'Socrates does not exist', 'Newman-1 does not exist', 'Noman does not exist', and even '{Noman-0, Nothan-0} does not exist'. In these other negative existentials, there is some sense in which the subject term refers to a definite nonexistent thing: a past, future, merely possible, or impossible object. The negative existentials say of these definite things, correctly, that they do not exist. By contrast, 'Nappy does not exist' and 'Curly-0 does not exist' have a completely different flavor and are true on altogether different grounds: In no sense is there a definite nonexistent thing referred to. Do these two sentences, then, deny existence of different things? If so, what things? How do they differ? 'Curly-0' is a different name from 'Nappy', but Curly-0 is not a different *thing* from Nappy. They are not *things* at all; they are nothing. Or perhaps I should say, there is no such thing as Curly-0, and likewise Nappy. As much as to say that Curly-0 and Nappy do not exist. That there are no such things is true, but what exactly is it?

One might be tempted to suppose that 'Nappy does not exist' expresses the proposition that there is no unique present emperor of France. This is essentially the approach of Russell. It directly conflicts with the theory of direct reference (entailing, for example, that 'Nappy' is not a rigid nondesignator), and has been discredited by the arguments supporting that theory. So with the Fregean semantic-ascent and intensional-ascent approaches to singular existentials. I shun the heavy-handed intensionality of these approaches, as well as the unexplained intensional machinery of Kripke's proposal to interpret 'Nappy does not exist' as a paraphrase of 'There is no true proposition that Nappy exists'. There is here a new homework problem.

Consider the slightly simpler issue of the meanings of sentences of the form of (1α) with α a thoroughly nonreferring name. Does 'Nappy is bald' express anything? Does 'Curly-0 is bald?' I believe the answer is clearly that they do. They are not mere

---

[52] But see note 43. I introduced 'Holmes$_1$' as a name having the thoroughly nonreferring use that the name 'Sherlock Holmes' originally has according to Kripke's theory. That alleged use is mythical. My introduction of the name thus misfired; no genuine use was attached to the name on which it may be said either to refer or not to refer. I might have fixed the reference of a new name, say 'Holmes$_3$' (not a disguised description), by the description 'the Holmesesque-Holmes$_2$'. Analogously, I might have introduced a name 'Vulcan$_3$' as a name for the planet, if there is one, whose gravitational force (rather than general relativity) correctly explains the irregularities in Mercury's orbit, and nonreferring otherwise. I would exploit a certain myth to obtain the reference-fixing description, but would have introduced the name in such a way that it does not refer instead to Babinet's mythical planet. Had I done this, authentic true negative existentials with thoroughly nonreferring names would have been generated.

strings of nonsense syllables. They have translations—very literal translations—into most natural languages (by resorting to use of the very names 'Nappy' and 'Curly-0'). Such translations preserve *something*. What? Not the proposition expressed, for these sentences express no proposition, or at least none that is a candidate for being true or false. I would propose that they be seen instead as expressing something severely disabled, the partially formed product of a failed attempt to construct a true-or-false proposition, something whose cognitive and semantic function is that of a truth-valued proposition but which is unable to fulfil its function for lack of an essential component. Think of the nondefective sentence 'Marlon Brando is bald' as expressing its semantic content in the manner of: 'This object is bald: Marlon Brando'. Then 'Nappy is bald' expresses the semantic content of 'This object is bald: __'. 'Curly-0 is bald' expresses the very same thing. Let us call it a *structurally challenged proposition*. It may be thought of for the present purpose as an ordered pair, or rather a would-be ordered pair, whose second element is the concept or property of baldness and whose first element is nothing whatsoever.[53]

Granted sufficient leeway, expressions like 'the proposition that Nappy is bald' and 'that Curly-0 is bald' may be taken to refer to the structurally challenged proposition expressed in common by their complement clauses. This is one crucial respect in which the present view differs from that of Kripke, who contends that 'Nappy is bald' and 'Curly-0 is bald' express nothing, and that their corresponding 'that' clauses are consequently thoroughly nonreferring. (See note 19.) On the view I am proposing, although Nappy does not exist, the structurally challenged proposition that Nappy is bald exists, and is identical to the structurally challenged proposition that Curly-0 is bald. Not all sentences of the form (1α) with α a nonreferring name or improper definite description express this structurally challenged

---

[53]The set-theoretic representation can be made formally precise in an intuitive way (for example by invoking partial functions). Cf. my discussion of *open propositions* in *Frege's Puzzle*, at pp. 155–156n. (The alternative terminology of 'structurally impaired proposition' is implicitly structurist, hence contrary to the inclusive spirit of the present essay, which celebrates cognitive structural diversity. I also resist the temptation to use the abbreviation '*SC*-proposition', for fear it might be mistaken as shorthand for 'Southern California proposition' and the idea the idea then summarily dismissed.)

It is reported in Almog, *op. cit.*, p. 618n15, that Kaplan, in an unpublished 1973 lecture commenting on Kripke, proposed that 'Vulcan does not exist' expresses a true "gappy proposition." Kaplan briefly mentions a similar idea in "Demonstratives," in J. Almog, J. Perry, and H. Wettstein, eds., *Themes from Kaplan* (Oxford University Press, 1989), pp. 481–563, at 496n23. Contrary to the view imputed to Kaplan, 'Vulcan does not$_C$ exist', taken literally, expresses on my view a false structurally *un*challenged singular proposition about the mythical planet (and my frequently be understood instead as expressing the true proposition that there is no Vulcanesque Vulcan$_2$).

Plantinga, in "On Existentialism," *Philosophical Studies*, 44 (1983), pp. 1–20, at 9, argues as part of a defense of serious actualism (note 29 above) that the singular proposition about William F. Buckley that he is wise might be regarded as existing but "ill-formed or even maimed" in a possible world in which Buckley does not exist. This is decidedly different from my view. The only defect suffered by Soc is that it does not exist; it is neither "ill-formed" nor "maimed." It is even true. In a possible world in which Buckley does not exist the proposition that he is wise is neither existent nor true, but it does not face the structural challenges of singular propositions about Nappy and Curly-0.

proposition. 'Socrates is bald' expresses that Socrates is bald, a proposition that does not exist but once did. 'Newman-1 is bald' expresses a different proposition, one that will exist but does not yet. 'Noman-0 is bald' expresses a proposition that might have existed but never will, and '{Nothan-0, Nathan Salmon} is bald' (properly interpreted) a proposition that could never exist. 'Sherlock Holmes is bald' and (1) express existing propositions that are untrue. None of these propositions are structurally challenged in the manner of ⟨___, baldness⟩. But all sentences of the form (1α) with α a thoroughly nonreferring name express this same structurally challenged proposition, *this one is bald:*   . None of these various propositions, structurally challenged and not, are true. I shall assume here that atomic structurally challenged propositions cannot be either true or false.[54]

Though both express the same structurally challenged proposition, 'Nappy is bald' and 'Curly-0 is bald' present their common semantic content to the mind of the reader in different ways. One presents it in the manner of 'This object is bald: the present emperor of France', the other in the manner of 'This object is bald: the possible bald man presently in Quine's doorway'. The reader takes the structurally challenged proposition differently, depending in this case on the actual words used to express it.[55] I have argued in previous work that the way in which a reader takes a given proposition has no bearing on semantics; what matters as far as semantics goes is the literal meaning of the sentence and what propositions are thereby semantically expressed. Though the way in which a proposition is taken is not semantics, it bears on cognitive psychology and plays an extremely important role in pragmatics, on which I have spoken elsewhere at some length. Structurally challenged propositions do not differ from their unchallenged cousins in this respect.[56]

---

[54] Frege's Principle of Compositionality for Reference, as he understood it, required that the usual truth-functional connectives observe their Kleene weak three-valued truth tables, on which any truth-functional compound with a non-truth-valued component is itself without truth value regardless of the truth values of the other components. Whereas Frege's argument for this may seem inconclusive at best, an analogous argument is more persuasive as regards truth-functional compounds with structurally challenged components. At the very least, atomic structurally challenged propositions do seem, intuitively, to lack the resources necessary to achieve truth value. If it is incorrect to say that Nappy is bald, it is equally incorrect to say that Nappy is not$_c$ bald, and for the very same reason. Mimicking Russell, if we enumerated the things that are bald, and then the things that are not bald, we should not find Nappy in either list. Even Russell, who loved truth value (and abhorred a synthesis), would probably have withheld falsity as well as truth from ⟨___, baldness⟩—unless he was prepared to label such things as Picadilly Circus and his own singleton false.

[55] The same point might be made by using Kaplan's '*dthat*' operator, on its originally intended interpretation. Cf. Kaplan's "Afterthoughts" to his "Demonstratives," *loc. cit.*, pp. 565–614, at 578–582. I am arguing that, on that original interpretation, the two sentences '*Dthat*[the present emperor of France] is bald' and '*Dthat*[the possible bald man presently in Quine's doorway] is bald' express the same thing, though each presents the structurally challenged proposition in its own special way.

[56] Thus one who believes that Carly-0 is bald thereby also believes (despite any denials) that Nappy is bald. Cf. *Frege's Puzzle*, at p. 7, and especially pp. 127–128. The present essay delivers on the promissory note issued there.

VII

Structurally challenged propositions provide content for the most intransigent instances of (4α). Even if (4α) does not express a nonexistent singular proposition (past, future, merely possible, or impossible), there is always the structurally challenged proposition. But if α is thoroughly nonreferring, all of (1α)–(4α) express structurally challenged propositions. It would seem that (4α) must then be neither true nor false, hence not true. But if α is nonreferring, (4α) is true. In philosophy, this is what is known as a *Headache.*[57]

I prescribe relief in the form of a new theory of singular existence, or rather of nonexistence. Although the intensional-ascent theory of existence improves upon Frege's semantic-ascent theory by capturing (or at least by approaching) the right modal intensions for singular existentials, there remains an intuitive difference between 'The present queen of England exists', which evidently mentions Queen Elizabeth II, and $'(\exists x)\Delta(^s(\imath y)$ (*Present-queen-of-England* $(y)^s$, $x)'$, which does not. There is an alternative to both approaches that, although still within the spirit of Fregean theory, has not to my knowledge been explicitly proposed before. We saw in section I that the distinction between choice and exclusion negation reveals an ambiguity in (2) for which there is no corresponding ambiguity in (1). According to Frege, one who utters (2) using 'not' in the sense of choice negation erroneously presupposes that there presently is a unique king of France. But one may use 'not' in the sense of exclusion negation to commit oneself only to the significantly weaker claim that no unique present king of France is bald. This same ambiguity occurs wherever 'not' does. One may thus take (3) to be analyzed by $(3'')$, as was the original idea, while taking (4) to be ambiguous between the following:

(9) $\sim_C(\exists x)[(\imath y)\,Present\text{-}king\text{-}of\text{-}France\,(y) = x]$
(10) $\sim_E(\exists x)[(\imath y)\,Present\text{-}king\text{-}of\text{-}France\,(y) = x].$

These correspond exactly to the two readings of the negation sign in $(4'')$. In the general case, on this theory, (3α) receives its usual analysis alternatively, the existence predicate may be regarded as primitive), while the 'not' in (4α) yields two readings. On one reading, (4α) means the same as $\ulcorner\alpha$ does not$_C$ exist$\urcorner$, on the other the same as $\ulcorner$The proposition that α exists is not$_C$ true$\urcorner$, or $\ulcorner$It is untrue that

---

[57] David Braun, in "Empty Names," *Noûs*, 27 (December 1993), pp. 449–469, at 460–465, develops Kaplan's idea of gappy propositions in connection with sentences like 'Vulcan is bald' and 'Vulcan does not exist'. See note 53 above. To repeat: Vulcan does exist, and such sentences as these express ordinary, structurally unchallenged propositions. Aside from this, Braun illegitimately makes the problem too easy for himself, arguing by analogy (in effect) that since all structurally unchallenged propositions have truth value so too do all structurally challenged ones, then asserting without further argument that atomic monadic singular propositions are false whenever there is nothing in the subject position that has the property in the predicate position—so that without any further ado, all atomic structurally challenged propositions are straightforwardly false. Against this, see note 54 above.

α exists⌐. Let us call this analysis of singular existentials and their negations *the choice/exclusion theory of nonexistence.*[58]

The choice/exclusion theory still has the consequence by Frege's lights that (3) is neither true nor F-false$_1$, and hence not false. But at least it is thus judged untrue (F-false$_2$). The choice/exclusion theory also has the consequence that (4) has a true reading while (3) does not. This might be deemed satisfactory.

It might even be deemed insightful. There is something odd about (4). If one wishes to correct the view that France presently has a king, it is more natural to do so by saying 'There presently is no king of France' (accompanied with an explanation that France is no longer a monarchy) or 'There is no such thing as the present king of France'. The former suggests (4'), the latter something like (8). By contrast, (4) itself seems to involve a faulty presupposition. We can use (4) to say something acceptable, but when we do, we seem to mean that it is untrue that the present king of France exists—precisely what (10) expresses. (This is what we mean, that is, unless someone whom we wish to enlighten about international politics has inadvertently created a mythical king of France, so that the description in (4) is used with invisible scare quotes to mean *the mythical object that Smith believes is presently king of France, thus depicted.*) Some of (4)'s oddness is present also in (3), and even in true singular existentials. If (1) presupposes (3'), as Frege and Strawson claim, then how could (3) fail to do so? (Compare Frege's comments about the name 'Sachse'.) If Britain were to dissolve its monarchy during the present queen's lifetime,

---

[58] As mentioned in note 16, Church cites (4) as an example of a true sentence in which a singular term has an *ungerade* occurrence. He also cites 'Lady Hamilton was like Aphrodite in beauty' and 'The fountain of youth is not located in Florida'. It is possible that Church held that the constructions '___ is located in Florida' and 'Lady Hamilton is like ___ in beauty' are (at least sometimes) *ungerade* devices. On such a view the un-negated sentences, 'The fountain of youth is located in Florida' and (3) would be F-false$_1$ sentences in which the subject terms have *ungerade* occurrences, the first expressing that the concept^s the fountain of youth^s determines something with a certain location. But it seems at least as likely, assuming that 'the fountain of youth' is nonreferring, that this sentence is neither true nor F-false$_1$, and the *ungerade* device in 'The fountain of youth is not located in Florida', and that in (4), is instead something common to both sentences.

In light of the fountain of youth's role in fable and myth (not to mention its impact on Ponce de Leon), Church's example might be better replaced with a sentence like 'The present king of France is not among the bald men of the world', which may be more readily accepted as true than (2). It is unclear whether Church would have held that this sentence, assuming it is true, means that the concept^s the present king of France^s does not determine something that is among the bald men of the world (analogously to the intensional-ascent theory of existence), or instead that the proposition ^{s}the present king of France is among the bald men of the world^s is not true (analogously to the exclusion theory of nonexistence). Church's abstention from citing (2) itself as another example of the same phenomenon may suggest the former interpretation—on which such expressions as 'located in Florida' and 'among the bald men of the world' are distinguished from 'bald' as *ungerade* devices. (C. Anthony Anderson conjectures that the relational aspect of '___ is located in___' 'and'___is like___in beauty' may have played a role in Church's view that they are *ungerade* devices. This would involve assimilating them to '___seeks___', which on Church's view expresses a relation between an object and a concept, thus distinguishing them from '___ is bald'. Cf. *ibid.,* p. 8n20. Anderson notes that '___ is among ___' is likewise relational.) On the other hand, the mere juxtaposition of two examples involving negation may suggest the latter interpretation. (It is possible that relational phrases like "located in Florida' and 'among the bald men of the world' have a greater tendency than 'bald' to induce the exclusion reading of their negation.)

'The present queen of England exists', uttered after the dissolution, would become untrue. But would it become straightforwardly false?

I propose combining the choice/exclusion theory of nonexistence with structurally challenged propositions. The resulting theory applies across the board to sentences with improper definite descriptions, nonreferring proper names, or other nonreferring terms. The negative existential 'Socrates does not exist' receives two readings: Soc, and *it is untrue that Socrates exists*. Neither proposition currently exists, but both are true. Similarly for 'Newman-1 does not exist' and 'Noman-0 does not exist'. The sentences 'Nappy does not exist' and 'Curly-0 does not exist' are also deemed ambiguous. On one reading, they each express the same structurally challenged proposition, one that is neither true nor false. On the other reading, they each express the same true proposition, that the structurally challenged proposition ⟨___, existence⟩ is untrue. Both readings, because of the involvement of structurally challenged propositions, are to some extent bizarre. The presence of distinct bizarre readings contributes towards the overall oddness of these negative existentials.

This theory relieves the Headache without capitulating to golden mountains. It also respects distinctions of content among intuitively nonsynonymous true negative existentials, like 'Socrates does not exist' and 'Noman does not exist'. And while it equates true negative existentials with thoroughly nonreferring names as expressing the same thing (or the same things), it respects their nonsemantic differences regarding how they present their common content. The theory diverges from Kripke's theory that a sentence like (2α) is sometimes true on the same ground as ⌜There is no proposition that α is bald⌝ and (4α) on the same grounds as ⌜There is no proposition that α exists⌝—whatever that ground is. There is no true proposition that Nappy is bald, or that Nappy exists, but these propositions exist. Instead (2α) sometimes means the same as ⌜It is untrue that α is bald⌝ and (4α) as ⌜It is untrue that α exists⌝, where the 'that' clauses always refer. Unlike Kripke's account, mine makes no intensional concessions that run against the grain of direct-reference theory.[59]

More important, the theory is intuitively correct as applied to a very wide range of sentences with nonreferring terms. The theory also coheres with Millianism to form a unified theory of content for singular terms, referring and not, and for sentences, existential and not. If there remain problematically true negative existentials for which the present theory does not provide a plausible account, I do not know which ones they are. Most importantly, if there are such, it may be that the Unified Metaphysico-Semantic Theory that some of us have sought exists only in fable and myth.

---

[59]The choice/exclusion ambiguity may extend also to the negation in 'Nappy is nonexistent', and even to the negations in 'Nappy is innocuous, since he is nonexistent'. The theory may even be sufficiently flexible to accommodate those who remain unconvinced concerning the nonexistent propositions mentioned above, like Soc. A skeptic concerning a particular nonexistent proposition may replace the offending proposition with the corresponding structurally challenged proposition, which does exist. It is not always possible to do so, however, while preserving truth value. The nonexistent proposition that Nothan, had he been born instead of me, would have been taller than I actually am is either true or false, but the corresponding structurally challenged proposition is evidently neither . Even if the latter is deemed to have truth value, then so must be the structurally challenged propositions corresponding to the nonexistent propositions that Nothan would have been shorter than I actually am and that Nothan would have been exactly the same height as I actually am. At least one of these existing structurally challenged surrogates fails to preserve the truth value of the nonexistent proposition it was put in to replace.

EMPTY NAMES

David Braun

The planet Mercury seems to deviate from the orbit that Newton's laws of motion and gravity predict for it. U. J. J. Le Verrier, a 19th century astronomer, thought the deviations were caused by an unobserved planet orbiting between Mercury and the Sun. Le Verrier wanted to name that planet 'Vulcan'. But, unfortunately for him, there was (and is) no such planet. So 'Vulcan' turned out to be an *empty name*— a proper name that fails to refer.

Empty names trouble philosophers who want to accept a Theory of Direct Reference for proper names. For according to these theories, a proper name has no semantic function other than referring to an individual. So these theories imply that 'Vulcan' has no semantic function. This suggests that the name has no meaning, and that sentences containing it say nothing. But these consequences seem unacceptable to many would-be Direct Reference theorists.

In this paper I describe two different theories of empty names that are consistent with Direct Reference. I believe both of these theories are defensible—but in the end I argue that one of them is more plausible and attractive than the other. By sketching these two theories, I hope to show would-be Direct Reference theorists that empty names may not pose the insuperable problems for Direct Reference Theory that many have supposed they do. Before I present these theories, I will say more about what Theories of Direct Reference are, describe the apparent problems that empty names raise for them, and criticize previous attempts to solve these problems.

1. Theories of Direct Reference for Proper Names

The works of Donnellan, Kripke, Kaplan, and others present (or at least strongly suggest) Theories of Direct Reference for proper names that differ in various ways.[1] What they have in common is the following thesis, which I call *The Fundamental Thesis of Direct Reference:*

> A proper name has no semantic function other than referring to an individual.

To put it in less technical terms: names never do anything (semantically speaking) other than refer. In particular, names do not describe individuals.[2]

---

[1] The term 'direct reference' comes from Kaplan (1989). Kripke describes, and comes close to explicitly endorsing, a Direct Reference view of proper names (or "Millianism") in (Kripke 1979, section I; and 1980, pp. 127, 134–5). Donnellan's views (esp. 1974, pp. 11–12, 20–1, 28–9) strongly suggest direct reference. Almog (1986), Kaplan (1989, pp. 497, 562), Salmon (1986), Soames (1987), and Wettstein (1986) explicitly advocate versions of Direct Reference for proper names.

[2] Kripke (1979, pp. 239–40) uses something like (a) to describe "a strict Millian view."

 (a) The sole linguistic function of a proper name is to refer to an individual.

 I have avoided using (a) to formulate Direct Reference Theory because it, together with (b) and (c), entails that 'Vulcan' is not a proper name.

 (b) An expression that does not refer does not have referring as one of its linguistic functions.

 (c) 'Vulcan' does not refer.

 A Direct Reference theorist could reasonably hold that 'Vulcan' is not a genuine proper name, even though it functions syntactically like one. But I prefer to formulate Direct Reference Theory so that it is consistent with holding that 'Vulcan' is a genuine proper name (one that has no semantic function).

Many Theories of Direct Reference make claims that go beyond The Fundamental Thesis. Here are two typical examples.

> The semantic value (or content, or meaning) of a proper name, if it has any, is the individual to which it refers.

> A sentence (or utterance of a sentence) that contains a proper name expresses a singular proposition, when it expresses any proposition at all.

These claims do not follow from The Fundamental Thesis—they are, instead, plausible additions to it. I wish to defend a Theory of Direct Reference which includes them. But they need a bit of explanation first.

An expression's semantic value is supposed to be an entity associated with the expression which is relevant to determining semantic properties of sentences (e.g., truth conditions). For those who accept The Fundamental Thesis, the obvious candidate for a proper name's semantic value is its referent.[3]

A proposition is traditionally thought to be a meaning, or semantic value, for a sentence (or utterance of a sentence). It in some way "contains or unifies" the semantic values of the sentence's constituents. A meaningful sentence *expresses* a proposition. When a person asserts a sentence, *what she says* is a proposition. A proposition is also supposed to be the primary bearer of truth and falsity. According to one view of propositions favored by many Direct Reference theorists (including myself), a proposition is an entity structured much like a sentence. It "contains" the semantic values of the words in a sentence which expresses the proposition. Thus a sentence that contains a proper name expresses a *singular proposition:* a proposition that contains an individual as a constituent. Propositions also contain the properties and relations to which words in a sentence refer. Direct Reference theorists often use sequences of individuals and relations to represent these propositions. For instance, the proposition expressed by 'Bush is human' might be represented by an ordered pair consisting of Bush and the property of being-human[4]:

⟨Bush, being-human⟩.

However natural the above additional theses are, a Direct Reference theorist who accepts The Fundamental Thesis could consistently reject them. He might

---

[3] When Direct Reference Theorists deny that names have meanings, they usually intend to deny that names have *descriptive* meanings. Some Direct Reference Theorists hold that proper names have several semantic values. Typically, they say that a name has both a linguistic meaning (a Kaplanian character) and a propositional content (relative to a context). The linguistic meaning is supposed to determine the name's propositional content in a context. Some Direct Reference theorists who use possible worlds as points of evaluation also assign intensions to names. In this paper, however, I will disregard these other (alleged) semantic values. This is justified in part by the fact that these other (alleged) semantic values are determined by the name's referent, and in part by the fact that I am ignoring all context sensitivity. (I reject the view that names themselves are context sensitive expressions.)

[4] The proposition expressed by a sentence containing a relational predicate, like 'Bush is taller than Reagan', might be represented by an ordered pair containing a sequence of objects in the "subject position": ⟨Bush, Reagan⟩, taller-than⟩. For a variety of arguments in favor of structured propositions see Almog (1986) and Soames (1987).

reject them because he thinks that there are no propositions, or he thinks that appealing to them in semantics is useless (or worse). (Similarly for semantic values, perhaps.) Let's call such a view "Fundamentalism."[5] There may be some advantages to Fundamentalism when it comes to dealing with empty names. A Fundamentalist need not worry about the meanings of empty names, or the propositions expressed by sentences containing them, because he thinks names never have meanings and sentences never express propositions. I think there are good reasons for rejecting Fundamentalism, but I do not have the space to give those reasons here. I will assume in this paper that we want our beliefs about empty names to be consistent with the doctrines of the more liberal Direct Reference sects.

2.   The Apparent Problems

Empty names raise several distinct problems for Theories of Direct Reference; they also create problems for theories of prepositional attitudes that are natural additions to Direct Reference. Before we can evaluate any theory of empty names, we should distinguish these problems as carefully as possible.[6]

One problem has to do with semantic values and propositions. According to Direct Reference, if 'Vulcan' does not refer, then it has no semantic value. Even worse, it seems that sentences containing 'Vulcan' cannot express propositions, since there is no semantic value to "fit into the subject position" of the proposition. These problems can be summarized in the form of an argument for two seemingly unacceptable conclusions ((1c) and (1e) below).

(1)   (a) The sole semantic value of a proper name, if it has any, is the individual to which it refers.

(b) 'Vulcan' is a proper name that does not refer.

So, (c) 'Vulcan' has no semantic value.

(d) A sentence containing a proper name that lacks a semantic value fails to express a proposition.

So, (e) 'Vulcan is a planet' and 'Vulcan does not exist' fail to express propositions.

I call this *The Problem of the Proposition Expressed*. Since propositions are supposed to be what sentences say, the main conclusion implies that the sentences 'Vulcan is a planet' and 'Vulcan does not exist' say nothing at all. It also implies that a person who asserts these sentences says nothing at all.

A closely related problem is *The Problem of Nonsense*. Suppose 'Vulcan does not exist' fails to express a proposition. Then it seems to follow that it is meaningless.

---

[5] Wettstein seems to accept Fundamentalism in (Wettstein 1988). Almog argues for Fundamentalism in (Almog 1991). (Obviously, Almog and Wettstein do not use the term 'Fundamentalism', and might even reject it.)

[6] Empty demonstratives create problems for Theories of Direct Reference similar to those raised by empty names. So do empty kind terms and empty property terms, if there are any. But I must set aside these problems here.

And therefore it is nonsense. Russell formulates this argument in the passage below.

> It is obviously a perfectly significant statement, whether true or false to say that Romulus existed. If Romulus himself entered into our statement, it would be plain that the statement that he did not exist would be nonsense, because you cannot have a constituent of a proposition which is nothing at all. (Russell 1956, p. 242)

Quine's character McX argues similarly.

> If Pegasus *were* not, McX argues, we should not be talking about anything when we use the word. Therefore it would be nonsense to say even that Pegasus is not. (Quine 1953, p. 2)

Clearly Russell's and McX's reasoning applies to any sentence containing a non-referring name. So we can formulate the following argument.

(2)   (a)   'Vulcan does not exist' and 'Vulcan is a planet' fail to express propositions.

     (b)   If a sentence fails to express a proposition, then it is nonsense.

So, (c)   'Vulcan does not exist' and 'Vulcan is a planet' are nonsense.

The next apparent problem is *The Problem of Truth.* If propositions are the primary bearers of truth, then a sentence must express a proposition in order to have a truth value. But according to the first argument, 'Vulcan does not exist' and 'Vulcan is a planet' do not express propositions. So 'Vulcan does not exist' is neither true nor false. But, obviously, it's true. (Some speakers also think that 'Vulcan is a planet' is false, but judgments about this vary.)

We might be able to formulate the same sort of problem without appealing to the notion of a proposition. (If so, The Problem of Truth is a problem even for the Fundamentalist.) Here's a plausible rule for finding truth conditions for simple name-predicate sentences: 'a is F' is true iff the referent of 'a' has the property to which 'is F' refers. Usually we can use this rule to derive a truth condition which does not mention words on "the right hand side." For instance: 'Mercury is a planet' is true iff the referent of 'Mercury' has the referent of 'is a planet', iff Mercury is a planet. But when a sentence contains an empty name like 'Vulcan', we cannot make a transition from talk about words to talk about objects. So we cannot say what the non-linguistic world must be like in order for this sentence to be true. This is a plausible reason for thinking that 'Vulcan is a planet' has *no* truth condition. Similarly for 'Vulcan exists'. So it seems that neither could be true; and it also seems that neither could be false, for how could a sentence have a (so-to-speak) "falsity condition" without having a truth condition?

Therefore it seems that (one way or another) we have a problem with truth. Let's again summarize the problem in the form of an argument.

(3)   (a)   If 'Vulcan' does not refer, then 'Vulcan does not exist' is neither true nor false.

     (b)   'Vulcan' does not refer.

So, (c)   'Vulcan does not exist' is neither true nor false.

The argument is nearly paradoxical when stated this baldly. For it seems that sentences of the form 'a exists' are true just in case 'a' refers, and false just in case 'a' fails to refer. So it seems that 'Vulcan does not exist' is true exactly when 'Vulcan' does not refer.

Thus far I have described some apparent semantical problems with empty names. These are the problems that empty names pose for Direct Reference Theory itself. There are also closely related problems with the *beliefs* of a person who sincerely utters these sentences. A person who sincerely utters a sentence believes what he says, and what he says is a proposition. Say that the proposition he believes is the *prepositional content* of his belief. Now suppose Fred sincerely utters 'Vulcan is a planet'. (Suppose he mistakenly thinks that Le Verrier was correct.) According to the following argument, he does not express any belief when he makes this utterance.

(4)   (a)   The prepositional content (if any) of the belief (if any) that Fred expresses by sincerely uttering 'Vulcan is a planet' is the same as the proposition expressed (if any) by 'Vulcan is a planet'.

(b)   'Vulcan is a planet' does not express a proposition.

So, (c)   The belief (if any) that Fred expresses by sincerely uttering 'Vulcan is a planet' has no prepositional content.

(d)   There are no beliefs that lack prepositional content.

So, (e)   Fred does not express any belief when he sincerely utters 'Vulcan is a planet'.

Similar conclusions hold for 'Vulcan does not exist'. But (4c) seems wrong. For if Fred has no belief "corresponding" to his sincere utterance of 'Vulcan is a planet', how could he be sincerely uttering that sentence? How could his action (his uttering the sentence) possibly be explained? Call this *The Problem of the Proposition Believed*.[7]

I will describe yet another problem with empty names, namely *The Problem of Differing Cognitive Values*, after I have attempted to deal with some of the above problems.[8]

---

[7] Another way to draw a connection between propositional attitudes and the problems with empty names (specifically, with The Problem of the Proposition Expressed) goes via the notion of *understanding*. Roughly, the problem is to explain how an auditor understands an utterance containing an empty name, if that utterance does not express any proposition that the auditor can grasp. See Keith Donnellan (1974, p. 7), Gareth Evans (1982, chapter 10), and Martin Davies (1981, pp. 94–103).

[8] There are two problems with empty names that I am setting aside here. Firstly, I am setting aside problems with empty names in modal contexts, belief reports, and non-extensional contexts. Secondly, I am setting aside The Problem of Discourse about Fiction. This is the problem of explaining how we (seemingly) express true propositions using (seemingly) non-referring names from fiction, e.g., by uttering (with the right intention) "Sherlock Holmes is a detective." I think that the utterances of "Holmes-like" sentences which seem true are those that are intended to be statements about fiction. I suspect they contain a covert fiction operator: in typical cases, an utterance of 'Holmes is a detective' says the same thing as 'In certain stories by Conan Doyle, Holmes is a detective'. So I suspect that utterances about fiction contain non-extensional contexts, and thus I am ignoring them here. (See Donnellan, 1974, for more on the distinction between discourse about fiction and discourse about reality.)

3. Some Unattractive Views of Empty Names

I believe that previous theories that have attempted to solve some of the problems with empty names have been unsatisfactory. I will describe four such theories, and criticize three of them. I do not think my criticisms conclusively show that these views are false and irreparable. My criticisms merely show why these views are unattractive, and thus motivate the theories I will present.

A *Meinongian View* maintains that 'Vulcan' *does* refer—not to any planet, nor to anything else that exists, but to a nonexistent object. So 'Vulcan' has a semantic value, sentences containing it express propositions, people who assert these sentences believe propositions, and so on. I will not attempt to criticize this view here. Like most philosophers, I will assume that, other things being equal, we should not hypothesize nonexistent objects to solve semantic problems.

The second view is *Descriptivism,* the sort of view commonly ascribed to Russell and Frege. According to it, proper names are synonymous with definite descriptions. So 'Vulcan' might be synonymous with 'the planet closer to the Sun than Mercury'; and a sentence like 'Vulcan is hot' might be synonymous with 'The planet closer to the Sun than Mercury is hot'. 'Vulcan' fails to refer on this view because nothing satisfies the description with which it is synonymous. But both the name and the description have a meaning, because the meaning of a description is (something like) a *property*. The property of being-the-planet-closer-to-the-Sun-than-Mercury exists, and can be a constituent of propositions, regardless of whether there is anything that satisfies it. So 'Vulcan is hot' expresses a descriptive proposition that is straightforwardly false, since the description is not satisfied. People who sincerely assert the sentence believe a descriptive proposition.

Donnellan and Kripke have presented powerful objections to Descriptivist views of *referring* names. The problems with empty names, however, might tempt one to hold a mixed view: Direct Reference for referring names and Descriptivism for empty names. But this mixed view is untenable. Firstly, it seems intolerable to say that the expression 'Vulcan' *turned out to be* a disguised description—but if only there had been a planet between Mercury and the Sun, it *would have been* a mere tag with *no* descriptive content. Secondly, many of Donnellan's and Kripke's counterexamples to Descriptivist views of referring names can be modified into counterexamples to Descriptivist views of empty names. I will sketch two such counterexamples. They might be called "the misdescription counterexample" and "the no uniquely identifying description counterexample."

First example: Suppose that astronomers who follow Le Verrier take the name 'Vulcan' to be synonymous with 'the planet closest to the Sun'. Then on the Descriptivist View, these astronomers refer to Mercury whenever they utter 'Vulcan'. So when they say 'Vulcan exists', they say something true. But they don't.[9]

---

[9] See Donnellan (1974, p. 24) for a similar example.

Second example: Suppose that a malicious Medieval historian made up the name 'Fred Derfel' and wrote in some document 'Fred Derfel helped sack Rome'. Suppose that we receive this document, take it to be reliable, and associate nothing else with the name. Then we would have an empty name with which no one associates a uniquely identifying description.[10]

The third view I call the *Metalinguistic View*. According to it, negative existentials are a special exception to Direct Reference Theory. In a negative existential, a name refers to itself. The sentence 'Vulcan does not exist' expresses the same proposition as

> 'Vulcan' does not refer.

The proposition expressed by both this and the negative existential has the name 'Vulcan' as a constituent, rather than an ordinary individual like a planet. This "metalinguistic proposition" is straightforwardly true or false, even though the name lacks a referent.[11]

On this view, an assertion which seems to be about the existence of an individual is really an assertion about a name and whether it refers. This has at least two unintuitive consequences. First, on this view the two sentences

> If Vulcan does not exist, then 'Vulcan' does not refer.
>
> If 'Vulcan' does not refer, then 'Vulcan' does not refer.

should express the same proposition. The latter sentence expresses a necessary proposition. But the former seems to express (at best) a contingent proposition, since it might have been the case that 'Vulcan' refers to something (e.g., Bush) though Vulcan does not exist.[12] Second, on this view, negative existentials that use different names (for instance, 'London does not exist' and 'Londres n'existe pas') cannot express the same proposition. This seems wrong. The advocate of the Metalinguistic View could reply in various ways; this makes it difficult to evaluate

---

[10] A Descriptivist would no doubt have replies to these two objections. For instance, she might reply that in the Ferd Derfel case, *we would* know a uniquely identifying description, namely 'the person to whom the author of this document referred using the name "Ferd Derfel"'. Kripke and Donnellan have attempted to answer similar Descriptivist replies when it comes to referring names. I do not have the space to give all of the analogous arguments, replies, and counter-replies here. But I claim that these analogous arguments and replies are as effective against Descriptivist views of *empty* names as the original Kripke-Donnellan objections are against Descriptivist views of *referring* names.

[11] The Metalinguistic View resembles Donnellan's view (1974). But Donnellan specifies only a truth condition for a negative existential—he does not attempt to specify the proposition expressed by a negative existential. His truth condition, however, is appropriate for the sentence '"Vulcan" does not refer', which expresses a metalinguistic proposition. (When specifying the truth condition, Donnellan says that a name like 'Vulcan' fails to refer when the historical chain leading to a use of it ends in a "block.")

[12] If the existence of the name 'Vulcan' is contingent, then we must use the following pair of sentences to press this modal objection.

> If the name 'Vulcan' exists, then if Vulcan does not exist then 'Vulcan' does not refer.
> If the name 'Vulcan' exists, then if 'Vulcan' does not refer then 'Vulcan' does not refer.

The second expresses a necessary truth; the first does not.

the force of these objections.[13] But the Metalinguistic View nevertheless has the unattractive feature that negative existentials are about words and semantical relations, though they don't appear to mention either. Similar objections hold for natural extensions of this view to predicative sentences containing empty names.

The fourth view I call the *Metapropositional View*. According to it, 'Vulcan does not exist' expresses the same proposition as

> There is no true proposition to the effect that Vulcan exists.

On this view, a negative existential is a disguised way of talking about propositions rather than talking "directly" about objects. The proposition expressed by the above sentence is allegedly true because there is no proposition to the effect that Vulcan exists.[14]

On this view, we apparently refer to the proposition that Vulcan exists when we say 'Vulcan does not exist'. But how can we, if there is no such proposition? The Metapropositional View seems to multiply our problems rather than solve them. Perhaps this last problem can be dodged by claiming that a higher-level proposition can contain a *seeming* reference to a lower-level proposition even if that latter proposition does not exist. Higher-level propositions would contain intensional elements, and the prepositional analog of existential generalization would not be valid for them. I see two problems for this view. First, there does not seem to be any motivation for admitting these intensional elements into higher-level propositions, while forbidding them from first-level propositions. So the Metapropositional theorist might as well hold that 'Vulcan does not exist' expresses a simple first-level proposition which contains an intensional element. Second, even leaving aside questions of levels, it is unclear what this intensional element is. Is it some kind of uniquely identifying property? We had good reasons to reject that answer. And it's not at all clear that we can get a more satisfactory answer here.

4. The No Proposition View: Beliefs

As I said before, I believe that there are two defensible views of empty names that are consistent with Theories of Direct Reference. I will now begin to sketch the first, which I call *The No Proposition View*. (The sketch I will give here will be, at

---

[13] Donnellan (1974, pp. 27–30) raises the problem of different languages. It is more likely to upset Direct Reference theorists than others. A Metalinguistic theorist might respond to the first objection by saying that 'Vulcan does not exist' expresses the same proposition as '"Vulcan" does not *actually* refer'. This sentence expresses a necessary truth. (So might '"Vulcan" does not refer *in English*'.) If 'Vulcan does not exist' is also necessarily true, then on this modified analysis, both of the conditional sentences mentioned in the text, when appropriately modified, express necessary truths, and the modal objection fails.

Even if the modal objection fails, one might still wonder whether 'Vulcan does not exist' and '"Vulcan" does not actually refer' are *logically equivalent*. Intuitively, it seems that the proposition expressed by the latter sentence entails that the name 'Vulcan' exists, whereas the proposition expressed by the first (if any) does not. But I have no theory of logical consequence for metalinguistic propositions that would justify these intuitions.

[14] Evans (1983, pp. 349–50) says that Kripke tentatively proposed this sort of view in his John Locke Lectures.

most, an outline of a complete theory.) According to The No Proposition View, 'Vulcan' has no semantic value or semantic function; and sentences containing 'Vulcan' fail to express propositions. This view embraces the conclusions of The Problem of the Proposition Expressed (namely (1c) and (1e)) which many find unacceptable.

It has to be admitted that embracing these conclusions is a disadvantage for The No Proposition View. But we should also admit that we do sometimes have conflicting intuitions about cases involving empty names. We are at least sometimes inclined to think that when someone utters 'Vulcan is a planet', she really says nothing (though she thinks that she says something).[15] My goal here is to show that a view that takes this (sometime) intuition seriously, as The No Proposition View does, can be made more plausible than most have been willing to admit.

There remain serious difficulties for The No Proposition View—namely, The Problems of Truth, Nonsense, and the Proposition Believed. It's hard to believe that 'Vulcan does not exist' has no truth value, and that someone who asserts it has no corresponding belief. It's also hard to accept that it is complete nonsense. In the next three sections, I will try to explain away these Problems from the perspective of The No Proposition View. I will begin with the cognitive problem, The Problem of the Proposition Believed. Though my main goal here is to deal with the semantic problems that Direct Reference has with empty names, a discussion of the cognitive problem will be a useful prelude to the semantic problems. Furthermore, we must have a plausible view about how empty names connect with prepositional attitudes in order to make any semantic view of empty names acceptable.

To deal with The Problem of the Proposition Believed, we must explain how it could be the case that 'Vulcan is a planet' fails to express a proposition, and yet Fred expresses one of his beliefs when he sincerely utters 'Vulcan is a planet'. How could (4c) be true and (4e) false? The answer is that (4d), the thesis that there are no beliefs that lack prepositional content, must be false. We must recognize a distinction between a belief, on the one hand, and a prepositional content, on the other hand. I think this is a distinction that we can make. Perhaps we already do. The word 'belief' seems ambiguous: it sometimes seems to mean a certain kind of mental state that occurs in the head, and at other times seems to mean a proposition towards which one takes an attitude.

I use the term 'belief' as a term for a mental state. A belief (or belief state, we might call it) is an enduring event-like entity that occurs in a brain (or mind). It is what "happens" in one's head when one believes a proposition. It occurs at a

---

[15] This intuition is stronger (for me) in the case of empty demonstratives. Suppose Sylvester is surrounded by a heavy fog. Suppose he points into the fog and says 'That's a tank'. Suppose further that there is no object in that direction. Then I have *some* inclination to say that Sylvester has said nothing. When I think about such cases, I am sometimes inclined to say the same thing about cases involving empty names. (Thanks to Richard Feldman for discussion of this point.)

time and location. It is a non-abstract entity that can stand in causal relations to sensations, bits of behavior, and other cognitive states.

The content of a belief is a proposition. It is not an event-like entity. It is not located in any brain. It is abstract. So beliefs and propositions are distinct entities. But beliefs *express* propositions, in much the same way that sentences express propositions. A person believes a proposition by having a belief (state) that expresses that proposition.[16]

Here is one way to picture how beliefs (or belief states) are involved when a person believes a proposition. Let's suppose that to have a belief (or to be in a belief state) is to have a token of a sentence-like representation in one's head in the right way. (An occurrence of a representation in one's head might be a certain kind of brain event.) These representations have syntactic structures—they are made up of words. A person is caused to have such a token mental representation by her sensations and other mental states; and an occurrence of a representation helps cause other mental states and actions (like utterances). So occurrences of these representations have the sorts of causes and effects that a belief is supposed to have. Furthermore, a mental representation can express a proposition. A representation does this iff it has the right sort of syntactic structure and its words refer to appropriate objects and relations. Let's suppose those words refer iff they stand in the right causal-historical relations to items in the world. So according to this "picture," a person stands in the believing relation to a proposition iff she has a belief (has a mental representation) that contains terms with the right causal-historical relations to the objects and relations that appear in the proposition.

On this picture, it's easy to see how a person (e.g., Fred) could have a belief that has no propositional content: he could have a mental representation that contains a token word that does not refer. That could happen if the token word does not stand in the right causal-historical relations to objects in the world.[17]

Even if the above mental representation theory of belief is wrong, it is still plausible to think that believing involves two distinct entities, a mental state (a belief) and a proposition. If this is correct, then it is possible, at least "in principle,"

---

[16] On this view, the believing *relation* might be analyzed as a three-place relation between a person, a proposition, and a belief state. See the next few paragraphs.

[17] In Fred, the occurrence of a mental representation might be a brain event. Clearly such a brain event could occur without having the right (causal-historical) relations for reference or for expression of a proposition. But it could still resemble a belief in nearly every other respect (e.g., in its causal role with respect to other mental states). The No Proposition View says that this sort of brain event is a genuine belief. Therefore a person could have a belief with no propositional content. Some might argue that a mental event without a propositional content cannot be a genuine belief. But they could still agree with the following: there are mental events that lack propositional content, but which have causes and effects just like contentful beliefs, and such an event could cause Fred's utterance of 'Vulcan is a planet'. This thesis is what's important to The No Proposition View's treatment of The Problem of the Proposition Believed.

for there to be beliefs that do not express any proposition. A person who has such a belief can be said to believe no proposition, or nothing at all.[18]

According to The No Proposition View, this is exactly what happens when people use empty names. Fred has a real belief which causes him to utter 'Vulcan is a planet'. The belief is a real event-like entity, which may cause other events, like utterances. But it has no prepositional content. So (4c) is true, but (4e) is false. Similarly, an astronomer may have a belief which causes him to utter 'Vulcan does not exist'. But neither his belief, nor his utterance, has a propositional content.

The cognitive states people have when they accept sentences containing empty names may cause further cognitive states that have normal propositional contents. For example, if Fred accepts 'Vulcan does not exist', he will probably also acquire another belief which disposes him to utter 'There is no planet closer to the Sun than Mercury'. This last belief has a normal propositional content. And Fred's having this last belief may prevent him from pointing telescopes towards areas in the sky where there are no planets. The causal influence that an 'empty belief" has on normal cognitive states, and on actions, may make it rational for a speaker to utter a sentence that contains an empty name, even if he knows that that sentence does not express a proposition.

We must be careful not to make the Descriptivist mistake here. Perhaps when an astronomer utters 'Vulcan does not exist' to Fred, he wants Fred to come to believe (among other things) that there is no planet closer to the Sun than Mercury. But this is not what the astronomer says by uttering 'Vulcan does not exist'. And this is not the content of the belief that causes the astronomer to utter 'Vulcan does not exist' The utterance and belief have no content on The No Proposition View.

So much for The Problem of the Proposition Believed. Now, with this background, we are ready to consider how The No Proposition View might handle another cognitive and semantic problem with empty names that I have yet to describe, *The Problem of Differing Cognitive Values*. In the 18th century, many people read poetry which they thought was written by a third-century Celtic bard named 'Ossian'. But there was no such poet—the poems were written by the 18th century poet James Macpherson. So 'Ossian' turned out to be an empty name. Now clearly Fred may sincerely assent to an utterance of 'Vulcan is a planet' and yet refuse to assent to an utterance of 'Ossian is a poet'. So it seems that these sentences are "associated" with different beliefs (in Fred) and have different cognitive values (for Fred). But, it might be argued, if these

---

[18] Thus according to The No Proposition View, it is possible for a person to have a belief without believing a proposition. For on this view, a belief is a non-relational, or at least head-internal, event (a brain event, for instance.) A person stands in the believing *relation* to a proposition iff (1) she has a belief, *and* (2) that belief expresses that proposition. But a person can have a belief that does not express a proposition. So a person can have a belief without (thereby) believing a proposition. Thus having a belief is a necessary, but not sufficient, condition for believing a proposition. So the property of having a belief is not the same as the property of standing in the believing relation to a proposition. Thus, on this view, one should not think of a belief as an instance of the property of believing some proposition or other.

sentences both fail to express propositions and the corresponding beliefs fail to have propositional contents (as The No Proposition View says), then Fred's belief that Vulcan is a planet cannot be different from his belief that Ossian is a poet. So if The No Proposition View were correct, Fred would not be able to assent to one sentence while refusing to assent to the other. So The No Proposition View must be false. These sentences must express propositions, and different ones at that.

But there is a mistake in this argument against The No Proposition View. The No Proposition View can allow a person to have many distinct beliefs that fail to express propositions. Fred may, for instance, have several distinct sentence-like mental representations that fail to express propositions. Having two such representations in the head may constitute having two distinct beliefs, even if both have the same content, or fail to have any content. These beliefs may cause different actions and cognitive states in Fred. One of them may dispose Fred to utter 'Vulcan is a planet' and another to utter 'Ossian is a poet'. Furthermore, his hearing 'Ossian does not exist' may cause different beliefs and cognitive changes in him than his hearing 'Vulcan does not exist'. This seems to be enough to account for Fred's assents and dissents, and perhaps also for the (alleged) differences in cognitive value between the sentences.[19]

5. The No Proposition View: No Nonsense

We can now see why according to The No Proposition View, it is either false or very misleading to say that "Vulcan does not exist' is nonsense. According to The No Proposition View, people who sincerely utter 'Vulcan does not exist' are caused to do so by real belief states (though these belief states lack propositional content). So they express genuine beliefs with those utterances. Furthermore, people who hear these sentences come to have beliefs about what these speakers say, and so those auditors in some sense understand those speakers. So there is a systematic connection between beliefs, on the one hand, and utterances and auditions of sentences containing 'Vulcan', on the other hand.

This systematic connection between beliefs, utterances, and hearings does not hold for paradigmatic examples of nonsense. Ungrammatical strings, like 'Hit boy girl the the' are not used to express beliefs, and are not uttered to affect the beliefs of others in the way that 'Vulcan' sentences are. Neither are nonsense sentences, like 'All mimsy were the borogoves'. So it seems that a sufficient condition for a sentence to "make sense" (not be nonsense) is that it have connections to belief states like those described above.

If this is right, then there are some sentences which fail to express propositions and yet make sense because of their connections to beliefs in hearers and speakers. Now (2b) says that all sentences that fail to express propositions are nonsense. This claim is false if 'nonsense' is used in the ordinary sense I tried to

---

[19] I go into more detail about the traditional problem of cognitive value, and how to solve it within a Direct Reference framework that countenances belief states, in (Braun 1991).

explain above. It is true, but extremely misleading, if 'nonsense' is used in a technical sense to mean 'lacks a semantic value'.[20]

6. The No Proposition View: Truth

Let's now leave behind the cognitive problems with empty names and turn to semantics. The No Proposition View has its most serious difficulties, in my opinion, with The Problem of Truth. I can think of two ways in which this view might deal with this problem.

The first way combines The No Proposition View with *The No Truth Value View*. This latter view simply accepts the conclusion that 'Vulcan does not exist' is neither true nor false. Of course, to accept this view we must somehow explain away the stubborn intuition that 'Vulcan does not exist' is true. But perhaps we can appeal to pragmatics to do this. Remember that the (contentless) belief caused in an auditor by an utterance of 'Vulcan does not exist' can itself cause various other beliefs. So an utterance of this sentence may have something like conversational implicatures. Perhaps in most cases when a person comes to have a belief which she would express by uttering 'Vulcan does not exist', she is also caused to believe that there is no planet that is closer to the Sun than Mercury. She may also typically come to believe that the name 'Vulcan' does not refer. These latter beliefs have normal propositional contents that are straightforwardly true. A typical speaker may also have beliefs with these true propositional contents. So perhaps speakers and hearers tend to think that these true implicated propositions are the same as the proposition allegedly asserted in an utterance of 'Vulcan does not exist'. This might explain why they mistakenly think that 'Vulcan does not exist' is itself true.

I have no strong arguments against this pragmatic explanation; but I seriously doubt that it adequately explains our judgments about truth. So I want to consider a second view, *The True Sentence View*. According to it, the *sentence* 'Vulcan does not exist' is true, even though it fails to express a proposition. On this alternative, we must reject the traditional view that only propositions, or objects that express propositions, can be true and false.

---

[20] I have sometimes heard the following sort of reaction to the previous two sections: "According to this view, there are utterances and beliefs that don't express propositions, but which 'act' just like those that do. So there are no *important* differences between utterances and beliefs that don't express propositions and those that do. So why not eliminate all talk of propositions from our theories?" This is not yet an argument against the existence of propositions (or against mentioning them in semantic theories), but perhaps we could get one by adding further premises and some principle of ontological economy. In any case, I do not have the space to deal with the many issues these remarks raise, or with the related doctrine of Fundamentalism. I am assuming here that some utterances and beliefs do express propositions. If this plausible assumption is correct, then there is (at least) a *semantic* difference between utterances and beliefs that express propositions and those that don't (arguably an important difference). So a semantic theory that fails to ascribe propositional contents to utterances and beliefs that have them omits some semantic truths, and is therefore incomplete.

Should we reject this traditional view? It is commonly said in its favor that there are many objects that are not true, but not false, either: the Eiffel Tower, for instance. A salient difference between the truth value bearers and the rest is that the former express propositions, while the latter do not. But this clearly does not show that expressing a proposition is a necessary condition for bearing a truth value. Surely there are important differences between the sentence 'Vulcan exists' and the Eiffel Tower. The sentence makes sense—it is systematically connected to people's beliefs. It is part of a language which people use in attempts to describe the way the world is. If it fails to be true, we might plausibly say that it fails in an attempt to describe the world. That seems like *a* notion of falsity. So perhaps we are not stretching the notions of truth and falsity too far by extending them to 'Vulcan exists' and 'Vulcan does not exist'.[21]

I think there are two reasons to hesitate, however. One is that the only sort of truth condition we can assign to the sentence 'Vulcan does not exist' is metalinguistic. (See note 21.) Secondly, and more importantly, we must deny some seeming platitudes in order to accept The True Sentence View. We would like to say that a sentence is true iff *what it says* is the case. And we want to say that the negation of a sentence is true iff what the embedded sentence says is not the case. But if we attribute truth to 'Vulcan does not exist', and yet hold that it says nothing, then we must deny these platitudes.

7. The Unfilled Proposition View

I believe that The No Proposition View is both defensible and consistent with Direct Reference. But I think that there is another theory of empty names which is also consistent with Direct Reference, and which is superior to The No Proposition View. Like The No Proposition View, it says that empty names have no semantic value—any view of empty names that can plausibly be said to be consistent with Direct Reference must say this. But unlike The No Proposition View, the alternative view allows sentences containing empty names to express semantical objects that (at the very least) strongly resemble propositions. To motivate and explain this view, I want to return to the Direct Reference theory of structured propositions.

Our intuitions concerning *aboutness* and *what is said* are among the strongest motivations for the structured proposition theory.[22] The proposition I express by uttering 'Bush is taller than Reagan' is *about* Bush, and Reagan, and

---

[21] Donnellan's (1974) official view of negative existentials is that some of them fail to express propositions and yet manage to be true. So he seems to accept The No Proposition View, combined with The True Sentence View. We can get the truth values we want (assuming the argument in the text is cogent) by applying the truth rule mentioned in section 2: 'a is F' is true iff the referent of 'a' has the property to which 'is F' refers. Since 'Vulcan' does not refer, 'Vulcan exists' is not true. We then infer that it is false (as argued in the text), and so its negation is true.

[22] There are other, more technical, motivations. For instance, the structured proposition view allows us to say that two logically equivalent sentences can express distinct propositions. See also (Almog 1986) and (Soames 1987).

the relation of being-taller-than. The structured proposition view recognizes this in a straightforward way, for on this view, Bush, Reagan, and the relation of being-taller-than are *constituents* of the proposition I express. Thus *what I say* is *about* those items. But obviously the proposition I express could not be a mere aggregate, or set, consisting of these three items, for if it were, the proposition expressed by 'Bush is taller than Reagan' would be the same as that expressed by 'Reagan is taller than Bush'. So the proposition I express by 'Bush is taller than Reagan' must contain something more than these three items.

The theory of structured propositions holds that there *is* something more, namely, a *structure:* a proposition consists of a structure, along with individuals and relations. On this view, a proposition consists of *two different kinds of entities*. There is first of all its structure, which is an entity that might be compared to a scaffolding or, even better, a tree. This structured entity contains positions or "slots", ready to be filled with individuals and relations. The rest of a proposition consists of individuals and relations. These items appear within a structure, occupying positions in a scaffolding, or decorating parts of a tree.

On this view, a proposition *reflects* a sentence in *two distinct ways*. A proposition, first of all, has a structure that reflects the syntax or grammatical structure of a sentence. Corresponding to argument positions in a sentence, there are argument positions in the proposition's structure; corresponding to predicate positions in the sentence, there are predicate positions in the proposition's structure. Thus the propositions expressed by 'Bush is taller than Reagan' and 'Reagan is taller than Bush' have a similar propositional structure, because the sentences have a similar grammatical structure. Secondly, a proposition reflects the semantic values of the words in a sentence. It does this simply by containing the semantic values of those words (the individuals and relations to which those words refer) in the right positions in the propositional structure. The propositions expressed by 'Bush is taller than Reagan' and 'Reagan is taller than Bush' differ because Bush and Reagan occupy different positions within the structures of the propositions expressed by those sentences.

It follows that a sentence has two semantical functions or "duties" with respect to structured propositions. First, a sentence *generates* a propositional structure containing positions ready to receive basic semantic values (individuals and relations). Sentences with the same syntactic structure generate the same type of propositional structure. Second, the words in the sentence generate basic semantic values to insert into those positions. The words do this merely by referring to individuals and relations. Two sentences with the same syntactic structure can generate different propositions by generating different basic semantic values.

Drawing these strands together, we can make the following observations. First, a propositional structure and the items filling positions in it are distinct entities; so it seems that there could be a propositional structure containing positions unfilled by either individuals or relations. Second, a sentence might successfully perform one of its semantical duties with respect to propositions, and fail in the other; specifically, a sentence might generate a propositional structure without generating basic semantic values to fill in that structure. Thus, we can conclude that the theory of structured propositions allows there to be sentences that express propositional structures with *unfilled positions*. Let's call such a propositional structure an *unfilled proposition*. According to *The Unfilled Proposition View*, sentences that make sense, and contain non-referring proper names, express unfilled propositions.[23]

The Unfilled Proposition View says that an empty name has no semantic value. Nonetheless, according to this view a sentence containing an empty name expresses something, namely an unfilled proposition. A person who utters such a sentence says and believes an unfilled proposition. The view also holds that these things that people say and believe have truth values. This is plausible for two reasons. For one thing, unfilled propositions strongly resemble completely filled propositions that bear truth values. For another, unfilled propositions "encode" important semantical facts about sentences containing empty names that make sense. As I noted in section 6, people can and have used those sentences in attempts to describe the world. Thus these sentences seem liable to (mis)represent in ways similar to sentences that express filled propositions. So the unfilled propositions that encode their semantical properties are plausible candidates for truth value bearers.

So much for motivating and outlining the view. I will now sketch in a few of its details. (My sketch will leave much work to be done.) To fill in this view, we need to be able to represent the elaborate syntactical structures of structured propositions, and allow for the representation of unfilled propositions. We could do this by modifying the sequence representations I gave earlier so that the various positions in a structure are themselves represented. This could be done by "adding more brackets." Suppose, for the moment, that we wish to represent only the subject positions in propositions. Then we might represent the proposition expressed by 'Bush is human' with

⟨{Bush}, being-human⟩.

This is simply the ordered pair consisting of Bush's singleton set and the property of being-human. But, informally, we can suppose that the brackets represent the

---

[23]The proposition expressed by a sentence like 'Vulcan is a planet' might also be called a *partially filled proposition* (or perhaps a *partial proposition*). David Kaplan discusses a similar notion in a footnote to his "Demonstratives" (Kaplan, 1989, p. 496), and in unpublished work (to which I have not had access). In the latter work Kaplan calls propositions with missing constituents *gappy propositions*. I wish to emphasize my debt to Kaplan's remarks in "Demonstratives"—they inspired the Unfilled Proposition View. But there may be differences between our views, and differences between the intuitions that motivate us. This is one reason why I have chosen not to use Kaplan's terminology.

One might ask why we should use an unfilled position in a proposition for "encoding" the fact that a sentence has a non-referring name. Why not use an arbitrarily selected object, like the Moon or the empty set? This would resemble Frege's view that we should simply *assign* a reference to empty names. There are two reasons to use unfilled positions. (1) It is natural and possible. (2) Arbitrarily selected objects have properties, so using them as referents for empty names leads to unintuitive results. For instance, if the empty set were our selected object, then the propositions expressed by 'Vulcan exists' and 'Vulcan is a set' would be true, unless we gave some novel theory of truth conditions for propositions.

subject position, which Bush fills. If a name in a sentence fails to refer, then the subject position is unfilled or unoccupied. We can represent the unfilled proposition expressed by 'Vulcan is a planet' with[24]

$\langle\{\}, \text{being-a-planet}\rangle.$

This sort of representation is perfectly adequate for the purposes at hand, but it may encourage a serious misunderstanding of The Unfilled Proposition View which is inconsistent with Direct Reference. On the Unfilled Proposition View, the semantic value of a proper name is just the individual to which it refers. The semantic value of 'Bush' is just Bush himself; it is *not* the singleton set {Bush}. Holding the latter would be inconsistent with the spirit of Direct Reference Theory. On The Unfilled Proposition View, the semantic value of a name appears *within* a propositional structure; in the sequence representation, the singleton set (the pair of brackets) helps represent this structure and is no part of the name's content. It follows that on this view, the semantic value of an empty name like 'Vulcan' is *not* { } (the empty set). 'Vulcan' has *no* semantic value on this view, just as Direct Reference requires.[25] We might be able to prevent this misunderstanding by using a different sort of representation of propositional structure. Trees would be particularly good (and might be more convenient in any case to represent the propositions expressed by complex sentences). We might represent the propositions expressed by 'Bush is human' and 'Vulcan is a planet' with something like the following:

---

[24] A sentence containing a relational predicate, like 'Bush is taller than Reagan', might be represented by $\langle\langle\{Bush\}, \{Reagan\}\rangle, \text{being-taller-than}\rangle$. The proposition expressed by 'Vulcan is identical with Vulcan' might be represented using a sequence of empty positions: $\langle\langle\{\}, \{\}\rangle, \text{being-identical}\rangle$.

[25] Kaplan's remarks in "Demonstratives" concerning "incomplete propositions" may be misleading in this respect. When writing about the use of braces to mark subject places in singular propositions, Kaplan says

> This technique can also be used to resolve another confusion in Russell. He argued that a sentence containing a nondenoting directly referential term . . . would be meaningless, presumably because the purported singular proposition would be incomplete. But the braces themselves can fill out the singular proposition, and if they contain nothing, no more anomalies need result than what the development of Free Logic has already inured us to. (Kaplan 1989, p. 496, fn. 13)

This passage may suggest that unfilled propositions are *complete*, because their subject positions are *occupied* (are filled out) by the empty set. This may suggest that on an unfilled proposition view, the semantic value of 'Vulcan' is { }. But this is contrary to Kaplan's intent (personal communication), and contrary to The Unfilled Proposition View.

The branches of these trees terminate in individuals and relations, not words; the right-hand tree has nothing under the Subj node. It is not very tempting to think that the semantic value of 'Vulcan' is some part of the right-hand tree. So it might be better to represent propositions with trees rather than sequences. But sequence representations are adequate, and are more convenient and familiar (to philosophers). Therefore I will continue to use them, despite my fear that they will mislead.

To complete our understanding of these propositions, we need to be clear about their truth conditions. The proposition ⟨{Bush}, being-human⟩ should be true iff Bush is human. (The humanity of Bush's singleton set is irrelevant.) We can state truth conditions for simple atomic propositions both to get this result and to cover unfilled propositions.

> If P is a proposition having a single subject position and a one-place property position, then P is true iff the subject position is filled by one, and only one, object, and it exemplifies the property filling the property position. If P is not true, then it is false.

Bush fills (or occupies) the subject position of ⟨{Bush}, being-human⟩. So that proposition is true iff Bush is human. If there is no occupant of the subject position of a proposition P, then P is not true, and so it is false. So atomic unfilled propositions, like ⟨{ }, being-a-planet⟩, are false.[26]

If atomic unfilled propositions are false, then propositional negation is straightforward. The negation of a false proposition, like

⟨⟨{ }, being-a-planet⟩, NEG⟩

is true iff the embedded proposition is false. So on The Unfilled Proposition View, we need not deny that a sentence is true iff what it says is the case, or that a negation of a sentence is true iff what the embedded sentence says is not the case. If we suppose negative existential propositions have a structure like

⟨⟨{ }, existence⟩, NEG⟩

then they are straightforwardly true. (Thus (3a) is false on this view.[27]) Notice that on The Unfilled Proposition View, there is only one true negative existential proposition. I return to this point below.

---

[26]This truth rule resembles Russell's truth condition for sentences containing definite descriptions. Just as Russell allows such sentences to fail to be true in two different ways, so this rule allows propositions to fail to be true in two different ways (intuitively speaking): (1) there can be exactly one occupant of the subject position, and it can fail to exemplify the property; (2) the subject position can fail to have exactly one occupant (by having, e.g., none).

This truth rule can obviously be generalized to cover propositions containing multi-place relations. This more general rule would entail that 'Vulcan is identical with Vulcan' expresses a *false* unfilled proposition. I have not formulated theories of necessary truth and logical truth here, but, given the above sorts of rules, atomic unfilled propositions should turn out to be *necessarily,* and *logically, false.*

[27]For those "keeping score": The Unfilled Proposition View also denies (1d), (4b), and (2a).

Thus goes propositional negation. There may be, in addition, predicate or property negation. It might be expressed by a sentence like

> Vulcan is a non-planet.

This is supposed to express a proposition attributing the complement of the property of being-a-planet to a subject:

> ⟨{ }, being-a-non-planet⟩.

This unfilled proposition is false, since the subject position has no occupant. So both 'Vulcan is a planet' and 'Vulcan is a non-planet' express false propositions.

A happy consequence of The Unfilled Proposition View is that 'Vulcan is a planet' and 'Ossian is a poet' express different propositions. A less happy consequence is that 'Vulcan is a planet' and 'Ossian is a planet' express the same unfilled proposition. So do 'Vulcan does not exist' and 'Ossian does not exist' (as I noted above). But, of course, a competent speaker could accept one member of these pairs and reject the other. So these pairs of sentences seem to differ in cognitive value.

To explain the cognitive differences between the sentences, without supposing they express different propositions, we must appeal to the theory of belief we developed above for The No Proposition View. Belief states, like sentences, can express unfilled propositions. The propositional content of a belief expressed by an utterance containing an empty name is an unfilled proposition. So the beliefs that a person expresses by sincerely uttering 'Vulcan does not exist' and 'Ossian does not exist' have the same unfilled propositional content. But they may nevertheless be distinct beliefs, for distinct beliefs may have the same unfilled propositional content. Hence a speaker might accept one of these sentences and reject the other, and may be disposed to make different inferences upon hearing them, and may act differently upon accepting them. Thus these sentences and beliefs may differ in cognitive (and causal) respects, without differing in any semantic respect.

8. Conclusion

The Unfilled Proposition View is consistent, in both letter and spirit, with Direct Reference theories for proper names. For the Direct Reference theory of structured propositions allows, and even encourages, the notion of an unfilled proposition. Furthermore, The Unfilled Proposition View embraces the Direct Reference requirement that an empty name have no semantic value. The unfilled Proposition View also satisfies many of our intuitions concerning empty names. We are (often) inclined to say that a sentence containing an empty name expresses a proposition, and that a person who sincerely utters such a sentence says and believes something. The Unfilled Proposition View agrees with these intuitions. The proposition expressed and believed is incomplete in some sense—but perhaps that is yet another intuitive advantage of the view. Finally, this view allows sentences containing empty names to be true or false in virtue of what they say, just as intuition requires.

The No Proposition View is also consistent with Theories of Direct Reference. But it lacks the above intuitive advantages of The Unfilled Proposition View. Nevertheless, if there were strong objections to The Unfilled Proposition View, I believe it might still be reasonable to adopt The No Proposition View. Thus I believe that some version of one of these two views will provide plausible solutions to the apparent problems that empty names pose for Theories of Direct Reference.[28]

REFERENCES

Almog, Joseph. (1986). "Naming without Necessity." *Journal of Philosophy,* 83, pp. 210–242.

Almog, Joseph. (1991). "The Subject-Predicate Class I." *Noûs,* 25, pp. 591–619.

Braun, David. (1991). "Proper Names, Cognitive Contents, and Beliefs." *Philosophical Studies,* 62, pp. 289–305.

Davies, Martin. (1981). *Meaning, Quantification, Necessity.* London: Routledge & Kegan Paul.

Donnellan, Keith. (1974). "Speaking of Nothing." *The Philosophical Review,* 83, pp. 3–31.

Evans, Gareth. (1983) *The Varieties of Reference.* Oxford: Oxford University Press, 1982.

Kaplan, David. (1989). "Demonstratives." In Joseph Almog, John Perry, and Howard Wettstein (eds.), *Themes from Kaplan,* pp. 481–614. Oxford: Oxford University Press.

Kripke, Saul. (1979) "A Puzzle about Belief," in Avishai Margalit (ed.), *Meaning and Use,* pp. 239–83. Boston: Reidel, 1979.

Kripke, Saul. (1980). *Naming and Necessity.* Cambridge, MA: Harvard University Press.

Quine, W. V. (1953). "On What There Is." In *From a Logical Point of View,* pp. 1–19. New York: Harper & Row.

Russell, Bertrand. (1956). "The Philosophy of Logical Atomism." In Robert Marsh (ed.), *Logic and Knowledge,* pp. 177–281. London: George Allen & Unwin.

Salmon, Nathan. (1986). *Frege's Puzzle.* Cambridge, MA: MIT Press.

Scott Soames. (1987). "Direct Reference, Propositional Attitudes, and Semantic Content." *Philosophical Topics,* 15, pp. 47–87.

Wettstein, Howard. (1986). "Has Semantics Rested on a Mistake?" *Journal of Philosophy,* 83, pp. 185–209.

Wettstein, Howard. (1988). "Cognitive Significance without Cognitive Content." *Mind,* 97, pp. 1–28.

---

[28]I am grateful to John Bennett, Earl Conee, Mark Crimmins, Michael Devitt, Richard Feldman, David Kaplan, Bernard Kobes, Gail Mauner, and Francis Jeffry Pelletier for many helpful discussions, comments, and criticisms. I wish to give very special thanks to Joseph Almog for numerous suggestions, and for many useful discussions on this topic, and other related topics. I presented earlier versions of this paper at the University of Rochester and the University of Alberta. I wish to thank the participants in the discussions that followed for their comments.

REFERENCE AND CONTINGENCY

Gareth Evans

"A logical theory may be tested by its capacity for dealing with puzzles, and it is a wholesome plan, in thinking about logic, to stock the mind with as many puzzles as possible, since these serve much the same purpose as is served by experiments in physical science."[1] This paper is an attempt to follow Russell's advice by using a puzzle about the contingent *a priori* to test and explore certain theories of reference and modality. No one could claim that the puzzle is of any great philosophical importance by itself, but to understand it, one has to get clear about certain aspects of the theory of reference; and to solve it, one has to think a little more deeply than one is perhaps accustomed about what it means to say that a statement is contingent or necessary.

The idea that there might be truths which are both contingent and *a priori* was thrown up by Kripke in the course of his celebrated discussion of the modal and epistemic categories to which the notions of the contingent and the *a priori* respectively belong.[2] There has been some discussion of the idea since Kripke raised it, all of it based upon the assumption that the existence of a statement which is both contingent and *a priori* would constitute an intolerable paradox. For example, Michael Dummett has argued that the fact that Kripke's views on reference and modality appear to lead to the recognition of the existence of *a priori* truths shows that something must be wrong with those views.[2a] In other recent discussions, attempts are made to dissolve the puzzle by showing that, properly understood, the problematical statements are not both contingent and *a priori*. There seem to me to be clear logical and semantical errors in all of these attempts, but more importantly, their starting-point seems incorrect. There is no paradox in the existence of statements which are both contingent and *a priori*, at least, not in the sense in which the problematical statements may be claimed to be contingent. There are two quite different conceptions of what it is for a statement to be contingent; statements may be, as we might say, *deeply contingent* or *superficially contingent*. Whether a statement is deeply contingent depends upon what makes it true; whether a statement is superficially contingent depends upon how it embeds inside the scope of modal operators. While it would be intolerable for there to be a statement which is both knowable *a priori* and deeply contingent, I shall try to show that there is nothing particularly perplexing about the existence of a statement which is both knowable *a priori* and superficially contingent, which is the most that the problematical statements may be claimed to be.

In Kripke's original presentation of the puzzle, and in all subsequent discussions, the problematical statements were formulated with the use of a very special

---

[1] B. Russell, "On Denoting", *Mind* 14 (1905), pp. 484–5.

[2] S. Kripke, "Naming and Necessity," in D. Davidson and G. Harman (eds.), *Semantics of Natural Languages* (Dordrecht): Reidel, 1972), pp. 253–355.

[2a] M. Dummett, *Frege* (London: Duckworth, 1973), p. 121.

kind of singular term, which I shall call 'a descriptive name': a name whose reference is fixed by description.[3] In fact, the puzzle about the contingent *a priori* does not have any special connection with the theory of reference, since it is easy to formulate statements with the same initially puzzling combination of characteristics without the use of singular terms at all. Indeed, it is one of the most serious deficiences in the existing attempts at a solution to the puzzle that they do not generalize to these other cases. Nevertheless, though the puzzle is not peculiar to them, and though they occur only infrequently in natural language, descriptive names are of some theoretical interest, and an understanding of their properties is essential to a critical appraisal of previous approaches to the puzzle. For these reasons, I shall devote the first part of this paper to an account of how descriptive names function. In Part II, I shall use this account to examine the previous attempts to dissolve the puzzle. In Part III, I attempt to get clear about the modal properties of statements, and in particular about the relation between the modal properties of a statement and its content. Finally, in part IV, I attempt to explain how it is possible for a statement to be both (superficially) contingent, and knowable *a priori*.

I

A descriptive name is a name whose reference is fixed by description. This formulation covers two points. First, a descriptive name is a referring expression; it belongs to that category of expressions whose contribution to the truth conditions of sentences containing them is stated by means of the relation of reference. Second, there is a semantical connection between the name and a description; the sense of the name is such that an object is determined to be the referent of the name if and only if it satisfies a certain description. If we borrow an idea of Frege's (as expressed by Dummett) and think of a statement of what an expression refers to as simultaneously showing, or displaying, its sense, then we may say that a descriptive name has a sense which is displayed by the statement that it refers to whatever it is that satisfies such and such a description. In this way, a descriptive name has a descriptive content.

Very few names which naturally occur in ordinary language can be regarded as descriptive names. It is difficult to hold of ordinary proper names that there is some particular description semantically associated with the name. It is more plausible to hold the view which Wiggins put as follows:

> The sense of a proper name simply consists in its having been assigned whatever reference it has been assigned; to know the sense of *n* is to know to which entity *n* has been assigned, a single piece of knowledge which may be given in countless different ways by countless different descriptions.[4]

Even when there is a community-wide association between a name and one description, as perhaps 'Homer' is now associated with the description 'The

---

[3] The term 'descriptive name' is also used by Strawson to refer to a type of definite description. See *Subject and Predicate in Logic and Grammar* (London: Methuen, 1974), p. 60.

[4] D. Wiggins, "Identity, Designation, Essentialism, Physicalism." *Philosophia* 5 (1975), p. 11.

author of *Iliad* and the *Odyssey*, it is more plausible to regard the association as constituting a bit of information, or misinformation, inherited from people who purported to use the name as an ordinary proper name, rather than as manifesting a general intention to use the name to refer to whoever in fact satisfies the description. A natural example of a descriptive name will occur only when a name is introduced in connection with some description. Kripke mentions 'Jack the Ripper' and 'Vulcan' as examples of such names; another example might be 'Deep Throat', used as a name for whoever in the White House was the source of Woodward and Bernstein's Watergate-related information. Nevertheless, no matter how rare examples may be, it would appear always to be open to create descriptive names by stipulation. For example, we might stipulate:

(D) Let us use 'Julius' to refer to whoever invented the zip,[5]

and, governed by such a stipulation, 'Julius' would appear to have the properties of a descriptive name. For present purposes, it is not necessary to concern ourselves with the situation that would arise if the name became associated with other predicates as a result of discoveries made using the stipulation. We need only consider the simple case—the initial period during which the name is unquestionably a 'one-criterion' name.

It is fairly easy to see how the view expressed by Wiggins leads to the claim that ordinary proper names are 'Russellian'—if they have no referent, they have no sense. On that view, understanding an ordinary proper name requires knowing of the referent that the name refers to it, and this knowledge cannot exist in the absence of a referent. After all, if the knowledge is capable of being given in countless different ways, there must be something which unifies them, and this can only be the fact that they are all ways of identifying the same object; in the absence of an object this principle of unification, and hence the single piece of knowledge, does not exist. But, given the close semantical connection between a descriptive name and a description, no such problem arises, and it is plausible to hold that such names are 'Fregean'—they have a sense whether or not they have a referent.[5a] It is sufficient to understand 'Julius' that one know that it refers to whoever invented the zip. This knowledge can certainly be possessed whether or not there is such a person, and possessing it, one is in a position to know exactly what conditions have to be satisfied for sentences containing the name to be true, and hence to understand them.

The only argument I know against the view that names introduced by description are Fregean was presented to me by Kripke. He supposed, I think correctly, that if one held that a speaker says something by uttering the sentence 'Julius is F' when the name is empty, then no better account could be given of what he said than this:

---

[5] In a slight regimentation, I shall take the English quantifier 'whoever' 'whatever' etc. to be free of existential commitment. By 'zip' I mean 'zip fastener'.

[5a] I no longer think the term 'Fregean' is appropriate for names which have a sense whether or not they have a referent, for reasons which I explain in my paper "Understanding Demonstratives" in *Meaning and Understanding*, eds. H. Parret and J. Bouveresse (Berlin and New York: W. de Gruyter, 1981), pp. 280–303.

he said that the man who invented the zip is F. But, Kripke argued, we cannot in general suppose that, when 'a' is a name whose reference is fixed by the description ϕ, that someone who utters the sentence 'a is F' says that the ϕ is F, since the statement that the ϕ is F may have different *modal* properties from the statement that *a* is F. I agree that sentences containing names embed differently under modal operators than do sentences containing descriptions, but it is perhaps the main point of this paper that the conclusion which Kripke draws from this fact follows only upon a questionable view of the connection between the content of an utterance and its modal properties. This important matter must be held over until part III.[6]

Russell held that there could not be a referring expression with the properties we are taking 'Julius' to possess. He wrote:

> Whenever the grammatical subject of a proposition can be supposed not to exist without rendering the propositions meaningless, it is plain that the grammatical subject is not a proper name, i.e., is not a name directly representing some object.[7]

Precisely because he held that sentences containing definite descriptions had determinate truth conditions whether or not the description was proper, he concluded that definite descriptions were not referring expressions, and he would surely have drawn the same conclusion about 'Julius'. Russell thought that it was a consequence of using the relation of reference to state the semantical contribution which an expression makes to sentences containing it that, in the event that the expression has no referent, those sentences would be deprived of truth conditions, and thus 'meaningless'. I think that Russell was wrong about this, but it is not a foolish view, and it is important for us to assure ourselves that there can be expressions of the kind the puzzle supposes names like 'Julius' to be. I feel this obligation particularly strongly since I agree with Russell, though not for his reasons, that definite descriptions are not referring expressions, and I also agree with him that other members of the category of referring expressions, to which I wish to regard 'Julius' as belonging, are such that, if they are empty, sentences containing them have no truth conditions. We must have at least some idea of what conception of

---

[6] As Kripke's inclination to argue in this way makes clear, my explanation of what it is for a name to have its reference fixed by description is almost certainly not the one intended by Kripke. I have made 'having a reference fixed by description' a semantical property of a word in a public language, whereas Kripke prefers to speak of a particular person, not necessarily the introducer of a name, fixing its reference by description. (I am grateful to John Dolan for reminding me of this.) It is a consequence of this that we cannot say that such-and-such a statement—here using a sentence in a public language—is knowable *a priori*, but only that such-and-such a sentence is *a priori* for X. If names like 'Julius' are Russellian, we will not even be able to state what X knows in a public language. Further, a sentence may be *a priori* for X, when it is not even true, namely when the name is empty. I am not sure what Kripke means by these relativized notions; they seem to come to something like: *what X means by S* or, *the belief X expresses by S*, is *a priori* true. If this is the case, then I do not think that the puzzle can be formulated, since I hold that it makes sense to say that what X means, or what X believes is contingent only relative to some way of expressing that belief in a public language. Since I see no incoherence in the idea of a descriptive name, I shall avoid Kripke's relativized notions.

[7] B. Russell, *Principia Mathematica* (2nd edn) (Cambridge: Cambridge University Press, 1968), p. 66.

reference includes 'Julius' as a referring expression, despite the fact that it is Fregean, and most referring expressions are not, and excludes 'the inventor of the zip', despite the very close similarity between it and the name 'Julius'.

Reference may be regarded as whatever relation it is between expressions and objects which makes the following principle true:

(P) If R $(t_1 \ldots t_n)$ is atomic, and $t_1 \ldots t_n$ are referring expressions, then R $(t_1 \ldots t_n)$ is true iff ⟨the referent of $t_1 \ldots$ the referent of t_n⟩ satisfies R.[8]

Satisfaction is also whatever relation makes (P) true; (P) simultaneously and implicitly defines reference and satisfaction in terms of truth. (P) invites the semantic theorist to identify a class of atomic sentences in which he can discern expressions of two characteristic types, and to deal with expressions of each type by means of two different semantic relations which fit together, according to (P), to yield the truth conditions of those sentences. This is all you know, and all you need to know, by way of a *definition* of reference, or of satisfaction. Then, it is natural to regard as a referring expression any expression whose semantic contribution to the sentence in which it occurs is stated by means of the relation of reference which is found in (P). Now, we should expect Russellian singular terms to have their semantic contribution stated in clauses such as:

(1) The referent of 'John' = John.

When there is no referent, no such clause can truly be stated, so that truth conditions for sentences containing the term cannot be derived: this is a formal representation of the fact that nothing is said by one who utters a sentence containing the term.[9] But it is not necessary that a clause for a referring expression should take this simple form. It is equally true that a clause like:

(2) (x) (Refers to ('Julius', x) ≡ x uniquely invented the zip)

uses only the relation of reference which is found in principle (P); taken together with the normal satisfaction clauses for atomic predicates, such a clause will enable us to derive truth conditions for sentences containing 'Julius' of the form:

(3) 'Julius is F' is true iff the man who invented the zip is F.[10]

Neither (2), nor anything used in the derivation of (3), presupposes the existence of a referent for 'Julius'. Hence, according to this theory, 'Julius' is Fregean.

---

[8] The status of the description 'the referent of t_i' is *sub judice*, but to understand (P) you need only your working masery of your language. A more realistic principle would need to take account of context dependence, but since our official business in no way depends upon context dependence, I have suppressed the complexities which stem from that source.

[9] For some of the consequences of using clauses like (1) in the theory of meaning, see J. H. McDowell, "On the Sense and Reference of a Proper Name," *Mind* 36 (1977), pp. 159–85.

[10] I contend that this statement of the truth conditions of 'Julius is F; is perfectly acceptable as a statement of its meaning or content, despite the fact that the sentence used on the right hand side embeds differently inside modal operators than the sentence quoted on the left. A theory incorporating such a theorem certainly need not misstate the truth conditions of any modal sentence, and as to content, I hold that the two sentences do have the some content, despite their modal differences. This is defended in part III.

The truth condition stated in (3) is not homophonic, but this is quite inessential to the approach, once we suppose the metalanguage to contain a name with the same sense as 'Julius'. However, at this point we must pay attention to an important logical consequence of the semantic status which we are in the course of securing for 'Julius'. It is a consequence of the fact that 'Julius' is Fregean that, when it is empty, not only are atomic sentences containing it significant (though not true) but there may also be *complex* sentences containing the name which are *true*. For example, unless we specifically prevent it, the general rule for sentential negation will apply to the sentence 'It is not the case that (Julius is F)'; and, since it states that a negated sentence is true iff the embedded sentence is not true, the result will be that the given sentence will be determined as true when the name 'Julius' is empty. A similar point applies to any truth-functionally complex sentence containing an atomic constituent of the form 'Julius is F'; given other constituents with suitably chosen truth values, such complex sentences may be true. It is therefore an immediate consequence of the recognition of a name like 'Julius' that we must either modify the classical clauses for the truth-functional connectives, or we must modify classical logic—specifically by restricting the rules of Existential Generalization (EG) and Universal Elimination (UE). Unrestricted, the rule of EG would enable us to pass from a true premises, such as '$-(F(Julius))$' to what might be a false conclusion, '$(\exists x) - F(x)$', when the name 'Julius' is empty. Similarly, the rule of UE would enable us to pass from a true premises, such as '$(x) (x = x)$', to a false conclusion: 'Julius = Julius' when the name 'Julius' is empty. Logics with the required restrictions are well known under the title of Free Logics.[11] I shall not go into details here. Since it will be convenient to allow names like 'Julius' to take wide, as well as narrow, scope, I shall suppose that we are working with a language with explicit scope indicators, and a rule of Existential Generalization which is sensitive, at least for these names, to their scope. Thus, I shall follow Russell's square bracket scope-indicating device, and distinguish:

$$[a]\ (P \lor F(a))$$

from:

$$P \lor [a]\ (F(a)),$$

and so on, with the logical theory permitting $(\exists x)\ A(x)$ to be inferred only from $[a]\ A(a)$.[12]

With this background, we can see that there is no obstacle to using the name 'Julius' to state its own semantic contribution, in the way which is characteristic of homophonic theories:

(4) (x) (Refers to ('Julius', x) $\equiv$ [Julius] $(x = $ Julius)).

---

[11] For an excellent text, see R. Schock, *Logics without Existence Assumptions* (Stockholm: Almqvist and Wicksell, 1968).

[12] Explicit scope-indicating devices are not necessary; in their absence, descriptive names would always be regarded as having narrowest scope, and wide-scope readings would be stated using the device: '$(\exists x)\ (x = a\ \&\ \ldots x \ldots)$'. See S. Kripke, "Is there a Problem about Substitutional Quantification?" in G. Evans and J. H. McDowell (eds.), *Truth and Meaning* (Oxford: Clarendon Press, 1976), pp. 373–4.

Using (4), we will be able to derive homophonic truth conditions for sentences containing the name 'Julius', but since the name has narrow scope in (4), and in the resulting statement of truth conditions, the semantic theory is not itself committed to the existence of a referent.[13]

We are half-way towards answering our question. We have an account of what unifies 'Julius' with other referring expressions, despite its difference from them. We have not yet explained why definite descriptions should not be regarded as referring expressions. There is no formal obstacle to treating descriptions in clauses similar to (2), and such theories have been constructed.[14] Since there are indefinitely many descriptions, we do not expect a clause in the theory of meaning giving the reference of each one. Rather, the theory would contain a recursive principle along the lines of:

> (5) $(\phi) (x)$ (Refers to ('the' $\frown \phi$, x) $\equiv$ $\underline{\text{Satisfies } (\phi, x)}$)),[15]

from which indefinitely many such statements of reference can be derived. Such a theory enables us to deduce a truth condition for sentences containing a description even when it is improper. Consequently, if the only objection to regarding descriptions as referring expressions stems from Russell's observation that, by uttering a sentence containing an improper description, one makes a perfectly intelligible move in the language game, then it would appear to have been met. However, it is not the only objection, for if we look at matters more closely, it becomes clear that a principle like (5) is not adequate to explain the behaviour of descriptions in all contexts.

The feature of the behaviour of descriptions which cannot be captured in this way comes out most clearly in modal contexts, and in order to explain it, we must work with some semantic theory adequate to deal with those contexts. Since possible-worlds semantic theories are both familiar and easy to work with, I shall put my points in their terms, but they should be capable of translation into any semantical framework. I certainly do not wish my use of possible-worlds semantics to be taken to indicate either that I believe it to be the correct semantical framework for modal sentences of natural languages, or that I believe it to be immune to philosophical objection.[16]

A possible-worlds semantic theory states the truth conditions of sentences of a language which contains modal operators in a metalanguage which dispenses with such operators in favour of explicit quantification over possible worlds. For

---

[13] It is not necessary to get involved here in the details of the truth theory; for some of them, see T. Burge, "Truth and Singular Terms," *Noûs* 8 (1974), pp. 309–25. Burge applies the same treatment to descriptions, which I do not want to do. His complicated restricted identity-substitution principle, (A8), seems unnecessary; the derivation of truth conditions need only exploit the extensionality of the description operator.

[14] See, e.g., T. Burge, *ibid.*

[15] I use underlining as a uniqueness operator. Thus: 'A $(\tau_1 \ldots \underline{\tau_i} \ldots \tau_n)$' abbreviates

'A $(\tau_1 \ldots \tau_i \ldots \tau_n)$ & (x) (A $(\tau_1 \ldots x, \ldots \tau_n) \supset x = \tau_i)$'.

[16] For an alternative approach to the semantics of modality, see C.A.B. Peacocke, "Necessity and Truth Theories," *Journal of Philosophical Logic* 7 (1978).

each n-place predicate, R, of the object language, there is in the metalanguage an $n + 1$ place predicate, R'; the additional argument-place being occupied by terms referring to, and variables ranging over, possible worlds. These predicates are connected *via* satisfaction clauses of the form:

$$(x_1) \ldots (x_n) \, (\text{Satisfies}_w \, (\text{'R'}, \langle x_1 \ldots x_n \rangle) \equiv R' \, (x_1 \ldots x_n w))^{17}$$

For example, an object satisfies 'Bald' *with respect to* a world w iff it is bald *in w*. The theory is so constructed that we are able to derive, for each sentence S, a theorem of the form:

$$(w) \, (\text{True}_w(S) \equiv \ldots)$$

with which the clauses for the modal operators connect in the familiar way:

$$(S) \, (w) \, (\text{True} \, (\text{'It is possible that'} \frown S) \equiv (\exists w') \, (\text{Alt} \, (w, w') \, \& \, \text{True}_w \, (S)))$$

('Alt' is some suitable 'alternativeness relation' defined over the set of possible worlds; its properties need not concern us.) A sentence is true *simpliciter* iff it is true$_{w^*}$, where 'w^*' refers to the actual world.

In the context of this semantic theory, the principle (P) must be modified to connect reference with the notion true$_w$.

(P') If R $(t_1 \ldots t_n)$ is atomic, and $t_1 \ldots t_n$ are referring expressions, then R$(t_1 \ldots t_n)$ is true$_w$ iff

⟨the referent of t_1 . . . the referent of t_n⟩ satisfies$_w$ R.

(From this principle, the principle (P) can be derived as a special case.) Once this change has been made, no other change needs to be made. Even in a modal language, all that is necessary to state the significance of names and other referring expressions is to state to what, if anything, they refer; the truth-with-respect-to-a-situation of a sentence containing a singular term depends simply upon whether or not its referent satisfies the predicate with respect to that situation. But, notoriously, this is not the case with definite descriptions. If we assign them a reference by means of a principle like (5), and connect this assignment with truth by means of (P'), if, in short, we treat them like other referring expressions, we capture only one of the readings of a sentence like:

The first man in space might have been an American,

namely that on which it is equivalent to the claim that Gagarin might have been an American. The whole sequence would be determined as true iff there is a possible world with respect to which the referent of the description, i.e., Gagarin,

---

[17] I subscript the satisfaction relation thus: 'Satisfies$_w$', and similarly with 'true$_w$', partly for ease of comparison with classical clauses, but also to emphasize that these relativized semantical relations are not got by the same process that gives us 'F'(x, w)' from 'F(x)'. The statement that a is bald in w ('Bald' (a, w)') can be understood as equivalent to the simple counterfactual: if w had been actual, a would have been bald, but the statement that a certain statement is true with respect to a world ('True$_w$(S)') is not equivalent to the simple counterfactual: if w had been actual, S would have been true. See below.

satisfies 'American'. In order to capture the other reading of this sentence, on which it is true iff there is a possible world in which the man who is first in space in *that* world is an American (in that world), some changes have to be made.

The only way of making those changes, while still attempting to treat descriptions as referring expressions, is by relativizing the relation of reference to a possible world. (5) must become:

(6) $(\phi)\,(x)\,(w)$ (Refers to$_w$('the' ϕ, x) $\equiv$ Satisfies$_w$ (ϕ, x))

and (P') must become:

(P") If R $(t_1 \ldots t_n)$ is atomic, and $t_1 \ldots t_n$ are referring expressions, then R$(t_1 \ldots t_n)$ is true$_w$ iff

⟨the referent$_w$ of t_1 . . . the referent t_w of t_n⟩ satisfies$_w$ R.

This can be done.[18] But it is at a high price, due to the fact that we must relativize the relation of reference in all cases. Simply in order to assimilate descriptions to other referring expressions, we introduce a major change in the semantic apparatus in terms of which we describe the functioning of those other expressions. As a consequence of this change, we ascribe to names, pronouns, and demonstratives semantical properties of a *type* which would allow them to get up to tricks they never in fact get up to; since their reference never varies from world to world, this semantic power is never exploited.

A similar point can be made when we take account of the existence of ambiguities which definite descriptions generate in tensed sentences, like:

The leader of the Conservative Party will be courageous.

To deal with this, essentially similar, ambiguity, the relation of reference must also be relativized to a time. Once again, this enrichment of the type of semantical assignment made to singular terms is unnecessary for all terms other than descriptions. Finally, the fact that a position inside a description can be bound by a higher quantifier, as in the sentence:

The father of each girl is good to her,

requires a relativization of the relation of reference to a sequence, or an assignment, π, to the empty singular term positions which the description may contain.[19]

---

[18] Has been done, by, e.g., R. Thomason and R. Stalnaker, "Modality and Reference," *Noûs* 2 (1968). 'An expression like "$(\imath x)\,\phi\,(x)$" is assigned a referent which may vary from world to world'. On such a view, the first reading considered is captured by giving the descriptive singular term wide scope with respect to the modal operator.

[19] This point is made in B. Mates's paper, "Descriptions and Reference," *Foundations of Language* 10 (1973), pp. 409–18. In fact, the objection can be dealt with if one uses 'Fregean' rather than 'Tarskian' treatments of the quantifiers; for this distinction, see my paper "Pronouns, Quantifiers and Relative Clauses (I)," *Canadian Journal of Philosophy* 7 (1977), 471–7. It should be stressed that the relativity to a time required to deal with the temporal flexibility of descriptions is quite different from that introduced by context-dependence, so that, treating descriptions as referring expressions imposes on the relation of reference a double relativity to a time.

Thus, if we are to include definite descriptions in the category of referring expressions, we are forced to describe the behaviour of all the members of that category in terms of the relation 'Refers to$_{w, t, \pi}(\tau, x)$' rather than the simple relation 'Refers to (τ, x)' which is otherwise perfectly adequate. This certainly does not constitute a knock-down argument against treating descriptions as referring expressions, but it does rather strongly suggest that the grouping that results on this treatment may not correspond to any natural, semantical, kind. This case is strengthened when we look at the other side of the story, and examine alternative approaches to descriptions. One approach looks especially promising. Every semantical theory must recognize the category of quantifiers, members of which occur in the sentences 'Every ϕ is ψ', 'Some ϕ is ψ', 'No ϕ is ψ', etc. We find that if we suppose the sentence 'The ϕ is ψ' to be built up in exactly the same way out of exactly the same type of semantic elements as the quantified sentences which it so closely resembles, we achieve a remarkably good fit with the behaviour it is observed to display. Even on a theory which attempts to treat descriptions as singular terms, we could introduce, with no complication of theory, a quantifier 'The', and the resulting sentences would be indistinguishable from those containing the supposed singular term. Such a theory could then be considerably simplified if it made do with just the quantifier 'The', and allowed the relation which deals with referring expressions to revert to its simple, unrelativized form. In other disciplines, such a consideration would strongly recommend the resulting theory, and I am not sure why the theorist of meaning should be unmoved by it.[20] In what follows, I shall treat 'The' as a quantifier; specifically, as a binary quantifier, taking two open sentences to make a sentence. 'The ϕ is ψ' is therefore formalizable as '$(\mathrm{I}x)\,(\phi(x);\,\psi(x))$', which I shall suppose to be provably equivalent to the Russellian expansion '$(\exists x)\,(\underline{\phi(x)}\,\&\,\psi(x))$'.[21]

I have assumed, in the argument I have just presented, that proper names, pronouns, and demonstrative expressions function as 'rigid designators'. I shall not defend this claim here; I shall only remark that it seems to be a fairly strongly marked feature of even such a name as 'Julius' that we do not use it so that the following comes out true:

> If you had invented the zip, you would have been Julius,
>
> If Julius had never invented the zip, he would not have been Julius.

However, if we adopt the recommendation of the previous paragraph, the behaviour which Kripke labels 'rigid designation' emerges as simply that of designation. A referring expression does not designate the same thing with respect to each

---

[20] I discuss the aspect of the methodology of semantic theories which I am here relying on in my paper "Semantic Structure and Logical Form," in Evans and McDowell, *op. cit.* For those who think that the proposal to treat 'The' as a quantifier need be accompanied by the butchering of the surface structure of English in which Russell so perversely delighted, see the treatment of quantifiers in my paper "Pronouns, Quantifiers and Relative Clauses (I)," *op. cit.*

[21] I have with these arguments finally come round to the position urged on me some years ago by Mr M. K. Davies.

possible situation; it simply designates, and the truth value of any sentence containing it depends upon what, if anything, it designates. The term 'rigid designation' carries with it the suggestion of 'non-rigid designation', and hence only really belongs in a theory in which the designation/reference relation is relativized and used in the treatment of both names and descriptions.

I began this line of thought with a doubt about the very possibility of a Fregean referring expression. I have tried to show that this doubt is groundless. If a name like 'Julius' is treated in clauses like (2), or (4), it will be Fregean, while if the relation of reference used in those clauses is connected to truth$_w$ *via* the principle (P'), it will behave as a 'rigid designator'. With this background, we can now consider the puzzle.

II

Given that the name 'Julius' is introduced into the language by means of the stipulation (D), it appears that someone can know that the sentence:

(S)   If anyone uniquely invented the zip, Julius invented the zip

is true, simply in virtue of knowledge he has as a speaker of the language. The problematical sentence is given this conditional form because the simple sentence:

(sub-(S)) Julius invented the zip

requires for its truth something which, it is supposed, (S) does not, namely that someone did uniquely invent the zip, and since this cannot be known *a priori*, neither can sub-(S).

At the same time, (S) appears to be contingent; there are possible worlds with respect to which it is false. Because 'Julius' is a referring expression, the truth with respect to a world of the consequent, sub-(S), requries the satisfaction with respect to that world of the predicate 'invented the zip' by the referent of 'Julius'— i.e. the man who actually invented the zip, if there is such a man. Hence, a world in which someone who did not actually invent the zip invents the zip is a world with respect to which the antecedent of the conditional is true, but the consequent, and thus the whole conditional, is false.

In order to bring out the puzzlement which this combination of characteristics ought, at least initially, to invoke, let me quote a passage of Kripke's:

> I guess it is thought that . . . if something is known *a priori* it must be necessary, because it was known without looking at the world. If it depended upon some contingent feature of the actual world, how could you know without looking? Maybe the actual world is one of the possible worlds in which it would have been false.[22]

And in a recent paper devoted to the puzzle, Donnellan poses the problem in similar terms:

> If a truth is a contingent one then it is made true, so to speak, by some actual state of affairs in the world, that, at least in the sort of example we are interested in,

---

22 Kripke, *op. cit.*, p. 263.

exists independently of our language and linguistic conventions. How can we become aware of such a truth, come to know the existence of such a state of affairs, merely by performing an act of linguistic stipulation?[23]

Donnellan attempts to solve the puzzle by showing that the problematical statement is not both contingent and capable of being known *a priori*. He summarizes his strategy as follows:

> I am going to invoke a distinction between knowing that a sentence expresses a truth and knowing the truth of what is expressed by the sentence. I am going to suggest that, as a result of the introduction of a name as a rigid designator by means of a description fixing the referent, we can come to know, perhaps even *a priori*, that certain sentences express truths, but we do not come to know *a priori* the truth of what they express.[24]

There undoubtedly exists a distinction between knowing that a sentence is true and knowing the truth it expresses—the passage from one bit of knowledge to the other is mediated by knowing what the sentence means. It is Donnellan's contention that someone who knows only the reference-fixing definition (D) does not understand the name 'Julius', nor sentences containing it. According to Donnellan, to understand the name, one must know *of* some object that it is the referent of the name, when such knowledge *of* an object requires a causal connection with it. (This last, causal, feature is inessential to his general strategy, which works provided any *a posteriori* knowledge is made a precondition of understanding the name. It is consistent with the strategy to adopt a criterion of 'knowledge *of*' according to which one knows *of* the shortest spy that he is a spy simply by knowing that the shortest spy is a spy; it remains the case that understanding the name will require *a posteriori* knowledge—that there exists an inventor of the zip—and so that one cannot have *a priori* knowledge of what (S) says.)[25]

This way of solving the puzzle obliges us to make sense of the idea that an expression can have a meaning in a language even though no past, present (and, possibly, future) speaker of that language knows what its meaning is. As Donnellan himself admits, this is not an idea with which we feel very comfortable. But apart from any reservations we may have about this idea in general, there is room for doubt about the use Donnellan makes of it to solve the puzzle. I shall make three points: one *ad hominem*, one substantive, and one promissory. First, the solution to the puzzle seems to me to take a needlessly complicated form. Given the strength of the premisses from which Donnellan proceeds, there is open

---

[23]K. S. Donnellan, "The Contingent *A Priori* and Rigid Designators," *Midwest Studies in Philosophy*, 2 (1977), p. 13.

[24]*Ibid.*, p. 18. As he acknowledges, Donnellan's solution to the puzzle follows that of A. Plantinga, *The Nature of Necessity* (Oxford: Clarendon Press, 1974), pp. 8–9, n. 1, and M. Levin, "Kripke's Argument against the Identity Thesis," *Journal of Philosophy* 72 (1975), p. 152, n. 2.

[25]This option is, in essentials, taken in S. Schiffer's paper "Naming and Knowing," *Midwest Studies in Philosophy* 2 (1977), pp. 28–41. See the passage cited on p. 198 below.

to him, and indeed he is really forced to take, a much, much shorter way with the puzzle. This comes clear when we take note of an obvious, but previously unmentioned, point: *there simply is no puzzle unless the use of free logic is accepted.* Unless a sentence containing the name 'Julius' can be formulated which is free of existential commitment, there is not even a candidate for the status of the contingent *a priori*, but within a classical framework, there are no such sentences. No matter how a name may be embedded in a sentence, in a classical language that name is accessible to existential quantification, and the truth of the whole sentence requires that the name refer. Since it is quite pointless, within a classical framework, to make the problematical sentence conditional in form, it must be presumed to be the intention of anyone offering these conditional sentences that they be taken to be sentences governed by a free logic in which the names take narrow scope. Using our earlier notation, and an otherwise obvious symbolization, (S) must be intended to be understood as having the form:

$$(\exists x) \, (\phi(\hat{x})) \supset [a] \, \phi(a)$$

It is a presupposition of the use of a free logic that there exist Fregean names, and hence a presupposition of the usual formulation of the puzzle, that names like 'Julius' be Fregean names. But Donnellan is prepared to impose upon understanding the name 'Julius' conditions which preclude it from being Fregean—the knowledge which Donnellan requires for really understanding the name cannot be in anyone's possession if the name is empty. Given that he was prepared to impose these requirements, I cannot see why he played along with the conditional form of (S), rather than exposing it as pointless, and I cannot see why he did not dismiss the supposed puzzle in a paragraph, stating that an unrestricted rule of Existential Generalization applies to any proper name, and that, for his part, he cannot see what all the fuss is about.

Anyway, both the position which Donnellan advanced, and this brusquer version of it, depend upon the claim that there cannot be descriptive names, and this brings me to my substantive point: I do not think that this is true. Donnellan does not advance any reason for his claim that a knowledge of (D) is not sufficient for understanding the name 'Julius'. On this crucial point, as though appealing to an unchallengable datum, he says simply:

> It is rather . . . that as these stipulations introduce names, they give the names no descriptive content.[26]

This will not do. It is one thing to hold that ordinary proper names have no descriptive content, quite another to hold that there can be no such thing as a descriptive name. Attempting the only demonstration to which these matters are susceptible, I have tried to show how a theory of meaning can be constructed

---

[26]Donnellan, *op. cit.*, p. 21. Donnellan's claim that names like 'Julius' have no descriptive content is particularly perplexing in the light of his earlier statement that such names are 'pegged to' descriptions. He also strongly suggests that the traditional description theory of names holds good of these names. See p. 17 of Donnellan.

which treats 'Julius' as a Fregean referring expression, and Donnellan gives no reason for thinking that this demonstration is defective.

By omitting to give reasons for one's views, one runs the risk that possibly quite erroneous speculations will be made as to what those reasons might be. I am going to suggest a line of thought which may have influenced Donnellan, though it must be stressed that there is only slight evidence of it in his paper. Suppose that x in fact invented the zip, and hence, is the referent of 'Julius'. Now, let us ask what makes a sentence like 'Julius is F' true. The only answer appears to be x's being F; the existence of that state of affairs in any world is a necessary and sufficient condition of the truth of 'Julius is F' with respect to that world. No state of affairs of the type *y's being the inventor of the zip and y's being F* when $y \neq x$ can make the sentence true, since it is not true with respect to a world incorporating any such state of affairs. Equally, it is not *x's being the inventor of the zip and being F* which makes the sentence true, since *x's being F* is enough to make the sentence true with respect to a world even if x is not the inventor of the zip in that world. (So much is simply to restate the rigidity of 'Julius'.) Consequently, if 'Julius is F' is true, what makes it true is the existence in the actual world of the state of affairs of *x's being F.* Now it seems reasonable to hold that someone who understands the sentence will know what state of affairs makes it true. In that it is made true by x's being in such-and-such a condition, the sentence is *about x*, and hence no one who is not aware of the connection between 'Julius' and x can understand the sentence, for he will not know what it is about. Since knowledge of (D) makes one aware of no such connection, knowledge of (D) is not sufficient for understanding the name.

I mention this argument now, though I will not try to explain what I think is wrong with it until the next section. It will suffice at this point to observe that the argument rests upon a connection between the content of a statement and its modal properties which no one who holds that there can be descriptive names has any reason to accept, and which there are good, independent reasons to reject. Those independent reasons stem from the fact that there are other sentences which have, at least the appearance of being both contingent and *a priori;* a solution to the conundrum in their case, and, I would argue, in all cases, depends upon rejecting the connection between content and modality upon which this argument turns. And this brings me on to my third, promissory point. Although I shall not give examples until Part IV, I claim that there exist examples of the contingent *a priori* which do not even appear to be amenable to treatment along Donnellan's lines. With these examples, it is out of the question to hold that those who are in a position to know that they are true *a priori* do not really understand them. This should make us even more reluctant to deny that there can be descriptive names, since it shows us that such a denial is not even part of a generally effective strategy on the puzzle we are trying to solve.

In what follows, I shall assume that a knowledge of (D) is sufficient for understanding the name 'Julius'. Donnellan may point out that, on such an assumption, (S) certainly does not say anything informative about the world, and this is undoubtedly correct. But saying this merely serves to identify the right puzzle, and

does not solve it. The puzzle is not how we can know *a priori* something informative or interesting about the world, but how we can know *a priori* something
contingent, and hence, how something contingent can be uninformative.

I have stressed that the puzzle does not even get off the ground unless we are
allowed to formulate (S) in a free logic, and in a way which gives the name 'Julius'
narrow scope. It may be thought that, understood in this way, (S) is no longer contingent. This seems to be the position of Stephen Schiffer, who wrote the following brief remarks on the puzzle. (I have altered the passage merely by substituting
my example for his.)

> Kripke cannot have it both ways. If (2) ['Ralph knows that Julius invented the zip
> if anyone did'] attributes to Ralph knowledge of a proposition that is contingent
> because the person who in fact invented the zip might not have, the 'Julius' in (2)
> refers to that person, and (2) attributes to Ralph *de re* knowledge of that person—
> specifically the knowledge that that person invented the zip if anyone did. Now I
> do not mind saying that the inventor of the zip is known by Ralph to have
> invented the zip, and if Ralph can reason a little, to have invented the zip if any-
> one did. But if Ralph has this knowledge, he has it just by virtue of knowing that
> some one person invented the zip, and not at all by virtue of having named the
> inventor of the zip 'Julius'. Yet Ralph's knowledge that some one person invented
> the zip is certainly something that he has only *a posteriori*, and so, therefore, is his
> knowledge, of the inventor of the zip, that the person invented the zip—if Ralph
> has that knowledge.[27]

This passage clearly implies that if there is a proposition which is contingent it
must be existentially committing, and hence, not *a priori*. Contrapositively, if (S)
is interpreted in such a way that it is not existentially committing, then it is not
contingent. *But this is just not true.* The sentence in which the name takes narrow
scope, is certainly contingent, at least in the sense that:

$$- \square \, [(\exists x) \, (\phi(x)) \supset [a] \, \phi(a)]$$

i.e.,

$$\lozenge \, [(\exists x) \, (\phi(\underset{\smile}{x})) \, \& - [a] \, \phi(a)]$$

It is no doubt true that, if (S) were contingent *because of* the contingency of
the possession by an individual of a certain, presumably conditional, property,
then (S) would have to be interpreted in a way which gave the name wide scope,
and Schiffer's way of solving the problem would become applicable. But I am not
aware that Kripke stipulated the *source* of the contingency of his problematical
sentence, and even if he had done so, the stipulation should be ignored, since it is
sufficient to generate the puzzle that the sentence be contingent, never mind how
or why it is contingent. It is true that the contingency of (S) crucially depends
upon the fact that 'Julius' is a referring expression; if we replace the name with the
description 'the inventor of the zip' in such a way that it too receives narrow scope,

---

[27]Schiffer, *op. cit.*, p. 29.

then the sentence is no longer contingent. But it does not follow from the fact that a sentence is contingent because it is formulated with the use of a referring expression, that its contingency is due to the contingent possession of a certain property by the object to which that expression refers.

The puzzle presented by (S) is a little more resistant to solution than it might first appear. The name 'Julius' can be understood by anyone who knows the reference-fixing definition, so a solution along Donnellan's lines is ruled out, while at the same time, simply observing that this is so does not dissolve the puzzle, for even when 'Julius' is interpreted as a descriptive name with narrow scope, (S) remains both contingent and knowable *a priori*.

III

As we have seen, a modal semantics associates with each sentence conditions under which it is true with respect to an arbitrary possible world. The notion 'true$_w$' is specifically designed to account for the way sentences embed inside modal contexts. If $\Diamond$(Q) is true, for example, then the true$_w$ relation for (Q) must be so characterized that there exists a world w such that (Q) is true$_w$. If we wish, we can think of the true$_w$ theorems as associating with each sentence a *function* from possible worlds to truth values, and it is customary to call such functions 'propositions'. As a preliminary to solving the puzzle presented by (S), we must get clear about the relation which exists between the *proposition* associated with a sentence and its *content,* or *what it says.* I shall not attempt to give an analysis of the notion of content here; I want to rely upon the intuitive sense according to which, if two sentences have the same content, then what is believed by one who understands and accepts the one sentence as true is the same as what is believed by one who understands and accepts the other sentence as true. On this, very strict, view of sameness of content, if two sentences have the same content, and a person understands both, then he cannot believe what one sentence says and disbelieve what the other sentence says. When two sentences meet this condition, I shall say that they are epistemically equivalent. Naturally, great difficulties arise when one attempts to apply the criterion in ordinary cases, but we shall be dealing exclusively with rather extraordinary cases—with 'one-criterion' words.

It is immediately evident that two sentences which express the same proposition can have different contents; after all, any two necessary truths are associated with the same function from worlds to truth values, as are the two sentences 'F(*a*)' and 'F(*b*)' when '*a* = *b*' is true. However, I think that it has generally been assumed that, if two sentences express different propositions, they must have different contents, or say different things, and this is the view I want to challenge. Just as we accept the situation which we may represent as follows:

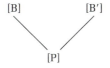

in which distinct statements are modally indistinguishable, so we must accept the situation:

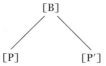

in which epistemically equivalent sentences are modally distinguishable. This may sound very grand, but it amounts to nothing more than this: that sentences with the same content might embed differently inside the scope of modal operators.

There is a position concerning negation and falsity which is parallel to the one I want to adopt, and although I am not at all sure I want to hold it, I think it is sufficiently familiar, and clear, to cast light upon the position I do want to hold. Upon at least one interpretation of Strawson's reply to Russell, he held that the sentence 'The ϕ is not F' is the unambiguous result of applying a negation operator, which I shall symbolize as 'N', to the sentence 'The ϕ is F', and that the sentence 'N(The ϕ is F)' is not true when the description is improper. However, Strawson pointed out, when 'N' is applied to the Russellian expansion 'Something is uniquely ϕ and it is F', the resulting sentence is true. Hence, 'The ϕ is F', and its Russellian expansion, embed differently under the operator 'N'. If one holds this view, one can continue to maintain that 'N' is a truth functional operator by adopting a three-valued logic, in which 'The ϕ is F' gets the value 1/2 ('neither true nor false') when the description is improper, and 'N' maps the value 1/2 on to itself.

On this view, the two sentences are associated with different functions from states of the world into truth values in the set {1, 1/2, 0}, and one can imagine a use of the notion of 'proposition' rather similar to that in the modal case, according to which this difference would mean that the sentences express different propositions. Nevertheless, it would be a great mistake to conclude from the fact that they are associated with different propositions, that the two sentences have different contents, or say different things. To draw this conclusion would place one in the hopeless position of casting around for an account of what it is that one who understands and accepts the sentence 'The ϕ is F' believes, other than that something is uniquely ϕ and F. There is simply no such account; the two sentences are epistemically equivalent. One should not allow oneself to be so misled by one's semantic theory. The division, among non-designated values, into the strictly false, and the neither true nor false, is simply designed to register the differences in the ways sentences embed under 'N', and there is no reason why those differences should not be due to differences in the way the sentences are constructed which are consistent with an identity of content.[28]

---

[28] My understanding of this position is due to Dummett's elaboration of it in *Frege*, Chap. 10. In fact, Strawson may have been arguing for the position which I believe he holds today, namely that the designation 'neither true nor false' is not an indication of a third truth value, but of a sentence's failing to say anything at all. However, it was precisely a reluctance to accept this that led Russell to formulate his theory of descriptions in the first place. I hope it is unnecessary to add that here and throughout when I speak of definite descriptions, I am concerned with 'pure' uses, when no link-up with antecedently existing identificatory knowledge is intended.

Whatever the merits of this position as an account of the way negation inter-acts with descriptions, it provides a parallel to the position I want to adopt in the case of modality. We know that the sentences 'Julius is F' and 'The inventor of the zip is F' are associated with different propositions—they have different true$_w$-conditions. Nevertheless, it seems clear that the two sentences are epistemically equivalent. Remember that we are interpreting the sentence 'Julius is F' in such a way that it is capable of being understood by one who knows only the reference-fixing stipulation (D), and that what it says must be capable of being specified in the absence of any referent. Given these conditions, I cannot imagine how the belief that Julius is F might be characterized which is not simultaneously a char-acterization of the belief that the inventor of the zip is F, i.e., that one and only one man invented the zip and he is F. Belief states are individuated by the evidence which gives rise to them, the expectations, behaviour, and further beliefs which may be based upon them, and in all of these respects the belief states associated with the two sentences are indistinguishable. We do not get ourselves into new belief states by 'the stroke of a pen' (in Grice's phrase)—simply by introducing a name into the language.[29]

In view of this, it seems to be just as much a mistake, leading to just as fruit-less a search, to argue from a difference of 'proposition' to a difference in content in this case, as it was seen to be in the previous case. Rather, we should accept that the two sentences are composed out of different parts of speech—a quantifier ver-sus a name—and that this is a difference in their construction to which modal operators are sensitive even though it leads to no difference in content.

If we had asked those working with a modal semantics why they believed that the situation represented by the second diagram could not arise, I think they might have given the following reply.

"One cannot simply say that two equivalent sentences can embed differently inside modal contexts, and leave matters there. The absolute notion of truth, and the relative notion, truth$_w$, cannot be as independent as this casual talk encourages us to imagine. A modal semantics must validate the theorem $Q \vdash \Diamond Q$, and this means that it is not only simpler, but theoretically indispensable, to be able to regard absolute truth as a special case of truth$_w$—i.e., as truth$_{w*}$, where w^* designates the actual world. Only if there is this connection between the concepts will it follow from the fact that a sentence is (absolutely) true, that there is a world with respect to which it is true. Hence we cannot have two separate parts of the semantic theory, one giving sentences absolute truth conditions, and thereby their content, and the other assigning true$_w$ conditions, and thereby explaining how the sentence will embed under modal operators. On the contrary, there is a single theory, assigning true$_w$

---

[29]I am ignoring what I take to be irrelevant complications which might arise if we take into account beliefs which arise about the name, or the stipulation. G. Harman argues in his paper "How to Use Propositions," *American Philosophical Quarterly* 14 (1977), pp. 174–5, that the introduction of a 'mental name' by a stipulation such as (D) enables someone to have thoughts and beliefs *about* the referent although his previous beliefs would have been merely existential or general. I cannot see any point in this suggestion other than the perhaps laud-able one of utterly discrediting the notion of 'belief about'.

conditions; the truth conditions, and the content of the sentence, must be derivable from that assignment. Hence, we must be able to regard each sentence as formulating a single property, or condition, which it demands of an arbitrary possible world—this is the function 'in intension'—and regard the content of a simple assertion made with the sentence as tantamount to the claim that the actual world satisfies this condition. Now, if two sentences are associated with different propositions, so that there are worlds with respect to which the one is true and the other is not, the associated properties which determine the functions from worlds to truth values must be different. How, then, could the two sentences have the same content, since one is tantamount to the claim that the actual world satisfies one property, and the other is tantamount to the claim that it satisfies a different property?"

The considerations offered in this reply certainly preclude any large-scale, or even very interesting, detachment of content and proposition. Nevertheless, there is a flaw in the argument—a gap which it leaves open, and which all the examples of the contingent *a priori* exploit. Consider for a moment the properties determined by the following two monadic predicate expressions:

(ξ) is as tall as John,

(ξ) is as tall as (ξ), or (ξ) is as tall as himself.

These are certainly different properties, in that there are objects which satisfy the second but which do not satisfy the first. But it is not correct to infer from this that, in all cases, the ascription of one property to an individual yields a statement with a different content from that which results from the ascription of the other property to that individual. When the two properties are ascribed to John, the results are the same, namely:

John is as tall as John.

Correspondingly, the argument advanced above will be fallacious just in the cases in which, to formulate the property of an arbitrary world which is associated with a sentence, one must make reference to what is actually the case. If a sentence is associated with such a property, then the way is open for it to be epistemically equivalent to a sentence which is associated with a distinct (non-co-extensive) property, and hence for sentences which have the same content to be associated with different propositions. In the case of 'Julius is F' and 'The inventor of the zip is F', this is exactly what we find. The former sentence requires of a world w that the man who invented the zip *in the actual world* be F in w, while the latter sentence requires of a world w that the man who invented the zip in w be F in w. Schematically the properties are

$$\lambda w\,[(\mathrm{I}x)(\phi'(x, w^*);\ \mathrm{F}'(x, w))]$$

and

$$\lambda w\,[(\mathrm{I}x)(\phi'(x, w);\ \mathrm{F}'(x, w))]$$

and these are certainly distinct. But the two sentences are epistemically equivalent, because, when applied to the actual world, they yield the same result:

$$(\mathrm{I}x)(\phi'(x, w^*);\ \mathrm{F}'(x, w^*)).$$

I conclude from this that the notion of epistemically equivalent sentences being associated with different propositions is a coherent one; that it has application to certain pairs of sentences in natural language, and that the sentences 'Julius is F' and 'The inventor of the zip is F' are such a pair.

If this conclusion is correct, it follows that we must use the notion of *what makes a sentence true* with a great deal of care, for, if it is used without care it will collapse the distinction between content and proposition which we have been at pains to describe. There are two ways in which one can use the notion of what makes a sentence true. One can follow traditional practice, as I shall do, and tie the notion to the content of a sentence, so that if two sentences are epistemically equivalent, they are verified by exactly the same state of affairs, and what one believes, in understanding the sentence and accepting it as true, is precisely that some verifying state of affairs obtains. On this conception, the same set of states of affairs makes the sentence 'Julius is F' true as makes the sentence 'The inventor of the zip is F' true. If $x, y, z \ldots$ is a list of all objects, then any member of the set:

> {*x's being the inventor of the zip & x's being F; y's being the inventor of the zip and y's being F; z's being the inventor of the zip & z's being F . . .*}

will suffice to make either sentence true.[30]

Alternatively, one can tie the notion of what makes a sentence true to the proposition it expresses by means of the principle: σ makes (Q) true iff, for any world w which comprises σ, (Q) is true$_w$. It was this conception of what makes a sentence true that we were using when we concluded on Donnellan's behalf that, if x in fact invented the zip, the state of affairs of *x's being F* alone made the sentence 'Julius is F' true. This is a perfectly legitimate way to use the notion of what makes a sentence true. What is not legitimate is to use the notion one way, and then slip into using it in the other way. Just such an illegitimate transition was made in the argument which we speculatively attributed to Donnellan. For that argument started from the claim that what makes 'Julius is F' true is *x's being F*— here relying upon the modal conception of what makes the sentence true—and concluded that the sentence is about x, conveys information about the existence of the state of affairs of *x's being F*, and hence, that someone who knew only the reference-fixing definition could not understand it.

When I use the notion of what makes a sentence true, I shall tie the notion to the sentence's content. But there is an ineliminable modal element in the notion of what makes a sentence true. For what can it mean to say that any one of a set of states of affairs renders a sentence true, other than that, if any one of them obtains, the sentence will be true, and that, if any one of them *had* obtained, the sentence *would have been* true? If this is so, to hold that the state of affairs of *y's being the inventor of the zip and being F*, for example, could serve to make the sentence 'Julius

---

[30] The problem presented by (S)—the fact that it is contingent—in no way depends upon the possibility that things might have existed which do not in fact exist, so there is no reason to quantify over possible but non-actual objects. '$x, y, z \ldots$' can here simply be a list of the objects that exist.

is F' true, would appear to commit one to the view that, had y invented the zip and been F, the sentence would have been true. But is this not inconsistent with the fact that the sentence 'Julius is F' is not true with respect to that situation?

I accept the counterfactual claim, but there is no inconsistency in doing so. The point only shows that 'true$_w$' must not be glossed as 'if w were actual, . . . would be true'.[31] But this is no matter; the notion 'true$_w$' is purely internal to the semantic theory, and needs no independent explanation. The counterfactual claim is true, because, had y invented the zip, y would have been the referent of 'Julius', and if he had also been F, then the referent of 'Julius' would have been F, and nothing more is required for the truth of the sentence. Notice that this is not a trivial counterfactual claim about the truth of a sentence identified merely as a sequence of expression types. On the contrary, in the circumstances mentioned, the sentence 'Julius is F' would have been true *as a sentence of English*. The hypothesis that y invented the zip no more involves the hypothesis of a semantical change in English than the hypothesis of its having rained on a day which was in fact dry does. The hypothesis that the name 'Julius' refers to y would involve a semantical change in English only if the reference-fixing definition (D) had established a semantical connection between the name 'Julius' and some particular person other than y. But we have seen that this is not the case. Even if someone did invent the zip, (D) does not introduce a semantical connection between 'Julius' and that person. Neither (D), nor the clauses (2) and (4) based upon it, are existentially committing, and knowledge of them cannot constitute knowledge of a relation between 'Julius' and some item; one cannot know of the existence of a relation between two things, not even a semantical relation, without knowing that those things exist. (D) instituted a semantical connection between a name and a description as fixing its reference, and that connection is preserved unchanged under the supposition that y is the inventor of the zip. Exactly the same theory of meaning serves to describe the language which would be spoken had y invented the zip, as describes the language which is actually spoken.

We are now in a position to reply to the argument of Kripke's against the Fregean status of names introduced by description which I mentioned earlier.[32] The argument rested on the claim that, even when the reference of 'a' is fixed by the description ϕ, one could not be taken to have said that the ϕ is F by uttering 'a is F' since the statement that a is F, and the statement that the ϕ is F have different modal properties. We can now see that this argument depends upon just the connection between content and proposition which I have challenged. It does not follow from the fact that one who utters the sentence 'a is F' says that the ϕ is F, that the sentence 'a is F' and 'The ϕ is F' will embed inside modal operators in the same way. We can regard the theorem:

'a is F' is true iff the ϕ is F

---

[31] This is why it is vital to distinguish 'true' (s, w), formed by the same process that gives us 'bald' (x, w), and 'true$_w(s)$'. See n. 16.

[32] See p. 940 above.

as showing the sense or content of the sentence '*a* is F' without arriving at the result that:

'Possibly (*a* is F)' is true iff Possibly (the ϕ is F).

While we have agreed that absolute truth conditions must be derivable from true conditions, there is no reason for supposing that true$_w$ conditions must be derivable from truth conditions, or content, but this is what Kripke's argument requires.

IV

The relationship which holds between what a sentence says and the proposition with which it is associated allows for the possibility that there be a wholly uninformative sentence which is nevertheless contingent. A sentence with this character could express *a priori* knowledge without engendering any paradox, since, in knowing it to be true, one thereby knows nothing about the world. To make this possibility clear, let us return to the sentences:

John is as tall as John,

John is as tall as himself.

If we ignore for a moment the worry that John might not exist (a worry which corresponds to nothing in the case of worlds), we can know both sentences to be true *a priori*. Now, the second sentence presents us with no problem, for we can think of it as ascribing to John a property possessed by every factual and possible object. But if we thought of the first sentence as ascribing to John the property of being the same height as John, as we are entitled to do, our *a priori* knowledge might give us pause, for this is certainly not a property which is possessed by every actual and possible object. We might worry: how can we know, *a priori*, without looking, that John has this property? How can we know without investigation that John is not one of the objects which lack this property?

No one would really find this perplexing. While it might appear on a causal inspection that one cannot know *a priori* that an object possesses a property not possessed by every object, with these examples in mind, we will readily amend the principle to hold that one cannot know *a priori* that an object possesses a property not possessed by every object, unless the specification of that property requires reference to that object. The same thing goes for properties of worlds. We can know *a priori* that the actual world possesses certain properties not possessed by every world so long as the specification of those properties requires reference to the actual world, or to what is actually the case.

The parallel with the sentences about John's height is also useful because it permits a very sharp characterization of the position adopted by Donnellan and those he was following. One holds a position parallel to Donnellan's in relation to the sentences about John's height if one maintains the view that, if a property is possessed by an object which is not possessed by every object, then it must hold in virtue of the existence of some state of affairs which can only be known to exist *a posteriori*—'by looking'. Presumably, the relevant state of affairs must be that of John's being a particular height—say 6 feet. So, one concludes that the sentence 'John is as tall as John' really says that John is 6 feet tall, that 'as tall as John' refers to the height of 6 feet, and that someone who does not know what height John is, and hence does not know to what height 'as tall as John' refers, does not really understand the sentence.

Sentences constructed with the operator 'Actually' provide very clear illustration of the way the possibility I have described can be exploited to yield harmless contingent *a priori* truths. Such sentences also help to free our minds from the idea that the puzzle about the contingent *a priori* has any particular connection with the theory of reference. I take 'Actually' to be an operator which yields a sentence true with respect to a world iff the sentence to which it applies is true *simpliciter*, and, correspondingly, that an object satisfies$_w$ 'Actually' A iff it satisfies$_{w^*}$ A.[33] The sentences Q, and ⌜Actually (Q)⌝ will be epistemically equivalent, but will embed differently under modal operators, and are hence associated with different propositions. For example, though the sentence:

> If you had painted the post with this paint, it would have been red,

said of a green post, might be true, the sentence:

> If you had painted the post with this paint, it would have been actually red,

said of the same post, would not be true.

Now, consider a sentence of the form:

$$(x) (F'x) \supset \text{Actually} (F'x)))$$

(e.g., 'If anything is red it is actually red'). This statement is clearly contingent; there are worlds with respect to which it is not true, viz. any world in which there are things which are not red in the actual world which are red. Nevertheless, it can clearly be known *a priori*. So there is a property which we can know *a priori* to be possessed by the actual world, but which is not possessed by every world. Is this disturbing? Not at all. For consider what property it is

$$\lambda w [(x) (F' (x, w) \supset F' (x, w^*))].$$

It is hardly surprising that we know *a priori* that the actual world possesses this property:

$$(x) (F' (x, w^*) \supset F' (x, w^*)).$$

This is an example of a contingent *a priori* truth which cannot be dealt with along Donnellan's lines; it can hardly be maintained that one who knows the meaning

---

[33]It is not important if this does not provide an exact description of the behaviour of the 'actually' operator of English; as with descriptive names, all that matters for the puzzle about the contingent *a priori* is that an operator with these properties can coherently be introduced into the language. For a treatment of a modal logic containing 'Actually' see J. Crossley and L. Humberstone, "The Logic of 'Actually'," *Reports on Mathematical Logic* 8 (1977), pp, 11–29; and M. K. Davies, *Truth, Quantification and Modality* (Ph.D. diss., Oxford, 1976).

of 'red', the quantifiers, and the 'actually' operator, does not understand these sentences, nor is it easy to see what bit of *a posteriori* knowledge would be required to really understand them.

This brings us very close to a solution to the puzzle presented by (S). The property (S) demands of an arbitrary possible world is

$$\lambda w \, [(\exists x) \, (\phi'(\underline{X}, w)) \supset [a] \, \phi'(a, w)].$$

Given the way the reference of '*a*' (i.e., 'Julius) is fixed, this is the property:

$$\lambda w \, [(\exists x) \, (\phi'^{\frown} (\underline{X}, w)) \supset (Ix) \, (\phi' \, (x, w^*); \, \phi'(x, w))].$$

This is certainly not possessed by every world, but the fact that we can know *a priori* that it is possessed by the actual world is once again quite unsurprising, for it amounts to the knowledge that:

$$(\exists x) \, (\phi' \, (\underline{X}, \, w^*)) \supset (Ix) \, (\phi'(x, w^*); \, \phi' \, (x, w^*))$$

and knowing this, we know absolutely nothing about the actual world.

To summarize the position we have arrived at, we can now see that perplexity occasioned by the contingent *a priori* status of (S) stems from a confusion between two different notions of contingency, which usually, but do not always, coincide. A sentence may be either superficially contingent or deeply contingent. A sentence (Q) is superficially contingent iff $\ulcorner \Diamond(Q) \urcorner$ is true, or, equivalently, there exists a world w such that it is not the case that (Q) is true$_w$. It is only in this sense that (S) is contingent. But it was wrongly assumed that (S), if contingent, was contingent in a different sense, captured by Kripke's phrase: "dependent upon some contingent feature of the actual world." We have the idea of a state of affairs, or a set of states of affairs, determined by the content of a sentence as capable of rendering it true, so that one who understands the sentence and knows it to be true, thereby knows that such a verifying state of affairs obtains. A deeply contingent statement is one for which there is no guarantee that there exists a verifying state of affairs. If a deeply contingent statement is true, there will exist some state of affairs of which we can say both that had it not existed the sentence would not have been true, and that it might not have existed.[34] The truth of the sentence will thus depend upon some contingent feature of reality.

(S) is not deeply contingent. A conditional sentence is rendered true by anything which falsifies the antecedent or verifies the consequent. Sub-(S), the consequent, is made true by the obtaining of any member of the set of states of affairs:

> {*x's being the inventor of the zip and inventing the zip; y's being the inventor of the zip and inventing the zip; z's being the inventor of the zip and inventing the zip. . .*}

which reduces to the set:

> (*x's being the inventor of the zip: y's being the inventor of the zip; z's being the inventor of the zip. . .*).

---

[34]Notice that in formulating the notion of deep contingency, one uses the notion 'true' (s, w)' and not 'ture$_w(s)$'.

The antecedent is falsified by the absence of every member of this set. Hence, (S) is made true by the absence of every member of this set or by the presence of any member of this set. Given that this is so, although (S) is true, and superficially contingent, it is not deeply contingent—there is no contingent feature of reality on which its truth depends.

(S) demands nothing of the actual world, which is why knowing it to be true *a priori* constitutes no paradox. Nevertheless, we have seen how it is possible for a sentence which demands nothing of the actual world to be false with respect to some possible world. This can arise when the condition which it demands of an arbitrary possible world is formulated in terms of what is actually the case. Thus a sentence can be superficially contingent without being deeply contingent, and with this comes the possibility of a perfectly innocent, if rather uninteresting, example of the contingent *a priori*.[35]

---

[35]The distinction between deep and superficial modal properties also has application to the case of the necessary *a posteriori*, but I must resist the temptation to elaborate. The distinction is adopted, and provided with a fascinating background which enables many further consequences to be drawn, in "Two Notions of Necessity" by M. K. Davies and L. Humberstone, in *Philosophical Studies* 38 (1980), pp. 1–30.

HOW TO MEASURE THE STANDARD METRE

Nathan Salmon

I

> There is *one* thing of which one can say neither that it is one metre long, nor that it is not one metre long, and that is the Standard Metre in Paris.—But this is, of course, not to ascribe any extraordinary property to it, but only to mark its peculiar role in the language-game of measuring with a metre-rule.

So says Wittgenstein (*Philosophical Investigations* §50). Kripke sharply disagrees:

> This seems a very "extraordinary property," actually, for any stick to have. I think [Wittgenstein] must be wrong. If the stick is a stick, for example, 39.37 inches long (I assume we have some different standard for inches), why isn't it one meter long? (*Naming and Necessity*, Harvard University Press and Basil Blackwell, 1972, 1980, at p. 54)

Kripke goes on to argue that it not only would be correct to say of the Standard Metre that it is exactly one metre long, but the very fact about the Standard Metre that it is exactly one metre long, although it is only a contingent fact, is in some sense knowable *a priori:*[1]

---

[1] The present discussion is predicated on the common myth that the unit of length, one metre, was at one time fixed by the length of a particular bar used as a standard and kept in Paris. In reality, the Standard Metre is kept in Sevres, near Paris, and is considerably greater than one metre in length; the term 'metre' was defined as the length between two particular scratches that had been carefully cut into the bar. (How far apart? Wittgenstein: "Don't ask." Kripke: "You want to know how far apart? One meter, what else?") The metre is no longer so defined. (Neither is the metre. Apparently it is now defined as the distance light travels in a certain fixed fraction of a second.)

We could make the definition more precise by stipulating that one meter is to be the length of S at a fixed time t_0. . . . [A] man who uses the stated definition [is] using this definition not to *give the meaning* of what he called 'the meter', but to *fix the reference*. . . . There is a certain length which he wants to mark out. He marks it out by an accidental property, namely that there is a stick of that length. Someone else might mark out the same reference by another accidental property. . . . Even if this is the *only* standard of length that he uses, there is an intuitive difference between the phrase 'one meter' and the phrase 'the length of S at t_0'. The first phrase is meant to designate rigidly a certain length in all possible worlds, which in the actual world happens to be the length of stick S at t_0. On the other hand, 'the length of stick S at t_0' does not designate anything rigidly. . . . [T]he 'definition', properly interpreted, does *not* say that the phrase 'one meter' is to be *synonymous* (even when talking about counterfactual situations) with the phrase 'the length of S at t_0' but rather that we have *determined the reference* of the phrase 'one meter' by stipulating that 'one meter' is to be a *rigid* designator of the length which is in fact the length of S at t_0. So this does *not* make it a necessary truth that S is one meter long at t_0. . . .

What, then, is the *epistemological* status of the statement 'Stick S is one meter long at t_0' for someone who has fixed the metric system by reference to stick S? It would seem that he knows it *a priori*. For if he used stick S to fix the reference of the term 'one meter', then as a result of this kind of 'definition' (which is not an abbreviative or synonymous definition), he knows automatically, without further investigation, that S is one meter long. On the other hand, even if S is used as the standard of a meter, the *metaphysical* status of 'S is one meter long' will be that of a contingent statement, provided that 'one meter' is regarded as a rigid designator: under appropriate stresses and strains, heatings or coolings, S would have had a length other than one meter even at t_0. . . . So in this sense, there are contingent *a priori* truths (*ibid.*, pp. 54–56)

. . . The case of fixing the reference of 'one meter' is a very clear example in which someone, just because he fixes the reference in this way, can in some sense know *a priori* that the length of this stick is a meter without regarding it as a necessary truth. (*ibid.*, p. 63)[2]

Wittgenstein's claim that the sentence in question is unassertable because of the Standard Metre's 'peculiar role in the language-game' goes much further than the doctrine held by the empiricists that such definitions are devoid of proper cognitive, extra-linguistic factual content. By contrast with Wittgenstein, the empiricists argued that the sentence does indeed express *a priori* knowledge, but only because it does not express a *matter of fact* and instead expresses a *relation of ideas* (or a linguistic convention devoid of cognitive, factual content, etc.). Kripke's claim that the metre sentence is contingent *a priori* is significant, in part, because it contradicts this empiricist tradition. If Kripke is correct, the metre sentence expresses a matter of contingent fact. My chief concern in this paper, however, is not with the relation of either Wittgenstein's or Kripke's views to the doctrine of

---

[2] In a footnote to this passage Kripke acknowledges that his claim that such sentences as 'Stick S is exactly one meter long at t_0' express *a priori* knowledge (for one who so fixes the reference of 'metre') may seem implausible, and that some version or variant of its denial may be true.

empiricism (vexing issues in themselves), but more directly with the apparent divergence between Kripke and Wittgenstein over the question of the assertability and epistemic justification of the metre sentence.

Either Wittgenstein is wrong or Kripke is wrong. For surely if one who defines 'metre' as the length of the standard S at t_0 can thereby know a priori that S is exactly one metre long at t_0, as Kripke claims, then pace Wittgenstein, one can correctly say of the standard that it is indeed one metre long at t_0. This follows from the trivial fact that knowledge entails truth and truth entails (is?) assertability. Who is right and who is wrong?

It must be admitted that Kripke has more plausibility on his side than Wittgenstein does. Still, my answer is that Kripke and Wittgenstein are probably both wrong to some extent. To the extent that Wittgenstein is wrong, some of what Kripke says is right. More interestingly, the extent to which Kripke is right suggests that in *some* sense, a significant part of what Wittgenstein says may also be right. Frankly, I suspect Wittgenstein is ultimately completely wrong regarding the Standard Metre. Nevertheless, some of what I shall say here provides a measure of support (of some sort) for Wittgenstein's paradoxical observations concerning the Standard Metre. Specifically, I shall propose an epistemic paradox that might, to some extent, vindicate Wittgenstein's enigmatic remark. I make no claim, however, to be faithfully capturing Wittgenstein's intent. In the passage from which Wittgenstein's remark was extracted, he is discussing issues concerning our use of language as a means of representation, and is not explicitly concerned with the epistemological issues I will enter into here.

II

I argued in *Frege's Puzzle*[3] that the disputed metre sentence is (apparently contrary to Wittgenstein) true, but (apparently contrary to Kripke) contingent a posteriori rather than contingent a priori. In judging the sentence contingent, I followed Kripke in gainsaying the traditional empiricist claim that such definitional sentences do not express matters of extra-linguistic fact, but I went further than Kripke by rejecting even the less controversial (not to say *un*controversial) doctrine that such sentences express a priori knowledge.[4]

I shall not rehearse the full argument for a-posteriority. Instead, I shall merely sketch the main premises, and leave their defence as a homework exercise for the reader. (Warning: This exercise should not be attempted by the

---

[3] Cambridge, Mass.: Bradford Books/MIT Press, 1986, at pp. 140–142.

[4] For a similar rejection of a-priority for definitional sentences like Kripke's metre sentence, see Michael E. Levin, "Kripke's Argument against the Identity Thesis," *Journal of Philosophy*. 72, 6 (March 27, 1975), pp. 149–167, at p. 152n: Alvin Plantinga, *The Nature of Necessity* (Oxford University Press, 1974), at pp. 8–9n: and Keith Donnellan, "The Contingent *A Priori* and Rigid Designators," in P. French, T. Uehling, and H. Wettstein, eds., *Contemporary Perspectives in the Philosophy of Language* (Minneapolis: University of Minnesota Press, 1979), pp. 45–60. My own argument, while not exactly the same as Donnellan's, owes a great deal to his and has much of the same flavour.

squeamish.) For this purpose let us call the length at t_0 of S (that is, the length one metre or 39.3701. inches), 'Leonard'. Leonard is an abstract quality, a species of the generic Lockean primary quality *length*. We assume that the measurement-term 'metre' is introduced in such a way that a phrase of the form $\ulcorner \alpha$ metres$\urcorner$, where α is a term referring to some number n, is itself a singular term referring to the length that is exactly n times as great as Leonard.[5] We assume further that the sentence 'The length at t_0 of S, if S exists, is one metre' has as its cognitive information content a Russellian *singular proposition* (David Kaplan) in which Leonard occurs directly as a constituent.[6] (This move in the argument presupposes a highly controversial theory of the nature of propositions, but Kripke is not prepared to reject it.) Let us call this singular proposition 'Peter'. For simplicity, we may assume that Peter has only two constituents: Leonard and the complex property of *being the length of S at t_0 if S exists*. (The fact that Peter actually has a somewhat more complex structure does not matter a great deal to the argument.) Peter is true in all and only those possible worlds in which the very stick S either does not exist at all, or does exist and has at t_0 the very length Leonard. To assert, believe, or know Peter is to assert, believe, or know of the length Leonard that if S exists, it is precisely *that* long at t_0. Therefore, the reference-fixer knows Peter, which is the cognitive content of the metre sentence, *a priori* only if he knows of Leonard without appeal to experience (beyond the experience needed merely to apprehend the proposition) that if S exists, it is precisely that long at t_0. That is, the reference-fixer knows the content of the metre sentence *a priori* only if he knows of Leonard that S, if it exists, is precisely that long at t_0, without his belief that this is so

---

[5] The phrase $\ulcorner \alpha$ metres$\urcorner$ probably should not be regarded as a simple proper name. Whereas the '2' in the phrase '2 metres' seems to be replaceable by a variable for existential generalization on a sentence like 'The length of S is 2 metres', it is certainly not thus replaceable in a genuine name like 'R2-D2'. In *Frege's Puzzle*, I made the somewhat artificial assumption that the term 'metre' itself was a proper name referring to Leonard. A more plausible account parses the word 'metre' and its pluralization 'metres,' as comprising a simple (non-compound) *functor* (like the 'squared' in the algebraic phrase 'three squared'), i.e., an operator that attaches to a singular term to form a new singular term. The functor would attach exclusively to number-terms ('three', '3', etc., with grammar determining the propriety of the singular or plural form) to form a compound term referring to a specific length. The function referred to is a systematic assignment of lengths to numbers, and has the entire class of length as its range. Measuring the length of an object is a way of determining the (or at least a) number corresponding to the given length. Thus units of measurement (such as the metre or the gram) for a generic quality (such as length or mass) are seen as systematic assignments of particular species of the genus to numbers (something like Gödel-numbering, or its converse). Although I shall not pursue the matter in this paper, the contrast between the two accounts of the logic of 'metre' is not altogether irrelevant to the issues discussed herein.

[6] I include the proviso 'if S exists' for the benefit of purists, who will point out that S's having Leonard as its length entails S's existence, and since one cannot know *a priori* that S exists, one therefore cannot know *a priori* that S has that length. The more cautious, conditional sentence does not entail S's existence, and indeed is a trivial consequence of 'S does not exist'. (This formulation presupposes a free logic.) In what follows, I will often ignore the complications that result from the inclusion of the proviso.

being justified by means of experience. Yet it would seem that no matter what stipulations one makes, one cannot know without resorting to experience such things as that S, if it exists, has precisely such-and-such particular length at t_0. It would seem that one must at least *look at* S's length, or be told that it is precisely that long, etc. Therefore, it would seem that the metre sentence is not *a priori* but *a posteriori*.[7]

Notice that someone who has heard of the stick S but has not yet seen it could still introduce the term 'metre' by means of the description 'the length of S at t_0'.[8] If the reference-fixer in this case has a wildly mistaken impression as to S's actual

---

[7] Gareth Evans, in "Reference and Contingency," *The Monist*, 62 (April 1979), pp. 161–189, defends Kripke's claim that such sentences as the metre sentence are *a priori*. Evans replaces Kripke's example with his own, in which a reference-fixer introduces the name 'Julius' for whoever uniquely invented the zip. Evans argues (pp. 172–173) that in putting forward such a sentence as 'If anyone uniquely invented the zip, Julius did' as not entailing the named entity's existence (see the preceding footnote), Kripke presupposes that the newly introduced name ('Julius') is a 'Fregean name', having descriptive content that may determine no referent. (The argument for this, which is largely implicit, appears to be that if the name contributed its referent, rather than a descriptive content, to the proposition expressed, then since a proposition cannot exist unless each of its constituents exist, the sentence could not be true with respect to a circumstance in which Julius does not exist.) Indeed, Evans defends the claim of a-priority by implicitly conflating the content of the sentence with something like that of the modally (nearly) equivalent, logically true sentence 'If anyone uniquely invented the zip, then the actual inventor of the zip did', in which the modal description 'the actual inventor of the zip', which has replaced the name 'Julius', has its indexical, modally rigid use. (See, for example, pp. 183–185, especially the last paragraph beginning on p. 184.) The alleged presupposition that the newly introduced name has descriptive content, in this sense, is something Kripke surely denies. Indeed, that proper names are not descriptive, in Evan's sense (even when their reference is fixed by description) might be regarded as the central thesis of *Naming and Necessity*. Cf. my *Reference and Essense,*Basil Blackwell and Princeton University Press, 1982), chapter 1, especially at pp. 14–16, 21–23. Contra Evans, the use of free logic involves no presupposition to the contrary. (The implicit argument for the presupposition is inapplicable to the phrase 'one metre' in any case, since Leonard presumably exists in every possible circumstance. More important, the argument is unsound; Peter does not exist in any possible circumstance in which S does not exist, yet it is true with respect to any such circumstance. Cf. *Naming and Necessity*, pp. 21n, 78. For related discussion, see *Reference and Essence*, pp. 35–40, and my "Existence," in J. Tomberlin, ed., *Philosophical Perspectives I: Metaphysics*, Atascadero: Ridgeview, 1987, pp. 49–108.) The central question before us is whether the metre sentence is *a priori* for the reference-fixer when the phrase 'one metre' is presumed to *lack* descriptive content, in the relevant sense, and is presumed instead to have been introduced in the way Kripke explicitly proposed. Evan's conflation of such a sentence with a logically true surrogate conflicts with one of the main premises of the argument just presented: that (something like) Leonard itself occurs directly as a constituent of the content of the metre sentence, rather than being represented therein by the content of a description, so that knowledge of the fact described by the metre sentence is *de re* knowledge of Leonard that S, if it exists, is that long at t_0. (As I have said, Kripke is not prepared to reject this premiss.) I do not deny that the corresponding logically true sentence 'The length at t_0 of S, if it exists, is the actual length at t_0 of S' is contingent *a priori*. By the same token, however, knowledge of the fact it describes is not *de re* knowledge concerning Leonard. (See footnotes 10 and 11 below.)

[8] David Kaplan recommended that Russell's friend who had a trying exchange with a touchy yacht owner might have done something exactly like this in order to convey what the yacht

length (and so uses the description *referentially*, in Donnellan's sense, to refer to a very different length), or has no opinion whatsoever regarding S's length (and so uses the description *attributively*), it would clearly be incorrect to describe him or her as knowing *a priori* of Leonard that S, if it exists, is exactly that long at t_0. It is only after the reference-fixer sees S's length for himself (or is told it, etc.) that the proposition Peter becomes a piece of knowledge. In his description of the reference-fixing situation, Kripke had in mind a case in which the reference-fixer sees S there in front of him and uses the description referentially to refer to that length.[9] In such a case, it is correct to say that the reference-fixer knows Peter, but, it would seem, only because he has had the experience needed to acquire this knowledge.

The reference-fixer can know without looking at (or being told, etc.) S's length that the length at t_0 of S, if it exists, is the length he means (in his present idiolect, as determined by his own overriding intentions) by 'one metre'. Perhaps this even qualifies as genuine *a priori* knowledge; it depends on whether one's knowledge of one's own intentions is ultimately justified by appeal to experience. For the sake of argument, let us agree that it is *a priori*. The reference-fixer could infer from this that the length at t_0 of S, if it exists, is one metre (and thereby know of Leonard that S, if it exists, is precisely that long at t_0) if only he knew of Leonard that the phrase 'one metre' refers to it (in his present idiolect, if S exists). But this

---

owner refused to understand him as saying. See Kaplan's "Bob and Carol and Ted and Alice," in J. Hintikka, J. Moravcsik, and P. Suppes, eds., *Approaches to Natural Language* (Dordrecht: D. Reidel, 1973), pp. 490–518, at p. 501. If Kripke were correct that doing so makes the specification of the length of the object an *a priori* truth, the yacht owner's original reply would still be apt and Kaplan's recommended strategy would be unsuccessful. There is considerable tension between this passage from Kaplan and some of his other writings—e.g., in "Dtha," in P. French, T. Uehling, and H. Wettstein, eds., *Contemporary Perspectives in the Philosophy of Language*, pp. 383–400, at p. 397, and especially in "Demonstratives," in J. Almog, J. Perry, and H. Wettstein, eds., *Themes from Kaplan* (Oxford University Press, forthcoming 1988), sections XVII ("Epistemological Remarks") and XXII ("On Proper Names")—wherein something close to Kripke's position is explicitly endorsed.

My own view (which is similar in this respect to Donnellan's—see footnote 4 above) is that Kaplan's examples ('the shortest spy', 'the first child to be born in the twenty-second century', 'the length of your yacht') might be used to *demonstrate* that the reference-fixer in Kripke's story does not know of Leonard *a priori* that it is the length at t_0 of S (or that 'one metre' refers to it, in his present idiolect, etc.). In this I agree with Kaplan's former view, enunciated in "Quantifying In," in L. Linsky, ed., *Reference and Modality* (Oxford University Press, 1971), pp. 112–144, at pp. 126–127, and especially 135. Unfortunately, the view has become controversial. In addition to Kaplan's more recent writings see Ernest Sosa, "Propositional Attitudes *De Dicto* and *De Re*," *Journal of Philosophy*, 71 (December 1975), pp. 883–896. Quine's views have also taken a turn towards a kind of latitudinarianism much like Sosa's. See his "Intensions Revisited," in P. French, T. Uehling, and H. Wettstein, eds., *Contemporary Perspectives in the Philosophy of Language*, pp.268–274, at pp. 272–273. (But see footnote 17 below.) A more extreme latitudinarian view has also been endorsed, for example by Stephen Schiffer in "The Basis of Reference," *Erkenntnis*, 13 (1978), pp. 171–206. (The paper, however, involves a curious inconsistency on that point, among the definition in note 4, the proposal on p. 202, and the example on pp. 203–204.) Kripke has an example that, I believe, decisively refutes extreme latitudinarianism.

[9] This was confirmed by Kripke in conversation.

is precisely what the reference-fixer apparently cannot know, without having an appropriate experience in which S plays a significant role. Pending this additional experience, all that the reference-fixer knows is the general proposition that the phrase 'one metre' refers (in his present idiolect) to whatever length S has at t_0, if S exists (and is non-referring otherwise).[10] In fact, the natural order of things is just the reverse: the reference-fixer would ordinarily rely on additional experience to discover first that S has Leonard as its length at t_0, and then infer that 'one metre' refers to Leonard. Both pieces of knowledge are apparently *a posteriori*.

---

[10] If this is correct, the reference-fixer cannot know, without some experiential contact involving S, such basic semantic facts about his own word 'metre' as that the phrase 'one metre' refers (in his present idiolect) to one metre (if S exists, and is non-referring otherwise), or that the metre sentence is true (in his present idiolect) if and only if S (if it exists) is one metre long at t_0. In this sense, without additional experience involving S the reference-fixer does not even understand his word 'metre' or any sentence, such as the metre sentence, using (as opposed to mentioning) the word—though he may be in a position to use the word in *asserting* (without apprehending) propositions involving Leonard. (Perhaps, for this reason, use of the phrase 'his idiolect' may not be fully appropriate here; pending suitable experience involving S, the reference-fixer has introduced a version of English that he himself does not fully understand. There may be a weaker sense of 'understand' in which the reference-fixer 'understands' the word 'metre' simply by knowing that it was introduced in such a way that 'one metre' refers to whatever length S has at t_0, if S exists. But understanding 'metre' in this weak sense does not give one the basic semantic knowledge that 'one metre' refers, if S *exists*, specifically to one metre.) He can know, without experiencing S and simply by knowing a bit of semantics, that the metalinguistic *sentences* 'The phrase "one metre" refers in my present idiolect to one metre' and "The sentence "S, if it exists, is one metre long at t_0" is true in my present idiolect if and only if S, if it exists, is one metre long at t_0' (in this perhaps extended sense of 'idiolect') are themselves true (in his present meta-idiolect). But his knowledge of these metalinguistic facts is in the same boat as his knowledge that the metre sentence itself is true. He knows that these sentences are true, but pending the additional experience, he does not understand them—he does not know what they mean or what facts they describe (in the stronger sense)— and he does not know those facts themselves.

Donnellan's argument mentioned supra in footnote 4 is criticized by Evans, *op. cit.*, at pp. 171–176 and *passim*. Evan's criticism, however, seems to be based on a serious misunderstanding of the argument. Specifically, Evans charges (p. 173) that Donnellan's argument (which is, in this regard, essentially the same as the one involving Leonard and Peter) gratuitously assumes the doubtful thesis that the name 'Julius' in Evans's example (see footnote 7 above) cannot have been introduced through fixing its reference by means of the description 'the inventor of the zip' in such a way that 'Julius' is thereby given descriptive content, since one cannot understand this name unless it has a referent. Evans counters that a successful introduction of this sort is indeed possible, and has the consequence that the reference-fixer understands the name 'Julius' whether or not it has a referent. (Donnellan uses a different example.) By contrast, Donnellan explicitly allows, at pp. 47–49, that 'Julius' *could* be introduced as a 'descriptive name', in Evans's sense, stipulated to be shorthand for 'the actual inventor of the zip'. Who is to stop us from doing so? To repeat a point made above, the relevant question is whether the metre sentence is *a priori* when the phrase 'one metre' is presumed *not* to have been introduced as a shorthand description, and is presumed instead to have been introduced in the way Kripke explicitly proposed, without taking on descriptive content. (Perhaps Evans denies the legitimacy, or even the possibility, of stipulating the use of the word 'metre' in this way. But who is to stop us from doing so?) Moreover, Donnellan's general argument allows that a speaker can understand the phrase 'one metre' (in a strong sense of 'understand'), so introduced, even if it is non-referring—simply by learning that it is non-referring. What the argument denies is that the general sort of semantic knowledge

If the claim that the metre sentence is a *priori* is to be maintained in the face of these considerations, its defence must come from fastening onto an important epistemic distinction: the distinction between experience that plays a peculiar role in the *epistemic justification* of a belief (which is relevant to the question of whether the knowledge is a *priori* or a *posteriori*), and experience that merely serves to place the believer in a position to apprehend the proposition in the first place (by giving him or her the requisite concepts, for example), and does not play the relevant role in the epistemic justification of the belief. Thus, for example, the fact that one must have some experience in order to acquire the concept of a bicycle, and so to apprehend the proposition that all bicycles are bicycles, does not alter the fact that the proposition is known *a priori*. One might maintain that the reference-fixer's visual experience of S in the introduction of 'metre' likewise enables the reference-fixer to apprehend Peter but plays no further role in justifying that belief.

The case for a-priority along these lines, however, is far from clear. The reference-fixer's visual experience of S *can* play an important role in enabling him to apprehend propositions directly concerning S, but it does play a crucial role in justifying his belief of Peter. Suppose the reference-fixer has got himself into a position of being able to apprehend propositions directly concerning Leonard somehow *other than* by looking at S and conceiving of Leonard as the length of S. He comes into the situation of the introduction of 'metre' already grasping the generic concept of length. Suppose that he conceives of Leonard as *'this length here',* pointing to some object other than S yet having the very same length. Even if the reference-fixer came to believe of Leonard (so conceived) that S, if it exists, is also exactly that long at t_0, but did so somehow solely through contemplation and reflection on his concepts without experiential justification (i.e., not by estimating S's length from its appearance, etc.), he still could not properly be said to *know* this of Leonard. At best, it seems more like extremely lucky guesswork. It is only by seeing S and its length that the reference-fixer comes to know that S (if it exists) is just that long.

Whereas the reference-fixer's visual experience of S certainly plays a crucial role in the justification of his belief of Peter, it is arguable that the experience *need not* play the *sort* of role that would disqualify the belief from being a *priori* knowledge. The issue is quite delicate; a great deal depends on the exact meaning of '*a priori*'. It is even possible that the issue is, to some extent, merely verbal. Ordinarily, at least, it would be quite odd to say that one can know *a priori* concerning a certain length that a particular stick (if it exists) is exactly that long. I conjecture that Kripke, in his

---

acquired through introducing the word 'metre' in the way Kripke envisages (the knowledge that the phrase 'one metre' refers to whatever length S has at t_0, if S exists, and is non-referring otherwise) is sufficient, without additional sensory experience involving S, for the more specific semantic knowledge of Leonard that 'one metre' refers (if S exists) to it. Contrary to the impression created by Evans, the question of whether the former knowledge qualifies as *understanding* the word 'metre' is quite irrelevant to the argument. (Use of the word 'understand' in this connection is apt to cause confusion, in light of the potential ambiguity alluded to in the preceding paragraph.)

discussion, either failed to distinguish properly between the *a posteriori* content of the metre sentence, i.e., Peter, and the arguably *a priori* truth that the length at t_0 of S is referred to (in the reference-fixer's present idiolect) as 'one metre' (or something similar, such as the proposition that the metre sentence is true in the reference-fixer's idiolect), or else he failed to appreciate that the reference-fixer's visual experience of S in the very introduction of the term 'metre' is a crucial part of the justification for the reference-fixer's belief of Peter.[11]

I claimed in *Frege's Puzzle* that actual measurement of S's length by someone is required in order for anyone to know that S has Leonard as its length. I did not mean that one must do the measuring oneself. One could be told S's length by someone else who actually measured it, etc. But I thought that at some point an actual measurement by someone was required. Kripke allows in his discussion

---

[11] In *Frege's Puzzle* I allowed (p. 180) that Kripke had given at least the outline of a mechanism for generating certain contingent *a priori* truths through fixing the reference of a name by means of a definite description, in cases where the description is of a special sort that involves a *de re* (or *en rapport*) connection with the thing described. One example might be 'If I am visually perceiving anyone in the normal non-illusory way, then I am perceiving Irving', where 'Irving' is introduced by the speaker as a name for whoever he is visually perceiving. (This is derived from a similar example proposed by Kripke in a lecture at a conference on Themes from David Kaplan at Stanford University in March 1984, in which Kripke responded to Donnellan's argument and developed and modified his position on the contingent *a priori*.) Kripke has suggested (in the Stanford lecture, and more recently in conversation) that his metre example can be bolstered through the use of a suitable description, perhaps 'the length of the stick presented to me in the normal way by this visual perception', used with introspective ostension to a particular veridical visual perception of S.

Although it is quite unlikely, the speaker *could* come to believe the proposition that is the content of such a sentence without proper epistemic justification: Suppose, for example, that the speaker, who is offering a reward for the return of his lost pet cat named 'Sonya', is shown several cats that are indistinguishable from Sonya, and looking coincidentally at Sonya, thinks to himself (with more hope than justification) 'If I am visually perceiving a cat, then I am visually perceiving a cat, then I am seeing none other than Sonya herself'—conceiving of Sonya not as '*this* cat I see here in front of me, whether or not it is Sonya' but in the more familiar, everyday manner in which he conceives of the beloved pet. Here the proposition in question is certainly not a piece of *a priori* knowledge, since it is not even a piece of knowledge. If the speaker were to come to believe this same singular proposition, this time conceiving of the cat in the former way rather than in the latter, the belief so formed would be epistemically justified in the appropriate manner. Since the speaker cannot be in a position to conceive of the cat correctly in the former way unless he sees the cat, his occurrent visual experience of the cat would therefore play a crucial role in the epistemic justification of the belief so formed. In some sense, the speaker would know of the cat in this case that she ('*this* very cat') is the cat he is looking at (if such exists), in part, by *looking* at her. Nevertheless, it is arguable that if the speaker conceives of the cat in the former way (as 'this cat I see here, whoever she is' and not as 'my pet Sonya', etc.), then he believes the singular proposition in question by virtue of the fact that he believes the more general proposition, which is knowable *a priori*, that if he is visually perceiving a cat, then he is perceiving *whichever cat he is perceiving*—together with the external fact that he is perceiving Sonya. If the visual experience does not play the sort of role here that would make the example *a posteriori* rather than *a priori*, then it is arguable that Peter is knowable *a priori* after all—*provided that S* is conceived of not as 'the stick I learned of earlier' but in the appropriate *de re* manner as 'this stick here' (or 'the stick I see here in the normal way', etc.), and Leonard is conceived of not as 'the length of the stick I learned of earlier' nor even (as in Kripke's original example) as 'the length of this stick here' but as 'this *length* here', with ostension to S's length *via* S itself. Otherwise, Peter is

that the inch may already be in use as a unit of length, independently of the introduction of the metre by the reference-fixer. One function that is filled by the institution of using a unit of length, such as the inch, is that it provides *standard* or *canonical names* for infinitely many otherwise unnamed abstract entities (the particular lengths), exploiting names already in use for the numbers ('39.37 inches', etc.). It seems plausible that if one is a member of a community of speakers for whom there are one or more units of length in use at a particular time, then at least in the typical sort of case, one would count as knowing exactly how long a given object is only if one is in a position to specify the object's length correctly by means of one of its standard names, given in terms of a conventional unit and the (or at least a) correspondingly appropriate numerical expression. It would follow that one counts as knowing exactly how long S is at t_0 only if one is able to specify S's length in some such manner as '39.37 inches' or '3.28 feet', etc. Having this ability would seem to depend on S's length having been previously measured— either by oneself, or by an informant, or by someone else who is the ultimate source of the information.

By the time *Frege's Puzzle* made its appearance in print, I realized that this piece of reasoning was flawed by overstatement. When one looks at an ordinary, middle-sized object, one typically sees not only the object; one typically also sees *its length*. To put it more cautiously, one typically thereby enters into a cognitive relation to the length itself, a relation that is analogous in several respects to ordinary visual perception, but that (because perceiving subjects may stand in the relation to abstract qualities like lengths) may not correspond exactly with the relation, standardly called 'seeing', between perceivers and the concrete objects they see. One also typically thereby sees (perhaps in some other extended sense) *the fact* that the object has that very length. Of course, merely perceiving an object will not always result in such empirical knowledge. Perhaps in order to see an object's length one must be able to take in the object lengthwise, from end to end, in one fell swoop. Perhaps the visual presentation cannot be under circumstances that create optical illusions (such as might be created by surrounding the object with miniature artifacts, each reduced to the same scale, etc.). Perhaps not. In any case, if the reference-fixer does indeed see S under the required circumstances, he can thereby know of its present length, Leonard, that S is presently exactly that

---

known by the reference-fixer only *a posteriori*. Against this, one may be inclined to maintain that, even if S and its length are so conceived, the reference-fixer knows only *a posteriori*, by seeing the stick's length, that the stick he sees in the normal way (if it exists) has the length he sees, so that Peter remains *a posteriori*. As I have said, though, the issue may be to some extent merely verbal. There is a great deal more to be said about this sort of case. (I am indebted to Eli Hirsch and to Kripke for fruitful discussion of these, and related matters. Kripke has informed me that he independently arrived at conclusions similar to many of those presented in this paper and discussed them in a lecture on these topics at Notre Dame University in 1986. I have not heard the Notre Dame lecture and am unsure as to the extent of agreement between us. There seems to be a good deal of convergence, though I have the impression that some significant differences between the account given in Kripke's Notre Dame lecture and the present treatment may remain.)

long.[12] No physical measurement is required beyond merely perceiving the object (taking it in lengthwise in one fell swoop, etc.). But some sensory experience in which S plays a crucial role seems to be required. The metre sentence is apparently *a posteriori*, even if physical measurement is not required for its verification.

The error in my argument for the necessity of measurement was the plausible assumption that to know of Leonard that S (if it exists) is exactly that long at t_0 is to know exactly how long S is at t_0 (provided it exists). I suppose that anyone who knows exactly how long a given object is ordinarily knows of its length that the object is exactly that long. But the converse is not universally true; one can know of an object's length, just by looking at the object (and its length, under appropriately favourable circumstances), that the object is exactly that long. Assuming there is a unit of length in use independently of the object in question, one does not thereby learn exactly *which* length the object's length is, as one would (for example) by physically measuring the object in terms of the conventional unit. Knowing exactly how long something is typically requires more than merely perceiving the object.

III

This brings us to Wittgenstein's paradoxical observation concerning the unassertability of the metre sentence. Wittgenstein claims that one can say of S neither that it is one metre long, nor that it is not one metre long. With part of this, there can be no quarrel. One assuredly cannot properly say of S that it is not one metre long, since that would be straightforwardly false. Why, then, can one not properly say of S that it is one metre long?

Let us modify Kripke's story slightly. Suppose there is no standard unit of length in use by the reference-fixer's community. Suppose the reference-fixer is a very clever caveman who is attempting to devise for the first time a precise method for specifying various lengths. He hits on the brilliant idea of establishing a convention of specifying every length whatsoever as a multiple (whole or fractional) of some one, specially selected length, which will serve as the standard unit of length. He arbitrarily selects for this purpose the length at that moment t_0 of a particularly straight and sturdy stick S that he picks up from among a pile of sticks and holds in his hands. He calls its length 'one metre'. His fellow tribesmen agree to his scheme. The length at t_0 of stick S, i.e. Leonard, happens to be 39.3701 inches, though of course, no one is in a position prior to the reference-fixer's flash of brilliance to specify its length using inches or any other unit of measurement, since there was no such thing until the historic moment t_0. Using a compass and a straightedge, the reference-fixer carefully scratches calibrations onto the stick, marking them '$1/_2$', '$1/_4$', '$3/_4$', etc., down to a very fine degree, say 128ths. The clever caveman knows that with this new tool, given any middle-sized object and sufficient time, anyone can now determine the object's length with a very high degree

---

[12] Thus I cannot accept the argument proposed on my behalf by Ralph Kennedy in "Salmon Versus Kripke on the *A Priori*," *Analysis*, 47, 3 (June 1987), pp. 158–161.

of precision. His people have a new prize possession, the only standard measuring rod on Earth. Soon the measuring rod is in such great demand that every household has its own, carefully crafted duplicate—each carefully measured against the original. A new institution has been born: measuring with a metre-rule.

Does the reference-fixer in this case know at t_0 that S is exactly one metre long? Yes, simply by looking at it. Surely he need not measure S against itself in order to determine its length as a multiple of the standard length. In fact, there is no clear sense to be made of the idea of measuring the standard itself by means of itself, or even against any of its facsimiles. Its length *is* the standard length, by stipulation. If the reference-fixer can know of S's length, Leonard, just by looking, that S is presently exactly that long, then in some sense he cannot fail to know that S's length is exactly one times that length—except by not seeing it under appropriately favourable circumstances. Physical measurement is not only unnecessary; the very notion is in some sense inapplicable to this case.[13]

But an interesting philosophical difficulty arises once we say that the reference-fixer does know that S is exactly one metre long. He has deliberately established a convention of measuring objects in order to determine their lengths, and of specifying those lengths as multiples of a standard unit of length. Within the framework of this institution or 'language-game', one counts as knowing *how* long something is (as opposed to merely knowing of its length that the object is that long), typically, if and only if one is in a position to specify its length correctly as a multiple of the standard length (for example, as '3 and $^{27}/_{32}$ metres')—within the degree of precision epistemically accessible to the community in the current state of scientific knowledge. It would seem that anyone who can correctly specify that a given object is exactly n metres long (with sufficient epistemic justification, understanding what the specification means, etc.) knows exactly how long that object is. Thus, if the reference-fixer knows that S is precisely one metre long, it would seem that he knows precisely how long S is. If Kripke's claim in this connection were correct, the reference-fixer would know exactly how long S is (provided it exists) *a priori*! This would be quite astonishing, but we have seen that Kripke's claim seems incorrect. In order to know that S is exactly one metre long, the reference-fixer must look at (or be told, etc.) S's length. However, we still get a rather curious result, not unlike Kripke's claim that the reference-fixer knows S's length *a priori*: if the reference-fixer knows without measuring and just by looking that S is precisely one metre long, then *he knows precisely how long S is without measuring and just by looking*.

---

[13] Of course, one may later measure the standard against (say) one of its duplicates in order to check whether the standard has *changed* in length over time (or, as Kripke and James Tomberlin pointed out, in order to verify that it is indeed the original standard)—provided one has reason to believe that the duplicate itself has not changed in length. But we are here concerned with how the reference-fixer knows *at t_0* of Leonard that S is that long *at t_0*. The fact that the length of the standard does not remain fixed over time introduces a host of issues that are largely irrelevant to the purposes of this paper. The problem I shall discuss would arise even if S did not change in length over time and even if the reference-fixer knew this. For simplicity, I shall simply presuppose that the reference-fixer knows that S's length remains constant.

Indeed, knowing that a given object's length is exactly n times that of another object (the standard) cannot give one knowledge of how long the first object is unless one already knows how long the second object is. If one knows only that the length of the first is n times that of the second without knowing how long the second object is, one knows only the proportion between the lengths of the two objects without knowing how long *either* object is. Thus, if measurement is ever to give one knowledge of how long an object is, one must already know how long the standard itself is. Yet we have just seen the reference-fixer could not have come to know exactly how long S is by actually measuring S. Physical measurement is out of the question. If he has this knowledge, he must have acquired it simply by *looking at* S's length, under appropriately favourable circumstances.

Suppose the reference-fixer wishes to know exactly how long his spear is. Can he tell just by looking at its length, without taking the trouble to measure? It would seem not. Now that there is an institution of measuring with a metre-rule, he can do much better than estimating the spear's length solely on the basis of its visual appearance. He can physically measure it. In fact, it would seem that he *must* physically measure the spear if he wishes to know *exactly* how long it is. Why is measurement not equally required in order for him to know exactly how long S is? Because of its unique role in the language-game of determining length with a metre-rule. Measuring the stick itself is, in some sense, impossible. There is nothing to measure S against that is not itself measured ultimately against S.

The caveman could try to do the same thing for the spear that he did for S. He could scratch calibrations into the spear at its midpoint, and so on, proposing the spear as a second and rival standard of measurement. Would this little exercise make it possible for the caveman to know exactly how long the spear is just by looking at it, as he can in the case of S? If so, then it would seem that he does not need to measure *anything*—or at least any ordinary middle-sized object—in order to know precisely how long it is. He need only look at it and propose to use its length as a new unit of length. Clearly, this would defeat the purpose of the institution of measuring: it would violate the rules of the language-game. No, if the caveman wishes to know exactly how long his spear is, he must do much better than merely look at it and perform a little ritual. He must measure it against the standard S, or by proxy against one of the many facsimile measuring sticks that have since been constructed, etc.

This makes S epistemically quite unique *vis à vis* the reference-fixer. No other object is such that he can know precisely how long it is just by looking at it. Once an institution of measuring lengths is put into operation, knowing how long an object is—at least if the object is something other than the standard itself—requires a little elbow grease. This is true even of the duplicate measuring sticks. But how could S have become knowable in a way that no other object is knowable? The measuring rod S was chosen entirely arbitrarily by the reference-fixer to serve a special purpose: all lengths are to be specified as multiples of its length. Despite its 'peculiar role in the language-game', it is still a stick, a physical object subject to the same natural laws and knowable in the same way as any other. If the reference-fixer had selected some other stick in place of S as the standard—as well he might have—the other stick would play the special role in the language-game. Its length, rather than Leonard, would be the one in terms of which all others are to be specified. In order to know precisely how long S is, one would simply have to measure it (or be told by someone who measured it, etc.). The reference-fixer's accidental selection of S as the standard could not have made it knowable in some direct way, quite different from the way it would have been knowable if it had not been selected in the first place. The reference-fixer cannot simply *legislate* that he knows exactly how long S is, any more than he can legislate that he knows exactly how long his spear is. The accidents and whims of human history and culture do not alter the nature of our epistemic relations to external objects. The laws of epistemology (if there are any such things) are *universal*. They do not play favourites by singling out this or that arbitrarily selected, inanimate object as epistemically special. If the laws of epistemology say *in order that thou knowest how long a physical object is, thou shalt measure it*, they do not make an exception in the case of some favourite stick.[14]

Thus as soon as we say that the reference-fixer knows that S is one metre long, we are embroiled in a paradox. The language-game of measuring with a metre-rule involves a simple criterion for knowing how long something is. In order for the reference-fixer to know how long anything is, he must be able to specify its length in metres *and* he must know how long the Standard Metre is. Saying that he knows that S is exactly one metre long attributes to him knowledge of exactly how long the Standard Metre is. But he could not have acquired this knowledge through measurement. If he has such knowledge, he can only have acquired it by simply looking at S. This would require S to be what it cannot be: knowable in a unique way in which no other object is knowable and in which it itself would not be knowable if it had not been arbitrarily selected as the standard. These considerations invite the skeptical conclusion that the reference-fixer does not know after all that S is exactly one metre long. This, in turn, leads to an even stronger skeptical conclusion. For if the reference-fixer does not know how long S is, he cannot know, and cannot even discover, how long *anything* is. Measuring an object's length using S only tells him the ratio of that object's length to the length of S.

The problem leads to an even more disturbing result. Suppose we grab the bull by the horns and deny that the reference-fixer knows the length of S or of anything else. Even if we say merely that S is *in fact* exactly one metre long, while not suggesting that the reference-fixer knows this, we pragmatically implicate that *we* know that S is exactly one metre long, thereby opening the door to the

---

[14] Thus, apparently, the reasoning in *Frege's Puzzle* would not have been overstated if Kripke's example had included the feature that there are no rival units of length defined independently of the metre. As I said at the end of section II above, if there is a rival system of measurement that supersedes the metric system, the reference-fixer's knowing of Leonard that S is exactly that long does not guarantee his knowing exactly how long S is. But where there is no rival system, to know that something is exactly n metres long is to know exactly how long it is, and knowing exactly how long something is apparently requires measurement. See footnote 19 below.

same skeptical paradox. For if we know that S is exactly one metre long, then (assuming S's length were the ultimate unit of length-measurement, in terms of which all other such units are ultimately defined) we must have come to know precisely how long S is simply by looking at its length, without measurement. This would make S inexplicably unique, differing in epistemic accessibility from all other objects, and from what it would have been if it had not been selected as the standard, solely by virtue of the special role it has arbitrarily come to occupy as the result of an accident of human history and culture. Since this is impossible, we are drawn to the skeptical conclusion that we do not know, and cannot discover, how long anything is! If this argument is sound, we are epistemically unjustified in saying of S that it is exactly one metre long at t_0. This comes very close to Wittgenstein's enigmatic claim.

There is a more general form of skepticism, of which the problem of the Standard Metre is only a special case. Analogous skeptical doubts can be raised in connection with other standards, such as the period of the earth's rotation on its axis, midnight Greenwich time, and so on. We may call the general form of skepticism exemplified by these examples *Does-anybody-really-know-what-time-it-is skepticism*.

This general problem arises in a particularly sharpened form in connection with the transcendental number π. Let us assume that the Greek letter 'π' was introduced as a standard name for the ratio of the circumference of a circle to its diameter, analogously to the introduction of 'metre'. We may then raise questions analogous to those raised in connection with the Standard Metre. First, do mathematicians know that π is the ratio of the circumference of a circle to its diameter? Notice that this is separate from the question of whether mathematicians know that 'π' refers to the ratio of the circumference of a circle to its diameter—which clearly should be answered affirmatively. What we are asking here is whether there is any number that mathematicians know to *be* the ratio of the circumference of a circle to its diameter. Questions arise concerning the various modes of acquaintance by which mathematicians are familiar with π. If mathematicians conceive of π as the ratio of the circumference of a circle to its diameter, or even as the sum of a particular convergent series, is their (or *our*) knowledge of π not merely what Russell called "knowledge by description"? Or are mathematicians also acquainted with π in some more direct fashion, something like the way in which we are acquainted with 3 or 4 (or even 3.1416)? Presumably, despite the doubts that this line of questions raises, many will insist that mathematicians do know of π that it is the ratio of the circumference of a circle to its diameter. Indeed, the conventional wisdom is that mathematicians know *a priori* that π is the ratio of the circumference of a circle to its diameter. Very well, then, do they know *exactly* what number this ratio is? What exactly is the value of 'π'? The very question seems to demand what it is impossible to produce: a specification of π by means of its full decimal expansion. Providing the decimal expansion of a particular constant is analogous to measuring a particular object to determine its length. It is not enough here (perhaps by contrast with the case of measuring) merely to be able to set upper and lower bounds within a desired (non-zero) margin of error. Whatever margin of error one chooses, there remain infinitely many numbers that have not yet been ruled out. Given that the ratio of the circumference of a circle to its diameter lies somewhere among infinitely many other numbers between these bounds, do mathematicians know which number it is? Since one cannot know the full decimal expansion of π, there seems to be a sense in which no one can know what number π is.[15] It would follow that no one knows, or can even discover, given the diameter of a circle as a rational number, what the circumference is, or what the internal area is, etc. The well-known formulas for computing these values yield only their proportion to the unknown quantity π.

The threat of Does-anybody-really-know-what-time-it-is skepticism gives a point (whether or not it is the intended point) to Wittgenstein's counsel that we not say of S that it is exactly one metre long. Our not saying this about S would indeed mark its peculiar role in the 'language-game' of determining how long objects are with a metre-rule. But how does this help to solve the paradox? It does not.[16]

IV

The paradox revolves around the epistemic notion of *knowing how long* a given object is. This concept is philosophically problematic in precisely the same way as the concept of *knowing who* someone is. In fact, both concepts should be seen as special cases of a more general epistemic notion: that of *knowing which F* a given *F* is, where '*F*' is some sortal. Knowing-who is the special case where '*F*' is 'person'; knowing-how-long is the special case where '*F*' is 'length.'[17] A number of philosophers have held that the

---

[15] Even more analogous to the case of the Standard Metre is the transcendental number e, defined as the base of the logarithmic function whose derivative is the reciprocal function. Just as all lengths are specified in the metric system as multiples of Leonard, so all positive numbers are specified via the Napierian (or 'natural') logarithmic function as powers of e.

[16] 'This was our paradox: no course of action could be determined by a rule, because every course of action can be made out to accord with the rule.' The problem discussed in and around *Philosophical Investigations* §201 is not the same as the epistemological problem just presented. Wittgenstein's (alleged) paradox concerns the concept of following a rule, such as the rule (set of instructions) for determining the length of an object with a metre-rule; Does-anybody-really-know-what-time-it-is skepticism concerns the distinct concept of knowing which thing of a certain kind (e.g., which length) a specially designated thing of that kind is, and in particular, the question of whether the rule for determining length using a metre-rule applies in exactly the same way to the Standard Metre. Even if we have a solution to Wittgenstein's (alleged) paradox, the latter problem still arises.

[17] The relation of knowing which *F*, for a particular *F*, is a relation between a knower and (using the terminology of *Frege's Puzzle*) a singular-term information value, that is, either an individual ('knowing which *F a* is') or an intensional representation thereof ('knowing which *F* the φ is'). As in the special case of length, a distinction should be maintained between knowing of a given *F* that it is α and knowing which *F* is α. One may know of a given thief, without knowing who he or she is but simply by witnessing the crime, that he or she is the person stealing a certain book from the library. This distinction has often been blurred. See, for example, Donnellan, *op. cit.*, at pp. 52, 57–58; Jaakko Hintikka *Knowledge and Belief* (Ithaca: Cornell University Press, 1962), at pp. 131–132, and *passim;* and Quine, *loc. cit.* The distinction is upheld in Stephen Boër and William Lycan, *Knowing Who* (Cambridge, Mass.: Bradford Books/MIT Press, 1986), at pp. 132–133; David Kaplan, "Opacity," in L. Hahn and P. A. Schilpp, eds., *The Philosophy of W. V. Quine* (La Salle: Open Court, 1986), pp. 229–289, at pp. 258–260; and Igal Kvart, "Quine and Modalities De Re: A Way Out?" *Journal of Philosophy*, 79, 6 (June 1982), pp. 295–328, at pp. 300–301. Cf. also the closing-paragraph of Section II above.

locution of 'knowing who' is highly interest-relative. Relative to some interests, simply knowing a person's name qualifies as knowing who he or she is: relative to other interests, it does not.[18] If this is correct, then the locution of 'knowing how long' is equally interest-relative. In some contexts, knowing a length's standard name in the metric system counts as knowing which length it is; in other contexts, it does not. One way of spelling out this idea (though not the only way) is to claim that the locution of 'knowing which F' is *indexical*, expressing different epistemic relations with respect to different contexts.[19]

Interest-relative notions can easily lead to paradox, if we shift our interests without noticing it. Epistemic notions, if they are interest-relative, lead to skeptical paradox. Someone whose epistemic situation remains unchanged may be correctly described, relative to one set of interests, as knowing something that, relative to another set, he or she cannot be correctly described as knowing. The appearance of contradiction is due to a sort of equivocation, similar to that typified by the sentence 'Now you see it; now you don't'. If the indexical (or interest-relative) theory of knowing which F is correct, the skeptic is not really denying what we claim when we claim to know something. The skeptic merely has different interests; he or she is changing the subject. There is no disagreement between us as to the facts of the matter.

It seems likely that the paradox outlined in the preceding section arises from some equivocation of this sort. In describing the caveman's situation, we invoke a notion of knowing-how-long for which a necessary and sufficient condition is, roughly, the ability to produce a standard name of the object's length, in terms of

---

[18] Cf. W. V. Quine, *op. cit.*, at p. 273.

[19] An alternative account would treat the locution 'knows which F' as non-indexical but implicitly ternary-relational, with an additional argument-place for a specification of a particular interest or purpose. Cf. the account given in Boër and Lycan, *op. cit.* (I am indebted to James Tomberlin for pointing out that the interest-relative theory need not take the form of an indexical theory.)

Kripke (in lecture) has proposed several examples that appear to demonstrate the dependency (in at least most contexts) of the concept of knowing which F on such contextual factors as one's training and whether a name has become standardized through cultural entrenchment. The thesis that knowing which F is (at least usually) dependent on such factors, however, is largely independent of the interest-relative theory (according to which someone whose cognitive relations to a given F remain unchanged might be correctly described relative to one set of interests as knowing which F the given F is, and relative to another set of interests as not knowing which F the given F is). I believe the former; I am inclined to believe the latter as well.

I am disinclined to believe the analogue of the interest-relative theory with respect to the separate phenomena of *de re* knowledge and *de re* belief. The view that *de re* belief is interest-relative is proffered by Ernest Sosa, *op. cit.*, and endorsed by Quine, *loc. cit. De re* belief, in my view, is simply belief of a singular proposition. In this (trivial) sense, my view makes *de re* belief into a species of *de dicto* belief, i.e. belief of a proposition. If the former notion were interest-relative, *ipso facto* so would be the latter. Cf. Kaplan, "Opacity" *loc.cit.*, and Kvart, *loc. cit.* Some philosophers have held that knowledge generally (knowledge of a proposition or fact, and not merely the special case of knowing which F) is indexical. See, for example, Alvin Goldman, "Discrimination and Perceptual Knowledge," *Journal of Philosophy*, 73, 20 (November 18, 1976), pp. 771–791; Stewart Cohen, "Knowledge, Context, and Social Standard," *Synthese* (forthcoming, 1987), and 'How to Be a Fallibilist,' in J. Tomberlin, ed., *Philosophical Perspectives II: Epistemology* (Atascadero: Ridgeview, forthcoming).

the standard unit, while understanding the meaning of that name. Within the confines of the caveman's language-game, knowing how long something is *just is* knowing the proportion of its length to Leonard. For every object but one, satisfying this condition requires actual physical measurement. but the reference-fixer *trivially* satisfies the necessary and sufficient condition for knowing how long S itself is, provided he sees its length. Knowing his own intention in introducing the term 'metre' gives the reference-fixer the ability to produce the standard name of S's length; seeing S's length gives him the understanding he needs of that standard name. (See footnote 10.) In the sense of 'measurement' in which knowing how long something is requires measurement against the standard, merely looking at the standard's length (under the appropriately favourable circumstances) counts as *measuring* the stick itself. In S's case, merely looking is a sort of limiting-case of measuring. The laws of epistemology are not violated; it is just that there are different ways of obeying them.

When we explicitly ask, on the other hand, whether the reference-fixer knows how long the standard itself is, we shift our focus from within the confines of his language-game to looking in on him from the outside. Without taking notice we have raised the ante. From our newer, broadened perspective, knowing how long S is seems to require physically measuring it against a higher standard—one that supersedes and overrides the reference-fixer's standard, one that (by hypothesis) is not available to the reference-fixer himself.

If we raise the same question with respect to our own, or our scientists', current standard, we may raise the ante beyond what anyone is currently in a position to pay. Perhaps there is a legitimate sense in which no one now knows *exactly* how long a metre is. Likewise, perhaps there is a sense in which no one *can* know exactly what number π is. But if there is a sense in which these instances of Does-anybody-really-know-what-time-it-is skepticism are true, what is true in this sense need not concern us. It is like shouting 'Fire!' in a crowded theatre merely because someone is lighting a cigarette. There is still the standard, everyday sense, in which everyone *of course* knows how long the Standard Metre is and everyone *of course* knows what number π is: the Standard Metre is exactly one metre long, and π is the ratio of the circumference of a circle to its diameter. We can expand on this by producing a metre-rule and thereby *showing* how long the Standard Merre is, or by producing a partial decimal expansion of π or instructions for computing its value to whatever number of places is desired. That is all one can have. To demand more than this is to change the rules of the game in such a way that nobody can win. At the other extreme, there are no doubt contexts in which it is true to say that the caveman knows how long his spear is just by looking at it. ('I'll get more respect when everyone sees how long my spear is.') The important fact is that we stand in such-and-such perceptual and cognitive relations to particular objects. In some (perhaps extended) sense of 'see', the caveman sees his spear's length by looking at the spear itself (lengthwise, in one fell swoop, etc.). Some of us are acquainted with π only by knowing an approximation to its decimal expansion. Perhaps there is even a (possibly metaphorical) sense of 'see' in which we may be said to see the ratio of the circumference of a circle to its diameter simply by looking at a diagram. In the end, what does it matter whether we dignify how we stand with the honorific 'knowing which *F*'?

If all of this is correct, there may be a better reason for not saying of the Standard Metre that it is exactly one metre long. In the circumstances of every-day, non-philosophical commerce, the proposition that the standard is just that long is something nearly everyone counts as knowing. But (in part for that very reason) merely uttering the sentence 'The Standard Metre is exactly one metre long' tends to raise the ante to a level at which its utterance becomes epistemically unjustified—and threatens to invoke the skeptic's favourite level, at which its utterance is in principle unjustifiable. If saying something that is trivially true leads us to say further things that sound much more alarming than they really are, it may be better to say nothing. In any even, this provides one sort of rationale for not saying of the Standard Metre that it is one metre long.

As I have said, however, I do not pretend that this rationale bears any significant resemblance to Wittgenstein's. It is unclear to me whether Does-anybody-really-know-what-time-it-is skepticism is connected with the issues discussed in and around *Philosophical Investigations* §50. If π occupies a unique role in the language-game of mathematics, analogous to the peculiar role of the Standard Metre in the language-game of measuring with a metre-rule, its peculiar role is (happily) not marked by any prohibition against saying that it is the ratio of the circumference of a circle to its diameter. Moreover, if the rationale I have suggested does bear some significant resemblance to Wittgenstein's, then his arresting remark itself is also something that sounds much more alarming than it really is, and in the absence of at least the minimal sort of explicit epistemological stage setting I have provided here, is probably better left unsaid.[20]

---

[20]I am grateful to Graeme Forbes, Eli Hirsch, Saul Kripke, Mark Richard and Timothy Williamson for their comments on an earlier draft.

THE NECESSARY APOSTERIORI

Scott Soames

A Framework for Our Discussion

The claim that there are genuine examples of the necessary aposteriori, and the corresponding claim that there are genuine examples of contingent apriori, are among the most important and far-reaching doctrines of *Naming and Necessity*. In this chapter, I will explain and evaluate the first of these claims, and the arguments that Kripke gives for it. . . . Kripke's discussion of these topics may properly be regarded as ground-breaking, and I will argue that many of his examples and arguments are illuminating. However, I will also indicate ways in which I believe he muddied the waters by saying certain things that are puzzling at best, and defective at worst. In the case of the necessary aposteriori, much of what he says can, I think, be taken to be straightforwardly correct, though, as we will see . . . , certain parts of his discussion unnecessarily weaken his case. In the case of the contingent apriori, considerably more reconstruction and revision is needed. Our aim . . . will be to clarify and correct these matters, in order to arrive at clear and defensible versions of the two doctrines.

In bringing out both the puzzling and the illuminating aspects of Kripke's discussion, I will . . . make use of a modest theoretical framework that goes beyond what he explicitly commits himself to in *Naming and Necessity*. The central assumptions of this expository framework are the following:

A1.   Some things are asserted, believed, and known. Propositional attitudes like assertion, belief, and knowledge are relations that hold between agents and the things that they assert, believe, and know.

A2.   The things asserted, believed, and known may be expressed by sentences, and designated by clauses such as *the statement that S, the assertion that S, the belief that S, the claim that S, the proposition that S*, or simply *that S*. I will call the things designated by these clauses *propositions*.

A3.   Propositions are bearers of (contingent or necessary) truth and falsity.

A4.   Propositions are not identical with sentences used to express them. Whatever they turn out to be, propositions are, roughly speaking, things which different sentences that "say" or express the same thing have in common.

A5.   Propositional attitude ascriptions—*x asserts/believes/knows/knows apriori/ knows aposteriori that S*—report that an agent asserts, believes, knows, knows apriori, or knows aposteriori the proposition designated by *that S*.

Kripke's discussion of the necessary aposteriori and the contingent apriori indicates his commitment to the view that (i) there are genuine cases in which some one thing is both necessarily true and knowable only aposteriori (on the basis of empirical evidence), and (ii) there are genuine cases in which some one thing is both contingent and knowable apriori (without appeal to such evidence). From the point of view of our modest theoretical framework, this is the view that there are some propositions—i.e., things capable of being asserted, believed, and known—that are both necessarily true and knowable only aposteriori, and there are other propositions that are both contingently true and knowable apriori. Although I will argue that this view is correct, I will also raise serious questions about Kripke's treatment of a substantial range of cases.

Genuine Instances of the Necessary Aposteriori: Explanation and Consequences for Our Conception of Inquiry

There is a natural and initially attractive conception of inquiry according to which ignorance about a given subject is a matter of lacking information about which, of certain relevantly different possible states the world could be in, it is actually in; and complete ignorance is a condition in which one doesn't know which, of all the possible states that the world could be in, it is actually in. According to this conception, when an agent is in this condition, (i) all metaphysically possible states of the world are epistemically possible—i.e., every way that the world could possibly be is a way that, for all the agent knows, it might actually be, and (ii) every epistemic possibility is a metaphysical possibility—i.e., every way that, for all the agent knows, the world might be is a way that the world really could be. Inquiry is the process of escaping from this position of ignorance. By investigating the world or relying on the testimony of others, the agent learns contingent truths that distinguish the way the world actually is from other ways it might possibly be, but isn't. Each time the agent learns one of these truths, he narrows down the class of metaphysical/epistemic possibilities compatible with what he knows, and within which he locates the way the world actually is. According to this conception, acquiring information is equated with narrowing down the range of metaphysically possible world-states that are compatible with what one knows. We may also speak of the truth of one proposition as providing information supporting the truth of another. On this conception, the truth of a proposition p provides information supporting the truth of a proposition q by ruling out certain possible ways in which q might fail to be true. Thus, the truth of p supports the truth of q only if the set of possible world-states with respect to which both p and the negation of q are true is non-empty.

There are two immediate consequences of this conception of inquiry. The first is that necessary truths are uninformative. Since they are true with respect to all possible world-states, knowledge of them provides no information, and is irrelevant to locating the way the world actually is within the range of possible ways it might be. Second, there are no necessary truths which, though knowable, are knowable only aposteriori. To say that a proposition q is knowable only aposteriori is to say that one can have the justification required to know q only if one has empirical evidence supporting its truth. However, according to the conception of inquiry just sketched, this is impossible. In order for the truth of any proposition p to support the truth of q, and hence to provide evidence for it, there must be possible world-states with respect to which q is untrue, which are ruled out by the truth of p. Since q is necessary, there are no possible world-states with respect to which it is untrue; hence there can be no evidence for q. This means that, on the conception of inquiry just sketched, there can be no necessary truths which, though knowable, are knowable only aposteriori.

Although a number of philosophers have taken this conception of inquiry, and the consequences that follow from it, to be plausible and even axiomatic, the conception is directly challenged by the framework developed by Kripke in *Naming and Necessity*.[1] This challenge is illustrated by the following examples.

1. Gregory Soames is not identical with (i.e., is not the same individual as) Brian Soames.

2. If Saul Kripke exists, then Saul Kripke is a human being.

---

[1] A good example of a philosopher who accepts this conception of inquiry, and extends it to provide a model of discourse, is Robert Stalnaker. See his "Assertion," *Syntax and Semantics 9* (1978): 315–32, reprinted in his *Context and Content* (New York: Oxford University Press, 1999), and his *Inquiry* (Cambridge, MA: MIT Press, 1984).

3. This table is not made out of clay.

4. If this table exists, then this table is made of molecules.

It seems evident that each of these sentences expresses a proposition that is knowable only aposteriori, on the basis of some sort of empirical evidence. In the case of (1), one needs to find out who Gregory and Brian are, and to assure oneself that they are different. In the case of (2), if the question were ever raised as to whether Kripke was a sophisticated robot, or an alien sent from another world, one would need empirical evidence to rule out these possibilities—though, of course, given their fanciful nature, not much evidence would be required. A similar point is true of (3), the justification of which might be provided by a cursory examination of the table. In the case of (4), the evidence required to know the truth that it expresses is much greater, and more sophisticated. Still, since in all four cases empirical evidence is required to know the truths expressed, all four propositions are knowable only aposteriori.

They are also necessary. In each case, the subject expression is a rigid designator—the names *Gregory Soames* and *Saul Kripke,* plus the demonstrative phrase *this table.*[2] Because of this, the sentences express necessary truths iff the properties they attribute to the referents of their subjects are essential properties—the properties of being non-identical with Brian Soames, of being human, of being not made out of clay, and of being made of molecules. These do seem to be essential properties; in fact they seem to be essential properties of anything that has them. For example, it is plausible to think that any individual who really is not the same individual as Brian Soames could not have existed while being the very same individual as Brian Soames. Because the name *Brian Soames* is itself a rigid designator, we can also make the point in another way: since the property of being non-identical is an essential property of any pair of things that have it, if two individuals (such as my two sons) really are non-identical, then there is no possible circumstance in which they are one and the same individual. Similar points hold for the other properties mentioned in these examples—anything that really is human could not have existed without being human, any object not made out of clay could not have existed while being (originally and entirely) made out of clay, and anything that really is made up of molecules could not have existed without being made up of molecules. Thus, sentences (1–4) all express necessary truths. Since they are also knowable only aposteriori, they are examples of the necessary aposteriori.

How can this be? How can a proposition that is necessary (and known to be necessary) be knowable only aposteriori? Kripke's answer appeals to our knowledge

---

[2] To say that an indexical phrase, like *this table,* is a rigid designator is to say, roughly, that when one uses it in context of utterance to refer to a particular thing, that thing remains its referent with respect to all possible world-states with respect to which we might evaluate a sentence containing it. So if I say, *This table is made of wood,* referring to the table t now directly in front of me, then I say something (express some proposition) which is true, when taken as a description of any possible world-state w, iff had the world been in state w, t (that very object) would have been made of wood. See David Kaplan, "Demonstratives," in Joseph Almog, John Perry, and Howard Wettstein, eds., *Themes from Kaplan* (New York and Oxford: Oxford University Press, 1989).

of which properties are essential. He argues, quite plausibly, that we know *apriori* that properties like non-identity, being human, being not made out of clay, and being made out of molecules are essential properties of the things that have them. So we know apriori that if things have these properties, then they have them necessarily. This means that the propositions expressed by (1–4) are such that we know apriori that *if* they are true, *then* they are necessarily true. Still, finding out that they are, in fact, true requires empirical investigation. This means that sometimes, in order to find out whether certain things are true with respect to all possible states of the world, and other things are true with respect to no possible states of the world, we first must find out what is true with respect to the actual state of the world. *Sometimes in order to find out what could and could not be, one first must find out what is.* This insight is incompatible with acceptance of the conception of inquiry sketched above. On that conception, necessary truths are uninformative, epistemic possibility is restricted to metaphysical possibility, and all inquiry is a matter of narrowing down the range of (metaphysically) possible states that the world could genuinely be in. Kripke's arguments may plausibly be taken to show that these views, and the conception on which they are based, are simply mistaken.

The central problem with the conception is its restriction of ways things could *conceivably* be to ways things could *really* be—i.e., its restriction of epistemic possibility to metaphysical possibility. This is something that Kripke rejects. Instead of identifying these two kinds of possibility, he sharply distinguishes them.[3] Once this is done, and both rigid designation and the existence of nontrivial essential properties of objects are accepted, the necessary aposteriori follows unproblematically.[4]

How, then, should we think of inquiry? Is there any way of modifying the original conception that retains its attractive features, while avoiding its errors? Although Kripke doesn't address this question explicitly, there is a natural strategy for doing this that makes use of materials he provides. Remember, for Kripke, possible states of the world are not alternate concrete universes, but abstract objects. They are maximally complete ways the real concrete universe could have been—maximally complete properties that the universe could have instantiated. Thinking of them in this way suggests an obvious generalization. Just as there are properties that certain objects could possibly have and other properties that they couldn't possibly have, so there are certain maximally complete properties that the universe could have had—possible states of the world—and other maximally complete properties that the universe could not have had—impossible states of the world.[5] If some of the properties that objects couldn't have had are, as our

---

[3] . . . this point requires further discussion. Near the end of lecture 3 of *Naming and Necessity*, Kripke responds to an objection to his conception of the necessary aposteriori in a way that may seem to cast doubt on his commitment to a sharp and robust distinction between epistemic and metaphysical possibility. In the end, I . . . argue that the passage is both misleading and something of an anomaly. . . .

[4] Essentially this explanation of the necessary aposteriori is given by Kripke on pp. 151–53 of "Identity and Necessity," in Milton Munitz, ed. (New York: NYU Press, 1971).

[5] For an explanation and defense of this conception of world-states (in response to a different problem), see Nathan Salmon, "The Logic of What Might Have Been," *The Philosophical Review* 98, 1 (1989): 3–34.

examples (1–4) indicate, properties that one can conceive them as having, then surely some maximally complete properties that the universe could not have had (some impossible states of the world) are properties one could conceive it as having. Given this, one could explain the informativeness of certain necessary truths as resulting from the fact that learning them allows one to rule out certain impossible, but nevertheless conceivable, states of the world. Moreover, one could explain the function played by empirical evidence in providing the justification needed for knowledge of the necessary propositions expressed by sentences (1–4); empirical evidence is required to rule out certain impossible, but nevertheless conceivable and epistemologically relevant, world-states with respect to which the propositions are false.[6] Thus, by expanding the range of epistemically conceivable states of the world to include some that are metaphysically impossible, one can modify the original conception of inquiry so as to accommodate Kripkean examples like (1–4). Whether or not the modification is sufficient to save the conception from further problems is a question to which we will return later.

Identity Statements and the Necessary Aposteriori

The Gap in Kripke's Argument

I now turn to what may be the most well-known examples that Kripke gives of the necessary aposteriori—identity statements involving rigid designators.

  5. Hesperus is Phosphorus.
  6. Hesperus is Hesperus.
  7. a = b.

If a sentence of the form (7) is true, then the term occupying the position of 'a' and the term occupying the position of 'b' refer to the same thing. If they are rigid designators, this means that they refer to the same thing with respect to all world-states in which that thing exists (and never refer to anything else). To keep things simple, let's ignore world-states in which the thing doesn't exist. Then we know that any true sentence of the form (7) in which the terms are rigid designators is a necessary truth; so (5) and (6) are necessary truths. (We take *is* in (5) and (6) to be the *is* of identity.) Of course, if we replace one of the names with a non-rigid designator, as in (8), then the example may be true without being necessary.

  8. The planet seen at a certain place in the evening sky in certain seasons is Hesperus.

In lecture 2 of *Naming and Necessity*, Kripke considers an objection to this view which he attributes to Quine.

> There's a dispute about this between Quine and Ruth Barcan Marcus. Marcus says that identities between names are necessary. If someone thinks that Cicero is

---

[6] Here, I assume that names and indexicals (unlike certain definite descriptions such as *the stuff out of which this table, if it exists, is constituted*) rigidly designate the same thing with respect to all world-states, possible or not.

Tully, and really uses 'Cicero' and 'Tully' as names, he is thereby committed to holding that his belief is a necessary truth. She uses the term 'mere tag'. Quine replies as follows, 'We may tag the planet Venus, some fine evening, with the proper name "Hesperus." We may tag the same planet again, some day before sunrise, with the proper name "Phosphorus." When we discover that we have tagged the same planet twice our discovery is empirical.[7]

Quine concludes from this that the statement expressed by (5) must be contingent—presumably because it is not knowable apriori. Kripke's reply is, essentially, that this objection rests on the incorrect assumption that necessity and aprioricity come to the same thing. Once this is recognized, the objection collapses.

There is, however, a slightly different objection that could be read into Quine's comment about our "discovering that we have tagged the same planet twice." This phrase suggests that perhaps what he has in mind is (9).

    9.   'Hesperus' and 'Phosphorus' refer (in our language) to the same thing.

The proposition expressed by (9) really is contingent, in addition to being knowable only aposteriori. However, the contingency of (9) is no argument against the necessity of (5), since the two sentences clearly express different propositions. Thus, Kripke's position remains intact.

Having considered these objections to his view that true identity statements involving names are necessary and aposteriori, Kripke devotes the last four pages of lecture 2 (the bottom of page 101 to the top of page 105) to explaining in detail why his view is correct. The section is too long to quote, so I will summarize it. The view Kripke presents goes essentially as follows: Let $a = b$ be a true identity sentence involving proper names. These names may either be ordinary names like *Cicero* and *Tully,* or special names like *Hesperus* and *Phosphorus* the understanding of which may involve associating them with reference-fixing descriptions. In either case, Kripke argues, the evidence available to a competent user of the names is insufficient to determine that they are coreferential. He illustrates this point by noting that there is a possible state of the world in which speakers are in an evidentiary situation that is qualitatively identical with the one which we actual speakers are in, and yet, in the merely possible situation, the names are used to refer to different things. For example, there is a world-state with respect to which speakers fix the referent of the name *Hesperus* just as we do in the actual world—by pointing to a bright object that appears in the evening in a certain part of the sky in certain seasons. Furthermore, speakers in that possible world-state fix the referent of the name *Phosphorus* by pointing to a bright object that appears in the morning in certain seasons. From a qualitative point of view, these speakers are in the same evidentiary situation regarding their uses of the names as we are. Yet their uses of the names refer to different things.

Kripke describes the case as follows:

---

[7] *Naming and Necessity*, p. 100.

The evidence I have before I know that Hesperus is Phosphorus is that I see a certain star or certain heavenly body in the evening and call it 'Hesperus', and in the morning and call it 'Phosphorus'. I know these things. There certainly is a possible world in which a man should have seen a certain star at a certain position in the evening and called it 'Hesperus' and a certain star in the morning and called it 'Phosphorus'; and should have concluded—should have found out by empirical investigation—that he names two different stars, or two different heavenly bodies. At least one of these stars or heavenly bodies was not Phosphorus, otherwise it couldn't have come out that way. But that's true. And so it's true that given the evidence that someone has antecedent to his empirical investigation, he can be placed in a sense in exactly the same situation, that is a qualitatively identical epistemic situation, and call two heavenly bodies 'Hesperus' and 'Phosphorus', without their being identical. So in that sense we can say that it might have turned out either way.[8]

Kripke intends this example to show that the evidence available to us in the actual state of the world, as well as to agents in qualitatively similar world-states, simply by virtue of being competent users of the names, is insufficient to show that the names are coreferential. We may express this idea as follows: Let E be the collection of metaphysically possible world-states in which the epistemic situation of agents regarding their uses of the terms *Hesperus* and *Phosphorus* is qualitatively identical with our actual epistemic situation. Kripke may have been thinking that for any proposition p, if it is not the case that p is true in all members of E, then p is a proposition which is not determined to be true by the qualitative evidence available to us, and so is one that we do not, and cannot, know apriori, simply on the basis of our mastery of the relevant terms or concepts. Let us grant this for the sake of argument. Well, one proposition that fails to be true in all members of E is the proposition that the names *Hesperus* and *Phosphorus* are coreferential; another closely related proposition is the one expressed by (10).

    10.   The sentence 'Hesperus is Phosphorus' expresses a truth in our language.

Thus, Kripke is in a position to conclude that the metalinguistic claim which says that the sentence 'Hesperus is Phosphorus' expresses a truth in our language is something that we cannot know apriori, but rather can come to be known only on the basis of empirical investigation.

So far so good. However, there is a problem. The lesson Kripke explicitly draws from this example is not that a certain metalinguistic claim is knowable by us only aposteriori, but rather that the claim that Hesperus is Phosphorus is knowable by us only aposteriori.

So two things are true: first, that we do not know *a priori* that Hesperus is Phosphorus, and are in no position to find out the answer except empirically. Second, this is so because we could have evidence qualitatively indistinguishable from the evidence we have and determine the reference of the two names by the positions of the two planets in the sky, without the planets being the same.[9]

---

[8] *Ibid.*, pp. 103–4.

[9] *Ibid.*, p. 104.

The problem is that Kripke's conclusion does not follow from his apparent premises. The proposition that Hesperus is Phosphorus is, as he insists, true in all
metaphysically possible world-states. So it is true in all members of the class E of
such world-states in which agents are in an epistemic situation qualitatively identical to ours. Since it is true with respect to those world-states, the principle that
only propositions true in all members of E are knowable by us apriori does not
rule out that we may know it apriori, even though it does rule out that we can
know apriori that 'Hesperus is Phosphorus' expresses a truth in our language.
Since the proposition expressed by (5) is *not* the same as the proposition
expressed by (10), showing the latter to be knowable by us only aposteriori is not
enough to establish that the former is knowable only in the same way.

   The point I am making depends on sharply distinguishing (5), on the one
hand, from (10), on the other. When explaining the *necessity* of (5), Kripke uses
his example of possible world-states in which agents are in an epistemic situation
qualitatively identical to ours to remind us that the contingency of (10) is irrelevant to the necessity of (5). According to Kripke, the agents in these world-states
use the sentence 'Hesperus is Phosphorus' to express a *different* proposition from
the proposition we actually use it to express. The fact that the proposition they use
it to express is false with respect to their states of the world does not show that the
proposition we actually use it to express is false at any world-state. What Kripke
fails to point out is that the same reasoning can be applied to the epistemic status
of the two examples. The proposition expressed by sentence (10) is knowable only
aposteriori. But how does that bear on the question of whether proposition (5) is
knowable apriori? The agents of Kripke's imagined world-states do not know the
proposition *they* use the sentence 'Hesperus is Phosphorus' to express, for the simple reason that the proposition that they use it to express is *false* with respect to
their world-states. But how does this show that the *different* proposition that *we*
use the sentence to express isn't known by us, or that it isn't known by us independent of empirical investigation? Until we can answer this question, we have no
way of viewing Kripke's discussion as supporting his conclusion that the claim
that Hesperus is Phosphorus is not knowable apriori and so qualifies as an example of the necessary aposteriori.

Kripke's Informal Strategy for Filling the Gap

Although there is undoubtedly a gap in Kripke's argument, it is not an inexplicable one. Throughout the passage, he exploits a very familiar and highly intuitive
connection between speakers' understanding and acceptance of sentences and our
ability to use those sentences to report what they believe. For example, if you
know that I fully understand and sincerely accept the sentence *Trenton is a town
in central New Jersey,* then normally you will feel justified in reporting that I believe
that Trenton is a town in central New Jersey. Similarly, if you know that I fully
understand the sentence but do not accept it—either because I am uncertain of its
truth or because I believe it to be false—then normally, and all other things being
equal, you will feel justified in reporting that I *don't* believe that Trenton is a town

in central New Jersey. The same is true of the sentence *Hesperus is Phosphorus.* In Kripke's example, before we made or learned of the astronomical discovery, we understood but did not accept the sentence; hence it is natural, and all but inevitable, to conclude that at that time we did not believe that Hesperus is Phosphorus. Moreover, as Kripke emphasizes with his evocation of agents in circumstances qualitatively identical to ours, we would not have been justified in accepting the sentence *Hesperus is Phosphorus* based on the evidence we had at that time. Because of this, it is natural to conclude that we wouldn't have been justified in believing that Hesperus is Phosphorus based on the evidence we then had. But if that is so, then knowledge that Hesperus is Phosphorus must require empirical justification, in which case it must not be knowable apriori that Hesperus is Phosphorus—exactly as Kripke concludes.

This, I believe, is what Kripke had in mind. Although there is much to be said for this pattern of reasoning, there is a potential puzzle lurking within it. In order to bring out the puzzle, I will first use our modest theoretical apparatus of propositions as objects of belief and knowledge to formulate explicit and generalized premises to fill the gap in Kripke's argument. Next, I will scrutinize these new premises and show that either their truth is highly doubtful, or they are not strong enough to allow Kripke to derive his conclusion. Having isolated sources of potential difficulty, I will return to the informal reasoning just sketched, expose the puzzle that lies behind it, and evaluate Kripke's conclusion about this putative example of the necessary aposteriori.

A Formal and Explicit Reconstruction of Kripke's Argument

The informal pattern of reasoning I have attributed to Kripke posits a close connection between our attitudes toward sentences and the beliefs those sentences are used to express. Using the terminology of propositions, we may express this thought as follows: Since sentences are vehicles for expressing propositions, the cognitive attitudes (belief, knowledge, etc.) that we bear to propositions expressed by sentences are mediated by the attitudes we bear to sentences that express them. Often, our believing a certain proposition goes hand in hand with understanding and accepting a sentence that expresses it. One initially plausible conception of the systematic connection between understanding and accepting a sentence, on the one hand, and believing the proposition it expresses, on the other, is stated by the following "strong disquotation" principle.[10]

STRONG DISQUOTATION

A sincere, reflective, rational individual i who understands a sentence S is disposed to accept S, and believe S to be true, iff i believes the proposition semantically expressed by S. Thus, if S is a sentence of English, then a reflective, rational individual i who understands S satisfies the formula *x believes that S* iff i accepts S, and believes S to be true; if S is not a sentence of English, but is translatable

---

[10] To avoid complications, we will understand this principle as restricted to sentences that don't contain indexicals like 'I', 'now', and so on.

into English as P (where S and P express the same proposition), then such an individual i satisfies *x believes that P* iff i accepts S, and believes S to be true.

Agents in an epistemic situation similar to ours before the astronomical discovery don't accept the sentence *Hesperus is Phosphorus,* and so they don't believe what they express by the sentence. Similarly, prior to the astronomical discovery we didn't accept the sentence, so, according to the principle, at that time, we didn't believe that Hesperus is Phosphorus. Moreover, the evidence available to both of us by virtue of our understanding the sentence is such that we would *not* have been *justified* in accepting the identity sentence on the basis of that evidence. With this in mind, one might formulate the following principle involving disquotation and justification:

STRONG DISQUOTATION AND JUSTIFICATION

A sincere, reflective, rational individual i who understands S and is in possession of evidence e would be justified in accepting S, and believing it to be true, on the basis of e iff i's possession of e is sufficient to ensure that i would be justified in believing the proposition semantically expressed by S. So, if S is a sentence of English, then i's possession of e is sufficient to ensure that i satisfies the formula *x would be justified in believing that S* iff i would be justified in accepting S, and believing S to be true, on the basis of e; if S is not an English sentence, but is translatable into English as P (where S and P express the same proposition), then i's possession of e is sufficient to ensure that i satisfies *x would be justified in believing that P* iff i would be justified in accepting S, and believing it to be true, on the basis of e.

If these two principles are accepted, then Kripke's argument at the end of lecture 2 can be reconstructed as follows:

(i) Since there are possible situations in which *Hesperus is Phosphorus* expresses something false, even though the agents in those situations are perfect reasoners who have evidence qualitatively identical with the evidence available to us simply on the basis of our linguistic competence, the evidence available to us simply on the basis of our linguistic competence does not justify our accepting the sentence.

(ii) So, by the strong disquotation and justification principle, the evidence available to us simply by virtue of our competence, plus our reasoning correctly about it, is not enough to justify us in believing that Hesperus is Phosphorus.

(iii) If the belief that Hesperus is Phosphorus were justifiable apriori, then it would be justifiable by the evidence available to us by virtue of our linguistic competence, plus our reasoning correctly about it.

(iv) So that belief is not justifiable apriori. Hence, it is not knowable apriori that Hesperus is Phosphorus.

This reconstruction of Kripke's argument has the virtue of being logically valid; the conclusion that it is not knowable apriori that Hesperus is Phosphorus is a logical consequence of Kripke's premises about the attitudes of agents toward the sentence *Hesperus is Phosphorus* plus the supplementary premise of strong disquotation and justification. Nevertheless, the argument is problematic—in part because there are reasons to suspect that the principles of strong disquotation and strong disquotation plus justification are untrue. One such reason is that these principles have the consequence that in order to believe a proposition, one must be disposed to accept every sentence one understands that semantically expresses it. Thus, the principles leave no room for the possibility that an individual might understand two sentences that semantically express the same proposition, without knowing that they do, and so might accept one of the sentences while not accepting the other. (In such a case the strong disquotation principle leads to the contradictory conclusion that the agent both believes and does not believe one and the same proposition.) Since there is reason to think that such possibilities are genuine, there is reason to reject the strong disquotation principles.[11]

One example of the problem with the strong disquotation principle is brought out by Kripke himself in his example of puzzling Pierre, discussed in his paper, "A Puzzle about Belief," published in 1979, nine years after he delivered the lectures that became *Naming and Necessity*.[12] Kripke's Pierre is a Frenchman who has grown up in Paris speaking French, who sees picture postcards of London and forms the belief that London is pretty, which he expresses by saying *Londres est jolie*. Later, he moves to London, learns English, not by translation but by immersion, and comes to live in a poor and unattractive part of the city. On the basis of his experience, he forms a belief that he expresses by saying *London is not pretty*. It is not that he has given up the belief he formed in Paris on the basis of the picture postcards. He still affirms *Londres est jolie* when speaking French to old friends, even though he does not accept the English sentence *London is pretty*. The reason for this disparity is that he doesn't realize that *Londres* and *London* name the same city. This doesn't mean that he fails to understand the two sentences. He understands the former as well as he and his French-speaking friends did while he was living in France, which was certainly well enough to assert and communicate his belief that London is pretty, and he understands the latter as well as his monolingual English-speaking neighbors in London do, who surely count as competent speakers. Moreover, the sentences are translations of one another; they mean the same thing and, it would seem, express the same proposition. But now we have a problem. By the strong disquotation principle (right to left direction) we

---

[11] For further discussion, see pp. 10–13 and chapter 3 of *Beyond Rigidity*. See also Nathan Salmon, "A Millian Heir Rejects the Wages of *Sinn*," in C. A. Anderson and J. Owens, eds., *Propositional Attitudes: The Role of Content in Logic, Language, and Mind* (Stanford, CA: CSLI, 1990), 215–47, at pp. 220–22. Also, Stephen Rieber, "Understanding Synonyms without Knowing That They Are Synonymous," *Analysis* 52 (1992): 224–28.

[12] Saul Kripke, "A Puzzle about Belief," in A. Margalit, ed., *Meaning and Use* (Dordrecht: Reidel, 1979); reprinted in N. Salmon and S. Soames, eds., *Propositions and Attitudes* (Oxford: Oxford University Press, 1988). Kripke's formulation of the strong disquotational principle in that article is more informal and less theoretically loaded than mine. Although these differences are not without consequence, and are well worth studying, I will not discuss them here. Suffice it to say that they do not affect the difficulties we are about to uncover.

get the result that Pierre does *not* believe the proposition expressed by *London is pretty,* since he understands but does *not* accept *London is pretty.* By a corresponding application of the strong disquotational principle (left to right direction) we get the result that he *does* believe the proposition expressed by *Londres est jolie.* Since the standard translation from French to English tells us that these sentences express the same proposition, we get the conclusion that Pierre both does and does not believe one and the same proposition. Since this is a contradiction, we have a *reductio ad absurdum* of the conjunction of the principle of strong disquotation with the standard (meaning-preserving) translation of French to English. This provides reason to doubt the strong disquotational principles.

One natural response to this problem is to replace the strong disquotational principles—which are biconditionals—by the following weak disquotational principles—which are merely conditionals.

WEAK DISQUOTATION

If a sincere, reflective, rational individual i who understands a sentence S is disposed to accept S, and believe it to be true, then i believes the proposition semantically expressed by S. If S is a sentence of English, i thereby satisfies the formula *x believes that S;* if S is not a sentence of English, but is translatable into English as P (where S and P express the same proposition), then i satisfies the formula x believes that P.

WEAK DISQUOTATION AND JUSTIFICATION

If a sincere, reflective, rational individual i who understands S and is in possession of evidence e would be justified in accepting S, and believing S to be true, on the basis of e, then i's possession of e is sufficient to ensure that i would be justified in believing the proposition semantically expressed by S. So, if S is a sentence of English, then i's possession of e is sufficient to ensure that i satisfies the formula *x would be justified in believing that S,* if i would be justified in accepting S, and believing S to be true, on the basis of e; if S is not an English sentence, but is translatable into English as P (where S and P express the same proposition), then i's possession of e is sufficient to ensure that i satisfies *x would be justified in believing that P,* if i would be justified in accepting S, and believing S to be true, on the basis of e.

When the principle of weak disquotation is substituted for that of strong disquotation in the story about Pierre, we no longer get the contradictory result that Pierre believes and does not believe the same thing. Instead, we get the weaker, and potentially defensible, result that he has contradictory beliefs; he believes that London is pretty by virtue of understanding and accepting the French sentence *Londres est jolie,* and he believes that London is not pretty (by virtue of understanding and accepting the English sentence *London is not pretty*).[13]

---

[13] Although Kripke himself draws no firm conclusion about the correctness or incorrectness of the principle of weak disquotation based on this case, he does find it puzzling and problematic that the principle leads to the result that Pierre—who may be fully rational and logical— has contradictory beliefs. For a defense of both weak disquotation and this result, see Nathan Salmon, *Frege's Puzzle* (Cambridge, MA: MIT Press), and my "Direct Reference, Propositional Attitudes, and Sematic Content," originally published in *Philosophical Topics* 15 (1987): 47–87; reprinted in Salmon and Soames, *Propositions and Attitudes.*

However, even if this result is acceptable, and the principle of weak disquotation and justification is substituted for that of strong disquotation and justification in our reconstructed version of Kripke's argument, the argument still does not go through. The problem now is that the conclusion no longer follows from the premises. In this argumentative scenario, all that follows from our not being justified in accepting the sentence (5), *Hesperus is Phosphorus*, solely on the basis of our understanding it, is that *if* the proposition it expresses can be known, or justifiably believed, apriori, then such knowledge or belief must arise from something other than understanding and accepting that very sentence. This leaves open the possibility that there might be some sentence other than (5) which both expresses the proposition that Hesperus is Phosphorus, and is such that one can be justified in accepting it, and believing it to be true, solely on the basis of one's understanding of it. Since nothing in our new reconstruction of Kripke's argument rules out this possibility, the version of the argument employing the weak disquotational principles does not entail his conclusion. Although the conclusion is entailed by the version of the argument employing the strong disquotational principles, there is little comfort in this, since, as we have seen, they appear to be false.

The Lesson to Be Learned: The Nontransparency of Meaning

Although the two formal reconstructions of Kripke's arguments fail in different ways, the source of the failure is the same in both cases—the nontransparency of meaning. Two sentences may mean the same thing, and hence semantically express the same proposition, even though a competent speaker who understands both sentences does not realize this, and so accepts one, and believes it to be true, while refusing to accept the other, and either believing it to be false, or suspending judgment on it. This was Pierre's situation with the sentences *Londres est jolie* and *London is pretty*. Since the principle of strong disquotation is incompatible with this seemingly obvious truth, it should, I believe, be rejected—in which case the first reconstruction of Kripke's argument must be judged unsound.

The second reconstruction of the argument—relying on weak disquotation— fails because it does not rule out the possibility that there might be some sentence S other than *Hesperus is Phosphorus* which semantically expresses the same proposition as it does, and which is such that understanding S is sufficient for accepting it and knowing it to be true. How, one might wonder, could there be such a sentence? Well, think again about names. If, as Kripke contends, names do not have descriptive meanings or senses, what do they mean? One natural thought is that the meaning of a name is its referent. If this thought is correct, then coreferential names like *Hesperus* and *Phosphorus* mean the same thing. But surely if two names mean the same thing, then substitution of one for another in a simple sentence like (5) should preserve the meaning of the sentence. By this reasoning, we may reach the conclusion that the sentences *Hesperus is Phosphorus* and H*esperus is Hesperus* mean the same thing, and hence semantically express the same proposition. Surely, it is reasonable to think that understanding *Hesperus is Hesperus* is sufficient for accepting it, and coming to know that it expresses a truth. Thus, it is natural to conclude that it is knowable apriori that Hesperus is Hesperus. But then, if the proposition that Hesperus is Phosphorus is nothing more than the proposition that Hesperus is Hesperus, it must be knowable apriori, contrary to Kripke.

Although this line of reasoning may initially seem far-fetched, and although it certainly goes beyond Kripke, there is nothing in *Naming and Necessity* to refute it. Moreover, once it has been recognized that meaning is not always transparent, one cannot object to the claim that *Hesperus is Hesperus* and *Hesperus is Phosphorus* mean the same thing—and hence semantically express the same proposition—simply by observing that it is possible for someone to understand both sentences, and yet not know that they mean the same thing. This surely is possible, but since meaning isn't transparent, this possibility doesn't establish that the sentences mean different things. Without establishing this, there is no way to use our disquotational principles to get Kripke's desired result.

Of course, Kripke didn't state any principles of strong or weak disquotation in *Naming and Necessity*, nor did he invoke our modest theoretical apparatus of propositions as objects of belief and knowledge. Hence, one might wonder about the relevance of our findings for his informal argument at the end of lecture 2. As we shall see, there is cause for concern.

His informal argument that it is not knowable apriori that Hesperus is Phosphorus is roughly the following:

(i) For someone who understands the sentence *Hesperus is Phosphorus,* sincerely accepting it and believing it to be true goes hand in hand with believing that Hesperus is Phosphorus—i.e., one who understands *Hesperus is Phosphorus* accepts it and believes it to be true iff one believes that Hesperus is Phosphorus.

(ii) Similarly, one who understands the sentence *Hesperus is Phosphorus* would be justified in accepting it and believing it to be true iff one would be justified in believing that Hesperus is Phosphorus.

(iii) In order to be justified in accepting *Hesperus is Phosphorus* and believing it to be true, it is not sufficient for one simply to understand it; in addition, one needs empirical evidence that the two names refer to the same thing.

(iv) Therefore, understanding the sentence *Hesperus is Phosphorus* is not sufficient for one to be justified in believing that Hesperus is Phosphorus; in order for one who understands the sentence to be justified in believing that Hesperus is Phosphorus, one must have empirical evidence that the two names refer to the same thing.

(v) Therefore, the statement that Hesperus is Phosphorus is not knowable apriori.

Principles (i) and (ii) are informal Kripkean counterparts of specific instances of the principles of strong disquotation and strong disquotation and justification.

Thus, in order to accept Kripke's informal argument, one must have good reason to believe that these principles are true.[14]

Let's just concentrate on (i), which is a particular instance of the following more general principle.

> (i*) Let S be an non-indexical sentence of English and let i be a competent speaker of English who understands S. Then, the attitude ascription *x believes that S* is true of i iff i accepts S.

Here is an example scenario that creates problems for (i*):

> A student at the local college, Martin Martin, is both the quarterback of the football team and the best math student in school. His math teacher, Professor McX, has graded his work and consulted other professors about him. On that basis, she forms the opinion that Martin is a brilliant mathematician, which she expresses by saying *Martin is a brilliant mathematician.* Since her class is large, she doesn't know him by sight, so when she decides to attend one of the football games on Saturday, and sees him turn in an astounding performance on the field, she does not realize that the talented quarterback she is watching is her student, Martin. Sitting in the stands with her friend Harriet, she makes numerous comments about Martin—pointing him out and saying things like *He is a wonderful athlete.* Later Harriet, who knows Martin's girlfriend, reports that Professor McX thinks that Martin is a wonderful athlete. Surely, Harriet's report is true; the professor does believe this. Yet, if one were to ask her: *Do you think that Martin is a wonderful athlete?* she would understand the question, but she would not assent. Although she understands the sentence *Martin is a wonderful athlete*, she has no basis for accepting it, since she doesn't realize that *Martin* is the name of the quarterback who impressed her so much. So, although she believes that Martin is a

---

[14] I do think that this much strong disquotation was implicit in Kripke's argument in *Naming and Necessity*. With this in mind, consider the following passage from footnote 44 of "A Puzzle about Belief": "some earlier formulations expressed disquotationally such as 'It was once unknown that Hesperus is Phosphorus' are questionable in light of the present paper (but see the previous note for this case)." The point here is that although it is unquestionable that it was once unknown that *Hesperus is Phosphorus* expressed a truth, we now see that we should not jump to the conclusion that it was once unknown that Hesperus is Phosphorus. This is questionable because it may just be that to know that Hesperus is Hesperus is to know that Hesperus is Phosphorus. But if that is so, then the argument at the end of lecture 2 of *Naming and Necessity* is undermined. I believe Kripke did not see this possibility at the time of the lectures. Nevertheless, footnote 44 continues: "I was aware of this question at the time *Naming and Necessity* was written, but I did not wish to muddy the waters further than necessary at that time. I regarded the distinction between epistemic and metaphysical necessity as valid in any case and adequate for the distinctions I wished to make." Three points: (*i*) although the distinction between different types of necessity (and possibility) is relevant for explaining many instances of the necessary aposteriori, it won't help here if knowing that Hesperus is Hesperus turns out to be the same as knowing that Hesperus is Phosphorus; (*ii*) in Kripke's argument at the end of lecture 2, he does not invoke the distinction between different kinds of necessity (or possibility), and (*iii*) although he may have been generally aware of the difficulties posed by Pierre-type examples for strong disquotational principles at the time of *Naming and Necessity*, it seems evident that he did not focus on their implications for his argument at the end of lecture 2, probably because at that time he did not take seriously the idea that *Hesperus is Hesperus* and *Hesperus is Phosphorus* might mean the same thing.

wonderful athlete, and although she understands the sentence *Martin is a wonderful athlete*, she does not accept it or believe it to be true.

This scenario casts doubt on (i*). But if (i*) is in doubt, then there may be reason to doubt (i) and (ii) as well. We need not here try to confirm or resolve those doubts, or to decide precisely what to say about potentially problematic cases like the one just sketched. It is enough to have shown that the premises needed, and tacitly used, in Kripke's argument are insecure, and cannot, without further investigation, be taken for granted in establishing his conclusion that it is not knowable apriori that Hesperus is Phosphorus.[15]

As we have seen, this is true whether the premises are formally stated using the theoretical apparatus of propositions as semantic contents of sentences and objects of propositional attitudes, or whether they are more informally and less abstractly formulated as (i) and (ii). Hence, we have little choice but to conclude that, despite the fact that there are other quite legitimate examples of the necessary aposteriori given in *Naming and Necessity*, Kripke's discussion at the end of lecture 2 does *not* establish that the statements made by identity sentences involving coreferential names are among them.

Final Assessment: A Dilemma

Despite this negative result, I suspect that many may be prepared to take it simply to be a datum that one can know that Cicero is Cicero, or that Hesperus is Hesperus, without knowing that Cicero is Tully, or that Hesperus is Phosphorus, and that this shows that sentences which differ only in the substitution of coreferential proper names may mean different things and semantically express different propositions. And if the sentences $a = a$ and $a = b$ semantically express different propositions, then at least the observation that the proposition expressed by the former is knowable apriori won't force the conclusion that the proposition expressed by the latter is too. So, even if we don't have an argument for the truth of *The proposition that $a = b$ is knowable only aposteriori*, accepting the alleged datum would allow one to block the most obvious line of argument for the falsity of that claim.

---

[15] My own view about this issue is that the sentence *Is it knowable apriori that Hesperus is Phosphorus?* may be used to ask different questions. If one uses it to ask whether the proposition semantically expressed by *Hesperus is Phosphorus* is knowable apriori, then the answer is *yes*. (For more, see below.) However, if one uses it to ask a question that could more explicitly be paraphrased as *Is it knowable apriori that the planet, Hesperus seen in the evening, is the planet. Phosphorus, seen in the morning?* then the answer is: that proposition is not knowable apriori, but it is also not necessary. In other work, I develop the idea that sentences are often used to assert more than their semantic contents, and sometimes these contents are not asserted at all. See *Beyond Rigidity*, and also "Naming and Asserting," in A. Szabo, ed., *Semantics and Pragmatics* (Oxford University Press, forthcoming). Following in the footsteps of my Ph.D. student Michael McGlone, I have come to believe that if this general idea is correct, then much of what is confusing about Kripke's puzzle about belief is due to the difficulty of keeping track of which propositions are being questioned and asserted in which contexts. For a recent note on this, see my "Saul Kripke, the Necessary Aposteriori, and the Two-Dimensionalist Heresy."

Fair enough. However, there is still a difficulty to be faced. We need some positive theory of the contributions made by proper names to the propositions semantically expressed by sentences containing them. If the alleged datum is to be accepted, then this account must make clear precisely in what respect the propositions expressed by sentences containing different but coreferential proper names can, and in certain cases do, differ. What makes this task daunting is that the old solution to this problem—namely, the view that names have descriptive semantic contents—seems to have been thoroughly discredited by Kripke's arguments. If this is right, if the idea that names have descriptive semantic contents really has been discredited, then, given the alleged datum, one cannot identify the semantic contents of names either with their referents, or with descriptive semantic information that may vary from one coreferential name to another. In what other way do coreferential names differ? Often, they have different spellings, pronunciations, or syntactic structures, and in theory one could appeal to these differences to distinguish the different propositions semantically expressed by sentences containing different names. Surely, however, we don't want to say that whenever speakers use words with different spellings, pronunciations, or syntactic structures, they must, thereby, differ in the propositions they assert or believe.

Consequently, one who accepts Kripke's anti-descriptivist arguments is left with a dilemma. There are two main options. According to the first option, one may accept the alleged datum that, typically, when sentences differ only in the substitution of one coreferential proper name for another, it is possible to assert, believe, or know the proposition semantically expressed by one of the sentences without asserting, believing, or knowing the proposition semantically expressed by the other. If one does take this option, then one must give some positive account of propositions and propositional attitudes that explains how this is possible. That doesn't seem easy.

According to the second option, one may reject the alleged datum and identify the semantic contents of names with their referents. If one does this, then one will be led to maintain that sentences which differ only in the substitution of coreferential names semantically express the same propositions, and, given this, one will find it very natural to conclude that attitude ascriptions involving such sentences are semantically equivalent. On this view, the proposition expressed by *Hesperus is Phosphorus* is identical with the proposition expressed by *Hesperus is Hesperus*. But then if (as many assume) the latter is knowable apriori, the former is too—in which case the claim that (5) is an example of the necessary aposteriori is false. This is the view defended by Nathan Salmon in *Frege's Puzzle*.[16] It is also the alternative I favor. However, it too faces a serious difficulty. The difficulty is to explain how, if the view is correct, speakers succeed in using sentences P and Q that differ only in the substitution of one coreferential proper name for another to assert and convey different information, and to express different beliefs—which

---

[16] Salmon, *Frege's Puzzle*.

they clearly do. In addition, it must be explained why speakers often do not regard an attitude ascription *n asserts/believes/knows that P* to be truth-conditionally equivalent to the corresponding attitude ascription *n asserts/believes/knows that Q*—which they often do not.

So the dilemma is either (i) to take it for granted that the sentences *Hesperus is Hesperus* and *Hesperus is Phosphorus* semantically express different propositions, and try to explain what this difference consists in, or (ii) to treat the two sentences as semantically expressing the same proposition, and try to explain how speakers use them to assert and convey different information, and to express and report different beliefs. The resolution of this dilemma is one of the most important unfinished legacies left to us by *Naming and Necessity*.[17]

A Further Note on Inquiry

At the beginning of the chapter, we considered a conception of inquiry according to which the point of rational belief formation is to locate the actual state of the world by eliminating merely possible world-states—i.e., maximally complete properties that the universe could have instantiated—incompatible with propositions one has come to know or believe on the basis of evidence. A revision of this conception was suggested in order to accommodate necessary aposteriori propositions expressed by sentences like (1–4). According to the revised conception, conceivable world-states—maximally complete properties that one can conceive the universe as instantiating (whether or not they could in fact be instantiated)—replace genuinely possible world-states in the model of inquiry. On this conception, the point of rational belief formation is to locate the actual state of the world by eliminating merely conceivable world-states incompatible with propositions one has come to believe on the basis of evidence. It is important to notice that our discussion in the previous section calls even this revised conception of inquiry into question. Suppose that it is possible to rationally believe a proposition p—like the proposition that London is pretty—by virtue of understanding and accepting a sentence P that expresses it, while also rationally believing the negation of p, by virtue of understanding and accepting the negation, ~Q, of a different sentence— without being in a position, or having the evidence necessary, to recognize the inconsistency. In this sort of case, it would seem that the fact that the agent believes p does not eliminate all conceivable world-states with respect to which the negation of p holds. On the contrary, when the agent considers such states, as they are presented by the sentence ~Q, they remain for him genuine epistemic possibilities. But if believing p doesn't eliminate the epistemic possibility that the

---

[17] In chapters 3 and 8 of *Beyond Rigidity*, I opt for (ii) and try to provide the basis for the needed explanations; these ideas are revised and extended in "Naming and Asserting." See Salmon, *Frege's Puzzle*, for a different defense of (ii). For defenses of (i), see Mark Richard, *Propositional Attitudes* (Cambridge: Cambridge University Press, 1990), and Larson and Ludlow, "Interpreted Logical Forms."

negation of p may be true, then the notion of eliminating conceivable states *incompatible* with what one believes becomes problematic, and the model of inquiry based upon it breaks down. Thus, if inconsistent beliefs of the sort discussed here are genuinely possible, then a conception of inquiry substantially different from those we have considered may be needed.[18]

---

[18] This point is related to arguments designed to show that propositions cannot be identified with sets of circumstances (metaphysically possible world-states, epistemically conceivable world-states, logically possible world-states, situations, etc.) with respect to which they are true. For such arguments, see my "Direct Reference, Propositional Attitudes, and Semantic Content."

A PUZZLE ABOUT BELIEF

Saul A. Kripke

In this paper I will present a puzzle about names and belief. A moral or two will be drawn about some other arguments that have occasionally been advanced in this area, but my main thesis is a simple one: that the puzzle *is* a puzzle. And, as a corollary, that any account of belief must ultimately come to grips with it. Any speculation as to solutions can be deferred.

The first section of the paper gives the theoretical background in previous discussion, and in my own earlier work, that led me to consider the puzzle. The background is by no means necessary to *state* the puzzle: As a philosophical puzzle, it stands on its own and I think its fundamental interest for the problem of belief goes beyond the background that engendered it. As I indicate in the third section, the problem really goes beyond beliefs expressed using names, to a far wider class of beliefs. Nevertheless, I think that the background illuminates the genesis of the puzzle, and it will enable me to draw one moral in the concluding section.

The second section states some general principles which underlie our general practice of reporting beliefs. These principles are stated in much more detail than is needed to comprehend the puzzle; and there are variant formulations of the principles that would do as well. Neither this section nor the first is necessary for an intuitive grasp of the central problem, discussed in the third section, though they may help with fine points of the discussion. The reader who wishes rapid access to the central problem could skim the first two sections lightly on a first reading.

In one sense the problem may strike some as no puzzle at all. For, in the situation to be envisaged, all the relevant facts can be described in *one* terminology without difficulty. But, in *another* terminology, the situation seems to be impossible to describe in a consistent way. This will become clearer later.

I. Preliminaries: Substitutivity

In other writings,[1] I developed a view of proper names closer in many ways to the old Millian paradigm of naming than to the Fregean tradition which probably was dominant until recently. According to Mill, a proper name is, so to speak, *simply* a name. It *simply* refers to its bearer, and has no other linguistic function. In particular, unlike a definite description, a name does not describe its bearer as possessing any special identifying properties.

---

[1] "Naming and Necessity," in D. Davidson and G. Harman (eds.), *The Semantics of Natural Languages* (Dordrecht: Reidel, 1971), 253–355 and 673–9. (Also as a separate monograph published by Harvard University Press and Basil Blackwell, 1972, 1980). "Identity and Necessity," in M. Munitz (ed.), *Identity and Individuation* (New York University Press, 1971), 135–64. Acquaintance with these papers is not a prerequisite for understanding the central puzzle of the present paper, but is helpful for understanding the theoretical background.

The opposing Fregean view holds that to each proper name, a speaker of the language associates some property or (conjunction of properties) which determines its referent as the unique thing fulfilling the associated property (or properties). This property(ies) constitutes the 'sense' of the name. Presumably, if '. . .' is a proper name, the associated properties are those that the speaker would supply if asked, "Who is '. . .'?" If he would answer ". . . is the man who——," the properties filling the second blank are those that determine the reference of the name for the given speaker and constitute its 'sense.' Of course, given the name of a famous historical figure, individuals may give different, and equally correct, answers to the "Who is '. . .'?" question. Some may identify Aristotle as the philosopher who taught Alexander the Great, others as the Stagirite philosopher who studied with Plato. For these two speakers, the sense of "Aristotle" will differ: in particular, speakers of the second kind, but not of the first kind, will regard "Aristotle, if he existed, was born in Stagira" as analytic.[2] Frege (and Russell)[3] concluded that, strictly speaking,

---

[2] Frege gives essentially this example as the second footnote of "On Sense and Reference." For the "Who is . . . ?" to be applicable one must be careful to elicit from one's informant properties that he regards as defining the name and determining the referent, not mere well-known facts about the referent. (Of course this distinction may well seem fictitious, but it is central to the original Frege–Russell theory.)

[3] For convenience Russell's terminology is assimilated to Frege's. Actually regarding genuine or 'logically proper' names, Russell is a strict Millian 'logically proper names' *simply* refer (to immediate objects of acquaintance). But, according to Russell, what are ordinarily called 'names' are not genuine, logically proper names, but disguised definite descriptions. Since Russell also regards definite descriptions as in turn disguised notation, he does not associate any 'senses' with descriptions, since they are not genuine singular terms. When all disguised notation is eliminated, the only singular terms remaining are logically proper names, for which no notion of 'sense' is required. When we speak of Russell as assigning 'senses' to names, we mean ordinary names and for convenience we ignore his view that the descriptions abbreviating them ultimately disappear on analysis.

On the other hand, the explicit doctrine that names are abbreviated definite descriptions is due to Russell. Michael Dummett, in his recent *Frege* (Duckworth and Harper and Row, 1973), 110–11, denies that Frege held description theory of senses. Although as far as I know Frege indeed makes no explicit statement to that effect, his examples of names conform to the doctrine, as Dummett acknowledges. Especially his 'Aristotle' example is revealing. He defines 'Aristotle' just as Russell would; it seems clear that in the case of a famous historical figure, the 'name' is indeed to be given by answering, in a uniquely specifying way, the 'who is' question. Dummett himself characterizes a sense as a "criterion . . . such that the referent of the name, if any, is whatever object satisfies that criterion." Since presumably the satisfaction of the criterion must be unique (so a unique referent is determined), does not this amount to defining names by unique satisfaction of properties, i.e., by descriptions? *Perhaps* the point is that the property in question need not be expressible by a usual predicate of English, as might be plausible if the referent is one of the speaker's acquaintances rather than a historical figure. But I doubt that even Russell, father of the explicitly formulated description theory, ever meant to require that the description must always be expressible in (unsupplemented) English.

In any event, the philosophical community has generally understood Fregean senses in terms of descriptions, and we deal with it under this usual understanding. For present purposes this is more important than detailed historical issues. Dummett acknowledges (p. 111) that few substantive points are affected by his (allegedly) broader interpretation of Frege; and it would not seem to be relevant to the problems of the present paper.

different speakers of English (or German!) ordinarily use a name such as 'Aristotle' in different senses (though with the same reference). Differences in properties associated with such names, strictly speaking, yield different idiolects.[4]

Some later theorists in the Frege–Russellian tradition have found this consequence unattractive. So they have tried to modify the view by 'clustering' the sense of the name (e.g., Aristotle is the thing having the following long list of properties, or at any rate most of them), or, better for the present purpose, socializing it (what determines the reference of 'Aristotle' is some roughly specified set of *community-wide* beliefs about Aristotle).

One way to point up the contrast between the strict Millian view and Fregean views involves—if we permit ourselves this jargon—the notion of propositional content. If a strict Millian view is correct, and the linguistic function of a proper name is completely exhausted by the fact that it names its bearer, it would appear that proper names of the same thing are everywhere interchangeable not only *salva veritate* but even *salva significatione:* the proposition expressed by a sentence should remain the same no matter what name of the object it uses. Of course this will not be true if the names are 'mentioned' rather than 'used': "'Cicero' has six letters" differs from "'Tully' has six letters" in truth value, let alone in content. (The example, of course, is Quine's.) Let us confine ourselves at this stage to *simple* sentences involving no connectives or other sources of intensionality. If Mill is completely right, not only should "Cicero was lazy" have the same *truth value* as "Tully was lazy", but the two sentences should express the same *proposition,* have the same content. Similarly, "Cicero admired Tully," "Tully admired Cicero," "Cicero admired Cicero," and "Tully admired Tully," should be four ways of saying the same thing.[5]

If such a consequence of Mill's view is accepted, it would seem to have further consequences regarding 'intensional' contexts. Whether a sentence expresses a necessary truth or a contingent one depends only on the proposition expressed and not on the words used to express it. So any simple sentence should retain its 'modal value' (necessary, impossible, contingently true, or contingently false) when 'Cicero' is replaced by 'Tully' in one or more places, since such a replacement leaves the content of the sentence unaltered. Of course this implies that coreferential

---

[4] See Frege's footnote in "On Sense and Reference" mentioned in n. 2, above and especially his discussion of 'Dr Gustav Lauben' in *"Der Gedanke."* (In the recent Geach-Stoothoff translation, "Thoughts," in *Logical Investigations*, (Oxford: Blackwell; 1977), 11–2, also in this volume.

[5] Russell, as a Millian with respect to genuine names, accepts this argument with respect to 'logically proper names'. For example, taking for the moment 'Cicero' and 'Tully' as 'logically proper names'. Russell would hold that if I judge that Cicero admired Tully, I am related to Cicero, Tully, and the admiration relation in a certain way: since Cicero *is* Tully, I am related in exactly the same way to Tully, Cicero, and admiration; therefore I judge that Tully admired Cicero. Again, if Cicero *did* admire Tully, then according to Russell a single fact corresponds to all of 'Cicero admired Tully', 'Cicero admired Cicero', etc. Its constituent (in addition to admiration) is the man Cicero, taken, so to speak, twice.

Russell thought that 'Cicero admired Tully' and 'Tully admired Cicero' are in fact obviously not interchangeable. For him, this was one argument that 'Cicero' and 'Tully' are *not* genuine names, and that the Roman orator is no constituent of propositions (or 'facts' or 'judgments') corresponding to sentences containing the name.

names are substitutable in modal contexts *salva veritate:* "It is necessary (possible) that Cicero . . ." and "It is necessary (possible) that Tully . . ." must have the same truth value no matter how the dots are filled by a simple sentence.

The situation would seem to be similar with respect to contexts involving knowledge, belief, and epistemic modalities. Whether a given subject believes something is presumably true or false of such a subject no matter how that belief is expressed; so if proper name substitution does not change the content of a sentence expressing a belief, coreferential proper names should be interchangeable *salva veritate* in belief contexts. Similar reasoning would hold for epistemic contexts ("Jones knows that . . .") and contexts of epistemic necessity ("Jones knows *a priori* that . . .") and the like.

All this, of course, would contrast strongly with the case of definite descriptions. It is well known that substitution of coreferential descriptions in simple sentences (without operators), on any reasonable conception of 'content,' *can* alter the content of such a sentence. In particular, the modal value of a sentence is not invariant under changes of coreferential descriptions: "The smallest prime is even" expresses a necessary truth, but "Jones's favourite number is even" expresses a contingent one, even if Jones's favourite number happens to be the smallest prime. It follows that coreferential descriptions are *not* interchangeable *salva veritate* in modal contexts: "It is necessary that the smallest prime is even" is true while "It is necessary that Jones' favourite number is even" is false.

Of course there is a '*de re*' or 'large scope' reading under which the second sentence is true. Such a reading would be expressed more accurately by "Jones's favourite number is such that it is necessarily even" or, in rough Russellian transcription, as "One and only one number is admired by Jones above all others, and any such number is necessarily even (has the property of necessary evenness)." Such a *de re* reading, if it makes sense at all, by definition must be subject to a principle of substitution *salva veritate,* since necessary evenness is a property of the *number,* independently of how it is designated; in this respect there can be no contrast between names and descriptions. The contrast, according to the Millian view, must come in the *de dicto* or "small scope" reading, which is the *only* reading, for belief contexts as well as modal contexts, that will concern us in this paper. If we wish, we can emphasize that this is our reading in various ways. Say, "It is necessary that: Cicero was bald" or, more explicitly, "The following proposition is necessarily true: Cicero was bald," or even, in Carnap's 'formal' mode of speech,[6] "'Cicero was bald' expresses a necessary truth." Now the Millian asserts that all these formulations retain their truth value when 'Cicero' is replaced by 'Tully,' even though 'Jones's favourite Latin author' and 'the man who denounced Catiline' would *not* similarly be interchangeable in these contexts even if they are codesignative.

---

[6] Given the arguments of Church and others, I do not believe that the formal mode of speech is synonymous with other formulations. But it can be used as a rough way to convey the idea of scope.

Similarly for belief contexts. Here too *de re* beliefs—as in "Jones believes, *of* Cicero (or: *of* his favourite Latin author) that he was bald" do *not* concern us in this paper. Such contexts, if they make sense, are by definition subject to a substitutivity principle for both names and descriptions. Rather we are concerned with the *de dicto* locution expressed explicitly in such formulations as, "Jones believes that: Cicero was bald" (or: "Jones believes that: the man who denounced Catiline was bald"). The material after the colon expresses the *content* of Jones's belief. Other, more explicit, formulations are: "Jones believes the proposition—that—Cicero—was—bald," or even in the 'formal' mode, "The sentence 'Cicero was bald' gives the content of a belief of Jones." In all such contexts, the strict Millian seems to be committed to saying that codesignative names, but not codesignative descriptions, are interchangeable *salva veritate*.[7]

Now it has been widely assumed that these apparent consequences of the Millian view are plainly false. First, it seemed that sentences can alter their *modal* values by replacing a name by a codesignative one. "Hesperus is Hesperus" (or, more cautiously: "If Hesperus exists, Hesperus is Hesperus") expresses a necessary truth, while "Hesperus is Phosphorus" (or: "If Hesperus exists, Hesperus is Phosphorus"), expresses an empirical discovery, and hence, it has been widely assumed, a contingent truth. (It might have turned out, and hence might have been, otherwise.)

It has seemed even more obvious that codesignative proper names are not interchangeable in belief contexts and epistemic contexts. Tom, a normal speaker of the language, may sincerely assent to "Tully denounced Catiline," but not to "Cicero denounced Catiline." He may even deny the latter. And his denial is compatible with his status as a normal English speaker who satisfies normal criteria for using both

---

[7] It may well be argued that the Millian view implies that proper names are *scopless* and that for them the *de dicto–de re* distinction vanishes. This view was considerable plausibility (my own views on rigidity will imply something like this for *modal* contexts), but it need not be argued here either way: *de re* uses are simply not treated in the present paper.

Christopher Peacocke ("Proper Names, Reference, and Rigid Designation," in Blackburn (ed.), *Meaning, Reference, and Necessity* (Cambridge, 1975); see section I), uses what amounts to the equivalence of the *de dicto–de re* construction in *all* contexts (or, put alternatively, the lack of such a distinction) to characterize the notion of rigid designation. I agree that for *modal* contexts, this is (roughly) equivalent to my own notion, also that for proper names Peacocke's equivalence holds for temporal contexts. (This is roughly equivalent to the 'temporal rigidity' of names.) I also agree that it is very plausible to extend the principle to all contexts. But, as Peacocke recognizes, this appears to imply a substitutivity principle for codesignative proper names in belief contexts, which is widely assumed to be false. Peacocke proposes to use Davidson's theory of intensional contexts to block this conclusion (the material in the 'that' clause is a separate sentence). I myself cannot accept Davidson's theory; but even if it were true, Peacocke in effect acknowledges that it does not really dispose of the difficulty (p. 127, first paragraph). (Incidentally, if Davidson's theory does block any inference to the transparency of belief contexts with respect to names, why does Peacocke assume without argument that it does not do so for modal contexts, which have a similar grammatical structure?) The problems are thus those of the present paper; until they are resolved I prefer at present to keep to my earlier more cautious formulation.

Incidentally, Peacocke hints a recognition that the received platitude—that codesignative names are not interchangeable in belief contexts—may not be so clear as is generally supposed.

'Cicero' and 'Tully' as names for the famed Roman (without knowing that 'Cicero' and 'Tully' name the same person). Given this, it seems obvious that Tom believes that: Tully denounced Catiline, but that he does not believe (lacks the belief) that: Cicero denounced Catiline.[8] So it seems clear that codesignative proper names are not interchangeable in belief contexts. It also seems clear that there must be two distinct propositions or contents expressed by 'Cicero denounced Catiline' and 'Tully denounced Catiline'. How else can Tom believe one and deny the other? And the difference in propositions thus expressed can only come from a difference in *sense* between 'Tully' and 'Cicero'. Such a conclusion agrees with a Fregean theory and seems to be incompatible with a purely Millian view.[9]

In the previous work mentioned above, I rejected one of these arguments against Mill, the modal argument. 'Hesperus is Phosphorus', I maintained, expresses just as necessary a truth as 'Hesperus is Hesperus'; there are no counterfactual situations in which Hesperus and Phosphorus would have been different. Admittedly, the truth of 'Hesperus is Phosphorus' was not known *a priori,* and may even have been widely disbelieved before appropriate empirical evidence came in. But these epistemic questions should be separated, I have argued, from the metaphysical question of the necessity of 'Hesperus is Phosphorus'. And it is a consequence of my conception of names as 'rigid designators' that codesignative proper names are interchangeable *salva veritate* in all contexts of (metaphysical) necessity and possibility; further, that replacement of a proper name by a codesignative name leaves the modal value of any sentence unchanged.

But although my position confirmed the Millian account of names in modal contexts, it equally appears at first blush to imply a *non-Millian* account of epistemic and belief contexts (and other contexts of propositional attitude). For I presupposed a sharp contrast between epistemic and metaphysical possibility: Before appropriate empirical discoveries were made, men might well have failed to know that Hesperus was Phosphorus, or even to believe it, even though they of course knew and believed that Hesperus was Hesperus. Does not this support a Fregean position that 'Hesperus' and 'Phosphorus' have different 'modes of presentation'

---

[8] The example comes from Quine, *Word and Object* (MIT Press, 1960), 145 Quine's conclusion that 'believes that' construed *de dicto* is opaque has widely been taken for granted. In the formulation in the text I have used the colon to emphasize that I am speaking of belief *de dicto.* Since, as I have said, belief *de dicto* will be our *only* concern in this paper, in the future the colon will usually be suppressed, and all 'believes that' contexts should be read *de dicto* unless the contrary is indicated explicitly.

[9] In many writings Peter Geach has advocated a view that is non-Millian (he would say 'non-Lockean') in that to each name a sortal predicate is attached by definition ('Geach', for example, by *definition* names a man). On the other hand, the theory is not completely Fregean either, since Geach denies that any definite description that would identify the referent of the name among things of the same sort is analytically tied to the name. (See, e.g., his *Reference and Generality,* (Cornell, 1962), 43–5). As far as the present issues are concerned Geach's view can fairly be assimilated to *Mill's* rather than Frege's. For such ordinary names as 'Cicero' and 'Tully' will have both the same reference and the same (Geachian) sense (namely, that they are names of a man). It would thus seem that they ought to be interchangeable everywhere. (In *Reference and Generality,* Geach appears not to accept this conclusion, but the *prima fact* argument for the conclusion will be the same as on a purely Millian view.)

that determine their references? What else can account for the fact that, before astronomers identified the two heavenly bodies, a sentence using 'Hesperus' could express a common belief, while the same context involving 'Phosphorus' did not? In the case of 'Hesperus' and 'Phosphorus', it is pretty clear what the different 'modes of presentation' would be: one mode determines a heavenly body by its typical position and appearance, in the appropriate season, in the evening; the other determines the same body by its position and appearance, in the appropriate season, in the morning. So it appears that even though, according to my view, proper names would be *modally* rigid—would have the same reference when we use them to speak of counterfactual situations as they do when used to describe the actual world—they would have a kind of Fregean 'sense' according to how that rigid reference is fixed. And the divergences of 'sense' (in this sense of 'sense') would lead to failures of interchangeability of codesignative names in contexts of propositional attitude, though not in modal contexts. Such a theory would agree with Mill regarding modal contexts but with Frege regarding belief contexts. The theory would not be *purely* Millian.[10]

After further thought, however, the Fregean conclusion appears less obvious. Just as people are said to have been unaware at one time of the fact that Hesperus is Phosphorus, so a normal speaker of English apparently may not know that Cicero is Tully, or that Holland is the Netherlands. For he may sincerely assent to 'Cicero was lazy', while dissenting from 'Tully was lazy', or he may sincerely assent to 'Holland is a beautiful country', while dissenting from 'The Netherlands is a beautiful country'. In the case of 'Hesperus' and 'Phosphorus', it seemed plausible

---

[10] In an unpublished paper, Diana Ackerman urges the problem of substitutivity failure against the Millian view and, hence, against my own views. I believe that others may have done so as well. (I have the impression that the paper has undergone considerable revision, and I have not seen recent versions.) I agree that this problem is a considerable difficulty for the Millian view, and for the Millian *spirit* of my own views in "Naming and Necessity." (See the discussion of this in the text of the present paper.) On the other hand I would emphasize that there need be no *contradiction* in maintaining that names are *modally* rigid and satisfy a substitutivity principle for modal contexts, while denying the substitutivity principle for belief contexts. The entire apparatus elaborated in "Naming and Necessity" of the distinction between epistemic and metaphysical necessity, and of giving a meaning and fixing a reference, was meant to show, among other things, that a Millian substitutivity doctrine for modal contexts can be maintained even if such a doctrine for epistemic contexts is rejected. "Naming and Necessity" never asserted a substitutivity principle for epistemic contexts.

It is even consistent to suppose that differing modes of (rigidity) fixing the reference is responsible for the substitutivity failures, thus adopting a position intermediate between Frege and Mill, on the lines indicated in the text of the present paper. "Naming and Necessity" may even perhaps be taken as suggesting, for some contexts where a conventional description rigidity fixes the reference ('Hesperus–Phosphorus'), that the mode of reference fixing is relevant to epistemic questions. I knew when I wrote "Naming and Necessity" that substitutivity issues in epistemic contexts were really very delicate, due to the problems of the present paper, but I thought it best not to muddy the waters further. (See nn. 43–4.)

After this paper was completed, I saw Alvin Plantinga's paper "The Boethian Compromise," *American Philosophical Quarterly* 15 (1978), 129–38. Plantinga adopts a view intermediate between Mill and Frege, and cites substitutivity failures as a principal argument for his position. He also refers to a forthcoming paper by Ackerman. I have not seen this paper, but it probably is a descendant of the paper referred to above.

to account for the parallel situation by supposing that 'Hesperus' and 'Phosphorus' fixed their (rigid) references to a single object in two conventionally different ways, one as the 'evening star' and one as the 'morning star'. But what corresponding *conventional* 'senses,' even taking 'senses' to be 'modes of fixing the reference rigidly', can plausibly be supposed to exist for 'Cicero' and 'Tully' (or 'Holland' and 'the Netherlands')? Are not these just two names (in English) for the same man? Is there any special *conventional, community-wide* 'connotation' in the one lacking in the other?[11] I am unaware of any.[12]

Such considerations might seem to push us toward the extreme Frege–Russellian view that the senses of proper names vary, strictly speaking, from speaker to speaker, and that there is no community-wide sense but only a community-wide reference.[13] According to such a view, the sense a given speaker attributes to such a name as 'Cicero' depends on which assertions beginning with 'Cicero' he accepts and which of these he regards as *defining*, for him, the name (as opposed to those he regards as mere factual beliefs 'about Cicero'). Similarly, for 'Tully'. For example, someone may define 'Cicero' as 'the Roman orator whose speech was Greek to

---

[11] Here I use 'connotation' so as to imply that the associated properties have an *a priori* tie to the name, at least as rigid reference fixers, and therefore must be true of the referent (if it exists). There is another sense of 'connotation', as in 'The Holy Roman Empire', where the connotation need not be assumed or even believed to be true of the referent. In some sense akin to this, classicists and others with some classical learning may attach certain distinct 'connotations' to 'Cicero' and 'Tully'. Similarly, 'The Netherlands' may suggest low altitude to a thoughtful ear. Such 'connotations' can hardly be thought of as communitywide; many use the names unaware of such suggestions. Even a speaker aware of the suggestion of the name may not regard the suggested properties as true of the object; cf. 'The Holy Roman Empire'. A 'connotation' of this type neither gives a meaning nor fixes a reference.

[12] Some might attempt to find a difference in 'sense' between 'Cicero' and 'Tully' on the grounds that "Cicero is called 'Cicero'" is trivial, but "Tully is called 'Cicero'" may not be. Kneale, and in one place (probably at least implicitly) Church, have argued in this vein. (For Kneale, see "Naming and Necessity," p. 283.) So, it may be argued, being called 'Cicero' is part of the sense of the name 'Cicero', but not part of that of 'Tully'.

I have discussed some issues related to this in "Naming and Necessity," pp. 283–6. (See also the discussions of circularity conditions elsewhere in "Naming and Necessity.") Much more could be said about and against this kind of argument; perhaps I will sometime do so elsewhere. Let me mention very briefly the following parallel situation (which may be best understood by reference to the discussion in "Naming and Necessity"). Anyone who understands the meaning of 'is called' and of quotation in English (and that 'alienists' is meaningful and grammatically appropriate), knows that "alienists are called 'alienists'" expresses a truth in English, even if he has no idea what 'alienists' means. He need *not* know that "psychiatrists are called 'alienists'" expresses a truth. None of this goes to show that 'alienists' and 'psychiatrists' are not synonymous, or that 'alienists' has *being called 'alienists'* as part of its meaning when 'psychiatrists' does not. Similarly for 'Cicero' and 'Tully'. There is no more reason to suppose that being so-called is part of the meaning of a name than of any other word.

[13] A view follows Frege and Russell on this issue, even if it allows each speaker to associate a cluster of descriptions with each name, provided that it holds that the cluster varies from speaker to speaker and that variations in the cluster are variations in idiolect. Searle's view thus is Frege–Russellian when he writes in the concluding paragraph of "Proper Names" (*Mind* 67 (1958), 166–73), "'Tully = Cicero' would, I suggest, be analytic for most people; the same descriptive presuppositions are associated with each name. But of course if the descriptive presuppositions were different it might be used to make a synthetic statement."

Cassius', and 'Tully' as 'the Roman orator who denounced Catiline'. Then such a speaker may well fail to accept 'Cicero is Tully' if he is unaware that a single orator satisfied both descriptions (if Shakespeare and history are both to be believed). He may well, in his ignorance, affirm 'Cicero was bald' while rejecting 'Tully was bald', and the like. Is this not what actually occurs whenever someone's expressed beliefs fail to be indifferent to interchange of 'Tully' and 'Cicero'? Must not the source of such a failure lie in two distinct associated descriptions, or modes of determining the reference, of the two names? If a speaker does, as luck would have it, attach the same identifying properties both to 'Cicero' and to 'Tully,' he *will*, it would seem, use 'Cicero' and 'Tully' interchangeably. All this appears at first blush to be powerful support for the view of Frege and Russell that in general names are peculiar to idiolects, with 'senses' depending on the associated 'identifying descriptions'.

Note that, according to the view we are now entertaining, one *cannot* say, "Some people are unaware that Cicero is Tully." For, according to this view, there is no single proposition denoted by the 'that' clause, that the community of normal English speakers expresses by 'Cicero is Tully'. Some—for example, those who define both 'Cicero' and 'Tully' as 'the author of *De Fato*'—use it to express a trivial self-identity. Others use it to express the proposition that the man who satisfied one description (say, that he denounced Catiline) is one and the same as the man who satisfied another (say, that his speech was Greek to Cassius). There is no single fact, 'that Cicero is Tully', known by some but not all members of the community.

If I were to assert, "Many are unaware that Cicero is Tully," *I* would use 'that Cicero is Tully' to denote the proposition that *I* understand by these words. If this, for example, is a trivial self-identity, I would assert falsely, and irrelevantly, that there is widespread ignorance in the community of a certain self-identity.[14] I *can*, of course, say, "Some English speakers use both 'Cicero' and 'Tully' with the usual referent (the famed Roman) yet do not assent to 'Cicero is Tully.'"

This aspect of the Frege–Russellian view can, as before, be combined with a concession that names are rigid designators and that hence the description used to fix the reference of a name is not synonymous with it. But there are considerable difficulties. There is the obvious intuitive unpalatability of the notion that we use such proper names as 'Cicero', 'Venice', 'Venus' (the planet) with differing 'senses' and for this reason do not 'strictly speaking' speak a single language. There are the many well-known and weighty objections to any description or cluster-of-descriptions theory of names. And is it definitely so clear that failure of interchangeability in belief contexts implies some difference of sense? After all, there is a considerable philosophical literature arguing that even word pairs that are straightforward synonyms if any pairs are—"doctor" and "physician," to give one

---

[14] Though here I use the jargon of propositions, the point is fairly insensitive to differences in theoretical standpoints. For example, on Davidson's analysis, I would be asserting (roughly) that many are unaware-of-the-content-of the following *utterance* of mine: Cicero is Tully. This would be subject to the same problem.

example—are not interchangeable *salva veritate* in belief contexts, at least if the belief operators are iterated.[15]

A minor problem with this presentation of the argument for Frege and Russell will emerge in the next section: if Frege and Russell are right, it is not easy to state the very argument from belief contexts that appears to support them.

But the clearest objection, which shows that the others should be given their proper weight, is this: the view under consideration does not in fact account for the phenomena it seeks to explain. As I have said elsewhere,[16] individuals who "define 'Cicero'" by such phrases as "the Catiline denouncer," "the author of *De Fato*," etc. are relatively rare: their prevalence in the philosophical literature is the product of the excessive classical learning of some philosophers. Common men who clearly use 'Cicero' as a name for Cicero may be able to give no better answer to "Who was Cicero?" than "a famous Roman orator," and they probably would say the same (if anything!) for 'Tully'. (Actually, most people probably have never heard the name 'Tully'.) Similarly, many people who have heard of both Feynman and Gell-Mann would identify each as 'a leading contemporary theoretical physicist'. Such people do not assign 'senses' of the usual type to the names that uniquely identify the referent (even though they use the names with a determinate reference). But to the extent that the *indefinite* descriptions attached or associated can be called 'senses', the 'senses' assigned to 'Cicero' and 'Tully', or to 'Feynman' and 'Gell-Mann', are *identical*.[17] Yet clearly speakers of this type can ask, "Were Cicero and Tully one Roman orator, or two different ones?" or "Are Feynman and Gell-Mann two different physicists, or one?" without knowing the answer to either question by inspecting 'senses' alone. Some such speaker might even conjecture, or be under the vague false impression, that, as he would say, 'Cicero was bald but Tully was not'. The premiss of the argument we are considering for the classic position of Frege and Russell—that whenever two codesignative names fail to be interchangeable in the expression of a speaker's beliefs, failure of

---

[15] Benson Mates, "Synonymity," *University of California Publications in Philosophy* 25 (1950), 201–26; reprinted in *Semantics and the Philosophy of Language*, L. Linsky (ed.) (University of Illinois Press, 1952). (There was a good deal of subsequent discussion. In Mates's original paper the point is made almost parenthetically.) Actually, I think that Mates's problem has relatively little force against the argument we are considering for the Fregean position. Mates's puzzle in no way militates against some such principle as: if one word is synonymous with another, then a sufficiently reflective speaker subject to no linguistic inadequacies or conceptual confusions who sincerely assents to a simple sentence containing the one will also (sincerely) assent to the corresponding sentence containing the other in its place.

It is surely a crucial part of the present 'Fregean' argument that codesignative names may have distinct 'senses', that a speaker may assent to a simple sentence containing one and deny the corresponding sentence containing the other, even though he is *guilty of no conceptual or linguistic confusion, and of no lapse in logical consistency*. In the case of two straightforward synonyms, this is not so.

I myself think that Mates's argument is of considerable interest, but that the issues are confusing and delicate and that, if the argument works, it probably leads to a paradox or puzzle rather than to a definite conclusion. (See also notes 23, 28, and 46.)

[16] "Naming and Necessity," pp. 291–3.

[17] Recall also n. 12.

interchangeability arises from a difference in the 'defining' descriptions the speaker associates with these names—is, therefore, false. The case illustrated by 'Cicero' and 'Tully' is, in fact, quite usual and ordinary. So the apparent failure of codesignative names to be everywhere interchangeable in belief contexts is not to be explained by differences in the 'senses' of these names.

Since the extreme view of Frege and Russell does not in fact explain the apparent failure of the interchangeability of names in belief contexts, there seems to be no further reason—for present purposes—not to give the other overwhelming *prima facie* considerations against the Frege–Russell view their full weight. Names of famous cities, countries, persons, and planets are the common currency of our common language, not terms used homonymously in our separate idiolects.[18] The apparent failure of codesignative names to be interchangeable in belief contexts remains a mystery, but the mystery no longer seems so clearly to argue for a Fregean view as against a Millian one. Neither differing public senses nor differing private senses peculiar to each speaker account for the phenomena to be explained. So the apparent existence of such phenomena no longer gives a *prima facie* argument for such differing senses.

One final remark to close this section. I have referred before to my own earlier views in "Naming and Necessity." I said above that these views, inasmuch as they make proper names rigid and transparent[19] in modal contexts, favour Mill, but that the concession that proper names are not transparent in belief contexts appears to favour Frege. On a closer examination, however, the extent to which

---

[18] Some philosophers stress that names are not *words* of a language, or that names are not *translated* from one language to another. (The phrase 'common currency of our common language' was meant to be neutral with respect to any such alleged issue.) Someone may use 'Mao Tse-Tung', for example, in English, though he knows not one word of Chinese. It seems hard to deny, however, that "*Deutschland,*" "*Allemagne,*" and "Germany" are the German, French, and English names of a single country, and that one translates a French sentence using "*Londres*" by an English sentence using "London." Learning these facts is part of learning German, French, and English.

It would appear that *some* names, especially names of countries, other famous localities, and some famous people, *are* thought of as part of a language (whether they are called 'words' or not is of little importance). Many other names are not thought of as part of a language, especially if the referent is not famous (so the notation used is confined to a limited circle), or if the same name is used by speakers of all languages. As far as I can see, it makes little or no *semantic* difference whether a particular name is thought of as part of a language or not. Mathematical notation such as '<' is also ordinarily not thought of as part of English, or any other language, though it is used in combination with English words in sentences of mathematical treatises written in English. (A French mathematician can use the notation though he knows not one word of English.) 'Is less than', on the other hand, *is* English. Does this difference have any semantic significance?

I will speak in most of the text as if the names I deal with are part of English, French, etc. But it matters little for what I say whether they are thought of as parts of the language or as adjuncts to it. And one need not say that a name such as '*Londres*' is 'translated' (if such a terminology suggested that names have 'senses', I too would find it objectionable), as long as one acknowledges that *sentences* containing it are properly translated into English using 'London'.

[19] By saying that names are transparent in a context, I mean that codesignative names are interchangeable there. This is a deviation for brevity from the usual terminology, according to which the *context* is transparent. (I use the usual terminology in the paper also.)

these opacity phenomena really support Frege against Mill becomes much more doubtful. And there are important theoretical reasons for viewing the 'Naming and Necessity' approach in a Millian light. In that work I argued that ordinarily the real determinant of the reference of names of a former historical figure is a chain of communication, in which the reference of the name is passed from link to link. Now the legitimacy of such a chain accords much more with Millian views than with alternatives. For the view supposes that a learner acquires a name from the community by determining to use it with the same reference as does the community. We regard such a learner as using "Cicero is bald" to express the same thing the community expresses, regardless of variations in the properties different learners associate with 'Cicero', as long as he determines that he will use the name with the referent current in the community. That a name can be transmitted in this way accords nicely with a Millian picture, according to which only the reference, not more specific properties associated with the name, is relevant to the semantics of sentences containing it. It has been suggested that the chain of communication, which on the present picture determines the reference, might thereby itself be called a 'sense'.[20] Perhaps so—if we wish[20]—but we should not thereby forget that the legitimacy of such a chain suggests that it is just preservation of reference, as Mill thought, that we regard as necessary for correct language learning.[21] (This contrasts with such terms as 'renate' and 'cordate', where more than learning the correct extension is needed.) Also, as suggested above, the doctrine of rigidity in modal contexts is dissonant, though not necessarily inconsistent, with a view that invokes anti-Millian considerations to explain propositional attitude contexts.

The spirit of my earlier views, then, suggests that a Millian line should be maintained as far as is feasible.

II. Preliminaries: Some General Principles

Where are we now? We seem to be in something of a quandary. On the one hand, we concluded that the failure of 'Cicero' and 'Tully' to be interchangeable *salva veritate* in contexts of propositional attitude was by no means explicable in terms of different 'senses' of the two names. On the other hand, let us not forget the

---

[20]But we must use the term 'sense' here in the sense of 'that which fixes the reference', not 'that which gives the meaning', otherwise we shall run afoul of the rigidity of proper names. If the source of a chain for a certain name is in fact a given object, we use the name to designate that object even when speaking of counterfactual situations in which some *other* object originated the chain.

[21]The point is that, according to the doctrine of "Naming and Necessity," when proper names are transmitted from link to link, even though the beliefs about the referent associated with the name change radically, the change is not to be considered a linguistic change in the way it *was* a linguistic change when 'villain' changed its meaning from 'rustic' to 'wicked man'. As long as the reference of a name remains the same, the associated beliefs about the object may undergo a large number of changes without these changes constituting a change in the language.

If Geach is right, an appropriate sortal must be passed on also. But see footnote 58 of "Naming and Necessity."

initial argument against Mill: If reference is *all there is* to naming, what semantic difference can there be between 'Cicero' and 'Tully'? And if there is no semantic difference, do not 'Cicero was bald' and 'Tully was bald' express exactly the same proposition? How, then, can anyone believe that Cicero was bald, yet doubt or disbelieve that Tully was?

Let us take stock. Why do we think that anyone can believe that Cicero was bald, but fail to believe that Tully was? Or believe, without any logical inconsistency, that Yale is a fine university, but that Old Eli is an inferior one? Well, a normal English speaker, Jones, can sincerely assent to 'Cicero was bald' but not to 'Tully was bald'. And this even though Jones uses 'Cicero' and 'Tully' in standard ways—he uses 'Cicero' in this assertion as a name for the Roman, not, say, for his dog, or for a German spy.

Let us make explicit the *disquotational principle* presupposed here, connecting sincere assent and belief. It can be stated as follows, where '*p*' is to be replaced, inside and outside all quotation marks, by any appropriate standard English sentence "*If a normal English speaker, on reflection, sincerely assents to 'p' then he believes that p.*" The sentence replacing '*p*' is to lack indexical or pronominal devices or ambiguities that would ruin the intuitive sense of the principle (e.g., if he assents to "You are wonderful," he need not believe that *you*—the reader—are wonderful).[22] When we suppose that we are dealing with a normal speaker of English, we mean that he uses all words in the sentence in a standard way, combines them according to the appropriate syntax, etc.: in short, he uses the sentence to mean what a normal speaker should mean by it. The 'words' of the sentence may include proper names, where these are part of the common discourse of the community, so that we can speak of using them in a standard way. For example, if the sentence is "London is pretty," then the speaker should satisfy normal criteria for using 'London' as a name of London, and for using 'is pretty' to attribute an appropriate degree of pulchritude. The qualification "on reflection" guards against the possibility that a speaker may, through careless inattention to the meaning of his words or other momentary conceptual or linguistic confusion, assert something he does not really mean, or assent to a sentence in linguistic error. "Sincerely" is meant to exclude mendacity, acting, irony, and the like. I fear that even with all this it is possible that some astute reader—such, after all, is the way of philosophy—may discover a qualification I have overlooked, without which the asserted principle is subject to counter-example. I doubt, however, that any such modification will affect any of the uses of the principle to be considered below.

---

[22]Similar appropriate restrictions are assumed below for the strengthened disquotational principle and for the principle of translation. Ambiguities need not be excluded if it is tacitly assumed that the sentence is to be understood in one way in all its occurrences. (For the principle of translation it is similarly assumed that the translator matches the *intended* interpretation of the sentence.) I do not work out the restrictions on indexicals in detail, since the intent is clear.

Clearly, the disquotational principle applies only to *de dicto*, not *de re*, attributions of belief. If someone sincerely assents to the near triviality, "The tallest foreign spy is a spy," it follows that he believes that: the tallest foreign spy is a spy. It is well known that it does *not* follow that he believes, *of* the tallest foreign spy, that he is a spy. In the latter case, but not in the former, it would be his patriotic duty to make contact with the authorities.

Taken in its obvious intent, after all, the principle appears to be a self-evident truth. (A similar principle holds for sincere affirmation or assertion in place of assent.)

There is also a strengthened 'biconditional' form of the disquotational principle, where once again any appropriate English sentence may replace '*p*' throughout: *A normal English speaker who is not reticent will be disposed to sincere reflective assent to '*p*' if and only if he believes that p.*[23] The biconditional form strengthens the simple one by adding that failure to assent indicates lack of belief, as assent indicates belief. The qualification about reticence is meant to take account of the fact that a speaker may fail to avow his beliefs because of shyness, a desire for secrecy, to avoid offense, etc. (An alternative formulation would give the speaker a sign to indicate lack of belief—not necessarily disbelief—in the assertion propounded, in addition to his sign of assent.) Maybe again the formulation needs further tightening, but the intent is clear.

Usually below, the simple disquotational principle will be sufficient for our purposes, but once we will also invoke the strengthened form. The simple form can often be used as a test for disbelief, provided the subject is a speaker with the modicum of logicality needed so that, at least after appropriate reflection, he does not hold simultaneously beliefs that are straightforward contradictions of each other— of the forms '*p*' and '~*p*'.[24] (Nothing in such a requirement prevents him from holding simultaneous beliefs that jointly *entail* a contradiction.) In this case (where '*p*' may be replaced by any appropriate English sentence), the speaker's assent to the negation of '*p*' indicates not only his disbelief that *p* but also his failure to believe that *p*, using only the simple (unstrengthened) disquotational principle.

So far our principle applies only to speakers of English. It allows us to infer, from Peter's sincere reflective assent to "God exists," that he believes that God exists. But of course we ordinarily allow ourselves to draw conclusions, stated in

---

[23]What if a speaker assents to a sentence, but fails to assent to a synonymous assertion? Say, he assents to "Jones is a doctor," but not to "Jones is a physician." Such a speaker either does not understand one of the sentences normally, or he should be able to correct himself "on reflection." As long as he confusedly assents to 'Jones is a doctor' but not to 'Jones is a physician', we *cannot* straightforwardly apply disquotational principles to conclude that he does or does not believe that Jones is a doctor, because his assent is not "reflective."

Similarly, if someone asserts, "Jones is a doctor but not a physician," he should be able to recognize his inconsistency without further information. We have formulated the disquotational principles so they need not lead us to attribute belief as long as we have grounds to suspect conceptual or linguistic confusion, as in the cases just mentioned.

Note that if someone says, "Cicero was bald but Tully was not," there need be *no* grounds to suppose that he is under *any* linguistic or conceptual confusion.

[24]This should not be confused with the question whether the speaker simultaneously believes *of* a given object, both that it has a certain property and that it does not have it. Our discussion concerns *de dicto* (notional) belief, not *de re* belief.

I have been shown a passage in Aristotle that appears to suggest that *no one* can really believe both of two explicit contradictories. If we wish to use the *simple* disquotational principle as a test for disbelief, it suffices that this be true of *some* individuals, after reflection, who are simultaneously aware of both beliefs, and have sufficient logical acumen and respect for logic. Such individuals, if they have contradictory beliefs, will be shaken in one or both beliefs after they note the contradiction. For such individuals, sincere reflective assent to the negation of a sentence implies disbelief in the proposition it expresses, so the test in the text applies.

English, about the beliefs of speakers of any language: we infer that Pierre believes that God exists from his sincere reflective assent to "*Dieu existe.*" There are several ways to do this, given conventional translations of French into English. We choose the following route. We have stated the disquotational principle in English, for English sentences; an analogous principle, stated in French (German, etc.) will be assumed to hold for French (German, etc.) sentences. Finally, we assume the *principle of translation: if a sentence of one language expresses a truth in that language, then any translation of it into any other language also expresses a truth (in that other language).* Some of our ordinary practice of translation may violate this principle; this happens when the translator's aim is not to preserve the content of the sentence, but to serve—in some other sense—the same purposes in the home language as the original utterance served in the foreign language.[25] But if the translation of a sentence is to mean the same as the sentence translated preservation of truth value is a minimal condition that must be observed.

Granted the disquotational principle expressed in each language reasoning starting from Pierre's assent to '*Dieu existe*' continues thus. First, on the basis of his utterance and the French disquotational principle we infer (in French):

> *Pierre croit que Dieu existe.*

From this we deduce,[26] using the principle of translation:

> Pierre believes that God exists.

In this way we can apply the disquotational technique to all languages.

Even if I apply the disquotational technique to English alone, there is a sense in which I can be regarded as tacitly invoking a principle of translation. For presumably I apply it to speakers of the language other than myself. As Quine has pointed out, to regard others as speaking the same language as I is in a sense tacitly to assume a *homophonic* translation of their language into my own. So when I infer from Peter's sincere assent to or affirmation of "God exists" that he believes that God exists, it is arguable that, strictly speaking, I combine the disquotational principle (for Peter's idiolect) with the principle of (homophonic) translation (of Peter's idiolect into mine). But for most purposes, we can formulate the disquotational principle for a single language, English, tacitly supposed to be the common language of English speakers. Only when the possibility of individual differences of dialect is relevant need we view the matter more elaborately.

---

[25] For example, in translating a historical report into another language, such as, "Patrick Henry said, 'Give me liberty or give me death!,'" the translator may well translate the quoted material attributed to Henry. He translates a presumed truth into a falsehood, since Henry spoke English; but probably his reader is aware of this and is more interested in the content of Henry's utterance than in its exact words. Especially in translating fiction, where truth is irrelevant, this procedure is appropriate. But some objectors to Church's 'translation argument' have allowed themselves to be misled by the practice.

[26] To state the argument precisely, we need in addition a form of the Tarskian disquotation principle for truth: For each (French or English) replacement for '*p*,' infer " '*p*' is true" from "*p*," and conversely. (Note that "'*p*' is true" becomes an English sentence even if '*p*' is replaced by a French sentence.) In the text we leave the application of the Tarskian disquotational principle tacit.

Let us return from these abstractions to our main theme. Since a normal speaker—normal even in his use of 'Cicero' and 'Tully' as names—can give sincere and reflective assent to "Cicero was bald" and simultaneously to "Tully was not bald," the disquotational principle implies that he believes that Cicero was bald and believes that Tully was not bald. Since it seems that he need not have contradictory beliefs (even if he is a brilliant logician, he need not be able to deduce that at least one of his beliefs must be in error), and since a substitutivity principle for coreferential proper names in belief contexts would imply that he does have contradictory beliefs, it would seem that such a substitutivity principle must be incorrect. Indeed, the argument appears to be a *reductio ad absurdum* of the substitutivity principle in question.

The relation of this argument against substitutivity to the classical position of Russell and Frege is a curious one. As we have seen, the argument can be used to give *prima facie* support for the Frege–Russell view, and I think many philosophers have regarded as such support. But in fact this very argument, which has been used to support Frege and Russell, cannot be stated in a straightforward fashion if Frege and Russell are right. For suppose Jones asserts, "Cicero was bald, but Tully was not." If Frege and Russell are right, I cannot deduce, using the disquotational principle:

(1) Jones believes that Cicero was bald but Tully was not,

since, in general, Jones and I will not, strictly speaking, share a common idiolect unless we assign the same 'senses' to all names. Nor can I combine disquotation and translation to the appropriate effect, since homophonic translation of Jones's sentence into mine will in general be incorrect for the same reason. Since in fact I make no special distinction in sense between 'Cicero' and 'Tully'—to me, and probably to you as well, these are interchangeable names for the same man—and since, according to Frege and Russell, Jones's very affirmation of (1) shows that for him there *is* some distinction of sense, Jones must therefore, on Frege–Russellian views, use one of these names differently from me, and homophonic translation is illegitimate. Hence, if Frege and Russell are right, we *cannot* use this example in the usual straightforward way to conclude that proper names are not substitutable in belief contexts—even though the example, and the ensuing negative verdict on substitutivity, has often been thought to support Frege and Russell!

Even according to the Frege–Russellian view, however, *Jones* can conclude, using the disquotational principle, and expressing his conclusion in his own idiolect:

(2) I believe that Cicero was bald but Tully was not.

I cannot endorse this conclusion in Jones's own words, since I do not share Jones's idiolect. I *can* of course conclude, "(2) expresses a truth in Jones's idiolect." I can also, if I find out the two 'senses' Jones assigns to 'Cicero' and 'Tully', introduce two names 'X' and 'Y' into my own language with these same two senses ('Cicero' and 'Tully' have already been preempted) and conclude:

(3) Jones believes that X was bald and Y was not.

All this is enough so that we can still conclude, on the Frege–Russellian view, that codesignative names are not interchangeable in belief contexts. Indeed this can be shown more simply on this view, since codesignative descriptions plainly are not interchangeable in these contexts, and for Frege and Russell names being essentially abbreviated descriptions, cannot differ in this respect. Nevertheless, the simple argument, apparently free of such special Frege–Russellian doctrinal premises (and often used to support these premises), in fact cannot go through if Frege and Russell are right.

However, if, *pace* Frege and Russell, widely used names are common currency of our language, then there no longer is any problem for the simple argument, using the disquotational principle, to (2). So, it appears, on pain of convicting Jones of inconsistent beliefs—surely an unjust verdict—we must not hold a substitutivity principle for names in belief contexts. If we used the *strengthened* disquotational principle, we could invoke Jones's presumed lack of any tendency to assent to 'Tully was bald' to conclude that he does not believe (lacks the belief) that Tully was bald. Now the refutation of the substitutivity principle is even stronger, for when applied to the conclusion that Jones believes that Cicero was bald but does not believe that Tully was bald, it would lead to a straightout contradiction. The contradiction would no longer be in Jones's beliefs but in our own.

This reasoning, I think, has been widely accepted as proof that codesignative proper names are not interchangeable in belief contexts. Usually the reasoning is left tacit, and it may well be thought that I have made heavy weather of an obvious conclusion. I wish, however, to question the reasoning. I shall do so without challenging any particular step of the argument. Rather it shall present—and this will form the core of the present paper—an argument for a paradox about names in belief contexts that invokes *no* principle of substitutivity. Instead it will be based on the principles—apparently so obvious that their use in these arguments is ordinarily tacit—of disquotation and translation.

Usually the argument will involve more than one language, so that the principle of translation and our conventional manual of translation must be invoked. We will also give an example, however, to show that a form of the paradox may result within English alone, so that the only principle invoked is that of disquotation (or, perhaps, disquotation plus *homophonic* translation). It will intuitively be fairly clear, in these cases, that the situation of the subject is 'essentially the same' as that of Jones with respect to 'Cicero' and 'Tully'. Moreover, the paradoxical conclusions about the subject will parallel those drawn about Jones on the basis of the substitutivity principle, and the arguments will parallel those regarding Jones. Only in these cases, no special substitutivity principle is invoked.

The usual use of Jones's case as a counter-example to the substitutivity principle is thus, I think, somewhat analogous to the following sort of procedure. Someone wishes to give a *reductio ad absurdum* argument against a hypothesis in topology. He does succeed in refuting this hypothesis, but his derivation of an absurdity from the hypothesis makes essential use of the unrestricted comprehension schema in set theory, which he regards as self-evident. (In particular, the class of all classes not members of themselves plays a key role in his argument.)

Once we know that the unrestricted comprehension schema and the Russell class lead to contradiction by themselves, it is clear that it was an error to blame the earlier contradiction on the topological hypothesis.

The situation would have been the same if, after deducing a contradiction from the topological hypothesis plus the 'obvious' unrestricted comprehension schema, it was found that a similar contradiction followed if we replaced the topological hypothesis by an apparently 'obvious' premiss. In both cases it would be clear that, even though we may still not be confident of any specific flaw in the argument against the topological hypothesis, blaming the contradiction on that hypothesis is illegitimate: rather we are in a 'paradoxical' area where it is unclear *what* has gone wrong.[27]

It is my suggestion, then, that the situation with respect to the interchangeability of codesignative names is similar. True, such a principle, when combined with our normal disquotational judgments of belief, leads to straightforward absurdities. But we will see that the 'same' absurdities can be derived by replacing the interchangeability principle with our normal practices of translation and disquotation, or even with disquotation alone.

The particular principle stated here gives just one particular way of 'formalizing' our normal inferences from explicit affirmation or assent to belief; other ways of doing it are possible. It is undeniable that we *do* infer, from a normal Englishman's sincere affirmation of 'God exists' or 'London is pretty', that he believes, respectively, that God exists or that London is pretty; and that we would make the same inferences from a Frenchman's affirmation of '*Dieu existe*' or '*Londres est jolie*'. Any principles that would justify such inferences are sufficient for the next section. It will be clear that the particular principles stated in the present section are sufficient, but in the next section the problem will be presented informally in terms of our inferences from foreign or domestic assertion to belief.

III. The Puzzle

Here, finally(!), is the puzzle. Suppose Pierre is a normal French speaker who lives in France and speaks not a word of English or of any other language except French. Of course he has heard of that famous distant city, London (which he of course calls '*Londres*'), though he himself has never left France. On the basis of what he has heard of London, he is inclined to think that it is pretty. So he says, in French, "*Londres est jolie.*"

On the basis of his sincere French utterance, we will conclude:

(4) Pierre believes that London is pretty.

I am supposing that Pierre satisfies all criteria for being a normal French speaker, in particular, that he satisfies whatever criteria we usually use to judge that a

---

[27]I gather that Burali-Forti originally thought he had 'proved' that the ordinals are not linearly ordered, reasoning in a manner similar to our topologist. Someone who heard the present paper delivered told me that König made a similar error.

Frenchman (correctly) uses '*est jolie*' to attribute pulchritude and uses '*Londres*'—standardly—as a name of London.

Later, Pierre, through fortunate or unfortunate vicissitudes, moves to England, in fact to London itself, though to an unattractive part of the city with fairly uneducated inhabitants. He, like most of his neighbours, rarely ever leaves this part of the city. None of his neighbours know any French, so he must learn English by 'direct method', without using any translation of English into French: by talking and mixing with the people he eventually begins to pick up English. In particular, everyone speaks of the city, 'London', where they all live. Let us suppose for the moment—though we will see below that this is not crucial—that the local population are so uneducated that they know few of the facts that Pierre heard about London in France. Pierre learns from them everything they know about London, but there is little overlap with what he heard before. He learns, of course—speaking English—to call the city he lives in 'London'. Pierre's surroundings are, as I said, unattractive, and he is unimpressed with most of the rest of what he happens to see. So he is inclined to assent to the English sentence:

(5) London is not pretty.

He has *no* inclination to assent to:

(6) London is pretty.

Of course he does not for a moment withdraw his assent from the French sentence, "*Londres est jolie*"; he merely takes it for granted that the ugly city in which he is now stuck is distinct from the enchanting city he heard about in France. But he has no inclination to change his mind for a moment about the city he still calls '*Londres*'.

This, then, is the puzzle. If we consider Pierre's past background as a French speaker, his entire linguistic behaviour, on the same basis as we would draw such a conclusion about many of his countrymen, supports the conclusion ((4) above) that he believes that London is pretty. On the other hand, after Pierre lived in London for some time, he did not differ from his neighbours—his French background aside—either in his knowledge of English or in his command of the relevant facts of local geography. His English vocabulary differs little from that of his neighbours. He like them, rarely ventures from the dismal quarter of the city in which they all live. He, like them, knows that the city he lives in is called 'London' and knows a few other facts. Now Pierre's neighbours would surely be said to use 'London' as a name for London and to speak English. Since, as an English speaker, he does not differ at all from them, we should say the same of him. But then, on the basis of his sincere assent to (5), we should conclude:

(7) Pierre believes that London is not pretty.

How can we describe this situation? It seems undeniable that Pierre *once* believed that London is pretty—at least before he learnt English. For at that time, he differed not at all from countless numbers of his countrymen, and we would have exactly the same grounds to say of him, as of any of them, that he believes that London is pretty: if any Frenchman who was both ignorant of English and never visited London believed that London is pretty Pierre did. Nor does it have any plausibility to suppose, because of his later situation *after* he learns English, that Pierre should *retroactively* be judged *never* to have believed that London is pretty. To allow such *ex post facto* legislation would, as long as the future is uncertain, endanger our attributions of belief to *all* monolingual Frenchmen. We would be forced to say that Marie monolingual who firmly and sincerely asserts, "*Londres est jolie*" may or may not believe that London is pretty depending on the *later* vicissitudes of her career (if later she learns English and . . .). No: Pierre, like Marie, believed that London is pretty when he was monolingual.

Should we say that Pierre, now that he lives in London and speaks English, no longer believes that London is pretty? Well, unquestionably Pierre *once* believed that London is pretty. So we would be forced to say that Pierre has *changed his mind, has given up his previous belief.* But has he really done so? Pierre is very set in his ways. He reiterates, with vigour, every assertion he has ever made in French. He says he has not changed his mind about anything, has *not* given up any belief. Can we say he is wrong about this? If we did not have the story of his living in London and his English utterances, on the basis of his normal command of French we would be *forced* to conclude that he *still* believes that London is pretty. And it does seem that this is correct. Pierre has neither changed his mind nor given up any belief he had in France.

Similar difficulties beset any attempt to deny him his new belief. His French past aside, he is just like his friends in London. Anyone else, growing up in London with the same knowledge and beliefs that he expresses in England, we would undoubtedly judge to believe that London is not pretty. Can Pierre's French past nullify such a judgement? Can we say that Pierre, because of his French past, does not believe that (5)? Suppose an electric shock wiped out all his memories of the French language, what he learnt in France, and his French past. He would then be *exactly* like his neighbours in London. He would have the *same* knowledge, beliefs, and linguistic capacities. We then presumably would be forced to say that Pierre believes that London is ugly if we say it of his neighbours. But surely no shock that *destroys* part of Pierre's memories and knowledge can *give* him a new belief. If Pierre believes (5) *after* the shock, he believed it before, despite his French language and background.

If we would deny Pierre, in his bilingual stage, his belief that London is pretty *and* his belief that London is not pretty, we combine the difficulties of both previous options. We still would be forced to judge that Pierre once believed that London is pretty but does no longer, in spite of Pierre's own sincere denial that he has lost any belief. We also must worry whether Pierre would *gain* the belief that London is not pretty if he totally forgot his French past. The option does not seem very satisfactory.

So now it seems that we must respect both Pierre's French utterances and their English counterparts. So we must say that Pierre has contradictory beliefs, that he believes that London is pretty *and* he believes that London is not pretty. But there seem to be insuperable difficulties with this alternative as well. We may suppose that Pierre, in spite of the unfortunate situation in which he now finds himself, is a leading philosopher and logician. He would *never* let contradictory beliefs pass. And surely anyone, leading logician or no, is in principle in a position to notice and correct contradictory beliefs if he has them. Precisely for this reason, we regard individuals who contradict themselves as subject to greater censure than those who merely have false beliefs. But it is clear that Pierre, as long as he is unaware that the cities he calls 'London' and '*Londres*' are one and the same, is in no position to see, by logic alone, that at least one of his beliefs must be false. He lacks information, not logical acumen. He cannot be convicted of inconsistency: to do so is incorrect.

We can shed more light on this if we change the case. Suppose that in France Pierre, instead of affirming "*Londres est jolie*," had affirmed, more cautiously, "*Si New York est jolie, Londres est jolie aussi*," so that he believed that *if* New York is pretty, so is London. Later Pierre moves to London, learns English as before and says (in English) "London is not pretty." So he now believes further, that London is *not* pretty. Now from the two premisses both of which appear to be among his beliefs ((*a*) If New York is pretty, London is, and (*b*) London is not pretty), Pierre should be able to deduce by *modus tollens* that New York is not pretty. But no matter how great Pierre's logical acumen may be, *he cannot in fact make any such deduction as long as he supposes that 'Londres' and 'London' may name two different cities.* If he *did* draw such conclusion, he would be guilty of a fallacy.

Intuitively, he may well suspect that New York is pretty, and just this suspicion may lead him to suppose that '*Londres*' and 'London' probably name distinct cities. Yet, if we follow our normal practice of reporting the beliefs of French and English speakers, *Pierre has available to him (among his beliefs) both the premisses of a* modus tollens *argument that New York is not pretty.*

Again, we may emphasize Pierre's *lack* of belief instead of his belief. Pierre, as I said, has no disposition to assent to (6). Lets us concentrate on this, ignoring his disposition to assent to (5). In fact, if we wish we may change the case: Suppose Pierre neighbours think that since they rarely venture outside their own ugly section, they have no right to any opinion as to the pulchritude of the whole city. Suppose Pierre shares their attitude. Then, judging by his failure to respond affirmatively to "London is pretty," we may judge, from Pierre's behaviour as an *English* speaker, that he lacks the belief that London is pretty: never mind whether he disbelieves it, as before, or whether, as in the modified story, he insists that he has no firm opinion on the matter.

Now (using the *strengthened* disquotational principle), we can derive a contradiction, not merely in Pierre's judgments, but in our own. For on the basis of his behaviour as an English speaker, we concluded that he does *not* believe that London is pretty (that is, that it is not the case that he believes that London is pretty). But on the basis of his behaviour as a *French* speaker, we must conclude that he *does* believe that London is pretty. This is a contradiction.[28]

---

[28]It is not possible, in this case, as it is in the case of the man who assents to "Jones is a doctor" but not to "Jones is a physician," to refuse to apply the disquotational principle on the grounds that the subject must lack proper command of the language or be subject to some linguistic or conceptual confusion. As long as Pierre is unaware that 'London' and '*Londres*' are codesignative, he need not lack appropriate linguistic knowledge, nor need he be subject to any linguistic or conceptual confusion when he affirms '*Londres est jolie*' but denies 'London is pretty'.

We have examined four possibilities for characterizing Pierre while he is in London: (*a*) that at that time we no longer respect his French utterance ('*Londres est jolie*'), that is that we no longer ascribe to him the corresponding belief; (*b*) that we do not respect his English utterance (or lack of utterance); (*c*) that we respect neither; (*d*) that we respect both. Each possibility seems to lead us to say something either plainly false or even downright contradictory. Yet the possibilities appear to be logically exhaustive. This, then, is the paradox.

I have no firm belief as to how to solve it. But beware of one source of confusion. It is no solution in itself to observe that some *other* terminology, which evades the question whether Pierre believes that London is pretty, may be sufficient to state all the relevant facts. I am fully aware that complete and straightforward descriptions of the situation are possible and that in this sense there is no paradox. Pierre is disposed to sincere assent to '*Londres est jolie*' but not to 'London is pretty'. He uses French normally, English normally. Both with '*Londres*' and 'London' he associates properties sufficient to determine that famous city, but he does not realize that they determine a single city. (And his uses of '*Londres*' and 'London' are historically (causally) connected with the same single city, though he is unaware of that.) We may even give a rough statement of his beliefs. He believes that the city he calls '*Londres*' is pretty, that the city he calls 'London' is not. No doubt other straightforward descriptions are possible. No doubt some of these are, in a certain sense, *complete* descriptions of the situation.

But none of this answers the original question. Does Pierre, or does he not, believe that London is pretty? I know of no answer to *this* question that seems satisfactory. It is no answer to protest that, in some *other* terminology, one can state 'all the relevant facts'.

To reiterate, this is the puzzle: Does Pierre, or does he not, believe that London is pretty? It is clear that our normal criteria for the attribution of belief lead, when applied to *this* question, to paradoxes and contradictions. One set of principles adequate to many ordinary attributions of belief, but which leads to paradox in the present case, was stated in section II; and other formulations are possible. As in the case of the logical paradoxes, the present puzzle presents us with a problem for customarily accepted principles and a challenge to formulate an acceptable set of principles that does not lead to paradox, is intuitively sound, and supports the inferences we usually make. Such a challenge cannot be met simply by a description of Pierre's situation that evades the question whether he believes that London is pretty.

One aspect of the presentation may misleadingly suggest the applicability of Frege–Russellian ideas that each speaker associates his own description or properties to each name. For as I just set up the case Pierre learnt one set of facts about the so-called '*Londres*' when he was in France, and *another* set of facts about 'London' in England. Thus it may appear that 'what is really going on' is that Pierre believes that *the city* satisfying *one* set of properties *is* pretty, while he believes that *the city* satisfying *another* set of properties *is not* pretty.

As we just emphasized, the phrase 'what is really going on' is danger signal in discussions of the present paradox. The condition stated may—let us concede for the moment—describe 'what really going on'. But they do not resolve the problem with which we began, that of the behaviour of names in belief contexts: Does Pierre, or does he not, believe that London (not the city satisfying such-and-such descriptions, but *London*) is pretty? No answers has yet been given.

Nevertheless, these considerations may appear to indicate the descriptions, or associated properties, are highly relevant somehow to an ultimate solution, since at this stage it appears that the entire puzzle arises from the fact that Pierre originally associated different identifying properties with 'London' and '*Londres*'. Such a reaction may have some force even in the face of the now fairly well-known arguments against 'identifying descriptions' as in any way 'defining', or even 'fixing the reference', of names. But in fact the special features of the case, as I set it out, are misleading. The puzzle can arise even if Pierre associates exactly the same identifying properties with both names.

First, the considerations mentioned above in connection with 'Cicero' and 'Tully' establish this fact. For example, Pierre may well learn, in France, '*Platon*' as the name of a major Greek philosopher, and later, in England, learn 'Plato' with the same identification. Then the same puzzle can arise: Pierre may have believed, when he was in France and was monolingual in French, that Plato was bald (he would have said, "*Platon était chauve*"), and later conjecture, in English, "Plato was not bald," thus indicating that he believes or suspects that Plato was *not* bald. He need only suppose that, in spite of the similarity of their names, the man he calls '*Platon*' and the man he calls 'Plato' were two distinct major Greek philosophers. In principle, the same thing would happen with 'London' and '*Londres*'.

Of course, most of us learn a *definite* description about London, say 'the largest city in England'. Can the puzzle still arise? It is noteworthy that the puzzle can still arise even if Pierre associates to '*Londres*' and to 'London' *exactly* the same *uniquely identifying* properties. How can this be? Well, suppose that Pierre believes that London is the largest city in (and capital of) England, that it contains Buckingham Palace, the residence of the Queen of England, and he believes (correctly) that these properties, conjointly, uniquely identify the city. (In this case, it is best to suppose that he has never seen London, or even England, so that he uses *only* these properties to identify the city. Nevertheless, he has learned English by 'direct method'.) These uniquely identifying properties he comes to associate with 'London' after he learned English, and he expresses the appropriate beliefs about 'London' in English. Earlier, when he spoke nothing but French, however, he associated *exactly* the same uniquely identifying properties with '*Londres*'. He believed that '*Londres*', as he called it, could be uniquely identified as the capital of England, that it contained Buckingham Palace, that the Queen of England lived there, etc. Of course he expressed these beliefs, like most monolingual Frenchmen, in French. In particular, he used '*Angleterre*' for England, '*le Palais de Buckingham*' (pronounced '*Bookeengam*'!) for Buckingham Palace, and '*la Reine d'Angleterre*' for the Queen of England. But if any Frenchman who speaks no English can ever be said to associate *exactly* the properties of being the capital of England etc. with the name '*Londres*', Pierre in his monolingual period did so.

When Pierre becomes a bilingual, *must* he conclude that 'London' and 'Londres' name the same city, because he defined each by the same uniquely identifying properties?

Surprisingly, no! Suppose Pierre had affirmed, '*Londres est jolie*'. If Pierre has any reason—even just a 'feeling in his bones', or perhaps exposure to a photograph of a miserable area which he was told (in English) was part of 'London'—to maintain 'London is not pretty', he need not contradict himself. He need only conclude that 'England' and '*Angleterre*' name two different countries, that 'Buckingham Palace' and '*le Palais de Buckingham*' (recall the pronunciation!), name two different palaces, and so on. Then he can maintain *both* views without contradiction, and regard *both* properties as uniquely identifying.

The fact is that the paradox reproduces itself on the level of the 'uniquely identifying properties' that description theorists have regarded as 'defining' proper names (and *a fortiori*, as fixing their references). Nothing is more reasonable than to suppose that if two names, *A* and *B*, and a single set of properties, *S*, are such that a certain speaker believes that the referent of *A* uniquely satisfies all of *S* and that the referent of *B* also uniquely satisfies all of *S* then that speaker is committed to the belief that *A* and *B* have the same reference. In fact, the identity of the referents of *A* and *B* is an easy *logical consequence* of the speaker's beliefs.

From this fact description theorists concluded that names can be regarded as synonymous, and hence interchangeable *salva veritate* even in belief contexts, provided that they are 'defined' by the same uniquely identifying properties.

We have already seen that there is a difficulty in that the set *S* of properties need not in fact be uniquely identifying. But in the present paradoxical situation there is a surprising difficulty even if the supposition of the description theorist (that the speaker believes that *S* is uniquely fulfilled) in fact holds. For, as we have seen above, Pierre is in no position to draw ordinary logical consequences from the conjoint set of what, when we consider him separately as a speaker of English and as a speaker of French, we would call his beliefs. He cannot infer a contradiction from his separate beliefs that London is pretty and that London is not pretty. Nor, in the modified situation above, would Pierre make a normal *modus tollens* inference from his beliefs that London is not pretty and that London is pretty if New York is. Similarly here, if we pay attention only to Pierre's behaviour as a French speaker (and at least in his monolingual days he was no different from any other Frenchmen), Pierre satisfies all the normal criteria for believing that '*Londres*' has a referent uniquely satisfying the properties of being the largest city in England, containing Buckingham Palace, and the like. (If Pierre did not hold such beliefs, no Frenchman *ever* did.) Similarly, on the basis of his (later) beliefs expressed in English, Pierre also believes that the referent of 'London' uniquely satisfies these same properties. But Pierre cannot combine the two beliefs into a single set of beliefs from which he can draw the normal conclusion that 'London' and '*Londres*' must have the same referent. (Here the trouble comes not from 'London' and '*Londres*' but from 'England' and '*Angleterre*' and the rest.) Indeed, if he *did* draw what would appear to be the normal conclusion in this case and any of the other cases, Pierre would in fact be guilty of a logical fallacy.

Of course the description theorist could hope to eliminate the problem by 'defining' '*Angleterre*', 'England', and so on by appropriate descriptions also. Since in principle the problem may rear its head at the next 'level' and at each subsequent level, the description theorist would have to believe that an 'ultimate' level can eventually be reached where the defining properties are 'pure' properties not involving proper names (nor natural kind terms or related terms, see below!). I know of no convincing reason to suppose that such a level can be reached in any plausible way, or that the properties can continue to be uniquely identifying if one attempts to eliminate all names and related devices.[29] Such speculation aside, the fact remains that Pierre, judged by the *ordinary* criteria for such judgments, *did* learn both '*Londres*' and 'London' by *exactly* the same set of identifying properties; yet the puzzle remains even in this case.

Well, then, is there any way out of the puzzle? Aside from the principles of disquotation and translation, only our normal practice of translation of French into English has been used. Since the principles of disquotation and translation seem self-evident, we may be tempted to blame the trouble on the translation of '*Londres est jolie*' as 'London is pretty,' and ultimately, then, on the translation of '*Londres*' as 'London.'[30] Should we, perhaps, permit ourselves to conclude that '*Londres*' should not, 'strictly speaking' be translated as 'London'? Such an expedient is, of course,

---

[29]The 'elimination' would be most plausible if we believed, according to a Russellian epistemology, that all my language, when written in unabbreviated notation, refers to constituents with which I am 'acquainted' in Russell's sense. Then no one speaks a language intelligible to anyone else; indeed, no one speaks the same language twice. Few today will accept this.

A basic consideration should be stressed here. Moderate Fregeans atempt to combine a roughly Fregean view with the view that names are part of our common language, and that our conventional practices of interlinguistic translation and interpretation are correct. The problems of the present paper indicate that it is very difficult to obtain a requisite socialized notion of sense that will enable such a program to succeed. Extreme Fregeans (such as Frege and Russell) believe that in general names are peculiar to idiolects. They therefore would accept no general rule translating '*Londres*' as 'London', nor even translating one person's use of "London' into another's. However, if they follow Frege in regarding senses as 'objective', they must believe that in principle it makes sense to speak of two people using two names in their respective idiolects with the same sense, and that there must be (necessary and) sufficient conditions for this to be the case. If these conditions for sameness of sense are satisified, translation of one name into the other is legitimate, otherwise not. The present considerations (and the extension of these below to natural kind and related terms), however, indicate that the notion of sameness of sense, if it is to be explicated in terms of sameness of identifying properties and if these properties are themselves expressed in the languages of the two respective idiolects, presents interpretation problems of the same type presented by the names themselves. Unless the Fregean can give a method for dentifying sameness of sense that is free of such problems, he *has no sufficient conditions for sameness of sense, nor for translation to be legitimate.* He would therefore be forced to maintain, contrary to Frege's intent, that not only in practice do few people use proper names with the same sense but that *it is in principle meaningless to compare senses.* A view that the identifying properties used to define senses should always be expressible in a Russellian language of 'logically proper names' would be one solution to this difficulty but involves a doubtful philosophy of language and epistemology.

[30]If any reader finds the term 'translation' objectionable with respect to names, let him be reminded that all I mean is that French sentences containing '*Londres*' are uniformly translated into English with 'London'.

desperate: the translation in question is a standard one learnt by students together with other standard translations of French into English. Indeed, 'Londres' is, in effect, introduced into French as the French version of 'London'.

Since our backs, however, are against the wall, let us consider this desperate and implausible expedient a bit further. If 'Londres' is not a correct French version of the English 'London,' under what circumstances can proper names be translated from one language to another?

Classical description theories suggest the answer: translation, strictly speaking, is between idiolects; a name in one idiolect can be translated into another when (and only when) the speakers of the two idiolects associate the same uniquely identifying properties with the two names. We have seen that any such proposed restriction, not only fails blatantly to fit our normal practices of translation and indirect discourse reportage, but does not even appear to block the paradox.[31]

So we still want a suitable restriction. Let us drop the references to idiolects and return to 'Londres' and 'London' as names in French and English, respectively— the languages of two communities. If 'Londres' is not a correct French translation of 'London', could any other version do better? Suppose I introduced another word into French, with the stipulation that *it* should always be used to translate 'London'. Would not the same problem arise for this word as well? The only feasible solution in this direction is the most drastic: decree that no sentence containing a name can be translated except by a sentence containing the phonetically identical name. Thus when Pierre asserts 'Londres est jolie', we English speakers can at best conclude, if anything: Pierre believes that *Londres* is pretty. Such a conclusion is, of course, not expressed in English, but in a word salad of English and French; on the view now being entertained, we cannot state Pierre's belief in *English* at all.[32] Similarly, we would have to say: Pierre believes that *Angleterre* is a monarchy, Pierre believes that *Platon* wrote dialogues, and the like.[33]

This 'solution' appears at first to be effective against the paradox, but it is drastic. What is it about sentences containing names that makes them—a substantial class—intrinsically untranslatable, express beliefs that cannot be reported in any other language? At best, to report them in the other language, one is forced to use a word salad in which names from the one language are imported into the other. Such a supposition is both contrary to our normal practice of translation and very implausible on its face.

---

[31] The paradox would be blocked if we required that they define the names by the same properties expressed in the same words. There is nothing in the motivation of the classical description theories that would justify this extra clause. In the present case of French and English, such a restriction would amount to a decree that neither 'Londres', nor any other conceivable French name, could be translated as 'London'. I deal with this view immediately below.

[32] Word salads of two languages (like ungrammatical 'semisentences' of a single language) need not be unintelligible, though they are makeshifts with no fixed syntax. "If God did not exist, Voltaire said, *if faudrait l'inventer.*" The meaning is clear.

[33] Had we said, "Pierre believes that the country he calls '*Angleterre*' is a monarchy," the sentence would be English, since the French word would be mentioned but not used. But for this very reason we would not have captured the sense of the French original.

Implausible though it is, there is at least this much excuse for the 'solution' at this point. Our normal practice with respect to some famous people and especially for geographical localities is to have different names for them in different languages, so that in translating sentences we translate the names. But for a large number of names, especially names of people, this is not so: the person's name is used in the sentences of all languages. At least the restriction in question merely urges us to mend our ways by doing *always* what we presently do *sometimes.*

But the really drastic character of the proposed restriction comes out when we see how far it may have to extend. In "Naming and Necessity" I suggested that there are important analogies between proper names and natural kind terms, and it seems to me that the present puzzle is one instance where the analogy will hold. Putnam, who has proposed views on natural kinds similar to my own in many respects, stressed this extension of the puzzle in his comments at the conference. Not that the puzzle extends to all translations from English to French. At the moment, at least, it seems to me that Pierre, if he learns English and French separately, without learning any translation manual between them, must conclude, if he reflects enough, that 'doctor' and *'médecin'*, and *'heureux'* and 'happy', are synonymous, or at any rate, coextensive;[34] any potential paradox of the present kind for these word pairs is thus blocked. But what about *'lapin'* and 'rabbit', or 'beech' and 'hêtre'? We may suppose that Pierre is himself neither a zoologist nor a botanist. He has learned each language in its own country and the examples he has been shown to illustrate *'les lapins'* and 'rabbits', 'beeches' and *'les hêtre'* are distinct. It thus seems to be possible for him to suppose that *'lapin'* and 'rabbit', or 'beech' and *'hêtre'*, denote distinct but superficially similar kinds or species, even though the differences may be indiscernible to the untrained eye. (This is especially plausible if, a Putnam supposes, an English speaker—for example, Putnam himself—who is not a botanist may use 'beech' and 'elm' with their normal (distinct) meanings, even though he cannot himself distinguish the two trees.[35] Pierre may quite plausibly be supposed to wonder whether the trees which in France he called *'les hêtres'* were beeches or elms, even though as a speaker of French he satisfies all usual criteria for using *'les hêtres'* normally. If beeches and elms will not serve, better pairs of ringers exist that cannot be told apart except by an expert.) Once Pierre is in such a situation, paradoxes analogous to the one about

---

[34]Under the influence of Quine's *Word and Object*, some may argue that such conclusions are not inevitable: perhaps he will translate *'médecin'* as 'doctor stage', 'undetached part of a doctor'! If a Quinean sceptic makes an empirical prediction that such reactions from bilinguals as a matter of fact can occur, I doubt that he will be proved correct. (I do not know what Quine would think, but see *Word and Object*, p. 74, first paragraph.) On the other hand, if the translation of *'médecin'* as 'doctor' rather than 'doctor part' in this situation *is*, empirically speaking, inevitable, then even the advocate of Quine's thesis will have to admit that there is something special about one particular translation. The issue is not crucial to our present concerns, so I leave it with these sketchy remarks. But see also n. 36.

[35]Putnam gives the example of elms and beeches in "The Meaning of 'Meaning'" (in *Language, Mind, and Knowledge* (University of Minnesota Press, 1975) also reprinted in Putnam's *Philosophical Papers*, ii (Cambridge University Press, 1975). See also Putnam's discussion of other examples on pp. 139–43; also my own remarks on 'fool's gold', tigers, etc. in "Naming and Necessity," pp. 316–23.

London obviously can arise for rabbits and beeches. Pierre could affirm a French statement with '*lapin*', but deny its English translation with 'rabbit'. As above, we are hard-pressed to say what Pierre *believes*. We were considering a 'strict and philosophical' reform of translation procedures which proposed that foreign proper names should always be appropriated rather than translated. Now it seems that we will be forced to do the same with all words for natural kinds. (For example, on price of paradox, one must not translate '*lapin*' as "rabbit"!) No longer can the extended proposal be defended, even weakly, as 'merely' universalizing what we already do sometimes. It is surely too drastic a change to retain any credibility.[36]

There is yet another consideration that makes the proposed restriction more implausible: even this restriction does not really block the paradox. Even if we confine ourselves to a single language, say English, and to phonetically identical tokens of a single name, we can still generate the puzzle. Peter (as we may as well say now) may learn the name 'Paderewski' with an identification of the person named as a famous pianist. Naturally, having learned this, Peter will assent to "Paderewski had musical talent," and *we* can infer—using 'Paderewski', as we usually do, to name the Polish musician and statesman:

(8) Peter believes that Paderewski had musical talent.

Only the disquotational principle is necessary for our inference; no translation is required. Later, in a different circle, Peter learns of someone called 'Paderewski' who was a Polish nationalist leader and prime minister. Peter is skeptical of the musical abilities of politicians. He concludes that probably two people, approximate contemporaries no doubt, were both named 'Paderewski'. Using 'Paderewski' as a name for the *statesman*, Peter assents to, "Paderewski had no musical talent." Should we infer, by the disquotational principle,

(9) Peter believes that Paderewski had no musical talent.

---

[36]It is unclear to me how far this can go. Suppose Pierre hears English spoken only in England, French in France, and learns both by direct method. (Suppose also that no one else in each country speaks the language of the other.) Must he be sure that 'hot' and '*chaud*' are coextensive? In practice he certainly would. But suppose somehow his experience is consistent with the following bizarre—and of course, false!—hypothesis: England and France differ atmospherically so that human bodies are affected very differently by their interaction with the surrounding atmosphere. (This would be more plausible if France were on another planet.) In particular, within reasonable limits, things that feel cold in one of the countries feel hot in the other, and *vice versa*. Things don't change their *temperature* when moved from England to France, they just *feel* different because of their effects on human physiology. Then '*chaud*', in French, would be true of the things that are called 'cold' in English! (Of course the present discussion is, for lack of space, terribly compressed. See also the discussion of 'heat' in "Naming and Necessity." We are simply creating, for the physical property 'heat', a situation analogous to the situation for natural kinds in the text.)

If Pierre's experiences were arranged somehow so as to be consistent with the bizarre hypothesis, and he somehow came to believe it, he might simultaneously assent to '*C'est chaud*' and 'This is cold' without contradiction, even though he speaks French and English normally in each country separately.

This case needs much more development to see if it can be set up in detail, but I cannot consider it further here. Was I right in assuming in the text that the difficulty could not arise for '*médecin*' and 'doctor'?

or should we not? If Peter had not had the past history of learning the name 'Paderewski' in another way, we certainly would judge him to be using 'Paderewski' in a normal way, with the normal reference, and we would infer (9) by the disquotational principle. The situation is parallel to the problem with Pierre and London. Here, however, no restriction that names should not be translated, but should be phonetically repeated in the translation, can help us. Only a single language and a single name are involved. If any notion of translation is involved in this example, it is homophonic translation. Only the disquotational principle is used explicitly.[37] (On the other hand, the original 'two languages' case had the advantage that it would apply even if we spoke languages in which all names must denote uniquely and unambiguously.) The restriction that names must not be translated is thus ineffective, as well as implausible and drastic.

I close this section with some remarks on the relation of the present puzzle to Quine's doctrine of the 'indeterminacy of translation', with its attendant repudiation of intentional idioms of 'propositional attitude' such as belief and even indirect quotation. To a sympathizer with these doctrines the present puzzle may well seem to be just more grist for a familiar mill. The situation of the puzzle seems to lead to a breakdown of our normal practices of attributing belief and even of indirect quotation. No obvious paradox arises if we describe the same situation in terms of Pierre's sincere assent to various sentences, together with the conditions under which he has learned the name in question. Such a description, although it does not yet conform to Quine's strict behavioristic standards, fits in well with his view that in some sense direct quotation is a more 'objective' idiom than the propositional attitudes. Even those who, like the present writer, do not find Quine's negative attitude to the attitudes completely attractive must surely acknowledge this.

But although sympathizers with Quine's view can use the present examples to support it, the differences between these examples and the considerations Quine adduces for his own skepticism about belief and translation should not escape us. Here we make no use of hypothetical exotic systems of translation differing radically from the usual one, translating '*lapin*', say, as 'rabbit stage' or 'undetached part of a rabbit'. The problem arises entirely within our usual and customary system of translation of French into English; in one case, the puzzle arose even within English alone, using at most 'homophonic' translation. Nor is the problem that many different

---

[37]One might argue that Peter and we do speak different dialects, since in Peter's idiolect 'Paderewski' is used ambiguously as a name for a musician and a statesman (even though these are in fact the same), while in our language it us used unambiguously for a musician-statesman. The problem then would be whether Peter's dialect can be translated homophonically into our own. Before he hears of 'Paderewski-the-statesman', it would appear that the answer is affirmative for his (then unambiguous) use of 'Paderewski', since he did not differ from anyone who happens to have heard of Paderwski's musical achievements but not of his statesmanship. Similarly for his later use of 'Paderewski', if we ignore his earlier use. The problem is like Pierre's, and is essentially the same whether we describe it in terms of whether Peter satisfies the condition for the disquotational principle to be applicable, or whether homophonic translation of his dialect into our own is legitimate.

interpretations or translations fit our usual criteria, that, in Davidson's phrase,[38] there is more than one 'way of getting it right'. The trouble here is not that many views as to Pierre's beliefs get it right, but that they all definitely get it *wrong*. A straightforward application of the principles of translation and disquotation to all Pierre's utterances, French and English, yields the result that Pierre holds inconsistent beliefs, that logic alone should teach him that one of his beliefs is false. Intuitively, this is plainly incorrect. If we refuse to apply the principles to his French utterances at all, we would conclude that Pierre never believed that London is pretty, even though, before his unpredictable move, he was like any other monolingual Frenchman. This is absurd. If we refuse to ascribe the belief in London's pulchritude only after Pierre's move to England, we get the counterintuitive result that Pierre has changed his mind, and so on. But we have surveyed the possibilities above: the point was not that they are 'equally good', but that all are *obviously wrong*. If the puzzle is to be used as an argument for a Quinean position, it is an argument of a fundamentally different kind from those given before. And even Quine, if he wishes to incorporate the notion of belief even into a 'second level' of canonical notation,[39] must regard the puzzle as a real problem.

The alleged indeterminacy of translation and indirect quotation causes relatively little trouble for such a scheme for belief; the embarrassment it presents to such a scheme is, after all, one of riches. But the present puzzle indicates that the usual principles we use to ascribe beliefs are apt, in certain cases, to lead to contradiction, or at least, patent falsehoods. So it presents a problem for any project, Quinean or other, that wishes to deal with the 'logic' of belief on any level.[40]

---

[38]D. Davidson, "On Saying That," in D. Davidson and J. Hintikka (eds.), *Words and Objections* (Dordrecht: Reidel, 1969), 166.

[39]In *Word and Object*, p. 221, Quine advocates a second level of canonical notation, "to dissolve verbal perplexities or facilitate logical deductions," admitting the propositional attitudes, even though he thinks them "baseless" idioms that should be excluded from a notation "limning the true and ultimate structure of reality."

[40]In one respect the considerations mentioned above on natural kinds show that Quine's translation apparatus is insufficiently sceptical. Quine is sure that the native's *sentence* "Gavagai!" should be translated "Lo, a rabbit!" provided that its affirmative and negative stimulus meanings for the native match those of the English sentence for the Englishman; scepticism sets in only when the linguist proposes to translate the *general term* 'gavagai' as 'rabbit' rather than 'rabbit stage', 'rabbit part', and the like. But there is another possibility that is independent of (and less bizarre than) such sceptical alternatives. In the geographical area inhabited by the natives, there may be a species indistinguishable to the nonzoologist from rabbits but forming a distinct species. Then the 'stimulus meanings', in Quine's sense, of 'Lo, a rabbit!' and 'Gavagai!' may well be identical (to nonzoologists), especially if the ocular irradiations in question do not include a specification of the geographical locality. ('Gavagais' produce the same ocular irradiation patterns as rabbits.) Yet 'Gavagai!' and 'Lo, a rabbit!' are hardly synonymous; on typical occasions they will have opposite truth values.

I believe that the considerations about names, let alone natural kinds, emphasized in "Naming and Necessity" go against any simple attempt to base interpretation solely on maximizing agreement with the affirmations attributed to the native, matching of stimulus meanings, etc. The 'Principle of Charity' on which such methodologies are based was first enunciated by Neil Wilson in the special case of proper names as a formulation of the cluster-of-descriptions theory. The argument of "Naming and Necessity" is thus directed against the simple 'Principle of Charity' for that case.

IV. Conclusion

What morals can be drawn? The primary moral—quite independent of any of the discussion of the first two sections—is that the puzzle *is* a puzzle. As any theory of truth must deal with the Lia Paradox, so any theory of belief and names must deal with the puzzle.

But our theoretical starting point in the first two sections concerned proper names and belief. Let us return to Jones, who assents to "Cicero was bald" and to "Tully was not bald." Philosophers, using the disquotational principle, have concluded that Jones believes that Cicero was bald but that Tully was not. Hence, they have concluded, since Jones does not have contradictory beliefs, belief contexts are not 'Shakespearean' in Geach's sense: codesignative proper names are not interchangeable in these contexts *salva veritate.*[41]

I think the puzzle about Pierre shows that the simple conclusion was unwarranted. Jones's situation strikingly resembles Pierre's. A proposal that 'Cicero' and 'Tully' *are* interchangeable amounts roughly to a homophonic 'translation' of English into itself in which 'Cicero' is mapped into 'Tully' and *vice versa*, while the rest is left fixed. Such a 'translation' can, indeed, be used to obtain a paradox. But should the problem be blamed on this step? Ordinarily we would suppose without question that sentences in French with '*Londres*' should be translated into English with London'. Yet the same paradox results when we apply this translation too. We have seen that the problem can even arise with a single name in a single language, and that it arises with natural kind terms in two languages (or one: see below).

Intuitively, Jones's assent to both 'Cicero was bald' and 'Tully was not bald' arises from sources of just the same kind as Pierre's assent to both '*Londres est jolie*' and 'London is not pretty.'

It is wrong to blame unpalatable conclusions about Jones on substitutivity. The reason does not lie in any specific fallacy in the argument but rather in the nature of the realm being entered. Jones's case is just like Pierre's: both are in an area where our normal practices of attributing belief, based on the principles of disquotation and translation or on similar principles, are questionable.

It should be noted in this connection that the principles of disquotation and translation can lead to 'proofs' as well as 'disproofs' of substitutivity in belief contexts. In Hebrew there are two names for Germany, transliteratable roughly as '*Ashkenaz*' and '*Germaniah*'—the first of these may be somewhat archaic. When Hebrew sentences are translated into English, both become '*Germany*'. Plainly a normal Hebrew speaker analogous to Jones might assent to a Hebrew sentence involving '*Ashkenaz*' while dissenting from its counterpart with '*Germaniah*'. So far there is an argument *against* substitutivity. But there is also an argument *for* substitutivity, based on the principle of translation. Translate a Hebrew sentence

---

[41] Geach introduced the term 'Shakespearean' after the line, "A rose/By any other *name,* would smell as sweet."

Quine seems to define 'referentially transparent' contexts so as to imply that coreferential names and definite descriptions must be interchangeable *salva veritate*. Geach stresses that a context may be 'Shakespearean' but not 'referentially transparent' in this sense.

involving '*Ashkenaz*' into English, so that '*Ashkenaz*' goes into 'Germany'. Then retranslate the result into Hebrew, this time translating 'Germany' as '*Germaniah*'. By the principle of translation, both translations preserve truth value. So: the truth value of any sentence of Hebrew involving '*Ashkenaz*' remains the same when '*Ashkenaz*' is replaced by '*Germaniah*'—a 'proof' of substitutivity! A similar 'proof' can be provided wherever there are two names in one language, and a normal practice of translating both indifferently into a single name of another language.[42] (If we combine the 'proof' and 'disproof' of substitutivity in this paragraph, we could get yet another paradox analogous to Pierre's: our Hebrew speaker both believes, and disbelieves, that Germany is pretty. Yet no amount of pure logic or semantic introspection suffices for him to discover his error.)

Another consideration, regarding natural kinds: Previously we pointed out that a bilingual may learn '*lapin*' and 'rabbit' normally in each respective language yet wonder whether they are one species or two, and that this fact can be used to generate a paradox analogous to Pierre's. Similarly, a speaker of *English* alone may learn 'furze' and 'gorse' normally (separately), yet wonder whether these are the same, or resembling kinds. (What about 'rabbit' and 'hare'?) It would be easy for such a speaker to assent to an assertion formulated with 'furze' but withhold assent from the corresponding assertion involving 'gorse'. The situation is quite analogous to that of Jones with respect to 'Cicero' and 'Tully'. Yet 'furze' and 'gorse', and other pairs of terms for the same natural kind, are normally thought of as *synonyms*.

The point is *not*, of course, that codesignative proper names *are* interchangeable in belief contexts *salva veritate*, or that they *are* interchangeable in simple contexts even *salva significatione*. The point is that the absurdities that disquotation plus substitutivity would generate are exactly paralleled by absurdities generated by disquotation plus translation, or even 'disquotation alone' (or: disquotation plus homophonic translation). Also, though our naïve practice may lead to 'disproofs' of substitutivity in certain cases, it can also lead to 'proofs' of substitutivity in some of these same cases, as we saw two paragraphs back. When we enter into the area exemplified by Jones and Pierre, we enter into an area where our normal practices of interpretation and attribution of belief are subjected to the

---

[42]Generally such cases may be slightly less watertight than the 'London'–'*Londres*' case. '*Londres*' just is the French version of 'London', while one cannot quite say that the same relation holds between '*Ashkenaz*' and '*Germaniah*'. Nevertheless:

(*a*) Our standard practice in such cases is to translate both names of the first language into the single name of the second.

(*b*) Often no nuances of 'meaning' are discernible differentiating such names as '*Ashkenaz*' and '*Germaniah*', such that we would not say either that Hebrew would have been impoverished had it lacked one of them (or that English is impoverished because it has only one name for Germany), any more than a language is impoverished if it has only one word corresponding to 'doctor' and 'physician'. Given this, it seems hard to condemn our practice of translating both names as 'Germany' as 'loose'; in fact, it would seem that Hebrew just has two names for the same country where English gets by with one.

(*c*) Any inclinations to avoid problems by declaring, say, the translation of '*Ashkenaz*' as 'Germany' to be loose should be considerably tempered by the discussion of analogous problems in the text.

greatest possible strain, perhaps to the point of breakdown. So is the notion of the *content* of someone's assertion, the *proposition* it expresses. In the present state of our knowledge, I think it would be foolish to draw any conclusion, positive or negative, about substitutivity.[43]

Of course nothing in these considerations prevents us from observing that Jones can sincerely assert both "Cicero is bald" and "Tully is not bald," even though he is a normal speaker of English and uses 'Cicero' and 'Tully' in normal ways, and with the normal referent. Pierre and the other paradoxical cases can be described similarly. (For those interested in one of my own doctrines, we can still say that there was a time when men were in no epistemic position to assent to 'Hesperus is Phosphorus' for want of empirical information, but it nevertheless expressed a necessary truth.)[44]

---

[43]In spite of this official view, perhaps I will be more assertive elsewhere.

In the case of 'Hesperus' and 'Phosphorus' (in contrast to 'Cicero' and 'Tully'), where there is a case for the existence of conventional community-wide 'senses' differentiating the two—at least, two distinct modes of 'fixing the reference of two rigid designators—it is more plausible to suppose that the two names are definitely not interchangeable in belief contexts. According to such a supposition, a belief that Hesperus is a planet is a belief that a certain heavenly body, rigidly picked out as seen in the evening in the appropriate season, is a planet; and similarly for Phosphorus. One may argue that translation problems like Pierre's will be blocked in this case, that '*Vesper*' must be translated as 'Hesperus,' not as 'Phosphorus'. As against this, however, two things:

(*a*) We should remember that sameness of properties used to fix the reference does *not* appear to guarantee in general that paradoxes will not arise. So one may be reluctant to adopt a solution in terms of reference-fixing properties for this case if it does not get to the heart of the general problem.

(*b*) The main issue seems to me here to be—how essential is a particular mode of fixing the reference to a correct learning of the name? If a parent, aware of the familiar identity, takes a child into the fields in the morning and says (pointing to the morning star), "That is called 'Hesperus,'" has the parent mistaught the language? (A parent who says, "Creatures with kidneys are called 'cordates,'" definitely has mistaught the language, even though the statement is extensionally correct.) To the extent that it is *not* crucial for correct language learning that a particular mode of fixing the reference be used, to that extent there is no 'mode of presentation' differentiating the 'content' of a belief about 'Hesperus' from one about 'Phosphorus'. I am doubtful that the original method of fixing the reference *must* be preserved in transmission of the name.

If the mode of reference fixing *is* crucial, it can be maintained that otherwise identical beliefs expressed with 'Hesperus' and with 'Phosphorus' have definite differences of 'content', at least in an epistemic sense. The conventional ruling against substitutivity could thus be maintained without qualms for some cases, though not as obviously for others, such as 'Cicero' and 'Tully'. But it is unclear to me whether even 'Hesperus' and 'Phosphorus' do have such conventional 'modes of presentation'. I need not take a definite stand, and the verdict may be different for different particular pairs of names. For a brief related discussion, see "Naming and Necessity," p. 331, first paragraph.

[44]However, some earlier formulations expressed disquotationally such as "It was once unknown that Hesperus is Phosphorus" are questionable in the light of the present paper (but see the previous note for this case). I was aware of this question by the time "Naming and Necessity" was written, but I did not wish to muddy the waters further than necessary at that time. I regarded the distinction between epistemic and metaphysical necessity as valid in any case and adequate for the distinctions I wished to make. The considerations in this paper are relevant to the earlier discussion of the 'contingent *a priori*' as well; perhaps I will discuss this elsewhere.

But it is no surprise that quoted contexts fail to satisfy a substitutivity principle within the quotation marks. And, in our *present* state of clarity about the problem, we are in no position to apply a disquotation principle to these cases, nor to judge when two such sentences do, or do not, express the same 'proposition'.

Nothing in the discussion impugns the conventional judgment that belief contexts are 'referentially opaque', if 'referential opacity' is construed so that failure of coreferential *definite descriptions* to be interchangeable *salva veritate* is sufficient for referential opacity. No doubt Jones can believe that the number of planets is even, without believing that the square of three is even, if he is under a misapprehension about the astronomical, but not the arithmetical facts. The question at hand was whether belief contexts were 'Shakespearean', not whether they were 'referentially transparent'. (Modal contexts, in my opinion, are 'Shakespearean' but 'referentially opaque'.)[45]

Even were we inclined to rule that belief contexts are not Shakespearean, it would be implausible at present to use the phenomenon to support a Frege–Russellian theory that names have descriptive 'senses' through 'uniquely identifying properties'. There are the well-known arguments against description theories, independent of the present discussion; there is the implausibility of the view that difference in names is difference in idiolect; and finally, there are the arguments of the present paper that differences of associated properties do not explain the problems in any case. Given these considerations, and the cloud our paradox places over the notion of 'content' in this area, the relation of substitutivity to the dispute between Millian and Fregean conclusions is not very clear.

We repeat our conclusions: Philosophers have often, basing themselves on Jones's and similar cases, supposed that it goes virtually without saying that belief contexts are not 'Shakespearean'. I think that, at present, such a definite conclusion in unwarranted. Rather Jones's case, like Pierre's, lies in an area where our normal apparatus for the ascription of belief is placed under the greatest strain and may even break down. There is even less warrant at the present time, in the absence of a better understanding of the paradoxes of this paper, for the use of alleged failures of substitutivity in belief contexts to draw any significant theoretical conclusion about proper names. Hard cases make bad law.[46]

---

[45] According to Russell, definite descriptions are not genuine singular terms. He thus would have regarded any concept of 'referential opacity' that includes definite descriptions as profoundly misleading. He also maintained a substitutivity principle for 'logically proper names' in belief and other attitudinal contexts, so that for him belief contexts were as 'transparent', in any philosophically decent sense, as truth-functional contexts.

Independently of Russell's views, there is much to be said for the opinion that the question whether a context is 'Shakespearean' is more important philosophically—even for many purposes for which Quine invokes his own concept—than whether it is 'referentially opaque'.

[46] I will make some brief remarks about the relation of Benson Mates's problem (see n. 15) to the present one. Mates argued that such a sentence as (*) 'Some doubt that all who believe that doctors are happy believe that physicians are happy', may be true, even though 'doctors' and 'physicians' are synonymous, and even though it would have been false had 'physicians' been replaced in it by a second occurrence of 'doctors'. Church countered that (*) could not

(*contd.*)

be true, since its translation into a language with only one word for doctors (which would translate both 'doctors' and 'physicians') would be false. If *both* Mates's and Church's intuitions were correct, we might get a paradox analogous to Pierre's.

Applying the principles of translation and disquotation to Mates's puzzle, however, involves many more complications than our present problem. First, if someone assents to 'Doctors are happy', but refuses assent to 'Physicians are happy', *prima facie* disquotation does not apply to him since he is under a linguistic or conceptual confusion. (See n. 23.) So there are as yet no grounds, merely because this happened, to doubt that all who believe that doctors are happy believe that physicians are happy.

Now suppose someone assents to 'Not all who believe that doctors are happy believe that physicians are happy'. What is the source of his assent? If it is failure to realize that 'doctors' and 'physicians' are synonymous (this was the situation Mates originally envisaged), then he is under a linguistic or conceptual confusion, so disquotation does not clearly apply. Hence we have no reason to conclude from this case that (*) is true. Alternatively, he may realize that 'doctors' and 'physicians' are synonymous; but he applies disquotation to a man who assents to 'Doctors are happy' but not to 'Physicians are happy', ignoring the caution of the previous paragraph. Here he is not under a simple linguistic confusion (such as failure to realize that 'doctors' and 'physicians' are synonymous), but he appears to be under a deep conceptual confusion (misapplication of the disquotational principle). Perhaps, it may be argued, he misunderstands the 'logic of belief'. Does his conceptual confusion mean that we cannot straightforwardly apply disquotation to his utterance, and that therefore we cannot conclude from his behaviour that (*) is true? I think that, although the issues are delicate, and I am not at present completely sure what answers to give, there is a case for an affirmative answer. (Compare the more extreme case of someone who is so confused that he thinks that someone's *dissent* from 'Doctors are happy' implies that he believes that doctors are happy. If someone's utterance, 'Many believe that doctors are happy', is based on such a misapplication of disquotation, surely we in turn should not apply disquotation to it. The utterer, at least in this context, does not really know what 'belief' means.)

I do *not* believe the discussion above ends the matter. Perhaps I can discuss Mates's problem at greater length elsewhere. Mates's problem is perplexing, and its relation to the present puzzle is interesting. But it should be clear from the preceding that Mates's argument involves issues even more delicate than those that arise with respect to Pierre. First, Mates's problem involves delicate issues regarding iteration of belief contexts, whereas the puzzle about Pierre involves the application of disquotation only to affirmations of (or assents to) *simple* sentences. More important, Mates's problem would not arise in a world where no one ever was under a linguistic or a conceptual confusion, no one ever thought anyone else was under such a confusion, no one ever thought anyone ever thought anyone was under such a confusion, and so on. It is important, both for the puzzle about Pierre and for the Fregean argument that 'Cicero' and 'Tully' differ in 'sense', that they would still arise in such a world. They are entirely free of the delicate problem of applying disquotation to utterances directly or indirectly based on the existence of linguistic confusion. See nn. 15 and 28, and the discussion in the text of Pierre's logical consistency.

Another problem discussed in the literature to which the present consideration may be relevant is that of 'self-consciousness', or the peculiarity of 'I'. Discussions of this problem have emphasized that 'I', even when Mary Smith uses it, is not interchangeable with 'Mary Smith', nor with any other conventional singular term designating Mary Smith. If she is 'not aware that she is Mary Smith', she may assent to a sentence with 'I', but dissent from the corresponding sentence with 'Mary Smith'. It is quite possible that any attempt to clear up the logic of all this will involve itself in the problem of the present paper. (For this purpose, the present discussion might be extended to demonstratives and indexicals.)

The writing of this paper had partial support from a grant from the National Science Foundation, a John Simon Guggenheim Foundation Fellowship, a Visiting Fellowship at All Souls College, Oxford, and a sabbatical leave from Princeton University. Various people at the Jerusalem Encounter and elsewhere, who will not be enumerated, influenced the paper through discussion.

ILLOGICAL BELIEF*

Nathan Salmon

I

My purpose here is to present a defense against some criticisms that have been leveled against various doctrines and theses I advanced in *Frege's Puzzle*[1] and to draw out some philosophically interesting applications and consequences of some of the central ideas utilized in my defense. The two principal objections I shall consider—one of which is offered by Saul Kripke and the other by Stephen Schiffer—as I reconstruct them, tacitly presuppose or assume one or both of a pair of closely related and largely uncontroversial principles concerning belief and deductive reasoning. The first is a normative principle, which I shall call *the belief justification principle*. It may be stated thus:

> Suppose x is a normal, fully rational agent who consciously and rationally believes a certain proposition p. Suppose also that x is consciously interested in the further question of whether q is also the case, where q is another proposition. Suppose further that q is in fact a trivial deductive consequence of p. Suppose finally that x fully realizes that q is a deductive consequence of p and is fully able to deduce q from p. Under these circumstances, x would be rationally justified in coming to believe q on the basis of his or her belief of p (and its deductive relationship to q), or alternatively, if x withholds belief from q (by disbelieving or by suspending judgement) for independent reasons, x would be rationally justified in accordingly relinquishing his or her belief of p.

The second principle is similar to this, except that it is descriptive rather than prescriptive. I shall call it *the belief closure principle:*

> Make the same initial-condition suppositions concerning x *vis-à-vis* the propositions p and q as given in the belief justification principle. Under these circumstances, if x consciously considers the question of whether q is the case and has adequate time for reflection on the matter, x will in fact come to believe q in addition to p on the basis of his or her belief of p (and its deductive relationship to q), unless x instead withholds belief from q (either by disbelieving or by suspending judgement) for independent reasons, and accordingly relinquishes his or her belief of p.

The belief justification principle, since it is normative rather than predictive, may seem somehow more certain and on sounder footing than the belief closure principle, but both principles are quite compelling. I shall claim that there are

---

* Part of the present paper was presented to the Pacific Division of the American Philosophical Association on March 26, 1987. It has benefitted from discussion with Stephen Schiffer and with Scott Soames. Thanks go also to Keith Donnellan and the participants in his seminar at UCLA during Spring 1987 for their insightful comments on *Frege's Puzzle*, and to the participants in my seminar at UCSB during Fall 1986 for forcing me to elaborate on my response to Kripke's objection to my position regarding his puzzle about belief.

[1] Cambridge, Mass.: Bradford Books/MIT Press, 1986.

situations that present straightforward counter-examples to both principles simultaneously. Specifically, I claim that these principles fail in precisely the sort of circumstances to which my objectors tacitly apply the principles.

First, a preliminary exposition of the project undertaken in *Frege's Puzzle* is in order. The central thesis is that ordinary proper names, demonstratives, other single-word indexicals or pronouns (such as 'he'), and other simple (noncompound) singular terms are, in a given possible context of use, Russellian "genuine names in the strict logical sense."[2] Put more fully, I maintain the following anti-Fregean doctrine: that the contribution made by an ordinary proper name or other simple singular term, to securing the information content of, or the proposition expressed by, declarative sentences (with respect to a given possible context of use) in which the term occurs (outside of the scope of nonextensional operators, such as quotation marks) is just the referent of the term, or the bearer of the name (with respect to that context of use). In the terminology of *Frege's Puzzle,* I maintain that the *information value* of an ordinary proper name is just its referent.

Some other theses that I maintain in *Frege's Puzzle* are also critical to the present discussion. One such thesis (which Frege and Russell both more or less accepted) is that the proposition that is the information content of a declarative sentence (with respect to a given context) is structured in a certain way, and that its structure and constituents mirror, and are in some way readable from, the structure and constituents of the sentence containing that proposition.[3] By and large, a simple (noncompound) expression contributes a single entity, taken as a

---

[2] See Russell's "Knowledge by Acquaintance and Knowledge by Description," Chapter X of Russell's *Mysticism and Logic and Other Essays* (London: Longmans, Green and Company, 1911), pp. 209–232, also in N. Salmon and S. Soames, eds., *Propositions and Attitudes* (Oxford University Press, Readings in Philosophy, 1988); and Russell's "The Philosophy of Logical Atomism," in his *Logic and Knowledge,* R. C. Marsh, ed. (London: George Allen and Unwin, 1956), pp. 177–281; also in his *The Philosophy of Logical Atomism,* D. Pears, ed. (La Salle: Open Court, 1985), pp. 35–155.

[3] This separates the theory of *Frege's Puzzle* together with the theories of Frege, Russell, and their followers, from contemporary theories that assimilate the information contents of declarative sentences with such things as sets of possible worlds, or sets of situations, or functions from possible worlds to truth-values, etc.

    Both Frege and Russell would regard declarative sentences as typically reflecting only *part of* the structure of their content, since they would insist that many (perhaps even most) grammatically simple (noncompound) expressions occurring in a sentence may (especially if introduced into the language by abbreviation or by some other type of explicit "definition") contribute complex proposition-constituents that would have been more perspicuously contributed by compound expressions. In short, Frege and Russell regard the prospect of expressions that are grammatically simple yet semantically compound (at the level of content) as not only possible but ubiquitous. Furthermore, according to Russell's Theory of Descriptions, definite and indefinite descriptions ('the author of *Waverley*', 'an author', etc.), behave grammatically but not semantically (at the level of content) as a self-contained unit, so that a sentence containing such an expression is at best only a rough guide to the structure of the content. Russell extends this idea further to ordinary proper names and most uses of pronouns and demonstratives. This makes the structure of nearly any sentence only a very rough guide to the structure of the sentence's content. The theory advanced in *Frege's Puzzle* sticks much more closely to the grammatical structure of the sentence. (But see the following paragraph in the text concerning abstracted predicates.)

simple (noncomplex) unit, to the information content of a sentence in which the expression occurs, whereas the contribution of a compound expression (such as a phrase or sentential clause) is a complex entity composed of the contributions of the simple components.[4] Hence, the contents of beliefs formulatable using ordinary proper names, demonstratives, or other simple singular terms, are on my view so-called *singular propositions* (David Kaplan), i.e., structured propositions directly about some individual, which occurs directly as a constituent of the proposition. This thesis (together with certain relatively uncontroversial assumptions) yields the consequence that *de re* belief (or *belief of*) is simply a special case of *de dicto* belief (*belief that*). To believe *of* an individual x, *de re*, that it (he, she) is F is to believe *de dicto* the singular proposition about (containing) x that it (he, she) is F, a proposition that can be expressed using an ordinary proper name for x. Similarly for the other propositional attitudes.

There is an important class of exceptions to the general rule that a compound expression contributes to the information content of a sentence in which it occurs a complex entity composed of the contributions of the simple components. These are compound predicates formed by abstraction from an open sentence. For example, from the "open" sentence 'I love her and she loves me'—with pronouns 'her' and 'she' functioning as "freely" as the free variables occurring in such open sentences of the formal vernacular as '$F(a, x)$ & $F(x, a)$'—we may form (by "abstraction") the compound predicate 'is someone such that I love her and she loves me'. Formally, using Alonzo Church's 'λ'-abstraction operator, we might write this '$(\lambda x)[F(a, x)$ & $F(x, a)]$'. Such an abstracted compound predicate should be seen as contributing something like an attribute or a Russellian *propositional function*, taken as a unit, to the information content of sentences in which it occurs, rather than as contributing a complex made up of the typical contributions of the compound's components.

In addition to this, I propose the sketch of an analysis of the binary relation of belief between believers and propositions (sometimes Russellian singular propositions). I take the belief relation to be, in effect, the existential generalization of a ternary relation, *BEL*, among believers, propositions, and some third type of entity. To believe a proposition p is to adopt an appropriate favorable attitude toward p when taking p in some relevant way. It is to agree to p, or to assent mentally to p, or to approve of p, or some such thing, when taking p a certain way. This is the *BEL* relation. I do not say a great deal about what the third relata for the *BEL* relation are. They are perhaps something like *proposition guises*, or *modes of*

---

[4] There are well-known exceptions to the general rule—hence the phrase 'by and large'. Certain nonextensional operators, such as quotation marks, create contexts in which compound expressions contribute themselves as units to the information content of sentences in which the expression occurs. Less widely recognized is the fact that even ordinary temporal operators (e.g., 'on April 1, 1986' + past tense) create contexts in which some compound expressions (most notably, open and closed sentences) contribute complexes other than their customary contribution to information content. See my "Tense and Singular Propositions," in J. Almog, J. Perry, and H. Wettstein, eds., *Themes from Kaplan* (Oxford University Press, forthcoming). The following paragraph in the text cites another largely overlooked class of exceptions.

acquaintance or familiarity with propositions, or *ways* in which a believer may take a given proposition. The important thing is that, by definition, they are such that if a fully rational believer adopts conflicting attitudes (such as belief and disbelief, or belief and suspension of judgement) toward propositions p and q, then the believer must take p and q in different ways, by means of different guises, in harboring the conflicting attitudes toward them—even if p and q are in fact the same proposition. More generally, if a fully rational agent construes objects x and y as distinct (or even merely withholds construing them as one and the very same—as might be evidenced, for example, by the agent's adopting conflicting beliefs or attitudes concerning x and y), then for some appropriate notion of a way of taking an object, the agent takes x and y in different ways, even if in fact $x = y$.[5] Of course, to use a distinction of Kripke's, this formulation is far too vague to constitute a fully developed *theory* of proposition guises and their role in belief formation, but it does provide a *picture* of belief that differs significantly from the sort of picture of propositional attitudes advanced by Frege or Russell, and enough can be said concerning the *BEL* relation to allow for at least the sketch of a solution to certain philosophical problems, puzzles, and paradoxes—including those in the same family as Frege's notorious 'Hesperus'–'Phosphorus' puzzle.[6]

In particular, the *BEL* relation satisfies the following three conditions:

(i) A believes p if and only if there is some x such that A is familiar with p by means of x and $BEL(A, p, x)$;[7]

---

[5] An appropriate notion of a way of taking an object is such that if an agent encounters a single object several times and each time construes it as a different object from the objects in the previous encounters, or even as a different object *for all he or she knows*, then each time he or she takes the object in a new and different way. This is required in order to accommodate the fact that an agent in such circumstances may (perhaps *inevitably will*) adopt several conflicting attitudes toward what is in fact a single object. One cannot require, however, that these ways of taking objects are rich enough by themselves to determine the object so taken, without the assistance of extra-mental, contextual factors. Presumably, twin agents who are molecule-for-molecule duplicates, and whose brains are in exactly the same configuration down to the finest detail, may encounter different (though duplicate) objects, taking them in the very same way. Likewise, a single agent might be artificially induced through brain manipulations into taking different objects the same way.

[6] The *BEL* relation is applied to additional puzzles in my "Reflexivity," *Notre Dame Journal of Formal Logic*, 27, 3 (July 1986), pp. 401–429; also in N. Salmon and S. Soames, eds., *Propositions and Attitudes*.

[7] I do not claim that a sentence of the form ⌐A believes p⌐ is exactly synonymous with the existential formula on the right-hand side of 'if and only if' in condition (*i*). I do claim that condition (*i*) is a (metaphysically) necessary, conceptually *a priori* truth. (See two paragraphs back in the text concerning the contents of predicates. It may be helpful to think of the English verb 'believe' as a *name* for the binary relation described by the right-hand side of (*i*), i.e., for the existential generalization on the third argument-place of the *BEL* relation.) My claim in *Frege's Puzzle* (p. 111) that belief may be so "analyzed" is meant to entail that condition (*i*) is a necessary *a priori* truth, not that the two sides of the biconditional are synonymous. (My own view is that something along these lines is all that can be plausibly claimed for such purported philosophical "analyses" as have been offered for ⌐A knows p⌐, ⌐A perceives B⌐, ⌐A (nonnaturally) means p in uttering S⌐, etc.)

(ii) A may believe p by standing in *BEL* to p and some x by means of which A is familiar with p without standing in *BEL* to p and all x by means of which A is familiar with p;

(iii) In one sense of 'withhold belief', A withholds belief concerning p (either by disbelieving or by suspending judgement) if and only if there is some x by means of which A is familiar with p and not-$BEL(A, p, x)$.

These conditions generate a philosophically important distinction between withholding belief and failure to believe (i.e., not believing). In particular, one may both withhold belief from and believe the very same proposition simultaneously. (Neither withholding belief nor failure to believe is to be identified with the related notions of disbelief and suspension of judgement—which are two different ways of withholding belief, in my sense, and which may occur simultaneously with belief of the very same proposition in a single believer.)

It happens in most cases (though not all) that when a believer believes some particular proposition p, the relevant third relatum for the *BEL* relation is a function of the believer and some particular *sentence* of the believer's language. There is, for example, the binary function f that assigns to any believer A and sentence S of A's language, the *way A takes the proposition contained in S* (in A's language with respect to A's context at some particular time t) were it presented to A (at t) through the very sentence S, if there is exactly one such way of taking the proposition in question. (In some cases, there are too many such ways of taking the proposition in question.)

This account may be applied to the comic-book legend of Superman and his woman-friend Lois Lane. According to this saga, Lois Lane is acquainted with Superman in both of his guises—as a mild-mannered reporter and dullard named 'Clark Kent' and as the superheroic defender of truth, justice, and the American way, named 'Superman'—but she is unaware that these are one and the very same person. Whereas she finds our hero somewhat uninteresting when she encounters him in his mild-mannered reporter guise, her heartbeat quickens with excitement whenever she encounters him, or even merely thinks of him, in his superhero guise. Consider now the sentence

(0) Lois Lane believes that Clark Kent is Superman.

Is this true or false? According to my account, it is true! For Lois Lane agrees to the proposition that Clark Kent is Superman when taking it in a certain way—for example, if one points to Superman in one of his guises and says 'He is him', or when the proposition is presented to her by such sentences as 'Clark Kent is Clark Kent' and 'Superman is Superman'. That is,

BEL[Lois Lane, that Clark Kent is Superman, f(Lois Lane, 'Superman is Superman')].

Lois Lane also withholds belief concerning whether Superman is Superman. In fact, according to my account, she believes that Superman is not Superman! For she agrees to the proposition that Superman is not Superman when taking it in the way it is presented to her by the sentence 'Clark Kent is not Superman'. That is,

> *BEL*[Lois Lane, that Superman is not Superman, *f*(Lois Lane, 'Clark Kent is not Superman')],

and hence, since Lois Lane is fully rational, it is not the case that

> *BEL*[Lois Lane, that Superman is Superman, *f*(Lois Lane, 'Clark Kent is Superman')].

II

It is evident that these consequences of my account do not conform with the way we actually speak. Instead it is customary when discussing the Superman legend to deny sentence (0) and to say such things as

> (1) Lois Lane does not realize that Clark Kent is Superman.

According to my account, sentence (1) is literally false in the context of the Superman legend. In fact, (1)'s literal truth-conditions are, according to the view I advocate, conditions that are plainly unfulfilled (in the context of the Superman legend). Why, then, do we say such things as (1)? Some explanation of our speech patterns in these sorts of cases is called for. The explanation I offer in *Frege's Puzzle* is somewhat complex, consisting of three main parts. The first part of the explanation for the common disposition to utter or to assent to (1) is that speakers may have a tendency to confuse the content of (1) with that of

> (1′) Lois Lane does not realize that 'Clark Kent is Superman' is true (in English).

Since sentence (1′) is obviously true, this confusion naturally leads to a similarly favorable disposition toward (1). This part of the explanation cannot be the whole story, however, since even speakers who know enough about semantics to know that the fact that Clark Kent is Superman is logically independent of the fact that the sentence 'Clark Kent is Superman' is true (in English, according to the legend), and who are careful to distinguish the content of (1) from that of (1′), are nevertheless favorably disposed toward (1) itself—because of the fact that Lois Lane bursts into uncontrollable laughter whenever the mere suggestion 'Clark Kent could turn out to be Superman' is put to her.

The second part of my explanation for (1)'s appearance of truth is that (1) itself is the product of a plausible but mistaken inference from the fact that Lois Lane sincerely dissents (or at least does not sincerely assent) when queried 'Is Clark Kent Superman?', while fully understanding the question and grasping its content, or (as Keith Donnellan has pointed out) even from her expressions of preference for the man of steel over the mild-mannered reporter. More accurately, ordinary speakers (and even most nonordinary speakers) are disposed to regard the fact that Lois Lane does not agree to the proposition that Clark Kent is Superman, when taking it in a certain way (the way it might be presented to her by the very sentence 'Clark Kent is Superman'), as sufficient to warrant the denial of sentence (0) and the assertion of sentence (1). In the special sense explained in the preceding section, Lois Lane withholds belief from the proposition that Clark Kent is Superman, actively failing to agree with it whenever it is put to her in so many words, and this fact misleads ordinary speakers, including Lois Lane herself, into concluding that Lois harbors no favorable attitude of agreement whatsoever toward the proposition in question, and hence does not believe it.

The third part of the explanation is that, where someone under discussion has conflicting attitudes toward a single proposition that he or she takes to be two independent propositions (i.e., in the troublesome 'Hesperus'–'Phosphorus', 'Superman'–'Clark Kent' type cases), there is an established practice of using belief attributions to convey not only the proposition agreed to (which is specified by the belief attribution) but also the way the subject of the attribution takes the proposition in agreeing to it (which is no part of the semantic content of the belief attribution). Specifically, there is an established practice of using such a sentence as (0), which contains the uninteresting proposition that Lois Lane believes the singular proposition about Superman that he is him, to convey furthermore that Lois Lane agrees to this proposition *when she takes it in the way it is presented to her by the very sentence 'Clark Kent is Superman'* (assuming she understands this sentence). That is, there is an established practice of using (0) to convey the thought that

> BEL[Lois Lane, that Clark Kent is Superman, f(Lois Lane, 'Clark Kent is Superman')].

III

The last part of the explanation just sketched may be clarified by considering an objection raised by Schiffer.[8] Schiffer sees my theory as attempting to explain ordinary speakers' dispositions to utter or to assent to (1) by postulating that in such cases a particular mechanism, of a sort described by H. P. Grice,[9] comes into play. The mechanism works in the following way: A speaker deliberately utters a particular sentence where there is mutual recognition by the speaker and his or her audience that the speaker believes the sentence to be false. The speaker and the audience mutually recognize that the speaker is not opting out of Grice's conversational Cooperative Principle (according to which one should make one's conversational contribution such as is required, at the stage at which it occurs, by the accepted purpose or direction of the conversation), and hence that the speaker is subject to the usual Gricean conversational maxims. Yet the speaker and audience also recognize that there is a *prima facie* apparent violation of the first conversational *maxim of Quality:* "Do not say what you believe to be false." The audience

---

[8] "The 'Fido'–Fido Theory of Belief," in James Tomberlin, ed., *Philosophical Perspectives 1: Metaphysics* (Atascadero: Ridgeview, 1987), pp. 455–480. Schiffer's article includes a rejoinder, in an appended postscript, to many of the arguments of the present article. I think it is useful, however, to include in the present article my own statements of the arguments and replies that Schiffer is rejoining in his postscript. It is left to the reader to evaluate the relative merits of my replies to Schiffer's objections and Schiffer's rejoinder to my replies.

[9] "Logic and Conversation," in P. Cole and J. L. Morgan, eds., *Syntax and Semantics*, volume 3 (New York: Academic Press, 1975), pp. 41–55; also in D. Davidson and G. Harman, eds., *The Logic of Grammar* (Encino: Dickenson, 1975), pp. 64–75; also in A. P. Martinich, ed., *The Philosophy of Language* (Oxford University Press, 1985), pp. 159–170.

infers, in accordance with the speakers intentions, that the speaker is using the sentence not to commit himself or herself to its literal content (which is taken to be false) but instead to convey, or to "implicate," some saliently related proposition, which is easily gleaned from the context of the conversation. In the case of sentence (1), on this account, the speaker employs this mechanism to implicate that Lois Lane does not agree to the proposition that Clark Kent is Superman when she takes it in the way it is presented to her by the very sentence 'Clark Kent is Superman'. Schiffer's criticism is that this account flies in the face of the obvious fact that ordinary speakers do not believe (1) to be false, but believe it true.

This criticism is indeed decisive against the explanation described above for our propensity to say such things as (1). But this is not the explanation I proposed in *Frege's Puzzle*. Oddly, the very example of sentence (1) comes from a particular passage in *Frege's Puzzle* that explicitly precludes Schiffer's interpretation:

> Now, there is no denying that, given the proper circumstances, we say things like 'Lois Lane does not realize . . . . that Clark Kent is Superman'. . . . When we make these utterances, we typically do not intend to be speaking elliptically or figuratively; we take ourselves to be speaking literally and truthfully. (p. 81)

My pragmatic account of the appearance of truth in the case of such sentences as (1) is meant not only as an explanation of the widespread disposition to utter or to assent to (1), but equally as an explanation of the widespread intuition that (1) is literally true, and equally as an explanation of the widespread belief of the content of (1). What is needed, and what I attempt to provide (or at least a sketch thereof), is not merely an explanation of the disposition of ordinary speakers to utter or assent to (1) given the relevant facts concerning Lois Lane's ignorance of Superman's secret identity, but an explanation why ordinary speakers who understand (1) perfectly well, fully grasping its content, sincerely utter it while taking themselves to speaking literally and truthfully, without being exactly similarly disposed toward such synonymous sentences as

Lois Lane does not realize that Superman is Superman

when they also understand these sentences perfectly well and the common content of these sentences is something these speakers believe.[10] The particular Gricean mechanism that Schiffer describes is no doubt part of the correct explanation in *some* cases of how ordinary speakers may use certain sentences to convey what these sentences do not literally mean. But the particular mechanism in question cannot yield a coherent account of why ordinary speakers believe that a given sentence is true. How would the alleged explanation go? "Here's why ordinary speakers believe that sentence S is true: They realize that it's false. This mutual recognition of its falsity enables them to use S to convey

---

[10] Contrary to a proposal Schiffer makes in his postscript, the observation that the content of (1) is something ordinary speakers believe, *per se*, does not yield an adequate explanation here. For ordinary speakers are not similarly disposed toward 'Lois Lane does not realize that Superman is Superman' although they fully grasp its content, which (on my view) is the same as that of (1).

something true. Their use of S to convey something true leads them to conclude that S *is* true." This alleged explanation is incoherent; it purports to explain ordinary speakers' belief that a given sentence is true by means of their belief that it is false. Clearly, no attempt to explain the widespread view that (1) is literally true can proceed from the initial hypothesis that ordinary speakers typically believe that (1) is literally false!

Schiffer's criticism concerns only the third part of the explanation sketched in the preceding section: the hypothesis that there is an established practice of using such a sentence as (0) to convey that Lois Lane agrees to the proposition that Clark Kent is Superman when taking it in the way it is presented to her by the very sentence 'Clark Kent is Superman'. I do not claim that this practice came about by means of a special Gricean mechanism requiring the mutual recognition by the speaker and his or her audience that sentence (0) is literally true. Quite the contrary, I suppose that many ordinary speakers, and most philosophers, would take the proposition that they use the sentence to convey to be the very content of the sentence. That is why they would deem the sentence literally false. Schiffer describes a particular mechanism that allows speakers to use a sentence to convey ("implicate") what it does not literally mean by means of a mutual recognition that what is conveyed cannot be what the sentence literally means. I had in mind an alternative mechanism that allows speakers to use a sentence to convey something stronger than what it literally means, thereby creating a mutual misimpression that what is conveyed is precisely what the sentence literally means. There is nothing in the general Gricean strategy (as opposed to the particular strategy involving Grice's first conversational maxim of Quality) that requires ordinary speakers to recognize or believe that the sentence used is literally false. Grice (*op. cit.*) describes several mechanisms that involve speakers' using a sentence mutually believed to be true to convey ("implicate") something further that the sentence does not literally mean, and Schiffer himself cites such a mechanism in the course of presenting his objection. Surely there can be such a mechanism that, when employed, sometimes has the unintended and unnoticed consequence that speakers' mistake what is conveyed ("implicated") for the literal content. Consider, for example, the conjunction 'Jane became pregnant and she got married', which normally carries the implicature that Jane became pregnant before getting married. Utterers of this sentence, in order to employ it with its customary implicature, need not be aware that the sentence is literally true even if Jane became pregnant only after getting married. Some utterers may well become misled by the sentence's customary implicature into believing that the sentence literally means precisely what it normally conveys—so that, if they believe that Mary became pregnant only after getting married, they would reject the true but misleading conjunction as literally false. A similar situation may obtain in connection with certain English indicative conditionals ("If you work hard, you will be rewarded") and universal generalizations ("All white male cats with blue eyes are deaf"), which carry an implicature of some salient connection between antecedent and consequent that is more than merely truth-functional "constant conjunction." (The implicated connection need not be the temporal relation of earlier-later, as in the conjunction case.) It is this general sort of situation, or something very similar, that I impute to propositional-attitude attributions.[11]

Frege's Puzzle makes the suggestion that, in a certain type of case, a simple belief attribution ⌜c believes that S⌝ may be routinely used to convey the further information (not semantically encoded) that (assuming he or she understands his or her sentence for S) x agrees to the proposition p when taking it in the way it is presented to x by the very sentence S, where x is the referent of c and p is the content of the nonindexical sentence S.[12] The book does not include the much stronger claim that the manner in which such a belief attribution is routinely used to convey this further information must exhibit all of the features that characterize Gricean implicature—let alone does it include the highly specific claim that the phenomenon in question is an instance of Gricean particularized conversational implicature.

I have not thoroughly explored the relation of Grice's many rich and fruitful ideas to the sort of project undertaken in *Frege's Puzzle;* obviously, there is a great deal more to be investigated. It should be clear, however, that there is nothing in Grice's general apparatus that makes the sort of explanation I have in mind in connection with propositional-attitude attributions altogether impossible. Quite the contrary, some of the central ideas of the Gricean program are obviously directly applicable.

---

[11] It is doubtful whether the conjunction and conditional cases, and the sort of situation I have in mind in connection with propositional-attitude attributions, qualify as cases of what Grice calls *particularized conversational implicature* (by far the most widely discussed notion of Gricean implicature); in a number of important respects, these cases better fit one or the other of Grice's two contrasting notions of *generalized conversational implicature* and *conventional* (nonconversational) *implicature.* Surely a great many speakers may be confused by the conventional or generalized conversational implicature of a sentence into thinking that the sentence literally says (in part) what it in fact only implicates. Grice's notion of particularized conversational implicature apparently precludes the possibility of this sort of confusion. (See the third essential feature of particularized conversational implicature cited *op. cit.* on p. 169 of Martinich.) In some cases, it may also be possible to cancel explicitly the conventional or generalized conversational implicature of a sentence. I am not suggesting that the case of propositional-attitude attributions is exactly analogous to the conjunction and conditional cases. (The issues here are quite delicate.)

[12] It might be thought that if ordinary speakers take a belief attribution ⌜c believes that S⌝ to express the assertion that x agrees to the proposition p when taking it in the way it is presented to x by the very sentence S, and they use the attribution to convey (or "implicate") precisely this proposition, then this proposition cannot help but *be* (part of) the content of the attribution. The fact that the attribution does not literally mean what it is used to convey is attested to by the validity of the inference from the conjunction 'Floyd claims that Superman is mild-mannered, and Lois believes anything Floyd says concerning Superman' to 'Lois believes that Superman is mild-mannered'. The inference would be invalid if its conclusion literally meant that Lois agrees that Superman is mild-mannered when she takes this proposition in the way it is presented to her by the very sentence 'Superman is mild-mannered'. The premise gives information concerning only what propositions Lois believes, not how she takes them in believing them. (Grice also insists, *op. cit.* p. 69 of Martinich, that the supposition that an erstwhile implicature of a particular construction has become included in the construction's conventional meaning "would require special justification.")

IV

In *Frege's Puzzle* I explicitly applied the various doctrines and these sketched in section I above to Kripke's vexing puzzle about belief.[13] Kripke considers a certain Frenchman, Pierre, who at some time t_1, speaks only French and, on the basis of deceptive travel brochures published by the London Chamber of Commerce and the like, comes to assent to the French sentence '*Londres est jolie*' (as a sentence of French), which literally means in French that London is pretty. At some later time t_2, Pierre moves to London and learns the English language by direct assimilation (not by translation in an ESL course). Seeing only especially unappealing parts of the city, and not recognizing that this city called 'London' is the very same city that he and his fellow French speakers call '*Londres*', Pierre comes to assent to the sentence 'London is not pretty' (as a sentence of English), while maintaining his former attitude toward the French sentence '*Londres est jolie*'. Kripke presses the following question: Does Pierre believe at t_2 that London is pretty? The puzzle arises from Kripke's forceful demonstration that both the assertion that Pierre does believe this, and the denial that he does, appear deeply unsatisfactory (for different reasons). Likewise, both the assertion that Pierre believes at t_2 that London is *not* pretty and the denial that he does appear deeply unsatisfactory.

What does my account say about Pierre's doxastic disposition at t_2 *vis-à-vis* the propositions that London is pretty and that London is not pretty? I maintain that he believes them both. For he understands the French sentence '*Londres est jolie*' when he assents to it, fully grasping its content. That content is the proposition that London is pretty. Since he agrees to this proposition when he takes it in the way it is presented to him by the French sentence, he believes it. Exactly the same thing obtains with regard to the negation of this proposition and the English sentence 'London is not pretty'. Hence he believes this proposition too. In fact, Pierre presumably also assents to the conjunctive sentence '*Londres* is pretty but London is not', as a sentence of Frenglish, i.e., French-cum-English (French-English "word-salad"). And he understands this sentence in Frenglish. Hence he even believes the conjunctive proposition that London is pretty and London is not pretty. If he is sufficiently reflective, he will even know that he believes that London is pretty and London is not pretty. For given adequate time to reflect on the matter he can, with sufficient linguistic competence and ample epistemic justification, assent to the sentence 'You, Pierre, believe that *Londres* is pretty but London is not', taken as addressed to him as a sentence of Frenglish. The tri-part explanation sketched in section II above may easily be extended to account for our propensity to say such thinzgs (in Frenglish) as 'Pierre does not realize that London is *Londres*' despite their falsity.

---

[13] "A Puzzle about Belief," in A. Margalit, ed., *Meaning and Use* (Dordrecht: D. Reidel, 1979), pp. 239–275; also in N. Salmon and S. Soames, eds., *Propositions and Attitudes*. Kripke's puzzle is addressed in appendix A of *Frege's Puzzle*, pp. 129–132.

Kripke objects to the sort of account I offer of Pierre's situation with some trenchant remarks. I quote at length:

> But there seem to be insuperable difficulties with [the position that Pierre believes both that London is pretty and that London is not pretty]. . . . We may suppose that Pierre, in spite of the unfortunate situation in which he now finds himself, is a leading philosopher and logician. He would *never* let contradictory beliefs pass. And surely anyone, leading logician or no, is in principle in a position to notice and correct contradictory beliefs if he has them. Precisely for this reason, we regard individuals who contradict themselves as subject to greater censure than those who merely have false beliefs. But it is clear that Pierre, as long as he is unaware that the cities he calls 'London' and *'Londres'* are one and the same, is in no position to see, by logic alone, that at least one of his beliefs must be false. He lacks information, not logical acumen. He cannot be convicted of inconsistency: to do so is incorrect.
>
> We can shed more light on this if we change the case. Suppose that, in France, Pierre, instead of affirming *"Londres est jolie,"* had affirmed, more cautiously, *"Si New York est jolie, Londres est jolie aussi,"* so that [according to this account] he believed that *if* New York is pretty, so is London. Later Pierre moves to London, learns English as before, and says (in English) "London is not pretty." So he now [allegedly] believes, further, that London is *not* pretty. Now from the two premises, both of which appear to be among his beliefs, (a) if New York is pretty, London is, and (b) London is not pretty, Pierre should be able to deduce by *modus tollens* that New York is not pretty. But no matter how great Pierre's logical acumen may be, *he cannot in fact make any such deduction, as long as he supposes that* 'Londres' *and* 'London' *may name two different cities.* If he *did* draw such a conclusion, he would be guilty of a fallacy.
>
> Intuitively, he may well suspect that New York is pretty, and just this suspicion may lead him to suppose that *'Londres'* and 'London' probably name distinct cities. Yet if we follow our normal practice of reporting the beliefs of French and English speakers, *Pierre has available to him (among his beliefs) both the premises of a modus tollens argument that New York is not pretty.* . . . (pp. 257–258)
>
> . . . Pierre is in no position to draw ordinary logical consequences from the conjoint set of what, when we consider him separately as a speaker of English and as a speaker of French, we would call his beliefs. He cannot infer a contradiction from his separate [alleged] beliefs that London is pretty and that London is not pretty. Nor, in the modified situation above, would Pierre make a normal *modus tollens* inference from his [alleged] beliefs that London is not pretty and that London is pretty if New York is. . . . Indeed, if he *did* draw what would appear to be the normal conclusion in this case. . . . Pierre would in fact be guilty of a logical fallacy. (p. 262)
>
> . . . The situation of the puzzle seems to lead to a breakdown of our normal practices of attributing belief. . . . [The view that Pierre believes both that London is pretty and that London is not pretty] definitely get[s] it *wrong.* [That view] yields the result that Pierre holds inconsistent beliefs, that logic alone should teach him that one of his beliefs is false. Intuitively, this is plainly incorrect. . . . [It is] *obviously wrong* . . . [a] patent falsehood. . . . (pp. 266–267)
>
> . . . when we enter into the area exemplified by . . . . Pierre, we enter into an area where our normal practices of interpretation and attribution of belief are

subjected to the greatest possible strain, perhaps to the point of breakdown. So is the notion of the *content* of someone's assertion, the *proposition* it expresses.

... Pierre's [case] lies in an area where our normal apparatus for the ascription of belief is placed under the greatest strain and may even break down. (pp. 269–270)

These passages indicate (or at least strongly suggest) that Kripke rejects as "plainly incorrect" the view, which I maintain, that Pierre believes at t_2 both that London is pretty and that London is not pretty.[14]

V

Schiffer raises a second objection to the theory advanced in *Frege's Puzzle*—one that is evidently similar in certain respects to Kripke's, but focuses more on the *de re* mode than on the *de dicto*. Schiffer's second criticism concerns such nesting (or second-level) propositional-attitude attributions as

(2) Floyd believes that Lois Lane does not realize that Clark Kent is Superman.

Schiffer tells a little story according to which Floyd is an ordinary speaker who is fully aware that the mild-mannered reporter is none other than the man of steel himself, and who is also aware of Lois Lane's ignorance of this fact. Schiffer argues that, whereas sentence (2) is straightforwardly true in the context of this little story—since Floyd believes that sentence (1) is true (and knows that if (1) is true, then Lois Lane does not realize that Clark Kent is Superman)—I am committed by my adherence to my central thesis (which Schiffer calls 'the 'Fido'–Fido theory of belief') to the falsity of (2), and further by my account of the dispositions of ordinary speakers to utter or to assent to (1), to the erroneous claim that Floyd does not believe that sentence (1) is true, and instead believes it to be false.

We have seen in Section III above that, contrary to Schiffer's interpretation, the explanation I offer for Floyd's propensity to utter (1) does not involve the obviously false claim that Floyd believes (1) to be false. How is it that I am committed to the claim that Floyd does not believe that Lois Lane does not realize that Clark Kent is Superman, and hence to the falsity of (2)? Schiffer argues that I am thus

---

[14] I believe that a careful reading of "A Puzzle about Belief" reveals that Kripke probably ultimately rejects his schematic *disquotation principle* (pp. 248–249). The schema might be rewritten in the form of a single general principle (instead of as a schema), as follows: *If a speaker, on reflection, sincerely assents to a particular sentence S that he fully understands (as a sentence of his language), then he believes the content of S (in his language with respect to his context).* By contrast with Kripke's original principle schema, in this variation the sentence S may contain indexical or pronominal devices, and need not be a sentence of English. Either version, if correct, would entail that, since Pierre is a normal English speaker who fully understands, and on reflection sincerely assents to, the English sentence 'London is not pretty', he believes that London is not pretty, and since Pierre is also a normal Frenglish speaker who fully understands, and on reflection sincerely assents to, '*Londres* is pretty', he also believes that London is pretty. It is this disquotation principle that is "subjected to the greatest possible strain, perhaps to the point of breakdown." In contrast to Kripke's skepticism, I endorse the disquotation principle and its consequences. In fact, the principle is virtually entailed by the first condition on the *BEL* relation given in section I above.

committed by invoking a certain principle that concerns *de re* belief, and which he has elsewhere called 'Frege's Constraint'.[15] Actually, the principle Schiffer explicitly cites is inadequate for his purposes, and should be replaced by a pair of principles which together entail the cited principle. The first might be called 'Frege's Thesis' and may be stated (using Schiffer's theoretical apparatus and terminology) as follows:

> If *x* believes *y* to be *F*, then there is an object *m* that is a mode of presentation of *y* and *x* believes *y* under *m* to be *F*.

The second principle, which I shall call 'Schiffer's Constraint', is the following (again stated using Schiffer's theoretical apparatus and terminology):

> If a fully rational person *x* believes a thing *y* under a mode of presentation *m* to be *F* and also disbelieves *y* under a mode of presentation *m* ⌜to be *F*, then *m* ≠ *m*⌝ and *x* construes *m* and *m'* as (modes of) presenting distinct individuals.

Together these two principles pose a serious obstacle to my taking the position, which seems undeniably correct, that sentence (2) is true. For Floyd, whom we may suppose to be fully rational, no doubt believes that Lois Lane realizes that Superman is Superman. Yet given that Floyd is aware of Superman's secret identity, there do not seem to be the two modes of presentation required by Frege's Thesis and Schiffer's Constraint in order for Floyd to believe furthermore that Lois Lane does not realize that Clark Kent is Superman.

VI

Let us consider first Kripke's argument against the view that Pierre believes at t_2 both that London is pretty and that it is not. I briefly addressed Kripke's objection in *Frege's Puzzle*. I shall elaborate here on certain aspects of my reply.[16]

Kripke's primary critical argument might be stated in full thus:

> *P1.* Pierre sees, by logic alone, that the propositions (beliefs) that London is pretty and that London is not pretty are contradictory.
>
> *P2.* If Pierre has the beliefs that London is pretty and that London is not pretty, then he is in principle in a position to notice that he has these beliefs.

Therefore,

> *C1.* If Pierre has the beliefs that London is pretty and that London is not pretty, then he is in principle in a position to see both that he has these beliefs and that they are contradictory.

---

[15] "The Basis of Reference," *Erkenntnis* 13 (July 1978), pp. 171–206, at p. 180.

[16] I treat logical attributes (such as the relation of deductive entailment and the property of contradictoriness) here as attributes of propositions, setting aside for the present purpose my contention that these attributes are primarily and in the first instance attributes of sentences in a language, and that whereas it is not incorrect, it can be quite misleading to treat them also as attributes of propositions.

P3. But Pierre, as long as he is unaware that the cities he calls 'London' and *'Londres'* are one and the same, is in no position to see that the propositions (beliefs) that London is pretty and that London is not pretty are simultaneously beliefs of his and contradictory, and hence is in no position to see that at least one of his beliefs must be false.

Therefore,

C2. As long as Pierre is unaware that the cities he calls 'London' and *'Londres'* are one and the same, it is incorrect to say that he has the beliefs that London is pretty and that London is not pretty.

An exactly similar argument may be stated, as Kripke proposes, replacing the belief that London is pretty with the more cautious belief that London is pretty if New York is, and replacing the logical attribute of contradictoriness with that of entailing that New York is not pretty. Furthermore, in this case we may replace the epistemic state of being in a position to see that at least one of the first pair of beliefs must be false with the disposition of being such that one would be logically justified in inferring that New York is not pretty from the second, more cautious pair of beliefs.

Both the displayed argument and the one obtained by making the suggested substitutions are extremely compelling. But they are fallacious. I do not mean by this that they proceed from false premises. I mean that they are invalid: the premises are all true, but one of the critical inferences is fallacious. Which one?

The fallacy involved may be seen more clearly if we first consider the following simpler and more direct argument:

If Pierre has the beliefs that London is pretty if New York is and that London is not pretty, then (assuming that he consciously considers the further question of whether New York is pretty, that he fully realizes that the proposition that New York is not pretty is a trivial and immediate deductive consequence of the propositions that London is pretty if New York is and that London is not pretty, that he has no independent reasons for withholding belief from the proposition that New York is not pretty, and that he has adequate time for reflection on the matter) he will come to believe that New York is not pretty on the basis of these beliefs, and he would be logically justified in doing so. But Pierre, as long as he is unaware that the cities he calls 'London' and *'Londres'* are one and the same, will not come to believe that New York is not pretty on the basis of his beliefs that London is pretty if New York is and that London is not pretty, and he would not be logically justified in doing so. Therefore, as long as Pierre is unaware that the cities he calls 'London' and *'Londres'* are one and the same, it is incorrect to say that he has the beliefs that London is pretty if New York is and that London is not pretty.

This argument is evidently at least very much like one of Kripke's, and it is valid. I have formulated it in such a way as to make obvious its reliance, in its first premise, on the belief closure and justification principles. (Let p be the conjunctive proposition that whereas London is pretty if New York is, London is not pretty, and let q be the entailed proposition that New York is not pretty.) I maintain that Pierre's inability to infer that New York is not pretty presents a bona fide counter-example to these principles, so that the first premise of this argument is false. The theses advanced in *Frege's Puzzle* show how Pierre's case may be seen as presenting a counter-example. Pierre fully understands the English sentence 'London is not pretty' and also the Frenglish sentence '*Londres* is pretty if New York is', grasping their content. In particular, he understands the Frenglish sentence to mean precisely what it does mean (in Frenglish): that London is pretty if New York is. (He does not misunderstand it to mean, for example, that *Rome* is pretty if New York is. If any French speaker who has never been to London can nevertheless understand French sentences containing the French name '*Londres*', Pierre understands the particular sentence '*Si* New York *est jolie, Londres est jolie aussi*' as well as its Frenglish translations.) When these sentences are put to him, he unhesitatingly assents; he agrees to the propositions that are their contents when he takes these propositions in the way they are presented to him by these very sentences. Hence he believes these propositions.

Pierre also fully understands the English sentence 'London is pretty if New York is', grasping its content. He is fully aware that the proposition so expressed, taken together with the proposition expressed by 'London is not pretty', collectively entail that New York is not pretty. Unfortunately for Pierre, he does not take this conditional proposition the same way when it is presented to him by the different sentences. He mistakes the proposition for two, logically independent propositions—just as he mistakes London itself for two separate cities. This is evidenced by the fact that he harbors conflicting doxastic attitudes toward the proposition. He believes it, since he agrees to it taking it one way (the way it is presented to him by the Frenglish sentence, or by its French translation), but he also withholds belief from it, in the sense specified in section I above, since he does not agree to it taking it the other way (the way it is presented to him by the English sentence). It is this confusion of Pierre's—his lack of recognition of the same proposition when it is presented to him differently—that prevents Pierre from making the logical connection between his two beliefs and drawing the *modus tollens* inference. He fails to recognize that his belief that London is not pretty is the negation of the consequent of his belief that London is pretty if New York is.

It is precisely Pierre's sort of situation, in which there is propositional recognition failure, that gives rise to counter-examples to the belief closure and justification principles. The principles can, of course, be weakened to rescue them from vulnerability to this sort of counter-example. One way to do this is to adjoin a further initial-condition supposition: that x recognizes that q is a deductive consequence of his or her belief of p. That is, we must be given not only that x recognizes both that he or she believes p and that p entails q, but furthermore that x also recognizes that p is both a belief of his or hers and entailing of q. Since he is a logician, Pierre knows that the compound proposition that *whereas London is pretty if New York is, London is not pretty* entails that New York is not pretty, and he also knows (taking this proposition in a different way) that this proposition is something he believes, but since he fails to recognize this proposition when taking it differently, he does not recognize that this proposition is *simultaneously* something that entails that New York is not pretty and something he believes.[17]

One might be tempted to defend these disputed instances of the belief closure and justification principles by arguing that if a normal, fully rational agent x knows both that a particular proposition p is something he or she believes and furthermore that p deductively entails another proposition q, then x can easily infer that p is simultaneously both something he or she believes and something that deductively entails q. Since the former conditions are already included as initial-condition suppositions in the belief closure and justification principles, the new initial-condition supposition would be entirely superfluous.

This purported defense of the belief closure and justification principles does not succeed. Notice how it is supposed to go. We might begin by noting that the argument form ⌜a is F and a is G; therefore a is both F and G⌝ is valid, since it is simply a special application of the 'λ'-transformation rule of *abstraction*, which permits the inference from a formula ϕ_a to ⌜$(\lambda_x)[\phi x](a)$⌝, i.e., to ⌜a is an individual such that ϕ_{it}⌝ (where ϕ_a is the result of uniformly substituting free occurrences of a for free occurrences of 'x' in ϕ_x—or for "free" occurrences of the pronoun 'it' in ϕ_{it}). In particular, then, there is a valid argument from 'x believes p, and p deductively entails q' to 'p is something that x believes and that deductively entails q'. We then invoke the belief closure and justification principles to argue that if x believes the conjunctive proposition that he or she believes p and p deductively entails q, then (assuming the rest of the initial conditions obtain) x will infer that

---

[17] Suppose x does not have the belief that p entails q, because (for example) x does not have the concept of logical entailment, but that x believes p and can nevertheless reason perfectly well, etc. Surely in some such cases we should expect that x would still come to believe q on the basis of his or her belief of p, and that x would be justified in doing so. One reformulation of the belief justification principle that seems both invulnerable to the sort of counterexample at issue in Pierre's case and more to the point makes explicit reference to the third relata of the *BEL* relation:

Suppose x is a normal, fully rational agent who fully understands a particular sentence S (as a sentence of x's language) and that $BEL[x, p, f(x, S)]$, where p is the content of S (in x's context). Suppose also that x is consciously interested in the further question of whether q is also the case, taking q the way he or she does when it is presented to x by the particular sentence S' (of x's language). Suppose further that x also fully understands S' (as a sentence of x's language). Suppose finally that S' is uncontroversially a trivial deductive consequence of S (in x's language) by logical form alone (without the help of additional analytical meaning postulates for x's language). Under these circumstances, x would be rationally justified in coming to stand in *BEL* to q and $f(x, S')$ on the basis of his or her standing in *BEL* to p and $f(x, S)$ (and the deductive relationship between S and S'), or alternatively, if for independent reasons x does not stand in *BEL* to q and $f(x, S')$, x would be rationally justified in accordingly ceasing to stand in *BEL* to p and $f(x, S)$.

where f is the function that assigns to an individual speaker and a sentence of his or her idiolect, the corresponding third relatum of the *BEL* relation (e.g., the way the speaker takes the proposition that is the content of the sentence when it is presented to him or her by that very sentence). Cf. note 14 above. I am assuming here that 'London is *Londres*' is not a logically valid sentence of Frenglish (Pierre's language), despite the fact that it is an analytic sentence of Frenglish. Cf. *Frege's Puzzle*, pp. 133–135.

An analogous principle may be given in place of the belief closure principle. These more cautious principles must be weakened even further to accommodate cases in which the function f is not defined, as in Kripke's 'Paderewski' case, *op. cit.*, pp. 265–266.

p is something that he or she believes and that deductively entails *q*, and *x* would be justified in doing so. This would be a *meta-application* of the belief closure and justification principles, an application to beliefs concerning inference and belief formation. But this meta-application of these principles is part of a purported justification of these very principles! The problem with this defense of the two principles is that, like the misguided attempt to defend induction-by-enumeration by citing inductive evidence of its utility, it presupposes precisely the very principles it is aimed at defending, and hence suffers from a vicious circularity. If we let *x* be Pierre, *p* be the conjunctive proposition that whereas London is pretty if New York is, London is not pretty, and *q* be the proposition that New York is not pretty, then the resulting instances of the belief closure and justification principles are precisely special instances whose truth is explicitly denied by the sort of account I advocate.

More generally, the theory advanced in *Frege's Puzzle* distinguishes sharply between a complex sentence ϕ_a and the logically equivalent sentence $\ulcorner (\lambda_x)[\phi x](a) \urcorner$ (or $\ulcorner a$ is such that $\phi_{it} \urcorner$) as regards their proposition content. I have argued elsewhere for this distinction in some detail in connection with sentences ϕ_a that involve multiple occurrences of the name *a*.[18] Thus, for example, Pierre no doubt believes (putting it in Frenglish) that *Londres* is prettier than London, and (according to my view) he thereby believes the proposition (putting it in proper English) that London is prettier than London, but he does not thereby believe the unbelievable proposition that London exceeds itself in pulchritude (that London is something that is prettier than itself). Likewise, Pierre believes the conjunctive proposition that London is pretty and London is not pretty, but he surely does not believe that London has the unusual property of being both pretty and not pretty.

The fallacy in Kripke's argument, as reconstructed above, occurs in the inference from the subsidiary conclusion *C1* and the additional premise *P3* to the final conclusion *C2*. More specifically, the argument would apparently involve an implicit and invalid intervening inference from *C1* to the following:

> *C1'*. If Pierre has the beliefs that London is pretty and that London is not pretty, then he is in principle in a position to see that these propositions (beliefs) are simultaneously beliefs of his and contradictory, and hence in a position to see that at least one of his beliefs must be false.

This intervening subsidiary conclusion *C1'* together with premise *P3* validly yield the desired conclusion *C2*. The implicit inference from *C1* to *C1'* is, in effect, a meta-application of one of the disputed instances of the belief closure and justification principles. Pierre is indeed in a position to know that he believes that London is pretty and that London is not pretty. Being a logician, he certainly knows that the propositions that London is pretty and that London is not pretty are logically incompatible. But he believes these facts about these propositions only when taking one of them in different ways, believing it to be two logically independent propositions, failing to recognize it as a single proposition. He is in no position to see or infer that these two propositions are simultaneously believed by him and contradictory.

---

[18] "Reflexicity," *loc. cit.*

There is a serious residual problem with the account given so far of Pierre's situation. There is an extremely compelling reason to deny that Pierre believes that London is pretty: when the sentence 'London is pretty' is put to him (after t_2), he sincerely dissents from it in good faith, while fully understanding the sentence and grasping its content. The theoretical apparatus of *Frege's Puzzle* makes it possible to dispel at least some of the force of this sort of consideration. Using that apparatus, where '*f*' refers to the function that assigns to a speaker and a sentence of the speaker's idiolect the corresponding third relatum of the *BEL* relation (e.g., the way the speaker would take the content of the sentence were it presented to the speaker at t_2 by that very sentence), we may say that at t_2

>   *BEL*[Pierre, that London is pretty, f(Pierre, '*Londres* is pretty')],

or in Frenglish,

>   *BEL*[Pierre, that *Londres* is pretty, f(Pierre, '*Londres* is pretty')],

whereas we must deny that at t_2

>   *BEL*[Pierre, that London is pretty, f(Pierre, 'London is pretty')].

Pierre believes the proposition that *Londres* is pretty, taking it as presented by those very words, but he also withholds belief from (in fact disbelieves) the proposition that London is pretty, taking it as presented by those very words. Pierre's doxastic disposition towards the proposition depends entirely on how the proposition is presented to him. The reason offered for denying that Pierre believes that London is pretty is a decisive reason for affirming that he disbelieves that London is pretty (and therefore that he withholds belief), but it is highly misleading evidence regarding the separate and independent question of whether he believes that London is pretty.[19]

---

[19] A reply exactly similar to this can be offered to Steven Wagner's central criticism (in "California Semantics Meets the Great Fact," *Notre Dame Journal of Formal Logic*, 27, 3 (July 1986), pp. 430–455) of the theory advanced in *Frege's Puzzle*. Wagner objects (at pp. 435–436) that the theory is incorrect to characterize someone who knows that 'Samuel Clemens' refers (in English) to Samuel Clemens as thereby knowing that 'Samuel Clemens' refers (in English) to Mark Twain, since any rational agent who knows the latter, and the trivial fact that 'Mark Twain' refers (in English) to Mark Twain, is *ipso facto* in a position to infer that 'Mark Twain' and 'Samuel Clemens' are co-referential, and that therefore 'Mark Twain is Samuel Clemens', and all of its Leibniz's-Law consequences, are true. (Wagner, at pp. 445–446, acknowledges the effectiveness of the sort of reply I am offering here, but finds it excessively reminiscent of the Fregean account of propositional-attitude attributions. There is considerable tension, however, between this reaction and some of his remarks on pp. 431–432. Cf. also note 5 above and *Frege's Puzzle*, pp. 2–7, 66–70, and especially pp. 119–126.)

On a related point, I argued in *Frege's Puzzle* (pp. 133–138) that the sentence 'Hesperus, if it exists, is Phosphorus' expresses a truth (in English) that is knowable (by anyone sufficiently *en rapport* with the planet Venus) *a priori*, by logic alone. One may also know, by principles of (English) semantics alone, that *if Hesperus, if it exists, is Phosphorus, then the sentence* 'Hesperus, if it exists, is Phosphorus' *is true (in English)*. But knowing these things does not *ipso facto* place one in a position to infer (and thereby to know by logic and semantics alone) that 'Hesperus, if it exists, is Phosphorus' is true (in English). The inability to draw this *modus ponens* inference (justifiably) is an instance of essentially the same phenomenon as Pierre's inability to draw the *modus tollens* inference.

VII

I turn now to Schiffer's criticism that I am committed to the falsity of the true sentence (2). I fully agree with Schiffer that sentence (2) is straightforwardly true in his little story involving Floyd, as long as Floyd understands sentence (1) when uttering it or assenting to it. In fact, far from being committed to the claim that (2) is false, the theory advanced in *Frege's Puzzle* is in fact committed to precisely the opposite claim that (2) is true! This virtually follows directly from the first condition on the *BEL* relation given in section I above, according to which it is sufficient for the truth of (2) that Floyd should agree to the content of (1) when taking this proposition the way it is presented to him by the very sentence (1).[20] On my view, then, Floyd does believe that Lois Lane does not realize that Clark Kent is Superman. In addition, I also maintain (as Schiffer correctly points out) that Floyd believes that Lois Lane does realize that Clark Kent is Superman—since Floyd believes the proposition that Lois Lane realizes that Superman is Superman, and on my view this just is the proposition that Lois Lane realizes that Clark Kent is Superman. Thus, I maintain that Floyd both believes and disbelieves that Lois Lane realizes that Clark Kent is Superman.

Schiffer has uncovered a very interesting philosophical problem here. Before presenting my solution, I want to emphasize the generality of the problem. The general problem is not one that is peculiar to my own theory of propositional-attitude attributions (contrary to the impression created by Schiffer's presentation of his criticism), but is equally a problem for the orthodox, Fregean theory, and indeed for virtually any theory of propositional-attitude attributions.

Consider an analogous situation involving straightforward (strict) synonyms. Suppose that Sasha learns the words 'ketchup' and 'catsup' not by being taught that they are perfect synonyms, but by actually consuming the condiment and reading the labels on the bottles. Suppose further that, in Sasha's idiosyncratic experience, people typically have the condiment called 'catsup' with their eggs and hash browns at breakfast, whereas they routinely have the condiment called 'ketchup' with their hamburgers at lunch. This naturally leads Sasha to conclude, erroneously, that ketchup and catsup are different condiments, condiments that happen to share a similar taste, color, consistency, and name. He sincerely utters the sentence 'Ketchup is a sandwich condiment; but no one in his right mind would eat a sandwich condiment with eggs at breakfast, so catsup is not a sandwich condiment'. Now, Tyler Burge, who has a considerable knowledge of formal semantics and who is well aware (unlike Sasha) that 'ketchup' and 'catsup' are exact synonyms, would claim that Sasha believes that ketchup is a sandwich condiment but that Sasha does not believe that catsup is, describing his view in

---

[20]In *Frege's Puzzle* I explicitly endorse (at pp. 129–130) Kripke's schematic disquotation principle. (Indeed, as pointed out in note 14 above, the principle is virtually entailed by the first condition on the *BEL* relation.) This disquotation principle (in turn) virtually entails the truth of (2) (in Schiffer's story), assuming Floyd fully understands (1) in assenting to it. Cf. also note 17 above.

exactly so many words.[21] Clearly, Burge believes that Sasha believes that ketchup is a sandwich condiment. (See note 23 below.) When queried, "Does Sasha believe that catsup is a sandwich condiment?", however, Burge sincerely responds "No," while fully understanding the question and grasping its content. Given Burge's mastery of English, there would seem to be every reason to say, therefore, that he also believes that Sasha does not believe that catsup is a sandwich condiment. Yet by an argument exactly analogous to Schiffer's, we are apparently barred, by Frege's Thesis and Schiffer's Constraint, from acknowledging this. For we have granted that Burge believes ketchup to be something Sasha believes is a sandwich condiment. If, while remaining fully rational, Burge also believed catsup (i.e., ketchup) *not* to be something Sasha believes is a sandwich condiment, there would be a violation of the conjunction of Frege's Thesis with Schiffer's Constraint. There are no relevant modes of presenting ketchup that Burge construes as (modes of) presenting different stuff, as are required by Frege's Thesis together with Schiffer's Constraint. The conjunction of Frege's Thesis with Schiffer's Constraint thus apparently prohibits us from acknowledging that Burge does indeed disbelieve what he sincerely claims to disbelieve—that Sasha believes that catsup is a sandwich condiment.

Some philosophers will conclude that, despite his insistence to the contrary, Burge really does not disbelieve that Sasha believes that catsup is a sandwich condiment, and when he protests that he does, he is operating under a misunderstanding of the phrase 'believes that'. What Burge really disbelieves, they claim, is something linguistic, for example that Sasha believes that the sentence 'Catsup is a sandwich condiment' is true in English, or that Sasha satisfies the sentential matrix 'x believes that catsup is a sandwich condiment' in English (i.e., that the open sentence 'x believes that catsup is a sandwich condiment' is true in English when Sasha is assigned as value for the free variable 'x').[22] Yet this seems plainly wrong—and therein lies the problem. Burge correctly understands the sentence 'Sasha believes that catsup is a sandwich condiment'. He understands it to mean (in English) that Sasha believes that catsup, i.e. ketchup, is a sandwich condiment. He knows enough formal semantics to know that the sentence does not mean instead that Sasha believes that the sentence 'Catsup is a sandwich condiment' is true in English, nor that Sasha satisfies the sentential matrix 'x believes that catsup is a sandwich condiment' in English. Burge sincerely dissents from this sentence (as a sentence of English) because of his philosophical views concerning belief (which assimilate the proposition so expressed with the false proposition that Sasha accepts, or would accept, the sentence 'Catsup is a sandwich condiment',

---

[21] See his "Belief and Synonymy," *Journal of Philosophy*, LXXV (March 1978), pp. 119–138.

[22] Cf. the discussion of Mates's famous problem concerning nested propositional-attitude attributions in Alonzo Church, "Intensional Isomorphism and Identity of Belief," in N. Salmon and S. Soames, eds., *Propositions and Attitudes*. Whereas I disagree with Church concerning Burge's beliefs, I fully endorse his argument that the sentences 'Burge disbelieves that Sasha believes catsup is a sandwich condiment' and 'Burge disbelieves that Sasha believes Ketchup is a sandwich condiment' cannot differ in truth value in English if 'ketchup' and 'catsup' are English synonyms.

understood in a certain way). Burge's sincere dissent surely indicates a belief on his part (even if it is confused) that Sasha does not believe that catsup is a sandwich condiment—in addition to his correct belief that Sasha does believe that ketchup is a sandwich condiment, and in addition to his (erroneous) linguistic belief that Sasha fails to satisfy the sentential matrix 'x believes that catsup is a sandwich condiment' in English. The problem is that this apparently conflicts with Frege's Thesis in conjunction with Schiffer's Constraint.

This time the objection is not an objection to my theory of belief attributions in particular. If Schiffer's second criticism of my theory of belief attributions is sound, any reasonable theory of belief attributions, even a Fregean theory, would be required to deny that Burge believes that Sasha does not believe that catsup is a sandwich condiment.[23] Yet surely we are not barred by the demands of reasonableness (and consistency) from acknowledging that Burge does indeed disbelieve what he claims to disbelieve. Since it proves too much, there must be something wrong with Schiffer's argument. What?[24]

---

[23]There is one potential difference between this case and that of sentence (2): Burge's belief that Sasha believes that ketchup is a sandwich condiment is very likely based, to some extent, on Sasha's readiness to assent to the sentence 'Ketchup is a sandwich condiment'. But whereas it is clear that Lois Lane fully understands the sentence 'Superman is Superman', and grasps its content, it is arguable that Sasha does not fully understand the sentence 'Ketchup is a sandwich condiment', since he takes it to be compatible with 'Catsup is not a sandwich condiment'. See the final footnote of Saul Kripke's "A Puzzle about Belief," concerning a "deep conceptual confusion" that arises from "misapplication of the disquotational principle" to speakers in situations like Sasha's. Kripke's view is that "although the issues are delicate, there is a case for" rejecting the claim that Burge believes that Sasha believes that ketchup is a sandwich condiment, on the grounds that Burge apparently misapplies the disquotation principle to Sasha's assent to 'Ketchup is a sandwich condiment', thereby betraying a misunderstanding of the term 'believe'. (Kripke adds that he does not believe that his brief discussion of this sort of situation ends the matter.)

Against this, the following should be noted. First, it is by no means obvious that Sasha fails to understand the term 'ketchup'; he has learned the term in much the same way as nearly everyone else who has learned it: by means of a sort of ostensive definition. If Sasha misunderstands the term 'ketchup', why does Lois Lane not similarly misunderstand the name 'Superman'? Second, even if Sasha's understanding of the term 'ketchup' is somehow defective, this does not make any difference to Burge's beliefs concerning Sasha's beliefs. Burge's philosophical views concerning belief allow that Sasha's grasp of the term 'ketchup', imperfect though it may be, is sufficient to enable him to form a belief that ketchup is a sandwich condiment. (See Burge's "Individualism and the Mental," in P. French, T. Uehling, and H. Wettstein, eds., *Midwest Studies in Philosophy IV: Studies in Metaphysics*, (Minneapolis: University of Minnesota Press, 1979), pp. 73–121.) Even if Burge's philosophical views are incorrect, they are views concerning belief. It would be implausible to claim that Burge's views in this connection *must* indicate a misunderstanding of the term 'believe' (as used in standard English), as opposed to advocacy of a somewhat controversial theory concerning (genuine) belief. Last but not least, even if Sasha's understanding of the term 'ketchup' is somehow defective, the claim that Sasha therefore fails to believe that ketchup is a sandwich condiment is fundamentally implausible. Suppose Sasha points to a bottle labeled 'KETCHUP', and sincerely declares, "This stuff here is a sandwich condiment." Does he nevertheless fail to believe that ketchup is a sandwich condiment, simply because he does not realize that 'ketchup' and 'catsup' are synonyms?

[24]The example of Sasha demonstrates that the difficulty involved is more general than it appears, arising not only on my own theory of propositional-attitude attributions but equally on a very wide range of such theories, including various Fregean theories. This feature is not peculiar to Schiffer's criticism. Although I cannot argue the case here, a great many criticisms

It is perhaps natural to point an accusing finger at Schiffer's Constraint. Since this principle (in conjunction with Frege's Thesis) apparently bars us—Fregeans, Russellians, and other theorists alike—from acknowledging what is patently true about Burge's beliefs, it would appear that it must be incorrect.

I was careful in *Frege's Puzzle* to avoid particular commitments concerning the nature of what I call 'proposition guises' or 'ways of taking propositions' or 'means by which one is familiar with a proposition'. However, I am prepared to grant, for present purposes, that *something* along the lines of Frege's Thesis and Schiffer's Constraint is indeed correct.[25] Does this, together with the doctrines and theses I advocate in *Frege's Puzzle,* lead to a commitment to the falsity of (2), as Schiffer argues? If so, then my position is strictly *inconsistent* since I also maintain that (2) is true.

Contra Schiffer, my granting that something along the lines of Frege's Thesis and Schiffer's Constraint is correct does not commit me to the falsity of sentence (2). For illustration, first instantiate the 'x' to Floyd, the 'y' to the fact (or proposition) that Clark Kent is Superman, and the 'F' to the property of *being realized by Lois Lane*. On my theory, the fact (or proposition) that Clark Kent is Superman is just the fact that Superman is Superman. The relevant instances of the two principles entail that, since Floyd both believes and disbelieves this fact to be realized by Lois Lane, if he is fully rational he must grasp this fact by means of two distinct modes of presentation of it, he must take this fact in two different ways. I am happy to say that Floyd does. In fact, my theory more or less requires that he does. Unless Floyd himself believes with me what Schiffer calls 'the 'Fido'–Fido theory of meaning', he may rationally proclaim 'The fact that Superman is Superman is trivial and something that Lois Lane realizes, whereas the fact that Clark Kent is Superman is neither; hence they are distinct facts'. As the discussion in section I made clear, whatever else my notion of a *way of taking* an object is, it is such that if Floyd believes that a proposition p is distinct from a proposition q, then Floyd takes these propositions in different ways (even if $p = q$). If Floyd is sufficiently philosophical, he may mistake the singular proposition about Superman that he is him, when it is presented to him by the sentence 'Clark Kent is Superman', for

---

that have been levelled against the sort of account I advocate—perhaps most—are based on some difficulty or other that is more general in nature than it first appears, and that equally arises on virtually any theory of propositional-attitude attributions in connection with the example of Sasha's understanding of the synonyms 'ketchup' and 'catsup'. The argument given here involving the terms 'ketchup' and 'catsup' is related to Kripke's "proof" of substitutivity using two Hebrew words for Germany, and to his argument involving 'furze' and 'gorse', in the conclusion section of "A Puzzle about Belief." All of these arguments are closely related to Church's famous arguments from translation. (See especially "Intentional Isomorphism and Identity of Belief.") I hope to elaborate on this matter in later work.

[25] For several reasons, I do not accept the letter of Schiffer's Constraint as here formulated, though I do accept its spirit. I believe that Schiffer shares some of my misgivings over the principle, as here formulated. He mentions potential problems arising from the 'F' in the statement of the principle, and the need for "modes of presentation" for properties. A related difficulty is noted below. In addition, I do not accept the Fregean notion of a purely conceptual *mode of presentation* of an entity as an adequate substitute for my notion of a *way of taking* the entity in question. See note 5 above.

some general proposition to the effect that the mild-mannered reporter having such-and-such drab physical appearance is the superhero who wears blue tights, a big 'S' on his chest, and a red cape, etc. Or instead he may mistake the proposition, so presented, for the singular proposition *taken in a certain way*, or what comes to the same thing, the singular proposition together with a certain way of taking it. This is how he takes the singular proposition when it is so presented. The fact that he knows this proposition to be true does not have the consequence that he sees it as the very same thing, in the very same way, as the corresponding thing (general proposition or singular-proposition-taken-in-a-certain-way) that he associates with 'Superman is Superman'.

Consider Frege in place of Floyd. On my view, Frege mistook the singular proposition about the planet Venus that it is it to be two different propositions ("thoughts"). He took this proposition in one way when it was presented to him by the sentence *'Der Morgenstern ist derselbe wie der Morgenstern'* (the German version of 'Morningstar is the same as Morningstar') and in another way when it was presented to him by the sentence *'Der Morgenstern ist derselbe wie der Abendstern'* ('Morningstar is the same as Eveningstar')—despite the fact that he was well aware that the names *'Morgenstern'* and *'Abenstern'* refer to ("mean") the same planet. That he took this proposition in two different ways is established by the fact that he took it to be two different propositions. Floyd is in a similar state with respect to the singular proposition about Superman that he is him—even if Floyd has not formed a specific view about the nature of propositions in general or about the nature of this proposition in particular, as long as he takes this proposition to be two different propositions. Anyone who does not consciously subscribe to the sort of theory advanced in *Frege's Puzzle* is likely to have different perspectives on a given singular proposition of the form x *is* x when it is presented in various ways, seeing it as a different entity each time.[26]

Let us return to Frege's Thesis and Schiffer's Constraint. Suppose instead that the 'y' is instantiated this time to Superman (or to Clark Kent) and the 'F' to the property of *being an individual x such that Lois Lane realizes that x is Superman*, or *being someone that Lois Lane realizes is Superman*. Surely Floyd believes Superman to have this property. (We ask Floyd, "You know that man who calls himself 'Superman'. Does Lois Lane realize that he is Superman?" If Floyd

---

[26]In *Frege's Puzzle* I wrote: "The means by which one is acquainted with a singular proposition includes as a part the means by which one is familiar with the individual constituent(s) of the proposition" (p. 108). Contrary to the interpretation advanced in Schiffer's postscript, I never suggested that the way an agent takes a structured complex object, such as a proposition, is made up *without remainder* of the ways the agent takes the separate constituents of the complex (with these ways-of-taking-objects structured in a similar way). The principal criticism of Schiffer's postscript challenges my contention that Floyd takes the singular proposition (or fact) about Superman that he is him in two different ways. It is difficult to understand, however, why Schiffer—who himself advanced (something along the lines of) Schiffer's Constraint in criticizing the theory of *Frege's Puzzle*—insists, as part of the same criticism, that the fact that a fully rational agent believes that whereas p is trivial, q is not, does not yield an adequate reason to conclude that this agent takes p and q in different ways (by means of different "modes of presentation").

REFERENCES

J. Almog, "Form and Content," *Noûs*, 19, 4 (December 1985):603–616.

T. Burge, "Belief and Synonymy," *Journal of Philosophy*, LXXV (March 1978):119–138.

T. Burge, "Individualism and the Mental," in P. French, T. Uehling, and H. Wettstein, eds., *Midwest Studies in Philosophy IV: Studies in Metaphysics* (Minneapolis: University Of Minnesota Press, 1979):73–122.

J. Barwise and J. Perry, "Shifting Situations and Shaken Attitudes," *Linguistics and Philosophy*, 8 (1985): 105–161.

A. J. Chien, "Demonstratives and Belief States," *Philosophical Studies*, 47 (1985): 271–289.

R. M. Chisholm, *The First Person* (Minneapolis: University of Minnesota Press, 1981).

A. Church, "Intensional Isomorphism and Identity of Belief," *Philosophical Studies* (1954):65–73; also in N. Salmon and S. Soames, 1988.

A. Church, "A Remark Concerning Quine's Paradox about Modality," in N. Salmon and S. Soames, 1988.

M. J. Cresswell, *Structured Meanings: The Semantics of Propositional Attitudes* (Cambridge, Mass.: Bradford Books/The MIT Press, 1985).

K. Donnellan, "Proper Names and Identifying Descriptions," in D. Davidson and g. Harman, eds., *Semantics of Natural Language* (Dordrecht: D. Reidel, 1972):356–379.

K. Donnellan, "Speaking of Nothing," *The Philosophical Review*, 83 (January 1974): 3–31; also in Schwartz, 1977, pp. 216–244.

G. Evans, "Pronouns, Quantifiers and Relative Clauses (I)," in M. Platts, ed., *Reference, Truth and Reality* (London: Routledge and Kegan Paul, 1980): 255–317.

G. Frege, *"Über Sinn und Bedeutung,"* *Zeitschrift für Philosophie und Philosophische Kritik*, 100 (1893): 25–50; in English in Frege, 1984, pp. 157–177; also in *Translations from the Philosophical Writings of Gottlob Frege*, translated by P. Geach and M. Black (Oxford: Basil Blackwell, 1952):56–78.

G. Frege, *"Der Gedanke,"* in English in Frege, 1984, pp. 351–372; also in Frege, 1977, pp. 1–30; also in N. Salmon and S. Soames, 1988.

G. Frege, *Logical Investigations* (New Haven: Yale University Press, 1977).

G. Frege, *Collected Papers on Mathematics, Logic, and Philosophy*, B. McGuinness, ed., translated by M. Black, V. H. Dudman, P. Geach, H. Kaal, E.-H. W. Kluge, B. McGuinness, and R. H. Stoothoff (Oxford: Basil Blackwell, 1984).

G. Frege, *Philosophical and Mathematical Correspondence*, G. Gabriel, H. Hermes, F. Kambartel, C. Thiel, and A. Veraart, eds., abridged by B. McGuinness, translated by H. Kaal (University of Chicago Press, 1980); excerpts in N. Salmon and S. Soames, 1988.

P. French, T. Uehling, and H. Wettstein, eds., *Contemporary Perspectives in the Philosophy of Language* (Minneapolis: University of Minnesota Press, 1979).

P. T. Geach, *Reference and Generality* (Ithaca: Cornell University Press, 1962).

P. T. Geach, "Logical Procedures and the Identity of Expressions," in Geach, *Logic Matters* (University of California Press, 1972):108–115.

H. P. Grice, "Logic and Conversation," in P. Cole and J. L. Morgan, eds., *Syntax and Semantics*, volume 3 (New York: Academic Press, 1975):41–55; also in D. Davidson and G. Harman, eds., *The Logic of Grammar* (Encino: Dickenson, 1975): 64–75; also in A. P. Martinich, ed., *The Philosophy of Language* (Oxford University Press, 1985): 159–170.

L. R. Horn, "Metalinguistic Negation and Pragmatic Ambiguity," *Language*, 61, 1 (1985):121–174.

D. Kaplan, "On the Logic of Demonstratives," in French et al. 1979, pp. 401–412; also in N. Salmon and S. Soames, 1988.

D. Kaplan, "Demonstratives," in J. Almog, J. Perry, and H. Wettstein, eds., *Themes from Kaplan* (Oxford University Press, forthcoming).

D. Kaplan, "Opacity," in L. E. Hahn and P. A. Schilpp, eds., *The Philosophy of W. V. Quine* (La Salle: Open Court, 1986):229–288.

S. Kripke, "Identity and Necessity," in M. Munitz, ed., *Identity and Individuation* (New York: New York University Press, 1971):135–164; also in Schwartz, 1977, pp. 66–101.

S. Kripke, *Naming and Necessity* (Harvard University Press and Basil Blackwell, 1972, 1980); also in D. Davidson and G. Harman, eds., *Semantics of Natural Language* (Dordrecht: D. Reidel, 1972):253–355, 763–769.

S. Kripke, "A Puzzle about Belief," in A. Margalit, ed. *Meaning and Use* (Dordrecht: D. Reidel, 1979): 239–275; also in N. Salmon and S. Soames, 1988.

D. Lewis, "Attitudes *De Dicto* and *De Se,*" *The Philosophical Review,* 88 (1979): 513–543.

D. Lewis, "What Puzzling Pierre Does Not Believe," *Australasian Journal of Philosophy,* 59, 3(1981):283–289.

L. Linsky, *Oblique Contexts* (Chicago: University of Chicago Press, 1983).

B. Loar, "Names in Thought," *Philosophical Studies,* 51 (1987): 169–185.

R. B. Marcus, "A Proposed Solution to a Puzzle about Belief," in P. French, T. Uehling, and H. Wettstein, eds., *Midwest Studies in Philosophy VI: The Foundations of Analytic Philosophy* (Minneapolis: University of Minnesota Press, 1981):501–510.

R. B. Marcus, "Rationality and Believing the Impossible," *Journal of Philosophy,* 80, 6 (June 1983): 321–338.

T. McKay, "On Proper Names in Belief Ascriptions," *Philosophical Studies,* 39 (1981): 287–303.

J. Perry, "Frege on Demonstratives," *The Philosophical Review,* 86 (1977): 474–497.

J. Perry, "The Problem of the Essential Indexical," *Noûs,* 13 (1979): 3–21; also in N. Salmon and S. Soames, 1988.

J. Perry, "Belief and Acceptance," in P. French, T. Uehling, and H. Wettstein, eds., *Midwest Studies in Philosophy V: Studies in Epistemology* (Minneapolis: University of Minnesota Press, 1980):533–542.

J. Perry, "A Problem about Continued Belief," *Pacific Philosophical Quarterly,* 61 (1980):317–332.

H. Putnam, "Synonymy, and the Analysis of Belief Sentences," *Analysis,* 14, 5 (April 1954): 114–122; also in N. Salmon and S. Soames, 1988.

H. Putnam, "Meaning and Reference," *The Journal of Philosophy,* 70, (November 8, 1973):699–711; also in Schwartz, 1977, pp. 119–132.

H. Putnam, "The Meaning of 'Meaning'," in K. Gunderson, ed. *Minnesota Studies in the Philosophy of Science VII: Language, Mind, and Knowledge* (Minneapolis: University of Minnesota Press, 1975); also in Putnam's *Philosophical Papers II: Mind, Language, and Reality* (Cambridge University Press, 1975), pp. 215–271.

W. V. O. Quine, "Reference and Modality," in Quine, *From a Logical Point of View,* (New York: Harper and Row, 1953):139–159.

W. V. O. Quine, "Quantifiers and Propositional Attitudes," *Journal of Philosophy,* 53, 5 (March 1, 1956): 177–187; also in Quine's *The Ways of Paradox* (New York: Random House, 1966):183–194.

M. Richard, "Direct Reference and Ascriptions of Belief," *Journal of Philosophical Logic*, 12 (1983): 425–452; also in N. Salmon and S. Soames, 1988.

M. Richard, "Attitude Ascriptions, Semantic Theory, and Pragmatic Evidence," *Proceedings of the Aristotelian Society*, 1, 87 (1986/1987):243–262.

B. Russell, "On Denoting," *Mind*, 14 (October 1905): 479–493; also in Russell, 1956, pp. 41–56.

B. Russell, "Knowledge by Acquaintance and Knowledge by Description," chapter X of Russell's *Mysticism and Logic and Other Essays* (London: Longman, Green and Company, 1911):209–232; also in N. Salmon and S. Soames, 1988.

B. Russell, "The Philosophy of Logical Atomism," in Russell, 1956, pp. 177–281.

B. Russell, *Logic and Knowledge*, R. C. Marsh, ed. (London: George Allen and Unwin, 1956).

N. Salmon, *Reference and Essence* (Princeton University Press and Basil Blackwell, 1981).

N. Salmon, *Frege's Puzzle* (Cambridge, Mass.: Bradford Books/The MIT Press, 1986).

N. Salmon, "Reflexivity," *Notre Dame Journal of Formal Logic*, 27, 3 (July 1986): 401–429; also in N. Salmon and S. Soames, 1988.

N. Salmon and S. Soames, eds., *Propositions and Attitudes* (Oxford University Press, Readings in Philosophy, 1988).

S. Schiffer, "Naming and Knowing," in P. French, T. Uehling, and H. Wettstein, eds., 1979, pp. 61–74.

S. Schiffer, "The Basis of Reference," *Erkenntnis*, 13 (1978):171–206.

S. Schiffer, "Indexicals and the Theory of Reference," *Synthese*, 49 (1981):43–100.

S. Schiffer, "The Real Trouble with Propositions," in R. J. Bogdan, *Belief: Form, Content, and Function* (Oxford University Press, 1986): 83–118.

S. Schiffer, "The 'Fido'-Fido Theory of Belief," in J. Tomberlin, ed., *Philosophical Perspectives 1: Metaphysics* (Atascadero: Ridgeview, 1987):455–480.

S. Schwartz, *Naming, Necessity, and Natural Kinds* (Cornell University Press, 1977).

S. Soames, "Lost Innocence," *Linguistics and Philosophy*, 8 (1985):59–71.

S. Soames, "Direct Reference, Propositional Attitudes and Semantic Content," in N. Salmon and S. Soames, 1988.

S. Wagner, "California Semantics Meets the Great Fact," *Notre Dame Journal of Formal Logic*, 27, 3 (July 1986):430–455.

D. Wiggins, "Identity, Necessity and Physicalism," in S. Korner, ed. *Philosophy of Logic* (University of California Press, 1976):96–132, 159–182.

D. Wiggins, "Frege's Problem of the Morning Star and the Evening Star," in M. Schirn, ed. *Studies on Frege II: Logic and the Philosophy of Language* (Stuttgart: Bad Canstatt, 1976):221–255.

SUBSTITUTION AND SIMPLE SENTENCES

Jennifer M. Saul

A great deal of attention has been devoted to propositional attitude contexts. Why? A key reason is that the substitution of co-referential names in otherwise identical sentences which ascribe propositional attitudes does not seem to preserve truth conditions. Little attention, however, has been paid to substitution of co-referential names in sentences which do not report propositional attitudes. Why? Because such substitutions are taken to be unproblematic. I will argue, however, that this is not right. There are simple sentences[1] which evoke anti-substitution intuitions quite similar to those evoked by attitude-reporting sentences.

Imagine that (1) is a truthful description of what happened on a Metropolis street:

(1) Clark Kent went into the phone booth, and Superman came out.

Substitution of co-referential names yields (1*), which seems false:

(1*) Clark Kent went into the phone booth, and Clark Kent came out.

What is going on? There is no propositional attitude verb in (1). There is not even a psychological verb of any kind. 'Go' is simply not the sort of verb that we expect to be involved in substitution failures. And yet it is. Here are some more examples of the same phenomenon:

(2) Clark Kent always arrived at the scene just after one of Superman's daring rescues.

(2*) Superman always arrived at the scene just after one of Clark Kent's daring rescues.

(3) Dan dresses like Clark Kent.

(3*) Dan dresses like Superman.

(4) She made a date with Superman, but found herself having dinner with Clark Kent.

(4*) She made a date with Superman, but found herself having dinner with Superman.

(5) Clark was in despair because Lois had fallen for Superman.[2]

(5*) Superman was in despair because Lois had fallen for Superman.

Existing accounts dictate that substitution of co-referential names preserves truth conditions in the above sentences. Why? Because existing accounts have not been concerned with simple sentences. It is only in attitude (or modal or quotational) contexts, according to these accounts, that something other than the reference of a name may be relevant to truth conditions.[3] The sentences above involve no such contexts.

---

[1] I will use 'simple sentences' to refer to sentences which contain no attitude, modal, or quotational constructions.

[2] This sentence is based on the following sentences at a (now sadly defunct) Lois and Clark Web Site: '. . . Lois fell for Superman. This sent Clark into a pit of despair because he had fallen head over heels for Lois the moment he met her.'

[3] This is true both of standard Fregean accounts and of more recent accounts invoking contextual variation. On the latter sort of account, the contextual variation is introduced by the presence of the attitude verb.

Another twist on this problem comes with consideration of sentences like (6) and (6*).[4]

(6) Superman was more successful with women than Clark Kent.

(6*) Superman was more successful with women than Superman.

If co-referential names must make the same contribution to the truth conditions of simple sentences, then it seems (6) and (6*) must have the same truth conditions. Since (6*) can't be true, (6) can't either.

And there are many pairs of sentences like this:

(7) Batman is more resistant to bullets than Bruce Wayne.[5]

(7*) Batman is more resistant to bullets than Batman.

(8) Lois kissed Superman before she kissed Clark Kent.

(8*) Lois kissed Superman before she kissed Superman.

(9) I never made it to Leningrad, but I visited St. Petersburg last week.

(9*) I never made it to Leningrad, but I visited Leningrad last week.

We can even generate a problem case with everyone's favourite extensional verb, 'hit':

(10) He hit Clark Kent once, but he never hit Superman.

(10*) He hit Clark Kent once, but he never hit Clark Kent.

The first question it makes sense to ask about these cases and the earlier ones is whether a Fregean account could be adapted in such a way as to accommodate them. It doesn't seem that it could. The Fregean response to attitude sentences is to take terms within belief clauses to refer to their customary senses. This allows a difference in truth conditions due to substitution of co-referential terms in such positions. The analogous solution to the problem posed here would be to allow terms in some simple sentences to refer to their customary senses. But the result of allowing 'Superman' and 'Clark Kent' to refer to their senses in the above sentences is nonsense. A sense cannot be successful with women. Parallel problems will arise for the candidates provided by other accounts, such as representations, words, or notions. Quotational solutions will also be unhelpful, since (6′) and (6″) are just as problematic as (6) and (6*):

(6′) The man called 'Superman' is more successful with women than the man called 'Clark Kent'.

(6″) The man called 'Superman' is more successful with women than the man called 'Superman'.

Perhaps we can arrive at a somewhat different account which will do the needed work. This might have the unfortunate consequence that cases like these receive an explanation different from that offered for attitude-reporting cases, but

---

[4] Chris Hookway called examples of this sort to my attention.

[5] The Bat-suit provides a kind of armour.

at least they would receive an explanation.[6] So what do we need? Well, if sentences like (6) are to have any chance of being true, 'Clark Kent' and 'Superman' must not co-refer. A natural way to accomplish this is via a semantics which makes use of temporal phases.[7] This is very appealing for sentences like (9). It seems reasonable to suppose that 'Leningrad' refers to one temporal phase of the city in Russia, while 'St. Petersburg' refers to another. If this is right, then (9) can be true. It's a little harder, of course, to make sense of 'Clark Kent' and 'Superman' picking out temporal phases, simply because there's more switching back and forth. There are also unclear cases: Which is he when he's in the shower? But these difficulties don't seem insurmountable.

The real problem with the temporal phase idea is that certain claims which seem clearly and importantly (at least to the philosophy of language) true must be ruled false:

> (11) Superman is Clark Kent.

'Superman' picks out one temporal phase, and 'Clark' picks out another. Since these temporal phases are distinct, (11) is false.

This is clearly not an acceptable result. One way of avoiding it is to say that, in (11), 'Superman' and 'Clark Kent' refer to individuals rather than temporal phases of individuals. But since we are already saying that in (6) they refer to temporal phases of individuals, we are forced to maintain that the reference of a name may vary with context, even when it is not embedded in an attitude construction. This means either that names will require a semantics akin to that for indexicals, or that they are ambiguous in a rather surprising way.[8]

There is an apparent alternative to finding a contextual variation in ambiguity in the semantics of names. This is to find an ambiguity in claims of identity, while upholding the simple temporal phase view.[9] We could take 'is' in (11) to mean 'is a stage of the same individual as', or 'occupies the same body as'. Either of these would of course yield the desired verdict for (11). Another use of 'is' might mean 'is the same temporal stage as'. Yet another might mean simply 'is identical with'. The appeal of this approach is that it minimizes the need for ambiguity claims. If we can accommodate our intuitions by postulating an ambiguity for a single verb, why should we postulate an ambiguity or context-dependence for all names?

---

[6] Alternatively, one could attempt to develop an account of attitude-reporting sentences based on the account of these cases.

[7] Ted Sider (1996) has, for unrelated reasons, recently defended a view according to which names refer to temporal stages.

[8] There is at least one possible precursor to the ambiguity view to be found in David Wiggins's discussion of 'Cleopatra's Needle'. He considers the idea of explaining an apparent example of relative identity as due to the ambiguity of the name 'Cleopatra's Needle'. On one reading, the name picks out a block of stone; on the other, a landmark. See Wiggins (1980: 34). Many others have defended the view that common names such as 'John' exhibit either ambiguity or context-dependence. This sort of variation is of a less surprising kind than that considered above.

[9] Stephen Makin suggested this idea.

The problem with this approach is that it is inadequate.[10] It deals only with sentences employing 'is', and there are other sorts of sentences which pose problems for the temporal stage view. Consider sentence (12), which seems true:

(12) Clark Kent can fly, though he conceals this fact.

On the simple temporal stage view, the temporal stages picked out by 'Clark Kent' are not ones that can fly. So (12) will be false. Further, no appeal to the tricky semantics of 'is' can help here.

The ambiguity and contextual variation views, on the other hand, can handle cases like (12). On such views, 'Clark Kent' needn't pick out a temporal stage in (12), even though it may do so elsewhere. Instead, it may pick out an individual, thereby allowing (12) to be true. We see now that if we are to uphold our intuitions about simple sentences, we will need to find a way to allow for substantial contextual flexibility. The context-dependent semantics or ambiguity claims that would be needed, however, will be undesirable to many.

An alternative way to handle contextual variation, of course, is via pragmatics. On this approach, we bite the bullet offered by standard theories. We maintain that substitution of co-referential names in simple sentences *cannot* alter truth conditions. If (1) is true, then (1*) is as well. Pragmatics, however, offers us a way to accommodate those intuitions which conflict with this. We accompany our favourite standard semantic account with the explanatory claim that such truth-preserving substitutions may well yield sentences which are quite misleading, due to false pragmatic implicatures. Despite its truth, we would be very unlikely to utter (1*) as a description of what occurred on that Metropolis street, because it will very likely convey something false. Evidence for this view comes from the fact that our anti-substitution intuitions appear to be cancellable, suggesting that they in fact result from pragmatic implicatures.[11] Consider sentences (1*) and (1**). Although (1*) seems false, (1**) seems true:

(1*) Clark Kent went into the phone booth, and Clark Kent came out.

(1**) Clark Kent went into the phone booth, and Clark Kent came out, but nobody recognized him.

Some of the cases discussed earlier may seem to pose extra problems for those who want to maintain that our anti-substitution intuitions are fuelled by pragmatics. They will need to offer a pragmatic explanation not just for the apparent falsity of sentences like (1*), but also for the apparent truth of sentences like (6), whose truth (on standard accounts) would guarantee that of (6*):

(6) Superman was more successful with women than Clark Kent.

(6*) Superman was more successful with women than Superman.

---

[10] It also, of course, makes some rather surprising claims about what we mean by 'is'.

[11] Apparent cancellability, of course, is not conclusive evidence of pragmatic implicatures. In fact, ambiguous or context-dependent terms may result in phenomena which very closely cancellation of implicatures. (For a discussion of this, see for example Crimmins (1992: 21–26).

Since (6*) can't be true, neither can (6). The pragmatic theorist must explain why it is that (6) seems true. This will presumably involve the claim that our intuitions about (6) result from a true implicature which it tends to carry. Although this is a complication, it doesn't seem an insuperable one.

The proponent of this response, however, now has a choice. She must decide whether or not to accept a perfectly parallel account of our intuitions about attitude reports, that offered by Salmon and Soames. (See Salmon 1986, for example.) According to them, substitution of co-referential names in attitude reports preserves truth conditions but may result in the generation of new, and misleading, pragmatic implicatures. It is these implicatures which result in our (mistaken) tendency to say that (6) may be true while (6*) is false:

(6) Lois believes that Superman can fly.

(6*) Lois believes that Clark Kent can fly.

This theory is supported by the fact that (6**) seems true, again indicating the cancellability of our intuitions:

(6**) Lois believes that Clark Kent can fly, though she'd never put it that way.

The main argument against Salmon and Soames's theory has been that it requires the violation of our intuitions about substitution. But the current approach to substitution in simple sentences requires what is apparently a perfectly parallel violation of intuitions, accompanied by a perfectly parallel appeal to pragmatics. The advocate of this approach owes us a reason for supposing that one set of intuitions deserves to be taken so much more seriously than the other.[12] Without such a reason, her objection to Salmon and Soames's approach loses much of its force. Alternatively, she may take these cases as evidence for the appropriateness of a pragmatic explanation of all our intuitions regarding substitution. It becomes, then, a reason to subscribe to Salmon and Soames's account.

Here, then, is the situation. We have two alternatives.

I. We can attempt to distinguish the truth conditions of (1) and (1*), and to allow for the truth of (6). We must, however, find a way to do this which allows us to maintain the truth of (11) and (12). This would seem to

---

[12] It is not as easy to provide such a reason as one might suppose. One reason, suggested to me by Scott Soames (on the Fregean's behalf), might be that assertion is an indicator of belief. Since (1) and (1*) express different propositions, for the Fregean, one might well believe what is expressed by (1) but not what is expressed by (1*). So it might be appropriate to utter (1) but not (1*) and one might mistakenly suppose that (1*) is false. But this runs into difficulties when we consider speakers who (like the readers of this paper) are perfectly aware of all the relevant identities. Such speakers will still quite often take (1) and (1*) to differ in truth conditions. This suggests speakers are taking more than the reference of a term to be relevant to the truth conditions of the proposition expressed by a sentence containing it. And this is quite mysterious for the Fregean, who holds that only reference can matter to the truth conditions of a simple sentence. Why should speakers apprised of all the relevant facts ascribe different truth values to (1) and (1*)? Since such speakers are not uncommon, the Fregean is left attempting to explain a systematic and widespread pattern of error.

require a semantics which allows the reference of a name to vary with context. Again, a decision would need to be made about the treatment of attitude sentences. If they are to be handled in a parallel manner, how will this work? If not, why should the cases be treated differently?

II. We can insist that the truth of (1) guarantees the truth of (1*) and that (6) cannot be true. This will require a pragmatic explanation of those intuitions which disagree. We will also need either to accept a similar explanation of intuitions about attitude sentences or to give a principled reason for explaining one set of intuitions via pragmatics and the other via semantics.

The point of this paper has been to undermine the thought that attitude-ascribing sentences are the only ones we should be thinking about if we are concerned with anti-substitution intuitions about names.[13] Other sentences, even ones which involve entirely non-psychological verbs, may provoke the very same sorts of intuitions. Consideration of them poses new problems both for accounts of attitude reporting and for accounts of names in general.[14]

REFERENCES

Crimmins, M. 1992. *Talk about Beliefs*. Cambridge, MA: MIT Press.
Salmon, N. 1986. *Frege's Puzzle*. Cambridge, MA: MIT Press.
Sider, T. 1996. "All the World's a Stage." *Australasian Journal of Philosophy* 74:433–57.
Wiggins, D. 1980. *Sameness and Substance*. Cambridge, MA: Harvard University Press.

---

[13] My focus here has been on examples involving names. It may be worth noting, though, that the same problems can arise with descriptions and demonstratives. Descriptions: 'The man in a suit went into the phone booth, and the man in a cape came out'. Demonstratives (pointing at superhero mug shots): 'That man went into the phone booth, and that man came out'.

[14] I am very grateful to David Braun, Chris Hookway, Stephen Makin, Teresa Robertson, Peter Smith, and Scott Soames for extensive and very helpful discussion of previous drafts of this paper. I am also grateful to Nigel Gibbions and David Harrison for their unique expert knowledge, and to the vast number of people who tolerated my endless questions about their intuitions regarding comic book plots.

HOW MUCH SUBSTITUTIVITY?

Graeme Forbes

In her paper (above, . . .), Jennifer M. Saul presents an ingenious defence of the Salmon/Soames 'naive' semantics for propositional attitude-ascriptions. This semantics permits substitution of co-referential terms in the content-sentences of attitude ascriptions, and explains away intuitions that such substitution is invalid by appeal to pragmatics. Saul's defence of this version of 'direct reference theory' is that substitution appears to fall in a certain range of 'simple' sentences much as it does in attitude ascriptions. However, moves analogous to ones familiar from the attitude case that would establish the genuineness of substitution-failure in simple sentences are plainly implausible. Hence a 'pragmatic' account of the anti-substitution intuitions for simple sentences becomes attractive. Why, then, resist such an account for attitude-ascriptions? Why not explain *all* intuitions of substitution failure uniformly, as being based on confusing what is literally said with what is not said but nevertheless conveyed?

In this note I will argue that there is a broadly Fregean account of substitution-failure in attitude ascriptions which *does* generalize to simple sentences, namely, the one developed in my 1990, 1993, 1996, forthcoming. The account is based on the idea that the mechanism which explains substitution-failure in propositional attitude ascriptions is a hidden version of the one visibly at work in Quine's example 'Giorgione is so-called because of his size' (1961p. 139); here 'Giorgione' refers in the normal way, but substitution alters the reference of the logophor 'so',[1] opening the door to change in truth-value. As a first approximation, then, from the true

(1) Lois has always believed that Superman can fly

we cannot infer that

(2) Lois has always believed that Clark Kent can fly

because in (at least one reading of) (1) there is a suppressed logophor:

(3) Lois has always believed *that Superman can fly*, so-labelled.

This hardly wears its meaning on its sleeve, and what makes the account Fregean is the way it is explained. (3) is interpreted as asserting

(4) The abstract situation of Superman's being able to fly is such that Lois has always believed her *so-labelled way of thinking of it*.

Propositions are understood as ways of thinking of abstract situations, as opposed to truth-values. Abstract situations are complexes of objects and properties, hence 'Superman' in (4) has its standard reference, in accordance with Davidson's 'semantic innocence' constraint.[2] But the same abstract situation can be thought of in different ways. For Lois, the propositions *that Superman can fly* and *that Clark Kent can fly* are two different ways of thinking of the same abstract situation, though, most of the time, she does not realize this. So far as this note is concerned, I shall write simply as if 'so-labelled' means that the words the ascriber

---

[1] A logophor is so-called because it is like an anaphor, except that it refers to its anchoring expression rather than to the latter's reference—'so' refers to 'Giorgione', not Giorgione.

[2] The situations are abstract in the sense of being abstracted from possible worlds: one and the same situation may obtain at some worlds and not at others. All other parameters, e.g., temporal ones where appropriate, are part of an abstract situation. For semantic innocence, see Davidson 1969, p. 172.

uses to specify the belief are the words Lois would herself use to express it (for a less crude account, see, e.g., my 1993). The upshot is that substitution in (1) fails because it changes the reference of the hidden logophor 'so' that is explicit in (4).

This analysis can be straightforwardly extended to what I call 'objectual attitudes', such as 'Lois admires Superman but not Clark', 'Lois saw Superman but not Clark', or

(5) Luthor fears Superman, but not Clark.

Here there is a cognitive attitude towards a material object rather than a proposition, but we can use the same apparatus to provide such statements with readings which resist substitution (see my 1996, §6). As a first step, (5) becomes

(6) Luthor fears Superman, so-labelled, but not Clark, so-labelled.

Again, the meaning is not obvious, but can be explained in terms of ways of thinking, this time of objects rather than abstract situations. For (6) I would offer

(7) Luthor fears Superman under Luthor's so-labelled way of thinking of Superman, but not Clark, under Luthor's so-labelled way of thinking of Clark.

If Luthor is afraid of Superman he must think of him in some way.[3] In fact he has two 'standing' ways of thinking of him, but is in the fearing relation only with respect to one of the two,[4] because the propositional attitudes which underlie his fear involve only the one labelled 'Superman'.[5]

Some of Saul's cases do not directly involve attitudes, but attitudes lurk under the surface, so an implicit 'so-labelled' is still plausible. For example,

(8) Clark Kent can fly, though he conceals this fact.

I suggest that 'conceals this fact' means 'conceals this fact, so-labelled'. 'Conceals' is not an attitude verb, propositional or objectual—concealing is an action. But Clark/Superman's goal in so acting is to prevent people from apprehending the

---

[3] Kripke has shown that 'famous deeds' accounts of ways of thinking of objects associated with proper names are not right, but there are alternatives; see Forbes 1990.

[4] In a regimentation there are at least two ways of accommodating the 'with respect to'. The most obvious is just to add an extra place to the objectual attitude verb 'fears': $fears\,(x, y, z)$, meaning x fears y under mode of presentation z. Probably a better alternative is to treat 'under mode of presentation z' as an operator which governs 'x fears y', subscripting 'z' with 'y'; see Forbes 1996, n. 26, for discussion.

[5] One of Saul's cases, 'Clark was in despair because Lois had fallen for Superman', involves one, perhaps two, objectual attitudes (despair possibly being 0-ary). *Falling for* is an objectual attitude, so 'Superman' cannot be substituted. But Saul holds that 'Clark' cannot be substituted either. However, I doubt if the conventional details of the story can justify this; after all, even when swooping out of the sky, Clark may be thinking 'This is no good, Lois loves only Superman, so-labelled'. Yet this is not to say that the subject-position of an attitude verb is always open to substitution; consider 'Clark often wishes that his clothes were more colourful, but Superman never wishes this'. See my discussion of (9) in the text for how I would explain this example.

fact that he can fly under a way of thinking of that fact which involves their ways of thinking of him labelled 'Clark Kent'. So the labelling of the fact is derivative from the content of ways of thinking of it, and while substitution in (8) does not change the fact, it would invoke a different way of thinking of it. This is the first illustration of how Saul's examples are grist to a Fregean mill.

Saul's most interesting cases are ones that do not seem to have any psychological aspect at all, for example,

(9) Clark went into the phone booth and Superman came out,

where substitution produces the apparently false

(10) Clark went into the phone booth and Clark came out.

But even in these cases it is plausible that failure of substitution is due to hidden logophor. When we deny that (10) follows from (9), this is because we are interpreting (9) as

(11) Clark, so-attired, went into the phone booth, and Superman, so-attired, came out.

Thus this non-psychological case actually *supports* a Fregean approach to attitudes: (11) is invoking *ways of dressing*, which can be related many-one to the clothed person, just as ways of thinking can be related many-one to the object of thought. The first 'so-attired' in (11) means 'attired in the "Clark Kent" way', in which the quotes are obligatory, since we are referring to the style Clark is affecting in situations where others apply 'Clark' to him.

Saul's other examples are amenable to the same kind of treatment. A way of dressing is perhaps a special case of a more general notion of a way of presenting oneself to others. So if we want to accept that Lois kissed Superman before she kissed Clark Kent, we can interpret it as meaning that Lois kissed Superman, so-presented, before she kissed Clark Kent, so-presented, and similarly for Superman's greater success with women than Clark's, for Lois's finding herself having dinner with Clark rather than Superman, and so on.

Saul observes that we can change intuitions about (10) if we put it this way:

(12) Clark went into the phone booth and Clark came out, but nobody recognized him.

Recognition is another objectual attitude, so the second 'Clark' in (12) cannot be substituted ('recognized him' means 'recognized him, so-labelled', where the 'so' refers to the second 'Clark'). So if

(13) Clark, so-attired, went into the phone booth, and Clark, so-attired, came out

gives the literal content of (10), then (10) is not a semantic constituent of (12), for the second 'so-attired' in (13) is not implicit in (12). But this is in line with Lewis's proposed mechanisms in [5] for "score-keeping in a language game": given the choice, we prefer to interpret an utterance of (12) so that it is true, and this requires some minor adjustment of interpretation.

Saul indicates sympathy for the view that the 'but nobody recognized him' clause is the cancellation of an anti-substitution intuition, suggesting that such intuitions "in fact result from pragmatic implicatures." In the same way, granted the acceptability of

(14) Lois has always believed that Clark Kent is Superman, but she wouldn't put it that way

we might conclude that resistance to

(15) Lois has always believed that Clark Kent is Superman

is based merely on its suggesting that she *would* put it that way. But direct reference theory misses a generalization here. If (14) is acceptable, then so is

(16) Oedipus wants to marry his mother, but he wouldn't put it that way.

Surely the 'but'-clauses in all three examples, (12), (14) and (16), are performing the same function. Yet direct reference theorists will not apply the 'literal truth/false implicature' model to (16), since they have no reason to say that 'Oedipus wants to marry his mother' is literally true: 'his mother' is a definite description, not a directly referential term, and so should not be substituted for 'Jocasta'. In (16), the 'but' clause indicates that 'his mother' occurs in a position that is open to substitution (it is *referentially transparent*, in the usual jargon). More carefully: 'his mother' is not substitutable in (16) taken as a whole, since it is within the scope of the logophor 'that way'; however, in any utterance of (16), the 'but' clause is a kind of commentary on what precedes it; what precedes it is understood as a completed assertion, and it is in this assertion that 'his mother' occurs transparently. Moreover, it is difficult to believe that in (12) and (14), the 'but' clause is playing a different role. So a uniform account of these three cases is to be preferred to an account that draws a distinction where there is no evident difference and treats (12) and (14) as involving cancellation of pragmatic implicature. However, on traditional approaches, a single account that encompasses all three examples will not be forthcoming, since the notion of transparent position is usually explained in terms of a limitation on the scope of some opacity-inducing operator that seems to govern the position, and there are no such operators in 'Clark went into the phone booth and Clark came out'. But on my analysis, a transparent position is one that does not fall within the extent of a 'so' or other logophor, and we can say that exactly this is the crucial point about all three of (12), (14) and (16). Considering the subsentence before the 'but'-clause in isolation, and then taking into account the 'but'-clause's commentary on it, we abandon the default interpretation of the initial subsentence that is natural to anyone who knows the story. In its place we impose an interpretation which does not read the relevant term as part of a characterization of manner or mode, be it of presentation or self-presentation.[6]

---

[6] Thanks to Kathrin Koslicki and Nathan Salmon for reaction to an earlier version of this paper.

REFERENCES

Davidson, D. 1969. On saying that. In *Words and Objections: Essays on the Work of W. V. Quine*, eds. D. Davidson and J. Hintikka. Dordrecht: Reidel.

Forbes, G. 1990. The indispensability of *Sinn*. *Philosophical Review* 99:535–63.

Forbes, G. 1993. Reply to Marks. *Philosophical Studies* 69: 281–95.

Forbes, G. 1996. Substitutivity and the coherence of quantifying in. *Philosophical Review* 105:337–72.

Forbes, G. Forthcoming. *Attitude Problems*.

Lewis, D. 1979. Scorekeeping in a language game. *Journal of Philosophical Logic 8*: 339–59.

Quine, W. V. 1961. Reference and Modality. In his *From a Logical Point of View*. New York: Harper and Row.

Saul, J. M. 1997. Substitution and simple sentences. *Analysis* 57:102–108.

REPLY TO FORBES

Jennifer M. Saul

First, a few words of clarification: "Substitution and Simple Sentences" (this issue) was not intended as a defence of the Salmon/Soames view, although it could certainly be used as part of such a defence. (I wouldn't mind giving a defence of the view, but I don't think that the paper does enough to qualify.) My real interest is in the problem it raises, which I think has been neglected in the philosophical literature. So I'm very pleased to see Forbes's reply ("How Much Substitutivity?," . . .), which uses the examples to defend quite a different view, a version of his own neo-Fregean one. Forbes's reply goes much further than I would have thought possible towards making a Fregean view accommodate the cases I discuss. Nonetheless, I think the problems that come with his proposal may outweigh its virtues. These problems serve well to show just how intractable the simple sentence puzzle cases seem to be for those who want to uphold our anti-substitution intuitions. It is quite difficult to extend an account of attitude-reporting sentences in such a way as to cover the problematic simple sentences as well.

In my paper, I was concerned with certain sorts of sentences, not involving attitude-reporting, for which substitution of co-referential names seemed counter-intuitive. Forbes is right that the most interesting of these cases are those with no plausible psychological component whatsoever, such as (1) and (1*):

(1) Clark Kent went into the phone booth, and Superman came out.

(1*) Clark Kent went into the phone booth, and Clark Kent came out.

Forbes's proposal for handling such cases invokes a quasi-Fregean notion of modes of self-presentation, presumably to be understood by analogy with the more standard modes of presentation. For this case, he suggests that we can solve our problems merely by invoking the fairly easily understood notion of ways of dressing (or modes of attire). His analysis of (1) and (1*) are as follows:

(1F) Clark Kent, so-attired, went into the phone booth, and Superman, so-attired, came out.

(1*F) Clark Kent, so-attired, went into the phone booth, and Clark Kent, so-attired, came out.

We are meant to take the first 'so-attired' as referring to the way of dressing that others associate with 'Clark Kent', and so on.

Ways of dressing seem easily enough understood, and this response to the problem appears fairly manageable. The problem, however, comes in with the fact that (as Forbes hints), ways of dressing cannot serve as a general solution. I'll spend a significant bit of time on the problems for modes of attire, since I think the move away from such a straightforward construal of modes of self-presentation is quite problematic. A first difficulty arises from the fact that ways of dressing may change. In fact, this discussion is well-timed, since a decision has evidently been made to change Superman's costume. Suppose that I want to inform someone of this change, after it has been made, but before it's widely known. I utter (2).

(2) Superman has changed his way of dressing, but Clark Kent hasn't.

(2) seems true, but on standard analyses it can't be: There's no psychological or modal verb, and the names are coreferential. (2*), with the same content according to such accounts, makes this clear.

(2*) Superman has changed his way of dressing, but Superman hasn't.

Forbes's modes of attire approach would yield:

(2F) Superman, so-attired, has changed his way of dressing, but Clark Kent, so-attired, hasn't.

(2*F) Superman, so-attired, has changed his way of dressing, but Superman, so-attired, hasn't.

Forbes's account seems to make room for a difference in content between the sentences, but another problem arises: It is quite hard to see how (2F) can be true. If the first 'so-attired' picks out the way of dressing historically associated with Superman, and I manage to refer to Superman at some point when he is dressed that way, then it's not true that he has changed his way of dressing. (I've been talking about Superman at a time that he's wearing the old costume.) If 'so-attired' picks out his new way of dressing, then it's not clear how my audience will understand what I'm saying, since she doesn't know about the change. This begins to show the difficulties for a modes of attire approach, but one might suppose that fancy work with temporal semantics could fix things up. (No matter what, some careful temporal semantics would probably be required for the account, since a key fact about modes of self-presentation is that different ones are adopted at different times.)

The modes of attire approach, however, really shows its limits when we come to cases where modes of attire can't even be invoked. At the risk of lowering the tone of the philosophical literature further than I already have, consider the possibility that (3) is true:

(3) Lois slept with Superman before she slept with Clark Kent.

Again, (3) seems as though it might be true, but standard approaches cannot yield this result. Attempting to make sense of this in terms of modes of attire gives us:

(3F) Lois slept with Superman, so-attired, before she slept with Clark Kent, so-attired.

I don't think we want to be committed to (3F) as an analysis of (3). The situation worsens if we imagine that Lois, due to her long-standing fascination with the Man of Steel, asks Clark to put on a little cape, take off those spectacles, etc. The less prurient might prefer to imagine Clark coming to a fancy-dress party as Superman, surely a possibility (and, it seems, a different one from Superman coming to a fancy-dress party as Superman). The difficulty is clear: There is much more to modes of self-presentation than ways of dressing.

The reason that this is such a concern is that modes of self-presentation are quite a mysterious thing. It is hard enough to makes sense of the standard Fregean or neo-Fregean modes of presentation, or ways of thinking. But at least we can understand that they are meant to be part of Fregean thoughts or propositions. For Forbes, they are psychological entities. It is much harder to see what a mode of self-presentation of the sort required might be, once we have discarded the thought that it is a way of dressing.

The only obvious way in which Clark, after he has taken off his spectacles and put on that cape, is presenting himself in a 'Clark'-like way, is that Lois thinks of him that way. This suggests the idea that a person is presented in a certain way just in case those around him would think of him in that way. But this is not right. For one thing, there may be nobody around. The intuition that (1) might be true while (1*) is false does not depend on the presence of observers.

The next thought is that the mode of self-presentation is dependent on the speaker's psychological state. Clark is presented in a 'Clark'-like just in case the speaker thinks that he is. But any speaker striving for truth and invoking 'Clark'-like modes of self-presentation will think that Clark is presented in a 'Clark'-like way. We can try to get around this: Say that Clark is presented in a 'Clark'-like way just in case the speaker, if she saw him, would think that he is. But we've already seen that appearance may not be the key to how a person is being presented. So what is key? What goes into a mode of self-presentation? We've seen that it can't be dependent on the psychological state of observers in the context, since there may not be any. Is it perhaps dependent on the psychological state of the person presented? But this seems wrong too: Surely Clark, emerging from the phone booth after a daring rescue, might think he is presenting himself as Clark, but have carelessly neglected to remove his cape, and thereby fail to present himself as Clark.[1]

---

[1] Notice also that any solution along these lines will involve uncovering a psychological component to the content of sentences which, prima facie, seem devoid of psychological content.

Another difficulty with modes of self-presentation understood as something other than ways of dressing is that we seem to be required to uncover a good deal of psychological content in claims which, on the face of them, don't involve any. It could be that this is right. But this would be surprising. The thought that the truth value for (1) depends even in part on anyone's psychological state is quite counterintuitive.

There is another move available to Forbes. Modes of self-presentation might well be understood as dependent on tendencies or dispositions to act in certain ways.[2] What distinguishes Clark Kent from Superman, no matter how he may be dressed, is that in times of crisis he'll reach for his notebook or dash for the phone booth, rather than simply flying off to a daring rescue. This is promising. It will make sense of Clark's behaviour with Lois, or at the fancy-dress party, and of how we will talk about that behaviour.

The problem with this approach is that tendencies or dispositions to behaviour, while an improvement, still won't do the needed work. Why? Because sometimes Superman doesn't behave like Superman. An evil genius might rob him of his special powers by way of some kryptonite-like substance, so he's no longer able to fly gallantly off. Or turn him evil, so that he no longer feels the inclination to do so. Despite the absence of Superman-like behaviours, or even dispositions to behave, these still seem like Superman modes of self-presentation. We might try to preserve this way of understanding modes of self-presentation by focusing on other Superman behaviours. But what would they be? Clark, at the fancy-dress party, might well answer to 'Superman' and not to 'Clark'. It's hard to see how we will find behavioural dispositions which can do the needed work of distinguishing modes of self-presentation.

Modes of self-presentation, appealing though they seem, are very hard to understand. They can't be analysed as ways of dressing, ways of thinking of oneself or other, or modes of behaviour. It's very hard, then, to get any kind of grip on what these things are. And yet they are crucial to Forbes's approach to my examples. If modes of self-presentation are needed to make sense of the cases I have suggested, then there is a very big project to be tackled. And this project will also have to involve a more detailed analysis of how and when modes of self-presentation come to be specified by particular claims.

Forbes's account of my cases is promising: It suggests a way that a Fregean might try to extend his account to cover non-attitude sentences. But it also demonstrates that this will not be a small matter. Before such an account can be said to succeed, we need to know a lot more about modes of self-presentation. I am not convinced that they can be explained in a way that will do the needed work. I am also not convinced that the benefit of accommodating our anti-substitution intuitions about these examples outweighs the theoretical difficulties that come with modes of self-presentation. The main thing I hope to have shown here is that it is still far from obvious how an account of attitude-reporting sentences might be extended to cover simple sentences as well.[3]

---

[2] Chris Hookway suggested this approach.

[3] I am grateful to Nick Clarke, Graeme Forbes, Chris Hookway, Ray de Rainville, Paul Sludds, and Peter Smith for comments, advice, and help in developing the examples used in this reply.

CREDITS

2: Ben Caplan, "On Sense and Direct Reference" from *Philosophy Compass* 1 (March 2006). Reprinted with the permission of the author and Blackwell.

84: Saul Kripke, "Identity and Necessity" from Milton K. Munitz, ed., *Identity and Individuation* (New York: NYU Press, 1971). Reprinted with the permission of the author.

107: Keith Donnellan, "Proper Names and Identifying Descriptions" from *Semantics of Proper Names,* edited by Matthew Davidson and Gilbert Harman (Dordrecht: Reidel Publishing Company, 1972), pp. 356–379. Reprinted with the permission of the author and Springer.

125: Michael Devitt, excerpt from *Designation.* Copyright © 1981 by Columbia University Press. Reprinted with the permission of the publisher.

126: Hilary Putnam, "The Meaning of 'Meaning'" in *Mind, Language, and Reality: Philosophical Papers, Volume 2.* Copyright © 1975 by Cambridge University Press. Reprinted with the permission of Cambridge University Press.

180: Mark Richard, "Taking the Fregean Seriously" in *Philosophical Analysis: A Defense by Example*, edited by David Austin (Boston, Kluwer, 1988), pp. 219–239. Reprinted with the permission of the author and Springer.

198: Nathan Salmon, "A Millian Heir Rejects the Wages of Sinn" from C. Anthony Anderson and Joseph Owens, eds., *Propositional Attitudes: The Role of Content in Logic, Language, and Mind* (Palo Alto: Center for the Study of Language and Information, 1990), pp. 215–247. Reprinted with the permission of the author.

236: David Kaplan, "Bob and Carol and Ted and Alice," in *Approaches to Natural Language*, by J. Hintikka et. al., eds., (Dordrecht: Reidel Publishing Company, 1973), pp. 490–518. Reprinted with the permission of the author and Springer.

266: Tom McKay, "On Proper Names in Belief Ascriptions" from *Philosophical Studies* 39 (1981): 287–303. Reprinted with the permission of the author and Springer.

280: Nathan Salmon, "Frege's Puzzle" (editor's title) from *Frege's Puzzle* (Cambridge: MIT Press, 1985 and Atascadero: Ridgeview Press,

1991), pp. 11–18 and 77–118. Copyright © 1991 by Nathan Salmon. Reprinted with the permission of the author.

327: Scott Soames, "Substitutivity" from *On Being and Saying: Essays for Richard L. Cartwright*, edited by Judith Jarvis Thomson. Copyright © 1987 by the Massachusetts Institute of Technology. Reprinted with the permission of The MIT Press.

356: Mark Crimmins and John Perry, "The Prince and the Phone Booth: Reporting Puzzling Beliefs" from *Journal of Philosophy* LXXXVI, no. 12 (1989): 685–711. Reprinted with the permission of the authors and *The Journal of Philosophy*.

379: Mark Richard, "Attitudes in Context" from *Linguistics and Philosophy* 16 (1993): 123–148. Reprinted with the permission of the author and Springer.

402: Stephen Schiffer, "Belief Ascription" from *Journal of Philosophy* (October 1992): 499–521. Copyright © 1992. Reprinted with the permission of the author and *The Journal of Philosophy*.

420: Graham Oppy, "Why Semantic Innocence" from *Australasian Journal of Philosophy* 70, no. 4 (December 1992): 445–454. Reprinted with the permission of the author and Taylor & Francis, Ltd., http://wwwtandf.co.uk/journals.

430: Michael Dummett, "Note on an Attempted Refutation of Frege" from *Frege: Philosophy of Language, Second Edition*. Copyright © 1973 by Michael Dummett. Reprinted with the permission of Harvard University Press and Gerald Duckworth & Co. Ltd.

462: Michael Devitt, "Against Direct Reference" from *Midwest Studies in Philosophy* 14 (1989): 206–240. Reprinted with the permission of Blackwell.

495: Jay David Atlas, "Why Water isn't H_2O, Much Less isn't Necessarily H_2O?" excerpted from "Reference, Meaning, and Translation" from *Philosophical Books* 21, no. 3 (July 1980). Reprinted with the permission of the author and publisher.

496: Brian Loar, "The Semantics of Singular Terms" from *Philosophical Studies* 30 (1976): 353–377. Reprinted with the permission of the author and Springer.